www.wadsworth.com

wadsworth.com is the World Wide Web site for Wadsworth and is your direct source to dozens of online resources.

At *wadsworth.com* you can find out about supplements, demonstration software, and student resources. You can also send e-mail to many of our authors and preview new publications and exciting new technologies.

wadsworth.com
Changing the way the world learns®

Music in Western Civilization

Music in Western Civilization

Craig Wright
Yale University

Bryan Simms
University of Southern California

THOMSON

SCHIRMER

Australia • Brazil • Canada • Mexico • Singapore • Spain • United Kingdom • United States

Music in Western Civilization
Craig Wright, Bryan Simms

Publisher: Clark Baxter
Senior Development Editor: Sue Gleason
Senior Assistant Editor: Julie Yardley
Editorial Assistant: Emily Perkins
Executive Technology Project Manager: Matt Dorsey
Executive Marketing Manager: Diane Wenckebach
Marketing Assistant: Rachel Bairstow
Marketing Communications Manager: Patrick Rooney
Project Manager, Editorial Production: Trudy Brown
Creative Director: Rob Hugel
Executive Art Director: Maria Epes

Print Buyer: Karen Hunt
Permissions Editor: Sarah Harkrader
Production Service: Johnstone Associates
Text and Cover Designer: Diane Beasley
Photo Researcher: Roberta Broyer
Copy Editor: Judith Johnstone
Autographer: Ernie Mansfield
Cover Image: Carlo Saraceni (1585–1620), *Saint Cecilia*. Galleria Nazionale d'Arte Antica, Rome, Italy. Scala/Art Resource, NY.
Compositor: Thompson Type
Text and Cover Printer: Quebecor World/Dubuque

Thomson Higher Education
10 Davis Drive
Belmont, CA 94002-3098
USA

For more information about our products, contact us at:
Thomson Learning Academic Resource Center
1-800-423-0563
For permission to use material from this text or product, submit a request online at
http://www.thomsonrights.com.
Any additional questions about permissions can be submitted by e-mail to **thomsonrights@thomson.com.**

BRIEF CONTENTS

DETAILED CONTENTS

Part II THE LATE MIDDLE AGES AND EARLY RENAISSANCE

Part III THE LATE RENAISSANCE

Part V   THE ENLIGHTENMENT AND THE CLASSICAL ERA

Part **VII**   THE EARLY TWENTIETH CENTURY

Part **VIII**　CONTEMPORARY MUSIC

PREFACE

The decision to write a new history of Western music must appear to others, as it occasionally still does to its authors, as an act of madness. Of course, we have taken up this challenge in order to create a book that will best serve our students and our own goals as teachers. But it seems appropriate at the outset to inform prospective readers—and even to remind ourselves—what these goals are and what specific things we think make this text better than other histories of Western music.

✸ THE "PLACE" OF MUSIC

Music is the expressive voice of a culture, and often that voice is clearest in one particular city, country, or region. For this reason, we have centered our discussion of music in the places where it took deepest root. For example, we link much of the presentation of medieval music to the city of Paris; Handel to London; Beethoven to Vienna; Richard Strauss to Berlin; jazz to Harlem. We have not attempted daring or esoteric connections. But by placing music in a culturally resonant setting, we can help our students to see and hear how the sociopolitical life of certain places not only gave rise to musical genres and styles but also broadened and shaped all of Western civilization. To accomplish our overarching goal, we made certain pedagogical decisions based on our many years of teaching music history.

✸ CONTENT AND ORGANIZATION

The most visible difference in the organization of this book is its arrangement of topics into 83 brief chronological chapters. The book includes everything we thought most important to cover, and its many brief chapters promote three main goals. First, the arrangement of chapters makes it easier for instructors to present the material to students in any order that best suits their courses. For example, we are accustomed to teaching the instrumental music of Bach before his vocal music. But instructors more comfortable leading with vocal music can easily do so by assigning Chapter 40 before Chapter 39. Second, as instructors all know, students do not invariably bring to their studies an unquenchable desire to read the assigned text material. We have found that assigning a smaller passage for every class session yields better results than long chapters. Third, short chapters allow time for supplementary or source readings, and thus promote a better-rounded treatment of the subject at hand.

To provide variety for the student while studying the basic materials and musical selections, we engage special topics in **Boxes.** These are always germane to the subject under discussion, and they give the student a momentary diversion on some relevant issue in the history of music. For example, students enjoy the quirky observations on sixteenth-century social dancing made by aging priest Thoinot Arbeau, so we have highlighted his *Orchésographie* in Chapter 22. Similarly, students are generally astonished to find that people were paid to attend opera performances in the nineteenth century and to applaud on cue, so a box in Chapter 62 explains the existence of the *claque*. Nine longer **Musical Interludes** appear between various chapters. These discussions—music printing in the Renaissance, the critical concept of romanticism, and the birth of rock, among others—deal with larger issues that characterize an entire musical and cultural age, and their greater length and placement between chapters reflect their added importance.

A comprehensive **Timeline** of composers interwoven with the important political, social, and artistic events of that era opens each of eight parts of the book. We intend each timeline to provide a visual synopsis of a major historical period and a cultural context for the many musical events that we will discuss in the chapters that follow.

At the root of any study of music history, of course, lies the music itself, and our 267 CD tracks represent the major genres, composers, and works in the history of Western music. The discussion in each chapter moves quickly from a geographical and cultural context to a close study of these works, which are placed in students' hands in the form of excellent recordings and scores. A **Listening Cue** in the text alerts the reader whenever the time is right to leave the text, pick up headphones and the Anthology, and grapple with the primary materials of music.

In our selection of music, we have emphasized the **coverage of women composers** by including works by Hildegard of Bingen, Beatriz de Dia, Barbara Strozzi, Elizabeth Jacquet de La Guerre, Clara Schumann, Alma Mahler, Lili Boulanger, Bessie Smith, Ruth Crawford Seeger, and Joan Tower. We are mindful that many important composers—male as well as female—have of necessity been omitted from our discussion to produce a text of reasonable size. We invite comments about our choices and have appended our e-mail addresses to the end of this preface for this and any other issues readers may wish to discuss with us. In rare instances, where we were unable to include a piece on the CD set, the Listening Cue directs the reader to the book's website or to the Internet.

❖ MATERIAL TAILORED TO YOUR COURSE

Most schools offer music history for music majors in a sequence covering one, two, or three semesters. A few lucky colleagues have four or more semesters to cover this subject. We both teach at schools that devote three semesters to the history survey, and we are well aware of the problems that arise in adapting any one text to sequences of different durations. But the emerging web economy has taught us and our students that we must provide greater choices.

Accordingly, we offer the book, the Anthology, and the thirteen CDs that accompany the text in combinations that match a typical two- or three-semester course—march time or waltz time, as it were. The book is also available, of course, as a single-volume text, in hardcover for durability over the course of a year or more. Students rightly complain if they must buy a book and then are assigned only part of it. Our flexible configuration of print and audio material allows instructors to require students to buy only as much material as they will actually use. The ISBN and order information for these several print and audio options appear on the back cover of the text.

For teaching formats that we have not anticipated but may best fit your unique course syllabus, please write your local Thomson-Schirmer sales representative to craft a print medium customized to your course. For help contacting this person, use the Rep Locator on the Schirmer home page: www.Wadsworth.com/music.

 ANCILLARIES

Several remarkable ancillaries accompany the text.

Anthology

Timothy Roden of Ohio Wesleyan University has joined us to create a splendid anthology of Scores. It contains all of the central works discussed in the text with the exception of a few jazz and modern pieces that lack scores. Tim has added informative introductory notes to each selection and supplied new translations for all works with texts in foreign languages. As mentioned earlier, the complete Anthology is available in two or three volumes.

Audio CDs and Web

Virtually every piece that we discuss in the text appears on one of thirteen audio CDs; recordings of a few works can be located on the book's website (www.Wadsworth.com/music). The recordings are of the highest quality; for example, much of the recorded medieval music comes from the prestigious Harmonia Mundi label. Recordings of hitherto unrecorded pieces have been specially commissioned from professional groups and performers, including The Washington Cornett and Sackbut Ensemble.

Workbook

Timothy Roden has also written a unique student workbook of analytical exercises and probing questions that will help students examine each piece of music in the Anthology and prepare for exams and quizzes. Nothing like it exists now, and by engaging the student, these exercises bring the music to life. The Workbook also includes an essay by Sterling Murray, "Writing a Research Paper on a Musical Subject," as well as a bibliography for students designed to help in the process of writing papers. The bibliography can also be found on the website (www.Wadsworth.com/music).

Instructor's Resource CD-ROM

An all-inclusive CD ROM contains ExamView computerized testing, as well as an electronic version of the Instructor's Manual/Test Bank. Also found here are PowerPoint presentations that include outlines for lectures, additional illustrations, musical examples in the text, audio clips, and other materials for use in the classroom.

 ACKNOWLEDGMENTS AND THANKS

A project this comprehensive and complex is naturally the work of many hands. We are grateful to colleagues who gave generously of their time, ideas, and good will to make this undertaking a success. Some read and critiqued large portions of the text, others answered specific questions, and still others graciously provided materials. We are sincerely grateful to all of the following for their help.

Jonathan Bellman, *University of Northern Colorado*

Jane Bernstein, *Tufts University*

Francisco Lorenzo Candelaria, *University of Texas, Austin*

Tim Carter, *University of North Carolina, Chapel Hill*

Cynthia J. Cyrus, *Blair School of Music, Vanderbilt University*

Jeffrey Dean, *The New Grove Dictionary of Music and Musicians*

Charles Dill, *University of Wisconsin, Madison*

Christine Smith Dorey, *Case Western Reserve University*

Lawrence Earp, *University of Wisconsin, Madison*

Robert Eisenstein, *University of Massachusetts and Mount Holyoke College*

Robert Galloway, *Houghton College*

David Grayson, *University of Minnesota*

James Grymes, *University of North Carolina, Charlotte*

Barbara Haggh-Huglo, *University of Maryland*

James Hepokoski, *Yale University*

Michael Holmes, *University of Maryland*

Derek Katz, *University of California, Santa Barbara*

Terry Klefstad, *Southwestern University*

Walter Kreyszig, *University of Saskatchewan*

James Ladewig, *University of Rhode Island*

Paul Laird, *University of Kansas*

Bruce Langford, *Citrus College*

Charles S. Larkowski, *Wright State University*

Lowell Lindgren, *Massachusetts Institute of Technology*

Dorothea Link, *University of Georgia*

Daniel Lipori, *Central Washington University*

Ralph Lorenz, *Kent State University*

Patrick Macey, *Eastman School of Music*

Thomas J. Mathiesen, *Indiana University*

Charles Edward McGuire, *Oberlin College Conservatory of Music*

Bryce Mecham, *Brigham Young University*

Donald C. Meyer, *Lake Forest College*

Sharon Mirchandani, *Westminster Choir College of Rider University*

Sterling Murray, *West Chester University*

Giulio Ongaro, *University of Southern California*

Leon Plantinga, *Yale University*

Keith Polk, *University of New Hampshire*

Hilary Poriss, *University of Cincinnati*

John Rice, *Rochester, Minnesota*

Anne Robertson, *University of Chicago*

Ellen Rosand, *Yale University*

David Rothenberg, *Colby College*

Ed Rutschman, *Western Washington University*

Christopher J. Smith, *Texas Tech University School of Music*

Tony C. Smith, *Northwestern State University of Louisiana*

Kerala Snyder, *Eastman School of Music*

Pamela Starr, *University of Nebraska*

Marica Tacconi, *Pennsylvania State University*

JoAnn Taricani, *University of Washington*

Susan Thompson, *Yale University*

Jess B. Tyre, *State University of New York at Potsdam*

Zachariah Victor, *Yale University*

Scott Warfield, *University of Central Florida*

Mary A. Wischusen, *Wayne State University*

Gretchen Wheelock, *Eastman School of Music*

Several colleagues who specifically asked to remain anonymous

Closer to home, we wish to thank our respective wives, Sherry Dominick and Charlotte E. Erwin, for reading and evaluating the text, for giving advice on many fronts, and, most of all, for their support and patience. Having ready access to the music libraries at Yale and the University of Southern California has been a special boon, and we are grateful to Kendall Crilly, Richard Boursy, Suzanne Lovejoy, and Eva Heater for help in acquiring materials, and to Karl Schrom and Richard Warren for advice with regard to recordings. Also offering invaluable assistance during the creation of new recordings were Richard Lalli and Paul Berry. At the end of the project we could not have done without the indefatigable labors of graduate students Pietro Moretti and Nathan Link in researching, editing, proofreading, and preparing materials for the instructor's CD; in the course of this project the students became the mentors.

Finally, the authors wish to thank the staff of Thomson-Schirmer that has helped to produce this volume. First of all, the guiding light, from beginning to end, was our publisher and friend, Clark Baxter; in many ways, this book is his. Joining Clark in this enterprise were a number of exceptionally talented people including Trudy Brown, who coordinated with great finesse the production of every part of this massive undertaking. Judy Johnstone merged, with her accustomed skill and forbearance, countless print and electronic chapters, images, and autography into a book that Diane Beasley's design has made exceptionally attractive. Sharon Poore and Sue Gleason helped us develop the manuscript itself. Julie Yardley worked closely with us and with Tim Roden on the ancillaries, especially on the Anthology. Emily Perkins, Clark's remarkable assistant, kept an ocean of paper and electronic material moving in the right direction, and on schedule. Matt Dorsey oversaw the development of the book's website and the Instructor's Resource CD-ROM. Finally, a word of thanks to Diane Wenckebach, who brought boundless energy and commitment to the marketing of this text, and who, with Patrick Rooney, prepared its promotional material.

Craig Wright
(craig.wright@yale.edu)

Bryan Simms
(simms@usc.edu)

Music in Western Civilization

ANTIQUITY AND THE MIDDLE AGES

*T*he period between 750 B.C.E. and about 1400 C.E. brought sweeping changes to the West. Our story of Western music begins during the age of antiquity in ancient Greece, where our democratic institutions, modes of critical thought, and the value we place on athletic contests and on the arts—especially music—find their roots. Greek music theory was later passed in voluminous amounts, sometimes by Roman interpreters, to the Middle Ages and the Renaissance. Monasteries provided centers of learning in the West during the early Middle Ages. They also preserved the great body of Western religious music, namely monophonic Gregorian chant, or

800 B.C.E.	700	600	500	400	300	200	100	0	100 C.E.	200	300

ANTIQUITY (800 B.C.E.–476 C.E.)

● 776 B.C.E. First Olympic Games include songs and hymns

c580–500 B.C.E. Pythagoras explores science of sound

c500–400 B.C.E. Euripides', Sophocles', Aeschylus', Aristophanes' plays include songs

Socrates (469–399 B.C.E.), continuing with Plato (c429–347 B.C.E.) and Aristotle (384–322 B.C.E.), expound ideas on music and education

Arithmetical basis of intervals and durations beginning fourth century B.C.E.

c6 B.C.E.–c30 C.E. Jesus Christ   Ambrose

1st century C.E. **Epitaph of Seikilos**

Corbis

432 B.C.E. *The Parthenon*

plainsong, intended for use with the Mass and canonical hours. Only after many centuries, around 900 C.E., was a written system of notation devised for Western plainsong. Shortly thereafter, polyphony emerged in England, France, and Spain. By 1300 C.E. Western musicians had not only developed a method for notating pitch but also one for regulating the increasingly complex rhythms of polyphony. On the eve of the Renaissance, in the late 1300s, composers began to turn away from this complexity and employ simpler rhythms and textures and more sonorous harmonies.

400	500	600	700	800	900	1000	1100	1200	1300	1400	1500

MIDDLE AGES (476–1450)

(340?–397) Ambrosian chant

c850–950 Earliest musical notation of plainchant and polyphony

c435 Martianus Capella develops *quadrivium*, including music

1100 John of St. Gall writes *De Musica* on 8 church modes

476 Western Roman Empire ends

King Richard I of England (1157–1199), trouvère

c612 St. Gall founded

Augustine of Hippo (354–430) *De Musica* on music and rhythm

Charlemagne (742–814)

Hildegard of Bingen (1098–1179)

800 C.E. Gallican chant merges with Roman

mid-1100s Beatriz de Dia, trobairitz

1200 Motet emerges in Paris

Boethius (c480–524) *De institutione musica*, compendium of Greek music theory

c1316 *Roman de Fauvel*

c1320 *La quinte estampie real*

Benedict of Nursia (c480–c550) establishes Benedictine order

Machaut, *Messe de Nostre Dame* (1360s)

Tuotilo of St. Gall (c850–915) composes tropes

1380s Philippus de Caserta, *Ars subtilior*

Notker Balbulus (c840–912) composes sequences

1030 Guido of Arezzo establishes musical staff and solfege

Gargoyle on Notre Dame of Paris, built 1163–1285. Leoninus and Perotinus the Great compose polyphony there.

Jean des Murs (c1290–c1351), *Ars novae musicae*

Philippe de Vitry (1291–1361), *Ars nova*

Jacques de Liège (c1260–c1330), *Ars antiqua*

Guillaume de Machaut (c1300–1377)

1348–1350 Black Death

1337–1453 Hundred Years' War

First clavichord 14th century

Baude Cordier (c1365–1398), circular canon

1378–1417 Great Western Schism

Chapter

1

Music in Ancient Greece

We in the West owe much to the ancient Greeks. Our democratic institutions, modes of critical thought, and the value we place on athletic contests and on the arts—especially music—trace their roots directly back to ancient Greece. In a real way, music in Western civilization began with the music and culture of that country.

Although Greece today is a rather small country, 2,500 years ago it exerted vast influence as the center of the civilized world in the West. Between 750 and 500 B.C.E. Greek colonists spread out around the shores of the eastern Mediterranean Sea (Map 1-1). Later, under the leadership of Pericles (c495–c429 B.C.E.), Greek political power was concentrated in the area around the city-state of Athens. During this period, called the Periclean Age, Athens saw the flowering of democratic principles as well as extraordinary artistic excellence. All male citizens had an equal voice in deciding affairs of state, and all citizens, male or female, enjoyed equal protection under the law. On a hill within Athens, an area called the Acropolis, the Greeks built a temple to the patron goddess of their city, Athena Nike (literally, Bringer of Victory). Here, in the Parthenon (see Part I timeline), architecture and sculpture expressed the qualities of beauty we have come to associate with classical art: symmetry, balance, an absence of excessive detail, and harmony in all things. During the fifth century B.C.E., Western drama had its beginnings in the powerful plays of Aeschylus, Sophocles, and Euripides. So too the philosophers of Athens, beginning with Socrates (469–399 B.C.E.) and continuing with Plato (c429–347 B.C.E.) and

✿ M A P   1 - 1

Ancient Greece.

Aristotle (384–322 B.C.E.), set the foundation for Western philosophical inquiry, which seeks to know the nature of reality. Thus, the Greeks of Athens established many of the political and intellectual systems, as well as the standards for beauty, that we still cherish today.

Sports and music, too, were basic to Greek life. Early on, festivals involving athletic competitions and music were offered in honor of the chief Greek god, Zeus, who was believed to dwell on Mount Olympus. From there, it was said, he hurled a thunderbolt that landed two hundred miles away, on what is called the plains of Olympia. On that spot in 776 B.C.E., and at four-year intervals thereafter, the best athletes of the world gathered to compete. From these games our modern Olympic Games have descended. The philosopher Socrates taught that music and gymnastics were the two essentials of every good education. His pupil Plato said in *Republic* that these two disciplines must be kept in proper balance, believing that too much music made the body weak and too much sport made the spirit insensitive.

But music was more than a mere counterbalance to athletic activity. All Greek poetry was sung, and most Greek drama was chanted, not spoken, to various metrical patterns. In these contexts, the Greeks refused to separate word from musical sound. Nor could dance be separated from her two sister muses, poetry and music. Greek vases frequently depict musical scenes in which the figures seem to move with the music. Figure 1-1 shows a line of lyre players stepping high as they sing and play. Such illustrations suggest that for the Greeks the sister arts of music, poetry, and dance were inextricably linked.

Réunion des Musées Nationaux/Art Resource, NY

🌿 **FIGURE 1-1**

Mid-sixth century amphora shows the close association among text, music, and movement. The players of the lyre seem to be executing the "fine high steps" described in a contemporary hymn.

✺ MUSIC IN GREEK SOCIETY

Music set the rhythm of Greek life. There were drinking songs, work songs, love songs, wedding songs, bridal chamber songs, funeral dirges, odes for heroic warriors, and hymns for the gods. Depending on the social context, Greek song might be performed by a chorus or by a solo singer, and it might be accompanied by a musical instrument such as the lyre, kithara (type of lyre), or aulos (wind instrument).

Public Religious Festivals

The ancient Greeks honored their gods by means of public religious festivals recurring every year, every two years, or every four years. The Olympic Games, as mentioned, was one such festival that was held on the plains of Olympia every four years before some 40,000 spectators who had walked to the site. In addition to athletic competitions and horse races, the games involved contests in poetry, dancing, and music. Related to the Olympic Games were the Panhellenic Games and the Pythian Games, both of which emphasized the arts. Prizes were awarded to the best performers on instruments such as the kithara and the aulos. All of these festivities, like our modern Olympic Games, were preceded by an elaborate procession with musical accompaniment during which a unison chorus sang praises to the gods. The stately **paean,** for example, was a hymn that celebrated the deeds of primary gods such as Zeus (the chief god) and Apollo (the god of the sun, of music, and of reason). On the other hand, the passionate **dithyramb** was a wild choral song, mingled with shouts, which did honor to playful Dionysus (the god of wine and fertility). Religious rites and bacchanals—both infused with music—were part of the original Olympics.

Music in the Theater

Public festivals also included Greek dramas. Drama gave poets, actors, and citizens of the chorus an opportunity to create large-scale musical structures on themes important to Greek life. At one annual festival held in Athens in honor of the god Dionysus, five comedies and three tragedies were presented over the course of five days. Prizes were awarded to the best playwright and the best actor. Greek theater usually allowed on stage two or three actors and an all-male chorus, numbering around fifteen. The chorus was far more important in ancient Greek drama than it is in the theater today. It commented on and moralized about the action occurring on stage (just as it would in later Baroque opera). The actors sang some parts and spoke others, while the chorus sang, gestured, and danced with dignity. A player of the aulos accompanied the chorus, in order to enhance the emotional response of the audience. Two papyrus scraps with musical notation for two plays by Euripides (d. 406 B.C.E.) are all that remain of the music of this once-great union of the musical and dramatic arts. Fortunately, one of these is the climactic Stasimon Chorus from Euripides' play *Orestes*. Euripides himself may have composed the music as well as the text. Because the papyrus is fragmentary, what we hear are really phrases from a Greek chorus, rather than the chorus in its entirety. Nonetheless, the fragment is sufficient to give us a sense of the power and the strange beauty of Greek dramatic music.

LISTENING CUE

EURIPIDES
Orestes (c408 B.C.E.)
Stasimon Chorus (fragment)

CD 1/1
Anthology, No. 1

Private Festivities: The Symposium

In addition to religious and dramatic festivals, Greek music was integral to everyday life. Work songs, love songs, and bawdy tunes appeared spontaneously. Other types of music-making occurred within carefully regulated domestic parties. Of these, the most elaborate was the symposium. The **symposium** was a tightly organized social gathering in which adult male citizens came together for conversation and entertainment—an after-dinner drinking party. Inside a well-to-do residence a special room accommodated seven or eleven couches set end to end along three of the walls. Reclining one or two to a couch, the men communicated, debated, and posed riddles across the open space in the center of the room. A symposiarch (master of ceremonies) laid down the rules for the evening and established the order of events. He decided the number of kraters (large wine bowls) to be drunk and set the proportion of water to wine for each krater (Fig. 1-2). (The ancient Greeks thought drinking undiluted wine barbaric.) A well-balanced mixture of wine and water brought relaxation and conviviality to the group. Everyone conversed. Some recited poetry to musical accompaniment. Professional musicians, dancers, and courtesans (prostitutes for aristocrats) provided entertainment as well as sexual favors. A well-conducted symposium was thought to be a highly civilized event providing liberation from everyday restraints within a carefully regulated environment. As Athenaeus wrote in his *Deipnosophistae* (*The Learned Banquet*):

 FIGURE 1-2

A fifth-century B.C.E. wine krater carries this image depicting a symposiast reclining on a couch as he is entertained by female aulete (player of the aulos).

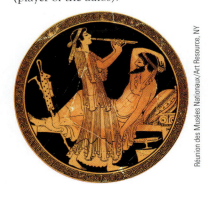

Réunion des Musées Nationaux/Art Resource, NY

> Drink with me, play music with me
> love with me, wear a crown with me,
> be mad with me when I am mad,
> and wise with me when I am wise.[1]

The primary musical entertainment at the symposium was the **skolion,** a song setting a brief lyrical poem. As a wreath of myrtle (symbol of the poetic muse) was
passed around the room, each guest in turn was asked to sing a skolion and to accompany himself on the lyre. Those who refused were thought to be uncultured.
Surviving today is a poem by Seikilos, written in the first century C.E., and long
thought to be one of the few skolia to survive with music (Ex. 1-1). Some scholars
call it an epitaph—a short piece of prose or verse eulogizing someone deceased.
Here, the four lines expound a fatalistic "eat-drink-and-be-merry" philosophy appropriate for a symposium. They inform a complete, albeit short, composition in
which the notation allows for an unambiguous transcription into modern symbols.

EXAMPLE 1-1[†]

1. As long as you live, shine   2. Grieve you not at all
3. Life is of brief duration   4. Time demands its end

🔘 LISTENING CUE

SEIKILOS   CD 1/2
Skolion or Epitaph (first century C.E.)   Anthology, No. 2
As long as you live

The ancient Greek musical notation clearly indicates the pitches and sets the
rhythmic durations. The basic unit of time was a short value called the **chronos**
(here, the eighth note). Two chronoi formed a long value called the **diseme** (quarter note) and three a triple-unit long called the **triseme** (dotted quarter). In the
skolion of Seikilos, the final syllable of each line is emphasized by means of a
triseme. The song spans an octave and is written in what some Greek music theorists called the Phrygian tonos (discussed below)—the equivalent of our white-note
scale on D. At the outset, the melody immediately reaches for the top-most note of
the Greek Phrygian mode and at the end concludes with the bottom-most note.
How are we to judge the impact of such a brief piece? Surely the effectiveness of the
skolion of Seikilos would depend entirely on the degree of enthusiasm and convic-
tion with which a wine-inspired singer might perform it.

[†]Adapted from Thomas J. Mathiesen, *Apollo's Lyre: Greek Music and Music Theory in Antiquity* (Lincoln,
1999), pp. 149–50.

❁ THE NATURE OF GREEK MUSIC

Musical Notation

Most Greek music was not written down but was transmitted orally from performer to performer, generation after generation. Much of the music that was written has been destroyed over time; very little Greek music survives today, no more than fifty pieces. Most are carved in stone monuments or written on papyrus. Moreover, many of these papyrus leaves are mere fragments. Consequently, our understanding of the sound of Greek music is limited. We can talk in general terms about the place of music in Greek society but it is very difficult to recreate its sounds.

The Greeks did, nevertheless, create a system of musical notation. Yet it was very different from our modern-day clefs, round note heads, and letter names for pitches. Instead, the Greeks assigned to each pitch a specific symbol derived from letters and grammatical signs. Several of these symbols can be seen positioned above the modern musical staff at the beginning of Example 1-1. Because the Greeks did not repeat a sign when reaching the octave, as we do, and because they divided the octave into many more than twelve pitches, Greek notation involved a great number of signs, more than sixty in just a three-octave span. To complicate matters further, the Greeks employed one set of symbols for vocal sounds and a second set of symbols for instrumental music, bringing the total number of signs to more than one hundred twenty. Given this complexity, it is no wonder that Greek musical notation was not adopted by later Western European musicians. Our present Western system of musical notation, which makes use of a staff and round notes with letter names, did not begin to evolve until more than a thousand years after the heyday of ancient Greek music (see Chapter 4).

Musical Instruments

Greek music, being closely tied to poetry and drama, was fundamentally vocal music and therefore literary in character. Both Plato and Aristotle stated that instrumental music was inferior to vocal music. Yet the Greeks did have musical instruments: percussion instruments similar to our timpani, and the snare drum, tambourine, and cymbals; wind instruments including a rudimentary flute; and a variety of plucked string instruments such as the psaltery and harp. (Oddly, they had few "stopped" or "fretted" string instruments like the violin or guitar.) Foremost among these Greek instruments were those of the family of the lyre (a plucked string instrument) and the aulos (a reed wind instrument). These were associated, respectively, with the restrained music for Apollo, and with the wilder, more excited sounds in honor of Dionysus.

The **lyre** was a medium-sized instrument usually fitted with seven strings of sheep gut and plucked by a plectrum of metal or bone (see Fig.1-1). The resonator at the bottom was simply a large turtle shell to which the strings were indirectly attached. The lyre rarely played solo melodies, being used most often to accompany a solo singer—usually the player himself—by providing a few stable pitches, perhaps a scale.

The largest of all Greek string instruments was the **kithara,** an especially big lyre. The kithara, too, usually had seven strings, but the resonator at the bottom was a sound-box made of wood rather than tortoise shell. Figure 1-3 shows a performer, head thrown back in song, singing to the sounds of a kithara. The right hand, which has just finished a stroke, strums the strings with a plectrum attached to the bottom of the sound-box with a string. By means of a wristband, the left forearm braces the

❁ FIGURE 1-3

A player of the kithara sings to his own accompaniment.

instrument against the body, while the left hand damps the strings. The kithara enjoyed high status in Greek society because it was most often used to accompany paeans offered to Apollo, the god of music. In Greek mythology, Apollo himself played the kithara and vanquished his enemy Marsyas, inventor of the aulos, in a famous musical battle of the gods.

The **aulos,** by contrast, was a wind instrument fitted with a round single reed or with a flat double reed. It consisted of two basic parts, the mouthpiece containing the reed(s) and the body or resonator. The resonator was made of wood or bone and was drilled through with a cylindrical bore and four or five finger holes. In later more advanced instruments, rudimentary key mechanisms were added so that additional finger holes might be set into the instrument and its range thereby extended. Paintings of the period show conclusively that the aulos was played in pairs (see Fig. 1-2); the left hand played one instrument, the right hand another. Together the two might produce ten or more pitches, and perhaps over-blowing would have allowed even more. In such cases, some rudimentary polyphony, playing in parallel fifths for example, was surely possible. While we might be tempted to think of the aulos as creating a sound similar to that of the modern clarinet or oboe, in fact it is really impossible to characterize the timbre of this early Greek woodwind instrument. A few instruments survive, but they can only be studied, not played. Contemporary writers, however, report that the aulos produced a high, clear, penetrating sound.

 ## MUSIC IN GREEK PHILOSOPHY

The Ethical Power of Music

Music was not only a pleasant amusement, improving the quality of life, but it could also affect human behavior, so the Greeks believed. For this reason both Plato (in *Laws*) and Aristotle (in *Politics*) declared music to be the most powerful of all the arts. To change a citizen's behavior, one need merely change the music! Thus, only the most upright sort of music should be taught to the youth of Athens. The Dorian mode (associated with Apollo) was thought appropriate because it was orderly and relaxed in its manner and rhythms, whereas the Phrygian (appropriate for Dionysus) was more frenzied and ecstatic, and more likely to encourage wanton behavior and drunkenness. Thus music had the force of law. In the words of Plato (*Republic*): "Our songs are our laws." Although the Greeks' attempts to regulate behavior by controlling music may seem repressive to us, do we not exhibit some of the same mentality in the "parental advisory" labels that go on some of today's compact discs?

To be sure, the ethical power of music, and the need to regulate it, was a notion deeply embedded in the Greek mythology. The following story recounts how the famous mathematician Pythagoras used music to save one member of his community from the crime of arson.

> Who is unaware that Pythagoras, by means of a spondaic melody, calmed and restored to self-control a youth of the city of Taormina who had become intoxicated by the sound of the Phrygian mode? For one night a prostitute was shut up in the house of the youth's rival, and he in his frenzy was about to set fire to it. Meanwhile Pythagoras, who was observing the motion of the stars, as was his custom, learned that the youth, agitated by the sound of the Phrygian mode and deaf to the many pleas of his friends, refused to desist from his crime. Pythagoras ordered that the mode be changed, and thus reduced the youth's fury to a state of perfect calm.[2]

Music of the Spheres

Notice in the preceding legend that **Pythagoras** (sixth century B.C.E.) was outdoors observing the motion of the stars. This is important, for Pythagoras was an astronomer and mathematician as well as a musician. As we shall see, because the sounds of music can be expressed as numbers, music was viewed as a science as well as an art in pre-modern times. Greek philosophy held that behind the surface appearance of everyday life rested universal truths that could be expressed in motion, in number, and in music. When the stars and planets rotated in balanced proportions, they made heavenly music—**music of the spheres** (see also Chapter 2). The soul on earth was to be in harmony with the heavens, so it too needed to embody a harmonious music. Body and soul resonate with earthly music (instruments and voices) because music consists of vibrations that are sympathetically felt by the body. If a mental or physical illness occurs, then a therapeutic music should be administered. This was the Greek world-view of music, and it persisted in the West until the time of Shakespeare and beyond.

❀ GREEK MUSIC THEORY

Greek philosophers spoke of a wondrous harmony throughout the universe. Music on earth was simply the audible expression of that harmony, and it sounded by means of mathematical ratios. By studying these ratios, we might comprehend truths about the sounds and secrets of the universe. But it remained for the Greek philosopher-musicians to explain how this worked—to demonstrate the arithmetical basis of musical intervals and durations. Thus, beginning with Aristoxenus in the fourth century B.C.E., continuing through Ptolemy, Cleonides, and Aristides Quintilianus in the centuries after Christ, and finally ending with Boethius about 520 C.E., a succession of great minds probed with astonishing rigor the nature of musical intervals, consonance and dissonance, and the scales. At no time in the history of music has the arithmetical basis of music been more thoroughly explored than under the penetrating eyes of the Greek theorists. These men were not interested in analyzing pieces of music. They were scientists seeking to understand the very essence and meaning of music. Aristoxenus, for example, was one of Aristotle's closest associates and a master of his methods of observation and classification; Claudius Ptolemy (flourished 127–148 C.E.) was an astronomer whose celestial observations were considered authoritative for the next fourteen hundred years. For these theorists, music was a science: pure, but not simple.

Intervals and Scales

Our understanding of musical intervals and our scale can be traced back to another myth involving the legendary Pythagoras. One day, when passing a forge, Pythagoras heard a blacksmith simultaneously bang two iron hammers and produce the sound of an octave. Investigating further, Pythagoras observed that the hammer giving the higher sound weighed exactly half that of the hammer producing the lower one. Hammers whose weights were in a 3:2 proportion produced the sound of a fifth, those in a 4:3 proportion produced a fourth. Inherent in a few simple mathematical ratios were the basic consonances of music. Pythagoras then went home, so the story goes, and replicated this experience with strings of different lengths.

In truth, iron hammers do not produce musical intervals in this fashion, and the pitches of strings depend not only upon their length but also their diameter and the tension placed upon them. But Pythagoras' principle was correct: strings or pipes with lengths having a 2:1 ratio produce an octave, 3:2 a fifth, 4:3 a fourth, and 9:8 a whole tone. Almost magically, the essence of music could be understood in ratios of four integers: 12:9:8:6.

Using these ratios, Greek theorists could construct a scale. They had no clefs or staff, simply the idea of ratios and intervals. With the aid of a device called the **monochord** (a single string stretched over a wooden block and anchored at each end; see Fig. 4-1) they took a string and divided it in parts to produce the intervals of an octave, fifth, fourth, and whole step. By applying these ratios at different points on the monochord, they created a regular succession of pitches—a scale. The building block within the scale was a **tetrachord** (a succession of four pitches) whose intervals begin with a semitone (S) followed by two full tones (T). Within the octave two successive tetrachords sounded above the pitch of the basic string. Today we would call the basic string (the lowest-sounding pitch) low A (the Greeks called it the **proslambanomenos**). The two tetrachords shared a common pitch and are thus conjunct tetrachords. Next, above this octave scale, two more conjunct tetrachords were added. The two tetrachords in the middle of the scale were separated by a whole tone and thus were disjunct. These four tetrachords, along with the proslambanomenos, formed the Greek **Greater Perfect System,** the framework of the Greek two-octave scale. Example 1-2 sets this within our modern great staff.

EXAMPLE 1-2

Proslambanomenos

Notice the similarities of the Greater Perfect System to our own white-key scale. From the Greeks' successive derivation of pitches from basic ratios (2:1, 3:2, 4:3 and 9:8) resulted a scale in which each octave-span contained seven pitches (five whole tones and two semitones), an arrangement that has endured to the present day. Thus from the very beginning of music theory, the scale has only a semitone between what we call E and F, and between B and C; the basic ratios of music required it be so.

Although the Greeks had no grid (staff) to indicate relative pitch height, their Greater Perfect System can be placed on our modern great staff. Moreover, the Greeks had scale patterns, just as we have our major and minor scales. They called each scale a **tonos** (plural, **tonoi**). Some Greek theorists identified as many as thirteen or even fifteen scales. The astronomer-musician Ptolemy, however, reduced the number to seven, one pattern for each of the seven species of diatonic scale within the octave. When placed within a modern representation of the Greater Perfect System, the seven tonoi appear as in Example 1-3.

EXAMPLE 1-3

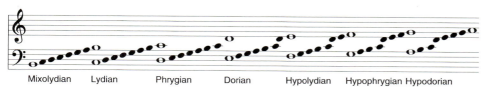

Mixolydian   Lydian   Phrygian   Dorian   Hypolydian   Hypophrygian Hypodorian

Greek theorists derived the names for these scales from the modes of singing associated with particular ethnic groups living around the Aegean Sea (Phrygia, for example, is in what is now western Turkey). Originally, these names may have reflected not only a scale pattern preferred in a particular region but also a style of singing, vocal quality, and mood that was favored there. Although Ptolemy's system contained seven scales, three were always thought more important: Lydian (corresponding to our diatonic C-C), Phrygian (D-D), and Dorian (E-E).†

The skolion of Seikilos mentioned earlier (Anthology, No. 2) would accord perfectly with Ptolemy's Phrygian tonos. Similarly, the Stasimon Chorus from Euripides' *Orestes* (Anthology, No. 1) is notated, according to Ptolemy's system, in the Phrygian tonos (transposed to E), but with chromatic inflections.

To accommodate chromaticism within the Greater Perfect System, the Greeks allowed for three different types of tetrachords, three "genera," as they were called. In all three genera the first and fourth pitches of the tetrachord were fixed (see capital letters below), while the inner two pitches were movable. The basic genus within the Greek system was called the **diatonic genus** (to the Greeks, "diatonic" meant "through the tones"). The diatonic genus reflected the primary tetrachord spanning the intervals S-T-T.

In its unaltered form, the Greater Perfect System is a succession of diatonic tetrachords, one disjunct point in the middle separating two conjunct tetrachords on either side. For chromaticism, however, another tetrachord was employed called the **chromatic genus** ("chroma" in Greek means "color"). A chromatic tetrachord consisted of two semitones and a minor third. It allowed more semitones to be inserted into the greater perfect system. Music demanding more subtle variations of pitch made use of the **enharmonic genus** ("enharmonic" means "in harmony" or "same sounding"). The enharmonic genus required a tetrachord consisting of a major third and two quartertones (pitches sounding nearly the same). Finally, as if the three genera were not enough, the Greeks further subdivided each genus into two "shades." Obviously, Greek melody was far more nuanced than our own, making use of what we call microtones—tones smaller than our semitones.

tetrachord of the diatonic genus: E, f, g, A

tetrachord of the chromatic genus: E, f, f♯, A

tetrachord of the enharmonic genus: E, e+, f, A

In practice a melody might be written in any one of the Greek tonoi, and the basic diatonic genus might be altered as well; that is, for greater expression, the chromatic or the enharmonic genus might be inserted momentarily. Moreover, entire melodies could be constructed using nothing but the chromatic or the enharmonic genus. Following is the Dorian tonos in each of the three genera.

Dorian tonos in the diatonic genus: E, F, G, A, B, C, D, E

Dorian tonos in the chromatic genus: E, F, F♯, A, B, C, C♯, E

Dorian tonos in the enharmonic genus: E, E+, F, A, B, B+, C, E

Today in music we have two distinctly different scalar patterns: major and minor. The Greeks, as we have seen, had multiple tonoi, further inflected by the various

†Later, in the Middle Ages, these names would be associated with different scale patterns.

shades of the diatonic, chromatic, and enharmonic genera. Today we clearly hear the difference between a piece in major and one in minor—recognizing that they have different moods. The ancient Greeks felt even more acutely the effects of their different tonoi and their shades. As Aristotle stated in his *Politics*:

> The musical scales differ essentially one from another, and those who hear them are differently affected by each. Some make men sad and grave, like the so-called Mixolydian. Others weaken the mind, like the relaxed scales. Yet others produce a moderate and settled mood, which appears to be the special effect of the Dorian. The Phrygian inspires enthusiasm![3]

 ## SUMMARY

Music informed life in ancient Greece to a surprising degree. Greek poets, philosophers, and scientists (themselves often musicians) frequently spoke of music. Because much Greek music was unwritten, and because much of what was written has been lost over time, there are only about fifty pieces (many fragmentary) surviving today. But Greek music theory was passed to the Middle Ages and Renaissance in voluminous amounts. Totaling more than a thousand dense pages and written over many centuries, ancient Greek music theory demonstrates a mathematical rigor and complexity that would never again be seen in the music theory of any people, East or West. Yet, not only does Greek music theory exhibit complexity but it also reveals that Greek music was in some ways richer and more subtle than our own. The Greeks enjoyed a greater number of scale patterns, for example, and employed microtones not possible on our modern keyboard.

Aspects of Ancient Greek Music Passed On to the West

1. A system of consonance and dissonance (octaves, fifths, fourths, and their multiples were consonances) that would remain unchanged until the fourteenth century
2. A system recognizing octave duplication and dividing each octave into seven pitches (five whole tones and two semitones)
3. The concept of scale patterns, each with its own name, incorporating different intervallic sequences
4. A system of tuning, called Pythagorean, that involved mathematically exact octaves, fifths, and fourths; it remained the only system of tuning discussed by music theorists until the late fifteenth century
5. Important musical terms such as "tetrachord," "diatonic," "chromatic," "enharmonic"

Aspects of Greek Music Passed to the Middle Ages But Then Gradually Abandoned

1. Notation: the Greeks had notational symbols for vocal music and a separate set of signs for instrumental music, but their system was cumbersome and was abandoned by the ninth century
2. Microtones
3. A belief in the music of the spheres
4. A belief that music is a quantitative science

What Was Not Passed On by the Ancient Greeks

1. A large musical repertory
2. Analysis of compositions

3. Instruments (only images survive, but few real artifacts)
4. A musical staff or clefs (the Greeks had no grid or staff; they thought only in terms of intervals and scale patterns)
5. A theory of musical rhythm (rhythm in Greek music, as discussed in the theory treatises, did not affect the development of written rhythmic notation in the West)

KEY TERMS

paean	lyre	proslambanomenos
dithyramb	kithara	Greater Perfect System
symposium	aulos	tonos
skolion	Pythagoras	diatonic genus
chronos	music of the spheres	chromatic genus
diseme	monochord	enharmonic genus
triseme	tetrachord	

Chapter 2

Antiquity to the Middle Ages: Music in Rome, Jerusalem, and the Early Christian World

 ROME

During the two centuries before the birth of Christ, the growing Roman Empire largely overran and absorbed the civilization of ancient Greece (Map 2-1). Typified by the brilliant general Julius Caesar (100–44 B.C.E.), the Romans personified military might, engineering skill, and administrative efficiency. Roman architecture, which endures today from the British Isles to the Near East, remains one of the wonders of the Western world. Roman dramatists such as Plautus and Terence gave us comic plays that are produced in schools today, just as Latin poems by Ovid and Virgil are still studied in Latin classes for their wit and elegance of style. But, oddly, the Romans left us little that is truly original by way of painting, sculpture, and music. Roman sculptures are often copies of earlier ones by Greek masters, and what little Roman painting survives seems to be equally derivative. With regard to music, once again the Romans borrowed heavily from the Greeks.

To be fair, it is difficult to know precisely what the music of ancient Rome was like, for not a note of it survives. Whereas approximately fifty examples of Greek music are extant from the Hellenic world, from the Romans there are none. This may suggest that Roman music was overwhelmingly oral in its transmission and not a written art. Roman historians comment about music in religious and civic ceremonies—in theatrical productions, during religious processions, and at athletic

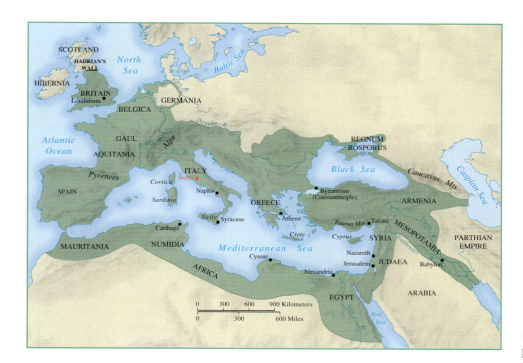

MAP 2-1
The Roman Empire, 117 C.E.

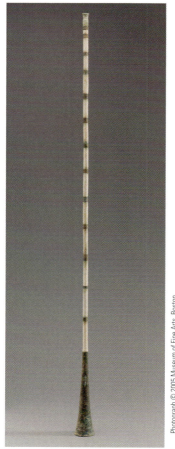

FIGURE 2-1
Roman *tuba*, preserved in the Instrument Collection of the Museum of Fine Arts, Boston.

contests. These same writers mention musical instruments, but the instruments they name are mainly those already played by the Greeks. The Romans in their turn adopted the simple wood flute, the lyre, the kithara, and the aulos, which they named the **tibia,** perhaps because of its bone-like appearance. In only one respect did the Romans exhibit what might be called a distinctly Roman musical instrument, and that was the trumpet.

Almost all writers, Greek and Roman, attribute the origin of the trumpet to the Etruscans, distant forebears of the Romans who lived in northern Italy nearly a thousand years before Christ. The Roman name for the trumpet was **tuba.** Images embedded in sculpture and pottery show that the *tuba* was a long, straight instrument with a cylindrical bore and a bell at the end. Writers say that it was made of bronze and iron, and was played with a bone mouthpiece (Fig. 2-1). Like the later straight-pipe trumpet of the Middle Ages, the *tuba* could play the fundamental pitch of its pipe as well as the harmonic series above it, depending on the capabilities of the player. The *tuba* served, among other things, to signal commands during battle, for its sound was said by various writers to be booming, roaring, loud, and clear. Given the military might of the Romans, it is not surprising that their principal contribution to music history was an instrument of war. From it developed the trumpet and, ultimately, beginning in the fourteenth century, the trombone.

As to music theory, here again the Romans owed a heavy debt to the Greeks. As much as 95 percent of what appears in early theoretical writings in Latin was culled from even earlier Greek sources. Among the Roman theorists of note was Augustine of Hippo (354–430 C.E.), who became a Christian theologian and was later canonized as St. Augustine. His *De Musica* (*On Music*) is a six-book study of rhythm in music and poetry. Martianus Capella (flourished c435 C.E.), who, like Augustine, lived in a Roman colony in North Africa, set forth a framework of seven intellectual

Cambridge University Library

✻ FIGURE 2-2

Boethius and Pythagoras.
Boethius sets pitches with a
monochord while Pythagoras
measures them with bells.

disciplines called the **seven liberal arts.** The first three—grammar, logic, and
rhetoric—formed the **trivium;** these deal with language, logic, and oratory. The
final four—arithmetic, geometry, astronomy, and music—constituted the **quadrivium;** they are scientific disciplines, for each uses number and quantitative reasoning
to arrive at the truth. Henceforth, and throughout the Middle Ages, music would
be classified among the sciences, not the language arts. Eventually, the "liberal arts"
were taken to mean subjects of study that free the mind for critical thinking rather
than prepare it for a particular trade or profession. The term is still used in this sense
within colleges and universities today.

No Roman music theorist was more important, and certainly none more dependent on Greek models, than Anicius Manlius Severinus Boethius (Fig. 2-2). **Boethius**
(c480–524 C.E.) was a descendent of an aristocratic family of Roman senators. His
birth came a few short years after barbarian Goths from north of the Alps swept
down and seized Rome in 476 C.E., thereby putting an end to the Roman Empire.
Eventually, Boethius became a minister in the government of the new Gothic king
Theodoric. But in 523 he was accused of treason and imprisoned; he was executed
the following year. In his short life Boethius wrote, among other works, a treatise on
each of the four disciplines within the quadrivium. His *Fundamentals of Arithmetic*
was adopted as the standard text for the study of mathematics throughout the
Middle Ages, and his *De institutione musica* (**Fundamentals of Music**) became the
required school text for music theory. When universities were formed in twelfth-
century Europe, the *Fundamentals of Music* became the established music text for
the liberal arts curriculum, and it remained so into the eighteenth century at the
universities of Oxford and Cambridge.

Boethius spoke and read Greek fluently. He read great amounts of Greek music
theory and translated it into his native Latin tongue. More than any other writer,
Boethius served as a conduit through which the great treasury of ancient Greek
music theory passed to medieval Europe. Specifically, he reaffirmed three important
tenets of Greek music theory. First, he reemphasized that music was a science and
that numerical ratios determine the pitches of the scale, melodic intervals, and consonances and dissonances. Second, by drawing from Plato and others, he posited
that the entire universe resonated with music. These harmonies, Boethius said,
could be divided into three general types: *musica mundana* (music of the spheres),
musica humana (music of the human body), and *musica instrumentalis* (earthly
vocal and instrumental music). Cosmic music (*musica mundana*) was the true music,
while earthly music (*musica instrumentalis*) was a poor approximation of these divine and unchanging proportions. Finally, Boethius set forth a distinction between
the *musicus* and the *cantor*—the musicologist who studies and understands music
as distinguished from the practitioner who performs it. All three of these concepts
were held dear by writers on music throughout the Middle Ages. Preserved today in
137 medieval manuscripts, Boethius' *Fundamentals of Music* remained the single
most influential work on the discipline of music for more than a thousand years.

✿ JERUSALEM AND THE RISE
OF EARLY CHRISTIAN MUSIC

Christ was a Jew, and so were his early followers. Thus it is not surprising that the
liturgy of the Christian Church had elements in common with the liturgical rites of
the Jewish Temple in Jerusalem. **Liturgy** is the collection of prayers, chants, readings, and ritual acts by which the theology of the church, or any organized religion,

is practiced. **Chant,** generally speaking, is the monophonic religious music that is sung in a house of worship. The first liturgical service to grow within the emerging Christian Church in Jerusalem was the commemoration of the Last Supper, a common evening meal shared in small groups around the city. A leader, serving as a priest, partook of the blood of Christ in the form of wine, and the faithful partook of the body in the form of bread. During this religious meal, worshipers prayed, sang psalms, and read passages of scripture, rituals also practiced in the Jewish Temple. But the early Christian Church did not derive its music directly from the Temple of Jerusalem. While the liturgies of the two religions arose from common elements (prayers, scripture-reading, and psalm-singing), the music of Jews and Christians developed along quite different lines. The issue is complicated by the fact that no music, Christian or Jewish, survives in written form from that period. Indeed, no written Jewish music with exact pitch notation survives at all much before 1700 C.E. Jewish music was passed along mainly by oral tradition. So, too, was Christian music for the first eight hundred years of its existence.

The service of the early Christians was very informal, with no fixed order of events. St. Paul suggests as much when he writes to the Corinthians (1 Cor. 14: 26–7): "When ye come together, every one of you hath a psalm, hath a doctrine, hath a tongue, hath a revelation, hath an interpretation." Early Christian liturgical texts, when written down, were primarily compiled in Greek, the universal learned language of the East. Much of the music must have been improvised or performed as the occasion demanded. What can be said with certainty is that, by the fourth century, faithful Christians gathered for services of prayer several times during the day. Singing at these services was led by a **cantor,** a person specially trained to lead the music of the community.

Not all Christians were in the city of Jerusalem, or any other city for that matter. As early as the third century a few particularly devout souls detached themselves from urban centers and went out to live as hermits in the desert, notably throughout Egypt and Syria. Some formed communities of monks and nuns whose chief liturgical activity was the recitation of the entire Book of Psalms. In the rituals of these desert hermits can be found the seeds of monasticism in the European Middle Ages.

The wanderings of hermits in the deserts of Egypt and Syria signified that Christianity was on the move, both west and east. Soon a Christian Church appeared in Alexandria, Egypt, that was called the Coptic Church. It developed its own liturgy and its own music, called Coptic chant. **Coptic chant,** the music of the Christian Church of Egypt, still exists today, passed along for nearly two thousand years entirely by oral tradition. Equally important, the liturgy of Jerusalem spread to the city of Byzantium (later Constantinople, and now Istanbul, Turkey). In 395 C.E. the aging Roman Empire was divided into two parts. Rome served as capital of the West and Byzantium of the East. A patriarch (the counterpart of the Roman pope) ruled over the Byzantine Church. This church, too, developed its own liturgy and a special dialect of chant called **Byzantine chant.** Unlike Coptic chant, Byzantine chant eventually came to be notated, and a body of music theory emerged to explain it. The chants of the Byzantine rite were organized into eight church modes, a practice later to be adopted by the Roman Church. Today's Eastern (Greek) Orthodox Church, as well as the Russian Orthodox Church, are institutions descended from the Byzantine Church.

Because the Apostles Peter and Paul were sent to preach in Italy, the Christian message arrived in Rome not long after the death of Christ. Here too the Church developed its own particular forms of devotion, in part because the persecuted Christians worshiped in secret. The style of liturgical singing in the early churches of Rome, today simply called **Roman chant,** was also passed along for centuries in

Cathedral de Leon, Spain

❀ FIGURE 2-3

An early example of Mozarabic chant coming from the cathedral of Leon, Spain. Although the music is for the feast of St. Aciscius, the pitches cannot be read with precision.

oral, but not written, form. Roman chant was the principal source from which Gregorian chant later would emerge.

In 312 C.E. the Roman Emperor Constantine converted to Christianity and the persecution of Christians in Rome ceased. If Christianity was not declared the official religion of the Empire, at least now it might compete on an equal footing with the older pagan gods. Historians estimate that in 300 C.E. only 10 percent of the populace of the Roman Empire was Christian; by 400 C.E. the number had risen to approximately 50 percent. Soon other independent Christian churches appeared in the West. By the late fourth century, Ambrose (340?–397 C.E.) established a separate church and liturgy in Milan in northern Italy. Here **Ambrosian chant** was sung, named in honor of the church's patron. Ambrose himself wrote a number of hymns that survive today. Surprisingly, the Ambrosian rite did not embrace the liturgical practices of nearby Rome, but drew upon those with origins in Jerusalem and elsewhere in the East.

So, too, pilgrims to the Holy Lands, both male and female, carried back to Spain some of the liturgical practices of Jerusalem. In 711 C.E. the Arab Moslems invaded Spain, but they did not entirely stamp out the old Christian music there, called **Mozarabic chant** (the word "Mozarabic" refers to Christians living under Moslem rule). Mozarabic chant survives today in more than twenty manuscripts dating from the ninth through the fourteenth centuries (Fig. 2-3). Unfortunately, it is nearly impossible to transcribe or perform Mozarabic chant because the notation does not specify clearly the distance between pitches.

Uncertainty also surrounds the Gallican chant sung north of the Alps in the early Middle Ages. **Gallican chant** is the Christian music of early-medieval Gaul, which roughly comprised modern-day France and parts of Switzerland. Gallican chant is believed to have been mostly improvised. When Charlemagne imported Roman chant into Gaul around 800 C.E. (see Chapter 3), the indigenous Gallican chant was almost entirely suppressed. At least fifty chants, however, survive today, having been copied down in later books of Gregorian chant. When compared to chants of other Western liturgies of this time, Gallican chant generally appears longer, more flowery, and more exuberant. A fine example of Gallican chant, one with great sweep and grandeur, is the Offertory of the Mass *Collegerunt pontifices* (*The Pontiffs Gathered*; Ex. 2-1). Gallican chant is important in the history of music because it played a primary role in the formation of Gregorian chant. During the ninth and tenth centuries, chant coming north from Rome mixed with the local Gallican chant to create Gregorian chant, the largest body of religious music ever created.

EXAMPLE 2-1

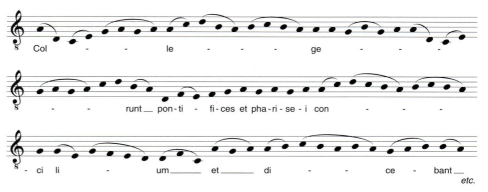

The pontiffs and pharisees gathered in council and said:

SUMMARY

Compared to the Greeks, the Romans made little contribution to the history of Western music. Roman music theory was essentially an elaboration and clarification of earlier Greek music theory. The *tuba*, a long straight-pipe military trumpet, seems to have been the only musical instrument created by the Romans.

The early Christian church had two centers: Jerusalem in the East, and Rome in the West. All of the music of the early Christian church was unwritten; it was in some measure improvised and largely communicated orally from one musician to the next. After 395 C.E., Byzantium gradually replaced Jerusalem as the center of the Eastern Church. The chant of the Byzantine Church, as well as Coptic chant, Ambrosian chant, and Mozarabic chant, had ties to the liturgical traditions of Jerusalem. Rome developed its own liturgy and music, called simply Roman chant. Gaul, the area north of the Alps, was Christianized by missionaries coming from Rome. Historically, the chant of that region, called Gallican chant, had strong ties to Rome. Later, in the eighth, ninth, and tenth centuries, Roman chant and Gallican chant would form a new dialect of chant called Gregorian chant.

KEY TERMS

tibia	*musica mundana*	Coptic chant
tuba	*musica humana*	Byzantine chant
seven liberal arts	*musica instrumentalis*	Roman chant
trivium	*musicus*	Ambrosian chant
quadrivium	*cantor*	Mozarabic chant
Boethius	liturgy	Gallican chant
Fundamentals of Music	chant	

Chapter

3

Music in the Monastery and Convent

When the Roman Empire fell to barbarian invaders around 476 C.E., the centers of civilization—the cities—began to disintegrate. Rome itself, which had a population of more than a million around the time of Caesar, had shrunk by the sixth century to fewer than a hundred thousand souls. Some devout Christians retreated to the countryside, where they set up centers of learning and worship called monasteries. In the Middle Ages a religious man living by himself was referred to by the Latin word **monachus** (a solitary person), and a woman as a **monacha**—today we would call them a monk and a nun. Their dwelling, too, was a solitary place, a monastery. In fact, monks and nuns did not live alone but in separate communities, separated by sex, ranging from a dozen like-minded souls to, sometimes, more than a hundred. Of course, there had been monks in the East shortly after the time of the Apostles, but they were few and far between, isolated hermits scattered about the deserts of Egypt, Palestine, and Syria. Now, during the sixth century, monasteries appeared everywhere on the Italian peninsula (Map 3-1). Soon missionaries went out from

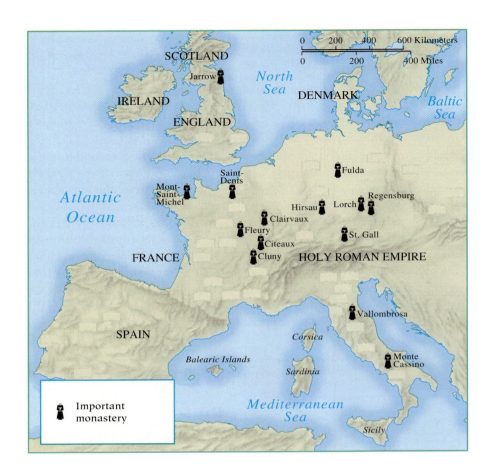

🌀 MAP 3-1

Important European monasteries
established before 1200.

Italy to establish new communities in Ireland and England, and from there other missionaries brought monasticism back to France, Germany, and Switzerland.

The force behind the monastic movement was Benedict of Nursia (c480–c550 C.E.), a Roman aristocrat who decided to exchange wealth for a life of religious poverty in the mountains south of Rome. About 530 C.E. Benedict compiled what is called the **Rule of St. Benedict,** a code of conduct to regulate daily life in a monastic community. It applied equally to both men and women. Those following the Rule of St. Benedict belonged to the Benedictine Order, and the founder's rule dictated their daily life.

Life in a rural monastery was not easy. Monks or nuns were required to profess vows of chastity, poverty, and obedience (obedience to the abbot or abbess in charge of the monastery or convent). The Benedictines spent most of the day in silence. They worked the land to feed their bodies, and prayed and chanted to save their souls. They were not so much interested in helping others as in personal salvation. Their life's goal was to overcome the sins of this world so as to enjoy eternal bliss in the next. If their vision of the world proved correct, they would rise among the elect on the Day of Judgment and sit everlasting with their Lord.

🌸 THE MONASTERY OF ST. GALL, SWITZERLAND

Of all the monasteries in the West, the most important for music is the Benedictine house of St. Gall, Switzerland (see Map 3-1). Certainly there are more early-music manuscripts preserved from St. Gall than from any other monastery. St. Gall was founded around 612 C.E. by an Irishman named Gallus, who arrived in the company of other Irish monastic missionaries to the Continent. In the northern foothills to the Alps, in what is now Switzerland, Gallus erected a simple wooden house of prayer and soon began to gather disciples around him. By 750 C.E. the number of monks at St. Gall had reached 53. About this time, these religious men constructed a **scriptorium** (writing room) for the production of books, some from which to study and others from which to sing. All books were, of course, copied by hand and some were beautifully illuminated with pictures (Fig. 3-1). About 850 C.E. the monks of St. Gall commissioned a drawing for an enlarged version of their monastery. From it we can reconstruct the **cloister,** the area around which the monks lived (Fig. 3-2).

As with other monasteries, St. Gall served as a center of learning. The Bible, of course, was copied and studied, but so were the writings of the great theologians, as well as Roman writers such as Virgil and Horace. Indeed, there were no universities or colleges in Western Europe at this time. We owe our knowledge of church music prior to 1000 C.E., as well as the preservation of the great works of Roman literature, to monasteries such as St. Gall.

Stiftsbibliothek St. Gallen

✻ THE CANONICAL HOURS: THE WORK OF THE LORD

At the heart of monastic life were the canonical hours, so-called because they were prescribed by the Rule of St. Benedict (the Latin word for rule is "canon"). The **canonical hours** (also called the **liturgical offices**) were a set of eight periods of worship occurring throughout the day. During these times the monks or nuns would cease their work and gather in the church for prayer, reading of scripture, and singing. The Rule of St. Benedict refers to these services as the "work of the lord" **(opus dei)** because they required as much or more attention and effort than physical labor. In reality, the exact times for manual work and for the celebration of the canonical hours varied from church to church and season to season. Following is a reconstruction of the daily activities at a typical monastery during the summer months.

❀ FIGURE 3-1

Early twelfth-century St. Gall manuscript showing the monk Luitherus presenting a book of chant to St. Gallus. Above them are early chant neumes, many different Alleluias for the Virgin Mary for use at different Masses.

Summer Schedule for a Benedictine Monastery

2 a.m.	Office of Matins in the church (about one hour), then back to bed
6 a.m.	Offices of Lauds in the church, followed by breakfast in the refectory
7 a.m.	Office of Prime in the church (about a half-hour) Business meeting of the monks in the chapter house Work or study
9 a.m.	Office of Terce in the church, followed by High Mass Work or study
12 noon	Office of Sext in the church, followed by main meal of the day Short nap or silent reading
3 p.m.	Office of Nones in the church (about a half-hour) Work or study
5 p.m.	Office of Vespers in the church (about a half-hour) Work or study
6 p.m.	Abbot's speech to the monks, followed by supper Period of conversation
7 p.m.	Office of Compline in the church (about half-hour) To bed (later in summer than winter)

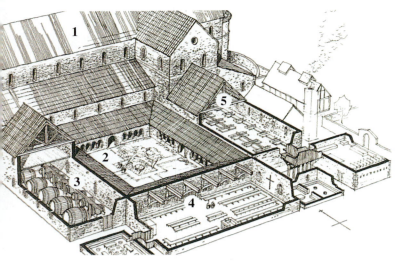

✻ FIGURE 3-2

Reconstruction of the monastery of St. Gall, showing the cloister (2), the cellar for wine and beer (3), the dining hall or refectory (4), and the dormitory (5). Adjacent to the church (1) were the scriptorium, where chant books were created, and the library, where books were stored and consulted.

Thus the canonical hours, along with the High Mass of the day, provided the framework for life in the monastery. Some hours were longer and more important than others. The night office of **Matins,** for example, required much singing, and on high feasts such as Christmas or Easter, might go on for four hours. Other services, such as Prime and Nones, were brief, involving little more than singing a few psalms and a hymn. Of the eight canonical hours, the late-afternoon service of **Vespers** is the most important for the history of music. As we shall see, Vespers involved singing, not only psalms and a hymn but also the Magnificat, a text that would remain a favorite with composers throughout the history of music. The liturgical day ended with the office of Compline, which usually concluded with a chant in honor of the Virgin Mary.

Taken altogether, medieval monastic life was an unceasing cycle of manual labor in the fields and spiritual labor before God in the church. Its unbending monotony challenged even the most devout of souls. Thus it was in the Middle Ages, and thus it is still today, in those few monastic communities around the world that continue to follow the rule of St. Benedict.

✾ GREGORIAN CHANT IN THE MONASTERY

The music sung daily at the eight canonical hours of prayer and at Mass was what we today call **Gregorian chant** (also, **plainsong**). Gregorian chant is a vast body of monophonic religious music setting Latin texts and intended for use in the Roman Catholic Church. Plainsong is entirely monophonic music sung in unison, and almost always without the accompaniment of instruments. It was composed over the course of fifteen hundred years—from the time of the Apostles to that of the Council of Trent (1545–1563), a conclave that brought sweeping reforms to the Church. Although Gregorian chant is named in honor of Pope Gregory the Great (c540–604), ironically, Gregory wrote little if any of this music. Pope Gregory was more a church administrator than a musician, and he merely decreed that certain chants should be sung on certain days of the liturgical year. Gregorian chant remained the official music of the Roman Catholic Church until the Second Vatican Council (1962–1965), when it lost its privileged status. Today plainsong is sung daily in only a few churches and monasteries. Yet because of its extraordinary beauty, Gregorian chant continues to be an object of great interest to historians and musicians alike.

Most Gregorian chant was created during the early years of the **Holy Roman Empire.** In 800 C.E. the Frankish warrior-king **Charlemagne** (742–814 C.E.) marched to Rome and had himself crowned emperor by Pope Leo III, thereby becoming the first Holy Roman Emperor. His aim was to resuscitate the western half of the old Roman Empire but to have it "holy"— under Christianity, not paganism as it had been in Caesar's day. To bring stability and political uniformity to his vast territories, Charlemagne mandated that the chant and liturgical traditions of the Church of Rome be imposed on all his lands, including those north of the Alps. Thus, religious music originating in Italy was carried north by Roman singers and, in the course of time, mixed with the local Gallican traditions. In addition, many new chants were composed in northern monasteries during this period. During the ninth century, plainsong first came to be called Gregorian chant, apparently to suggest that it enjoyed the ancient authority of the papacy.

In sum, the core of what we still call Gregorian chant was created north of the Alps during the ninth and tenth centuries, and it was an amalgam of Italian, French, and German religious music. During the next hundred years, the newly refurbished and enlarged repertory was carried back to Italy, and to Spain and England as well. On any given day, monks in central Italy, for example, would sing the same chants, in more or less the same way, as those in southern England or northern Germany. Although the Holy Roman Empire soon lost its political cohesion, the liturgy and music of the church continued to provide a common cultural thread throughout the entire Middle Ages. Indeed, Gregorian chant provided the West with its first international musical repertory.

GREGORIAN CHANT FOR VESPERS

Why sing? The purpose of singing in the monastery was for the entire community to offer praises to God in a heartfelt, joyful way. Each monk or nun gave voice to the communal song; they sang as if with one voice in a unison chorus. Above all, chanting in the monastery involved singing the **Psalter,** the book of one hundred fifty psalms found in the Old Testament—that portion of the Bible mainly compiled by Jewish teachers before Christ's ministry on earth. According to the Rule of St. Benedict, all one hundred fifty psalms had to be rendered to God each week, ninety at Matins, thirty at Vespers, and so forth. The act or process of singing the psalms is called **psalmody.** Because Vespers was the canonical hour to have the greatest impact on later Catholic and Protestant church music, the psalmody of Vespers will serve as an example for all eight canonical hours.

When the monks or nuns entered the church for Vespers, they said and sang a small number of preliminary chants and prayers. But the bulk of the service consisted of singing four psalms on Sunday, another four on Monday, another four on Tuesday, and so on. After the psalms came a hymn appropriate for the season and, finally, the Magnificat. The clergy were divided and placed on benches or choir stalls on either side of the church. Everyone was required to sing, no matter how poor the voice. A **cantor** (chief musician) sat with one of the two groups and led the singing. He began the psalm so as to give the pitch to the full monastic community and his side of the aisle completed the first verse—each psalm has many verses. The second psalm verse was sung by the other side of the choir, and so on. Such a method of musical performance, in which a divided choir alternately sings back and forth, is called **antiphonal singing.** Once all the verses of a psalm had been sung antiphonally, a two-verse **doxology** ("Gloria Patri," a standard formula of praise to the Holy Trinity) was added at the end. But there is more to psalmody. The entire psalm and its doxology were surrounded by another chant. That is to say, a short chant specific to the day came before the psalm and was repeated after it. Because that short chant began and concluded the antiphonal singing of the psalm, it came to be called an **antiphon.** The following shows the process of singing just one psalm.

> Antiphon (begun by the cantor and completed by all)
> Verse 1: begun by the cantor and completed by his side of the choir
> Verse 2: sung by the opposite side of the choir

Verse 3: sung by the cantor's side of the choir
Verse 4: sung by the opposite side of the choir
etc. through the remaining verses
Doxology: first verse sung by one side of the choir
second verse sung by the opposite side of the choir
Antiphon (sung by all)

Psalms were chanted to very simple repeating patterns, rather than elaborate melodies. These simple recitation formulas are called the **psalm tones.** Each psalm tone begins with an intonation sung by the cantor, continues with a recitation on a single pitch followed by a pause (mediation), and, after more recitation on the recit- ing tone, concludes with a termination. The mediation helps separate the two units of syntax of each verse, and gives the singers a chance to breathe. Example 3-1 shows the parts of a psalm tone in diagrammatic form.

EXAMPLE 3-1

After the first verse, each successive verse is sung in the same fashion, except that the intonation is not repeated. Because each psalm had as few as a half-dozen verses or as many as twenty, the amount of time needed to sing a psalm varied con- siderably. The first psalm sung each Sunday at Vespers, Psalm 109 *Dixit Dominus* (My *Lord said unto me*) requires about four minutes. The Rule of St. Benedict stipu- lates that four psalms should be sung in this fashion, each with its antiphon, at every Vespers service. The antiphon-psalm-antiphon unit was the bedrock of this and every canonical hour.

Following the singing of four psalms at Vespers, all the monks chanted a hymn. In the Middle Ages, as now, a **hymn** was a relatively short chant with a small num- ber of phrases, often four, and a rather narrow vocal range (Ex. 3-2). One melody served for as many as five or six stanzas of text, as is true for the Christmas hymn *Jesu, Redemptor omnium* (*Jesus, Redeemer of All*). Like the psalms, the hymn was sung antiphonally, each side of the choral community taking a stanza in turn.

EXAMPLE 3-2

Jesus, redeemer of the world, who was the light before the beginning...

Finally, the office of Vespers concluded with the singing of the **Magnificat,** the culmination of the service. The Magnificat is a **canticle,** a particularly lyrical and memorable passage of scripture usually drawn from the New Testament of the Bible. The Magnificat is the canticle of Mary, and it comes from the Gospel of St. Luke (1: 46–55), in which Mary joyfully responds to the news that she will bear the son of God ("My soul doth magnify [*magnificat*] the Lord"). The Magnificat is sung much like a psalm, except that its recitation pattern is slightly more ornate than that of a psalm tone (Ex. 3-3). The particularly beautiful quality of the text, and its emphasis on Mary, has endeared the Magnificat to church composers, including Monteverdi, Bach, and Mozart.

EXAMPLE 3-3

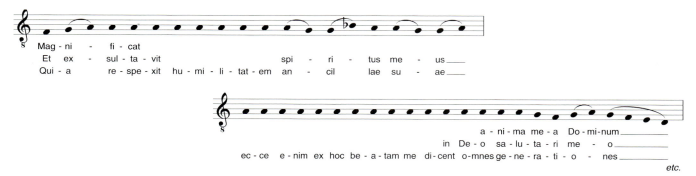

Mag - ni - fi - cat
Et ex - sul - ta - vit   spi - ri - tus me - us____
Qui - a   re - spe - xit hu - mi - li - tat - em an - cil   lae su - ae____

a - ni - ma me - a Do - mi - num_____
in De - o sa - lu - ta - ri me - o_____
ec - ce e - nim ex hoc be - a - tam me di - cent o - mnes ge - ne - ra - ti - o - nes_____

etc.

My soul magnifies the Lord and my spirit rejoices in God my Savior, for he has regarded the low estate of his handmaiden. For behold, henceforth all generations will call me blessed.

The following is a summary of the important parts of the canonical hour of Vespers.

> Brief introductory prayers and petitions:
> Antiphon-Psalm-Doxology-Antiphon
> Antiphon-Psalm-Doxology-Antiphon
> Antiphon-Psalm-Doxology-Antiphon
> Antiphon-Psalm-Doxology-Antiphon
> Hymn
> Antiphon-Magnificat-Doxology-Antiphon

Vespers was, and is, sung each day in the evening at Benedictine monasteries around the world (Fig. 3-3).

❊ FIGURE 3-3

Nuns of the Benedictine convent of Regina Laudis, in Bethlehem, Connecticut, singing chant.

Abbey of Regina Laudis Archives

LISTENING CUE

CHANTS OF VESPERS
Antiphon, *Tecum principium*
Psalm, *Dixit Dominus*
Hymn, *Jesu, Redemptor omnium*

CD 1/3–4
Anthology, Nos. 3, 4

❊ GREGORIAN CHANT FOR THE MASS

The central and most important religious service each day in the monastery was the **Mass.** The term comes from the final dismissal of the service: "Go, [the congregation] is dismissed" ("Ite, missa est"). The high point of the Mass is the sacrament of the Eucharist (taking communion). Before, during, and after the ritual of the Eucharist, chants are sung, scripture read, and prayers said. The chants are of two sorts, Proper and Ordinary. The **Proper of the Mass** consists of chants whose texts change each day to suit the religious theme, or to honor a particular saint on just that one day. The **Ordinary of the Mass,** on the other hand, includes chants with unvarying texts, and these can be sung almost every day of the year. All Masses include Ordinary and Proper chants. Later, from the late Middle Ages onward, when a composer such as Dufay, Mozart, or Beethoven sat down to write a polyphonic Mass, he set only the Ordinary chants. Setting just the Ordinary allowed the choir to perform the polyphonic Mass more than on just one day each year. The Mass, of course, was not created all at once by any single church father or theologian. Rather, parts were added to it gradually over a period of roughly eight hundred years, from the time of the Apostles until after the reign of Charlemagne (d. 814 C.E.). The following shows the standard parts of the Mass.

Proper of the Mass	Ordinary of the Mass
Introit (an introductory chant for the entrance of the celebrating clergy)	
	Kyrie (a petition, in Greek, for mercy)
	Gloria (a hymn of praise to the Lord)
(reading of the Epistle)	
Gradual (a reflective chant)	
Alleluia or **Tract** (a chant of thanksgiving or penance)	
Sequence (a chant commenting on the text of the Alleluia)	
(reading of the Gospel)	
	Credo (a profession of faith)
Offertory (a chant for the offering before the ritual of communion)	
	Sanctus (an acclamation to the Lord)
	Agnus dei (a petition for mercy and eternal peace)
Communion (the chant accompanying communion)	
	Ite, missa est (short dismissal)

Every Mass begins with the singing of an **Introit,** a chant that accompanies the entry of the priests and abbot or bishop into the church and up to the high altar. Notice that singing an Introit is much like singing a psalm. The Introit for Mass on Christmas Day, *Puer natus est nobis* (*A boy is born to us*), begins with an antiphon intoned by the cantor and completed by the full choir (Ex. 3-4). Next comes, not a full psalm but a single verse of a psalm, then the doxology, and finally the antiphon is repeated by the choir in full. Thus, singing an Introit is a kind of abbreviated psalmody: instead of singing many verses of a psalm, the choir chants only one. The psalm verse of the Introit, beginning "Cantate Domino cantium novum" ("Sing to the Lord a new song"), is an example of what is called **syllabic chant**—there is usually only one note for each syllable of text. The antiphon of the Introit provides an example of **neumatic chant**—there are often three, four, or five notes for each syllable of text. The *Kyrie* that follows the Introit in the Mass has many notes per syllable and exemplifies **melismatic chant** (a **melisma** is a lengthy vocal phrase setting a single syllable). Generally speaking, the more important services (Matins, Vespers, and the Mass) have the most melismatic chants.

EXAMPLE 3-4

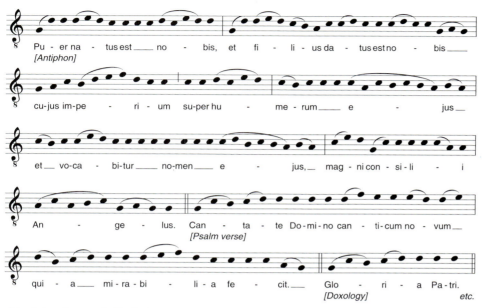

Pu - er na - tus est __ no - bis, et fi - li - us da - tus est no - bis __
[Antiphon]

cu-jus im-pe - ri - um su-per hu - me - rum __ e - jus __

et __ vo-ca - bi-tur __ no-men __ e - jus, mag - ni con - si - li - i

An - ge - lus. Can - ta - te Do-mi-no can - ti-cum no - vum __
[Psalm verse]

qui - a __ mi-ra-bi - li-a fe - cit. __ Glo - ri - a Pa-tri.
[Doxology] etc.

A boy is born to us, and a Son is given to us; whose government is upon His shoulder;
and His name shall be called the Angel of great counsel. Sing ye to the Lord a new song,
because He hath done wonderful things. Glory be to the Father… [A boy is born to us…]

The **Kyrie** of the Mass, an ancient Greek text, is the only portion of the Mass not sung in Latin. Here the congregation petitions the Lord for his mercy and does so in threefold exclamations:

> "Kyrie eleison" ("Lord have mercy upon us") three times
>
> "Christe eleison" ("Christ have mercy upon us") three times
>
> "Kyrie eleison" ("Lord have mercy upon us") three times

The musical structure of the *Kyrie* often mirrors this tripartite arrangement. In the *Kyrie* for the Christmas Mass (Anthology, No. 6), each musical phrase is to be sung three times, as indicated by the symbol "iij."

For both the *Gloria* and *Credo*, the full choir sings from beginning to end, once a soloist has set the pitch. The **Gloria** (Anthology, No. 7) is a hymn of praise going back to early Christian times, while the **Credo** is a profession of faith formulated as the result of the Council of Nicaea in 325. Both are lengthy chants because they set long texts, yet the *Gloria* is more neumatic than the highly syllabic *Credo*. The text of the *Gloria* was sung to any one of approximately fifty melodies during the Middle Ages, while the *Credo* was usually chanted to just one, the widely known melody given below.

EXAMPLE 3-5

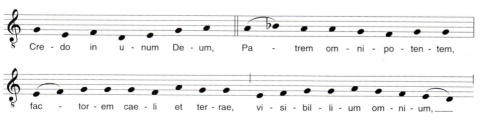

Cre - do in u - num De - um, Pa - trem om - ni - po - ten - tem,

fac - tor - em cae - li et ter - rae, vi - si - bil - li - um om - ni - um, __

(Continued on next page)

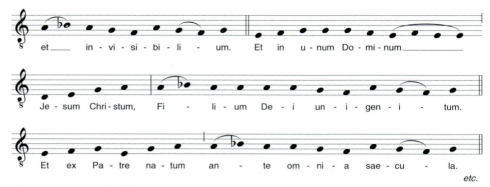

I believe in one God, the father almighty, maker of heaven and earth, and of all things visible and invisible. And in one Lord Jesus Christ, the only begotten Son of God, begotten of the Father before all worlds…

Placed between the *Gloria* and *Credo* are two chants of unusual length and breadth, the Gradual and the Alleluia. The **Gradual** is so-called because it was originally sung from an elevated position, a step (Latin "gradus") in the choir area of the church. The Gradual consists of two parts: an antiphon and a psalm verse. But because the psalm verse is not sung by the chorus antiphonally, the opening chant is not called an antiphon. Instead, it is called a **respond;** the full chorus prefaces and responds to the psalm verse, which is sung by a soloist. Accordingly, the Gradual exemplifies **responsorial singing** (choral respond, solo verse, choral respond). The Gradual *Viderunt omnes fines terrae* (*All the ends of the earth have seen;* Anthology, No. 8) exhibits the sweeping range of many graduals. All Graduals are melismatic chants. Notice, for example, the fifty-two-note melisma on the syllable "Do" of the word "Dominus" (Ex. 3.6). Here in the verse, standing high for all to see, the soloist is able to "showcase" his virtuosic skills as he literally sings praise to the Lord (which is what "Dominus" means in Latin). Following this elaborate solo, the full chorus is meant to repeat the respond, although not all monastic choirs do so today.

EXAMPLE 3-6

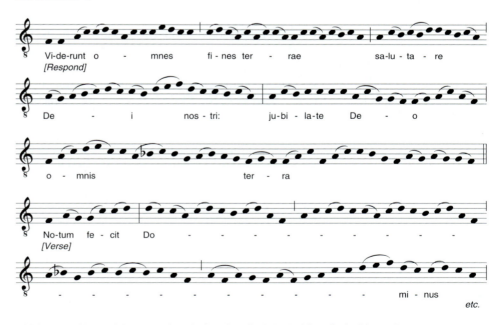

All the ends of the earth have seen the salvation of our God; sing joyfully to God, all the earth.
The Lord hath made known…

The **Alleluia,** of course, is a cry of joy (Hallelujah!). It, too, is a responsorial chant as well as a highly melismatic one. The most distinctive part of the Alleluia is a melisma on the final syllable "a" of "alleluia." It is called the **jubilus** because at this moment the full choir and community celebrates with jubilation the redemptive life of Christ. The verse of the Alleluia is sung by a soloist, as can be seen in *Alleluia. Dies sanctificatus* (*Alleluia. Day Sanctified*; Anthology, No. 9). To this the full chorus again responds with "Alleluia." Thus, the structure of the Alleluia is Alleluia-verse-Alleluia (respond-verse-respond). Finally, both the Gradual and the Alleluia are reflective chants during which there is no "action" in the service. Here all attention is turned to the singing of the sacred text, a fact that likely accounts for the greater length and elaborate, melismatic style.

Although the ritual of communion is theologically the high point of the Mass, the chants attending this rite are less melismatic than the preceding Gradual and Alleluia. The Offertory and Communion chants are now stand-alone antiphons, which, in the course of time, have been stripped of their psalm verses. The *Sanctus* and *Agnus dei* are rather similar in musical style to the *Kyrie*. Indeed, like the *Kyrie*, the *Agnus dei* is a threefold petition to the Lord. To conclude the Mass, the priest sings forth "Go, the congregation is dismissed," to which the community replies "Deo gratias" ("Thanks be to God").

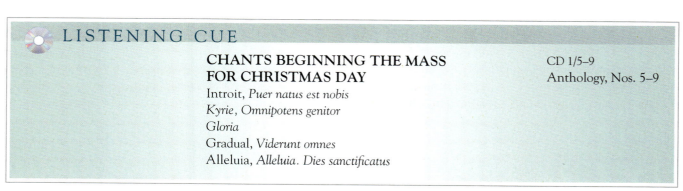

 LISTENING CUE

CHANTS BEGINNING THE MASS
FOR CHRISTMAS DAY

CD 1/5–9
Anthology, Nos. 5–9

Introit, *Puer natus est nobis*
Kyrie, *Omnipotens genitor*
Gloria
Gradual, *Viderunt omnes*
Alleluia, *Alleluia. Dies sanctificatus*

SUMMARY

Religious life in the West during early Middle Ages was centered in monasteries and convents. The Rule of St. Benedict regulated life within these communities, including the singing of Gregorian chant, or plainsong. Gregorian chant is a vast body of monophonic religious music consisting of thousands of melodies. The repertory was gradually assembled over the course of many hundreds of years by clerics of several different lands, primarily in Italy, Germany, Switzerland, and France. The music for the Western Latin Church assumed its virtually final shape within the confines of the Holy Roman Empire during and after the reign of Charlemagne (768–814 C.E.). Partly because of this long and diverse history, and partly because plainsong serves many functions within the liturgy, Gregorian chant has many diverse musical styles. Some chants are narrow in range and very syllabic (the psalm tones) and others are melismatic and involve a wide vocal range (the Graduals and Alleluias).

Despite the diversity of musical styles, there are several qualities common to all chants. All Gregorian chant is sung in unison (even if doubled at the octave by choirboys or female voices during those rare occasions when monks and nuns sang together). Chant tends to move stepwise, avoiding large leaps, so that the full community can easily participate in the singing. Chant is written without regular rhythms, and it has no meter (you can't tap your foot to it). Finally, chant does not try to convert the listener by overt musical gestures, as a Beethoven symphony might. On the contrary, when sung correctly, chant seems to float, spirit-like, through the air. Its aim is to create a quiet, nonconfrontational environment in which the faithful soul might experience a transcendental union with the divine. In the medieval world, chant was not to be enjoyed for itself, but to lead to God.

KEY TERMS

monachus	Psalter	Introit
monacha	psalmody	syllabic chant
Rule of St. Benedict	cantor	neumatic chant
scriptorium	antiphonal singing	melismatic chant
cloister	doxology	melisma
canonical hours (liturgical offices)	antiphon	*Kyrie*
	psalm tone	*Gloria*
opus dei	hymn	*Credo*
Matins	Magnificat	Gradual
Vespers	canticle	respond
Gregorian chant (plainsong)	Mass	responsorial singing
Holy Roman Empire	Proper of the Mass	Alleluia
Charlemagne	Ordinary of the Mass	jubilus

Chapter 4

Music Theory in the Monastery: John of St. Gall and Guido of Arezzo

Almost all educated musicians of the Middle Ages were churchmen or churchwomen, because the monasteries, and later the cathedrals, were the sole centers of learning. These church musicians borrowed greatly from ancient Greek music theory. Among other things, they adopted the Greek system of consonance and dissonance, a diatonic scale with the octave divided into seven pitches (five whole tones and two half-tones), and a musical vocabulary including words such as "chromatic" and "tetrachord." But the ancient Greeks were essentially interested in the science of the sound, not in the performance and analysis of music. Medieval musicians, on the other hand, looked upon music theory less as an arcane science, and more as a tool to aid in the daily singing of the canonical hours and Mass. Medieval monks needed a theory that could explain and facilitate their principal activity in life, singing praises of the Lord, the *opus dei* (the work of the Lord). They also needed a system to capture and preserve the music they sang. Perhaps because Charlemagne wanted the services of the church to be the same everywhere in the Empire, Carolingian clerics created a musical notation that allowed them to write down the plainsong of the church and send it from place to place.

 THE EIGHT CHURCH MODES

By the year 900 C.E. the repertory of Gregorian chant had grown to nearly 3,000 melodies. To keep track of all this music, church musicians first began to group chants by function within the liturgy and by category of melodic pattern—that is to say, by "mode." Every melody was placed in one of just eight melodic groups, or modes. To give these groups identity, theorists borrowed ethnic names from the ancient Greeks, names such as Dorian and Phrygian. The scale patterns to which these names were assigned, however, were entirely different from the patterns used by the Greeks. Moreover, initially different medieval theorists proposed different names or numbers for the modes. Around 1100 a monk from St. Gall, called **John of St. Gall** (also known as John Cotton), wrote a treatise entitled *De Musica (On Music)*. In it he set forth the eight church modes in a system with numbers to which were added Greek names, and these have remained in use for chant down to the present day. The modality of a melody—the scale-group in which it belonged—was determined by two factors: the range of the chant and its final note. John identifies the eight **church modes** as in Example 4-1.

EXAMPLE 4-1

Number	Name	Range	Final Pitch	Type
1	Dorian		D	authentic
2	Hypodorian		D	plagal
3	Phrygian		E	authentic
4	Hypophrygian		E	plagal
5	Lydian		F	authentic
6	Hypolydian		F	plagal
7	Mixolydian		G	authentic
8	Hypomixolydian		G	plagal

As can be seen, the eight church modes consist of four pairs: the Dorian, Phrygian, Lydian, and Mixolydian. The first mode within each pair is called the **authentic mode** and the second, the **plagal** (meaning "derived from") **mode**. The plagal modes are all a fourth below their authentic counterpart. (The prefix "hypo" in Greek means below, as in hypodermic needle—a needle that goes beneath the skin.) Yet, although the plagal modes are lower than the corresponding authentic ones, each pair has the same final. In simple terms, we have a regular-sounding Dorian mode and a lower-sounding one, for example. Although the range of each chant was in principle only an octave, in practice a melody might embrace one note on either side of that octave. Finally, it is worth remembering that there was no such thing as absolute pitch in the music of the Middle Ages. A choir director had the freedom to transpose any chant, no matter what its mode, into a range that was comfortable for the singers.

CHANT NOTATION

Musicians of the earliest Western church created chant without a system of written notation. Following certain formulas, cantors composed melodies in their heads to fit a given Latin text and then taught them orally to other clerics. But how might music be sent from place to place, or how might it be preserved for future monks and nuns, if the cantor were not present? The limitations of the oral tradition gradually encouraged the development of a system of written musical notation. In this development, however, the notational signs of the ancient Greeks proved to be useless; they were simply too numerous and complex. Indeed, by the year 900 Western musicians had abandoned Greek notation almost entirely. They were engaged in devising a new way to notate music. What they ultimately created—the staff, note heads, and letter names for the pitches—has remained the basis of Western musical notation down to the present.

During the Carolingian era (768–987), Western Europe was transformed from an almost entirely oral culture to one more grounded in written symbols. At first the musical monks simply wrote signs on parchment to indicate that the voice was to go up or down. (They may have been imitating the grammatical accents and punctuation marks found in Greek and Latin texts at this time.) The signs themselves were generally not higher or lower but, like modern texts' accents in French, for example, they suggested whether the voice should go up or down (acute = up, grave = down, circumflex = up-down). Often several pitches were contained within one sign. Signs for single pitches as well as for groups were called **neumes** (see Ex. 4-2). At the beginning, around 900 C.E., the neumes were just laid out on the parchment above the text, as a way of reminding the singer how a melody ought to be sung (see Fig. 3-1). The neumes suggested whether the music went up or down. But how far up or down?

MUSICAL STAFF AND PITCH NAMES

By 1000 C.E. musicians had begun to answer the question "how far up or down" by setting neumes on horizontal lines placed one on top of the other, signaling the beginning of our modern musical staff. In addition, the lines and spaces between were given letter names, starting with low A. Sometimes the horizontal lines indicating A, F, or C were color-coded to make pitch identification easier. At first there were only two lines, but by the twelfth century the number had grown to four. The neumes themselves were also changed so as to emphasize precise pitches and not the space between; curving lines were replaced by square note heads connected by lines. Sometimes the connecting lines were omitted. Simultaneously, theorists began to speak of a pitch sign not only as a neume (a collection of pitches) but also as a **nota**—a symbol on a line or space representing a single, precise pitch. Soon the notes came to be thought of in terms of the letters marking the lines and spaces (the note A or the note D). Example 4-2 shows the opening chant for the Mass of Christmas Day, the Introit *Puer natus est nobis* (*A boy is born to us*): (a) in early non-heightened neumes—the notes are all pretty much on the same horizontal plane—from St. Gall; (b) in later heightened neumes with a staff using a C clef from late-medieval England; (c) in modern chant neumes from a modern edition of plain-chant called the *Liber usualis*; and (d) transcribed into standard modern musical notation.

EXAMPLE 4-2

a.

Puer   natus   est   nobis,   et   filius   datus   est   nobis:

b.

Pu-er   na - tus   est   no   -   bis, et fi   -   li   us da - tus est no   -   bis:

c.

Pu-er   na - tus   est   no   -   bis,   et fi   -   li   us da - tus est no   -   bis:

d.

Pu - er na   tus est   no   -   bis,   et   fi   -   li - us da   -   tus est no   -   bis:

❋ FIGURE 4-1
Guido and his pupil Theodor picking out pitches on a monochord. Miniature from a twelfth-century manuscript.

The leader in the creation of the musical staff and note names was an Italian monk named **Guido of Arezzo** (c991–c1033; Fig. 4-1). In a music theory treatise called the **Micrologus** (*Little Essay*; c1030), Guido set forth all that a practicing church musician needed to know to sing the liturgy: the scale, intervals, church modes, how to transpose, and even a bit about singing simple polyphony. The *Micrologus* became, in today's terms, a bestseller, second only to Boethius' *Fundamentals of Music* as the most popular treatise on music in the Middle Ages. In another writing (a preface to a book of chant) Guido set forth his new system for a musical staff and note names. Guido was proud of his invention; now, he said, it no longer took days to teach novices a new chant orally (by rote memorization); instead, they could look at a chant written in chalk on a slate board or in ink on a piece of parchment and know what pitches to sing. Guido's invention—placing notes on a staff— had made it possible for musicians to sight sing!

❋ HEXACHORDS

But the musical staff and note names were not Guido's only contributions to music history. In the famous *Letter to Brother Michael*, Guido set forth the beginnings of a system that is today known as **solfege**—singing different pitches to the syllables "do, re, mi, fa, sol, la, ti, do." (From the middle syllables "sol" and "fa" comes the Italian "solfeggio," and from it the English "solfege.") Guido derived these syllables from lines of a Latin hymn to St. John the Baptist. Each phrase of the hymn began with a vowel and started on a successively higher degree of the scale (Ex. 4-3).

EXAMPLE 4-3

UT que-ant la - xis **RE**-so-na-re fi-bris **MI** - ra ge-sto - rum **FA**-mu-li tu-o - rum,

SOL - ve pol-lu-ti **LA**-bi-i re - a-tum, San - cte Jo - an-nes.

So that your servants may sing with all their voice the wonders of your deeds,
clean the guilt from our stained lips, O Saint John.

Thus the pitch C also became known as "ut," D as "re," E as "mi," and so forth. But why were solfege syllables needed? Why two names ("C" and "ut," for example) for each note?

Solfege syllables solve a problem inherent in the diatonic scale. In the eight church modes (and in our major and minor scales) some consecutive pitches are only half the distance apart compared to others (a half step as opposed to a whole step). To the vast throng of musically illiterate monks of the Middle Ages, this was a serious problem. If all notes looked equidistant, how did you know when to sing just half a step? By reducing the number of pitches from eight to just six, and by following a constant pattern of TTSTT (T = tone, S = semitone), Guido was able to isolate the semitone. The half step would always fall in the middle, between the syllables "mi" and "fa." Isolating the half step removed uncertainty from the minds of beginning singers as to the whereabouts of whole and half steps in the diatonic scale. All successive intervals were whole steps, except between "mi" and "fa." Guido then laid out these six-note units starting on the notes C, F, and G across the full diatonic scale. Guido's six-note pattern is a hexachord. In the course of time the hexachord placed on C was called the **natural hexachord**, the one set on F the **soft hexachord**, and the one on G the **hard hexachord**. The soft hexachord was so-called because it included a rounded symbol for "b" (whence our flat sign ♭), whereas the hard hexachord derived its name from the fact that it was signaled by a square natural sign ♮ for "b." The following example shows the diatonic scale (with both B♭ and B♮) as it was in Guido's day. Upon it the three hexachords are situated and repeated so as to cover the full range of the scale.

EXAMPLE 4-4

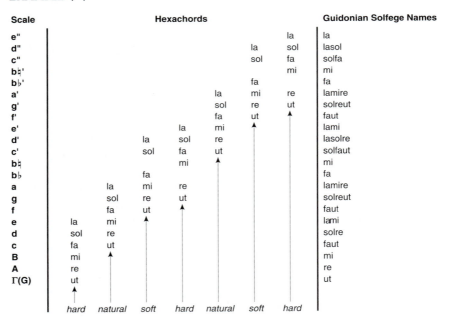

The Guidonian system of hexachords remained the standard framework for sight-singing Gregorian chant and later polyphony into the seventeenth century, at which time "ti" (or sometimes "si" or "pha") was added, and the rule of the hexachord gave way to that of the octave. By then singers had gradually learned to deal with two half-steps, and the octave replaced the hexachord as the basic unit of musical measurement.

✿ THE GUIDONIAN HAND

To facilitate sight-singing with hexachords, Guido added a further innovation, the **Guidonian hand** (Fig. 4-2). In truth, it is not certain whether Guido himself devised the musical hand or later theorists simply attributed its innovation to him—the medieval mind loved to ascribe many diverse inventions to a few male authority figures.

In the Middle Ages the human hand, usually the left hand, served as a mini-calculator on which a variety of computations might be performed. By pointing to the lines and joints of the left hand with the index finger of the right, a medieval monk or nun would be able to calculate the day on which Easter would fall the coming year, the sequence of the signs of the Zodiac, the number of days in each of the twelve months, the arrival of the next full moon, the letters of the alphabet (for those who were deaf), and, from the eleventh century onward, the notes of the scale. The left hand was thus the original Palm Pilot computer.

Biblioteca Ambrosiana, Milan

Example 4-5 demonstrates how the syllables of the Guidonian hexachords might be applied to a particular chant, in this case a *Kyrie* (given in full in the Anthology, No. 6). The melody begins in a range best sung in the hard hexachord. In the second phrase, however, it goes lower, and a new hexachord must be chosen, specifically the natural hexachord. On the opening pitch of the second phrase, for example, the singers would "mutate" hexachords, as it was called, the "re" of the hard hexachord giving way to the "la" of the natural.

EXAMPLE 4-5

hard: re re ut re fa mi re ut re   re
                    natural: la sol fa re mi   mi sol la re   mi sol fa mi fa re re

For musicians, the hand provided not only a mnemonic aid but also a portable musical staff that could be easily carried into rehearsals of the monastic choir. Each of the notes of the Guidonian scale, from low G to high E, was mentally inscribed on the hand. The choirmaster needed only point with the index finger to the spot on the hand, and the choir would know which pitch to sing. Before organs became widespread in church (the fourteenth century) and long before the advent of the piano, the hand provided, if not a keyboard, at least a "hand-board," for teaching music.

Why did the choirmaster need to point to his hand and not simply have the monks sing from books? Because there were no books, or at least very few books. In the Middle Ages a single volume of chant might take a year or more to copy (to say nothing of the lives of many sheep, which were necessary to make parchment, the basic writing material of the Middle Ages). In most monasteries and convents, usually only the cantor personally owned a music book. When music was written in a classroom, then as now, it was most often done with chalk on a small slate board. If the music teacher had a book, a voice, and a hand, that was sufficient to teach religious vocal music following Guido's new system.

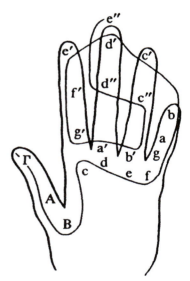

✿ FIGURE 4-2

(a) In this thirteenth-century Italian manuscript, a monk points at the joints of his hand to indicate musical pitches. (b) In modern times, the Guidonian hand may be represented like this.

SUMMARY

Memory and oral learning were enormously important in the ancient world and during the Middle Ages. The musicians of the early church composed plainsong without a system of written notation. Cantors created chants in their heads to fit a given Latin text and taught them orally to other clerics. Only after many centuries, around 900, was a system of notation devised for Western plainsong. Notation allowed for the production of chant books, and with these the repertory could be passed from one church to the next. A staff (horizontal lines) with pitches identified by letter names appeared in rudimentary form around 1000. By 1200 it consisted of four lines of what would later be called the F or bass clef. In order to organize the vast repertory of Gregorian chant, church melodies were grouped in one of the eight modes. To facilitate the learning of chant, a system of hexachords emerged, initiated by Guido of Arezzo. This made it easier for beginning musicians to sing up and down the diatonic scale by isolating the interval of a half-step ("mi" to "fa"). The hexachords were then superimposed on the hand so novices and musicians generally could more easily teach and learn new melodies. Most church music was taught literally "by hand" in the Middle Ages and not by reading from manuscripts. The Guidonian hand remained in use in some areas until the end of the seventeenth century.

KEY TERMS

John of St. Gall	nota	soft hexachord
church modes	Guido of Arezzo	hard hexachord
authentic mode	*Micrologus*	Guidonian hand
plagal mode	solfege	
neume	natural hexachord	

Chapter 5

Later Medieval Chant: Tropes, Sequences, and the Liturgical Drama of Hildegard of Bingen

By 1000 C.E. the liturgy and music of the Western Catholic Church had assumed a form it would retain for the next five hundred years and more. The various canonical hours, as well as the Proper and Ordinary of the Mass, were all firmly in place. Yet musicians continued to feel a need to express themselves. They did so by creating three new genres, or types, of chant: tropes, sequences, and liturgical dramas. Tropes and sequences were not sung every day, but only on about thirty high feasts of the church year. Liturgical dramas (church plays) were even less frequently inserted into the liturgy, usually only on a half-dozen important days around Christmas and Easter. These new chants did not change the basic shape of the services of the church. They simply made the musical portions of these services longer and more splendid.

 TROPES

A **trope** is an addition of music or text, or both, to a pre-existing chant. Musicians inserted tropes into the liturgy to elaborate upon the religious theme of an older, pre-existing chant, which remained unchanged. Most tropes were added to chants of the Proper of the Mass, especially the Introit. The new music and text might alternate with the old, or it might come entirely before it, and thereby serve as a musical preface. The trope *Hodie cantandus est nobis* (*Today we sing of a child*; Anthology, No. 10) introduces the Introit for Mass on Christmas morning. It was composed by **Tuotilo of St. Gall** (c850–915 C.E.) around the year 900. Tuotilo was a talented monk who has left us paintings, ivory carvings, and poetry, in addition to a collection of tropes for the high feasts of the church year. Elaborating on the meaning of the Christmas Introit, the trope *Hodie cantandus est nobis* proclaims that the Christ Child was born of a heavenly father and an earthly mother, his coming predicted long ago (Ex. 5-1). Thus tropes more fully explain the theology inherent in the chants to which they are added. As is typical of tropes, the musical style of *Hodie cantandus est nobis* is very similar to that of the Introit it introduces, *Puer natus est nobis* (*A boy is born to us*).

EXAMPLE 5-1

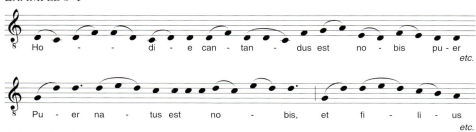

Today we sing of a child…
A boy is born to us, and a Son is given to us…

Sources also attribute to Tuotilo of St. Gall the most famous of all *Kyrie* melodies, *Omnipotens genitor* (Ex. 5-2). Some medieval chant manuscripts include an additional text in Latin for this *Kyrie*—in other words, the *Kyrie* has been troped, or elaborated upon. There is uncertainty, however, as to which came first, the version of the melody with Latin text or the more melismatic version without it. Nevertheless, today scholars refer to the Latin texted version as a *Kyrie* trope—a *Kyrie* with added text.

EXAMPLE 5-2

Almighty father, God, creator of all things, have mercy.
Font of love, source of goodness, everlasting light, have mercy.
May your love save us, good ruler, have mercy.

🔘 LISTENING CUE

TUOTILO OF ST. GALL
Introit trope, *Hodie cantandus est nobis* (c900)
Kyrie trope, *Omnipotens genitor* (c900)

CD 1/10–11
Anthology,
Nos. 10, 11

❉ SEQUENCES

The **sequence** began life much like the trope, as an addition of music with text to a pre-existing chant. The sequence did not precede another chant, but followed it, hence the Latin name "sequentia" ("a following thing"). Specifically, the sequence follows the Alleluia of the Mass. From the ninth century onward, sequences were appended to the Alleluia on high feast days as a way of extending through music the joy associated with the word "Hallelujah."

The story of the sequence begins once more at St. Gall with a famous writer of sequences, **Notker Balbulus** (c840–912; Fig. 5-1). (*Balbulus* means "stammerer" in Latin, and Notker actually referred to himself as "the toothless stammerer" [*balbulus et edentulus*]). Despite his physical challenges, Notker was a fine poet and musician, and he compiled a collection of sequences called the *Liber hymnorum*. In the preface to his book, Notker recounts the story of its genesis. About 850 a monk of the monastery of Jumièges north of Paris fled his abbey to escape marauding Vikings. Seeking refuge, he arrived at St. Gall carrying a few notated sequences. Notker thought he could compose better texts, and he set about the task. In the end he compiled a collection of forty sequences. This he showed to his master, Marcellus, who had them copied out individually on parchment rolls (medieval sheet music) so that they could be taught to other monks. From there, Notker's creations spread across the Holy Roman Empire.

The opening work in Notker's book of sequences is *Natus ante saecula* (*Born before the ages*) for high Mass on Christmas Day. As with all sequences, it is an entirely syllabic chant. As Notker himself said: "Each movement of the melody must have its own syllable." It also possesses another distinctive feature of the sequence: **double verse structure.** Each musical phrase is sung twice to accommodate a pair of verses. One side of the choir sings the first verse, the other repeats this music with the second verse. Thus sequences exemplify antiphonal singing. Example 5-3 gives only the first two of six double versicles of Notker's sequence *Natus ante saecula*.

❀ FIGURE 5-1
With inkwells by his right arm, monk and musician Notker Balbulus sharpens his quill and prepares to write.

Jagiellonian Library, Krakow

EXAMPLE 5-3

Na - tus an - te sae - cu - la de - i fi - li - us in - vi - si - bi - lis, in - ter - mi - nus,
Per quem fit ma - chi - na cae - li ac ter - rae, ma - ris et in his de - gen - ti - um.

Per quem di - es et ho - rae la - bant et se i - te - rum re - ci - pro - cant,
Quem an - ge - li in ar - ce po - li vo - ce con - so - na sem - per ca - nunt:

The Son of God, born before time, invisible, and without end.
Through him heaven, earth, and sea and all the things in them were informed.
Through him days and hours pass and repeat their course.
Of him the angels in heaven always sing with harmonious voice.

Today the most famous of all medieval sequences is the **Dies irae** (*Day of Wrath*). It was written during the thirteenth century and serves as the sequence for the

Requiem Mass (Mass of the Dead) in the Roman Catholic Church. The text speaks of the hellfire that threatens every soul on the Day of Judgment. Over the centuries numerous composers, most notably Mozart, Berlioz, and Verdi, have set the sequence *Dies irae* in spectacular fashion. Consequently, the melody has come to be associated with the macabre and spooky, and has been used in such horror films as *The Shining, Nightmare before Christmas,* and *Sleeping with the Enemy.* As verses one and two of the sequence show, clearly the *Dies irae* is frightening only because of the words—the mostly stepwise melody is very typical of medieval syllabic chant (Ex. 5-4). This demonstrates a point about Gregorian chant: rarely is there an attempt to emphasize or intensify particular words through special musical processes—a text that speaks of descending into Hell is just as likely to go up as down. Chant is a somewhat abstract medium that does not try overtly to "convince" the listener, only to provide an environment for individual contemplation.

EXAMPLE 5-4

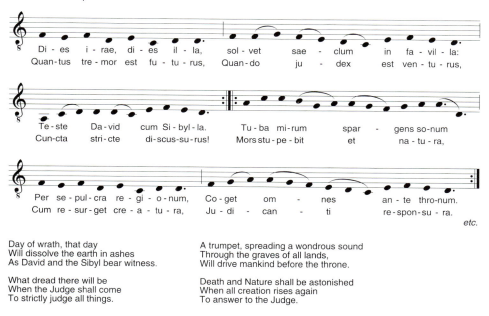

Di - es i - rae, di - es il - la, sol - vet sae - clum in fa - vil - la:
Quan-tus tre - mor est fu - tu - rus, Quan - do ju - dex est ven - tu - rus,

Te - ste Da - vid cum Si - byl - la. Tu - ba mi - rum spar - gens so - num
Cun - cta stri - cte di - scus - su - rus! Mors stu - pe - bit et na - tu - ra,

Per se - pul - cra re - gi - o - num, Co - get om - nes an - te thro - num.
Cum re - sur - get cre - a - tu - ra, Ju - di - can - ti re - spon - su - ra.

etc.

Day of wrath, that day	A trumpet, spreading a wondrous sound
Will dissolve the earth in ashes	Through the graves of all lands,
As David and the Sibyl bear witness.	Will drive mankind before the throne.
What dread there will be	Death and Nature shall be astonished
When the Judge shall come	When all creation rises again
To strictly judge all things.	To answer to the Judge.

LISTENING CUE

ANONYMOUS

Dies irae (c1250)

CD 1/12

Anthology, No. 12

Tropes and sequences, being somewhat later additions to the music of the church, were not as fixed and unchanging as were the older parts of the Mass and canonical hours. Tropes fell completely out of fashion in the thirteenth century and then virtually disappeared. Sequences, on the other hand, only grew in popularity. Finally, during the Renaissance, these lengthy musical additions came to be viewed with suspicion as fabrications of the superstitious Middle Ages: thus sequences were cast out of the church by the reform-minded Council of Trent (1545–1563). Only five sequences were allowed to remain in the liturgy of the Roman Catholic Church, among them the justly famous *Dies irae* for the Requiem Mass.

MUSIC IN THE CONVENT: THE CHANT AND LITURGICAL DRAMA OF HILDEGARD OF BINGEN

Medieval society was broadly divided into three groups: those who worked (the peasants), those who fought (the nobles), and those who prayed (the clergy). Roughly a quarter of the population was clerical, and nearly one-half of these people were women. Celibate Christian women had banded together in cloistered groups since at least the fourth century. In the sixth century they, too, began to follow the monastic life prescribed in the Rule of St. Benedict. They lived in what was then called a monastery, but today is most often referred to as a **convent** or a **nunnery.** Here, almost entirely removed from all male associations, they worked, prayed, and sang. An abbess governed the convent, and the main female singer, the **cantrix,** directed the choir. Nuns sang the same chants and read the same lessons as the monks, but they could not celebrate the sacrament of the Mass (for that a priest had to be called). Cloistered nuns also received training in singing, according to the rules of music theory of that day. Some musical exercises added to a Psalter from an English convent suggest what this instruction might have been like. The nuns practiced scales and leaps—but all (except at the end) within the confines of a single hexachord (Ex. 5-5).

EXAMPLE 5-5

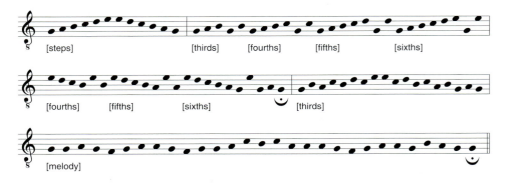

In the secular world, however, women were encouraged to be seen but not heard; they were silently to mouth the psalms in church, but not pronounce or sing them! Parish and cathedral churches, for example, were different from monasteries, and here women had no role whatsoever in the service. This interdiction derived from a biblical admonition of St. Paul: "A woman must be silent in church."

The life of **Hildegard of Bingen** (1098–1179) demonstrates that sometimes a woman might rise above her traditionally subordinate position within the church to become a figure of renown, even veneration. Hildegard was born on the banks of the Rhine River in 1098. The tenth daughter of a minor nobleman and his wife, her parents gave her over to the church at the age of eight. At fourteen Hildegard chose to profess vows of chastity, poverty, and obedience, and formally join the convent. There she studied the Rule of St. Benedict, the liturgy, and the seven liberal arts, in order to understand the scriptures. When her abbess died in 1136, Hildegard herself was chosen mother superior. Later, she founded a new and larger community of nuns on the slopes of a mountain called Rupertsberg, near the small town of Bingen. It was for this convent that she composed most of her seventy-seven chants and her liturgical drama. Indeed, we have more monophonic chants surviving from the pen of Hildegard of Bingen than from any other single figure during the Middle Ages, male or female. But Hildegard was far more than a musician and church administrator. She was also a botanist, zoologist, pharmacologist, theologian, preacher, and religious visionary. Indeed, she wrote books in each of these and other areas of endeavor—thirteen in all. Toward the end of her life, clergymen, nobles, kings, and even the pope sought her opinion in various matters of church and state.

From an early age, Hildegard possessed unusual spiritual gifts. During moments that we might today identify as severe migraine headaches, she heard voices and saw visions accompanied by great flashes of light: a serpent-like Satan devouring the petals of a scarlet rose, or the blood of Christ streaming in the heavens, for example. These she gathered into a single volume called **Scivias** (***Know You the Ways***), which reads much like the Book of Revelation, the phantasmagorical conclusion of the New Testament. Hildegard's visions also found their way into her musical compositions. More than any other religious poet of the Middle Ages, her musical texts are filled with extraordinarily colorful images. Hildegard's poems are not so much verbal structures as pictures transferred to words. Flowers, serpents, blood, drops of dew, all commingle to almost surreal effect. Toward the end of her life, Hildegard arranged her music in a book called **Symphonia,** of which two manuscript copies are preserved today. Hildegard took no credit for what she created: "The words I speak come from no human mouth. I saw and heard them in visions sent to me . . . I am carried along as a feather on the breath of God."

Hildegard's music consists mainly of hymns, antiphons, and sequences for saints important in her region (Disibod, Rupert, Ursula, and others) as well as for Christ and the Virgin Mary. Typical of Hildegard's life in general, her chants do not conform to the accepted norms of the time. For example, she does not always stay within the confines of the prescribed church modes, her antiphons are not always neumatic but sometimes wildly melismatic, and her sequences do not strictly follow double-verse form. Viewing herself merely as a conduit for the voice of God, Hildegard seems to have had little concern for the norms of Gregorian chant that had been established here on earth.

One thing in the music of Hildegard, however, is consistent with the chant of her day: the structure of the text determines the shape of the music. Hildegard's words form a phrase, and she provides each phrase with its own music. The verbal phrases taken together convey the meaning of the sacred text; the musical phrases cohere into a compelling composition. Take, for example, Hildegard's antiphon for St. Ursula, O rubor sanguinis (O, Redness of Blood; Ex. 5-6). It is written in the Dorian mode, but with a B♭ so as to avoid the tritone F-B. In the Middle Ages, musicians sought to avoid the dissonant tritone, which came to be called the **diabolus in musica** (devil in music). The chant starts on D and ends on D. Every separate phrase of text ends on A (the reciting pitch in the Dorian mode) or D. The text dictates the structure of the music. Normally antiphons are neumatic in style (two, three, or four notes per syllable). But the spirit often moved Hildegard to write melismatic exclamations, such as we see on "O" and the thirty-one-note melisma on "numquam" ("never") as the antiphon gradually wends its way back to the final pitch of the Dorian mode. There is rhapsodic beauty, even ecstasy here, but it unfolds within a clear musical structure.

EXAMPLE 5-6

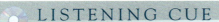

O redness of blood, which flowed down from on high…

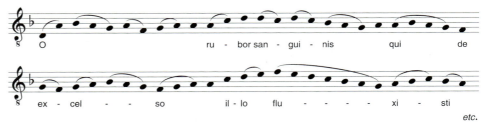

LISTENING CUE

HILDEGARD OF BINGEN
O rubor sanguinis (c1150)

CD 1/13
Anthology, No. 13

Perhaps the most extraordinary musical creation of Hildegard is her **Ordo virtutum (Play of the Virtues),** a collection of some eighty chants that form a full-length music drama. Specifically, it is a **liturgical drama**—a religious play-with-music intended to be inserted into the liturgy, usually before Mass. Many liturgical dramas were at first simple tropes (additions to the pre-existing liturgy); eventually they grew so elaborate as to stand as separate, independent dramas. Almost all religious plays of the Middle Ages had a scriptural basis, drawing upon some event described in the Bible (the story of Daniel escaping from the lion's den or King Herod slaughtering the innocent children, for example). But Hildegard's *Ordo virtutum* is not drawn from any story in the Bible. Instead, hers is an original work that, according to the prologue, God created and commanded she record. The protagonist in these ninety minutes of musical theater is the human Soul, a woman who represents everywoman. The Soul is torn between the difficult road to spiritual salvation, recommended by the Virtues, and the easy path of worldly fame and fortune urged by the Devil.

🌿 FIGURE 5-2

A twelfth-century illumination depicting Hildegard of Bingen receiving divine inspiration, perhaps a vision or a chant, directly from the heavens. To the right, her secretary, the monk Volmar, peeks at her in amazement. This illumination was painted twenty-one years after her death.

Otto Miller Verlages, Salzburg

The climax of the drama centers on a confrontation between the Soul and the Devil, who encourages the Soul to know and enjoy the pleasures of the human flesh. The Soul sings of her fears and weaknesses. Satan shouts but cannot sing—Hell is a noisy place and its lord is unmusical. The Virtues, on the other hand, sing alluringly of a life removed from the temptations of this world. Needless to say, in this earliest Christian morality play the Virtues ultimately win out. The triumphant final chorus gathers together the Virtues and every Soul. All are urged to witness the suffering and sacrifice of Christ and to follow his example.

Hildegard's *Ordo virtutum* was likely first performed in her convent at Rupertsberg in 1152. The roles of the Soul and the fourteen Virtues were presumably sung by fifteen of the approximately fifty nuns in residence. Abbess Hildegard herself surely played the part of the narrator, while the only male at the convent, her secretary Volmar (Fig. 5-2), likely portrayed the Devil. By excluding all male characters except Satan, Hildegard's *Ordo virtutum* reinforces the first rule of the convent: a woman of virtue is married only to Christ.

LISTENING CUE

HILDEGARD OF BINGEN
Excerpts from *Ordo virtutum* (c1150)

CD 1/14
Anthology, No. 14

SUMMARY

By 1000 C.E. the Mass and canonical hours had assumed their final form. Thereafter, the new chants added to the liturgy usually came in one of three types: trope, sequence, or liturgical drama. Tropes were inserted almost everywhere in the liturgy, though most often they came at the beginning of the Introit of the Mass. Sequences were always inserted after the Alleluia of the Mass as a way of extending this moment of jubilation. Sequences are longer pieces than tropes, usually follow a prescribed form (double verses), and are invariably syllabic. Liturgical dramas are religious plays-with-music inserted into the service, usually before Mass. Tropes and liturgical dramas fell out of fashion later in the Middle Ages. Sequences, however, remained in favor into the Renaissance. Ultimately, all but five were removed from the Catholic liturgy by the reforming authorities of the Council of Trent (1545–1563).

Hildegard of Bingen (1098–1179) was one of the most remarkable figures of the Middle Ages. A polymath who wrote lengthy books on many subjects, she has left us a collection of nearly eighty chants preserved in her *Symphonia* as well as a lengthy liturgical drama entitled *Ordo virtutum*, the earliest morality play to be set entirely to music. Hildegard's texts are extraordinarily vivid, and the music to which she sets them is beautifully effusive.

KEY TERMS

trope
Tuotilo of St. Gall
sequence
Notker Balbulus
double verse structure
Dies irae

Requiem Mass
convent
nunnery
cantrix
Hildegard of Bingen
Scivias (Know You the Ways)

Symphonia
diabolus in musica
Ordo Virtutum (Play of the Virtues)
liturgical drama

Troubadours and Trouvères

Not all music in the Middle Ages was religious. There were songs for the knights as they rode into battle, songs for the men in the fields and the women around the hearth, and songs and dances for the nobles in their castles. Unfortunately, most of this secular music, and virtually all of it coming from the common folk, is now lost because it was never written down. Only the church music is preserved in any significant amount, because only the men and women of the church were trained in musical notation and educated generally. Even the nobility was more or less illiterate in Latin, the universal language of the Western church. This was the state of affairs in the West until the high Middle Ages of the twelfth and thirteenth centuries.

During the high Middle Ages the court first emerged as a center for the patronage of the arts. Kings, dukes, counts, and princes assumed greater responsibility for defense, commerce, and justice—affairs previously handled largely by the church. To enhance the ruler's prestige and show that he or she was a person of refinement and sensibility, the noble often engaged bands of trumpeters to herald an arrival, instrumentalists to provide dance music for festivals of the court, and singers and poets to create lyric verse. Simultaneously, vernacular tongues began to emerge from the shadow of Latin and become literary languages in their own right. Poetry in French, German, Italian, and Spanish first appears at this time. Some poems were meant to be recited, others sung.

Southern France was the center of this new courtly art. The poet-musicians who flourished there went by the name of **troubadour** (for men) and **trobairitz** (for women). Both terms derived from the verb "trobar," which meant "to find" in their vernacular tongue. Thus the troubadours and trobairitz were finders or inventors of new modes of verbal and vocal expression. Their tongue, the language of southern France, was called **langue d'oc** (also **occitan**). By the early thirteenth century the art of the troubadours had spread to the north. Here the poet-musician was called a **trouvère** (both masculine and feminine) from the word "trouver" (again, "to find"). The language of the north was called **langue d'oïl.** (Both "oc" and "oïl" meant "yes" in medieval French.) A song of the south was called a **canso,** while one of the north was a **chanson.** By gathering many songs into a single volume, the musicians of the north created a **chansonnier** (a book of songs). The scribes of the first chansonniers, whether troubadour or trouvère, simply borrowed the musical notation of the monastery and brought it into the castle. All told, the troubadours created approximately 2,600 courtly poems, about a tenth of which survive today with music. Similarly, the trouvères have left us 2,100 poems, about 1,400 of which have melodies.

The social standing of the troubadours and trobairitz was varied. Many were noblemen or noblewomen—dukes or countesses, for example. Others, however, were the humble servants of such aristocrats. Contrary to popular belief, a troubadour was not a carefree minstrel wandering from town to town. He was a serious verse-technician, usually attached to a single court, who wrote a particular kind of love poetry about **fin'amors** (ideal love). Fin'amors expressed the values of chivalric society as they applied to the art of love, the love of a knight or a poet for his lady. The noble poet-musician placed his beloved woman on a pedestal and swore to honor and obey her, as a vassal would a lord. From this great flowering of troubadour poetry emerged a new view of women in courtly society. The female was now thought to be the more virtuous, purer, yet weaker sex, worthy of both veneration and protection. But the woman, too, had her point of view. Included among the southern repertory are about forty poems by trobairitz, though unfortunately for only one has the music been preserved.

Countess Beatriz de Dia wrote the sole extant song by a trobairitz. She lived in southern France during the middle of the twelfth century. Though married to Count William of Poitiers, she fell in love with a fellow troubadour, Raimbaut of Orange (1146–1173). Her song *A chantar m'er* (*I must sing*) laments her failure in love, despite her self-proclaimed charms. Almost all troubadour and trouvère songs are strophic, and this one has five stanzas. Were we to strip away the text, the melody alone might at first be taken for a chant from the church. Like chant, troubadour and trouvère music is monophonic and has no regular rhythmic pattern or meter. So, too, the song moves predominantly in step-wise motion and has a strong sense of a church mode (in this case, the Dorian mode). Nevertheless, the Countess de Dia's canso exhibits a repetitive formal plan (**ABABCDB**). Such clear-cut repetition schemes are common in the music of the troubadours and trouvères, but virtually unknown in the chant of the church. Often it is the rhyme scheme of the vernacular poem that creates regularity in the music. Throughout the high Middle Ages and into the Renaissance, the secular music of the court will exhibit formal repetitions far more than the sacred music of the church.

LISTENING CUE

BEATRIZ DE DIA
A chantar m'er (c1175)

CD 1/15
Anthology, No. 15

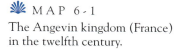

MAP 6-1
The Angevin kingdom (France) in the twelfth century.

✿ THE COURT OF ELEANOR OF AQUITAINE

More than any other place, the art of the troubadours and trouvères flourished at the court of **Eleanor of Aquitaine** (c1122–1204). Eleanor was arguably the most remarkable woman of the high Middle Ages, and certainly the most powerful. Her grandfather, Duke William IX (1071–1126) of Aquitaine, was the first recorded troubadour—the first to leave us love songs in the vernacular tongue. From her father, Duke William X, Eleanor inherited the duchy of Aquitaine in southwestern France. In 1137 she married Louis of France and, when he succeeded to the French throne that year, Eleanor became queen. But the temperaments of the royal couple were ill-suited: Louis thought Eleanor strong-willed and promiscuous; Eleanor considered Louis a pious wimp. By mutual consent, their marriage was annulled in March 1152. Eight weeks later Eleanor married Henry of Anjou, who in 1154 succeeded to the throne of England as King Henry II. Now Eleanor was queen of England, as well as countess of Anjou, and duchess of Normandy and Aquitaine. The territorial holdings of Eleanor and Henry extended from Scotland through England and down through western France to Spain (see Map 6-1). Because the geographic center of this realm was the French county of Anjou, these holdings came to be called the **Angevin kingdom.** In land and population, the twelfth-century Angevin kingdom was far better endowed than the kingdom of France.

Queen Eleanor and King Henry moved frequently, and usually separately, to rule their vast lands. Her preferred abode was the castle of Chinon near Anjou. Here Eleanor drew poets and musicians and encouraged her own children to pursue these arts. At her court was Marie de France, the first writer, male or female, to put the legend of King Arthur into verse.

Foremost among the troubadours at Chinon was **Bernart de Ventadorn** (c1135–c1195). We know something of the life of Bernart owing to the chansonniers that preserve his compositions. In these song books, the works of each composer are grouped separately and prefaced by a small portrait of the artist, as well as a brief biographical sketch called a *vida.* Here is the beginning of the "vita" of Bernart de Ventadorn.

> Bernart de Ventadorn was from the Limousin, from the castle of Ventadorn. He was poor by birth, the son of a servant who fired the ovens for baking bread at the castle. But he became handsome and clever and knew well how to sing and make songs, and became courteous and wise. His lord, the Viscount, liked him and did him great honor. The Viscount had a wife, young, noble and joyful; she liked Bernart and his songs, and fell in love with him and he with her; and he made songs and verses for her, about the love he had for her and her worthiness. Their love lasted a long time before anyone noticed. But when the Viscount found out, he separated Bernart from her, and his wife was locked up and guarded. She was made to advise Bernart to leave and go far away. And he left and went to the Duchess of Normandy—Eleanor of Aquitaine—who was young and of great valor, and who understood merit and words of praise. The songs of Bernart pleased her well, and she received him and welcomed him warmly. For a long time he stayed at her court, and he was enamored of her and she of him, and he made many fine songs about her.[1]

Bernart of Ventadorn has left forty-five poems, of which eighteen are supplied with melodies. By far his most popular song is *Can vei la lauzeta (When I see the lark).* It was copied and translated into four other languages, including Spanish and German. The "Lark" here refers to Eleanor of Aquitaine. The *vida* of Bernart, again, tells us something about how this song came to be:

> Bernart de Ventadorn called Eleanor of Aquitaine "Lauzeta" because of a knight who loved her and whom she called "Rai" [short for Raimond]. One day the knight came to the duchess and entered her room. Eleanor, seeing him, lifted the front of her skirt and put it over his head, and fell back onto the bed. Bernart de Ventadorn saw all this, because one of the lady's maids had shown him where to hide. On this subject Bernart made the song *Can vei la lauzeta.*[2]

Given these events, no wonder the song *Can vei la lauzeta* is full of bitterness. The idealistic poet Bernart has been deceived. In seven eight-line stanzas he gives vent to his feelings: the joy of love has left his heart because the "lark" has done what is forbidden her—she has broken the rules of *fin'amors*. To the final stanza, Bernart adds an **envoi,** literally a "send-off." Here he calls forth the image of the knight Tristan, the great lover in medieval legend:

Tristans, ges no'm auretz de me,	Tristan, you will hear no more of me,
Qu'en m'en vau, chaitius, no sai on.	For I am going sadly away, I do not know where
De chantar me gic e'm recre,	I am going to stop singing,
E de joi d'amor m'escon.	And I flee from the joy of love.

Indeed, Bernart de Ventadorn did go away. His *vida* says that he withdrew from the secular court of Eleanor of Aquitaine and ended his days in a monastery. Ulti-

FIGURE 6-1

Tomb of Eleanor of Aquitaine and her son Richard the Lionheart at Fontevraud Abbey. At far left is the tomb of Eleanor's husband, Henry II. Notice that Eleanor holds a book, a symbol intended to suggest that she was both learned and a person of authority within the convent.

mately, Eleanor of Aquitaine, too, withdrew to a monastery. In her eighties she took up residence among the Benedictine nuns at Fontevraud near Chinon. Her funeral monument remains there today (Fig. 6-1), along with those of her husband, King Henry, and son, Richard.

LISTENING CUE

BERNART DE VENTADORN   CD 1/16

Can vei la lauzeta (c1165)   Anthology, No. 16

 **TROUVÈRES**

Eleanor of Aquitaine had eleven children. Her eldest daughter was Marie of Champagne, herself a patroness of poets. Of Eleanor's five sons her favorite was Richard, who ultimately became King Richard I of England (1157–1199). Richard set to music poetry written in the *langue d'oïl*, for he spoke the language of the north, as did his father, King Henry II of England. Thus Richard was a trouvère—indeed, one of the first. Contemporaries called him **Richard the Lionheart,** for he displayed great courage during the third crusade to the Holy Lands. On his journey home, however, King Richard was ambushed, taken prisoner, and held for ransom. To while away the hours, Richard wrote verse and set it to music. His most famous song is *Ja nus hons pris ne dira (Truly, a captive doesn't speak his mind)*. Obviously written during his period of captivity (1192–1194), it is a beautiful complaint: the lords of the Angevin kingdom have failed to produce the ransom that will set him free. Each of the six stanzas is carried by music in the simplest of musical forms (**AAB**).

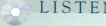

LISTENING CUE

RICHARD THE LIONHEART   CD 1/17

Ja nus hons pris ne dira (1192–1194)   Anthology, No. 17

 FIGURE 6-2

A thirteenth-century miniature from the court of King Alfonso the Wise, showing a medieval fiddle (the rebec) on the left and a lute on the right. Both instruments were brought into Spain by the Arabs and then carried northward into the lands of the troubadours and trouvères.

By the beginning of the thirteenth century, imitations of the French love song were being written in Italian, German, Spanish, and even English. In Germany a poet-musician writing love songs in the native tongue was called a **Minnesinger** and the song he created a **Minnesang** ("song of love" in old high German). Spain, however, was geographically closer to southwestern France than any other country, and the mixing of troubadour poetry with the melodic traditions of Arabic Spain produced a distinctive new vocal genre. A medieval Spanish or Portuguese monophonic song is called a *cantiga.* Hundreds of these were created on subjects of love, epic heroism, and everyday life, but few of these secular poems are preserved today with music. One special group of some four hundred songs surviving with music goes by the name **Cantigas de Santa Maria.** About 1270 this anthology was collected, and perhaps some songs composed, by **Alfonso the Wise,** king of Castile, Spain. While the texts of these *cantigas* all honor the Virgin Mary and tell of her miracles, their musical style is more secular than sacred. Many incorporate the **AAB** form often used by both troubadours and trouvères, and some are believed to be pre-existing secular songs just outfitted with sacred words. Most remarkable, however, are the beautiful illuminations contained in the various manuscripts of Alfonso's *cantigas*. These depictions constitute a rich source of information about medieval musical instruments, as can be seen in Figure 6-2. Here, before a backdrop of Arabic geometric patterns, we see clear illustrations of the lute (an instrument of Arabic origin), and a medieval fiddle. Such instruments, which are discussed in further detail in Chapter 11, undoubtedly were used in the performance of Spanish songs at the court of King Alfonso.

 SUMMARY

Not all music in the Middle Ages was religious. Secular love music also existed in Western Europe but was not written down until the late twelfth century. The courtly tradition of creating love poems with music was centered in France. The troubadours and trobairitz held forth in southern France during the twelfth century, and they were succeeded in the thirteenth century by the trouvères in northern France. Most troubadour and trouvère songs are syllabic, mainly stepwise melodies setting poems in strophic form. The French tradition of the monophonic courtly chanson inspired the rise of the German *Minnesang* and the Spanish *cantiga.* Equally important, the monophonic canso and chanson of the troubadours and trouvères established the genre of the courtly love song, and from this tradition would emerge the pan-European polyphonic chanson of the late Middle Ages and Renaissance.

 KEY TERMS

troubadour	trouvère	chanson
trobairitz	langue d'oïl	chansonnier
langue d'oc, occitan	canso	*fin'amors*

Early Polyphony

Western music has one distinctive characteristic: polyphony. By contrast, Chinese music, Indian music, Korean music, Japanese music—all of these venerable musical traditions—have enormously intricate melodies, ones filled with subtle microtones not present in the melodies of the West. Similarly, sub-Saharan African music employs rhythms so complex as to make those of Westerners look childish by comparison. But for music making with many simultaneously sounding pitches—polyphony—no musical tradition is richer than that of the West. To be sure, Western classical music has cultivated polyphony (expressed in both harmony and counterpoint) to a degree unknown in other musical cultures. One consequence of this can be seen, for example, in the colossal orchestral scores of Gustav Mahler and Richard Strauss. But how, when, and where did this Western obsession with polyphony begin?

Perhaps polyphony began when individuals singing in different vocal ranges noticed their harmoniously different sounds and began to cultivate them; perhaps it began when people singing the same tune in slightly different ways created polyphonic intervals from time to time; perhaps polyphony emerged when a group sang a round and enjoyed the resulting polyphonic sound. Obviously, we do not know where or why polyphony first appeared, but very likely singing polyphonically is as innate to human expression as singing itself.

❈ ORGANUM IN MUSIC THEORY SOURCES

What we do know is that the first documented appearance of polyphonic music comes from a Benedictine abbey in northwestern Germany and dates from the 890s. It is found in a music theory treatise entitled **Musica enchiriadis** (**Music Handbook**) that describes a type of polyphonic singing called organum. Soon the term **organum** (pl., **organa**) came to be used generally to connote polyphony. As one theorist explained, polyphony is called organum because voices singing in harmony show "a resemblance to the instrument that is called the organ."[1]

The author of the *Musica enchiriadis*, identified as Abbot Hoger (d. 906) in the earliest sources, does not address his discussion of organum to composers, nor does he intend it for music theorists who wish to analyze music. Instead, Abbot Hoger's sole aim is to teach church singers how to improvise polyphonic music on the spot—to take a given piece of Gregorian chant and make it sound more splendid by adding one or more additional lines around it. This sort of improvised polyphony would be cultivated in Western churches for nearly a thousand years, up to the time of the French Revolution. Thus, the *Musica enchiriadis* and other similar treatises taught musicians, not the rules of composition but a technique for improvising music extempore.

Exactly how did this work? Most organum described in the *Musica enchiriadis* is called **parallel organum** (organum in which all voices move in lockstep, up or down, with the intervals between voices remaining the same). In its most basic form, parallel organum proceeds with only two voice parts. One, called the ***vox principalis*** (principal voice), is a pre-existing chant to be enhanced; the other, called the ***vox organalis*** (organal voice), is a newly created line to be added to the chant. The intervals at which the two voices proceed, not surprisingly, are the primary consonances of the early Middle Ages: the octave, the fifth, and the fourth. The *Musica enchiriadis* allows for parallel organum at either the fourth or the fifth below the plainsong; thus, the *vox organalis* always moves along with the *vox principalis* at the interval of either a fourth or a fifth below. What is more, both voices may be doubled an octave above or below. Thus four-voice parallel organum is also permissible (Ex. 7-1).

EXAMPLE 7-1

Vox principalis

Sit glo - ri - a Do - mi - ni,   in sae - cu - la...

Vox organalis

May the glory of the Lord, throughout the ages...

Singing in parallel fourths or fifths often results in a dissonant tritone, as when F and B sound together. To avoid the tritone, the author of the *Musica enchiriadis* urges the organal voice to remain stationary at those potentially dangerous moments. In Example 7-2, the organal voice would normally start on D in parallel organum at the fourth, but here starts on G so as not to create an F-B tritone while the principal voice rises through B. Such a moment is called organum with **oblique motion** (one voice repeating or sustaining a pitch while another moves away or toward it).

EXAMPLE 7-2

Vox principalis

Vox organalis   Te   hu - mi - les   fa - mu - li   mo - du - lis   ve - ne - ran - do   pi - us.

The humble servants, venerating you with pious melodies.

More than a century passes before we find further discussions of polyphony. They appear in the writings of two music theorists of the eleventh century, Guido of Arezzo and John of St. Gall, both of whom we have previously met. Guido introduced the musical staff with pitch-letter names as well as a system of hexachords and a musical hand that facilitated sight-singing; John was the first to expound a complete system for the eight church modes as we know them today. In his *Micrologus* (c1030) Guido devotes the last of nineteen chapters to polyphony. He does not advocate four-voice organum, only two-voice organum, with the *vox organalis* usually a fourth below. He, too, was concerned about avoiding the offensive tritone. He advocates parallel organum whenever possible, but where a tritone might lurk it should be avoided by means of oblique motion. Guido was the first theorist to be concerned about the cadence, which he called the **occursus**—a running together.

Example 7-3 demonstrates not only oblique motion at a final cadence, but also contrary motion. In brief moments such as these, with the voices moving against one another, we see the earliest signs of what will later be called counterpoint.

EXAMPLE 7-3

Vox principalis

Vox organalis   Ve - ni ad do - cen - dum   nos   vi - am pru - den - ti - ae

Come to teach us the path of wisdom.

John of St. Gall devotes only one chapter of his *De Musica* (c1100) to organum, but he has two important things to say: (1) contrary motion and voice crossing in organum are to be encouraged, and (2) the *vox principalis* (the chant) should appear beneath, not above, the *vox organalis*. Hereafter, from the late eleventh through the sixteenth century, the given Gregorian chant is placed toward the bottom of the musical texture as voices are added around it. The old chant serves as a scaffold supporting the newly added voices.

❋ ORGANUM IN PRACTICAL SOURCES

Our best information about early polyphony comes from music theorists who were intent on instructing medieval singers how to improvise organum around a given chant. But contemporary manuscripts survive that contain written polyphony as well. The earliest of these comes from a Benedictine monastery at Winchester, England, and dates from c1000 C.E. The collection is called the **Winchester Troper,** because it contains mainly tropes—a troper is a chant manuscript mainly preserving additions to the liturgy called tropes (see Chapter 5). The Winchester Troper dates some thirty years before the invention of the musical staff, and its pitches are written in unheightened neumes. Moreover, the two-voice polyphony is not notated in one manuscript. Since the singers already knew the chant by memory, only the newly composed voice was notated in the Winchester Troper. Consequently, because the notation does not specify relative pitch and because the two voices are not placed one on top of the other in the same book, it is impossible today to sing the music with any confidence. All we can say is that, from the Winchester Troper, singers could generate a repertory of about 150 two-voice organa—*Kyries* and Alleluias for the Mass, for example. The Winchester Troper was clearly not a prescriptive document for sight-reading, but a memory aid—the singers had all of this organum in their heads and just needed a reminder from time to time.

In contrast to the notational uncertainty of the Winchester Troper, the next significant collection of organum can be read with great clarity. Surviving today from southern France is a repertory of about sixty-five pieces of two-voice organum. It is called **Aquitanian polyphony** because many of the works come from various monasteries in the region of Aquitaine in southwestern France (see Map 6-1). Most are tropes, sequences, and a later musical form called the conductus (see Chapter 9). All pieces date from the twelfth century. Fortunately, with the Aquitanian repertory we can read the pitches with no difficulty. Yet the rhythm still poses a problem; the notation seems not to imply rhythmic durations. We can transcribe the notes as a series of eighth-notes, for example, but the music was most likely performed extempore:

FIGURE 7-1

Viderunt Hemanuel, a two-voice organum of the twelfth century coming from southern France. Notice the alphabetical pitch indicators to the left of each staff.

Bibliothèque Nationale, Paris

one singer (the bottom voice) simply held and waited for the other (top part) to sing the more complex line. Indeed, many Aquitanian pieces exemplify passages of what is called **sustained-tone organum**—the bottom voice holds a note while the faster-moving top voice embellishes it in a florid fashion. In Aquitanian polyphony, sustained-tone organum most often occurs at cadence points at the ends of musical lines.

A fine example of Aquitanian polyphony is the anonymous two-voice *Viderunt Hemanuel* (Fig. 7-1). This is a two-voice trope of the Gradual of the Mass for Christmas, *Viderunt omnes* (see Chapter 3 and Anthology, No. 8), and it would have been sung at a monastery on Christmas morning. The bottom voice begins like the Gradual chant *Viderunt omnes* while the top voice is newly composed. Intervals of thirds and sixths are plentiful in the middle of phrases but more consonant fifths and octaves always sound at the beginnings and ends. At several end points the bottom voice holds while the top voice cascades a full octave down the scale to form a final cadence, a clear instance of sustained-tone organum (see Ex. 7-4). Aquitanian polyphony gives the distinct impression of being music that is rhythmically free, luxuriant, even sensual. There is little that is prescribed in the written score other than the pitches. The ultimate effect of a performance depended greatly upon the tempo, rhythms, and vocal nuances the singers chose to employ.

EXAMPLE 7-4

They saw Emmanuel…
Israel in ruin…

Related to the repertory of Aquitanian polyphony is a small collection of some twenty pieces preserved today at the cathedral of **Santiago (St. James) de Compostela,** Spain. Next to Rome, the pilgrimage site of greatest importance in medieval Europe was the cathedral of Santiago, for it was believed to house the relics (bones) of the Apostle James. So important was it that a grand street in Paris was (and is still) called Rue St. Jacques, and each year along this road thousands of pilgrims went south on their way out of Paris walking toward Compostela in northwestern Spain. It is estimated that, in all, 500,000 pilgrims took this and various other routes to Compostela annually. Thousands still do so today, sleeping in monasteries and youth hostels along the way.

Surviving today at the church of St. James in Compostela is a manuscript called the **Codex Calixtinus,** written around 1150 and once believed to be the work of Pope Calixtus II. It contains a service for St. James, which includes twenty polyphonic pieces, mostly for Mass and Vespers. Once again, the musical notation does not suggest rhythms, only relative pitches. The singers must fit the two parts together as the spirit and the meter of the text move them. The Codex Calixtinus is an important monument in the history of Western music because it is the first manuscript to ascribe composers' names to particular pieces (Fig. 7-2). Among the composers named in the manuscript is **Master Albertus of Paris.** To him is attributed one of the earliest three-voice compositions in Western music, *Congaudeant Catholici* (*Let the faithful rejoice*), the beginning of which is given below. Master Albertus did, in fact, exist; he was the cantor of the cathedral of Notre Dame of Paris in the mid twelfth century. Thus it is to Paris and the music of the so-called Notre Dame School that we now turn.

FIGURE 7-2
Congaudeant Catholici from the Codex Calixtinus. Two voices are notated in different-colored ink on the bottom staff and one voice only on the top staff.

EXAMPLE 7-5

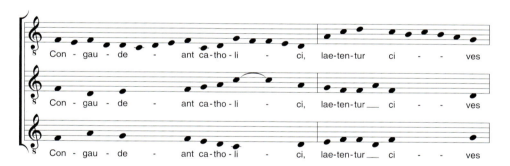

Let the faithful rejoice...

 LISTENING CUE

MASTER ALBERTUS OF PARIS
Congaudeant Catholici (c1150)

CD 1/19
Anthology, No. 19

SUMMARY

The first discussions of polyphony in any musical culture appear in northwestern Europe in the ninth century. Early polyphony was called organum, and our knowledge of it comes from two different types of sources: theory treatises and music manuscripts. The treatises begin by emphasizing parallel organum but increasingly come to recognize the need for oblique and contrary motion to avoid the dissonant tritone. Organum, unlike monophonic chant, was not an everyday affair. Singers wishing to adorn the liturgy in a special way employed it on the highest feast-days of the church year. In all early organum—in England, France, and Spain—the general tendency was to assign polyphony to those chants traditionally sung by soloists, such as the tropes and the difficult responsorial chants. Simple syllabic chants, such as psalms and hymns, continued to be sung chorally in monophonic Gregorian chant.

The largest collections of early written organum are found in the Winchester Troper (c1000 C.E.), which contains about 150 pieces that cannot accurately be deciphered, and a twelfth-century repertory from medieval Aquitaine (southwestern France), which includes about sixty-five compositions, some in sustained-tone, florid style. The Codex Calixtinus, a manuscript preserved at the pilgrimage church of St. James in Compostela, Spain, contains twenty examples of organum dating about 1150. It is the first source to ascribe compositions to particular composers.

KEY TERMS

Musica enchiriadis (*Music Handbook*)	*vox organalis*	sustained-tone organum
organum (pl., organa)	oblique motion	Santiago de Compostela
parallel organum	occursus	Codex Calixtinus
vox principalis	Winchester Troper	Master Albertus of Paris
	Aquitanian polyphony	

Chapter 8

Music in Medieval Paris: Polyphony at Notre Dame

Today Paris is breathtaking, arguably the most beautiful, sophisticated, and visually stunning city in the world. But it was not always this way. At the time of the collapse of the Roman Empire (fifth century C.E.), Paris was home to no more than a few thousand souls who huddled on an island (the *Île de la Cité*) in the middle of the Seine River. The early Merovingian kings (ruled c500–751) made Paris their first city; but Holy Roman Emperor Charlemagne, the founder of the Carolingian dynasty, moved his capital to Aachen in western Germany around 790. When Charlemagne died in 814 he left gifts to the twenty-one most important cities in his empire—Rome, Milan, Cologne, even Arles—but nothing to insignificant Paris. Forgotten, Paris declined further. Not until the tenth century, upon the extinction of the Carolingian line and the ascent of a new dynasty of French kings (the Capetians), did the center of government return to Paris. Two centuries later the city experienced a renaissance.

During the twelfth century a new style of architecture emerged in Paris and surrounding territories, one that replaced the older, heavy, Roman-dominated (Romanesque) style. Today we call this new, lighter manner **Gothic architecture,** but contemporaries called it *opus francigenum* ("work in the French style"). Churches in cities near Paris and in Paris itself were built or rebuilt in the new Gothic style. In the main these were urban cathedrals, not rural monasteries. As the new church steeples reached toward the heavens, they signified a rising urban power.

Also in the twelfth century, education moved from the monastery to the cathedral, from the country to the city. In Paris church schools appeared next to the cathedral and eventually spilled over onto the south (left) bank of the Seine River. Here theologians taught the seven liberal arts so that clerical students might read and correctly interpret the scriptures. Spellbinding teachers such as Peter Abelard (1079-1142) attracted thousands of students from across the length and breadth of Europe. In 1215 a university was recognized by the Pope, a *Universitas magistrorum et scholarium* (university of masters and scholars), as it was called. Soon overrun by students, the population of Paris swelled, from 25,000 in the early twelfth century, to 80,000 in the mid-thirteenth, to nearly 200,000, according to a census of 1329. Paris had become the largest and most important city in northern Europe.

❖ NOTRE DAME OF PARIS

At the center of it all, geographically and spiritually, was Notre Dame. Like most cathedrals in France, the one in Paris was dedicated to the Blessed Virgin Mary, Our Lady (*Notre Dame*). Typical of most Gothic cathedrals, the campaign to construct Notre Dame took more than a century. The church we see today was begun about 1163 but was not finished until more than a hundred years later (Fig. 8-1). Today, eight hundred years after the fact, we have become accustomed to the size and beauty of Notre Dame, standing ten stories tall (108 feet). In the Middle Ages, however, visitors to Paris were stunned. Notre Dame towered over the surrounding buildings like a colossus. A vision of the house of the Lord, celestial Jerusalem, had been placed on earth, indeed in the very center of the city.

By far the largest building in any major medieval city was the cathedral. The western end of the church was called the **nave.** This was the public part of the church. People came and went as they pleased. Goods and services were bought and sold, pilgrims slept on the floor, preachers preached, and heralds made public announcements. The nave functioned as town hall and civic auditorium, all contained within the west end of the Lord's temple. But where were the musicians?

Most music was made in the east end of the church, in the area called the **choir,** which included the high altar. In fact, the name for this part of the church was derived from the group of singers (Latin *chorus*) that performed therein. The clergy, as many as a hundred at a time, sat in stalls divided in half—half sat on the north side of the choir aisle and half on the south. Six to eight choirboys occupied benches on the floor. Everyone—the full clerical community—sang the basic Gregorian chant. For solos in the chant and for singing polyphony, however, specialists were needed. At Notre Dame this more professional choir of specially trained singers numbered about a dozen. When these soloists performed polyphony, they stepped down from their choir stalls and gathered around a single

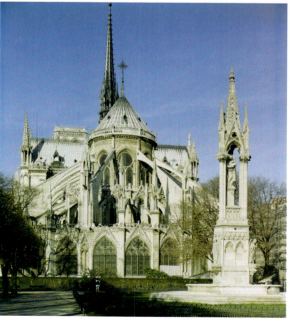

❀ FIGURE 8-1
East end of Notre Dame Cathedral, a fine example of Gothic architecture.

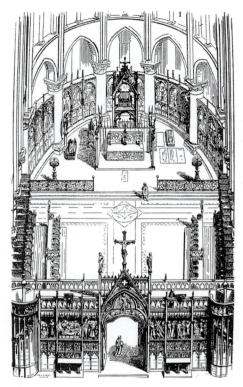

🌸 FIGURE 8-2

Hypothetical reconstruction of
original choir of Notre Dame of
Paris executed by the architectural historian Viollet-le-Duc
in the nineteenth century.
The medieval roodscreen at the
very front was torn down in
the eighteenth century during
the Enlightenment. Note the
choir stalls for the clergy to the
left and right of the main aisle.

lectern in the center of the choir (Fig. 8-2). Here they sang the organum
made famous throughout Europe by the composers of Notre Dame.

🌼 LEONINUS AND THE *MAGNUS LIBER ORGANI*

Among the many students drawn to the University of Paris in the late thirteenth century was an Englishman with a particular interest in music. After
his studies in Paris he returned to England and wrote a music theory treatise commenting on contemporary music in Paris. We do not know his
name and therefore call him Anonymous IV, because later his treatise was
published as the fourth in a series of anonymous writings on music.[†] In the
course of a discussion of the principles of musical notation, Anonymous IV
inserts the following brief history of polyphonic music at Notre Dame.

> And note that Magister Leoninus, according to what was said, was the best
> creator of organum (*optimus organista*), who made a great book of organum
> for both the Mass and canonical hours to adorn the divine service. And
> this was in use until the time of Perotinus the Great, who abbreviated it
> and made many better substitute clausulae or sections, because he was the
> best composer of discant, better than Leoninus . . . . This Magister Peroti-
> nus composed the best four-voice works, such as *Viderunt* and *Sederunt*, with
> an abundance of artful harmonic color; and similarly he composed the most
> noble three-voice works, such as Alleluia *Posui adiutorium*, *Nativitas*, etc.

And he made three-voice conducti [see Chapter 9], such as *Salvatoris hodie*, and two-
voice conducti, among them *Dum sigillum summi patris*, as well as monophonic conducti, such as *Beata viscera* among many others. The book or books of Magister
Perotinus were in use in the choir of the cathedral of Notre Dame in Paris until the
time of Magister Robertus de Sabilone and from his time until the present day.[1]

Anonymous IV says three important things: (1) that there was a composer named
Leoninus who wrote a great book of polyphony called the **Magnus liber organi** to
make the Mass and the canonical hours more splendid; (2) that Leoninus was succeeded by Perotinus the Great, who altered the contents of the *Magnus liber organi*
and also wrote, among other things, his own three- and four-voice music; and (3) that
this Gothic polyphony was sung in the choir of Notre Dame of Paris for as long as a
century, until the time that he, Anonymous IV, set pen to parchment about 1280.
By happy coincidence, three music manuscripts survive from the thirteenth century
that contain almost all of the music Anonymous IV mentions. Let us start with
Magister Leoninus and his great book, the *Magnus liber organi*.

Magister Leoninus (Latin for "Little Leo") flourished during the period
1160–1201. He was educated in Paris, earning the degree master of arts (thus "Magister" Leoninus). He was also a priest, poet, and canon (high-ranking official) of the
cathedral of Notre Dame. Anonymous IV calls Leoninus "*optimus organista*," meaning the best singer-composer of organum. Indeed, his *Magnus liber organi* contains
nearly a hundred pieces of two-voice organum. He composed it, as Anonymous IV
attests, so as to make the divine service at Notre Dame more splendid on the high
feasts of the church year—on Christmas, Easter, and the feast of the Assumption of

[†]The all-female early-music performing group called Anonymous IV derived its name from this medieval theorist.

the Virgin, for example. For the Mass he did not set all of the Ordinary and Proper, but only the two responsorial chants of the Proper, specifically the Gradual and the Alleluia, melismatic chants in which soloists played a leading part. Similarly, for Vespers and Matins, Leoninus set in two-voice polyphony only the lengthy and difficult responsories. All other music at Notre Dame remained monophonic chant. As we review the parts of the Mass, the boldface type shows where Leoninus adorned this morning service:

ORDINARY	PROPER
	Introit
Kyrie	
Gloria	
	Gradual
	Alleluia
Credo	
	Offertory
Sanctus	
Agnus dei	
	Communion

Recall that the Gradual and the Alleluia of the Mass were lengthy, florid chants in which soloists stepped forward to sing a verse within the context of choral respond (see Chapter 3). Leoninus added polyphony only to the solo portions of these two responsorial chants—his organum was difficult music far beyond the skill of the average, musically challenged cleric. Taking the Gradual *Viderunt omnes* for Mass at Christmas as an example, we can see how Leoninus allocated his polyphony to the chant. How many new parts, or voices, did Leoninus create? Only one: the top voice—the lower voice was a pre-existing Gregorian chant then already centuries old.

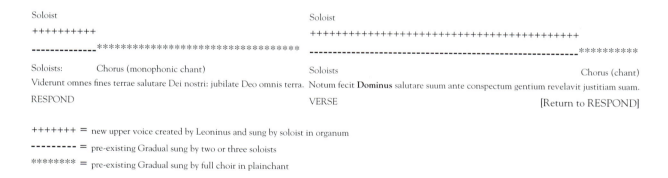

Soloist
++++++++++
-------------***********************************

Soloist
+++
--**********

Soloists: Chorus (monophonic chant)
Viderunt omnes fines terrae salutare Dei nostri: jubilate Deo omnis terra.
RESPOND

Soloists   Chorus (chant)
Notum fecit **Dominus** salutare suum ante conspectum gentium revelavit justitiam suam.
VERSE   [Return to RESPOND]

+++++++ = new upper voice created by Leoninus and sung by soloist in organum

-------- = pre-existing Gradual sung by two or three soloists

******** = pre-existing Gradual sung by full choir in plainchant

To begin the piece (and set the pitch for all), the soloists commenced in organum ("Viderunt omnes"). A single soloist sang the top part while a small group of soloists, probably two or three, sang the chant. Then the full choir, perhaps as many as a hundred voices, concluded the respond in monophonic chant. The soloists then performed the verse in polyphony, again with just one on top. Toward the end, the full choir joined in to render the last word or two in chant. Finally, the respond was repeated. Almost all of the approximately one hundred two-voice organa in Leoninus' *Magnus liber organi* were performed in this way.

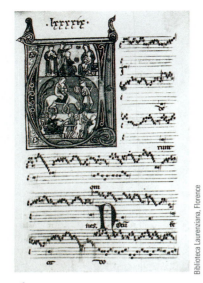

Biblioteca Laurenziana, Florence

✿ FIGURE 8-3

A thirteenth-century manuscript preserving Leoninus's organum for Christmas, *Viderunt omnes*. Leoninus' newly created voice is notated on each of the odd-numbered staves, while the slower-moving Gregorian chant appears below it on each of the even-numbered staves.

Leoninus was a composer and singer. He may have served as the soloist who negotiated the difficult upper part. Figure 8-3 shows his two-voice organum for *Viderunt omnes* as it appears in a thirteenth-century manuscript coming from Paris; indeed, one compiled within the shadow of the cathedral. It begins with a large illuminated initial for the letter "V" with scenes from the Christmas season (top to bottom): the adoration of the three kings, the flight into Egypt, and the slaughter of the innocents. Next comes the music, set on the page in pairs of staves. On the top is Leoninus' added voice; supporting it below in long notes is the chant *Viderunt omnes*. Because the bottom voice holds or draws out the notes of the chant, it is called the **tenor** (from the Latin *teneo*, to hold). While the tenor holds the chant, the upper voice undulates and cascades around it with vocal flourishes. From time to time the voices momentarily pause on a consonance, namely the octave, fifth, fourth, or unison. In general, the style of Leoninus' two-voice piece is that of older sustained-tone organum, which now is called ***organum purum*** (pure organum). *Organum purum* is florid two-voice organum.

Yet Leoninus also created something very new. Look carefully at the bottom of the Figure 8-3. Suddenly, on the syllable "do" (the beginning of "dominus" = Lord), the tenor begins to move more rapidly, almost as quickly as the upper voice. At the same time, notice how the upper voice, which had been moving up and cascading down, is now organized into neat little units of two or three notes. Instead of pure organum we now hear **discant,** a style of music in which both voices move at roughly the same rate and are written in clearly defined rhythms (see Ex. 8-2). Each separate section making use of discant style is called a **clausula** (section, phrase, or "musical clause"). "Dominus" is a clausula. What is radically new here is the introduction of music with a strong rhythmic profile. There is contrast and excitement in the music of Leoninus as it moves from polyphony to monophony and from the older, florid style of pure organum to the newer Gothic style of discant with its clearly articulated rhythms.

LISTENING CUE

LEONINUS

Viderunt omnes (c1170)

CD 1/20

Anthology, No. 20

To execute the rhythmically precise discant clausulae in *Viderunt omnes* requires that the singer read a new type of musical notation. This is called **modal notation,** and it came into music gradually, beginning around 1150–1170. By the early thirteenth century it had evolved into a system of six **rhythmic modes.** The rhythmic modes were simple patterns of repeating rhythms: one pattern for mode one, another for mode two, and so on. Variants of these patterns could be created by extending or subdividing elements of these six. Music theorists such as Anonymous IV set out the six basic patterns of modal notation as given below. The important point is this: In mensural notation (from which our modern system derives), each sign has a separate and distinct shape and thereby denotes a specific value. In older modal notation, the context determines the rhythm; the performer looks at the context of an entire passage (a group of ligatures) and extrapolates an unvarying rhythm to be applied from beginning to end (Ex. 8-1).

EXAMPLE 8-1

Mode	Combination	Example	Transcription
I	*32222*		
II	*22223*		
III	*1333*		
IV	*3331*		
V	*333*		
VI	*433*		

In modal notation, individual square notes are grouped into units of two, three, or perhaps four notes. Each group is called a **ligature** (from the Latin "ligare," to bind). The order of ligatures signals to the singer the rhythmic mode to be applied. For example, a ligature of three notes might be followed by several ligatures of two notes. This indicates that the singer is to sing the pattern for mode 1 throughout the entire passage. If, however, the performer sees a succession of two-note ligatures followed by one of three notes, he sings the passage in rhythmic mode 2. In modal notation there are no durational values inherent in any one symbol or ligature. The performer scans the passage, recognizes the mode to be applied, and then sings it with the implied rhythmic pattern. Look again at Leoninus's *Viderunt omnes* (see Fig. 8-3) at the discant clausula on "dominus." The music is given in modal notation in Example 8-2a and the singer sings as in the modern notation found in Example 8-2b.

EXAMPLE 8-2A   EXAMPLE 8-2B

For the history of music, this was a monumental development. Now it was possible to indicate and control rhythm, as well as pitch, with precision. Modal notation was in favor for more than a hundred years, from roughly 1150 to 1280 when, because of the somewhat rigid nature of the patterns, it was gradually replaced by a more flexible system called mensural notation, in which each symbol signifies one, and only one, duration (see Chapter 10).

Rhythm in music is primeval. What was new and exciting for Leoninus and his colleagues at Notre Dame of Paris was the capacity to notate and control it. Never before did any culture have a system to write down complex rhythmic patterns. Not surprisingly, the musicians of Notre Dame decided to play with their new discovery. Composers began to isolate particular sections of the organum, specifically the discant clausulae, and apply different rhythmic and melodic solutions. For the clausula "Dominus," for example, they composed more than a dozen alternatives. These were compositional essays—attempts to explore new rhythmic opportunities. Some were written in mode 2, others in 3, 4, and 5. Some of these creations were later inserted into the pre-existing organum of Leoninus, thereby creating what is called a **substitute clausula,** one clausula written in discant style intended to replace another. Example 8-3 shows the beginnings of just two of the substitute clausulae that might be inserted in *Viderunt omnes* in place of the original clausula "Dominus." In these musical experiments there was an element of adventure and amusement. One clever follower of Leoninus created a substitute for "Do-mi-nus" which he entitled "Nus-mi-do." Appropriately, he made the chant in the tenor go backwards—the first written example of retrograde motion in the history of music!

EXAMPLE 8-3

PEROTINUS THE GREAT

Perotinus the Great (c1160–c1236) took the rhythmic innovations of Leoninus and used them to create polyphonic works of unprecedented length, complexity, and grandeur. Yet we know little of his life. Like Leoninus, he was called by the diminutive (Little Peter), had a degree from the University of Paris, and was associated with Notre Dame. He may have been the Petrus Succentor who served as canon and then choirmaster at the cathedral from 1198–1238. Anonymous IV names seven compositions by him, and he likely wrote hundreds more. His settings of the Graduals *Viderunt omnes* and *Sederunt principes* were sung at Notre Dame in 1198 and 1199, respectively. So little biography for so great a composer!

Perotinus' *Viderunt omnes* and *Sederunt principes* are extraordinary compositions. Each is long, extending more than ten minutes, and each is written for four voices. Few pieces of polyphony before this time had been composed for three or four voices. Leoninus wrote for only two voices, and thus it was not necessary to regulate all aspects of rhythm at all times; the performers could simply look at one another and sense when each was moving to the next harmony. But, when the texture was increased to three or four voices, stricter rhythmic discipline was required to coordinate all parts. Thus Perotinus dispensed with the older, improvisatory style and created a new type of organum. The tenor still holds out the chant in long notes, but all of the upper voices proceed in strict rhythms. Occasionally, when the chant is especially melismatic, Perotinus shifts into discant style, the tenor now moving with the same degree of rhythmic organization as the upper voices.

Most remarkable, the great four-voice organa of Perotinus display a unique modular construction. He creates units of carefully shaped phrases, each two, three, four, or more of what we would call measures in length. These phrases are interchangeable, that is, a unit in the **duplum** (second voice) may appear a few measures later in the **triplum** (third voice), and then shortly thereafter in the **quadruplum** (fourth voice). Modules are also repeated within one and the same voice. Example 8-4 shows the beginning of Perotinus' setting of the old Christmas Gradual *Viderunt omnes*. All four voices begin with a held note on an open fifth chord built on F. Then, while the tenors hold this pitch, the upper voices sing through a succession of phrases each four units (in $\frac{3}{8}$ meter) in length. Rhythmic mode 1 is in play. The duration of sound in one part is carefully coordinated with that in all others. The boxes show the repetitions and interlocking exchanges of the musical modules. Notice also that, at the beginning of each phrase, two and sometimes all three upper voices have a pitch that is dissonant (a major seventh) with the tenor F; by the end of the four-unit phrase, however, all voices have reached a perfect consonance with the tenor on the open-fifth chord with which the piece began.

EXAMPLE 8-4

Notice also in Perotinus' *Viderunt omnes* how the voices are all in a rather narrow range, usually within the octave above the tenor. Thus there is no clear differentiation of sonority by register; each unit looks and sounds like all the others, like so many interlocking stones on a great Gothic wall. Notice as well not only the shifts between organum and discant but also the moments when the tenor presents a new syllable of text. Perotinus calls attention to these important points by creating a crunching dissonance and then moving to a pure, open fifth, an effect especially stunning inside a stone church with sonorous acoustics. Much of the power and strength of his work derives from the tension, and ultimate resolution, of the dissonance-consonance conflict. Finally, note the feeling of rest and repose that descends when, after the excitement of the polyphony of Perotinus, the full clerical community returns with the sounds of the ancient chant. The Lord has revealed his righteousness, and the world is at peace on Christmas day.

LISTENING CUE

PEROTINUS THE GREAT
Viderunt omnes (1198)

CD 1/21
Anthology, No. 21

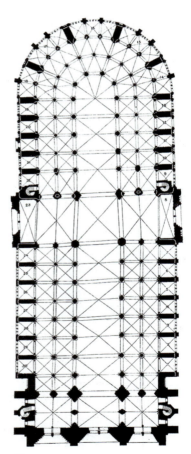

🌿 F I G U R E 8 - 4

The floor plan of the cathedral of Paris reveals the almost endless repetition of a few basic geometric patterns, just as the great four-voice organum of Perotinus repeats various melodic patterns.

The importance of Perotinus in the history of Western music can hardly be exaggerated; he can fairly be called the first modern composer. Whereas previous performer-creators of liturgical polyphony, including Leoninus, had sought to capture and notate what was at heart a free improvisatory vocal style, Perotinus undertook a radically new approach to musical organization. He replaces the expansive and wide-ranging melismas of earlier composers with shorter, complementary blocks of sound, and these in turn are balanced, shaped, and interposed to produce a brilliantly original musical architecture. Indeed, the analogy to architecture is appropriate here. Consider Figure 8-4, which shows the floor plans of Notre Dame of Paris. Notice how the full design is created by replicating again and again a few simple geometric patterns. Like the musical phrases in *Viderunt omnes*, these units are reciprocal and interchangeable. Finally, like an architect conceiving an entire edifice in the abstract and then drawing a blueprint, Perotinus thinks about the long-term implications of each musical decision. He composes each voice with an immediate eye toward the others, as well as toward what might come later in the piece. The architectonic quality of *Viderunt omnes* suggests that here we are dealing with a composer in the modern sense of the word, an artist who had a plan and who designed *a priori* all parts of his composition. The composer has replaced the improviser.

Notre Dame of Paris has now survived more than eight centuries. Yet never was Notre Dame more important in the history of music than during the period 1160–1260. Leoninus, Perotinus, and their colleagues created a huge musical repertory, more than a thousand pieces. So numerous were their compositions and so influential their style that historians later came to speak of the **Notre Dame School.** There had been other, earlier centers of organum, in monasteries in England and in southern France, as we have seen (Chapter 7). But the polyphonic pieces created in these churches were comparatively few and were unique to them; almost never did an organum from one center reappear in a manuscript produced at another. By the thirteenth century things began to change. The fledgling University of Paris was attracting theology students from across Europe. When these masters and scholars returned to their native lands, they carried with them not only what they had learned of scholastic theology but also the most up-to-date music from Paris. The works of Leoninus and Perotinus came to be heard in Spain, Germany, England, Italy, the Low Countries, and even Poland. Now for the first time it was possible to speak of an international repertory of polyphonic music.

SUMMARY

During the late twelfth century, Paris became the center of music, as well as architecture and theology, for Western Europe. All that was new in music could be seen in the compositions of two leading figures, Leoninus and Perotinus. Leoninus compiled a *Magnus liber organi* containing nearly one hundred two-voice organa, mostly settings of the Gradual and Alleluia to adorn the Mass on high feast days. Perotinus updated this and composed many new pieces for three and four voices. Perhaps the most impressive musical works of the high Middle Ages can be found in the four-voice organa of Perotinus. These are long, complex works that would have required a great deal of "pre-planning," or composition as we think of it today. Large-scale, multi-voice composition had been made possible by a new development: rhythmic control. By means of a system of rhythmic modes, Leoninus and Perotinus developed a way to regulate rhythm through musical notation. The innovative style of the Notre Dame School spread throughout Western Europe, thereby becoming the first international repertory of polyphonic music.

KEY TERMS

Gothic architecture	*organum purum*	substitute clausula
nave	discant	Perotinus
choir	clausula (pl., clausulae)	duplum
Leoninus	modal notation	triplum
Magnus liber organi	rhythmic modes	quadruplum
tenor	ligature	Notre Dame School

Music in the Cathedral Close and University: Conductus and Motet

Leoninus and Perotinus created organa to adorn the liturgy celebrated in the choir of Notre Dame on high feasts. But they and their later musical colleagues also wrote polyphony that was not so strictly tied to the church. New musical genres such as the conductus and motet were equally at home in the cathedral, outside the church in the adjoining close, and at the university.

Situated next to almost every medieval cathedral was an independent urban enclave called the **close.** The close was a gated community for the men employed in the cathedral: canons, chaplains, vicars, musicians, choirboys, sacristans, and vergers, as well as several hundred assistants and servants, most male but a few female. As a territory free from control of the king, the close at Notre Dame of Paris enjoyed its own weights and measures, police force, and jail. Within its walls sat several dozen houses for the clergy, the cathedral school where music was taught, and the dormitory for the choirboys. Figure 9-1, the earliest surviving map of Paris,

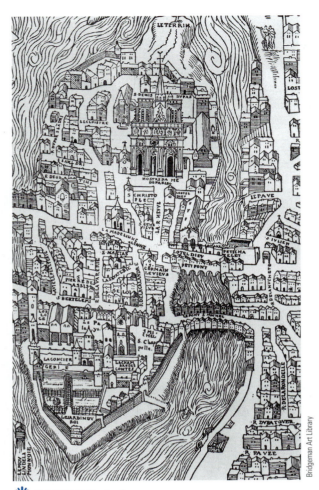

🌿 FIGURE 9-1

Île de la Cité and close of Notre Dame of Paris as they appear in the earliest map of Paris. The area of the close is to the left of the cathedral.

Bridgeman Art Library

shows the *Île de la Cité,* the cathedral, and the close ("le cloistre") to the north (left) of the church.

Of all the clerics to reside in the close of Notre Dame, none was more famous, or infamous, than **Peter Abelard.** Abelard, a nobleman turned cleric, set up shop as a professor of logic in the close of Notre Dame in 1114. Soon he obtained lodging in the house of canon Fulbert, and was given charge of the education of Fulbert's niece, the gifted **Héloise.** The relationship led to one of the most passionate and scandalous romances of the Middle Ages, culminating in the birth of a child and the castration of Abelard. Banned from the close, he became a monk, she a nun. Despite the shame and pain, their love affair produced an outpouring of poetry and music from the pen of Abelard, as Héloise reveals in the first of her famous letters to him:

> You had besides, I admit, two special gifts whereby to win at once the heart of any woman—your gifts for composing verse and music, in which we know other philosophers have rarely been successful. This was for you no more than a diversion, a recreation from the labors of your philosophic work, but you left many love-songs and verse which won wide popularity for the charm of their words and tunes and kept your name continually on everyone's lips. The beauty of the melodies ensured that even the unlettered did not forget you.[1]

Although the words and music of a hymn and six laments by Abelard are preserved, none of the love songs that the great philosopher wrote in the close of Notre Dame has survived.

The scandal of Abelard and Héloise, along with related disorders, caused the churchmen of Notre Dame to expel the unruly scholars and masters from the close. In the course of the twelfth century, the schools moved across the Seine and onto the left bank. In 1215 the pope gave formal recognition to the new *Universitas*—a unified collection of all the schools and colleges under a single administrative head. By then, there were approximately ten thousand students enrolled at the university of Paris, about one-fifth of the total population of the city.

Life in a medieval university was very different from university life today. To begin with, all students were male, usually ranging in age from fourteen to twenty-two. To the extent that women received an education in the Middle Ages, this occurred in the home or in a convent. Students paid their money directly to the master for the instruction they received, and the teacher's income was proportional to the number of students he attracted. Lectures were given in Latin, and on the streets students spoke the international language of all scholars, again Latin (hence the term "**Latin Quarter**" of Paris). There were few textbooks, and what books the student possessed he copied by hand, section by section, from an exemplar rented from a local bookstore. Most learning was done by oral repetition and rote memory. After six years of study, including one term devoted to Boethius' *the Fundamentals of Music,* a student could petition to be examined. If successful, he was admitted to the group of masters licensed to teach the seven liberal arts—he had graduated.

At the head of the University of Paris was the chancellor of the cathedral of Notre Dame. In matters of education he spoke for both the cathedral and the university. During the years 1217–1236 the head of the University of Paris was Philip of Nemours, called **Philip the Chancellor** (c1160–1236). From Philip's pen flowed no fewer than seven hundred sermons for the cathedral and the university. He was also a poet and apparently a composer of some merit. Seventy compositions with religious or moralistic texts by Philip survive today. Most of Philip's creations can be classified among one of two new musical genres that arose during these years: the conductus and the motet.

CONDUCTUS

The term **conductus** derives from the Latin infinitive *ducere*, to lead. From a related word *educere* (to lead forward or elevate) come our words "educate" and "education." As the name suggests, the conductus was sung as the clergy moved from place to place or was engaged in some other type of kinetic activity, such as dance. The prefix "con" may also imply that this music was sung as part of a gathering of clergy, perhaps for a festal or convivial event. Thus conducti[†] appear as processional pieces to convey celebrants from one spot to another within the church, as musical accompaniments to the movements of characters in liturgical drama, and as songs to lead the clergy into and out of the church. They are not part of the formal liturgy (Mass and canonical hours). Conducti are written for one, two, three, and occasionally four voices. Their texts are metrical Latin poems arranged in successive stanzas. Most are serious and moralistic in tone. Many conducti, however, have ties to the Christmas and New Year's season. As such, these seasonal conducti served as the medieval equivalent of today's Christmas carols—joyous pieces, often with a refrain, sung by a group in the church or in the close.

A good example of a lighter conductus can be seen in the anonymous three-voice *Orientis partibus* (Ex. 9-1). Known throughout the musical world today as the *Song of the Ass*, it parodies the solemnities of the Christmas season. To understand its meaning, we must set the context in which this conductus was sung.

For the medieval clergy, most of the fun of Christmas came, not on Christmas day but during the following week, when the services of the church were handed over to the younger clergy to celebrate in place of their superiors. The most raucous revels came on Circumcision (1 January), also known as the **Feast of Fools,** when the youngest of the adult clerics took charge of the church. Standing in the choir and at the high altar, the youths engaged in a blasphemous mockery of the liturgical service. Some dressed as women, others threw bones across the choir aisle, while the "celebrant" lit an old shoe and censed the altar with its smoke. Before all this began, however, the youths processed around the town and then back into the church. Leading the procession was an ass, the humble beast of burden that had carried Mary and her baby to Bethlehem (see Fig. 8-3). Picture in your mind's eye several dozen inebriated teenagers driving a frightened donkey up the aisle of Notre Dame on New Year's Eve. As they proceeded, they sang a conductus, one that imitated the hey-hawing ("Hez, va") of the ass and concluded with a reference to what this beast did most often on the floor.

[†]In the Middle Ages "conductus" appears as both a second- and fourth-declension noun. The plural, thus, can be either "conducti" or "conductus."

EXAMPLE 9-1

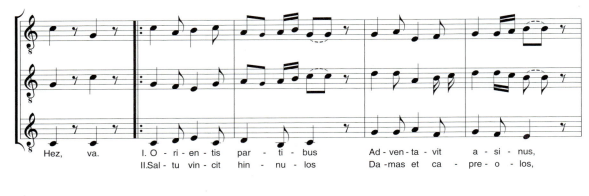

Hez, va. / I. O - ri - en - tis par - ti - bus / II. Sal - tu vin - cit hin - nu - los / Ad - ven - ta - vit a - si - nus, / Da - mas et ca - pre - o - los,

Pul - cher et for - tis - si - mus, / Su - per dro - me - da - ri - os, / Sar - ci - nis a - ptis - si - mus. / Ve - lox Me - dy - a - ne - os, / Hez, [va,] hez, sire as - ne, hez! / Hez, [va,] hez, sire as - ne, hez!

From Orient lands
Came an ass,
Handsome and most strong,
An excellent beast of burden
Hey, ho, hey, Sir Ass, hey!

With a leap he out-jumped the stag
The antelope and deer
Faster than dromedaries
From Media
Hey, ho, hey, Sir Ass, hey!

    Orientis partibus (c1200) is a short, simple conductus. Yet in many ways it is typical of the genre. The text setting is syllabic, and all parts sing a single text simultaneously. The text itself is metrical and strophic, each of its seven strophes ending with a refrain. It speaks to the asinine moment, but is full of sacred allusions to scripture. Notice the tuneful nature of the tenor. As in other genres of polyphony in the Middle Ages, the tenor came first and the other voices were built upon it. But what is most important in the conductus is that the tenor is not a pre-existing chant, but a newly composed melody. This is the first polyphonic music in which the composer has free rein to create all the voices. The style of the conductus is that of discant—all voices move at about the same rate and create consonances on the strong beats. In *Orientis partibus*, the first rhythmic mode predominates, synchronized to the troachic meter of the Latin poetry. At the end of each musical phrase the upper voices cadence with the tenor, thereby clarifying the structural division of the work. *Orientis partibus* is immediately accessible because the tenor sounds strongly tonal to our ears, centered as it is around what we would call a C major triad. Medieval ears, however, would have heard this as a piece in the Lydian mode (with B♭) transposed to C. Perhaps because of the tuneful, tonal quality of the tenor, the medieval *Orientis partibus* survives today in many books of Christmas carols under the title *The Friendly Beast*.

LISTENING CUE

ANONYMOUS
Orientis partibus (c1200)

CD 1/22
Anthology, No. 22

Orientis partibus is exceptional for its humor, specifically for its parody of the liturgy of Christmas. Far more typical, however, are the serious moralistic conducti of Philip the Chancellor. His texts range from pious prayers to the Virgin to stinging condemnations of corrupt clergymen, kings, and popes. In his sermons and poems he fought for the rights of the chancellor of the university, fending off the encroaching masters (the faculty) and their ally, the pope. His conductus *Dic, Christi veritas* (*Speak, Christian Truth*) shows how Philip used the musical genre of the conductus as a bully pulpit from which to excoriate his enemies, namely the masters, as well as the pope, who rarely came to his aid in these academic disputes. *Dic, Christi veritas* is a rhetorical composition, one in which text and music work together for maximum effect. The effect is achieved by means of what the music theorists of the day referred to as a **cauda** (pl., **caudae**)—literally a "tail" (whence our word "coda"), a long melisma on a single syllable. A *cauda* might come anywhere—beginning, middle, or end—of a conductus to set off key words. The most distinctive *cauda* in *Dic, Christi veritas* comes at the end of the first stanza where Philip the Chancellor depicts the rantings of the pope with a lengthy melisma on "fulminante" ("fulminating")—a rare moment of word painting in medieval music. *Dic, Christi veritas* may have been sung as the Chancellor processed to the pulpit to deliver a sermon. Yet it could also stand alone outside the church, for this conductus is itself both a sermon and a lecture in music.

LISTENING CUE

PHILIP THE CHANCELLOR
Dic, Christi veritas (c1230)

CD 1/23
Anthology, No. 23

 MOTET

Medieval Paris was also home to another new genre of music that emerged around 1200, the motet. Originally a **motet** (diminutive of the French *mot* meaning "word") was a discant clausula (see Chapter 8) to which sacred words were added. Recall that a discant clausula was simply a self-contained section of organum in discant (note-against-note) style involving just one or two words in the original chant. With the motet, however, things are different. Instead of all voices singing just one word in melismatic fashion, each upper voice declaims its own new poetic text. These new words comment upon the significance of the single Latin word sung by the tenor. Throughout the Middle Ages theologians had taken a passage of scripture and expanded upon it, offering their own views as to the meaning of the holy writ. Now this practice, called "glossing," was applied to music. The upper voice or

✳ FIGURE 9-2

The motetus and tenor (bottom
system) of the motet *El mois
d'avril/O quam sancta/Et gaudebit*
as it appears in a manuscript compiled in the area of Paris around
1300. In the upper minature a
cleric venerates a statue of the
Virgin, while the lower scene
depicts events associated with
spring.

voices glossed the meaning of the tenor. For example, while the tenor
voice sang the word "Lord," a second voice (now called the **motetus**)
would speak of Christ's birth and the hope for humankind that the Lord
brings, while the third voice (still called the triplum) would relate the
Lord's ultimate fate on the cross. Thus the early motet was polytextual,
involving at least two Latin texts and sometimes three or four, in cases of
three- or four-voice motets. Soon French texts were inserted along with
those in Latin. In the course of the thirteenth century the motet gradually replaced organum and conductus as the preferred genre of musical
composition. By 1300 more than a thousand motets had been created.
One manuscript alone, called the Montpellier Codex (Fig. 9-2), contains
345 motets, some with Latin upper voices, some with French, and some
with both languages sung simultaneously.

To understand the historical development of the motet, consider the
text of the Alleluia *Alleluia. Non vos reliquam* and Example 9-2a–c. The
clausula (and subsequent motets) grew out of the words "Et gaudebit"
("And it will rejoice") of the chant. Example 9-2a shows the beginning of
the two-voice discant clausula *Et gaudebit* as it appears in the *Magnus liber
organi*. The clausula belonged to organum added to the Alleluia of the
Mass for Ascension, that joyful day on which Christ ascended into heaven.
The Alleluia text borrows from John (14:18)—*Alleluia. Non vos relinquam
orphanos; vado et venio ad vos et gaudebit cor vestrum* (Alleluia. I will not
leave you orphans; I come and go among you, and your heart, it will rejoice). Thus the spiritual theme of these motets is Christian rejoicing.

Alleluia - - - .   Non vos relinquam orphanos; vado et venio ad vos **et gaudebit** cor vestrum.
Organum-chant. Organum - **clausula** - organum

EXAMPLE 9-2A

Example 9-2b shows the beginning of the same piece but with text now added to
the upper voice, thereby creating a motet. The new text in this motetus voice sings
the praises of the Virgin and of the joy of the angels, and it ends with an obvious
expansion of the spiritual theme of the tenor (*Et gaudebit*): *Gaude in filio, gaudens
ego gaudeo in Domino* (Rejoice in the Son, rejoicing I will rejoice in the Lord).

EXAMPLE 9-2B

Example 9-2c shows the same two-voice motet, but now with a third voice. The text here is in old French and speaks of the beauties of spring. At first glance, this poem seems to have little to do with the spiritual message of the tenor.

EXAMPLE 9-2c

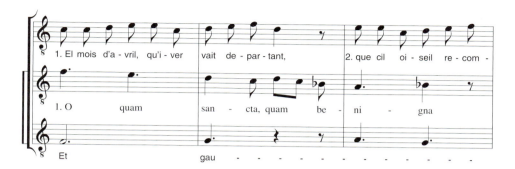

In the month of April, when winter begins to depart and the birds begin again their song,
one morning I was riding through the woods . . .
Oh, how holy, how benign, shines the mother of the Savior . . .
And [my heart] will rejoice.

Let us examine more carefully this anonymous three-voice bilingual motet *El mois d'avril/O quam sancta/Et gaudebit*, written in Paris around 1230. Once again, we see the basic principle of medieval composition at work: a phrase of Gregorian chant provides a scaffold for the entire composition. That is to say, the pitches of a pre-existing chant, placed in the tenor, determine the harmonies created by the upper voices—the motetus and triplum form consonances with the tenor on strong beats and dissonance off the beat. The favored consonances are the unison, fifth, and octave, with the fourth also appearing from time to time. Notice that the three voices are moving at different rates of speed. The French triplum has more text than the Latin motetus and thus must move in shorter note values. In fact, the triplum is in rhythmic mode 6, the motetus in mode 1, and the slow moving tenor in mode 5 (on the medieval rhythmic modes, see Chapter 8). Here the modes are slightly obscured because of extensions and subdivisions of the basic modal patterns. At the beginning, for example, the tenor extends or elongates the mode 5 pattern, changing two dotted quarter-notes into a single dotted half-note. What results in the tenor is an unvarying rhythmic pattern four bars in length.

Most important, the entire tenor melody is repeated, starting in measure thirty-six. The decision to repeat the tenor required the composer to write the piece a second time, providing a new musical response above the same tenor melody and rhythm. The texts of the upper voices respect, indeed emphasize, the sectional division within this motet. Part I (bars 1–35) of the motetus offers praises to the Virgin Mary, extolling her virtues; Part II (bars 36–70) is a supplication to Mary, imploring her to pray to Christ on behalf of the sinners of this world. Similarly, Part I of the triplum tells of a wandering knight who visits a magical garden, whereas Part II describes the wondrous maiden he found there. But how did a knight and a maiden get into this story of Christ's ascension?

To understand the full meaning of the motet *El mois d'avril/O quam sancta/Et gaudebit* we must enter into the mindset of a medieval university student. A literal reading of the story of the handsome knight and the beautiful maiden (*El mois d'avril*) suggests an earthly love. A medieval university cleric, however, would have understood it much differently, applying an allegorical interpretation to the text, just what the theologians taught at the University of Paris. The magical garden is the sacred garden of Gethsemane; the maiden is not any maid but the Virgin Mary; the fine spring day in April is the period around Ascension; and the new love is the love for the newly risen Christ. Mary has given herself to Christ and, in the end, so will every faithful Christian. Motet texts of this type can be read at two levels, the literal and the allegorical. The students and masters of the day delighted in multiple meanings just as they delighted in multiple texts. The polytextual motet of the Middle Ages is as subtle intellectually as it is pleasing musically.

Given the intellectual quality of the medieval motet, for whom was it written? Who was the audience? Music theorists of the period tell us that the motet was created for an educated elite. Johannes de Grocheio, for example, writing in Paris around 1300, says that the motet was intended for the "literati"—a literate class who could properly understand it. In the thirteenth century there was only one literate, elite class: the clerical students and masters who lived at the cathedral and university. Only they could have appreciated, for example, the richness of the Latin poem in the motetus (*O quam sancta*) with its biblical references to Jacob's ladder and the tree of Jesse. In sum, the polytextual motet was created for clerical recreation and edification, to be sung in private moments in private residences. This is religious music, but not necessarily music for the church, and certainly not for the masses.

LISTENING CUE

ANONYMOUS MOTET   CD 1/24
El mois d'avril/O quam sancta/Et gaudebit (c1230)   Anthology, No. 24c

Music of the Notre Dame School began at the cathedral and gradually spread beyond its confines, to the close, to the university, and then to other countries. As it did so, new genres of music, the conductus and motet, were created. By the second half of the thirteenth century polyphony began to lose its historical connection to the cathedral. Motet tenors were no longer drawn exclusively from the repertory of cathedral chants that had served Leoninus for the *Magnus liber organi*, for example. Instead, tenor tunes came from other chants, from trouvère melodies, from popular songs, from street cries, and from new melodies fashioned for the occasion by the composer.

By the end of the thirteenth century, the subject matter of the motet in Paris ranged from the esoteric to the frivolous. Similarly, no one motet style dominated.

Instead, we find remarkable diversity of borrowed tenors and formal procedures, as the motet runs the gamut from high to low art. A more popular style can be found in the three-voice *On parole de batre/A Paris/Frese nouvele,* a simple piece which extols the simple pleasures of medieval Paris. As both motetus and triplum voices assure us, Paris was renowned for its food, wine, and beautiful women. In keeping with the urban theme, here the tenor is a street cry—the call of a wandering peddler of the sort who could still be heard on the streets of Paris into the 1970s. This medieval street vendor is hawking fresh strawberries and ripe blackberries. The musical structure of his cry is as basic as his merchandise: the same eight-bar phrase is heard four times. We are now very far from the esoteric allegory of cathedral close and university. While it may be going too far to call this the "rap music" of the high Middle Ages, nonetheless this motet shows that, in late thirteenth-century Paris, popular urban polyphony was alive and well.

EXAMPLE 9-3

On pa-ro-le de batre et de van-ner et de fo-ïr et de han-ner;

A Pa-ris soir et ma - tin truev[e] on bon pain et bon

Fre - se nou - ve - le, mue-re fran-ce, mue-re, mue-re

They talk of threshing and winnowing, of digging and cultivating
In Paris morn and night one can find good bread and good clear [wine]
Fresh strawberries, ripe black berries…

LISTENING CUE

ANONYMOUS MOTET
On parole de batre/A Paris/Frese nouvele (c1280)

CD 1/25
Anthology, No. 25

SUMMARY

The art music of the thirteenth century is marked by the appearance of two new musical genres, the conductus and motet. The conductus was not part of the canonical liturgy but something of an "add-on"—it was most often sung as the clergy moved from place to place. In musical style the conductus might be from one to as many as four voices. The conductus does not make use of a pre-existing Gregorian chant. All voices are newly composed, even the tenor, and all sing the same Latin text. The subject matter of the conductus ranges widely, from holiday carol texts to political sermons. The musical style, however, is consistently discant.

The motet came into being around 1200 and soon became the most favored type of polyphonic music of the thirteenth century. It began life within the service of the church, when clerics added a text to the upper voice of a two-voice clausula within an organum. Soon, however, more voices were added, with texts in French as well as Latin. The upper texts glossed (commented upon) the spiritual theme carried by the pre-existing chant in the tenor. Gradually, the motet moved away from the liturgy inside the cathedral to the close and university, where clerics enjoyed it for both spiritual enlightenment and entertainment. By the end of the thirteenth century, popular refrains, even street cries, had made their way into the motet, occasionally transforming it into a type of urban popular music.

KEY TERMS

close

Peter Abelard

Héloise

Universitas

Latin Quarter

Philip the Chancellor

conductus

Feast of Fools

cauda (pl., *caudae*)

motet

motetus

Chapter 10

In the Parisian Master's Study: Music Theory of the *Ars Antiqua* and *Ars Nova*

In the Middle Ages people did not think of the world as we do today. To begin with, they believed that the sun revolved around the earth, that Jerusalem sat at the exact center of the earth, and that the world was no more than seven thousand years old, extending back only a few years before the Flood. Reality was explained by the Bible, not science, and it was flexible. The time needed to boil an egg was calculated by the length of time necessary to say a *Miserere* (Psalm 50). The New Year might begin on 1 January, 25 March, or Easter, depending on where you lived. Time was regulated by the seasons, by night and day, or perhaps by a sundial if it were not dark or too cloudy. An "hour" of the day was longer in the summer than during the winter (the span of daylight was divided by twelve no matter how long an hour might last). Everywhere the progress of time was marked by the unfolding of the liturgy of the church and announced to the people by the ringing of bells. Needless to say, this was an inexact measurement that depended upon local religious traditions. Evening (Vespers), for example, might be signaled in one town at one time and many, many minutes later in another. What difference did it make?

Around 1300 all this began to change. Within fifty years on either side of this date, mechanical clocks were invented, cannons fired, organs placed in Gothic cathedrals, and nautical charts written—all inventions dependent upon the precise measurement of time, distance, space, or pitch. Clocks and organs were most often placed in the nave of the church, so that all the people could see and hear these astonishing technological innovations. Harmony, whether produced by instrument or by voice, was possible because pitches could be precisely measured and adjusted so as to achieve a harmonious sound. Music theorists since Greek antiquity had measured two pitches against each other, seeing in them a worldly manifestation of divine number. In order for three or four voices to sing separate parts, however, time had to be precisely measured. Music theory throughout the thirteenth century was concerned with the measurement of time. By the end of the century both harmonic intervals and musical time were rationalized within coherent systems of pleasing regularity.

Once again Paris, and specifically the University of Paris, was the epicenter of these important developments—the music theorists of the day were almost all masters at the university. These musicians were perhaps as much "teacher-reporters" as what we would call music theorists. They prepared lectures on music for the students of the various schools and colleges. They delivered these orally, but over the decades their various pronouncements on music were arranged in logical fashion by students or other masters and written down. The masters were concerned with measuring and classifying pitch, but more so with rhythm.

❋ FRANCO OF COLOGNE AND THE *ART OF MEASURED SONG*

The clearest exposition of the music theory of the thirteenth century is found in Franco of Cologne's *Ars cantus mensurabilis* **(Art of Measured Song). Franco of Cologne,** sometimes called Franco of Paris, was a German who had come to Paris to teach around 1280. His treatise contains the first fully systematic classification of harmonic intervals, one that he frames in terms of consonance and dissonance in the following way:

CONSONANCES

Perfect consonances:	*Intermediate consonances:*	*Imperfect consonances:*
unison and octave	fifth and fourth	major and minor thirds

DISSONANCES

Imperfect dissonances:	*Perfect dissonances:*
minor seventh, major sixth, whole tone	minor sixth, semitone, tritone, major seventh

From our modern perspective, it is surprising to find the fourth classified here as a consonance (by the fifteenth century it will come to be viewed as a dissonance). Similarly, it is surprising to see that the sixths, which sound "sweet" to us, were dissonant to medieval ears; a minor sixth, for example, was thought to be just as dissonant as a semitone!

Most important, Franco's hierarchy of consonance and dissonance suggests that music was developing much like philosophy and logic at this time. Intellectuals divided material, even musical intervals, into categories, sets, and then subsets. They created a revolutionary approach to "information management" by constructing chains of hierarchical categories and relationships. This mode of thinking is called **scholasticism,** and it rose to prominence at the University of Paris during the thirteenth century. When we prepare an outline with topics and subtopics, headings and subheadings, we engage in a scholastic exercise.

Time, too, could be divided and subdivided into many separate parts. If the newly invented clock allowed the day to be broken into exact hours, minutes, and seconds, so the theorist might divide music into temporal units such as the double long, the long, and the short. The smaller units were interchangeable subsets of the larger. Franco of Cologne organized these into reciprocal relationships and explained temporal duration in music in terms of an overarching system. Franco recognized three basic note shapes: the **long** (◻), the **breve** (◻) and the **semibreve** (◻). Each unit stood in a triple relationship to the unit nearest it so as to honor, Franco said, the Holy Trinity—the fundamental meter of all written music was still triple, as in the days of modal rhythm. This was the theory, although Franco allowed that in practice a long or a breve could be made duple (reduced by a third) by a neighboring note. He also acknowledged the presence of the duplex long, a value equal to two longs. The important point, however, is that from Franco onward each note has a unique shape and a specific duration (Ex. 10-1).

EXAMPLE 10-1

| Duplex Long = 2 Longs | Long = 3 Breves | Breve = 3 Semibreves |

Rests, too, have their own symbols (Ex. 10-2).

EXAMPLE 10-2

| Duplex Long | Long | Breve | Semibreve |

By giving each note value and rest its own distinctive sign, Franco signaled the end of the older, contextual system for indicating rhythmic duration in the Notre Dame era. In brief, modal notation (contextual notation) now gave way to **mensural notation** (symbol-specific notation). Again, Franco's system can fairly be called "scholastic" because, like the famous *Summa theologica* of Parisian master Thomas Aquinas (1225–1274), it is both comprehensive and hierarchical, progressing in categories from largest to smallest values. Time in music was now thought of as a continuum involving division and further subdivision. The next generation of Parisian masters would extend Franco's scholastic system to radical lengths.

✺ JEAN DES MURS AND PHILIPPE DE VITRY: THE *ARS NOVA*

Significantly, both masters Jean des Murs and Philippe de Vitry were Parisian mathematicians as well as music theorists. As we have often seen, the medieval mind might occupy itself equally with the manipulation of numbers, the motion of the stars and planets, or the duration of musical sounds. **Jean des Murs** (c1290–c1351) was an astronomer, mathematician, musician, and convicted murderer (for which crime he was exiled to Cyprus for seven years). **Philippe de Vitry** (1291–1361) was a mathematician, astronomer, poet, diplomat, and bishop, as well as composer. Each compiled an important musical treatise. Jean des Murs called his *Notitia artis musicae* (*Knowledge of the Art of Music*), but it also went under the title *Ars novae musicae* (*Art of New Music*). Philippe de Vitry's work simply went by the name *Ars nova* (*New Art*). That the title *Ars nova* was given to these treatises suggests that Jean and Philippe were keenly aware of the power and originality of their ideas; they knew that they were creating a new art, an *avant garde* that would soon affect polyphony generally. Thus later historians have given the title *Ars nova* to all music of the first half of the fourteenth century. But what is new about the *Ars nova*?

The *Ars nova*—music of the first half of the fourteenth century—is characterized by four innovations: (1) The theorists acknowledge a new short note value, the **minim,** as a subdivision of the semibreve. In the course of the thirteenth century the duration of each note in performance had become longer, and this had necessitated the addition of a new note sign (the minim) to express a shorter value. (2) For the first time in the history of music, musicians divide durations into duple as well as triple units (Ex. 10-3). The long, for example, might consist of either two or three breves, and the breve of two or three semibreves. What we call duple meter is now sanctioned by music theory. This further extends the scale of musical time. Note values now run from the triplex long to the minim (the very shortest conceivable unit of time). Duple or triple divisions were possible at all levels of duration. When duple divisions were in play, a **dot** could be added after the note to turn it temporarily into a triple value; thus the dot, adding 50 percent to the value of the note, enters music history at this time. Taking the division of the notes, duple or triple, from largest to smallest: the division of the long was called the **mode** (*modus*), that of the breve the **time** (*tempus*), and that of the semibreve **prolation** (*prolatio*). (3) By coloring certain notes red, triplets and hemiola could be introduced in what were otherwise duple meters. (4) Meter signatures (time signatures) now appear for the first time in the history of music. To signal to performers what relationships hold sway in a composition (duple or triple), signs are placed at the beginning of the work. Originally there were six signs indicating a duple or triple division for the mode, time, and prolation. Soon, however, those for mode were dropped, leaving these four time signatures. One of these signatures, the C indicating "common time," is still in use today.

EXAMPLE 10-3

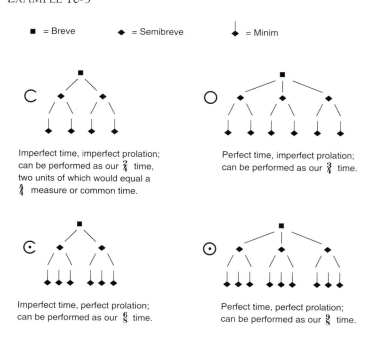

The practical result of all this was that the musicians of the *Ars nova* saw before them a brave new world of rhythmic flexibility. A composition need not have the same monorhythmic sound from beginning to end; it need not thump along in repetitive patterns like the discant of Leoninus and Perotinus. Rhythmic textures could change with surprising rapidity. Although the tempo would remain the same, the music might seem to speed up and then suddenly slow down, faster here, slower there, as radically longer or shorter values were introduced. The shortest note in the system (the minim) was eighty-one times faster (shorter) than the longest note (the triplex long). Musicians had gained total control over the second of the two fundamental parameters of music: pitch and time. The composer could create and express on parchment, in the most precise and detailed terms, these two axes, pitch written vertically and time horizontally. The West had its first graph, and it was created in music. The composer, consciously or not, stood at the forefront of science.

But not all musicians were pleased. One in particular, the music theorist **Jacques de Liège** (c1260–c1330), inveighed against the radical innovations of the *Ars nova* with its duple relationships and small note values. He preferred instead the earlier style of Parisian music, with its uniform pace and clear ternary units—the sort of music that we have seen in the motet *El mois d'avril/O quam sancta/Et gaudebit* (see Chapter 9). Jacques dubbed this older repertory the *Ars antiqua.* Battle lines were drawn between the conservative music of the thirteenth century and the radical new music of the fourteenth—between the *Ars antiqua* and the *Ars nova.* Even **Pope John XXII** charged into the fray to defend conservative church music. In his bull *Docta sanctorum patrum* (*Teachings of the Holy Fathers*; 1324) he fumed:

> But certain exponents of a new school, who think only of the laws of measured time, are composing new melodies of their own creation with a new system of notes, and these they prefer to the ancient, traditional music; the melodies of the Church are sung in semibreves and minims and with gracenotes of repercussion. . . . These composers, knowing nothing of the true foundation upon which they must build, are ignorant of the church modes, incapable of distinguishing between them, and cause great confusion. The great number of notes in their compositions conceals from us the plainchant melody, with its simple well-regulated rises and falls that indicate the character of the church mode. These musicians run without pausing. They intoxicate the ear without satisfying it; they dramatize the text with gestures; and, instead of promoting devotion, they prevent it by creating a sensuous and indecent atmosphere. . . . Consequently, we intend to prohibit, cast out, and banish such things from the Church of God.[1]

But the pope's opinion had little sway. The music of the *Ars nova* continued to develop unchecked. Why? Because, as history shows, it is futile to legislate progress or regulate personal preference in the arts. In fact, in this specific instance, the voice of the pope grew fainter and fainter, as the authority of the church generally declined during the fourteenth century. The balance of power in the arts—in poetry and literature as well as music—was shifting away from the church to the courts of secular rulers.

SUMMARY

The single most important development in Western music in the thirteenth century was the movement away from a system of notation based on context (modal notation) to one based on specific signs (mensural notation). By the end of the century, there were four basic note values as expounded by Franco of Cologne: duplex long, long, breve, and semibreve. But these values began to slow down (last longer), so yet a new smaller value, the minim, was introduced around 1300 to carry the faster-moving notes. Musicians continued to be fascinated with the possibilities of measuring and controlling time, and they experimented with rhythm in the main musical genre of the day, the motet. Music theorists Jean des Murs and Philippe de Vitry pro-moted several rhythmic innovations, including duple meter, triplets, and hemiola, and the use of time signatures. A wide range of durations as well as a greater variety of patterns were now possible. This new style of music (*Ars nova*) was far more com-plex rhythmically than thirteenth-century music (*Ars antiqua*) with its simple pat-terns, all in triple meter. By the end of the fourteenth century musicians would take the rhythmic innovations of the *Ars nova* to extraordinary extremes.

KEY TERMS

Art of Measured Song	mensural notation	time
Franco of Cologne	Jean des Murs	prolation
scholasticism	Philippe de Vitry	Jacques de Liège
long	minim	*Ars nova*
breve	dot	*Ars antiqua*
semibreve	mode	Pope John XXII

Chapter

Music at the Court of the French Kings

11

Notre Dame of Paris sits on the east end of an island (*Île de la Cité*) in the Seine River, and has traditionally served as a symbol of religious and spiritual authority in French life. The government and the courts, however, have historically been situ-ated at the west end of the island. In medieval times, secular power rested with the kings who resided there in a fortified palace. By the early fourteenth century, the royal compound included, among other buildings, apartments for the king and his courtiers, a donjon, a meeting hall for parliament, and a two-story chapel, the fa-mous Sainte-Chapelle that still stands today. Yet the largest and most impressive part of the royal palace was the Grande-Salle. Measuring 70 meters in length and 27 meters in width, it was then the largest hall in Western Eu-rope. Here, surrounded by mounted statues of the ancient rulers of France, the king welcomed heads of state and gave royal banquets. All such events were adorned with secular music of various sorts.

The Grande-Salle was built during the reign of King Philip IV (1285–1314) by his chief financial minister Enguerran de Marigny (c1275–1315). Marigny had risen to a position of great power at court, but had accumu-lated equally powerful enemies along the way; moreover, he was skim-ming money from the king's treasury. Immediately upon the death of his royal protector in 1314, Marigny was accused of corruption, tried, con-victed, and hanged high above Paris on the gallows at Montmartre. So sensational were these events that they gave rise to a long poetic satire called the *Roman de Fauvel*. In one copy of the *Roman de Fauvel* (Fig. 11-1), the story is brought vividly to life through the addition of illustrations and music. With its 135 monophonic and 34 polyphonic compositions, and its pictures, this version of the *Roman de Fauvel* constitutes the most im-portant music manuscript of the first half of the fourteenth century.

FIGURE 11-1

A plate from the *Roman de Fauvel*, showing Fauvel the ass, in the top panel, on his wedding night.

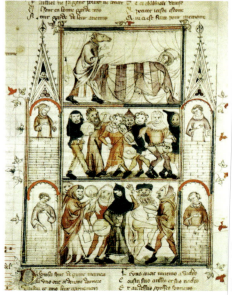

Bridgeman Art Library

✤ THE ROMAN DE FAUVEL

The **Roman de Fauvel** (*Tale of Fauvel*) is a fable about political power gone awry. In it Enguerran de Marigny and his corrupt henchmen are collectively portrayed as a witless ass, Fauvel. The animal's name is an acronym derived from the first letters of six worldly sins—*Flaterie*(flattery), **A**varice (avarice), *Vilanie* (villainy), *Variété* (fickleness), **E**nvie (envy), and *Lascheté* (loose morals) = FAUVEL. Most of the poem was written in 1314 by Gervès de Bus, though the poet Chaillou de Pesstain and the composer Philippe de Vitry made insertions a few years later. All three men were young notaries at the French royal court. Thus they had the "inside scoop" on what was happening behind the back of old King Philip IV. They intended their satirical creation to serve as a warning to the next ruler to root out graft and corruption; if the king would only follow the poet's advice, he could not fail to become an excellent ruler. In Fauvel's world, Lady Fortune has turned everything upside down: lawyers pervert the law; justices are unjust; and pope and king bow down, fawning before Fauvel. (Our expression "to curry favor" is derived from "to curry Fauvel.") Most of the *Roman de Fauvel* is a poetic recitation to be delivered in medieval French by a narrator, perhaps with simple improvised instrumental accompaniment in the background. The following selected lines give a taste of this political morality tale.

De Fauvel que tant voi torcher	I see so many people curry Fauvel
Doucement sans lui escorcher,	Softly without skinning him,
Sui entréz en merencolie,	I've fallen into a melancholy state
Pour ce qu'est beste si polie. . . .	Because he is so well groomed. . . .
Fauvel ne gist mès en l'estable,	Fauvel no longer lives in a stable
Il a meson plus honorable:	He has a more honorable house
Haute mengoere demande	A high manger he requests,
Rastelier bel et assez viande	A handsome haystack and plenty of food.
Il s'est herbergiéz en la sale,	He lodges himself in the great hall
Pour miex demonstrer sa regale. . . .	The better to show that he is royal. . . . .
Fortune, contraire a raison,	Fortune, contrary to reason,
L'a fait seigneur de sa meson;	Has made him lord of her house
En lui essaucer met grant peine,	And taken great pains to raise him
Car ou palais roial le maine;	Because in the Palais Royal she leads him
De lui fere honorer ne cesse. . . .	To have him honored without ceasing. . . .
Vicontes, prevos et baillis;	Viscounts, provosts, and sheriffs
A bien torcher ne sont faillis;	To curry well, not are lacking;
Bourgois de bours et de cités	Bourgeoisie of the towns and cities
Torchent par grans subtilités,	Curry with such great subtlety,
Et villains de ville champestre	And rustics from the country towns
Sont empres Fauvel pour li pestre.	Gather round Fauvel to ask for favors.

💿 LISTENING CUE

GERVÈS DE BUS
Roman de Fauvel (1314)

CD 1/26
Anthology, No. 26

Music regularly interrupts the poetic narrative of the *Roman de Fauvel*, as singers comment upon the events unfolding before them. In the anonymous two-voice *Quare fremuerunt gentes* (*Why do the people rage*), for example, they ask why the people are discontent. The answer: because never have they seen such corruption and discord. *Quare fremuerunt gentes* is a reworking of a century-old conductus, here refashioned and bedecked with all of the rhythmic finery of the *Ars nova*. Each metrical unit consists of three breves; each breve is divided into two semibreves, and each of these in turn into three minims. Thus the mensuration that governs is perfect mode, imperfect time, and perfect prolation. Note values of widely different duration allow for passages of rapid movement, effected by minims, to be set against clearly articulated points of arrival, signaled by longs. This use of widely divergent rhythmic durations is typical of the exploring spirit of the composers of the *Ars nova*.

EXAMPLE 11-1

Why do the people and nations rage? Because they did not see the monsters with their own eyes…

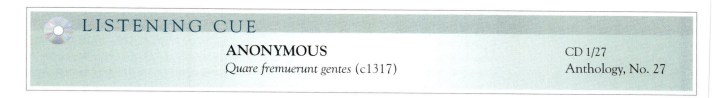

LISTENING CUE

ANONYMOUS

Quare fremuerunt gentes (c1317)

CD 1/27

Anthology, No. 27

PHILIPPE DE VITRY

"The only true poet among the French"—this is how the renowned Italian poet Petrarch characterized **Philippe de Vitry** (1291–1360).[1] We have already seen that Vitry was a notary at the royal court and an influential music theorist (see Chapter 10). He was also a mathematician, astronomer, politician, soldier, and diplomat, and he ended his career as the bishop of the city of Meaux. Typifying the medieval intellectual with diverse interests, Vitry was living proof that we need not wait until the Renaissance to meet "the Renaissance man."

Vitry's involvement in royal politics can be seen in one of his contributions to the illustrated *Roman de Fauvel*. His three-voice motet *Garrit Gallus/In nova fert/Neuma* is an animal allegory. The text speaks of the rooster, chicken, and lamb (the French people), who are devoured by the wicked fox (Enguerran de Marigny) because the blind lion (King Philip IV) does not see the deceit. To this scalding political satire Vitry adds biblical and classical references, creating a dense web of textual allusions. His music is equally complex. The tenor voice employs a new technique called isorhythm.

In **isorhythm** (same rhythm) a rhythmic pattern is repeated again and again in a line, usually in the tenor voice. Here in Vitry's motet a rhythmic pattern of ten measures is stated six times in the tenor. The rhythmic pattern, or unit, is called a **talea** (a segment or slice). There are three statements of the talea, and then the melody of the tenor is sung a second time to another three statements of the talea. In an isorhythmic motet the melodic unit is called the **color**. Thus, in this motet, two statements of the color coincide with six of the talea, as can be seen in the example below.

EXAMPLE 11-2

In Vitry's motet, the upper voices offer their complaint at a blistering pace but the isorhythmic regularity of the tenor holds the work tight. Isorhythm presupposes forethought and careful planning. Every rhythm of the tenor is predetermined. Like fugal procedure in the eighteenth century or twelve-tone technique in the twentieth, isorhythm helped the medieval composer give structure to a lengthy musical composition. Eventually, with the next generation of composers, not only the tenor but also the upper voices will come under strict isorhythmic control.

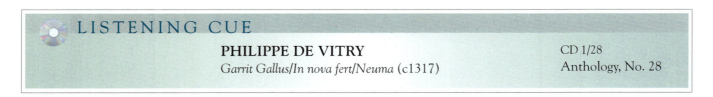

LISTENING CUE

PHILIPPE DE VITRY   CD 1/28
Garrit Gallus/In nova fert/Neuma (c1317)   Anthology, No. 28

✿ ROYAL DANCES

The kings of France welcomed and amused their guests in the Grande-Salle of the royal court. King Charles V, for example, entertained Holy Roman Emperor Charles IV and a group of eight hundred courtiers there in 1378 (Fig. 11-2). In good weather the king and his entourage might repair to the royal garden at the westernmost tip of the island. Here shaded walkways, soft grass benches, colorful flowers, and succulent fruits were to be found. Yet whether in the Grande-Salle or in this royal garden of delights, the most popular musical entertainment was dancing.

Broadly speaking, people in the Middle Ages enjoyed two types of dances, each with a distinctive form. One type was a song and dance called the **carole**. It made use of a musical form called strophe plus refrain, in which a series of stanzas would each end with the same refrain. The singers and dancers grouped in a circle. As they danced around, a soloist sang each successive strophe of text, while everyone else joined in for the refrain (Fig. 11-3). The subject matter of the carole might have to do with Christmas or Easter, spring, the month of May, or love. A second type of dance was called the **estampie** or "stomp" (likely derived from the Old French *estampir,* to stamp or make resound). The estampie, like all medieval dances in Western Europe, was originally a sung dance. That is to say, the dancers of the early estampie sang a text, usually a poem about love, as they danced. During the thirteenth and fourteenth centuries, the text was often dropped, leaving a purely instrumental piece, either monophonic or polyphonic. A French chronicler of the fourteenth century emphasizes the instrumental nature of the estampie, and perhaps the choral quality of the carole: "And as soon as [the minstrels] had stopped the estampies that they beat, those gentlemen and ladies who had amused themselves dancing began, without hesitation, to take hands for carolling."[2]

This and other evidence suggests that the carole was danced and sung by a group holding hands, alternating male and female. The estampie, however, was for couples. We know nothing about the choreography of the estampie, beyond the fact that couples of all ages danced in stately procession.

The most characteristic feature of the estampie is its musical structure. It comprises a succession of couplets, or pairs of musical phrases. Each pair is called a **punctum** (phrase, pl. **puncta**) and, although the puncta of the dance may be of different lengths, all end with the same music, a refrain. Most important, this concluding refrain has both an **open** and a **closed ending.** Thus the form of the estampie can be represented: **AxAyBxByCxCyDxDy** etc. (Ex. 11-3). It is here in the repertory of medieval dance music that first and second endings appear for the first time in the history of music.

We do not know for which French king *La quinte estampie real* (*The Fifth Royal Estampie*) was composed, only that it appears as the fifth in a collection of eight estampies, all called "royal." Typical of the estampie, the melodic range here is narrow, and there are no chromatic inflections. The four puncta appear to be constructed by linking small melodic-rhythmic units. Medieval performers may well have improvised, or elaborated upon, such dance tunes as the occasion demanded. As with all French estampies, this one enjoys a solid modal grounding. Indeed, part of the charm of *La quinte estampie real* is the continuous interplay between the C-grounded first ending and the A-based second. A theorist of the fourteenth century would say that this interchange was between the Lydian mode (with B♭ and transposed to C) and Dorian (with B♭ and transposed to A). Later, in the sixteenth century, theorists would designate these modes as Ionian and Aeolian. Today we would simply call them major and minor.

Bridgeman Art Library

❋ FIGURE 11-2

Holy Roman Emperor Charles IV and his nephew French King Charles V at a banquet given in honor of the emperor in 1378.

❋ FIGURE 11-3

To the accompaniment of shawms and a bagpipe, dancers execute a carole in a garden while holding hands.

Bodleian Library, University of Oxford

EXAMPLE 11-3

Finally, what is perhaps most striking about medieval dance music is how little of it is preserved. No more than fifty instrumental pieces prior to 1450 have survived. What does that say—that there were few dances and little music? Likely not. Rather it suggests that the dances played by the minstrels of the court belonged to a tradition of improvised music that was passed orally from one generation of musicians to the next without benefit of written notation. Indeed, the first evidence that instrumentalists were required to read written notation does not appear until much later, in the 1470s.

Instrumental music was not a sacred object to be preserved in a splendid manuscript. Much of it survives as an after-thought to music history; it was added at the end or copied in the margins of manuscripts of vocal music. Instrumental music did not require a great deal of pre-compositional planning, but came alive during performance. It was everyday music, which might be written down, but more likely was not. In this sense, medieval instrumental music has more in common with our modern-day jazz than it does with the ancient Mass and motet.

MUSICAL INSTRUMENTS AT COURT AND IN CHURCH

FIGURE 11-4

Vielle as depicted in an illumination from late thirteenth-century Paris. The medieval vielle had a very flat bridge and was often used for playing chords by employing drones and multiple stops.

What instruments played dance music at the French royal court during the thirteenth and fourteenth centuries? Music theory treatises, poems, and paintings reveal that in Paris, as elsewhere throughout Europe, a great variety of instruments were heard. Most likely to accompany an estampie was the **vielle** (Fig. 11-4), a large five-string fiddle capable of playing the entire Guidonian scale. Players of the vielle are mentioned performing alone, in pairs, or occasionally in groups of four, as a contemporary poem recounts: "Then the servants hurried and quickly took away the napery [table linen]. Four minstrels of the vielle played a new estampie before the lady."[3] The harp, psaltery, and gittern (an early cousin of the lute) likewise played at court, though the sounds of these soft-stringed instruments may have been too faint to accompany a party of energetic dancers. Indeed, louder sounds were needed if the dance took place out of doors. Thus such instruments as the pipe and tabor (fife and drum), played by one or two persons, as well as a bagpipe and two shawms, often appear in illustrations of dances (see Fig. 11-3). The **shawm** (an ancestor of the modern oboe) was a double-reed instrument with a loud penetrating tone; by the late fourteenth century it came in two sizes, treble and tenor pitched a fifth below. Trumpets were present but they did not play dance music; rather, they sounded fanfares and heralded pronouncements.

Bodleian Library

Prior to 1300 the only "keyboard" instrument that existed was the organ, but it was rare and, in truth, used sliders and not keys. Sliders were flat pieces of wood that could be pulled in and out to allow air to pass through the pipes. The invention of the keyboard was a technological innovation of the fourteenth century. Now, instead of sliding boards in and out, keys could be pushed to let air rush through the pipes to make sound. The keyboard was added to both the portative and positive organ, which differed only in size. The **portative organ** was a small movable instrument that sounded at courtly entertainments, though more often to accompany singers than dancers. The organist played with one hand and pumped the bellows with the other (or an assistant might pump the bellows; Fig. 11-5). The **positive organ** was a large stationary instrument that began to appear in large numbers shortly after 1300. Because the positive organ was considered to be one of the technological wonders of the day, it was usually attached high on a wall in the nave of the church for all the populace to see and hear. The organ at this time was called, as it is today, "the king of instruments." It was the only musical instrument officially sanctioned within the church by ecclesiastical authorities, all others being viewed as worldly profanations of sacred space.

Finally, the fourteenth century witnessed the development of the **clavichord** (literally "key-string"), a keyboard instrument that makes sound when a player depresses a key and thereby pushes a small metal tangent in the shape of a "T" upward to strike a string. The clavichord was initially called the **chekker,** likely from the medieval English word for counting board, which had a checkered look. The first mention of the chekker is found at the court of the king of France in 1360, when King John II received one as a gift from the English King Edward III. From the French royal court in this period comes our earliest surviving collection of keyboard music, called the **Robertsbridge Codex.** This manuscript preserves three estampies and arrangements of three motets from the *Roman de Fauvel*, music typically heard at the French royal court during the mid fourteenth century. The music of the second estampie sounds fresh yet untutored, being full of lively rhythms but endless parallel octaves as well.

FIGURE 11-5

A fifteenth-century domestic scene in which a gentleman plays a portative organ, assisted by a lady who pumps the bellows. Today, wind pressure is created in the organ by means of electronically activated pumps.

EXAMPLE 11-4

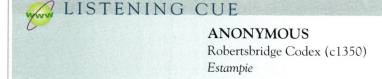
LISTENING CUE

ANONYMOUS
Robertsbridge Codex (c1350)
Estampie

Thomson-Schirmer
Website
Anthology, No. 30

SUMMARY

Historians have long recognized the fourteenth century as a period of decline in the power of the church and a corresponding increase in the influence of the secular court. During this period no court was more brilliant than that of the French kings.

The two principal northern European composers of the fourteenth century, Philippe de Vitry and Guillaume de Machaut (see Chapter 12), both had strong ties to the French monarchy. The most important music manuscript of the first half of the fourteenth century, the *Roman de Fauvel*, is a scathing attack on the power and corruption within the court. It contains several isorhythmic motets of Vitry, a genre of music that reflects the continued desire of composers to give structure to their music by the precise measurement and repetition of units of musical time. The French court was also home to dances, called caroles and estampies, as well as the first surviving pieces for keyboard in the history of music.

KEY TERMS

Roman de Fauvel	estampie	portative organ
Philippe de Vitry	punctum (pl., puncta)	positive organ
isorhythm	open ending	clavichord
talea	closed ending	chekker
color	vielle	Robertsbridge Codex
carole	shawm	

Chapter 12

Fourteenth-Century Music in Reims: Guillaume de Machaut

FIGURE 12-1

The poet-composer Guillaume de Machaut at work, one of the earliest portraits of a Western artist.

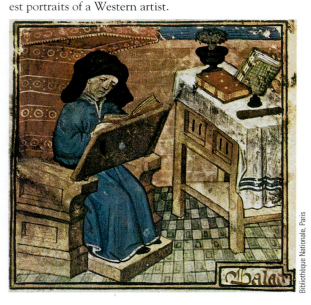

Bibliothèque Nationale, Paris

With its 200,000 inhabitants, Paris was by far the largest city in Western Europe in the mid fourteenth century. But it was not the only French town of musical and artistic importance. Situated a hundred miles to the northeast of the capital, the city of **Reims** could boast a cathedral as large and impressive as Notre Dame of Paris. Here, at Notre Dame of Reims, all kings of France were crowned. Today we think of Reims as the home of great champagne. In the Middle Ages it was known as the city that crowned the French king. Among the 20,000 residents of Reims in the mid fourteenth century was Guillaume de Machaut (c1300–1377; Fig. 12-1), the most renowned poet and musician of the age. Machaut himself sang in two royal coronations, that of King John II in 1350 and Charles V in 1364.

Guillaume de Machaut was born about 1300, educated in the schools of the cathedral of Reims, and apparently obtained the degree master of arts, probably at the University of Paris. Around 1323 he became the secretary of John, duke of Luxembourg and king of Bohemia, in whose service he traveled widely—to Bohemia (Czech Republic), Poland, and perhaps to Lithuania and Russia as well. In 1337 Machaut was appointed a canon at the cathedral of Reims and began to adopt a more settled life. During his mature years he spent most of his time writing lyrical verse and music on commission for members of the French royal family. Kings John II and Charles V were among his principal patrons. In all, Machaut composed 23 motets, 19 lais (monophonic songs using the form of the sequence), 42 ballades, 22 rondeaux, 33 virelais, a hocket, and a four-voice polyphonic Mass, as well as fifteen long narrative stories and a collection of 280 short poems that he chose not to set to music—a sizable body of music and poetry! By 1350 Machaut had begun to gather this enormous literary and musical *oeuvre* into neatly organized manuscripts. Machaut is the first composer in the history of music for whom we possess a "complete works"—almost all of his music survives. He died in Reims in 1377 and was buried in the nave of the cathedral.

MACHAUT, THE BLACK DEATH, AND THE HUNDRED YEARS' WAR

Guillaume de Machaut was the companion and confidant of kings. As a man of the times, he personally experienced some of the horrific events that marked what one historian has called "the calamitous fourteenth century." In 1348 a bubonic plague known as the **Black Death** swept Europe, carried by fleas hosting upon rats. A human victim would develop a high fever and soon buboes would appear (black welts in the armpits and around the groin). Death was as sudden as it was sure. By 1351 fully a third of the population of Western Europe, perhaps 20 million people, had died. Among them was Bonne of Luxembourg, mother of King Charles V of France, for whom Machaut wrote a memorial motet *Trop plus est bele/Biauté paree/Je ne sui mie certeins*. In one of his narrative poems, Machaut reveals that he spent the winter of 1337–1349 shut up in his house in Reims. In this fashion he survived the plague while many of his friends, he tells us, were "mors et en terre mis" (dead and buried).

A decade later another calamity came to the gates of Reims, the **Hundred Years' War** (1337–1453). The English kings wanted to control not merely the western side of modern France (the old Angevin kingdom; Map 6-1) but all of it. And because the English and French royal houses had intermarried, the king of England had a distant hereditary claim to the French throne, should the French king die leaving no male heir. The hostilities that resulted—sporadic bloody battles interrupted by fragile peaces—occurred between 1337 and 1453. They ended only after **Joan of Arc** rallied the French royal forces and led the dauphin (the future king Charles VII) to be crowned at Reims.

Indeed, Reims was central to the Hundred Years' War, for, to be king of France, an aspirant had to be crowned in Reims. To this end, the English King Edward III led a large army across northern France to the walls of the city in the fall of 1359. The nearly 60-year-old poet-composer Guillaume de Machaut put on armor and mounted the ramparts prepared to enter battle. (The famous English poet Geoffrey Chaucer was captured by the French during the same campaign.) After forty days of futile assaults on Reims, the English king raised his siege and marched away. Machaut commemorated these events in three isorhythmic motets. In one, *Christe qui lux es/Veni creator spiritus/Tribulatio proxima*, his triplum speaks of those "Who tear us apart in the wars that have now arisen," while his motetus cries "Our enemies surround us"—a fitting description of the English siege of Reims.

Because the walls of Reims held firm, King Edward III of England never became king of France. The crown remained in the French royal house, passing to Charles V at Notre Dame of Reims on 19 May 1364. Machaut himself participated in the coronation ritual; the canons of Reims traditionally played an important role in the ceremony, leading the new king into the church. Indeed, Machaut seems to have composed a work specifically for the event. It is entitled *Hoquetus David* (the French king was often called David in these years by way of analogy to the biblical king of that name). **Hocket** is both a contrapuntal technique and a musical genre. It occurs when the sounds of two voices are staggered by the careful placement of rests, thereby creating a highly syncopated piece. The term "hocket" derives from the Latin word *hoquetus* (hiccup), and indeed the sound is similar to a musical hiccup. In Machaut's *Hoquetus David,* an isorhythmic tenor is fashioned from the end of *Alleluia. Nativitas,* which speaks of the kings of the Old Testament. Tenor talea and color overlap in a highly complex fashion (see Anthology, No. 31). But although the tenor is crafted with arithmetic precision, the profiles of both talea and color are almost wholly inaudible to the listener. As is often the case in medieval music, a mathematical structure rests unheard beneath the audible surface. What catches our ear is not the isorhythmic tenor, but the snappy hocketing above in the duplum and triplum. Hocketing was a popular technique during the thirteenth and fourteenth centuries, but it disappeared thereafter. Most hockets are without texts. They might be sung by voices alone or performed on instruments. Wind instruments, with their aggressive attacks, are particularly effective at bringing out the syncopations. Example 12-1 offers a small sample of the technique of hocket from *Hoquetus David.*

EXAMPLE 12-1

LISTENING CUE

GUILLAUME DE MACHAUT   CD 2/1
Hoquetus David (c1364)   Anthology, No. 31

✳ MACHAUT AND THE *FORMES FIXES*

The troubadours and trouvères had bequeathed to Western Europe a great treasury of lyrical love poetry set to music (see Chapter 6). Many of these monophonic songs and dances were composed in just a few patterns, or musical forms. By the early fourteenth century, most French secular art songs were written in one of just three forms: ballade, rondeau, and virelai. Because each of these forms was always prescribed, or fixed, in advance (like a *prix fixe* menu), they were called the *formes fixes* (fixed forms). The French *formes fixes* are not religious pieces but secular songs and dances setting texts in medieval French. Thus there is no pre-existing Latin tenor, as is true for motets and hockets: in *formes fixes* pieces all voices are newly composed. Guillaume de Machaut did not invent these forms; rather, he popularized them, cultivating these to the exclusion of all other secular musical forms. For Machaut, and continuing for composers a hundred years later, almost all secular music setting a French text was composed in one of these three fixed forms.

A **ballade** is a song setting a poem with from one to three stanzas, or strophes. Each stanza usually contains seven or eight lines of text, and the last line serves as a refrain (a highlighted résumé at the end of the stanza). In addition, lines one and two are sung to the same music as lines three and four, usually with first and second endings for each pair; lines five through seven or eight have new music. Thus the musical form of each stanza of a ballade is **AAB.** The text below is the first strophe of Machaut's three-stanza ballade *Je puis trop bien*, with boldface letters indicating the musical sections and italic type showing the textual refrain.

Machaut's *Je puis trop bien* (*I can well compare*) is an excellent example of a piece composed in **ballade style** (Ex. 12-2). Here a treble voice sings a text to a lyrical melody while a slower moving tenor and contratenor provide a harmonic support. The lower voices may also be sung, or they may be played on musical instruments. Noteworthy here is the new attention given to the upper voice, the melody. It is more tuneful, rhythmically flexible, and melismatic than in previous secular polyphonic music. Now for the first time the melody voice is called the **cantus,** meaning "the song," perhaps because the singer can luxuriate on a single syllable so as to enjoy the sheer beauty of the human voice. The syllables on which these vocalises occur in the cantus are usually not important to the meaning of the poem; in much medieval music, musical line and poetic intent work independently. The tenor provides a foundation, and the contratenor fills out the harmony. In ballade style we see for the first time a true accompanied song. The text of the song recalls the story of the ancient Greek sculptor Pygmalion, who creates a statue so beautiful he falls in love with it. The same story served as the basis of George Bernard Shaw's play *Pygmalion* and the Broadway musical *My Fair Lady*.

Je puis trop bien madame comparer	**A**	I can well compare my lady
A l'ymage que fist Pymalion		To the statue Pygmalion made
D'yvoire fu, tant belle et si sans per	**A**	Of ivory so beautiful and without equal
Que plus l'ama que Medee Jazon.		That he loved it more than Jason did Medea.
Li folz toudis la prioit,	**B**	Mad with love, he cried out,
Mais l'ymage riens ne li respondoit.		But the image did not respond.
Einssi me fait celle qui mon cuer font,		Thus does she treat me, the one who melts my heart,
Qu'ades la pri et riens ne me respont.	(refrain)	*For I pray to her ever, but she does not respond.*

EXAMPLE 12-2

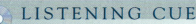

LISTENING CUE

GUILLAUME DE MACHAUT
Je puis trop bien (c1355)

CD 2/2
Anthology, No. 32

The virelai and rondeau are generally more playful than the serious ballade. Indeed, these *formes fixes* originated with the troubadours and trouvères as monophonic dances that involved choral singing. The **rondeau** consists of two musical sections, **a** and **b.** At the outset everyone sang a text refrain to these two sections. Then a soloist sang a new line of text to **a,** to which the chorus responded with part of the refrain set to **a.** Next the soloist sang two new lines to **a** and **b,** followed by a concluding choral refrain. The complete form of a rondeau was thus **ABaAabAB** (the capital letters indicate the refrain). Below is the text of Machaut's three-voice rondeau *Ma fin est mon commencement et mon commencement ma fin* (My end is my beginning and my beginning my end). It is famous in the history of music because the text suggests the mode of performance: the cantus voice goes forward while the tenor sings the same music backward against it; a contratenor, only half as long as the other two voices, sings to its end and then returns to the beginning. Here retrograde motion is ingeniously joined to a clear example of rondeau form. The numbers below represent units of time (modern measures) in Machaut's famous rondeau.

Cantus:	1	5	10	15	20	25	30	35	40
Tenor:	40	35	30	25	20	15	10	5	1
Contratenor:	1	5	10	15	20	15	10	5	1

Ma fin est mon commencement	**A**	*My end is my beginning*
Et mon commencement ma fin.	**B**	*and my beginning my end.*
Et teneüre vraiëment	**a**	This much is clear.
Ma fin est mon commencement	**A**	*My end is my beginning*
Mes tiers chans iij fois seulement	**a**	My third voice sings three times only
Se retrograde et einsi fin.	**b**	in retrograde, and then is done.
Ma fin est mon commencement	**A**	*My end is my beginning*
Et mon commencement ma fin.	**B**	*and my beginning my end.*

The form of the **virelai** can simply be represented as **AbbaA.** There are two musical sections (**a** and **b**) as well as a textual refrain (**A**) sung to music **a.** Unlike the rondeau, the virelai may have more than one stanza. For a three-stanza virelai, such as Machaut's monophonic *Douce dame jolie*, the form that results is **AbbaAbbaAbbaA.** Machaut's *Douce dame jolie* (*Fair sweet lady*) is a simple poem of unrequited love set to an equally simple, but charming melody.

Douce dame jolie,	(refrain)	**A**	*Fair sweet lady*
Pour Dieu ne pensés mie			*for God's sake never think*
Que neulle ait signourie			*that any woman rules*
Seur moy, fors vous seulement.			*my heart, except you alone.*
Qu'adès sans tricherie, chierie		**b**	I have cherished you long
Vous ay, et humblement			and served you faithfully
Tous les jours de ma vie servie		**b**	All the days of my life
Sans vilein pensement.			without a base thought.

Helas! Et je mendie	a	Alas! I must do without
D'esperance et d'aïe,		hope and help, and thus
Dont ma joie est fenie,		my joy has ended,
Se pité ne vous en prent.		unless you pity me.
Douce dame jolie . . . . (refrain)	A	*Fair sweet lady . . .*

LISTENING CUE

GUILLAUME DE MACHAUT
Douce dame jolie (before 1350)

CD 2/3
Anthology, No. 33

Originally, both the virelai and the rondeau were dance pieces in which a soloist sang the verses and a chorus the refrain. In the course of the fourteenth century, however, a new performance practice emerged in which a single voice sang the choral refrain as well as the verses. A lively dance had become more intimate chamber music.

 ## MACHAUT AND THE MASS OF OUR LADY

By far Machaut's most famous work is his *Messe de Nostre Dame* (*Mass of Our Lady*), one of the greatest artistic achievements of the Middle Ages. Composed for four voices during the 1360s, Machaut's Mass is revolutionary on several counts. It is the first complete treatment in polyphony of the Ordinary of the Mass. Prior to this, to create a polyphonic Mass, composers had usually chosen to set the responsorial chants of the Proper of the Mass (see Chapter 8). Because these earlier Mass settings were therefore proper to a specific day in the liturgical calendar, each could, in principle, be performed only once a year. By composing music for the Ordinary of the Mass (chants heard at nearly every Mass) Machaut created a composition that was appropriate for, and thus could be performed on, many days of the year. In addition, Machaut's *Mass of Our Lady* is the first **cyclic Mass,** meaning that all of the movements of the Mass are linked together by a common musical theme (see Anthology, No. 34). A distinctive motive occurs in each of the six movements of the Mass (*Kyrie, Gloria, Credo, Sanctus, Agnus dei,* and *Ite missa est*), and this recurring gesture binds together into a coherent unit what would otherwise be six separate, disconnected movements. Taken in sum, Machaut's Mass movements constitute a work that requires nearly twenty-five minutes to perform, by far the longest polyphonic composition before the fifteenth century.

The sound of Machaut's Mass is brilliant, indeed startling, because of a new approach to choral sonority. In earlier polyphony, two, three, or four voices were written in approximately the same range, within an octave or so of what we call middle C. Now Machaut has expanded the vocal texture to two full octaves. The cantus (triplum) sings in a high range and stays there; the tenor does similarly in a tenor range. Between these Machaut adds a third voice, as well as a fourth one, both called contratenor. The lower contratenor works in conjunction with the tenor and often goes below it, providing a true bass within the four-part harmony. Soon after Machaut's time the contratenor below the tenor would be called the **contratenor**

bassus, whence our term "bass," and the contratenor above the tenor **contratenor altus,** whence our term "alto" voice. Here for the first time we have a clear separation of the vocal parts by range. Something akin to true four-part harmony has been created, and this generates a fuller, richer choral sound.

Machaut's sound is exhilarating for other reasons as well. The listener senses a formal rigidity, perhaps because of the isorhythm and pre-existing chant in the slow-moving tenor; yet hocket and frequent syncopation add an element of daring to the upper two voices (Ex. 12-3a). The contrapuntal fabric bristles with unprepared dissonances. Throughout it all, Machaut poses and resolves conflicting forces, creating a *concors discordia* (harmony through discord) typical of medieval art: sustained chords vie with quick-moving hockets; rich triads yield to hollow open fifths; and biting double leading tones pull to perfect consonances (Ex. 12-3b).[†] The sound that results is one of extraordinary excitement and power.

EXAMPLE 12-3A   EXAMPLE 12-3B

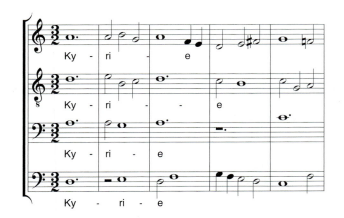

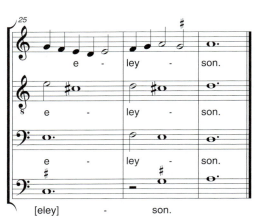

Guillaume de Machaut composed his Mass to honor the Virgin Mary, and he established an endowment of 300 French *livres* (a huge donation in the fourteenth century) so that it might be performed every Saturday of the year. Upon his death in 1377 prayers for his departed soul were added to the Mass, and both Mass and prayers were celebrated weekly before a statue of the Virgin in the nave of the cathedral of Reims. It was here that the composer had asked to be buried. By endowing such a votive service Machaut was simply conforming to the religious beliefs of the age. He hoped to reduce the length of time his spirit might languish in Purgatory and ensure that it arrived at the gates of St. Peter well recommended by the Virgin.

[†]For a description of the double leading-tone cadence, see Musical Interlude 1.

SUMMARY

During the fourteenth century, musicians continued to exploit the potential of musical rhythm first explored by the composers of the *Ars nova*. Isorhythm remained a structural force in both motet and Mass. French musicians, led by the preeminent figure of Guillaume de Machaut, consolidated their secular polyphonic music into just three fixed forms: ballade, rondeau, and virelai. The ballade was the most serious in tone of the three, while the rondeau and virelai were generally lighter pieces that only gradually gave up their ties to sung dance. Machaut made use of large-scale isorhythmic structure in his motets and in his most important work, the *Mass of Our Lady*. In this four-voice Mass, he places the voices in distinctly different registers, thereby creating a new, expanded sense of tonal sonority. Machaut's *Mass of Our Lady* is the first complete polyphonic setting of the Ordinary of the Mass, and it established a precedent; hereafter, when composers created a polyphonic Mass, they almost always set only the Ordinary of the Mass.

KEY TERMS

Reims	hocket	rondeau
Guillaume de Machaut	*formes fixes*	virelai
Black Death	ballade	cyclic Mass
Hundred Years' War	ballade style	contratenor bassus
Joan of Arc	cantus	contratenor altus

Chapter

13

Avignon, Symbolic Scores, and the *Ars Subtilior*

 ## PAPAL AVIGNON

In 1335 the renowned Italian poet **Francesco Petrarch** (1304–1374) called the city of Avignon in France "this profane Babylon that knows no shame."[1] Petrarch, an official of the papal court, was writing from Avignon because the popes had moved the papacy there from Rome. As a result, the population of this once-small southern French town (Map 13-1) swelled from 5,000 in 1300 to 120,000 by 1340. People squeezed themselves together within the protective walls of the city, which encircled no more than six square miles (an area about the size of Central Park in New York). They lodged in any available space along narrow tortuous streets, along the ramparts, even in cemeteries. Crime and prostitution were rampant. Soon, however, these urban ills were temporarily relieved by another: in 1348 the Black Death killed 62,000 souls, spreading rapidly among the densely packed citizens. Avignon was a microcosm of all that might go wrong in a medieval city. Thus Petrarch

 M A P 1 3 - 1
Avignon.

Bridgeman Art Library

✤ FIGURE 13-1

Avignon, France, Palace of the Popes. The towers at the palace were a continuation of families' towers in Italian city-states where families had sought refuge during the furious vendettas of the Middle Ages.

✤ FIGURE 13-2

Long view of the chapel of Pope Clement VI within the Palace of the Popes.

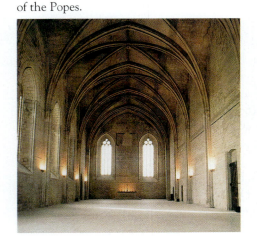

equated it with ancient Babylon, the city of luxury and vice. Following his example, historians now call the period in which the papacy resided in Avignon the **Babylonian Captivity** (1309–1403). But how did it come to pass that the popes had left Rome? How did it happen that the most progressive music of the late fourteenth century was written, not in Paris or Rome, but in the southern French city of Avignon?

Throughout much of the Middle Ages, the papacy was not in Rome; the Eternal City was the symbolic center of the Church but often not its physical home. At the height of the Roman Empire the population of Rome was more than a million; by 1350 it had shrunk to about 20,000. Rome was in ruins. Warring families as well as crime, both organized and disorganized, made it dangerous. Not surprisingly, the popes preferred safer, more salubrious cities in Italy (Florence, Pisa, and Genoa) and in southern France (Lyon, Vienne, and Avignon), and so they moved from place to place. Indeed, the medieval papal court (the pope and his retinue of about three hundred officials and servants) moved almost as often as today's circus.

Thus when Pope Clement V entered Avignon in March 1309 he did not expect that he and his successors would remain there for nearly a hundred years. But remain they did. In 1378 an Italian pope, Gregory XI, attempted to return the papacy to Rome, but he died just after arriving there. Under pressure from the Roman mobs, one group of cardinals elected an Italian as the next pope, while a pro-French group chose a Frenchman, who immediately returned to Avignon. The **Great Western Schism** had begun, and it would remain until 1417.

The Avignonese popes were mindful of their prestige and so built a worthy palace (Fig. 13-1). Contemporaries called it "the most beautiful and most fortified house in the world." The papal banquet hall was 162 feet in length. The chapel, constructed between 1345 and 1352 by Pope Clement VI, was the largest palace chapel in the world (Fig. 13-2). Appropriately called the **Clementine Chapel,** it served as a model for the one that Pope Sixtus IV would later build at the Vatican, the Sistine Chapel (see Fig. 25-2). In the Clementine Chapel, the Avignonese popes heard Mass as the papal chapel sang chant and polyphony. Indeed, during the Babylonian Captivity the word **cappella** begins to assume two separate and distinctly different meanings: a building consecrated for religious worship, as well as an organized group of highly trained musicians who sang at these services.

Given its location roughly halfway between Paris and Rome, papal Avignon became a crossroads for arts and ideas. Poets, painters, and musicians sojourned there, or simply passed through. Composer-theorists Philippe de Vitry and Jean des Murs were both in Avignon during the 1340s. When Vitry was there in 1342 he composed an isorhythmic motet, *Petre Clemens/Lugentium*, in honor of the election of Pope Clement VI. The Great Western Schism (1378–1417) did little to dim the allure of Avignon. Some composers continued to live there permanently as members of the papal chapel, some were employed in the service of the thirty-two cardinals who resided with the Avignonese pope, and others simply visited the city in the retinues of counts, dukes, and kings. At the end of the fourteenth century, Avignon was the center of the most progressive music then written in the West.

❀ BAUDE CORDIER AND SYMBOLIC SCORES

Among the musicians passing through Avignon at the end of the fourteenth century was **Baude Cordier.** Cordier's music is marked by unusual rhythmic sophistication, as can be seen in his French rondeau *Tout par compas suy composés* (*All by a compass am I composed*). This is an ingenious piece on several counts. As is immediately apparent (Fig. 13-3), the shape of the music bears out the title of the piece, for it is written in circular notation on lines drawn by a compass. Other scores in this period are shaped like a heart, a harp, and a labyrinth to symbolize, through music, the meaning of the text. Indeed, the late fourteenth century was a fanciful age in which musical shapes, rhythmic symbols, riddle canons, and pseudonyms helped create an almost make-believe world of sound.

The name Cordier literally means "String Man," and it apparently served as the professional nickname of Baude Fresnel (c1365–1398), a harper employed by Duke Philip the Bold of Burgundy. In 1391 and 1395 Cordier traveled with Duke Philip to Avignon. His presence there is confirmed by the text of the rondeau *Tout par*

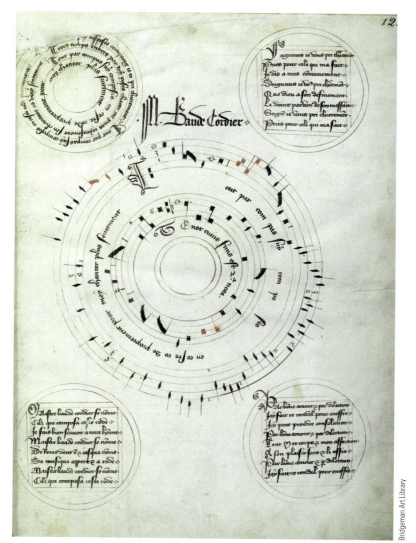

❀ **FIGURE 13-3**

Baude Cordier's symbolic score *Tout par compas suy composés.* There are four rondeau poems in the four corners. The refrain of that in the upper left (*Tout par compas suy composés*) is also set beneath the music of the outer circle. The outer circle generates a two-voice canon, or round (hence the symbolism). The inner circle is a tenor support for the two-voice canon.

compas suy composés. At each of the four corners of the manuscript (see Fig. 13-3) is a stanza of text; each is encompassed by a circle, and each is fixed in the poetic form of a rondeau. The stanza at the bottom left literally says that Cordier's music was known as far as Rome but, in fact, it refers to Avignon. For in this period the Avignonese popes advanced the doctrine of **Ubi papa, ibi Roma** (Wherever is the pope, there be Rome). The palace of the popes in Avignon was called "Rome" in the official documents of the day.

Maistre Baude Cordier se nomme	**A**	*His name is master Baude Cordier*
C'ilz qui composa ceste rode.	**B**	*Who composed this round.*
Je sui bien scavoir a toute homme,	**a**	I make it known to all,
Maistre Baude Cordier se nomme	**A**	*His name is master Baude Cordier*
De Reims est et jusqu'à Romme	**a**	From Reims, whose music circulates
Sa musique appert et a rode.	**b**	To Rome and is known.
Maistre Baude Cordier se nomme	**A**	*His name is master Baude Cordier*
C'ilz qui composa ceste rode.	**B**	*Who composed this round.*

Line two calls this piece a "rode" (Latin *rota*) or round, and so it is in two senses: it goes around, three times completely; and it is a round, or canon. In Latin the word **canon** literally means "rule." In music the rule is that a second voice must duplicate exactly the pitches and rhythms of the first, as in "Row, row, row your boat," for example. Here, the leading voice begins at about eleven o'clock as we view the music (see Fig. 13-3). After one measure a second voice enters and follows the melody exactly, note for note, thereby creating the canon. Beneath this canonic duet a tenor provides a harmonic foundation. The text set beneath the music instructs the voices to make three full turns around the circle as they sing. The three trips around the circle come in the rondeau form as follows: 1 (**AB**), 2 (**ab**), and 3 (**AB**).

Tout par compas suy composés	**A(1)**	*All with a compass am I composed*
En ceste rode proprement		*Properly, as befits a round*
Pour moy chanter plus seurement.	**B**	*To sing me more surely.*
Regarde com suy disposés	**a**	Look how I am disposed,
Compaing, je te pri chierement.		Companion, I pray you kindly.
Tout par compas suy composés	**A**	*All with a compass am I composed*
En ceste rode proprement.		*Properly, as befits a round.*
Trois temps entiers par toy posés	**a(2)**	Three times you go around me entirely
Chacer me pues joyeusement,		You can chase me joyfully,
S'en chantant as vray sentiment.	**b**	If in singing you're true to me.
Tout par compas suy composés	**A(3)**	*All with a compass am I composed*
En ceste rode proprement		*Properly, as befits a round*
Pour moy chanter plus seurement.	**B**	*To sing me more surely.*

LISTENING CUE

BAUDE CORDIER
Tout par compas suy composés (c1391)

CD 2/5
Anthology, No. 35

Finally, look carefully once again at the original manuscript of Cordier's rondeau (see Fig. 13-3). Notice that there are symbols and numbers situated in both the cantus and tenor parts. These are mensuration signs (time signatures) and indicators of proportions (see below). They control the temporal flow of the music and give this already artful piece great rhythmic complexity.

PHILIPPUS DE CASERTA: THE *ARS SUBTILIOR*

Just how complex rhythm became at the end of the fourteenth century can be seen in the music of **Philippus de Caserta,** an Italian composer working in Avignon during the reign of Pope Clement VII (1378–1394). In fact, Caserta's two-stanza ballade *Par les bons Gedeons (By the Good Gideon)* is written in honor of Pope Clement VII. Here the tenor establishes a solid rhythmic foundation, sounding firmly on the beat in modern $\frac{2}{4}$ time. Against it, the contratenor altus offers a light rhythmic counterpoint, providing syncopations and occasional moments of hocket. Above this framework, Caserta sets a flowing but difficult cantus. This melodic line is challenging to any singer, owing to the variety of rhythmic and metrical patterns that the voice must employ against the other voices: 4 against 1, 3 against 2, and 4 against 3. Long stretches of syncopation create polyrhythms that in turn suggest **polymeter,** two or more meters sounding simultaneously. In measures 23–25, for example, the cantus appears to be in $\frac{3}{4}$ while the lower voices are in $\frac{2}{4}$. Moreover, one and the same meter can be set against itself. In measures 10–16 all voices are in $\frac{2}{4}$, yet the cantus enters an eighth-note after the other two voices, thereby creating a lengthy passage of metrical syncopation (Ex. 13-1). This sort of music has been dubbed the **Ars subtilior** (more subtle art)—a style of music radiating out from Avignon to other parts of southern France and into northern Italy during the late fourteenth century. The *Ars subtilior* is marked by the most subtle, sometimes extreme, rhythmic relationships.

EXAMPLE 13-1

 LISTENING CUE

PHILIPPUS DE CASERTA
Par les bons Gedeons (c1385)

CD 2/6
Anthology, No. 36

Philippus de Caserta was not only a composer but also a music theorist. In his *Tractatus figurarum (Treatise on Note-Shapes;* c1385) he offers one of the earliest discussions of the **sincopa** (syncopation). Syncopation is, in effect, a temporary shift of the downbeat, just as occurs in twentieth-century ragtime and jazz. The rhythmic pattern of one voice can be shifted so that it is out of sync with that of another. Certainly a good deal of the rhythmic subtlety found in Cordier's *Tout par compas suy composés* and Caserta's *Par les bons Gedeons*, as we have seen, is due to syncopation. But not all of it. The most complex passages are those involving **proportions,** time signatures often written as fractions that modified the normal value of notes.

Proportions in early music often produced "irrational" groupings of notes (groupings not involving an exact doubling or tripling of the note value). The characteristic division of the beat in one voice might differ from that in another. For example, in the music of the *Ars subtilior*, three eighth-notes in the cantus might sound against two in the tenor, or four against three, five against two, or nine against four. Proportions create polymeters that may last for only a beat or two, or for several measures. They make it difficult for performers to stay together because the parts are in metrical conflict. Below are two passages from the *Ars subtilior* repertory typifying such moments of difficulty (Exs. 13-2a, 13-2b). They approach the limits of what vocal performers can execute.

EXAMPLE 13-2A   EXAMPLE 13-2B

In the music of the *Ars subtilior,* proportional changes are most often assigned to the cantus voice. To signal to the performer when to apply proportions, musicians introduced a host of new note-shapes. In his *Treatise on Note-Shapes,* Philippus de Caserta set forth several new notational forms (*figurae*). Example 13-3 shows first the standard note shapes of the *Ars nova* and then several new *figurae* of Caserta and his colleagues of the *Ars subtilior.*

EXAMPLE 13-3

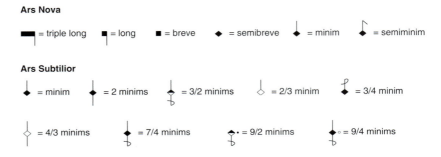

Not surprisingly, these odd-looking shapes were never widely adopted. Instead, musicians soon began to indicate proportions by writing arabic numerals, such as $\frac{4}{3}$ or $\frac{5}{2}$, in the score. Nonetheless, these shapes reveal to what extremes musicians were willing to go in search of rhythmic novelty. They also suggest just how far musicians had come. In little more than a century, rhythm in Western music had progressed from the simple triple-meter patterns of the *Ars antiqua* music of Leoninus and Perotinus to the astonishing intricacies of the *Ars subtilior*.

SUMMARY

During the early fourteenth century, musicians of the *Ars nova* began to unleash the full potential of rhythm. They discovered that sounds might have many different durations and relationships, and that these could be used for expressive purposes. By 1350 there were six different note values (ranging from triple long to semiminim), and duple or triple relationships were possible among them all. Musicians pushed these rhythmic discoveries to greater lengths, ultimately creating the intricate rhythms and complex proportions of the *Ars subtilior*. Early on, in 1324, the Avignonese Pope John XXII inveighed against such rhythmic excesses (see Chapter 10). Yet, ironically, Avignon and the region around it soon became the center for rhythmic experimentation in music, as can be seen in the compositions of Baude Cordier and Philippus de Caserta. It was almost as if composers had found a new musical toy (rhythm) and were intent on driving their elders crazy with it. Indeed, at no time in the history of music before the twentieth century did composers go to such rhythmic extremes as during the late fourteenth century. Soon, having reached the practical limits of what is rhythmically performable, the avant-gard (*Ars subtilior*) of Western European music retreated. Composers began to do away with difficult syncopations and to employ simpler rhythms and textures and more sonorous harmonies. In these developments we see harbingers of a musical Renaissance.

KEY TERMS

Francesco Petrarch	Baude Cordier	*Ars subtilior*
Babylonian Captivity	*Ubi papa, ibi Roma*	*sincopa*
Great Western Schism	canon	proportions
Clementine Chapel	Philippus de Caserta	
cappella	polymeter	

From Medieval Manuscript to Modern Performance

When we listen to a piece of medieval music today, we are likely to think it sounds as it did during the Middle Ages. But how do we know? Surely the performers are doing their best to be faithful to the written score, but does that written document provide sufficient information to generate a faithful rendition of something seven hundred years old? In truth, the recordings we hear reflect a great deal of speculation by the modern editors and performers. Musicians today must make many more decisions when they engage the repertory of early music than they do when performing a symphony by Mahler or a ballet by Stravinsky, for example. The reason for this is easy to understand: the medieval manuscript contains only the barest of information. It is a mere sketch for a performance, and the farther back we go in music history, the more this is true.

Complicating things further is the fact that improvisation, and unwritten music generally, played an enormous role in the Middle Ages. Medieval culture was to a great extent an oral culture, not a visual one, as ours is. A teacher at a cathedral school in medieval France would read a prescribed text, and the pupil would memorize it orally and aurally. Only after the student had learned the entire text by ear (or by heart) would he be given a written version of it—the textbook—as a status symbol of his learned accomplishment. In medieval music, some entire repertories—organum and instrumental music, for example—grew out of a tradition, not of *a priori* composition as we know it, but the practice of spontaneous improvisation following various rules and procedures commonly accepted at that time. Today we, too, have entire repertories of music—jazz, much rock, hip-hop, funk, and rap—that involve traditions of spontaneous musical creation that use the ear but are not dependent on written notation.

As the Middle Ages unfolded, the growing complexity of the music caused more and more of it to be committed to a written format. More voices and a greater interdependence among them made it increasingly necessary to have a notated blueprint to keep everyone together. Consider the progress of medieval music: in the seventh century C.E. an important music theorist, Isidore of Seville, wrote: "Unless sounds are remembered by man, they perish, for they cannot be written down."[1] Yet two centuries later, monks and nuns had started to do just that—to capture and write down the melodies of the church (see Ex. 4-2). A basic staff was in place by the beginning of the eleventh century, and in the twelfth century churchmen devised a system to regulate and record rhythmic durations (see Ex. 8-1). By the fourteenth century, the heyday of Vitry, Machaut, and the *Ars subtilior,* a way to capture sounds not only existed but had also become enormously complicated, as we have seen (see Ex. 13-3 and Anthology, Nos. 35 and 36). This transition—from a completely oral music, and the belief that music could not be preserved, to the creation of complicated musical scores—is one of enormous importance and far-reaching implications. The composer gradually began to replace the improvising performer as the determinant force in a musical creation. As the centuries progressed, the composer gained more and more control over the way the music sounded. The dominance of the composer and a heavy dependence on a written score are two distinctive aspects of Western art music that separate it from the art music of other cultures around the world. These two distinctive Western characteristics first appeared during the Middle Ages.

Despite the increasing control of the composer and the growing importance of the written score, a medieval music manuscript is a far cry from our modern orchestral score, which contains various stylistic marks in virtually every measure. The medieval performer had to make decisions regarding a long list of musical elements, which were never notated. Medieval notation specified just pitch and duration, and even these only in a relative way. Following are listed the many elements that medieval performers had to regulate, which are also those that modern performers must confront in order to make early notated manuscripts come to life as sounding music.

PITCH

Pitch was the first element of music to be notated, and this occurred in the late ninth and early tenth centuries. Nevertheless, medieval pitch was only relative (the pitch of a written note was determined in relation to the pitch of other written notes). There was no such thing as absolute pitch. Indeed, an "international" standard for precise pitch was not finalized until the twentieth century. Medieval musicians simply transposed the music, whether plainchant or polyphony, secular or sacred, into a range that comfortably fit the voices and instruments at hand. Pieces 38 and 40 in the Anthology, for example, have been transposed by modern editors to make them easier to sing. Medieval musicians would have done this as well, just by singing and playing higher or lower at sight.

 ## DURATION AND TEMPO

Similarly, medieval musicians developed a system to notate different rhythms in the twelfth century, but only for relative durations (how long this note is compared to that one). This system, however, said nothing about how long the notes should be. Presumably a long should be long and a breve short, but how long or how short? Not before 1496 did a music theorist (Gaffurius, *Practica musicae*) suggest any sort of absolute standard for duration, and even that wasn't very precise: the beat (then the semibreve) should go at the rate of the heartbeat of a person breathing normally. Composers did not begin to specify tempo markings until the seventeenth century, and even then they did so in an inexact way with terms such as *allegro* (fast) and *adagio* (slow). The ability to specify the exact duration of the beat (the tempo in music) came only with the advent of the metronome in the early nineteenth century.

 ## VOLUME AND EXPRESSION

Here again indications for how loud or soft the music should be do not appear written into manuscripts and prints until the early seventeenth century. Expression marks such as "gravely" or "gaily" don't generally appear until the eighteenth. The medieval composer left it entirely to the performers to adjust the volume and shape the phrase to suit the demands of the music at any given moment.

PRONUNCIATION AND TEXT UNDERLAY

Needless to say, English, French, Italian, Spanish, and even Latin are not pronounced today as they were during the Middle Ages. Singers today need to study languages and perhaps work with a **philologist** (a scholar of early languages) to approximate a correct pronunciation of earlier texts. One key to correct pronunciation is the rhyming patterns within medieval poetry. Sometimes, too, the text is missing from a part in a vocal piece, often the alto or tenor. Does this mean that the part is to be played on an instrument, or rather that the scribe assumed the performer would insert the text in the untexted voice? That depends on local scribal practices. For Anthology, No. 38, for example, a literary account says that the upper two parts were sung, but the only surviving manuscript to preserve the piece has no text in the lower of these two voices (the alto). Thus we have supplied the text for the alto part, allocating the syllables according to the example of other texted pieces of this period and region.

✿ ORNAMENTATION

Given the importance of improvisation in the music of the Middle Ages and Renaissance, it is not surprising that medieval musicians added embellishment to the notated music. Should not modern performers do the same? For an idea of the sort of ornamentation that instrumentalists added, compare the beginning of the vocal version of Jacopo da Bologna's *Non al suo amante* (Anthology No. 37) with a slightly later written instrumental version of it, also from Italy (Exs. 1-1a, 1-1b). Again, the instrument on which the ornamented version is to be played is not specified in the manuscript; rather, the choice is left to the performer.

EXAMPLE 1-1A

EXAMPLE 1-1B

✿ ACCIDENTALS (ADDING MUSICA FICTA)

Not only did medieval performers have to supply their own ideas about tempo, dynamics, expression, pitch, and many other things but they also sometimes had to insert accidentals into the written score. Sometimes the composer (or scribe) wrote in all the accidentals, sometimes not. It was up to the performer, and now the modern editor, to supply missing accidentals according to various rules of music theory of the period. Notice in the preceding example how a B♭ is provided in the vocal version, but not in the instrumental one. In the latter case flats have been added by the modern editor, as indicated by the fact that they are written above the note, not before it. Two melodic rules require the B♭ here. The first is simple: wherever possible, perfect consonances such as the fourth should be kept perfect (hence the F-B ambitus of the melody requires a B♭). Second and more complex: a melodic line in which the hexachord is exceeded by only the step above "la" in the Guidonian system should always be sung as a half-step (thus here in a melody in the natural hexachord a B♭ is required).

Other rules for adding accidentals emerged from the growing awareness of counterpoint and voice leading during the fourteenth century. Indeed, our term **counter-**

point begins to appear at this time and is derived from the Latin expression *punctus contra punctum* (one note moving against another note). When writing for two or more voices, certain intervals were to be avoided. The augmented octave and the tritone, for example, were proscribed; in fact, the disagreeable tritone eventually came to be known as the **diabolus in musica** (the devil in music). Other intervals were highly desirable at certain moments in contrapuntal part writing. The aim was to have the voices get as close as possible to the most common perfect intervals, which at this point in history were the unison, fifth, and octave. At cadences, for example, thirds moving to fifths were to be major thirds, and sixths moving to octaves should be major sixths. To make these thirds and sixths major usually required the insertion of accidentals by the performers. Such accidentals, with the exception of B♭, were not to be found on the limited medieval scale as developed by Guido of Arezzo (see Chapter 4). Because these accidentals were theoretically "off the scale" and had to be imagined, they were called **musica ficta** (false music), as opposed to the notes on the medieval scale, which were called *musica recta* (correct music).

Recall that the earlier Guidonian system made use of three hexachords: the natural starting on C, the soft on F with a B♭, and the hard on G with a B♮ (Chapter 4). Thus in Guido's eleventh-century scale, B♭ was the only allowable chromatic note. Now, in the early fourteenth century, musicians began to place hexachords on pitches other than C, F, and G. By starting on other pitches, but keeping the interval pattern of the hexachord intact (1, 1, 1/2, 1, 1), they produced other accidentals such as F♯, C♯, and E♭. By 1375 a fully chromatic keyboard was in place. Nevertheless, because all chromatic notes other than B♭ were new additions to the system, they still were considered false, or *ficta*, notes.

To see how *musica ficta* works, consider the final cadence of the first *Kyrie* of Machaut's *Mass of Our Lady* (Ex. 1-2). The *ficta* C♯ in the bass in the first measure (bar 25) should be added by the performers so as to avoid an augmented octave with the C♯ that Machaut wrote in the alto voice. The *ficta* C♯ in the alto in measure two (bar 26) was also placed in the manuscript by Machaut, yet the *ficta* G♯ in the bass and in the soprano should be added by the performers for two reasons: to avoid a tritone and to make the third expanding to a fifth a major third. Music theorists said that voices should be "less distant from that location which they intend immediately to reach."[2] Accordingly, the G♯ and C♯ change a minor third and minor sixth to a major third and major sixth, and thus make these voices closer to the notes A and D they intend to reach in the final D-A-D chord. They thereby form what is called a **double leading-tone cadence,** here in the Dorian mode. Double leading-tone cadences create the biting, pungent sound characteristic of much fourteenth-century music.

EXAMPLE 1-2

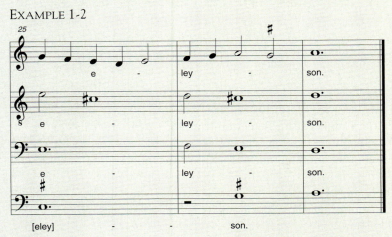

with rhythmic complexities, they are nevertheless enamored

LISTENING CUE

FRANCESCO LANDINI
Or su, gentili spirti (c1389)

CD 2/8
Anthology, No. 38

SUMMARY

The polyphonic music created in Florence and other northern Italian cities during the trecento consists mainly of secular songs, a total of more than six hundred madrigals, caccias, and ballatas. The majority of these are preserved in a single manuscript, the Squarcialupi Codex, a compendium assembled in Florence about 1415. Almost all songs set texts written in Italian, which emerges in this period as an important literary and poetic language. Trecento music has rhythms that are more regular than the French music of this period. At the same time, it often luxuriates in long melismas for the soprano or uppermost voice at the end of lines of text. By the end of the century, however, some French influences—specifically greater syncopation, and first and second endings—can be seen in the ballata. The repertory culminates in the three-voice ballatas of Francesco Landini, which combine Italian lyricism with French rhythmic subtlety. Simultaneous thirds and sixths (6/3 chords) become more frequent in Landini's music, especially at cadences. These create a sonority that will become basic to the music of the emerging Renaissance: parallel 6/3 chords. In addition, the overwhelmingly secular nature of the repertory suggests that the focus of composers is turning away from religious music to music for purely human pleasure, recreation, and delight. In this more secular, less sacred world can be seen the beginnings of musical humanism—music not offered solely to God, but made by humans to be enjoyed by humans.

KEY TERMS

city-state	ritornello	Landini cadence
Squarcialupi Codex	caccia	Giovanni Boccaccio
trecento	ballata	*Decameron*
madrigal	ripresa	

15

Music at the Cathedral of Florence

Like the Colosseum in Rome, the cathedral of Florence (Fig. 15-1) serves as a cultural icon for all of Italy. When the gigantic dome was finished in 1436, the authorities in Florence called upon a Frenchman, not a native Italian, to create new music for the ceremony of dedication. They did so in part because Italy had no strong tradition of large-scale polyphonic church music. Italian sacred music during the Middle cities, among them Milan, Pisa, Ferrara, Venice, Siena, and Florence, controlled their own destinies. Most were ruled by despots. Florence, however, was a republic. Its citizens elected the government, established rules of commerce, and hired an army. By 1340, 100,000 people lived within the high city walls, though 40,000 of these would perish during the Black Death of 1348. Florentine society was not rigidly hierarchical, as was generally true elsewhere in the Middle Ages. No sections of the city were reserved for the rich, no ghettoes inhabited solely by the poor. Individuals of talent could move freely among all classes. Thus physicians conversed with architects, and musicians dined with wealthy bankers. A growing pride in civic accomplishment, and a new emphasis on individual achievement marked Florence and the early Renaissance generally.

✿ TRECENTO MUSIC AND THE SQUARCIALUPI CODEX

Florentine pride and respect for individual creativity can clearly be seen in the sumptuous **Squarcialupi Codex,** a music manuscript containing 354 compositions (Fig. 14-1). Its large size, rich colors, and brilliant gold leaf typify the tradition of Florentine excellence in the arts and crafts. Copied about 1415, the Squarcialupi Codex is a retrospective anthology of music important in Florence during the **trecento** (short for *mille trecento*, or the century of the 1300s) in which the arts flourished. It derives its name from one of its first owners, Antonio Squarcialupi (1416–1480), organist at the cathedral of Florence. All the songs included here are settings of Italian texts, for during the trecento this vernacular tongue emerged as a major literary and poetic language. Some pieces are monophonic, some for two voices, and others for three. Together they represent the sum total of the written song repertory of trecento Florence.

The compositions preserved within the Squarcialupi Codex belong to one of three musical genres: the madrigal, the caccia, and the ballata. These are the Italian *formes fixes*. The fourteenth-century **madrigal** was originally a poem in the vernacular tongue (Italian, not Latin) to which music was added for greater emotional effect. The poem, usually about love, consists of two (sometimes three) three-line stanzas followed by a two-line **ritornello** (refrain). It was Petrarch who elevated and popularized the madrigal as a poetic form. By the mid fourteenth century his madrigals were given musical accompaniment by composers working in northern Italy, among them Jacopo da Bologna.

Jacopo da Bologna (c1310–c1386) took Petrarch's madrigal text *Non al suo amante* (*Not to her lover*) and set it in typical madrigal style for two voices. The text consists of two three-line units, each sung to the same music, followed by a ritornello. Thus the musical form of this and all trecento madrigals is **AAB.** Rhythmically, the voices in Jacopo's madrigal are rather square, even mechanical; section **A,** for example, has not a single instance of syncopation, as frequently found in the contemporary songs of Machaut, for example. However, lyricism abounds in the florid upper voice, which begins and ends each line with a melisma. If the Italians are not concerned with rhythmic complexities, they are nevertheless enamored

✿ FIGURE 14-1

A page of the Squarcialupi Codex showing the blind organist Francesco Landini playing the organ and the music of his ballata *Musica son.*

with long, almost sensual, musical lines. Typical of the madrigal, here the ritornello is in a different musical meter from that of the preceding stanzas ($\frac{3}{4}$ instead of $\frac{4}{4}$). Petrarch, as was his custom, concludes this madrigal poem with a vivid image, allowing composer Jacopo da Bologna to underscore it through a change to triple meter. Their madrigal ends with a lovely oxymoron: the lover experiences a shiver of passion in the heat of the noonday sun.

EXAMPLE 14-1

Non al suo amante più Diana piacque	**A**	Not to her lover did Diana ever more please
Quando per tal ventura tutta ignuda		As when, through good fortune,
La vidi in mezzo de le gelide acque.		He saw her naked in the midst of the cool waters.
Ch'a me la pastorell'alpestre e cruda,	**A**	As did please me the cruel shepherdess,
Posta a bagnar un leggiadetretto velo,		Washing her white veil, which protects
Ch'a l'aura il vago e biondo capel chiuda.		Her fine blond hair from blowing free.
(ritornello)	**B**	
Tal che mi fece quand'egli arde 'l cielo,		Thus it made me, now when the sky is fiery,
Tutto tremar d'un amoroso gielo.		All tremble with the chill of love.

LISTENING CUE

JACOPO DA BOLOGNA
Non al suo amante (c1350)
(text by Francesco Petrarch)

CD 2/7
Anthology, No. 37

The caccia and the ballata constitute the two other genres of secular music in trecento Italy. A **caccia** is a piece involving a musical canon in the upper two voices supported by a slower moving tenor. In Italian, *caccia* means "hunt," and many of the texts recreate vivid hunting scenes. For example, an archer may chase a doe through a wooded landscape, accompanied by musical shouts, and perhaps hocket. Often such texts are merely allegories of an amatory pursuit, as the lover pursues the beloved. The canonic quality of the upper voices exemplifies the process of the hunt, one voice chasing after the other at an exact interval of pitch and time.

As the name suggests (from the Italian *ballare*, to dance) the **ballata** was a dance song with a choral refrain. Its musical and poetic form is very similar to the French virelai: **A** (ripresa) **b** (piede) **b** (piede) **a** (volta) **A** (ripresa). The terms *piede* (foot), *volta* (turn) and **ripresa** (refrain) recall the origins of the ballata as a monophonic dance. The Florentine composer Francesco Landini was the first to write two- and three-voice ballatas. During the second half of the trecento, the ballata replaced the madrigal as the most popular Italian musical genre. Landini has left us thirteen madrigals and only one caccia, but 140 ballatas.

 ## FRANCESCO LANDINI

By all standards, Francesco Landini (c1325–1397) was the most important composer of the trecento. As a child he was blinded by smallpox. To compensate, he developed his aural faculties, becoming proficient on a number of string, wind, and keyboard instruments. In time he also became a leading Florentine intellectual, a respected authority on politics, religion, ethics, and even astronomy. Sometime during the 1360s the king of Cyprus crowned Landini poet laureate, thereby acknowledging his excellence in verse as well as music. Thus, in his portrait in the Squarcialupi Codex (see Fig. 14-1) Landini wears the laurel wreath around his cap. In his hands he holds a portative organ, the instrument on which he excelled above all others. From 1365 until his death Landini was organist at the church of San Lorenzo in the center of Florence. It was here that he was buried in 1397, and here that his tombstone can be seen today.

The society that enjoyed Landini's music is described in two important literary works, Giovanni Boccaccio's *Decameron*, which recreates events in Florence in 1348, and Giovanni da Prato's *Il Paradiso*, set in 1389. The *Decameron* is a collection of one hundred short stories, told by ten persons over the course of ten days. Music, and the women who make it, play an important role in these novellas (see Box). Giovanni da Prato's *Il Paradiso* is a similar collection of stories told by a group of Florentine intellectuals who gather in the homes of leading citizens. Francesco Landini is among the guests, and is introduced by da Prato with the following words:

> At that time, wondrous to recount, still flourished Francesco of the Organs, a theorist and practical musician. Blind almost since birth, he showed himself to be of such divine intellect that in all the most abstract aspects of music he understood the most subtle proportions of musical numbers, and realized them with such sweetness on his organ that it seemed unbelievable even when one heard it. Moreover, he discussed with every artist and philosopher not only his music but also all the liberal arts because he was knowlegible [sic] in all of them.[2]

As was the custom, the circle of friends moves to a garden where Landini, like the other guests, is asked to tell a story. When he has finished, two young ladies step forward to sing a ballata he composed:

> And soon with the approval of all, and especially the musician Francesco himself, two young ladies began to sing a ballata to the accompaniment of Biagio di Sernello, with such grace and angelic voices that not a single man or woman was unmoved; and soon the birds, up among the cypresses, came near and imitated the singing with even greater sweetness. The words of the ballata are these: *Or su, gentili spiriti* [sic].[3]

This eyewitness description shows that the upper two parts of Landini's ballata were sung by young women, while a gentleman sang the tenor or played that line on an instrument. Other accounts demonstrate that instruments such as the vielle and lute might accompany, or even replace, one or more voices. The poem that

Landini set is likely his own, and its high quality suggests that he well merited the title "poet laureate" bestowed upon him by the king of Cypress.

EXAMPLE 14-2

(ripresa) Or su, gentili spirti, ad amar pronti,	A	Come now, gentle spirits, ready to love,
Volete voi vedere 'l Paradiso?		Do you want to see Paradise?
Mirate d'esta petra 'l vago viso.		Admire the beautiful face of this [precious] stone.
(piede) Nelle sue luce sancte ard' e sfavilla	b	Victorious love burns and glows
Amor victorioso, che divampa		In her holy eyes, which inflames he who
Per dolcezza di gloria chi la mira.		Gazes upon her through the sweetness of glory.
(piede) Ma l'alma mia, fedelissima ancilla	b	But my soul, most faithful helpmate,
Piatà non trova in questa chiara lampa		Finds no pity in this clear light,
E null'altro che lei ama o disira.		Nor does it love or desire anything else than her.
(volta) O sacra iddea, al tuo servo un po' spira	a	O holy image, to your servant show some
Mercé; mercé sol chiamo, già conquiso:		Mercy; already conquered, mercy I alone ask:
Dé, fallo pria che morte m'abbia anciso.		Come, do this before death kills me.
(ripresa) Or su, gentili spirti. . . .	A	Come now, gentle spirits. . . .

Landini's *Or su, gentili spirti* demonstrates several stylistic features of late-trecento music. The principal vocal line is still the cantus, but now this part is more fluid, rhythmically less rigid, than in earlier trecento music. Evidently, Landini was much influenced by the French *Ars nova*. Syncopations occur frequently and sometimes run across the bar line. Primitive-sounding parallel fifths are still present. Yet parallel thirds and sixths appear in greater abundance, lending to the music a sweeter sound typical of the emerging Renaissance. At cadences, the sixth in the outer voices expands to an octave. Landini liked to ornament these cadences by adding a lower neighbor-tone to the upper part as it moves up to the octave. So prevalent is this cadential gesture in his music that it has come to be called the **Landini cadence.** The final cadence of *Or su, gentili spirti* has both syncopation in the cantus

Women Making Music in Boccaccio's *Decameron*

Giovanni Boccaccio was inspired to write his ***Decameron*** by the horrific events of 1348, when "into the distinguished Florence, more noble than any Italian city, came a deadly pestilence."[4] Like all Florentines, Boccaccio suffered greatly from the Black Death, but he survived, thanks to the assistance of several woman friends. To repay their kindness, he determined to create a set of stories that would center around women. Thus was born *Decameron*, a work of fiction in which a group of wealthy young Florentines briefly escape to the Tuscan hills. Their life of idyllic beauty in the countryside contrasts sharply with the city below that is festering with the plague. *Decameron* means "ten days," and Boccaccio's book is a collection of one hundred stories, told over ten days by ten persons, each day's activities concluding with a ballata that is both sung and danced. Seven of the ten characters are women. They sing ballatas, play musical instruments, and lead the dancing (Fig. 14-2). Indeed, to judge from the *Decameron* and other contemporary writings, women predominated in the performance of secular songs and dances throughout the trecento.

But women were not taught to be composers, partly because they were not given instruction in musical notation. A lady could learn by rote to sing and play an instrument such as the vielle, psaltery, or harp, or to dance. But in the Middle Ages musical notation was written in arcane symbols and explained in a language that remained the preserve of the church. All medieval music theory treatises were written in Latin, which women generally did not study. Nor were women allowed to enroll in the university—neither in church-controlled universities such as that in Paris nor in municipally supported ones such as in Florence. Conse-

quently, they were deprived, among other things, of the study of ethics and moral philosophy. Boccaccio says that his *Decameron* intends to correct this inequity. A moral can be drawn from each of his one hundred tales, as well as from the texts of his ten ballatas that conclude each day, and, from these, women can learn the ways of the world. In this fashion, Boccaccio says, "I will make up in part the wrong done [to women] by Fortune."[5]

Bibliothèque Nationale, Paris

FIGURE 14-2

Queen Pampinea in the garden in an illustrated copy of *Decameron*. The women dance; the men watch.

and a Landini cadence. As you can see, the first line of Landini's text invites the participants to enjoy love and thereby experience Paradise, the general theme of Giovanni da Prato's *Il Paradiso*.

EXAMPLE 14-3

LISTENING CUE

FRANCESCO LANDINI
Or su, gentili spirti (c1389)

CD 2/8
Anthology, No. 38

SUMMARY

The polyphonic music created in Florence and other northern Italian cities during the trecento consists mainly of secular songs, a total of more than six hundred madrigals, caccias, and ballatas. The majority of these are preserved in a single manuscript, the Squarcialupi Codex, a compendium assembled in Florence about 1415. Almost all songs set texts written in Italian, which emerges in this period as an important literary and poetic language. Trecento music has rhythms that are more regular than the French music of this period. At the same time, it often luxuriates in long melismas for the soprano or uppermost voice at the end of lines of text. By the end of the century, however, some French influences—specifically greater syncopation, and first and second endings—can be seen in the ballata. The repertory culminates in the three-voice ballatas of Francesco Landini, which combine Italian lyricism with French rhythmic subtlety. Simultaneous thirds and sixths (6/3 chords) become more frequent in Landini's music, especially at cadences. These create a sonority that will become basic to the music of the emerging Renaissance: parallel 6/3 chords. In addition, the overwhelmingly secular nature of the repertory suggests that the focus of composers is turning away from religious music to music for purely human pleasure, recreation, and delight. In this more secular, less sacred world can be seen the beginnings of musical humanism—music not offered solely to God, but made by humans to be enjoyed by humans.

KEY TERMS

city-state	ritornello	Landini cadence
Squarcialupi Codex	caccia	Giovanni Boccaccio
trecento	ballata	*Decameron*
madrigal	ripresa	

Chapter 15

Music at the Cathedral of Florence

Like the Colosseum in Rome, the cathedral of Florence (Fig. 15-1) serves as a cultural icon for all of Italy. When the gigantic dome was finished in 1436, the authorities in Florence called upon a Frenchman, not a native Italian, to create new music for the ceremony of dedication. They did so in part because Italy had no strong tradition of large-scale polyphonic church music. Italian sacred music during the Middle

Ages and early Renaissance was overwhelmingly monophonic Gregorian chant, the age-old music of the Western Church. By the early fifteenth century a few polyphonic Masses and motets began to appear in Italian music manuscripts. But most of these were the work of French and English composers, not native Italians. Just as Gothic architecture was brought down to Italy from France in this period, so too musicians and musical genres, such as the isorhythmic motet, were imported from the north.

Among the northern musicians who came to Italy in this period was Guillaume Dufay (c1397–1474), a native of the region of Cambrai in northern France. (His name should be pronounced with three syllables "Du-fa-y" for in his day it rhymed with the French word "me-lo-die.") During the 1420s and 1430s Dufay served a number of patrons, working his way up to become the pope's **magister cappellae** (leader of the chapel). During the summer of 1434, Pope Eugenius IV and his court were chased from Rome by unruly mobs and took up residence in Florence. Thus it was convenient for the citizens of Florence to call upon their pope and his principal musician, Dufay, to celebrate the completion of the cathedral of Florence in 1436.

The dome of the cathedral of Florence is one of the architectural wonders of the Western world. The citizens of fifteenth-century Florence planned to construct a church with an enormous dome that would loom large as testimony to the glory and power of their republic. But no dome this size had been constructed since Roman times. The challenge was to build a colossal structure that would go upward and then progressively inward, but not collapse, and do so without supports. (At Notre Dame of Paris, and all other Gothic churches, the high vaults were built above a wooden scaffold that supported them from beneath; then, when the mortar of the vaults had dried, the scaffold was removed.) But no trees were large enough to go across the expanse planned for the dome of Florence (140 feet across), and steel beams did not exist. To solve this engineering problem, the Florentine architect **Filippo Brunelleschi** (1377–1446) went to Rome to study the ancient Pantheon. Using the secrets of classical architecture, he then built for the Florentines a dome with a double shell, the inner shell lightening the load of the outer one. Further, he contained the outward thrust of the bricks by tying them together with bands of stones linked together by iron rings.

On the morning of 25 March 1436, the pope and the citizens of Florence gathered to celebrate Brunelleschi's accomplishment. To make the ceremony more splendid, Guillaume Dufay composed a motet, *Nuper rosarum flores* (*Recently roses*). Because this was a solemn state occasion, Dufay chose to make it an isorhythmic motet, creating one of the last pieces in this medieval genre; throughout history composers have made use of old-fashioned, conservative musical styles for ceremonial and state occasions.

Dufay built his motet upon the opening phrase of a chant, *Terribilis est locus iste* (*This is a redoubtable place*), the Introit of the Mass for the dedication of a church. This melody resounds with double force because two tenors sing the notes of the chant, tenor I a fifth lower than tenor II. Both melody and rhythm in the tenors are stated four times, once in each of the four sections of the motet. Each of these sections begins with a duet in the upper two voices and to these the two tenor parts are

CORBIS

❀ FIGURE 15-1
The cathedral of Florence with its giant dome designed by Filippo Brunelleschi was dedicated in 1436.

soon joined. In medieval notation each section is twenty-eight longs in length (twenty-eight double whole-notes, i.e., twenty-eight bars in modern notation). Mensuration signs (medieval time signatures) control the length of each section. In Section I the long lasts for six semibreves (six half-notes in modern notation), in Section II for four, in Section III for two, and in Section IV for three. Thus the four sections unfold with a durational ratio of 6:4:2:3.

I	II	III	IV
Duet then	Duet then	Duet then	Duet then
four voices	four voices	four voices	four voices
28 × 6 half-notes	28 × 4 half-notes	28 × 2 half-notes	28 × 3 half-notes

But there are more numbers at work in Dufay's motet. Each section consists of fourteen bars of two-voice and fourteen bars of four-voice music. The two tenors each sing the same fourteen notes of the chant in each of the four sections. The motet text, which speaks of the dedication of the church, consists of four stanzas each of seven lines and each line has seven syllables. The numbers 1, 2, 4, 7, 14, and 28 inform the entire motet. Thus, *Nuper rosarum flores* is no less architectonic (constructed by a master builder) than the architecture of the cathedral.

In fact, *Nuper rosarum flores* mirrors the proportions of the cathedral. The cathedral of Florence was built according to a measurement called the *braccio* (a length of about 22 inches, or an arm's length, from the Italian word for "arm"). The nave of the church is 72 *braccia* wide (outside wall to outside wall), 72 *braccia* long, and 72 *braccia* high. Brunelleschi's dome, moreover, is 72 *braccia* in diameter and 2 × 72 (144) *braccia* high. The numbers basic to Dufay's motet, 6, 4, 2, 3, when multiplied, also equal 144. Dufay's motet is the only piece by a major composer in the history of music to attempt to replicate the proportions of a building through sound.[1]

We estimate that some 20,000 citizens of Florence crowded into their new cathedral on the day of its consecration. Did they hear the intended unity of music and architecture as they listened to Dufay's motet under Brunelleschi's magnificent dome? Did they sense any of the other musical symbolism inherent in this music (see Box)? Perhaps not. The steady stream of small note values and the unequal distribution of the text obscure the changing proportions among the four sections. Meaning in early music often lurks unseen or unheard beneath the surface, accessible only to an intellectual few. What apparently struck the people of Florence was the grand sonorities of the music. Here is what one eye-witness said of the music that day:

> All the places of the Temple resounded with the sounds of harmonious symphonies [of voices] as well as the concords of diverse instruments, so that it seemed not without reason that the angels and the sounds and singing of divine paradise had been sent from heaven to us on earth to insinuate in our ears a certain incredible divine sweetness.[2]

This "incredible divine sweetness" may refer to the new sonorities of Dufay's motet. *Nuper rosarum flores* has none of the dissonant parallel seconds and sevenths of fourteenth-century music. Gone, too, are all antiquated parallel fifths and octaves. (Here in the early fifteenth century music theorists decree for the first time that perfect intervals should not come one after the other in direct succession.) Moreover, intervals are now carefully regulated so that dissonance does not occur on a strong beat, but rather off the beat in some sort of passing fashion. Any dissonance that does fall on the beat is carefully prepared and resolved. In this motet of the late Middle Ages and early Renaissance we see the rules of counterpoint and good part-writing beginning to take shape.

Musical Number Symbolism

Meaning in music of the Middle Ages and Renaissance was conveyed as much through **number symbolism** as it was through overt explanation. Numbers came to possess rich theological associations. Christ was represented by 8 and, by extension, 888; Satan by 666, according to the Book of Revelation; the Virgin Mary by 7, because of her seven sorrows, seven joys, seven acts of mercy, seven virginal companions, and seven years of exile in Egypt; the temple by 4 and 7 because of its four cornerstones and seven pillars of wisdom; the Trinity by 3; and so forth. Silent, unseen numbers informed all of God's creations, including Dufay's motet.

Dufay chose the structural proportions 6:4:2:3 to mirror not only the cathedral of Florence but also the ancient temple of Solomon in Jerusalem, the prototype and spiritual authority of all churches throughout Christendom. The Bible (I Kings: 6) tells us that Solomon's temple measured 60 cubits in length (divided into 40 and 20 cubits for the nave and sanctuary, respectively) by 20 cubits in width and 30 cubits in height. It was begun in the fourth year of Solomon's reign and took seven years to complete. The service of dedication occurred in the seventh month of the seventh year and required twice seven days.

In *Nuper rosarum flores*, Dufay has wedded the symbolic numbers of the biblical temple to those of the Virgin, to whom the cathedral of Florence was dedicated. He thereby created a perfect union, one centering around 28, the number inherent in the four sections of his motet. Since ancient times, 28 was recognized as a perfect number ($1 \times 28 = 2 \times 14 = 4 \times 7$; $1 + 2 + 4 + 7 + 14 = 28$).

We may not hear any of this number symbolism, but that is how the intellectuals of the Middle Ages and Renaissance understood the world, how they perceived the theological concepts of the universal church and the Virgin. The numbers were embedded in the music and that was all that mattered. Early music often conveys meaning through abstractions rather than overt, mimetic expression. Yet some twentieth-century composers also engaged in number symbolism. For a discussion of the "Golden Section" in the music of Béla Bartók, see the Box in Chapter 71.

Finally, Dufay graces his motet with abundant thirds and sixths (Ex. 15-1). Parallel sixths, for example, often form the structural backbone of the piece. In addition, the composer frequently places the third of a chord in the soprano voice to give it prominence. In the final chord of the piece he ends on a third, as if to say "I like this new sound," but then moves away to a more traditional ending with an open-fifth chord. Not for another seventy years would composers actually finish with the sweeter-sounding third. Last of all, notice such important phrases as "the temple, majestic in its engineering" and "this same most enormous temple." Here Dufay requires the alto part to divide, thereby momentarily creating a richly sonorous five-voice texture. This is truly a grand motet for what was and remains the largest dome in the pre-modern world.

EXAMPLE 15-1

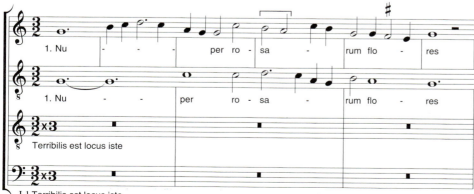

I,1 Terribilis est locus iste

Section I: 28 × 6 half-notes

(Two voices) Nuper rosarum flores	Recently roses given by the pope
Ex dono pontificis	Have not ceased to adorn,
Hieme licet horrida,	Cruel winter having past,
Tibi, virgo celica,	The Temple,
Pie et sancte deditum	Majestic in its engineering,
(Four voices) Grandis templum machinae	Dedicated to the Virgin
Condecorarunt perpetim.	In piety and holiness.
Hodie vicarius	Today the vicar
Jesu Christi et Petri	Of Jesus Christ and successor
Successor Eugenius	Of Peter, Eugenius,
Hoc idem amplissimum	This same most enormous Temple
Sacris templum manibus	With sacred hands
Sanctisque liquoribus	And holy oils

Section II: 28 × 4 half-notes

(Two voices) Consecrare dignatus est.	Has deigned to consecrate.
Igitur, alma parens	Therefore, sweet parent
Nati tui et filia	And daughter of your son,
Virgo decus virginum,	God, virgin of virgins,
(Four voices) Tuus te Florentiae	To you your devoted
Devotus orat populus	Populace of Florence petitions
Ut qui mente et corpore	So that whoever begs for something,
Mundo quicquam exorarit,	With pure spirit and body,

Section III: 28 × 2 half-notes

(Two voices) Oratio-	May, by
(Four voices) ne tua	your prayer
Cruciatus et meritis	And the merits,
Tui secundum carnem	Owing to his carnal torment,

Section IV: 28 × 3 half-notes

(Two voices) Nati domini sui	Of your son, their lord,
(Four voices) Grata beneficia	Be worthy to receive
Veniamque reatum	Gracious benefits and
Accipere mereatur.	Forgiveness of sins.
(Four voices) Amen.	Amen.

LISTENING CUE

GUILLAUME DUFAY
Nuper rosarum flores (1436)

CD 2/9
Anthology, No. 39

SUMMARY

The early fifteenth century is a period of gradual transition between the Middle Ages and the Renaissance that is revealed in painting, architecture, and music. The architect Filippo Brunelleschi, for example, went to Rome to study structural designs from classical antiquity, and he used these to create a renaissance in architecture, specifically at the cathedral of Florence. But only half of the cathedral of

Florence is Renaissance in style. The nave of the church was constructed during the fourteenth century in the older Gothic-style architecture. Thus art historians say that the west half of the church (the nave) is medieval and the east half (the choir covered by the dome) is Renaissance in style. So too Dufay's motet *Nuper rosarum flores* has qualities of the old and the new. It is medieval in the sense that the composer builds upon the older framework of isorhythmic structure and uses medieval number symbolism. The motet is of the Renaissance, however, in that Dufay embraces the sweeter sounds of thirds and sixths, avoids parallel fifths and octaves, and carefully controls all dissonances. Significantly, the final cadential phrase "Amen" (mm. 169–170) is added on to, and lies beyond, the medieval isorhythmic structure. This powerful final moment of choral homophony points most clearly toward the newer, more richly sonorous harmonies of the Renaissance.

KEY TERMS

magister cappellae   Filippo Brunelleschi   number symbolism

Chapter

16

Music in England

Before the fifteenth century, England had no single great musical figure, like Guillaume de Machaut in France or Francesco Landini in Italy. Nor were there any English cities with a population of more than 10,000 except London (Map 16-1), which in 1300 counted 75,000 souls, about a third of the number in Paris at this time. England was fundamentally a rural society. About ninety percent of its six million inhabitants were engaged in one way or another in agriculture. They worked the lands of the lords or those of the church. Monasteries exerted an especially strong presence in this rural environment. Thus English music written during the thirteenth and fourteenth centuries consists mostly of compositions for monastic communities. Almost all pieces are anonymous—religious music written by nameless monks who lived and died in the service of the church.

From the moment Frenchman William the Conqueror seized England in 1066 until the early fifteenth century, the kings of England spoke French at their court. French culture dominated English high society in other ways as well. French-born and French-educated clerics held the major offices of church and state. English students flocked to the University of Paris. When Oxford University was established in the 1300s, its founders modeled the new institution on the older French one. So too in music, things French informed English institutions. Organum from Paris was heard at the English royal chapel; and the French conductus provided a model for composition in the English monasteries.

At the same time, however, a few distinctly English musical practices coexisted with imported French styles. From time immemorial the English

 MAP 16-1
England during the early Renaissance.

had a love of unaccompanied polyphonic singing; the Winchester Troper, dating from around 1000, preserves some of the West's earliest organum (see Chapter 7). And England enjoyed its own special dialect of Gregorian chant, called **Sarum chant** from the old Latin name of the cathedral town of Salisbury; the melodies and texts of this English repertory were different from the more "standard" chant sung on the Continent.

❁ RONDELLUS AND ROTA

One distinctly English musical practice is a technique called **rondellus.** In rondellus, two or three voices engage in voice exchange or, more correctly, phrase exchange. Each voice starts with its own phrase and then they switch. After each part has sung all phrases, the voices begin new phrases and then switch again, as the following scheme demonstrates:

Voice 1	a	b	c	d	e	f
Voice 2	b	c	a	e	f	d
Voice 3	c	a	b	f	d	e

Rondellus technique was part of a long unwritten tradition of choral singing. Welsh people in the western part of England are known to have sung rondellus in the twelfth century when, according to one observer, "you could hear as many songs (phrases) as you could see heads, yet they all accord in one consonant polyphonic song."[1] A rondellus might stand as an independent song, or the technique might be worked into a motet or conductus. Finally, the simple process that generates a rondellus (singing in a round) may imply that at least some of this English music was improvised on the spot. The English love of singing glees and catches (canons or rounds) continued well into the nineteenth century.

❁ FIGURE 16-1

The Summer Canon, with its two-voice pes at the bottom.

British Library

The most famous of all medieval English compositions makes use of rondellus technique as well as canon. It is entitled *Sumer is icumen in* (*Summer is coming in*), or simply the **Summer Canon,** and was written about 1300 (Fig. 16-1). Here, the bottom two voices engage in a brief rondellus, continually exchanging a short, two-bar phrase. The English called a bottom voice that continually repeats a **pes.** Thus in the Summer Canon the pes is a rondellus. Above the pes unfolds a four-voice canon in which each new voice enters at a distance of two measures in modern notation. Once the first voice reaches the end, it and its followers are instructed to return to the beginning to start again in a potentially never-ending cycle. The English called this type of canon that endlessly circles back to the beginning a **rota** (Latin for wheel, from which the English word "round"). The Summer Canon, or rota, is not only the first canon but also the first circular canon in the history of music. In addition, it is also the first surviving composition for six voices. Like most simple canons, this one works because the strong beat of each metrical unit (downbeat of each measure) creates, or implies, one and the same chord, in this case what we today call an F major triad, here transposed to D to make it easier to sing.

The original manuscript of the Summer Canon (Fig. 16-1) shows two texts written below the music (Ex. 16-1). The upper one is in Middle English (*Sumer is icumen in*) and the lower is in Latin (*Perspice Christicola*). The English text tells of the exuberant sights and sounds of a rural spring:

the singing cuckoo, the bleating lamb, the lowing cow, and the farting goat, among them. The Latin text speaks of the death and resurrection of Christ on Easter Sunday (see below). While these themes might at first seem unrelated, both joyfully celebrate the eternal process of rebirth and regeneration that occurs each spring. All the while, the singers sing of this ceaseless re-creation as they continually repeat their endless round. The anonymous Summer Canon is a delight to sing (try it with a few friends), and it also demonstrates several qualities of early English music: a folksy tune, a predilection for canon, a preference for many voices, and a love of consonant, often triadic, sonorities.

EXAMPLE 16-1

Middle English	Modern English
Sumer is icumen in,	Summer is coming in
Lhude sing cuccu!	Loudly sing, cuckoo!
Groweth sed and bloweth med	Seeds sprout and the meadow blooms,
And springeth the wde nu.	And new wood growth appears.
Sing cuccu!	Sing cuckoo!
Awe bleteth after lomb,	Ewe bleats after lamb,
Lhouth after calve cu.	Cow lows after calf,
Bulluc sterteth, bucke verteth,	Bullock leaps, he-goat farts,
Murie sing cucu!	Merrily sing cuckoo!
Wel singes thu cuccu.	Well sing you cuckoo.
Ne swik thu naver nu!	Don't ever stop!

Latin	Modern English
Perspice Christicola,	Observe, worshipers of Christ
que dignatio!	what gracious condescension!
Celicus agricola	How the heavenly husbandman
pro vitis vicio,	for the sin of the vine [in Eden]
filio	not sparing his son

non parcens exposuit	exposed him
mortis exicio.	to the pains of death.
Qui captivos semivivos	Those half-dead captives
a supplicio	sentenced [to Purgatory]
vite donat	he restores to life
et secum coronat	and crowns them next to him
in celi solio.	on the heavenly throne.

Pes: Sing cuccu!

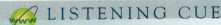

LISTENING CUE

ANONYMOUS
Sumer is icumen in (c1300)

Thomson-Schirmer Website
Anthology, No. 40

❋ ENGLISH FABURDEN AND CONTINENTAL FAUXBOURDON

The English passion for choral singing and consonant sound can be heard in a style of music called faburden. **Faburden** arose when singers improvised around a given chant: one voice sang above the plainsong at the interval of a fourth, and another sang below it at a third; at cadences the bottom voice would drop down to form an octave with the top one (Ex. 16-2). The sound that resulted was a succession of parallel 6/3 chords punctuated by occasional 8/5 chords at the beginnings and ends of phrases. Singers declaimed the sacred text simultaneously in the free rhythm of plainsong. Below is the process of faburden as singers of the fourteenth and fifteenth century might have improvised it around a *Kyrie* (Anthology, No. 6).

EXAMPLE 16-2

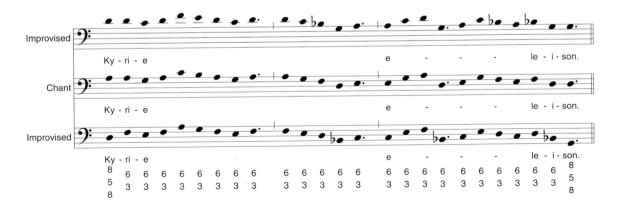

Because faburden was an improvisatory technique, almost no written examples of it survive—we know it was popular because music theorists tell us so. The importance of faburden is that English composers incorporated this unwritten improvisatory style into their more formal written works. Indeed, much of the English music that survives from the early fifteenth century is overrun with parallel 6/3 chords. This same technique is sometimes more generally referred to as **English discant**—adding two improvised voices upon a chant so as to increase its sonority. What results is a euphonious stream of consonant chords.

Most late-medieval English polyphony, whether strict faburden or the more general English discant, was composed for three voices, each of which had a different name. The lowest part was called, of course, the tenor. The middle voice was often called the "meane" (middle, as in "mean average") and the highest part the **treble** (perhaps from "triple" because this was the third voice). The term "meane" was of no lasting importance, but not so the term "treble." From this word comes our general musical term "treble," meaning top part. In the course of time, English-speaking musicians also came to refer to the highest clef in music, the G clef, as the "treble clef."

Three-voice faburden originated in England and was carried into France in the fifteenth century by the followers of the English kings. Soon Continental composers developed a related style called fauxbourdon. In **fauxbourdon** singers of sacred music improvised at pitches a fourth and a sixth below a given plainsong. Thus in faburden the chant is in the middle voice, but in fauxbourdon it is on top. Both styles, however, produce parallel 6/3 chords. Many written-out examples of this improvisatory process survive in fifteenth-century French, Italian, and German manuscripts. Sometimes the composer would lightly ornament the chant (marked by "x" in Ex. 16-3) on the top as well as the bottom part, so as to break the monotony of the parallel 6/3 chords. Rather than writing out the middle voice, however, he then simply inserted the word *fauxbourdon* in the score, thereby telling the middle part to sing a fourth below the chant. In the fauxbourdon applied by Guillaume Dufay to the following popular Christmas hymn, we are midway between improvisation and composition.

EXAMPLE 16-3

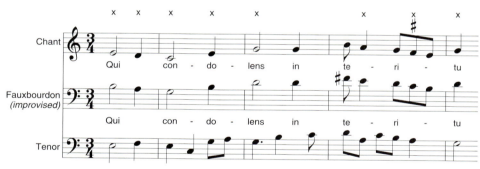

You whose suffering...

Both English faburden and Continental fauxbourdon suggest that, in addition to the composed music preserved in written form, late medieval musicians engaged in a great deal of improvised singing. What little we can glimpse today of these improvisatory practices is likely only the tip of an iceberg that went deep into the ancient tradition of English choral song.

KING HENRY V: THE OLD HALL MANUSCRIPT AND THE CAROL

Of all the late-medieval kings of England, **Henry V** (r. 1413–1422) was the most dashing and successful. He has been immortalized by Shakespeare (*Henry V*), whose kingly creation, in turn, has been portrayed in several twentieth-century films. Henry conquered northern France, and would have taken all of it had he not died

British Library

❧ FIGURE 16-2

A polyphonic *Gloria* ascribed to King Henry in the Old Hall Manuscript.

suddenly in 1422. Though Henry was a valiant soldier, he also possessed a taste for literature, poetry, and music. He supported two important chapels, one that traveled with him around England and to the Continent and one that was resident at Windsor Castle, the traditional home of the English kings and queens just west of London. Among the musicians employed by the royal family was Leonel Power (c1380–1445), a composer important in the history of the unified Mass cycle (see Chapter 17). In addition, King Henry V himself seems to have been something of a composer.

Surviving today are a polyphonic *Gloria* and *Sanctus* ascribed to "Roy Henry," presumed to be Henry V. Both are preserved in an important music manuscript compiled during the 1420s. It is called the Old Hall Manuscript (now in the British Library, but formerly at the College of St. Edmund in Old Hall, England). The **Old Hall Manuscript** contains 147 compositions, mostly Mass movements and motets, many by composers serving the royal household (Fig. 16-2). Several motets in honor of the warrior St. George may link the book to the chapel of St. George on the grounds of Windsor Castle. Not only is the Old Hall Manuscript the largest collection of English polyphony from the late fourteenth and early fifteenth centuries, it also contains music of the most advanced English style, a style that would soon come to influence music in France and Italy. England at this moment in history was no longer an isolated island, but a potent force in both music and politics.

In 1415 King Henry V of England invaded northern France, landing at Harfleur near the mouth of the Seine River. His army was small, fewer than 10,000, and it relied on an infantry of fast moving archers and pike-men. The French army was nearly four times as large, but depended upon the mainstay of the older medieval military: knights in heavy armor. When the two forces clashed on a muddy field near Agincourt on 25 October, the agile English made numerical inferiority work to their advantage and cut the lumbering French to shreds. With the French defenses weakened, Henry V gradually moved south. In 1419 he captured Paris and was declared regent of France.

Henry V's stunning victory at the **Battle of Agincourt** was soon celebrated in song, in a genre of music called the carol. The English **carol** was a strophic song for one to three voices, all of which were newly composed. It began with a refrain, called the **burden,** which was also repeated after each stanza. What results is a common musical form called **strophe plus refrain.** Usually the strophe, or stanza, was sung by a soloist while all the singers joined in with the burden, or refrain. The text was in Latin or English (or a combination of the two) and usually dealt with Christmas, Easter, the Virgin Mary, or the saints. More than 120 polyphonic carols survive from fifteenth-century England. Some were inserted into the liturgy, at the end of Mass or an office, and others served as popular spiritual recreation at home. Our modern Christmas carol—often a strophic song with refrain graced with a few words of Latin—traces its ancestry to the English carol of the fifteenth century.

Not all carols were for Christmas, however. Some were political and nationalistic. Witness the anonymous **Agincourt Carol,** which celebrates the victory of Henry V over the French (Ex. 16-4). It begins with a two-voice refrain (or burden), to be sung by all. Thereafter comes a verse performed by soloists, and finally an expanded version of the refrain, now for a chorus of three voices. The harmonic framework consists of 5/3, 6/3, and 8/5 chords, but here the essential note-against-note sonorities are animated through melodic ornamentation. In the exciting Agincourt Carol, the English exhibit pride in their monarch as well as their traditional love of choral singing and full, harmonious sounds.

Vestiges of English Traditions in the "Country" Music of Today

The musical form strophe plus refrain appears in the music of many western European countries by the late Middle Ages, but it is perhaps most deeply rooted in English music, especially in the carol. Over the course of the centuries, strophe plus refrain would continue to provide formal structure for much of the popular and folk music of the British Isles.

During the seventeenth and eighteenth centuries, English, Scottish, and Irish settlers brought their folk music to America, and to the Appalachian region in particular. Much of the "folk" and "country" music we hear today still relies on the late-medieval form of strophe plus refrain. In addi-

tion, American "country" music often perpetuates the ancient English love of euphonious singing. The next time you hear a medley of "country" tunes, especially hymns and gospel music, notice that many of them have a melody accompanied quietly by one or two other singers who move in identical rhythms in thirds, sixths, and fifths (singing in harmony) against the lead voice. This practice, too, has its origins in the ancient discant-like improvised folk singing of the British Isles. Both strophe-plus-refrain form and tight vocal harmony can be heard on many of the tracks of the Grammy Award–winning soundtrack for the film *O Brother, Where Art Thou?*

Burden I (two voices):   Deo gratias, Anglia, redde pro Victoria!
        (England, give thanks to God for the victory!)

Stanza I: Our king went forth to Normandy
        With grace and might of chivalry;
        There God for him wrought marv'lously
        Wherefore England may call and cry. Deo gratias.

Burden II (three voices):   Deo gratias, Anglia, redde pro Victoria!

EXAMPLE 16-4

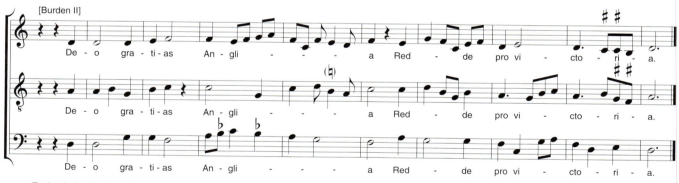

England, give thanks to God for the victory.

LISTENING CUE

ANONYMOUS
Agincourt Carol (c1420)

CD 2/10
Anthology, No. 41

JOHN DUNSTAPLE AND THE *CONTENANCE ANGLOISE*

Among the English musicians who traveled to France in the wake of the invasion of King Henry V was John Dunstaple (c1390–1453). He may have sung in the chapel of King Henry and been at Agincourt, for the royal chapel accompanied the

English army. Dunstaple was not only a composer but also an astronomer and mathematician, and he thus stood squarely in the medieval tradition that associated music and the sciences. He left us approximately sixty compositions, mostly polyphonic Mass movements and motets. One isorhythmic motet (*Veni creator spiritus/Veni sancte spiritus*) is of special note because it is **pan-isorhythmic**; isorhythm is applied to all voices, not merely the tenor.

Most of Dunstaple's compositions are preserved in manuscripts coming, not from England, but from the Continent. Indeed, Dunstaple's Continental influence is confirmed by a French poet, Martin Le Franc, writing around 1440. Le Franc reports that the leading French composers, Dufay and Binchois, followed Dunstaple and adopted the *contenance angloise* (English manner). But what is the "English manner" that the French found so appealing?

A hint may be found in Dunstaple's motet *Quam pulcra es* (*How beautiful thou art*). The music makes use of **pan-consonance**; almost every note is a member of a triad or a triadic inversion and not a dissonance. Likely this dissonance-free environment is one stylistic feature of the *contenance angloise* that Dufay and Binchois adopted from Dunstaple. Notice also that Dunstaple gives the text an almost entirely syllabic setting in which the voices clearly declaim the text. Words such as "Veni" ("Oh come") are highlighted through music for rhetorical effect. Here we see some of the earliest signs of a growing affinity between word and sound, one that will become more pronounced as the Renaissance gains force.

Dunstaple drew the text of *Quam pulcra es* from the **Song of Songs** (also called the Song of King Solomon), a particularly lyrical book in the Old Testament of the Bible. Throughout the ages Jewish rabbis and Christian exegetes have interpreted these surprisingly sensuous texts as allegories; the beautiful woman of *Quam pulcra es* can be seen as the nation of Israel, the entire Christian community, or the Blessed Virgin Mary. Often in English churches motets drawing from the Song of Songs were sung in front of a statue of the Virgin at the end of the liturgical day. Here the sensual poetry and pure, dissonance-free music of the *contenance angloise* were intended to inspire an almost mystical spiritual union with the Virgin.

EXAMPLE 16-5

Quam pulcra es et quam decora,	How beautiful thou art, and fair,
Carissima in deliciis.	My beloved, in thy delights.
Statura tua assimilata est palme	Thy stature is like a palm tree,
Ubera tua botris	Thy breasts like unto round grapes.
Caput tuum ut Carmelus	Thy head is like Mount Carmel and
Collum tuum sicut turris eburnea.	Thy neck like a tower of ivory.
Veni, dilecte mi	Oh come, my beloved;
Egrediamur in agrum et videamus	Let us go into the fields and see

Si flores fructus parturierunt	If the blossoms have borne fruit,
Si floruerunt mala punica	If the pomegranates have flowered
Ibi dabo tibi ubera mea.	There I will give to you my breasts.
Alleluia.	Alleluia.

LISTENING CUE

JOHN DUNSTAPLE
Quam pulcra es (c1420)

CD 2/11
Anthology, No. 42

SUMMARY

At no time before the arrival of the Beatles in the 1960s was English music more influential than during the fifteenth century. Fifteenth-century English music represented a culmination of centuries of indigenous choral practices. These include a fondness for two seemingly opposite styles: a preference for contrapuntal techniques such as rondellus and rota yet a love for strongly homophonic textures such as those produced by faburden and exhibited in the carol. Faburden helped establish the chord we call the "triad" as a building block of music and transform the interval of a sixth from a dissonance to a consonance in the eyes and ears of Continental musicians. Some of these practices were not limited to England—parallel 6/3 chords can be found in the Italian music of Landini, for example—but they were heard with greater frequency in England. Perhaps most important for the future of Renaissance music, Dunstaple and his colleagues were the first to begin to tie text to tone, to underscore the meaning of the word through an appropriate musical gesture. Finally, faint echoes of medieval English musical practices can still be heard today, in that institution we call the Christmas carol and in authentic Appalachian "folk music."

KEY TERMS

Sarum chant	treble	strophe plus refrain
rondellus	fauxbourdon	Agincourt Carol
Summer Canon	Henry V	pan-isorhythmic
pes	Old Hall Manuscript	*contenance angloise*
rota	Battle of Agincourt	pan-consonance
faburden	carol	Song of Songs
English discant	burden	

Chapter

Music at the Court of Burgundy

17

Today Western Europe looks very different than it did more than five hundred years ago (Map 17-1). In the fifteenth century there was no Spain, Italy, Germany, Belgium, or the Netherlands as we know them. What we now call Spain, for example,

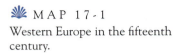 MAP 17-1

Western Europe in the fifteenth century.

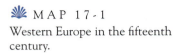 MAP 17-2

Burgundian lands in 1477.

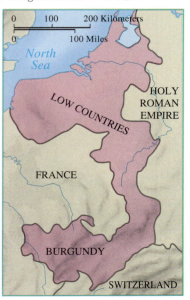

was three smaller kingdoms (Navarre, Castile, and Aragon), and Italy consisted of a patchwork of territories and independent city-states. Much of central Europe, including modern Germany, was embraced by the Holy Roman Empire; but this empire, as every student of history knows, was neither holy, nor Roman, nor an empire—it was a loose confederation of some two hundred principalities, all to varying degrees under the control of an elected German prince. Scotland was largely independent of England, yet the king of England still held territories in France. France, only two-thirds the size of its modern self, had been weakened politically and economically by the Hundred Years' War. Into this vacuum of power marched the dukes of Burgundy. They were cousins, increasingly distant and hostile, of the kings of France. By the mid-fifteenth century they had made Burgundy an independent state and the most powerful military force in Europe.

We think of Burgundy as an agricultural region in eastern France that produces great wine. But in the fifteenth century it was much more. By 1477 the dukes of Burgundy had inherited, purchased, and conquered large portions of present-day northern France and the Low Countries (Belgium, Luxemburg, and the Netherlands; Map 17-2). Thus it is preferable to speak more broadly of the **Burgundian lands,** rather than simply the duchy of Burgundy. The court of Burgundy and the Burgundian lands are important at this moment in music history for two reasons. First, the court was an important center for the patronage of the arts, and music in particular. At its height in the mid fifteenth century it comprised more than four hundred attendants, including cooks, heralds, poets, painters, minstrels, trumpeters, and a chapel of about twenty singers. Second, within the Burgundian lands were born nearly all of the great polyphonic composers who flourished in the West between 1425 and 1550.

Figure 17-1 shows the two most famous musicians of the court of Burgundy. To the left is Guillaume Dufay (c1397–1474), and to the right, Gilles Binchois (c1400–1460). These two, along with the Englishman John Dunstaple, were the most important composers in Europe in the decades before 1450. We have met Dufay before in Florence as a member of the papal chapel (see Chapter 15). In this portrait Dufay stands next to an organ, the quintessential instrument of the church, perhaps to suggest that he was primarily a church musician. Binchois holds a harp, the instrument of the educated courtier, perhaps to suggest that he associated more with a worldly court.

FIGURE 17-1

Guillaume Dufay and Gilles Binchois as depicted in a manuscript copied c1440.

GILLES BINCHOIS AND THE BURGUNDIAN CHANSON

For nearly thirty years, from roughly 1430 until his death in 1460, Gilles Binchois was a singer and composer in the chapel of Duke Philip the Good (r. 1419–1467). As an ordained priest and chapel singer, he wrote religious music—Masses and motets, and simpler liturgical forms such as hymns. Yet, as a composer of sacred music, Binchois broke no new ground. He composed no large-scale cantus firmus Masses, for example, of the sort that Dufay would make famous (see below). Binchois was a musical jeweler—he created small gems and he did so in the genre of the French chanson.

Chanson is simply the French word for song, be it monophonic or polyphonic. The troubadours and trouvères had written monophonic chansons. Machaut had composed more than sixty polyphonic ones. Now, during the fifteenth century, the French polyphonic chanson became the dominant genre of secular music. More than four hundred of them survive, not merely in manuscripts from France, but also from Spain, England, Italy, and Germany—such was the dominance of the French language and culture in this period. When performers sang and played a chanson, they did so from an oblong sheet of paper or parchment called a **rotulus** (Latin for "roll"); this was the sheet music of the late Middle Ages and early Renaissance (see Fig. 18-2). Chansons were also sometimes copied together in a single volume called a **chansonnier,** a collected anthology of chansons (Fig. 17-2). A chansonnier might contain as few as twenty to as many as two hundred songs by many different composers. Gilles Binchois composed nearly sixty chansons, each written in one of the three French *formes fixes* (ballade, rondeau, or virelai). As is true of most pop songs today, those of Binchois are about affairs of the heart, even though he was a priest. Indeed, most composers of secular art music in this period were clerics in holy orders, because the church still had a monopoly on formal education as well as on the secrets of musical notation.

Gilles Binchois's chanson *Dueil angoisseus (Anguished mourning)* is about love lost. It is a setting of a ballade by the Burgundian poet **Christine de Pisan** (c1364–c1430), who had lost her husband at an early age and here laments his passing; thus, this poem affords us the chance to hear about love from the woman's perspective (see Box, Chapter 18). Pisan's ballade has three stanzas, though we will concern ourselves only with the first. As typical of ballade settings, Binchois assigns the eight lines of text to the musical structure **AAB**.

FIGURE 17-2

Opening of the Cordiforme Chansonnier. As its name "heart-shaped" suggests, both the form and the content deal with affairs of the heart (love songs).

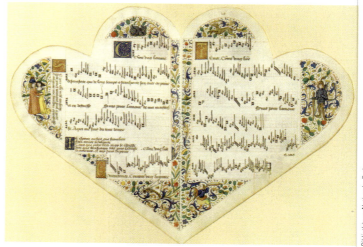

Dueil angoisseus, rage demesuree,	**A**	Anguished mourning, immeasurable rage	
Grief, desespoir plein de forsennement,		Grief, despair full of madness	
Languor sans fin et vie maleuree,	**A**	Languor without end, a life accursed,	
Plaine de plour, d'angoisee et de tourment.		Full of lamentation, anguish, and torment.	
Coeur doloreux qui vit obscurement,	**B**	A dolorous heart which lives in darkness,	
Tenebreux corps sur le point de partir,		A shadowy corpse on the point of death,	
Ay sans cesser continuellement,		These have I without cessation,	
Et si ne puis ne garir ne morir.	(refrain)	*And so can neither recover nor die.*	

Knowing that the text is a lament by a woman who has lost her one true love, the modern listener will be struck by the almost cheerful tone of the music—but cheerful to our ears only. Early music had its own notions of beauty. Musicians had not yet developed the convention that grief and pain were to be expressed musically by the minor mode and painful dissonances, for example. On the contrary, here the Lydian mode with an added B♭ (our major mode) rules most of the piece. An intensely personal text is matched by an intensely beautiful melody. Indeed, Binchois surpassed composers of his generation in his lilting, seemingly effortless melodies that move gracefully through a succession of short, well-directed phrases. Gone are the rhythmic complexities of the *Ars subtilior* and the rigid structure of isorhythm. Here, all is simplicity and grace. Yet each line has a role to play: the cantus carries the melody, the slower-moving tenor provides a support below, and the contratenor moves alternately above and below the tenor, filling out the texture. All three parts can be sung, or just the cantus alone, with the lower two parts played on instruments such as the vielle and lute (Ex. 17-1).

EXAMPLE 17-1

Anguished mourning, immeasurable rage,
Languor without end, a life accursed,

LISTENING CUE

GILLES BINCHOIS
Dueil angoisseus (c1435)

CD 2/12
Anthology, No. 43

Notice the final cadence of Binchois's *Dueil angoisseus* (Ex.17-2b). Whereas in the fourteenth and early-fifteenth centuries the basic three-voice cadence involves a double leading tone with a third pulling to a fifth and a sixth expanding to an octave

(Ex. 17-2a), now in the mid fifteenth century the contratenor has been placed below the tenor so as to achieve a wider, richer sonority. In that lower position the only note that is consonant with the interval of a sixth above (and which will not create forbidden parallel octaves or fifths) is a fourth below the ultimate final note of the cadence (here C below the final F). When only three voices are present, the contra-tenor often jumps an octave to fill in the texture of the final chord, producing what is called a **Burgundian cadence** (octave-leap cadence), as seen in Example 17-2b. In the newer four-voice writing used later by both Binchois and Dufay, however, the presence of both bass and alto contratenors makes it unnecessary for the bass to jump an octave. Still, the only consonant note to which it can move in the final octave-fifth chord is the final or "tonic" (Ex. 17-2c). Thus what we today call a "dominant-tonic" (V-I) cadence arose in the mid-fifteenth century partly as a desire for greater sonority and partly as a result of a part-writing constriction.

EXAMPLES 17-2A, 17-2B, AND 17-2C

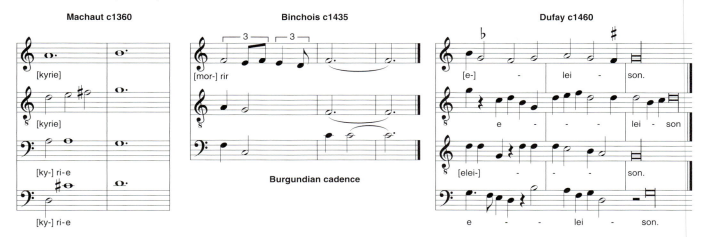

❀ GUILLAUME DUFAY: A LAMENT AND A MASS FOR THE CHRISTIAN SOLDIER

Although Guillaume Dufay was never officially a member of the musical chapel of the dukes of Burgundy, nevertheless he was a frequent visitor to their court. In 1439 he is referred to as a "familiar" of Duke Philip the Good. When Dufay died in 1474 he left six books of music to Duke Charles the Bold (r. 1467–1477), a bequest that signals an unusually close relationship between prince and composer. Dufay was born in the area around Cambrai, France, about the year 1397. Although he was the illegitimate son of a single woman and a priest, he rose to become a trusted friend of the major rulers of the day. In addition to being a "familiar" of the dukes of Burgundy, Dufay served at various times as master of the chapel of Pope Eugenius IV (see Chapter 15), as private counselor to the duke of Savoy, as a canon of the cathedral of Cambrai, and as a con-fidant of the Medici rulers in Florence. The Medici referred to Dufay as "the chief or-nament of our age"; Dufay's intellect and artistic talent brought him into contact with the major players on the political stage of mid fifteenth-century Europe.

On 29 May 1453 the Christian world suffered a grievous loss when the Ottoman Turks defeated the Byzantine Christians and captured their capital, Constantinople (today Istanbul, Turkey). Now the Turkish Muslims not only controlled the Near East but they also began to push farther into the Balkans and to threaten Italy by sea. The pope in Rome called upon the rulers of the West to mount a holy war against these so-called infidels. But among the Christian princes only Duke Philip the Good of Burgundy responded enthusiastically.

In February 1454, Duke Philip summoned his knights and courtiers to the town of Lille in northern France. His aim was to rally support for the crusade, and to this end he staged the **Feast of the Pheasant,** where the guests ate pheasant, then an exotic bird imported from the Muslim East. Though heavy with ethnic symbolism, the Feast of the Pheasant proved to be one of the great parties of the fifteenth century. The banquet hall was organized around three large tables. On one was a mock church "in which was a sounding bell and four singers who sang and played on organs when their turn came." Another table supported a huge pastry so formed that it could house "twenty-eight living persons playing on divers instruments." At a third table "three children and a tenor sang a very sweet chanson, and when they had finished a shepherd played on a bagpipe in a most novel fashion." Later, two gentlemen came forward, hidden within the costume of a stag.

> Then entered a wondrously great and beautiful stag. Mounted upon the stag was a young lad, about twelve years old. The boy held the two horns of the stag with his hands. As he entered the hall be began the upper part of a chanson in a very high, clear voice; and the stag sang the tenor, without there being any other person except the boy and the artifice of said stag. The song that they sang was named *Je ne vis onc-ques la pareille* [ascribed to Binchois in one chansonnier and to Dufay in another].[1]

Finally, an elephant was led into the hall and upon its back was a little castle in which was a man disguised as a woman to represent the figure of the Holy Mother Church. In falsetto voice he sang a lament bemoaning the fall of Constantinople and appealing for aid from Duke Philip and his knights.

Guillaume Dufay composed four polyphonic laments on the fall of Constantinople, though only one survives; it is entitled *Lamentatio sanctae Matris Ecclesiae Constantinopolitanae* (*Lament for the Holy Mother Church of Constantinople;* 1454). This four-voice lament is a cross between a motet and a chanson. Such a hybrid is called a **motet-chanson,** a genre in which a vernacular text in an upper voice is sung simultaneously with a Latin chant in the tenor. Here in the cantus, the Virgin Mary melodiously pleads in French for aid ("O merciful fountain of all hope") for the Holy Mother Church, while the tenor chants a passage in Latin from the Lamentations of Jeremiah (1: 2) of the Old Testament: "All her friends have deserted her, among all her lovers she hath none to comfort her." Just as the Jews were endangered during the first Babylonian Captivity (597 B.C.E.), now it is the Latin Church of the West that is threatened.

EXAMPLE 17-3

I come to lament at your sovereign court...
All her friends have deserted her...

GUILLAUME DUFAY
Lamentatio sanctae Matris Ecclesiae
Constantinopolitanae (1454)

CD 2/13
Anthology, No. 44

In the end, the dukes of Burgundy did little to help the church. No Burgundian crusade set forth, no sword was raised in battle, no Turk slain. Yet the militant spirit of the moment did have a musical resonance. Surviving today in music manuscripts of the late fifteenth century and beyond are more than thirty-five polyphonic Masses built on a favorite melody, the **L'Homme armé tune** (*Armed Man* tune; Ex. 17-4). No other melody has been borrowed as often for religious purposes. Significantly, many of these Armed Man Masses were written by Burgundian composers. While the text of the Armed Man tune is a call to arms, the music forms an unexpectedly bouncy triple-meter melody in **ABA** form.

EXAMPLE 17-4

The armed man, the armed man, should be feared.   **A**
Everywhere the cry has gone out,
Everyone should arm himself   **B**
With a breastplate of iron.
The armed man, the armed man, should be feared.   **A**

Clearly, this jaunty tune is a secular song, not a sacred Gregorian chant. But how was it possible to use a popular tune in a sacred Mass or motet for the church? In the late Middle Ages and early Renaissance, profane songs could be given sacred meaning. For example, the distraught woman described in Binchois's song *Comme femme desconfortée* (*Like a woman disconsolate*) becomes the tearful Virgin Mary at the cross when the melody is used in a motet for the church during Holy Week—the tune still has meaning even though the original words are now removed. Likewise, when placed in a Mass, the soldier of the Armed Man tune becomes the Christian soldier—be he a crusader about to fight the Turk, or every Christian soul who daily wages war with the devil in this world of sin and temptation. In a larger theological sense, the Armed Man, the ultimate warrior, is Christ himself who, according to scripture, defeated the forces of evil by his act of sacrifice on the cross. When he arose in a fifteenth-century Mass, the Armed Man was Christ and all those good Christians who marched with him.

Sometime during the late 1450s, Guillaume Dufay took the *L'Homme armé* tune and made it serve as a tenor scaffold in a new setting of the Ordinary of the Mass. In so doing he created what is called a **cantus firmus Mass**—a cyclic Mass in which the five movements of the Ordinary are unified by means of a single **cantus firmus** (a Latin adjective meaning "firm" or "well-established"). Thus a cantus firmus is a well-established, previously existing melody, be it a sacred chant or a secular song. By employing one and the same cantus firmus in all five movements of the Ordinary of the Mass, a composer could effect unity. Invariably, the composer placed the cantus firmus in long notes in the tenor voice. The five movements of the Mass, each of which has a different text, were thus tied together by a common melody and a common theological theme—in this case the ideal of the Christian soldier fighting a war against the forces of evil. In Dufay's *Missa L'Homme armé*, the Armed Man cantus firmus appears in the tenor once in the *Kyrie*, twice in the *Gloria*, three times in the *Credo*, twice in the *Sanctus*, and three times in the *Agnus dei*. Significantly, in the final two statements in the *Agnus dei*, Dufay makes the Armed Man tune move backward and then forward to the end. Dufay was just one of many composers of the period who used retrograde motion to symbolize Christian faith in the round-trip journey of the Lord: Christ (the Lamb of God, or "Agnus dei") journeyed to earth, descended into Hell to defeat the forces of Satan, and then returned to Heaven. Thus, cantus firmus technique brought not only musical unity to the five sections of the Ordinary of the Mass but also theological unity, sometimes by symbolic means. Example 17-5 shows the beginning of Dufay's *Kyrie* with the *L'Homme armé* tune serving as a cantus firmus in the tenor.

EXAMPLE 17-5

LISTENING CUE

GUILLAUME DUFAY	CD 2/14–15
Kyrie of the *Missa L'Homme armé* (c1460)	Anthology, No. 45a-b

 ## SUMMARY

Music at the court of Burgundy was dominated by two composers, Gilles Binchois and Guillaume Dufay, and it emphasized two musical genres, the chanson and the cantus firmus Mass. Continuing to compose in the secular *formes fixes* established by Machaut during the fourteenth century, Gilles Binchois composed about sixty ballades, rondeaux, and virelais, all relatively short pieces but many with exceptionally beautiful melodies. Although likely invented by English composers such as John Dunstaple and Leonel Power, the cantus firmus Mass reached maturity in the hands of Dufay around 1460, becoming a five-movement work full of contrapuntal artifice yet united by a single religious theme. The symbol-laden cantus firmus was placed in long notes in the tenor. So dominant did the cantus firmus Mass become that it quickly replaced the isorhythmic motet as the large-scale musical structure in which a composer might demonstrate profound technical mastery. In fact, after 1450 no more isorhythmic motets were composed. Finally, in the music of the court of Burgundy and elsewhere in this period, we begin to see a cadence that we now call dominant-tonic (V-I)—the first hints of functional harmony as we know it.

 ## KEY TERMS

Burgundian lands	Christine de Pisan	*L'Homme armé* tune
chanson	Burgundian cadence	cantus firmus Mass
rotulus	Feast of the Pheasant	cantus firmus
chansonnier	motet-chanson	

Chapter

Music at the French Royal Court

18

Who has not heard of **Joan of Arc** (c1412–1431), the miraculous Maid of Orléans who rescued France from the English? Joan's heroics occurred in the last stages of the Hundred Years' War. In 1415 the English army, under King Henry V (1387–1422), had won a stunning victory at the Battle of Agincourt (see Chapter 16). From there the English invaders had gone on to capture large portions of northern France. Henry's son, King Henry VI (1421–1471), was eventually crowned king of France at Notre Dame of Paris. The French claimant to the throne, the future Charles VII, was pushed out of Paris and took up residence 200 miles south in the Loire Valley. Owing to the heroism of Joan of Arc, Charles was led to Reims and crowned king there on 16 July 1429. Thus there were two kings of France, one

French, one English. Gradually, Charles gained allies among the nobility and re-pelled the English. In 1436 the French retook Paris, and by 1450 most of northern France had been returned to the French crown.

The lands of the French kings may have been restored, but not their confidence. King Charles VII (r. 1429–1461) and his successor Louis XI (r. 1461–1483), still fearful of Paris, continued to reside in the beautiful Loire Valley as they expanded their royal authority. Just as the French royal court enjoyed a resurgence at this time, so too did the royal chapel. By 1451 King Charles had engaged fourteen singers to celebrate the Mass and Vespers daily in plainchant and polyphony. Only one of these musicians was a composer of renown, but that one, Johannes Ockeghem (c1410–1497), enjoyed unusual longevity and influence.

JOHANNES OCKEGHEM AND MUSICAL CANONS

Johannes Ockeghem, too, was born in Burgundian lands, in the hamlet of St. Ghis-lain south of Brussels. By 1451 he had moved further south and joined the French royal chapel. There he remained as a singer for nearly fifty years, working his way up, from chaplain to first chaplain (1454), to master of the chapel (1465), and finally "to counselor and master of the chapel of the king" (1477). Perhaps because of his central position at the French royal court, Ockeghem seems to have influenced the development of many major composers of the day. Dufay was his friend and confidant, and many composers whom we shall meet (Josquin, Basiron, Busnoys, and Tinctoris) studied directly or indirectly with this much-loved figure. A visitor to the French court in 1470 said the following about Ockeghem:

> I am sure that you would not dislike this man, so pleasing is the beauty of his person, so noteworthy the sobriety of his speech and of his morals, and his graciousness. He alone of all the singers is free from vice and abounding in all virtues.[1]

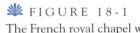

FIGURE 18-1

The French royal chapel with Johannes Ockeghem (presumably) at far right, wearing glasses.

Bridgeman Art Library

Figure 18-1 is a later illustration of the French royal chapel. The elderly gentleman to the far right is likely Ockeghem, since we know that he served the chapel until a ripe old age, wore spectacles, and, in addition, sang bass.

Surviving today from the pen of Johannes Ockeghem are twenty-five chansons, six motets, and fifteen Masses—not a large *oeuvre* for a man who lived so long and was held in such high esteem by his musical colleagues. Yet in each of these three genres Ockeghem demonstrated exceptional technical skill, a fact that may account for his great fame in his own time. His twenty-five chansons are important because as a group they show the first systematic attempt to structure compositions by using **imitation** (one voice duplicates the notes and rhythms of another for a brief span of time). Other composers, extending back into the fourteenth century, had used imitation from time to time, but the generation of Ockeghem and his pupils Philippe Basiron and Antoine Busnoys (see below) was the first to employ it consistently as a structural tool. From the mid-fifteenth century onward, imitation would come to dominate the texture of written polyphonic music to the point that the entire Renaissance might well be called "the age of imitative counterpoint." We will see shortly an imitative chanson by Ockeghem's pupil Antoine Busnoys. For the moment let us concentrate on an extreme application of imitation, imitative technique as found in Ockeghem's three-voice *Prenez sur moi* (*Take from me*; Ex. 18-1).

Usually when we speak of imitation we refer to only a short span of exact imitation, a measure or so. When, however, the imitation is exact from the beginning to the end of a piece, a stricter form of counterpoint, canon, is at work. We have met musical canons before. They first appear with the famous English Summer Canon of about 1300 (see Chapter 16) and continue with the French *chace* and the Italian *caccia* of the fourteenth century. But in these earlier canons only the upper voices are canonic. The lower voice stands apart from the canon, supporting it with various notes from below. Now, with the generation of Ockeghem and his pupils, fully canonic writing takes hold.

Ockeghem's three-voice *Prenez sur moi* was one of his most popular chansons. It is something of a musical game, or at least a musical pun. The text is ostensibly a love song in the form of a rondeau, and the first voice begins "Take from me your example of love." And take from the leader the subsequent voices do; the second and third voices enter in turn and duplicate exactly the pitches and rhythms of the first, thereby producing a three-voice canon. Note that the voices do not enter at simple intervals of unison, fifth, or octave, but rather at successively higher fourths. Although the complete song is a three-voice canonic rondeau with lyrics, it can be performed with equal effect simply as a three-voice instrumental piece.

EXAMPLE 18-1

Take from me your example of love...

LISTENING CUE

JOHANNES OCKEGHEM
Prenez sur moi (c1460)

CD 2/16
Anthology, No. 46

As this canon and other works indicate, Johannes Ockeghem was a master of musical artifice, posing and solving difficult technical problems in music. In fact, Ockeghem is said to have written a canonic piece for no fewer than thirty-six voices, the sacred motet *Deo gratias*. Among Ockeghem's Masses, two are famous for their erudite construction. The *Missa Cuiusvis toni* (*Mass on Whichever Mode*) is composed so that it can be performed in any one of the eight church modes. Ockeghem notates the Mass only once, but requires the performers to read the music in any one of four different clef combinations, thereby covering the four pairs of authentic and plagal modes. Clearly, this was a test to see how well singers were able to read different clefs.

The epitome of Ockeghem's ingenious constructions, however, is found in his *Missa Prolationum* (*Mass of the Prolations*). Indeed, it has been called the most extraordinary contrapuntal achievement of the fifteenth century. Here the four voices simultaneously sing two two-voice mensuration canons. A **mensuration canon** is one in which two voices perform the same music at different rates of speed; they start at the same time, but one moves through the notes faster—and progressively away from the other in time. In early music, one and the same note shape could have different values depending on the mensuration sign (meter signature) specified by the composer; for example, a long note in a perfect time (triple meter) would be held for three beats but in imperfect time (duple meter) for only two beats. Thus the voice in duple meter sang through the notes more quickly and moved progressively ahead. In the *Kyrie* of Ockeghem's Mass, for example, cantus and altus begin in unison and sing a canon in extended $\frac{2}{4}$ and $\frac{3}{4}$ time, respectively; the tenor and the bass are likewise in unison and sing a second canon in $\frac{6}{8}$ and $\frac{9}{8}$. In the original manuscript only the higher voice is notated for each pair; it was up to the performers to extract from this notation the two missing canonic voices. In Example 18-2 the music is realized in modern edition for all four voices. A mensuration canon is extremely difficult to construct and Ockeghem has two working together simultaneously. Even the great contrapuntalist J.S. Bach never fashioned musical canons this complex or technically difficult.

EXAMPLE 18-2

<table>
<tr><td>💿</td><td colspan="3">LISTENING CUE</td></tr>
<tr><td></td><td>JOHANNES OCKEGHEM
Kyrie of the Missa Prolationum (c1475)</td><td>CD 2/17
Anthology, No. 47</td></tr>
</table>

Obviously Ockeghem intended his *Missa Prolationum* to be a brain teaser for performers, and he was not alone in playing these erudite musical games. A spirit of playful artifice is a hallmark of this generation of musicians. Ockeghem's pupil Antoine Busnoys is credited with having written a set of six Masses on the *L'Homme armé* tune (see Chapter 17). In these, the melody is made to go forward, backward (retrograde), upside-down (inversion), and upside-down and backward (retrograde inversion). To effect these permutations, the composer gives instructions to the performers by means of riddle canons (enigmatic rules) written in the language of ancient Greek music theory. In all of music history, no generation of composers was more intent on posing and then solving such esoteric musical puzzles. In fact, there is little in the twelve-tone music of the twentieth century (see Chapter 69) that had not already been worked out during the fifteenth century by Ockeghem, Busnoys, and their ingenious colleagues.

A MUSICAL JOKE FOR THE FRENCH KING

The ingenuity of composers in this period was sometimes put to use just for fun. French King Louis XI (1461–1483) clearly loved music, and he paid the master of his chapel, Johannes Ockeghem, handsomely. Toward the end of his reign he hired the young Josquin des Prez (see Chapter 21) and commissioned him to set in polyphony psalm texts with special meaning for him. And when Louis was ill, having suffered a stroke, he asked for his instrumentalists to play quietly beneath his window. But, despite his passion for music, Louis seems to have had little talent. A sixteenth-century music theorist, Heinrich Glarean, tells the story of how the king asked a singer of the court, apparently Josquin, to write a piece in which he, too, could participate.

> Some relate such [humorous] stories about Josquin des Prez, and it is of such a kind which we are now going to tell. Louis [XI], the French king, is said to have had a very inadequate voice. He had formerly been pleased by some song and asked the chief of his singers if there was anyone who would compose a song in several voices in which he could also sing some part. The singer, wondering at the demand of the King, whom he knew to be entirely ignorant of music, hesitated a while and finally decided what he would answer. "My King," he said, "I shall compose a song in which your Majesty will also be given a place in the singing." The following day, after the King had had breakfast and was to be refreshed with songs, according to royal custom, the singer produced this song, composed in four voices. . . .
>
> He had composed the song so that two boys would sing very lightly and delicately the *cantus*, taken from a single theme, evidently so that the exceedingly thin voice of the King would not be drowned out. He had given the King the next voice, notated on one continual tone in the range of the alto, a range which would be suitable to the royal voice. . . . And so that the King would not waver in pitch, the composer, who was going to sing the bass, arranged this bass voice so that at regular intervals he would support the King at the octave, on the alternate tone of the *tempus*. But the octave is like the unison, through which octave the voice of the King was helped exceedingly. The King laughed merrily at the trick and gladly dismissed the composer with a present.[2]

Fortunately, this musical joke survives today in a manuscript copied in France about 1510. It is called "The French Song of Louis XI, King of France" and carries a simple, rustic text *Guillaume se va chaufer* (*William is going to warm himself*). As you can see, the king was, in fact, apparently tone deaf, for he sang only a single long pitch on D. Against him, the two choirboys produced a short, continually repeating canon, while the bass supported the king with octaves and fifths below. Surely this is the only piece in the history of music written for a royal monotone. But even in this short, humorous piece, the composers of the royal court were able to work in a clever canon.

EXAMPLE 18-3

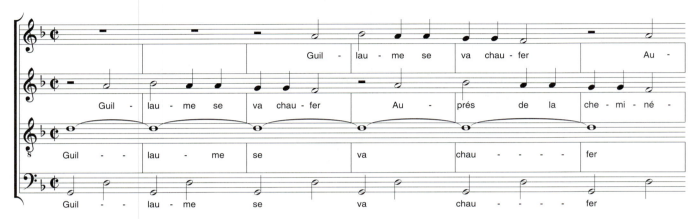

William is going to warm himself.

LISTENING CUE

JOSQUIN DES PREZ
Guillaume se va chaufer (c1482)

CD 2/18
Anthology, No. 48

PHILIPPE BASIRON AND THE PARAPHRASE MOTET

Philippe Basiron (c1449–1491) was a singer at the king's Sainte-Chapelle in the central French town of Bourges. Although not a major figure in the history of music, his compositions were nonetheless known in Spain, Italy, and Bohemia (Czech Republic) as well as France. Basiron's significance rests in the fact that he was an early practitioner of paraphrase technique, though in truth he borrowed this from earlier English composers and from his apparent mentor at the French court, Johannes Ockeghem. In **paraphrase technique** a composer takes a pre-existing plainsong (Gregorian chant) and embellishes it somewhat, imparting to it a rhythmic profile; the elaborated chant then serves as the basic melodic material for a polyphonic composition. Unlike cantus firmus technique, in which the borrowed melody is usually placed in long notes in the tenor, with paraphrase technique the ornamented chant can appear in any and all voices, though most often it is heard in the cantus. The paraphrased chant might appear in a motet, thereby creating a **paraphrase motet.** Similarly, paraphrase technique might be applied to all five movements of a polyphonic Mass. A Mass in which the movements are united by a single paraphrased chant is called a **paraphrase Mass.** Josquin des Prez's famous *Missa Pange lingua* is such a Mass, one in which a continually ornamented hymn tune, Thomas

Aquinas's hymn *Pange lingua*, permeates all voices and binds all five movements into a unified whole.

Basiron's *Salve, Regina* (sometimes attributed to Ockeghem himself) takes the famous Marian antiphon of that name as its point of departure. The beautiful *Salve, Regina* (*Hail queen*) melody was one of the most popular chants of the Middle Ages and Renaissance; in many locales it was sung daily at the end of the canonical hours before retiring for the night. A comparison of the chant with Basiron's polyphonic setting shows how he added rhythmic energy, even syncopation, to the chant, while keeping its melodic contour essentially intact. Here the paraphrased chant appears almost exclusively in the cantus, the lower three voices providing counterpoint and structural support. Later in the fifteenth century, composers will be more inclined to allow the paraphrased melody to migrate to all voices in the polyphonic complex. The virtue of Basiron's setting, however, is that no matter how rich the supporting harmonies below, the borrowed melody is always clearly audible on top.

EXAMPLE 18-4

LISTENING CUE

PHILIPPE BASIRON
Salve, Regina (c1475)

CD 2/19
Anthology, No. 49

ANTOINE BUSNOYS AND THE IMITATIVE CHANSON

The fact that such a fine composer as Antoine Busnoys is little known today simply underscores the fact that in the late fifteenth century there were many great composers; Busnoys was only one star in a bright firmament. Antoine Busnoys (c1435–1492) was apparently born in the hamlet of Busnes in the Burgundian lands of northern France. By 1461 he had journeyed south and was employed as a singer in the town of Tours, the abode of the king of France and his chapel master Johannes Ockeghem. Indeed, for the coronation of King Louis XI in 1461, Busnoys composed a motet-chanson *Resjois toi terre de France/Rex pacificus*. Shortly before 1467, Busnoys left the orbit of the French king and became a singer at the court of the king's arch-rival, Duke Charles of Burgundy.

Like his mentor Ockeghem, Busnoys delighted in musical cryptograms. In one motet, *Anthoni usque limina*, he wrote the instructions for performance in Latin and Greek around a picture of a bell; this musical puzzle has never been satisfactorily solved. In four chansons Busnoys makes use of literary codes to allude to a special lady. For example, *Je ne puis vivre ainsy tousjours* (*I cannot live like this forever*) contains an **acrostic** (a poem in which the first letters of each line form a word or phrase). Here the first letters of each line produce the name Jaqueljne d'Aqvevjle" (Jacqueline de Hacqueville). The lady secretly signaled here may have been a devotee or lover of Busnoys, or she may have been the author of the text (see Box). Regardless, *Je ne puis vivre ainsy tousjours* is a charming virelai (**AbbaA**) of one stanza, with the music of section **a** in triple meter and that of **b** in duple. Typical of the newer-style chanson of the Ockeghem-Busnoys generation, the texture is infused with imitation, which in turn creates an equality of rhythmic and melodic activity among the voices. A hallmark of Busnoys's personal style can be seen at the very beginning of the chanson, when each voice rises quickly up the scale to the distance of a tenth, thereby clarifying the mode of the piece; Busnoys would say that it is in the Lydian mode (with a B♭) transposed to C; we would call it simply C major.

Je ne puis vivre ainsy tousjours	**A**	I cannot live like this forever
Au mains que j'aye en mes dolours		Unless I have in my distress
Quelque confort,		Some comfort,
Une seule heure ou mains ou fort;		A single hour, more or less
Et tous les jours		And every day
Léaument serviray Amours		Loyally I will serve Love
Jusqu'a la mort.		Until death.
Noble femme de nom et d'armes	**b**	Noble woman of name and arms
Escript vous ay ce dittier-cy,		I have written you this ditty
Des jeulx pleurant à chaudes larmes	**b**	With crying eyes full of warm tears
Affin qu'aiez de moi mercy.		That you may have mercy on me.
Quant a moy, je me meurs bon cours	**a**	As to me, I waste away apace
Vellant les nuyt, faisant cent tours,		Awake at nights, tossing a hundred times,
En criant fort:		And crying loudly:
Vengence! a Dieu, car a grant tort		Vengeance! by God, because wrongly
Je noye en plours		I drown in tears
Lorsqu'au besoing me fault secours,		While in need I lack succor
Et Pitié dort.		And Pity sleeps.
Je ne puis vivre ainsy tousjours	**A**	I cannot live like this forever . . . .

LISTENING CUE

ANTOINE BUSNOYS
Je ne puis vivre ainsy tousjours (c1460)

CD 2/20
Anthology, No. 50

Women Poets and Performers

While it may seem that early music was an all-male activity, often it was not. The text of Binchois's chanson *Dueil angoisseus* (see Chapter 17) was written by Christine de Pisan (c1364–c1430) and that of Busnoys's *Je ne puis vivre ainsy tousjours* possibly by Jacqueline de Hacqueville. Pisan was a single mother and a feminist before her time, compiling a lengthy chronicle of the deeds of illustrious women throughout Western history. Jacqueline de Hacqueville was apparently a lady-in-waiting at the French royal court. One of the pastimes of such women was the composition of poetry. The ladies serving at the court of King Charles VII of France were criticized for "staying up too late writing rondeaux and ballades." However, when women wrote love poetry they sometimes employed the female voice and sometimes they adopted the male perspective (referring to the lover as "he" and the beloved as "she"). In addition, although women were proscribed from singing in church, except in convents, they were encouraged to do so at court. The majority of illustrations of secular music-making in the fifteenth century prominently shows women as performers. They appear as singers, presumably of the cantus part, or as instrumentalists (usually playing string instruments), or as both. Clearly, women participated formally and informally in secular music-making, but they were "off the books" because they occupied the somewhat ill-defined position of "ladies-in-waiting." All the official musical positions at court—those of chaplain, minstrel, trumpeter, and organist—still went to men.

Bridgeman Art Library

 FIGURE 18-2

A garden of love wherein two gentlemen and two ladies perform a chanson. Both ladies are singing from a rotulus (sheet music).

SUMMARY

Like their contemporaries at the court of Burgundy, composers in the orbit of the French king in the Loire Valley—Ockeghem, Josquin, Basiron, and Busnoys, among them—composed chansons, Masses, and motets. They were concerned with developing new localized formal devices, such as imitation, as well as large-scale structural procedures, such as cantus firmus and paraphrase techniques. By applying imitation to all the voices within a composition, stratification between voices was reduced; by its very nature imitation makes all vocal parts, if not exactly equal, at least rather similar in their melodic content and rhythmic activity. The royal composers also began to popularize the paraphrase motet and the paraphrase Mass. In these a single pre-existing chant was taken, lightly ornamented, and then spun through the various voice parts, appearing most prominently in the cantus. Johannes Ockeghem and his pupils also explored more esoteric textual and musical procedures such as acrostics, mensuration canons, and modal transpositions, as well as inversion and retrograde motion. Rarely in the history of music have composers been more interested in learned contrapuntal processes.

KEY TERMS

Joan of Arc   paraphrase technique   paraphrase Mass
imitation   paraphrase motet   acrostic
mensuration canon

Chapter 19

Music in the Low Countries

During the fifteenth century, the region that we now call the Low Countries fell mostly within the Burgundian lands (see Chapter 17). In fact, the dukes of Burgundy derived most of their wealth from these northern territories, the countries of modern-day Belgium, the Netherlands, and Luxemburg. Towns such as Ghent, Bruges, Brussels, and Antwerp enjoyed bustling trade by boat with England and by land with Italy. These cities, not those in France or Germany, formed the commercial center of northern Europe. The dominant language was what is now called Dutch (also called Flemish). In these Dutch- or Flemish-speaking cities new churches sprang up and fine musical choirs appeared. Commerce fostered support for religious institutions, and these, in turn, supported education. Many churches began to sponsor a **choir school**—a school that took in boys at about the age of six, gave them an education with a strong emphasis on music and especially singing, and prepared them for a lifetime of service within the church. These schools and the intense musical education they provided may account for a remarkable historical fact: most of the major composers of learned polyphony in western Europe during the period 1425 to 1550 were born in the Burgundian Low Countries. These musicians are sometimes called Burgundian composers, sometimes Franco-Flemish composers, or sometimes just the Netherlanders. In addition to Binchois, Dufay, Ockeghem, and Busnoys, they include, among others, Jacob Obrecht, Josquin des Prez, Heinrich Isaac, Cipriano de Rore, Adrian Willaert, and Orlande de Lassus. Some of these musicians served the court of Burgundy, some the court of the king of France, and others migrated south to gain fame and fortune at courts in Italy. But many musicians avoided the vicissitudes of court life. They stayed at home in the Low Countries, earning a stable living as church singers or city instrumentalists. One musician who did so was Jacob Obrecht.

JACOB OBRECHT AND THE MULTIPLE CANTUS FIRMUS MASS

Jacob Obrecht was born in 1457 or 1458 in Ghent, the son of a trumpeter who served his city for more than thirty years. Young Jacob may have been trained as a trumpeter, learning to play fanfares and to improvise on well-known tunes. Yet, for most of his adult career, Obrecht was a choir director in churches in and around the Low Countries: in Bergen op Zoom, Cambrai, Bruges, and Antwerp. He composed many of his nearly three dozen Masses, for example, for the urban church of St. Donatian in Bruges. Not until 1504 did Obrecht yield to the temptation to accept a more lucrative position at a secular court, specifically as *magister cappellae* for Duke

Hercules d'Este in Ferrara, Italy. It was an unwise decision; Obrecht died in Ferrara shortly after his arrival, the victim of a sporadic outburst of bubonic plague.

Perhaps as no other composer in the history of music, Jacob Obrecht was a master at combining several melodies, either simultaneously or successively. When several secular tunes are brought together, the process creates a genre of music called a **quodlibet** (Latin for "whatever you like"). Obrecht wrote many of these popular medleys, several in his native language of Dutch. (The practice of writing quodlibets for the amusement of an urban public, which begins here in the late fifteenth century, continued to the time of Bach and beyond.) In a more serious vein, Obrecht often combined several cantus firmi in a single motet or Mass. In his Mass for St. Martin, for example, he incorporates no fewer than nine chants taken from the liturgy of St. Martin; as the singers sing these in succession they allude to the major events in the life of the saint, thereby creating a sort of musical *curriculum vitae*. When two or more cantus firmi sound simultaneously or successively in a Mass a **multiple cantus firmus Mass** results. In all, Obrecht composed approximately thirty chansons, thirty-four motets, and thirty-five Masses. About a dozen of his sacred works, both motets and Masses, make use of multiple cantus firmi.

Obrecht's most impressive multiple cantus firmus Mass is his *Missa Sub tuum presidium* (*Mass Under Your Protection*), a Mass in honor of the Virgin Mary. As the following chart shows, Obrecht at first borrows only a single sacred cantus firmus, then two, three, and four as more and more voices are added in succeeding movements of the Mass. The climactic *Agnus dei* calls for seven voices, four to sing various cantus firmi simultaneously and three to sing free counterpoint against them. (Perhaps it is not mere coincidence that the Mass concludes with seven voices, for seven was the symbolic number for Mary.) The principal cantus firmus of the Mass, the antiphon *Sub tuum presidium*, was sung in many churches before a favorite painting of the Virgin Mary; for faithful Catholics, the Virgin served as the great protector of humankind. Other chants allude to other attributes of Mary and Christ. In the *Credo*, for example, the composer sets two cantus firmi in the highest two voices, *Sub tuum presidium* and another borrowed petition to the Virgin, *Audi nos* (*Hear us*). Beneath these the lower three voices weave a dense web of counterpoint. Just as the Virgin protects the people beneath her, so the chants sound down from on high. Yet of such beauty is Obrecht's *Missa Sub tuum presidium* that one barely notices that the composer has built a musical scaffold of extraordinary complexity. If you think this is easy, take three or four folk songs or pop tunes and adjust the rhythms so that all three or four will sound simultaneously and make good harmony—and then write free counterpoint against these in three other voices!

Structure of Jacob Obrecht's *Missa Sub tuum presidium*

	Kyrie	*Gloria*	*Credo*	*Sanctus*	*Agnus dei*
Cantus 1	S	S	S	S	S
Cantus 2	—	—	CF	CF	CF
Alto 1	—	—	—	—	CF
Alto 2	O	O	O	O	O
Tenor 1	—	—	—	CF	CF
Tenor 2	O	O	O	O	O
Bass	—	O	O	O	O

S   Cantus firmus taken from antiphon *Sub tuum presidium*
CF   Other sacred cantus firmi
O   Free counterpoint setting text of Ordinary of the Mass
—   Voice is silent

MUSICAL INSTRUMENTS

Not all music in the cities of the Low Countries was vocal in nature. Towns throughout northern Europe employed instrumentalists, mostly wind players, to signal the approach of an invading army, salute a visiting nobleman, or herald an important announcement. Wind bands for these communal events performed in the market square, from the city gates, from the belfry of the highest church, and from the balcony of the town hall. Our tradition of literally broadcasting sacred tunes from church belfries began in this era in the Low Countries and Germany. As a result, toward the end of the fifteenth century the separation of secular and sacred repertories by place of performance began to break down. In Bruges in 1483, for example, trumpets and shawms were permitted to play at services in the church nave, sometimes adding secular tunes to the otherwise-sacred repertory. Conversely, sacred chants and motets were taken out into the streets and performed as part of religious processions, thereby linking music to civic spectacle. Motets of Obrecht, for example, are known to have been performed outdoors by wind bands in cities from Bruges to Venice.

Civic and courtly instrumental music at this time centered around dancing and the early-Renaissance equivalent of chamber music. Trumpets and shawms were needed here for dancing, but so too were lutes, vielles, recorders, and even the harpsichord for quieter music. The first detailed description of a **harpsichord** comes from the Low Countries about 1440. Dating more than two hundred and fifty years before the advent of the piano, this instrument was designed by Henri Arnaut de Zwolle (c1400–1466), master of medicine, astronomy, and astrology to Duke Philip the Good of Burgundy. As can be seen in Figure 19-1, Zwolle describes four key-jack mechanisms, and his nearly-three-octave keyboard (B to a") is fully chromatic. Like the portable organ, the early harpsichord could easily be carried from place to place and was meant to be played when set upon a table top. On it a single performer could easily play an arrangement of a dance piece or a popular song.

Throughout the fifteenth century, instruments were classified according to one of two types: *haut* (loud) or *bas* (soft). The **hauts instruments** included trumpets, shawms, bagpipes, drums, and tambourine. The straight-pipe military trumpet (*trompette de guerre*) and the folded trumpet with slide (*trompette des menestrels*) were made of brass, or sometimes silver. The slide trumpet, also known as the **sackbut** (from the French *sacque-boute* meaning roughly "push-pull"), was the precursor of our modern trombone. The shawm, ancestor of the modern oboe, was a brilliant-sounding double-reed instrument that played in one of two ranges, treble and tenor (pitched

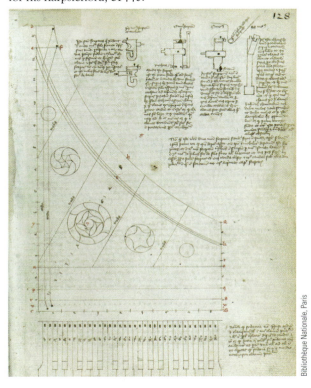

FIGURE 19-1
Henri Arnaut de Zwolle's plans for his harpsichord, c1440.

Bibliothèque Nationale, Paris

❄ FIGURE 19-2

An ensemble of *hauts instruments* (two shawms and a sackbut) accompanying a *basse danse* as represented in a miniature executed for the duke of Burgundy, 1468–1470.

a fifth below). The typical wind band consisted of a sackbut along with two or three shawms and perhaps an accompanying drum (Fig.19-2). Later, by around 1500, the wind band was sometimes joined by a **cornett,** a wooden, lip-vibrated wind instrument with finger-holes and a cup-shaped mouthpiece that produced a soft trumpet sound, but with a somewhat wooden or hollow tone. The cornett sounded in the range of the soprano voice.

Unlike the *hauts instruments*, the **bas instruments** constituted no set group. These soft instruments (recorder, vielle, lute, harp, psaltery, portative organ, and harpsichord) might appear individually or in any one of a number of possible combinations. These were best used as chamber instruments, their quickly diminishing sounds being less well suited for the noisy dance hall and the outdoor pageant. Women frequently played string instruments, but rarely wind instruments, with the exception of the flute. Usually only one instrument played a given musical line; there was no doubling or tripling of parts. Finally, most of the instrumentalists of the period may not have been able to read musical notation. Certainly much of this instrumental repertory was improvised, and performers most likely learned by aural memory, not by reading music.

✻ THE BASSE DANSE

When Duke Charles the Bold of Burgundy died at the battle of Nancy in 1477, he left no male heir. The Burgundian lands in the Low Countries passed to Charles's daughter, Mary of Burgundy. More for protection than love, Mary immediately married Maximilian I of the house of Hapsburg, who was soon to be Holy Roman Emperor (r. 1493–1519). The children of Maximilian and Mary in turn married the offspring of Ferdinand and Isabella of Spain (patrons of Christopher Columbus), and thus the Low Countries came under Spanish rule. During this gradual transition from Burgundian to Hapsburg-Spanish control, the old court of Burgundy was

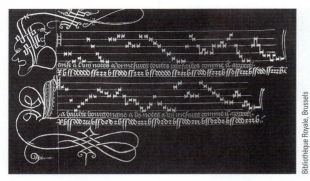

Bibliothèque Royale, Brussels

🌸 FIGURE 19-3

A *basse danse* book from the court of Margaret of Austria. The parchment has been dyed black, and the writing is executed in gold and silver ink.

directed by **Margaret of Austria** (1480–1530), daughter of Mary and Maximilian. Ruling from the town of Mechlin, Margaret served as official regent of the Low Countries from 1507 to 1530.

Like her father and grandfather before her, Margaret of Austria was a great patron of music. She was skilled as a singer and keyboard player, and she wrote poetry, some of which was set to music by court composers. But Margaret was also a victim of bad luck, for she was thrice married and thrice widowed. A shroud of mourning thus descended upon her Burgundian-Hapsburg court, and even joyful activities such as dancing assumed a moribund tone. Witness the famous *basse danse* book of Margaret of Austria: its parchment has been dyed black (Fig. 19-3).

The **basse danse** was the principal aristocratic dance of court and city during the early Renaissance. As its name "low dance" suggests, the *basse danse* was a slow, stately dance in which the dancers' feet glided close to the ground (see Fig. 19-2). Proceeding in a line of couples, the participants executed any one of four choreographic gestures (see Ex. 19-1): a single step (s), a double step (d), a step backward (r), or a shake (b), all preceded by a reverential bow by the gentleman (R). Margaret of Austria's *basse danse* book (see Fig. 19-3) preserves fifty-eight dance tunes, each with its own name. The titles often allude to the musician who created the tune, or the region in which the melody originated. Music was provided by a standard wind band. The sackbut played the tune in slow notes of equal value. During each note the dancers executed one of the four steps of the choreography. As the tune progressed, shawms and perhaps a cornett wove a polyphonic accompaniment above, much like a jazz quartet of today in which a piano and saxophone improvise above the fundamental bass notes provided by the double bass or guitar.

One of the most popular dance tunes around the year 1500 was *La Spagna* (*The Spanish Tune*; Ex. 19-1). It survives in more than two hundred polyphonic arrangements, ranging from settings for solo lute to Mass movements for multiple voices. In fact, the setting by Heinrich Isaac was also made to serve as a movement in a Mass by that composer. Written arrangements such as *La Spagna* capture in notation, after the fact, what was at first an improvisatory dance tradition. Later, in the early sixteenth century, the *basse danse* would be followed by a faster dance called the *tordion*. But although the *basse danse* was slow and stately, the music for it, as demonstrated by this version of *La Spagna*, could be very lively indeed!

EXAMPLE 19-1

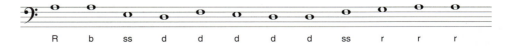

R   b   ss   d   d   d   d   d   ss   r   r   r

💿 LISTENING CUE

HEINRICH ISAAC
La Spagna (c1500)

CD 2/22
Anthology, No. 52

SUMMARY

Composers in the Low Countries during the late fifteenth century continued to write large-scale compositions, specifically the sacred motet in Latin and the five-movement Latin Mass. To bring unity to these large-scale works, composers used cantus firmus, paraphrase, or multiple cantus firmus technique, thereby creating, for example, a cantus firmus Mass, a paraphrase Mass, or a multiple cantus firmus Mass. Jacob Obrecht was the master of the multiple cantus firmus Mass. In these, several borrowed melodies would appear both successively and simultaneously.

Instruments proliferated and instrument makers flourished in cities of the Low Countries during the late fifteenth century. *Bas instruments* provided most of the softer, quieter instrumental music for court and private home. The louder *hauts instruments*, on the other hand, were especially well suited for playing dance music, the principal dance of the era being the stately *basse danse*. Instrumentalists also began to play polyphonic motets both inside and outside the church. They simply sounded the notes and omitted the text. Here, for the first time in the history of music, instruments other than the organ—specifically the shawm, cornett, and sackbut—began to be associated with music of the church.

KEY TERMS

choir school	harpsichord	*bas instruments*
quodlibet	*hauts instruments*	Margaret of Austria
multiple cantus firmus	sackbut	*basse danse*
Mass	cornett	

THE LATE RENAISSANCE

*S*trictly speaking, the word *renaissance* means "rebirth," but it also connotes "recovery" and "rediscovery." Nineteenth-century historians invented the term to describe the great flowering of intellectual and artistic activity that occurred first in Italy and then elsewhere in Europe during the years 1350–1600. In the early part of this period, roughly 1350–1475, music underwent profound changes. Such stylistic changes continued and even accelerated during the late Renaissance (1475–1600). Yet, what specifically was "reborn," or at least new, about the music of the late Renaissance? First, the Renaissance unleashed the expressive, indeed rhetorical, power of music as the result of the

1350	1400	1450	1500

EARLY RENAISSANCE (1350–1475)   **LATE**

Johannes Gutenberg (c1400–1468), inventor of printing with movable type

Emperor Maximilian I (1459–1519)

Lorenzo the Magnificent (b. 1449), Medici prince

Girolamo Savonarola (1452–1498), perhaps the most famous, or infamous, writer of laude

Josquin des Prez (c1450–1521), Renaissance

Ottaviano Petrucci (1466–1539),

● 1470 Buxheim Organ Book

Hercules d'Este (r. 1471–1505),

Michelangelo

Claudin de Sermisy

Pierre Attaingnant

Sistine Chapel,
constructed 1477–1481

CORBIS

Martin Luther
(1483–1546)

Bridgeman Art Library

humanists' concern with literature. Music increasingly came to intensify the meaning of the text. Second, there was with the Renaissance a growing sense that music might be not only for religious solace and salvation but also for personal enrichment and entertainment. Third, a new technology (music printing) made possible the widespread dissemination of written music to a much broader segment of society and generally increased musical literacy. Fourth, the Renaissance witnessed a gradual shift in the perception of music as a discipline among the sciences to one among the fine arts. Finally, attending this new view of music as a fine art was an increased awareness of the composer as an individual—indeed an artist—worthy of special honors and financial rewards.

1500	1550	1600	1650

RENAISSANCE (1475–1600)

● 1524 Johann Walter (1496–1570) publishes *Geistliche Gesangbüchlein*

● 1530 Madrigal arises in Italy   ● 1567 Giovanni Pierluigi da Palestrina (1525–1594) composes *Mass for Pope Marcellus*

of Austria

who wrote texts of carnival songs

Queen Elizabeth I (r. 1558–1603) of England

1545–1563 Council of Trent

Carlo Gesualdo (1561–1613) publishes 7 books of madrigals and 3 volumes of motets

composer

John Dowland (1563–1626), greatest composer of English lute ayres

Venetian printer first to publish polyphonic music

William Shakespeare (1564–1616)

containing 256 compositions for organ

patron of musicians   **Queen Mary (r. 1553–1558)**

Claudio Monteverdi (1567–1643), important composer of late madrigals and early operas

(1475–1564)

(c1490–1562), composer of Parisian chansons

1589 *Orchésographie*, a treatise on dance, is published by Thoinot Arbeau (Jehan Tabourot)

(c1495–c1552), official printer of music for the French crown

Jacques Arcadelt (c1505–1568), early proponent of madrigal

Thomas Tallis (c1505–1585) composes for Catholic, Anglican, and Puritan faiths

King Henry VIII (r. 1509–1547) of England, musician, composer, and church reformer

King Francis I (r. 1515–1547) of France, brings Italian Renaissance to France

Orlande de Lassus (1532–1594) composes in all genres of his day

William Byrd (1543–1623), preeminent composer under Queen Elizabeth

1555 Peace of Augsburg

Thomas Morley (1557–1602), important composer and theorist in London

El Greco (1541–1614), "Christ Clasping the Cross" (1600–1605)

Musical Interlude

Musical Humanism and the Renaissance

Although the historians who coined the term "renaissance" greatly exaggerated the difference between the old "dark" Middle Ages and the newly "revivified" Renaissance, they had a point. Observers of the day were aware that something new was in the air. As the important music theorist **Johannes Tinctoris** (c1435–1511) said in his *Art of Counterpoint* (1477): "There is no composition written over forty years ago which is thought by the learned as worthy of performance." What mattered to Tinctoris was all that was new. To be sure, the Renaissance brought with it a new way of looking at things. During the period 1475–1600, music generally would come to be governed by strict rules of counterpoint. Perhaps more important, musicians came to believe that in vocal music a composition should reflect the meaning of its text in the fullest and most vivid manner. This new attitude about text and tone, and about music generally, was derived largely from the study of the arts and letters of ancient Greece and Rome, a discipline called *studia humanitatis*.

Humanism was the study of ancient texts and monuments with the aim of extracting a model for thinking and acting in the emerging society of the Renaissance. It began in the fourteenth century with Francesco Petrarch's (see the introduction to Part II) exploration of the literature of ancient Rome. Now in the late fifteenth century scholars intensified their interest in the poetry, philosophy, and arts of classical Greece and Rome and tried to make the principles found therein work for the present day. By learning from the past, humanists expected to create a society full of truth and beauty populated by morally upright citizens.

Implicit in humanism is the notion that human beings have the capacity to shape their world. If the Middle Ages had placed great emphasis on God and relegated man to a minor, faceless role in a great divine pageant, the Renaissance placed its faith in human achievement and individual creativity. The fact that Michelangelo sculpted his David (1501–1504) as a huge figure fully nude—something never done in medieval religious art—suggests a new artistic imperative (Fig. 1). Humans must give free rein to their creative instincts and fashion a world, not so much in the image of God as in the image of man. These were lofty aspirations, but how specifically did they affect the composition and performance of music in this period?

For musicians the study of the musical artifacts of antiquity was less direct than it was for other disciplines. The reason was simple: as far as they knew, no music survived from ancient Greece and Rome. Instead, the musical humanists studied the writings in music theory of classical Greece and the attitudes about music held by the ancient philosophers such as Plato and Aristotle (see Chapter 1). Greek music theory greatly influenced Renaissance theory and brought about changes both in theory and practice, as we shall soon see. Musicians of the Renaissance eagerly embraced the ancient belief that music could affect the emotions. Plato had told stories of how music had calmed the agitated spirit and made the warrior brave. Accordingly, Renaissance musicians tried to create a more affective, more emotionally expressive music. Because the poet and the musician were one and the same in Greek society, Renaissance musicians came to insist upon a closer union between text and tone. During the sixteenth century, composers developed a vocabulary of

❧ FIGURE 1

Michelangelo's giant statue *David* (1501–1504) expresses the heroic nobility of man in near-perfect form. Like Leonardo da Vinci, Michelangelo made a careful study of human anatomy.

Bridgeman Art Library

fine poet, and he encouraged Isaac and others to set his words to music. The genre of music Lorenzo seems to have enjoyed most is the carnival song.

Carnival season comes immediately before Lent. To understand the fun and frivolity of the Italian carnival, think of *Mardi gras* in New Orleans or *carnaval* in Rio with masked revelers, music, and dance, all fueled by appropriate drink. In Renaissance Florence the leading revelers were called *mascherati* (masqueraders), men and boys in costume (frequently, in "drag"). They would go about the city singing songs appropriate for the moment. Sometimes they would stop in a city square or beneath the window of an important lady, and her lover would pay them to sing. Figure 20-1 shows five Florentine *mascherati* so performing. To their left stands Lorenzo de' Medici, purse prominent. Lorenzo wrote poems that he then had set to music to serve as a **carnival song** (*canto carnascialesco*). Most carnival songs are short, homophonic pieces in three vocal parts. Texts usually deal with everyday life on the streets of Florence and are sometimes sexually explicit. One of the best known of the carnival songs was the *Canto de' profumieri* (*Song of the Perfume Sellers*). Here simple, declamatory music accommodates a refrain and seven strophes of text. The refrain introduces the *mascherati*, who in this case claim to be a group of gentlemen merchants of the Spanish town of Valencia. The first two stanzas extol their wares, including soothing oils that bring relief to women in the heat of love, a clear *double entendre*. The text of this carnival song was by Lorenzo the Magnificent. The music was likely improvised by singers in the streets; only later, when it had become part of the oral tradition of Florence, was the musical version written down.

Biblioteca Riccardiana, Florence

FIGURE 20-1
Lorenzo de' Medici and carnival singers.

EXAMPLE 20-1

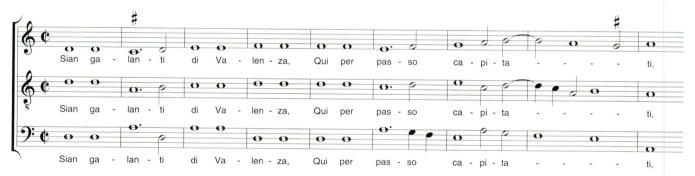

We are the gallants of Valencia, who in passing are smitten...

LISTENING CUE

LORENZO DE' MEDICI
Sian galanti di Valenza (c1490)

CD 3/1
Anthology, No. 53

Florence was and remains a city of extremes—of wealth and poverty, tradition and novelty, passion and piety. The secular carnival song had its sacred counterpart in the lauda. A **lauda** (Italian for "a song of praise"; pl., **laude**) was a simple, popular sacred song written, not in church Latin but in the local dialect of Italian. From its beginning in the thirteenth century, the lauda had been sung by members of a

confraternity, a society of laymen devoted to one or another aspect of Christian faith, such as the Virgin Mary or the Holy Cross. Florence had no fewer than twelve such confraternities, and performing laude was an essential part of their fraternal life. Hundreds of their lauda texts survive, but few melodies. The reason for this is simple: most laude were sung to pre-existing melodies, and many different texts could be sung to the same tune. A prescription at the top of a text would instruct the brothers to sing the lauda "just as to the Song of the Fisherwoman" or "just as to the Song of the Perfume Sellers." The newly fashioned piece was called a **contrafactum** (pl., **contrafacta**)—something fabricated from something else, in this case a religious piece from a very secular one. (In a similar manner the reform-minded Lutherans would soon make contrafacta by retexting popular songs with religious texts, thereby creating Lutheran chorales.) Lorenzo the Magnificent also wrote lauda texts, and his lauda *O maligno, e duro core* (*O, malignant, evil heart*) was to be sung to the *Song of the Perfume Sellers*. As comparisons of just the refrains show, the number of syllables per line (eight) and the rhyme scheme (**abba**) of the lauda was the same as that of the carnival song; thus one tune easily works for both texts.

Lauda	Rhyme scheme	Carnival song
O maligno e duro core,	a	Sian galanti di Valenza,
Fonte d'ogni mal concetto,	b	Qui per passo capitati,
Che non scoppi a mezzo il petto,	b	D'amor già presi e legati
Che non t'apri di dolore.	a	Delle donne di Fiorenza.
(O, evil, bitter heart,		(We are the gallants of Valencia
Source of all malicious thought,		Who in passing are smitten,
Who bursts from the breast not even a little,		Taken and tied by the love
And opens not for sadness.)		Of the ladies of Florence.)

Perhaps the most famous, or infamous, writer of laude was **Girolamo Savonarola** (1452–1498). Savonarola was a Dominican friar, a member of a monastic order that still exists today. Born and raised in Ferrara, Italy, Savonarola came to Florence in 1482. By 1490 he had advanced to become the principal religious orator of the city. Preaching to thousands in the nave of the gigantic cathedral (see Fig. 15-1), the friar railed against the laxity of the clergy, including the pope, as well as against the idleness of the aristocracy. Part populist, part rabble-rouser, and part religious fanatic, Savonarola's critical attacks earned him a following among many reform-minded citizens of Florence.

By 1497 the devout Savonarola had become the most powerful figure in the city and, needless to say, he didn't think much of carnival season. In 1497, and again in 1498, Savonarola instigated a practice now known as the **bonfire of the vanities.** Instead of going through the streets singing carnival songs, his supporters went from house to house collecting "useless" worldly items including women's hats, wigs, masks, rouge pots, mirrors, chessboards, perfumes, pictures, cards and dice, books, musical instruments, and music manuscripts. These they burned in a huge bonfire in the Piazza della Signoria (the central square of Florence; Fig. 20-2). Such bonfires were a powerful symbol of the friar's fanaticism and his belief that the Florentines must lead simple, virtuous lives if they themselves hoped to avoid the eternal bonfire of Hell. Savonarola was, to say the least, anti-humanist.

But Savonarola was not entirely anti-music. He himself was the author of twelve lauda texts, and each of these was supplied with music by means of a contrafactum; a carnival song provided music for a lauda. Savonarola's numerous followers went through the streets of Florence lamenting the sinful world as they sang his laude. Savonarola's most popular lauda text, *Giesù, sommo conforto* (*Jesus, highest solace*), survives with an anonymous popular tune serving as a cantus. Against this, a tenor provides a harmonic support while an alto adds simple counterpoint, mostly in parallel thirds often above the cantus. Originally, the duet between the cantus and altus might have been improvised, and it is easy to imagine that this entire setting faithfully records what was essentially an oral, improvisatory practice. Such an approach did not create a musical masterpiece, but it was sufficient to convey Savonarola's spiritual message: every good Florentine should be willing to join Christ on the cross and burn with "holy fire," as the text of this lauda says.

Bridgeman Art Library

Ultimately, such a fiery fate befell Savonarola himself. Followers of the pope and the Medici family united and took him prisoner. As punishment for having rendered "false prophecies," Savonarola was tied to an elevated crucifix in the Piazza della Signoria and burned to death on 23 May 1498 (Fig. 20-2).

FIGURE 20-2

Savonarola instituted the "bonfire of the vanities" to rid the city of objects of personal adornment and enjoyment. Eventually, the citizens of Florence rid themselves of Savonarola by subjecting him to the same fate. This anonymous painting shows the burning of Savonarola and two of his followers.

EXAMPLE 20-2

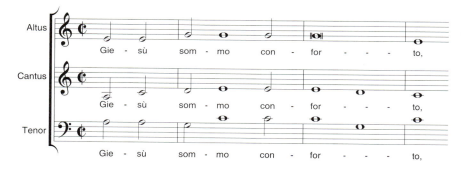

Jesus, highest solace…

LISTENING CUE

GIROLAMO SAVONAROLA
Giesù, sommo conforto (c1495)

CD 3/2
Anthology, No. 54

THE FROTTOLA

In addition to the carnival song and lauda, another genre of Italian popular music arose during the quattrocento, the frottola. The term **frottola** (pl., **frottole;** believed to derive from the Latin "frocta," a collection of random thoughts) was used as a catch-all word to describe a polyphonic setting of a wide variety of strophic Italian poetry. Although the frottola flourished between the years 1470 and 1530, its roots lie in a tradition of improvisatory, solo singing that arose in Italy during the 1400s. A singer would recite poetry while accompanying himself on a string instrument. This practice was especially popular among Italian aristocrats. Lorenzo de' Medici was fond of improvisatory singing and accompanied himself on a Renaissance fiddle called the **lira da braccio**, a bowed five-string instrument tuned in fifths and played on the shoulder (Fig. 20-3). Improvisation of this sort should be seen as

❄ FIGURE 20-3

Lira da braccio of 1563. The *lira da braccio* was similar in design and function to the medieval vielle (see Fig. 11-4 and Fig. 2 on p. 149). It had five strings and two drone strings off the fingerboard.

a humanistic effort to recover the simplicity associated with the music of classical antiquity. With a *lira* in hand, the Renaissance musician appeared as ancient Orpheus reborn. In his influential *The Book of the Courtier* (1528), Baldassare Castiglione argues that the ability to sight-read polyphonic music is important. But even more desirable is the capacity to perform self-accompanied solo song:

> In my opinion, the most beautiful music is in singing well and in reading at sight and in fine style, but even more in singing to the accompaniment of the *lira*, because nearly all the sweetness is in the solo and we note and follow the fine style and the melody with greater attention in that our ears are not occupied with more than a single voice, and every little fault is the more clearly noticed—which does not happen when a group is singing, because the one sustains the other. But especially it is poetic recitation with the *lira* that seems to me most delightful, as this gives the words a wonderful charm and effectiveness.[2]

The frottola began life in this fashion, as poetry sung to an improvised string accompaniment; the performer would sing successive strophes of the text while bowing an accompaniment. It first took deep root in the northern Italian city of Mantua, where two Italians, Marchetto Cara (c1465–1525) and Bartolomeo Tromboncino (born 1470–died after 1535), perfected the genre. Some Franco-Flemish musicians working in Italy also turned to the frottola from time to time. Josquin des Prez wrote at least three, the best known of which is *El grillo* (*The Cricket*).

As Josquin's work shows, by 1490 the frottola could be fully sung, as well as performed by a solo voice with accompanying instrument(s). Here four singing parts are all assigned the same lively rhythms, a procedure that creates a highly homophonic texture. Curiously, just as rock guitarists in the 1950s and 1960s accompanied tunes almost exclusively in root-position chords, so here Josquin makes use of nothing but root-position triads in his harmony. This again suggests the ancestry of the frottola, that originally it was a poem sung to the accompaniment of simple chords bowed on a *lira da braccio* or strummed on a lute. The text of *El grillo* is typical of the lighter, sometimes comic, quality of the frottola. On one level, the subject of the poem, the cricket, can be taken to represent a singer who sings for love rather than for money. On the other hand, a *double entendre* may lurk here; the cricket's "long cry" and his singing "when the weather is hotter" may suggest a coarser interpretation. Either way, the music and the text are a long way from the lofty expression of the courtly Burgundian chanson. *El grillo* has the same zest for life and lighter musical style as the Florentine carnival song.

EXAMPLE 20-3

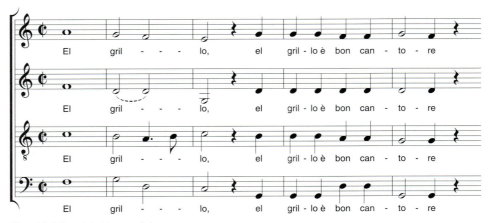

The cricket, the cricket is a good singer…

El grillo è bon cantore	The cricket is a good singer
Che tiene longo verso.	Who has a long cry.
Dale beve grillo canta.	The cricket sings of drinking.
El grillo è bon cantore.	The cricket is a good singer.
Ma non fa come gli altri ucelli,	But he is not, like other birds,
Come li han cantata un poco,	When they have sung a little,
Van' de fatto in altro loco,	Go off elsewhere,
Sempre el grillo sta pur saldo.	The cricket stays still.
Quando là maggior el caldo	When the weather is hotter
Alhor canta sol per amore.	Then he sings for love.
El grillo è bon cantore	The cricket is a good singer
Che tiene longo verso.	Who has a long cry.
Dale beve grillo canta.	The cricket sings of drinking.
El grillo è bon cantore.	The cricket is a good singer.

 LISTENING CUE

JOSQUIN DES PREZ   CD 3/3
El grillo è bon cantore (c1500)   Anthology, No. 55

THE EARLY MADRIGAL IN FLORENCE

The **madrigal,** like the frottola, was a catch-all term used to describe settings of Italian verse. Earlier (see Chapter 14) we met the Italian trecento madrigal, a strophic secular piece for two or three voices in **AAB** form. The sixteenth-century madrigal, however, is musically unlike its earlier namesake. The sixteenth-century madrigal is invariably **through composed** (new music for every line of text), rather than strophic. Moreover, it employs a variety of textures and compositional techniques—simple homophonic declamation, imitative counterpoint, and extended melismatic passages among them. Thus, the madrigal is capable of a much wider range of expression than the usually uniform, strophic frottola. So too the madrigal displays a more serious tone, for the poetic texts are of a higher quality. The lofty aspiration of the madrigalists can be seen in the fact they often took their texts from the finest poets in the Italian language, their favorite being the great Francesco Petrarch (see introduction to Part II).

Given the importance of the madrigal to Italian musical culture during the Renaissance, it is ironic that most of the composers first associated with the genre were French or Flemish. Chief among them was Jacques Arcadelt (c1505–1568), a Frenchman who was active in Florence during the 1530s and spent much of his later career in the service of the pope in Rome. While in Florence, Arcadelt became one of the chief proponents of the madrigal. His first essays into the genre were published in 1538 or 1539 under the title *Primo libro di madrigali d'Archadelt* (*The First Book of Madrigals by Arcadelt*). The collection was so popular it was reprinted more than fifty times, and it secured Arcadelt's reputation as the preeminent composer of the early madrigal.

Opening Arcadelt's *Primo libro di madrigali* is his enduring *Il bianco e dolce cigno* (*The gentle white swan*). Typical of the madrigal, it sets a single stanza of poetry written in seven- or eleven-syllable lines. The subject is love and death. Legend has it that the swan sings a last song before dying—hence the term "swan song," meaning one's last act. The death of a beautiful white swan is not a happy image, yet here this conceit is sharply contrasted to the death of the speaker who dies with "joy and desire." Once again we have a *double entendre*, for in Renaissance poetry "death" was a metaphor for sexual release. Poetic antitheses and extremes of emotion such as these lie at the heart of madrigal poetry. They afford the composer the opportunity for equally diverse and extreme musical expression, but how does this play out in the music?

Il bianco e dolce cigno begins with soft, tranquil music worthy of the noble swan. The initial image of the swan quickly gives way to the "weeping" ("piangendo") of the narrator, which is underscored by an almost painfully surprising chord built on the flat seventh degree of the scale. Perhaps for rhetorical effect, this striking musical moment is immediately repeated. Similarly, a few bars later (mm. 21–23) the painful joy of a blessed "death" is highlighted by a flood of suspensions (dissonances releasing to consonances). Finally, the notion that a thousand such deaths would be desirable is conveyed through music by a passage of pervasive imitation, the phrase "di mille morti il dì" ("a thousand deaths a day") being sung by the voices seemingly a thousand times. Obviously, in the madrigal, as in no other musical genre of the Renaissance, there is a tight bond between text and music.

EXAMPLE 20-4

The gentle white swan dies singing, and I, weeping, approach the end of my life.

Il bianco e dolce cigno	The gentle white swan
Cantando more, e io	dies singing, and I,
Piangendo giung'al fin del viver mio,	weeping, approach the end of my life.
Stran'e diversa sorte,	Strange and diverse fates,
Ch'ei more sconsolato,	that he dies disconsolate,
E io **moro beato,**	and I die happy.

Morte che nel morire	Death, that in the [act of] dying
M'empie di gioia ela e di desire.	fills me wholly with joy and desire.
Se nel morir, altro dolor non sento,	If in dying I feel no other pain,
Di mille mort'il dì, sarei contento.	I would be content to die a thousand deaths a day.

LISTENING CUE

JACQUES ARCADELT
Il bianco e dolce cigno (c1538)

CD 3/4
Anthology, No. 56

The use of striking chord shifts, musical repetition, controlled dissonance, and abrupt textural changes to highlight the meaning of the text is called **text painting** in music; the music overtly sounds out the meaning of the text, almost word by word. Text painting (also called **word painting**) became all the rage with madrigal composers, in Italy and later in England. Even today such musical clichés as sighs and dissonances for "harsh" words are called **madrigalisms.**

Just how far composers of the Italian madrigal might go along the path of overt text expression can be seen in a five-voice setting of the same text, *Il bianco e dolce cigno*, by Orazio Vecchi (1550–1605). Vecchi's remake is an homage to, and perhaps even a parody of, Arcadelt's famous setting (Ex. 20-5). Both works are in the same mode (what would then be called the Ionian mode transposed to F), and Vecchi quotes the opening five bars of the earlier work (mm. 1–9). However, the entrance of the upper two voices in bars 6 and 7, which feature a playful melisma on "canTANdo," signals an entirely different tone and expressive intent. The remainder of the work is saturated with abrupt changes in texture and with word painting. Here Vecchi seems to want to make this piece do everything a madrigal "should" do and then some. Vecchi so exaggerates the moments of word painting that the madrigal becomes comic, as if poking fun at itself. As highly social music for both male and female singers, the madrigal intended to please performers and listeners alike. If it was funny as well as fun, so much the better.

EXAMPLE 20-5

The gentle white swan dies singing…

LISTENING CUE

ORAZIO VECCHI
Il bianco e dolce cigno (1589)

CD 3/5
Anthology, No. 57

SUMMARY

During the fifteenth century, composers from northern Europe thoroughly dominated the creation of learned polyphonic music in Italy (Masses, motets, and chansons). But there was much native music-making as well. Quattrocento Italian music tended to be lighter in style and more popular in expression. Because Italian music was often improvised on the spot, little of it was written down. Music with the Italians, and the Florentines in particular, involved perpetuating popular traditions in which complicated counterpoint had no place. The carnival song and the lauda were part of this vigorous, more spontaneous, Italian approach to music. The frottola, too, began life as an improvised genre, albeit inside the court rather than on the streets of the city. Yet in musical style it likewise manifests aspects of native Italian popular music: abundant root-position chords, snappy rhythms, and light, sometimes frivolous, texts. The madrigal, which arose in Italy about 1530, had a more serious tone and was part of a general movement in the Renaissance to elevate vernacular poetry to a higher status. The madrigal originated in Florence and then spread to other Italian cities, and eventually the Low Countries and England. The extent of its dominance in sixteenth-century musical life can be measured in the fact that many thousands were published. Above all, the madrigal is marked by an exceptionally close relationship between music and word.

KEY TERMS

quattrocento
Lorenzo de' Medici
   (the Magnificent)
carnival song
lauda (pl. laude)
confraternity

contrafactum
   (pl., contrafacta)
Girolamo Savonarola
bonfire of the vanities
frottola (pl., frottole)
lira da braccio

madrigal
through composed
text painting (word
   painting)
madrigalism

Chapter

21

Josquin des Prez and Music in Ferrara

Political power in Renaissance Italy was concentrated in three separate areas: the kingdom of Naples in the south; the papal lands, with Rome at its heart, in the center of the peninsula; and the city-states in the north (see Map 14-1). Florence, Milan, and Venice were the most important northern city-states. But other smaller cities claimed attention, and one of the most important of these was **Ferrara.** Owing to a central location and a succession of strong rulers, Ferrara became a center of musical activity. Ferrara, unlike Venice and Florence, was not a republic. In the late fifteenth century it was ruled by a succession of despots, all members of the d'Este family. The d'Este were a rough, sometimes brutal, bunch but they did know a good composer when they heard one. The important musicians who at one time or another associated with the d'Este family included major composers such as Josquin des Prez, Adrian Willaert, Cipriano de Rore, and Carlo Gesualdo. By the end of the sixteenth century, the population of Ferrara had grown to about 60,000, and the court of Ferrara employed as many as forty full-time musicians, both singers and instrumentalists.

✤ JOSQUIN DES PREZ

Although the Renaissance produced many fine composers, Josquin des Prez (c1450–1521) is surely among the very best (Fig. 21-1). His fame was so great that at a time when composers from previous generations quickly became forgotten, his music continued to be published some fifty years after his death. Today ardent admirers place Josquin des Prez alongside Bach, Mozart, and Beethoven in the Pantheon of great composers. Josquin (as he was known by his contemporaries) wrote in all the musical genres of his day: approximately twenty Masses, seventy motets, seventy secular songs (chansons and frottole), as well as a few instrumental pieces carry his name. Martin Luther favored Josquin's music above that of all other composers: "Josquin is master of the notes, which must express what he desires; other composers can do only what the notes dictate."[1] The Florentine humanist Cosimo Bartoli compared Josquin to the great Michelangelo (1475–1564), who decorated the ceiling of the Sistine Chapel where Josquin was once a singer:

✤ FIGURE 21-1
The only surviving likeness of Josquin des Prez.

British Library

> Josquin may be said to have been a prodigy of nature, as our Michelangelo Buonarroti has been in architecture, painting, and sculpture; for, as there has not thus far been anyone who in his compositions approaches Josquin, so Michelangelo among all those who have been active in these arts, is still alone and without a peer; both Josquin and Michelangelo have opened the eyes of all those who delight in these arts or are to delight in them in the future.[2]

Yet despite his greatness, the details of Josquin's life are still somewhat sketchy. His full name was Josquin Lebloitte dit (called) des Prez and he was born in northern France—we are not sure where—around 1450. In his youth, Josquin seems to have been a choirboy in the northern French town of St. Quentin, then a singer at the court of René d'Anjou in Provence in southern France, and later an employee of King Louis XI of France in Paris and Tours (see Chapter 18). By 1484 Josquin had migrated to Italy, and here he moved rather often between the courts at Milan, Mantua, Ferrara, and the papal curia in Rome. The records of the papacy show that Josquin sang in the Sistine Chapel between 1489 and 1495, and his name, which he carved on the wall of the singers' gallery, can still be seen there today (artistic license, or graffiti?). Eventually, Josquin left Rome and entered the service of Duke Hercules of Ferrara.

✤ JOSQUIN'S MUSIC FOR DUKE HERCULES OF FERRARA

At the end of the fifteenth century, Ferrara was ruled by Hercules d'Este (r. 1471–1505). Hercules was a professional soldier whose army was often hired to fight for other, larger Italian city-states such as Florence and Milan. Thus, the most famous

© Alinari/Art Resource, NY

✿ FIGURE 21-2

A portrait of Josquin's patron in Ferrara, Duke Hercules d'Este in full military armor.

portrait of Hercules shows him in full battle armor (Fig. 21-2). Yet Hercules was also a devoutly religious man, attending Mass daily, going on religious pilgrimages, and washing the feet of the poor during Holy Week. Throughout his life Hercules modeled his conduct after his namesake Hercules, the hero of classical Greek mythology. Images of the ancient Hercules appeared everywhere at the court of Duke Hercules—painted on walls, woven into tapestries, stamped on coins, and sculpted as statues for the ducal garden. Why all this Herculean imagery? During the Renaissance the hero Hercules became something of a role model for Christian rulers because he had fought and defeated the forces of evil in Greek antiquity. Hercules, both modern duke and ancient hero, was a warrior who ultimately chose a life of piety. As a sign of his piety, and of his love of music, Duke Hercules supported a chapel that in 1503–1504 counted thirty-one singers and three organists, the largest in western Europe at that time. Chief among them was Josquin des Prez.

The esteem in which Josquin was held can be judged from letters of 1502, when Duke Hercules was in need of a new director for his court chapel. The duke had recruiters searching for the best composer of the day, and had narrowed the choice down to two musicians: Josquin des Prez and the renowned Heinrich Isaac, court composer for the Holy Roman Emperor. One recruiter urged the duke to hire Josquin, whose presence, it was suggested, would make the Ferrarese chapel the equal of that of a king:

> My Lord, I believe that there is neither lord nor king who will now have a better chapel than yours if Your Lordship sends for Josquin . . . and by having Josquin in our chapel I want to place a crown upon this chapel of ours.[3]

Yet another agent felt Josquin, although the better composer, was too temperamental an artist:

> To me [Isaac] seems well suited to serve Your Lordship, more so than Josquin, because he is more good-natured and companionable, and will compose new works more often. It is true that Josquin composes better, but he composes when he wants to and not when one wants him to, and he is asking 200 ducats in salary while Isaac will come for 120—but Your Lordship will decide.[4]

To his credit, Duke Hercules chose the moody, more expensive Josquin, who became ducal chapel master in 1503.

Josquin's *Missa Hercules Dux Ferrarie*

Josquin des Prez composed a four-voice Mass in honor of Hercules, and he did so in a novel fashion, knowing that the duke liked to see his name everywhere. Josquin took the Latin title "Hercules dux Ferrarie" and extracted the vowels (e, u, e, u, e, a, i, e). These he equated with the Guidonian solfege syllables to produce the pitches "re," "ut," "re," "ut," "re," "fa," "mi," and "re," and he made these serve as the cantus firmus of the Mass (Ex. 21-1). A cantus firmus extracted from the vowels of a name is called a *soggetto cavato dalle vocali* ("subject cut out from the vowels"). It can simply be called a **soggetto cavato** ("a cut-out subject"—you can make one of your own name). Josquin's *Missa Hercules dux Ferrarie* is one of the first compositions to use this procedure. Like the Guidonian hexachord itself (see Chapter 4),

the *soggetto cavato* could, in principle, appear in its natural form set on C, in the soft
form set on F (with B♭), or in the hard form set on G (with B♮).

EXAMPLE 21-1

In fact, Josquin uses the *soggetto* only in its natural and hard positions. He strings
the two together to form a twenty-four-note cantus firmus (Ex. 21-2). In the course
of the Mass this twenty-four-note unit appears twelve times, perhaps as a symbolic
reference to the twelve labors of the ancient hero Hercules.

EXAMPLE 21-2

Josquin's *Missa Hercules dux Ferrarie* begins with a statement of the cantus firmus in
the soprano, so as to introduce the *soggetto* and make it clearly audible. Thereafter,
the cantus firmus is assigned to the tenor, which does nothing other than sing the
vowels of *Hercules dux Ferrarie* for the duration of the Mass; Josquin wanted to make
sure we knew for whom this Mass was written! It seems likely that the ducal tenors
sang the syllables of the duke's name rather than the text of the Ordinary. In fact,
Hercules himself may have sung the motto with his tenors, since he is known to
have "sung solfege on books of Masses for his amusement." The *Sanctus* may be
taken as typical of Josquin's Mass as a whole (Ex. 21-3). At the conclusion of this
movement the motto appears without interruption and in short note values, which
creates the sense of driving excitedly toward the end.

EXAMPLE 21-3

LISTENING CUE

JOSQUIN DES PREZ
Sanctus of the *Missa Hercules dux Ferrarie* (c1503?)

CD 3/6

Anthology, No. 58

In the *soggetto cavato* Josquin had found a simple new way to unify all five parts of the Ordinary of the Mass and at the same time honor a generous employer. The *Missa Hercules dux Ferrarie* was first printed in 1505, the year of the duke's death, and the act of publication was seen as a tribute by a great composer to a famous patron. Although Josquin was the first to create a musical *soggetto cavato*, the process continued for centuries. Bach, Schumann, Berg, and Shostakovich were among the later composers who in similar ways fashioned themes, and sent coded messages, by means of musical letters.

Josquin's Motet *Miserere Mei, Deus*

In his day, Josquin des Prez was renowned above all else as a composer of motets. The unique quality of Josquin's motets rests in the relationship between music and text. Josquin is among the first composers to assess the meaning of the words of each section of a sacred text and craft music that captures the emotional content of those words. This is an important development in the history of music. It signals the end of the abstract, emotionally noncommittal music-text relationship of the Middle Ages, and the beginning of a new kind of expressive music designed to reflect and enhance the meaning of the words. Such text-specific music was inherent in the early madrigal of the 1530s, as noted in Chapter 20. It first appeared, however, around 1500 in the motets of Josquin des Prez.

One of Josquin's most powerful motets is his *Miserere mei, Deus* (*Have mercy upon me, O Lord*). It was inspired by, and modeled upon, a sermon by Girolamo Savonarola (1452–1498).[5] As we have seen (see Chapter 20), Savonarola, a native of Ferrara, was a religious fanatic who had gained control of Florence late in 1494. He urged spiritual reform and ordered that objects of idle pleasure, including musical instruments and music manuscripts, be burned in the central square of Florence. Ultimately, Savonarola was arrested, tried for heresy, and himself burned on a cross in the central square. While awaiting his execution, Savonarola penned a sermon in which he assumes the voice of a penitent soul who has sinned against God. The words of the sermon are periodically interrupted by a refrain, the opening line of Psalm 50, *Miserere mei, Deus*.

Psalm 50 is one of the seven so-called **Penitential Psalms,** seven psalms among the one hundred fifty of the Psalter that are especially remorseful in tone and sung in the rites of the Catholic Church surrounding death and burial. Savonarola's sermon quickly came to the attention of Duke Hercules of Ferrara, himself something of a religious fanatic. Hercules commanded his chapel master Josquin des Prez to create a musical counterpart to Savonarola's meditation on impending death.

In constructing his great work, Josquin drew inspiration from the psalm tone (see Ex. 3-1) to which *Miserere mei, Deus* is traditionally sung at the burial service. At the heart of the psalm tone is a **recitation** (reciting) **tone,** a constantly repeating pitch followed by a mediation. Here the mediation is an upper neighbor tone. Such an up-down motion, particularly by a half-step, has been traditionally associated with sighing or lamenting. This mournful reciting tone provides a structural grid for the motet, appearing as a cantus firmus in the tenor (Ex. 21-4).

EXAMPLE 21-4

Mi - se - - re - re me - i De - us   Becomes with Josquin   Mi - se - re - re me - i De - us

Josquin's *Miserere mei, Deus* begins with second tenor, bass, soprano, and alto presenting the reciting tone in turn and then continuing with imitative counterpoint. The tenor soon enters with the reciting tone in long notes starting on the pitch e'. At the end of the first verse it returns with words "Miserere mei, Deus" on the reciting tone, but now a pitch lower, starting on d'. Here all voices join in with the cry "Have mercy upon me, O Lord," as if all humanity were petitioning for forgiveness. In this fashion the motet proceeds: duets and trios present the verses of the psalm and each verse ends with the choral refrain "Miserere mei, Deus" led by the tenor, each time beginning on a pitch a step lower. Josquin divides the twenty verses of Psalm 50 into three parts, consisting of eight, seven, and five verses per part. The reciting tone "Miserere mei, Deus" falls by step (starts a step lower each time) in part one, rises by step in part two, and falls again in part three. One might hear this as a repentant sinner falling to his knees, rising, and then falling once again before the Lord. Every time the tenor enters with its phrase, all other voices join his mournful cry.

How does Josquin paint, through music, the deeply sorrowful tone of the text? First of all, he makes plentiful use of the sorrowful quality of the reciting tone with its rise and fall. Moreover, he sometimes isolates a single word, setting it off on either side by rests, so as to highlight the meaning of that word, as he does in verse one on the petition "dele" ("remove [my sin]"). Also, Josquin uses "word painting" from time to time to emphasize the meaning of the text. For example, at the beginning of verse two all the voices sing together with a full choral sound on the word "amplius" ("more fully"). Finally, the entire psalm is oriented around the Phrygian mode, a scale that has historically possessed a strangely mournful quality, likely owing to the half-step relationship between scale degrees one and two. Exploiting these text expressive techniques within a masterful treatment of counterpoint leads to a work of extraordinary beauty and power. Josquin's *Miserere mei, Deus* is one of the greatest choral works ever written. In it we clearly hear how one composer achieved a primary goal of Renaissance humanists and musicians: to endow music with the persuasive power of rhetoric.

LISTENING CUE

JOSQUIN DES PREZ

Miserere mei, Deus (1503)

CD 3/7

Anthology, No. 59

A few months after Josquin composed this motet, the bubonic plague returned to Ferrara. The composer fled the city and left Italy for good, returning to the small town of Condé, his family's home, on the border of modern-day France and Belgium. There he died, a much-respected musician, in 1521. But the legend of Josquin only continued to grow.

JOSQUIN AND AN ARTIST'S TEMPERAMENT

Upon the death of Josquin at least a half-dozen composers penned musical tributes to his memory. Publishers issued more and more of his chansons, Masses, and motets, making Josquin the most published composer of his age. Indeed, in Germany printers began issuing motets falsely under Josquin's name in order to capitalize on his reputation. This led one important figure, thought to be Martin Luther, to remark wryly: "Now that Josquin is dead, he is putting out more work than when he was still alive." Josquin is the first composer in the history of music for whom we have contemporary anecdotes, stories that reveal something of the personality and working habits of a truly exceptional composer. The Swiss music theorist Heinrich Glarean says, for example, that Josquin worked laboriously on his compositions, revising them and holding them back for many years before releasing them to the public. Another Swiss humanist, Johannes Manlius, reports that each time Josquin composed a new work he would give it to the choir to try out. As they sang, he would walk around, listening to the harmony. When he heard something he disliked, he would say "Be quiet, I will change that." To a singer who was so bold as to add notes to what the master had written, Josquin angrily responded: "You ass, why did you add those embellishments? If I had wanted them, I would have written them myself. If you want to correct musical works that have been composed in a natural or plain style, then write your own, but don't change my works."[6] Like other composers of the Renaissance, including Dufay and Obrecht (see Chapters 15, 17, and 19), Josquin would sometimes insert his own name, and information about himself, into the text of a motet. And let us not forget that Josquin was said to compose only when he wished and demanded a salary twice that of his principal competitor (Heinrich Isaac). In sum, Josquin comes across as one of a new breed, the artist of the Renaissance: moody, egotistical, demanding of himself and others, and supremely confident in the rightness of his own human creations.

 ## SUMMARY

Ferrara, Florence, and Venice were among the northern Italian city-states that encouraged the arts, and especially music, during the Renaissance. Ferrara in particular had a rich musical history, extending from the composer Josquin des Prez at the beginning of the sixteenth century to Carlo Gesualdo at the end. Josquin des Prez is one of the greatest composers in the history of music. In his nearly twenty Masses he used many erudite procedures (canon, retrograde motion, and *soggetto cavato*, for example) yet surrounds them with such beautiful sounds that these technical devices are barely noticeable—ingenious craftsmanship embedded within sublime sound. In his seventy-odd motets, Josquin reveals himself a master of text expression, one of the earliest composers to create musical gestures that intensify the meaning of individual words and phrases of the text. Numerous documents and anecdotes from Josquin's own day show that his contemporaries accorded him and his music a degree of respect like that of no other composer.

 ## KEY TERMS

Ferrara
soggetto cavato

Penitential Psalms
recitation tone

Musical Interlude

Music Printing in the Renaissance

Before the year 1450 all books in the West were written by hand; that is why they are called "manuscripts" (a combination of the Latin "manus" and "scriptus"). During the 1450s, however, a German craftsman working in the city of Mainz perfected a new method to produce books. His name was **Johannes Gutenberg** (c1400–c1468). Gutenberg invented printing with **movable type,** and it works in the following way. Hundreds of small pieces of metal type are cut, each containing a letter of the alphabet; these are arranged to form words in a series of lines that in turn create a page; after completion of the appropriate number of pages, the type is locked into an iron frame, called a "forme," and then is ready to be placed in the press. The type is then covered with ink and a sheet of paper pressed against it. When all the sheets for that forme are printed, the pieces of type can now be disassembled and reused to produce other formes. Finally, when all the sheets of a book are printed, they are arranged in order, and sent to a bookbinder to be stitched together.

Figure 1 shows a Renaissance printing press at work, as a sheet is pressed down tightly onto a metal forme full of movable, and reusable, type. Printing significantly reduced the amount of time needed to produce a book, and therefore its cost. A book was no longer something owned only by the nobility and high-ranking clergy, but could be had by lawyers, doctors, and tradesmen as well. Printing with movable type remained the standard method for generating books and newspapers until the advent of the computer-compositor in the late twentieth century.

Johannes Gutenberg printed mainly religious works, including the famed "Gutenberg Bible." The first examples of printed music also involved the sacred, specifically monophonic Gregorian chant. Printing polyphonic music, however, was a more difficult task because of the complexity of the different rhythmic values. It would not be until 1501—some fifty years later—that printing polyphonic music with movable type was successfully achieved.

The Germans had invented book printing in the West, and they soon carried the idea to Italy, specifically to Venice, where it became a huge commercial success. In fact, Venice became the center of publishing not only for Italy but also for all of Europe. Here technology went hand in hand with learning, for publishing and debating ancient Greek and Roman texts became, of course, the principal activity of Renaissance humanists. During the sixteenth century about 35,000 different titles were published in Venice, each with a press run of about 1,000, resulting in the publication of approximately 35 million books!

In 1501 the first book of polyphonic music from movable type was printed in Venice by **Ottaviano Petrucci** (1466–1539). He called it the **Odhecaton,** a Greek term meaning one hundred songs ("od" is Greek for "song," as in "melody" and "prosody"). Most of the songs in this collection were not by

FIGURE 1

A French printing shop about the year 1530. On the right, proofreaders check the text for errors.

Italians but were works of the great northern masters of counterpoint such as Ockeghem, Busnoys, Obrecht, and Josquin. During the next two decades Petrucci went on to publish additional collections of songs, as well as Masses, motets, and frottole. Yet no matter what he printed, Petrucci executed everything with great care and clarity.

Petrucci's music prints are uniformly elegant because he used a complicated process called **multiple-impression printing**. First, he printed the lines of the staff horizontally across the page. Then he carefully pressed down the sheet a second time on a new metal plate and printed the notes onto the staff. Finally, he pressed the page down yet a third time to add text, title, composer's name, and any written instructions. Multiple-impression printing was time consuming, making the price fairly high and the number of buyers comparatively low. Indeed, Petrucci's press runs were modest; usually he printed no more than 500 copies of any one collection of songs or Masses.

An economical way of printing music was not realized in Italy or Germany, but in France, specifically in Paris during the late 1520s. Here **Pierre Attaingnant** (c1494–c1552), a printer and book seller living in the university quarter of the Left Bank, popularized a method called single-impression printing. In **single-impression printing** both the note and a small vertical section of the staff are fashioned onto a small piece of movable, reusable type. Dozens of such small pieces are needed to represent every possible pitch and rhythmic value, including multiples of them necessary to create many lines of music at once. A typesetter would set down staff, music, and text all in one forme, and press the sheet of paper only once, thereby substantially reducing production time and cost. The finished product had slight disjunctions where the individual pieces of type fit together. Compare the smooth look of a Petrucci print with the more utilitarian result of Attaingnant, where the breaks in the staff appear as small, jagged lines (Figs. 2 and 3). Attaingnant's method was not elegant, but it got the job done. With the single-impression method, music printing

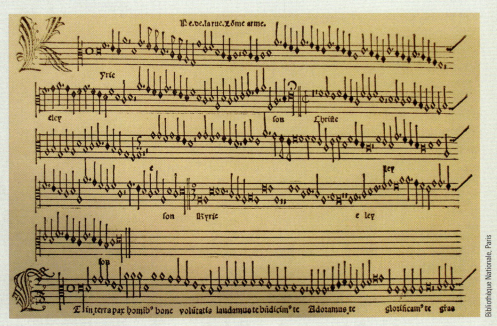

✺ FIGURE 2

The soprano part of a Mass by Pierre de la Rue in Petrucci's print of 1503.

became a commercially viable enterprise, and it quickly spread throughout Europe to become the usual mode of production of music books during the Renaissance. Single-impression printing remained the norm for printing music until the late seventeenth century, when the process of musical engraving gradually came to replace it.

Most early prints of music, whether from the press of Petrucci in Venice or Attaingnant in Paris, were issued not in score but in what are called part books. A **part book** is a volume that contains the music of one voice part and only one voice part. Even the new printed books were expensive. If you were a soprano, did you really need the alto's music? If you sang bass, why pay for what the tenor would sing? (Some well-to-do collectors, of course, bought sets with all the parts.) Because it was easier and cheaper for the printer to lay out the voice parts in separate books, the part book helped further reduce the cost of printing, and this stimulated a mass market for music. The part book format remained the main vehicle for disseminating vocal music until the middle of the seventeenth century, when printing music in score became more common.

Much as printing affected intellectual life in general during the Renaissance, so printing music affected musical life. Printed part books contributed to the growth of musical literacy, not so much at court or in church, but at home. "How to" manuals encouraged ordinary men and women to learn to read musical notation, to sing, and to play an instrument. Here, for the first time in music history, we see the appearance of the musical amateur. Moderately priced musical anthologies provided the music the amateur needed.

Finally, the fact that printing music required skilled craftsmen to cut the fonts of type, pressmen to manufacture the books, and shops in which to sell them, suggests that printing music was very much an urban phenomenon dependent on technology and commerce. Large cities such as Venice, Rome, and Paris became centers of the music publishing business, and the fledgling industry grew along with the ever-increasing urban populations. During the Renaissance a printer such as Petrucci or Attaingnant acquired the press and the fonts of type, gathered the musical compositions and arranged them into a pleasing collection, printed the books, and sold them in the same shop where he printed them. Music lovers came to the shop, acquired the music, and took it home to perform. This model of the urban music store, where printed music could be bought for performance in the home, remained in place until a mere fifty years ago. It was gradually replaced by the record store and then the CD store, where it was possible to buy music that others had performed and to listen to their performances at home. Now even the music shop has become obsolete. Most music today is performed by others—by professionals—and is downloaded from the Internet.

Boston Athenaeum

 FIGURE 3

The soprano part of a Mass by Jean Mouton in Attaingnant's print *Viginti missarum musicalium* of 1532. Note the wavy lines created by the many small pieces of movable type.

KEY TERMS

Johannes Gutenberg
movable type
Ottaviano Petrucci
Odhecaton

multiple-impression
  printing
Pierre Attaingnant

single-impression
  printing
part book

Chapter 22

Music in Renaissance Paris

During the late Middle Ages (1150–1350), Paris was at the center of all that was new in polyphonic art music. The composers of organum, motets, and conductus, as well as the later isorhythmic motets, were, at least at first, nearly all Parisians. They wrote Europe's most "cutting edge" music. But the Black Death of 1349–1350 and the Hundred Years' War (1337–1453) brought calamity to late medieval Paris, and not until the Renaissance did the capital of France finally recover.

When Paris did regain its former glory it did so under the aegis of an especially powerful, yet artistically sensitive, king: **Francis I** (ruled 1515–1547) (Fig. 22-1). Almost single-handedly, he brought the Italian Renaissance north to France. To adorn the royal court, Francis hired some of the greatest Italian artists of the day (Leonardo da Vinci and Benvenuto Cellini among them). He encouraged the study of classical literature in both Latin and ancient Greek by founding a college in Paris that still exists today (the *Collège de France*). The number of students living in the university section of Paris—the Latin Quarter on the Left Bank—grew to nearly 16,000. For religious music, King Francis supported a large chapel of the best singers and composers he could find; for secular entertainment he employed lutenists, string players, chamber singers, trumpeters, and shawmists, among others. His singers were mostly French, but many of his instrumentalists were imported from Italy. Yet perhaps the greatest contribution Francis made to the growth of art music in Renaissance Paris was his support for the fledgling music industry of Paris, specifically his sponsorship of the new industry of music publishing. For Francis, art, industry, and technology progressed hand in hand.

As we have seen (Musical Interlude 3), the commercial music business as we know it first began in Paris with **Pierre Attaingnant** (c1494–c1552), a book printer and seller with a shop on the Left Bank. In 1528 King Francis gave Attaingnant a copyright on the music he published and a patent on the technology that made it possible. In 1537 the king named Attaingnant the official printer of music for the crown. Attaingnant had received, in effect, a monopoly to print music, at least in and around Paris. It must have been a lucrative business, because Attaingnant produced music book after music book, more than 170 different titles in all.

❀ F I G U R E   2 2 - 1
King Francis I as painted by Jean Clouet about 1525.

Bridgeman Art Library

❀ THE PARISIAN CHANSON

What kind of music did Attaingnant print? He issued books for all kinds of music-making, from large, luxurious choir books of polyphonic Masses for professional church choirs, to cheaper, small-size books containing collections of motets, lute music, keyboard music, and dances for instrumental ensembles. But, above all, Attaingnant printed anthologies of polyphonic chansons, a total of more than a hundred of them. Each book contained about thirty songs, and for each he ran off about 500 to 1,000 copies. Most chansons were for four voices, a few for three. Like the Italian printers before him, Attaingnant published these songs (as well as his motets) not in score, but in part books. A singer need not purchase an entire set, only the music for his or her vocal part (Fig. 22-2).

In all, Pierre Attaingnant printed more than two thousand separate secular chansons. Many of these songs are of a type referred to as the **Parisian chanson.** Before 1500 the poetry of the French chanson was essentially a courtly affair that spoke of ideal love in a somewhat abstract way. For nearly two centuries it followed the rigid rules and rhyme schemes of the *formes fixes.* The musical setting, too, was abstract, meaning that there was little attempt to write music to convey the sense of particular words, or to capture the natural rhythm of the text. Often the text could be set almost anywhere beneath the music with no specific tying of the words to particular notes. In the newer Parisian chanson, however, the rhythm of the text begins to animate the rhythm of the music. Now, almost every note has its own syllable, and the duration of that note is often determined by the length or stress of the syllable. Similarly, the subject matter of the lyrics is far more "down to earth" in tone. These chansons sometimes speak of love, but love of a less ideal, more physical sort—of lusty lovers or libidinous priests and their all-too-willing companions, for example. Some songs depict drinking scenes, others, particularly those of Clément Janequin (c1485–c1560), are medleys of battle sounds or the street cries of Parisian vendors. Many texts are funny, some obscene.

The musical style of the Parisian chanson is almost entirely syllabic, because the stresses of the words largely determine the duration of the notes. All four voices often declaim the text together, thereby creating a generally chordal texture. Homophonic declamation now takes precedence over linear counterpoint. Pitches are frequently repeated in snappy recitation called **patter-song**—the rapid delivery of text on repeated notes. The form of the song flows naturally from the particular structure of the text. Indeed, every song seems to have its own form. By 1530 the stiff, medieval *formes fixes* had been driven from the scene, replaced by a multitude of formal types; the old courtly chanson gave way to a more flexible, urban (and urbane) popular song.

Bridgeman Art Library

✤ FIGURE 22-2

Tapestry from Bourges, France, depicting four singers performing a chanson from part books. As the scene suggests, this was music for all literate musicians to enjoy, female as well as male.

CLAUDIN DE SERMISY

The master of the new Parisian chanson was Claudin de Sermisy (c1490–1562). Claudin (as he was known in his day) was primarily a church musician. Between 1508 and 1562 he served as a singer and then master of the royal chapel for three successive French monarchs. Though an ordained priest, Claudin's fame now rests, not on his religious music, but on his 169 surviving secular songs. Like Paul McCartney in the twentieth century, Claudin was one of the greatest melody writers of his day.

It is no surprise, therefore, that Claudin's chansons dominate Pierre Attaingnant's inaugural publication, the *Chansons nouvelles* of 1528, and that the second song in that set was his *Tant que vivray* (*As Long as I Live*). The seductive melody and infectious rhythm suggest why *Tant que vivray* went on to become one of the hit tunes of the sixteenth century, the object of many reprints, not just in Paris but in places like England, Italy, the Netherlands, and Spain. Here the structure of the text determines the structure of the music, each line beginning with a new idea and ending in a clear cadence (Ex. 22-1). Notice, again, how the rhythm of the text determines the rhythm of the music. Except for the short melisma in the cantus and tenor in bar 10, the piece is entirely syllabic—each syllable generates one note, but no more. At the very beginning, the poetic unit is that of a dactyl (long-short-short-long), and for that Claudin creates a corresponding rhythm: "Tant que vivray" (♩♩♩♩). Toward the end, the dactyls come faster as short, four-syllable lines pile one on top of the other in patter-song style, and likewise the musical rhythms reflect the increased verbal speed: "Son alliance, c'est ma fiance" (♩♪♪♩♩). Yet while the music reflects the rhythm of the text, it does not overtly sound out its meaning, as is true of many Italian madrigals. *Tant que vivray*, like most Parisian chansons, is strophic, and multiple stanzas cannot accommodate text painting.

EXAMPLE 22-1

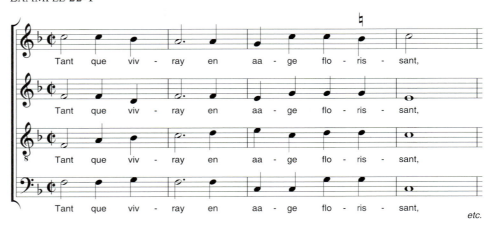

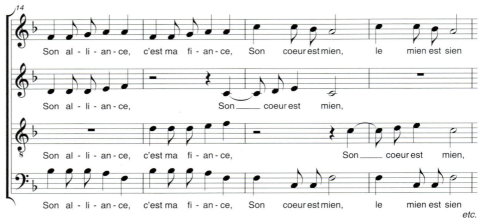

As long as I live in the prime of life,...
Her allegiance, that is my faith, her heart is mine, and mine is hers.

LISTENING CUE

CLAUDIN DE SERMISY
Tant que vivray (c1528)

CD 3/8
Anthology, No. 60a

✦ INSTRUMENTAL ARRANGEMENTS

The popularity of Claudin's *Tant que vivray* can be judged by the fact that it was not only reprinted many times as a vocal piece but also arranged for a variety of instruments: solo keyboard, lute, lute and voice, and even for three lutes; of course, it could also be played as a four-part instrumental piece simply by eliminating the text. No sooner did Pierre Attaingnant publish the song as a four-voice vocal piece in 1528 than the very next year he printed an arrangement of it for solo voice with lute accompaniment as well as another for lute alone. The version for solo lute is called a lute **intabulation,** in part because it is written in lute **tablature.** (Lute tablature is explained in Chapter 23 in connection with Ex. 23-2.) An intabulation implies that a preexisting polyphonic vocal piece has been arranged for a single instrument.

The lute intabulation of Claudin's *Tant que vivray* takes into account the technical and sonorous limitations of that instrument. First of all, the alto part has been removed, a standard practice when reducing a four-part song to a more manageable number of lines on a solo instrument (Ex. 22-2). But, more important, because no lute can sustain for long the delicate sound of the plucked strings, embellishment is added. To fill in sonic voids—the long notes in the original song—figural ornamentation is inserted, mainly in and around the melody line.

EXAMPLE 22-2

etc.

🌐 LISTENING CUE

CLAUDIN DE SERMISY

Tant que vivray arranged for lute (1529)

Thomson-Schirmer Website
Anthology, No. 60b

In Attaingnant's arrangement for voice and lute, on the other hand, the voice now carries the melody. Consequently, the lute is free to restore the original alto line and need not supply as much sound-filling ornamentation (Ex. 22-3). Needless to say, what Attaingnant and his arranger have given us by way of lute accompaniment is only one possibility. A talented instrumentalist would have improvised many alternative accompaniments as the singer sang subsequent strophes of the song. Instrumental music at this time was only gradually moving from a mainly aural and improvisatory tradition to one of written musical notation or, in this case, written musical tablature.

EXAMPLE 22-3

LISTENING CUE

CLAUDIN DE SERMISY
Tant que vivray arranged for voice and lute (1529)

CD 3/9
Anthology, No. 60c

In 1531 the always enterprising Pierre Attaingnant issued Claudin's *Tant que vivray* in yet another arrangement, this time for keyboard. A translation of the title of that print reads: *Twenty-one chansons reduced to tablature for organ, harpsichord, clavichord, and similar musical instruments.* Clearly, the publisher wanted to sell as many volumes as possible by making it known that this music could be played on any sort of keyboard instrument. A quick glance at the keyboard version of Claudin's *Tant que vivray* shows that Attaingnant's arrangement makes use of all of the old-fashioned, stereotypical organ embellishments of the fifteenth century and grafts them onto the chanson (Ex. 22-4). These older keyboard figures include the quick turn around the initial note of the piece, simple scales, and seemingly aimless "noodling" (see bar 8). Occasionally, the keyboard ornamentation results in out-dated parallel fifths (entry to bar 8) and parallel octaves (bar 21, see Anthology, No. 60d). In truth, this keyboard transcription, burdened with antiquated features, possesses none of the charm or airy grace of the lute arrangement or the vocal original. In general, one can safely say that the keyboard music of the early sixteenth century only rarely attains the generally high level of musical excellence found in the secular and sacred vocal music of that period.

EXAMPLE 22-4

etc.

Finally, a group of instruments might perform Claudin's popular *Tant que vivray* simply by playing, rather than singing, the vocal lines. In sixteenth-century Paris a family of viols (see Chapter 23) or of recorders, or of a flute for the melody with recorders below, would have been common. Attaingnant mentions what he calls the "German flute" (our transverse flute; Fig. 22-3) as well as the recorder. All instrumentalists, with the possible exception of the bass part, were expected to improvise around the written chanson lines. Indeed, today's performers of early music do this as a matter of course when recreating the sounds of the Renaissance. When improvising in the style of the Renaissance, modern instrumentalists employ, among other things, the ornamental patterns set forth in Attaingnant's own lute and keyboard transcriptions.

DANCE MUSIC

Parisian chansons had direct, pleasing rhythms, and often these songs, when played by an instrumental ensemble, served well as dance music. Claudin's *Tant que vivray*, for example, was transformed, later in the century, into a duple-meter Italian dance known as the *passamezzo*. Popular chansons, however, were not the only kind of music used for dancing. Beginning in 1529 Attaingnant issued a series of volumes containing pieces specifically created to be dance music. Most of the collections were filled with dance pieces for an instrumental consort—for a quartet of viols or of recorders, for example. Attaingnant's first publication for instrumental consort, *Six Gaillardes et six Pavanes avec Treze chansons musicales a quatre parties* (*Six Galliards and Six Pavanes with Thirteen Songs in Four*

FIGURE 22-3

A lutenist playing from a rotulus (sheet music) and a player of a transverse flute, performing from a printed part book, execute a Parisian chanson about 1540. Notre Dame of Paris can be seen in the background.

Parts; 1530), contains just what the title says: a dozen dances along with thirteen songs that could be sung or played as dance music. That the dances are entirely pavanes or galliards suggests the importance of these two dance types. By the mid sixteenth century the pavane and galliard had supplanted the *basse danse* and the *tordion* (see Chapter 19) as the most favored pair of what might fairly be called the "couples" type of ballroom dances.

The pavane gradually replaced the fifteenth-century *basse danse* as the primary slow dance of the court. Like the earlier *basse danse*, the **pavane** is a slow, gliding dance performed by couples holding hands, but it is in duple rather than triple meter. The stately quality of the pavane is indicated by the fact that it also served— and still serves today in some regions of France—as wedding music while entering the chapel, as well as processional music for ecclesiastics entering and exiting the church. The pavane is perhaps the simplest of all Renaissance dances. It consists of only four steps, as described in the introduction to Anthology, No. 61. The music, too, was rigorously organized into phrases of four bars in our modern notation, which could be extended to eight- or twelve-bar units.

The anonymous third pavane from Attaingnant's *Second Livre de danceries* (*Second Book of Dances*; 1547) is comprised of such four-bar phrases (Ex. 22-5). Each beat and each step of the dance occupies a half note (semibreve) in a measure of cut time. Finally, each four-, eight- or twelve-bar section is repeated, and the entire piece could be repeated as many times as necessary, according to the will and stamina of the dancers.

EXAMPLE 22-5

Thoinot Arbeau: The Dancing Priest

Most of what we know about dance in sixteenth-century France comes from an unexpected source, an elderly canon and priest of Langres, in the eastern part of France. His name was Jehan Tabourot (1520–1595) but he chose to write about dance under the *nom de plume* of an anagram of that name: **Thoinot Arbeau.** In 1589 Arbeau published a lengthy treatise on dance called *Orchésographie,* the name of which is derived from the fact that in the theater of ancient Greece the chorus sang and danced in what was called "the orchestra." It may seem strange that a man of the cloth would write about dance, but male clerics frequently danced in the pre-modern church, just as spiritual men such as shamans and dervishes have in other cultures throughout the ages.

Arbeau writes his dance treatise in the form of a master-pupil dialogue. His pupil is a young law student who, like Beethoven some two hundred years later, wished to improve his social graces by taking dancing lessons. Arbeau patiently describes the popular dances of the day, laboriously detailing the steps for each. He tells us what is in fashion and what is not. From him we glean unexpected information about the performance practices of the day: that a harpsichord playing octaves regularly in its low range could simulate and replace a drum beat; that a tambourine might also give the beat; that a solo violin might accompany a dance; or that, if instruments were not at hand, singers could sing a tune for the dancers. Arbeau specifically recommends the dance music "of the recently deceased Pierre Attaingnant" and gives his address in Paris, should the reader wish to buy dance music from his shop.

Arbeau provides an amusing insight into the social mores of the day. The pupil is encouraged to improve himself because "by learning fencing, dancing, and tennis you may be an agreeable companion to ladies and gentlemen alike." Ladies should do likewise because "they lead sedentary lives, intent upon their knitting, embroidery, and needlework, and are subject to a variety of ill-humours, which have need to be dispelled by some temperate exercise." After dancing, the gentlemen are permitted to kiss their mistresses "to ascertain if they are shapely or emit an unpleasant odor as of bad meat." Finally, Arbeau, who was sixty-nine when he wrote his treatise, suggests how to deport oneself on the dance floor:

When you dance in company never look down at your feet to see whether you are performing the steps correctly. Keep your head and body erect and appear self-possessed. Spit and blow your nose sparingly, or if needs must, turn your head away and use a fair white handkerchief. Converse affably in a low, modest voice, your hands at your sides, neither hanging limp nor moving nervously. Be suitably and neatly dressed, your hose well secured and your shoes clean; and remember this advice not only when you are dancing the galliard but in performing all other kinds of dance as well.[1]

ORCHESOGRAPHY

RÉVÉRENCE

❋ FIGURE 22-4

A couple executing a "révérence" as depicted in Thoinot Arbeau's *Orchésographie* (1589), as reproduced in the English edition of Mary Steward Evans, p. 80.

The pavane was usually followed by the **galliard,** a fast leaping dance in triple meter. The basic unit of this dance and its music involves six beats and six steps in $\frac{6}{4}$ time. The galliard proceeds at a much faster tempo than the pavane, and the beat is now carried by the quarter note (minim), as can be seen in the third galliard from Attaingnant's *Second Livre de danceries* (Ex. 22-6). Most important, the steps of the galliard are much different from those of the pavane. The galliard involves a succession of fast steps with periodic leaps (*sauts*) into the air. Each step takes place within the space of a single quarter note. The principal leap (*saut majeur*) occurs on beat five of the six-beat phrase, and this accounts for the frequent use of rhythmic hemiola, with stress suddenly coming on beats three and five of the six-beat phrase. Thus if the stately pavane was a slow dance for the old, the leaping galliard was a show dance for the young. An athletic couple would enter the dance floor together but then dance separately as one or the other took the lead. Queen Elizabeth I of England was famous as a dancer of the galliard and a related dance called the volta, in which the woman was tossed so high that she "will feel her brain reeling and her head full of dizzy whirlings" (see Fig. 27-1).[2] With leaps by solo dancers, the galliard and similar dances must have approached what we today call ballet.

EXAMPLE 22-6

LISTENING CUE

ANONYMOUS
Pavane and Galliard (1547)

CD 3/10 and
Thomson-Schirmer Website
Anthology, Nos. 61a, 61b

Ultimately, in the course of the sixteenth century, other dances were added to, or replaced, the pavane and galliard. The allemande, for example, made its first appearance in an Attaingnant print in 1557, and Arbeau discusses the courante and gavotte in his treatise of 1589. The practice of stringing together several dances, each with its own tempo, meter, and mood, intensified in France and Italy after 1550, and eventually led to the Baroque instrumental suite, which culminated around 1720 in those of Bach and Handel.

SUMMARY

Paris regained its position as an important cultural and artistic center in the first half of the sixteenth century. King Francis I (r. 1515–1547) encouraged the growth of scholarship and the cultivation of music as well as the medium by which to disseminate both, namely printing. Between 1528 and 1557 the firm of Pierre Attaingnant published virtually all of the music that survives today from Paris in the first half of the sixteenth century, to wit, Masses, motets, instrumental dances, and, especially, popular songs. During this period, composers in and around Paris developed a new style of polyphonic song called the "Parisian chanson." Here the subject matter is topical and speaks of everyday life in a realistic way. The poetic text determines the overall structure of the music, and the rhythm of the poem usually sets the rhythm of the music as well. Pierre Attaingnant also published instrumental arrangements of songs, as well as ten collections of dances for lute, keyboard, or instrumental consort. These include the older *basse danse* as well as the newer pavane and galliard. The pavane is a slow, stately dance in duple meter constructed of four-bar phrases, while the galliard, made up of six-beat units, is a faster dance in triple meter involving quick steps and athletic leaps. Combining several dances of different moods and styles ultimately led to the Baroque dance suite.

KEY TERMS

Francis I	intabulation	Thoinot Arbeau
Pierre Attaingnant	tablature	*Orchésographie*
Parisian chanson	pavane	galliard
patter-song		

Chapter **23**

Renaissance Instruments and Instrumental Music

The greatest glories of Renaissance music, without doubt, are to be found in its vocal pieces, specifically in the Masses, motets, madrigals, and chansons of composers such as Josquin, Lassus, Palestrina, and Byrd, for example. Measured purely in terms of musical sales, vocal music was more in demand in the Renaissance than instrumental music. Around 1550 music publishers produced about fifteen prints of vocal music for every one of instrumental. But there is an explanation for this seeming imbalance: before 1500 almost all instrumental music was performed by aural memory and not from written scores, and after 1500 much of it continued to be performed in this way. Also, lute intabulations and keyboard scores were generally more expensive to print than vocal part books. Nevertheless, the sixteenth century was an important moment in the history of instrumental music. The printing press enabled instrumental music to circulate farther afield than before. Finally, new instruments appeared, including the guitar, viol, and violin, and new instrumental genres were created, such as the prelude, ricercar, and fantasia.

✤ KEYBOARD INSTRUMENTS

Organ

The organ was first widely introduced into churches only during the late Middle Ages, specifically in the fourteenth century. Most organs were "show pieces" embodying the newest technology in metallurgy and scientific measurement. For that reason organs were usually put in the people's part of the church at the back (west end), where they could be seen and heard by all. By the sixteenth century, many churches in Europe had two organs, a large one at the back and a smaller one in the area of the church called the choir (east end). This second instrument could more easily accompany singers near the altar. The largest of the church organs had two keyboards for the hands and a pedal keyboard as well. Smaller portative organs possessing a single keyboard were also present in the dwellings of monks and canons (high-ranking churchmen) in monasteries and cathedrals, as well as in residences of the aristocracy and well-to-do (see Fig. 11-5). On these domestic organs, performers played keyboard arrangements of both sacred vocal music and popular songs. The monks enjoyed a good tune as much as their secular brethren.

In fact, one of the largest sources of Renaissance organ music was once owned by a monastery. It is called the **Buxheim Organ Book,** Buxheim being the site of a monastery that still exists today near Munich in southern Germany. The manuscript (Fig. 23-1) was written about 1470 and contains 256 compositions for organ, almost all of them anonymous arrangements of sacred and secular vocal music. Notice that the Buxheim Organ Book is written in **keyboard tablature,** a combination of note symbols (for the fast-moving upper part) and pitch-letter names (for the lower parts). In principle, tablature in music directs the performer's fingers to a specific spot on an instrument, in this case a key called A or F, for example. Tablature of this sort continued fashionable for three centuries, and was sometimes used by J.S. Bach when he composed for the organ.

Notice also in Figure 23-1 that for the first time we see what appear to be bar lines, or measure lines, in the music. The lines are not always consistently placed, but they generally mark off units (measures) of equal duration. Bar lines are found in keyboard and lute tablatures much earlier than they appear in vocal music, perhaps because composers thought it necessary to show vertical alignment in music where the notes are superimposed in score format. To hear an organ from the Renaissance, go to CD 3/13.

Clavichord, Harpsichord, and Virginal

The **clavichord** is a medieval instrument (see Chapter 11) that produces sound when a tiny metal tangent in the shape of a "T" is pushed into the string from beneath. The tangent does not so much pluck as caress the string by vibrating against it from below. Consequently, the sound of the clavichord is very quiet, the softest of any musical instrument. Yet in one important way it is the most expressive of the keyboard instruments; because the tangent remains in contact with the string, the performer can push slightly up or down on the key and create a vibrato, as on the violin.

✤ FIGURE 23-1

An anonymous setting of the chant *Salve, Regina,* written in keyboard tablature and preserved in the Buxheim Organ Book. Notice the presence of measure or bar lines.

Bayerische Staatsbibliothek, Munich

The **harpsichord** first appeared in the Low Countries around 1440 (see Chapter 19). It creates sound when a key is depressed, and this in turn pushes a lever upward. Attached to the lever is a plectrum or pick (then made of crow's quill, today made of plastic) that plucks the tight wire string. A **virginal** is a smaller harpsichord with the strings running at right angles to the keys. (For more on the virginal, see the discussion of the Fitzwilliam Virginal Book, Chapter 27.) In the Renaissance these keyboard instruments did not have legs or a stand, but were simply set upon a table (Fig. 23-2). The harpsichord was best known in Italy, the virginal in northern Europe, and the clavichord everywhere.

Although the organ, clavichord, harpsichord, and virginal differ greatly in size and sound, they all shared the same musical repertory during the Renaissance. Publishers encouraged this "one size fits all" approach to keyboard music because they sold more copies of the printed score. A uniform method also applied to fingering for all keyboard instruments. This approach to fingering differed greatly from what we do today on the organ, harpsichord, and piano. Renaissance performers had essentially a "thumbless" approach to the instrument. Even when running up and down the scale, they would avoid using the thumb and would continually cross 2 over 3 or vice versa, as can be seen in Example 23-1. To see how this looked in practice, turn to Figure 27-2, which shows a young woman playing a virginal using this 2-3 technique. To hear a clavichord, go to CD 7/8; to hear a harpsichord, go to CD 3/22.

EXAMPLE 23-1

🌊 F I G U R E 2 3 - 2

Emperor Maximilian I in his music room, from Hans Burgkmair the Elder's woodcut entitled *Maximilian I Surrounded by His Court Musicians and Instruments* (c1514). On the table we see a keyboard instrument, most likely a clavichord. Above it is a viol, and next to it on the lower left, a crumhorn. Many other instruments, including organ, harp, drums, lute, sackbut, shawm, recorder, and transverse flute, are also visible.

  STRING INSTRUMENTS

During the Renaissance the medieval psaltery, harp, and vielle gradually disappeared, supplanted by members of the viol and violin families, while the medieval lute only grew in popularity.

Lute

The **lute** is a pear-shaped instrument with six sets of strings called courses, then usually made of animal gut, now of wire. The most distinctive feature of the lute is the peg box that turns back at a right angle to the fingerboard (Fig. 23-3). Wrapped around the fingerboard at measured intervals are thin strips of leather that create frets, as on a modern guitar. These make it possible to mark and play the half-steps of the scale with ease. The performer stops the string at a fret to produce the desired pitch.

During the sixteenth century, the lute became the most popular of all musical instruments. Although the lute has many strings, and thus takes a long time to tune, it enjoys one distinct advantage—you can walk around with it. The French publisher Pierre Attaingnant issued more than ten times as many lute collections as he did those for keyboard. Similarly, in England surviving lute pieces outnumber keyboard works about 4 to 1, there being roughly sixteen hundred lute pieces but only about four hundred for keyboard.

Lute music, like keyboard music in the Renaissance, was written in a special type of notation called tablature. **Lute tablature** directs the fingers to stop strings at specific frets so as to produce sounds. Example 23-2 provides a diplomatic facsimile of a page of French lute tablature as printed in Paris by Pierre Attaingnant in 1529, along with modern transcription (above). A staff of six spaces serves to represent the six courses, or strings, of the lute. The top space visually indicates the highest sounding string. The lute, then as now, is usually tuned G, c, f, a, d', g', and thus the highest space represents the open string g' above our middle c'. All open strings are indicated by the letter "a", all first frets by "b", and so forth. The duration of each pitch is set by a simple system of vertical stems with each additional flag on a stem indicating a duration half as long as that of the next higher value. Exact duration matters less on the lute than on other instruments, because the sounds die away so quickly. The essential features of Renaissance lute tablature are still in use in guitar notation today. To hear the sound of the lute, go to CD 3/9.

Bridgeman Art Library

✿ FIGURE 23-3
Young ladies performing a chanson by Claudin de Sermisy. The singer in the back reads from a rotulus (sheet music) accompanied by a small lute and transverse flute. The flutist plays from a soprano part book, and two other part books are stacked before her.

EXAMPLE 23-2

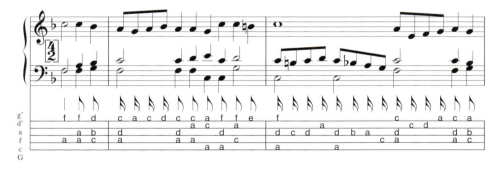

New String Instruments from Spain: *Vihuela* (Spanish Guitar) and the Viol

The lute entered western Europe via Spain, having been brought there by the Arabs in the early Middle Ages. During the late fifteenth century, two new fretted string instruments related to the lute emerged in Spain and then, like the lute, spread around the West. These were the *vihuela* (Spanish guitar) and the viol.

The **vihuela** is a plucked string instrument with a waisted body, and a long pole-neck that serves as a fingerboard (Fig. 23-4). Our modern classical guitar is a direct descendant of the *vihuela*. Because the *vihuela* was plucked, it was often called the *vihuela de mano* (hand guitar). Related to it was a similar Spanish instrument called the *vihuela de arco* (bowed guitar) that was better known in its day as the viol.

Contrary to general opinion, the viol was not a medieval instrument, but one that developed in Spain around 1475. The **viol** (see Fig. 24-2) had six strings and was fretted and tuned like the lute and *vihuela,* but it was bowed and not plucked. It came in three sizes—treble, tenor, and bass—and was played with the instrument resting on the lap and legs. Thus the viol is often called by the Italian name **viola da gamba** (leg viol). Having entered Italy from Spain, the viol quickly spread to all of northern Europe, including England. Throughout the Renaissance it served as the principal bowed string instrument for high art music. Only in the Baroque period did the viols yield in prominence to the members of a different string family, that of the violin. To hear the sound of a viol, go to CD 3/10.

Violin

The violin is only slightly younger than the viol. Violins first appear in northern Italy around 1520 in towns such as Cremona, Brescia, Mantua, and Ferrara. Indeed, Cremona became the center of violin building, made famous by generations of the Amati family, who standardized its shape and size. Unlike the viol, which is played off the chest or the legs, the violin is held off the shoulder. From its inception, the violin was smaller than the viol, and this may account for the diminutive name *violino* (little viol), from which the final "o" was eventually dropped, giving us in English "violin." Naturally, its small size caused the violin to produce higher pitches, and its tone generally was brighter and more penetrating. The early violin had only three, or sometimes four, strings and did not make use of frets. It was tuned in fifths (g, d', a' or g, d', a', e") instead of fourths, as was generally true of the viols. Because of its brighter, more penetrating sound, the violin was preferred for dance music. In the course of time, larger, lower-sounding instruments of the violin family were developed, namely the viola and the violoncello. The modern double bass, however, is not a relative of the violin family, but is a descendent of the viol, being tuned not in fifths but fourths.

Throughout the sixteenth century, the viol, not the violin, was considered the aristocrat of string instruments. Members of the violin family were thought more low class, appropriate for professional and semi-professional musicians to play for dancing in taverns or cavorting through the streets. Because of their "wilder" associations, the Roman Catholic Church sometimes ordered violins destroyed. Not until the seventeenth century, during the Baroque period, would the violin become the dominant bowed string instrument, the *sine qua non* for the early orchestra.

✿ WIND INSTRUMENTS

Recorders and flutes

Recorders were usually called *fleuste* (French), *flauto* (Italian), or *flöte* (German) during the Renaissance. What we today call the flute (the transverse flute) was known as the **German flute,** *fleuste d'Allemande* (Fig. 23-3). Recorders and flutes were made of wood, or occasionally of ivory. Recorders came in many sizes, from smaller than soprano down to the great-bass. Each had a range of about an octave and a sixth, and each sounded an octave higher than written. When a group of recorders, or viols, or any instruments of the same family played together they produced a **consort**—an

✿ **FIGURE 23-4**

A representation of Orpheo (Orpheus) playing a *vihuela* (Spanish guitar) from the *Libro de musica de vihuela* of Luis Milán (1535/1536).

ensemble of instruments all of one family. When instruments of different types played together, as was the case in the loud wind band, what resulted was called a **broken consort** (or mixed ensemble). Generally speaking, Renaissance instrumentalists did not double musical lines; a five-part piece was played by five instruments, and a three-part piece by a trio, for example.

The Renaissance Wind Bands: Trumpet, Sackbut, Shawm, Crumhorn, and Cornett

During the early Renaissance two bands of wind instruments emerged from the group originally called the *hauts instruments* (see Chapter 19). One was an ensemble of trumpets, which sometimes combined with kettledrums (early timpani). This group was ceremonial, its music essentially restricted to fanfares. During the sixteenth century, though, some trumpeters developed the ability to play very high, in the so-called **clarino register.** Later, in the Baroque period, the clarino register was exploited by such composers as Torelli, Handel, and Bach (see Chapter 33).

A second ensemble, more important musically, also developed at this time: the loud wind band. By about 1500 it usually included two or three shawms and one or two sackbuts, and thus was a broken consort. As we have seen (Chapter 19), the sackbut was the predecessor of the modern trombone and the shawm of the oboe. In fact, already in 1589 Thoinot Arbeau (see Chapter 22) refers to the shawm as the "**hautboys**" (oboe). In the course of the Renaissance, the loud wind band expanded to as many as eight players and new instrumental colors were added, mainly the sound of the crumhorn and cornett. The **crumhorn** (curved horn) is a capped double-reed wooden instrument with a curving shape (see Fig. 23-2). It has a range of a tenth and produces a buzzing sound similar to the noise of a kazoo. The **cornett** is also a wooden instrument with fingerholes, but is played with a mouthpiece and sounds in the soprano range. Its tone is something like that of a soft trumpet but with a more hollow, "wooden" sound, and it blends particularly well with the sackbut.

During the late Renaissance the loud wind band went by various names, among them *alta cappella* (loud choir) in Italy and *Stadtpfeifer* (town pipers) in German-speaking lands. Figure 23-5 shows a group of town pipers playing during a religious progression in Antwerp. Clearly visible are (right to left) sackbut, tenor shawm, alto shawm, cornett, tenor shawm, and an early bassoon. Most important, from the early sixteenth century onward, many wind bands accompanied church choirs in the performance of sacred music during religious services. Wind instruments, particularly cornett and sackbut, came to enjoy a special association with sacred music during the Renaissance, and they would continue to do so through the time of Mozart. To hear the instruments of a Renaissance wind band, go to CD 2/22 or CD 3/11.

✿ **FIGURE 23-5**

Detail from painting by Denis van Alsloot of a religious procession in Antwerp showing, from right to left, sackbut, tenor shawm, alto shawm, cornett, tenor shawm, and early bassoon.

© Museo del Prado, Madrid

✿ INSTRUMENTAL GENRES

The Renaissance witnessed the creation of several new musical genres that sprang forth because of the quickening interest in instrumental music. Many of these genres would remain in vogue for centuries hereafter.

Arrangements, Intabulations, and Variations

Chansons, madrigals, motets, and Masses—the four principal genres of Renaissance vocal music—were often arranged for keyboard, lute, or guitar. We have seen how one arranger refashioned Claudin de Sermisy's chanson *Tant que vivray* for lute and for keyboard, for example (see Chapter 22). Such arrangements were called intabulations simply because they were written in lute or keyboard, or even guitar, tablature. When adapting a vocal work for instrument, the arranger invariably made use of the ornamental style of instrumental writing favored at the time (see Ex. 22-4). Ornaments had the practical advantage of sustaining sounds that would quickly decay on softer instruments.

In addition to instrumental arrangements, composers wrote variations on preexisting melodies, be they the ancient chants of the church or the hit tunes of the day. Such variations were not transcriptions or arrangements of preexisting works, but entirely new compositions. By the end of the sixteenth century, many composers were also writing variations on popular bass lines and harmonic patterns. For an example of a set of variations on a popular tune, see Thomas Morley's setting of *Goe from my window* (Chapter 27).

Dances

Dance music, of course, had been popular during the Middle Ages (see Chapter 11)—indeed, since time immemorial. During the early Renaissance, dances came to be grouped in pairs. A slow duple dance was followed by a fast triple one: the *basse danse* by the *tordion* (see Chapter 19), for example, and the pavane by the galliard (see Chapter 22). Toward the end of sixteenth century the allemande would come to precede the pavane and galliard. Thus the nucleus of the Baroque dance suite, later exploited by Corelli, Handel, and Bach (see Chapter 34), was already in place by the end of the Renaissance.

Prelude

As the name suggests, a **prelude** is a preliminary piece, one that comes immediately before and introduces the main musical event. An organ prelude might precede a Magnificat at Vespers, for example, or a lute prelude might introduce a lute intabulation of a chanson. The prelude had its roots in earlier improvisatory practices. It often opens with chordal strumming and follows with freely running scales or moments of light imitation. But the prelude had a function, perhaps several. While playing, the performer might make sure that the strings of the instrument were in tune. At the same time, the player could establish the mode of the piece to follow and even prefigure some of its themes. Finally, a prelude could stop conversation in its tracks and call attention to the fact that serious music was about to begin.

Ricercar

Originally the ricercar was closely related to the prelude. Indeed, the Italian word *ricercare* (to seek out) suggests much the same function as the prelude: in a short preliminary piece the performer searches for the mode and the themes of the larger piece to follow. By the mid sixteenth century, however, the ricercar had changed noticeably. Composers in Italy, influenced by the sacred vocal music of the day, now wrote fully independent pieces that contained a number of imitative sections, each with its own imitative theme. A **ricercar** can be defined as an instrumental piece, usually for lute or keyboard, similar in style to the imitative motet of the sixteenth century. During the next several centuries, composers such as Frescobaldi, Pachelbel, and Bach would continue to breathe new life into a musical genre that had originated during the Renaissance. To hear a slightly later ricercar, go to CD 4/15.

Fantasia

The word fantasia suggests a kind of music in which the composer might give free rein to the imagination. Indeed, in its early stages during the first decades of the sixteenth century, the fantasia was a freeform, seemingly spontaneous creation. By mid-century, however, the fantasia, like the ricercar, had evolved into a predominantly imitative, motet-like piece. Thus a definition of the Renaissance **fantasia** must reflect its changing style: an instrumental piece that at first allowed the composer to indulge flights of chordal or scalar fancy, but that gradually evolved into work displaying imitative counterpoint from beginning to end. Ironically, as the fantasias of Bach and Mozart demonstrate, the fantasia later shed its imitative skin and reverted back to its earlier, freer, more whimsical form.

Consider the fantasia for Spanish guitar (*vihuela*) by Miguel de Fuenllana (c1510–c1585) published in Seville, Spain, in 1554. With its predominantly imitative texture, it typifies the contrapuntal fantasia of the mid sixteenth century. Fuenllana works out four different imitative themes in succession. The first theme unfolds in four-voice imitation in the ranges of soprano, then alto, tenor, and finally bass; yet immediately the soprano and alto lines vanish. This is typical of the fantasia, and particularly of those for lute and guitar in which the sound dies quickly—the imitative voices seem to enter and disappear at will.

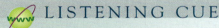

LISTENING CUE

| **MIGUEL DE FUENLLANA** | Thomson-Schirmer Website |
| Fantasia (1554) | Anthology, No. 62 |

Canzona

Originally, "canzona" was simply an Italian word designating a French chanson, more specifically the Parisian chanson of the mid sixteenth century. By the end of the century, however, a **canzona** denoted a freely composed instrumental piece, usually for organ or instrumental ensemble, which imitated the lively rhythms and lightly imitative style of the Parisian chanson. Canzonas seem to have been particularly favored by the wind bands of northern Italy, especially in Venice. The canzona composed by the Venetian organist Claudio Merulo (1533–1604) exemplifies the genre (Ex. 23-3). Although no specific instruments are called for in the score, this canzona contains the kind of music that cornetts, shawms, and sackbuts can execute well. The performers must sharply attack repeated pitches, but rarely do they play scales where speed and intonation may be an issue. Notice the repeating notes at the beginning. This is an opening rhythmic figure found in almost all canzonas: long, short, short. Notice also how the composer pairs the imitative entries so that an echo often results, a particularly exciting effect in a resonant church. In this late-Renaissance canzona by Merulo, as in most, pulsating sound is all that is needed to animate the music.

EXAMPLE 23-3

 LISTENING CUE

CLAUDIO MERULO
Canzona 5 (c1600)

CD 3/11
Anthology, No. 63

SUMMARY

By the sixteenth century many, but by no means all, of the instruments with which we are familiar today had already come into existence. Some of these, namely the sackbut (our modern trombone) have changed very little since the Renaissance. Others, such as the organ, guitar, violin, recorder, flute, shawm (modern oboe), bass shawm (bassoon), and trumpet were in place but would continue to undergo a process of evolution well into the nineteenth century. Other instruments existed in rudimentary form but were not used for art music—notably the hunting horn (the later French horn). Still others, among them the piano and clarinet, would not emerge until the eighteenth century. Yet, not all Renaissance instruments remained popular. The viol, cornett, and crumhorn fell victim to changing musical tastes. By the mid eighteenth century they had become something like musical dinosaurs, nearly extinct.

During the Renaissance several new genres appeared that remained exclusively associated with instrumental music. Of these, only the instrumental transcription did not continue to thrive during the Baroque era. The other genres—variations, the newly emerging dance suite, the prelude, ricercar, fantasia, and canzona—were intensely cultivated during the Baroque era and far beyond. Today when we practice and perform a canzona by Gabrieli, a dance suite by Handel, a prelude by Bach, or a fantasia by Mozart, Schubert, or Schumann, we perpetuate venerable musical genres that originated during the Renaissance.

KEY TERMS

Buxheim Organ Book
keyboard tablature
clavichord
harpsichord
virginal
lute
lute tablature
vihuela

viol
viola da gamba
violino
German flute
consort
broken consort
clarino register
hautboys

crumhorn
cornett
prelude
ricercar
fantasia
canzona

Music Theory in the Renaissance

Medieval music theory had been concerned with practical issues: singing the notes of the scale, identifying the consonant and dissonant intervals, and explaining the complicated notation used to signify rhythmic durations in music. Renaissance music theory is practical as well. It too was concerned with how the composer should write music and how the performer should sing or play it. But Renaissance theorists also inquired into the meaning of music. Why do we have music? What is unique about it? Why does it move us the way it does? In posing these questions, the theorists explored the aesthetics and emotive power of music, just as had the ancient Greeks. They also tried to reconstruct the particulars of ancient Greek music theory.

THE REBIRTH OF ANCIENT GREEK MUSIC THEORY

Beginning shortly before 1500, musicians began to embrace the writings on music of the ancient Greek theorists. In this they demonstrated the same humanistic desires as their fellow scholars in the other arts and sciences. Many Greek texts on music were now translated into Latin for the first time. Some musical humanists learned enough Greek to study the ancient texts in the original language. Greek terminology was again adopted by the theorists. During the late Middle Ages, for example, the modes had usually been identified simply by numbers (mode 1, mode 2, and so on); now the ancient Greek ethnic names—Dorian, Phrygian, and the like—were again commonly invoked. The complicated issue of tuning, whether that of Pythagoras or others, again came to the fore (see below). Finally, the ancient Greek genera—diatonic, chromatic, and enharmonic—were revisited. One theorist in particular, **Nicola Vicentino** (1511–c1576), championed the reinstitution of the chromatic and the enharmonic genera as a way to re-impose the power of ancient Greek music (on the genera, see Chapter 1). To this end he composed madrigals with microtonal inflections that sought to capture the shadings of the enharmonic genus in particular. He also constructed a strange new keyboard instrument called the arcicembalo. The **arcicembalo** was a harpsichord that had two keyboards, each with three rows of keys (Ex. 4-1). The two keyboards supplied thirty-six keys within each octave, an ample number to accommodate the microtonal inflections of the Greek genera. Surely a nightmare to tune, the arcicembalo did not catch on. Yet it suggests the lengths to which Renaissance musicians might go to capture the specifics, as well as the general spirit, of ancient Greek music.

EXAMPLE 4-1

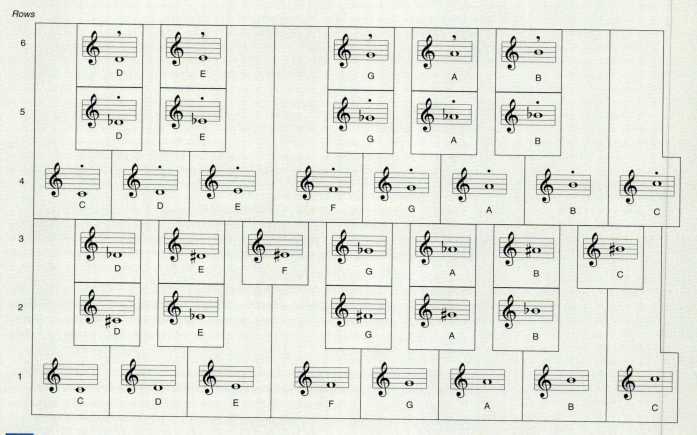

NEW RULES FOR HARMONY AND COUNTERPOINT

Where did we get the rules for harmony and counterpoint that we study today? Most originated with the composers and theorists of the Renaissance. During the Middle Ages, theorists were occupied in large measure with identifying the consonances and dissonances. As a rule, they prescribed that consonances fall on strong beats but they allowed great freedom as to how dissonance might come between consonances. Renaissance theorists, beginning with **Johannes Tinctoris** (c1435–1511), set up precise rules as to where, in what way, and for how long dissonance might last. Below is an example of three-voice counterpoint from Tinctoris's *The Art of Counterpoint* (1477). It shows how passing tones, neighboring tones, suspensions, and even a chain of suspensions should be created (Ex. 4-2). The beat is called the **tactus.** As a general rule, dissonance should come between one tactus and the next. If it comes on the tactus (beat), it should be prepared by the same pitch and sound for one tactus at most. All dissonance should be approached and left by stepwise motion, although a leap away from dissonance is occasionally tolerated.

The octave, unison, and fifth remain the primary musical consonants. Yet from the fifteenth century onward, theorists legislate that perfect consonances should not come in succession—no parallel fifths or octaves. Why? Because such sounds lack variety and diminish the integrity of the individual voices. Thirds and sixths are now considered imperfect consonances. The fourth, however, which had been a consonance during the Middle Ages, is increasingly treated as a dissonance and handled with care. Often it appears in what we today call a "4-3" suspension. Indeed, it is at this time that the concept of a suspension, called a **syncope** by Renaissance musicians, is first described by music theorists. Example 4-2 has a 9-8 and then a 4-3 suspension properly prepared and resolved in the upper voice.

EXAMPLE 4-2

Tinctoris was the first to set out strict rules of counterpoint. Later, these would be refined by other theorists such as Pietro Aaron (c1480–c1554) and Gioseffo Zarlino (1517–1590). Zarlino recognized two forms of what later would be called the triad (major and minor); he posited that the major was particularly appropriate for heroic sounds, and the minor for sad, plaintive music. The rules for chords and counterpoint further came to be codified in musical practice, particularly in the contrapuntally conservative compositions of Giovanni Pierluigi da Palestrina (1525/26–1594). By the end of the sixteenth century the pristine compositional style of Palestrina had become the model for good counterpoint. Implicit everywhere in Palestrina's music is the notion that contrary motion is to be preferred to similar motion among the outer voices, and that large leaps should be followed by a stepwise movement in the opposite direction—cardinal rules of counterpoint that we still follow today. Indeed, Palestrina's contrapuntal precepts, distilled into a teaching manual by Johann Fux in 1725, were studied and taught by Bach, Haydn, Mozart, and Beethoven, among others, into the nineteenth century and beyond.

❈ NEW MODES

During the Middle Ages, tonal structure was controlled and determined by the eight church modes (see Chapter 4), and this continued to hold true into the 1550s. But, as early as the 1470s, Renaissance theorists showed an interest in analyzing particular pieces so as to identify the modal structure of a work. Theorists now provided the names of pieces by well-known composers such as Dufay and Josquin and asked the reader to consider the modal structure of these works.

Modality in Renaissance music, the theorists tell us, should be judged by the progress of the tenor line. The final note and the range of the tenor are important considerations, but so are the position of melodic fourths and fifths within the tenor line as well as the pitches of the internal cadences. By analyzing music according to these criteria, a musician can determine the mode of a Renaissance composition.

Here, for the first time in the history of music, theorists seem to be as much interested in musical analysis—understanding and assigning value to works of art—as they are in giving prescriptive rules to composers and performers.

Equally important, Renaissance theorists expanded the number of modes, or what we would call scales. In 1547 a Swiss musical humanist named **Heinrich Glarean** (1488–1563) published his *Dodecachordon (Twelve-String Instrument)*. It acknowledged the presence of two new modes, both running up and down the white keys, one beginning on A and the other beginning on C (Ex. 4-3). By supplying each of these two new modes with a plagal partner, Glarean raised the number of modes from eight to twelve. Reaching back to Greek music theory for names, he called the first of these the **Aeolian** mode and the second the **Ionian.** Their plagals he called Hypoaeolian and Hypoionian.

EXAMPLE 4-3

Number	Name	Range	Final Pitch	Type
9	Aeolian		A	Authentic
10	Hypoaeolian		A	Plagal
11	Ionian		C	Authentic
12	Hypoionian		C	Plagal

Glarean thought he had rediscovered the ancient Greeks' system of modes—no matter that his modes were rather different from the scales the Greeks associated with these names. The important fact is that the major (Ionian) and minor (Aeolian) modes were now officially recognized. In the course of the next two centuries, these two new modes would gradually come to be used to the exclusion of all others, foreshadowing the dominance of the major and minor scales today.

❄ NEW TUNINGS AND TEMPERAMENTS

A fully chromatic keyboard with twelve half-step pitches within each octave was recognized in western Europe by the end of the fourteenth century. However, the distance between these half-steps was by no means equal. Renaissance theorists fought over what type of tuning a musician should use. Those favoring the oldest Greek method argued for what is called **Pythagorean tuning,** a process in which the octaves, fifths, and fourths are tuned in perfect 2:1, 3:2, and 4:3 ratios. While this produced fine-sounding fifths and fourths, the half-steps were not equal. Some Renaissance theorists favored a system called **just tuning,** in which the major and minor thirds were also tuned according to strict ratios (5:4 and 6:5). Just intonation reflected the growing importance of thirds and sixths in Renaissance music. But just intonation resulted not only in unequal half-steps, but unequal whole steps as well. The distance from C to D was much greater than that from D to E, for example.

Some basic triads, those around C, were beautifully tuned in perfect intervals, but those far away from C were badly out of tune. To remedy these defects, practicing musicians began to shave just a bit off the perfect fifths. The result was a **temperament**—the tuning of intervals in something slightly more or less than strict mathematical ratios.

By the early sixteenth century, however, some musicians were advocating a division of the octave into twelve equal half-steps, each with the ratio of approximately 18:17. This was called **equal temperament.** The composer Adrian Willaert (c1490–1562) wrote a motet that progressed entirely around the circle of fifths without sounding out of tune; this was possible only with equal temperament. But equal temperament did not immediately carry the day. Most harpsichords and organs continued to be tuned in Pythagorian or just tuning, or some variant thereof, well into the eighteenth century. (On the adoption of equal temperament in the eighteenth century, see Chapter 39.)

Finally, during the Renaissance there was no such thing as standardized pitch—an A in one locale might be as much as a whole step lower or higher than that pitch in another place. A set of three recorders pitched in f-c-f' made in one town might be slightly sharper or flatter than those of a similar set made by another craftsman in a neighboring city, but the players could adjust in several ways. There were rules and standards in the Renaissance, but that did not stop the process of music-making.

KEY TERMS

Nicola Vicentino	syncope	Pythagorean tuning
arcicembalo	Heinrich Glarean	just tuning
Johannes Tinctoris	Aeolian	temperament
tactus	Ionian	equal temperament

Chapter 24

Music in Three German Cities: The Protestant-Catholic Confrontation

Throughout its history, the country we now call Germany has assumed many territorial forms. During the late Middle Ages and Renaissance, German-speaking lands belonged only to a loose confederation of two hundred principalities and city-states called the **Holy Roman Empire** (Map 24-1). These lands and cities owed allegiance to the Holy Roman Emperor. There was no fixed capital of the Empire, nor in fact were there any German-speaking cities of any significant size before the sixteenth century. Perhaps for this reason, polyphonic music was not as rigorously cultivated in Germany as it was in the Low Countries, France, England, or Italy. As we have seen, the creation of polyphonic music was mainly either a courtly or an urban phenomenon. While Germany had its own dialects of Gregorian chant, what poly-

MAP 24-1
The Holy Roman Empire, c1500.

phonic art music there was in medieval Germany was often derived from the genres and styles of music coming from France.

In the later fifteenth century, however, German commerce, technology, and culture generally began to flourish. The printing industry, for example, first saw the light of day in the 1450s in the German town of Mainz. Eventually, as the quickening pace of commerce encouraged the growth of German cities, music printing began to appear in such centers as Leipzig, Nuremberg, Augsburg, and Munich.

Some of these German printers issued both religious music and religious pamphlets. They were soldiers engaged in the war of words fought between the reform-minded Protestants and the tradition-based Roman Catholics. The Protestant Reformation, as we shall see, occurred first in German-speaking lands, before spreading to Switzerland, France, the Low Countries, and England. Generally speaking, the southern (Alpine and Italian) parts of the Empire remained Catholic, while those cities and principalities to the north tended to go over to the Protestant side. Thus Alpine Innsbruck stayed in the Catholic fold, the more-northern Augsburg became Protestant, while Munich was geographically and spiritually somewhere between the two.

INNSBRUCK: MUSIC UNDER EMPEROR MAXIMILIAN I

Surrounded by snow-capped mountains, the beautiful Alpine city of Innsbruck, Austria, owes its importance to its location. Since Roman times it has sat on the main route between Germany and Italy, where that road goes across a bridge (German, "Brücke") traversing the fast-moving river Inn. In the fifteenth century, Innsbruck and the surrounding lands, called the Tyrol, were under the control of the Hapsburg family, whose greatest figure was **Emperor Maximilian I** (1459–1519). In 1477 Maximilian married Mary of Burgundy, thereby uniting the old Burgundian territories in the Low Countries to the Hapsburg lands in Germany and Austria. Eventually, Maximilian left the government of the Low Countries to his daughter Margaret (see Chapter 19), while he ruled the German and Austrian parts of the Empire from Innsbruck, Augsburg, or Vienna. Among these, Innsbruck was the preferred residence: as Maximilian said, "Innsbruck and the Tyrol are the center of the German Empire." It was here that he built a mausoleum to honor his accomplishments, and it was here that he brought his chapel.

At the center of religious and musical life at the Hapsburg court was the **Hofkapelle** (German for "court chapel"), a group of approximately twelve singers responsible for the religious music of the court. In 1496 Maximilian added a jewel to the crown of imperial singers when he hired the illustrious composer Heinrich Isaac (c1450–1517). Though born in the Low Countries, Isaac had spent many years in Florence as the principal musical ornament at the court of the ruling Medici family. But in 1494 the Medici were expelled from Florence, leaving Isaac temporarily unemployed. Two years later Maximilian recruited him for his chapel. For the next twenty years Isaac moved with the imperial court from Innsbruck, to Vienna, to Augsburg, to Constance, and elsewhere throughout the German-speaking part of the Empire. Ultimately, old and sick, Isaac was given leave to return to Florence, where he died in 1518.

Although reform-minded German Protestants began their verbal attack on the power and privileges of Rome during the early sixteenth century, Emperor Maximilian steadfastly remained a Catholic. Thus the religious music that Heinrich Isaac composed for the imperial court was polyphony for the traditional Catholic liturgy. Maximilian was fond of large-scale projects, and sometime during the early 1500s he encouraged Isaac to set polyphonically all of the Proper chants of the Catholic Mass for the major feasts of the church year. Ultimately, nearly three hundred fifty motet-like compositions appeared in Isaac's collection. It is called the **Choralis Constantinus** because it sets in polyphony chants from the German diocese of Constance. The *Choralis Constantinus* was the first systematic attempt to provide polyphony for the entire church year since the twelfth-century *Magnus liber organi* of Leoninus (see Chapter 8).

Heinrich Isaac wrote not only serious Catholic church music for the imperial Hofkapelle but also more light-hearted secular music. When in Innsbruck, the versatile Isaac set in polyphony popular strophic songs in the local vernacular tongue, in this case German. A popular or art song in German is simply called a **Lied** (pl., **Lieder**). Isaac wrote thirty-four polyphonic Lieder, almost all during his years of service to Maximilian. In these he took a simple preexisting popular tune and reworked it in one of two ways. The first way was the more traditional German approach, that of the Tenorlied. In a **Tenorlied** the preexisting tune is placed in the tenor and two or three other voices enhance it with lightly imitative polyphony. Thus the Tenorlied continues the tradition of the tenor cantus firmus. Isaac's second approach to setting a German Lied was to place the tune in the cantus and support it with chords below. In this second type of setting, with the melody on top and all voices beginning and ending phrases at the same time, we see an early manifestation of the four-part chorale style later used so effectively by J. S. Bach (see Chapter 40).

Examples 24-1a and 24-1b show the beginnings of two different settings by Heinrich Isaac of the same popular tune. The first is in the style of the Tenorlied, with the tune in the tenor; here, the alto closely imitates the tenor. The second, and later, setting by Isaac provides a more homophonic harmonization, with the melody now in the cantus.

EXAMPLE 24-1A

EXAMPLE 24-1B

Innsbruck, I must now leave you, I'm going on my way...

The popular tune that Isaac employed, one still well known by every citizen in Innsbruck today, is a love song, addressed not to a man or woman, but to a city. As the title and text show, in *Innsbruck, ich muss dich lassen (Innsbruck, I must now leave you)*, a musician laments his departure from this beloved place, a sentiment Isaac must have felt as he moved all too often with Emperor Maximilian from one imperial German city to another. Soon Protestant Germans would alter the text to make the music serve as a religious piece, creating *O Welt, ich muss dich lassen (O World, I must now leave you)*.

LISTENING CUE

HEINRICH ISAAC
Innsbruck, ich muss dich lassen (c1510)

CD 3/12
Anthology, Nos. 64a
and 64b

Among the musicians at Innsbruck in these years was the organist Paul Hofhaimer (1459–1537), who first arrived there in 1478. For more than thirty years Hofhaimer served the family of Emperor Maximilian I, first in Innsbruck and later in Augsburg. When Maximilian died in 1519, Hofhaimer assumed the post of organist at the cathedral of Salzburg, a position that Mozart would occupy some two hundred sixty years later.

Contemporaries agreed that Hofhaimer had no equal as an organist. They marveled at his powers of invention as he improvised at the keyboard. Unfortunately, only a small portion of Hofhaimer's improvisatory art comes down to us in notated form. His *Salve, Regina*, one of two surviving sacred pieces for organ, is built on the old Gregorian antiphon in honor of the Virgin Mary. As in much organ music of the Renaissance, Hofhaimer's setting makes use of **alternatim** technique—the verses of the chant are assigned to alternating performing forces. Here, the first verse is given to the organ, the second to a choir to sing in monophonic chant, the third back to the organ, and so on. A glance at the score of *Salve, Regina* (Ex. 24-2) will show that Hofhaimer makes use of cantus firmus technique here as well. He has the ancient chant *Salve, Regina* (see Ex. 18-4) sound forth in long notes in the range of the tenor voice. Above this cantus firmus the right hand plays an array of ornamental patterns; from the very beginning, keyboard music has always demanded more of the right hand than the left. The right-hand figuration is technically demanding, yet sometimes mechanical and repetitive. We must remember, however, that the organ at this time had no centuries-old tradition behind it, as was true for vocal music. Even in the fifteenth century, church organs were something of a novelty. Much of the allure of the organ came, not from the beauty of the part-writing, but from the unusual brilliance and power of the instrument itself—from sound rather than idea.

EXAMPLE 24-2

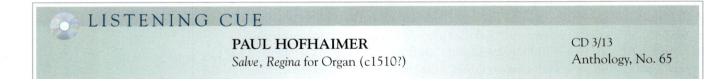

LISTENING CUE

PAUL HOFHAIMER
Salve, Regina for Organ (c1510?)

CD 3/13
Anthology, No. 65

✸ THE REFORMATION: MUSIC IN AUGSBURG

One of the cities that Heinrich Isaac, Paul Hofhaimer, and their patron Emperor Maximilian I often visited was Augsburg, Germany. Because Augsburg was a republic (free city) beholden to no prince and situated near the geographical center of the Empire, it was an ideal site for meetings of the imperial Diet. The **Diet** (or **Reichstag**) was a legislative assembly that met almost annually to voice opinions on the finances of the Empire and on affairs of state. So often did Emperor Maximilian convene the Diet in Augsburg, and his court reside there for extended periods, that the citizens jokingly came to call him "Burghermeister" (mayor) of the city. Figure 24-1 shows the imperial Hofkapelle in Augsburg about 1518 with a Mass in progress. To the center right, Maximilian kneels in prayer; in the lower right, the singers of the Hofkapelle group before a large music manuscript; and to the left, seated at the organ, is imperial court organist Paul Hofhaimer.

In the early sixteenth century, Augsburg was a thriving commercial center of more than 25,000 inhabitants, the most progressive city in southern Germany. Foremost among the citizens was Jacob Fugger, appropriately nicknamed "the Rich" (1459–1525). Fugger and his descendants were money lenders, the first family north of the Alps to institute the now-popular practice of "private banking" for rulers such as Emperor Maximilian. They were also patrons of intellectuals and artists, and they collected music manuscripts and printed part books, many of which survive today. In 1514 Jacob Fugger lent a large sum of money to Pope Leo X to rebuild St. Peter's Basilica in Rome. To repay him, Leo sold indulgences to true-believing Catholics; this led Protestant reformers to protest the "commercialization of the Gospel." But, as fate would have it, the staunchly Catholic Fuggers came to be linked to the radical reformer Martin Luther; in 1512 they chose as the site of their private chapel in Augsburg the small monastic church of St. Anne, a church that Luther would soon come to call home.

On 31 October 1517, **Martin Luther** (1483–1546) nailed his **Ninety-Five Theses** (objections to current church practices) to the door of the castle church in Wittenberg, Germany. This defiant act was an important moment in the **Reformation**—the religious revolution that began as a movement to reform Catholicism and ended with the establishment of Protestantism. Soon Luther's theses were widely circulated, and he was called to Augsburg, to the church of St. Anne, to defend himself against the charge of heresy brought by the pope. In brief, Luther and other Protestant theologians wished to bring an end to the following church practices:

- The selling of indulgences—a forgiveness of sin sold by the church with the promise that the buyer, and members of his family, might thereby spend less time in Purgatory after death
- The selling of church services (such as last rites and funeral services)
- The selling of church offices to the highest bidder
- The excessive veneration of saints, which was seen as idolatry
- The growth of religious holidays, especially saints' days, on which commercial activity could not take place
- The use of writings other than the Bible (medieval legends of the saints, for example) as sources of religious truth
- The insistence that leaders of the church remain celibate (unmarried)
- The existence of monks and nuns and thus monasteries and convents

Augsburg, with a tradition of independent thinking, was particularly sympathetic to Luther's views. On Christmas Day 1524, the church of St. Anne celebrated the Mass according to the reformed version of Martin Luther. Two years later, in 1526, Luther published this as his *Deudsche Messe* (German Mass). It encouraged the use of the German language rather than Latin and allowed a larger role for the congregation in the service. Luther was concerned that each person understand and

❀ FIGURE 24-1
Emperor Maximilian I hears Mass in his chapel at Augsburg around 1518.

participate in the service in his own language. Unlike the Catholic Church, which tried to effect a uniform Mass from one church to the next, Luther allowed Protestant churches a great deal of local freedom as to how the service might unfold. Rural communities tended to say the Mass in German, while more "learned" city churches retained much Latin. In the university town of Leipzig, for example, reformed churches continued to sing portions of the service in Latin beyond the time of Bach. Nevertheless, the Lutheran service everywhere differed from the Catholic in several important ways:

- The Mass and the canonical hours were reduced to just the Mass and an evening service.
- The vernacular language was allowed to replace Latin within the service.
- The congregation, and not just the trained choir, was expected to sing during the service.
- The Gloria of the Mass was omitted.
- Simple hymns replaced several parts of the Proper of the Mass.
- Sermons were regularly preached at both Mass and the evening service.

Martin Luther had a fine voice, played flute and lute, could compose pleasing melodies, and could harmonize a tune in four parts. He had come to love the splendor and richness of Gregorian chant from his years of service as a Catholic priest, and he especially enjoyed the polyphony of Josquin des Prez (see Chapter 21). Thus Luther was not disposed to remove music from the service of the reformed church, only to simplify it, making it more accessible to the people. To that end, he and his followers began to assemble a body of church music that centered around the chorale.

A **chorale** is a monophonic spiritual melody or religious folksong, what many Christian denominations today would simply call a "hymn." Chorale melodies are usually simple and their text strophic. To fashion a collection of tunes appropriate for the new Protestant churches, the reformers pressed into service many old Gregorian chants, changing their texts from Latin to German. In this way the Easter chant *Victimae Paschali laudes* (*Hail the Paschal Victim*) became the chorale tune *Christ lag in Todesbanden* (*Christ Lay in Death's Dark Prison*), for example. Popular tunes became chorales, too, by switching the text from profane to sacred. ("Why should the Devil have all the good tunes?" was asked at the time.) Thus, the charming melody *Innsbruck, ich muss dich lassen* became the sacred tune *O Welt, ich muss dich lassen*, as we have seen. Such a transformation—secular piece to sacred, or sacred to secular—is called a **contrafactum** (pl., **contrafacta**). Perhaps the most famous example of a German contrafactum is the conversion of the love song *Mein Gmütt ist mir verwirret* (*I'm all shook up*) into the chorale *O Haupt voll Blut und Wunden* (*O Sacred Head Now Wounded*), which later became the central chorale of J.S. Bach's *St. Matthew Passion* (1727). Others chorales were newly composed. Luther himself created about twenty new chorale tunes, setting them to simple German texts that explained the Scriptures.

Of the chorales composed by Martin Luther, the most famous is *Ein feste Burg ist unser Gott* (*A Mighty Fortress Is Our God*). As with many of his chorales, Luther shaped the music into an **AAB** form. The melody has a simple rhythm, is predominantly step-wise without difficult leaps, has short clear-cut phrases and a strongly implied tonal center—all qualities designed to make the tune easy to learn and remember. The text, again by Luther himself, is simply his German adaptation of Psalm 46, *God is our refuge*.

EXAMPLE 24-3

| Ein | fe - ste Burg | ist | un - ser | Gott, ein | gu - te | Wehr und | Waf | - fen. |
| Er | hilft uns frei | aus | al - ler | Not, die | uns jetzt hat be | - trof | - fen. |

Der al - te bö - se Feind, mit Ernst er's jetzt meint, gross Macht un viel

List sein grau - sam Rüst - ung ist, auf Erd' ist nicht seins Glei - chen.

Ein feste Burg ist unser Gott
Ein gute Wehr und Waffen.
Er hilft uns frei aus aller Not
Die uns jetzt hat betroffen.
Der alte böse Feind
Mit Ernst er's jetzt meint,
Gross Macht und viel List
Sein grausam Rüstung ist,
Auf Erd' ist nicht seins Gleichen.

A   A mighty fortress is our God
      A bulwark never failing.

A   Our helper he amid the flood
      Our mortal ills prevailing.

B   For still our ancient foe
      Does seek to work us woe,
      His craft and power are great
      And armed with cruel hate,
      On earth is not his equal.

LISTENING CUE

MARTIN LUTHER
Ein feste Burg ist unser Gott (1529)

CD 3/14
Anthology, No. 66a

To spread the new music among his followers, Luther encouraged the publication of his chorales as broadside sheets (sheet music) and in printed hymnals. He also urged a colleague, **Johann Walter** (1496–1570), to set the chorales in polyphony, so as to create a repertory for trained church choirs. In 1524 Walter published his ***Geistliche Gesangbüchlein*** *(Little Book of Spiritual Songs)*. This collection of settings of thirty-eight Protestant hymns and five Latin motets became the first monument of Protestant church music. Walter's *Gesangbüchlein* provided a core repertory for Lutheran church choirs, and over the course of the century it appeared in many different editions. Its purpose, however, was as much pedagogical as it was theological. The preface by Luther himself explains:

> And therefore [these songs] were arranged in four parts [some in fact are written in three voices and others in five] to give the young—who should at any rate be trained in music and other fine arts—something so that they will put aside love ballads and dirty songs, and learn wholesome things in their place, thus combining the good with the pleasing, as is proper for the young.[1]

Accordingly, these chorale settings were taught in Lutheran schools as part of a student's education in the arts. Once the chorale setting had been learned by heart in school, it might be sung in the service of God in the church.

In a later edition of the *Geistliche Gesangbüchlein*, Johann Walter published a four-voice setting of Luther's *Ein feste Burg ist unser Gott*. The chorale tune is placed in the tenor, following the tradition of the Tenorlied. Above and below it, the other three voices provide a chordal support and lightly animated counterpoint. For modern ears it is difficult to hear the chorale because the tenor is covered by the surrounding voices. Yet sixteenth-century listeners, long familiar with tenor cantus firmus technique, would have had no difficulty perceiving the chorale and its intended message: God alone is a refuge for devout Protestants.

LISTENING CUE

MARTIN LUTHER

Ein feste Burg ist unser Gott (1529)
Arranged by Johann Walter

CD 3/15
Anthology, No. 66b

Augsburg continued to be a hotbed of religious conflict as most, but by no means all, of its citizens converted to Lutheranism. At the Diet of Augsburg in 1530, supporters of Luther presented to the new emperor, Charles V, what has come to be called **The Augsburg Confession,** the definitive doctrinal statement of the Lutheran faith. (Exactly three centuries later Felix Mendelssohn would commemorate this event in his *Reformation* Symphony and quote Luther's famous hymn *Ein feste Burg ist unser Gott*.) In 1555 supporters of Luther and Catholic Emperor Charles V agreed to the **Peace of Augsburg.** This treaty marked a milestone in the history of Western political processes, for it was the first attempt to grant Protestants and Catholics alike a measure of religious freedom within the same city.

❋ ORLANDE DE LASSUS AND THE COURT OF MUNICH

If Innsbruck remained steadfastly Catholic and Augsburg became a stronghold of Lutheranism, the city of Munich, Germany, found itself somewhere in the middle, both in terms of religion and geography (see Map 24-1). Though situated just north of the Alps, sixteenth-century Munich, the capital of the duchy of Bavaria, still felt the pressure of Protestant reform. In the 1560s the leader of the Munich court chapel, Ludwig Daser, was a Protestant; its foremost composer, Orlande de Lassus (1532–1594), was a Catholic; and the leader of the court, Duke Albrecht V, vacillated between the two religions, ultimately siding with the Catholics.

Like the art of the great German painter Albrecht Dürer, the music of Orlande de Lassus found favor with Protestants as well as Catholics. Orlande de Lassus (known to Italians as Orlando di Lasso) was by far the most famous composer of his day. His music was published in all of the important printing centers of Europe, including Venice, Rome, Nuremberg, Antwerp, Paris, and London, as well as Munich. An international figure, he wrote more than two thousand works in all genres of his day: sixty Masses, more than one thousand motets, and countless Italian madrigals, French chansons, and German Lieder. Yet Lasso was above all a great master of the motet. When it came to writing religious music, the more diversified nature of the motet text suited his expressive genius.

Orlande de Lassus was not born in Germany, but in the Low Countries near the small town of Mons, south of Brussels. As a youth, Lassus was a choirboy at the church of St. Nicolas in Mons, and tradition has it that he was kidnapped three times owing to the beauty of his voice. He spent his early adulthood as a singer in Italy, and his first publication, a collection of madrigals and chansons, appeared when he was only twenty-three. In 1558 Lassus was recruited to be a tenor in the chapel of Duke Albrecht of Bavaria in Munich; here he stayed for the remainder of his life, working his way up to master of the chapel and personal confidant of the duke. Figure 24-2 shows the chapel of Albrecht, along with the instrumentalists of the court, as if they were all about to provide chamber music for a ducal banquet. In fact, this banquet hall, especially built by Albrecht for such ceremonial occasions, was often a place for music-making, for what the Germans call *Tafelmusik* (chamber music, both vocal and instrumental, for the dinner table).

Duke Albrecht was not only a lover of music but also of the visual arts. During the 1550s he constructed next to his residence in Munich an art gallery (the first art gallery north of the Alps) to house the treasures from classical antiquity that he had purchased in Rome—an appreciation of ancient art symbolic of the Renaissance. The rooms above the art gallery were configured to serve as a library, and here the duke put the splendid books he purchased or commissioned. The most lavish of the ducal books is a two-volume set of Penitential Psalms newly composed by Lassus—lavish because each page of Lassus's music is surrounded by color paintings of the biblical scenes and themes expressed by the psalms (Fig. 24-3). So artistically splendid was this pair of books that Duke Albrecht kept them in the new library, rather than with the music books in the chapel. This was sacred music in the service of the visual arts, but what music it was!

Many aspects of Lassus's musical style are immediately audible in his Penitential Psalms: the richness in harmonic color, quick changes in texture, rapid shifts in the number of voices, and forceful yet clear text declamation. Lassus's music is more compact, more harmonically conceived, and more economical in utterance than that of his contemporaries. His aim was not to weave together long strands of imitative counterpoint, but rather to convey the intensity of a bold text through an equally bold musical gesture, as he does superbly in his Penitential Psalms. Lassus's expressive, text-oriented style can be heard nowhere better than in his settings of the Penitential Psalms.

The **Psalter** (150 psalms of the Old Testament) is one of the great treasures of both the Christian and Jewish faiths. Early in the history of the Christian church, seven psalms were given special attention. They are called the **Penitential Psalms** because their texts express a sense of sin and because they petition God for mercy in an especially personal, heartfelt way. In the liturgy of the Catholic Church, the Penitential Psalms were traditionally sung on Ash Wednesday, during Holy Week, and as part of the Office of the Dead. (For Josquin's setting of the Penitential Psalm *Miserere mei, Deus*, see Chapter 21). Protestants, however, found these biblical texts provided a means for a direct appeal to the Lord; an individual might plead for mercy in the

Bayerische Staatsbibliothek, Munich

❋ FIGURE 24-2

An illumination, painted by Hans Mielich (c1560), that appears at the front of a luxurious manuscript containing the Penitential Psalms of Orlande de Lassus. Lassus is seated at the harpsichord. Behind and around him are the instrumentalists of the court and, behind them, the chapel singers.

Bayerische Staatsbibliothek, Munich

quiet and solitude of the home, without the liturgical ritual of the established church. Lassus was the first composer to set all of the Penitential Psalms in polyphony. In so doing, he created one of the great monuments of Renaissance choral music.

The sixth of the seven Penitential Psalms (Psalm 129) begins: *De profundis clamavi ad te Domine: Domine, exaudi vocem meam (From the depths I cried to you, O Lord: Lord hear my voice)*. The illustrations accompanying Lassus's music (see Fig. 24-3) depict those heroes who throughout sacred history have been imprisoned and have implored the Lord for deliverance, among them Joseph in the dungeon of the Pharaoh, Daniel in the den of the lions, and Jonah in the belly of the whale—all Old Testament precursors of Christ. At the outset, Lassus's music too poignantly expresses deep despair as the basses fall down to great F and climb back up an octave only to plummet again—an excellent example of text painting in music. Clearly, Lasso was greatly affected by his early exposure to the Italian madrigal. Furthermore, because the Penitential Psalms, like all other psalms, comprise a succession of short verses, the music for them is made up of short sections, each one setting one verse of text. Accordingly, in *De profundis clamavi*, Lassus continually changes the number of voices and moves boldly from one harmony to another as he proceeds from one verse to the next (Ex. 24-4). In this way the distinction between verses is clear and the text emphatically expressed.

❋ FIGURE 24-3

The soprano and bass parts of Orlande de Lassus's motet *De profundis*.

EXAMPLE 24-4

From the depths I cried to you, O Lord:

LISTENING CUE

ORLANDE DE LASSUS

De profundis clamavi (c1560)

CD 3/16

Anthology, No. 67

For the first twenty years of their existence, Lassus' seven Penitential Psalms were kept in Duke Albrecht V's library above his art gallery; this was his private music. Members of the court called it **musica reservata,** text-sensitive music reserved for a small circle of connoisseurs. Only after the death of the duke in 1579 did the Penitential Psalms receive their first public performance. Lassus and the singers of the ducal chapel sang them in a darkened gymnasium of a Jesuit college in Munich during Holy Week 1580.

EPILOGUE: THE PSALTER IN OTHER PROTESTANT COUNTRIES

The Book of Psalms was important to Catholics like Lassus, but even more so to Protestants in Germany and elsewhere. Some extreme reformers such as Ulrich Zwingli (1484–1531) in Switzerland banned all music from the church. Others, however, allowed music in the sanctuary, but limited it exclusively to singing the Psalter. One such reformer was John Calvin (1509–1564), a Frenchman exiled to the Swiss town of Geneva. Calvin believed that polyphonic Masses and motets sung by a trained choir distracted the faithful from the Word of God. For him the only true church music was the Psalter sung monophonically in unison by the congregation. To this end, Calvin published what is called **The Geneva Psalter** (1539; revised 1551) containing a translation of all one hundred and fifty psalms into metrical and rhyming French. Many of the psalms were supplied with simple melodies, most created by the Geneva musician Louis Bourgeois (c1510–c1560). Among them was the pleasing tune for Protestant Psalm 134: *Or sus, serviteurs du Seigneur* (*Ye servants of the Lord of might*; Ex. 24-5).

EXAMPLE 24-5

Or sus, ser-vi-teurs du Sei-gneur, Vous qui de nuict en son hon-neur
De-dans sa mai-son le ser-vez, Lou-ëz-le_et son Nom es-le-vez.

Ye servants of the Lord of might,
Who in his house do watch by night,
Attending there, your selves address,
The Lord our God to praise and bless.

Two decades later the Psalter was translated into poetic English. It too was published, not in England but in Geneva, Switzerland, where English reformers had temporarily taken refuge during the reign of Catholic Queen Mary I (1553–1558). In this collection the melody of Louis Bourgeois was also made to serve Psalm 100, which subsequently became known in the English-speaking world as "Old Hundreth" (*All people that on earth do dwell*; Ex. 24-6).

EXAMPLE 24-6

All peo-ple that on earth do dwell, Sing to the Lord with cheer-ful voice.

The principals behind the English Psalter were Thomas Sternhold and John Hopkins and their collection, the **Sternhold and Hopkins Psalter,** enjoyed enormous popularity, appearing in nearly five hundred editions in the course of the next hundred years; in these, a small number of melodies did service for the many "Englished" psalm texts. When the Pilgrims (English reformist refugees) landed on the shores of America in 1620, they carried with them the Sternhold and Hopkins Psalter. Even today, psalm settings from this book as well as the Geneva Psalter appear in Protestant hymnals. Thus has the Book of Psalms inspired music for worship for Jews, Catholics, and Protestants over the span of more than three thousand years.

 ## SUMMARY

German-speaking lands had a long tradition of monophonic Gregorian chant. Yet composed polyphonic art music did not become deeply rooted there until the Renaissance. With the growth of German cities, and especially with the advent of music printing, polyphonic music in the German tongue began to flourish. The German song (Lied) was set in polyphony by a number of composers, most notably Heinrich Isaac. Composers placed the tune in the tenor, thereby producing a Tenorlied. Having more in common with the French chanson than the Italian madrigal, the strophic Tenorlied rarely indulged in word painting or bold chromatic harmonies. It was unadorned, pleasing music designed to appeal to the general public.

So too was the music of the early Protestant church. Martin Luther and his followers reduced the complexity of the Catholic service, introduced German into the Mass, and allowed for congregational singing of a new type of religious song called the chorale. Like hymns today, the strophic German chorale was intentionally simple and tuneful so that all could sing it. Lutheran musicians, especially Johann Walter, set chorale tunes in a four-voice, lightly imitative style, usually with the chorale in the tenor. Later the chorale migrated to the soprano, which is where it appears in the four-part chorale harmonizations of J.S. Bach.

Southern-most Germany and Austria remained Roman Catholic during the Renaissance. Composers working in these lands continued to write in the traditional genres of religious music—the Mass and motet, both still using the Latin language. The most prominent of these was Orlande de Lassus at the court of Munich. Having been influenced at an early age by the Italian madrigal, Lassus made use of text painting and harmonic coloring in his sacred music for the Catholic service. Lassus's style generally is more vivid, direct, and rhetorical than the somewhat ethereal, abstract style then coming forth from Counter-Reformation Rome.

 ## KEY TERMS

Holy Roman Empire	Tenorlied	Reformation
Emperor Maximilian I	*alternatim* technique	chorale
Hofkapelle	Diet (Reichstag)	contrafactum
Choralis Constantinus	Martin Luther	(pl., contrafacta)
Lied (pl., Lieder)	Ninety-Five Theses	Johann Walter

Geistliche Gesangbüchlein
The Augsburg
  Confession
Peace of Augsburg

Tafelmusik
Psalter
Penitential Psalms
musica reservata

The Geneva Psalter
Sternhold and Hopkins
  Psalter

Rome and the Music of the Counter-Reformation

Rome was the greatest city on earth at the height of the Empire, during the reigns of Julius Caesar and his successors. It fell into disarray and often chaos in the Middle Ages, only to regain much of its former splendor in the fifteenth and early sixteenth centuries. Indeed, Rome epitomized the rebirth expressed by the term "Renaissance." Just how bad had things become in the Eternal City? By the fourteenth century the population of Rome, which once numbered more than a million, had shrunk to about 20,000; the great monuments of the Empire lay in ruin, covered by debris and vines; the papacy was no longer in Rome, having moved to Avignon (see Chapter 13); and, at night, wolves roamed the streets, looking for the latest victims of plague or malaria.

Things began to improve, however, when Pope Martin V returned the papacy to Rome in 1420. Clergymen now journeyed to the city to receive the benefits and privileges that only a pope could bestow. Pope Nicholas V declared 1450 a jubilee year, and thousands of spiritual pilgrims flocked to Rome, bringing not only their questing souls but also the money of the tourist. Gradually, streets were refurbished, monuments were restored, and fallen statues resurrected. New construction began in the area of the Vatican on the western edge of the city. Pope Sixtus IV built the Sistine Chapel between 1477 and 1481, and popes Julius II, Leo X, and Paul III began to erect a new St. Peter's Basilica, which would take a century to complete. By the sixteenth century the papacy had regained administrative and financial control over religious practices in much of western Europe. From Rome went orders as to how the universal church should be administered; to Rome came the money contributed by the faithful.

In the early sixteenth century, after nearly a century of improving fortunes, the papacy ran headlong into an implacable foe: Martin Luther. Luther and his fellow reformers sought to bring an end to the persistent corruption within the Roman Catholic Church: the sale of indulgences, graft in appointing church officers, and personal excess by the popes. The very worldly nature of the papacy can be seen in Figure 25-1, which shows a joust going on near the papal apartments as the new St. Peter's rises in the background; the pope was a warlord as well as a spiritual leader. By the time the Protestant Reformation had run its course, most of Germany, Switzerland, the Low

🌸 FIGURE 25-1

A joust in progress inside the gardens of the papal apartments at the Vatican. The Sistine Chapel is at the top. Workers constructing the new St. Peter's Basilica can be seen in the background at the upper right.

Countries, and all of England, as well as parts of France, Austria, Bohemia, Poland, and Hungary, had gone over to the Protestant cause. The established Roman Catholic Church was shaken to its very foundation.

In response to this religious challenge, the Church of Rome began to clean its own house. The cleansing applied not only to matters of spirituality and church administration but also to art, liturgy, and music. Nudity in religious paintings, musical instruments within the church, secular tunes in the midst of polyphonic Masses, and married church singers were now deemed inappropriate to a truly pious environment.

The movement that fostered this reform within the established Roman Church is called the **Counter-Reformation.** Its spirit was institutionalized in the **Council of Trent** (1545–1563), a congress of bishops and cardinals held at the small town of Trento in the Italian Alps. Although the assembled prelates debated many aspects of reform within the Church of Rome, the liturgy and its music occupied much of their time. In essence, they put the contrapuntal style of sacred music on trial. They considered banning all polyphony from the church. What bothered the Catholic reformers most about the church music of the day was the incessant entry of voices in musical imitation, which created an overlapping of lines that obscured the text; in other words, excessively dense counterpoint was burying the sacred word of the Lord. As one well-placed bishop said derisively:

> In our times they [composers] have put all their industry and effort into the writing of imitative passages, so that while one voice says "Sanctus," another says "Sabaoth," still another says "Gloria tua," with howling, bellowing, and stammering, so that they more nearly resemble cats in January than flowers in May.[1]

This states what sacred polyphony should not be. But how should good music for the church sound? In September 1562 deputies of the Council declared the following:

> All things should indeed be so ordered that the Masses, whether they be celebrated with or without singing, may reach tranquilly into the ears and hearts of those who hear them, when everything is executed clearly and at the right speed. In the cases of those Masses which are celebrated with singing and with organ, let nothing profane be intermingled, but only hymns and divine praises. The whole plan of singing in musical modes should be constituted not to give empty pleasure to the ear, but in such a way that the words be clearly understood by all, and thus the hearts of the listeners be drawn to desire of heavenly harmonies, in the contemplation of the joys of the blessed.[2]

GIOVANNI PIERLUIGI DA PALESTRINA

Clarity of the text—the word of the Lord—was of primary importance to the church fathers at the time of the Counter-Reformation. Immediately, composers such as Giovanni Pierluigi da Palestrina (1525/26–1594) set about to produce polyphonic Masses that demonstrated that sacred polyphony for four, five, or six voices could be written in a clear, dignified manner. Among these works was Palestrina's **Mass for Pope Marcellus** (1567), a Mass which later generations came to view as the model of the clear, serene style of the Counter-Reformation. For his role in maintaining a place for composed polyphony within the established Church, Palestrina, rightly or wrongly, came to be called "the savior of church music."

Palestrina was born in the small hill town of that name outside Rome. He spent almost his entire professional life as a singer and composer at various churches in and around the Vatican: St. Peter's Basilica, St. John Lateran, St. Mary Major, and the **Sistine Chapel** (the pope's private chapel within his apartments; Fig. 25-2). Al-

FIGURE 25-2

Interior of the Sistine Chapel. The high altar and Michelangelo's *Last Judgment* are at the far end; the balcony for the singers is at the lower right, just on the other side of the choir screen.

though Paul IV, one of the more zealous of the reforming popes, dismissed him from the Sistine Chapel in 1555 because he was a married layman not conforming to the rule of celibacy, Palestrina returned to papal employment at St. Peter's in 1571, holding the title *maestro di cappella* (master of the chapel) and ultimately *maestro compositore* (master composer). In the course of his lengthy career as a church musician, Palestrina composed more than 700 sacred works, including 104 polyphonic Masses. All of this music was conceived for voices alone. It was the custom in most Roman churches at this time to sing polyphony without the accompaniment of musical instruments. The Sistine Chapel in particular had never made use of instruments, even the organ. The expression *"a cappella Sistina"* (in the style of the Sistine Chapel) eventually would be reduced simply to **a cappella**—singing without instrumental accompaniment. Palestrina's music is invariably performed *a cappella*.

The *Sanctus* of Palestrina's *Missa Aeterna Christi munera* (*Mass: Eternal Gifts of Christ*) epitomizes the musical spirit of the Counter-Reformation that then radiated from Rome. Palestrina's *Sanctus* unfolds slowly and deliberately with long notes gradually giving way to shorter, faster-moving ones, but without catchy rhythms or a strong beat. The sober mood is created in part by the careful use of imitative counterpoint. Each phrase of text is assigned its own motive, which appears, in turn, in each voice. A motive used in this fashion is called a **point of imitation.** Palestrina's *Sanctus* has four points of imitation (mm. 1, 13, 23, and 30). The first enters in the order soprano, alto, tenor, bass, and the music works to a cadence. While the soprano and bass conclude the cadence, the alto and tenor begin the second point of imitation. Soon this section cadences in the soprano and alto as the bass and tenor enter with the third point. Palestrina was a master at sewing a cadence to the beginning of a new point of imitation (Ex. 25-1). The listener experiences not only a sense of satisfaction on arrival at the cadence but also a feeling of ongoing progress as the new point pushes forward. Notice the individual musical lines. Each voice moves primarily in step-wise motion. The largest leap is an octave, which occurs only in ascending motion. Diminished and augmented intervals are prohibited. Dissonance occurs off the beat or, if on the beat, is carefully controlled. This conservative style of writing continued an old tradition, going back to Ockeghem and Josquin, that would soon come to be called the **prima pratica** (first practice)—a traditional style for church music that is in contrast to the freer writing found in some madrigals of the late sixteenth century. In this conservative style, the Church of Rome found the musical embodiment of the restrained spirit of the Counter-Reformation.

EXAMPLE 25-1

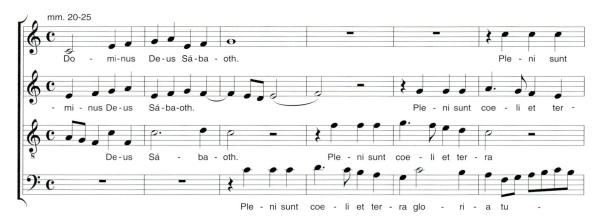

mm. 20-25

Do - mi-nus De-us Sá-ba - oth.   Ple - ni sunt

- mi - nus De-us   Sá-ba-oth.   Ple - ni sunt coe - li et ter -

De-us   Sá - ba-oth.   Ple - ni sunt coe - li et ter - ra

Ple - ni sunt coe - li et ter - ra glo - ri - a tu -

Lord God of Sabaoth, the heavens are full of your glory…

💿 **LISTENING CUE**

GIOVANNI PIERLUIGI DA PALESTRINA   CD 3/17

Sanctus of the *Missa Aeterna Christi munera* (1590)   Anthology, No. 68

❀ FIGURE 25-3

The high altar of St. Peter's Basilica and, above it, the Latin inscription beginning *Tu es Petrus* and ending *regni caelorum*. Palestrina set this text on several occasions.

Scala/Art Resource

The **Vatican,** the compound in which the pope resides today, derives its name from the old Roman name of the hill (*mons Vaticanus*) on which it sits. The site was chosen to be the seat of the Church of Rome because in 324 C.E. Emperor Constantine, the first Christian emperor, had built a church there, where the earliest Christians venerated the bones of St. Peter, Christ's apostle to Rome. Today on this site we see the largest church in the world, the gigantic **St. Peter's Basilica.** Designed in part by Michelangelo, it is a Renaissance replacement for Constantine's Roman church. Thus, St. Peter has been the object of devotion in the area of what we call the Vatican for nearly two millennia.

The source of the Apostle Peter's special status within the Roman Church is found in the Bible where, in the Gospel according to St. Matthew (16:18–19), Christ says to Peter: "Tu es Petrus et super hanc petram aedificabo ecclesiam meam" ("You are Peter and upon this rock I will build my church"). This decree that Peter be the foundation of the church is inscribed in giant letters in the dome of St. Peter's Basilica (Fig. 25-3). The scene of Christ presenting the keys of the church to Peter also appears in a fresco painted on a wall of the Sistine Chapel. Similarly, the theme of this transfer of power from Christ to Peter resounds in much music by Palestrina.

Palestrina worked at various times in both St. Peter's Basilica and in the Sistine Chapel. Not surprisingly, he composed three motets setting the text *Tu es Petrus* (*You are Peter*), one each for five, six, and seven voices. The six-voice motet makes use of points of imitation, but it also employs a less strict musical process called **rhythmic imitation** (Ex. 25-2). Here each voice in turn sings the same rhythmic motive, but to melodic motives that differ slightly in pitch.

EXAMPLE 25-2

[I will build] my church…

Rhythmic imitation creates roughly the same effect as strict imitation, but it does not require the same contrapuntal rigor. Generally speaking, in the late sixteenth century, the more voices for which a composer writes, the greater the likelihood he will use rhythmic imitation rather than strict imitation.

Palestrina composed motets not only for six voices but also for eight, divided into two choirs of four parts each. In Palestrina's *Tu es Petrus* the six voices are often divided into two groups of three, a harbinger of the double chorus style that became popular for sacred music in both Rome and Venice at the end of the sixteenth century. Throughout this motet, one group of voices will respond to the music of another, often in a chordal declamatory style. The musical lines are not long and undulating, but short and energetic. Important phrases of text are repeated again and again for special emphasis. The motet *Tu es Petrus* demonstrates that Palestrina relied not only upon imitation but also upon straightforward chordal declamation to project the meaning of a sacred text. To make the word of the Lord clearly audible to all was a spiritual imperative for composers of the Counter-Reformation.

LISTENING CUE

GIOVANNI PIERLUIGI DA PALESTRINA   CD 3/18
Motet *Tu es Petrus* (1573)   Anthology, No. 69

Sometime about 1585 Palestrina composed a six-voice *Missa Tu es Petrus* in which he borrowed musical material from his six-voice motet *Tu es Petrus*. For example, the beginning *Kyrie* of the Mass draws from the opening of the motet, specifically the music of "Tu es Petrus" (Ex. 25-3); and, in the *Christe,* Palestrina takes from the music of "aedificabo Ecclesiam meam." Earlier composers had also borrowed previously existing material, specifically when making use of cantus firmus technique or of paraphrase technique. Here, however, a different process is involved, one called parody technique. In **parody technique** a composer borrows, not merely a pre-existing melody from another work, but an entire polyphonic complex. That is to say, in parody technique one or more short passages involving several simultaneously-sounding voices are taken over by another composer. The new composer then goes on to elaborate upon and add to the borrowed material, thereby creating an entirely new composition.

EXAMPLE 25-3A   EXAMPLE 25-3B

Today "to parody" usually means "to make fun of," but that is not the case with the term "parody technique." Rather, the second composer pays homage to the first by suggesting that the earlier model is worthy of emulation. For that reason, parody technique is sometimes called **emulation technique.** One composer emulates another by borrowing portions of a musical mentor's polyphonic work. In the case of *Tu es Petrus,* however, Palestrina is simply emulating himself.

LISTENING CUE

GIOVANNI PIERLUIGI DA PALESTRINA   CD 3/19
Kyrie of the *Missa Tu es Petrus* (c1585)   Anthology, No. 70

Finally, toward the end of sixteenth century, it was not uncommon for the soprano part in the choirs of the Sistine Chapel and St. Peter's Basilica to be sung by one or more castrati. The **castrato** was a type of high-voice male singer created by castrating boys who showed promising voices before they reached puberty. Castrati sang in church choirs and, later, in opera houses in Italy and elsewhere until the early twentieth century (see also Chapter 38). They first entered the Sistine Chapel in 1562, and many of the earliest ones came from Spain, which at the time had close musical ties with Rome.

 ## SPANISH MUSIC DURING THE COUNTER-REFORMATION

Rome was the epicenter of the Counter-Reformation, but other cities in Italy also adopted the clear, conservative style of church music. So too did other countries, most notably Spain. Throughout the sixteenth century there were close political and artistic ties between Spain and Italy. And, because there had been a history of Spanish popes during the early sixteenth century, the Sistine Chapel in particular welcomed Spanish singers. Cristóbal de Morales (c1500–1553), Francisco Guerrero (1528–1599), and Tomás Luis de Victoria (1548–1611) were three important Spanish composers who came to Rome to learn the style of the musical Counter-Reformation. Victoria may have studied with Palestrina himself during the 1560s. To the uninitiated, his style of composition is virtually indistinguishable from that of Palestrina. Indeed, Victoria is the Spanish Counter-Reformation composer *par excellence*. His dark, austere, somewhat mysterious sound provides a musical equivalent to the paintings of El Greco (1541–1614; see timeline for Part III). Like El Greco, who painted almost no secular subjects, Victoria wrote no secular music. Both Victoria and Palestrina composed serenely beautiful sacred vocal music appropriate for the solemn mood of the Counter-Reformation Church.

SUMMARY

The Counter-Reformation was born of a desire to rid the Church of Rome of administrative abuses—and secular influences generally. In specifically musical terms, it proscribed the use of popular tunes in Masses and motets, and it encouraged the clearest possible exposition of the sacred text. Simple contrapuntal imitation and straightforward chordal declamation were the preferred means of expression. Above all, the musical style of the Counter-Reformation was conservative in its harmony and counterpoint. Indeed, the "rules" of good voice-leading and part-writing for music came to be extracted from the music of Palestrina, Victoria, and their contemporaries. Later, during the Baroque period, these practices would be codified into method books of counterpoint that were studied by great composers such as Bach and Mozart. The conservative style of church writing, first called the *prima pratica* and later the *stile antico* (old or traditional style), provides the foundation for the study of modal and species counterpoint in universities even today. Thus, for the first time in music history, a historical style became the basis of a pedagogical theory.

KEY TERMS

Counter-Reformation	point of imitation	parody technique
Council of Trent	*prima pratica*	(emulation
Mass for Pope Marcellus	Vatican	technique)
Sistine Chapel	St. Peter's Basilica	castrato
a cappella	rhythmic imitation	

Chapter 26

Music in Elizabethan England: Early Vocal Music

Prior to 1560 the winds of the Renaissance were slow in reaching the British Isles. England had experienced little of the humanistic study of classical authors that flourished in Renaissance Italy. The architecture of the period was a particularly English brand of flamboyant gothic and small-window manor house, rather than the broad, grand, symmetrical style of the Italian Renaissance. English composers in general concentrated on liturgical texts for use in the services of the Catholic Church. Their secular vocal pieces showed little of the close cooperation between music and word that was then evident in the Italian madrigal. When the Renaissance finally came to England—in the plays of Shakespeare, the poetry of Edmund Spenser, the architecture of Inigo Jones, and the music of William Byrd and John Dowland, for example—it arrived late, but stayed longer, well into the seventeenth century. Shakespeare, for example, lived from 1564 until 1616. For much of the Bard's life, England was ruled by a wise and temperate monarch, Elizabeth I, who encouraged the arts and letters generally and loved music in particular. To understand how this extraordinary woman became the sole ruler of England, we return to the early sixteenth century and the tumultuous reign of Henry VIII.

❀ HENRY VIII AS MUSICIAN AND CHURCH REFORMER

During most of the first half of the sixteenth century, England was governed by a single dominant figure, King **Henry VIII** (r. 1509–1547). Henry did nothing in moderation. At his court he employed no fewer than fifty-eight musicians, many of whom were skilled instrumentalists brought over from the Continent. He owned fifty-six keyboard instruments, twenty "horns" of various sorts, nineteen bowed string instruments, thirty-one plucked strings, and no fewer than 220 wind instruments of various kinds. Moreover, Henry himself was a musician. He sang and played the recorder, flute, lute, and even cornett, and he danced with enthusiasm. What is more, Henry was a composer of some thirty-five secular pieces. Among the best of these—and certainly the best-known in Henry's day—is his *Pastyme with Good Companye* (Ex. 26-1). Its robust, vigorous sound reflects the assertive personality of the king.

EXAMPLE 26-1

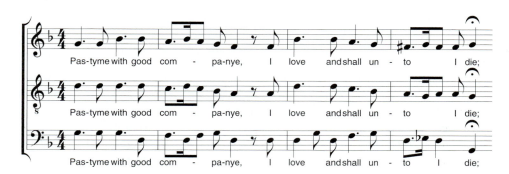

Pastyme with Good Companye is a fine example of an English **partsong**—a strophic song with English text intended to be sung by three or four voices in a predominantly homophonic musical style. With its lively, dance-like rhythms and chordal texture, the English partsong has much in common with the Parisian chanson of the 1530s (see Chapter 22). In fact, Henry seems to have purloined the melody for this piece from a chanson (*De mon triste et desplaisir*) by the Parisian composer Jean Richafort.

LISTENING CUE

KING HENRY VIII

Pastyme with Good Companye (c1520)

CD 3/20

Anthology, No. 71

Henry VIII was a larger-than-life figure with an immense appetite: he devoured food; he devoured women; and, ultimately, he devoured the Roman Catholic Church. In 1528 Henry, in dire need of a male heir, asked Pope Clement VII to annul his nineteen-year marriage to Catherine of Aragon (daughter of Ferdinand and Isabella of Spain). When the pope refused, Henry proceeded to divorce Catherine and marry Anne Boleyn, the second of his six wives. Soon the pope retaliated, excommunicating Henry and, in effect, all English citizens. Henry responded by establishing a new Church of England with himself, the king, as its Supreme Head. He adopted some of the beliefs of the Protestants on the Continent. For example, Henry came to view all monasteries and convents as leeches on society and closed them. Some churchmen in England, influenced particularly by the Calvinists in Switzerland and France, went even further than Henry wished to go toward religious reform; they insisted upon a complete break with the liturgy of the Church of Rome and argued for a new, far simpler, religious service. Consequently, by 1547, the last year of Henry's reign, there were three branches of formalized religion in England, comprising the Church of Rome as well as two Protestant offshoots—the Church of England (later called the Anglican Church, and related to the Episcopal Church in America), and the more progressive, reform-minded group of Protestantism called the Puritans. After Henry's death, church composers working in England wrote for one, or all, of these three religious persuasions.

This was the religious situation in England when on 17 November 1558, Princess Elizabeth Tudor, daughter of Henry and Anne Boleyn, ascended the throne of England. As Queen **Elizabeth I** she ruled for forty-five years, until her death in 1603. She was called "the Virgin Queen" because she never married. There were eager suitors enough, but for political reasons Elizabeth chose to remain single, fashioning an image of herself as a wise and learned monarch devoted to the interests of her subjects. Alone among her sex, she held the unique position of a woman who exercised power successfully in a deeply patriarchal world.

Religion, and the music that accompanied it, occupied much of Elizabeth's attention during her long reign. Political survival dictated that the queen steer a middle course between the reactionary conservatives of the Catholic faith and radical reformers among the Puritans. In her own chapel, Elizabeth followed the newly truncated service adopted by the Anglican Church—instead of Mass and eight canonical hours observed by Catholics, she attended an Anglican service. The Anglican service consisted of **Morning Prayer** (a compression of Matins and Lauds), Mass, and **Evensong** (a similar compression of Vespers and Compline). Sometimes her large chapel of thirty-two men and twelve boys sang in Latin using the same

The Education of a Renaissance Queen

Elizabeth Tudor was exceptionally well prepared to be ruler of England. Her father Henry VIII, recognizing that she was an unusually bright child, provided tutors in almost every conceivable subject (Fig. 26-1). She studied architecture, mathematics, the fundamentals of astronomy, and geography. But special emphasis was placed on foreign languages. By her adolescence she could speak and write French, Italian, and Latin almost as well as she could English, and she had also acquired some Greek. For practice, she read Cicero and Livy in Latin and the New Testament in Greek. Later, when queen, Elizabeth was known to give, on the spur of the moment, a lengthy harangue to Parliament in fluent Latin. As monarch, she found time to read history three hours a day. She was, in short, a natural scholar. For amusement Elizabeth would ride horseback, play chess, dance, and make music, all skills she learned at an early age. As one of her tutors said of Elizabeth when she was eighteen:

> Her mind has no womanly weakness and her perseverance is equal to that of a man and her memory long keeps what it quickly picks up. She talks French and Italian as well as she does English and has often talked to me readily and well in Latin, moderately in Greek. When she writes in Greek and Latin, nothing is more beautiful than her handwriting. She delights as much in music as she is skilful in it.[1]

Indeed, Elizabeth's skills in music and dance, as we will see, were considerable.

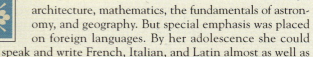

FIGURE 26-1

A portrait of Princess Elizabeth Tudor at the age of thirteen, attributed to William Scrots. She holds a book, and another rests on a lectern, both prominently displayed to symbolize Elizabeth's extraordinary capacity for learning.

style of elaborate counterpoint preferred by the Catholics on the Continent. At other times the royal chapel sang simple polyphonic psalm settings of the sort favored by reformed congregations of Calvinists and Puritans. If nothing else, composers in the service of Elizabeth needed to be versatile.

THOMAS TALLIS AND THE ENGLISH PSALM

Thomas Tallis (c1505–1585) was one such versatile composer; he wrote music for all three faiths—Catholic, Anglican, and Puritan. Tallis has left us a stunning set of Lamentations suitable for the Catholic Church during Holy Week, as well as many anthems (see below) in English and motets in Latin, including one for forty voices (*Spem in alium*)—all appropriate for the Church of England. Yet today Tallis is known equally well for simple psalm settings of the sort favored by the Puritans.

As we have seen, the English Puritans were greatly influenced by the Calvinist religion on the Continent, which endorsed no music in the service except simple psalms sung in the vernacular tongue. English reformers soon translated the Psalter into English and supplied it with simple tunes. The most popular of these was the Sternhold and Hopkins Psalter (see the end of Chapter 24), but it was not the only such book. In 1567 Matthew Parker, a clergyman close to Queen Elizabeth, produced another translation and asked royal composer Tallis to provide the music. Parker's volume, *The Whole Psalter Translated into English Metre*, took the Latin prose of the Book of Psalms and turned it into English poetry. Tallis provided music for eight of the translated psalms, one for each of the old church modes (Ex. 26-2). But, because many of the psalms had a common meter, Tallis's eight musical settings were able to accommodate most of the one hundred fifty psalms in Parker's book; one setting served many psalms. Below is Parker's metrical translation of Psalm 2 as set by Tallis, preceded by the Latin previously used in England, and followed by the later English as it appeared in the early-seventeenth-century King James version of the Bible.

Ps. 2: Latin of Vulgate Bible
Quare fremuerunt gentes,
et populi meditati sunt inania?
Astiterunt reges terrae,
et principes convenerunt in unum,
adversus Dominum,
et adversus Christum ejus.

Ps. 2: Parker's translation, set by Tallis
Why fum'th in sight the Gentiles spite,
in fury raging stout?
Why tak'th in hand the people fond,
vain things to bring about?
The kings arise, the Lords devise,
in counsels met thereto,
against the Lord with false accord,
against his Christ they go.

Ps. 2: King James Version
Why do the heathen rage
and the people imagine a vain thing?
The kings of the earth set themselves
and the rulers take counsel together,
against the Lord, and against his
Anointed.

EXAMPLE 26-2

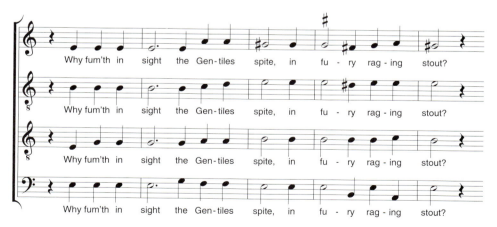

Appropriate for the simple musical needs of the English reformed church, Tallis's *Why fum'th in sight* is a straightforward, chordal setting of Psalm 2 for four voices. Like the reformers of the German Lutheran Church, who often borrowed from the chant of the Church of Rome when fashioning a chorale tune, Tallis here adopted a melody from the medieval Catholic liturgy. His tune is nothing other than a reworking of the old Gregorian psalm tone for the Phrygian mode (mode 3). In

Parker's book, Tallis describes the Phrygian mode as one that "doth rage and roughly brayth." And, like German musicians who often placed the tune in the tenor voice when setting a chorale, Tallis puts his melody in the tenor. Finally, just as the German chorale tune migrated over the centuries from the tenor to the soprano, Tallis's melody eventually moved to the highest voice. Today an arrangement of Tallis's psalm setting, with the melody in the soprano, can be found in the hymnal of both the Anglican (Episcopal) and Lutheran church. The tune continues to be well known to lovers of later orchestral music, for in 1910 the English composer Ralph Vaughan Williams made it the basis of his hauntingly beautiful *Fantasy on a Theme of Thomas Tallis* (see Chapter 61).

LISTENING CUE

| **THOMAS TALLIS**
Psalm 2 (1567) | Thomson-Schirmer Website
Anthology, No. 72 |

 ## WILLIAM BYRD AND THE ENGLISH ANTHEM

When Tallis died in 1585, his place as the preeminent composer of the Elizabethan age devolved to his pupil William Byrd (1543–1623). Byrd faithfully served Elizabeth for forty-five years, and she in turn rewarded and protected him. Protection was needed, for Byrd was a Catholic in an increasingly anti-Catholic country. He, like all Romanists, was forced to practice his faith in secret at small, clandestine gatherings in private homes and chapels. The music that Byrd wrote for these underground Catholic services includes three polyphonic Masses, for three, four, and five voices, respectively. He also composed many motets setting Latin texts. Several of these recount the fall of Jerusalem, because, for Byrd and other English Catholics, the decline of the homeland Catholic Church was tantamount to the fall of Jerusalem in biblical times.

Despite his personal faith, duty required that Byrd write motets for the Anglican Church. These works, reflecting the reformed service, used English instead of Latin texts, and were called anthems. Thus an **anthem** is a sacred vocal composition, much like a motet but sung in English, in honor of the Lord or invoking the Lord to preserve and protect the English king or queen. Most anthems were composed for Morning Prayer or Evensong, some in honor of the monarch. Later, Henry Purcell and George Frideric Handel would write anthems for church and crown. One of Handel's *Coronation Anthems*, "Zadok the Priest," has been performed at the coronation of every English king and queen since its creation in 1727.

Byrd's anthem *O Lord, make thy servant, Elizabeth* was written for Elizabeth I, sometime around 1570. Byrd has simply reshaped a few lines from the beginning of Psalm 21 to make them apposite for his royal patron, turning "the King" into "our Queen."

Psalm 21, verses 1, 2, and 4:	**Byrd's text in honor of Elizabeth:**
The King shall joy in thy strength, O Lord.	O Lord, make thy servant, Elizabeth our Queen to rejoice in thy strength;
Thou hast given him his heart's desire, and hast not withholden the request of his lips.	Give her her heart's desire, and deny not the request of her lips.

He asked life of thee, and thou gavest
in him,
even length of days for ever and ever.

But prevent her with thine everlasting
blessing,
and give her a long life, ev'n for ever
and ever.
Amen.

Appropriate for the royal subject matter, Byrd adorns this text with a large-scale, five-voice setting. In musical style, this Anglican anthem is similar, in the most general way, to the learned, imitative polyphony created by Catholic composers on the Continent at this time, among them Lassus and Palestrina. There are moments of choral declamation for emphasis, such as the opening entreaty "O Lord," that remind us of Lassus. But throughout most of the anthem Byrd spins out points of imitation, first on the words "Give her her heart's desire" and then on "And give her a long life," a contrapuntal technique reminiscent of Palestrina. But there are also moments here that sound distinctly English. Look carefully at measures 14, 15, and 42, where a crunching dissonance occurs. In each case a B♭ in the soprano sounds against a B♮ in the alto. Both conflicting notes are correct, however, and indeed are required by the rules of proper voice leading—the line with the flat is moving down, that with the natural is moving up, ultimately to serve as a leading tone at the cadence (Ex. 26-3).

EXAMPLE 26-3

Such moments of harmonic (but not melodic) conflict were heard on the Continent at this time, but were especially relished by English composers throughout the sixteenth and seventeenth centuries. The sound is called the **English cross (false) relation**—the simultaneous or adjacent appearance in different voices of two conflicting notes with the same letter name. The intensity, even shock, of such conflicting moments adds expressive power to the music.

Finally, Byrd's anthem for Queen Elizabeth ends with a quiet "Amen," and this too is a peculiarity of the English music at the time. German Lutheran chorales never end with "Amen" because these texts are not derived from the psalms. In the medieval Catholic liturgy, psalms end with a lengthy doxology concluding with "Amen." English Protestants shortened the doxology to simply the last word "Amen" (the old Hebrew "and so be it"). English composers in turn gave this short, emphatic conclusion special attention, developing what we call the **Amen cadence.** They usually set the word "Amen" as a **plagal cadence,** a term drawn from the Greek word *plagalis*, meaning "derived from" or "not direct." Today we describe the plagal cadence as a IV-I chordal movement with the bass in root position falling down by the interval of the fourth. In Byrd's anthem, the main body of the piece ends with a V-I authentic cadence; the appended "Amen," however, ends with a IV-I plagal, or Amen, cadence (Ex. 26-4).

EXAMPLE 26-4

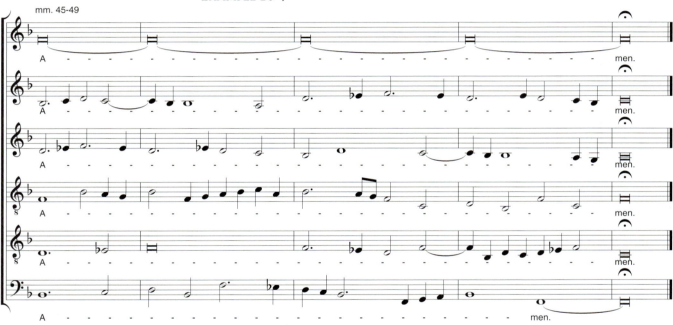

LISTENING CUE

WILLIAM BYRD
O Lord, make thy servant, Elizabeth (c1570)

CD 3/21
Anthology, No. 73

SUMMARY

The Renaissance came late to England but lasted longer, well into the seventeenth century. During the Middle Ages, English polyphonic music was cultivated widely in monasteries and cathedrals around the country. During the Renaissance, however, the composition and performance of written art music was centered around the person of the king or queen, first Henry VIII and then his daughter Elizabeth I. Most of the English Renaissance occurred during the reign of Elizabeth, and without this remarkable monarch there likely would have been no golden age of English music. Elizabeth was a practical ruler who tolerated Puritan, Anglican, and Catholic music alike. Her chapel singers, Thomas Tallis and William Byrd, were both versatile composers able to create simple psalm settings, or more elaborate English anthems and Latin motets as the occasion demanded.

KEY TERMS

Henry VIII	Morning Prayer	English cross (false) relation
partsong	Evensong	Amen cadence
Elizabeth I	anthem	plagal cadence

Chapter

27

Music in Elizabethan England: Instrumental Music and Later Vocal Music

Early in her reign, in 1575, Queen Elizabeth had favored her two chapel composers Thomas Tallis and William Byrd with a special privilege: a monopoly on the printing of music in England. This was a way to augment a musician's salary without draining a queen's purse. Armed with their new commercial authority, Tallis and Byrd immediately issued a collection of religious music called *Cantiones sacrae* (1575). In the preface they thanked their benefactor with seemingly fulsome praise: "Her Royal Majesty, the glory of our age, is accustomed always to have Music among her pleasures. Not content simply to hear the venerable works of others, she herself sings and plays excellently." Flattery this was not.

Like her father, King Henry VIII, Queen Elizabeth I was enamored of music. She too apparently tried her hand at composition, for in 1598 she related to the French ambassador that as a girl she had "composed measures [dance steps] and music and played them herself and danced them." And she kept on dancing, almost to her end (Fig. 27-1). In 1599 the Spanish ambassador reported that the 66-year-old "head of the Church of England and Ireland was to be seen in her old age dancing three or four galliards."[1] As to her performing skills, Elizabeth sang and played the lute and harpsichord. Her music making seems to have transpired, not so much in public, but more in the solitude of her privy chamber, as the following report of the Scottish ambassador suggests:

> That same day after dinner [I was taken] up to a quiet gallery that I might hear some music, where I might hear the Queen play upon the virginals. After I had hearkened a while, I took by the tapestry that hung before the door of the

FIGURE 27-1
A painting believed to show Queen Elizabeth dancing the volta with the Duke of Leicester.

☙ FIGURE 27-2

The title page of *Parthenia* (1612), a collection of keyboard music by Byrd, Gibbons, and Bull, showing a young performer seated at a virginal. Notice the prominent use of "2-3 fingering" with the thumb little engaged.

chamber, and seeing her back was toward the door, I entered within the chamber, and stood a pretty space hearing her play excellently well. But she left off immediately, so soon as she turned her about and saw me. She appeared to be surprised to see me, and came forward, seeming to strike me with her hand; alleging she used not to play before men, but when she was solitary, to shun melancholy.[2]

Indeed, more than one visitor to the English court reports that the queen played on an instrument with strings "of pure gold and silver." That instrument was called a virginal.

❋ ENGLISH KEYBOARD MUSIC

A **virginal** (often "virginals") is a diminutive harpsichord possessing a single keyboard with the strings placed at right angles to the keys (Fig. 27-2). The instrument was small enough to rest easily on a table. Because of its modest size, sound, and cost, it was the ideal beginning instrument for young girls—hence the term "virginal." Indeed, it is clear from paintings and drawings of the period that women played the virginal far more often than men, who tended to prefer the lute.

A young woman can be seen seated at a virginal on the cover of *Parthenia* (1612), the first collection of keyboard music printed in England and one of the earliest English examples of musical engraving, a new method for printing music (see Fig. 27-2). Behind this title page are twenty-one keyboard works by William Byrd, Orlando Gibbons (1583–1625), and John Bull (1562–1628), all three employed at one time or another as singers or organists at the royal chapel. A much larger collection of keyboard music is preserved today in a manuscript at the Fitzwilliam Museum in Cambridge, England. Copied during the early seventeenth century, this giant anthology is now called the **Fitzwilliam Virginal Book** (c1615). In previous centuries it was known, incorrectly, as Queen Elizabeth's Virginal Book, because so much of the music emanated from her royal court.

Among the 297 compositions in the Fitzwilliam Virginal Book are many keyboard fantasias, settings of dances such as the pavane and galliard, descriptive pieces including William Byrd's *The Bells*, and even intabulations of a few Italian madrigals and French chansons. But almost all the compositions in this collection, in one way or another, employ **variation technique,** a procedure in which successive statements of a theme are changed or presented in altered surroundings.

Typical of these is a set of variations composed by Thomas Morley (1557–1602) on the popular song *Goe from my window*.[3] Morley's setting of *Goe from my window* gives seven variations of the tune. As with most variations on top hits in Elizabethan England, the tune itself is not given prominently at the beginning. By contrast, later composers—Bach, Beethoven, Haydn, and Mozart, among others—always give the listener the tune clearly before they begin to vary it. But, in the Renaissance, when aural traditions were more strongly ingrained, composers thought it unnecessary to provide the unadorned melody. Everyone knew the tune, so they just started with the first variation. Because we do not know the tune, the melody of *Goe from my window* is given in Example 27-1.

EXAMPLE 27-1

In truth, Morley focuses his attention more on the harmonic pattern supporting *Goe from my window* than on the tune itself. The challenge he sets himself is to create seven equally compelling versions of the same harmonic plan. At the same time, Morley seems intent upon improving the performer's technique in one way or another. Variation four, for example, emphasizes the need to play parallel sixths cleanly, while six and seven develop the ability to play scales rapidly and evenly, first in the right hand and then the left. Yet there is more here than mere mechanical figures: Morley's variation one has rich chords and fine part-writing, while his variation two begins with a masterful demonstration on how to create a chain of suspensions. Moreover, variation five contains a remarkable driving, leaping bass that seems to prefigure those of Handel and Bach more than a century later (Ex. 27-2). This is keyboard music of a very high quality. Could Queen Elizabeth ever have played up to tempo music with such complexity and technical difficulty? Judging from what contemporaries said of her musical skills, likely yes.

EXAMPLE 27-2

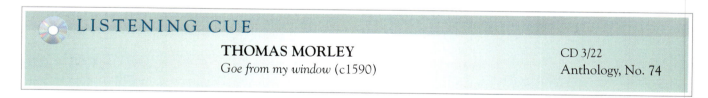

LISTENING CUE

THOMAS MORLEY
Goe from my window (c1590)

CD 3/22
Anthology, No. 74

THE ENGLISH MADRIGAL

As the years went by, Elizabeth found it difficult to keep up the image of the youthful virgin queen. Servants applied wigs, teeth whiteners, perfumes, and powders to this end. Courtiers, too, were expected to do their part to perpetuate the myth of the ageless queen. Playwrights like Ben Jonson curried favor by means of plays and masques (elaborate court entertainments that praise the ruler through music and dance). Composers were left to flatter the queen through the verse of their madrigals.

In 1601 Thomas Morley fashioned a remarkable volume of royal adulation when he engaged twenty-three colleagues to join him in creating a collection of madrigals to honor Queen Elizabeth. The resulting set of twenty-five pieces (Morley provided two) was published under the title **The Triumphes of Oriana**—Oriana and Gloriana being two names the Elizabethans had adopted for their beloved queen. To promote her patriotic cult, Morley demanded that each contributor end his madrigal with the acclamation "Thus sang the nymphs and shepherds of Diana / Long live fair Oriana."

That Morley might call upon so many English madrigalists suggests the great popularity of the madrigal in England. Indeed, England was the only country outside Italy to develop a native variety of the madrigal. Madrigals performed outside Italy were usually Italian pieces sung in Italian, not in the native tongue. At first English composers too were strongly influenced by the Italian madrigal, but gradually they transformed the genre into something distinctly English. Simultaneously, the English adopted and adapted a lighter form of sixteenth-century Italian vocal music called the balletto, transforming it into the English ballet with dance-like rhythms and a "fa, la, la" refrain. In 1588 this vogue for Italian music was first made manifest in England in print with **Musica transalpina** (*Music across the Alps*). Although the thirty-three madrigals contained herein were mainly by Italian composers, the Italian texts were replaced by English translations. Two years later, a second publication of this sort appeared under the title *Italian Madrigals Englished*. Soon English composers, many employed at the royal court, began to issue madrigal collections of their own, including Morley's *The Triumphes of Oriana*.

Typical among the madrigals in *The Triumphes of Oriana* is the six-voice *As Vesta Was from Latmos Hill Descending* by Thomas Weelkes (1576–1623), a gentleman of the royal chapel. The text, likely created by Weelkes himself, is a rather confused mixture of images from classical mythology: the Roman goddess Vesta, descending the Greek mountain of Latmos, spies Oriana (Elizabeth) ascending the hill; the nymphs and shepherds attending the goddess Diana desert her to sing the praises of Oriana. This is doggerel with a meaning: Elizabeth is in the ascent. As Vesta descends from her temple of vestal virgins, Oriana takes her place; even the attendants of Diana, goddess of the hunt and chastity, pay homage to this virgin queen. The descriptive text provides many opportunities for madrigalisms (word painting). The music descends, ascends, runs, mingles imitatively, and offers "mirthful tunes" to Elizabeth as the text commands. In many ways *As Vesta Was from Latmos Hill Descending* is typical of the English madrigal. English composers rarely engage in the extremes of emotionalism and chromatic intensity, as the Italian madrigalists Gesualdo and Monteverdi do (see Chapter 28), for example. English madrigals can be serious, but more often they are light, fun, and even funny. Yes, this madrigal for Queen Elizabeth is an example of political flattery. But, with word painting that is sometimes over the top, it also lampoons the Italian musical tradition from which the English madrigal sprang.

LISTENING CUE

THOMAS WEELKES   CD 3/23
As Vesta Was from Latmos Hill Descending (1601)   Anthology, No. 75

The Triumphes of Oriana was just one of more than forty books of madrigals published in London between 1588 and 1627, each volume usually containing some twenty pieces or more. The composers who fashioned this great outpouring of English secular music—among them Byrd, Morley, Weelkes, Wilbye, and Gibbons—have been dubbed the **English Madrigal School,** and their collective creations constitute one of the glories of the English Renaissance.

❁ THE ENGLISH LUTE AYRE

The popularity of the English madrigal coincided with the end of the Elizabethan Renaissance. Equal-voice counterpoint had long typified music of the Renaissance, but it was not the wave of the future. The future of music, both in England and on the Continent, was to be found in the expressive solo song. The solo art song first flourished in England just before and after 1600, toward the end of Queen Elizabeth's reign, and it appeared in two forms. In one, called the **consort song,** the voice is accompanied by a group of independent instruments, usually a consort of viols. In the other, called the **lute ayre,** the soloist is accompanied by a lute and possibly a bass instrument such as the *viola da gamba*. Both consort song and lute ayre are strophic—the same music serves each of two, three, or four stanzas. It was the job of the solo singer to employ the expressive nuances of the voice to make each stanza sound distinctive. The madrigal, by contrast, was rarely strophic; each word or phrase needed its own very special music. Madrigals were no longer published in England, or elsewhere, after the early decades of the seventeenth century; but the lute ayre, and the solo song generally, flourished in England and on the Continent throughout much of what is called the Baroque era in music.

The principal proponent of the lute ayre in England was John Dowland (1563–1626). Indeed, Dowland (pronounced "Doe-land") is now recognized as the finest English composer of lute songs as well as of music for solo lute. Unlike most of the great Elizabethan composers, Dowland did not enjoy a position at court, at least not at first. Instead, he traveled widely and worked on the Continent in France, Germany, Italy, and even Denmark. Queen Elizabeth heard Dowland's music on many occasions, and in 1596 she sent a messenger to Germany to wish him "health & soon return." Yet Dowland was known to be a difficult person, and not until 1612, well after Elizabeth's death, was he appointed royal lutenist. Between 1597 and 1612, Dowland published four collections of lute ayres. His *Second Booke of Songs or Ayres* (1600) contains *Flow my tears*, a song so powerful that it created something of a sensation. Countless arrangements for keyboard, lute, and instrumental consort survive in more than a hundred manuscripts of the period. The melody became, in effect, Dowland's "signature tune," for he began to sign himself "John Dowland de Lacrimae" (*Lacrimae* being the Latin for "tears"). Dowland published *Flow my tears* with an optional part for *viola da gamba*, which might double the lowest notes of the lute and thereby add weight to the powerful bass he had created. The plaintive melody with strong bass support can most clearly be heard at the words "And tears, and sighs, and groans" (mm. 11–12) where an ascending sequence begins low in the bass and rises spectacularly out of the depths of despair (Ex. 27-3). No wonder this exceptional song became all the rage during the Elizabethan age.

EXAMPLE 27-3

mm. 9-13

Since pi - ty is fled, And tears, and sighs, and groans my wea - ry days, my wea - ry days

LISTENING CUE

JOHN DOWLAND
Flow my tears (1600)

CD 3/24
Anthology, No. 76

Some of Dowland's most expressive lute ayres have qualities of the solo monody emerging in Italy during the Baroque era (see Chapter 29). He writes an intense solo vocal line and creates a texture with a strong polarity between melody and bass. What Dowland does not compose is a vocal line with elaborate, virtuosic embellishments. Despite some forward-looking elements, *Flow my tears* belongs to the tradition of the unadorned Renaissance air, not the vocally demanding Baroque aria we will soon meet.

SUMMARY

Queen Elizabeth's court witnessed the creation of the first repertory of keyboard music of high artistic quality and high technical difficulty. Royal composers Byrd, Gibbons, and Morley, among others, wrote lengthy keyboard works, almost all of which use variation technique in one way or another. They intended these to be played on the dominant keyboard instrument of the day, a small harpsichord called the virginal.

Secular vocal music also flowered with Elizabeth's encouragement, the principal genres being the madrigal and the lute ayre. Although at first derived from the style of the Italian madrigal, English madrigals can be lighter, less serious in tone, and less chromatic in design than their Italian counterparts. The lute ayre remained a principal vehicle for solo singing throughout the seventeenth century. The most intense of John Dowland's lute ayres exhibit an expressive solo voice as well as a strong polarity between vocal melody and bass support. These features are also apparent in the solo monody emerging in Italy around the turn of the seventeenth century.

 KEY TERMS

virginal
Fitzwilliam Virginal
  Book

variation technique
The Triumphes of Oriana
Musica transalpina

English Madrigal School
consort song
lute ayre

Chapter 28

The Later Madrigal in Ferrara and Mantua: Gesualdo and Monteverdi

Sixteenth-century Italy witnessed a resurgence of written art music by native composers. If Italian courts in fifteenth-century Italy had been dominated by northern Franco-Flemish composers such as Dufay and Josquin, now at the end of the sixteenth century the Italian scene was ruled by native composers. The advent of the frottola and especially the madrigal gave new energy to musical settings of poetry in the Italian language. The madrigal in particular only continued to grow in popularity. More than a thousand individual collections, each containing about twenty madrigals, were printed between 1530 and 1620. Some Italian madrigals were even printed with Italian texts outside of Italy, specifically in German-speaking lands, England, Denmark, and the Low Countries. Thus the madrigal became the first genre of Italian music to be exported around Europe, as opera and the concerto would be during the seventeenth century. The popularity of the madrigal signaled that Italy was becoming the center of the Western musical world, a position it would continue to enjoy through the eighteenth century.

The birthplace of the madrigal was Florence, but soon popular enthusiasm carried it to Venice, Rome, Ferrara, and Mantua (see Map 14-1). Ferrara and Mantua were city-states but, unlike Florence, not republics. Instead, they were ruled by hereditary, autocratic families, namely the d'Este family in Ferrara and the Gonzaga clan in Mantua. To their court in Ferrara the d'Estes attracted musicians such as Josquin, Cipriano de Rore, and the nobleman-composer Carlo Gesualdo, while the Gonzagas patronized the frottolist Marchetto Cara and, later, the great Claudio Monteverdi.

THE MADRIGAL IN FERRARA

The court of Ferrara had been a beacon for northern composers since the mid fifteenth century (see Chapter 21). Guillaume Dufay provided music for the Ferrarese rulers as early as the 1430s. Josquin des Prez became a singer there in 1503 and was followed by another northerner, Jacob Obrecht, who died of the plague in Ferrara in 1505. In 1515 Obrecht's countryman, Adrian Willaert, moved south to enter the service of the d'Este duke, where he remained until 1527. Willaert was a prolific composer who, as we have seen, experimented with a radically new approach to tuning called "equal temperament" (see Musical Interlude 4). Two of Willaert's pupils, Cipriano de Rore, a northerner, and Nicola Vicentino, an Italian, likewise shared their mentor's enthusiasm for experimental music. We have previously met Vicentino's chromatic keyboard instrument called the arcicembalo, a harpsichord with thirty-six keys (pitches) within each octave (see Musical Interlude 4). Cipriano de Rore's interest in experimental chromatic music can be seen in his *Calami sonum ferentes* published in 1555 (Ex. 28-1). Melodic chromaticism is immediately evident here, as each line rises up the scale in half-steps. But even more novel is the harmony. Chords are built not only on the seven notes within the mode but also on tones that are foreign to it. At the outset, the chromatically rising bass (mm. 8–10) creates chords built on E, F, F♯, G, and A in immediate succession. The results are startling to the ear.

EXAMPLE 28-1

Those who set forth the sweet sounds of the flute with Sicilian rhythm...

During the second half of the sixteenth century, Ferrara maintained its reputation as the center of the musical avant-garde, in both composition and performance. The most forward-looking aspect of musical performance at Ferrara was the **concerto delle donne** (ensemble of ladies). During the 1570s the duke and duchess of Ferrara encouraged performances by a trio of singers, all of whom were women of the minor nobility. Then, in 1580, in an obvious attempt to elevate the standards of musical performance, the duke dismissed the original three singers. In their place he hired three, and sometimes four, women of middle-class background, all with exceptionally fine voices. To maintain propriety, the members of the *concerto delle donne* were classified as ladies in waiting to the duchess, not among the ranks of paid musicians; professional women musicians were still viewed with mistrust at this time, being thought little better than street entertainers. In fact, however, the *concerto delle donne* comprised vocalists of the highest quality and constituted the first professional ensemble of women employed by a court. The excellence of their singing impressed visitors coming to Ferrara, and soon similar all-female vocal groups could also be heard in Rome, Florence, and Mantua.

At Ferrara the *concerto delle donne* performed for the duke and duchess each afternoon, singing usually for two hours. (Playing cards and board games, reading poetry, and listening to live music were the ways in which the aristocracy amused itself in the days before TVs and DVDs.) Each of the ladies of the *concerto delle donne* also played a string instrument—the harp, lute, viol, or harpsichord—that might provide an accompaniment to their singing. They were supported by a single bass singer and sometimes joined by a tenor. Yet, as the following eyewitness accounts suggest, often the ladies had need of neither the bass nor the tenor voice:

> **8 September 1582:** Wednesday after having dined, the duke passed a good deal of time listening to those ladies sing from ordinary music books. Even in that kind of singing the ladies were beautiful to hear, because they sing the low parts an octave higher.

> **29 July 1584:** And then [the duke] favored me [an emissary from Florence] by allowing me to hear for two hours without break his *concerto delle donne*, which is truly extraordinary. Those ladies sing excellently, both when singing by memory and when singing at sight from part books they are secure. The duke favored me continually by showing me written out all the pieces that they sing by memory, with all the virtuosic passages that they do.[1]

As these reports suggest, the *concerto delle donne* did not perform for the full court, but only for the ducal family and a very few important guests. In fact, these concerts went by a special name, **musica secreta** (secret music). At other courts this chamber music was sometimes called *musica reservata* (reserved or private music; see Chapter 24). But, whether termed *musica secreta* or *musica reservata*, this was progressive chamber music reserved for a small, elite audience.

The exclusive nature of *musica secreta,* and the intense emphasis on the text, led to a style of composition that was more virtuosic and dramatic. For example, when singing madrigals in these private chamber concerts, the ladies often performed florid vocal passages either written by the composer or improvised on the spot. So, too, textures became more extreme through the contrast of highs against lows and very long notes against very short ones. Moreover, madrigals appear for single solo voice with instrumental accompaniment. Finally, this elitist chamber music tended to encourage chromatic writing, sometimes of the most intense sort. The result? The equal-voice imitative polyphony commonly found in the madrigal and motet of the earlier sixteenth century began to give way to a more fragmented, dramatic style. The earlier conservative style of composition was called the *prima pratica,* while the newer, text-driven, dramatic style went by the name *seconda pratica*, for reasons we will soon see.

A good example of the new, dramatic madrigal is *O docezze amarissime d'amore* (*O sweet bitterness of love*) by Luzzasco Luzzaschi (c1545–1607), a composer resident in Ferrara from the 1560s onward. Measures 10–14 exhibit widely varying rhythms, difficult vocal passages, and a moderate degree of chromaticism (Ex. 28-2). Yet the music is animated by the sort of text painting we have come to expect in the madrigal: the word "gioisco" ("I enjoy") inspires rapturous melismas, while later the command "fuggite" ("flee") generates flighty imitation. With its three demanding parts for soprano (and optional keyboard accompaniment), this madrigal was a vocal showcase for the ladies of Ferrara.

EXAMPLE 28-2

Why is grief with me if I take pleasure in it…

❋ CARLO GESUALDO

Carlo Gesualdo (1561–1613) is perhaps the most notorious figure in the history of music. He was an aristocrat, prince of the small territory of Venosa east of Naples and dutiful husband of the Marchesa of Pescara, Maria d'Avalos. But on the night of 16 October 1590 Gesualdo discovered his wife and her lover in what was then referred to as "flagrant violation and flagrant sin" and stabbed them both to death. Gesualdo was not punished by any civil court; death was thought an appropriate reward for adulterous women in Renaissance Italy. Instead of going to prison or the gallows, Gesualdo simply repaired to his country villa until the scandal blew over. Here, in semi-isolation, he was able to cultivate all the more intensely his passion for music.

Exactly when and how Gesualdo learned music is not entirely clear, but music became his obsession. During his isolation, Gesualdo composed at least two books of madrigals. By the time of his own death in 1613 he had published seven such books, as well as three volumes of motets and other religious works in Latin. In 1594 Gesualdo was able to rehabilitate his reputation by marrying Leonora d'Este, niece of Duke Alfonso d'Este of Ferrara, and for most of the years 1594–1596 he resided there. Letters to and from Ferrara at this time show that Gesualdo was a somewhat compulsive figure whose craving for music was so strong he could not endure even a single evening without it, as a Ferrarese court official suggests:

15 February 1594: [Gesualdo] discourses on hunting and music and declares himself an authority on both of them. Of hunting he did not enlarge very much since he did not find much reaction from me, but about music he spoke at such length that I have not heard so much in a whole year. He makes open profession of it and shows his works in score to everybody in order to induce them to marvel at his art. He has with him two sets of music books in five parts, all his own works, but he says that he has only four people [in his entourage] who can sing, for which reason he will be forced to take the fifth part himself . . . This evening after supper he sent for a harpsichord . . . so that he could play on it himself along with the guitar, of which he has a very high regard. But we could not find a harpsichord for which reason, so as not to pass an evening without music, he played the lute for an hour and a half.[2]

During his three years in Ferrara, Gesualdo published his first four books of madrigals. Books three and four in particular show the influence of the progressive musical style of Ferrara and of the singing of the *concerto delle donne*. Books five and six, not published until 1611 and 1613, demand even greater aural skills and vocal bravura. Typical of these pieces is the remarkable five-voice madrigal *Moro, lasso* (*I die, miserable*).

Let us first consider its text. As is customary with the madrigal, the poem is a single stanza with lines of seven or eleven syllables. It is also rather short and aphoristic; that is to say, it is packed with intense words and vivid images. Finally, it makes use of oxymoron—two words that mean the opposite. At the beginning of *Moro, lasso* death confronts life: the lover wishes to die because the beloved will not let him live. Gesualdo preferred short, vivid texts full of such antitheses. A brief text allowed him to work through each word very slowly and express it through music as intensely as possible. He gives each word or phrase its distinct meaning by switching textures (from slow chordal-declamatory passages to rapid imitative ones, for example), as well as by means of sudden strong dissonances, and, most important, bold chromatic shifts. These lightning-quick changes of musical style capture the opposite meanings contained in an oxymoron. The opening chords shock because of their chromatic relationship (chords built on C♯, C, and B come in immediate succession). They lend a feeling of uncertainty and strangeness to the music. *Moro, lasso* is intense, chromatic, passionate, often beautiful, and, like Gesualdo himself, sometimes bizarre.

EXAMPLE 28-3

I die, miserable in my despair, and the one who can give me life…

Moro, lasso, al mio duolo	I die, miserable in my despair
E chi mi può dar vita	And the one who can give me life
Ahi, che m'ancide e non vuol darmi aita!	Ouch, that one kills me and gives no aid!
O dolorosa sorte,	Oh, dolorous fate,
Chi dar vita mi può, ahi, mi dà morte.	The one who can give me life, alas, gives only death.

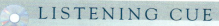

LISTENING CUE

CARLO GESUALDO
Moro, lasso (published 1613)

CD 3/25
Anthology, No. 77

Needless to say, the late madrigals of Gesualdo are not for the timid amateur singer. Rather, the rapid ascents, wide ranges, and difficult leaps suggest a repertory intended for highly skilled professional performers. The chromatic sections in particular challenge the fearless singer to find and cling to the right pitch in the midst of an unsettled sea of harmonic change. When performed without the support of instruments, the madrigals of Gesualdo can be among the most difficult works in the entire repertory of *a cappella* vocal music. Indeed, not before the advent of "atonal" music in the twentieth century do we find chromatic vocal lines as challenging as these. It is not surprising, then, that the modern Russian composer Igor Stravinsky became fascinated with Gesualdo's music, "recomposing" three of Gesualdo's madrigals to create his tribute *Monumentum pro Gesualdo di Venosa* (1960).

MUSIC IN MANTUA: ISABELLA D'ESTE

Like Ferrara, Mantua was a Renaissance city-state of between fifty and sixty thousand citizens ruled by an aristocratic, music-loving family, in this case the Gonzagas. A link between the two cities was forged in 1490 when **Isabella d'Este** (1474–1539; Fig. 28-1), daughter of the Duke of Ferrara, married Francesco Gonzaga, son of the Marquis of Mantua. Isabella moved to Mantua and took with her many of the musical traditions of the Ferrarese court. As a youth she had studied Latin and could recite passages from the poets of Roman antiquity—part of the humanistic curriculum of the Renaissance. Because her husband was a military general often far from home, Isabella frequently ran the affairs of state for Mantua and its subordinate lands. But when business was done, Isabella turned to the arts for recreation and spiritual solace. She was not, however, content merely to listen to the musicians, professional and amateur, of her court. She, too, joined in the music-making. Isabella had a fine soprano voice and made sure her voice teacher at Mantua was a soprano as well. (Because only males served as singing teachers at this time, she found a man who sang in the soprano range in falsetto voice.) Isabella also acquired a singing method book, which contained a program of study and exercises. By the 1490s she had learned to play the harpsichord, clavichord, *lira da braccio*, lute, viol, and *vihuela de mano* (Spanish guitar). All of these instruments she kept in a specially constructed music room at court.

Besides music, Isabella was a connoisseur of the visual arts. She collected ancient Greek and Roman sculpture and commissioned paintings from the most prominent artists of the day, including Andrea Mantegna, Titian, and Leonardo da Vinci (see

FIGURE 28-1

Isabella d'Este was a great patron of both musicians and artists. Here she is seen in a portrait commissioned from Leonardo da Vinci.

Tiroler Landesmuseum Ferdinandeum, Innsbruck

FIGURE 28-2

Portrait of Claudio Monteverdi by Bernardo Strozzi (1581–1644). Strozzi also painted the singer and composer Barbara Strozzi (see Chapter 31).

Fig. 28-1). Similarly, Isabella both wrote and collected poetry and commissioned composers, principally the frottolist Marchetto Cara (c1465–1525), to set this verse to music. Cara's frottola *Forsi che sì, forsi che no* (*Perhaps yes, perhaps no*), which sets the motto of the Gonzaga family, is a typical fruit of Isabella's patronage. Given Isabella's commitment to the arts, it is not surprising that Mantua became a principal center for musical composition during the sixteenth century.

CLAUDIO MONTEVERDI

The cultivation of music continued at Mantua well into the seventeenth century, as can be seen in the career of Claudio Monteverdi (1567–1643; Fig. 28-2). Monteverdi arrived in Mantua in 1591 to be a string player in the ducal orchestra. By 1601 he had worked his way up the musical ladder to become *maestro della musica* at court. In this capacity, Monteverdi provided myriad musical services for the Gonzaga family. He composed, he played, he taught composition and singing, he conducted, and eventually he mounted operas and ballets. Although Monteverdi wrote an important Mass and Vespers service for the church, he was best known in his day as a composer of secular music, including nine books of madrigals and several important early operas. As the years went by, Monteverdi found his duties at Mantua excessively heavy and his pay exceedingly light. Consequently, in 1613 he moved on to Venice to become *maestro di cappella* of the basilica of St. Mark, where he extended his distinguished career into the 1640s.

As a composer of madrigals in Mantua, Monteverdi became embroiled in what is known as the **Artusi-Monteverdi controversy.** Giovanni Maria Artusi (c1540–1613) was a churchman and conservative music theorist. While visiting Ferrara in 1598 he heard several newly composed madrigals, among them *Cruda Amarilli* (*Cruel Amarillis*) by Monteverdi, and was horrified by the "errors" in counterpoint and harmony that he found. In 1600 Artusi published *Delle imperfettioni della moderna musica* (*On the Imperfections of Modern Music*) in which he goes almost measure by measure through Monteverdi's *Cruda Amarilli* pointing out its "mistakes." These "errors" have come about, according to Artusi, because composers such as Monteverdi have given free rein to the ear and not followed reason, that is, the traditional rules of harmony and counterpoint. Even so, he believes, such passages are offensive to the ear.

> They are harsh to the ear, and offend rather than delight it. They bring confusion and imperfection to the good rules of harmony left by those who have established the principles of the science of music. Instead of enriching, augmenting, and ennobling harmony by various means, as so many noble spirits have done, they have created a situation in which the beautiful and purified style is indistinguishable from the barbaric.[3]

Monteverdi responded to Artusi in the preface to his Fifth Book of Madrigals (1605; Fig. 28-3) and more fully (using his brother to speak for him) in the preface to his *Scherzi musicali* (1607). Here, the composer defends his progressive musical style in firm and forceful tones. In a famous phrase he declares that "harmony (music) must be the servant of the words" and not the other way around. He calls his new text-driven approach to musical composition the **seconda pratica,** and dis-

STVDIOSI LETTORI.

Non vi marauigliate ch'io dia alle ftampe quefti Madrigali fenza prima rifpondere alle oppofitioni, che fece l'Artufi contro alcune minime particelle d'effi, perche fend'io al feruigio di quefta Sereniffima Altezza di Mantoa non fon patrone di quel tempo che tal'hora mi bifognarebbe : hò nondimeno fcritta la rifpofta per far conofcere ch'io non faccio le mie cofe à cafo, & tofto che fia refcritta vfcirà in luce portando in fronte il nome di SECONDA PRATICA, ouero PERFETTIONE DELLA MODERNA MVSICA, delche forfe alcuni s'ammireranno non credendo che vi fia altra pratica, che l'infegnata dal Zerlino ; ma fiano ficuri, che intorno alle confonanze, & diffonanze, vi è anco vn'altra confideratione differente dalla determinata , la qual con quietanza della ragione , & del fenfo diffende il moderno comporre , & quefto hò voluto dirui fi perche quefta voce SECONDA PRATICA talhora non foffe occupata da altri , fi perche anco gli ingegnofi poffino fra tanto confiderare altre feconde cofe intorno all'armonia , & credere che il moderno Compofitore fabrica fopra li fondamenti della verità.   Viuete felici.

TAVOLA DELLI MADRIGALI:

Cruda Amarilli	1	Che dar più vi pofs'io	13
O Mirtillo Mirtillo anima mia	2	M'è piu dolce il penar	14
Era l'anima mia	3	Ahi come a un vago fol	16
Ecco Siluio. Prima parte.	4	Troppo ben può	17
Ma fe con la pietà. Secon.par.	5	Amor fe giufto fei	19
Dorinda hà dirò. Terza par.	6	T'amo mia vita	20
Ecco piegando.Quarta par.	7	A fei voci.	
Ferir quel petto. vlt. par.	8	E cofi à pocoà poco.	21
Ch'io t'ami. Prima parte.	10	A noue voci.	
Deh bella e cara. Secon.par.	11	Sinfonia. Quefti vaghi.	22
Ma tu piu che mai. vlti. par.	12		

❊ FIGURE 28-3

The preface to the fifth book of madrigals by Claudio Monteverdi, in which the composer defends his text-driven approach to the madrigal, referring to it, as can clearly be seen, in capital letters as *SECONDA PRATICA*. Notice also that he places *Cruda Amarilli* as the first madrigal in the collection, something of an "in your face" response to the music theorist Artusi.

Albi Rosenthal

tinguishes it from the older, more conservative *prima pratica*, in which composers often followed the rules of counterpoint regardless of the text (see Chapter 25). The emotional content of the text was of such importance that it justified, indeed required, violations of the standard rules for part-writing in the sixteenth century. But what rules did Monteverdi violate?

The gist of the Artusi-Monteverdi controversy concerns what are called unprepared dissonances—dissonant seconds, fourths, diminished fifths (tritones), and sevenths sounding against the lowest pitch without proper preparation. Taking the offending passages in *Cruda Amarilli* in turn, as did Artusi: in bar 13 the soprano jumps in with a second against the bass (Ex. 28-4a); in bar 19 the quinto (fifth part) rises to a seventh against the bass; in bar 21 the bass itself enters to form a diminished fifth against the tenor; in bar 36 the alto leaps down to create a seventh against the bass, and then the tenor and soprano do the same (Ex. 28-4b).

EXAMPLE 28-4A

EXAMPLE 28-4B

According to Artusi's strict interpretation, each of these spots violates conventional rules of harmony for preparing and resolving dissonance. Monteverdi, on the other hand, believes that each "violation" is justified by the text at that moment. The words "ouch" (m. 13), "bitterly" (mm. 19 and 21), "wasp" (mm. 36–38), and "fierce" (m. 41) require such dissonances—dissonances made all the more stinging, bitter, and fierce precisely because they are not prepared. Are these unprepared dissonances offensive to the ear, as Artusi believes, or do they intensify the meaning of the text, as Monteverdi contends? You be the judge.

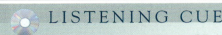

LISTENING CUE

CLAUDIO MONTEVERDI
Cruda Amarilli (1598; published 1605)

CD 3/26
Anthology, No. 78

In truth, Monteverdi's unprepared "barbarities" may not be as shocking as Artusi alleges. Monteverdi saw himself, not as a radical innovator but as part of a long continuum of composers. In his reply to Artusi, Monteverdi applied the label *seconda pratica* to the madrigals of text-expressive composers extending back over the last fifty years. Modern historians, however, have seized upon the term as a way to focus attention on the debate between the old and new musical practices around 1600—to contrast the law-abiding music of Palestrina (*prima pratica*) against the illicit, text-driven music of Monteverdi (*seconda pratica*). Ultimately, Monteverdi's vision proved correct, for it is from the *seconda pratica* that the new music of the Baroque emerged.

 SUMMARY

Music in late sixteenth-century Italy was marked by an intensification of interest in the textually explicit madrigal. One of the hallmarks of the Renaissance, as opposed to the earlier Middle Ages, was the creation of text-reflective music that forged a close bond between text and tone. Renaissance composers developed a system of onomatopoeic gestures to express text through music. Explained in the simplest terms, the word "ouch" would require a dissonance, and "peace" a soothing major triad, for example. Composers made use of these gestures to varying degrees, and by the end of the century a separation of compositional styles had developed. On the one hand, a conservative contrapuntal idiom was evident, especially in religious music. Called the *prima pratica,* it included the Masses and motets of Ockeghem and Josquin, and eventually those of Palestrina as well. Proceeding with a carefully regulated control of harmony and counterpoint, the *prima pratica* too showed a concern for clear text declamation but did not engage in detailed text painting. At the same time, a second, more progressive musical style developed in northern Italian city-states such as Ferrara and Mantua. Typified by the madrigals of Gesualdo and Monteverdi, this *seconda pratica* delighted in extremes of textures, difficult vocal writing, bold chromatic progressions, and, occasionally, unprepared dissonance—all with the aim of supercharging an already vivid text. Ultimately, this progressive second practice proved to be the path to the future.

Finally, the private concerts of chamber music that emerged at the end of the sixteenth century in Ferrara, Mantua, Florence, and Rome reshaped the relationship between performers and audience. Since its beginnings in Florence and Rome, the sixteenth-century madrigal had been sung largely for the pleasure of the singers themselves—the singers and audience being one and the same. This was social music, in which amateurs eagerly sang music that was not too difficult to read. Toward the end of the century, however, the progressive madrigal became so vocally demanding that professional singers were needed. This resulted in a separation between highly skilled, solo performers and a non-participating, generally aristocratic audience, a division that set the stage for early Baroque opera.

KEY TERMS

concerto delle donne	Isabella d'Este	seconda pratica
musica secreta	Artusi-Monteverdi controversy	

1670 Heinrich Biber (1644–1704), violin virtuoso, enters employment at court of archbishop of Salzburg

daughter of Giulio Strozzi, publishes 8 volumes of vocal music

appointed Kapellmeister at German court of Dresden

Antonio Vivaldi (1678–1741), violinist and composer important in development of concerto

Jean-Philippe Rameau (1683–1764), composer and theorist

Giuseppe Torelli (1658–1709), violinist, writes trumpet concertos for St. Petronio's basilica in Bologna

Johann Sebastian Bach (1685–1750)

BAROQUE MUSIC

234

Chapter

29

Early Baroque Music

Music historians agree, with unusual unanimity, that Baroque music first appeared in the early seventeenth century in northern Italy, in cities such as Florence, Mantua, and Venice. Around 1600 the choral polyphony of the Renaissance gradually gave way to a new exuberant style of solo singing that musicians of the day called "the new music." Later, this new music was given a new name: Baroque.

Baroque is the term used generally to describe the art, architecture, and music of the period 1600–1750. It derives from the Portuguese word *barroco*, meaning a pearl of irregular shape then used in jewelry and fine decoration. Critics applied the term "Baroque" to indicate a rough, bold sound in music and excessive ornamentation in the visual arts. To the philosopher Jean-Jacques Rousseau (1712–1778), "A baroque music is that in which the harmony is confused, charged with modulations and dissonances, the melody is harsh and little natural, the intonation difficult, and the movement constrained." Thus originally the term "Baroque" had a pejorative meaning. It signified the extravagant, the excessive, even the bizarre. Only during the twentieth century, with a newfound appreciation of the painting of Peter Paul Rubens (1577–1640) and the music of Antonio Vivaldi (1678–1741) and J.S. Bach (1685–1750), among others, has the term "Baroque" come to assume a positive meaning in Western cultural history. Today we admire Baroque art for its drama, opulence, intense expression, and grandeur.

The period of Baroque art roughly corresponds with what political historians call the **Age of Absolutism.** The theory of absolutism held that a king enjoyed absolute power by reason of divine right. Rulers were said to govern with absolute authority so that citizens might live in a well-ordered society. The pope in Rome, the Holy Roman Emperor, the kings of France and Spain, and, to a lesser extent, the king of England were the most powerful absolute monarchs of the seventeenth century. Much Baroque art, architecture, and music came into being to reflect and extend their absolute power. In almost every way, the church and the aristocratic court remained the principal patrons of the arts, in Italy and elsewhere.

Most striking about many monuments of Baroque art, such as St. Peter's Square in Rome or the palace of Versailles outside of Paris, is their vast scale. The buildings and grounds are massive. St. Peter's Square, designed by Gian Lorenzo Bernini (1598–1680), is so enormous that it seems to swallow people, cars, and buses (Fig. 29-1). The palace of Versailles, built by French King Louis XIV (1638–1715), is not merely a building but was once an entire city under a single roof, designed to be home to several thousand court functionaries (see Part IV timeline).

The music composed for such vast expanses could also be grandiose. No longer was every part played by a single instrument, as had been the case generally during the Renaissance. By the end of the seventeenth century many parts were doubled so as to increase the volume of sound. The orchestra playing for the opera

❀ FIGURE 29-1
St. Peter's Square, Rome, designed by Bernini in the mid seventeenth century. St. Peter's Basilica, the largest church in the world, is in the center; the smaller Sistine Chapel is to the right.

Archiv fur Kunst Und Geschichte, Berlin

and ballet at the court of King Louis XIV at Versailles some-times numbered more than eighty instrumentalists, although such an ensemble was exceptional. In Rome and elsewhere composers wrote choral works for twenty-four, forty-eight, and even fifty-three separate vocal parts. These vocal works were generally intended for the great Baroque churches in Italy and Austria, and this style of music for multiple choruses with in-strumental accompaniment has come to be called the grand, or colossal, Baroque.

Yet the art and architecture of the Baroque era is marked by strong contrasts. Buildings of enormous scale, for example, are usually adorned by much ornamental detail. Artists filled the long lines and vast spaces of the palaces and churches with abundant decoration. Monumental space created a vacuum, and into this rushed the artist with intense, dramatic energy. In creating his *Throne of St. Peter* for the interior of that basil-ica in Rome, the sculptor Gian Lorenzo Bernini filled the ex-panse with twisting forms that energize the otherwise static architecture (Fig. 29-2). Similarly, a Roman ceiling painting entitled *Glorification of Pope Urban VIII* by Pietro da Cortona (1596–1669) epitomizes the size and exuberance of the Baroque art (Fig. 29-3). The architectural space is filled with figures that writhe and clouds that swirl. The painting is monu-mental yet packed with countless energetic details.

This same approach to artistic expression is found in the music of the Baroque era. Composers too created large-scale compositions and filled them with energetic figures. In both vocal and instrumental music, strong chordal blocks support highly ornamental melodic lines. The florid melodies add energy and

Bridgeman Art Library

❄ FIGURE 29-2
Bernini's *The Throne of St. Peter* within St. Peter's basilica. This is not the high altar of St. Peter's, merely a rear chapel, which sug-gests the enormous size of the basilica. Bernini responded to the architectural scale by filling the chapel with exuberant decoration.

Bridgeman Art Library

❄ FIGURE 29-3
Pietro da Cortona, *Glorification of Pope Urban VIII*. This ceiling fresco, executed in Rome in 1633–1639 for the family of the pope, is both energetic and monumental.

excitement to what would otherwise be a purely static harmonic background. Notice in the following excerpt from Giulio Caccini's aria *Ardi, cor mio* (*Burn, O my heart*) of 1602 how the energetic vocal line is supported by a solid bedrock of simple chords (Ex. 29-1).

EXAMPLE 29-1

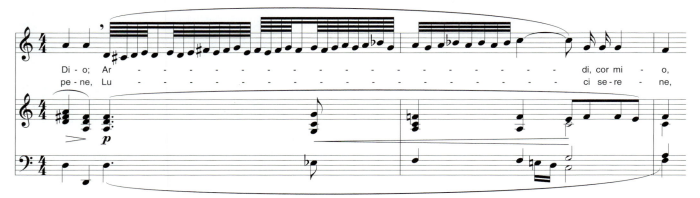

Di - o; Ar - di, cor mi - o,
pe - ne, Lu - ci se - re - ne,

❋ CHARACTERISTICS OF EARLY BAROQUE MUSIC

Toward the end of the sixteenth century the madrigal was the most progressive genre of music in Europe. The more forward-looking of the madrigal composers—Gesualdo and Monteverdi among them—wrote experimental works that broke many of the established rules of counterpoint. They valued the text and its meaning above purely musical procedures. In 1600 Monteverdi was attacked in print by a conservative music theorist named Giovanni Maria Artusi and he responded in kind, thereby creating what has come to be called the **Artusi-Monteverdi controversy** (see also Chapter 28)—a war of words over what was more important, music or text. Monteverdi called his new text-driven approach the *seconda pratica* (second practice). This he distinguished from the more traditional *prima pratica*, the conservative, mainly church style that dutifully followed the traditional rules of linear counterpoint. Later, musicians would refer to the conservative church style as the *stile antico* (old or traditional style) and the newer *seconda pratica* as the *stile moderno* (modern style). Composers continued to write in both *antico* and *moderno* styles throughout the seventeenth century.

Monteverdi and his progressive colleagues believed that music had the power to move the soul, as had ancient Greek music. Their faith that the language of music could express many and varied emotions led to an aesthetic theory called the Doctrine of Affections. The **Doctrine of Affections** held that different musical moods could and should be used to influence the emotions, or affections, of the listeners. A musical setting should reinforce the intended "affection" of the text. As early as 1602 the composer Giulio Caccini, in his *Le nuove musiche* (*The New Music*), referred to "moving the affections of the soul." Later music theorists would advocate a unity of affections, holding that each piece of music should project only a single affection, be it anger, hate, sorrow, joy, or love (see Chapter 34). Indeed, Baroque music generally does not change quickly from one mood to another, as might a polyphonic madrigal in the Renaissance or a symphony from the later Classical period. The Baroque artist—whether painter, sculptor, or musician—created emotional units that were clearly defined, distinctly separate, and long-lasting.

Vocal Expression and Virtuosity

During the Renaissance, vocal music was mostly ensemble music—works for groups of vocalists, even if there were only one singer on a part. In the early Baroque, however, emphasis shifted from vocal ensemble to accompanied solo song. Vocal groups might be a useful way to convey the abstract religious thoughts of the multitudes but, to communicate raw human emotions, direct appeal by an individual soloist was now thought more effective. Solo madrigals, solo arias, and solo recitatives were all designated by a single word: **monody** (from Greek terms meaning "to sing alone"). The vogue of monody was simply a continuation of the attempts of poets, scholars, and musicians to emulate the music of ancient Greece by making the words intelligible and enhancing their effect. In Chapter 30 we shall discuss several types of monody (see Anthology, Nos.79–81). For the moment it is enough to say that emphasis on the solo voice quickly led to a more flamboyant style of singing (see Ex. 29-1). Soon the vocal virtuoso would emerge, the star of the court theater and the operatic stage.

Harmonic Conception and the Basso Continuo

During the Renaissance the prevailing texture for music, vocal as well as instrumental, involved imitative counterpoint. In a Renaissance Mass, motet, or madrigal, for example, several equal parts spin out a web of polyphony, one line imitating another in turn. Early Baroque music has a fundamentally different orientation. Instead of having three, four, or five contrapuntal lines, composers now emphasized just the top and bottom parts, using the other voices to add chordal enrichment in the middle. If much of Renaissance music was created polyphonically and horizontally, working line by line, that of the early Baroque period is more homophonically conceived, its chords springing up vertically from the bass.

✺ FIGURE 29-4

A Lady with Theorbo (c1670) by John Michael Wright. The bass strings are at the top of the instrument and off the fingerboard. Each bass string plays just one note of a low, diatonic scale. The theorbo was often used to play the basso continuo in the seventeenth century.

In the early 1600s, composers acknowledged the new importance of the bass, and they gave it a new name: **basso continuo** in Italian (commonly called "thorough bass" in England). The basso continuo was a bass line that provided a never-ending foundation, or "continuous bass," for the melody above. Early in the Baroque, the basso continuo might be played by a single solo instrument such as the lute or the **theorbo**—a large lute-like instrument with a full octave of additional bass strings descending in a diatonic pattern such as F-E-D-C-B'-A' (Fig. 29-4). Gradually, a low melody instrument such as the *viola da gamba*, cello, or bassoon came to reinforce the bass line. Thus the basso continuo often consisted of an ensemble of two instruments; while one performer played the written bass line, another played a harmony above the bass on a chord-producing instrument—organ, harpsichord, lute, theorbo, or even guitar, for example. (For a clear example of the sound of the basso continuo, turn to the Anthology, No. 85.) The chord-playing instrument linked the melody on top to the bass below by improvising on the spot in a flexible, expressive way. But how did the player know what chords to improvise?

The harmonies of the basso continuo were usually indicated by a notation called **figured bass**—a numerical shorthand placed with the bass line that tells the player which unwritten notes to fill in above the written bass note. Figured bass is similar in intent to the numerical code found in "fake books" used by modern jazz pianists that indicate which chords to play beneath the written melody. Today, music theory courses in conservatories and universities around the world still teach, and test, the capacity to realize (play chords above) a figured bass at sight (Ex. 29-2).

EXAMPLE 29-2

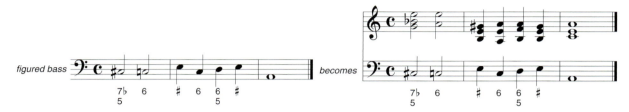

A musician who has mastered the ability to realize a figured bass has a solid understanding of chordal harmony. Indeed, in the early Baroque, chordal harmony was becoming increasingly important. More and more, composers were conceiving music as a series of chordal units, or chord progressions. In addition, they came to write these chord progressions within just the major and minor keys.

Major and Minor Tonalities

In the course of the seventeenth century, two scale patterns, major (the Ionian mode) and minor (the Aeolian mode), came to be employed to the virtual exclusion of all of the other church modes of the Renaissance and before. The old Dorian and Phrygian modes, for example, became less and less important. (For more on the increasing importance of major and minor tonalities, see Musical Interlude 5 following Chapter 36.) Of course, privileging just the major and minor modes meant that melodies were written mostly in just these two scales. But it affected harmony as well. Modal polyphony of the Renaissance had emphasized triads that were often only a second or a third apart; the new tonal polyphony of the Baroque, on the other hand, tended increasingly to construct chords upon notes of the scale that were a fourth or a fifth apart. Viewed from the perspective of harmony alone, the seventeenth century can be seen as a period in which modal harmony gradually gave way to tonal harmony. The difference between the two approaches can be seen by comparing two progressions centering on the home pitch E (Exs. 29-3a, 29-3b), the first by Renaissance composer Thomas Tallis and the second by Baroque composer Arcangelo Corelli.

EXAMPLE 29-3A   EXAMPLE 29-3B

Modal harmony (Tallis, 1567)   Tonal harmony (Corelli, c1690)

As harmonies were reduced to just the major and minor modes, the listener could more easily focus on the distinct properties of each. Composers could play the dark minor mode off against the bright major, or vice versa, to create the emotional effects and shadings of color so important in Baroque music in particular and Baroque art generally.

Instrumental Color and Musical Dynamics

The Baroque era is a crossroads in the progressive development of musical instruments. Some instruments of the Renaissance, such as the lute, theorbo, cornett, recorder, and *viola da gamba*, were peaking in popularity and would disappear with the Baroque era. Others, particularly the members of the violin family, including the violoncello (or cello), were relatively new and would grow in popularity during the Baroque period. In the early 1600s, however, all of these instruments were available and were called for by composers at various times. A variegated ensemble in which a theorbo, *viola da gamba,* cornett, sackbut, violin, recorder, transverse flute, bassoon, cello, and harpsichord played together was not uncommon. The early Baroque orchestra was not yet dominated by members of the violin family; instead it was remarkable for its diverse, colorful sounds.

Similarly, diversity of sound came to include the volume of sound. Certainly there were louds and softs in the music of the Middle Ages and Renaissance. Yet not until around 1600 did composers specify levels of volume in their music. At first they did so in a very simple way: they merely wrote *piano* or *forte* in the score. Generally, in Baroque instrumental music, dynamics do not change gradually within a section of a piece. Rather, a single dynamic range, whether loud or soft, holds fast until abruptly replaced by another. Setting loud against soft, winds against strings, soloist against chorus, major against minor—all these helped create the brilliant colors and strong contrasts that mark Baroque music.

Idiomatic Writing for Instruments and Voice

Finally, Baroque music welcomes for the first time truly idiomatic writing for both instruments and voice. In the Renaissance, melody was more or less all of one type. It was a direct, uncomplicated line that could be performed by either a voice or an instrument. Indeed, Renaissance publishers exploited the generic quality of melody, eagerly advertising their newest print as "suitable for both voices and instruments." Beginning about 1600, however, instrumental style began to diverge from vocal. Composers recognized that the violin, for example, can play a scale faster than the human voice can sing one. Thus they began to write idiomatic (well suited) music for particular instruments—rapid scales for the violin or repeating notes of a triad for brass instruments, for example. Vocal music, too, began to go its own way. Composers wrote vocal lines with starkly different levels of rhythmic activity and with trills and other ornaments that highlighted the acrobatic ability of the voice. Nowhere could this distinctly idiomatic vocal style be more clearly heard than in the newly emerging opera.

SUMMARY

In Western cultural history the term "Baroque" identifies an artistic style that flourished during the years 1600–1750. Baroque art, architecture, and music are characterized by vivid colors, strong contrasts, and grand designs. Around 1600 the choral polyphony that had dominated the Renaissance gave way to an exuberant style of solo singing. If Renaissance music was mostly conceived contrapuntally and horizontally, line by line, that of the early Baroque period is organized more homophonically and vertically, chord by chord. Attention came to be focused almost entirely on an expressive melody supported by a strong bass. Tonality increasingly came to be limited to just the major and minor modes. Throughout the Baroque era, idiomatic writing created two distinctly different styles, one for instruments and another for voices.

KEY TERMS

Baroque	*seconda pratica*	theorbo
Age of Absolutism	Doctrine of Affections	figured bass
Artusi-Monteverdi controversy	monody	
	basso continuo	

Chapter

30

The Birth of Opera: Florence, Mantua, and Venice

Today opera is an enormously popular medium. While symphony orchestras struggle to stay in business, opera companies flourish, and demand for the best singers pushes ticket prices to the roof. Yet, oddly, opera emerged rather late in the history of Western art music, around 1600. By way of comparison, both China and Japan had had a flourishing tradition of opera since at least 1300. True, something approaching sung drama had existed in the West in the liturgical drama of the medieval church. But liturgical drama flowered only briefly around 1200 and then died, leaving no successor. The opera that we listen to today, and for which there are passionate devotees around the world, emerged in northern Italy about the year 1600.

Opera literally means "work." Musically speaking, the term was first employed in the Italian phrase *opera drammatica in musica* (a dramatic work, or play, set to music). In opera the lines of the actors and actresses are not merely spoken, but sung. At first this sounds like a very odd thing to do; human beings do not sing out their day-to-day conversations ("Please pass the peas as soon as possible," for example). But the fundamental premise of opera is that sung music can heighten the emotional intensity of a dramatic text. The text that conveys the story of the opera is called the **libretto,** and it is written in poetic verse. By combining music, poetry, drama, scenic design, and dance, opera can be the most powerful of all forms of art. Some consider it the supreme expression of the human spirit.

✤ EARLY OPERA IN FLORENCE

Opera in the West first appeared at the court of the Medici princes in Florence, Italy, at the turn of the seventeenth century. In quick succession came *Dafne* (1598) by Jacopo Peri, *Euridice* (1600) again by Peri, and *Euridice* (1602) by Giulio Caccini. All three early operas set a libretto by the Florentine court poet Ottavio Rinuccini (1562–1621). The stories of Dafne and Apollo and of Euridice and Orpheus are based on ancient Greek myths. In fact, most early operas set a libretto drawn from mythology because the creators of opera were trying to recapture the spirit of ancient drama while carrying the listener to a magical world far from reality. The first operas of Peri and Caccini did not emerge out of thin air, however. Rather, they were the result of nearly twenty-five years of discussion and experimentation about the nature of ancient Greek music.

As early as the 1570s, a group of prominent Florentines had gathered in the home of Count Giovanni Bardi (1534–1612) to discuss the literature, science, and arts of the day. Later, one of Bardi's protégés dubbed this society the **Florentine camerata** ("club" or "circle"). Bardi was a soldier by profession, but an antiquarian by passion. Fellow camerata members included the translator and textual scholar Girolamo Mei (1519–1594) and the musician-scientist Vincenzo Galilei (c1528–1591). Galilei is important to history and music on several counts: he was the father of the famous astronomer Galileo Galilei (1564–1642); he was one of the earliest to advocate equal temperament as the most practical way of dealing with tuning in music; and he was one of the first to argue for a new style of solo singing, as stated in his *Dialogo della musica antica, et della moderna* (*Dialogue on Ancient and Modern Music*, 1581). Bardi, Mei, Galilei, and their colleagues shared a common purpose, to create a modern music that approximated the vocal declamation of ancient Greek tragedy. Though they lacked the actual music from ancient Greece, they knew that Greek drama had been sung, or at least declaimed in a musical manner. What the camerata advocated was a new type of vocal delivery called *stile rappresentativo*. **Stile rappresentativo** (dramatic style or theater style) was vocal expression somewhere between song and declaimed speech. The singer emphatically declaimed the text so that the pitches and rhythms of the voice matched exactly the rhythms, accents, and sentiments of the text. What began as an antiquarian study of Greek musical practices became a model for contemporary composition.

In 1589 the leaders of the camerata presented their new experimental style of singing to an aristocratic audience drawn to Florence for the wedding of the grand duke of Tuscany, Ferdinando de' Medici. The principal wedding entertainment was a play. Between each of the acts of the play, however, Bardi and his associates inserted a sung diversion, called an intermedio, a sung play within a play. Figure 30-1 shows Jacopo Peri (1561–1633) portraying the role of the mythological singer Arion in the fifth intermedio of 1589. Typical of such late Renaissance court entertainments, each intermedio was fully sung, yet each was an isolated dramatic scene; they did not form a unified sung drama.

Nine years later Jacopo Peri created the first true opera, *Dafne* (1598), a unified multi-scene drama entirely sung. Unfortunately, only fragments of *Dafne* have survived. The first completely preserved opera dates from two years later: Peri's setting of the story of Orpheus and Euridice, simply called *Euridice* (1600). The story of Orpheus and Euridice is important in the history of opera because numerous composers would set it to dramatic music over the next three centuries.

The **Orpheus legend** tells the tale of Orpheus (Orfeo in Italian), the son of Apollo, the Greek god of the sun and of music. (As mentioned, our word "music" comes from the muses who attend Apollo.) Orpheus, himself a demi-god, falls in love with the beautiful human Euridice. No sooner are they married than she is fatally bitten by a snake and carried off to Hades (the realm of the dead). Orpheus vows to descend into the Underworld and restore his beloved to earthly life. This he nearly accomplishes by exploiting his divine powers of musical persuasion, for Orpheus can make the trees sway, calm savage beasts, and even overcome the furies of Hades with the beauty of his expressive song.

🌱 **F I G U R E 30 - 1**

Composer-singer Jacopo Peri portraying the mythological poet-singer Arion in Florence in 1589.

In his preface to the published score of *Euridice*, Jacopo Peri explained his approach to setting a text "in the manner of the ancient Greeks and Romans":

> I recognized that in our [Italian] language certain words are uttered in such a way that they allow a harmony to be built on them, and that in the course of speech, one passes through many other words that are not stressed, until one eventually returns to another word capable of sustaining a new consonant harmony. Having in mind those affects and stresses that we use to create lamenting, rejoicing, and similar emotions, I set the bass moving at the same pace as human speech, now faster, now slower, according to the affections, and held it firm through dissonances and consonances until, running through the various notes, the voice of the singer arrived at a syllable stressed in ordinary speech that then allows a new harmony.[1]

Exactly the sort of music Peri describes can be heard at the climax of *Euridice*, when Orfeo, having descended into Hades to rescue Euridice, confronts the horrors of that region. In a vocal solo entitled "Funeste piagge" ("Deadly shores") the composer drives rapidly through lines of text, often with quickly repeating pitches. At strategic moments, however, usually at the ends of lines where rhyming words appear, he underscores the text through long notes. The bass moves more rapidly or slowly as the text requires. Along the way dissonance is treated freely—not prepared or resolved according to the traditional rules of counterpoint. The excerpt from "Funeste piagge" in Example 30-1 exemplifies both monody (the term used generally to describe accompanied solo song at the turn of the seventeenth century) as well as the more specific *stile rappresentativo* (the dramatic or theatrical style). The chords above the basso continuo have been realized by a modern editor following the indications of Peri's figured bass.

EXAMPLE 30-1

While with sad accents I lament with you my lost love; and you, oh, pitying my anguish…

Jacopo Peri had a rival on the operatic stage in Florence: the composer, singer, and singing teacher Giulio Caccini (1551–1618). No sooner had Peri performed his *Euridice* (October 1600) than Caccini rushed into print with his own setting of the same libretto (January 1601). Caccini was intent on making sure his *Euridice* was seen to be as timely and as novel as Peri's. In the preface to his *Euridice*, Caccini was quick to point out that he too had set to music the fable of *Euridice* in the *stile rappresentivo* and he too had supported the recited parts with a basso continuo. He also announced that he would soon explain a new method for singing ornaments that he had invented.

The next year, Caccini made good on his promise by publishing **Le nuove musiche** (*The New Music*, 1602). Ironically, not all of *Le nuove musiche* was new music. It is, in fact, an anthology of solo madrigals and strophic solo songs gathered over time. Several of the madrigals, Caccini claims in his preface, had been greeted with "warm applause" when heard by the Florentine camerata as early as 1590. What is truly new about *Le nuove musiche* is Caccini's description of the vocal techniques that grace his monodies. Caccini was the first to describe early Baroque vocal ornaments and the first composer to write them directly in the score. The preface to *Le nuove musiche*, therefore, provides invaluable information on performance practices for modern performers seeking to re-create the true spirit of early Baroque vocal music. His instructions apply equally well to chamber singing and to early Baroque opera, because at that time both used the same techniques of singing.

Caccini has much to say about vocal execution, and his comments guide those singers who re-create Baroque opera today: Singers should inflect longer notes by means of slight crescendos and diminuendos, moments that he calls exclamations (*esclamazioni*); at that time musicians had no symbols to indicate crescendo and diminuendo. (Yet Caccini urges caution with the crescendo because the pitch may go sharp as the voice gets louder.) Singers are encouraged to fill in larger melodic intervals with running scales (*passaggi*). Singers may also vary the written rhythms to add lightness to the music. Most important, singers are urged to insert idiomatic vocal ornaments at cadences for emphasis, but to do so in moderation. To explain the principal two cadential ornaments, Caccini includes the following example (Ex. 30-2). His *trillo* is a repeating percussive effect placed on a single pitch, whereas his *gruppo* is the counterpart of our modern neighbor-note trill.

EXAMPLE 30-2

The monodies that follow the preface of *Le nuove musiche* exemplify Caccini's thoughts on vocal execution. The madrigal *Filli, mirando il cielo* (*Phyllis, admiring the heavens*), for example, is filled with well-placed vowels that offer opportunity for brief crescendos and diminuendos, and it ends with an elaborate *trillo* and *gruppo*. Indeed, the last line "What torment I shall have when my face turns sallow and my hair silver" is set three times with increasingly elaborate ornamentation. The principles of ornamentation set forth here apply not only to solo madrigals such as this but to all Florentine monodies including, as mentioned, those of early opera.

LISTENING CUE

GIULIO CACCINI
Le nuove musiche (1602)
Filli, mirando il cielo

CD 4/2
Anthology, No. 80

EARLY OPERA IN MANTUA: MONTEVERDI'S *ORFEO*

"There is no lover of music who does not keep Orfeo's songs before him at all times."[2] This contemporary remark attests to the popularity of the newborn opera generally and to the legend of Orpheus in particular. Soon another important composer, Claudio Monteverdi, took up the legend of Orpheus and Euridice. Monteverdi, as we have seen (see Chapter 28), was a composer who wrote madrigals in the manner of the *seconda pratica,* the progressive style that flourished around 1600. During the early 1600s, Monteverdi was director of music at the northern Italian court of Mantua. He apparently got the idea of writing an opera on the Orpheus legend when he heard Peri's *Euridice* in Florence in the fall of 1600. By 1607 Monteverdi was ready to stage his own version of the tale, one built on a new libretto by Alessandro Striggio (1573–1630). Monteverdi's *Orfeo* is Mantua's answer to Florentine operas based on the same subject.

Monteverdi intended his Mantuan *Orfeo* to be a chamber opera heard by a small and elite audience. At the first performance on 24 February 1607 about two hundred aristocrats crowded into a standing-room-only chamber measuring just 30 × 40 feet. (The room, on the ground floor of the ducal palace in Mantua, survives today, but serves as a gift shop!) Monteverdi divides his *Orfeo* into five short acts that together last no more than ninety minutes.

Orfeo opens with a brief fanfare entitled "toccata." A **toccata** (literally a "touched thing") is an instrumental piece, for keyboard or other instruments, requiring the performer to touch the instrument with great technical dexterity. In other words, it is an instrumental showpiece. Here the full orchestra puts on the show. Monteverdi requires a remarkable variety of instruments that feature many distinctly different sounds, as is typical of early Baroque ensembles: strings including violins and viols, recorders, trumpets, trombones, cornetts, harpsichord, theorbo, harp, organ, and reed organ. At no time, however, do all the instruments sound together. In the opening toccata, for example, the trumpets lead the way, racing up and down the scale in brilliant fashion. In his printed score Monteverdi instructs that the toccata be sounded three times: presumably first to get the attention of the audience, then to announce the arrival of the patron, the duke of Mantua, and finally to signal that the action is about to begin.

LISTENING CUE

CLAUDIO MONTEVERDI
Orfeo (1607)
Toccata

CD 4/3
Anthology, No. 81a

Compared to earlier settings of the Orpheus legend, Monteverdi's *Orfeo* is a richer, more opulent score. The luxuriant sound is created partly by the large number and variety of instruments, and partly by the diverse kinds of music Monteverdi creates; his opera has a mix of choral songs, choral dances, instrumental dances, instrumental interludes, and, most important, solo singing of various kinds. The accompanied solo singing, the monody, is stylistically the most progressive music, and he saves it for the dramatic high points of the opera.

The first such moment of high drama comes midway through Act II, when Orfeo learns that his new bride Euridice has been killed by a snake and carried off to the Underworld. Two shepherds relate how the hero took the news. They do so in a style of monody that will soon be called *stile recitativo* ("recited style"). **Recitative** is musically heightened speech. When it is accompanied only by basso continuo, it is usually called **simple recitative** (*recitativo semplice* in Italian). Recitative in opera usually tells the audience what has happened. Because recitative attempts to mirror the natural stresses of oral delivery, it is often made up of rapidly repeating notes followed by one or two longer notes at the end of phrases, after which the reciter might pause to catch a breath. Thus the Second Shepherd relates the bitter news (Ex. 30-3).

EXAMPLE 30-3

At the bitter news the unfortunate one was turned to stone...

Orfeo now reacts to this thunderbolt. He tells us how he feels by using a more flexible, expressive style of monody that will soon be called "arioso." **Arioso style** is a manner of singing halfway between a recitative and a full-blown aria. It involves fewer repeating pitches and is more rhythmically elastic than a purely declamatory recitative, but is not as song-like and expansive as an aria. In Orfeo's arioso-style "Tu se' morta, mia vita" ("You are dead, my life"), Monteverdi uses expressive vocal intervals, changing rhythms of speech, and bitter harmonies to intensify the hero's grief (Ex. 30-4).

EXAMPLE 30-4

You are dead, my life, and I breathe,...

At the peak of his misery and rage, Orfeo vows to go where no human has ever tread: he will descend into Hades and rescue his bride. Here he confronts Caronte (Charon), the guardian of the Underworld. Now Orfeo must use all of his vocal skills to pacify the frightful guard (Fig. 30-2). His song, the central number in the opera, is the aria "Possente spirto" ("Powerful spirit"). An **aria,** Italian for "song" or "ayre," is more florid, more expansive, and more melodious than a recitative or arioso. It tends to have less rapid-fire delivery and more melismas (one vowel luxuriously spread out over many notes), as can be seen in Example 30-5. Occasionally, an aria is set for two or three singers, in which case the terms "duet" or "trio" are appropriate. Finally, an aria invariably sets a short poem made up of several stanzas. In fact, a closed strophic poem created by the librettist became a cue to the composer to create a lyrical aria. The text of "Possente spirto" has three strophes each with three eleven-syllable lines rhyming **aba.** Here is the first of these stanzas.

Possente spirto e formidabil nume,	**a**	Powerful spirit and formidable god
Senza cui far passaggio à l'altra riva	**b**	without whom no bodiless soul,
Alma da corpo sciolta in van presume.	**a**	onto the shore of Hades has trod.

EXAMPLE 30-5

The following two stanzas make use of the same melody and bass, somewhat varied each time. What results is a **strophic variation aria,** an aria in which the same melodic and harmonic plan appears, with slight variation, in each successive strophe. Composers of the early seventeenth century seized upon strophic variation form as a way of giving variety to the otherwise utterly repetitive strophic form.

Finally, an aria in a Baroque opera, unlike a recitative, is often accompanied by more than just the basso continuo, and, the later we go in the seventeenth century, the more this is true. Early in the Baroque, however, treble instruments accompanying the aria melody were rather rare, and Monteverdi was one of the first to experiment with this procedure. In his "Possente spirto" Orfeo's appeal to Caronte is accompanied at various times by organ, theorbo, violins, cornetts, and harps. With its expansive solo singing and rich accompaniment, the aria provides the musical high points of this and almost every opera.

🌸 FIGURE 30-2

Monteverdi's aria "Possente spirto" with the vocal part in both an ornamented and an un-ornamented version. Why two versions? Perhaps Monteverdi needed to show the less experienced singer how to ornament this melody, leaving it to the more advanced singer to add ornaments to the simple, unadorned version at will. Notice that the printer is still making use of single-impression printing, a technique developed in Paris nearly a hundred years earlier (see Chapter 22). This accounts for the "wavy" lines on the staves.

💿 **LISTENING CUE**

CLAUDIO MONTEVERDI

Orfeo (1607)

Recitative, "A l'amara novella"

Arioso, "Tu se' morta, mia vita"

Aria, "Possente spirto"

CD 4/4–6

Anthology,

No. 81b-d

In truth, the terms just used to describe the expressive monody heard in Monteverdi's *Orfeo* were not coined in connection with this opera. The word "aria" was frequently employed to describe solo songs in strophic form in the late Renaissance, whereas the terms "recitative" and "arioso" did not become commonplace until the 1630s. Nevertheless, Monteverdi's use of different styles of monody is an important innovation. *Orfeo* is the first opera to differentiate styles of singing clearly so as to underscore different sorts of dramatic events. He shows that declamatory recitative can be used to deliver impersonal narration, whereas the more expansive aria is best saved for intense personal expression and rhetorical persuasion. As we shall see, the stylistic distinction between recitative and aria, and their different dramatic functions, will become even more pronounced in later Baroque opera.

EARLY OPERA IN VENICE

In 1613 Claudio Monteverdi quit his job as director of music in Mantua and moved to Venice. He had composed two path-breaking operas for the Mantuan court, *Orfeo* (1607) and *Arianna* (1608), but had received neither appreciation nor remuneration. "I have never in my life suffered greater humiliation of the spirit than when I had to go and beg the treasurer for what was mine," he said. Disgusted with Mantua, Monteverdi accepted the much coveted position of *maestro di cappella* (director of music) at St. Mark's Basilica in Venice (see Fig. 31-1), the most prestigious musical post in Italy. Naturally, his new job at this famous church required that he compose much religious music, and this he did for the next thirty years. In 1640, however, Monteverdi returned to the operatic stage, lured there by the sudden appearance of, not one but two, new opera houses in Venice.

When the citizens of Venice first embraced opera in 1637, they did so very differently than elsewhere in Italy. In Florence, Mantua, and Rome, opera was sponsored by aristocratic courts as a way to enhance the prestige of the prince. In Venice, on the other hand, opera became the enterprise of wealthy merchant families who saw it as a way to make money. To be commercially successful, however, an opera had to play night after night in a large theater. Thus the patrician families of Venice created theaters especially for opera. The audience was not a select group of two hundred aristocratic guests, but a fee-paying crowd of as many as 1,500 drawn from a cross section of society: merchants, soldiers, clerics, students, and the like. Soon several opera houses were competing head-to-head, much like Broadway theaters today. Between 1637 and 1678 Venetian audiences saw more than one hundred fifty operas in nine different theaters. To make the business of opera efficient (and to abide by the religious customs of the city), opera in Venice was confined to the carnival season (roughly from after Christmas to the beginning of Lent), when the population of Venice swelled to nearly 150,000. The leveling of social classes, in the streets and in the opera house, was facilitated by the fact that during carnival everyone wore masks. Opera was no longer the private preserve of an elite group. It had become a public spectacle.

The very public nature of opera in Venice soon led to changes. Star singers became more important as opera lovers became enamored with the special qualities of one or another of the leading voices of the day. Competition between opera houses in Venice inflated the salary of the singers, who soon were earning twice as much as the best composers. More and more, composer and librettist were forced to tailor the music to suit a leading singer's vocal range, capacity for ornamentation, and dramatic skills. In addition, stage machinery and elaborate sets created an air of the spectacular (Fig. 30-3). Angels flew across the sky and naval vessels did battle on the high seas of the stage. With its emphasis on glitzy sets and lavish costumes, Venetian opera had all the trappings of a modern-day mega musical.

By 1640 Claudio Monteverdi had reached the age of seventy-two and become the grand old man of Venetian music. Yet, that year, having apparently finished no new operas in more than three decades, he returned to the stage, first with *Il ritorno d'Ulisse in patria* (*The Return of Ulysses*), followed by *Le nozze d'Enea* (*The Marriage of Aeneas*, 1641) and *L'incoronazione di Poppea* (*The Coronation of Poppea*, 1642). *Poppea*, as this last opera is known, would be the final composition of Monteverdi's long and distinguished career.

Many believe *Poppea* to be the greatest opera of the seventeenth century. Certainly, it is a very different sort of opera from those that preceded it. The subject matter is not drawn from Greek mythology but Roman history. It celebrates, not the virtues of the ruling class, but their vices. The somewhat sensational plot goes as follows: The Roman emperor Nero lusts for the beautiful Poppea, a lady of the court; to achieve his desires, he sentences to death his wise but prudish counselor Seneca, banishes his own wife Ottavia, and places the ambitious Poppea triumphantly on the throne of all Rome.

In many ways, the realistic dramaturgy of Monteverdi's opera resembles that of his older contemporary, William Shakespeare. Sovereigns share the stage with servants; high tragedy alternates with low comedy; and wise advice goes unheeded by passionate young lovers. But unlike the works of Shakespeare, where ill deeds are condemned if not punished, here vice triumphs over virtue. Poppea is crowned empress and revels in her triumph in a final love duet with Nero. In this duet "Pur ti miro" ("I adore you") the guilty lovers are left on stage to sing a seemingly endless chain of voluptuous dissonance-to-consonance progressions. This ravishing conclusion encapsulates the passionate, sensuous nature of their love and the entire opera as well. Above all, it demonstrates just how far opera had progressed since Monteverdi left Mantua. The orchestral writing is luxuriant and the musical numbers are distinctively different so as to highlight the special qualities of the principal characters. Most important, a clear stylistic distinction exists between recitative and aria—the one syllabic and declamatory, the other florid, even rhapsodic.

FIGURE 30-3
Ships sail on the high seas as gods descend from the heavens in Giacomo Torelli's stage set for the opera *Bellerofonte* (Venice, 1642).

LISTENING CUE

CLAUDIO MONTEVERDI? (see Box)	CD 4/7
L'incoronazione di Poppea (1642)	Anthology, No. 82
Duet, "Pur ti miro"	

Venetian opera did not end with the death of Claudio Monteverdi in 1643 but lived on in the hands of his pupil Francesco Cavalli (1602–1676) and follower Antonio Cesti (1623–1669). Cavalli composed thirty-three operas, the best known of which was the often-performed *Giasone* (1649), which deals the myth of Jason and the Argonauts. Of the twelve or so operas attributed to Cesti, certainly the most

Did Monteverdi Write the Finale? Does It Matter?

Today, when a composer finishes an opera the creative process usually ends and the score becomes the blueprint for the performance. That was true for the earliest court operas from Florence and Mantua as well. But beginning with public opera in seventeenth-century Venice, composers, librettists, and impresarios (producers) started to tinker with the score, making additions and cuts, right up to the premier and even after. Requirements of the particular theater, the cast, and the tastes of the audience had to be met. As with new Broadway shows today, a mid-century Venetian opera was not so much a finite work of art as a continuing work in progress.

There is reason to believe that the final duet, "Pur ti miro" ("I adore you"), may have been added later to Monteverdi's *Poppea*, and perhaps was not composed by Monteverdi at all. The text of the duet does not appear in the separately published libretto and it can be argued that the musical style differs slightly from Monteverdi's norm. Could the duet have been the work of Monteverdi's pupil Francesco Cavalli, whose hand can be seen elsewhere altering Monteverdi's score, or perhaps that of an admirer, Benedetto Ferrari, who wrote the text of the duet (and possibly the music)? Conversely, did Monteverdi himself write "Pur ti miro" to Ferrari's text and append it to his own score in order to make the finale of *Poppea* even more glamorous?

This issue of authenticity of "Pur ti miro" leads us to ask: Does it matter who creates a work of art? Would the *Mona Lisa* be any less beautiful were it painted, not by Leonardo da Vinci, but by someone else named Leonardo? Authorship should not matter, of course, unless we are more concerned with the life of the composer than the created work, more concerned with biography than art. Whether by Monteverdi or someone in his circle, "Pur ti miro" is an exquisite aria (duet), one perfectly exemplifying mid-century Venetian opera.

spectacular was *Il pomo d'oro* (*The Golden Apple*); in 1668 it received a lavish production with twenty-four different stage sets at the court of the Holy Roman Emperor in Vienna. Generally speaking, the operas of Cavalli and Cesti contain fewer choruses and instrumental interludes and more arias for the star singers. In addition, they distinguished more clearly between the recitative and the aria. Arias became not only more numerous but longer. These trends—more emphasis on solo singing in opera, more and longer arias, and more vocal display—would accelerate during the second half of the seventeenth century. Singers were wresting control of opera away from the composer.

SUMMARY

Nowhere was the new Baroque style more clearly evident than in a new genre of music that emerged around 1600: opera. Fully sung dramatic works were at first dominated by a style of monody called *stile rappresentativo*. Gradually, a distinction emerged between the declamatory recitative used for narration, and the more florid, melodious aria intended for personal expression. Florence, Italy, was the home of early opera, but the genre soon spread to Mantua, Rome, Naples, and Venice, and then north of the Alps. What began as a small-scale courtly experiment in Florence within fifty years had become a large-scale public spectacle. The opening of public theaters for opera in Venice in the 1630s accelerated the growing tendency to turn the operatic spotlight entirely upon the aria and the star singers. By 1650 the framework for Baroque opera was fully in place involving: (1) a multi-act, fully sung drama setting either a mythological or historical subject, and (2) a clear distinction between recitative and aria. Already by mid-century the balance of power within the opera theater was beginning to shift, with less importance placed on the composer and more on the star singers.

KEY TERMS

opera	Orpheus legend	simple recitative
libretto	*Le nuove musiche*	arioso style
Florentine camerata	toccata	aria
stile rappresentativo	recitative	strophic variation aria

Chapter

31

The Concerted Style in Venice and Dresden

Venetia, Venetia, chi non ti vede non ti pretia! This sixteenth-century proverb can roughly be translated as: To appreciate Venice, you have to see it! The proverb is still true today. Venice remains a fantasyland of maze-like walkways and exotic buildings, all perched precariously above the waters of a lagoon. Venice was formerly a republic directed by a Doge (duke or chief magistrate) and an oligarchy of leading families. By 1630 the city had a population of 102,000 and was already a mecca for tourists and spies. Visitors came in search of the exotic, the foreign (the city enjoyed a thriving trade with the Near East), and the forbidden (prostitution and gambling flourished). They also came for the music. From the late 1630s onward, opera held sway at several opera houses during carnival season (see Chapter 30). By mid-century, 144 organs could be found in 121 different churches. Religious music in churches, civic music in processions of the Doge, and, later, public concerts at orphanages for females could be heard year-round.

The focus of civic and spiritual life in Venice, then and now, was the **basilica of St. Mark,** where the bones of the Evangelist Mark were believed to be buried. Because St. Mark's served as the chapel of the Doge, the political leader, it functioned as the goal of processions on occasions of state as well as religious festivals. St. Mark's has an architectural plan unique among the major churches of the West. It is built in the form of an equal-sided Greek cross, likely because in its early history Venice had strong ties to the Byzantine Empire in the East.

Beginning in the mid sixteenth century, Venetian musicians exploited the unusual architectural plan of St. Mark's by composing *cori spezzati*—literally "broken choirs," music for two, three, or four choirs placed in different parts of a building. At first these separate ensembles at St. Mark's were situated in the two choir lofts to the left and right of the main aisle (Fig. 31-1). Later, on days of special ceremonial importance, they were also stationed in other elevated galleries that adjoined the central dome. By positioning musicians in groups at points around the central axis of the church, the authorities of St. Mark's created something akin to multiphonic

✻ FIGURE 31-1

A view of singers in a gallery at St. Mark's Basilica drawn by Canaletto in the eighteenth century. A matching gallery for musicians was at the opposite side of the church.

Bridgeman Art Library

surround sound for special, festive motets. Into these musicians' galleries crowded not only singers, but instrumentalists as well.

Seventeenth-century Venice was at the forefront of technology. The city was the European center for printing generally, and for music printing in particular, as well as for shipbuilding, glass production, and the fabrication of musical instruments. Recorders, shawms, cornetts, sackbuts, viols and violins, harpsichords, and clavichords were all produced in Venice for use there or for export to other cities in Italy and north of the Alps. The tradition of polychoral religious music at St. Mark's joined happily with the civic interest in musical instruments to foster a new style of music, the concerted style.

Stile concertato is Italian for "concerted style." It is a term broadly used to identify Baroque music marked by grand scale and strong contrast, either between voices and instruments, between separate instrumental ensembles, between separate choral groups, or even between soloist and choir. Our term "concerto" derives from the same word and has the same connotation, "to act together," perhaps within the spirit of friendly competition. The first publication that employed the word "concerto" was printed in Venice in 1587: *Concerti . . . continenti musica di chiesa* (*Concertos . . . containing church music*). The church music contained herein was the creation of two organists and composers at St. Mark's, Andrea Gabrieli (1533–1585) and his nephew Giovanni. A clear example of the concerted style can be seen in Example 31-1, the beginning of a polychoral *Gloria* by Giovanni Gabrieli. Here simple chordal units create an echo-like effect. Generally speaking, the composers at St. Mark's and other large Baroque churches avoided complex counterpoint and quick harmonic changes in favor of short units of homophonic declamation in which the text is clearly audible. Textual clarity is particularly important in a large, stone building such as St. Mark's which, then and now, has "muddy" acoustics.

EXAMPLE 31-1

And peace on earth…

GIOVANNI GABRIELI AND THE CONCERTED MOTET

Giovanni Gabrieli (c1554–1612) was among the first composers fully to exploit the sonic opportunities afforded by the architecture of St. Mark's. Gabrieli had studied with Lassus in Munich and knew well the tradition of the expressive Latin motet. Yet, as a native of Venice, he was intimately familiar with the Doge's windband of cornetts and trombones, as well as the newly emerging violin. In his *Sacrae symphoniae* (*Sacred Symphonies*, 1597), Gabrieli became the first composer in the history of music to indicate dynamic levels in a musical score. Specifically, his *Sonata pian e forte* requires the instruments to play soft and loud at various times; one four-voice choir of cornett and trombones alternates with another of violin and trombones in short bursts of louds and softs. Gabrieli was also one of the first composers to use the term "sonata" (for more on the sonata, see Chapter 33). One sonata by Gabrieli, published posthumously in 1615, is scored for twenty-two separate instrumental parts (mostly violins, cornetts, and trombones), plus basso continuo. For the early seventeenth century, this was a large-scale orchestra.

Giovanni Gabrieli was also the first composer to write idiomatically for particular instruments and specify the instruments in the score. In his motet *In ecclesiis* (*In the Churches*), which appeared in the second volume of *Sacred Symphonies* (1615), he explicitly stipulates the makeup of three separate ensembles: choir 1, an instrumental sextet requiring violin, three cornetts, and two trombones; choir 2, a group of four solo voices (soprano, alto, tenor, and bass); and choir 3, a four-voice chorus covering the same parts. To this is added a basso continuo played by the organ and perhaps a bassoon. Because the concertato style is evident everywhere in the motet *In ecclesiis*, we call it a **concerted motet.** Gabrieli assigned the soloists (choir 2) difficult parts, often with long melismas. To the chorus (choir 3) he gives a completely different kind of music: merely a chordal refrain on the word "Alleluia," a sign of collective rejoicing. The instruments (choir 1) have their own timbre, one distinct from the voices. Sometimes they play entirely by themselves, while at others they merely double the vocal parts; sometimes the instruments insert their own lines independent of the voices. When this occurs, a highly complex texture results with fourteen independent musical strands. *In ecclesiis* is a concerted motet full of luxuriant sounds designed to make more splendid one of the grand occasions of state that culminated beneath the domes of St. Mark's.

LISTENING CUE

GIOVANNI GABRIELI
In ecclesiis (c1612)

CD 4/8
Anthology, No. 83

CLAUDIO MONTEVERDI AND THE CONCERTED MADRIGAL

We have met Monteverdi twice before, first as a creator of a new-style madrigal at the end of the Renaissance (see Chapter 28), and then as the main progenitor of a new musical genre, opera (see Chapter 30). To this might be added the fact that in 1610 he composed a spectacular *Vespers* that brought the new dramatic style into the church. Herein lies the important point: Claudio Monteverdi, more than any other composer, set the standard for early Baroque music. First in Mantua and then in Venice, he led the avant-garde toward the creation of new musical genres and styles.

Monteverdi moved to Venice in 1613 to succeed Giovanni Gabrieli as the principal composer of the basilica of St. Mark. His new job required him to compose religious works and to oversee the performance of music generally in the church. After three years his superiors were pleased with Monteverdi's work. They extended his contract for ten years into the future at an annual salary of 400 ducats (he earned another 200 from freelance work fulfilling commissions from other Venetian churches). The extension was offered, so the contract stipulated, in order to assure that Monteverdi "live and die in the service [of this church]." And this is precisely what happened. Monteverdi served as *maestro di cappella* at St. Mark's until his death in 1643 at the age of seventy-six.

Sadly, most of the music Claudio Monteverdi composed for St. Mark's has been lost. It existed only in manuscript copies. By contrast, Monteverdi's secular music, intended for the large domestic market, was published and thus survives mostly intact. In all, Monteverdi wrote nine books of madrigals; the first five date from his years in Mantua, and the last four from his time in Venice. In the earlier madrigals, five voices sing continually with a uniform texture from beginning to end (see *Cruda Amarilli*, Chapter 28). In the later Venetian madrigals, however, instruments appear, and textures and timbres are strongly contrasting; all are characteristics of the **concerted madrigal.**

The concerted madrigal appears most prominently in Monteverdi's eighth book (1638). He entitled the collection *Madrigali guerrieri, et amorosi* (*Madrigals of War and Love*). Indeed, most of the pieces are about love and battles of the heart. In his preface Monteverdi says:

> I have come to realize that the principal passions or affections of our mind are three: anger, moderation, and humility; so the best philosophers declare. The very nature of our voice suggests this by having a high, low, and middle range. The art of music also points clearly to these three emotions in its terms "agitated," "soft," and "moderate" [*concitato, molle,* and *temperato*]. In all the works of earlier composers I have found examples of the "soft" and the "moderate," but never of the "agitated," a type of music nevertheless described by Plato in the third book of his *Republic* in these words: "Create a harmony that would fittingly imitate the words and accents of a brave man who is engaged in warfare."[1]

In other words, Monteverdi intends to create a new style of music, **stile concitato** (the agitated style), one particularly suited to warlike music. In truth, there had been martial music earlier during the Renaissance, but Monteverdi's agitated warlike music is more direct and insistent. To create it, he tells us, he simply took whole notes and divided them into machine gun–like short notes—sixteenth notes all firing on the same pitch.

The madrigal *Hor che 'l ciel e la terra* (*Now that the heavens and earth*) from the eighth book shows clearly how Monteverdi incorporates *stile concitato* to create bellicose sounds. It is scored for six voices, two violins, and basso continuo. The text is by the venerable Francesco Petrarch (see Chapters 13 and 14), a favorite poet of madrigal composers. It speaks of a quiet night, when the heavens, the earth, and the sea are calm; yet the lover battles the pains of unrequited love. He is both lover and warrior, supple yet violent. At the words "War is my state, full of rage and pain" (Ex. 31-2), Monteverdi unleashes a barrage of notes in *stile concitato*, continually repeating the word "guerra" (war).

EXAMPLE 31-2

War, war, war is my state...

Monteverdi's *Hor che 'l ciel e la terra* is both old and new. By 1638 the madrigal as a genre was then a hundred years old and at the end of its history. Monteverdi's attempt to capture a particular emotion (agitation) following the dictates of Plato is the last gasp of the Renaissance humanists who sought to re-create the affective powers of ancient Greek music. On the other hand, there is much here in the modern Baroque style. In this Baroque concerted madrigal, a basso continuo supports the voices, and here there are two violins as well. Not only do the violins accompany the voices, they also play independently from time to time. Most important, there is strong textural contrast as is typical of the concerted madrigal. All six voices begin and end in chordal harmony. Along the way we hear a duo alternate with interjections from the full chorus, as well as a four-voice chorus set in opposition to a six-voice one. Most striking is the moment when the two violins take charge in *stile concitato* on the word "guerra" ("war"). In this late madrigal by Monteverdi, the coolly uniform texture of the Renaissance gives way to the opulent sonic variety of the Baroque.

LISTENING CUE

CLAUDIO MONTEVERDI
Hor che 'l ciel e la terra (1638)

CD 4/9
Anthology, No. 84

✤ BARBARA STROZZI AND THE EARLY BAROQUE CANTATA

The life of Barbara Strozzi (1619-1677) shows yet another aspect of the colorful world of seventeenth-century Venice: the cultured literary salon where chamber music flourished. Barbara Strozzi (Fig. 31-2) was the illegitimate daughter of Giulio Strozzi, a merchant, diplomat and noted poet who provided texts for Monteverdi, among others. Barbara studied music with opera composer Francesco Cavalli (see Chapter 30) and began to compose herself. In 1637 her father Giulio founded a literary society called the Accademia degli Unisoni (Academy of the Like-Minded) to showcase his daughter's musical skills. Intellectual academies for males only (as was the custom at this time) were popular in Italy because they offered a place to debate the social, moral, and artistic issues of the day. The minutes of the Academy of the Like-Minded show that Barbara sang at their meetings as well as suggested topics that the members of the club might debate. In all, she published eight volumes of vocal music, mostly solo madrigals, arias, and cantatas with basso continuo.

Whereas opera was the dominant form of theatrical music of the Baroque era, the cantata became the primary genre of vocal chamber music. The word **cantata** literally means "something sung," as opposed to the sonata, "something sounded" or played on an instrument. Because it was usually performed before a select group of listeners in a private residence, this genre is called the **chamber cantata** (see also Chapter 32). In the seventeenth century the Italian cantata was usually a piece of accompanied solo vocal music that most often dealt with a secular topic: tales of unrequited love, stories from ancient history and mythology, or discussions of the pressing moral issues of the day. (Later, Bach and his fellow German composers would transform the cantata into a religious work for the church; see Chapter 40.) The cantata grew out of, and ultimately replaced, the monodic madrigal of the early seventeenth century. A solo madrigal will typically last three to four minutes, but a cantata by Barbara Strozzi or one of her contemporaries usually runs eight to twelve minutes or even more. The greater length of the cantata is caused by its sectional design, one in which singing in aria, recitative, and arioso style can come in any order. A single work could thus encompass more moods, or points of view. Aria, recitative, and arioso style yield to one another almost imperceptibly. In fact, a flexible mixture of the three styles typifies the cantata of 1620 to 1680. To hold the various sections together—to bring unity to the cantata—composers of the mid seventeenth century often employed a repeating bass line, or *basso ostinato*.

In Italian "*ostinato*" is the word for someone or something obstinate, stubborn, or even pigheaded. Thus a **basso ostinato** is a bass line that insistently repeats, note for note. Seventeenth-century musicians favored short patterns that had fanciful-sounding names such as *passamezzo antico, folia, passacaglia,* and *ciaconna*. Above these popular bass lines composers wrote vocal and instrumental variations (much like composers do today above the blues pattern). The beloved English ballad *Greensleeves* is built above a repeating *passamezzo antico,* and from the pen of Corelli we have a well-known violin piece above a repeating *folia* bass.

EXAMPLE 31-3

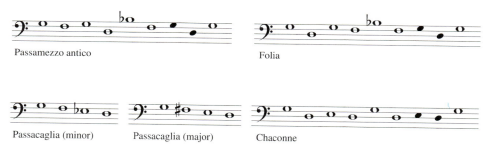

Passamezzo antico

Folia

Passacaglia (minor)   Passacaglia (major)   Chaconne

FIGURE 31-2
A portrait of Barbara Strozzi painted in the 1630s by Bernardo Strozzi, perhaps a relative.

The *ciaconna* (called *chaconne* in French) and *passacaglia,* both of Spanish origin, originally were separate and distinct bass melodies. But during the seventeenth century the distinction between them began to blur. The two terms came to be used indiscriminately to indicate almost any repeating bass pattern of short duration.

Just how a *basso ostinato* might provide a unifying structure within a lengthy cantata can be seen in Barbara Strozzi's *L'Amante Segreto: Voglio morire* (*The Secret Lover: I wish to die*) from her collection *Cantate, ariette e duetti* of 1651. Here a four-note descending *passacaglia* bass regulates the flow of most of the piece. Such descending tetrachordal figures, almost always in triple meter, are common in the Baroque period. Most often they are associated with pain, tears, and lamentation. Accordingly, such a tetrachordal *ostinato* is called a **lament bass.** (We will encounter it again in Dido's Lament by Purcell and in the "Crucifixus" of the B-Minor Mass by Bach.) Here the "Secret Lover" cannot reveal his feelings to his beloved, and wishes to die. An aria-like vocal line spins out the lover's despair above the repeating bass in the basso continuo (Ex. 31-4a). Yet periodically, the aria and supporting *ostinato* stop and a passage of declamatory recitative appears so as to move the "plot" along (Ex 31-4b). This is typical of the early Baroque cantata by Strozzi and her contemporaries: triple-meter arias alternate with duple-meter recitatives. Thus in a cantata, *stile concertato* is effected not so much by alternating units of contrasting timbres, but rather by changing to distinctly different vocal styles. What Barbara Strozzi has created is a variegated showpiece for soprano voice.

EXAMPLE 31-4A

I wish to die…

EXAMPLE 31-4B

As if she wished to say "Reveal, reveal your pain,"…

LISTENING CUE

BARBARA STROZZI   CD 4/10
L'Amante Segreto: Voglio morire (1651)   Anthology, No. 85

✿ THE CONCERTED STYLE MOVES NORTH: HEINRICH SCHÜTZ IN DRESDEN

Venice is only 225 miles from Munich, Germany, about the same distance it is from Rome. Indeed, as the northern-most large Italian city, Venice had frequent commerce—musical and otherwise—with the German and Austrian cities to the north.

Most important among these were Munich, Dresden, and Vienna. Monteverdi dedicated his eighth book of madrigals to the Holy Roman Emperor in Vienna, as did Barbara Strozzi her *Cantate* of 1651. Musicians from Italy went north to study, and vice versa. Both Andrea and Giovanni Gabrieli had gone to Munich to sit at the feet of Lassus in the 1560s and 1570s. Yet in the next generation, the most promising German composer, Heinrich Schütz, came to Venice to study, first with Gabrieli and again later with Monteverdi. When he returned to the court of Dresden, Germany, in 1629, Schütz carried with him seven cornetts of various sizes and numerous collections of Italian music. Paintings, too, flowed north from Italy. Today one of the finest holdings of Italian art of the Renaissance and Baroque is in the former court collection in Dresden, including the famous portrait of Barbara Strozzi (see Fig. 31-2). Similarly, the equally renowned portrait of Monteverdi (see Fig. 28-2) found a home in Innsbruck, Austria. Paintings, instruments, music, musicians, and musical styles—the concerted style in particular—moved from Italy to German-speaking lands during the first half of the seventeenth century.

Heinrich Schütz (1585–1672) was among the first of a long line of seventeenth- and eighteenth-century composers who made their way to Italy to learn the Italian style (Handel and Mozart would follow). Schütz, who came from the area of central Germany not far from Dresden, had shown musical talent as a youth. Consequently, a patron sent him to study with the renowned master Gabrieli in Venice. As Schütz later recounted:

> Since at that time a very famous if elderly musician and composer [Giovanni Gabrieli] was still alive in Italy, I was not to miss the opportunity of hearing him and gaining some knowledge from him. And the aforementioned Princely Highness ordered that a yearly stipend of 200 thalers be presented to me for the journey. Then (being a young man, and eager to see the world besides) I quite willingly accepted the recommendation with submissive gratitude, whereupon I set out for Venice in the year 1609, against my parents' wishes [they intended a career in law for young Schütz].[2]

After two years of tuition with Gabrieli, Schütz published the fruits of his study (a book of madrigals in Italian) and then returned to Germany.

In 1615 Schütz joined the chapel of the Elector[†] of Saxony in Dresden, then the largest musical institution in the largest city in Germany. By 1621 he had been appointed **Kapellmeister**—chief of music at court, the German equivalent of *maestro di cappella* (chapel master) in Italy. The job required that he supervise the selection and performance of the singers and instrumentalists, and oversee the education and musical preparation of the choirboys. Schütz also began to publish sacred music for the court, but his professional activities were severely hindered by the wars of religion that swirled around Saxony, specifically the Thirty Years' War.

The **Thirty Years' War** (1618–1648) was one of the great conflicts in the history of early-modern Europe. It consisted of a series of declared and undeclared wars fought essentially between the Protestants and the Catholics over political control—and religious dominance—in central Europe. On one side were the Protestants, led by the northern German princes and the king of Sweden. Arrayed against them were the Catholic forces of southern Germany and Austria, led by the Holy Roman Emperor. Hostility quickly grew into a "world war," or at least "pan-European war," as France and Denmark joined the Protestants and Spain aided the Catholic Emperor. Saxony, with Dresden as its capital, was politically and geographically caught in the

---

[†]In German history, an elector was one of nine powerful princes with the right to vote in the election to choose the Holy Roman Emperor.

middle. Musical institutions at Dresden and elsewhere in Germany were devastated. Schütz himself began to write for smaller musical forces, fearing there were no German ensembles left capable of performing fully concerted scores for voices and instruments. Even as Kapellmeister, his own salary often went unpaid.

Schütz's publications reflect these troubled times. Two early collections of polychoral motets, *Psalmen Davids* (1619) and *Symphoniae sacrae* Part I (1629), are large-scale works. But his *Kleine geistliche Konzerte* (*Little Sacred Concertos*; 1639 and 1641), written during the middle of the Thirty Years' War, suggests that only reduced forces were now available. Around the end of the war, however, Schütz was hopeful enough to publish large-scale works, specifically his *Symphoniae sacrae* Parts II and III (1647 and 1650). Schütz composed vocal music almost exclusively, most of it setting German texts. His religious music is most often not in the Latin of the Roman Catholic Church but in the German of the Protestant Church—Dresden and its court adhered to the Lutheran doctrine. Schütz was also the first composer to write an opera in German, specifically his *Dafne* (now lost) of 1627. In 1629 Schütz undertook a second trip to Venice, this time to study with Monteverdi, the master of the opulent Venetian style in general and early opera in particular. There, to quote his own words, Schütz learned "fresh devices" used by the newest Venetian composers "to tickle the ears of today."

Schütz's knowledge of the dramatic conventions of opera and the Venetian concerted motet can be seen in his *Saul, Saul, was verfolgst du mich?* (*Saul, Saul, Why doest thou persecute me?*). Published in 1650 as part of the *Symphoniae sacrae* Part III, Schütz's motet sets five short lines from the New Testament book of Acts (26:14–18). Here the Bible recounts how Christian-persecutor Paul, addressed by the Hebrew name Saul, was confronted on his way to Damascus, Syria; a blast of divine light knocks him dumb. The voice of Jesus asks:

> Saul, Saul, why doest thou persecute me? It is hard for thee to kick against the pricks . . . [go preach to] the Gentiles, unto whom now I send thee, to open their eyes, and to turn them from darkness to light, and from the power of Satan unto God.

Saul converts to Christianity, adopts the Christian name Paul, and goes on to write the New Testament epistles (letters) attributed to him. Painters of the early Baroque, among them Caravaggio (Fig. 31-3), were fond of depicting this scene with strong contrasts of light and dark to emphasize this dramatic moment of divine illumination.

Dramatic contrast also lies at the heart of Schütz's motet. A choir of six soloists is set against two four-voice choruses. Two violins and a basso continuo of organ and double bass are the only instruments specified, though others such as cornetts and trombones could double the two choruses if they were available. Throughout the score, the texture switches quickly among passages in *cori spezzati*, monody, and six-voice concerted madrigal style. Equally important, Schütz employs dynamic markings of *forte*, *piano*, *mezzopiano*, and *pianissimo*. As we have seen, his teacher in Venice, Giovanni Gabrieli, was the first to

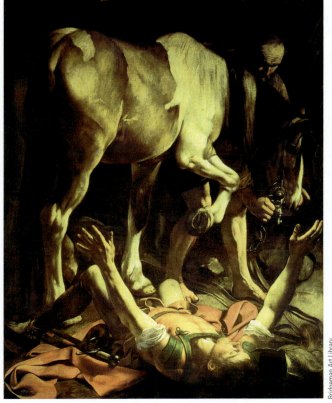

✺ FIGURE 31-3

Caravaggio, *Conversion of Saint Paul,* 1601. Caravaggio's depiction of Saul's transformation on the road to Damascus uses stark contrast between light and dark to suggest a ray of divine revelation coming from above. This sort of dramatic juxtaposition is typical of both Baroque art and music.

Bridgeman Art Library

include dynamic markings in a musical score. At the very end of *Saul*, Schütz removes the double choruses and asks the soloists to conclude by singing in succession *forte*, *mezzopiano*, and finally *pianissimo*. Clearly, his intent was to end the motet with a *diminuendo*, even though in 1650 there was no musical term or sign for this effect. Thus not only by alternating vocal and instrumental forces but also by the use of different dynamic levels does Schütz masterfully re-create the dramatic conversion of Saul/Paul on the road to Damascus.

LISTENING CUE

HEINRICH SCHÜTZ

Symphoniae sacrae (1650)

Saul, Saul, was verfolgst du mich?

CD 4/11

Anthology, No. 86

SUMMARY

In the early Baroque a new musical style developed, *stile concertato*. The concerted style employed distinctly separate units of voices and instruments to create vivid contrasts. Composers applied the concerted style to several different genres of music, most notably to the motet and madrigal. The solo chamber cantata also developed at this time, but here the concerted style was less pronounced because no chorus was involved. St. Mark's Basilica was the epicenter of musical life in Venice. The polychoral concerted motets of Gabrieli and Monteverdi exploited the particular acoustics of the church. The concerted madrigal and cantata, however, were intended for homes of the well-to-do and the literary academies that enlivened Venetian life.

By 1650 the musical tide had fully turned around. During the Renaissance, northern composers such as Dufay and Josquin brought the newest styles of learned art music to Italy; during the Baroque, however, Italian musicians became the leaders, and they carried the Italian style northward across the Alps. Thus the progressive Venetian concerted style of Gabrieli and Monteverdi made its way to Germany, specifically to the important court centers in Dresden and Vienna. The culmination of the concerted style north of the Alps can be found in the dramatic polychoral works of Heinrich Schütz, Kapellmeister to the Elector at Dresden.

KEY TERMS

basilica of St. Mark

cori spezzati

stile concertato

concerted motet

concerted madrigal

stile concitato

cantata

chamber cantata

basso ostinato

ciaconna (*chaconne*)

passacaglia

lament bass

Kapellmeister

Thirty Years' War

Chapter 32

Religious Music in Baroque Rome

Rome is a city of churches. It is also the home of the largest single organized church in the world, the Roman Catholic Church, which numbers approximately 700 million adherents. So important is the Catholic Church to Rome that it occupies its own nation-state, the Vatican, in the middle of the city. Here resides the pope as well as the numerous cardinals and other officials who direct the affairs of the Church. Within the Vatican are the Sistine Chapel, an interior sanctuary serving the pope, as well as the larger and more public St. Peter's Basilica. St. Peter's, by far the largest church in the world, provides a gathering place for thousands of the faithful during moments of extraordinary religious display. As is true for most of the largest churches in Rome, St. Peter's was completed during the Baroque era. By 1650 the city already possessed no fewer than 250 churches—basilicas such as St. Peter's, parish churches, chapels, and oratories, as well as numerous monasteries and convents.

Naturally, this concentration of religious institutions led to an emphasis on religious art and music. As nowhere else, art and music in Baroque Rome was overwhelmingly sacred, and the men who sponsored it were predominantly high-ranking church officials, specifically the pope and his attending cardinals. In truth, the papacy was very much a family affair. During the first half of the seventeenth century, for example, cultural life in Rome was dominated by Pope Urban VIII (1623–1644) and his three nephews. Urban appointed two of these nephews cardinals—hence the term "nepotism," from the Italian "*nipote*" for "nephew." This unique situation—family sponsorship of almost all high culture in the name of the Church—led to styles of sacred music particular to Rome as well as to one new musical genre, the sacred oratorio.

Art and music in seventeenth-century Rome expressed the spirit of the **Counter-Reformation,** the Church's aggressive response to the Protestant Reformation (for the Counter-Reformation in the Renaissance, see Chapter 25). The Catholic reformers purified the sanctuary by banning secular tunes and painting over nudity in religious art, and they limited corruption by curtailing the sale of indulgences (payment of money for remission of sin). Yet the Counter-Reformation Church also clung to the traditional Catholic practices: the centralization of power in Rome, celibacy for the clergy, a limited role for women, the veneration of images, and the continued support of monasteries and convents. The newly strict Church also strengthened the Inquisition (a Church court with the power of imprisonment) and imposed censorship by means of the Index of Prohibited Books. To foster the teachings of the Church, the popes promoted the work of a relatively new religious order, the **Jesuits.** Jesuit priests established colleges to impart a sense of a true Catholic life by means of education. Today, the Jesuit rule is still the principal sponsor of Catholic universities in the United States and around the world.

By the 1620s the Catholic Church had achieved something of a victory. Territory north of the Alps was no longer being lost to the Protestants, and some regions had even been reclaimed for the Church of Rome. A mood of triumph and celebration came over the Eternal City. Colleges and large churches sprang up everywhere. Into a few large churches on the high feast days went groups of musicians, sometimes as many as a hundred and fifty of them. Taking the largest view, music in Baroque Rome can be seen as belonging to one of three distinctly different types:

(1) a conservative style of vocal polyphony called *stile antico* (the old or traditional style) sung by the papal chapel; (2) a newer style of concerted music intended for a few vast churches and called "the colossal Baroque"; and (3) a highly progressive style in which the innovations of opera (aria and recitative) were manifest in sacred operas, oratorios, and cantatas.

❋ THE CAPPELLA PONTIFICIA SISTINA AND THE *STILE ANTICO*

During the seventeenth century, the pope's (pontiff's) private vocal ensemble came to be called the **cappella pontificia sistina** (papal Sistine Chapel). As the last name suggests, the home of this group was the Sistine Chapel, which had been constructed during the late fifteenth century (see Chapter 25). In 1625 there were thirty-four singers on the chapel's roster, and thus in principle about eight singers for each vocal part. All singers were male clerics, with the soprano and alto parts allocated about equally to both castrati and falsettists. Yet, despite these impressive numbers, rarely did the entire group perform at once. The long hours needed each day to sing through the lengthy cycle of the Mass and offices required that the singers perform in shifts, usually with no more than one on a particular vocal part.

The *cappella pontificia sistina* employed a distinctive mode of performance and a unique musical repertory. All music was vocal music sung *a cappella* (no instruments, not even the organ, participated). The core of the chapel's music was a conservative repertory centering on the compositions of Palestrina and others engaged at the Sistine Chapel during the Renaissance and early Baroque. This conservative style, at first called the *prima pratica*, emphasized imitative counterpoint and followed strict rules of sixteenth-century part writing. More recent composers of the chapel—among them Tomás Luis de Victoria (1548–1611), Felice Anerio (c1560–1614), Stefano Landi (1587–1639), and Gregorio Allegri (1582–1652)—perpetuated this traditional style well into the seventeenth century. Because the *prima practica* increasingly looked backward rather than forward, the conservative music emanating from the papal chapel came to be dubbed the **stile antico** (old or traditional style).

By far the most famous example of *stile antico* music written for the papal chapel is the *Miserere*, composed by Gregorio Allegri in 1638. In truth, were it not for his *Miserere*, Allegri would be virtually unknown today. But this one piece, a setting of Psalm 50 (*Miserere mei, Deus; Have mercy upon me, O Lord*), captivated the imagination of listeners for two hundred and fifty years, including the likes of Goethe, Mozart, Mendelssohn, Ralph Waldo Emerson, and Samuel F. B. Morse (the inventor of Morse Code). Allegri's *Miserere* owed its appeal to the unusual atmosphere in which it was performed in the Sistine Chapel. The Penitential Psalm *Miserere* was the musical high point of each of the three most solemn days of Holy Week: Maundy Thursday, Good Friday, and Holy Saturday. The morning offices of these three days were (and are still) called the **Tenebrae service** (Latin for "darkness"), because the service was sung in almost total darkness. To represent the blackness of the world in which the light of Christ had been extinguished, the candles around the chapel were blown out one by one, leaving the pope and his cardinals prostrate on the floor as the voices of the *cappella pontificia* resounded from on high. The effect of the *a cappella* singing of the castrati and falsettists, as reported by countless visitors, was an eerie, ghostly sound like no other.

Despite its fame, Allegri's composition is a rather simple piece that represents a type of music called **falsobordone**. *Falsobordone* originated in Spain and Italy around 1480. Like its earlier cousin *fauxbourdon* (see Chapter 16), *falsobordone* was at first an improvisatory technique used by church singers. In early *falsobordone*, three voices chanted along with the psalm tone to produce four-voice, root-position chords (Ex. 32-1), an easy way of making simple chant sound more splendid. By the seventeenth century, however, both the psalm tone and improvisation had been largely abandoned, resulting in a newly composed piece for four or even five voices, as can be seen in the opening of Allegri's *Miserere* (Ex. 32-2). The voices chanted in simple psalm-tone style employing root-position chords with slightly ornamented cadences.

EXAMPLE 32-1

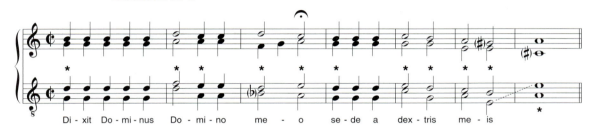

Di - xit Do - mi - nus Do - mi - no me - o se - de a dex - tris me - is

The Lord said to my Lord, "Sit on my right [hand]."

EXAMPLE 32-2

Have mercy upon me, O Lord, according to thy great [mercy].

Ironically, the thing that made Allegri's *Miserere* famous was not included in his score: vocal ornamentation. To Allegri's simple *falsobordone* foundation, soloists added unwritten, but carefully calculated counterpoint. As the generations went by, the nature of the ornamentation changed, as did, in fact, Allegri's written score. Nevertheless, visitors to the Sistine Chapel—from musicians such as Mozart, Mendelssohn, and Liszt to writers like Goethe, Shelly, and Dickens—came to marvel at Allegri's *stile antico* music and the eerie beauty of the Tenebrae service.

Mozart Pirates Allegri's *Miserere*

The *cappella pontificia sistina* was a closed men's club. It was a private all-male singing group, controlled by the pope, which elected its own members and selected its own musical repertory. In general, the papal chapel sang only Gregorian chant approved by the pope or polyphony composed by its own members, past or present. After 1638 Allegri's *Miserere* became a popular favorite with the faithful throngs who crowded into the back of the Sistine Chapel to witness the Tenebrae service annually just before Easter. But Allegri's motet was never published or even copied outside the chapel itself. Successive popes banned its reproduction on pain of excommunication. By the eighteenth century, however, pirated editions had begun to leak out. One of those who secretly copied the *Miserere* was the 14-year-old Wolfgang Amadeus Mozart.

How much music can you retain on first hearing: three seconds, seven seconds, ten seconds? It all depends on the capacity of your musical ear and your ability to process and retain musical patterns—on your innate musical talent. Needless to say, Mozart possessed extraordinary talent and he was able to write down by memory the essentials of all of Allegri's *Miserere* during just one performance. Mozart and his father, Leopold, were in Rome in April 1770 and, like many tourists, went to the Sistine Chapel to observe the famous Tenebrae service culminating with Allegri's *Miserere*. But let Mozart's father tell the story:

You have often heard of the famous *Miserere* in Rome, which is so greatly prized that the performers in the chapel are forbidden on pain of excommunication to take away a single part of it, to copy it or to give it to anyone. But we have it already! Wolfgang has written it down and we would have sent it to Salzburg in this letter, if it were not necessary for us to be there to perform it. But the manner of performance [the ornamentation] contributes more to its effect than the composition itself. So we shall bring it home with us. Moreover, because it is one of the secrets of Rome, we do no wish to let it fall into other hands, lest we incur, directly or indirectly, the punishment of the Church.[1]

Mozart's sister adds that Wolfgang returned to the Sistine Chapel two days later, hiding his pirated copy in his hat, and made a few corrections to his score.

In truth, remarkable as Mozart's accomplishment was, it may not be quite as astonishing as it first appears. Although Allegri's setting of Psalm 50 can take eight to twelve minutes to perform, depending upon the tempo, it consists of fewer than thirty bars of original music: a five-part *falsobordone* section alternates with a four-voice *falsobordone* section, and between each of these come verses of monophonic chant (see Anthology, No. 87). The amount of original polyphonic music to be copied, in either five or four parts, runs about one minute and thirty seconds. In addition, because the *falsobordone* sections repeat in successive verses, Mozart had a chance to hear each polyphonic section five times. How much of the improvised ornamentation he tried to capture is anyone's guess.

LISTENING CUE

GREGORIO ALLEGRI
Miserere mei, Deus (1638)

CD 4/12
Anthology, No. 87

ST. PETER'S BASILICA AND THE COLOSSAL BAROQUE

A **basilica** is a special, grand church that happens not to be a cathedral (not the seat of a bishop). St. Peter's Basilica is special, of course, because on this site, directly below the high altar, are believed to be the bones of Peter, the Apostle, to whom Christ gave the authority to build the Church. Emperor Constantine had constructed a sanctuary on this site around 324 C.E., and a new, more magnificent building was begun in the sixteenth century. The central dome of the new St. Peter's, designed by Michelangelo, was completed in 1586; the nave and the great façade went up during the early decades of the seventeenth century. At the height of activity in 1611, more than eight hundred men worked at the site, sometimes at night by torchlight. Pope Urban VIII consecrated the structure in 1626, exactly one hundred years after the first cornerstone had been set. This was a triumphant moment for the Church. St. Peter's symbolized a newfound optimism of the clergy and people of Rome. The Counter-Reformation had purified the Church, and now its splendor could be revealed for all the world to see. St. Peter's was simply the largest visible symbol of this triumphant moment in Roman Church history.

Given its great size and acoustical resonance, it is in no way surprising that the music heard in St. Peter's was very different from that at the smaller Sistine Chapel. Indeed, the vast scale of the basilica invited composers to exploit size to achieve sonic magnificence. Accordingly, the musicians of St. Peter's, who formed an ensemble separate and independent from the singers of the Sistine Chapel, turned to large-scale compositions in the concerted style. Composers at St. Peter's—Paolo Agostini (c1583–1629), Virgilio Mazzocchi (1597–1646), and Orazio Benevoli (1605–1672), for example—wrote Masses and motets for as many as twelve choirs of voices and instruments. We have come to call this idiom of large-scale multiple-choir music for voices and instruments the **colossal Baroque.** Colossal Baroque church style usually involves four or more choirs, both answering each other and sometimes singing together in impressive tutti passages. Echoing units of choral sound provide the fundamental building blocks, and from these one or more solo voices occasionally emerge. This is concerted music, but concerted music on the largest possible dimension. For example, in 1639 musicians from St. Peter's and other choirs around Rome performed a work by Virgilio Mazzocchi, in honor of the patron saint. A contemporary reported that the piece was executed by "twelve or sixteen choirs"—apparently there were so many that it was impossible to count them all with confidence. Moreover, "an echo choir was placed at the top of the dome [and] in the space of that vast temple it was wonderfully effective." Obviously, Mazzocchi wished to achieve a heavenly effect by having at least one choir echo down from the top of Michelangelo's gigantic dome (Fig. 32-1). For this performance musicians stood on the floor, in the galleries above the floor, and on high in the cupola (dome). Instruments, specifically violins, cornetts, and trumpets, are reported in the dome as early as 1637. On these days honoring the patron saint, St. Peter, the church itself served as a giant resonator for both voices and instruments.

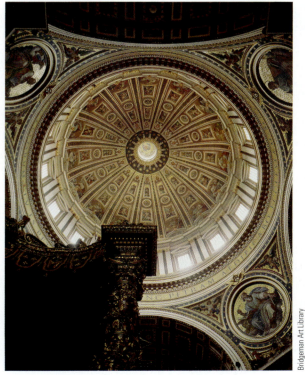

✻ FIGURE 32-1

Interior of the dome of St. Peter's Basilica. This grand church, the largest in Christendom, was dedicated in 1626.

Bridgeman Art Library

Unfortunately, little of the music in the style of the colossal Baroque survives. These were large pieces designed for specific events and usable within only a few specific churches. None of the large scores was ever published, and only a few manuscript copies are preserved. To get a sense of the sound of the colossal Baroque, therefore, we must turn to a Mass composed for the Catholic cathedral of Salzburg, Austria, where the colossal style had spread. This anonymous Mass, called simply the *Missa Salisburgensis* (*Salzburg Mass*), was first attributed to the Roman composer Orazio Benevoli of St. Peter's, and more recently to the German Heinrich Biber. Most likely, the Mass was composed in 1682 to celebrate the eleven-hundredth anniversary of the founding of the diocese of Salzburg. Despite its likely Austrian origin, however, the *Missa Salisburgensis* arises from the spirit of the Roman colossal Baroque, because during the seventeenth century both the Roman musical style and musicians trained in Rome held sway at this Austrian church. A glance at the gigantic score (Anthology, No. 88) will show that the composer wrote for seven separate musical ensembles and a total of fifty-three independent parts. The choirs were placed around the church, with two trumpet groups somewhat removed from the singers.

To avoid creating a sonic muddle with so many different parts, the composer of the *Missa Salisburgensis* employed only a few basic chords and changed them only very slowly. Because large Baroque churches generally had a long **reverberation time** (the time it took the sound to die out), composers of the colossal Baroque style in particular avoided quick harmonic changes. Otherwise, the simultaneous reverberation of two different chords would yield a dissonance. Of necessity, then, the harmony of the *Missa Salisburgensis* is conservative and the counterpoint very basic. The sound, however, is simply magnificent.

 LISTENING CUE

UNKNOWN

Kyrie of the *Missa Salisburgensis* (1682?)

CD 4/13

Anthology, No. 88

ORGAN MUSIC BY GIROLAMO FRESCOBALDI

Except at the Sistine Chapel, instruments usually accompanied choral singing in the larger Baroque churches. The primary church instrument was the organ, which sounded both by itself and with the singers, providing a basso continuo and helping to keep the voices on pitch. Owing to the city's intense religious activity, Rome had more church organs than any European city; at least two hundred organs had been installed by 1640, and individual organists owned numerous portative organs that they transported from church to church as needed.

The foremost organist in Rome during the first half of the seventeenth century was Girolamo Frescobaldi (1583–1643; Fig. 32-2). By the end of his life Frescobaldi was universally recognized as the greatest organ composer, not just in Italy but in all of Europe. Frescobaldi was born in Ferrara, but by as early as 1601 had moved to Rome. Here he remained, with few absences, for more than forty years. Like many organists today, Frescobaldi was employed at more than one church, and he combined an active career as a teacher with his work as a composer and performer. He also received income for being "musician in residence" to a succession of wealthy clerical patrons, notably Cardinal Francesco Barberini, nephew of Pope Urban VIII. Yet Frescobaldi's principal post, from 1608 until his death in 1643, was organist at St. Peter's Basilica.

As organist at St. Peter's, Frescobaldi performed at the massive displays of concerted polychoral music that marked the feasts honoring St. Peter. He also participated in the more usual music-making at the basilica, playing organ at Sunday and feast-day Masses. For these services, Frescobaldi would have regularly improvised music, such as toccatas, ricercars, and canzonas, to introduce or

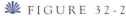 FIGURE 32-2

An engraving showing the likeness of Girolamo Frescobaldi. The inscription reads, "Girolamo Frescobaldi of Ferrara, organist of the basilica of St. Peter in the Vatican, thirty-six years of age."

Bridgeman Art Library

replace the choral singing during Mass. The organist might also alternate with the choir, playing a solo in place of the choral chant or polyphony. When the organ played alternate verses of the *Kyrie* or *Gloria*, for example, the result (see Chapter 24) was a performance using ***alternatim* technique.**

In 1635 Frescobaldi published a collection of Mass music to serve St. Peter's and other churches, his ***Fiori musicali*** (*Musical Flowers*). It includes organ music for Mass for most of the Sundays and feast days of the church year. Each Mass begins with an organ prelude, and is followed by an *alternatim* setting of the *Kyrie*. Then come other organ solos, in which the instrument replaces the choir in the Proper of the Mass. A Mass in which an organ alternates with, or entirely replaces, the choir is simply called an **organ Mass.** The heyday of the organ Mass was the seventeenth century, and Frescobaldi was its principal exponent.

For an example of an organ Mass from Frescobaldi's *Fiori musicali*, let us turn to the opening piece, the *Toccata avanti la Messa* (*Toccata before the Mass*). A **toccata,** as we have seen (see Chapter 30), is an instrumental work designed to show off the creative spirit of the composer as well as the technical skill of the performer. Although the term sometimes applies to pieces for other instruments, "toccata" most often signifies a freeform keyboard piece in which a "touching" of the keyboard is needed to demonstrate digital dexterity. The opening toccata of this particular organ Mass is shorter than most, being compressed into just thirteen measures (Ex. 32-3). Frescobaldi extended his keyboard figuration into the middle and lower ranges of the instrument, a far different practice from Renaissance keyboard music, in which the figuration is confined mostly to the highest register. Notice the two G sharps in this toccata (mm. 4 and 5) that pull toward the note (A) a fifth away from the home pitch (D); this is clear evidence of a growing awareness of what we today call functional tonality and secondary dominant chords.

EXAMPLE 32-3

A *Kyrie* using *alternatim* technique comes next, and here the organ plays the first verse and the choir chants the next, continuing thus through all nine verses of the *Kyrie*. Each independent organ section in an *alternatim* organ Mass is called an **organ verset,** a short piece that replaces a liturgical item otherwise sung by the choir. The organ versets in this *Kyrie* make use of *cantus firmus* technique; here (Ex. 32-4) the ancient *Kyrie* chant sounds in long notes, not in the tenor, but in the highest line.

EXAMPLE 32-4

Whereas the organ versets of the *Kyrie* employ an old technique from the Renaissance, the following organ ricercar is radically new. In this organ Mass, the ricercar replaces the Offertory usually sung by the choir. A **ricercar,** as we have seen (see Chapter 23), is an instrumental piece, usually for lute or keyboard, that is similar in style to the sixteenth-century imitative motet. Frescobaldi's newer ricercar, however, is very different from its sixteenth-century forebear. To begin with, it is monothematic. The composer has fashioned a single distinct subject and a countersubject (an important counterpoint to the subject; see Ex. 32-5, bar 3). Moreover, when the second voice imitates the subject at the interval of a fifth above, it changes the subject so as to keep the music in the home tonality, thus producing a **tonal answer** (Ex. 32-5, bar 3). Finally, the second section of the ricercar presents a new countersubject, which appears both in a normal and an inverted form. In every measure of this ricercar either the subject or a countersubject can be heard—a remarkably dense web of counterpoint. Developing a contrapuntal piece from a single subject and its countersubjects points directly toward the German fugue of the eighteenth century. In fact, J. S. Bach knew Frescobaldi's *Fiori musicali* well, for he obtained a manuscript copy as early as 1714 and kept it with him to the end of his life.

EXAMPLE 32-5

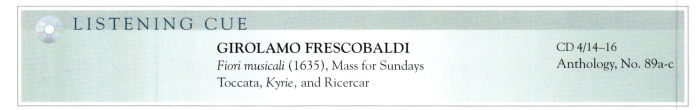

🔘 LISTENING CUE

GIROLAMO FRESCOBALDI
Fiori musicali (1635), Mass for Sundays
Toccata, *Kyrie*, and Ricercar

CD 4/14–16
Anthology, No. 89a-c

SACRED OPERA AND ORATORIO: GIACOMO CARISSIMI'S *JEPHTE*

Rome was predominantly a city of religious music, but not exclusively. During the early seventeenth century, opera spread from its home in Florence to Mantua, Venice, Naples, and Rome. Traditional secular operas using plots drawn from classical mythology, such as Stefano Landi's *La morte d'Orfeo* (*The Death of Orpheus*, 1619), saw the light of day in Rome. Even comic opera had a hearing, as evidenced by *Chi soffre speri* (*Who suffers may hope*, 1637), an opera by Virgilio Mazzocchi and Marco Marazzoli based on a story by Boccaccio.

But opera in Rome was not like opera in other cities. First of all, Rome produced a far higher percentage of sacred, or Christian, operas. As early as 1600, Emilio de' Cavalieri's sacred music drama *Rappresentatione di Anima, et di Corpo* (*Representation of Soul and Body*) was performed in a Roman church. In 1631 Stefano Landi set to music a libretto treating the life of St. Alexis (*Il Sant'Alessio*); in subsequent years it was performed spectacularly at the palace of Cardinal Francesco Barberini in a huge hall seating three thousand spectators. Typical of Christian opera, the libretto for *Il Sant'Alessio* was written by a priest, Giulio Rospigliosi (1600–1669), who went on to become Pope Clement IX (1667–1669). In a way unique to Rome, most opera, secular or sacred, was sponsored by clergymen—usually not by the pope himself, but by his cardinals in their lavish palaces. Also peculiar to Rome was the absence of female singers; women were not allowed to appear on stage in Rome or in papally controlled lands (though they could do so in "extraterritorial" foreign embassies!). Thus, Roman opera usually made use of castrati and boys for the highest parts. Finally, religious scruples here as elsewhere dictated that opera, as with spoken drama, be heard during the festive season of carnival, but not during the solemn time of Lent.

To satisfy the Roman desire for dramatic music during Lent, patrons and musicians developed a new musical genre: **oratorio.** Conforming to the solemn tone of Lent, oratorio put away lavish sets, costumes, and choreography. The dramatic text, either in Italian or Latin, usually elaborated upon a story found in the Old Testament, one recounting a tale of sacrifice and self-denial concordant with the spirit of Lent. Oratorio differs from opera because the singers are not in costume and do not fully act out their dramatic roles. A narrator simply reports what happens. Nevertheless, the fundamental musical processes of opera—recitative, aria, and chorus—also animate oratorio. Choruses (even if sung by only one on a part) loom larger in oratorio than in opera, for the chorus often carries a moral message delivered by the people to the people.

As the Italian term "oratorio" suggests, an oratorio was performed in an **oratory,** a prayer hall set aside just for praying, preaching, and devotional singing. Each oratory in Rome was supported by a **confraternity,** a fraternal order emphasizing religious devotion and charity. The most prestigious Roman confraternity was that of the Most Holy Crucifix, a brotherhood of educated noblemen. Every Friday during Lent its members gathered in their oratory in the center of Rome to hear one or more oratorios, works often composed by Giacomo Carissimi.

Giacomo Carissimi (1605–1674) served for more than forty years as director of music at the German College in Rome, an important Jesuit institution of higher learning. In addition to Masses and motets, Carissimi also wrote about a hundred and fifty secular cantatas. He is remembered today, however, mainly for his fourteen surviving oratorios. Most are based on stories from the Old Testament recounting deeds of heroic characters such as David killing Goliath or Jonah escaping from the belly of the whale. Rather than simply quote verbatim from scripture, the text of an oratorio embroiders upon the story; a more elaborate text allowed for a more vivid musical setting.

Just how Carissimi might bring a biblical story to life can best be judged in his oratorio *Jephte* (c1648), which embellishes upon events in the Old Testament book of Judges 11. There are three principal characters, the *Historicus* (narrator), Jephte, and his nameless daughter, as well as a chorus representing the people of Israel. Jephte is the leader of the Israelites, about to do battle against the Ammonites. He promises

God that if victory be granted, he will sacrifice upon his return the first living creature to greet him. This welcomer proves to be his own daughter. Dutifully, the daughter retreats to the mountains to lament her fate and bravely commends her soul to God. Her willingness to sacrifice was meant to inspire every good Christian during Lent.

In mid seventeenth-century oratorio, just as in early opera, the distinction between vocal styles is not always clearly drawn. Generally speaking, simple recitative is used to report events, and arioso style (more expressive recitative) appears for moments of greater intensity, while the aria projects poetic texts of special beauty or feeling. This is true of the climax of *Jephte*, where the daughter's lamentation ("Plorate, colles") is in four sections, each beginning syllabically like a recitative, but ending with a long melisma, as might an aria. Also typical of an aria, the text is often repeated for rhetorical emphasis. At first the daughter repeats her own words, then voices from the chorus provide a mountain echo. The daughter's lamentation is followed by a choral treatment of the same subject ("Plorate, filii Israel"), one of the most beautiful choruses ever written. At the beginning the basses descend in a repeating tetrachord, or lament bass, the musical symbol of despair and suffering. Toward the end, however, they rise by step while the upper voices fall down in a chain of mournful suspensions (Ex. 32-6). Such beauty is timeless, and nearly a century later Handel "borrowed" Carissimi's music and made it serve in his own oratorio *Samson* (1743); the Latin words "Plorate, filii Israel" ("Weep, children of Israel") were simply changed to the English "Hear, Jacob's God."

EXAMPLE 32-6

★ = suspension

LISTENING CUE

GIACOMO CARISSIMI

Jephte (c1648)

"Plorate, colles" (solo)

"Plorate, filii Israel" (chorus)

CD 4/17–18

Anthology, No. 90a-b

THE CHAMBER CANTATA: A CHRISTMAS CANTATA BY ALESSANDRO SCARLATTI

Late seventeenth-century Rome saw the culmination of the chamber cantata, a genre that had originated in northern Italy and is exemplified in the works of Barbara Strozzi (see Chapter 31). As the name suggests, a **chamber cantata** was performed for a select audience in a private residence. By the end of the century it consisted of a succession of movements for solo voice and accompaniment that alternated between rapid declamation (recitative) and florid song (aria). Most cantatas were in Italian and spoke of love, though some revisited events in Roman history and a few embraced sacred subjects. Compared to an opera or an oratorio, a chamber cantata usually required only a single voice, was accompanied only by basso continuo and a few strings at most, and incorporated only a small number of recitatives and arias. Thus, while an opera or oratorio might extend well beyond an hour, the briefer chamber cantata usually lasted no more than fifteen minutes. Owing to its brevity and concentration, it was customary for a cantata to be repeated several times to allow the audience to savor the poetry and the music. At the end of the seventeenth century no composer in Rome was more celebrated as a creator of chamber cantatas than Alessandro Scarlatti.

Alessandro Scarlatti (1660–1725) belonged to a large family of musicians and was himself the father of the famous keyboard composer Domenico Scarlatti (see Chapter 43). It is not entirely certain with whom Scarlatti studied, but by 1680 he had been appointed composer-in-residence to exiled Queen Christina of Sweden, an important Roman patroness. After her death in 1689, Scarlatti eventually assumed a similar role at the court of Cardinal Pietro Ottoboni, great-nephew of Pope Alexander VIII. With their support, Scarlatti progressed to become the leading composer of opera in Rome, and later in Naples.

Patrons such as Queen Christina and Cardinal Ottoboni sponsored not only operas and oratorios but also chamber cantatas. Cardinal Ottoboni had responsibility for arranging to have Christmas cantatas performed annually on Christmas Eve in the papal apartments at the Vatican. Here, between the celebration of Christmas Vespers and the midnight Mass, the pope and perhaps twenty-five guests enjoyed spiritual refreshment in the form of a Christmas cantata and then moved on to an abundant meal.

We do not know precisely when, where, or for whom Alessandro Scarlatti composed his beautiful Christmas cantata *Oh di Betlemme* (*O Bethlehem*), but surely it was written around 1700 for one of the patrician houses in Rome. In the surviving manuscripts the cantata is identified simply as a *Cantata pastorale. . . . per la Natale* ("Pastoral cantata . . . for the Nativity"). In this work, as in many of his more than six hundred cantatas, Scarlatti developed a new structure for the aria.

In the 1690s Alessandro Scarlatti established the ***da capo* aria,** a formal arrangement that would come to enjoy enormous popularity. The text of the aria, usually consisting of just a single stanza, was assigned to two contrasting musical sections, and at the end of the second the first would return exactly, thus producing **ABA** form. The reprise of **A,** of course, was not written out, but simply signaled by the inscription "*da capo*" (take it from the top or, literally, "from the head").

Scarlatti's *Oh di Betlemme* makes exclusive use of the *da capo* aria—all three arias are molded in that form. The cantata begins with a brief instrumental introduction followed by a recitative, "Oh di Betlemme" ("O Bethlehem"), in which the singer contrasts the humble former status of Bethlehem, site of the nativity, with its present glory. The aria that follows, "Dal bel seno d'una stella" ("From a fair bosom of a star"), sets only four lines of text; the first two evoke the image of the sun (and Son), while the third and fourth refer to the Virgin Mary. To form the *da capo* structure, Scarlatti simply allocates his music to the text in pairs of lines, as shown below. He then emphasizes the distinction between **A** and **B** in two ways: he shifts tonalities from D major to B minor (the relative minor), and he assigns an instrumental ritornello to section **A,** but not **B.** As the term suggests, an instrumental **ritornello** (refrain) is a distinctive musical phrase that comes at the beginning of the aria and returns frequently thereafter. Here, in the charming aria "Dal bel seno d'una stella," the instrumental ritornello, played by a solo violin, establishes a dialogue with the voice. Thus, in *Oh di Betlemme*, Alessandro Scarlatti shows clearly why he is important to the history of the Italian cantata and to vocal music generally: he established the form and style of the chamber cantata, which would remain the norm for this genre in the first half of the eighteenth century; and he crafted a particular musical form, the *da capo* aria, that would continue to be favored by composers of operas, oratorios, and cantatas to the very end of the Baroque era.

Dal bel seno d'una stella	**A**	From a fair bosom of a star
Spunta a noi l'eterno sole.		Rises for us an eternal sun.
Da una pura verginella	**B**	From a pure maiden
Nacque già l'eterna prole.		is born an eternal son.
Dal bel seno d'una stella	**A**	From a fair bosom of a star
Spunta a noi l'eterno sole.		Rises for us an eternal sun.

LISTENING CUE

ALESSANDRO SCARLATTI
Cantata *Oh di Betlemme* (c1700?)
Recitative, "Oh di Betlemme"
Aria, "Dal bel seno d'una stella"

CD 4/19–20
Anthology, No. 91a-b

 ## SUMMARY

More than any European city, Rome was and is dominated by the Roman Catholic Church, and this simple fact accounts for the preeminence of religious music there. During the seventeenth century, at the end of the Counter-Reformation, the fortunes of the Church reached a high point, as symbolized by the completion of St. Peter's Basilica, consecrated in 1626. Generally, the size and function of the church determined the nature of the music to be performed. Three musical styles predominated: (1) a dignified, conservative style of vocal polyphony called *stile antico* (old or traditional style) sung by the papal chapel in the Sistine Chapel; (2) a harmonically conservative style of concerted polychoral music called the colossal Baroque that was intended for a few vast spaces such as St. Peter's Basilica; and (3) a highly progressive style in which the innovations of opera (aria and recitative) were manifest in sacred operas, oratorios, and cantatas, many of which were performed in private residences of aristocratic churchmen. Organ music, most notably that of Girolamo Frescobaldi, also grew in importance at this time as a way of providing sonic variety for what otherwise was a religious service of exclusively vocal music.

Opera was known in early seventeenth-century Rome, but Roman opera usually emphasized moral and especially Christian themes. The religious orientation of

Rome also contributed to the creation of oratorio, a new musical genre. Although oratorio made use of the same conventions as opera (recitative, aria, and chorus), its message was spiritual and its plot usually drawn from dramatic events of the Old Testament, as is the case of the oratorios of Giacomo Carissimi. The chamber cantata, too, involved neither costumes nor histrionics. A lone singer sang a succession of recitatives and arias, accompanied by a basso continuo and a few strings at most. Alessandro Scarlatti solidified the general form and style of the Italian cantata, as well as popularized *da capo* form, a structure that would become the norm for the late Baroque aria in cantata, oratorio, and opera alike.

KEY TERMS

Counter-Reformation	reverberation time	tonal answer
Jesuits	*alternatim* technique	oratorio
cappella pontificia sistina	*Fiori musicali*	oratory
stile antico	organ Mass	confraternity
Tenebrae service	toccata	chamber cantata
falsobordone	organ verset	*da capo* aria
colossal Baroque	ricercar	ritornello

Chapter 33

Instrumental Music in Italy

Instrumental music came into its own in the Baroque era. During the sixteenth century (late Renaissance) composers had written much instrumental music, and a variety of colorful instruments played it (see Chapter 23). Yet, not until the seventeenth century (early Baroque) did composers write for instruments in a truly idiomatic way, in a way that matched particular musical figures with the strengths of each separate instrument. Not until then was instrumental music printed in abundance. Indeed, during the seventeenth century, publishers began to issue as much instrumental music as vocal music, and by the eighteenth century, publishers' catalogues show a preponderance of instrumental music for sale. New instruments, new styles of playing, and new genres of pieces, including the sonata and concerto, all sprang forth during the seventeenth century.

The place of origin of these innovations was northern Italy (Map 33-1). Northern Italy saw the rise of the violin—the Baroque instrument *par excellence*. The first great violinmakers were all northern Italians and so, too, were most of the composers who satisfied the rapidly growing demand for music for this instrument. From northern Italy the violin and its music spread to the rest of Italy, and eventually to the rest of Europe as well.

 MAP 33–1

Northern Italy in the seventeenth century.

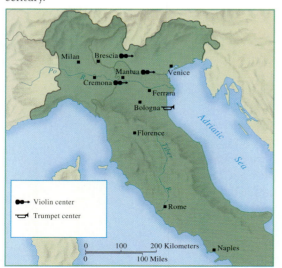

THE VIOLIN FAMILY

As we have seen (see Chapter 23), the violin originated in the sixteenth century as a "low-class" instrument used for playing dance music in inns and taverns. Appearing first in such northern Italian towns as Cremona and Brescia, the violin quickly spread to larger northern cities like Mantua and Venice, and eventually south to Rome and Naples. **Cremona** is crucial to the development of the violin. Claudio Monteverdi, the first great composer to write consistently for the violin, was a native of the city. Here, too, were born and lived many of the great violin-makers, including Antonio, Girolamo and Nicolò Amati, and Pietro and Giuseppe Guarneri, as well as **Antonio Stradivari** (c1644–1737). Today instruments by these exceptional Cremonese artisans are so highly prized that they fetch millions of dollars at auction houses in London and New York.

All members of the violin family have four strings and are tuned in fifths, the violin g-d'-a'-e". Violas and cellos are simply larger-sized violins. The cello developed from an early bass violin called the *violone* (large bass violin) tuned B♭', F, c, g. After 1650 a somewhat smaller instrument, tuned C, G, d, a, became popular, so the diminutive expression "cello" was appended to *violone* creating "violoncello," or "small large bass violin," which we now abbreviate as "cello."

The double bass emerged only at the end of the seventeenth century. Its ancestor was not the violin, but the viol, and it retains to the present day two viol-like characteristics: it is tuned in fourths (rather than fifths, as with the violin, viola, and cello); and it is often played with an "underhand" viol bowing, not "overhand" as used for violin, viola, and cello. Then, as now, the double bass sounded an octave below written pitch, and usually doubled the cello an octave lower. By the end of the seventeenth century, the violin, viola, cello, and often the more distantly related double bass, had come to form the nucleus of the Baroque orchestra.

FORMATION OF THE BAROQUE ORCHESTRA

The symphony orchestra as we know it today had its origins in Italy during the seventeenth century. At its beginning, the early Baroque orchestra was something of a "mixed bag" of instruments. The ensemble accompanying Monteverdi's *Orfeo* (1607), for example, consisted of violins and viols, recorders, trumpets, cornetts, sackbuts (trombones), harpsichord, theorbo, harps, organ with metal pipes, and organ with reed pipes. It was an ensemble of soloists; players did not normally double on the same instrumental part. The sound was diverse and colorful, but not especially powerful.

After the mid seventeenth century, however, several instruments important in the Renaissance—viol, cornett, sackbut (trombone), shawm, and theorbo—began to lose favor.[†] In their place stepped forward the instruments of the violin family to form a core ensemble, and to this group other instruments were gradually added. As the seventeenth century progressed, composers came to specify oboes, bassoons, flutes, trumpets, and, last, horns along with the strings. A single harpsichord (or organ in church) gradually replaced the theorbo and other plucked string instruments as the provider of a chordal support in the basso continuo. By the end of the century more than one player—two, three or even four—might sometimes execute one and the same string part. Yet, even with some parts doubled, what resulted was

---

[†] The large *viola da gamba* remained popular into the eighteenth century as a bass instrument in ensembles and as a solo instrument. The shawm evolved into the modern oboe. The sackbut, generally called the trombone during the Baroque era and thereafter, continued to be heard in church music and provide special effects in the opera theater. It was not added to the symphony orchestra, however, until the time of Beethoven.

The Violin Then and Now

What makes a great violin? They all look remarkably similar, with a common shape and common features, characteristics that were established in the sixteenth century. But the type and place of origin of the wood chosen for the front (usually spruce) and the back (usually maple), the way the wood is cured and then carved, the way the pieces are assembled, the type of final varnish applied—these are just a few of the features that separate a superb instrument from a mediocre one. Antonio Stradivari was among the greatest of the Cremonese violinmakers. Some six hundred fifty Stradivari instruments survive today: violins, violas, cellos, and even guitars. Today professional virtuosos such as Joshua Bell or Midori are willing to pay millions of dollars for the magnificent sound of a Stradivari.

In truth, the Stradivari violin sold today in New York or London is not precisely the one Stradivari made; all Stradivari violins have been rebuilt and significantly modified over the centuries. The size and general shape of the Baroque and modern instruments are the same, but the Baroque violin had a shorter fingerboard, and thus could not play pitches as high as can the modern instrument (Fig. 33-1). The bridge was lower, in part because there was less tension placed on the strings. Strings were made of animal gut (often cat intestine) sometimes spun around with a thin thread of brass or silver wire for added resonance. The Baroque violin bow had a narrower band of horsehair and was under less tension than its modern counterpart. Finally, there was no chin rest in the seventeenth century, and the violin was often played off the shoulder rather than under the chin (Fig. 33-2). With gut strings and less tension on both instrument and bow, the Baroque violin had a light, clean sound, not nearly as loud and rich as that produced by the modern violin. The Baroque violin was prized because it could play rapidly and could clearly articulate the lively rhythmic patterns of the new Baroque style.

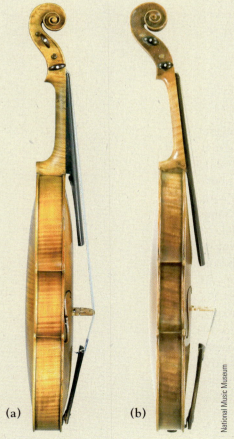

(a)   (b)

National Music Museum

❋ FIGURE 33-1

Baroque violin (a) compared to modern one (b), side view.

Elvehjem Museum of Art

❋ FIGURE 33-2

Young Man Playing a Violin, attributed to Pietro Paolini, c1620. Note that the instrument is played off the shoulder rather than under the chin.

a modest-size orchestra with no more than twenty-five players. By way of example: eighteen instrumentalists were on the payroll at the basilica of St. Mark in Venice in 1643; twelve were employed at the basilica of St. Petronio in Bologna about 1680. By contrast, King Louis XIV (r. 1643–1715) sometimes augmented his core of twenty-four string players to more than eighty for performances of court ballet and opera at Versailles, and Cardinal Ottoboni once employed an orchestra of a hundred to play for a sacred opera in Rome. These large orchestras, however, were very much the exception rather than the rule.

In sum, during the seventeenth century the instrumental ensemble gradually coalesced around the instruments of the violin family (violin, viola, and cello) with a low string instrument such as the double bass sometimes added. After mid-century, oboes and bassoons might also double the strings, and a trumpet sound forth for extra brilliance. Beneath them all was the basso continuo held together by a harpsichord or, in church, by an organ.

CHURCH AND CHAMBER MUSIC

Today we distinguish between orchestral music (music with more than one on a part played before a large audience) and chamber music (music with just one on a part played before a small audience). In the Baroque era, the line separating orchestral and chamber music was not as clearly drawn. Most instrumental ensemble music, regardless of the place of performance and size of the audience, was played by just one performer on each part. Similarly, the same sonata or sinfonia might be performed in a church accommodating several thousand or a salon seating only a handful of listeners.

In an age in which there were no public concert halls and few public opera houses, church and chamber were the only two venues for ensemble music. Indeed, in the second half of the seventeenth century, composers gradually began to identify music as **da chiesa** (of the church) and as **da camera** (of the chamber). Thus were born the *sonata da chiesa* and the *sonata da camera*. The chamber sonata was usually made up of a series of dance-like movements, each of which had the name and character of a particular dance such as allemande, courante, and gigue. The church sonata included fewer pieces with dance rhythms, and the titles of the movements were simply tempo markings such as *grave, adagio, allegro,* or *presto*; it was thought inappropriate to have the movements of a piece destined for the church associated with secular dances.

SALOMONE ROSSI AND THE EARLY BAROQUE SONATA

A **sonata** (something to be sounded) is a piece for a single instrument or small instrumental ensemble. The term was first used in Venice around 1600 to indicate a composition intended specifically to be played or sounded, as opposed to one that was to be sung (a cantata). At first a sonata might be written for four, five, or as many as twenty-two, instrumental parts. It consisted of a single movement, which often had distinct sections with different tempos and moods. Thus around 1600 there was little difference between an early-Baroque sonata and a late-Renaissance canzona. In the course of the seventeenth century, however, the sonata took on its own distinctive features and the canzona gradually disappeared. In brief, the sonata experienced a gradual reduction of the number of parts, leaving just the solo sonata and trio sonata (see below); simultaneously, it expanded from a single movement, with separate sections, to multiple movements. Two important figures in this development were Salomone Rossi and Arcangelo Corelli.

To learn that violinist Salomone Rossi (c1570–c1630) was a native of Mantua is not surprising; northern Italian cities such as Cremona, Brescia, and Mantua were among the first to embrace the newly popular violin. More remarkable is the fact that Rossi was a Jew who flourished within the Christian court of Duke Vincenzo Gonzaga at Mantua. Duke Vincenzo showed the esteem in which he held Rossi by exempting him from wearing the identifying yellow star, a requirement of most other Jews in Italy at this time. Not only did Rossi compose instrumental music for the Mantuan court, he also created *Hashirim asher lish'lomo* (*The Songs of Solomon*, 1622), the first print to set Hebrew texts to music. The intent of this collection of thirty-three polyphonic settings of Hebrew psalms and hymns was to provide music for the synagogues thriving within the strictly defined Jewish zones (ghettos) in northern Italian cities such as Ferrara, Mantua, and Venice. Nevertheless, it is not for his vocal music for the synagogue, but rather for his contribution to the instrumental sonata, particularly the trio sonata, that Rossi is today considered most influential.

Salomone Rossi published four collections of instrumental ensemble music in the early decades of the seventeenth century. In these he moves away from the instrumental canzona of the late Renaissance (see Chapter 23) with its four-voice imitative texture. Instead, Rossi prefers a top-bottom texture with a duet for two violins on top and a basso continuo below. He clearly was influenced by the lyrical vocal monody and duets that he heard in the operas and concerted motets of his colleague at Mantua, Claudio Monteverdi. Indeed, a flamboyant vocal style for one or two high instruments dominates Rossi's sonatas. Yet Rossi goes beyond this vocally inspired manner, adding dashing turns, quick repeated notes, and rapid runs to exploit the idiomatic capabilities of the violin; such figures can be played faster and cleaner on the violin than they can be sung. Supporting the acrobatic upper parts is a rock-solid basso continuo that clearly sets out the direction of the harmonies.

Typical of Rossi's early Baroque sonatas is his *Sonata sopra l'aria di Ruggiero* (*Sonata on the song Ruggiero*). *Ruggiero* was a popular tune of the late Renaissance that continued to fascinate learned composers well into the seventeenth century. It possessed not only a melody but also a distinctive bass pattern. In fact, it was one of several bass patterns of the early seventeenth century that often served as a *basso ostinato*, a bass line repeating over and over, above which the composer built a set of variations (see Ex. 31-3). Rossi's *Sonata sopra l'aria di Ruggiero* consists of eight variations upon the *Ruggiero* bass (Ex. 33-1), the last of which is repeated at a faster tempo. Most of Rossi's variations involve a rapid interplay between the two upper violins. At times, the growing competition between them leads to virtuosic display. However, at strategic points (the beginning, and beginnings of variations four and seven), Rossi inserts passages of longer note values that have the effect of creating a much slower tempo. This alternation of slow/fast/slow/fast became a hallmark of the sonata. Here the alternation occurs within a single substantive movement. By the late seventeenth century the sections with differing tempos and moods would be separated and made to stand as independent movements, some of substantial duration, others very brief. Rossi and contemporaries such as Dario Castello and Biagio Marini intuited that the future of the sonata would rest in a multi-movement format.

EXAMPLE 33-1

LISTENING CUE

SALOMONE ROSSI
Sonata sopra l'aria di Ruggiero (1623)

CD 4/21
Anthology, No. 92

ARCANGELO CORELLI: SOLO SONATA AND TRIO SONATA

From the northern centers of Cremona and Mantua, the violin, and music for it, spread south to the rest of Italy. One important conduit was the composer Maurizio Cazzati (1616–1678), who carried the northern idioms from Mantua to Bologna. Bologna, on the main road south to Rome, soon became a center for the composition and performance of instrumental music. Opportunity for employment at the gigantic basilica of St. Petronio provided a special lure. Among the violinists attracted there was Arcangelo Corelli (1653–1713). Corelli learned his craft in Bologna, but by about the age of twenty had moved farther south to Rome. In Rome he became the darling of the aristocratic salon, admired for the rigor and precision of his playing.

Rome in the late seventeenth century was a city of about 150,000 people, and many contradictions. The Holy City had more than two hundred temples of worship, yet houses were crowded together, sanitary conditions appalling, and crime rampant. Virtually everyone of any means carried a sword, pistol, or dagger. Nonetheless, art and music flourished under the sponsorship of patrons with strong religious convictions. Corelli's first patron was Christina, exiled queen of Sweden, who in 1654 had renounced the Protestant religion and her throne, and moved to Rome to embrace Catholicism. To her Corelli dedicated his first publication, Opus 1 (1681), a set of twelve trio sonatas. Another important patron was young Pietro Ottoboni (1667–1740), who had been elevated to the rank of cardinal by his uncle, Pope Alexander VIII (more nepotism, as discussed in Chapter 32). Ottoboni collected paintings and musical instruments, and maintained an orchestra in his splendid Palazzo della Cancelleria in the center of Rome. In 1690 he engaged Corelli to serve as its *maestro di concerto* (concert master).

Corelli was the first composer in the history of music to make his reputation exclusively as an instrumental composer. He did not compose a great deal, but almost all of what he wrote was instrumental, not vocal, music. Corelli published four sets of trio sonatas, two *sonate da chiesa* (Opus 1 and Opus 3) and two *sonate da camera* (Opus 2 and Opus 4); a set of twelve solo sonatas for violin (Opus 5); and a collection of twelve ensemble concertos (Opus 6). Both of the latter publications contain examples of *da chiesa* as well as *da camera* format. Corelli was also the first composer to achieve international fame primarily from musical publications, because whatever was printed first in Italy under his name was quickly pirated by printers in Amsterdam and London. His solo sonatas in particular became enormously popular; forty-two editions of Opus 5 appeared before 1800, including arrangements for other instruments such as recorder. Appearing in Corelli's violin sonatas are modern bowing practices and frequent use of **multiple stops,** playing two or more notes simultaneously as chords. Corelli set the standard for composers throughout Europe at the turn of the eighteenth century, and his style was often imitated.

To be sure, the sonata was at the heart of Corelli's creative activity, and in his hands this genre became standardized both with regard to instrumentation and form. Earlier sonatas had been written for ensembles of various sizes, from one to as many as twenty-two instrumental players. With Corelli, however, the norm took two types: the solo sonata and the trio sonata. These two instrumental combinations became standard for composers until the end of the Baroque era around 1750. The **solo sonata** comprised a line for a single melody instrument (usually a violin) and basso continuo, while the **trio sonata** had two treble instruments (usually two violins) and continuo. (Because the basso continuo often required two instruments—one playing chords and the other the bass line—the solo sonata actually involved three players, and the trio sonata four.)

Form, too, now coalesced into a stereotypical pattern. Sonatas, whether solo or trio, usually consisted of a succession of four movements alternating slow/fast/slow/fast. All movements were in the same key (or relative major or minor). Sonatas intended for church (*da chiesa*) had movements simply labeled with a tempo marking such as *allegro* or *adagio*; sonatas for the private chamber (*da camera*) usually had not only a tempo indicator but also a title of a dance such as allemande or gigue. These were not real dances, but stylized pieces intending to conjure up in the mind of the listener a sonic image of the dance in question.

Corelli also standardized form within movements through a new emphasis on tonality. He developed a strategy of dividing the music of a movement into two balanced sections and repeating each. The first begins in the tonic key and ends on a dominant chord; the second begins on that dominant and works its way back to the tonic. In this process Corelli helped create what is now known as **binary form,** a structure consisting of two complementary parts, the first moving to a closely related key and the second beginning in that new key but soon returning the music to the tonic. In other words, it uses tonality to clarify form. Binary form became the standard form for single movements in sonatas and dance suites throughout the Baroque era.

In Corelli's music, tonality not only regulates the larger formal plan but also directs the smaller, more localized, harmonic event. Corelli's harmonies sound modern to our ears because they are often composed of triads, the roots of which are a fifth apart. Corelli also modulates, using melodic sequence, around the circle of fifths. One chord moves to the next in a purposeful, well-directed fashion, in a chord progression. The feeling of chords pulling one to another is often created by the use of chromatic inflection. The dominant chord has a leading tone that pulls to the tonic and a secondary chord often has a chromatic inflection (usually a sharp) that leads by half-step to the dominant pitch (see Ex. 33-3). What we hear in Corelli is a strong sense of functional tonality as we know it—the kind of harmonic movement still studied in music theory classes today.

In 1694 Corelli published his Opus 4, a set of *sonate da camera* dedicated to his art-loving patron, Cardinal Ottoboni. All twelve sonatas are trio sonatas scored for two violins and basso continuo (here, cello and harpsichord). In addition, all twelve sonatas proceed in a sequence of movements with alternating tempos: slow/fast/slow/fast. Sonata No. 1 in C Major opens with a slow *Preludio* (Prelude), which gives the players a chance to warm up while it sets the general mood of the sonata. Movement two is entitled *Corrente* (from the Italian *correre*, "to run") and proceeds in a fast triple meter. The fourth and final movement is also brisk and carries the title *Allemanda* (literally, "the German dance"). In the *Allemanda* the bass moves consistently in eighth notes, often up or down the scale (Ex. 33-2). A bass moving in a steady pace in this fashion is called a **walking bass.** Here, however, the fast tempo transforms it into something akin to a running or sprinting bass.

EXAMPLE 33-2

Between the fast *Corrente* and the brisk concluding *Allemanda,* Corelli places a slow *Adagio* in A minor, the relative minor key. Notice how, toward the end, a steadily rising bass line moves by half-step chromatic inflection to the tonic (Ex. 33-3). Combining the steady motion of a walking bass with chromatic inflections that pull to neighboring chords, or to those a fifth away, is just one way in which Corelli lends to his music a newfound sense of tonal direction.

EXAMPLE 33-3

In sum, Corelli is important in the history of music for developing modern violin techniques such as multiple stops, for standardizing the Baroque sonata as either a solo sonata or trio sonata, for popularizing binary form, for impressing a four-movement format on the whole, and for creating a purposeful harmonic language, one that other composers throughout Europe would soon eagerly adopt. Today, Corelli remains the only instrumental composer to be buried in Rome's famous Pantheon, a hall of fame for Italy's most illustrious artists and statesmen.

LISTENING CUE

ARCANGELO CORELLI
Opus 4, No. 1 (1694)
Preludio, Corrente, Adagio, Allemanda

CD 4/22–25
Anthology, No. 93a-d

TRUMPET MUSIC BY GIUSEPPE TORELLI: THE BEGINNINGS OF THE SOLO CONCERTO

The violin and members of the violin family were not the only instruments to thrive in seventeenth-century Italy. The harpsichord, which had been around since the fifteenth century, became the workhorse of the Baroque ensemble, holding together the basso continuo. And melody instruments, such as the oboe, flute, and trumpet, saw a body of solo music created especially for them. For the trumpet in particular, the period of the seventeenth and early eighteenth centuries was a glorious moment. The trumpet, of course, had existed in Europe since Roman antiquity (see Chapter 2). But it flourished during the seventeenth century, perhaps because of the growing interest in brilliant instrumental sounds during the Baroque era. Trumpet makers in London, England, and Nuremberg, Germany, produced large numbers of quality instruments; and composers such as Henry Purcell in London and Giuseppe Torelli in Bologna created pieces that exploited its brilliant upper register as well as the advanced playing techniques of virtuoso performers.

During the seventeenth century the most important center for trumpet music was Bologna, Italy. The city had a long history of interest in civic music played by municipal trumpeters, one that extended back into the Middle Ages. Increasingly, trumpet music, and music generally in Bologna, was concentrated in the gigantic basilica of St. Petronio, a church far larger than either the Sistine Chapel in Rome or the basilica of St. Mark in Venice. Music at St. Petronio's entered a golden era with the appointment of Maurizio Cazzati as *maestro di cappella* in 1657. Cazzati, inspired by the skill of several trumpeters in Bologna, published the first sonatas for solo trumpet in 1665. By the early eighteenth century, the music library at St. Petronio's comprised hundreds of instrumental works by Cazzati and other composers, including some eighty-three pieces for trumpet. Foremost among the composers of trumpet music in this collection was Giuseppe Torelli. Indeed, judging from the number of pieces surviving under his name in Bologna and elsewhere (approximately forty-five), Torelli was the preeminent composer of trumpet music of the entire Baroque era.

Giuseppe Torelli (1658–1709) was born in Verona, near Venice, but moved to Bologna and a position at St. Petronio's in 1684. He remained in Bologna, except for a brief sojourn in Berlin and Vienna around 1700, for the remainder of his life. Ironically, Torelli was himself a violinist, not a trumpeter. He published two early sets of trio sonatas for strings (1686) as well as two somewhat-later sets of string concertos (1692 and 1698). The concertos of 1692 are important because they are among the first to specify that the orchestral string parts are to be multiplied—as many as three or four players are to reinforce each orchestra line. Yet, following in the footsteps of Cazzati, Torelli also chose to write for the virtuoso trumpeters of Bologna, who filled St. Petronio's with brilliant sound on the high feast days of the church year.

Between 1684 and his death in 1709, Torelli wrote nearly four dozen trumpet pieces for St. Petronio's. Most were performed as a prelude to the Mass or as a substitute for the Mass Offertory on the feast of St. Petronio (4 October), the patron saint of Bologna. Some of these pieces Torelli called sonatas, others sinfonias, and still others concertos. Some he wrote in the slow/fast/slow/fast movement format typi-cal of a sonata, and others in the fast/slow/fast arrangement that was coming to be common for the sinfonia. By 1700 the term **sinfonia** was used to designate a three-movement instrumental overture, one that might preface an opera or a Mass. In truth, Torelli employed the terms "sonata," "sinfonia," and "concerto" without distinction; there is no difference in form or musical process from one genre to the next. Indeed, this indiscriminate use of the terms is a hallmark of Italian instrumen-tal music around 1700.

Consequently, Torelli's Sinfonia in D Major for trumpet should be heard as a three-movement sinfonia, but one possessing early signs of the solo concerto (on the concerto, see below under Antonio Vivaldi). It opens with an orchestral pre-sentation of a theme that will return repeatedly in the first movement (Ex. 33-4). When the trumpet enters, it emphasizes a rising fourth motive (Ex. 33-5), and it alone plays lengthy trills. Thus a distinction is made between the music assigned the soloist and that given the orchestra. Moreover, the trumpet's rising fourth mo-tive is clearly drawn from the opening theme played by the orchestra. These two procedures—differentiating the music of the soloist from that of the orchestra, and having the soloist expand upon material derived from a recurring orchestral theme (ritornello)—are hallmarks of the emerging Baroque concerto. They will become especially prominent in the mature concertos of Antonio Vivaldi.

EXAMPLE 33-4

EXAMPLE 33-5

By contrast, the trumpet is entirely silent during the slow second movement. Here, Torelli writes a short, simple succession of chords and ends with a half-cadence that leads directly into the finale. Above most of these chords Torelli has placed a small dash, the sign for *spiccato*. **Spiccato** (Italian for "sharp") requires the performers to play in a detached fashion, but not quite as short as *staccato*. Compared to nor-mal playing, *spiccato* produces less resonance but greater clarity, a desirable feature in a large, resonant church such as St. Petronio's, where the reverberation time is an astonishing twelve seconds.

Finally, there is a distinction here as to what the violin can play and what the trumpet cannot. In measures 20–24, the violin leads a modulation that touches on chords moving around the circle of fifths: B-E-A-D. This is effected by means of chromatic notes, some of which, such as g#', c#", and d#", are not easily available on

National Music Museum

❀ FIGURE 33-3

Two trumpets by Johann Wilhelm Hass, Nuremberg, c1690–1700. Trumpets like these were frequently purchased by Italian trumpeters.

a trumpet pitched in D. Thus this modulatory passage is assigned to the strings but not the trumpet. The Baroque trumpet could play *in* keys such as tonic and dominant, but it could not easily move *through* different keys.

Recall that the trumpet during the seventeenth century is a natural instrument without keys or valves (Fig. 33-3). The notes it can produce are those of the harmonic series. Most trumpets around 1700 were pitched with a fundamental that sounded low D, and therefore most compositions for them in the Baroque are in the key of D major. Example 33-6 shows the notes of the harmonic series, and thus the pitches available to a natural trumpet pitched in D. Notice that the notes g♯', c♯'', and d♯'', among others, are not present in this series. In addition, some of the harmonics (7, 11, 13, and 14) are not in tune and only approximate the black notes written in the example. A skilled performer, however, could blow more or less hard to produce a sharp or flat inflection (B♮ or C for harmonic 7, for example). As the trumpet entered the highest harmonics, a fully chromatic scale resulted. Only in this highest register could the trumpet play conjunct melodies and not merely jump around in fourths and fifths. Playing in this high register, called the **clarino register,** was a special technique of Baroque trumpeters. By 1760, however, this brilliant upper-register playing had became something of a lost art. The trumpet parts written by Baroque composers Torelli, Purcell, and Bach are much more difficult than those composed by Classical masters Haydn, Mozart, and Beethoven.

EXAMPLE 33-6

LISTENING CUE

| **GIUSEPPE TORELLI** | CD 5/1–3 |
| Trumpet Sinfonia in D Major (c1700) | Anthology, No. 94 |

❀ ANTONIO VIVALDI: SOLO CONCERTO AND CONCERTO GROSSO

The seventeenth century witnessed the advent of several new musical genres, among them opera, oratorio, cantata, sonata, and concerto. In the early seventeenth century, the term "concerto" appeared in many contexts and meant many things. Generally, it connoted a composition that involved opulent, contrasting sound created by diverse musical forces, whether instrumental or vocal. In this sense it was closely related to the early Baroque term *concertato*, music marked by strong contrasts (see Chapter 31). Only during the last two decades of the seventeenth century did the word **concerto** come to denote a purely instrumental piece for ensemble in which one or more soloists both complemented and competed with an orchestra.

The most prolific composer of Baroque concertos was Antonio Vivaldi. In fact, Vivaldi has left us nearly five hundred concertos. Roughly three hundred fifty of these are for one solo instrument or another, and thus they belong to the category **solo concerto.** Of the solo concertos most (some two hundred thirty) are for violin, but some are for bassoon, cello, oboe, flute, recorder, and even mandolin. Vivaldi himself was a virtuoso violinist. He was one of the first to showcase his skill as a soloist at the end of a movement of a concerto. In 1715 a visitor from Germany to Venice heard the master play such an improvised conclusion.

> Towards the end Vivaldi played a solo accompaniment—splendid—to which he appended a cadenza which really frightened me, for such playing has never been nor can be: he brought his fingers up to only a straw's distance from the bridge, leaving no room for the bow—and that on all four strings with imitations and incredible speed. With this he astounded everyone, but I cannot say that it pleased me, for it was not so pleasant to listen to as it was skillfully executed.[1]

Thus the instrumental **cadenza**—a technically demanding, rhapsodic, improvisatory passage near the end of a movement—entered the concerto in the early eighteenth century in the music of Vivaldi and other contemporary Italian composers.

Antonio Vivaldi (1678–1741) was a native of Venice and became an important figure in that city's long and distinguished musical history (see Chapter 31). His father was a barber and part-time violinist on the payroll of the basilica of St. Mark, the principal church of the city. The young Vivaldi's proximity to St. Mark's naturally brought him into contact with the clergy. Although a violin virtuoso at an early age, he entered Holy Orders and gained the priesthood in 1703. Yet Vivaldi's life was by no means confined to the realm of the spirit. He concertized on the violin throughout Europe; he wrote and produced nearly fifty operas, which brought him a great deal of money; and for fifteen years he lived with an Italian opera soprano. The worldly pursuits of *il prete rosso* (the red-haired priest) eventually provoked the wrath of the Church of Rome, and in 1737 Vivaldi was forbidden to practice his musical artistry in certain papally controlled lands. This ban seems to have affected his income as well as his creativity. He died poor and obscure in 1741 in Vienna, where he had moved in a futile effort to resuscitate his career.

Despite his frequent travels, Vivaldi's career was centered in Venice. From 1703 until 1740 he served variously as a violinist, music teacher, and composer-in-residence at the *Ospedale della Pietà* (Hospice of Mercy). The Hospice of Mercy was a combination orphanage, convent, and music conservatory providing for the care and education of young women. It was one of four such charitable institutions in Venice that accepted abandoned, mostly illegitimate, girls, who, as several reports state, "otherwise would have been thrown in the canals." All girls received religious training and some instruction in domestic crafts (cooking, embroidery, lace-making, and the like). The more musically talented were given lessons on instruments and required to practice as much as four hours a day. Each Sunday afternoon the all-female orchestra offered public performances for tourists and well-to-do Venetians alike. The girls appeared in the chapel of the orphanage standing on high in a special gallery, a musicians' loft, and played to the outside world through a grill (Fig. 33-4). The report of a French diplomat in 1739 is typical of the impression they made.

> These girls are brought up at the expense of the state and trained solely to excel in music. Moreover, they sing like angels and play the violin, the flute, the organ, the oboe, the cello, and the bassoon; in short, there is no instrument, however unwieldy, that can frighten them. They are cloistered like nuns. It is they alone who perform, and about forty girls take part in each concert. I vow

✻ FIGURE 33-4
Women musicians perform behind a grill at an eighteenth-century Venetian orphanage.

Photo Costa

to you that there is nothing so diverting as the sight of a young and pretty nun in a white habit, with a bunch of pomegranate blossoms over her ear, conducting the orchestra and beating time with all the grace and precision imaginable.[2]

Vivaldi composed many of his concertos specifically for his female pupils at the Hospice of Mercy in order that they might develop and demonstrate their musical skills. Some of these concertos he published, but most he left in manuscript copies at the time of his death. Among the works Vivaldi published are a set of twelve concerti grossi, comprising Opus 3, entitled *L'estro armonico* (*Harmonic Whim*, 1711) and a group of twelve solo concertos, comprising Opus 8, called *Il cimento dell'armonia e dell'inventione* (*The Contest between Harmony and Invention*, 1725). The first four concertos of this latter set are the famous **The Four Seasons.** In these, Vivaldi writes some of the earliest program music, for the composer inserts a poem about each season into the first violinist's part and then fashions music to match the poetic images (singing birds, a gathering storm, a babbling brook, and so on). Today Vivaldi's *The Four Seasons* concertos are perhaps the most popular of all Baroque compositions—standard background music in restaurants and coffee houses, as well as films and TV commercials.

Less popular today, but more influential in Vivaldi's day, are the concertos contained in the *L'estro armonico*. This collection, which greatly influenced the leading composers of the day, has been called "the single most important collection of instrumental music to appear during the whole of the eighteenth century."[3] Most of the twelve concertos are of the concerto grosso type. In a **concerto grosso** a larger body of performers, namely the full orchestra, contrasts with a smaller group of soloists. The larger ensemble is sometimes called the concerto grosso ("large concerto"), but more commonly identified as the **ripieno** (Italian for "full"). The smaller group of two, three, or four soloists is called the **concertino** ("little concerto"). In the Baroque era these soloists were not expensive stars brought from afar, but the regular first-chair players of the orchestra. When they were not serving as soloists, these leaders simply melted back into the ripieno to play the orchestral parts.

As with the solo concerto, the Baroque concerto grosso is in three movements, fast/slow/fast. The serious first movement is usually composed in a carefully worked-out structure called **ritornello form.** The Italian word **ritornello,** as we have seen (see Chapter 32), simply means "return" or "refrain." Vivaldi employs ritornello form in both his solo concerto and concerto grosso. A piece in ritornello form begins with a distinct main theme, the ritornello, which returns again and again, invariably played by the *ripieno*. Between statements of the ritornello, the *concertino* (or soloist in a solo concerto) comes forward to expand and elaborate upon musical ideas contained or suggested within the ritornello. The *concertino* also provokes modulations to more distant keys. In general, the *ripieno* provides tonal stability, while it is up to the *concertino* to push the piece farther afield tonally. The tension between these two different sound masses and between the tonal zones of the two groups is what gives the concerto grosso its exciting, dynamic quality.

A classic example of a concerto grosso is the eighth within Vivaldi's *L'estro armonico* (Opus 3, No. 8, in A Minor). No less a person than the young J.S. Bach transcribed it for organ so as to study and absorb Vivaldi's style. The opening movement is in ritornello form. Here the ritornello is comprised of four distinct parts. Part 1 (Ex. 33-7a) begins with three strong chords followed by a descending scale played in unison by the strings (unison string writing is a favorite device of Vivaldi). Part 2 (Ex. 33-7b) presents a repeated figure that soon gives way to a descending melodic sequence (frequent use of melodic sequence is another hallmark of

Vivaldi's style). Part 3 (Ex. 33-7c) is marked by a gesture idiomatic to the violin (rocking back and forth with slurred down bows); while Part 4 (Ex. 33-7d) inserts a striking chord (B♭ chord in A minor) as the violins saw away. All four sections are energized by small repeating rhythmic cells, thereby creating the motor-like rhythms that typically propel Vivaldi's music forward. Now the *concertino* (here two violins and cello) takes over from the *ripieno*, and it interjects an insistent, repeated figure borrowed from Part 1 of the ritornello. Thereafter the movement unfolds as a succession of increasingly ornate elaborations of bits of the ritornello played by the *concertino* and returns of one or more sections of the ritornello performed by the *ripieno* (see below). The *concertino* sounds daring and adventuresome; the *ripieno* solid and secure. The interplay between the two goes to the very heart of the concerto, a spirited give-and-take between opposing musical forces.

EXAMPLES 33-7 A–D

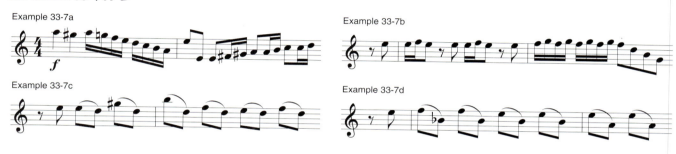

Example 33-7a

Example 33-7b

Example 33-7c

Example 33-7d

Formal diagram of Vivaldi, Opus 3, No. 8, 1st movement

Ritornello part:	1–4		4		2		1		3		1		2+4		4
R (*ripieno*) or c (*concertino*):	R	c	R	c	R	c	R	c	R	c	R	c	R	c	R
Key:	a		a	C			d		a		a		a		a

 LISTENING CUE

ANTONIO VIVALDI
Opus 3, *L'estro armonico* (1711)
Concerto Grosso, No. 8, First movement

CD 5/4
Anthology, No. 95

SUMMARY

During the seventeenth century, instrumental music became just as important as vocal music, judging from the amount of music published. For the first time in the history of music, composers began to write idiomatically for instruments. By mid-century the sonata had become the dominant genre of instrumental music, though by the end of the century another new genre, the concerto, began to compete for pride of place. At first the sonata was a single-movement composition with sections having different tempos and moods. Similarly, the early sonata might involve as many as twenty-two individual parts. The sonatas of Salomone Rossi, while still embodying a single movement, reduce the instruments to just two high parts and a basso continuo. Arcangelo Corelli standardized the Baroque sonata as either a solo sonata or a trio sonata, and as either *da chiesa* or *da camera*. He impressed a four-movement format on each sonata and binary form on each movement within each sonata. Corelli also created a purposeful harmonic language by using chromatic inflections, secondary dominant chords, and abundant melodic sequences. Giuseppe Torelli wrote trumpet sonatas, sinfonias, and concertos in which can be seen the beginnings of the solo concerto: a separation of material assigned to soloist and opposing orchestra. Antonio Vivaldi popularized both the solo concerto, as exemplified by *The Four Seasons*, and the concerto grosso. In both genres Vivaldi often employs ritornello form to set up a dialogue involving theme and key between the full orchestra (*ripieno*) and a single soloist, or a group of soloists (*concertino*).

KEY TERMS

Cremona	binary form	*The Four Seasons*
Antonio Stradivari	walking bass	concerto grosso
da chiesa	sinfonia	*ripieno*
da camera	*spiccato*	*concertino*
sonata	clarino register	ritornello form
multiple stops	concerto	*ritornello*
solo sonata	solo concerto	
trio sonata	cadenza	

Chapter

34

Instrumental Music in Germany and Austria

Italy was the fountainhead of Western art music during the seventeenth century. Almost all of the new musical genres of the Baroque era—opera, concerted motet, oratorio, cantata, sonata, sinfonia, and concerto—originated there. So dominant was Italy during this period that the terminology the Italians developed for music soon spread to other countries, and it remains fundamentally the one we use today. Terms for dynamics (such as *piano, forte, fortissimo*), for tempo (*allegro, adagio,* and *moderato*), for processes (*ostinato, obbligato, staccato,* and *spiccato*), and even for instruments (violin, viola, cello) were popularized in Italy during the seventeenth century. But other nations had their own distinctive musical styles and practices. In German-speaking lands (mainly modern Germany and Austria; Map 34-1), intensely contrapuntal pieces and those built upon a sacred melody (either Catholic or Protestant) were especially favored. As we have seen, German musicians journeyed to Italy to study the latest Italian musical styles and, similarly, Italian musicians were much prized at German and Austrian courts. With such comings and goings on the Continent, musical styles (Italian, German, French, and Spanish) inevitably became intertwined, and we are sometimes at pains to know exactly which musical characteristics originated where. Some German-speaking composers restricted themselves

MAP 34-1
Northern Europe in the seventeenth century.

to a distinctly Germanic style. Others were proficient at adopting or adapting several national idioms. One such cosmopolitan master was Johann Froberger.

JOHANN FROBERGER AND THE BAROQUE DANCE SUITE

Who was Johann Froberger (1616–1667) and why should we care? Froberger was a German musician who worked mainly in Austria, spent years studying in Italy, and traveled extensively as a virtuoso performer in France and England. He is important to the history of music because he established the dance suite as an important genre of music for string keyboard instruments (harpsichord and clavichord). Handel and Bach later composed keyboard suites building on Froberger's model; young Bach in particular copied keyboard pieces by Froberger to learn his craft, and held him in high esteem throughout his life. Dance suites for keyboard and instrumental ensembles proliferated during the Baroque era and then disappeared after 1750, only to enjoy a renaissance during the twentieth century in the hands of Debussy, Strauss, Respighi, Schoenberg, Stravinsky, and others.

Johann Froberger was born in Stuttgart, Germany, the son of a court musician. In 1634 he moved to the Austrian capital of Vienna and three years later was appointed organist to the imperial court. That same year, Froberger received a stipend from the emperor, which allowed him to study for several years in Rome with the renowned keyboardist and composer Girolamo Frescobaldi (see Chapter 32). Froberger was again given leave from the imperial court in 1651–1652, when he visited London and Paris, meeting and absorbing the musical styles of the leading Parisian composers in particular. He returned to imperial service in Vienna in 1653, but was released in 1657 when a new emperor came to the throne. He ended his days as artist-in-residence for the aristocratic family that his father had once served in Stuttgart.

Froberger composed almost exclusively keyboard music. Those compositions belonging to the Italian tradition (canzonas, toccatas, and ricercars, for example) he intended mainly for organ, while those showing French influence (mostly the dance suites) were designed for harpsichord or clavichord. In Paris, Froberger had come under the sway of the French school of lutenists centering around Denis Gaultier (see Chapter 36), and he transferred their style to the harpsichord. The French, of course, had enjoyed a long history of composed dance music, and by the seventeenth century their earlier dance pair of pavane and galliard (see Chapter 22) had been greatly expanded. Sometimes as many as a dozen dances were organized by key into a group, and it was left to the performer to pick and choose a set to create the desired mood. Our English word "suite" simply means a succession of pieces coming in an order pleasing to performer and audience. The audience listened but did not dance. These were stylized dances in which the composer aimed to capture in music the spirit of the dance in question. As one musician of the day commented, they are written "for the refreshment of the ear alone."[1]

Johann Froberger crystallized the dance suite by creating some thirty suites that usually had the same four dances: allemande, courante, sarabande, and gigue.[2] Subsequent composers such as Handel and Bach would add one or more other dances, but these four dances henceforth remained the backbone of the suite. A **dance suite** can therefore be defined as an ordered set of dances (often on the sequence of allemande, courante, sarabande, and gigue) for solo instrument or ensemble, all written in the same key and intended to be performed in a single sitting.

Below are listed the main traits of these four core dances as well as those of other dances sometimes inserted into the suite as fashion or fancy demanded:

- **Allemande.** The name suggests the place of origin of this dance ("allemande" is French for "German"); a stately dance in $\frac{4}{4}$ meter at a moderate tempo with an upbeat and gracefully interweaving lines that create an improvisatory-like style
- **Courante.** A lively dance ("courante" is French for "running") characterized by intentional metrical ambiguity created by means of hemiola—measures of two beats with triple subdivision $\frac{6}{4}$ interplay with those of three beats with duple subdivision $\frac{3}{2}$
- **Sarabande.** A slow, stately dance in $\frac{3}{4}$ with a strong accent on the second beat
- **Gigue.** A fast dance in $\frac{6}{8}$ or $\frac{12}{8}$ with a constant eighth-note pulse that produces a galloping sound; the gigue is sometimes lightly imitative and often used to conclude a suite
- **Minuet.** An elegant dance of French origin in triple meter and performed at a moderate tempo; the only Baroque dance to remain popular in the Classical period
- **Bourrée.** A fast dance in $\frac{4}{4}$ (or in cut time) with a quarter-note upbeat that usually follows a slower dance in $\frac{3}{4}$ such as the sarabande
- **Gavotte.** Another dance of French origin marked by a moderate tempo, duple meter, and four-bar phrases
- **Hornpipe.** An energetic dance of English origin, derived from the country jig, in either $\frac{3}{2}$ or $\frac{2}{4}$

Froberger's Suite No. 6 in C Major is typical of his thirty keyboard suites. It also demonstrates a unique peculiarity of his music: Froberger had a penchant for composing a highly expressive lament as a response to personal or national tragedy. When he witnessed a well-known French lutenist take a fatal tumble down a flight of stairs, he composed a lament in honor of the fallen musician; and when he had been robbed by pirates on his way from Paris to London in 1652 he composed a "plaint" (musical complaint). Sometimes Froberger's laments were independent, free-standing pieces, as is true for the one he composed on the death of Emperor Ferdinand III in 1657. In other instances, Froberger placed the descriptive piece at the opening of a suite, where it serves as an allemande. In Suite No. 6 in C Major, the allemande is entitled *Lamento sopra la dolorosa perdita della Real Maestà di Ferdi-*

Österreichische Nationalbibliothek

✿ FIGURE 34-1

Autograph keyboard score from the end of the opening *Lamento* (*Allemande*) of Johann Froberger's Suite No. 6 in C Major. These final two staves conclude with a three-octave C-major scale ascending to heaven. (Turn sideways to better see the faces of the angels.)

nando IV Rè de Romani (*Lament on the occasion of the sad loss of his Royal Majesty Ferdinando IV, King of the Romans*). The son and heir of Froberger's employer, Ferdinand IV, died unexpectedly in 1654. Froberger's lament is full of painful dissonance and ends with a run up the C major scale, a graphic depiction of the hoped-for ascent of the young man's soul. Indeed, Froberger's autograph manuscript, preserved today in Vienna (Fig. 34-1), shows the soul-bearing scale being welcomed by the light of three heavenly angels. The remaining dances of the suite are all in the same mood, key, and form as the opening *Lamento* (*Allemande*).

🔵 **LISTENING CUE**

JOHANN FROBERGER

Suite No. 6 in C Major (1654)

Lamento (*Allemande*), *Courante*, *Sarabande*, *Gigue*

CD 5/5–8

Anthology, No. 96a-d

✿ BIBER AND KUHNAU: THE PROGRAMMATIC SONATA

Johann Froberger wrote mainly suites for solo keyboard, while Heinrich Biber, a contemporary virtuoso violinist, composed mainly sonatas for violin and basso continuo. In the late seventeenth century, the suite and the sonata had much in common. Both were multi-movement instrumental works with the movements generally in one key, and both were comprised of a succession of dances (the suite always, the sonata often). Moreover, both suite and sonata began to display programmatic influence. In **program music** some external influence or non-musical event affects the general spirit and the specific details of an instrumental composition. We have just seen how the expected upward spiritual journey of King Ferdinand IV received musical depiction at the end of the opening movement of Froberger's Suite No. 6.

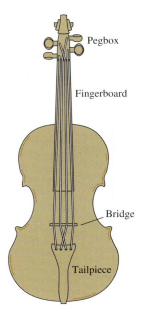

❋ FIGURE 34-2

Twice-crossed strings on the violin suggests the theme of Christ's resurrection. This arrangement is one possible way to effect the *scordatura* required for Biber's sonata for the resurrection.

❋ FIGURE 34-3

The image of the resurrection accompanying Biber's sonata of that name. In the autograph manuscript of Biber's "Mystery" Sonatas, each sonata is prefaced by an engraving that suggests the spiritual meaning of the music to follow. The rather dramatic ascent of Christ from the sepulcher may explain the agitated music with which this sonata opens.

So too in Heinrich Biber's "Mystery" Sonatas, things outside of music shape (provide a program for) a lengthy musical creation.

Heinrich Biber (1644–1704) was a Bohemian-born virtuoso violinist. In 1670 he entered employment at the court of the archbishop of Salzburg in northern Austria (where Mozart and his father would serve some hundred years later), and in 1684 he became Kapellmeister (a coveted position neither Mozart attained). Salzburg was a German-speaking city, but, like most of those in Austria and southern Germany, it sat squarely within the spiritual realm of the Roman Catholic Church. Thus Italian music, and especially Roman-style church music, was very much in favor here. Biber wrote *a cappella* Masses in *stile antico* as well as more flamboyant, large-scale *stile concertato* Masses. He is probably the author of the colossal, fifty-three part *Missa Salisburgensis* (*Mass of Salzburg;* c1682), once ascribed to the Roman master Orazio Benevoli (see Chapter 32).

Despite his skill as a composer of sacred music, Biber is best known today for his instrumental pieces, specifically his programmatic "Mystery" Sonatas composed for Salzburg about 1674. The **"Mystery" Sonatas,** also known as the **"Rosary" Sonatas,** are a set of fifteen sonatas for solo violin and continuo that project through music the sacred devotion of the rosary (votive prayers coming in fifteen groups). During the recitation of each of these groups, the faithful Catholic meditates upon one of fifteen events associated with the life of Christ or the Virgin Mary, keeping count of the prayers by means of rosary beads. Thus the program for the fifteen "Mystery" Sonatas follows a sequence of fifteen miraculous, or mysterious, events in the lives of Christ and Mary: the annunciation, visitation, nativity, crucifixion, resurrection, and ascension, for example. The violinist projects each mystery by means of a solo sonata with one to four movements.

Yet there is another "mystery" in the "Mystery" Sonatas, and that has to do with the tuning of the violin. Biber instructs that the violinist must tune the instrument a different way for each of the fifteen sonatas. The first sonata requires the standard violin tuning with the strings in fifths (g-d'-a'-e"). Subsequent sonatas instruct that the strings must be set at an interval of a third or a fourth, or even an octave, apart. Tuning a string instrument to something other than standard tuning is called *scordatura* (from an Italian word literally meaning "mistuning"). The purpose of *scordatura* is to make certain passages easier to play, to produce special effects, and to make the instrument sound more brilliant by emphasizing the resonance of particular strings. Biber's "Mystery" Sonatas provide the most extensive use of *scordatura* in the entire repertory of Western music.

Exactly how *scordatura* works, and how it helps project the meaning of Biber's "Mystery" Sonatas, can be seen in Sonata No. 11, *The Resurrection.* Here the violinist must tune the strings to g-g'-d'-d". This may be accomplished one of two ways: (1) by simply switching the two inner strings and tuning them in octaves with the adjacent outer string; or (2) by tuning them g-d'-g'-d" but twice crossing the inner two strings thereby producing g-g'-d'-d" (Fig. 34-2). This crossing of the instrument adds a visible sign of the resurrection (see the cross on Christ's standard in Fig. 34-3).

No violinist could have learned to play these *scordature* in the "Mystery" Sonatas without great labor. To simplify things, Biber writes out his music as if the violinist has the standard tuning in mind (g-d'-a'-e"). This creates an apparently nonsensical collection of notes on the page (top line in Ex. 34-1), but, owing to the *scordatura,* the written notes are mysteriously transformed into pitches that will sound harmonious with those of the basso continuo (second line in Ex. 34-1).

EXAMPLE 34-1

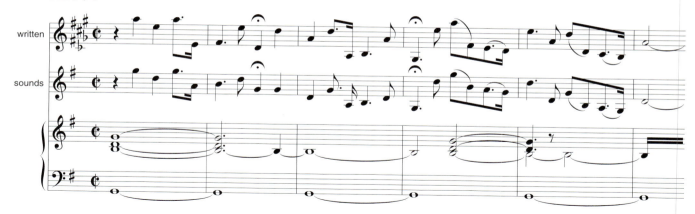

A *scordatura* emphasizing G's and D's, as in Sonata No. 11, naturally works well in the key of G, for here the G-string and D-string are open strings (not stopped), and the tonic and dominant chords sound especially resonant. Sonata No. 11, in fact, is written almost entirely in G major. Notice also that Biber is fond of writing multiple stops to create his virtuosic violin style. This adds to the resonant sound, but it also gives the impression of two, or sometimes three, independent lines working together; polyphony, even when projected on a melodic instrument like the violin, is very much a hallmark of German Baroque music.

Finally, consider the core of this sonata—the stately second movement. Here Biber has constructed a lengthy chaconne upon a popular Latin hymn *Surrexit Christus hodie* (*Christ has risen today*). The hymn first appears in the basso continuo as a chaconne bass, and upon it Biber then constructs a set of variations for the violin. By means of this hymn the "program" of the sonata is communicated to the faithful. Lest the listener miss the point, the movement concludes with the violin playing the hymn in octave double-stops and the continuo an additional octave below (Ex. 34-2)—an emphatic affirmation of the mystery of Christ's resurrection.

EXAMPLE 34-2

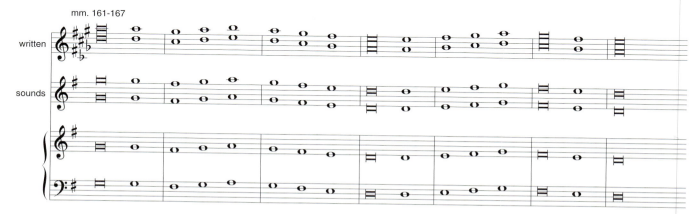

LISTENING CUE

HEINRICH BIBER
"Mystery" Sonatas (c1674)
The Resurrection, Movements 1–2

CD 5/9–10
Anthology, No. 97a-b

Heinrich Biber, working at the Catholic court of the archbishop of Salzburg, Austria, was not the only composer to embrace the programmatic sonata. To the north, in the Protestant town of Leipzig, Germany, Johann Kuhnau (1660–1722) did the same. Kuhnau was the cantor of the St. Thomas Church, the immediate predecessor of the great Bach in that position in Leipzig. Kuhnau wrote sacred vocal music for the St. Thomas Church (almost all of it unpublished), and two collections of sonatas and two sets of suites for keyboard (all four published). Today Kuhnau's reputation rests almost exclusively on his last published work for keyboard, a set of six sonatas entitled *Musicalische Vorstellung einiger biblischer Historien* (*Musical Representation of a few Biblical Histories*; 1700). Each sonata in the set attempts to illustrate a particular event from the Old Testament: the combat between David and Goliath, Saul cured by David through music, and Jacob's death and burial, for example. To guide the listener, Kuhnau adds a synopsis of each story in phrases of Italian. Thus the first sonata is entitled *Il combattimento trà David e Goliath* (*The Battle between David and Goliath*) and opens with the phrase "Le bravate di Goliath." The dramatic events within the story are depicted musically by a series of self-contained movements, each having a sound distinctly appropriate to the narrative. Example 34-3 suggests the way in which Kuhnau's explicitly pictorial music works.

EXAMPLE 34-3A

The bravado of Goliath [pompous, dotted rhythms]

EXAMPLE 34-3B

The quavering of the Israelites in the face of the giant and their prayer made to God. [trembling chords that fall down and to which is soon added the chorale tune *Out of the Deep I Cry to Thee*]

EXAMPLE 34-3C

The courage of David and his eagerness to prevail over the pride of his terrifying enemy through his confidence found with the help of God. [David steadfastly remains in the key of C major]

The Doctrine of Affections

In the winter of 1645–1646 the French philosopher René Descartes (1596–1650) published an essay entitled *Les Passions de l'âme* (*Passions of the Soul*), in which he sought to classify and explain the full spectrum of human emotions. With each description of an emotion came a physiological diagnosis, as here in the case of sadness:

> *The definition of Sadness.* Sadness is a disagreeable languor in which consists the discomfort and unrest which the soul receives from evil. . . .
>
> *The movement of the blood and spirits in Sadness.* In sadness, the openings of the heart are much contracted by the small nerve which surrounds them, and the blood of the veins is in nowise agitated, which brings it to pass that very little of it goes toward the heart and yet the passages by which the juice of the food flows from the stomach and the intestines towards the liver remain open, which causes the appetite not to diminish at all, excepting when hatred, which is often united to sadness, closes them.[3]

Obviously, Descartes's understanding of the workings of the mind and body was somewhat different from our own. But his views greatly influenced intellectuals generally and music theorists in particular, both French and German. One such theorist was Johann Mattheson (1681–1764) of Hamburg, Germany, who codified a theory of *Affektenlehre,* or what came to be called the Doctrine of Affections. The **Doctrine of Affections** embodies the Baroque belief that emotions are objective phenomena that can be represented by analogous tones and rhythms. As Mattheson explains in his *Der vollkommene Capellmeister* (*The Complete Music Director;* 1739):

Those who are learned in the natural sciences [i.e. Descartes] know how our emotions function physically, as it were. It would be advantageous to the composer to have a little knowledge of this subject. Since, for example, joy is an *expansion* of our vital spirits, it follows sensibly and naturally that this affect is best expressed by large and expanded intervals. Sadness, on the other hand, is a *contraction* of those same subtle parts of our bodies. It is, therefore, easy to see that the narrowest intervals are the most suitable. Love is a *diffusion* of the spirits. Thus, to express this passion in composing, it is best to use intervals of that nature. Hope is an *elevation* of the spirit; despair, on the other hand, a *casting down* of the same. These are subjects that can well be represented by sound, especially when other circumstances (tempo in particular) contribute their share. In such a manner one can form a concrete picture of all the emotions and try to compose accordingly.[4]

Of course, composers had long been writing music that gave expression to the emotions, in the text painting of the Renaissance madrigal and in the laments and revenge arias of Baroque opera and cantata, for example. Eighteenth-century musician Mattheson is simply providing a theory, or doctrine, for this phenomenon of the "affects" of music well after the fact. This posterior description demonstrates a maxim in music history: theory follows practice. The important point, however, is that when overt musical depiction entered the seventeenth-century sonata, it proved that music without text (instrumental music) could sway the emotions just as much as music with text. Instrumental music had taken on the same emotive power as vocal music.

EXAMPLE 34-3D

And so it goes. This music is overtly descriptive, indeed onomatopoeic, because it sounds out its own meaning. One French composer even went so far as to set in musical tones the gruesome stages of a Baroque kidney-stone operation (without anesthesia)! To our modern ears, program music of this sort is almost comical, like melodramatic silent film scores or even cartoon music. But around 1700 the insertion of such intensely emotional music into the sonata had a profound result. The programmatic sonatas of Biber and Kuhnau deepened the emotional content of the genre, making the sonata far richer and more satisfying than a series of merely pleasing dance pieces. Instrumental music was appropriating the sort of expressive, and sometimes extravagant, gestures that had been the exclusive preserve of vocal music. Gravity and intensity of expression were the legacy the sonata composers of the Baroque bequeathed to those of succeeding generations, specifically to C.P.E. Bach, Haydn, and Mozart.

DIETERICH BUXTEHUDE AND THE NORTH GERMAN ORGAN TRADITION

The pipe organ is known as the king of instruments, in part because in medieval times it was the only instrument sanctioned within the walls of the church. In truth, organs in churches did not become widespread until the fourteenth century, but thereafter most large institutions in the West had at least one, and often two, instruments to support religious music-making. Building an organ requires precise woodworking skills and a knowledge of metallurgy, physics, and acoustics—all attributes German artisans have traditionally possessed. During the years 1650–1750, north Germany produced some of the most remarkable organs ever fabricated. By the early eighteenth century, large organs with three or four manuals (keyboards) and thousands of pipes had been installed in north German port cities such as Hamburg and Lübeck.

At this time, the commercial cities around the Baltic and North Seas (see Map 34-1) formed a distinct region with regard to politics, culture, and music. Here emerged a particular style of organ composition and performance, one beginning with Jan Sweelinck (1562–1621) in Amsterdam and extending to Jan Reincken (1643?–1722) in Hamburg and to Dieterich Buxtehude (c1637–1707) in Lübeck. The practices of the north German organists greatly influenced J. S. Bach, who heard and played for Reincken and studied with Buxtehude.

Dieterich Buxtehude was the greatest of the north German organ composers. He was born in Denmark, but by 1668 had become organist at the church of St. Mary in Lübeck, Germany, where he remained until his death. (Both Bach and Handel apparently had the opportunity to succeed Buxtehude in this post, but both declined because local custom required the new incumbent to marry his predecessor's daughter!) At the time of Buxtehude's arrival, Lübeck was an important shipping center of nearly 30,000 people, a free city loosely linked to the Holy Roman Empire. At Lübeck's center stood its largest church, St. Mary's, which was Lutheran, like all churches in the city; by 1670 the city fathers had expelled most Catholics, Calvinists, and Jews. St. Mary's had two organs, one near the high altar at the east end of the church for votive services and funerals, and the other a gigantic all-purpose instrument at the west end. A guidebook to the church of 1697 says the following about the organs and music at St. Mary's:

> On the west side, between the two pillars under the towers, one can see the large and magnificent organ, which, like the small organ, is now presided over by the world-famous organist and composer Dieterich Buxtehude. Of particular note is the great Abend-Music, consisting of pleasant vocal and instrumental music, presented yearly on five Sundays between St. Martin's and Christmas, following the Sunday vesper sermon, from 4 to 5 o'clock, by the aforementioned organist as director, in an artistic and praiseworthy manner. This happens nowhere else.[5]

The **Abendmusik** proudly advertised in the guidebook was an hour-long concert of sacred music with arias and recitatives—something akin to a sacred opera or oratorio. A single religious theme unfolded in music over the course of five late-afternoon performances on the Sundays immediately before and during Advent (prior to Christmas). Large crowds flocked to the *Abendmusik* at St. Mary's Church. A report from an early eighteenth-century observer suggests, however, that the populace may have been attracted by things other than great music and the opportunity for spiritual enlightenment.

> The composer [Buxtehude] has never failed also to give an artistic and beautiful setting. However, . . . it is also a great inconvenience that the *Abendmusiken* are held at such an unfriendly and bleak time of the year, namely in the middle of the winter, so that after one has already spent three hours in the cold [for Vespers and the Vespers sermon] one must freeze for a fourth hour as well [for the *Abendmusik*]. The atrocious noise of the mischievous young people and the unruly running and romping about behind the choir take away all the enjoyment that the music might have given, to say nothing of the sins and wickedness that takes place under cover of darkness and poor light.[6]

Such a report reminds us of the limited opportunities for fun and recreation during the long, bleak winters of northern Europe before electricity and central heating. Communal religion, enhanced by voices, instruments, and the organ, was then the chief form of public entertainment. So popular did the *Abendmusik* become at St. Mary's that a special police guard was hired to help maintain order. Among those auditors attracted to these Sunday concerts at St. Mary's was young J.S. Bach, who in 1705 walked some 280 miles to hear them (see also Chapter 39) and who later modeled his own six-part Christmas Oratorio on Lübeck's *Abendmusik*.

Sadly, most of the music Buxtehude composed for the *Abendmusik* has been lost, though the many cantatas surviving under his name are sufficient to give us a sense of his sacred music. Similarly, although Buxtehude composed hundreds of organ pieces (toccatas, preludes, fugues, and chorale settings), fewer than eighty works have escaped the ravages of time. To get an idea of the type of organ piece he wrote in Lübeck, we turn to Buxtehude's *Wie schön leuchtet der Morgenstern* (*How Brightly Shines the Morning Star*), built on a chorale of that name. Recall that a chorale is a monophonic spiritual melody or religious folksong of the Lutheran church—what many Christian denominations today would simply call a hymn (see Chapter 24). The chorale *Wie schön leuchtet der Morgenstern* was one of two melodies composed, or at least adapted, by Lutheran pastor Philipp Nicolai in 1599 (the other is discussed in Chapter 40). Here the shining light of the Lord is equated with the bright star leading to the Christ child, and so this chorale was often heard at Advent and during the *Abendmusik* in Lübeck. The entire chorale is given as Example 34-4.

EXAMPLE 34-4

How brightly shines the Morning Star, With mercy beaming from afar; The host of heav'n rejoices;
O Righteous Branch, O Jesse's Rod! Thou Son of Man and Son of God! We, too, will lift our voices;
Jesus, Jesus! Holy, holy, yet most lowly, Draw thou near to us; Great Emmanuel, come and hear us.

North German organists made a specialty of projecting the Lutheran chorale on their large and colorful instruments. Buxtehude's forty-seven chorale settings constitute the main part of his organ music. Building on the chorale *Wie schön leuchtet der Morgenstern*, Buxtehude creates a **chorale fantasia,** a lengthy composition for organ that takes a chorale tune as a point of departure but increasingly gives free rein to the composer's imagination. In this case, the chorale is first placed in long notes in the bass with two-voice counterpoint set against it (Ex. 34-5a). Then the tune appears a second time, in the treble with the counterpoint coming below. Because the organ can create very different sorts of sonic colors and assign them to separate musical lines on separate keyboards, the chorale tune can be made to stand out distinctively no matter where in the texture it appears. For that reason, chorale settings are more effective on organ than on harpsichord or clavichord. But, as Buxtehude's piece progresses, his creative fancy more and more obscures the tune. Example 34-5b demonstrates how the composer transforms the opening of the chorale into an energetic fugue subject. Example 34-5c shows how he turns the descending scale at the end of the tune into a concluding theme in first three- and then four-voice counterpoint. This is an impressive composition! Remarkably, north German organists such as Buxtehude were expected to improvise such chorale fantasias on the spot as part of every audition. Without this skill, they could not get a job.

EXAMPLE 34-5A

EXAMPLE 34-5B

EXAMPLE 34-5C

LISTENING CUE

DIETERICH BUXTEHUDE
Wie schön leuchtet der Morgenstern (c1690)

CD 5/11
Anthology, No. 98

JOHANN PACHELBEL AND THE SOUTH GERMAN TRADITION

Who has not heard Pachelbel's Canon? Although he is popularly known today only through this one composition, Johann Pachelbel (1653–1706) was a prolific composer who wrote hundreds of pieces, vocal as well as instrumental. Pachelbel was born in Nuremberg, in southern Germany, studied in the Catholic church tradition in Vienna, worked in the central German Lutheran town of Eisenach (where he befriended the Bach family), and ended his days at the Lutheran church of St. Sebaldus back in Nuremberg (see Map 34–1). Pachelbel himself was keenly aware that he had been trained in the south German and Austrian tradition, not that of the north. What exactly differentiated the north and south German styles?

To contrast the two, compare the beginning of Buxtehude's setting of *Wie schön leuchtet der Morgenstern* (see Ex. 34-5) with that of Pachelbel (Ex. 34-6). First, however, keep in mind that Buxtehude's is a chorale fantasia (with the tune in G), while Pachelbel's is a chorale prelude (with the tune in F), and that north and south German composers wrote both types of pieces. A **chorale prelude** is a work for organ that sets a Lutheran chorale tune, surrounding it with counterpoint and florid embellishment. It is called a "prelude" because the organist played it immediately before the congregation sang the chorale in the Sunday service. (For more on the German chorale prelude, see Chapter 39.) Different from the lengthy chorale fantasia, the chorale prelude sounds the tune just once, enough to remind the faithful of the melody they are about to sing. A typical chorale fantasia takes six or seven minutes to perform, while the average chorale prelude lasts only half that time. So, what is the stylistic difference between the two German traditions? The southern style is a bit more tuneful. Pachelbel's counterpoint flows gently along, whereas Buxtehude's denser counterpoint is marked by a high degree of virtuosic and improvisatory-like gestures. In Pachelbel's chorale prelude, melody and counterpoint are joined in equal measure. It is primarily this greater fondness of lyricism that sets apart the south German tradition from the more rigid north German one.

EXAMPLE 34-6

LISTENING CUE

JOHANN PACHELBEL
Wie schön leuchtet der Morgenstern (c1690)

CD 5/12
Anthology, No. 99

This same mixture of counterpoint and pleasing melody marks Pachelbel's most famous work, his Canon in D Major (c1690). The Canon is part of a brief instrumental suite consisting of just a canon and a concluding gigue. The canonic process unfolds in three violin parts, one imitating another at the temporal interval of two measures. Below the canon, a basso continuo sets forth a relentless two-bar *basso ostinato*, which appears twenty-eight times. As the *ostinato* churns away beneath, the canon above gathers rhythmic energy and ascends to ever-higher peaks (Ex. 34-7). Though a musical commonplace for us today, Pachelbel's Canon amply demonstrates that in this south German music rigorous counterpoint (a three-voice canon) can generate soaring lyricism.

EXAMPLE 34-7

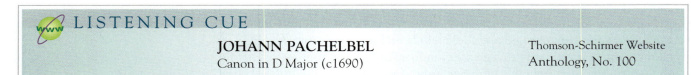

 LISTENING CUE

JOHANN PACHELBEL
Canon in D Major (c1690)

Thomson-Schirmer Website
Anthology, No. 100

SUMMARY

Composers in Germany and Austria were important in the development of seventeenth-century instrumental music. Johann Froberger established the dance suite as the primary genre of music for string keyboard instruments (harpsichord and clavichord). Through programmatic works such as his "Mystery" Sonatas for violin, Heinrich Biber added greater gravity and breadth of expression to the sonata. Here we see an early demonstration that purely instrumental pieces could project the same sort of deep emotional expression as did the texted vocal music of the Baroque period.

Historically, the Germans and the French have excelled in organ-making, the German skill in crafting precision instruments of all sorts proving a special advantage in this regard. The organ's multiple keyboards and separate groups of pipes not only encouraged the creation of multiple musical lines but also made it possible to project a religious melody (chorale tune or chant) with distinct clarity. The north German organ tradition, exemplified by the chorale fantasia of Dieterich Buxtehude, is thus marked by intense counterpoint, the use of a chorale tune, as well as plenty of virtuosic display showing vestiges of improvisation. The south German tradition, evident in the chorale prelude of Johann Pachelbel, tempered the Nordic rigor with increased lyricism. The great German organ composer of the next generation, J.S. Bach, would fashion a synthesis of these northern and southern styles.

KEY TERMS

dance suite	bourrée	*scordatura*
allemande	gavotte	Doctrine of Affections
courante	hornpipe	*Abendmusik*
sarabande	program music	chorale fantasia
gigue	"Mystery" Sonatas	chorale prelude
minuet	("Rosary" Sonatas)	

Music in Paris and at the Court of Versailles: Vocal Music

Chapter
35

Today the French are a proud and sometimes prickly lot, though in fairness they have an extraordinary amount about which to be proud and prickly. Their nationalism, belief in the superiority of their culture, and suspicion of foreign influence is not something unique to modern times. In fact, it is built upon ancient cultural icons extending back to the *Marseillaise* of the Revolution, to Joan of Arc, and to the great Gothic cathedrals—all French creations. But no French man or woman was ever grander, prouder, or more regal than King Louis XIV (Fig. 35-1), the Sun King (*Roi soleil*), source of light for all the French people, or so he said.

Louis XIV personified the absolute monarch. Indeed, his exceptionally long and authoritarian reign (1643–1715) inspired the political theory of **absolutism**—that ultimate power in the state rested in the hands of a king who claimed to rule by divine right. Whatever Louis wanted, Louis got. Wherever Louis was, there was the French government. As he himself famously said: "I *am* the State!" ("L'État, c'est moi!"). Louis strengthened and expanded the nation, pushing its borders to their modern limits and making France the leading power in Europe. He set the standard for monarchs across Europe, to the point that the second half of the seventeenth century and early years of the eighteenth have come to be seen as the "Age of Louis XIV" or the "Age of Absolutism."

As an example of the *grandeur* to which Louis aspired, consider **Versailles** (see Part IV timeline). In 1669 the Sun King determined to build a new home for himself and consolidate his power some twelve miles southwest of Paris. Over the course of twenty years, forests were cleared, rivers diverted, lakes created, and a colossal palace—actually, a complete city—was constructed by a workforce approaching 36,000. When finished, Versailles stood as a monumental symbol of the French absolutist

 FIGURE 35-1
King Louis XIV as painted by Hyacinthe Rigaud about 1700. The portrait captures the king's sense of majesty and authority.

state. It was also home to thousands of governmental officials, courtiers, and artists. Here ballets and operas were staged, orchestral dance suites performed, and Masses and motets sung in the royal chapel. Toward the end of his reign, Louis XIV employed between 150 and 200 musicians at any given time. Louis controlled and centralized the creation of art music, much as he did governmental administration.

Consequently, musical talent was not scattered around the cities of France. It was concentrated at the king's court, whether at Versailles or the several much-smaller royal residences in Paris, such as the Louvre, the Tuileries, and the Palais Royal. Moreover, the royal musicians usually were not Italians, as was the case at many other European courts at this time, but were mostly French men and women.

The extent of French bias against foreign influence can be seen in the people's reaction to Italian opera. Italian opera was gradually conquering most of late-seventeenth-century Europe. Cardinal Mazarin, an Italian-born prelate who directed the French government during Louis XIV's minority, tried to establish an Italian opera company in Paris by bringing Italian opera there several times between 1645 and 1662. But French listeners did not warm to fully sung drama offered in a foreign language (Italian) in which the highest vocal parts were often sung by castrated males (castrati). "We almost died of boredom," said a lady of the court.[1] Instead, the French preferred their own special genre of theatrical music called *ballet de cour*, one that emphasized not vocal virtuosity, but dance, choral singing, and spectacle.

✳ BALLET DE COUR

If the English historically have been obsessed with choral church music and the Italians with opera, the French have been enamored with dance. Indeed, the roots of modern ballet are to be found in a distinctive French genre of theatrical display called *ballet de cour*. A **ballet de cour** (court ballet) was a type of ballet danced at the French royal court from the late sixteenth to the late seventeenth century in which members of the court appeared alongside professional dancers. Sets of dances and choruses, simple airs (called *airs de cour*), instrumental interludes, pantomime, and lavish scenery all combined to project a loosely assembled dramatic theme. Much of the *ballet de cour* was taken up with eye-popping "production numbers" involving large groups of similarly costumed singers and dancers. Invariably, the ballet opened with a prologue in which allegorical figures sang the praises of the king and the wisdom of his rule. And similarly it concluded with a *grand ballet*, a final grand dance in which the *grands seigneurs* (great lords) of the court, and often the king himself, danced. In all, Louis XIV appeared in some eighty roles in forty major ballets. Through such carefully choreographed exercises, Louis could affirm aspects of an elitist culture then important to the French monarchy: rank, formality, protocol, discipline, and a sense of style.

As for the music of the *ballet de cour*: some of it was choral music sung during dances, and some of it was a special type of French solo song called the **air de cour**— a simple, strophic song for single voice or a small group of soloists. In addition to this vocal music, the *ballet de cour* included purely instrumental music involving sets of dances popular at that time (see Chapter 34): galliards, minuets, bourées, courantes, sarabandes, and the like. These were played by the French court orchestra, which was built around a core of string instruments called the **Vingt-quatre violons du roi**: twenty-four instruments of the violin family (six violins, twelve violas, and six *basse de violons* [oversize cellos]). In the tradition of seventeenth-century French orchestral music, the *Vingt-quatre violons* played five-part music consisting of treble and bass as well as three middle parts played by the twelve violas divided into groups of four. To these could be added harpsichords, trumpets, drums, and the *Douze grands hautbois* (twelve great oboes) of the royal wind band. On occasion, the orchestra for the *ballet de cour* grew to eighty instrumentalists, a size appropriate for the lavish spectacles of the Sun King.

The image of Louis as Sun King first appeared publicly in a *ballet de cour* presented on 3 February 1653 in which the fifteen-year-old king danced the role of the Rising Sun (Fig. 35-2). Louis equated himself with the Greek god of the sun, Apollo, who watched over the arts and sciences generally, and music in particular. Appearing alongside the king that evening was a young Italian-born choreographer and musician named Jean-Baptiste Lully. Lully himself would soon create some twenty-six *ballets de cour*, more than any other composer. The association of King Louis and composer Lully, and the meteoric rise of Lully, date from that moment.

FIGURE 35-2
Louis XIV as the Sun in the *Ballet de la Nuit*, 1653.

Réunion des Musées Nationaux/Art Resource, NY

JEAN-BAPTISTE LULLY AND *TRAGÉDIE LYRIQUE*

Giovanni Battista Lulli (1632–1687) was born in Florence and recruited as a youth to serve as an Italian teacher and dancing master to a cousin of the French king. After he caught the attention of Louis XIV in 1653, the king appointed him *Compositeur de la musique instrumentale* (1653). Other titles followed, including *Maître de la musique de la famille royale* (Master of Music for the Royal Family) in 1662. That same year, Lulli became a naturalized French citizen under the name of Jean-Baptiste Lully. With the king's unflinching support, the enterprising and often ruthless Lully gradually gained exclusive authority over public vocal music. Lully's hegemony reached the point that almost no piece of polyphonic art music could be performed before the French aristocracy without his permission. Lully himself had become an absolutist. He might well have said: "La Musique, c'est moi!"

One of the musical institutions over which Lully gained exclusive control was the *Académie royale de musique*. King Louis XIV established this company (under a slightly different name) in 1669 as a way to encourage the growth of French opera, just as he had founded similar academies to foster painting (1648), dance (1661), literature (1663), the sciences (1669), and architecture (1671). The **Académie royale de musique** was, in effect, an opera company directly licensed and indirectly financed by the king. It performed in the center of Paris at the Palais Royal and was, in everything but title, the Paris Opéra. France now had a national opera company, but it had no French operas to perform. During the 1670s, Lully set about to remedy this deficiency, and in so doing created a new and unique genre of theatrical music, French *tragédie lyrique*.

French theater reached its zenith during the second half of the seventeenth century, in the comedies of Molière (1622–1673) and in the classical tragedies of Pierre Corneille (1606–1684) and Jean Racine (1639–1699). For musical theater, the court enjoyed its own special brand of ballet (*ballet de cour*), as we have seen. Now Lully brought a new kind of entertainment to the stage: French opera, first called *tragédie en musique*, then **tragédie lyrique.** To create this distinctly French style of opera, Lully fused classical French tragedy with traditional French ballet (*ballet de cour*). This new genre, French opera, embraced ballet. Accordingly, the action of the opera might be interrupted at any moment by a ***divertissement,*** a lavishly choreographed diversionary interlude with occasional singing. Thus *tragédie lyrique* was not a solo singer's opera, like Italian opera, but a dancing actor's opera. Indeed, the principal singers were called *acteurs* and *actrices* in keeping with the tradition of French classical theatre. Lully's librettist, Philippe Quinault (1635–1688), drew his subjects from ancient Greek and Roman mythology and from tales of medieval chivalry. But no matter what the plot, the aim was always the same: to praise the king and reaffirm the values of the prevailing aristocratic culture.

Perhaps no *tragédie lyrique* better represents this genre than Lully's five-act *Armide* (1686), the last of his thirteen French operas. King Louis XIV, inspired by an earlier Italian poem, suggested this tale of medieval chivalry and magic-induced love to Lully. The stage is set near Jerusalem during the First Crusade (1095–1099). The sorceress Armide reluctantly falls in love with the most heroic of all the crusaders, Renaud, and then captures his affection by means of a magic spell. Ultimately, Renaud (a shill for King Louis XIV) comes to his senses and rejects Armide, choosing Duty over the illusion of Love.

Armide opens with a **French overture**, a distinctive type of instrumental prelude created by Lully. (Our English word "overture" comes from the French "ouverture," an opening.) A French overture begins with a slow section in duple meter marked by stately dotted rhythms (suggesting the pomp and grandeur of the court), followed by a fast triple-meter section in imitative counterpoint, and finally a return to the slow, stately style of the opening. Because most later composers like Handel and Bach dropped the slow third section, the French overture came to be known as a two-section piece: slow and dotted, then fast and fugal. Thereafter, throughout the remainder of the Baroque period, a French overture could be used to introduce an opera, ballet, oratorio, or instrumental dance suite.

Following the French overture and a prologue obliquely praising the king, the action begins. In Lully's day, *Armide* was known as "the lady's opera" because sorceress Armide dominates the stage. To love or to kill the hero Renaud, that is her dilemma. Armide's inner conflict is most clearly evident at the end of Act II in a scene beginning "Enfin il est en ma puissance" ("Finally, he is in my power"). Here she intends to stab the sleeping Renaud, but love holds her back. Armide expresses her uncertainty in a new type of singing developed by Lully called ***récitatif ordinaire*** (ordinary recitative). Ironically, this sort of recitative is anything but ordinary. Although still accompanied only by continuo, it is noteworthy for its length, vocal range, and generally dramatic quality. Here we see clearly the difference between Italian recitative of the period and recitative in Lully's *tragédie lyrique*. While the Italian recitative involves rapid declamation within a rather narrow range (see Anthology, No. 91a), French *récitatif ordinaire* is far more elastic. There are rapid passages that recall Italian simple recitative, but also expansive moments that sound much like a florid aria. Notice also the frequent changes of meter. Poet Quinault has fashioned verse with lines of irregular length. Composer Lully sets them within measures of changing length so that the ends of the lines (always stressed in French) come on downbeats (Ex. 35-1). Lully had carefully studied French declamation, as projected on the Parisian stage by actors in the plays of Corneille and Racine. In this example of *récitatif ordinaire*, Lully captures the drama of the moment not only by assigning Armide erratic melodic leaps that suggest confusion but also by inserting unexpected rests that imply hesitation—to kill or not to kill Renaud.

EXAMPLE 35-1

Finally, he is in my power, this superb conqueror. The charm of sleep brings him within my vengeful spell…

For the first performance of *Armide* in 1686, the role of Armide was sung by soprano Marie Le Rochois (1658–1728), who gained something of a cult following because of the way she played this scene. As one fan observed:

> Dagger in hand, ready to pierce the breast of Renaud, Fury animated her features. [Yet] Love took hold of her heart. The one and the other agitated her in turn, pity and tenderness succeeded at the end, and Love was left the victor. What true and beautiful poses! What different movements and expressions in her eyes and on her face during this soliloquy of twenty-nine lines ["Enfin il est en ma puissance"]. . . One can say that it is the greatest piece in all our opera and the most difficult to perform well.[2]

Of course, Armide yields to her heart. To reflect this decision, Lully changes the music from *récitatif ordinaire* to a resolute, yet dance-like air in the style of an *air de cour* (Ex. 35-2). In Lully's French opera, dancers are never far from the center of the action. Moving to the strains of this charming air, magical zephyrs now transport Armide and Renaud to a place where they may enjoy the pleasures of love (Fig. 35-3). Ultimately, Renaud abandons Armide to heed the call of duty. The enraged Armide sets fire to her palace and escapes high across the stage in a flying chariot, bringing the opera to a spectacular end.

✳ FIGURE 35-3
Armide uses her seductive powers to capture the heart of Renaud in a painting by François Boucher, created about 1733.

Lully Kills Himself Conducting

Jean-Baptiste Lully died shortly after the creation of *Armide*, and he did so in a very odd way. On 8 January 1687 Lully went to a Parisian church to conduct a religious work, his *Te Deum*, in a performance involving more than a hundred musicians. To keep them together, he used a large pointed baton to signal the beat, and in so doing he stabbed himself in the foot. The foot became infected and, little more than two months later, Lully died from gangrene. (Ironically, the performance of the *Te Deum* was organized to give thanks for the recent recovery of King Louis XIV from illness.)

While waving a large stick or staff through the air may seem a strange way to set a beat, this was a common practice when conducting religious music in the seventeenth century. With smaller, single choirs of the Renaissance, it was entirely possible to follow visually the motion of the hand of a leader, and many paintings of the period show a choir director manually giving the beat in the air. With the advent of multiple choirs and polychoral music in the Baroque, however, distances between singers increased and coordination of voices became more of a challenge. A large staff, visible at a great distance, was needed. (Even today experienced performers know that, when multiple groups are separated by distance, or perhaps even placed offstage, it is essential not to listen to the sound, which arrives late, but rather to watch the conductor's beat.) At French churches in the seventeenth century, conductors were urged to strike the beat ("Frappez la mesure"). A Frenchman in Rome in 1638 reports that he saw ten choirs held together by a principal conductor who struck the beat (*battoit la principale mesure*) while ten assistant conductors, one with each of the ten choirs, duplicated his motions. This Baroque practice—musicians watching a staff at a great distance—is still used today in marching bands, where performers follow the beat given by a drum major.

EXAMPLE 35-2

Come, come, support my desires, demons, transform yourselves into favorable winds.

LISTENING CUE

JEAN-BAPTISTE LULLY   CD 5/13–14
Armide (1686)   Anthology, No. 101a–b
Overture
"Enfin il est en ma puissance"

To sum up: French *tragédie lyrique*, created by Jean-Baptiste Lully, was a new genre of opera that fused elements of *ballet de cour* and traditional French tragic theater. Differing markedly from Italian opera, it possessed the following characteristics:

- **Structure:** requires five acts, following the model of traditional French and English tragedy, rather than the three acts of Italian opera
- **Libretto:** draws on mythological or chivalric topics to create a thinly disguised allegory praising the king and reaffirming the elitist values of the court and the aristocracy generally

- **Overture:** begins with a French overture, not an Italian overture (a sinfonia)
- **Singing:** done mainly in *récitatif ordinaire*; involves little of the virtuosic vocal display then coming into Italian opera
- **Voices:** uses female sopranos, never castrati
- **Chorus:** plays a major role in large-scale choral-dance scenes
- **Dance:** is as important as singing to the overall impact of the work; choreographed *divertissements* regularly interrupt the flow of the drama
- **Spectacle and special effects:** brought about by lavish costumes and elaborate stage machinery, all designed to please the audience and satisfy the ego of the king

RELIGIOUS MUSIC

The fact that Jean-Baptiste Lully was mortally wounded when conducting a lengthy motet (his own *Te Deum*) proves, if nothing else, that not all music at the French court was opera and ballet. As King Louis XIV entered old age, he assumed an increasingly pious life, and his court took on a more devout decor. Not just Lully but other, younger composers were now encouraged to provide sacred music for the king and his relatives. Among these composers were Marc-Antoine Charpentier (1643–1704), who wrote eleven Masses and some 207 motets of various sorts, and Michel-Richard de Lalande (1657–1726), who specialized in writing *grands motets* for the court, some seventy-seven in all. Such works might be heard in religious services at the chapel of Versailles, at many of the Jesuit churches and colleges around Paris, or at the king's Sainte-Chapelle on the Île de la Cité, where Charpentier served as music director from 1698 until his death. When monopolistic Lully departed the scene, Italian-style church music had a chance to gain a foothold. Charpentier studied with Giacomo Carissimi for three years in Rome (see Chapter 32), and he introduced Italian oratorio into France. The sacred cantata, also bearing a strongly Italian imprint, likewise came to France at this time, owing in part to the work of Elizabeth Jacquet de La Guerre (1665–1729).

ELIZABETH JACQUET DE LA GUERRE AND THE CANTATE FRANÇAISE

King Louis XIV was not averse to hiring talented female artists. There were professional female dancers in his *ballet de cour*, leading *actrices* in the French opera, and even female sopranos in the royal chapel—this at a time when women did not generally appear as solo singers in churches throughout Europe. About 1670 King Louis heard a five-year-old prodigy named Elizabeth Jacquet sing and play harpsichord, and he granted her a place at court as a performing musician under the care of his principal mistress, Madame de Montespan (Louis's piety came later). A journal of the day commented on her ability to compose and to transpose a piece to any key upon demand. At the age of nineteen, Jacquet left Versailles to marry the organist Marin de La Guerre and thereafter assumed the name Elizabeth Jacquet de La Guerre (Fig. 35-4). She established herself in Paris, giving lessons and concerts, and continuing to compose. Jacquet de La Guerre's output was not large, but what she produced was of high quality, notably her suites for solo harpsichord and her violin sonatas. She also wrote an opera, a *tragédie lyrique* entitled *Céphale et Procris* (1694), the first composed in France by a woman. Her twelve cantatas in French on subjects drawn from the Old Testament are testimony to the growing popularity of the cantata in France in the early years of the eighteenth century.

❀ FIGURE 35-4

Posthumous medallion honoring Elizabeth Jacquet de La Guerre, created in 1732. The reverse of the portrait shows her seated at a harpsichord with the motto "I competed for the prize against the great musicians," implying that she was the equal of her male competitors.

Library of Congress

"One talks only of cantatas, only cantatas are advertised at the street corners," said an observer of contemporary Parisian life.[3] Here is evidence that early eighteenth-century France witnessed a flowering of the cantata, both secular and sacred. The cantata, like its instrumental counterpart the sonata, was a product of Italy that by 1700 had made its way over the Alps. By 1730, some 1,200 cantatas had appeared in print in France. Needless to say, the **cantate française,** as it was called, set a French, not an Italian, text. But, in other ways, it was identical to the late seventeenth-century Italian cantata (see Anthology No. 91a–b). A soloist told a story in simple recitative and then, intermittently, the same singer reflected upon these events in ensemble-accompanied arias or in arias with basso continuo only. Succumbing to the Italian rage for the *da capo* aria developed by Alessandro Scarlatti, most of the arias were in **ABA** form. Librettists drew upon either classical mythology (for the secular cantata) or scripture (for the sacred cantata). These were dramas in miniature, for a single character, occasionally two. Thus a *cantate française* can be defined as a piece of chamber music projecting a short mythological or scriptural drama; the story, sung in French, unfolds in a succession of recitatives and arias for solo voice (or duet) accompanied by basso continuo and, occasionally, a small orchestra.

Elizabeth Jacquet de La Guerre published three books of *cantates françaises*, in 1708, 1711, and 1715, respectively. Both of the first two are entitled *Cantates françaises sur des sujets tirez de l'Ecriture* (*French cantatas drawn from subjects from Scripture*). Both portray events in the lives of heroes and heroines of the Old Testament, and both were dedicated to the grandest of all contemporary patrons, King Louis XIV. Like all sacred cantatas, they were intended to provide music for private spiritual reflection, be it in a grand salon or a modest home.

Perhaps it is not surprising that Jacquet de La Guerre, a woman working in the mostly male profession of music, had a special fondness for heroic female characters in biblical history and therefore named cantatas after them: the daughter of Jephte, Judith, Esther, Rachel, and Suzanna, to be specific. We have met the dutiful daughter of Jephte before in Giacomo Carissimi's oratorio of that name (see Chapter 32). Jacquet de La Guerre goes over the same thematic ground as Carissimi but uses neither multiple characters nor a chorus to comment on the action; hers is a cantata, not an oratorio. Her libretto is not in Italian but French, a French that has a certain restrained quality owing to its third-person narrative. Jacquet de La Guerre adopts for all her arias the Italian-born *da capo* aria form (**ABA**). Moreover, she creates luxuriant Italian-style vocal lines with lengthy melismas in the arias (Ex. 35-3) and supports the rapidly shifting emotions of the recitative with rich, Italianate harmonic changes (Ex. 35-4). In sum, Jacquet de La Guerre effects an impressive synthesis of Italian "passion" and French "cool." French musicians of the time referred to this union as "*les goûts réunis*" (the two styles united).

EXAMPLE 35-3

Jephté returns full of glory…

EXAMPLE 35-4

The daughter of Jephté, full of joy, exits from the palace and hastens before him; you will see her all too soon, unfortunate father, alas!

 LISTENING CUE

ELIZABETH JACQUET DE LA GUERRE	CD 5/15–16
Jephté (1711)	Anthology, No. 102a-b
Aria, "Jephté revient"	
Recitative, "La Fille de Jepthé"	

 SUMMARY

French musical institutions flourished, both in Paris and at the royal palace of Versailles, during the long and absolute rule of King Louis XIV (1643–1715). French *ballet de cour* was a unique blend of ballet and choral singing, interspersed with airs and instrumental interludes, all of which was intended to glorify the monarchy. Beginning in 1673, Jean-Baptiste Lully created a new genre of musical theater called *tragédie lyrique*, French national opera with a distinctly Gallic flavor. Noticeably different from the then-dominant Italian opera, French *tragédie lyrique*, typified by Lully's *Armide* (1686), begins with a French overture and is marked by a style of vocal music in which the singer carefully declaims a French text in a flexible and expansive style of recitative called *récitatif ordinaire*. The heroic-tragic drama is regularly interrupted by *divertissements* involving ballet, solo and choral singing, and instrumental dances. *Tragédie lyrique* depends less on virtuoso singers and more on actors who can sing and dance. Both *ballet de cour* and *tragédie lyrique* employed complex machinery and lavish costumes to create visual effects that astonished and moved their audiences while affirming princely power.

The cantata in the French language (*cantate française*), setting either a religious or a secular subject, enjoyed a brief vogue in the salons of early eighteenth-century Paris. Among the principal creators of the *cantate française* was Elizabeth Jacquet de La Guerre, who delighted in bringing to life the stories of heroic women of the Old Testament. In a French cantata, as with an Italian one of this period, a single performer, or two at most, relates a tale from scripture or classical mythology by means of a series of recitatives and arias. It is thus a drama in miniature, lasting only about ten minutes. Unlike French *tragédie lyrique*, which kept its distance from Italian opera, the *cantate française* borrowed heavily from the Italian vocal idiom, particularly the form and virtuoso style of singing of the *da capo* aria.

KEY TERMS

absolutism	*Vingt-quatre violons du roi*	*divertissement*
Versailles	*Académie royale de*	French overture
ballet de cour	*musique*	*récitatif ordinaire*
air de cour	*tragédie lyrique*	*cantate française*

Chapter 36

Music in Paris and at the Court of Versailles: Instrumental Music

For the French royal court and the well-to-do of Paris, the seventeenth century witnessed a flowering of vocal music within the new genres of *ballet de cour*, French opera (called *tragédie lyrique*), and the *cantate française*. Yet the Baroque era was also a golden age for instrumental music in France. In this period the French were leaders in the construction of lutes, harpsichords, and organs. Music for the lute, and for the harpsichord in particular, reached a zenith, not only in the history of French Baroque music but also in Baroque music generally.

 ## THE GAULTIERS: FRENCH LUTE MUSIC

During the late Renaissance, the lute had been the most popular of all "learned" musical instruments, considered to be the descendent of the Greek lyre of Apollo and Orpheus. Recall, for example, that for Renaissance Paris roughly ten times more music was published for the lute than for the harpsichord (Chapter 23). The lute continued to enjoy favor during the early Baroque era, especially at the French royal court. Queen Anne (wife of Louis XIII) took up the instrument and so too did Cardinal Richelieu, leader of the French government during the regency of this young king. "It would be difficult to imagine anything more ridiculous than to see him [Richelieu] take his lessons from [lutenist] Gaultier." Though a lute-playing cardinal seemed absurd to this contemporary observer, Richelieu's lessons suggest how pervasive the lute had become in seventeenth-century French aristocratic circles. For the French courtier, playing lute and dancing were two necessary social graces.

The teacher of Cardinal Richelieu, Ennemond Gaultier (1575–1651), was one of a half-dozen musicians working at this time in and around Paris named Gaultier (or Gautier). Equally famous was his younger cousin Denis Gaultier (1597?–1672). The older, and then the younger, Gaultier dominated lute playing in Parisian salons at mid-century. Both seem to have composed only for lute and both seem to have written mainly dance pieces belonging to suites for lute.

The dance suite in France grew out of the practice of pairing dances such as the pavane and galliard during the Renaissance (see Chapter 22). The vogue of the *ballet de cour* (see Chapter 35) made dancing fashionable and brought new dances to prominence, including the allemande, courante, sarabande, and gigue (see Chapter 34). By 1630 these had spread to the repertory for lute and were grouped together in loosely organized suites according to key and/or tuning.

Throughout the Renaissance the standard tuning for the lute involved mainly fourths (G-c-f-a-d'-g'), much like today's guitar tuning (E-A-d-g-b-e'). During the seventeenth century, however, other tunings emerged. Perhaps more important, strings were added to the bass to generate the pitches F, E, E♭, D, and perhaps C'—this so that the lute could participate more effectively as a basso continuo instrument. At mid-century a suite of dances was often preceded by an indication of the tuning appropriate for the group of pieces to follow.

Denis Gaultier's *La Rhétorique des dieux* (*The Rhetoric of the Gods;* c1652) is a sumptuous culmination of the long history of French music for the lute (Fig. 36-1). *La Rhétorique des dieux* is not a widely disseminated print of lute music, but a unique manuscript put together by a group of music-loving admirers of Denis Gaultier. Here are found twelve suites by Gaultier (some incomplete) arranged in pairs of modes—Dorian and Hypodorian, Phrygian and Hypophrygian, and so on—covering all twelve of the late Renaissance church modes. Most of the pieces are dances, but some have emblematic titles and descriptions suggesting to the listener the meaning of the music. For example, one piece is entitled *Apollo the Orator* and is followed by the following lines: "Apollo [god of music] having assumed the human form of Gaultier, displays here all the powers of his eloquence, and by force of his [musical] persuasion makes his listeners pay the keenest attention." Gaultier is the musical "orator" through whom the gods communicate to those on earth.

Commencing the third suite of *La Rhétorique des dieux* is an allemande with the title *Tombeau de Madamoiselle Gaultier* (correctly translated *Lament for Gaultier's Wife*). Here Gaultier speaks to his wife, but only after he is dead! A **tombeau** (French for "tomb") is an instrumental piece commemorating someone's death. Gaultier wanted to commemorate his own demise and leave his wife a brief musical monument of himself; she did, in fact, outlive the composer. The Gaultiers (Ennemond and Denis) were the first to write *tombeaux*, though the tradition continued in France well into the twentieth century. For

🌿 FIGURE 36-1

The title page of *La Rhétorique des dieux* (c1652), in which one god holds the title of the work interlined with lute tablature and another plays a lute containing as many as ten strings and/or courses (pairs of strings).

Staatliche Museen du Berlin

this *tombeau* in honor of himself, Denis selected the Phrygian mode, an apposite choice considering the long association of the Phrygian mode and lamentation (see, for example, Josquin's *Miserere*, Chapter 21). But there is more, for Gaultier begins and ends in F♯ minor. In the Baroque era F♯ minor was a highly remote and indeed unusual key, which would have sounded out of tune and thus painful.[1] The full impact of the Phrygian mode, however, may have been lessened by the addition of chromatic inflections and leading tones which have the effect of transforming the Phrygian mode into the more modern melodic minor scale, here transposed to F♯. In fact, the music throughout *La Rhétorique des dieux* conforms more to the newly emerging major-minor tonality than it does to the older sound of the twelve church modes.

A glance at the score of Denis Gaultier's *Tombeau* reveals a musical texture typical of lute music of the period, one called *style brisé*. **Style brisé** (literally "broken style") is a modern term for a type of discontinuous texture in which chords are broken apart and the notes enter one by one. Voices seem to dart in and out. Such a texture is inherent in lute music because the sounds of the lute are delicate and quickly evaporate. Consider the opening of the *Tombeau* (Ex. 36-1). Sometimes there seem to be four voices in the texture, sometimes only two or just one, as on the downbeat of bar four. We hear a bit of plucking here, a bit there—as appropriate to the lute. Yet, in this fragmented environment, a compelling melody is not easily established. In bars 15–17, for example, melody seems to be sacrificed to the pleasures of chordal strumming (Ex. 36-2). Such a style is well suited to the lighter sound and generally lighter musical repertory of the lute, though musicians soon came to adopt it as well for the harpsichord. J.S. Bach's famous opening prelude to the first book of The Well-Tempered Clavier (Ex. 36-3) adopts *style brisé* but transforms it into particularly German rigid arpeggio patterns.

EXAMPLE 36-1

EXAMPLE 36-2

EXAMPLE 36-3

LISTENING CUE

DENIS GAULTIER
La Rhétorique des dieux (c1652)
Tombeau de Madamoiselle Gaultier

CD 5/17
Anthology, No. 103

Adding more and more strings to its lower range made the already-difficult lute even more challenging to play. Larger lutes had as many as twenty-one strings to tune, a time-consuming process. "I have had the pleasure of hearing many a lute tuned, but few played," remarked an exasperated listener of the day. In the second half of the seventeenth century the easily strummed guitar and the colorful, powerful harpsichord replaced the lute as the chamber instrument of choice in France.

❋ THE COUPERINS: FRENCH HARPSICHORD MUSIC

After the Bach family, the Couperin clan forms the most illustrious of all musical dynasties. During the reign of Louis XIV and beyond there were at least a dozen Couperins, both male and female, who made a living as organists, string players, harpsichordists, and composers in Paris. Of these, the most distinguished were Louis Couperin (1626–1661) and his nephew François (1668–1733) called Le Grand ("the Great"). The professional seat of the Couperin family was the parish church of St. Gervais, still standing on the Right Bank of Paris near the Seine River. For nearly 175 years, one Couperin or another served as organist at this splendid Baroque church. In addition, the more talented among them, including Louis and François, were instrumentalists at the royal court.

Louis Couperin is remembered today for one important achievement: he popularized the unmeasured prelude. An **unmeasured prelude** (*prélude non mesuré*) is an opening piece without indications for rhythmic duration or metrical organization. In other words, it has no bar lines and is rhythmically free. The ancestor of the unmeasured prelude for harpsichord was the unmeasured lute prelude. Here a performer moved his fingers freely over the strings to warm up and check the tuning. By the mid seventeenth century, harpsichord composers had adopted the genre as an effective way to open their keyboard suites.

Louis Couperin's unmeasured Prelude in A Minor is the best known of the fourteen that survive under his name. Inspiration for it likely came from the German composer Johann Froberger, for a manuscript preserving this Prelude in A Minor calls it "Prélude à l'imitation de Monsieur Froberger." Froberger, it will be recalled, visited Paris in 1651–1652 and helped standardize the harpsichord suite (see Chapter 34). The opening of the first section of Couperin's prelude (Ex. 35-5), in fact, seems to be an "unmeasuring" of the opening of Froberger's Toccata No. 1 in A Minor (compare Exs. 36-4 and 36-5). Here the unmeasured prelude loosens the already loose toccata.

EXAMPLE 36-4

EXAMPLE 36-5

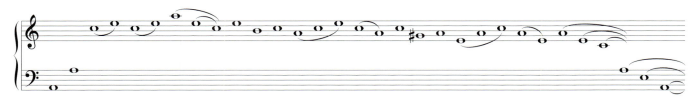

Publishers eventually tired of dealing with the bizarre-looking notation of the unmeasured prelude. Composers, however, continued to embrace the newfound freedom of the genre in various ways throughout the eighteenth century. J.S. Bach's well-known Chromatic Fantasy was conceived in this freer spirit, and his son C.P.E. Bach wrote unbarred fantasias (see Chapter 43). A French composer summed up the main virtue of the unmeasured prelude when he said "because it is unmeasured, one plays it as one wishes."[2]

It was with good reason François Couperin (1668–1733) was called Le Grand ("the Great"). He surely was the greatest of the Couperins and, arguably, of all French Baroque instrumental composers. J.S. Bach copied Couperin's harpsichord music into the keyboard tutorial he prepared for his wife (the Anna Magdalena Bach Book); Johannes Brahms was one of the co-editors of the first complete edition of Couperin's harpsichord music; and both Debussy and Ravel composed pieces in his honor, the latter writing a belated *Tombeau de Couperin* (see Chapter 67).

François Couperin was born and died in Paris and, like his forebears and descendants, served as organist at the church of St. Gervais. But he also was a leading musician at the court of Louis XIV during the declining days of the Sun King, serving as *organiste du roi* and then as the king's personal harpsichordist. Couperin composed most of his sacred music—including the exquisitely beautiful *Leçons de ténèbre* for Holy Week—for the king's chapel at Versailles. Likewise, Couperin wrote most of his chamber music for the court, including his *Concerts royaux* (*Royal Concerts*, 1722) and *Les Goûts réunis* (*The Tastes United*, 1724), an exercise in melding Italian and French musical idioms. Couperin further showed his love of the Italian style in a trio sonata entitled *Apothéose de Corelli* (1724), yet he quickly followed this with one complimentary to the French style called *Apothéose de Lully* (1725).

In his day François Couperin was considered second to none as a teacher of the harpsichord, and among his pupils were the children and grandchildren of the king. In 1716 Couperin published the fruit of his years of teaching: *L'Art de toucher le clavecin* (*The Art of Playing the Harpsichord*). The **clavecin** (French for harpsichord) was then the favorite chamber keyboard instrument, and some French *clavecins* of the period were large and ornate (see Box, p. 317). **The Art of Playing the Harpsichord** is a pedagogical manual in which Couperin leads the *clavecin* student through a discussion of fingering, ornamentation, and other aspects of performance. His comments on fingering show him to be of the old school, in which the third finger crosses over the second or fourth running down or up the scale (the thumb still does not pass under). But most important is Couperin's discussion of ornamentation.

Ornamentation is an indispensable part of almost all Baroque music. Generally speaking, Baroque ornamentation falls into two broad types: that in which an entire line of music is embellished (as in Italian vocal music, for example); and that in which individual notes are decorated (as in French lute and harpsichord music, for example). No musical repertory was more heavily ornamented than French harpsichord music. The ornaments, what the French call **agréments,** are not written out in full in the keyboard score. Rather, they are indicated by a variety of symbols, and it is up to the performer to insert these *agréments* into the music. Couperin's manual tells the performer how to do it. Below are just a few of the *agréments* Couperin presents.

EXAMPLE 36-6

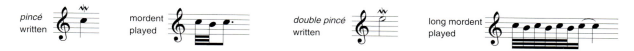

The length of the mordent can be adjusted to the fit the length of the note to which it is applied: the longer the note, the longer the mordent. Most important, the mordent starts on the note, not above it.

EXAMPLE 36-7

Contrary to the mordent, the trill starts above the note. It, too, is to be adjusted to the length of the note it ornaments.

EXAMPLE 36-8

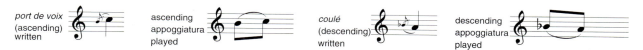

The *port de voix* is a lower, and the *coulé* an upper, appoggiatura. The first note, written as a smaller grace note, is a dissonant note against the bass and must assume at least half of the duration of the larger written note that follows. Finally, all of these ornaments start on the beat, never before it.

In addition to these *agréments*, Couperin discusses performance techniques that are part of the unwritten tradition in French Baroque music. Foremost among these are **notes inégales** in which a succession of equal notes moving rapidly up or down the scale are played somewhat unequally, such as "long-short, long-short." Related to this is the practice of **overdotting,** in which a dotted note is made longer than written, while its complementary short note(s) is made shorter. The performance of *notes inégales* and overdotting appears to have involved more art than science, and was likely much less mathematically exact than the following examples suggest. Couperin does not explain either technique in precise detail, but he makes clear that in French Baroque music, what you see on the page is not always what you play.

> We [French] write [music] differently from the way we play it, which causes foreigners to play our music less well than we play theirs. On the other hand, the Italians write their music in the true note values in which they intended them [to be played]. For example, we dot groups of eighth-notes moving by step [*notes inégales*] despite the fact that we write them as equal notes.[3]

EXAMPLE 36-9

Deciding how to interpret the *agréments* and whether to utilize the practices of *notes inégales* and overdotting are just some of the decisions that a performer must make when engaging Couperin's harpsichord music. Below is one possible realization of two sections of a Prelude by Couperin (Exs. 36-10a and 36-10b). Couperin's original, with his ornamental symbols, appears in the lower system. *Agréments*, *notes inégales*, and overdotting have been applied in the upper one. This realization suggests just how highly nuanced French Baroque harpsichord music can be, and offers a good example of French rococo style. **Rococo** is a term used to describe the decorative arts and the music of mid eighteenth-century France, with all their lightness, grace, and highly ornate surfaces (Fig. 36-3). Perhaps because of the airy yet brilliant sound of the harpsichord, Couperin's rococo style is very idiomatic to this keyboard instrument.

EXAMPLE 36-10A

EXAMPLE 36-10B

The graceful lines of Couperin's art can best be found in the four collections of harpsichord music he published during his lifetime, each entitled *Pièces de clavecin* (1713, 1717, 1722, and 1730). Containing a total of two hundred twenty pieces, these four books constitute the bulk of the harpsichord music that Couperin wrote and that made him famous in his day. Each book is comprised of a handful of suites (called *ordres*), made up mostly of dance pieces. Like the suite, an "**ordre**" is a group of pieces loosely associated by feeling and key. Couperin's *ordres*, however, differ from the usual suite in that they are filled not only with the standard keyboard dances but also with numerous character pieces—pieces that try to capture the personality of an individual, a place, or an aspect of nature or society.

Take *La Favorite* (piece for the Favorite One) from Couperin's third *ordre* (*Pièces de clavecin*, Book I, 1713). The Favorite One may have been the Dauphin, the much

The Eighteenth-Century French Harpsichord

The harpsichord, as we have seen (Chapter 23), first appeared in the Low Countries around 1440 and soon spread south to neighboring France. By the mid eighteenth century, Paris had replaced Antwerp as the European center of harpsichord fabrication and restoration. Among the notable makers of Parisian harpsichords were Jean and Claude Jacquet, earlier relatives of composer Elizabeth Jacquet de La Guerre (see Chapter 35). The Jacquets were succeeded by four generations of the Blanchet family, who started building harpsichords in Paris in 1689 and continued until the Revolution (1789).

While the basic mechanism of the harpsichord remained unchanged—depressing a key caused a plectrum of quill or leather to pluck a metal string—the instrument became increasingly large and complex during the seventeenth and eighteenth centuries. Parisian harpsichord makers were among the first to standardize a two-manual instrument. A second (upper) keyboard was particularly useful in executing pieces involving cross-handed playing (left hand moving over or on top of the right), a technique often required in the music of both Louis and François Couperin. In addition, the bottom keyboard was equipped with two sets of strings: a larger one (called 8',

though the length of the longest string was actually less than eight feet) and a smaller one (called 4', and sounding an octave higher). The upper keyboard had its own set of 8' strings. Moreover, the two keyboards could be made to play together by means of a "coupler." Thus the large French harpsichord of the eighteenth century might play with one of five string sets or combinations and produce as many sound colors: 8' alone (bottom or top); two 8' together (top and bottom manuals coupled); 8' and 4' together (bottom); 8', 8' and 4' together (bottom and top coupled); or 4' alone (bottom). Finally, the keyboard of the instrument was gradually enlarged from four octaves (C to c"') to five (F' to f"'). Some of François Couperin's earliest *ordres* require such a five-octave instrument.

Figure 36-2 shows a five-octave, two-manual harpsichord made by François Blanchet the Elder in Paris about 1740. It typifies the kind of *clavecin* on which Couperin would have played. The notes of his *La Favorite*, for example, would fit easily within its five-octave compass. Moreover, a performer could clearly elucidate the rondeau structure of *La Favorite* by playing the refrain with the keyboards coupled together, while executing the contrasting "couplets" on a single manual that produced a softer sound.

Yale University Collection of Musical Instruments

❋ FIGURE 36-2

A two-manual harpsichord built by François Blanchet the Elder in Paris c1740.

---

loved eldest son of Louis XIV, who died of the measles in 1712. A sense of loss is conveyed by the bass line of the main theme, which is a chromatic descending tetrachord, a traditional sign of lamentation throughout the Baroque era (see Chapter 31). The piece, as stated by Couperin himself, is a chaconne in the form of a rondeau—"chaconne" because the tetrachord returns repeatedly and thus forms a chaconne bass, yet "rondeau" because the chaconne bass disappears from time to time to allow other musical ideas to come forward. A **rondeau** in the Baroque era is therefore a composition based on the alternation of a main theme (refrain) with subsidiary sections called **couplets** (couplets) to allow musical diversity. Here the refrain and the various couplets create the pattern **ABACADAEAFA.** Couperin's magnificent chaconne-rondeau, four minutes in length, shows that French harpsichord music of the period is not just marked by abundant surface decoration but, if need be, it can project monumental gravity as well.

LISTENING CUE

FRANÇOIS COUPERIN
Pièces de clavecin . . . premier livre (1713)
La Favorite

CD 5/18
Anthology, No. 104

 FIGURE 36-3

"The Harlequin Family" by J. J. Kändler, c1740, a superb example of rococo decoration. Here the passage of time is surrounded by an elegant embellishment and the figures of Harlequin (right) and Columbine (left). Harlequin's smile is somewhat grotesque; the mask of Columbine is that of a bird.

A dancing bear, a beehive, the pleasures of St. Germain-en-Laye, and a famous opera soprano—these are a few of the people, places, and things François Couperin brings to life in the character pieces found within his twenty-seven *ordres*. He also pokes fun at the king's mistresses, the secret societies of the idle rich, and the pretensions of the musicians' union in Paris. One of Couperin's most arresting miniature portraits is his *L'Arlequine* from the twenty-third *ordre* (*Pièces de clavecin*, Book IV, 1730).

Harlequin is a clown from the tradition of Italian *Commedia dell'arte* (improvised slapstick comedy). A troupe of *Commedia dell'arte* players, with clowns Harlequin, Columbine, and Pierrot, was in residence in Paris in the early decades of the eighteenth century. All three clowns wore masks to be funny, certainly, but also to hide a buffoon's pain and humiliation. In a world in which the aristocracy had little to do—the absolute king ran the government absolutely—courtiers tried to while away the hours by creating a make-believe world. This they did with clowns and masks. Harlequin was both comical and grotesque, his smile frightening (Fig. 36-3). Perhaps that is why Couperin has marked his *L'Arlequine* to be performed "*grotesquement*." The piece starts cheerfully enough. But it ends with a swing around the circle of fifths that includes three successive major seventh chords—a shockingly dissonant sound to eighteenth-century ears and a very modern one to ours. Surely, Couperin inserts this unusual harmonic moment to emphasize the grotesque nature of Harlequin's persona. In character pieces such as *L'Arlequine*, Couperin shows himself to be not only a composer of superb music but also a sharp critic of the courtly society, one full of pretension and masquerade.

LISTENING CUE

FRANÇOIS COUPERIN
Pièces de clavecin . . . quatrième livre (1730)
L'Arlequine

CD 5/19
Anthology, No. 105

SUMMARY

Large volumes, both printed and in manuscript, of high-quality lute music were created in mid seventeenth-century France by Ennemond and Denis Gaultier. The Gaultiers wrote mainly dance pieces, grouped in loosely organized suites, which were often marked by *style brisé*, a broken texture in which the notes of chords are played one after the other and the musical lines dart in and out. *Style brisé* was well suited to the evanescent sound of the lute, yet it was soon brought into the repertory of the harpsichord as well.

French harpsichord music of the late seventeenth and eighteenth centuries is one of the glories of that country's musical patrimony. Members of the Couperin family, Louis and François, set the standard. Louis popularized the unmeasured prelude, a genre that allowed the performer great interpretive freedom. His more important nephew, François Couperin, developed the *ordre*—a suite-like collection of dances and character pieces as well. For his *Pièces de clavecin* Couperin composed two hundred twenty harpsichord works arranged into twenty-seven *ordres* and published in four separate books (1713, 1717, 1722, and 1730). His *Art of Playing the Harpsichord* is a teaching manual that sets out in detail the master's recommended manner of fingering and ornamenting these pieces. Couperin's harpsichord works are always elegant and carefully crafted, sometimes monumental, and sometimes filled with musical irony that serves as social commentary on the aristocratic society of eighteenth-century France.

KEY TERMS

tombeau

style brisé

unmeasured prelude

clavecin

The Art of Playing the Harpsichord

agréments

notes inégales

overdotting

rococo

ordre

rondeau

couplet

Musical Interlude

From Ancient to Modern: Aspects of Baroque Music Theory

During the seventeenth century, scientists and philosophers revolutionized some of the most fundamental concepts of Western intellectual thought. In this century, Johannes Kepler (1571–1630) formulated the laws of planetary motion; Galileo Galilei (1564–1642), the son of a musician, posited a heliocentric universe; René Descartes (1596–1650) argued for a mathematically based understanding of the material word; and Isaac Newton (1642–1727) discovered the laws of gravity and optics. So significant was this scientific and philosophical revolution that historians call this the **Age of Reason** and mark the seventeenth century as the beginning of the "modern era" in Western history.

In music, too, old modes of thinking about musical structure were replaced by new paradigms during the seventeenth and early eighteenth centuries. This revolution can be seen as a transition from the ancient to the modern world, for most of the theoretical models put forth by Baroque musicians—musical systems and the terms to describe them—are still used by students and professional musicians when they discuss music today. As in most moments in the history of music, Baroque theorists were simply attempting to formulate a rational explanation for the new music they heard. Much of the theory they posited, however, remains with us today.

MODALITY YIELDS TO TONALITY

The modal scales grew out of the eight tones used for singing the psalms in the medieval church, though their names (Dorian, Phrygian, and the like) had been borrowed from the ancient Greeks. Initially there were eight church modes, but these were expanded to twelve during the late Renaissance. Similarly, the modes were first used as a way of defining and directing monophonic chant, though by the Renaissance they provided a framework and direction for polyphonic compositions, both vocal and instrumental. Pieces composed modally seem, to modern ears, to "float" in harmonic space, shifting side to side and cadencing on unexpected pitches. A piece need not even end with the final or fundamental pitch of the mode sounding in the bass.

During the seventeenth century, however, composers increasingly limited their compositions to just two modes: Ionian on C and Aeolian on A. French music theorists were the first to call these two patterns **major** (*majeure*) and **minor** (*mineur*), because the former scale began with a larger third than the latter. They also recognized that the two patterns might be transposed to other pitches so long as accidentals were included to keep the major or minor scale pattern intact. Around 1650, Denis Gaultier wrote a minor-key piece transposed to F♯, for example (see Anthology, No. 103). By 1725 almost all art music was written in either a major or minor key. Even the esteemed George Frideric Handel noticed that the older church modes had become totally obsolete, as he wrote to a friend around 1725:

> As concerns the Greek modes [church modes], I find that you have said everything that there is to say. Their knowledge is doubtless necessary to those who want to practice and perform ancient music [the music of the sixteenth and seventeenth centuries], which formerly was composed according to such modes; however, since now we have been freed from the narrow bounds of ancient music, I cannot perceive what use the Greek modes [church modes] have in today's music.[1]

When defining a central pitch within a melody, theorists began to replace the old Latin term "*finalis*" with words such as "tone" and "key" (in English), "*tonique*" (French), and "*tuono*" (Italian). That central tone was the first note of a seven-note scale (repeating at the octave). Even this concept of a seven-note unit was revolutionary from a pedagogical perspective, for the old way of teaching music involved the ancient system of Guidonian hexachords organized around six-note units (see Chapter 4). During the seventeenth century the natural, soft, and hard hexachords were challenged by a single seven-note pattern (the term for the seventh pitch was "pha," "si," or "ti," among others). A century later, "do" replaced "ut" as the opening syllable, to complete our present system of "do, re, mi, fa, so, la, ti, do."

CHORD INVERSION, FUNCTIONAL HARMONY, AND THE CIRCLE OF FIFTHS: A CLOSED MUSICAL UNIVERSE

During the Baroque era, musical space, like the physical universe observed by Kepler, Galileo, and Newton, became organized in a systematic way that was radically new. Many musical thinkers were involved in this process of reformulating the sonic world of music. But the most innovative and comprehensive thinker about musical harmony was **Jean Philippe Rameau** (1683–1764). Rameau was a composer as well as a theorist. Indeed, his nearly thirty works for the French musical stage and numerous *Pièces de clavecin* rank him as the most important composer in France of the generation after François Couperin. Because Rameau was a composer, he felt himself well positioned to conceptualize and explain to his fellow musicians the new tonal music of the eighteenth century:

> I could not help thinking that it would be desirable (as someone said to me one day while I was praising the perfection of our modern music) for the knowledge of musi-

cians of this century to equal the beauties of their compositions. It is not enough to feel the effects of a science or an art. Rather, one must fashion a theory in order to render them intelligible.[2]

The foundation of Rameau's theory is set forth in his lengthy **Treatise on Harmony** (*Traité de l'harmonie*), which he published in 1722. Just as Newton had approached the physical sciences through mathematics (*Mathematical Principles of Natural Philosophy*, 1687), so Rameau embraced sounding number, the physical division of string, and later the overtone series, as a way to determine what he called the fundamental bass (root) of a collection of pitches in a chord. In a group of pitches involving two consecutive thirds, such as E, G, C, E, G, C, for example, the fundamental pitch, no matter what actually sounded in the bass, was always C (the bottom note of the only perfect fifth in the aggregate). What Rameau codified was the revolutionary principal of **chord inversion** (Ex. 5-1). To this he added other corollaries, in his *Treatise on Harmony* and later works: that the primary chords in music are the triad and seventh chord; that the basic movement within a succession of chords proceeds through fundamental bass notes a fifth apart; that the fundamental tone (tonic) exerts an almost gravitational force that pulls chords to it; that cadences are perfect or imperfect to the degree that they yield to this force of the pulling fifths. Explicit or strongly implied in Rameau's theory were concepts such as the triad, seventh chord, perfect and imperfect cadences, tonic, dominant, subdominant, and mediant pitches, functional harmonic progressions, and chord inversions—all terms and concepts commonly used by later music theorists.

EXAMPLE 5-1

As the eighteenth century progressed, Rameau and other theorists gradually came to adopt an equal tempering of the scale, and this facilitated the completion of a uniform theory of harmony based on the **circle of fifths.** In his *Treatise on Harmony*, Rameau had emphasized the importance of the interval of the fifth as the primary catalyst for moving the fundamental bass through a harmonic progression. In 1711, and then again in 1728, the German composer and theorist Johann David Heinichen (1683–1729) published a "Musical Circle," showing how a composer might proceed around the tonal globe moving by fifths (with relative minor keys interspersed; Fig. 1). Such a movement by fifths, however, might occur only if the scale were "well tempered" or, even better, tuned to equal temperament in which there is exact enharmonic equivalence (F♯ equals G♭, for example). A closed musical circle such as Heinichen's shows the desire of early eighteenth-century composers to play chords and chord progressions in all possible keys.

FIGURE 1

Johann David Heinichen's "Musicalischer Circul" from his *Der General-Bass in der Composition* (1728) demonstrates visually the process of moving around the circle of fifths.

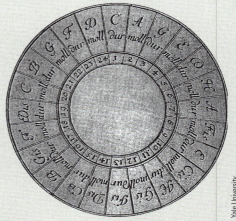

SUMMARY

The seventeenth and early eighteenth century witnessed a radical reformation of the way in which the pitch content of music was organized and explained. Teachers of music began to replace the hexachord with the octave as the standard unit of measure, and composers gradually reduced the twelve church modes to just two tonalities (major and minor). At the same time, composers also began to transpose these two tonalities to all twelve pitches of the chromatic scale. This created a self-contained tonal universe regulated by movements of a fifth. Within each key, chords a distance a fifth apart pulled toward one another. By means of modulation, a tonal center could be moved to another center a fifth away and then to another, also a fifth away, and so on, allowing a journey that passed through all twelve chromatic keys of the scale and miraculously arrived back at the beginning (because twelve superimposed fifths result in a unison in equal temperament). This early eighteenth-century organization of tonal space into twenty-four keys (twelve major and twelve minor) revolving around a circle of fifths was as revolutionary for music as was Newton's theory of gravity or Kepler's theory of planetary motion for astrophysics. Indeed, Rameau, influenced by the work of Newton, spoke of a gravitational pull moving the subdominant and dominant to the tonic. And, like most of Newton's laws, this remarkable eighteenth-century construct—a closed network of twenty-four keys forming a unified harmonic system—has endured down to the present day.

KEY TERMS

Age of Reason	Jean Philippe Rameau	chord inversion
major	*Treatise on Harmony*	circle of fifths
minor		

Music in London: Henry Purcell

The seventeenth century was a tumultuous time in English politics. In 1649 the English Parliament seized the king (Charles I) and had him beheaded. Civil war raged between the forces favoring a monarchy and those supporting a more democratic form of government. The royalists regained power in 1660, only to have Parliament depose another king (James II) in 1688, this time by forcing him into exile. Now Parliament invited new rulers, William and Mary, to mount the throne as king and queen. The power of the king and the court was greatly curtailed, while that of Parliament, with its House of Lords and House of Commons, grew proportionally. Individual liberties and democratic self-government expanded (although women were not allowed to vote until 1928!). By the end of the seventeenth century, England had established the first broadly representative government in the West since ancient Greece.

The partial transfer of power from court to commoner that marked the seventeenth century eventually affected music in the Baroque period. Serious opera, for example, rarely flourished in England, in part because it was expensive to produce and received little support from the weakened court. Oratorio, on the other hand, did thrive, because it was less costly to mount and thus appealed to the practical English Puritans. So, too, public concerts and public theaters prospered, because they brought in revenue from daily ticket sales and attracted the increasingly affluent middle class. By 1700 the center of social and artistic life had shifted from the court to public houses (pubs) and public theaters.

London, of course, was the capital and center of art and music for all of England. Its population now numbered nearly 500,000, making it by far the largest city in Europe. Musical life in London was concentrated in three areas. West of the city center was the area of Westminster, where Parliament met. Here, too, stood an old Benedictine monastery called **Westminster Abbey,** providing a venue for ceremonies of state, all with appropriate musical pomp. To the east of Westminster Abbey was Whitehall, where the king and his court resided and entertained, and where the royal chapel sang. Closer to the center of London, then as now, was the theater district. Plays with music, and the occasional opera, were performed here in theaters such as Dorset Garden and Drury Lane, which still exists today.

❋ HENRY PURCELL AND THEATER MUSIC

Henry Purcell (1659–1695) was a child of this changing political and musical environment. Purcell's father was a singer in the royal chapel, and the young Henry too began his career as a chorister in this choir. Here he received instruction in singing, notation, theory, composition, and playing keyboard instruments. After his voice broke in 1673, Purcell became keeper of the royal instruments, then organist at Westminster Abbey and the royal chapel, and finally "composer-in-ordinary" to the court. Toward the end of his life, as the political power and musical interest of the king and queen declined, Purcell increasingly turned his attention to theater music outside the court, where there was more money to be made.

The history of opera in England is somewhat different from that of opera on the European Continent. The Italians and Germans had cultivated opera since the early decades of the seventeenth century. But the English, particularly the Puritans, were skeptical about all-sung opera. Non-stop singing in a theater seemed unnatural to the practical English, especially when it happened in a foreign language. Moreover, the English enjoyed a rich history of purely spoken drama, best exemplified by the plays of Shakespeare. Instead of opera, the English preferred spoken plays (with incidental songs), masques, and semi-operas. The **masque** was an elaborate courtly entertainment using music, dance, and drama to portray an allegorical story that shed a favorable light on the royal family; thus, in many ways, the masque was similar to French *ballet de cour* (see Chapter 35). The **semi-opera** was a spoken play in which the more exotic, amorous, or even supernatural moments in the story were sung or danced. Only rarely was there fully sung opera, such as the excellent *Venus and Adonis* (1685) by John Blow, Purcell's teacher.

Henry Purcell likely acquired his love of the theater at a young age. Since the Middle Ages the roles of women in theatrical productions in Europe had invariably been performed by boys dressed as women; not until 1660 did a woman appear on the public stage in England. For theatrical productions at the English court, the choirboys of the royal chapel often served as female impersonators, and the young Purcell may have got his start in such a role. Regardless of what brought him there, Purcell's compositions for the stage are considerable. They run the gamut of musical theater genres, from simple songs inserted into plays, to incidental music, to semi-opera and fully sung opera. The best known of these today is his only fully sung opera, *Dido and Aeneas*.

Dido and Aeneas (1689)

Purcell's *Dido and Aeneas* apparently received its first performance in 1689 at a school for young women in the London suburb of Chelsea. The school was run by Josias Priest, a friend of Purcell, who was also a choreographer and man of the London theater. The girls presented one major stage production annually, something akin to the senior class play of today, and Priest seems to have provided a role for each and every pupil. They sang in the numerous choruses or danced in the equally frequent dance numbers. All nine solo parts save one (the role of Aeneas) were written for female voices, with the more important solo roles featuring professional singers imported from nearby London.

Appropriately for a school curriculum steeped in classical Latin, the libretto of *Dido and Aeneas* is drawn from Virgil's *Aeneid*. Surely the girls had studied this epic poem in Latin class, and even memorized parts of it. Surely too they knew the story of the soldier-of-fortune Aeneas who seduces proud Dido, queen of Carthage, but then deserts her to fulfill his destiny—sailing on to found the city of Rome. The tale concludes as the abandoned Dido sings an exceptionally beautiful lament, and then runs herself through with a sword (Fig. 37-1). All that remains is for a final chorus to lament her fate.

Dido and Aeneas is an opera in miniature, a chamber opera lasting little more than an hour. Within the three brief acts the music glides quickly between recitative, arioso, and full-blown aria. The climax of the opera comes in the final scene, which culminates in Dido's death. It begins with a brief recitative, "Thy hand, Belinda." Normally recitative is a business-like process that moves the dialogue along through direct, simple declamation. But this one is special. In the stepwise scale that descends an octave, touching almost every chromatic note along the way, we can feel the resignation of the abandoned Dido as she sinks into the arms of her servant Belinda. Here, too, we glimpse one of Purcell's greatest skills: the magical way he sets the English language. He understood where the accents fell in the text of his libretto and gave these stressed syllables greater length and metrical weight in the music; here, the accented syllables generally come on beats one and three, as can be seen in the opening lines "Thy hand, Belinda! Darkness shades me."

❀ FIGURE 37-1

A detail from the painting *The Death of Dido* by Guercino (1599–1666). The servant Belinda bends over the dying Dido, who has fallen on her sword, atop what will become her funeral pyre.

EXAMPLE 37-1

Thy hand, Be - lin - da; dark - ness shades me, On thy bo - som let me rest, More I would, but Death in - vades me; Death is now a wel - come guest.

The aria that follows, known as Dido's lament, is one of the most famous pieces in operatic literature. It is constructed of two beautifully shaped musical phrases that carry the following two lines of text:

> When I am laid in earth, may my wrongs create
>   no trouble in thy breast.
> Remember me, but ah! forget my fate.

Each of the two lines is repeated, as are many individual words and pairs. Such repetition of text is typical of an aria, but not a recitative. It is one means by which the composer depicts emotion. The heroine can vocalize, but cannot clearly articulate her feelings in complete sentences. The listener cares less about proper grammar and more that the text and music are emotionally charged. No fewer than six times does Dido plead with Belinda, and with us, to remember her. And, indeed, we do remember, for Dido's plaintive lament is one of the most moving arias in all of opera.

Purcell constructed the lament "When I am laid in earth" on a *basso ostinato*. As we have seen (see Chapter 31), the term *basso ostinato* is an extension of the Italian word *ostinato*, meaning "obstinate," "stubborn," or "pig-headed." In this case, it refers to the fact that the bass line repeats over and over. English composers of Purcell's day called the *basso ostinato* the **ground bass,** because the repetitive bass provided a solid foundation on which an entire composition could be built, or grounded. The repeating pattern might be only a few notes, or several measures, in length.

The ground bass Purcell composed for Dido's lament is five measures long and is heard eleven times. Note that the first half of the musical pattern consists of a chromatic descent that passes through a tetrachord (G, F♯, F, E, E♭, D); the second half moves the harmony from dominant back to tonic. As we have seen (Chapter 31), composers of the Baroque period often used a descending tetrachordal bass as a musical symbol to suggest grief, lamentation, and impending death. Thus, when the basso continuo alone played the descending tetrachord at the beginning of this aria, the audience would have understood the tragic character of the music even before the singer uttered a word. Eight statements of the ground bass then support the repeating phrases of the voice. At the end of Dido's final line, the singer breaks off, as if unable to articulate her sorrow further. But the strings press on, carrying Dido's inconsolable grief across two final statements of the ground bass.

EXAMPLE 37-2

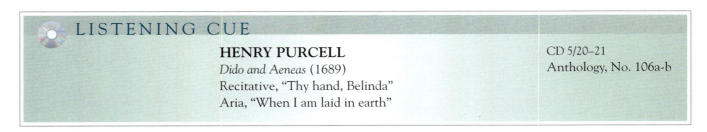

When I am laid, ___ am laid ___ in earth, may my wrongs ___ cre - ate...

LISTENING CUE

HENRY PURCELL
Dido and Aeneas (1689)
Recitative, "Thy hand, Belinda"
Aria, "When I am laid in earth"

CD 5/20–21
Anthology, No. 106a-b

✿ PURCELL'S ODES AND FUNERAL MUSIC FOR QUEEN MARY

William and Mary (for whom the College of William and Mary is named) were crowned king and queen of England in Westminster Abbey on 11 April 1689. Purcell marched in the procession, composed some of the coronation music, and played organ during the sacral ceremonies. Indeed, Purcell was a busy man that day. It seems that his organ loft gave a good view of the king and queen below, and Purcell made the enormous sum of five hundred pounds selling admission. But the treasurer of the abbey asked for the money back when he learned of the composer's unsanctioned activity. Purcell was not punished further because, as the authorities of the abbey noted, he was "in truth the most excellent musician of his time."

As the years went by, neither William nor Mary proved to be a generous patron of music. Parliament drew their purse strings tight. Moreover, William was a Calvinist (generally called a Puritan in England), and this rather austere branch of Protestantism had little love of music in or out of church. For only one event annually, the queen's birthday, was Purcell required to compose a work for the court.

Art Music Displaced by Folk Music

The music of Henry Purcell belongs to the repertory of what we now call "classical music." Although in its day this kind of brilliant orchestral music and virtuosic singing was appreciated by most of the populace, it was still very much "high art." Yet, even high-born royalty sometimes longed for more commonplace music, if we can trust a story told about Purcell and Queen Mary.

> Having in mind one afternoon to be entertained with music [Queen Mary] sent Mr. Gostling [a singer in the royal chapel] to Henry Purcell and Mrs. Arabella Hunt [see Fig. 37-2], who had a very fine voice, and an admirable hand on the lute, with a request to attend her; [and] they obeyed her commands. Mr. Gostling and Mrs. Hunt sang several compositions of Purcell, who accompanied them on the harpsichord; at length the queen beginning to grow tired, asked Mrs. Hunt if she could not sing the old Scots ballad *Cold and Raw*. Mrs. Hunt answered yes, and sang it to her lute. Purcell was all the while sitting at the harpsichord unemployed, and not a little nettled [annoyed] at the queen's preference of a vulgar ballad to his music.[1]

This anecdote reminds us that a rich tradition of largely unwritten popular music, much of it what we now call Anglo-Irish folk music, coexisted with written art music in England at this time. The Scottish folksong *Cold and Raw*, which apparently originated in the 1500s, was passed along orally for centuries and eventually written down. Several versions of it are currently audible via the internet, some played by electronic synthesizers! To hear one or more of these, simply search under the song title *Cold and Raw*. If the queen found it a pleasant diversion from high art music, you may too.

❀ FIGURE 37-2
Mrs. Arabella Hunt, a much admired soprano in her day, and performing partner of Henry Purcell.

When writing for the royal court, whether for the birthday, wedding, or welcoming of a ruler, English composers traditionally employed a genre of music called the ode. The **ode** is a multi-movement composition, usually lasting about twenty minutes, containing an instrumental introduction, choruses, duets, and solo arias. The ode has no recitative, however, because there is no drama or action to narrate. Instead, the successive movements offer lyrical hymns of praise to a member of the royal family. In a few cases, odes were also written in honor of St. Cecilia, the patron saint of music.

Henry Purcell composed twenty odes for the English royal family and four in praise of St. Cecilia. Six of the royal odes mark the birthday of Queen Mary (30 April), one for each of the six years Mary ruled. The best of these is the last, *Come, ye sons of art* (1694). The text was newly created by Nahum Tate, who had also fashioned the libretto for Purcell's *Dido and Aeneas*. In successive movements it invites "ye sons of art" (musicians) to celebrate Mary's "triumphant day." First the trumpet, then the "hautboy" (oboe), viol, lute, harp, flute, and finally Nature herself are asked to bring forth their special sounds of praise for the queen. The trumpet is represented by two altos who step forward to sing the duet "Sound the trumpet." On either side of the duet Purcell places the title chorus "Come, ye sons of art" to serve as a spirited choral refrain. In Purcell's day, as was the tradition in the Middle Ages and Renaissance, the alto voice was sung by a male in head voice, or falsetto. Today this high, falsetto alto part is performed by a singer called a **countertenor.** Here two countertenors sing music that is appropriately full of major-key fanfare motifs of the sort usually played by trumpets.

But there is irony in the duet "Sound the trumpet." No trumpets actually sound. Instead, as the countertenors sing in trumpet style, the two trumpeters of the orchestra sit silent. Purcell intended this to be an "in joke," for in his day the two royal trumpeters were named John and William Shore, which surely brought a smile at the words "you make the list'ning shores rebound." More-modern musicians, however, have put the trumpet back in Purcell's vocal duet; the music has been arranged for soprano and trumpet and recorded by, among others, trumpeter Wynton Marsalis.

EXAMPLE 37-3

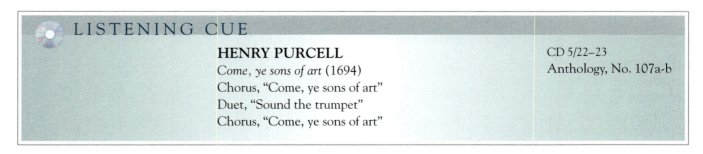

LISTENING CUE

HENRY PURCELL
Come, ye sons of art (1694)
Chorus, "Come, ye sons of art"
Duet, "Sound the trumpet"
Chorus, "Come, ye sons of art"

CD 5/22–23
Anthology, No. 107a-b

Despite Purcell's best wishes, Queen Mary did not live long. An epidemic of smallpox swept London in the fall of 1694, and on 21 December the queen fell ill.

Doctors prescribed various draughts and potions, subjected her to bleeding, and applied red-hot irons to blister her temples. Not withstanding (or perhaps because of) these treatments, she died a week later. The solemn task of composing the music for her funeral fell to Purcell. Like most of her subjects, Purcell seems to have been sincerely fond of his patron and queen. Indeed, her burial occasioned the same sort of outpouring of national grief as did the funeral of Princess Diana in 1997, which was also held in Westminster Abbey, where Purcell's music fittingly was heard once again. For Mary's service the composer fashioned some of the most beautiful burial music ever written. At the center of the service stood an English choral anthem, the famous *Thou knowest Lord, the secrets of our Hearts*. Preceding and concluding the anthem was a march and a canzona. The march is worthy of special attention, for it is the earliest instrumental funeral march to survive.

Purcell's funeral march is noteworthy also for the instruments that played it: four flat trumpets. The **flat trumpet** was a slide trumpet (like the early trombone), but one for which the sliding tube extended backward over the player's left shoulder, rather than extending forward from the right. Actually, little is known about the flat trumpet and no original survives today. Apparently, the name derives from the fact that the slide made it easier for the trumpet to play in minor keys, which employ a "flat" third scale degree. Surely the capacity to play in minor as well as major accounts for the appearance of the flat trumpet in the funeral music for Queen Mary; the traditional non-slide natural trumpet playing in the usual brilliant keys of C, D, or E♭ major would have been out of place at this somber event. Purcell's march is nothing more than five homophonic chord progressions, each three bars in length. Why then did it bring "tears from all," as an eyewitness reported? Likely because of the rich harmonies, the slow and stately tempo, and the mournful tones of the flat trumpets. The more sprightly canzona sounds less like a funeral dirge than a dance, owing to the rapidly moving notes and lightly imitative texture. Its dance-like character is occasioned by an age-old tradition that holds that burials should end with hopeful, lively music, because the dead are said to dance with the angels in heaven in the life beyond. On our accompanying CD recording, modern reproductions of flat trumpets can be heard.

LISTENING CUE

HENRY PURCELL
Funeral Music for Queen Mary (1695)
March and Canzona

CD 5/24–25
Anthology, No. 108a-b

Less than a year after the death of Queen Mary, Purcell himself died, possibly of tuberculosis. He was barely thirty-six and at the height of his powers. Once again, Purcell's funeral music sounded forth, this time for his own obsequies in Westminster Abbey. He was buried at the foot of the organ, where his memorial plaque can still be read today.

SUMMARY

Like Mozart and Schubert, Henry Purcell composed a remarkable amount of music during his tragically short life. A fully sung opera, *Dido and Aeneas,* numerous semi-operas, and incidental interludes and songs for plays constitute the bulk of his music for the theater. For the English royal family he composed church anthems, twenty birthday odes, and music for Queen Mary's funeral. Whether writing for theater or court, Purcell's scores show his special gifts for melody, infectious dance rhythms, impeccable handling of the English language, and an unfailing freshness of sound. Like his successor, Handel, much of Purcell's finest writing is to be found in his choruses.

KEY TERMS

Westminster Abbey	ground bass	countertenor
masque	ode	flat trumpet
semi-opera		

Chapter 38

Music in London: George Frideric Handel

George Frideric Handel was German-born but spent most of his life in London, becoming in his time a beloved English institution. Handel and his music were arguably the single most important force for cultural unity in England during the entire eighteenth century, even following the composer's death in 1759.

Handel was born in Halle, Germany, in 1685, the same year as J.S. Bach. His father, a surgeon-barber (the two professions were often joined in Handel's day), wanted the son to be a lawyer. But the young Handel's love and obvious talent for music soon led to a change in plans and a rigorous musical education as organist, harpsichordist, and composer. At eighteen Handel moved to the populous north German city of Hamburg, where he played second violin and then harpsichord in the opera orchestra. There he began to study German opera, which was then heavily influenced by the musical style and theatrical conventions of Italian opera. His principal mentor was Reinhard Keiser (1674–1739), the foremost composer of opera in the German language. In 1706 Handel set off for Italy to learn the Italian traditions firsthand, and there he remained for four years, listening to and composing cantatas and operas in Italian. This Italian experience, one not shared by his contemporary, Bach, gave to Handel's subsequent vocal music an accent thoroughly Italianate. Back in Germany in 1710, Handel accepted a position at the court of the elector of Hanover at an annual salary of 1,000 thaler. The terms of his employment allowed for ample travel, so the composer soon set off for England.

As a friend of Handel said in 1713: "In these times, whoever wishes to be eminent in music goes to England. In France and Italy there is something to learn, but in London there is something to earn."[1] Indeed, the already-famous Handel arrived in England with the aim of making money by bringing Italian opera to London. As we have seen, London, with its population of 500,000, was the largest city in Europe. But opera in England had had a checkered history, owing, among other things, to the English aversion to all-sung drama (see Chapter 37). Yet public demand for real opera sung by top-flight Italian virtuosi was starting to grow, and in 1711 Handel satisfied it with *Rinaldo,* the first fully sung Italian opera designed specifically for London and the first to use an all-Italian cast. Conveniently forgetting his obligations in Germany, Handel remained in London, writing Italian opera and using his music to ingratiate himself with the ruling monarch, Queen Anne. But Anne died in the summer of 1714. As fate would have it, Handel's employer in Germany, the elector of Hanover, acceded to the English throne as King George I. Thus were patron and errant musician reunited. Now the most famous composer in England was a German, and so was the king.

Given his connections to the royals, Handel naturally was the first composer called upon when need arose for festive music to entertain the court or to mark its progress. Thus Handel wrote odes and anthems and, ultimately, the *Coronation Service* for the royal family. Among the purely instrumental works Handel composed for the court are his *Water Music* (1717) and *Music for the Royal Fireworks* (1749). For the general public he published sets of concerti grossi, solo concertos for organ and orchestra, and numerous keyboard suites. All the while, Handel worked tirelessly to make Italian opera a staple of English musical life. Encountering increasing financial problems with opera, however, the composer eventually turned his attention to oratorio. Through oratorio, Handel won the hearts and minds of the court and the well-to-do (mostly high-church Anglicans) as well as the common people of England (mostly Puritans). By the time of his death in 1759, Handel had become a cultural monument to which most people could relate with enthusiasm, albeit a few with cynicism (Fig. 38-1). Embracing his ceremonial music for the English monarchy as well as his ever-popular oratorios, the English developed a special bond with Handel's music and responded to it as one people.

FIGURE 38-1

Handel did not do things in moderation—he composed 42 operas and at least 22 full-length oratorios. He consumed food and drink with the same enthusiasm as he soaked up national musical styles. This caricature by Joseph Goupy, done in 1754, pokes fun at the composer for his gluttony (food and wine cask) and his penchant for loud music (trumpet, horn, and drum by his left foot).

HANDEL AND THE DANCE SUITE

The versatile Handel composed in virtually every genre of music known in Western Europe during the early eighteenth century. Aside from *Messiah,* today his most popular composition is his dance suite *Water Music.* Recall that a **dance suite** is a collection of dances all in a single key for one instrument or another, be it a solo instrument or a full orchestra (see Chapter 34); moreover, in the Baroque era the dances of a suite were almost invariably in binary form, **AB.** The suite may begin with a prelude or a French overture, and then continue with a succession of dances, usually ranging in number from four to seven. Of course, listeners did not actually dance to these pieces; they were stylized abstractions. But it was the job of the composer to bring each one to life, making it recognizable to the audience by incorporating the salient elements of rhythm and style from each particular dance.

Bach wrote dance suites for orchestra, for harpsichord, and for solo cello. Handel composed suites for orchestra, specifically *Water Music* and *Music for the Royal Fireworks.* He also published eight suites for harpsichord in 1720 and nine more in 1733. (Handel's famous *The Harmonious Blacksmith,* a title bestowed in the nineteenth century, appears in the fifth suite of the first collection.) Both collections for harpsichord are entitled *Suite de Pièces*, reminding us that our English word "suite" comes directly from the French word of the same spelling, meaning "succession" of pieces.

Water Music (1717)

The English royal family, historically, has had a problem with its image. To win favor with the public, the monarchy has traditionally given outdoor concerts, as Queen Elizabeth II did by inviting pop musicians to perform at Buckingham Palace in 2002. Handel's *Water Music* was created for an earlier bit of royal image-building. In 1717 King George I, a direct ancestor of the present queen, was an unpopular monarch. He refused to speak a word of English, preferring his native German. He fought with his son, the Prince of Wales, and banned him from court. London thought King George dimwitted, "an honest blockhead," as one contemporary put it.

To improve his standing in the eyes of his subjects, the king's ministers planned a program of public entertainments, including an evening of music that all the people of London could hear and enjoy. Thus on 17 July 1717, the king and his court traveled by boat up the Thames River. Indeed, so numerous were the boats that it seemed "the whole River in a manner was cover'd." Next to the king's boat was a barge carrying about fifty musicians. As an eyewitness reports, they included "trumpets, horns, hautboys [oboes], bassoons, German flutes [transverse flutes], French flutes [recorders], violins and basses." The account continues: "The music had been composed specially by the famous Handel, a native of Halle [Germany], and His Majesty's principal Court Composer. His Majesty approved of it so greatly that he caused it to be repeated three times in all, although each performance lasted an hour—namely twice before and once after supper."[2] The king and his party did not return to London and the royal residence at St. James until nearly four-thirty in the morning.

To create an hour of music Handel wrote three successive dance suites: one in F major featuring the horn, one in D major highlighting the trumpet, and one in G major and minor centering on the flute. Yet because Handel's complete autograph score of *Water Music* has been lost, and because the surviving contemporary manuscript copies and the early prints do not agree, modern editions differ in the number of movements, titles, and keys. A commonly accepted sequence for the entire work follows.

Suite No. 1 in F Major	Suite No. 2 in D Major	Suite No. 3 in G Major and Minor
1. Overture	10. (Overture)	15. (Sarabande)
2. Adagio e staccato	11. Alla hornpipe	16. Raguadon
3. (Allegro)-Andante-(Allegro)	12. Minuet	17. Minuet
4. (Minuet)	13. Lentement	18. (Andante)
5. Air	14. Bourrée	19. (Country Dance I/II)
6. Minuet (and trio)		
7. Bourrée		
8. Hornpipe		
9. (Allegro)		

The sound of Handel's *Water Music* is both distinctive and historic. It is one of the first English scores to include parts for horn. Although horns had been welcomed into orchestras in Germany, France, and Italy well before 1700, the instrument was introduced into English ensembles only after this date. Oddly, although the home of the horn was Germany and Bohemia (Czech Republic), the English came to call the instrument the **French horn,** having become acquainted with it during visits to the French court of King Louis XIV. Only in the English language is it so named (it is known simply as "the horn" in other countries). The early eighteenth-century French horn was a natural instrument (with no valves) and had a smaller bell, and thus a smaller sound, than the modern horn. Composers frequently assigned a characteristic musical figure called **horn fifths** to the French horn and trumpet, in which the instruments slide back and forth through sixths, fifths, and thirds, sometimes ornamenting along the way as can be seen in Example 38-1 from the Minuet of Suite No. 1. Needless to say, both the French horn and trumpet are featured in *Water Music* because the sound of these brass instruments carries well across outdoor expanses.

EXAMPLE 38-1

LISTENING CUE

GEORGE FRIDERIC HANDEL
Water Music, Suite No. 1 (1717)
Minuet and Trio
Hornpipe

CD 5/26–27
Anthology, No. 109a-b

Water Music proved to be immensely popular; it was played in pubs and in public gardens in London and throughout the British Isles. The work was arranged for small ensemble, for flute and harpsichord, and for solo harpsichord. In short, it conquered England. Today, Handel's *Water Music*, Bach's Brandenburg Concertos, and Vivaldi's *The Four Seasons* constitute the most popular instrumental music of the first half of the eighteenth century.

HANDEL AND OPERA

Handel enjoyed great success when he became one of the first to bring all-sung Italian opera to London during the years 1711–1717, and this inspired a bolder venture. In 1719 he became the musical force behind a remarkable capitalistic enterprise: the formation of a publicly-held stock company for the production of Italian opera. The principal investor was the king, and thus Handel's opera company was called the **Royal Academy of Music.** Handel wrote most of his best operas for the Academy, yet it went bankrupt in 1728 and again in 1734. To understand how this could happen, we must understand something of the economics of Baroque opera, specifically *opera seria.*

Handel composed some forty-two operas, most of which fall into the category of *opera seria.* **Opera seria** (literally, serious opera, as opposed to comic opera) was fully sung Italian opera of the most elaborate and expensive sort. The plots of *opera*

The Castrato in Handel's Operas

Today pop singers make fortunes, and each star has his or her fanatics. Opera singers have cult followings too, and they earn the most money among "serious" musicians. Over the years, tenor Luciano Pavarotti has commanded a hundred thousand dollars for each appearance at Madison Square Garden or Foxwoods Casino, and soprano Renée Fleming (see Fig. 48-2) appears regularly on the David Letterman Show.

Yet the cult of the singer is not new. In the late Baroque era, star singers were the most adored, and by far the best paid, of musicians. Among the men, the most prized was the virtuoso castrato. The castrato, as we have seen, was a male singer who had been castrated, usually between the age of eight and ten; his body would grow but his larynx and vocal cords would remain small, like those of a woman—all this in hopes that he could be trained to sing beautifully in the soprano or alto range. Audiences on the Continent were greatly enamored with the sound of the castrato, for it combined the high range of a female voice with the power of the male frame. Some could hold a note for a full minute and had a range of an incredible three octaves. The popularity of the castrato was enhanced by the fact that on the Baroque stage, high standing was represented by singers, whether male or female, of high vocal range; the roles of Julius Caesar and Alexander the Great, for example, were sung by castrati, and basses and tenors were usually given only minor parts. Castrati gradually disappeared from the operatic stage during the second half of the eighteenth century, but they continued to sing in Italian churches throughout the nineteenth. The last castrato, papal singer Alessandro Moreschi, died in 1921.

Among the most famous castrati of Handel's day was Francesco Bernardi, called **Senesino** (c1690–1759) because he came from Siena, Italy (Fig. 38-2). Senesino was engaged to sing at the Dresden opera in 1717, where he received a carriage—the eighteenth-century equiva-lent of a limousine—and an annual salary of 7,000 thalers (Bach's base salary about that time was 400 thalers). Senesino's temper tantrums got him fired from the opera at Dresden, and he moved on to London. In the course of the next two decades he sang heroic roles in some twenty operas by Handel, including that of Caesar in *Giulio Cesare*. Opinion of the English public was divided about Senesino, and castrati in general. One observer noted that "Senesino is daily voted the greatest man that ever lived," while another referred to him as a "squeaking Italian." Today the role of Caesar is sung in one of three ways: by a male in chest voice with the part transposed down an octave, by a male singing in falsetto voice (a countertenor), or by a low female voice called **contralto** (a low alto).

🌸 FIGURE 38-2

A caricature of the principal singers in a scene from an opera by Handel showing the castrato Senesino (left) and soprano Cuzzoni (center).

seria are usually derived from historical events or mythology, and involve larger-than-life figures—kings, queens, gods, and goddesses. There is little drama on stage. The action is often not seen by the audience, but reported by third parties, generally in the form of recitatives. The leading characters do not act so much as react. One after the other, they step forward to sing a self-contained aria, each expressing one of several stock emotions—hope, anger, hate, frenzy, despair, and vengeance, among others. Above all, *opera seria* is a singers' opera. In Handel's day it provided a platform for those singers who possessed the vocal equipment to quiet a restless, often noisy crowd by the power, range, and beauty of their singing. For this to occur, highly trained virtuosi—the best in the world—were needed. But virtuoso singers, then as now, are expensive. The great sopranos and castrati were each paid £1,500 per season, far more than Handel himself. It was Handel's job to recruit these virtuosi (all Italian) from opera houses around Europe. English money was used to buy the best vocal talent Italy had to offer.

Giulio Cesare (Julius Caesar, 1724)

The greatest Italian voices of the day sang the leads in *Giulio Cesare*, an unusually successful *opera seria* that Handel composed in 1724 for his Royal Academy in London. The libretto recounts an episode in Caesar's life in which he pursues and then defeats his rival Pompey, in Egypt. Cleopatra, who rules Egypt jointly with her brother Ptolemy, conspires to seduce the newly arrived Caesar and gain his help in eliminating her despised brother. All this Cleopatra accomplishes, aided by a generous supply of confidants, servants, disguises, and theatrical tricks. By the end of this nearly three-hour opera, she becomes queen to a Roman emperor.

In the 1724 production of *Giulio Cesare*, the famous castrato Senesino (see Box and Fig. 38-2) sang the soprano part of Caesar, while the equally famous female soprano Francesca Cuzzoni sang the role of Cleopatra. In the aria "V'adoro, pupille" ("I Adore You, O Eyes") from Act II of *Giulio Cesare*, Cleopatra must exert all her charms to win the heart of Caesar, and her music, accordingly, must enchant and captivate. To create seductive sounds, Handel not only constructed an exquisite melody but also called for unusual orchestral instruments—the *viola da gamba*, the theorbo (a large, lute-like instrument), and the harp for heavenly accompaniment. As is true for most arias in *opera seria*, "V'adoro, pupille" is a *da capo* aria (**ABA**; see Chapter 32), though here the return to **A** is interrupted by a bit of recitative delivered by the now-enraptured Caesar. Conventions of the *da capo* aria required the singer portraying Cleopatra to ornament the reprise of **A** to add variety as well as to show off her voice. Example 38-2 gives the beginning of **A** as Handel wrote it (top) and suggests how a singer might have ornamented it (bottom).

EXAMPLE 38-2

LISTENING CUE

GEORGE FRIDERIC HANDEL
Giulio Cesare (1724)
Aria, "V'adoro, pupille"

CD 5/28
Anthology, No. 110

With beauty such as this, how could Handel's opera company have gone bankrupt? The exorbitant cost of the principal singers has already been mentioned, but there were other factors contributing to the demise of fully sung opera. Among these was the rise of ballad opera (see Chapter 41), a genre of musical theater alternating spoken

Opera Then and Now

In some ways eighteenth century opera was similar to opera today. Handel's company was funded by a combination of subscriptions and daily ticket sales. Operas were given in a public theater to a paying audience during a season that ran from November into June. Singers were expensive and temperamental. Handel constantly fought with his leading castrato, Senesino; he threatened to throw the diva Cuzzoni out a window when she refused to sing an aria he had written; and Cuzzoni and another prima donna, Bordoni (see Chapter 41), once engaged in a hair-pulling fight onstage. Much was spent on costumes and scenery, but comparatively little on the orchestra. Opera's main drawing cards, then as now, were social glamour and star singers.

There were important differences as well. Most operas performed by Handel's Royal Academy of Music were new works, often composed by Handel himself. Today, opera companies mostly perform "revivals" of previously composed operas—by Handel, Mozart, Verdi, or Wagner, for example.

Moreover, in Handel's day the composer was expected to tailor the music to the voices of the singers in a particular production. If an aria was too high or too low, too difficult or not showy enough, Handel would quickly take up the pen to change it. Today's composers, needless to say, are less accommodating.

Finally, what went on in the opera house was much different. The opening overture was played to call the audience to its seats, not when the audience was seated and quiet. The curtain stayed up between the acts, because other performers stepped on stage to play or dance during intermission. Handel is known to have performed his organ concertos between the acts of his oratorios, and Vivaldi played violin concertos between the acts of his operas. How much of this the audience took in is anyone's guess. Clearly, walking and talking during the performance were more tolerated then; to make a mundane comparison, Handel's opera audience probably behaved like the crowd at a baseball game today.

---

dialogue with traditional ballads. The popularity of ballad opera, the eighteenth-century counterpart of today's Broadway musical, lured people away from Handel's more high-brow art. Finally, in 1733 a second *opera seria* company, called the "Opera of the Nobility," began operation in London in direct competition with Handel's Academy. Eventually both companies failed, and Handel increasingly turned his attention to oratorio.

HANDEL AND ORATORIO

Oratorio, like opera, was born in seventeenth-century Italy. The very name "oratorio" suggests that it originated in an oratory, a large chapel for prayer. As we have seen (see Chapter 32), an oratorio was a large-scale, multi-movement composition setting a sacred text. Oratorio was not part of the regular worship services of the church, but provided extra-liturgical enlightenment and, especially, enjoyment for the faithful. Indeed, by the time of Handel, the oratorio had become in most ways little more than an unstaged opera with a religious subject. Handel originally intended his oratorios to be spiritual substitutes for opera during the six-week Lenten season before Easter, when secular entertainments such as opera were usually not permitted.

To be sure, oratorio and opera in eighteenth-century London had much in common. Oratorio, like opera, was performed in a public theater before a paying audience. Both usually begin with an overture, are divided into three acts, and consist mostly of recitatives and arias. Finally, both oratorio and opera tell a dramatic story by using individual characters and a chorus.

But there are important differences between oratorio and opera. First of all, oratorio, unlike *opera seria,* is not sung in Italian but in the language of the local people.

In the case of Handel's oratorios, they were sung in English. Moreover, oratorio does not involve staging, costumes, or acting; instead, the audience must picture in its mind's eye the drama that is described on stage. Similarly, oratorio does not require expensive operatic voices and the vocal writing generally is less extravagant than in opera. Finally, oratorio, unlike opera, does not draw upon historical events or tales from classical mythology, but on religious subjects, usually those recorded in scripture. The religious nature of oratorio requires moralizing, and this is done best by the collective forces of a chorus; thus, in oratorio, the chorus is generally far more important than in opera.

Given these qualities, it is easy to see why oratorio appealed to Handel. He could do away with the irascible and expensive castrati and prima donnas. He no longer had to pay for elaborate sets and costumes. He could draw on the English love of choral music, a tradition that extended well back into the Middle Ages (see Chapter 16). In addition, social forces were favoring oratorio. The aristocracy and its wealth, the support network for opera from its inception, was weakening in England. Increasing in importance was a new, untapped market of middle-class consumers—the faithful of the Puritan, Methodist, and growing evangelical sects in England, who viewed the pleasures of foreign opera with distrust, even contempt. Similarly, the subject matter of English oratorio—biblical stories of oppressed peoples who threw off the shackles of domination—was not lost on this rising middle class, who saw themselves overburdened by a corrupt government. The enterprising Handel was quick to see that oratorio was a cost-effective way to use music to bring religious enlightenment to his countrymen, remain politically correct, and still make a handsome profit.

Messiah (1741)

Between 1732 and 1751, when he stopped composing because of blindness, Handel wrote twenty-two oratorios. The majority of these depict heroic figures from the Old Testament, among them Joseph, Susanna, Samson, Esther, Joshua, and the people of Israel captive in Egypt. Yet Handel's most popular oratorio, then as now, is Messiah, which draws on passages from the Old and New Testament concerning the idea of a messiah. Handel composed Messiah in only three-and-a-half weeks during the summer of 1741. It was first performed in Dublin, Ireland, the following April as part of a charity benefit, with Handel conducting. Having heard the dress rehearsal, the local press waxed enthusiastic about the new oratorio, saying that it "far surpasses anything of that Nature, which has been performed in this or any other Kingdom." Such a large crowd was expected for the work of the famous Handel that ladies were urged not to wear hoopskirts, and gentlemen were admonished to leave their swords at home. In this way an audience of 700 could be squeezed into a hall possessing only 600 seats!

Pleased with his artistic and financial success in Dublin, Handel took Messiah back to London, made minor alterations, and performed it in the public theater at Covent Garden. In 1750 he again offered Messiah, this time in the chapel of the Foundling Hospital for orphans, and again there was much popular acclaim for Handel, as well as much profit for charity. In time, Handel gave a conducting score and instrumental parts of Messiah to the hospital and paid for an organ there, so that the oratorio might be given annually. The performances of Messiah at the Foundling Hospital did much to convince the public that Handel's oratorios were appropriate for churches and for charitable fund-raisers. As the music historian and friend of

Handel, Charles Burney, said at the time: "[*Messiah*] has fed the hungry, clothed the naked, fostered the orphan, and enriched succeeding managers of Oratorios, more than any single musical production of this or any country."[3] And so it does to the present day.

In a general way, *Messiah* tells the story of the life of Christ. It is divided into three parts (instead of three acts): (1) the prophecy and birth of Christ; (2) his crucifixion, descent into Hell, and resurrection; and (3) the Day of Judgment and the promise of eternal life. Handel usually performed *Messiah* immediately after Easter. Today it is also offered during the season of Advent before Christmas.

Messiah is comprised of fifty-three musical numbers. Nineteen are for chorus, sixteen are solo arias, sixteen are recitatives, and two are purely instrumental pieces. The large number of choruses reflects the importance of the chorus generally in Handel's oratorios. By contrast, while the arias are important, they tend not to be the big *da capo* show pieces heard in Handel's operas. Ornamentation and vocal display was less important in oratorio than opera, and consequently Handel ultimately included only two *da capo* arias in the entire score. Instead, Handel created for *Messiah* a variety of smaller aria forms in which he tried to create a musical shape and mood appropriate for each aria text.

Typical of the simpler text-specific arias in *Messiah* is the lovely "He shall feed his flock," which invokes the image of Christ, the gentle shepherd of his flock, and of shepherds generally. For this calm and comforting text, Handel fashioned appropriately soothing music. Indeed, "He shall feed his flock" is a perfect example of what is called a **pastoral aria,** a slow aria with several distinctive characteristics: parallel thirds that glide mainly in step-wise motion, a lilting rhythm in compound meter, and a harmony that changes slowly and employs many subdominant chords. The tradition of the pastoral in music extends well back into the seventeenth century and includes, among other pieces, Corelli's "Christmas" concerto from his Opus 6. Bach and later composers, among them Beethoven and Schumann, would also compose pastoral works. Thus Handel's aria "He shall feed his flock" is part of a long continuum in music history in which shepherds, and particularly those of Christmas, are supplied with a lilting style of music called the pastoral.

EXAMPLE 38-3

LISTENING CUE

GEORGE FRIDERIC HANDEL

Messiah (1741)

Aria, "He shall feed his flock"

CD 6/1

Anthology, No. 111a

Despite the beauty of its arias, the true glory of *Messiah* is to be found in its choruses. Handel was arguably the finest composer for chorus who ever lived. Nowhere is his choral mastery more evident than in the justly famous "Hallelujah" chorus, which concludes Part II of *Messiah* (Fig. 38-3). Here the multitude shouts for joy, for Christ has been victorious on the cross and has ascended triumphantly to reign in heaven.

The power of the "Hallelujah" chorus is generated by several forces: the rhythmically incisive setting of the word "Hallelujah" makes for an exciting exclamation; the repetition of this word throughout builds a feeling of communal participation in a great dramatic pageant; and a variety of choral styles—unison, chordal, fugal, and chordal and fugal together—creates a kaleidoscope of colors and textures. The music is at once complex and very clear. So moved was King George II when he first heard the great opening chords, as the story goes, that he rose to his feet in admiration, thereby establishing the tradition of the audience standing for the "Hallelujah" chorus—for no one sat while the king stood. With its brilliant writing for trumpets in the bright key of D major, this movement might well serve as a royal coronation march, though in *Messiah*, of course, it is Christ the King who is crowned.

The British Library

🌼 F I G U R E 3 8 - 3

The autograph of the full score of Handel's *Messiah* showing the beginning of the "Hallelujah" chorus.

💿 LISTENING CUE

GEORGE FRIDERIC HANDEL
Messiah (1741)
"Hallelujah" chorus

CD 6/2
Anthology, No. 111b

For the first performance of *Messiah* in 1742, Handel's musical forces were rather diminutive: an orchestra of about twenty (mostly strings) and a chorus of eight choirboys for the soprano and five adult males on each of the alto, tenor, and bass lines. As for the soloists, women sang the alto and soprano solos in *Messiah*, and indeed in all Handel's oratorios. (By contrast, the soprano solos in Bach's religious music were invariably sung by a choirboy.) For the performances of *Messiah* at the Foundling Hospital in London during the 1750s, the orchestra grew to thirty-eight players by the addition of doubling instruments (oboes, bassoons, and horns). Later, for the Handel Commemoration of 1785 in Westminster Abbey, about five hundred performers participated, equally divided between chorus and orchestra. In the course of the next hundred years, the chorus swelled to as many as four thousand, with a balancing orchestra of five hundred.

So too grew Handel's stature in the hearts and minds of the English. When he died in April 1759, he left an enormous estate of 20,000 pounds, much of which he bequeathed to charity. He was buried with full honors in Westminster Abbey, with three thousand persons in attendance. Today a sculpture of the composer holding an aria from *Messiah* stands in the Abbey directly opposite a memorial to another giant of English cultural history, William Shakespeare.

SUMMARY

In some ways the music of George Frideric Handel represents a continuation of the English musical tradition. Henry Purcell and his generation wrote wonderfully expressive choral anthems for the church and brilliant trumpet parts to adorn court festivals, as well as evocative music for the theater. But Handel greatly enriched this tradition. As a world traveler with an unsurpassed ear, he had grown up with the sound of the densely contrapuntal German fugue; when in Rome he absorbed the cohesive harmonic language and well-directed basses of Corelli; and, again in Rome, he embraced the Italianate vocal style of the cantata, opera, and oratorio. By combining these sounds with the English choral tradition, Handel achieved a remarkably rich synthesis of national styles. His oratorios in particular show a melding of English choral traditions with the operatic conventions of aria and recitative. Most important, Handel had a flair for the dramatic gained from a lifetime in the theater. He could seize the emotional core of any text, convert it to musical expression, and maintain it with intensity over long spans of time. The vividness, intensity, and grandeur of Handel's music mark it as a positive, life-affirming force.

KEY TERMS

dance suite	Royal Academy of Music	contralto
French horn	*opera seria*	oratorio
horn fifths	Senesino	pastoral aria

Chapter 39

Johann Sebastian Bach: Instrumental Music in Weimar and Cöthen

Johann Sebastian Bach and George Frideric Handel are today the best-known composers of Baroque music. Yet their lives could hardly have been more different. Handel was a man of the world, traveling freely around the European Continent and back and forth to England. Handel had no children, indeed never married. His base of operation was London, a city of a half-million inhabitants. Bach, by contrast, was a devoted father to twenty children and something of a stay-at-home, rarely venturing beyond his familial roots in central Germany. He worked in towns with as few as 3,500 citizens. Handel was a man of the theater, while Bach remained mainly within the precincts of the church.

Yet Bach was keenly attuned to the musical currents of his day, taking great pains to keep in touch with changing musical styles and shape them according to his own intensely rigorous musical intellect. Perhaps more than Handel, Bach used strict constructivist processes to create musical projects of almost superhuman design, such as his Brandenburg Concertos and The Art of Fugue. Whereas Handel wanted his music to sound good, to be heard and enjoyed by all, Bach wanted his music to be good in an almost divinely perfect way; he composed, so he said, "for the greater glory of God alone." By means of intellectual rigor and supreme technical mastery, Bach brought Baroque music to a glorious culmination.[†]

Johann Sebastian Bach came from a long line of musicians who lived and worked in central Germany (Map 39-1). A family tree of this clan includes nearly sixty musical Bachs, extending from the late sixteenth century into the nineteenth. Of these, Johann Sebastian was simply the most talented and industrious. Bach was born in the small town of Eisenach, Germany, in 1685. His father, Ambrosius, directed a town band of five wind players. Bach senior also played the violin, and seems to have taught his son violin, viola, and cello. Young Bach also learned to play the organ, and by the age of fifteen was already composing for that instrument. When Johann Sebastian's parents both died prematurely, he was sent to live with his older brother Johann Christoph in the nearby town of Ohrdruf. There he seems to have learned his trade by secretly copying the works of the masters from a book his brother kept shut away in a cupboard.

As a youth, Johann Sebastian Bach studied music, the humanities, and theology in private Lutheran church schools at Eisenach, Orhdruf, and finally Lüneburg in northern Germany. In all, Bach received twelve years of formal education, more than any other Bach until that time. To pay his way, Bach sang as a choral scholar in various church-school choirs. At Lüneburg, for example, he was a soprano, and then a bass after his voice broke at age fifteen (puberty came later in those earlier centuries). With his formal education completed at the age of seventeen, Bach went forth to make his way in the musical world.

Over the course of the next six years (1702–1708), Bach worked in a number of musical positions, including that of church organist in the small town of Arnstadt (see Map. 39-1). His desire to learn the latest styles resulted in a now-famous story. At age twenty, Bach asked for a leave of absence from his job as organist in Arnstadt

MAP 39-1
Central and north Germany in Bach's day.

[†]Like Handel, Bach composed a large number of pieces, more than 1,200. Handel's most important works are vocal compositions and thus are identified simply by their title. Bach, however, wrote a great deal of instrumental music. To avoid confusion among these pieces, twentieth-century musicologists developed a system of grouping his compositions by genre and numbering them. Thus when we buy music by Bach or attend a performance, we usually see an identifying number for the piece in question preceded by the letters **BWV (Bach Werke Verzeichnis),** which is simply German for "Bach Work List." The BWV number for Bach functions much like the "K." numbers used for Mozart's works (see Chapter 47).

to journey to Lübeck, where he could hear the newest organ pieces as well as the famous *Abendmusik* of Dieterich Buxtehude (see Chapter 34). Accordingly, in November 1705, Bach set forth to walk the entire 280-mile distance between Arnstadt and Lübeck. Although his superiors in Arnstadt had given him a leave of a month, Bach walked back into Arnstadt four months after he had left. He was reprimanded not only for truancy but also for the elaborate way he was now playing his chorale preludes on the organ—with so much ornamentation no one could recognize the chorale tune! Evidently, the small town authorities did not like the fancy stuff young Bach had learned from Buxtehude in the big city. Eventually, Bach left Arnstadt and moved on to more promising positions, first in Mühlhausen and then in Weimar.

✱ BACH IN WEIMAR: THE ORGAN MUSIC

During his years in the city of Weimar (1708–1717), Bach wrote most of his great works for organ. In fact, in his day Bach was known more as a virtuoso organist and organ expert than as a composer. At the time, the organ had come to occupy a central place in the religious music of the Lutheran church and in German society generally. In the Lutheran service the organ accompanied the choir and congregation, yet also sounded as a solo instrument, one that could rival a full orchestra in volume and tone color. Moreover, the Germans, then as now, had a tradition of excellence in the manufacture of precision instruments, and they produced pipe organs of the highest quality.

The *Orgelbüchlein*

Among Bach's organ compositions dating from his nine years in Weimar is the **Orgelbüchlein,** a collection of forty-six pieces written mostly between 1708 and 1713. It is called the *Orgelbüchlein* (*Little Organ Book*) because the manuscript measures only 6 x 7 inches. Each of the forty-six pieces is a **chorale prelude,** which, as we have seen (Chapter 34), is an ornamental setting of a pre-existing chorale tune intended to be played on the organ before the singing of the chorale by the full congregation. The performance of the prelude served to recall the chorale tune in the minds of the faithful before they tried to sing it themselves. The title page of the *Orgelbüchlein* suggests that Bach intended to achieve three things with this collection of chorale preludes: (1) to provide the organist with a repertory of pieces to play in church; (2) to show the organist-composer how to construct a chorale prelude on a given tune by providing multiple examples; and (3) to develop the technical facility of the organist by requiring an extensive use of the pedal. In organ music prior to the *Orgelbüchlein,* the bass line could, if the performer wished, be played manually (by the hands) not *pedaliter* (by the feet). Here, in all forty-six pieces, at least one voice must be played by the pedals. Thus users of the *Orgelbüchlein* learned how to coordinate hands and feet, perhaps the most difficult organ technique of all.

Just how challenging a chorale prelude within the *Orgelbüchlein* might be can be seen in "In dulci jubilo" ("In Sweet Jubilation"), a piece intended for Christmas. Originally the melody of "In dulci jubilo" was a Gregorian chant, a hymn sung in Latin in the Roman Catholic Church. In the sixteenth century, the Lutheran Protestants transformed it into a chorale tune by replacing the Latin text with one that combined German and Latin. Even today this jaunty Christmas carol is sung around the world, most often to the English words "Good Christian men rejoice."

The Organ in Bach's Day

The pipe organ, as is well known, makes sounds when air is forced through graduated rows of pipes, usually constructed of metal but sometimes of wood. Pipes of the same type are grouped together and produce a particular sound, and each group of similar-sounding pipes is called a **rank.** Some ranks are made to sound like violins, others like trumpets or horns, and still others like flutes or oboes. Every rank of pipes is activated by pulling out a small wooden knob called a **stop.** A rank of pipes can sound by itself or in combination with other ranks. Thus the fullest sound is made by "pulling out all the stops." The rows, or ranks, of pipes were placed in wooden chests, and one chest usually contained the big pipes for the lowest bass notes. Each of the chests was linked to one or more keyboards at the console of the organ, and a foot (pedal) keyboard was supplied for the bass notes. In Bach's day an assistant was needed to pump the bellows and thereby force air into the pipes, a task nowadays performed by an electrical pump.

Figures 39-1 and 39-2 show the organ at the New Church in Arnstadt, Germany. Dating from the early eighteenth century, it is the only organ Bach himself played that survives to the present day. The organ possesses two manuals and a pedal keyboard, and thus is a mid-size instrument by Bach's standards. A few large north German organs in Bach's time included more than fifty ranks of pipes and four manual keyboards plus one for the feet. One particular virtue of the organ rests in its multiple keyboards, which facilitate playing contrapuntal pieces. By assigning a particular rank of pipes with a distinctive tone color to a particular keyboard, the composer could project three, four, or five individual lines at once, all clearly differentiated from one another by means of their contrasting timbres.

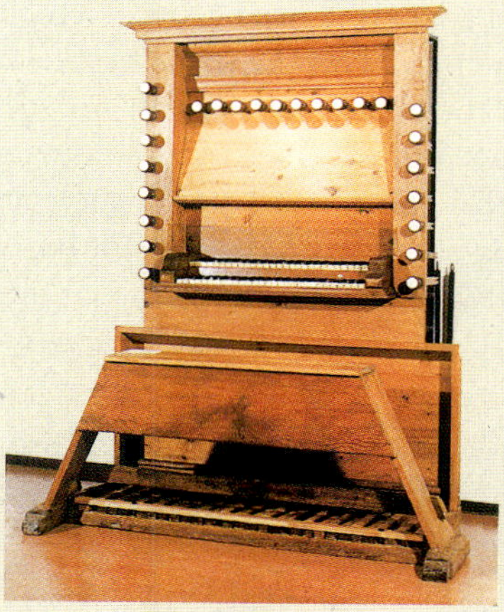

FIGURE 39-1
The console of the organ on which Bach played in the New Church at Arnstadt, Germany, now preserved in a local museum. The console with its keyboards served as the "central processor" for the instrument and sent information to the pipes indicating which were to sound.

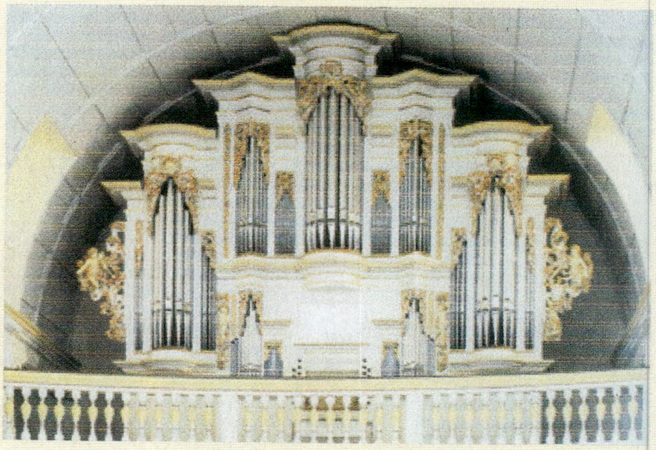

FIGURE 39-2
The pipes of the organ at Arnstadt remain today as they were in Bach's day, although the console of the instrument (Fig. 39-1) with its keyboards has been removed and replaced with a more modern one.

When Bach composed a chorale prelude, he usually placed the tune in the soprano and embellished it, lightly or heavily, with appropriate counterpoint. Here, the melody is indeed in the soprano and Bach does supply counterpoint, but he adds one other important element: canon. In truth, Bach was not the first to set "In dulci jubilo" in canon; earlier German composers had recognized that this melody could easily be set against itself at the distance of a measure because each downbeat is a member of the tonic triad. But Bach was not a man to allow himself to be outdone by any composer. Thus, for his setting of "In dulci jubilo," he created two canons—one between the soprano and bass featuring the chorale melody, and another between the alto and tenor serving as counterpoint against the tune. "In dulci jubilo" is one of the earliest manifestations of Bach's lifelong interest in canon.

EXAMPLE 39-1

At the end of "In dulci jubilo," Bach appends a brief coda in which the parts undulate above a constantly held low note played on the pedal keyboard of the organ. Because of its original association with the pedal of the organ, any such sustained or continually repeated pitch, usually placed in the bass and sounding while the harmonies change around it, is called a **pedal point.** Bach often concludes his keyboard works with such a sustained or repeating bass. Here a pedal point begins in the tenor range and three measures later the left hand adds its own "pedal point" an octave lower.

EXAMPLE 39-2

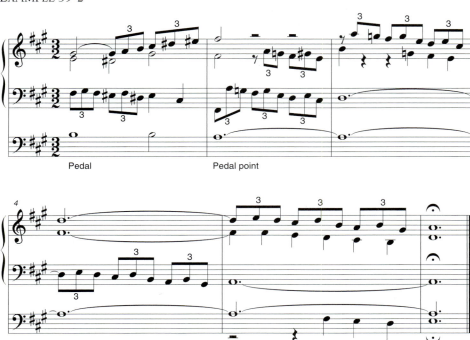

LISTENING CUE

JOHANN SEBASTIAN BACH	CD 6/3
Orgelbüchlein (c1710)	Anthology, No. 112
"In dulci jubilo" (BWV 608)	

Musical symbolism was an important part of Bach's expressive world. In the chorale prelude "In dulci jubilo" he surely chose to include a canon, indeed a double canon, because the text of the original Latin hymn ended with the plea to Christ: "Trahe me post te" ("Lead me after you"). Bach employs a different sort of musical symbolism in another famous chorale prelude from the *Orgelbüchlein*, "Durch Adams Fall ist ganz verderbt" ("Through Adam's Fall All Mankind Fell"). As the chorale tune sounds on high in the soprano, the alto and tenor provide contrapuntal embellishment below. The bass, however, has a different agendum. It falls precipitously in jagged, dissonant sevenths, thereby playing out through music Adam's "fall" into sin.

EXAMPLE 39-3

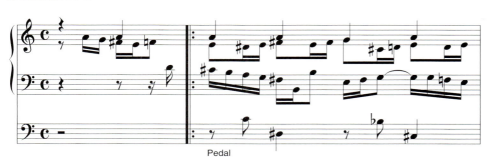

LISTENING CUE

JOHANN SEBASTIAN BACH	CD 6/4
Orgelbüchlein (c1710)	Anthology, No. 113
"Durch Adams Fall ist ganz verderbt"	
(BWV 637)	

BACH IN CÖTHEN: CHAMBER AND ORCHESTRAL MUSIC

By 1717 Bach had attained full maturity as a musician. He was also an ambitious man fully aware of his talents and his responsibility to his increasingly large family. To better his station in life, Bach now traveled to the court town of Cöthen (see Map 39-1) and successfully auditioned for the job of director of music. When Bach returned to Weimar to collect his family and possessions, Duke Wilhelm of Weimar had him thrown in jail for a month. The duke was not pleased that his musician had "jumped ship" to another court without ducal permission; musicians before Beethoven were little more than indentured servants. When released from jail on 2 December 1717, Bach fled to the court of Cöthen, where he remained for the next six years (1717–1723).

The position Bach assumed at Cöthen was very much a step up for him. He was appointed **Kapellmeister,** the term used in the Baroque and Classical periods to refer to the chief musician, not just of the chapel, but of the entire court. Cöthen, with a population of only 3,500, was not a big city. Nevertheless, it was ruled by an enlightened prince, Leopold of Anhalt-Cöthen, who loved music, played violin, and sang a passably good bass. Having served primarily as an organist at Weimar, Bach was engaged at Cöthen mainly to compose instrumental music. Indeed, his finest chamber and orchestral music dates from these years.

The Two- and Three-Part Inventions

Early in his career, Bach developed a reputation as a superb teacher. Even in Weimar he had attracted nearly a dozen pupils, some coming from great distances and boarding in the master's home. Not coincidentally, as teaching became an important part of his musical life, Bach began to assemble volumes of pedagogical materials for his pupils to play. The *Orgelbüchlein* was one such musical primer for organists. During the years 1720–1723 he compiled another collection of didactic pieces for keyboard players, which we now call the Two- and Three-Part Inventions (the Three-Part Inventions are also called the Sinfonia). The **Two- and Three-Part Inventions** (1723) are two sets of contrapuntal pieces along the lines of simple fugues. Each collection contains fifteen works and each of these is in a separate key (Bach avoids the keys farthest harmonically from C major). These "mini-fugues" require the player to develop a lyrical playing style and to use all five fingers equally; up to this time keyboardists had neglected the thumb (see Chapters 23 and 27). But Bach had a larger pedagogical plan in mind: having mastered two-voice and then three-voice contrapuntal pieces, the student would progress to even more digitally demanding material, the preludes and fugues of The Well-Tempered Clavier.

The Well-Tempered Clavier

Ever since its creation, The Well-Tempered Clavier (*Das wohltemperirte Clavier* in German) has served as the holy grail for harpsichordists and pianists; it is music of such rarified beauty and technical challenge that mastery of it can be a lifelong quest. **The Well-Tempered Clavier** is a collection of preludes and fugues by Bach in two books, one composed in Cöthen about 1720–1722 and the other in Leipzig during the late 1730s. Each volume contains twenty-four pairs of preludes and fugues arranged by key in ascending order—a prelude and fugue in C major is followed by one in C minor, and in turn by one in C♯ major and then C♯ minor, and so on. In this way all twelve pitches of the octave are supplied with a prelude and fugue in a major and minor key. The title implies that Bach now believed a keyboard instrument could, and indeed should, be tuned to play in all tonalities. Bach was gradually moving from a system of unequal temperament to something close to **equal temperament**—a division of the octave into twelve equal half-steps such as we have on the keyboard today (see Box, p. 349). By "clavier" Bach most likely intended to specify the harpsichord, although a performer in his day might try these pieces on the organ or clavichord as well.

To focus on only one prelude and fugue from The Well-Tempered Clavier is to do an injustice to the great variety of styles and designs throughout the collection. Yet the prelude and fugue in C minor from Book I deserves special attention. The prelude begins with blazing sixteenth notes in perpetual-motion style, giving the impression of a highly skilled player improvising a toccata on the spot. The arpeggiated chords change relentlessly, and the performer must jump with a wing and a prayer in hopes of landing on the right notes to begin each new figural pattern. Thumb and fifth finger in particular get a workout here. Finally, although the prelude is in a minor key, it concludes with a bright-sounding major triad. Such a shift from minor to major at the end of a piece is called a **Picardy third.** Musicologists don't know where or why this term was first used, but Baroque composers frequently ended minor-key pieces with a tonic major chord.

To this prelude Bach joined a companion fugue in C minor, a contrapuntal classic that has been analyzed by many musicians, including Bach himself. It begins with a theme, which in the case of a fugue we call the **subject.** This subject is an energetic one, its lively rhythms reminiscent of Italian instrumental music of the day. Typical of fugal composition, each voice presents the subject in turn in an opening section called the **exposition.** Sounding against this subject from time to time is a unit of thematically distinctive material called the **countersubject,** a counterpoint to the subject (Ex. 39-4). The fugue in C minor is a three-voice fugue (in this case alto, soprano, and bass), so once all three voices have presented the subject the exposition is complete. Next comes a free section, called an **episode,** based on motives derived from the subject. Episodes usually involve melodic sequences and

EXAMPLE 39-4

EXAMPLE 39-5

modulation, and this one carries the tonality by step from the tonic C minor up to the relative major E♭. Thereafter, single statements of the subject in different keys alternate with modulating episodes. The epicenter of this particular fugue is found in the episode at measures 17–19, where Bach composes **invertible counterpoint**; the motive which had been in the bass (A) is moved to the alto and the alto motive (B) is placed in the bass (Ex. 39-5). Notice also that motive B is none other than the original countersubject. Finally, the tonality swings around the circle of fifths before the bass and then soprano return with two statements of the subject in a last affirmation of the tonic key. Bach concludes this keyboard work, once again, with a pedal point and a Picardy third. Because no two fugues are alike, they are difficult to define. But a working definition of the term **fugue** might be as follows: a contrapuntal composition for two, three, four, or five voices, which begins with a presentation of a subject in imitation in each voice (exposition), continues with modulating passages of free counterpoint (episodes) and further appearances of the subject, and ends with a strong affirmation of the tonic key. Below is a visual approximation of how this C-minor fugue by Bach unfolds.

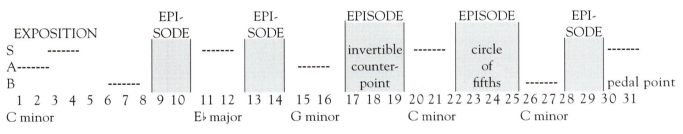

------- statement of the subject

LISTENING CUE

JOHANN SEBASTIAN BACH
The Well-Tempered Clavier (1722)
Prelude and Fugue in C Minor (BWV 847)

CD 6/5–6
Anthology, No. 114

Other Chamber Music

Much of Bach's chamber and orchestral music was written during his years in Cöthen (1717–1723). His position as Kapellmeister required that he compose for, as well as lead, the court orchestra, and that he also provide music for solo performances. In Bach's musical world, solo pieces, works for small ensembles, and even orchestral

Pitch and Tuning in Bach's Day

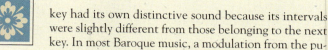

In Bach's day there was no such thing as standardized pitch. Indeed, the "rule" that concert pitch should be built around an "A" vibrating 440 times per second was not universally mandated until the International Organization for Standardization did so in 1955. The pitch A above middle C was set in Paris in Lully's time (c1675) at about 410 vibrations per second. A tuning fork associated with Handel gives the same A at 422.5. Things were even more variable in Bach's Germany, for here there was one pitch for the organs in church, and another for the instruments of the court or town orchestra. Yet despite the lack of a uniform standard for tuning (A 440, for example), a general trend emerged during the eighteenth century. Tuning slowly evolved from a tuning or temperament with unequal intervals in the various keys (see Musical Interludes 4 and 5) to one of equal temperament with equal intervals.

There were advantages and disadvantages to both the old and new system of tuning. In unequal temperaments, each key had its own distinctive sound because its intervals were slightly different from those belonging to the next key. In most Baroque music, a modulation from the purity of C major to the tension of E major, for example, was a more exciting journey than today. Similarly, a piece in F major sounded very different from one in A major. But the newer equal temperament had its advantages. The composer could modulate through many different keys, indeed all of them, without encountering unpleasant dissonance. Moreover, enharmonic equivalence was now possible; the key of C♯ major sounded exactly like that of D♭ major. Equal temperament was more bland, but more versatile.

In truth, we do not know if Bach's expression "well-tempered" means equal-tempered, or just something very close to equal-tempered. But The Well-Tempered Clavier is an important milestone in the long transition from a scale tuned in unequal intervals to the one tuned in equal intervals that we use today.

compositions were considered to be chamber music because all such music was performed in a domestic music room, or chamber (Fig. 39-3).

Among Bach's chamber pieces are a set of six sonatas for violin, another collection of three sonatas for *viola da gamba*, and yet another group of three for flute, all accompanied by obbligato harpsichord. The term **obbligato** (obliged or mandatory) indicates that a composer has written a specific part for an instrument and intends it to be played as written. Apparently, Bach was reluctant to allow other musicians to realize the figured bass parts to his sonatas. Instead, he often wrote out his own demanding keyboard accompaniments. For violinists and cellists, however, Bach's most important chamber music is to be found in his unaccompanied suites, sonatas, and partitas (**partita** is simply a word that Bach used as a synonym for suite). Here the string instrument is entirely alone.

The six unaccompanied violin sonatas and partitas are especially important. They provide violinists today with a basic repertory for both teaching and performance, just as The Well-Tempered Clavier does today for pianists and the six cello suites for cellists, and no self-respecting violinist can be without the set. Bach himself was a violinist, and his son C.P.E. Bach said that even into his old age his father played the instrument "cleanly and penetratingly." Bach's aim in his set of six works for solo violin is to build technique. Among other things, the player must learn to execute double, triple, and even quadruple stops (to play two, three, or four notes almost

❋ FIGURE 39-3
The recently refurbished Crystal Room at the palace of Cöthen where Bach's Brandenburg Concerto No. 5 was first performed.

Deutsches Staatsbibliothek, Berlin

simultaneously), as well as to maintain several polyphonic lines at once. Bach was determined to show that the violin could play a multi-voice fugue just as effectively as a keyboard instrument, so he made the second movement of each solo sonata a fugue. As Example 39-6 shows, while demonstrating that a violin can play a fugue, Bach also forces the performer to improve technique by stretching to get several notes in tune at once.

EXAMPLE 39-6

The Brandenburg Concertos

Among the concertos Bach composed while in Cöthen is a justly famous set of six called the **Brandenburg Concertos.** Bach's job at Cöthen required him to lead the court orchestra, conducting either from the harpsichord or the first violinist's desk. The Cöthen orchestra consisted of a group of about fifteen specialists, many of whom had come from the area of Berlin (see Map 39-1). In March 1719, Bach himself went to Berlin to pick up a large new harpsichord that Prince Leopold had ordered. While there, he met the Margrave Christian Ludwig of Brandenburg (1677–1734)—Brandenburg is a territory very near Berlin—who expressed an interest in Bach's music. When he returned to Cöthen, Bach assembled a set of six concerti grossi (some written earlier) and eventually sent them to the Margrave with a flowery dedication. Here Bach writes in French, the courtly language of the period, and with a groveling yet *gallant* tone typical of dedications at this time.

> As I [Bach] had the pleasure a couple of years ago of being heard by Your Royal Highness, in accordance with your commands, and observing that you took some delight in the small musical talent that Heaven has granted me, and as, when I took my leave of Your Royal Highness, you did me the honor of requesting that I send you some of my compositions, I have therefore followed your most gracious commands and taken the liberty of discharging my humble obligation to Your Royal Highness with the present concertos which I have adapted to several instruments. I beg you mostly humbly not to judge their imperfections by the standards of that refined and delicate taste in music that everyone knows you to possess, but rather to accept, with benign consideration, the profound respect and most humble devotion that I attempt to show by this means. . . . I desire nothing more than to be employed on occasions more worthy of you and your service, being with unparalleled zeal,
> Sire,
> Your Royal Highness's
> most humble and most obedient servant,
> Cöthen, 24 March 1721   Jean Sebastien Bach[1]

Most likely, the always-ambitious Bach was angling for a better job. Although no offer of employment was forthcoming from the Margrave, the collection of six concertos still today carries the name "Brandenburg."

In his dedication Bach refers to "the present concertos which I have adapted to several instruments." These words allude to the fact that he designed the Brandenburg Concertos to showcase a variety of orchestral colors. Recall that the concerto grosso consists of a basic orchestra of all players, called the *ripieno* (full) or tutti (all), and from this emerges a small core of soloists, called the *concertino*, to develop and decorate the primary musical themes (see Chapter 33). The various solo groups Bach features in the six Brandenburg Concertos (1721) are as follows.

Key	Movements	Concertino
No. 1 (BWV 1046) F major	[Allegro]-Adagio-Allegro-Minuet	2 horns, 3 oboes, bassoon and *violino piccolo*
No. 2 (BWV 1047) F major	[Allegro]-Andante-Allegro	Trumpet, recorder, oboe, and violin
No. 3 (BWV 1048) G major	[Allegro]-Adagio-Allegro	3 violins, 3 violas, and 3 cellos
No. 4 (BWV 1049) G major	[Allegro]-Andante-Presto	Violin and 2 recorders
No. 5 (BWV 1050) D major	Allegro-Affettuoso-Allegro	Harpsichord, violin, and flute
No. 6 (BWV 1051) B♭ major	[Allegro]-Adagio-Allegro	2 violas, 2 *viole da gamba*, and cello

Let us concentrate on Concerto No. 5, for in this work Bach himself surely functioned as the harpsichord soloist during performances at Cöthen. Concerto No. 5 pits the full orchestra against a *concertino*, consisting of harpsichord, violin, and flute. As with most concerti grossi, the first movement is written in ritornello form, a musical plan popularized by Corelli and Vivaldi. In principle, ritornello form demands that the *ripieno* (tutti) play the ritornello while the *concertino* executes either motives derived from the ritornello or free material that complements it. With Bach, however, the separation between ritornello theme and concertino excursion is not as clear-cut as it had been with Corelli and Vivaldi (see Chapter 33). In Bach's more complex design, the distinction between the large ensemble and the small group of soloists is less pronounced. Nonetheless, Bach's ritornello theme is typical of Baroque melodies in three distinctive ways (Ex. 39-7): it is idiomatic to the violin (repeated notes are easy to play on string instruments); it is lengthy and somewhat asymmetrical; and it possesses a driving rhythm that propels the music forward. As the first movement proceeds, the violin and flute gradually fall by the wayside to allow the harpsichord to carry all the solo material. What had started as a concerto grosso has become a showpiece for solo harpsichord. Bach has written, in fact if not in name, the first true solo concerto for keyboard. Only a virtuoso of the highest order can play the extremely difficult passage-work found toward the end of the movement. But Bach was just this sort of keyboard virtuoso. Picture in your mind's eye the orchestra at Cöthen playing in the prince's music room (see Fig. 39-3). At the center of it all was Bach, seated at the large, new harpsichord he had brought from Berlin, and astounding the members of the court with his bravura playing.

EXAMPLE 39-7

LISTENING CUE

JOHANN SEBASTIAN BACH
Brandenburg Concerto No. 5 in D Major
  (BWV 1050; 1721)
First movement

CD 6/7
Anthology, No. 115

SUMMARY

Johann Sebastian Bach wrote many important vocal works, including some three hundred cantatas for the Lutheran church. But the majority of his nearly 1,100 works are for instruments of one kind or another. In his day Bach was known more as a virtuoso organist than as a composer. Bach also played cello, viola, and violin, and early in his career was hired at a court as a violinist. Throughout his life Bach was also a renowned teacher. Many of his best-known instrumental pieces were conceived of, and are still used today, as sets of instructional works. They intend to develop the technical skills and overall musical understanding of the performer. Among Bach's pedagogical projects are the *Orgelbüchlein* (a series of chorale preludes intended to cover the entire church year), the Two- and Three-Part Inventions, the two books of The Well-Tempered Clavier, the six violin sonatas and partitas, and the six cello suites. Bach's complete understanding of the idiomatic capabilities and distinctive colors of the instruments of the Baroque orchestra can best be seen in his Brandenburg Concertos. In this one collection of six concerti grossi, Bach demonstrates a mastery of virtually every instrumental combination and type of orchestral scoring known in his day.

KEY TERMS

BWV (Bach Werke
  Verzeichnis)
Orgelbüchlein
chorale prelude
rank
stop
pedal point
Kapellmeister

Two- and Three-Part
  Inventions
The Well-Tempered
  Clavier
equal temperament
Picardy third
subject
exposition

countersubject
episode
invertible counterpoint
fugue
obbligato
partita
Brandenburg Concertos

Chapter 40

Johann Sebastian Bach: Vocal Music in Leipzig

In the spring of 1723, Bach moved to the city of Leipzig, and there he remained until his death in 1750. Leipzig, with 30,000 inhabitants, was a large German city by the standards of the day, and it boasted an important university where Bach's sons (but not daughters) might enroll. The position that Bach assumed in Leipzig was that of **cantor** (director of church music) at the St. Thomas Church, the largest and most important church in this Lutheran city. While the post of cantor was a prestigious one, the incumbent was nonetheless a civil servant selected by and answerable to the Leipzig town council. Surprisingly, Bach was not the first choice of the city fathers. Only after the well-known composer Georg Philipp Telemann (1681–1767) and the now obscure Christoph Graupner (1683–1760) declined the post, did the members of the town council reluctantly turn to Bach. When he assumed the position in Leipzig, it was understood that Bach would henceforth turn his attention away from instrumental music for the court and would instead concentrate on religious vocal music for the church.

Bach's job in Leipzig was not an easy one. He was required to play the organ at weddings and funerals, teach music and sometimes even Latin grammar to the boys of the choir school of St. Thomas, and superintend the liturgical music of the four principal churches of the city. But by far the most demanding duty of his position as cantor was to provide about a half-hour of new music for the church each Sunday and religious holiday, a total of about sixty days a year. In so doing, Bach brought an important genre of religious music, the Lutheran chorale cantata, to the highest point of its development.

THE LUTHERAN CHORALE CANTATA

When Bach arrived in Leipzig in 1723, he set about composing a cycle of cantatas for the entire church year. In fact, over the next few years he created five such cycles, nearly 300 cantatas in total (although only about two hundred of these survive today). The cantata was the musical high point of the Sunday service. In Bach's time, St. Thomas Church celebrated a Sunday Mass as prescribed two centuries earlier by Martin Luther (1483–1546). Attended by some 2,000 of the faithful, the St. Thomas service began at seven o'clock in the morning and lasted nearly four hours. Following a few introductory chants and prayers, a celebrant read the day's scriptural message from the Gospel. The organist then played a chorale prelude to remind the congregation of the chorale melody of the day and give the instrumentalists an opportunity to tune. At this point, the choir and instrumentalists performed the cantata under Bach's direction. The cantata served as a musical elaboration upon the spiritual theme of the Gospel. Thereafter, a preacher ascended the pulpit (Fig. 40-1) to offer an hour-long sermon discussing the moral and practical implications of this spiritual message. Later that afternoon, the choir and instrumentalists repeated the cantata at a Vespers service at the St. Nicolas Church across town, where an equally large congregation awaited Bach's music.

Typical of the cantatas Bach composed for Leipzig is *Wachet auf, ruft uns die Stimme* (*Awake, A Voice Is Calling*; BWV 140), a work built upon a chorale tune of the same name. A chorale, as we have seen (see Chapter 24), is simply the German version of what most English-speaking communities would call a hymn. *Wachet auf* is a texted chorale tune written in the sixteenth century and widely used by musicians in the Lutheran church before Bach took it up. The structure of the tune is typical of chorale melodies (Ex. 40-1). It is

FIGURE 40-1

Interior of the St. Thomas Church in the mid nineteenth century, looking across the parishioners' pews toward the high altar. Notice the pulpit on the right from which the sermon would be delivered.

composed of seven phrases that unfold in a pattern **AAB,** specifically **A** (1, 2, 3), **A** (1, 2, 3) **B** (4-7, 3).

EXAMPLE 40-1

A. Awake, a voice is calling
   From the watchmen from high in the tower
   Awake, Jerusalem!
   Midnight is the hour
   They call us with a clarion voice
   Where are the Wise Virgins?

B. Get up, the Bridegroom comes
   Stand up and take your lamps
   Alleluia
   Prepare yourselves
   For the wedding
   You must go forth to meet him!

Because it is based upon a chorale tune, Bach's *Wachet auf* is called a chorale cantata, a genre of music that arose in Germany in the late seventeenth century. The **chorale cantata** is a sacred vocal genre that employs the text and tune of a preexisting Lutheran chorale in all or several of its movements. *Wachet auf* makes use of a traditional chorale melody during each of its three choral movements, which present the hymn's three textual stanzas in succession. The intervening movements, consisting of recitatives and duet-arias, represent Bach's newly composed settings of the lyrical poems by one of his contemporaries, and use neither the chorale tune nor its text. Thus, Bach creates a formal symmetry, with the chorale-based choral movements at the beginning, middle, and end, flanking each of the recitative-aria pairs and providing a structural framework for the composition as a whole.

			Movement:			
1	2	3	4	5	6	7
Chorus	Recitative	Aria (duet)	Chorus	Recitative	Aria (duet)	Chorus
1st stanza			2nd stanza			3rd stanza

Bach was a devoted husband, a loving father to twenty children, and a respected burgher of Leipzig. His cantata *Wachet auf* clearly shows his faith in the religious traditions of his German Lutheran community. Bach composed it in 1731 for a service on a Sunday immediately before Advent (four Sundays before Christmas). The text of the cantata announces the coming of a bridegroom toward his hopeful bride. Christ is the groom. A group of ten virgins represents the bride and, by extension, the entire Christian community. Their story, the Parable of the Wise and Foolish Virgins, is told in the Gospel of St. Matthew (25:1–13); five of the Virgins have brought oil for their lamps and are prepared to meet the coming Christ, but five have not. Both the Gospel and Bach's cantata proclaim this central message: Here

Bach's Choir and Orchestra: Where Were the Ladies?

During the seventeenth century, women frequently appeared as soloists on the operatic stage and occasionally in vocal and instrumental music-making at court. As the eighteenth century progressed, women also began to sing religious music in churches and theaters. But the Lutheran church was a conservative institution in Bach's day. Aside from a few small rural churches where ladies were allowed to appear as "choral adjuncts," women played no role in the performance of Lutheran church music. Ultimately, this traditionalist attitude affected the way the Bach family conducted its business.

When Bach arrived in Leipzig in 1723, he was accompanied by his four children and his second wife, Anna Magdalena Bach (his first wife had died unexpectedly in 1720). Anna Magdalena was a gifted singer who had been employed by the court of Cöthen at a salary almost as great as that of her new husband. But moving to the Lutheran church position in Leipzig forced her to give up her career as a performer. Henceforth, Anna Magdalena would serve as the nucleus of what might be termed "Bach Incorporated"—that industrious group of some dozen or so children, relatives, and students who copied each new Bach cantata and all the necessary parts in preparation for the coming Sunday service. In their quarters next to the St. Thomas Church (Fig. 40-2), Anna Magdalena copied manuscript after manuscript for her husband. She may have assisted him with rehearsals as well.

The actual public performance of a cantata by Bach, however, was an all-male affair. In 1730 Bach stipulated clearly the nature of the orchestra and chorus he required for his sacred vocal music. He drew his instrumentalists from a pool of a dozen string and wind players employed by the town, and these men were supplemented by students from the (all-male) University of Leipzig. Although Bach wanted an orchestra of some twenty players, fifteen seems to have been the norm, and sometimes even fewer were on hand. As to the singers, for the standard four-part choir Bach required at least three singers on each part, though he said he preferred four for a total of sixteen singers. Often, however, many fewer were actually on hand. All of the vocalists—soloists as well as choral singers—were boys or young men from the St. Thomas choir school or the nearby university. Thus the alto and soprano choral parts in Bach's sacred music were sung by males (young men in falsetto voice and boys), and the difficult soprano solos were executed by a solitary choirboy. Indeed, the ladies never did get a fair hearing.

Bach-Archiv, Leipzig

❀ FIGURE 40-2
Leipzig, the St. Thomas Church (center), and the choir school (left), from an engraving of 1723, the year in which Bach moved to the city. Bach and his large family occupied two floors of the choir school, and it was here that the composing, copying, and rehearsing of his music took place.

in the season of Advent all good citizens of Leipzig should put their spiritual houses in order, for Christ will soon be with them.

The spiritually attuned listener can hear the inexorable march of Christ in the opening movement of cantata *Wachet auf*. Here Bach creates a chorale fantasy that is both dramatic and monumental. First the orchestra announces Christ's arrival by means of a three-part ritornello (Ex. 40-2). The ritornello conveys a feeling of growing anticipation. The increasingly numerous sixteenth notes suggest the urgent movement of the faithful surging forward to meet the coming Christ. Then the ancient chorale melody enters on high in the sopranos; it is the voice of tradition, perhaps the voice of God. In long, steady notes, it enjoins the populace to prepare to receive the Lord. Beneath this the voices of the people—the altos, tenors, and basses—scurry in rapid counterpoint, eager to meet their savior. Lowest of all is the bass of the basso continuo. It moves steadily ahead, mainly in stepwise motion in notes of similar value. This walking bass enhances the meaning of the text, underscoring the steady approach of the Lord. The enormous complexity of the movement, with its dense textural layering and rich symbolism, shows why musicians, then and now, view Bach as the greatest contrapuntalist who ever lived.

EXAMPLE 40-2

LISTENING CUE

JOHANN SEBASTIAN BACH
Cantata BWV 140, *Wachet auf, ruft uns die Stimme* (1731)
Movement 1

CD 6/8
Anthology, No. 116a

Movement 2 is a recitative for tenor solo, a narrator who announces the imminent arrival of Christ, the bridegroom. This is an example of simple recitative because the accompaniment is limited to a basso continuo, featuring in this case the organ and bassoon. Generally speaking, in his sacred vocal works Bach assigns the role of the narrator, or evangelist, to a tenor.

Movement 3 is a lengthy duet for soprano (the Soul) and bass (Christ). In German sacred music of the Baroque period, the role of Christ is traditionally assigned to a bass. Here Bach ornaments the charming soprano-bass duet with a lengthy ritornello played by a ***violino piccolo*** (a small violin usually tuned a minor third higher than the normal violin).

Movement 4 calls upon the chorale melody once again. Now Bach places the tune (and the second stanza of the chorale text) in long notes in the tenor voice alone. The tenors are the watchmen of Zion who call Jerusalem (Leipzig) to awake. Beneath this chorale the bass plods forward, mostly in unwavering quarter notes. This classic example of a Baroque walking bass again suggests the inevitable coming of Christ. Against the tenor and bass the violins and violas play a hauntingly beautiful ritornello (Ex. 40-3). It is exactly twelve bars long and subdivided into six two-bar groups—an unusually symmetrical construction for Bach. Perhaps because of the symmetrical, lyrical style of the ritornello, this movement has become one of Bach's most beloved compositions. Indeed, it was one of Bach's favorites too, for it was the only cantata movement that he published.[1] All the rest of his Leipzig cantatas were left in handwritten scores at the time of his death.

EXAMPLE 40-3

> **LISTENING CUE**
>
> **JOHANN SEBASTIAN BACH**
> Cantata, *Wachet auf, ruft uns die Stimme*
> Movements 2, 3, and 4
>
> CD 6/9–10 and
> Thomson-Schirmer Website
> Anthology, No. 116b-d

Movement 5 is an **accompanied recitative** in which the bass soloist (representing Christ) invites the anguished Soul to find comfort in him. Unlike the tenor's simple recitative (movement 2), this movement features strings providing a lush chordal accompaniment, creating a halo-like effect to surround the words of Christ—another example of musical symbolism in Bach.

Movement 6 is a duet between Christ and the Soul, who are once again represented by the bass and soprano soloists. Bach wrote no operas, and indeed by the time he arrived in 1723 the Leipzig opera house had closed for good. But he frequently went to nearby Dresden (see Map 39-1), where the court sponsored a flourishing opera, one of the best in Europe. In movement 6, Bach comes as close as he ever will to composing an operatic love duet. In fact, the piece is a perfect *da capo* aria of the sort that might be found in a Baroque *opera seria*.

Movement 7 is a four-part harmonization of the chorale tune that sets the third and final stanza of the chorale text. Here the full congregation joined in the singing of the chorale, likely not by reading from a hymnal but by singing the tune from memory. In this concluding movement, all of the instrumental parts double the vocal lines, a technique termed ***colla parte*** (with the part). Here too all the spiritual energy of Leipzig was united in Bach's simple but expressive harmony.

EXAMPLE 40-4

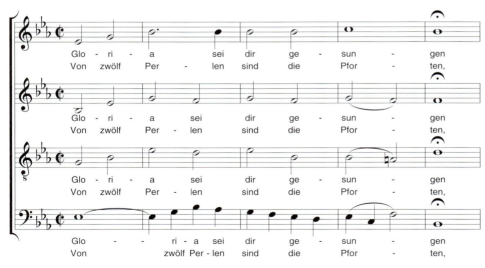

May glory be sung to you…
The gates are of twelve pearls…

Bach's Four-Part Chorale Harmonizations and Teaching Music Theory Today

Today in colleges, universities, and music conservatories around the world, the study of music theory is grounded in a thorough investigation of four-voice chorale harmonizations by Johann Sebastian Bach. Almost all students majoring in music, for example, study Bach chorales to learn how to write, and thereby understand, proper chord progressions, modulations, and voice leadings. They compose the "missing" three voices (bass, tenor, and alto) below ancient chorale melodies in the style of Bach. Thus the model of Bach, established nearly three hundred years ago, lies at the core of much theory pedagogy today. But would Bach have approved?

Indeed, he would have, for this was precisely the method of teaching Bach himself employed. C.P.E. Bach, the master's second son, said this about his father's approach to teaching harmony: "His pupils had to begin their studies by learning pure four-part thorough [figured] bass. From this he went to chorales; first he added the basses to them himself, and they had to invent the alto and the tenor. Then he taught them to devise the basses themselves."[2] Bach also encouraged his students to copy into their notebooks four-part chorale settings from his passions and cantatas (such as, for example, the final movement of the cantata *Wachet auf*). Owing in part to these notebooks of Bach's students, 371 of Bach's chorale settings have been preserved for us to study today. Thus, in a sense, we are all students of Bach.

LISTENING CUE

JOHANN SEBASTIAN BACH	CD 6/11–13
Cantata, *Wachet auf, ruft uns die Stimme*	Anthology, No. 116e-g
Movements 5, 6, and 7	

In addition to some three hundred cantatas, Johann Sebastian Bach is said to have composed five passions and a Christmas oratorio, all large-scale works. A **passion** is a musical depiction of Christ's crucifixion as recorded in the Gospels; it is traditionally performed on Good Friday. By Bach's time, a passion had become virtually identical to an oratorio, except that it dealt with just one subject, the death of Christ. Of Bach's five passions, only two survive, the St. John Passion (1724) and the St. Matthew Passion (1727). The former requires about two hours to perform, and the latter two-and-a-half. Perhaps for that reason, members of the Bach family called the St. Matthew setting the "Great Passion." It requires three choirs and two small orchestras, each with a colorful variety of instruments. Many believe the St. Matthew Passion, with no fewer than sixty-eight expressive movements, to be Bach's greatest dramatic work.

BACH'S LATER MUSICAL PROJECTS

By 1730 Bach had tired of the weekly grind of creating new music for the church each Sunday. He did not relinquish his position at the St. Thomas Church, but gave it less time as he turned his attention to other musical activities. In late March 1729, Bach assumed directorship of the Collegium Musicum in Leipzig. A **collegium musicum** was an association of musicians, usually university students, who came together voluntarily to play the latest music before the public in a large café or beer hall. (The name "collegium" is still used today by performing groups in colleges and universities, although now the emphasis is not on a repertory of modern music, but on early music as played on reproductions of historical instruments.) Bach directed the Collegium Musicum of Leipzig, on and off, for at least a dozen years. It provided an opportunity for him to compose and perform orchestral music—concertos and orchestral suites—something that his recent preoccupation with church music in Leipzig had not allowed him to do.

Not only did Bach turn to projects beyond the St. Thomas Church in his last decades but he also looked beyond the city limits of Leipzig. In 1733 he composed a *Kyrie* and *Gloria* for the court in Dresden, which would later serve as the opening movements of his great B-Minor Mass (see below). Another work destined for Dresden at this time is Bach's **Goldberg Variations** (BWV 988), a virtuosic set of thirty variations preceded and concluded by a simple air, the air and each variation based on the same thirty-two-bar harmonic pattern. The collection derives its name from a gifted pupil of Bach, Johann Goldberg, who worked for one of Bach's patrons in Dresden. It seems that the patron was something of an insomniac and asked Bach for music that Goldberg might play to alleviate the tedium of his sleepless nights.

In 1747 Bach undertook his last substantial journey, a trip to Berlin to visit his son, Carl Philipp Emanuel Bach. C.P.E. Bach was employed as a keyboardist at the court of King Frederick the Great of Prussia (1712–1786), who himself was a musical enthusiast, being a skilled flautist. Bach arrived in the evening, when Frederick, as was his custom, was playing chamber music with his court musicians. Immediately the king went to a keyboard to play a melody he had composed, and asked Bach to improvise a fugue on it on the spot. This Bach did in a way such that the king and his courtiers alike "were seized with astonishment," as a newspaper of the day reported. But Bach himself was not satisfied. When he returned home to Leipzig he set about making the royal theme serve as the unifying element, not merely in a single fugue, but in a collection of pieces: a trio sonata, two fugues (called ricercars), and ten puzzle canons. Bach called his royally inspired collection **The Musical Offering** (BWV 1079) and dedicated it to His Majesty with appropriately inflated praise of the king's musical talent. In truth, however, The Musical Offering reveals how the genius of Bach was needed to unlock the full musical potential of the king's original idea.

Bach's other great encyclopedic work is The Art of Fugue, which he began about 1740 and had not quite finished at the time of his death a decade later. **The Art of Fugue** (BWV 1080) is a collection of fugues and canons, all derived from the same subject (Bach's own) and all apparently intended for keyboard. Here we see exemplified almost every contrapuntal technique known to musicians. When published after his death, it consisted of fourteen fugues and four canons, all written in score and most for four voices. Bach intended the final fugue to be a quadruple fugue, but it breaks off shortly after the exposition of the fourth subject. Appropriately, this last subject is built upon the four pitches B♭, A, C, B♮, which in German musical notation spells the word BACH.

The Goldberg Variations, The Musical Offering, and The Art of Fugue demonstrate Bach's focus on large-scale musical projects during the last decade of his life. In each of these he brought one particular form of composition—variation, puzzle canon, or fugue—to a level of excellence that was never surpassed.

B-Minor Mass

Bach's last composition, his **B-Minor Mass** (BWV 232), is perhaps the grandest of all of these large-scale projects, for here he brought the tradition of the Baroque Latin Mass to a glorious culmination. As we have seen, Bach had composed the *Kyrie* and *Gloria* for the court of Catholic Dresden back in 1733. Now, in 1748, in old age and declining health, the master determined to extend the work by adding a *Credo*, *Sanctus*, and *Agnus*, and thus create a complete setting of the Ordinary of the Mass as sung for centuries in the Roman Catholic Church. For these additional movements, Bach did not compose entirely new music. Instead, he refashioned movements of cantatas and Masses that he had written years before. For example, a *Sanctus* written in 1724 became the opening of the *Sanctus* of the B-Minor Mass; a movement of a cantata of 1714 (*Weinen, Klagen* [*To Whine and Wail*, BWV 12]) was reworked to serve as the "Crucifixus" of the *Credo*. Bach borrowed from this earlier cantata because its subject matter (weeping) was signalled by a descending tetrachordal bass, the Baroque emblem of mourning. The vocal parts of the "Cruci-fixus" are thus filled with dissonant, painful tritones and augmented seconds, all created in the score by the use of many sharps (but no flats). The sharp, of course, is cruciform or cross-like, in shape; this is the way Bach's musical symbolism works.

EXAMPLE 40-5

Today we may be scandalized that Bach chose to re-use so much previously written material in what would be his last great work. But virtually all composers of the Baroque period engaged in this practice. (Handel was an especially notorious "borrower.") It gave the artist a chance to review an earlier work, revise it, and thereby improve the score. For Bach in particular, this process of musical review provided yet another opportunity to perfect his art, and Bach was nothing if not a perfectionist.

LISTENING CUE

JOHANN SEBASTIAN BACH
B-Minor Mass (BWV 232; 1749)
Credo, "Crucifixus" (begun 1714; final form 1749)

CD 6/14
Anthology, No. 117a

The turn to the relative major at the end of the "Crucifixus" sounds a note of hope to be realized in the next movement, "Et resurrexit" ("And He arose").

The theme of Christ's resurrection now receives an appropriately triumphant setting. With large orchestra and brilliant trumpets sounding in a sprightly triple meter, the music seems to dance joyfully toward heaven. Unlike the "Crucifixus," which was refashioned from much-earlier music, the "Et resurrexit" was apparently newly composed. Indeed, these notes must have been among the last that Bach wrote. Thus what we call the great B-Minor Mass is a compilation of pieces that Bach had composed over the course of three decades. It represents a culmination of all that he had learned about writing sacred music for the church.

LISTENING CUE

JOHANN SEBASTIAN BACH
B-Minor Mass (1749)
Credo, "Et resurrexit" (1749)

CD 6/15
Anthology, No. 117b

Bach's B-Minor Mass is a massive five-movement sacred work that takes some two hours to perform. During the composer's lifetime, the Mass was never heard in its entirety. It was inappropriate for the Lutheran church because it contains portions of the Mass text not used in the Lutheran service; likewise, it was unsuitable for the Catholic liturgy due to its length and the freedoms taken with the text. Nor could it have been sung simply as a concert—concerts of purely religious music as we know them did not exist in Bach's day. Today the B-Minor Mass is performed in concert halls around the world. It is appreciated less as a Catholic Mass and more as a work that transcends denominations. Like Beethoven's Ninth Symphony, Bach's B-Minor Mass is his ecumenical gift to all humanity.

SUMMARY

When Johann Sebastian Bach died during the summer of 1750, apparently of a stroke, he and his music were soon forgotten. With its heavy reliance on traditional chorale tunes and dense counterpoint, his creations were thought to be too old-fashioned and rigid, even pedantic. Yes, Bach's music is often difficult. He was intent on discovering and exploiting the musical potential of every idea, and he took no shortcuts. In so doing, Bach created grand projects that demonstrate the special qualities of almost every musical genre and form except opera—organ prelude, prelude and fugue, solo sonata, concerto grosso, cantata, passion, variation set, puzzle canon, and Latin Mass. These encyclopedic projects offer a splendid summation of music of the Baroque era.

But as early as the 1730s new musical currents were in the air, those of the Enlightenment. The public wanted lighter textures, simple phrasing, and tuneful melodies. Although Bach's sons adjusted to the tastes of the day, "the old Wig," as one of them irreverently called him, did so only sporadically. Thus, shortly after 1750, the mention of the name "Bach" would likely have conjured up the image of one or the other of his fashionable sons, not the great polyphonic master. Yet, a small group of musicians, including Mozart, Beethoven, Schumann, and Mendelssohn, kept the knowledge of Bach's extraordinary music alive. When Mendelssohn performed Bach's St. Matthew Passion in 1829 as part of a centenary commemoration, a "Bach revival" was underway. From that time on, musicians have never ceased to admire Bach's music for its internal integrity, grand design, and superhuman craftsmanship.

  KEY TERMS

cantor
chorale cantata
violino piccolo
accompanied recitative

colla parte
passion
collegium musicum
Goldberg Variations

The Musical Offering
The Art of Fugue
B-Minor Mass

THE ENLIGHTENMENT AND THE CLASSICAL ERA

*H*istory is a seamless flow. When politicians act, artists create, and philosophers think, they do so without concern for periodicity. Historians look back and group together earlier leaders, artists, and thinkers within a fixed historical period because common themes seem to unite their aims and modes of expression—ones distinctly different from what came before and after. Music historians, for example, find it convenient to mark the end of the Baroque period at 1750 with the death of Bach. But choosing this or any other year oversimplifies an evolutionary process. Need-

1650	1700	1750

BAROQUE PERIOD (1600–1750)   **ENLIGHTENMENT**

Tsar Peter the Great (r. 1682–1725)

King Frederick

Antoine Watteau (1684–1721), French painter

Domenico Scarlatti (1685–1757), Italian composer

c1700 Bartolomeo Cristofori (1655–1732) invents the piano in Florence, Italy

Giovanni Battista Sammartini (c1700–1775), leader in creation of concert

Johann Stamitz (1717–1757), composer and

Empress Maria Theresa of Austria (1717–1780)

1725 *Concert spirituel* founded in Paris

Johann Christian Bach

Carl Ditters von

Giovanni Paisiello

André Grétry

Joseph Haydn (1732–1809)

Bridgeman Art Library

Wolfgang Amadeus Mozart (1756–1791)

CORBIS

Ludwig van Beethoven (1770–1827)

CORBIS

less to say, composers did not stop writing in one musical style one day and start in a new one the next. Often elements of baroque music coexisted with those of the emerging Classical style. The decades from 1730 to 1770 were a time of gradual transition. This period of musical change coincided with an intellectual era called the Enlightenment, a philosophical, scientific, and political movement that dominated eighteenth-century thought. Similarly, the years 1770–1820 encompass the music of Haydn, Mozart, and Beethoven, three composers with sometimes very different musical styles. Yet their modes of expression, which build upon traditional principles of balance and proportion, have much in common. The music of all these composers comprises the Classical era.

Part V

| 1750 | 1800 | 1850 |

(1730–1770)   CLASSICAL PERIOD (1770–1820)

the Great of Prussia (r. 1740–1786)

Napoleon Bonaparte (1769–1821)

Franz Schubert (1797–1828), composer

♦ **1776 Adam Smith publishes *Wealth of Nations***

1796–1815 Napoleonic Wars

symphony

conductor of Mannheim orchestra

Carl Czerny (1791–1857), composer and one of Beethoven's best students

● 1805 *Fidelio* premieres at the Theater-an-der-Wien

● 1810 Metronome invented in Vienna

1814–1815 Congress of Vienna

(1735–1782), composer (son of J. S. Bach)

Dittersdorf (1739–1799), composer and friend of Mozart

(1740–1816), composer of Italian *opera buffa*

(1741–1813), French opera composer

Johann Wolfgang von Goethe (1749–1832), German poet

Lorenzo da Ponte (1749–1838), librettist

Antonio Rosetti (1750–1792), composer of symphonies

Antonio Salieri (1750–1825), official court composer to Emperor Joseph II

Muzio Clementi (1752–1832), pianist and rival to Mozart

Ignace Pleyel (1757–1831), pupil of Haydn and composer

Luigi Cherubini (1760–1842), composer of opera

Catherine the Great (r. 1762–1796)

Chapter 41

Music in the Age of Enlightenment: Opera

The **Enlightenment** was a philosophical, scientific, and political movement that dominated eighteenth-century thought. Ultimately, it brought about wholesale social revolution, transforming a society that had been ruled mainly by court and church into one governed by more democratic institutions. During the Enlightenment, also called the Age of Reason, scientists gave free rein to the pursuit of truth and the discovery of natural laws. Faith in human reason replaced faith in divine intervention. This era saw the rise of a natural religion called Deism, the belief that a Creator made the world, set it in motion, and left it alone thereafter. Much of this philosophy sprang from the *Principia mathematica (Mathematical Principles)* of Isaac Newton (1642–1727), which postulates that the universe runs according to natural laws such as gravity. Social scientists like Hume in England and Voltaire in France tried to extend these natural scientific laws into the realm of political action. They attacked the privileges and abuses of the established court and church. Gradually, age-old customs and beliefs (or superstitions) were pruned away. In many French churches, medieval stained glass was removed in favor of clear glass, a literal act of "enlightenment."

Most important, the principles of the Enlightenment incited a revolt against the monarchy and the *status quo*. At first the attack came from the written word, not the sword. A French *Encyclopédie*, by far the most comprehensive work of its kind to date, was produced between 1751 and 1772; the first *Encyclopedia Britannica* appeared in 1768. The twenty-eight volume *Encyclopédie* was compiled by a group of French freethinkers called **les philosophes**, including the important trio Denis Diderot (1713–1784), Jean-Jacques Rousseau (1712–1778), and François-Marie Arouet, known as Voltaire (1694–1778). They espoused the principles of social justice, equality, religious tolerance, and freedom of speech. Voltaire, in particular, made fun of the habits and privileges of both clergy and aristocracy. The frilled cuffs, pink stockings, and powdered wig of the courtier were an easy target for his pen. A more natural appearance, one appropriate to a tradesman, merchant, or manufacturer, was his ideal. Pretension and privilege should yield to common sense and social equality, although some (women and slaves) would still be decidedly less equal.

Needless to say, the notion that all persons (or at least free men) were created equal put the thinkers of the Enlightenment on a collision course with the defenders of the existing social order. Spurred on by economic self-interest and the principles of the philosophers, an increasingly numerous and self-confident middle class in America and France rebelled against the monarchy. The American Revolution began in 1776 and the French Revolution in 1789. The Enlightenment philosophers had done their work.

Jean-Jacques Rousseau, a leading Enlightenment philosopher, advocated that all government should be based on the consent of the governed rather than the divine right of kings. For Rousseau, nature was the source of all good art, and the "noble savage" was far superior to the civilized courtier. Rousseau was also a musician. As a youth he taught music and worked as a music copyist when money was scarce. He later wrote the articles on music for the *Encyclopédie* and compiled a *Dictionnaire de musique* (1768) with 900 entries, the first modern musical dictionary. Throughout his *Dictionnaire*, Rousseau argued that musical expression should be simple and natural, relying on melody as the main vehicle of communication. For Rousseau, issues of the heart were equal to those of the head.

But Rousseau, not satisfied to be a musical philosopher, also tried his hand at composition. Among his surviving works is a comic opera called *Le Devin du village* (*The Village Soothsayer*, 1752), for which he created both libretto and music. Rousseau's story line, in which true love (assisted by a bit of magic) triumphs over wealth and status, reflects his democratic leanings. The overture ends with a simple dance (a piano reduction is given in Ex. 41-1). Rousseau's phrases are short and arranged in neat four-bar units. His texture is light, being concentrated on the outer voices; the first and second violins generally skip along in pleasing parallel thirds. Finally, with the expression mark "Gai" he asks the performers to play with a carefree spirit.

EXAMPLE 41-1

Music historians use the French term **galant** style (rather than "Enlightenment style") to describe eighteenth-century music such as this, music that is graceful, light in texture, and generally symmetrical in melodic structure. The *galant* ideal of a graceful melody with a simple accompaniment is indeed fully harmonious with the Enlightenment values of naturalness, clarity, and simplicity. But the *galant* idiom was just one of many styles to be heard during the Enlightenment.

MUSIC OF THE ESTABLISHMENT: ENLIGHTENMENT OPERA SERIA

To appreciate the plurality of musical styles that existed during the Enlightenment, we begin by visiting the electoral-royal court of Dresden, Germany. Dresden was seat of the Elector of Saxony.[†] In the early eighteenth century, the elector was

---

[†]As we have seen, in German history, an elector was one of nine powerful princes with the right to vote in the election to choose the Holy Roman Emperor.

Gemäldegalerie, Dresden

❧ FIGURE 41-1

Soprano Faustina Bordoni, wife of composer Johann Hasse, who sang the title role in his opera *Cleofide*. She and her rival Francesca Cuzzoni developed the stereotype of the *prima donna*: a singer with a superb voice, a high salary, and a demanding and often difficult temperament.

named August the Strong, and he held the titles king of Poland and duke of Saxony. In 1719 Elector August built a new opera house seating 2,000 spectators. He also hired the best singers he could find (all Italian), including an expensive castrato called Senesino (see Box in Chapter 38). In 1731 August engaged what might be called the first "power couple" in the history of music, composer Johann Hasse (1699–1783) and his wife, soprano **Faustina Bordoni** (1697–1781). Hasse was a north German educated in Italy, whose services as a composer of opera were in demand throughout much of the Continent; Bordoni (Fig. 41-1) was the leading soprano, the great *prima donna* (leading lady) of the age, and she commanded fees far greater than his.

Hasse and Bordoni made their operatic debut in Dresden in 1731 with an *opera seria* entitled *Cleofide*. Not only was *Cleofide* Hasse's first opera for Dresden, it was also one of the first in which he would set a text by **Pietro Metastasio** (1698–1782), the principal librettist for eighteenth-century *opera seria*. Like Gilbert and Sullivan in the nineteenth century and Rodgers and Hammerstein in the twentieth, Metastasio and Hasse worked as a team to create many works for the musical stage—in this case, nearly thirty operas. Metastasio's strength was his ability to fashion clearly shaped drama and equally crystalline poetry. But Metastasio did not provide texts only for Hasse. His libretti were set nearly four hundred times by other composers of eighteenth-century *opera seria*, including Handel, Gluck, and even Mozart on occasion.

The libretto of Hasse's *Cleofide* concerns the life of Alexander the Great, and like many *opere serie*, the plot is a thinly disguised allegory that praises the virtues of a magnanimous ruler. When the ancient warrior-king Alexander the Great stepped on stage in Dresden, the audience was encouraged to see the modern warrior-king August the Strong, for both had territorial ambitions to the east. The heroine Cleofide (sung by Bordoni), queen of a region of India, is in love with Poro, king of another region of India. Cleofide confesses her love in a famous aria, "Digli ch'io son fedele" ("Tell him that I am faithful"), not knowing that he, disguised as his own general, hears her confession. The magnanimous Alexander (sung by a castrato) agrees to their marriage, even though he fancies the bride for himself. All of this is typical of late-Baroque *opera seria*; the plots are complicated, characters appear in disguise, and male leads usually have high, womanly voices. As the eighteenth century progressed, Metastasio himself worked to reduce the number of characters and simplify the plot, bringing the libretto more in line with Enlightenment ideals of clarity and simplicity. As to the music, it centered on the *da capo* aria and the vocal ability of the soprano and castrato. *Cleofide* is very much a singer's opera. Essential characteristics of Enlightenment *opera seria* include the following.

- The libretto is a thinly disguised allegory that praises the heroic actions of the ruler.
- The opera has a happy ending (*lieto fine* in Italian), thanks to the intervention of a god or a magnanimous monarch.
- Elaborate scenery is required, sometimes including horses, elephants, and camels on stage.
- Castrati sing the roles of young romantic leads; tenors or basses sing the parts of male authority figures such as fathers.

- The music consists almost exclusively of simple recitatives and florid *da capo* arias.
- Attention is focused on beautiful melodies and the vocal skill of the leading singers.
- The *prima donna* and the castrato reign supreme, receiving fees many times that of the composer.

The premiere of Hasse's *Cleofide* in Dresden on 13 September 1731 was a gala event. In the audience were two significant guests: Johann Sebastian Bach and the future King Frederick (the Great) of Prussia. Bach, as we have seen, was then cantor in nearby Leipzig, and he took every opportunity to go to the Dresden opera house to hear what he called "the lovely Dresden ditties." Frederick of Prussia, as we will see, was a music-loving monarch who took up the flute as well as composition. Later, Frederick established his own opera company in Berlin and composed an ornamented version of "Digli ch'io son fedele" for a performance of *Cleofide*. In fact, we possess three versions of this aria: Hasse's original (Ex. 41-2, top), a slightly ornamented version said to have been created by Faustina Bordoni herself (Ex. 41-2, middle), and the king's even more florid rendition (Ex. 41-2, bottom). We now call such florid figuration assigned to the soprano voice **coloratura,** and refer to singers of such passagework as coloratura sopranos.

EXAMPLE 41-2

Tell him that I am faithful, tell him that he is my treasure, tell him that he is my treasure…

LISTENING CUE

JOHANN ADOLF HASSE
Cleofide, (1731)
Aria, "Digli ch'io son fedele"

CD 6/16
Anthology, No. 118

Although librettist Metastasio reduced the number of characters found in Baroque *opera seria* and simplified the plot in accordance with the spirit of Enlightenment, *opera seria* was still a serious art form for the elite. Above all, Metastasio's libretti reaffirmed the values of the ruling aristocracy: loyalty, benevolence, and enlightened rule. Perhaps as an antidote to this high-art seriousness, a new genre of musical theater arose that we now broadly call comic opera. Throughout the eighteenth century these two types of opera—traditional *opera seria* and the newer, lighter comic opera—would vie for supremacy on the operatic stage.

❋ MUSIC AND SOCIAL CHANGE: COMIC OPERA

Comic opera was a simpler, more direct type of musical theater that made use of comic characters, dealt with everyday social issues, and emphasized values more in step with those of the middle class. Arising in several countries in Europe at the same time, comic opera went under various names: ballad opera (England), *opera buffa* (Italy), *opéra comique* (France), and *Singspiel* (Germany). In each of these countries, comic opera assumed a distinctly local form. Whereas *opera seria* was sung only in Italian, comic opera was usually performed in the native tongue. Using the local language brought comic opera closer to the ordinary citizen.

English Ballad Opera: *The Beggar's Opera*

The first important challenge to the *opera seria* establishment was John Gay's *The Beggar's Opera*, produced in London in 1728. In this three-act work, John Gay (1685–1732) populates the stage, not with heroic kings but common criminals. The criminals must be able to sing simple tunes, but need not trouble themselves with recitative because Gay's dialogue is simply spoken in the vernacular of the audience. At the outset a beggar steps forward and speaks for Gay himself: "I hope I may be forgiven, that I have not made my Opera throughout unnatural, like those in vogue; for I have no Recitative." The "unnatural" opera then "in vogue" in London was, of course, the *opera seria* of Handel that was playing at the King's Theater.

The Beggar's Opera poked fun at aristocratic Italian opera and the established government. Whereas *opera seria* began with a formal three-section sinfonia or a two-part French overture, the overture to *The Beggar's Opera* quotes the tune *The Happy Clown*, a satirical lampoon of reigning prime minister Robert Walpole. While *opera seria* had lengthy *da capo* arias, *The Beggar's Opera* uses popular songs. Many of the tunes are English, Scottish, or Irish folk songs, generally called ballads. A **ballad** is a traditional, usually strophic, song that tells a lengthy story. *The Beggar's Opera* is a **ballad opera**—a comic opera using re-texted ballads (or other popular songs) and spoken dialogue rather than recitative.

The plot of *The Beggar's Opera* concerns the love of Polly Peachum for handsome Captain Macheath. It unfolds within the world of lowlife London, where there is no honor among thieves, and less among the nobility. Polly's mother is a prostitute, her father a fence and an informer, and Macheath a mugger. Mr. and Mrs. Peachum are scandalized to find that Polly has married Macheath. They fear that his criminal line of work, though praiseworthy, will not prove lucrative enough for her (and them). What is worse, a lawyer will now be needed to settle Polly's dowry. To the tune of *A Soldier and a Sailor*, Mr. Peachum pillories the legal profession:

> Your wife may steal your rest, sir,
> A thief your goods and plate . . .
> If lawyer's hand is fee'd, sir,
> He steals your whole estate.

And so fly the verbal barbs in this satire of eighteenth-century law and morality. As to the music, it charms through the innocence and timeless beauty of the ballad melodies. Polly's song "Oh, ponder well! be not severe" is a re-texting of the English ballad "The children in the wood," which had been well-known since Shakespeare's time (Ex. 41-3). The ballad melody is only eight bars long and the vocal range quite limited; in Gay's ballad operas, the leads need not be great singers, just good actors.

EXAMPLE 41-3

LISTENING CUE

JOHN GAY
The Beggar's Opera (1728)
Dialogue and Songs from Act I

CD 6/17–20
Anthology, No. 119a-d

The *Beggar's Opera* was a huge success. It ran for sixty-two performances (then a record) in a West End London theater operated by one John Rich (wags said that Rich had been made gay and Gay rich). By the end of the century, Gay's ballad opera had been carried to colonial cities such as Boston, Philadelphia, Richmond, Charlestown, and Williamsburg (it was said to be George Washington's favorite opera). In 1928 Bertold Brecht and Kurt Weill built their *Dreigroschenoper* (*Threepenny Opera*) on Gay's story and characters (see Chapter 70), and made Macheath famous through his song "Mac the Knife."

Opera Buffa

If the English had their ballad opera in this period, the Italians had **opera buffa**. Literally, *opera buffa* means buffoonish (comic) opera. In the seventeenth century, comic operas had been few and far between. There were, however, comic scenes played out by lower-caste characters within Italian serious opera, just as earlier there had been scenes of comic relief within Shakespeare's plays. Around 1700 separate comic scenes came to be performed between the acts of an *opera seria*. A musical diversion between the acts of an opera or a play is called an **intermezzo.** By 1710 full-length comic operas had appeared in Naples. In contrast to *opera seria, opera buffa* involved a wide spectrum of social classes, from peasants and servants to noblemen. Moreover, it usually included a comic bass part, but no high-flying castrato (except in Rome where women were banned from the stage and castrati assumed their roles). The musical high points featured short airs, as opposed to lengthy *da capo* arias. Of the many comic operas originating in Italy at this time, by far the best-known today is Pergolesi's *La serva padrona* (*The Maid Made Mistress*, 1733).

Small, sickly, and crippled Giovanni Battista Pergolesi lived only twenty-six years (1710–1736). After his premature death from tuberculosis, greedy music publishers and sympathetic music historians attributed more music to Pergolesi than he had actually written. In truth, his musical output comprised only a handful of operas, four cantatas, a few sonatas, and some religious music, including a well-known *Stabat Mater* (1736). Pergolesi composed *La serva padrona* as a brief two-act intermezzo to be played between the acts of one of his longer, serious operas. *La serva padrona* has only two singing characters: Serpina (soprano), a clever chamber maid, and Uberto (bass), her elderly, lecherous lord. In the course of this fast-moving farce, the impertinent Serpina dupes Uberto into marrying her and thus becomes "The Maid Made Mistress." Here comic opera turns the established social order on its head.

The interplay between the maid and the master is at its best toward the end of Act I. In a spirited recitative the two protagonists exchange insults. In *opera buffa,* unlike ballad opera, the dialogue is not spoken but is delivered in fast-paced simple recitative. Recitative periodically yields to lyrical singing, however, as can be seen in a duet, "Lo conosco a quegl'occhietti" ("I see it in your eyes"), that typifies Pergolesi's naturally effervescent style. Employing a carefree *galant* idiom, Pergolesi captures in music the spirit of the two characters: she is high-strung, flighty, yet supremely self-confident; he is lowdown, slow-witted, and not so resolute, equivocating between major and minor. With its driving rhythmic energy, quick interchanges between characters, and rapid shifts between major and minor, this duet foreshadows the glorious ensemble finales fashioned by Mozart at the end of the century.

Most important, the immediate popularity of *La serva padrona* announced that a new musical genre, *opera buffa,* had arrived. The appeal of English ballad opera was limited to England and its colonies. Italian *opera buffa,* on the other hand, soon spread throughout continental Europe and beyond, gradually becoming a serious rival to *opera seria* for the public's affection. By 1760 *La serva padrona* had been staged in more than sixty theaters in cities as disparate as St. Petersburg and Barcelona, Vienna and Baltimore. In this case, an upstart maid (*opera buffa*) had become mistress of the opera house.

LISTENING CUE

GIOVANNI BATTISTA PERGOLESI	CD 6/21–22
La serva padrona (1733)	Anthology, No. 120a-b
Recitative, "Io non só chi mi tien!"	
Duet, "Lo conosco a quegl'occhietti"	

The War of the Buffoons: *Opéra Comique*

In 1752 a troupe of traveling Italian players carried *La serva padrona* to Paris, capital of the Enlightenment. Here Pergolesi's *opera buffa* ignited, not merely a controversy but a paper war over the relative merits of Italian and French musical style. The battle came to be called **La Guerre des Bouffons** (The War of the Buffoons—drawn from the term "clownish" in *opera buffa*) and it raged, on and off, for several years. More than sixty pamphlets were written, on one side or the other, by the major social critics of the day. The issue was this: What sort of opera was appropriate for the French stage? Should it be the traditional opera of the French court (the old *tragédie lyrique*; see Chapter 35), or the newer, lighter-style opera (Italian *opera buffa*) that portrayed everyday characters? On the conservative side were King Louis XV, the followers of Lully and Rameau, and the defenders of French classical theater; on the populist side were the freethinking *philosophes* and the social egalitarians.

Not surprisingly, liberal Jean-Jacques Rousseau marched into these opera wars on the progressive (pro-Italian) side. Indeed, he did something unusual for a Frenchman: he criticized the French language as being unmusical. In a pamphlet entitled *Lettre sur la musique française* (1753), Rousseau opined that French vocal music ran the risk of being "insipid and monotonous." In his view, the high-flown language of French classical drama had too many mute syllables and too few sonorous vowels; Italian was a more musical language. A year earlier Rousseau had demonstrated how a simpler poetic style and a more natural melody might better serve the French musical stage. He created a light opera entitled *Le Devin du village* (*The Village Soothsayer*, 1752), one of the first of a type that we now call *opéra comique*. French **opéra comique,** similar to its Italian cousin *opera buffa*, has characters from the everyday world. They sing in a fresh, natural style, and the dialogue is generally spoken, but sometimes (as in *Le Devin du village*) it is delivered in recitative. The principals sing either simple airs or popular melodies called *vaudevilles* (whence the English term "vaudeville" for a popular review or show). Consider Rousseau's simple air (here a duet) for the principals of *Le Devin du village*, the shepherds Colin and Colette. Most of the time they sing basic triads or skip down the scale in a dance-like rhythm. These are not psychologically differentiated characters; they have almost the same name and say almost the same words. Moreover, they sing almost the same music, Colin's usually duplicating Colette's at the interval of a sixth (Ex. 41-4). Rousseau even allows parallel octaves (see bar 7). In Rousseau's rustic *opéra comique*, academic rules of counterpoint were out of place. Indeed, counterpoint itself was judged "unnatural" by Rousseau.

EXAMPLE 41-4

(*continued on next page*)

coeur et ma foi. Qu'un doux ma - ri - a - ge m'u - nisse a - vec toi.

coeur et sa foi. Qu'un doux ma - ri - a - ge m'u - nisse a - vec toi.

Forever, Colin pledges my (his) heart and faith; in this sweet marriage I am united with you...

LISTENING CUE

JEAN-JACQUES ROUSSEAU
Le Devin du village (1752)
Duet, "À jamais Colin"

CD 6/23
Anthology, No. 121

The opera wars flared up again in Paris during the 1770s. An Italian composer, one Niccolò Piccinni (1728–1800), had been brought to Paris to create an Italianate alternative to the *tragédies lyriques* that continued to play on the Parisian stage. In response, the pro-French party brought in a champion of its own, Christoph Willibald Gluck, to revitalize French music drama. The "Piccinnists" now did battle with the "Gluckists" in notes and words. The quarrel even caught the attention of the American minister to France, Benjamin Franklin, who said wryly: "Happy people! thought I, you live certainly under a wise, just, and mild government, since you have no public grievances to complain of, nor any subject of contention but the perfections and imperfections of foreign music."[1] Franklin does not say if he was a Piccinnist or a Gluckist.

❀ FIGURE 41-2
Christoph Willibald Gluck composing at a clavichord.

Bridgeman Art Library

❀ THE REFORM OPERAS OF GLUCK

Christoph Willibald Gluck (1714–1787; Fig. 41-2), though born in what is now the Czech Republic, seems to have lived as a citizen of all Europe. At least he spent extended periods in all the operatic capitals of Europe, including Vienna, Milan, Naples, London, Prague, Dresden, Hamburg, and Paris. Gluck composed almost nothing but opera, about forty-five in all. In 1752 Gluck settled more or less permanently in Vienna, where he came to occupy official musical positions at the court of Empress Maria Theresa (1717–1780). It was here that he helped to create a new style of opera—serious opera, in Italian, but opera very different from Baroque *opera seria*.

By 1760 Vienna had become a remarkably cosmopolitan city. Italian opera had long dominated the Viennese court. Indeed, Pietro Metastasio, the greatest *opera seria* librettist of the eighteenth century (see above), was the official court poet. In 1761 Vienna became home to another important Italian librettist, Ranieri Calzabigi (1714–1795). At the same time, French culture had made strong inroads in Vienna, for here, as elsewhere throughout Europe, the French language enjoyed the status of the primary language of cultured society. In 1755 Gluck had become director of a French opera and dance company installed at the Viennese court. Calzabigi himself had spent a decade in Paris and knew well French *tragédie lyrique*, which placed great weight on the ballet and the chorus. In 1762 Gluck and Calzabigi teamed up to create a new type of opera that historians call "reform opera." **Reform opera** sought to combine the best features of the Italian and French traditions, to yoke Italian lyricism to the French concern for intense dramatic expression.

The first of the reform operas by Gluck and Calzabigi carried the title *Orfeo ed Euridice*. The plot is familiar. Indeed, it is yet another telling of the story with which opera had begun more than a hundred and fifty years earlier: the Orpheus legend (see Chapter 30). The Italian libretto crafted by Calzabigi, however, distilled the action down to its essential elements. The opera starts, not by introducing Orfeo and Euridice but by his mourning her death. Calzabigi also reduced the number of characters to just three (Orfeo, Euridice, and Cupid). Gluck's contribution was no less radical. He did away with the old *da capo* aria and greatly reduced the importance of elaborate, coloratura singing. As Gluck said about his new approach to opera:

> I resolved to free [opera] from all the abuses which have crept in either through ill-advised vanity on the part of the singers or through excessive complaisance on the part of composers, with the result that for some time Italian opera [*opera seria*] has been disfigured and far from being the most splendid and most beautiful of all stage performances has been made the most ridiculous and most wearisome.[2]

As the role of the virtuoso soloist diminished, that of the chorus increased greatly. Equally important, Gluck exploited a type of recitative new to the eighteenth century: obbligato recitative. As its name implies, in **obbligato recitative** (also known as **accompanied recitative**) the orchestra is necessary (obligatory) to the desired musical effect. Not only does the orchestra provide accompaniment for the singer but it also plays significant musical motives on its own. Throughout Gluck's *Orfeo ed Euridice*, the orchestra accompanies all arias and all recitatives. Thus the boundary between aria and recitative is less distinct, and the contrast between the sections, or "numbers," within the opera is less clear. *Orfeo ed Euridice* unfolds continually, one number flowing almost imperceptibly into the next, leaving the audience little opportunity to applaud (and stop the action). Attention is focused on the musically enhanced drama rather than on the vocal displays of the soloists, and clarity and direct expression of the text assume paramount importance. The extent to which Gluck transformed opera can be gauged by comparing the qualities of Hasse's earlier Enlightenment opera *Cleofide* (see above) with Gluck's reform opera *Orfeo ed Euridice*. Qualities of Gluck's reform opera include the following.

- The overture generally sets the mood of the opera to follow.
- The vocal style is far less florid, with little improvised ornamentation.
- The focus is on the expressive potential of the text.
- *Da capo* arias are eliminated and strophic forms favored.
- Obbligato recitative (accompanied recitative) is used extensively.
- Arias and recitatives are less strictly separated.
- The plot of the libretto is simplified, the number of characters reduced.
- The chorus assumes an important role and participates in the drama.
- Dance assumes a dramatic role.
- The orchestra is more important and provides more varied sounds.

In many ways, Gluck's reforms gave back to opera the character it possessed at the very beginning of its history (c1600): restrained, yet expressive singing is fully integrated with choral music and dance.

The most dramatic moment in *Orfeo ed Euridice* occurs at the beginning of Act II, as Orfeo descends into the Underworld to reclaim his beloved Euridice. For this inferno scene, Gluck assembled an uncommonly large and colorful orchestra. In addition to the expected strings and winds (pairs of oboes, bassoons, and horns), he includes unusual instruments such as the harp and two ancient wind instruments, namely the cornett and trombone. The sweet-sounding harp accompanies Orfeo as he pleads with the furies, who block his way in the Underworld. They in turn are supported by the demonic sounds of blaring cornett and trombone. When the chorus of furies rebuffs Orfeo with shouts of "no, no," these wind instruments contribute to the cacophony with biting diminished-seventh chords. For the eighteenth century, this was literally the sound and fury of Hell. Ultimately, Orfeo's musical pleading softens the demonic spirits; the trombones withdraw and the infernal voices become quiet. Expressive, yet controlled, singing has vanquished the hellish sounds of chorus and orchestra, and Orfeo is free to pass.

LISTENING CUE

CHRISTOPH WILLIBALD GLUCK
Orfeo ed Euridice (1762)
Aria, "Deh placatevi"
Chorus, "Misero giovane"

CD 7/1–2
Anthology, No. 122a-b

Toward the end of *Orfeo ed Euridice*, the hero succumbs to his human failing. Fearful that Euridice does not follow, he turns to see if she is there—the single act expressly forbidden by Cupid. Again, the gods carry Euridice away. Orfeo laments his loss, first in an obbligato recitative and then in a full-blown aria. The aria, the famous "Che farò senza Euridice" ("What will I do without Euridice"), rejects *da capo* form and vocal display. Instead, this strophic song is full of what Gluck himself called "beautiful simplicity" that captures the poignancy of the moment. Orfeo's overweening curiosity—a very human failing—has stripped him of his prize. Ultimately, the god Cupid takes pity on these mortals and reunites them, an act of clemency that would have been appreciated by Enlightenment audiences.

LISTENING CUE

CHRISTOPH WILLIBALD GLUCK
Orfeo ed Euridice (1762)
Obbligato recitative, "Ahimè! Dove trascorsi?"
Aria, "Che farò senza Euridice"

CD 7/3–4
Anthology, Nos. 122c-d

Within ten years Gluck's *Orfeo ed Euridice* had made its way to theaters in Italy, Germany, Sweden, and England, and the composer had become a celebrity. In 1774 he brought *Orfeo ed Euridice* to Paris and added more ballets to please Parisian taste. Knowing the French aversion to the castrato voice, he also transposed the alto castrato part of Orfeo down into the range of high tenor. Paris loved this new French arrangement, now titled *Orphée et Eurydice*. Here was opera that combined the best of both Italian and French music drama. It had melody, but melody that was dignified; it had chorus and ballet, but both were integrated in the drama, not merely spectacular interruptions. Even the critical Jean-Jacques Rousseau praised the opera:

"To spend a couple of hours in the enjoyment of so great a pleasure persuades me that life is worth living."[3]

SUMMARY

Italian *opera seria*—the traditional opera of the established aristocratic court—continued to thrive throughout the Enlightenment but was not uncontested. *Opera seria* glorified the status quo and the absolute ruler. Its stage was decorated with expensive sets and populated with high-priced castrati and divas who specialized in vocal virtuosity. Librettist Pietro Metastasio, often working with composer Johann Hasse, attempted to reduce the number of characters, simplify the plot, and concentrate the action. Their Enlightenment *opera seria*, however, was still informed by, and strongly reinforced, aristocratic values. By 1730 a rival to *opera seria* appeared on the stage in several European countries: comic opera. Although comic opera assumed a distinctly different guise in each country in which it appeared, the various national forms nonetheless had many common characteristics. They

- Were designed to appeal to more middle-class sensibilities.
- Had characters from everyday life, even lowlife, populate the stage.
- Satirized the upper classes or foreigners who threatened the simple, honest way of life.
- Contained spoken dialogue (or rapid-fire simple recitative) in the native language of the country.
- Preferred actors who could sing to expensive singers who could act.
- Abounded with pantomime and slapstick comedy.

The differences among the national dialects of comic opera were: English ballad opera employed simple tunes, many of them ballads (traditional folk songs), to which new text was added as appropriate for the plot; Italian *opera buffa* did not use spoken dialogue but fast-moving simple recitative; French *opéra comique* preferred pre-existing airs and popular melodies called *vaudevilles*; and German *Singspiel* (see Chapter 48) frequently employed folk songs for the sung portions and sometimes favored magical or supernatural events in the plot.

Comic opera, a new and different genre, attacked *opera seria* from without. The reform opera of Christoph Willibald Gluck tried to alter it from within. True to the spirit of the Enlightenment, the reform opera of Gluck emphasized simple design and natural expression. Reform opera was still serious grand opera with characters of noble intentions. Yet in reform opera the dictates of dignity and moderation created a drama centered on the expression of intense human emotions, rather than the vocal exploits of star singers.

KEY TERMS

Enlightenment
les philosophes
galant style
Faustina Bordoni
prima donna
Pietro Metastasio

coloratura
comic opera
ballad
ballad opera
opera buffa
intermezzo

La Guerre des Bouffons
opéra comique
reform opera
obbligato recitative
   (accompanied
   recitative)

Chapter 42

Music in the Age of Enlightenment: Orchestral Music

Society underwent profound changes during the Enlightenment as power and wealth increasingly devolved from the aristocracy to the middle class. The introduction of comic opera with characters from all ranks of society, as we have seen, was a musical reaction against exclusively aristocratic *opera seria*. In the field of instrumental music, too, social transformation led to change in the type of music produced and the kind of person who played and heard it. By the mid eighteenth century, economic progress had brought prosperity to the growing middle class. Now the bookkeeper, physician, cloth merchant, stock trader, and student collectively had enough disposable income to organize and patronize their own concerts. High art music, which we call "classical music," moved beyond the court and church to become popular entertainment. The day of the public concert had arrived.

PUBLIC CONCERTS

The city of Paris, home to Voltaire, Rousseau, and other freethinking egalitarians, was the epicenter of the Enlightenment. Not surprisingly, therefore, Paris saw the first and most numerous public concert series. Foremost among these was the **Concert spirituel** founded in 1725. Originally formed to give a public hearing to religious music sung in Latin, its repertory soon came to emphasize purely instrumental symphonies and concertos. Concerts were advertised to the public by means of flyers distributed in the streets. To make its offerings accessible to several strata of society, it also instituted a two-tiered system of prices (four *livres* for boxes and two *livres* for the pit), with children under fifteen admitted at half price. Women were almost as numerous in the audience as men. Thus, we can trace to the mid eighteenth century the practice of middle-class citizens buying tickets and attending public performances of high art music.

London, too, participated in the advent of public concerts during the eighteenth century. Here, concerts were at first centered in the Vauxhall Gardens, something akin to an eighteenth-century theme park located on the south bank of the Thames River. Visitors paid a daily admission fee, bought exorbitantly priced food and drink, and wandered freely among various amusements. The musical fare included free concerts in a centrally located bandstand. Leopold Mozart, father of Wolfgang, took his family to the Vauxhall Gardens when visiting London in 1762. Here he found both pleasing music and a new spirit of democracy in the air:

> In the middle is a kind of high open summerhouse in which is to be heard an organ and music on trumpets, drums and all instruments. . . . Here each person pays only one shilling and for this shilling has the delight of seeing many thousands of people and the most beautifully illuminated garden; and of hearing beautiful music. More than six thousand people were present when I attended. . . . Here everyone is equal, and no lord allows any person to uncover [doff a hat] before him; having paid their money [to enter], all are upon equal terms.[1]

In Vienna, the music of Wolfgang Mozart, as well as Haydn and Beethoven, would later sound at public concerts in the Burgtheater (Court Theater). This Viennese hall, which had opened in 1741, welcomed paying customers of whatever class, as long as they dressed and behaved properly. Although the nobility still occupied the best seats (Fig. 42-1), opening the doors of culture to the general public fostered a leveling between classes. The featured artists were usually composer-performers who offered the public a variety of music: their latest symphony, a concerto, and an aria or two, and perhaps a fantasia or set of variations for solo keyboard.

THE EARLY SYMPHONY: GIOVANNI BATTISTA SAMMARTINI IN MILAN

The word "symphony" descends from the ancient Latin term *symphonia*, which connotes a harmonious sound. By the 1620s, the Italian term "sinfonia" was applied more specifically to an instrumental ritornello at the beginning or in the middle of a vocal work. Soon the title "*sinfonia avanti l'opera*" became a simple way to designate the opening instrumental overture to an opera. Thereafter, for the next hundred years, the symphony developed mainly in the context of the Italian opera overture. By the late seventeenth century, the typical Italian symphony/overture had acquired three sections that came in immediate succession, fast/slow/fast. The middle portion was very brief and in a contrasting key, whereas the finale often made use of a light dance idiom. Finally, by the 1730s, composers in Italy had begun to write symphonies as free-standing instrumental works, a development that signaled the decline of the Baroque concerto grosso. Thus the **concert symphony** as we know it today—a three- or four-movement instrumental work projecting the unified sounds of an orchestra—was a creation of the more egalitarian Enlightenment. The emphasis shifted from just a few "stars" of the Baroque concerto grosso to the larger orchestral team of the Enlightenment symphony. Henceforth the symphony would constitute the weightiest composition at a public orchestral concert. So closely associated did the orchestra become with the genre of the concert symphony that still today we call it a "symphony orchestra."

The leader in the creation of the concert symphony was Giovanni Battista Sammartini (c1700–1775). Despite his very Italian-sounding name, Sammartini was the son of a French oboist (Saint-Martin) who had immigrated to Milan, Italy. The son too played oboe, and violin and organ as well. Sammartini spent his entire career in Milan as a church musician. Toward the end of his life he held the post of *maestro di cappella* (director of church music) at no fewer than eight churches simultaneously. Sammartini's activity in the church did not preclude him from writing symphonies. Indeed, in this period, symphonies and even concertos were often included as preludes to or interludes during religious services. Sammartini's symphonies were also heard at outdoor public concerts that he himself directed.

In all, Sammartini left some eighty symphonies. Most are in three movements (fast/slow/fast), with the last movement often a minuet finale. Some of his early symphonies from the 1730s are "trio symphonies"—symphonies with only two independent violin parts and a bass line for viola, cello, and double bass, each playing the same notes an octave apart in its own register. More common is the four-part symphony for four independent string parts, with the cellos and basses doubling on the bass line. If a woodwind sound was desired, oboes or flutes would simply double the violin parts. Only in the symphonies from the last decade of his life (1765–1775)

❋ FIGURE 42-1

A performance at the Burgtheater in Vienna in 1785. The nobility occupied the frontmost seats on the floor, but the area behind (to the left of) the partition was open to all. So, too, in the galleries, the aristocracy bought boxes low and close to the stage, while commoners occupied higher rungs as well as the standing room in the fourth gallery. Ticket prices depended, then as now, on proximity to the performers.

did Sammartini write independent oboe parts and separate the cellos and basses into two independent lines.

Sammartini's Symphony in D Major (J-C 14)[†] is a fine example of the *galant* symphony in its formative stages. Each of the three movements is brief, lasting approximately three minutes, a minute-and-a-half, and two minutes, respectively. Typically, the first movement is the longest and most substantive. Its form is binary, as in the movements of the Baroque dance suite. But there are two innovations here. First, Sammartini introduces a clear-cut second theme coinciding with the appearance of the dominant key. Second, and perhaps more important, the beginning of part **B** is greatly expanded; the first theme and transitional material are transformed as the music pushes through two related keys. This creates what might be called "expanded binary form," with part **B** now being significantly longer than part **A** (fifty-two measures, compared to twenty-eight). The beginning of part **B,** in fact, is similar to what we will later call a "development section" because of its elaboration of earlier themes. This portion of binary form will take on increasing importance throughout the eighteenth century. The first movement of Sammartini's Symphony in D Major can be diagrammed as follows:

Theme:	‖: 1st	transition	2nd	:‖:	1st	1st and trans. developed		2nd :‖
Key:	D major		A major		A major	B minor	E major	D major
Part:	‖: A			:‖:	B			:‖
Measure:	1–8	9–20	21–28	:‖:	29–36	37–72		73–80 :‖

As to the *galant* features of this movement, notice the first theme at the very opening of the movement (Ex. 42-1). It is a simple D major triad set out as a descending arpeggio and played in unison. The pattern is immediately repeated in halved note values and then halved again as the theme gains rhythmic energy. These opening four bars, which end on the dominant, form an **antecedent phrase**; it is immediately answered by a four-bar complementary unit called the **consequent phrase** that returns the music to the tonic. Such symmetrical phrasing is typical of the *galant* idiom as well as the Classical style to come.

EXAMPLE 42-1

[†]J-C refers to the system for numbering Sammartini's symphonies provided in Newell Jenkins and Bathia Churgin, *Thematic Catalogue of the Works of Giovanni Battista Sammartini* (Cambridge, Massachusetts, 1976).

Playing in an Eighteenth-Century Orchestra

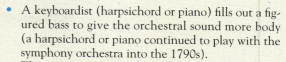

Needless to say, the orchestra in the age of Enlightenment was smaller than the modern symphony orchestra; even the biggest ensemble generally had no more than forty players. The more subdued timbre of the string instruments resulted in part from the strings themselves, which were made of animal gut, not of wire, and from the design of the bridge, which put less tension on the strings. Furthermore, bows had less horsehair and were more "bowed" (convex rather than concave) in shape. There were other important differences as well, as implied in Johann Quantz's *Essay on Playing the Flute* (*Versuch einer Anweisung die Flöte traversière zu spielen*) of 1752, a three-hundred page treasure trove of information about mid eighteenth-century performance practices.

Johann Quantz (1697–1773) was one of the great flautists of the age. He had spent long years associated with orchestras in Dresden and Berlin. He had also traveled widely, to London and Paris, among other places, and had heard Sammartini's orchestra in Milan. Here are a few of the differences between playing in an orchestra then and now, as suggested by Quantz:

- The principal violinist should serve as conductor (a non-playing conductor, baton in hand, doesn't appear before the orchestra until the nineteenth century).

- A keyboardist (harpsichord or piano) fills out a figured bass to give the orchestral sound more body (a harpsichord or piano continued to play with the symphony orchestra into the 1790s).
- The principal violinist gets the pitch from the keyboard (not the oboe) and then sounds it for the other players.
- The pitch varies greatly from region to region; pitch is lower in France and Italy, for example, than in Germany, but even in Germany what they called an A in concert orchestras was approximately a full step lower than our A 440 today.
- The orchestra should memorize the first few bars of the piece so as to watch the conductor and effect a cleaner, more emphatic beginning.
- The players should add ornaments (trills and appoggiaturas, for example) to the written score, but these must be carefully rehearsed by the conductor.
- The players should stand during an orchestral concert; only those who must sit (the keyboardist and cellos) may do so.
- The players should tap the beat with the front of the foot, even during rests, to keep a steady tempo.

Finally, Quantz provides a seating chart for a mid-size orchestra (below). Presumably, this was just one of several possibilities at the time.

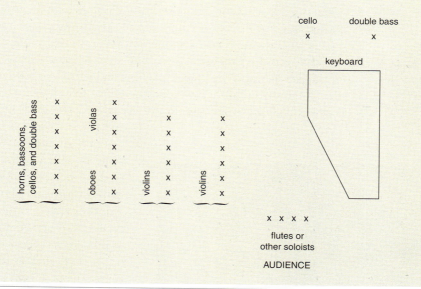

LISTENING CUE

GIOVANNI BATTISTA SAMMARTINI
Symphony in D Major (c1740)
First movement, *Allegro*

CD 7/5
Anthology, No. 123

✺ THE RISE OF ORCHESTRAL DISCIPLINE: JOHANN STAMITZ IN MANNHEIM

By the 1750s, the Italian symphony had moved north across the Alps. Here it took deep root and grew into the Classical symphony as we know it today. One important northern center for its development was Mannheim, Germany. In the mid eighteenth century, Mannheim was the capital of the Palatine, a territory running south-north along the Rhine River. Its ruler was Elector Carl Theodore (1724–1799), a lover of music and books. The palace from which Carl Theodore governed is an impressive complex (it now houses the University of Mannheim). At its center is a grand stairway leading up some two-hundred steps to the Hall of Knights (*Rittersaal*; Fig. 42-2), where concerts were held.

The Mannheim orchestra in the mid eighteenth century boasted a distinguished conductor and composer, Johann Stamitz (1717–1757). The Czech-born Stamitz had come to Mannheim in 1741 to be a violinist in the court orchestra. Indeed, Stamitz was apparently a virtuoso on all string instruments; at a concert in June 1742 he was the featured soloist, in turn, on violin, viola, cello, and double bass. Within a decade, Stamitz became director of the orchestra at Mannheim and distinguished himself as a composer. His works number fifty-eight symphonies and nearly two dozen concertos, including twelve for solo flute and one for clarinet, probably the first clarinet concerto ever written.

At Mannheim, Stamitz assembled an all-star orchestra. He hired a number of celebrated woodwind players and entire families of Czech hornists and trumpeters—the area around Prague was renowned for its brass players at this time. Stamitz taught and coached until he molded the orchestra into the most disciplined ensemble in Europe. The fame of the Mannheim orchestra lasted well beyond Stamitz's premature death. One observer of the day called it "an army of generals." Mozart's father said of it in 1763: "Ah if only the court music [at Salzburg] were regulated as it is in Mannheim! The discipline that reigns in that orchestra!"[2]

What was this orchestral discipline of which the elder Mozart speaks? Observers of the day mention the precise playing, and particularly the uniform bowing among the strings. In addition, the orchestra specialized in novel dynamic effects: *fortissimo* followed by *piano*, for example. At Mannheim, the louds seem to have been louder and the softs softer. But nothing impressed listeners in the Hall of Knights more than what is called a **Mannheim crescendo,** a gradual increase from very soft to very loud with a repeating figure over a pedal point. Another special effect was the **Mannheim rocket,** as it was later called—a triadic theme that bursts forth as a rising arpeggio. Orchestral gestures such as these, when precisely executed, were known to bring the audience to its feet.

Dramatic orchestral effects are clearly audible in Johann Stamitz's own symphonies, but other distinctive features are noteworthy as well. First, Stamitz was the earliest composer consistently to incorporate a fourth movement in his symphonies. After the opening *allegro* and the slow second movement, he

FIGURE 42-2

Hall of Knights at Mannheim. In the mid eighteenth century this lavish two-story room served as a concert hall for the twice-weekly, semi-public concerts of the Mannheim court.

inserted a minuet and trio (see Chapter 45), which he followed with a fast finale (*presto* or *prestissimo*). Second, Stamitz expanded the orchestral score, making the winds obligatory. His symphonies of the 1750s are set out for eight parts: four strings, two horns, and two oboes (flutes or clarinets may substitute for the oboes). His horns not only provide a harmonic backdrop for the strings, but often step forth with solos. Similarly, whereas most previous composers used the oboes simply to double the violins, Stamitz frequently gives them their own independent lines. Later, Mozart would sometimes call for four woodwind instruments simultaneously: clarinets, flutes, and bassoons, as well as oboes. Mozart, who had spent much time in Mannheim as a youth and would go on to write superb orchestral parts for woodwinds, learned much about orchestration from Mannheim composers such as Stamitz.

Stamitz's Symphony in E♭ Major was published in 1758 in a collection of six symphonies called *La Melodia Germanica*. Here neither binary form nor any expansion of it shapes the music. Instead, thematic ideas seem to be conceived as orchestral gestures. They appear, and then reappear, in an unpredictable order so as to dramatize the effects of precision playing. Example 42-2 shows a portion of the first theme, in which the melodic material seems to be generated solely to service an orchestral effect; the strings churn away while the dynamic level rises from *pianissimo* to *fortissimo*—a fine example of a Mannheim *crescendo*.

EXAMPLE 42-2

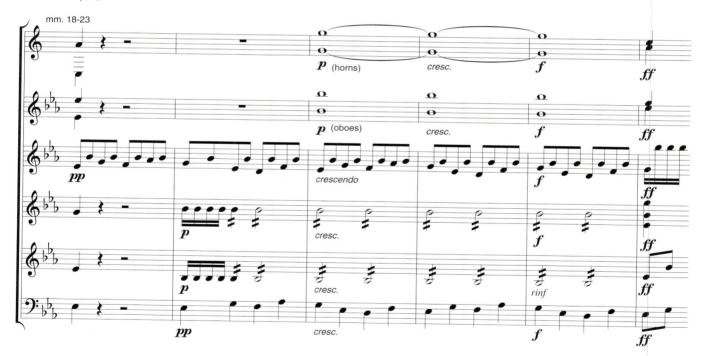

LISTENING CUE

JOHANN STAMITZ
La Melodia Germanica, No. 3 (c1755)
Symphony in E♭ Major
First movement, *Allegro assai*

CD 7/6
Anthology, No. 124

How Fast Is *Allegro*?

Composers began placing tempo markings in music during the seventeenth century. As time progressed, the instructions became more elaborate, so that by 1750 expressions such as *Allegro ma non troppo*, *Adagio spiritoso*, and *Adagio pesante*, among others, were used. But how fast is *Allegro*, and how slow *Adagio*? Even in the scientific age of the Enlightenment, a standardized mechanism for measuring musical time had yet to be devised. Johann Quantz (see earlier Box), an experienced orchestral player, proposed using a device that musicians had employed since at least 1500 for setting a beat in a musical performance: the human pulse. The musician checked his pulse and then set the beat by getting it in sync with a specific note value (half-, quarter-, or eighthnote) depending on the tempo marking of the composer.

To simplify things, Quantz set out four basic categories for tempos: *Allegro assai* (very fast), *Allegretto* (moving), *Adagio cantabile* (a songful *adagio*), and *Adagio assai* (very slow). All other tempo markings, he stipulated, were more "an expression of the dominant passions in each piece than a real tempo marking." He did, however, allow for a moderate middle tempo between the first two, which resulted in five primary tempos. To each of these he assigned a speed according to "the pulse beat at the hand of a healthy person," or 80 beats per minute. The modern equivalents of Quantz's tempo markings can be summarized as:

Allegro assai	160 beats per minute
Allegro moderato	120 beats per minute
Allegretto	80 beats per minute
Adagio cantabile	40 beats per minute
Adagio assai	20 beats per minute

Quantz was quick to admit that his system lacked uniformity. He knew that in every musician the pulse changed according to the time of day, the amount of that person's activity and food consumed, and other variables. A rate of 80 pulse beats per minute was most likely to be found, he said, "in a jovial and high-spirited yet rather fiery and volatile person" after he had eaten lunch! A musician who was "low-spirited, or melancholy, or cold and sluggish" could set the tempo slightly faster than his pulse. Quantz knew that this was not very scientific, and he concluded his discussion of tempo with the following remark: "Beyond this, if someone could discover a simpler, more accurate, and more convenient device [than the pulse] for learning and establishing tempos, he would do well to communicate it to the public immediately."

This "more convenient device" would come, but musicians had to wait until the invention of the metronome in Vienna around 1810.

SUMMARY

During the Enlightenment (1730–1770), the public concert hall began to rival the aristocratic salon as the preferred performing venue for art music. Even the nobles of the court, such as the elector of Mannheim, sponsored performances in larger halls and opened the doors to more visitors, thereby creating what might be called "semi-public" concerts. As concerts for the public became more numerous, the symphony gradually supplanted the Baroque concerto grosso as the principal genre of orchestral music. The more egalitarian spirit of the age facilitated the growth of the orchestra, which emphasized a united ensemble sound more than soloistic skills. The tripartite Italian opera overture grew into the three movement concert symphony (fast/slow/fast), best seen in the eighty-some symphonies of Giovanni Battista Sammartini. By 1750 the Italian symphony had crossed the Alps to German-speaking cities such as Mannheim. Here Johann Stamitz expanded the symphony to four movements, added dramatic effects to the score, and improved ensemble discipline by demanding uniform bowing and precise changes in dynamics.

KEY TERMS

Concert spirituel
concert symphony
antecedent phrase

consequent phrase
Essay on Playing the Flute
Johann Quantz

Mannheim *crescendo*
Mannheim rocket

Music in the Age of Enlightenment: Keyboard Music

In 1776 the Englishman Adam Smith published his *Wealth of Nations*, a landmark study of the creation of capital. Here for the first time was an account of **capitalism**, an economic system in which the means of production of goods are privately owned and bring ever-increasing wealth to private individuals. In the eighteenth century, London was the European center of capitalism, for the English had profitably explored and exploited new markets around the world. They also enjoyed relatively free trade and comparatively little royal control. Other European cities prospered as well. For the newly affluent merchant, lawyer, and stock trader, it was important to create a domestic situation in which the lady of the house did not work; how else might she be distinguished from women of lower social classes? Moreover, the beginning of the Industrial Revolution ushered in an era in which items women had traditionally made at home (soap, candles, and clothes, for example) were increasingly produced in factories and sold in shops. Greater wealth, then, brought with it increased leisure time, which provided middle-class women the opportunity to make music in the home.

 ## DOMESTIC KEYBOARD MUSIC FOR WOMEN

A smattering of French, an eye for needlepoint, some skill at the keyboard—these were the signs of good breeding necessary to a gentlewoman of the Enlightenment. The spirit of democracy may have been in the air, but this was still very much a sexist age. Serious learning was deemed beyond the ken of a woman, and the notion that a woman might attend university was considered absurd. Only one career awaited, that of wife and mother. To improve marital prospects, domestic refinements were required. And, as a German social critic said in 1773: "Among the *galant* arts that are expected of a young lady, music figures the most important of all."[1]

What sort of music might a young lady perform in those days? Keyboard music, of course. Wind instruments distorted the face. The violin required the upper torso to twist. The cello necessitated the legs to be spread; perish the thought! The guitar and mandolin were decorous enough, but by far the most favored instruments were the harpsichord and piano. Consequently, as almost every painting of the period shows, a woman making domestic music in the mid eighteenth century did so demurely seated at a keyboard, joined perhaps by a singer.

Composers quickly rushed to supply this emerging market with pieces such as "sonatas for the fair sex," "songs particularly adapted for ladies with pianoforte accompaniment," and "keyboard pieces for the cultured lady." It was assumed that ladies would not wish "to bother their pretty little heads with counterpoint and harmony." All that was needed was a tuneful melody and a few supporting chords to flesh it out. In 1775 the accommodating Johann Reichardt published his *Songs for the Fair Sex* with the more difficult notes in smaller note heads to be omitted "if the pretty little hand won't stretch."

Needless to say, a repertory aimed at amateur performers, whether male or female, encouraged a lighter, less complicated style than the more professionally oriented keyboard music of the Baroque era. More melody and less counterpoint was the general trend. In truth, a simpler kind of music had already been produced in Italy around 1730. This Italian *galant* style of keyboard music can be seen in the forty-odd harpsichord sonatas of Domenico Alberti (c1710–1746). Alberti would be forgotten today had not other composers adopted a particular component of this style, an accompaniment pattern we now call the Alberti bass. An **Alberti bass** animates simple triads by playing the notes successively in a pattern, as shown in Example 43-1. For the keyboardist, this was an easy formula to play. Should the Alberti bass prove too difficult, an even simpler method was at hand: repeat the bass note, but in alternating octaves, as shown in Example 43-2. A rumbling octave bass became a favorite technique of both Italian and German composers of the eighteenth century. The Germans called it the **murky bass.** Composers of the eighteenth century, including the young Beethoven, used both the Alberti bass and the murky bass as a way of energizing what was at heart a simple, homophonic accompaniment. Such "bass filler" patterns made the keyboard music of the day more accessible, and made the average amateur performer sound more technically skilled than she was.

EXAMPLE 43-1 Domenico Alberti, Opus 1, No. 3 (1748), first movement

EXAMPLE 43-2 J. C. Bach, Opus 5, No. 1 (1766), third movement

THE ADVENT OF THE PIANO

During the Enlightenment a new instrument, the piano, began to replace the harpsichord as the workhorse of musical performance. The harpsichord, which first appeared in France in the fifteenth century (see Chapter 19), produces sound when strings are plucked, but the plucking always has the same force, and thus produces the same volume of sound. A different kind of keyboard instrument, the piano, was invented in Florence, Italy, around 1700 by Bartolomeo Cristofori (1655–1732). To replace the harpsichord's plucking apparatus, Cristofori invented a mechanism to strike the string with a soft hammer and have it then fall quickly and quietly back to its resting position. Each blow could now be carefully controlled by the force of the player's finger. The instrument could play *piano* as well as *forte*—hence the term **pianoforte** (see Box in Chapter 47).

The original piano had a narrow range and a small tone. But its ability to regulate instantly the volume of each note gave it a major advantage over the harpsichord. Successive phrases of a musical "question and answer" could be shaded in varying degrees of soft and loud, which constituted an important factor in a music that increasingly came to be made up of short, complementary phrases. Moreover, the piano could also emphasize the melody at the expense of the accompaniment, something only possible on a harpsichord if the instrument had two keyboards. With a range of articulations including staccato and legato, it also could produce a variety of subtle nuances. Finally, the piano could play gradations of sounds—diminuendos and crescendos—to make the music more exciting.

Figure 43-1 shows a sample page from the first music ever published for piano, Lodovico Giustini's *Sonate da cimbalo di piano, e forte* (Florence, 1732). A glance at the score, covered with marks such as "pia." and "for." and "più for.," confirms that the composer took full advantage of the sonic capabilities of the new instrument. From 1750 onward, most keyboard music was advertised as "appropriate for both harpsichord and piano," even if it were better suited for one than the other. No intelligent publisher could afford to ignore a substantial share of the growing market, and no self-respecting keyboardist could avoid performing on both instruments.

FIGURE 43-1

Lodovico Giustini, *Sonate da cimbalo di piano, e forte* (Florence, 1732) was the first keyboard score to be intended explicitly for piano. Clearly evident are the markings "*pia.*" and "*for.*" calling for the dynamic levels *piano* and *forte*.

DOMENICO SCARLATTI IN MADRID

Domenico Scarlatti (1685–1757) was born in Naples, the son of opera and cantata composer Alessandro Scarlatti (see Chapter 32). Young Scarlatti's domain, however, was not to be vocal music, but music for the keyboard. In his earliest years, Domenico showed himself to be something of a harpsichord prodigy, and at the age of fifteen he was appointed keyboardist to the king of Naples. In 1719 Scarlatti's career took a surprising turn for an Italian musician deeply steeped in Italian musical ways: he became composer to King João V of Portugal and moved to Lisbon. Scarlatti's principal charge at the Portuguese court was to serve as music teacher and mentor to the king's daughter, Maria Barbara. A marriage in 1729 placed Maria Barbara in line to be queen of Spain, and both she and Scarlatti moved to Madrid. Scarlatti spent his last decades in the Spanish capital writing keyboard sonatas for his patroness and other members of the royal court, creating some 555 sonatas in all.

Most surprising for a keyboard prodigy such as Scarlatti, he published no music for keyboard until he was fifty-three years old! His first publication, called *Essercizi* (1738), contains thirty sonatas, each of only one movement. The title *Essercizi* suggests that these pieces were to serve as exercises to develop specific keyboard skills, much as would the etude in later centuries. (Similarly, in this period the English often called their sonatas "lessons," implying that some technical advantage was to be gained from the study of such pieces.) In the preface to his *Essercizi*, however, Scarlatti downplays the difficulties of these works and suggests that his temperament, as his contemporaries noted, was congenial with the more playful mood of the *galant* age: "Do not expect, whether you are an amateur or a professional, to find any profound intention in these compositions, but rather an ingenious jesting with art by means of which you may attain freedom in harpsichord playing."

Scarlatti's "ingenious jesting with art" is fully evident in his Sonata in A Major (Kirkpatrick No. 26[†]) from the *Essercizi*. As with almost all of Scarlatti's sonatas, the form here is binary (**AB**), with both sections repeated. The harmonic plan, too, has the conventional movement of I-V in **A** and V-I in **B**. Scarlatti's playfulness can be heard at the very beginning, where a downbeat sounds like an upbeat in an off-kilter example of metrical displacement (Ex. 43-3A). But the real surprises come at the junctions between I and V in part **A** and between V and I in part **B**. At the first of these moments Scarlatti includes crunching downbeat dissonances (Ex. 43-3B). This is the famous Scarlatti *acciaccatura.* In Italian, "acciaccatura" denotes something bruised or battered, and here the composer batters the listener with these dissonant downbeat chords. Scarlatti experts believe he derived this unusual effect from hearing dissonant chords strummed on Spanish guitars. Indeed, few composers fell more deeply under the intoxicating spell of the Spanish guitar music than Scarlatti. Likewise, the juncture between V and I in part **B** has a distinctly Spanish sound. Here the harmony rocks back and forth between two chords built on bass notes a major second apart, a sure sign of modal music indigenous to old Spain (Ex. 43-3C). Finally, everywhere throughout this sonata we see another hallmark of Scarlatti's flamboyant style, **hand-crossing.** Continually, the left hand must cross over the right to create an exciting three-level texture (left hand, right hand, and left over). Hand-crossing looks difficult but is often rather easy to do, and it gives to the music the appearance of playful daring.

EXAMPLE 43-3A

[†]While there are at least three numbering systems for the sonatas of Domenico Scarlatti, the most widely recognized one is that of Ralph Kirkpatrick, which appeared in his book *Domenico Scarlatti* (Princeton, 1953).

EXAMPLE 43-3B

mm. 37-42

EXAMPLE 43-3C

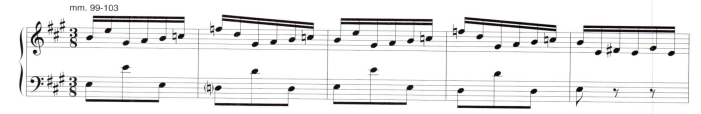

mm. 99-103

Did Scarlatti intend his sonatas for the harpsichord or piano? The preface to the *Essercizi* explicitly mentions the harpsichord, perhaps because at that time the piano was a relative newcomer. Yet Scarlatti's patroness and protégé, Queen Maria Barbara of Spain, owned three pianos on which her music master surely played. Thus, although Scarlatti expected his sonatas to be played on the harpsichord, it is not historically inaccurate to play them on the piano.

LISTENING CUE

DOMENICO SCARLATTI
Essercizi (1738)
Sonata No. 26 in A Major

CD 7/7
Anthology, No. 125

THE CLAVICHORD IN BERLIN: CARL PHILIPP EMANUEL BACH

During a long reign (1740–1786), King **Frederick the Great** made his realm, the north German kingdom of Prussia, a major player in European affairs. He also transformed Berlin (see Map 39-1) from a sleepy hamlet of 10,000 into a cosmopolitan capital of 100,000, full of art and learning. Frederick was an enlightened leader who spoke French fluently, wrote poetry and music, and brought the philosopher Voltaire to his court. He also built an opera house on a site that the Berlin Opera has occupied ever since. Yet Frederick also became a great military leader, one whose territorial acquisitions laid the foundation for the modern state of Germany. From the age of seven, Frederick received lessons in keyboard playing and figured bass realization. Eventually he even tried his hand at composition (see Chapters 40 and 41). Frederick also played the flute, and, when he became king in 1740, one of his first acts was to lure the flautist Johann Quantz (see Chapter 42) to the royal court in Berlin. The next year he engaged as keyboardist C.P.E. Bach, one of J.S. Bach's talented sons. During the day, King Frederick drilled his troops. Each evening, between the

Bildarchiv Preussischer Kulturbesitz/Art Resource, NY

FIGURE 43-2

Flautist and monarch Frederick the Great plays chamber music at his court. Carl Philipp Emanuel Bach is at the keyboard, and the king's teacher, Johann Quantz, stands on the extreme right.

hours of seven and nine, however, he played flute sonatas and concertos (Fig. 43-2), most composed by his teacher Johann Quantz and accompanied by C.P.E. Bach at the keyboard.

Carl Philipp Emanuel Bach, the second son of J.S. Bach, moved from Leipzig to Berlin in 1741 to serve as personal accompanist to the flute-playing king of Prussia. Here he remained for more than twenty-five years, performing in the monarch's evening musicales, accompanying in the court opera orchestra, and composing. Bach wrote in all musical genres of the day except opera and Catholic Mass. But he had been trained by his father as a keyboardist, and keyboard music lies at the heart of his creative work.

By the mid eighteenth century, demand for keyboard music for amateurs, and especially women, was increasing. Bach capitalized on this quickening enthusiasm for middle class music-making by issuing a stream of artistically and commercially successful keyboard sonatas. Principal among these are his *Six Easy Sonatas* (1766), six sonatas *For Use by Ladies* (1770), and six collections of sonatas *For Connoisseurs and Amateurs* (1779–1787). The last sets, *For Connoisseurs and Amateurs*, were particularly lucrative—taken together some 6,300 copies were printed, an astonishingly large number for the eighteenth century.

Coinciding with the growing demand for amateur music was the need for instructional manuals dealing with matters of musical performance. Johann Quantz satisfied the desires of flutists, as we have seen (Chapter 42), with his *Essay on Playing the Flute* (1752). In 1756 Leopold Mozart, father of Wolfgang, would write a best-selling violin method. By far the most influential instruction book for keyboard in the eighteenth century was C.P.E. Bach's two-part **Essay on the True Art of Playing the Keyboard** (*Versuch über die wahre Art das Clavier zu spielen*, 1753 and 1762). Clementi and Haydn would later learn from Bach's book, as would the young Beethoven. In his lengthy *Essay*, Bach tries to give both soloist and accompanist all the practical information the keyboard performer might need concerning musical intervals, key signatures, figured bass realization, ornamentation, improvisation, accompanying techniques, and fingering. At the end of his method book, Bach appends six three-movement sonatas in ascending order of difficulty that were designed to develop keyboard technique.

To appeal to the largest number of buyers for his sonatas, C.P.E. Bach referred to his instrument by the generic term "clavier," meaning simply "keyboard." Sometimes C.P.E. played on the harpsichord and sometimes on the newer piano; his royal patron owned fifteen! But C.P.E. Bach's favorite instrument was the quieter clavichord, which, while much softer than the harpsichord or piano, allowed for far greater expressivity. Said an observer of Bach's playing: "To know Bach completely one must hear the wealth of his imagination, the profound sentiment of his heart, his constant enthusiasm as he improvises on his clavichord."[2]

Bach's style of playing and his style of composition—his "profound sentiment of his heart"—came to be associated with the *empfindsamer Stil*. **Empfindsamer Stil** (German for "Sensitive Style") is a term applied to the hyper-expressivity that

The Clavichord

The clavichord first appeared in the fourteenth century, and its popularity in the West continued unabated until the late eighteenth century (see Chapter 23). The harpsichord and piano produce sound when a device plucks or strikes the string and then falls back. On the clavichord, however, a metal "T" called a tangent pushes against the string and continues to do so as long as the key is depressed. This allows the performer to hold and "wiggle" the key up and down and produce a vibrating sound that the Germans called **Bebung**—"quaking." Composers indicated this trembling effect in the score by placing dots with a slur over them above the note (Ex. 43-4). *Bebung* was the perfect vehicle for expressing the throbbing heart, panting breast, or quivering hand in music in the *empfindsamer Stil*.

The clavichord was smaller than either the piano or the harpsichord and was accordingly less expensive. Usually the clavichord was encased in a rectangular box with strings running at right angles to the keyboard. Because it was smaller, composers could carry one in their baggage when traveling, as Mozart often did. Because it was quiet to the point of being almost inaudible, the clavichord was a good practice instrument in schools, convents, and seminaries. Finally, because of its low volume, the clavichord was the best keyboard instrument for very private music-making by the solitary soul. It could express the quiet grief so dear to sensitive hearts in the age of *Empfindsamkeit* (sensitivity). The following *Ode to My Clavier* (here, meaning clavichord) was published in Germany the year after Part I of Bach's *Essay* on keyboard playing. It is not a great poem, but it expresses well the "heart on sleeve" sentimentality that marked the poetry and music of the *empfindsamer Stil*.

Ode To My Clavichord by Wilhelm Zachariae (1754)

Oh Echo of my sighing soul,　　　Help me, gentle strings,　　　Yes, sadness I condone.
My faithful strings set in array,　Help remove these painful things.　I love the saddest part,
Now troubling day gives way　　But no! leave me to my pain,　　And if I cry alone,
To night—all sorrow's goal.　　Comfort I do distain.　　　　I vent my loving heart.[3]

---

affected northern European arts generally in the second half of the eighteenth century. True to the Enlightenment, this "cult of feeling" was not inspired by religious ecstasy but by ordinary domestic experience. Jane Austen's later *Sense and Sensibility*—full of heart-rending family scenes and dramatic reconciliations—typifies the sentimental style in English literature. In music, this intimate and often passionate voice can best be heard in the keyboard pieces of C.P.E. Bach. As he said toward the end of his autobiography: "I believe that music must, first and foremost, stir the heart." True to his vow, when Bach played, "He looked like one inspired. His eyes were fixed, his under-lip fell, and drops of effervescence distilled from his countenance." [4]

Another fine example of *empfindsamer Stil* can be found in C.P.E. Bach's Fantasia in C Minor (Helm No. 75/iii and Wotquenne No. 63.6/iii[†]). It appears as the final movement of the last of six sonatas appended to his keyboard method book. The **fantasia** of the eighteenth century is a rhapsodic, improvisatory work, often unbarred, in which the composer gives free rein to the musical imagination without concern for conventional musical forms. It is in the fantasia that we most fully experience C.P.E. Bach's *Empfindsamkeit*: long asymmetrical lines, unpredictable rhythms, abrupt harmonic shifts, and sudden dynamic changes. In truth, C.P.E. Bach is not a typical composer of the *galant* style. His long, irregular phrases often go against the grain of the simpler *galant*, with its short, balanced, repeating phrases. Bach was known to

---

[†]There are two standard catalogues of the works of C.P.E. Bach, that of E.E. Helm, *Thematic Catalogue of the Works of Carl Philipp Emanuel Bach* (New Haven, CT, 1989), and an earlier one of A. Wotquenne: *Thematisches Verzeichnis der Werke von Carl Philipp Emanuel Bach (1714–1788)* (Leipzig, 1905).

improvise at the clavichord for hours on end, and indeed the Fantasia in C Minor sounds like an expressive improvisation committed to paper (Ex. 43-4). We can be sure that he intended it for the clavichord because the score contains signs calling for *Bebung*, a trembling ornament that can only be played on a clavichord.

EXAMPLE 43-4

* asterisk indicates *Bebung*

LISTENING CUE

CARL PHILIPP EMANUEL BACH
Fantasia in C Minor for clavichord (1753)

CD 7/8
Anthology, No. 126

Growing tired of King Frederick's increasingly conservative musical taste, and having seen no increase in his pay for a sixteen-year period, C.P.E. Bach left Berlin and moved to Hamburg in 1768. Here he took charge of the music in the five major Protestant churches of this north German city. On the side, Bach instituted a series of public subscription concerts (six or twelve concerts in each series), in which he featured himself at the keyboard. While he was promoting public concerts for a paying audience in Hamburg, his half-brother J.C. Bach was doing the same in London.

✻ THE PIANO IN LONDON: JOHANN CHRISTIAN BACH

C.P.E. Bach was known as "the Berlin Bach," while his half-brother J.C. Bach was called "the London Bach." Although he was the youngest son of J.S. Bach, Johann Christian Bach (1735–1782) was anything but a chip off the old Bach: the son moved to Italy, converted from Lutheran to Catholic, wrote operas, and ended up composing tuneful piano pieces in London. As this famously practical Bach said, "My brother (C.P.E.) lives to compose, but I (J.C.) compose to live."

Arriving in London in 1762, J.C. Bach used his German connections to get himself appointed music master to the English royal family, itself of German descent. And, just as his brother accompanied the flute-playing Frederick the Great in Berlin, so J.C. Bach sometimes accompanied the flute-playing English king George III (against whom the American colonies would soon rebel). In 1764 J.C. Bach and another German musician, Carl Abel, began a series of public concerts in London. A music lover could buy a ticket to a subscription series of up to fifteen concerts, at which the two featured their most recent compositions, along with those of other fashionable composers. The **Bach-Abel concerts** continued for nearly twenty years, and became a model for the public concert series in London and elsewhere throughout Europe. Also in 1764, J.C. Bach met and befriended the Mozarts, who were in London as part of a European tour to showcase the seven-year-old Wolfgang's talents. Bach and Mozart played together on a single keyboard, Wolfgang sitting on Bach's lap: "Herr Johann Christian Bach, the Queen's teacher, took the son between his legs, the former played a few bars, and the other continued, and in this way they played a whole sonata."[5] Young Mozart studied the music of J.C. Bach and later acknowledged the artistic debt he owed him. Indeed, there was a great affinity between the emerging Classical style of Mozart and the *galant* style of J.C. Bach.

Johann Christian Bach's music represents the essence of the *galant* style. His melodies are smooth and graceful, his accompaniments simple, and his textures light and airy. Moreover, Bach's melodies are not technically difficult, a fact that was seen as appealing to amateurs. Said an Englishman of the time: "In general his compositions for the piano forte are such as ladies can execute with little trouble; and the allegros [more] resemble bravura songs, than instrumental pieces."[6] In his keyboard music, J.C. Bach rarely calls on the right hand to play more than a single melodic line, and this produces a *cantabile* (singing) melody, as can be seen in Example 43-5. An Italianate Alberti bass in the left hand, providing a simple, direct harmonic accompaniment, supports the easily flowing tune in the right. Although the rapidly moving bass looks difficult, it is really rather simple, since very few chords are involved and thus few changes of hand position are required. In fact, the thumb of the left hand plays only two notes.

EXAMPLE 43-5

Soon after arriving in London, J.C. Bach took advantage of the flourishing music trade to publish collections of symphonies, keyboard concertos, and keyboard sonatas. Among these, the six he issued as Opus 5 in 1766 represent a landmark—they are the first sonatas published in London to indicate on the title page the option of performance by piano. Moreover, Bach was the first musician to play the piano as a solo instrument in public in England, which he did at one of the Bach-Abel concerts in 1768. As Bach's friend, the historian Charles Burney, observed: "After the arrival of John Christian Bach in this country, and the establishment of his concert[s] . . . all the harpsichord makers tried their mechanical powers at piano-fortes."

Of the sonatas in J.C. Bach's Opus 5, the second in D major shows particular evidence of being conceived for piano rather than harpsichord. Not only are there marks of "piano" and "forte" written in the score, but there are also striking contrasts of texture that can best be brought out on the piano. The opening movement, for example, alternates dramatic chordal units with a quieter two-bar *cantabile* melody (Ex. 43-6). Perhaps most important, Bach lengthens the binary form considerably, a harbinger of the longer piano sonata of the Classical era. There are two distinctly different themes in section **A,** and the beginning of section **B** is expanded

The Piano Comes to England

In 1760 London was not only Europe's most populous city but it was also the richest. Exploration, free trade, and emerging capitalism caused commerce to flourish. The gentrified middle class had money and time to spare for the finer things in life. One thing many well-to-do Londoners came to covet was a pianoforte. In 1750 the piano was almost unknown in England; by 1800 it had replaced the harpsichord entirely, putting harpsichord makers out of business. Part of the attraction of the piano was its size and price. During the 1760s an enterprising German émigré, Johannes Zumpe, began to manufacture what is known as the **square piano,** a small box-shaped piano with strings running at right angles to the keys that could be set upon a table or a simple stand (Fig. 43-3). Zumpe's diminutive pianos sold for less than half the price of large harpsichords. Said an observer of the day: "There was scarcely a house in the kingdom where a keyed instrument had ever had admission, but was supplied with one of Zumpe's piano-fortes for which there was nearly as much call in France as in England. In short he could not make them fast enough to gratify the craving of the public."[7]

During this time the English term "grand" piano originated, and it did so in a strange way. In 1777 Robert Stodart applied for an English patent for a combination piano and harpsichord. He called his instrument "grand" to distinguish it from the smaller square model of Zumpe. Almost immediately, however, the term **grand piano** was applied solely to a large piano with sturdy legs and strings running roughly in the same direction as the keys. By the 1780s, the English piano-maker John Broadwood referred to his five- or six-foot-long pianos as "grands," and the term has remained in use ever since.

🌀 FIGURE 43-3

Johann Zoffany's painting of 1775 represents members of two British families as they gather for music-making. The woman plays a square piano by Johannes Zumpe and the man a cello.

---

into a full-blown development. In fact, this movement is written not in Baroque binary form, but instead in one that will dominate the Classical period: sonata form (see Chapter 44).

EXAMPLE 43-6

LISTENING CUE

JOHANN CHRISTIAN BACH

Piano Sonata in D Major, Opus 5, No. 2 (1766)
First movement, *Allegro di molto*

Thomson-Schirmer Website
Anthology, No. 127

Later, in 1772, Wolfgang Amadeus Mozart paid homage to his early mentor, J.C. Bach. He arranged three of the Opus 5 sonatas (Nos. 2–4) as piano concertos, thereby creating what are now known and enumerated as Mozart concertos K. 107, 1–3. Mozart's alterations were by no means elaborate; he mainly provided Bach's keyboard score with accompanying orchestral parts and added cadenzas for the soloist. Needless to say, if Mozart could make a Classical concerto out of a *galant* sonata, there was little distinction between late *galant* and early Classical styles. At this moment in music history, Classical style simply emerged from the *galant*.

SUMMARY

Amateur music-making flourished during the Enlightenment as the middle class grew with an expanding European economy. Keyboard music in particular enjoyed favor with women who had increased leisure time. The harpsichord ceded pride of place during the eighteenth century to the pianoforte, owing to the piano's greater capacity for contrasts and shadings of volume as well as nuanced articulation. The leading keyboard genre was the sonata, whether the one-movement type associated with Domenico Scarlatti or the far more common three-movement kind of C.P.E. Bach and his younger brother, J.C. Bach. Scarlatti and C.P.E. Bach project two distinctly personal views of *galant* style. The former's writing is flamboyant and extroverted, showing off the skills of the performer including hand-crossing; the latter is more introverted and often unpredictable, with long themes and irregular phrases. The compositional style of J.C. Bach is closer to the core of *galant* style, with its graceful, balanced phrases composed of short motivic ideas supported by simple harmonies. There is a great affinity between the *galant* style of J.C. Bach and the emerging language of Classical music, especially as expressed by Mozart.

KEY TERMS

capitalism	hand-crossing	*Bebung*
Alberti bass	Frederick the Great	fantasia
murky bass	*Essay on the True Art of*	Bach-Abel concerts
pianoforte	*Playing the Keyboard*	square piano
acciaccatura	empfindsamer *Stil*	grand piano

Chapter 44

Classical Music in Vienna

The music of Haydn, Mozart, and the young Beethoven dominates our view of the late eighteenth century. These composers, along with Franz Schubert (1797–1828), form what historians refer to as the **Viennese School,** for indeed all four of these great musicians capped their careers in Vienna. Perhaps at no time in the history of music were so many extraordinary composers found within the walls of a single city. What is more, these composers interacted with one another in a variety of ways: Mozart was a close friend of Haydn; Haydn taught Beethoven; and Schubert was a torchbearer at Beethoven's funeral.

Musical style, too, had a cohesion rarely found in the history of music. Universal musical principles were at work in an age that greatly valued universal ideals. Composers working in Naples, Madrid, Berlin, Paris, and London, influenced by those in Vienna, tacitly reached a consensus as to how music was supposed to sound. The style they created we now call "Classical" music.[1] Whereas "classical" (lower case "c") suggests all Western art music, "Classical" (with a capital "C") has come to denote the high art music of the period roughly 1770–1820. In no city did that art music reach a higher level than in Vienna.

Vienna was then the capital of the old Holy Roman Empire (see Map 49-1). As such, it served as the administrative center for a large part of Europe, including portions of modern-day Germany, Italy, Croatia, Bosnia, Serbia, Slovakia, Poland, Czech Republic, and Hungary, in addition to all of Austria. Vienna was surrounded by vast agricultural lands, with no other large cities for hundreds of miles. The aristocracy from disparate territories, even Russia, congregated in Vienna, especially during the long winter months when there was little agricultural work to be supervised. In 1790, the heyday of Haydn and Mozart, Vienna had a population of roughly 215,000. The nobility numbered about 3,250, and they were attended to by some 40,000 footmen, maids, and other servants. The unusually high percentage of aristocrats among the population may partly account for the fact that art music was so intensely cultivated in the city. The nobles patronized music, often enjoying it together with middle-class citizens at public or semi-public concerts.

With so much patronage to offer, Vienna attracted musicians from throughout Europe, including Christoph Willibald Gluck (1714–1787) from Bohemia (Czech Republic), Antonio Salieri (1750–1825) from Italy, Joseph Haydn (1732–1809) from Rohrau in lower Austria, Wolfgang Amadeus Mozart (1756–1791) from Salzburg in upper Austria, and Ludwig van Beethoven (1770–1827) from the German Rhineland. Vienna was a crossroads for human transit and thus a melting pot of culture. Here high art music from many regions coalesced into a universal musical style that would set the standard for all of Europe.

✾ CLASSICAL STYLE

What are the musical characteristics of Classical style? Many are the same as those found in *galant* music of the earlier Enlightenment: clarity, simplicity, formal balance, and naturalness. Formal patterns are clearly articulated and readily apparent to the ear. Architecture of the late eighteenth century conveys many of these same qualities to the eye. It too is marked by balance, harmonious proportions, and an absence of ornate decoration. Because the designs of many eighteenth-century public buildings were taken directly from classical Rome, this style is called **Neoclassical architecture** (Fig. 44-1). Around the turn of the nineteenth century, Neoclassical architecture was carried to the United States by Thomas Jefferson and others. Today it can be seen in many state capitols, universities, and government buildings, particularly in Washington, D.C. Just as this architectural style has become "classic," continuing to give pleasure to succeeding generations, so too has the music of Haydn, Mozart, and Beethoven.

An excerpt from the famous *Andante* middle movement of Mozart's Piano Concerto No. 21 in C Major (K. 467) exemplifies the clarity, expressive grace, noble simplicity, and balanced contrasts that characterize the Classical style in music. Here Mozart fashions two three-bar phrases: the first is an antecedent phrase that carries the music forward and ends on the dominant harmony, while the second unit is a consequent phrase that complements the first three bars but brings the music back home to the tonic (Ex. 44-1). Subsequent phrases are grouped in three two-bar phrases. The piano presents a melody that is light and airy, yet perfectly balanced. It is also both singable and memorable; indeed, this melody was turned into a popular movie theme (the "love song" from *Elvira Madigan*). A light harmonic support is fashioned by repeating, first a tonic triad, then a dominant-seventh chord, and finally the tonic triad again. This accompaniment supports, but does not interfere with, the graceful melody. Gone entirely is the heavy bass line of the Baroque basso continuo. Gone too is the sometimes-asymmetrical melody of the Baroque that was often more instrumental than vocal in character.

FIGURE 44-1

The façade of Schoenbrunn Palace near Vienna was completed in 1744–1749 with the encouragement of Austria Empress Maria Theresa (1717–1780). The symmetrical units, long lines, and freedom from excessive ornaments are typical of Neoclassical architecture.

EXAMPLE 44-1

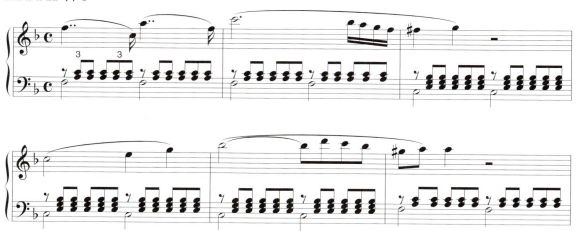

CLASSICAL FORMS

Classical music resounds with pleasing proportions, owing to balanced lines and uncluttered textures. In addition, large-scale musical forms are at work. In the Classical era, perhaps more so than any other period, certain tried-and-true musical forms regulated nearly all art music. Rare was the symphony, concerto, or sonata written during the period 1770–1820 that was not shaped according to a conventional musical form. Most of these forms, however, were not new. Some, such as rondo form and theme-and-variations form, go back to the Middle Ages, while ternary form and rounded binary form flourished during the Baroque period. Only one new form, sonata, emerged during the second half of the eighteenth century. Yet it came to dominate musical structure during the Classical period and continued to be an important formal procedure into the twentieth century.

Rounded Binary Form

Baroque composers usually used binary form (**AB**) in their sonatas and dances. Classical composers generally preferred rounded binary form (**ABA'**). Here **A** ends by establishing a new key (usually the dominant or relative major), while **B,** beginning in a non-tonic key, at first contrasts with **A** but gradually gives way to an altered reprise of **A** (hence **A'**) with a return to the tonic key. In the Classical period, minuets and scherzos are almost always written in rounded binary form, with **A** and then **BA'** repeated (‖:A:‖:BA':‖). Perhaps more important, it is from rounded binary form that the larger sonata form emerged.

Sonata Form

The most important formal innovation of the Classical period is **sonata form.** Classical composers most often employed this form when writing a fast (*allegro*) first movement of a Classical sonata, quartet, or symphony. They also often invoked it when writing fast finales and, less frequently, slow second movements. Sonata form can best be understood as an expansion of rounded binary form. Composers began to extend the **A** portion of rounded binary form by including a second, often contrasting, theme in the dominant (or, in minor-key pieces, relative major) key. The passage of modulation between the tonic and the new key in sonata form we call the **transition** or **bridge.** Often too some distinctive thematic material is added at the end of **A** to serve as a closing theme. The entire **A** section is called the **exposition,** because the primary thematic material of the movement is "exposed" or presented there. Likewise, the **B** section is now expanded and made to provide more contrast to **A.** Here the themes of the exposition are varied or developed in some fashion, hence the name **development.** The development is usually full of counterpoint and rapid modulations, much like an episode in a fugue. Harmonically, it is the most unstable section of sonata form. Only toward the end of the development, in the **retransition,** does tonal stability return, often in the form of a dominant pedal point. The dominant chord then gives way to the tonic and the simultaneous return of the first theme. This return signals the beginning of the **recapitulation.** Though essentially a revisiting of previous material (**A**), the recapitulation is by no means an exact repeat. Composers invariably rewrote the transition in the recapitulation to ensure that the second theme remained in the tonic key. Moreover, most composers took advantage of the recapitulation to offer a "second pass" at the thematic material—to vary it by means of slight thematic alterations or enrich it by adding complementary contrapuntal lines. It was the convention in the eighteenth century in both binary and sonata form movements to repeat both **A** (exposition) and then **BA** (development and recapitulation). Today, however, performers do not always honor such repeats (see Box).

Finally, optional elements may appear at either end of sonata form. Many of the mature symphonies of Mozart, and especially Haydn, have brief introductions before the exposition. Almost without exception these are slow, stately prefaces full of provocative or puzzling chords designed to set the listener wondering what sort of

Should I Repeat?

Symphonies, quartets, and sonatas in the Classical period began, and often ended, with a movement in sonata form. Almost all call for a repeat of the exposition by means of repeat signs, and many require a repeat of the development-recapitulation as well. Today performers and conductors usually honor the first repeat, but rarely the second. Does dropping the second repeat conform to eighteenth-century practice? In some cases, yes. To be specific, a few musicians of the day were growing impatient with this practice of a double repetition, as the French opera composer André Grétry (1741–1813) implied in 1797:

> A sonata is a speech. What would we think of someone who, dividing his speech in half, delivered each half twice? [For example:] "I came to your house this morning; yes, I came to your house this morning; to talk with you about some business; to talk with you about some business." This is nearly the effect that musical repeats have.[1]

As early as the 1780s, Haydn and Mozart began to dispense with the second repeat (development and recapitula-tion) in some, but not all, of their works. The autograph of Mozart's Symphony in G Minor (No. 40), for example, indicates a second repeat in the finale but not in the first movement. Similarly, Mozart calls for the second repeat in the first movement of his Piano Sonata in B♭ Major (K. 570), but gives no such indication in the first movement of his Sonata in D Major (K. 576). Such omissions are likely intentional, but should not be taken as a license to omit all written repeats. Because Mozart carefully specified his intentions in his scores, a performer who wishes to be faithful to him should use a historically accurate edition and follow the composer's repeat signs as indicated.

By the nineteenth century, the second repeat had almost entirely disappeared. The mature Beethoven usually required a repeat of the exposition, but not the development and recapitulation. The tradition of the first repeat, however, long held firm. Composers such as Brahms and Dvořák were still calling for a repeat of the exposition in sonata-form movements as late as the 1880s.

---

musical adventure is about to unfold. A **coda** (Italian for "tail"), on the other hand, might be appended to the recapitulation. Its function is to add extra weight to the end of the movement to give it a feeling of conclusion. Like tails, codas may be short or long; however, they always end in the tonic key.

The diagram of sonata form, below, aims to show the basic principles underpinning sonata form. As with all models of this sort, it represents a simplified abstraction of what is in fact a lengthy, complex, and often unpredictable musical process. In practice, most pieces do not conform to this model in all particulars. The ensuing chapters discuss many movements in sonata form within string quartets, symphonies, and sonatas of Haydn, Mozart, and Beethoven—yet the application of sonata form within each work is unique.

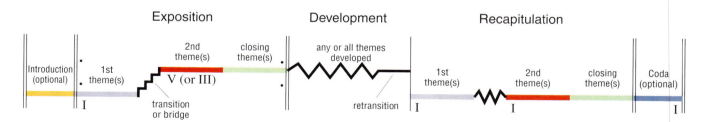

Ternary Form

In the Classical period, composers made frequent use of strict ternary form (**ABA**), as well as a more varied version of it. In strict ternary form, the **A** section begins and ends in the tonic; this is different from binary and rounded binary form, in which **A** ends in the dominant. **B** carries the music to a complementary key such as the dominant, relative major, or parallel minor, and the returning **A** repeats the first section (**A**) note for note. Strict ternary form, broadly applied, was especially favored by Classical composers for the third movements of symphonies and string quartets, in which minuet-trio-minuet or scherzo-trio-scherzo sequences were common. In the more varied version of ternary form, the reprise of **A** was considerably rewritten. Classical composers often employed varied ternary form for their slow movements, as did Beethoven in his Symphony No. 3, The "Eroica" (Anthology, No. 141).

Theme-and-Variations Form

In theme-and-variations form, the composer chooses a theme and then varies it, by altering the melody, harmony, and/or rhythm, or by ornamenting or embellishing around it. Composers of the Classical period preferred to write variations on simple tunes—popular or patriotic songs, folk melodies, or tunes of their own making. Mozart, for example, wrote variations on what we now call "Twinkle, Twinkle Little Star," while Beethoven composed a set on "God Save the King." The simplicity of such melodies as these allowed composers greater freedom in the process of variation. Originally, a work in theme-and-variations form was a one-movement, free-standing piece. But, in the 1760s, Haydn had brought theme-and-variation form into the multi-movement symphony and quartet. Here it usually served as a formal plan for fast finales, and was sometimes found in slow movements, as is the case in Haydn's famous Symphony No. 94, The "Surprise" (Anthology, No. 130).

Rondo Form

The rondo of the Classical period perpetuates a formal procedure that extends back into the Middle Ages (see Chapter 12). During the Baroque era, the "rondeau" was popular, particularly in France, as a one-movement instrumental dance or keyboard piece (see Anthology, No. 104). Enlightenment composers such as J.C. Bach brought the form into the multi-movement symphony and sonata. A typical Classical **rondo** sets a refrain (**A**) against contrasting material (**B, C,** or **D**) to create a pattern such as **ABACA, ABACABA,** or even **ABACADA.** Almost all true rondos include at least three statements of the primary structural unit or refrain (**A**) and at least two contrasting sections (**B** and **C**). The rondo usually projects a playful, exuberant mood, and for that reason the form often served as the last movement of a sonata or symphony, to bid a happy farewell to the audience. Mozart, for example, wrote four concertos for French horn, and the finale of each is in rondo form. Similarly, Beethoven used rondo form in the finales of all five of his piano concertos (see Chapter 49).

CLASSICAL GENRES

Form regulates the flow of most art music, and Classical music is no exception. Classical composers Haydn, Mozart, and Beethoven carefully positioned all of the elements of musical expression—themes, harmonic relationships, instrumental colors, textures, and dynamics—in ways that enhance formal clarity. Form provides a structure for each movement. But most compositions of the Classical period are multi-movement works. Classical composers grouped movements together to conform to an established genre—a broad category, or type, of music. Among other things, a musical genre implied a particular performing force as well as a place of performance. The symphony, for example, was usually performed by a full orchestra in a large princely chamber or public concert hall, while the quartet was played by four soloists in the home. Following are brief descriptions of the principal genres of Classical instrumental music. Genres of vocal music, namely, opera, oratorio, and Mass, will be discussed in Chapters 46 and 48.

Symphony

During the eighteenth century, the symphony gradually replaced the solo concerto and concerto grosso as the leading genre of large-scale instrumental music. Haydn, Mozart, and Beethoven each wrote more symphonies than concertos, and concerts featuring the music of these masters would invariably begin and end with one of their symphonies. Beethoven, for example, in his public debut in Vienna on 2 April 1800, presented a concert that began with a symphony by Mozart and ended with his own Symphony No. 1. The overall symphonic output of the eighteenth century was immense; one scholar has catalogued more than 12,000 symphonies produced between about 1720 and 1810. From the mid eighteenth century onward, the symphony formed the heart and soul of almost every orchestral concert. That is why the large orchestral ensemble is still called a symphony orchestra.

Concerto

During the Baroque era, two types of concertos could be found: the solo concerto and the concerto grosso. During the Classical period, the concerto grosso largely disappeared, leaving only the solo concerto, which Classical composers preferred to write for solo violin or keyboard. By the time Mozart arrived in Vienna in 1781, the piano was well on its way to replacing the harpsichord as the solo instrument in the keyboard concerto. Haydn, Mozart, and Beethoven all wrote concertos for piano as well as for violin. Of the piano concertos, the twenty-three concertos of Mozart and the five of Beethoven are the best known today (see Anthology, Nos. 136 and 140).

Divertimento and Serenade

Originally the term "divertimento" simply meant a musical diversion and comprised a variety of types of chamber music including the string quartet. But, in time, the **divertimento** came to imply a lighter style of music and a five-movement format: fast/minuet and trio/slow/minuet and trio/fast. The term **serenade** was generally used interchangeably with divertimento. Both types were played not only indoors but also outdoors as evening entertainment. Open-air concerts in the summer helped give Vienna its reputation as a musical city. The term "serenade" also implied that the music was appropriate for serenading a lady on her birthday or name day. Early in his career young Haydn earned money by serenading in the streets of Vienna.

Some divertimenti and serenades were composed for strings alone. One such piece is Mozart's famous *Eine kleine Nachtmusik* (*A Little Night Music*, 1787). It was originally written in five movements (the first minuet has been ripped out of the autograph score) for four string parts: two violins, viola, and cello, with double bass perhaps doubling the cello. But wind ensembles were also active participants in this genre (Fig. 44-2) because their sounds project well outdoors. At first, pairs of oboes, French horns, and bassoons formed the standard ensemble; later, after 1780, a pair

🌀 FIGURE 44-2

A large *Harmonie* employed at the German court of Oettingen-Wallerstein consisting of pairs of flutes, clarinets, oboes, and French horns, supported by bassoon and double bass. Musicologist Sterling Murray, an expert on Oettingen-Wallerstein, dates this silhouette to 1783–1784 because a second bassoonist joined the ensemble in 1785.

of clarinets was added. Because in the eighteenth-century orchestra the winds played mostly harmony (German "Harmonie") and not melody, such an independent wind band came to be called a **Harmonie** in late eighteenth-century Vienna, and the music for it was designated **Harmoniemusik.** Mozart wrote a number of excellent divertimenti and serenades for *Harmonie*, including his Serenade in C Minor, created in 1782 for the emperor's wind band.

String Quartet

Joseph Haydn wrote his first string quartets in the late 1750s, and would bring the genre to its first maturity. With the addition of a viola line to the old Baroque trio sonata texture, along with an animated cello part, the quartet featured four more-or-less evenly matched instrumental parts. The function of a string quartet was somewhat different from that of the symphony or concerto, in that it was designed for a private or semi-private performance in the aristocratic salon or the middle-class parlor. This domestic music, always played one-on-a-part, came to be called "chamber music."

Sonata

The Classical **sonata** was a type of domestic instrumental chamber music in two, three, or, more rarely, four movements for soloist or small ensemble. In Vienna in particular, young women of refinement were expected to play the piano. They acquired, and then demonstrated, their skills by playing piano sonatas. The easiest and shortest of these was sometimes dubbed **sonatina** (Italian for "little sonata"). Sonatas and sonatinas by Haydn, Mozart, Clementi, and others flooded the market. Although most were intended as teaching pieces, Beethoven designed many of his piano sonatas to serve as vehicles to showcase his own virtuosity. Accordingly, his sonatas are more technically demanding than those of Haydn or Mozart. In addition, Haydn, Mozart, and Beethoven all wrote violin sonatas. Yet, here again a distinction must be made. The accompanied sonatas of Haydn and Mozart often demand more of the keyboard player than the violinist. Indeed, in Mozart's earliest sonatas for violin and piano, the violin is optional (Ex. 44-2). Not until the violin sonatas and cello sonatas of Beethoven do the soloist and pianist consistently behave as equal partners.

EXAMPLE 44-2 Mozart, Violin Sonata in G Major (K. 9), III

In the Classical era, each of these instrumental genres carried implications with regard to form. To illustrate the relationship between genre and form in Classical music, a list of well-known compositions by the Classical masters follows, along with an indication of their forms, movement by movement. The symphony and string quartet usually consisted of four movements, whereas the sonata and concerto usually had just three. In all of these genres, the first movement was almost always in sonata form. In the four-movement genres (symphony and quartet), the third movement was usually a ternary-form dance (minuet-trio-minuet or scherzo-trio-scherzo), each section of which (minuet, scherzo, or trio) was in rounded binary form. The pieces listed below demonstrate how the three foremost Classical composers—Haydn, Mozart, and Beethoven—chose to allocate musical form within the various genres of instrumental music.

Genre of Composition		Form of Composition		
Symphony, Quartet, and Serenade	*1st movement*	*2nd movement*	*3rd movement*	*4th movement*
Haydn, Symphony No. 94, the "Surprise"	sonata	theme & variations	ternary	sonata
Haydn, String Quartet, the "Emperor"	sonata	theme & variations	ternary	sonata
Mozart, Symphony in G Minor (K. 550)	sonata	sonata	ternary	sonata
Mozart, Serenade, *Eine kleine Nachtmusik*	sonata	ternary	ternary	rondo
Beethoven, Symphony No. 3, the "Eroica"	sonata	ternary	ternary	theme & variations
Piano sonata	*1st movement*	*2nd movement*	*3rd movement*	
Haydn, Sonata No. 52 in E♭ Major	sonata	ternary	sonata	
Beethoven, the "Pathétique"	sonata	rondo	rondo	
Piano concerto	*1st movement*	*2nd movement*	*3rd movement*	
Mozart Piano Concerto in G Major (K. 453)	sonata	ternary	theme & variations	

 ## THE CLASSICAL ORCHESTRA

The story of the Western orchestra between 1750 and 1820 is essentially one of growth. A typical orchestra around 1750 included strings, two oboes, two bassoons, and two horns, as well as an accompanying keyboard instrument (then the harpsichord), and to this ensemble could be added trumpets and timpani on festive occasions. Joseph Haydn's experience with several Classical orchestras may be taken as representative. When Haydn first signed on at the Esterházy court in 1761, his princely patron's orchestra numbered only about sixteen players, though this ensemble was gradually increased to twenty-five; in the 1780s, Haydn's symphonies were played in public concerts in Paris by a group of more than seventy; for his concerts

Photograph courtesy of Richard J. Martz Horn Collection

❋ FIGURE 44-3

The natural French horn of the eighteenth century with crooks that, when inserted, alter the pitch of the instrument.

in London in 1795, an orchestra of about sixty was on hand. Obviously, as the performance site for the symphony moved from the private salon to the public auditorium, the volume of sound needed to be increased to fill the larger hall.

Most of this increase occurred in the string section. Mozart mentions an orchestra of some eighty players including forty violins, ten violas, eight cellos, and ten double basses, for a public concert at the Burgtheater in Vienna in 1781. Although this was an exceptionally large ensemble brought together for a special benefit concert, it suggests that, for times of public display, the Baroque orchestra with two or three string players per part would no longer please.

Color was added to the ensemble through the addition of more woodwinds. The orchestra at Mannheim had led the way in this regard (see Chapter 42). Instead of a pair of oboes (or flutes or clarinets) and bassoons, now pairs of oboes, clarinets, flutes, and bassoons became the norm for the largest ensembles. The woodwinds gave variety to the sound and could be used to add contrapuntal weight to the texture. Mozart in particular exhibited great care in his woodwind parts, usually composing a separate line for each instrument within the pair, rather than having both instruments double on one line.

As to the brasses, two French horns were part of every ensemble, although occasionally four horns were required. These horns were still natural instruments, without valves (Fig. 44-3). Chromatic pitches could be played by inserting the hand into the bell of the instrument (hand-stopping). If the player needed to change key, he inserted a **crook** (a small piece of pipe) that altered the length of tubing within the instrument and consequently its pitch. Finally, to create an especially festive, brilliant sound, trumpets and drums might appear. Trumpets too were natural instruments that were usually pitched in the "bright" keys of D or C.

In sum, private aristocratic orchestras in the Classical period remained small, but ensembles for public halls, especially in Vienna, Paris, and London, sometimes became quite large, featuring as many as eighty musicians in special cases. But, what was the norm? Perhaps the orchestra Mozart assembled for his public concerts in Vienna in 1783 can be taken as the typical "mid-size" orchestra. The ensemble counted six first violins, six seconds, four violas, three cellos, and three double basses; to these were added pairs of flutes, oboes, clarinets, and bassoons, four horns, two trumpets, and timpani—a total of thirty-seven players.

❋ CLASSICAL COMPOSERS

Viewed from a modern perspective, the Classical period was dominated by three composers: Haydn, Mozart, and Beethoven. There were, of course, many other artists active at the time, some of whom were very successful. While Haydn's music was widely disseminated and respected, Mozart's was less well known. Even in Vienna, Mozart's operas were less popular than those of such now-obscure figures as Vicente Martín y Soler (1754–1806) and Giovanni Paisiello (1740–1816). Haydn and Mozart had their competitors. Mozart's nemesis, as portrayed in the film *Amadeus*, was Antonio Salieri (1750–1825), who served as official court composer to Emperor Joseph II. Mozart also had a rival in Muzio Clementi (1752–1832), and the two engaged in a famous keyboard duel in 1781. Clementi has left us many sonatas and sonatinas, which most beginning and intermediate pianists still play today. Other important figures of the day include Ignace Pleyel (1757–1831), Haydn's pupil and sometime rival, and Antonio Rosetti (1750–1792), whose Requiem Mass was performed at a memorial service for Mozart. To these can be added Carl Ditters von Dittersdorf (1739–1799), who sometimes played string quartets with Mozart and Haydn in Vienna, and Haydn's younger brother Michael (1737–1806), who for years worked in Salzburg with Wolfgang and Leopold Mozart. Michael Haydn's Symphony in G Major (1783) was long thought (mistakenly) to be a symphony by Mozart. As this confusion shows, these were able musicians whose compositional skill was not that much less than the great Viennese masters. The best compositions of Haydn, Mozart, and Beethoven, however, reached a level all their own.

SUMMARY

The term "Classical period" denotes the art music composed during the late eighteenth and early nineteenth centuries, roughly 1770–1820. The epicenter for the Classical style was Vienna. Haydn, Mozart, Beethoven, and Schubert collectively have come to be called the Viennese School. Classical composers were remarkably consistent with regard to the musical genres they adopted and the musical forms they employed within these genres. Of the forms, the newest and most important is sonata. It became the structural backbone of almost all first movements within the instrumental genres, and of many final movements as well. The genres and forms popularized in the second half of the eighteenth century remained important throughout the nineteenth and even into the twentieth century. The orchestra increased in size and color during the Classical period, owing in particular to the addition of woodwinds. The orchestral showpiece was the symphony, and from the Classical period onward it is possible to speak in terms of the "symphony orchestra." Joseph Haydn was a great innovator in the genres of string quartet and symphony; Wolfgang Amadeus Mozart created works of extraordinary beauty in every genre; and Ludwig van Beethoven took the genres and forms created by his predecessors and gave them unheard-of expressive powers.

KEY TERMS

Viennese School	retransition	*Harmonie*
Neoclassical architecture	recapitulation	*Harmoniemusik*
sonata form	coda	sonata
transition (bridge)	rondo	sonatina
exposition	divertimento	
development	serenade	

Joseph Haydn: Instrumental Music

The story of Joseph Haydn's life is a rags-to-riches tale spanning many decades. Haydn was born into humble circumstances, yet by dint of talent and hard work became the most famous composer in Western Europe. His long career bridged the span between the late Baroque and early Romantic periods; he started composing while J.S. Bach was still working on his B-Minor Mass and lived to hear Beethoven's early-Romantic symphonies. Haydn excelled in writing instrumental music, single-handedly creating what we now call the string quartet, and accelerating the development of the symphony, making it the showpiece of the public concert hall.

THE LIFE OF JOSEPH HAYDN (1732–1809)

Joseph Haydn was born in 1732 in a farmhouse in Rohrau, Austria, about twenty-five miles east of Vienna (Map 45-1). His father, a wheelwright, played the harp but could not read music. When the choir director of St. Stephen's Cathedral in Vienna happened to be scouting for talent in the provinces, he heard the boy soprano Haydn sing, and brought him back to the cathedral in Vienna. Here Haydn remained as a choirboy, studying the rudiments of composition and learning to play the violin and keyboard. When his voice broke at the age of seventeen, he was abruptly dismissed. During the next eight years Haydn eked out what he called "a wretched existence," working as a freelance performer and teacher in Vienna. In 1761 Haydn's years of struggle ended when he was engaged as director of music at the Esterházy court.

The **Esterházy family** was the richest and most influential among the German-speaking aristocrats of Hungary, with estates covering some ten million acres south-east of Vienna. Over a period of more than thirty years, Haydn worked for three Esterházy princes, the most important of which was Nikolaus Esterházy, who played

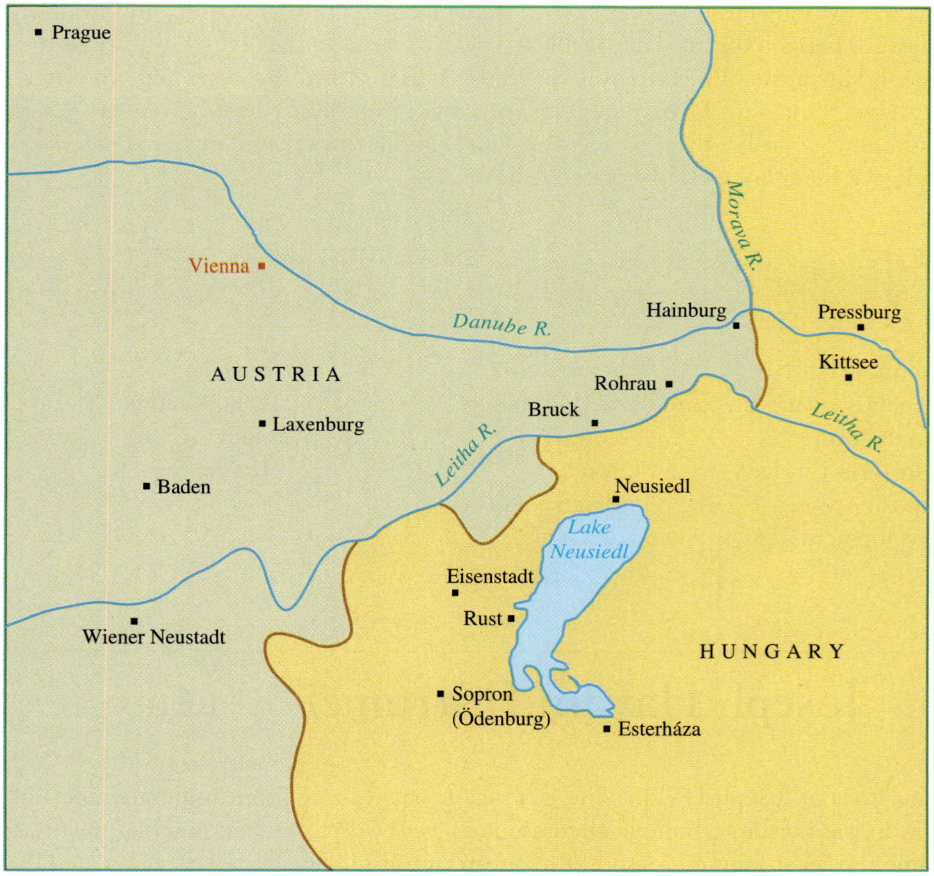

MAP 45-1
Haydn's world.

the **baryton** (a *viola da gamba*–like instrument with six strings) and for whom Haydn wrote 126 baryton trios. The contract Haydn signed at the Esterházy court in 1761 provided a handsome salary, lodging, board at the table of court staff, and the blue and gold servant's livery of court employees (Fig. 45-1). It also regulated Haydn's musical activities:

> [He] and all the musicians shall appear in uniform, and the said Joseph Haydn shall take care that he and all the members of the orchestra follow the instructions given, and appear in white stocking, white linen, powdered, and with either a pigtail or a tiewig . . . .
>
> The said [Haydn] shall be under obligation to compose such music as his Serene Highness may command, and neither to communicate such compositions to any other person, nor to allow them to be copied, but he shall retain them for the absolute use of his Highness, and not compose for any other person without the knowledge and permission of his Highness.[1]

As the contract makes clear, Haydn could compose only for his Esterházy patron, and the works he produced belonged to the prince, not the composer—such was the subservient position of composers generally in eighteenth-century society. Yet Haydn was more than satisfied with his position at the Esterházy court. Except for a few weeks during the winter season when the ruler and his retainers visited Vienna, the court resided in the princely estates southeast of the city. This mostly isolated life away from the musical world forced Haydn to become inventive, as he noted when recalling his days with Prince Nikolaus: "I was cut off from the world, nobody in my vicinity could upset my self-confidence or annoy me, and so I had no choice but to become original."[2] The desire to "take risks" and create novel effects never deserted the composer.

For most of the 1760s, Haydn wrote mainly instrumental music for the Esterházy court—symphonies, concertos, and baryton trios in which Prince Nikolaus could perform. During the 1770s, however, Haydn turned his attention increasingly to opera. Here, too, he composed according to the tastes of his patron, for during this decade Prince Nikolaus undertook to complete a massive new court complex called Esterháza south of Vienna (see Map 45-1). When finished, Esterháza would approach in size the colossal palace of Versailles and boast a large, free-standing opera house (Fig. 45-2) for which Haydn composed some dozen operas in Italian. But, despite his success with opera and his later Masses and oratorios, Joseph Haydn is remembered today primarily as a composer of instrumental music: symphonies, string quartets, concertos, and keyboard sonatas.

✵ FIGURE 45-1

Portrait of Joseph Haydn at about the age of thirty, wearing a wig and the blue livery of the Esterházy court. With the kind permission of Professor Daniel Heartz.

✲ HAYDN'S EARLY AND MIDDLE SYMPHONIES†

Joseph Haydn has been called the "father of the symphony," but this honor is not entirely merited. As we have seen (see Chapter 42), many other composers were actively writing symphonies during the 1740s and 1750s. Nonetheless, Haydn wrote

---

†As is true for Bach and Mozart, there is a thematic catalogue of the compositions of Joseph Haydn, in this case one prepared by the Dutch musicologist Anthony Hoboken (1887–1983): *Joseph Haydn: thematisch-bibliographisches Werkverzeichnis* (Mainz, 1957–1978), 3 vols. Thus, a work of Haydn is often identified in the literature by a **Hoboken (Hob.) number.** For the symphonies of Haydn, however, the Hoboken numbering system has been so commonly adopted (Haydn Symphony No. 104 equates to Hob.I:104) that usually no Hoboken number appears. Finally, Hoboken has classified the works of Haydn chronologically by genre; roman number I stands for the symphonies and III for the string quartets, for example.

❋ FIGURE 45-2

The palace of the Esterházy family southeast of Vienna, where Joseph Haydn lived 1766–1790. It was modeled on the grand French palace of Versailles west of Paris.

Pesci, Esterhása Castle, Orszagos Müemleki Felügeloség

more works in this genre than any other composer, 108 in all. Haydn's first symphonies (1757–1760) are in three movements (fast/slow/fast). By the time Haydn joined the Esterházy court in 1761, however, a four-movement format had become his norm. Following the example of Johann Stamitz at Mannheim, Haydn inserted a minuet in third position. Originally a **minuet** was a triple-meter dance that was often added toward the end of the Baroque dance suite (see Chapter 34). In the Classical period, this dance was invariably written in rounded-binary form and coupled with a matching rounded-binary movement called the trio, to form a **minuet and trio** (at first the trio was more lightly scored than the minuet, being often written for just three instruments, hence its name). Thus, Haydn's usual sequence of movements within a symphony proceeded fast/slow/minuet and trio/fast.

Typical of the best of Haydn's early symphonies is a set of three (Nos. 6–8) that he composed in 1761, soon after arriving at the Esterházy court. He named them *Le Matin* (*Morning*), *Le Midi* (*Noon*), and *Le Soir* (*Evening*), and in each he sought to create an appropriate musical mood for the corresponding time of the day. *Le Matin*, for example, opens with a slow introduction that depicts a sunrise; the upper parts slowly rise and then hold on high, as the dynamic level grows from *pianissimo* to *fortissimo*. Writing a slow introduction to the fast opening movement of a symphony becomes common with Haydn at this time, and in his late symphonies it becomes the norm. In addition, Haydn composed his symphonies Nos. 6–8 in a special orchestral style called **concertante,** a concerto-like approach in which individual instruments regularly emerge from the orchestral texture to function as soloists. The newly instituted orchestra at Esterházy was small, consisting of only about sixteen musicians, including the string section, two horn players, a bassoonist, and two oboists who might also double on flute. Evidently, Haydn wanted to please his patron by writing in a way that best displayed the talents of the orchestra. In *Le Matin*, for example, the main theme of the first movement is carried by a solo flute (Ex. 45-1), and the return to it at the recapitulation is announced by a jaunty French horn solo. In the context of the modest Esterházy orchestra, these wind solos would have projected particularly well.

EXAMPLE 45-1

🔊 LISTENING CUE

JOSEPH HAYDN
Symphony No. 6 in D Major,
Le Matin (1761)
First movement, *Adagio; Allegro*

CD 7/9
Anthology, No. 128

Clearly, Haydn's aim in his "times-of-the-day" symphonies was to create a descriptive set along the lines of Vivaldi's earlier *Four Seasons*. This was not the only occasion on which Haydn would call upon extra-musical phenomena to inform his symphonies. Various later symphonies also suggest an outside stimulus, judging from their nicknames (given by later commentators). Among these are the "Hornsignal" (Symphony No. 31), "Funeral" (No. 44), "Farewell" (No. 45), "Passion" (No. 49), and "Fire" (No. 59). The **"Farewell" Symphony** is today the best known of these programmatic works, perhaps owing to the anecdote that gave rise to its title. It seems that Prince Nikolaus had stayed at Esterháza longer than expected, and his musicians were eager to return to their wives and families closer to Vienna. To make the point, Haydn concludes the symphony by asking the players, one by one, to extinguish their candles and walk off the stage, leaving only two violinists to play at the end. The prince got the message, as the story goes, and the musicians were soon allowed to return to their winter quarters.

Haydn Goes Hunting

What did the great composers do for recreation and amusement? Beethoven took long walks, musical sketchbook in hand, almost daily, no matter how foul the weather. Mozart played endless games of billiards (he had a billiard table in his bedroom) and went horseback riding in the Prater Park in Vienna for exercise. Joseph Haydn too tried horseback riding, but when he took a nasty spill in 1760 he vowed never to remount. Haydn was small and unassuming, and his physical stature sometimes disappointed those who loved his music. Once Haydn was singled out in a crowd of admirers, but at least one person refused to believe the small man could be the great composer: "That's not Haydn—it can't possibly be! Haydn must be a fine, big, handsome man and not that insignificant little one you've got there in the middle."[3]

In his old age Haydn was fond of telling stories about his earlier days on the Esterházy estates. His first biographer, G. A. Griesinger, says the following about his outdoor activities: "Hunting and fishing were Haydn's favorite pastimes during his stay in Hungary, and he never forgot that he once brought down with one shot three hazel-hens, which later appeared on the dinner table of the Empress Maria Theresa (1717–1780). Another time he aimed at a hare, but only shot off its tail; yet the bullet continued and killed a pheasant that chanced to be close by; then Haydn's dog, pursuing the hare, strangled itself in a snare." Evidently, hunting with Haydn could be dangerous sport.[4]

Aside from the unusual nature of its programmatic content, the "Farewell" Symphony is also important in the history of music because its style typifies a group of Haydn's works dating from the late 1760s and early 1770s, whose expressive character has been called *Sturm und Drang*. The term **Sturm und Drang** ("Storm and Stress") originated not in music but in German literature. It suggests a mode of expression that sought to frighten, stun, and overcome with emotion. Its anti-rational approach was, of course, at variance with the Enlightenment emphasis on order and rational thought in all things. In fact, the *Sturm und Drang* movement had less affinity to the balanced Classical idioms of the eighteenth century than to the more passionate Romantic art of the nineteenth century. As a specifically musical term, *Sturm und Drang* refers to a small but significant group of works written around 1770 that are marked by agitated, impassioned writing, such as Mozart's Symphony No. 25 and Haydn's symphonies Nos. 44, 45, and 49. All are characterized by minor keys, angular themes, syncopation, string tremolos, sudden dynamic shifts, and violin lines that race up and down the scale. In Haydn's case, this intense, stressful sound gradually disappears as he turns increasingly to opera during the later 1770s.

HAYDN'S STRING QUARTETS

Joseph Haydn is also called the "father of the string quartet," and here the honor is entirely justified, for Haydn almost single-handedly fashioned the genre in its modern form. In all, he composed sixty-eight quartets scored for two violins, viola, and cello. To appreciate Haydn's accomplishment, we must recall that small-ensemble writing at the end of the Baroque era was dominated by the string trio sonata—usually two violins over a basso continuo (bass line with chordal support by the harpsichord). The first violin carried the melody above a heavy bass. Between 1750 and 1770, Haydn gradually refashioned what was essentially a "top and bottom" texture into one with four more-or-less equal voices, the lowest of which was a cello; the old basso continuo was reduced to a single cello line.

Haydn also brought a new mood to the string quartet. His earliest quartets of the 1750s have the feel of the light, outdoor, five-movement divertimento. By the 1770s, however, the tone of his quartets had become more serious and the individual movements more weighty. Like the symphony, the quartet now consisted of four movements, including a minuet in either second, or, increasingly, third position. Yet, unlike the symphony, which often excels in dramatic effects that only a large orchestra can create, the string quartet emphasizes a continual motivic development, and this motivic working out occurs almost equally in all four parts.

Haydn's set of six string quartets Opus 20, written around 1772, was something of a landmark for the genre, exhibiting the two most prominent characteristics of the Classical string quartet: an approximately equal-voiced texture and a generally serious tone. Two of the six (Nos. 3 and 5) are in minor keys, and the generally dark quality of the set places it firmly within Haydn's *Sturm und Drang* period of the early 1770s. Moreover, three of the quartets (Nos. 2, 5, and 6) have fugal finales. The use of fugal procedure within the string quartet makes these works sound both serious and "learned." Haydn was not only a playful, capricious composer but also, when he chose to be, a very cerebral one. The finale of Opus 20, No. 5, is, in Haydn's words, a "Fuga a due soggetti" ("Fugue with two subjects"), while the fugal finale of No. 6 has three subjects, and No. 2 has four. In these finales, Haydn displays such erudite contrapuntal techniques as musical inversion, canon, and stretto.

Almost ten years elapsed before Haydn issued his next collection of string quartets, a set of six numbered Opus 33. In 1779 Haydn had signed a new contract with Prince Nikolaus Esterházy that allowed him to sell his music to whomever he wished. The Opus 33 quartets seem to be a product of this new arrangement. Haydn himself solicited sales of the set by writing to potential buyers, advertising that the quartets were "written in an entirely new and special way." Now, for the first time in his quartets, the movement that had been called "minuet" is entitled **scherzo** (Italian for "joke" or "jest"). These scherzi, in fact, do play jokes on the listener, because the downbeat of the dance is frequently placed out of sync with the minuet's three-beat meter, creating syncopations and hemiolas. The Opus 33 quartets are Haydn's first mature quartets to be imbued with this playful, more popular, style. Opus 33, No. 2, for example, is referred to as the "Joke" Quartet because it concludes unexpectedly in the middle of a phrase; the players simply stop, leaving listeners to wonder if the piece is really at an end. Opus 33, No. 3, is nicknamed the **"Bird" Quartet** because the strings sound distinctly like birds chirping and pecking their way across the musical landscape.

Despite its playful tone, the opening movement of the "Bird" Quartet (Opus 33, No. 3) is a carefully crafted composition in sonata form. At the outset, melody and harmony are set forth in a way that blurs the distinction between leading voice and accompaniment; this greater integration of melody and accompaniment is one of the hallmarks of quartet style. The exposition contains three themes (first, second, and closing), each of equal weight yet each presenting "the sprightly bird" in a distinctly different pose. The substantive development makes use of all three themes and is almost as long as the exposition itself. Everywhere, well-proportioned sections support a melodic unfolding full of light-hearted charm. What is characterized as the "popular" quality of Haydn's music can perhaps best be seen in his closing theme (Ex. 45-2). Here a tuneful, stepwise melody sounds forth in the first violin, with the quick grace-notes adding avian charm to the sound.

EXAMPLE 45-2

Finally, in the coda, Haydn drives to the end with the opening bars of the first theme, a gambit that his pupil Beethoven will later exploit in his own symphonies and sonatas. The Opus 33 quartets influenced Mozart as well, for they served as a point of departure for a set of six that Mozart wrote during 1782–1785 (see Chapter 47) and, appropriately enough, dedicated to his good friend Joseph Haydn.

LISTENING CUE

JOSEPH HAYDN
Opus 33, No. 3, The "Bird" Quartet
(Hob.III:39; 1781)
First movement, *Allegro moderato*

CD 7/10
Anthology, No. 129

Haydn continued to write string quartets to the very end of his composing years. Indeed, the incomplete string quartet Opus 103, which he abandoned in 1803, marks his last composition in any genre. Among the late quartets is a set of six, Opus 76, composed in 1797, which includes the so-called Emperor Quartet.

The **"Emperor" Quartet** (Opus 76, No. 3) reflects the political and military events of the Napoleonic Wars (1796–1815), which made their way right to Haydn's doorstep. In 1796 the armies of Napoleon invaded the Austrian Empire and this, in turn, ignited a firestorm of patriotism in Vienna, the Austrian capital. But the Austrians were at a musical disadvantage: the French had their *Marseillaise* and the English their *God Save the King* (which Haydn had heard repeatedly in London), but the Austrians had no national anthem around which to rally. Thus Haydn was commissioned to compose an appropriate tune, and he created the melody for the text *Gott erhalte Franz den Kaiser* (*God Preserve Emperor Franz*) in honor of the reigning Austrian Emperor Franz II (Ex. 45-3). Called **The Emperor's Hymn,** it was first sung in theaters throughout the Austrian realm on the Emperor's birthday, 12 February 1797.

EXAMPLE 45-3

God preserve Emperor Franz, our good Emperor Franz.
Long life to Emperor Franz, in the brightest splendor of happiness.
Garlands of laurel bloom for him wherever he goes, as a wreath of honor.
God preserve Emperor Franz, our good Emperor Franz.

Capitalizing on the popularity of his tune, Haydn soon made it serve as a basis of a theme-and-variations set in the second movement of his string quartet Opus 76, No. 3 (Hob.III:77), now called the "Emperor" Quartet. In this movement the theme is stated by the first violin and harmonized by simple chords. Then four variations follow. In these the second violin, cello, viola, and again first violin each has its turn to present the tune amidst increasingly ornate embellishment.

As we might suspect, Haydn's patriotism was not sufficient to keep Napoleon's armies at bay. Nor was the Austrian army. The French had surrounded Vienna in 1805 and would do so again in 1809. Indeed, in the spring of 1809 a cannon ball fell adjacent to Haydn's house, shaking the composer and terrifying his servants. But Haydn retained faith in his emperor and his tune, and he played a piano arrangement of it daily. In fact, *The Emperor's Hymn* was the last music Haydn played before he died in the early hours of 31 May 1809.

The popularity of *The Emperor's Hymn* ended neither with Haydn's death nor with the final defeat of Napoleon in 1815, nor even with the death of Emperor Franz II in 1835. So alluring was Haydn's melody that, with altered text, it became a Protestant hymn and then, in 1853, the national anthem of Austria. Austria gave up the tune after its defeat in World War II, but, with amended text, Germany took it up in 1950! And so today Haydn's timeless melody serves as the German national anthem.

HAYDN'S SONATAS AND CONCERTOS

Today Joseph Haydn is known primarily for his string quartets and symphonies. But he also wrote more than sixty keyboard sonatas and more than thirty concertos for various instruments. In Haydn's case, we say "keyboard" sonatas because it is not always certain whether a particular sonata was composed for the harpsichord, clavichord, or pianoforte. Haydn seems to have switched to the newer piano in the early 1770s. One sonata in particular, No. 20 in C minor (Hob.XVI:20; 1771), includes a rapid alternation of pianos and fortes, which could be executed on the piano (or clavichord), but not on the harpsichord (Ex. 45-4). This passage also reveals a characteristic feature of Haydn's keyboard sonatas: highly variegated rhythms. In general Haydn's writing for solo keyboard is marked by frequent changes of note values and rhythmic patterns. So too Haydn's sonatas tend to be freer and more unpredictable in the unfolding of the melodic material; they belong more to the expressive tradition of the north German sonata and fantasia of C.P.E. Bach than to the smooth, elegant Italian-style sonata of J.C. Bach.

EXAMPLE 45-4

Although Haydn's keyboard sonatas are now played less often in recital than those of his younger contemporaries Mozart and Beethoven, they do have strong advocates among professional pianists today. Most favored among these are the aforementioned No. 20 in C minor, a passionate work belonging to the composer's *Sturm und Drang* period, and No. 52 in E♭ major (Hob.XVI:52). This last sonata, which dates from Haydn's final stay in London in 1794, was written for the female virtuoso Therese Jansen Bartolozzi. When this work was finally published in London in 1800, it was entitled "Grand Sonata for the Piano Forte," and its proportions are indeed grand. Remarkable for a sonata in E♭, it has a slow movement in the key of E major (Ex. 45-5). The pianist ends the first movement on a solid E♭ major triad and directly proceeds to open the middle movement with an equally solid, but entirely shocking, E major triad. Haydn may have been a grandfatherly figure by 1794, but he could still behave like an *enfant terrible*.

EXAMPLE 45-5

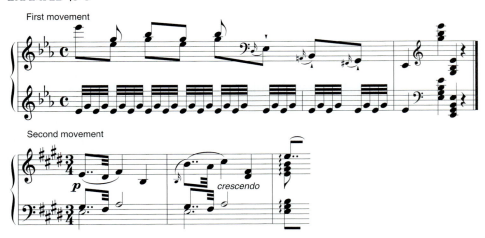

Surviving from Haydn's hand are ten solo concertos for various string and woodwind instruments (at least seven others have been lost). Most important among these are the Cello Concerto in D Major of 1784 and the Trumpet Concerto in E♭ of 1796. The latter piece is especially well known today, owing to a Grammy-winning recording by Wynton Marsalis. Haydn also composed more than a dozen keyboard concertos, most of which are early works of the 1750s and 1760s that were conceived for the harpsichord rather than piano. Mozart augmented his income by mounting concerts at which he would be the featured soloist in one of his own piano concertos. Haydn, while a competent pianist, was no virtuoso, and, as we shall see, filled his purse during the 1780s and 1790s, not by writing concertos but mainly by composing symphonies.

SUMMARY

Joseph Haydn wrote a great deal of vocal music in his long career, including at least fifteen Italian operas, fourteen Latin Masses, and two important oratorios. Yet he is remembered today primarily for his instrumental music: his sixty-eight string quartets, 108 symphonies, fifty-two piano sonatas, and numerous concertos, including a celebrated one for cello and another for trumpet. Haydn created the modern string quartet, transforming the old trio sonata into a new genre, and converting what had been a top-bottom texture held together by a basso continuo into a sonority of four more-or-less equal lines. Homophony now blends with counterpoint so as to lessen the distinction between melody and accompaniment. After Haydn, the string quartet remained the most common form of chamber music, and nearly every important subsequent composer wrote for this medium.

Haydn did not create the symphony, but in the course of forty years managed to revolutionize it. In 1750 the symphony had only begun to emerge as an independent instrumental genre. By the end of the century, it had become the preeminent means of musical expression for a large ensemble, one rivaled only by opera. Most of Haydn's early symphonies were written at the Esterházy court for a small orchestra of sixteen, and they often have no more than three or four independent lines playing at once (the remaining instruments simply doubled). During the 1770s, Haydn composed his symphonies, in particular, in an emotional style called *Sturm und Drang,* and these works are marked by minor keys, angular themes, syncopation, string tremolos, and sudden dynamic shifts. Haydn enjoyed a long and productive career, and he continued to compose quartets, symphonies, and sonatas until the age of seventy.

KEY TERMS

Esterházy family	minuet and trio	scherzo
baryton	concertante	"Bird" Quartet
Hoboken (Hob.) number	"Farewell" Symphony	"Emperor" Quartet
minuet	*Sturm und Drang*	*The Emperor's Hymn*

Chapter

46

Joseph Haydn: Late Symphonies and Vocal Music

By 1780 Joseph Haydn had become one of the foremost composers in Europe, primarily through pirated copies of his music. The previous year, Haydn had signed a new, less restrictive, contract with his patron, Prince Nikolaus Esterházy, which freed the composer from his prior obligation to compose solely for the prince. Free to write for anyone and publish wherever he wished, he now sold his music to publishers in a number of prominent European cities, including Vienna, Paris, and London. The opportunity to publish abroad brought Haydn handsome fees, and growing fame brought him equally remunerative commissions. Consequently, in his maturity and old age Haydn enjoyed fame and, if not fortune, at least considerable financial security (Fig. 46-1). His first important foreign commission came from Paris, and it occupied much of Haydn's time during the mid-1780s.

THE PARIS SYMPHONIES

Haydn's music had been known in Paris since the 1760s. By the 1780s, his symphonies were played there far more than those of any other composer, and in 1785 he received a lucrative commission from the *Loge Olympique*, a society of musically inclined Free-masons. These artistically enlightened Parisian amateurs requested six symphonies to be performed by their orchestra. For each symphony, Haydn would receive twenty-four Louis d'Or and an additional five Louis d'Or for publication rights. The six symphonies Haydn subsequently created (Nos. 82–87) are now called the **Paris Symphonies.**

The orchestra of the *Loge Olympique* in Paris was more than three times the size of that of Haydn's Esterházy patron back in Austria. The Paris ensemble counted nearly seventy strings, including forty violins and ten double basses, as well as pairs of winds. Perhaps for this reason, the Paris Symphonies show a Haydn eager to re-place complex counterpoint with dramatic orchestral effects. From time to time the violins suddenly surge forward *fortissimo* and the textures and dynamics shift radi-cally. Of course, the Paris Symphonies were intended, not for a private salon but for a large public concert hall and a paying audience. This may account for the broadly popular nature of many of the themes. Phrasing tends to be uncomplicated, even folksy, often fashioned in two- or four-measure pairs. Indeed, the slow movement of Symphony No. 85 is a set of variations built on an old French folk song, *La gentille et jeune Lisette* (*Young, Sweet Lisette*), itself a model of classical balance (Ex. 46-1).

🌸 F I G U R E 4 6 - 1
The mature Joseph Haydn in the act of composition. His left hand tries out an idea at the keyboard (likely a clavichord), while his right hand is poised to write it down. Haydn said the following about his compositional process: "I sat down and began to fanta-size, according to whether my mood was sad or happy, serious or playful."

EXAMPLE 46-1

Symphony No. 85 became the favorite of Reine (Queen) Marie-Antoinette (who was later to lose her head during the Revolution of 1789–1799), and thus it is known as "La Reine." Two other Paris Symphonies also acquired fanciful names: Symphony No. 82 is known as "L'Ours" ("The Bear"), because the finale is said to suggest the lumbering dance of a circus bear; while No. 83 is called "La Poule" ("The Hen"), re-putedly because of the "clucking" sound of the violins in the first movement. Clearly, Haydn was playing to popular taste in these Parisian works. Haydn's next five symphonies (Nos. 88–92) also have connections to Paris, although the last of these (No. 92) has come to be called the "Oxford" Symphony because it was performed in July 1791 when Haydn received an honorary degree at Oxford University in England.

 ## THE LONDON SYMPHONIES

How did Haydn come to be in England? In 1790 Haydn's long-time patron Nikolaus Esterházy died and, after nearly thirty years of service, Haydn was now a free man—he was "pensioned off." Immediately, Haydn was approached by a foreign musician who knocked at his door and declared: "I am Salomon of London and have come to fetch you. Tomorrow we will arrange a contract."[1] The visitor was Johann Salomon, a German violinist and concert promoter living in London, who proposed that Haydn travel to London and participate in a venture that promised both financial gain and public acclaim. Thus, the aging Haydn, now nearly sixty, departed Vienna in December 1790; those seeing him off in a tearful farewell included Wolfgang Amadeus Mozart. Haydn resided in London during 1791–1792 and again in 1794–1795. His principal assignment there was to provide Salomon with twelve new symphonies. Haydn was to be paid both for the performances and the publication rights. These twelve symphonies, which Haydn composed from 1791 to 1795, have come to be called the **London Symphonies.** From his activities in London, Haydn netted 24,000 Austrian gulden, the equivalent of more than twenty years' salary at the Esterházy court. His trips to London made him financially secure for life, and the London Symphonies crowned his career as a symphonic composer.

As with the earlier Paris Symphonies, several of the London Symphonies have received fanciful titles. No. 100 is called the "Military" Symphony, for example, because the score requires instruments from a military band, namely cymbals, triangle, and bass drum; No. 101 is named the "Clock" owing to the "tick-tock" accompaniment in the *Andante* movement; and No. 96 takes its name the "Miracle" supposedly because a large chandelier crashed during the premiere in London and—miraculously—no one was hurt! But among the "titled" London Symphonies, none is better known than the "Surprise" Symphony.

The **"Surprise" Symphony** (No. 94) was exceptionally well received by the London audience at its premiere on 23 March 1792. The first movement provides a vivacious dance in $\frac{6}{8}$ meter; the third movement is a rollicking minuet with trio; and the brilliant finale forms an appropriately rousing conclusion. Yet both the name and the fame of the symphony come from its second movement marked *Andante*. In his last years, Haydn gave his biographers two different accounts as to why he had hidden a "surprise" inside this movement. In one, the composer says that he wanted simply "to surprise the public with something new, and to make a [London] début in a brilliant manner. . . ." In the second account, Haydn says more specifically that during the second half of the Salomon concerts, the London audience was prone to fall asleep. To call it to attention, he prescribed that the full orchestra play a sudden *fortissimo* at the end of the very quiet first phrase. "The sudden thunder of the whole orchestra shocked the sleepers, all awoke and looked at each other with surprised expressions"—whence the acquired title.[2]

Reviewers of the day were struck not only by this novel effect but also by the "simple, profound and sublime" quality of music. Haydn's *Andante* does indeed embody a simple binary theme (**AB**), beginning with a tonic triad followed by a dominant seventh chord (Ex. 46-2), which serves as the basis for a set of variations. Yet this commonplace opening allows for a shocking change of harmony and mood in the exact middle of the movement, the location of which creates an overall balance despite radical contrast.

EXAMPLE 46-2

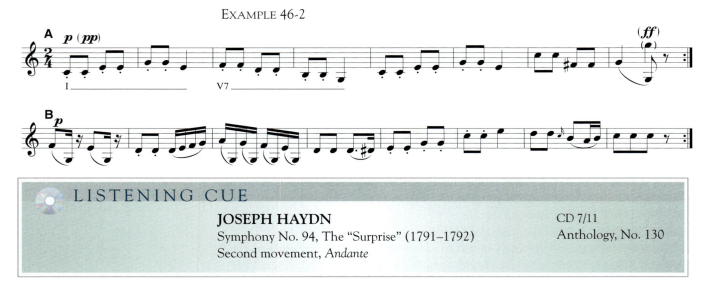

<table>
<tr><td>💿</td><td colspan="2">LISTENING CUE</td></tr>
<tr><td></td><td>JOSEPH HAYDN
Symphony No. 94, The "Surprise" (1791–1792)
Second movement, Andante</td><td>CD 7/11
Anthology, No. 130</td></tr>
</table>

When Joseph Haydn returned to London in February 1794 for an additional series of Salomon's concerts, he opened the season with a new symphony in E♭ major, No. 99. The critic of the *Morning Chronicle* could barely contain his enthusiasm: "[The new symphony] is one of the grandest efforts of art that we ever witnessed. It abounds with ideas, as new in music as they are grand and impressive; it rouses and affects every emotion of the soul; [and] it was received with rapturous applause."[3] Perhaps it was the elegiac slow movement, or the pleasing minuet, or even the contrapuntally complex finale that delighted the London critic. But when the program was repeated a week later, the first movement gave such special pleasure that it was immediately encored; in the eighteenth century, the audience not only applauded after each symphonic movement but also demanded the immediate repeat of a movement it found exceptionally pleasing.

What might have been the "new ideas" that impressed the London critic? In the first movement, the novelty is not in the construction of the melodies, but in the orchestration and the unusual, even eccentric, approach to harmony and form. Here, for the first time (1794), Haydn makes use of clarinets in a symphony (though Mozart had done so as early as 1778). These, in addition to pairs of flutes, oboes, bassoons, horns, and trumpets, as well as timpani, help create a rich, imposing orchestral sound. The movement's numerous harmonic and formal surprises include a dominant pedal point in the introduction that sits on the "wrong" note for the key of E♭; an expected "second theme" in the dominant key that turns out to be none other than the first theme transposed (a technique not uncommon to Haydn's sonata-form compositions); and a recapitulation that omits almost entirely the all-important first theme. But most striking here are the abrupt contrasts between stable passages of music (the tonally secure first theme and closing theme, for example) and those that are unstable owing either to syncopated accents marked *sforzando* or to chromatically sliding chords. Once again with Haydn, unity is born of diversity and contrast.

<table>
<tr><td>💿</td><td colspan="2">LISTENING CUE</td></tr>
<tr><td></td><td>JOSEPH HAYDN
Symphony No. 99 in E♭ Major (1794)
First movement, Adagio; Vivace assai</td><td>CD 7/12
Anthology, No. 131</td></tr>
</table>

Haydn Wins Over His Orchestra

Great artists are often known for their tempers, eccentricities, and egos. Beethoven was legendary for having tantrums in front of musicians and patrons alike. Gustav Mahler was reputed to be a tyrannical conductor. Even the composer of serene sacred music, Josquin des Prez, would fly into a rage when singers tampered with the notes he had composed. By contrast, Haydn seems to have been more diplomatic—or perhaps more cunning!—than most great artists.

When Haydn arrived in London he spoke scarcely a word of English. His principal charge was to compose and perform his new symphonies before a large paying audience at the Hanover Square Rooms in central London. Haydn himself conducted the orchestra of seasoned freelance professionals, including many Germans and Italians, from his position seated at the keyboard. (A keyboard instrument, either harpsichord or piano, still sometimes accompanied the symphony orchestra, a legacy of the Baroque basso continuo.) Professional orchestral players, then as now, are a notoriously hard-nosed, unsympathetic group. As reported in an early biography, one dictated by Haydn himself, the composer used almost every trick imaginable to get the London musicians to play their best.

[Haydn] had set out a symphony that began with a short *Adagio*, three identical-sounding notes opening the music. Now when the orchestra played the three notes too emphatically, Haydn interrupted with nods and "Sh!

Sh!" The orchestra stopped, and [Johann] Salomon had to interpret for Haydn. They then played the three notes again but with no happier result. Haydn interrupted again with "Sh! Sh!." In the ensuing silence a German cellist quite near to Haydn expressed his opinion to his neighbor, saying in German, "If he doesn't like even the first three notes, how will it be with the rest!" Haydn was happy to hear Germans speaking, took these words as a warning, and said with the greatest courtesy that he was requesting as a favor something that lay wholly within their power, and that he was very sorry that he could not express himself in English. Perhaps they would allow him to demonstrate his meaning on an instrument. Whereupon he took a violin and made himself so clear by the repeated playing of the three tones that the orchestra understood him perfectly. Haydn did not in the future let the matter rest there. He implored, as small children do, by holding up both hands, called now this one, now that one "my treasure" or "my angel." He often invited the most important players to dinner, so that they appeared gladly for private rehearsals in his home. He praised them and interwove reprimand, when it was necessary, with praise in the subtlest fashion. Such behavior won him the affection of all musicians with whom he came in contact, so that out of love for him they rose to the level of inspiration required for a performance of a Haydn work.[4]

THE LATE VOCAL MUSIC

Joseph Haydn received his first formal musical instruction at the Cathedral of St. Stephen in Vienna while serving as a choirboy during the 1740s. From this experience he gained a thorough knowledge of the music and liturgy of the Roman Catholic Church. Haydn, Mozart, and Beethoven all lived in Catholic Austria and followed, with different degrees of fervor, the Roman Catholic faith. Thus, throughout his long life Haydn composed sacred music for the church, including Latin motets and full settings of the Ordinary of the Mass. As did Mozart and Beethoven, Haydn gave special attention to religious music toward the end of his life.

When Haydn returned to Vienna in September 1795, he resumed his relations with the Esterházy court. His responsibilities were less demanding than before, now being reduced to a single requirement: each year he was to produce a polyphonic Mass for the name-day of Maria Esterházy, wife of the prince. Thus, he composed and directed a total of six Masses for the Esterházy court, which were performed annually on 8 September (the Feast of the Nativity of the Virgin Mary). These Masses are large-scale works requiring full orchestra and chorus with soprano, alto, tenor, and bass soloists. A Mass with orchestra and chorus in eighteenth-century Austria was as much a festive concert as it was a religious service. This was especially true of these late Masses of Haydn, in which the orchestra often adopts both symphonic style and symphonic forms. Best known today among Haydn's Masses are his *Mass in the Time of War* (1796) and *Lord Nelson Mass* (1798), both associated in the public mind with events of the Napoleonic Wars that then engulfed Austria.

Toward the end of his creative life, Haydn composed two sacred oratorios, **The Creation** (1796–1798) and *The Seasons* (1801). During his stay in London, Haydn had been impressed by the massive choral performances of Handel's oratorios in Westminster Abbey. This experience encouraged him to try his hand at English oratorio; indeed, he brought the original English-language libretto of *The Creation* with him when he returned from London to Vienna in 1795. For the next three years he fine-tuned the libretto and composed the score, setting the words in both English and German and thereby creating a bilingual work that could be performed in either language to suit the audience. *The Creation* received its first public performance on 19 March 1799, in the Burgtheater in Vienna (see Fig. 42-1). Like Handel's *Messiah*, Haydn's *The Creation* became a staple of charity fund-raising; Haydn himself frequently conducted subsequent performances to raise money for worthy causes.

As its name suggests, *The Creation* recounts the story of the creation of the world as told in the Book of Genesis. Like Handel's *Messiah*, it is divided into three parts, each of which consists of various choruses, arias, and recitatives. Moreover, each part ends with a rousing chorus, in which the multitudes proclaim the glory of God. "The Heavens Are Telling," which concludes Part One, can be taken to be Haydn's response to Handelian choral writing. The declamation is clear and forceful, passages of homophony alternate with those of imitative polyphony, and a textual refrain ("the heavens are telling") serves to unify the movement. Haydn had carried the genre of the large-scale symphony to England; in return he brought English oratorio to the Continent.

EXAMPLE 46-3

LISTENING CUE

JOSEPH HAYDN
The Creation (1796–1798)
"The Heavens Are Telling"

CD 7/13
Anthology, No. 132

In the same year that Haydn conducted the premiere of *The Creation*, he complained to his German publisher about his declining health and waning powers of concentration:

> Some days my enfeebled memory and the un-strung state of my nerves crush me to the earth to such an extent that I fall prey to the worst sort of depression, and am quite incapable of finding even a single idea for many days there-after; until at last Providence revives me, and I can again sit down at the pianoforte and begin to scratch away.[5]

Indeed, Haydn's productivity diminished and, after giving up work on his last string quartet in 1803, he composed no more. The public, however, continued to shower him with praise and various honors, including a performance of *The Creation* in 1808 to mark his seventy-sixth birthday (Fig. 46-2). When Haydn finally expired on 31 May 1809, Europe lost a beloved cultural icon.

❀ FIGURE 46-2

Haydn's farewell. This watercolor records the performance of *The Creation*, conducted by Antonio Salieri, given in Vienna on 27 March 1808 to mark Haydn's 76th birthday. Haydn himself attended, but had to be transported into the hall in a chair (he is the seated figure in lowest center to which all eyes are turned). Haydn stayed up to the end of Part I, ending with "The Heavens Are Telling," and then, old and frail, asked to be carried from the hall. This was his last public appearance.

Erich Lessing/Art Resource, NY

SUMMARY

The late symphonies of Joseph Haydn consist mainly of the Paris Symphonies (Nos. 82–87) and the London Symphonies (Nos. 93–104), which date from the 1780s and 1790s, respectively. All are large-scale, four-movement symphonies remarkable for their variety and sometimes for their formal and harmonic daring. Haydn's Paris and London Symphonies were performed in those cities by large orchestras, sometimes consisting of seventy or more players. Taking full advantage of these big ensembles, his scores now reflect a richer, more spacious texture, sometimes with as many as ten or twelve independent lines sounding together. They also call for unexpected orches-tral effects, such as the sudden *fortissimo* in the midst of the quiet opening of the "Sur-prise" Symphony. The critical acclaim that greeted Haydn's Paris and London Symphonies cemented his position as the most renowned composer in Europe. During the 1790s and early 1800s, Haydn, now in his sixties, still managed to create six large polyphonic Masses and two full-length oratorios. In these late symphonies, Masses, and oratorios, Haydn once again reveals his unique gift. He could combine the con-ventional with the unexpected, the serious with the jocular, and the learned with the popular, thereby creating music that appealed to prince and commoner alike.

KEY TERMS

Paris Symphonies
London Symphonies

"Surprise" Symphony
The Creation

Chapter 47

Wolfgang Amadeus Mozart: Instrumental Music

Mozart lived barely thirty-six years. Yet, because he had an insatiable appetite for composing, he left us an astonishing amount of music.[†] The published complete edition of Mozart's music includes some one hundred twenty often-thick volumes. Mozart seems to have composed in his head far faster than he could write the notes on paper. Moreover, he excelled in all genres of music of his day, composing operas, piano concertos, symphonies, and chamber works that must be counted among the greatest works ever written in these categories. For this reason, Mozart has been rightly called "the most universal composer in the history of Western music."[1]

✺ THE LIFE OF WOLFGANG AMADEUS MOZART (1756–1791)

Mozart was a child prodigy. Unlike Haydn, whose career developed slowly and lasted long, Mozart's star shot suddenly across the musical firmament and disappeared just as quickly. He was born in 1756 in the mountain town of Salzburg, Austria, and died in 1791 in Vienna. Whereas Haydn's father could not read music, Mozart's father, Leopold, was a composer and well-known violin pedagogue, and his older sister Nannerl was a talented keyboard performer. Leopold noticed almost immediately that his son had an extraordinary ear and a preternatural facility for music generally. At the age of six, the young Mozart was playing the piano, violin, and organ, as well as composing. Soon Leopold abandoned his own ambitions and focused the energies of the entire family on nurturing the talent of their *Wunderkind* Wolfgang.

In 1763 the Mozart family began a show tour—part educational, part moneymaking—around the major capitals of Europe. In Vienna, Wolfgang played for and sat on the lap of Empress Maria Theresa. Then the family went to Munich, Brussels, Paris, London, Amsterdam, and Geneva, playing for royalty all along the way. At times the "traveling Mozarts" came perilously close to resembling a circus act. On demand, Wolfgang would sight-read difficult music, improvise on a tune requested by the audience, or play blindfolded or with the keyboard covered with a cloth. After three years the Mozarts made their way back to Salzburg. But father and son soon departed on multi-year visits to the major cities of Italy, and in each the boy gave at least one concert to cover expenses. In Rome, in 1770, Pope Clement XIV dubbed the fourteen-year-old Mozart a Knight of the Golden Spur, the first musician in two hundred years to be so honored. Although the aim of this globe-trotting was to acquire fame and fortune, the result was that Mozart, unlike Haydn, was exposed at an early age to a wealth of musical styles—French Baroque, English choral, German polyphonic, and Italian vocal. His keen ear absorbed them all, and ultimately they increased both the substance and the universal appeal of his music.

Mozart spent most of the 1770s in his native Salzburg. Still a prodigy but no longer a child, he earned a living from his position as violinist and organist for the Archbishop of Salzburg. The reigning Archbishop Colloredo, however, did not

---

[†]More than six hundred compositions survive from Mozart's pen. In 1784 he began to keep track of them in a little book he called "Verzeichnis aller meiner Werke" ("List of all my works"). This thematic catalogue later served as the basis for a more complete inventory of Mozart's works done by the German botanist and mineralogist Ludwig von Köchel (1800–1877). A Köchel or "K" number identifies Mozart's compositions in roughly chronological order.

spend generously on the arts and had little appreciation of Mozart, genius or not (the composer referred to his patron as the "Archboobie"). Provided only with a place in the orchestra, a small salary, and his board, Mozart at Salzburg, like Haydn at Esterháza, ate with the cooks and valets. For a Knight of the Golden Spur who had dazzled kings and queens, this was humble fare indeed, and Mozart chafed under this system of aristocratic patronage. After several unpleasant scenes in the spring of 1781, the twenty-five-year-old composer cut himself free of the archbishop and set out to make a living as a freelance musician in Vienna.

The mid-1780s witnessed the peak of Mozart's productivity and the creation of many of his greatest works. He had a full complement of pupils (all female), played several concerts a week, and enjoyed lucrative commissions as a composer. Piano concertos, string quartets, and symphonies flowed from his pen seemingly as fast as he could write them down. In little more than a year (1786–1787) he created two of the greatest operas ever written: *Le nozze di Figaro* (*The Marriage of Figaro*) and *Don Giovanni*.

Mozart died unexpectedly on 5 December 1791. Several theories—kidney failure and rheumatic fever among them—have been put forward as possible causes. Despite later rumors, Mozart was not poisoned by Antonio Salieri or anyone else. Mozart's early death is all the more tragic because in 1791 his career was flourishing. His *Singspiel* (German comic opera), *Die Zauberflöte* (*The Magic Flute*), had been a hit with middle-class patrons at a suburban Vienna theater; his *opera seria, La clemenza di Tito* (*The Clemency of Tito*), was well received by the court in Prague; and his Requiem Mass, for which a mysterious patron had made a handsome down payment, was nearly completed. The astonishing grandeur and pathos of the Requiem, left unfinished at the time of Mozart's death, suggest an artist still in full command of his creative powers.

SYMPHONIES

Mozart composed symphonies throughout his life, completing a total of forty-one, according to the traditional count.[2] Many of these he wrote as a mere youth during his travels about Europe. Numerous others were the products of his years as a frustrated court employee in Salzburg. His final six symphonies came into being in Vienna between 1782 and 1788. They, along with the late symphonies of Haydn, represent the culmination of the Viennese symphonic style.

The Oscar-winning film *Amadeus* begins with the opening of Mozart's striking Symphony No. 25 in G Minor (K. 183), known as the **"Little" G-Minor Symphony** (to distinguish it from the later, longer Symphony No. 40 in G Minor; K. 550). This selection, written in Salzburg in 1773, provides an appropriate way to introduce Mozart, for in this work the young composer exhibits his own distinctive voice in the genre of the symphony. The piece represents Mozart's first symphony in a minor key. Indeed, the minor mode, agitated syncopations of the strings, and dramatic fall of a diminished seventh (Ex. 47-1) all show Mozart writing in the *Sturm und Drang* style of the early 1770s. But more important is Mozart's approach to the instruments of the orchestra. The urgent, jagged first theme almost immediately transforms into a lyrical melody for solo oboe—a wonderful example of the "dramatic" quality of Classical music by which one mood can quickly give way to another. In addition, Mozart writes for four natural French horns (see Fig. 44-3), one pair in G and the other in B♭; this allows him to modulate to different keys and still include the colorful sound of the horn. With its passion and intensity, rapid shifts between major and minor, and colorful writing for the winds, the "Little" G-Minor Symphony is a small masterpiece. These same Mozartean characteristics would appear more fully developed in his last six symphonies written for Vienna.

EXAMPLE. 47-1

In 1781 Mozart lamented, "[In Salzburg] there is no stimulus for my talent. When I play or when any of my compositions is performed, it is just as if the audience were all tables and chairs."[3] As we have seen, Mozart felt unappreciated in provincial Salzburg, where his patron, the archbishop, placed little value on his talent. Consequently, in the spring of 1781 at the age of twenty-five, Mozart broke loose and established himself as an independent, freelance musician in Vienna. Writing symphonies was only a small part of Mozart's creative life in Vienna, yet the six he produced there can be counted among the finest examples of the Classical symphony. The first three of these later took names from the patron or the city for which the work was destined, while the last two are known by titles given them by later commentators. Mozart's final six symphonies are:

- Symphony No. 35 in D Major, the "Haffner" (K. 385) (written in 1782 for a wealthy Salzburg family)
- Symphony No. 36 in C Major, the "Linz" (K. 425) (written in 1783 for a performance in Linz, Austria)
- Symphony No. 37, in G Major (Only the slow introduction to the first movement is by Mozart, the rest is the work of Michael Haydn, younger brother of Joseph Haydn.)
- Symphony No. 38 in D Major, the "Prague" (K. 504) (written in 1786 for a performance in Prague)
- Symphony No. 39 in E♭ Major (K. 543) (written in 1788, likely for performance at Mozart's subscription concerts in Vienna)
- Symphony No. 40 in G Minor, the "Great" (K. 550) (written in 1788, likely for performance at Mozart's subscription concerts in Vienna)

- Symphony No. 41 in C Major, the "Jupiter" (K. 551) (written in 1788, likely for performance at Mozart's subscription concerts in Vienna)

The people of Prague, now the capital of Czech Republic, had a special love for Mozart's music. Two of his operas (*Don Giovanni* and *La clemenza di Tito*) enjoyed premieres there, and Mozart's **"Prague" Symphony** was destined for that city as well. The first movement of the "Prague" is one of Mozart's finest symphonic creations. Certainly it is one of his most difficult to perform, owing to the density of the texture and the demands placed on the woodwinds. To the usual complement of strings, Mozart adds pairs of flutes, oboes, bassoons, horns, and trumpets, as well as timpani. The winds in particular add contrapuntal density as they weave an intricate polyphonic web around the melodic line carried by the strings. Mozart also injects a new element of chromaticism; again the woodwinds enrich the texture by inserting chromatic scales, as can be seen in bars 28–31 of the first movement (Ex. 47-2).

EXAMPLE 47-2

Mozart's colorful use of woodwinds and his penchant for chromaticism is heard again in his celebrated **Symphony No. 40 in G Minor,** sometimes called the "Great" G-Minor Symphony to distinguish it from the earlier "Little" G-Minor

Symphony (1773). This was one of three symphonies (his last three) that Mozart wrote in the short span of six weeks during the summer of 1788. All three were apparently intended for performance at subscription concerts Mozart planned to give that fall in the casino of Vienna; Mozart often performed there because, then as now, the casino offered large public rooms and attracted people with money.

Symphony No. 40 is one of the most performed of all eighteenth-century symphonies, indeed of all symphonies. It is not a festive composition (and hence features no trumpets or drums), but rather an intensely brooding work that suggests desperation, even tragedy. The first movement starts quietly with an insistent accompaniment that precedes the haunting violin melody. The second theme in particular is a beautifully scored dialogue between strings and woodwinds. Yet the summit of woodwind writing occurs in the retransition immediately before the recapitulation. Here the strings stop entirely to allow the upper woodwinds to cascade down in a chromatic sequence above a bassoon pedal point, for a rainbow of sound that returns us to the opening theme (Ex. 47-3). Originally the symphony had no clarinets, but Mozart added them later to increase the richness of the wind writing. Indeed, Mozart took great pains with his orchestration, and his scores are more complex than those of any of his Classical contemporaries. The winds in particular are always carefully "voiced," and rarely simply double the string parts. Ultimately, Mozart's colorful writing for winds formed the basis for the orchestration of Haydn's London Symphonies as well as those later composed by Beethoven and Schubert.

EXAMPLE 47-3

LISTENING CUE

WOLFGANG AMADEUS MOZART   CD 7/14
Symphony No. 40 in G Minor (K. 550; 1788)   Anthology, No. 133
First movement, *Allegro*

In what was to prove to be his final symphony, Symphony No. 41 in C Major, Mozart returned to the festive sounds of the large orchestra and a bright major key. The title **"Jupiter" Symphony** was not given by Mozart. Rather, it was bestowed by Haydn's friend Johann Salomon (see Chapter 46), apparently because Mozart's use of trumpets and timpani, as well as stately dotted rhythms, evoked images of nobility and godliness for eighteenth-century listeners. Of the four movements of the "Jupiter," the most famous is the finale, which contains perhaps the greatest technical *tour de force* in all of music. Here Mozart begins as usual in standard sonata form, presenting five themes: two in the first theme group, one in the transition, and two in the second theme group (Ex. 47-4).

EXAMPLE 47-4

In the development section, Mozart marches these five themes through various contrapuntal drills, including musical inversion, invertible counterpoint, and stretto. Yet it is in the coda that a Mozartean miracle occurs: quintuple invertible counterpoint. It turns out that Mozart had designed each of these five themes so that they might all be heard simultaneously and their vertical position continually reshuffled—one great final display of contrapuntal ingenuity. Below is given the superimposition of the themes as Mozart composed it (Ex. 47-5a) and, for clarity of presentation, an abstraction of this transposed to C (Ex. 47-5b).

EXAMPLE 47-5A

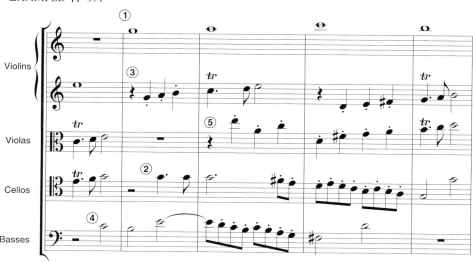

EXAMPLE 47-5B

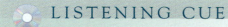

LISTENING CUE

WOLFGANG AMADEUS MOZART
Symphony No. 41 in C Major
(K. 551, 1788)
Fourth movement, *Molto allegro*

CD 7/15
Anthology, No. 134

CHAMBER MUSIC

Today we think of chamber music as music for a small instrumental group, played in a small to mid-size room or hall, with one performer to a part. In Mozart's day, however, the distinction between "chamber" and "orchestral" music was not so easily made. Mozart's small ensemble pieces were played both indoors and outdoors, sometimes with one musician to a part and sometimes with more. Mozart composed a number of divertimenti and serenades for wedding receptions, balls, university celebrations, outdoor serenading, and other sorts of public entertainments. He seems to have used the terms "divertimento" and "serenade" interchangeably to signal a composition usually in five movements and often displaying a lighter mood (see Chapter 44). Some were for winds alone (*Harmoniemusik*; see Chapter 44), some for strings, and some for a mixture of the two groups.

Best-known among Mozart's serenades is his *Eine kleine Nachtmusik* (K. 525, 1787) scored for four string parts. It can be played by a full string ensemble with basses doubling the cello line, or simply by the four instruments of a string quartet. Although the autograph score is dated 10 August 1787, we do not know the precise occasion for which Mozart composed this bit of night entertainment. Certainly nothing demonstrates better the simplicity and pleasurable intent of the serenade than the famous opening melody of the first *Allegro* that outlines first a tonic triad and then a dominant-seventh chord (Ex. 47-6).

EXAMPLE 47-6

Mozart composed some two dozen string quartets, but his six **"Haydn" Quartets** (1782–1785) form the core of his work in this genre. As we have seen (Chapter 45), Joseph Haydn was the creator of the string quartet, and in 1781 he published his influential Opus 33 set of quartets in Vienna. This same year, Mozart moved to Vienna, studied these quartets, and began to compose his own set of six, which he published in 1785 and dedicated to Haydn. Haydn and Mozart had become fast friends in these years, and they sometimes played quartets together in Mozart's apartment. It was at one of these gatherings in early 1785 that Haydn said to Leopold Mozart, then visiting from Salzburg: "Before God and as an honest man, I tell you that your son is the greatest composer known to me either in person or by name."[4]

In his touching dedication to the "Haydn" Quartets, Mozart refers to Haydn as his "very dear friend" and to the quartets as "the fruit of a long and arduous study." Judging from the unusually high number of revisions Mozart made to his manuscripts, he did indeed labor mightily on these quartets in an effort to digest Haydn's method of thematic integration. In the end, Mozart produced a set of six quartets that are distinctly different from one another: K. 387 in G major, K. 421 in D minor, K. 428 in E♭ major, K. 458 in B♭ major (the "Hunt"), K. 464 in A major, and K. 465 in C major (the "Dissonance").

The final work in the collection, the **"Dissonance" Quartet,** derives its title from the *Adagio* introduction to the first movement, a passage famous for its harmonic audacities. Here, Mozart leads the listener through a bizarre harmonic labyrinth as the harmony slides down chromatically by half-steps; the ensuing C-major first theme of the exposition sounds all the more shocking for its tonal clarity. (For study purposes, the opening of this quartet can be found in the Anthology, No. 135.)

Not to be forgotten among Mozart's chamber works are several fine quintets, including K. 452 for piano and winds, K. 581 for clarinet and strings, and K. 515 and 516 for strings alone. This last piece is an extraordinary work, one of only a handful of pieces that Mozart wrote in G minor. As this quintet and his two famous symphonies in the same key show, Mozart saved G minor for pieces of great intensity.

✿ PIANO AND VIOLIN SONATAS

When Mozart moved to Vienna in the spring of 1781, he intended to make his living as a composer. But, like so many other creative musicians throughout history, he soon took on private students as a way to pay the bills. In a letter of early 1782,

Mozart reveals that he had to squeeze composition into the beginning and end of the day, because the best hours were taken up with giving piano lessons:

> My hair is always done by six o'clock in the morning and by seven I am fully dressed. I then compose until nine. From nine to one I give [piano] lessons. Then I lunch unless I am invited to some house where they lunch at two or even three o'clock. . . . I can never work before five or six o'clock in the evening, and even then I am often prevented by a concert. If I am not prevented, I compose until nine.[5]

In these years, Mozart had had three or four pupils at a time, all of them women. Throughout the eighteenth century most keyboard sonatas were directed toward amateurs for performance in the home, and most of these consumers were women (see Chapter 43). For his female pupils, for patrons, and sometimes for himself, Mozart composed a total of eighteen sonatas for solo piano and twenty-eight sonatas for piano and violin. The Piano Sonata in C Major (K. 545) was clearly intended as a teaching piece for beginning students (and is still used as such today); when Mozart entered the piece in his list of compositions in 1788, he labeled it "for beginners." As with most Classical keyboard sonatas, K. 545 is in three movements. At the outset we see Mozart writing in a simple *galant* style typical of the Classical era (Ex. 47-7). The melody is graceful, arranged in units of two-plus-two measures, while the left-hand accompaniment is a standard Alberti bass, and the texture is light. All of these—balanced phrases, Alberti bass, and transparent textures—are musical fingerprints by which we identify the Classical style, and all are found abundantly in Mozart's piano sonatas.

EXAMPLE 47-7

Some of Mozart's best pupils, Barbara Ployer and Josepha Auernhammer among them, were the equals of male performing professionals. For these female virtuosos, and for himself, Mozart wrote more technically demanding sonatas. The Sonata in A Major (K. 331) of 1783 is such a work. The final movement (Ex. 47-8), the famous "Alla Turca," is a rousing rondo in **ABCBAB**+coda form. Here Mozart explicitly aims to imitate the sounds of **Turkish music,** the noise of Turkish military percussion instruments, which were introduced into European music in the eighteenth century during the Turkish Wars. Some pianos of the day were equipped with special devices to effect the sounds of the "Turkish" music, such as bass drum, cymbals, and the like. These could make the Turk sound all the more terrifying.

EXAMPLE 47-8

Pianoforte or Fortepiano?

Does one say "pianoforte" or "fortepiano"? In writings about music, we see both, but which is more correct? The piano was invented around 1700 by Bartolomeo Cristofori in Florence, Italy (see Chapter 43). At first it was called "cimbalo di martelletti" (harpsichord with little hammers) and it could "fa' il piano e il forte" (play soft and loud). Eventually, these words were compressed into a single noun, "pianoforte." During the 1760s, German performers began to reverse the words, creating "fortepiano," but Mozart, judging from his letters, continued to prefer "pianoforte," though he often used the then-generic word "cembalo" (keyboard) as well. But, whether called pianoforte or fortepiano, Mozart's instrument was much smaller and more delicate than the modern concert grand.

Mozart began playing the piano, as opposed to the harpsichord, during the 1770s. He admired the instruments of Andreas Stein of Augsburg for their light, even tone. Stein's instrument also included a knee lever, the forerunner of the modern damper pedal, which empowered the player to raise the dampers and allow the strings to resonate. When Mozart purchased his own instrument in Vienna around 1783, he chose a piano by the Viennese maker Anton Walter. This instrument is preserved today in the Mozart family museum in Salzburg (Fig. 47-1). In 1785 Mozart also acquired a pedal board, with strings and pedal keyboard, that could be positioned beneath his Walter piano (Fig. 47-2). This allowed him to reinforce the bass notes of his keyboard music and extend them by five notes. Mozart played the two instruments together, much as he might an organ. When he performed in Vienna, whether at the municipal theater or casino, movers apparently transported Mozart's piano with pedal board to the concert site.

The piano of the late eighteenth century was rather small by modern standards. Similar in shape, size, and weight to the harpsichord, Mozart's piano had a range of only five octaves (F' to f''') plus five lower notes provided by the pedal. Moreover, the key depth was only about 3 mm, and roughly 10 to 15 grams of force were needed to depress it (as compared to a key depth of 9 mm on a modern piano and a required force of about 55 grams). This would have encouraged a light, rapid style of playing. Finally, the hammer on Mozart's piano was a small wooden one covered with leather (as opposed to the much larger one covered with softer felt on the modern piano). The light hammers and efficient damper mechanism allowed the crisp attacks and subtle nuances of articulation called for in Mozart's keyboard scores.

FIGURE 47-1
Mozart's piano, now preserved in the Mozart Museum, Salzburg. The composer purchased the instrument in Vienna, in about 1783, from the manufacturer, Anton Walter.

FIGURE 47-2
An early piano with pedal keyboard of the type once owned by Mozart. This instrument was made in Salzburg in 1798 by Johann Schmidt.

We must not forget that Mozart was not only a composer and pianist but also a virtuoso violinist who astonished listeners at the age of six. His father Leopold, moreover, was a leading violin pedagogue. Mozart's twenty-eight violin sonatas, as was usual in the Classical period, often placed more technical demands on the pianist than on the violinist. Indeed, Mozart considered the violin, not the piano, to be the accompanying instrument. Perhaps most remarkable is the Sonata in E Minor (K. 304), Mozart's only violin sonata in a minor key. Written during a disastrous trip to Paris in 1778, the final movement is full of pathos and despair. Perhaps Mozart composed it as an act of homage to his mother, who had died in Paris, leaving the son to report the sad news to his father back in Salzburg.

CONCERTOS

The piano concertos take us into the world of Mozart, the public performer. If Mozart created many of his piano sonatas for teaching purposes in the home, he fashioned his piano concertos for himself and his very best students to play in public. A prodigious pianist, Mozart was certainly one of the first in music history to make his mark as a touring virtuoso on the instrument. Although the solo keyboard concerto was known to composers of the late Baroque era, they were few in number. Just as it can be fairly said that Haydn created the string quartet, so Mozart can be considered the father of the modern piano concerto.

The years 1783–1788 marked the high point of Mozart's popularity in Vienna. Not coincidentally, Mozart composed more than half of his twenty-three original piano concertos during these five years. The Viennese musical public wanted to hear brilliant passagework and dazzling displays of keyboard virtuosity. The piano concerto was the test-track for such display. At each of his public concerts Mozart offered one or two of his latest creations. He alone selected the program. He also rented the hall, hired and paid the orchestra, publicized the concert, directed the moving of his piano, and sold tickets from his apartment. Sometimes all went well for concert-promoter Mozart, as suggested by the following review:

> **Vienna, 22 March 1783:** Tonight the famous Knight Herr Mozart held a musical concert for his own benefit at the Burgtheater in which pieces of his own music, which was already very popular, were performed. The concert was honored by the presence of an extraordinarily large audience and the two new concertos and other fantasies which Herr Mozart played on the Forte Piano were received with the loudest approval. Our Monarch [Emperor Joseph II], who contrary to his custom honored the entire concert with his presence, joined in the applause of the public so heartily that one can think of no similar example. The proceeds of the concert are estimated at 1600 gulden.[6]

Like the Baroque keyboard concerto, Mozart's piano concertos are always in three movements (fast/slow/fast). Generally, the first movement sets the substantive tone for the work, the second offers a contrasting lyrical "song," and the third provides a light, dance-like sendoff. Most important to the development of the concerto genre was Mozart's employment of a new form for the fast first movement. The commonly used term "double-exposition" form derives from the fact that the materials of the exposition are played twice, first by the orchestra and then by the pianist with orchestral accompaniment. But one must distinguish between two very different sorts of expositions: one is "passive" and the other "active." Indeed, a better term for the form of the first movements of Mozart's concertos is **concerto-sonata form** (see page 433). First the orchestra presents its exposition entirely in the tonic, and is thus introductory ("passive") in function; then the soloist enters in the tonic but provides the crucial ("active") modulation to the secondary key area, thereby providing the same tonal "drama" found in conventional sonata form. The active solo exposition is a distinctly different section, for here the performer has the freedom to add new themes into the mix, as well as to elaborate (or omit) some of the orchestra's themes. Toward the end of the solo exposition, the full/tutti orchestra returns with selected bits of its opening theme, a throwback to the ritornello principle of both the old Baroque concerto grosso and the *da capo* aria (see Anthology, No. 91b, for example). Thus, Mozart integrates the older ritornello procedure with the new principles of sonata form. The diagram below shows how a movement in concerto-sonata form begins. Remember that this diagram is an abstraction, and many concertos deviate from the model in one way or another.

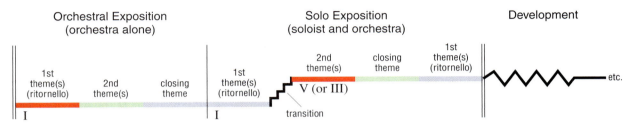

Mozart composed perhaps a half-dozen piano concertos that might rightly appear in any list of the greatest concertos ever written. The serene G major (K. 453), heroic C major (K. 467), demonic D minor (K. 466), wind-dominated E♭ major (K. 482), and tragic C minor (K. 491) are among his very best. Yet surely one of the brightest lights in this shining constellation is the Piano Concerto in A Major (K. 488) of 1786.

Probably written for his star pupil, Barbara Ployer, the Concerto in A Major has always been one of Mozart's most popular compositions. The first movement offers a seemingly endless supply of graceful melodies, and both it and the closing movement appear in the bright key of A major (a particularly resonant key for strings). Yet, for the slow second movement, Mozart chooses a key found almost nowhere else in his oeuvre, the starkly dark key of F♯ minor, whose somber tone contributes to the unearthly beauty of this *Adagio*.

The essence of Mozart's concerto style, however, can be seen in his sparkling musical "dialogues." Lightning-quick exchanges between soloist and accompanying orchestra were entirely new to the concerto. In these, Mozart reveals the full potential of the genre, showing that soloist and orchestra might not simply speak "in turn," but instead banter back and forth in the most playful and pleasing way. "Anything you can do, I can do better." "No you can't." "Yes I can"—the antagonists seem to say. In Mozart's contest between interactive forces there is no winner—except the listener.

 LISTENING CUE

WOLFGANG AMADEUS MOZART
Piano Concerto in A Major (K. 488; 1786)
First movement, *Allegro*

CD 8/1
Anthology, No. 136

 SUMMARY

Mozart was a prolific composer who wrote an astounding amount of music in his fewer than thirty-six years. His compositions, catalogued by Ludwig von Köchel (K), number more than six hundred. They range from early piano sonatas composed at the age of six (1762) to his unfinished Requiem Mass (1791). The traditional numbering system for Mozart's symphonies counts forty-one, though in fact he composed nearly sixty. In addition, he wrote eighteen piano sonatas, twenty-four string quartets, and twenty-three piano concertos. Mozart can rightly be seen as the creator of the piano concerto, and he established concerto-sonata form as the norm for the first movement of that genre.

Mozart's mature concertos and final six symphonies display a rich, distinctly Mozartean array of orchestral sounds. They are dramatic, often because of quick shifts between the major and minor mode, as well as colorful, owing especially to the brilliant woodwind writing. Finally, they frequently show two other characteristics of Mozart's style: intense chromaticism and dense counterpoint. In their drama, color, and intensity, Mozart's late instrumental works not only carry the Viennese Classical style to new heights but they also prefigure the music of the Romantic era.

KEY TERMS

Köchel (K) number	Symphony No. 40	"Dissonance" Quartet
"Little" G-Minor	in G Minor	Turkish music
Symphony	"Jupiter" Symphony	concerto-sonata form
"Prague" Symphony	"Haydn" Quartets	

Chapter 48

Wolfgang Amadeus Mozart: Vocal Music

Mozart was fascinated by the magic of the theater. Scarcely was there a moment in his career when he was not looking for a good libretto to set, writing an opera, or overseeing the production of one. In all, he composed twenty operas. Eight are of the older Italian *opera seria* kind, seven in the newer Italian comic *opera buffa* style, and five of the simpler German type called **Singspiel**, a German light comic opera with spoken dialogue rather than recitatives. Mozart's first *Singspiel*, entitled *Bastien und Bastienne* (1768), was written when he was twelve and intended for Vienna. It apparently premiered in the summer home of the famous Dr. Franz Anton Mesmer (1733–1815), the inventor of the theory of animal magnetism (whence, "to mesmerize"). Of the operas Mozart composed before moving to Vienna in 1781, the most impressive is *Idomeneo* (1780). *Idomeneo* is an *opera seria*—the plot involves an ancient mythological story and requires both chorus and ballet. Yet Mozart removes the often statue-like stiffness of *opera seria* by giving the characters more natural music to sing. Although *Idomeneo* has been called "the greatest *opera seria* of the eighteenth century," its emphasis on strong character development through music hints at the masterpieces of Mozart's last decade.

Soon after settling for good in Vienna in 1781, Mozart received a commission directly from Emperor Joseph II: he was to create a German opera for the Emperor's German-speaking subjects. Mozart's response was a *Singspiel* entitled *Die Entführung*

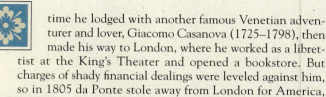

Lorenzo da Ponte: Librettist to Mozart

The life story of Lorenzo da Ponte should be the subject of a movie (as Mozart's was for *Amadeus*), because it was filled with extraordinary contradictions and improbable adventures. His birth name was not Lorenzo da Ponte, but Emmanuele Conegliano. Born in northern Italy of Jewish parents, he converted to Catholicism in 1763, adopted the name of the local bishop (Lorenzo da Ponte), entered a seminary, and became a Catholic priest. Having studied Latin and Italian in the seminary, da Ponte took a job as a tutor of literature and languages in Venice, but his love of liberal politics and married women soon got Father da Ponte banned from that city. Making his way to Vienna, he gained an introduction to Emperor Joseph II through Antonio Salieri, imperial court composer and rival of Mozart. Da Ponte soon became the official court librettist ("Poet to the Imperial Theaters"), and both Salieri and Mozart made use of his talents. But when Joseph died in 1790 and Mozart the following year, da Ponte's fortunes declined. For a short time he lodged with another famous Venetian adventurer and lover, Giacomo Casanova (1725–1798), then made his way to London, where he worked as a librettist at the King's Theater and opened a bookstore. But charges of shady financial dealings were leveled against him, so in 1805 da Ponte stole away from London for America, one step ahead of his creditors. After a brief stop in New York, he established himself in Sunbury, Pennsylvania, as a merchant, distiller, and occasional gunrunner during the War of 1812. Eventually, da Ponte returned to New York City, where in 1826 he mounted a production of Mozart's *Don Giovanni*, the first opera by Mozart to be performed in America. About this same time he also became the first professor of Italian literature at Columbia University. Upon his death in 1838, da Ponte bequeathed his personal library to Columbia, where it remains the nucleus of the Italian collection to the present day.

FIGURE 48-1
Lorenzo da Ponte (1749–1838)

aus dem Serail (*The Abduction from the Seraglio*). Like all operas of the *Singspiel* type, here the dialogue is simply spoken (there are no recitatives). The comic plot concerns the somewhat clumsy rescue of two young women from the harem of a Turkish lord. Obviously Mozart was capitalizing on the fact that in late eighteenth-century Vienna, things Turkish were all the rage. There were Turkish dress styles, Turkish hairdos, Turkish stories, and, as we have seen (Chapter 47), Turkish music. To satisfy the public's appetite for Turkish exoticism, Mozart made sure that his new opera not only had a Turkish plot, but also contained plenty of Turkish music—percussive marches and choruses with bass drum, cymbal, and triangle.

Beginning in 1785 Mozart had the good fortune to join forces with a gifted librettist, the larger-than-life figure **Lorenzo da Ponte** (1749–1838). Ultimately, da Ponte ended up in America selling guns to the British, mounting the first full production of a Mozart opera in the United States, and founding the Italian Department at Columbia University (see Box). But he was first and foremost a poet and librettist. During the 1780s da Ponte and Mozart created three operatic masterpieces, *Le nozze di Figaro* (1786), *Don Giovanni* (1787), and *Così fan tutte* (1790). Each is an *opera buffa*, yet each is infused with a newly serious tone. Social revolution, amorality and murder, and human frailty and infidelity are examined in turn. Mozart's fluid musical style was well suited for blending comedy with tragedy. As often with life (and Mozart), we don't know whether to laugh or cry.

Le nozze di Figaro (*The Marriage of Figaro*) is based on a radical work of the French playwright Beaumarchais, a play that fanned the flames of the French Revolution (1789). For six years the French king's ministers had prevented it from reaching the stage. When it finally did in 1784, the play took Paris by storm. In Austria a frightened Joseph II quickly banned the work from his Empire, but librettist Lorenzo da Ponte convinced him to allow a softened version to come to the stage in Vienna as an opera. What was so seditious about the play and libretto derived from it? In *Le nozze di Figaro* a clever, good-hearted, mostly honest manservant (Figaro) outwits a philandering, mostly dishonest nobleman (Count Almaviva). Perhaps most revolutionary of all is the close friendship between Countess Almaviva and her maid Susanna. It is this unlikely pair of women who ultimately teach the Count a lesson.

Social tension is immediately apparent at the outset of the opera. In the palace of the Count, Figaro has been measuring a bedroom for himself and his betrothed, Susanna. To his dismay, he learns that the room they have been given is right next to the Count's. The Count wishes to exercise his ancient *droit de seigneur*—the lord's claim to sexual favors from a servant's fiancée. In the aria "Se vuol ballare" ("If you want to dance") Figaro tells us that, should the Count wish to fool around, Figaro will call the tune. In fact, Figaro refers to the Count with a derisive diminutive "Signor Contino"—which, given his tone of voice, might be translated roughly as "you little twerp." Musically, the aria begins with straightforward, indeed foursquare music, showing Figaro to be a well-balanced, rational, yet resolute fellow. In the middle section, however, where the libretto reveals that the servant might need trickery to defeat the master, the music accordingly invokes slippery chromaticism and the sinister sound of the minor mode. Finally, in the closing *presto* section, Figaro's anger gets the better of him. Fulminating with rage, he loses control of his deliberate "dance."

LISTENING CUE

WOLFGANG AMADEUS MOZART
Le nozze di Figaro (1786)
Aria, "Se vuol ballare"

CD 8/2
Anthology, No. 137a

In Act II of *Le nozze di Figaro* we meet Countess Almaviva, the victim of the Count's womanizing (Fig. 48-2). What sort of person is she? Mozart tells us in music that she is a woman who bears sorrow with great serenity and dignity. In traditional *opera seria*, a soliloquy such as this would call for dazzling coloratura—a soloist alone on stage needs to do something sensational. But Mozart is not so much interested in vocal display as character development through music. Over long, legato lines of arching beauty, the Countess asks that the god of love bring her relief, "Porgi, amor." The text is simple, not extravagant, and so is the vocal range and style. The Countess's stature is portrayed instead in the richness of the orchestral scoring, most especially in the lush wind writing. Throughout *Le nozze di Figaro* Mozart sets high style against low, fast against slow, loud against soft, major against minor, and male against female. Nowhere in *Le nozze di Figaro* is there an aria in which virtuosic coloratura singing is heard; everywhere there is balance and control, the essence of Classical style.

LISTENING CUE

WOLFGANG AMADEUS MOZART
Le nozze di Figaro (1786)
Aria, "Porgi, amor"

CD 8/3
Anthology, No. 137b

In the subsequent aria, "Voi, che sapete" ("You ladies who know"), Mozart develops yet another character type—the petulant adolescent. Here we meet Cherubino, a lad of fourteen who is in love with the Countess, and with Susanna, and with all women all at once. His music is light, bouncy, and generally charming, yet full of mood swings (to distant keys in the aria's middle). At the climax Cherubino clamors upward in excited melodic sequence, only to dissolve in frustration back to the tonic. The part of adolescent Cherubino was intended by Mozart to be sung by a woman dressed as a man. It is thus called a **trouser role.** Such cross-dressing was common on the eighteenth-century stage, and it brought a certain erotic charge to the action.

The aria "Voi, che sapete" demonstrates another aspect of Mozart's musical genius: the capacity to write music of exquisite beauty from the simplest of materials (Ex. 48-1). It begins with an unremarkable four-bar antecedent phrase, followed by a matching four-bar consequent phrase. Yet together the two form a perfect pair, one made all the richer by the luxuriant accompaniment, again, for woodwinds (here clarinet, oboe, bassoon, and flute). Yet there is more, for when Cherubino enters he (she) inserts a new four-bar phrase in the middle of the previous two. So perfectly crafted is this new phrase that we hardly notice its insertion. All is sublimely beautiful, yet sublimely simple. To paraphrase Mozart's own words, there seems to be "not one note too many, nor one too few."[1]

❋ FIGURE 48-2
Renée Fleming singing the role of Countess Almaviva.

EXAMPLE 48-1

(continued on next page)

Insert

Don - ne, ve - de - te, s'io l'ho nel cor,

Consequent

Don - ne, ve - de - te, s'io l'ho nel cor.

You ladies who know about love, tell me if I have it in my heart.

LISTENING CUE

WOLFGANG AMADEUS MOZART
Le nozze di Figaro (1786)
Aria, "Voi, che sapete"

CD 8/4
Anthology, No. 137c

Despite the charm and beauty of his arias, it is in his ensembles that Mozart carries vocal music for the stage to unequaled heights of complexity and intrigue. The ensemble played to Mozart's strengths. As we have seen in his piano concertos (see Chapter 47), no one was better at composing rapid-fire dialogue in music. Likewise, no one was better at handling the intricacies of plot and action as one character after another appeared on stage. Having two, three, four, and more individuals press their points of view simultaneously helped push the dramatic action along; rather than having things happen in succession, they could come all at once. Compared to other operas, fast-paced *Figaro* contains relatively few solo arias and many more vocal ensembles. Three of the four acts end with an energetic **ensemble finale**—a rousing way to bring down the curtain.

To sample just a bit of Mozart's ensemble technique, we examine a section of the ensemble finale that closes Act II, a group song for independent soloists that goes on for an astonishing twenty-five minutes. On stage at this point are Figaro, Susanna, the Count and Countess, and Antonio, the gardener. Antonio is annoyed that someone has trampled his flowers; the Count suspects the culprit is Cherubino, who may have jumped out the Countess's window; Figaro, Susanna, and the Countess have reason to protect Cherubino. Thus there are many points of view to be heard. Here Antonio sings only on a single pitch, showing that he is a rustic fellow of no refinement. Figaro is musically agitated, then triumphant; the Count is triumphant, then agitated. The ladies sing together in interlocking thirds, thereby demonstrating their solidarity through music. Each twist in the plot is underscored in the music by a corresponding change in key and style. These are the musical mechanisms by which Mozart works his magic in his complex ensemble finales.

LISTENING CUE

WOLFGANG AMADEUS MOZART
Le nozze di Figaro (1786)
Ensemble, "Vostre dunque"

CD 8/5
Anthology, No. 137d

Mozart teamed with da Ponte to fashion two other *opere buffe*, *Don Giovanni* and *Così fan tutte* (*Thus do they all*). *Don Giovanni* tells the story of a philandering, indeed murdering Don Juan, a nobleman whose deviant behavior makes the peasants he exploits seem all the more noble. The music Mozart created for this lurid tale may be even more powerful than that of *Le nozze di Figaro*. In fact, many believe *Don Giovanni* to be the greatest opera ever written. While *Così fan tutte*, too, has much beautiful music, the libretto has little of the sensationalism or social bite of *Don Giovanni* or *Le nozze di Figaro*.

In his last year (1791), Mozart composed two operas that show his remarkable versatility. One, *La clemenza di Tito* (*The Clemency of Tito*) is an *opera seria* commissioned for the crowning of Emperor Leopold II in Prague as king of Bohemia; needless to say, for the installation of a king, old-style *opera seria*, and old-style values, were chosen above social revolution. The second opera, *Die Zauberflöte* (*The Magic Flute*), is very different. *Die Zauberflöte* is a German *Singspiel*, yet here the music ranges from the most vocally demanding sounds of Italianate opera to the naively simple style of German folk song. The libretto was the product of actor-singer-showman Emanuel Schikaneder, and he called for all the special effects the eighteenth century could muster—magical instruments, a fire-breathing snake, a flaming temple, and the like. Yet the end has distinctly Masonic overtones that promote universal brotherhood. From the start Mozart and Schikaneder aimed to appeal to a popular rather than a courtly audience. Accordingly, they mounted their production, not at the court theater in central Vienna, but at a suburban theater beyond the city walls in a neighborhood where the tickets were cheaper and the audience sat on wooden benches. This was the Viennese equivalent of "off-Broadway." *Die Zauberflöte* hit the target audience to the financial gain of all, and to this day remains one of Mozart's most universally appealing operas.

REQUIEM MASS

Mozart became ill in the fall of 1791. He took to his bed about 20 November and died in the early morning of 5 December (see also Chapter 47). All fall he had been working on a Requiem Mass, which had been commissioned by a mysterious messenger. (Not until 1964 was it fully revealed that an Austrian nobleman had requested the work with the aim of honoring his recently deceased wife, passing off Mozart's score as his own composition.) Realizing that he was dying, Mozart eventually came to see this requiem as burial music for himself.

The **Requiem Mass** is the funeral music for the Roman Catholic Church. As such it makes use of several movements from the traditional Ordinary and Proper of the Mass that have existed since the Middle Ages (see Chapter 3). To these is added a medieval chant particular to the burial service, the sequence *Dies irae* (*Day of Wrath*). The **Dies irae** (discussed at length in Chapter 5) is by far the longest and most textually expressive movement within the Requiem Mass. Over the centuries many composers have set the requiem in polyphony, paying special attention to the *Dies irae*. Mozart, Berlioz, and Verdi are just a few of the composers to capture in sound the "hellfire and brimstone" quality of this apocalyptic text:

Dies irae, dies illa,	Day of wrath, that day,
Solvet saeclum in favilla,	When the ages shall be reduced to ash
Teste David cum Sibylla.	As foretold by David and the Sibyl Prophet.
Quantus tremor est futurus,	What terror will occur
Quando judex est venturus,	When the eternal Judge arrives,
Cuncta stricte discussurus.	To loosen the chains of those in Hell.

For frightening words such as these, Mozart creates appropriately terrifying music. Subsequent verses, too, have music that does honor to the vivid text. In the verse "Tuba mirum" ("Wondrous trumpet"), for example, Mozart creates what is perhaps the most famous trombone solo in the entire literature. Although the trombone was featured in the unearthly scenes of such operas as Gluck's *Orfeo* and Mozart's *Idomeneo*, it would not be admitted into the symphony orchestra until the time of Beethoven. Yet within the music for the church, it had a long history extending back to the sacred Masses and motets of the Renaissance. Mozart calls for the trombone at this point in his requiem (Ex. 48-2) because the text itself calls for the trumpet (or trombone) to sound the Last Judgment.

EXAMPLE 48-2

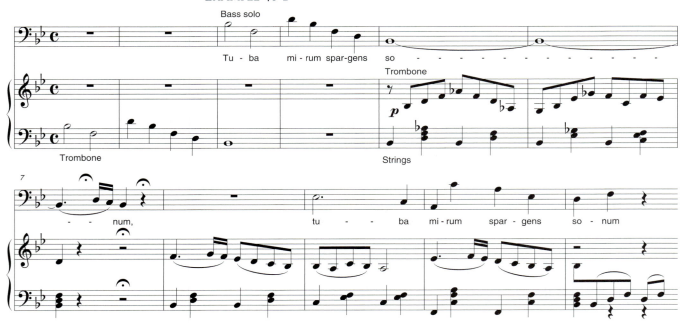

The trumpet sends forth its wondrous sound.

Perhaps the most graphic moment in Mozart's Requiem is found in the "Confutatis" of the *Dies irae*. Here the text erects a contrast between the cries of the hellish pain of the damned ("Confutatis" = those confounded) against the heavenly sounds of the elect ("Benedictis" = those blessed). Mozart places the damned down low in a minor key, supported by an agitated accompaniment. They sing with a jagged vocal line that incorporates a tritone (the *diabolus in musica*, the tonal devil). The elect, on the other hand, dwell in a higher, quieter realm of major, where any dissonance is quickly resolved. In Mozart's vision of the cosmos, there is vivid contrast, yet balance, even between Heaven and Hell.

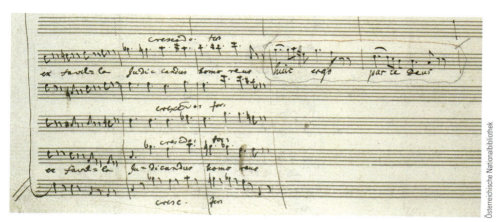

🌸 FIGURE 48-3
The last notes written by Mozart, toward the opening of the "Lacrimosa" of the Requiem Mass.

Österreichische Nationalbibliothek

💿 LISTENING CUE

WOLFGANG AMADEUS MOZART
Requiem Mass (1791)
"Confutatis"

CD 8/6
Anthology, No. 138a

Mozart did not complete his Requiem. It was left to his students, most notably Franz Xaver Süssmayr (1766–1803), to compose a few unfinished portions and flesh out the orchestration. Where Mozart stopped can be determined by a glance at the autograph score (Fig. 48-3), specifically toward the end of the *Dies irae* in a section called "Lacrimosa dies illa" ("Ah, that day of tears and mourning"; Ex. 48-3). Here Mozart writes a melody that ascends in a mostly chromatic scale for more than an octave, like the just man or woman rising from ashes of Hell. At this point death took the pen from the master's hand. The version completed by pupil Süssmayr is generally used in performances today.

EXAMPLE 48-3

(continued on next page)

When the just person rises from the ashes to be judged…

 LISTENING CUE

WOLFGANG AMADEUS MOZART	CD 8/7
Requiem Mass (1791)	Anthology, No. 138b
"Lacrimosa" (completed by Süssmayr)	

 **SUMMARY**

Given the highly dramatic quality of Mozart's music, it is not surprising that he was attracted to the dramatic potential of musical theater in its most elaborate form: opera. In all, Mozart composed some twenty operas. His universality in this genre can be seen in the fact that he has left us examples of traditional *opera seria*, German *Singspiel*, and *opera buffa*. Moreover, his operas *Le nozze di Figaro*, *Don Giovanni*, and *Così fan tutte*, all with librettos by Lorenzo da Ponte, mix elements of *seria* and *buffa*. Mozart's special gift as an operatic composer was his uncanny ability to portray each dramatic situation and each character vividly through music. The various characters are often united in cumulative fashion in ensemble finales, where the differing points of view are heard simultaneously in a brilliant display of musical and dramatic counterpoint. Mozart also composed much splendid music for the Roman Catholic Church. By far his best-known religious work is his Requiem Mass with its graphic setting of the text of the *Dies irae* movement. Commissioned under mysterious circumstances and composed during his final weeks, Mozart came to look upon this Requiem Mass as music for his own funeral.

KEY TERMS

Singspiel
Lorenzo da Ponte

trouser role
ensemble finale

Requiem Mass
Dies irae

Chapter

49

The Early Music of Beethoven

In November 1792, Ludwig van Beethoven, then twenty-one years of age, arrived in Vienna to study with Joseph Haydn and to expand his musical horizons (Map 49-1). He had traveled some five hundred fifty miles from his hometown in Bonn, where he had already showed such prodigious skill as a composer and pianist that his teacher compared him to Mozart. From this time until his death in 1827, Beethoven remained a permanent resident of Vienna. His career there coincided with a period of political and social unrest and changing musical tastes, and it was beset by the composer's own personal adversities.

Despite these distractions, Beethoven created a body of musical works that is recognized throughout the world as unique and enduring. His compositions have

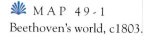 MAP 49-1
Beethoven's world, c1803.

continually delighted and inspired listeners, with no periods of waning interest, no significant revisionist thinking that has questioned their importance, no lessening of their profundity after repeated hearings. His music has shown a universal greatness, equally perceptible to audiences of all periods and in all places. It is as important to classical music in the twenty-first century as it was in the twentieth or nineteenth, and its appeal is as evident to listeners in Asia and Africa as it is to those in Austria, where the music was created.

Why is it that we all like Beethoven's music? One reason is that he wrote music with all of us in mind, whatever our tastes or background. People who are new to classical music will all respond to his Fifth Symphony because he composed this work so that it would be likable by just such listeners. It is full of life (we all know what that's like) and everyone can follow its pacing, marked by passages of rest that erupt into great climaxes, or moments when two conflicting forces seem to have locked horns, ultimately leading to the triumph of the more positive of these opponents.

Beethoven seemed to address more experienced listeners in his string quartets, and others still in works like the *Missa solemnis* and Piano Sonata in C Minor, Op. 111, which hint at some higher universe beyond the one of struggle and conflict so realistically portrayed in the Fifth Symphony. Another appealing thing about Beethoven's music is its balanced mixture of elements, like a fine wine that has just the right proportion of sugar and tartness. One moment Beethoven will write the most exquisite melody—think of the slow movement of the "Pathétique" Piano Sonata—and the next moment he puts any thought of beautiful melody aside so as to concentrate on motion and rhythm, which can erupt in such muscular displays as in the scherzo of the Ninth Symphony. Beethoven wrote music for everyone.

In light of Beethoven's special significance to the history of music, a discussion of his life and works will occupy the next three chapters of this book. These chapters conform to a customary division of his creative life into three periods—early, middle, and late—each of which is set off by important events in the composer's personal life and by distinguishable musical styles. The first period begins at the time of his arrival in Vienna in 1792 and extends until about 1802, a time of crisis when the composer had to face the prospect of losing his hearing. This period is preceded by an apprenticeship during the composer's earlier years in Bonn. The middle period extends from about 1802 until roughly 1814, and the late period—filled with works unprecedented in form and range of expression—follows this and continues until only months before his death on 26 March 1827.

❀ YEARS OF APPRENTICESHIP: 1770–1792

Beethoven was born in 1770 in the German city of Bonn, probably on December 16; his baptismal certificate is dated the following day. Like Bach and Mozart before him, he was raised in a family of musicians. His father was a singer who worked for the ruler (or "elector") of an archdiocese that lay on the west bank of the Rhine River near the large city of Cologne. Its seat of government was some fifteen miles to the south, in the smaller city of Bonn. Under the instruction of another court musician, **Christian Neefe,** Beethoven at the age of eleven began to compose, and he increasingly attracted attention for his skill as a keyboard player.

In 1784 a new elector, Maximilian Franz, came to power in Bonn, and the thirteen-year-old Beethoven was then given a salary as assistant court organist. He seemed destined to follow in the footsteps of his father and grandfather—and those of established musicians like Joseph Haydn—as a court employee. The music-loving Maximilian Franz had strong ties to Vienna and its musicians. He was a brother of the reigning Hapsburg monarch, Joseph II, and he had grown up in Vienna, where he knew and admired Mozart. ("He thinks the world of me," Mozart smugly reported to his father.)

In 1787 the elector sent Beethoven to Vienna to study with Mozart, although Beethoven almost immediately returned, due to the illness of his mother. After her death later in that year, he was forced to take over the guardianship of his two younger brothers and his alcoholic father, although his musical achievements continued. Carl Junker heard Beethoven play in 1791 and published this report:

> I heard him extemporize in private; yes, I was even invited to propose a theme for him to vary. The greatness of this amiable, light-hearted man, as a virtuoso, may in my opinion be safely estimated from his almost inexhaustible wealth of ideas, the altogether characteristic style of expression in his playing, and the great execution which he displays. . . . In short, he is more for the heart—equally great, therefore, as an *adagio* or *allegro* player. Even the members of this remarkable [Bonn] orchestra are, without exception, his admirers, and all ears when he plays.[1]

In 1792 Maximilian Franz again attempted to invest in the future of music at his court by financing another trip for Beethoven to Vienna. Mozart had died the year before, so this time arrangements were made for him to have lessons with Joseph Haydn, who had examined some of Beethoven's recent music on a leg of his first trip to London in 1790–1792. Bonn's young genius left for Vienna in the first days of November, never to return. Just before his departure, Count **Ferdinand Waldstein,** one of his most influential supporters in Bonn, wrote prophetically in Beethoven's album:

> Dear Beethoven! You are going to Vienna in fulfillment of your long frustrated wishes. The genius of Mozart is mourning and weeping over the death of its pupil. It found refuge but no occupation with the inexhaustible Haydn. Through him it wishes to form a union with another. With the help of assiduous labor you will receive *Mozart's spirit from Haydn's hands.*[2]

Waldstein's sentiments show the esteem in which Mozart's works were held in Bonn—an admiration that Beethoven fully shared—but a surprisingly condescending judgment of Haydn, then widely recognized as the world's greatest living composer.

Beethoven was well-advanced as a composer when he went to Haydn. He had written about fifty works during his apprenticeship period in Bonn and, although many of these were published at the time, none is a mature composition. Most involve piano, including sonatas, variations, a concerto, small pieces, and chamber music. There are also works for winds, songs, and arias, and, most important, two cantatas whose texts observe the death in 1790 of Emperor Joseph II and the crowning of his successor, Leopold II. Most of these compositions are now identified by **WoO numbers** (*Werk ohne Opuszahl,* work without opus number), which were assigned to them in the standard catalog of Beethoven's music compiled in 1955 by Georg Kinsky and Hans Halm.

❋ BEETHOVEN'S WORLD IN 1792

Beethoven's trip from Bonn to Vienna in November 1792 coincided with the beginning of a twelve-year period of warfare between France and its European neighbors. Only months before, France was gripped by a general insurrection, after which its monarchy was abolished and a republican form of government established. These measures brought to a climax the **French Revolution,** which had begun in 1789. Armies from German lands, primarily Prussia and Austria, marched on France at this time to try to protect the French king and the Austrian provinces in what is now Belgium, but they failed in both objectives.

Beethoven's trip to Vienna was filled with adventure. The roads on which he traveled to the east were occupied by German soldiers heading west to meet the French. Near the city of Koblenz (just south of Bonn), Beethoven's carriage made a mad dash through army troops, for which Beethoven gratefully gave his driver an extra payment.

When Beethoven reached Vienna after about a week, he was temporarily separated from warfare, although by 1805 French armies had reached even Vienna. His friends in Bonn were not so lucky, since the city was quickly overrun by the French. His former employer Maximilian Franz permanently fled into exile.

✸ VIENNA: 1792–1802

Ferdinand Waldstein's slighting attitude toward the "inexhaustible Haydn" seems to have carried over into Beethoven's studies, which he undertook with Haydn for about one year after arriving in the Austrian capital. Although outwardly maintaining a respectful attitude, Beethoven made it no secret to friends that he was disappointed with the instruction he was receiving from Haydn, and he later sought out more systematic training in counterpoint from Johann Albrechtsberger and Johann Schenk, in violin playing from Ignaz Schuppanzigh, and in vocal composition from Antonio Salieri.

The profession of music in Vienna in 1792 still had many antiquated features when compared to the artistic opportunities available in a city like Paris or London. In Vienna, a serious musical culture existed primarily in the private houses and palaces of the aristocracy. The music-loving nobility sometimes maintained their own private orchestras and chamber ensembles. They hired teachers and coaches, sponsored concerts, presented visiting performers, encouraged new music, and provided a forum for interchange among artists and skilled amateurs. In the public sphere, opera remained the most lucrative genre for a successful composer, and large churches—such as the magnificent Cathedral of St. Stephen in the center of the city—presented music that could be heard by the general public. Public concerts tended to focus on the works of an individual composer or performer, and these were often gala events mixing orchestral and vocal selections in which soloistic playing was typically limited to improvisation. Until well into the nineteenth century, public concerts in Vienna were limited by the lack of a suitable auditorium. Theaters were used for concerts, but they were available only on relatively few dates—primarily during Lent and before Christmas—and they were usually rented directly by a featured artist rather than by any established concert-presenting agency.

Beethoven's preliminary contacts with Bonn's music-loving aristocracy and his irresistible prowess on the piano opened the doors of Vienna's aristocrat musical culture to him. His piano playing—especially his **improvisations**—became legendary. His student **Carl Czerny** recalled his playing:

> Nobody equaled him in the rapidity of his scales, double trills, skips, etc.—not even Hummel. His bearing while playing was masterfully quiet, noble, and beautiful, without the slightest grimace (only bent forward low, as his deafness grew upon him). . . . He made frequent use of the pedals, much more frequent than is indicated in his works.

His playing of the scores of Handel and Gluck and the fugues of Seb. Bach was unique, in that in the former he introduced a full-voicedness and a spirit which gave these works a new shape.[3]

Czerny especially praised Beethoven's legato playing, which he found refreshingly different from the "hammered, detached staccato technique of Mozart's time." Beethoven himself often remarked that he wished to make the piano sing. The instrument that Beethoven preferred during his early period was one made for him by Johann Andreas Streicher and his wife, Nannette Stein. This was considerably smaller and lighter than the modern grand piano, and it used the nuanced "Viennese action" that had small hammers covered with leather and light dampers that were lifted by a knee lever rather than a pedal. Its normal range was from F (two octaves and a fifth below middle C) to F or G five octaves above. The modern piano, by comparison, has a range of more than seven octaves.

PIANO MUSIC AND THE "PATHÉTIQUE" SONATA

During his first decade in Vienna, Beethoven composed primarily for his own instrument, the piano. He wrote twenty of his thirty-two mature piano sonatas between 1794 and 1802, and there are also thirteen sets of variations, numerous small piano pieces, two piano concertos, and chamber music with piano (mainly instrumental sonatas and piano-string trios). The piano sonatas are the centerpieces of this body of works. Here, Beethoven inherited a genre already cultivated by Mozart and Haydn, although from the very beginning—the three sonatas of Opus 2, published in 1796—Beethoven treats the sonata as though confident of his ability to surpass these great forebears. His sonatas have a range of emotion, a diversity of formal structure, and a technical difficulty that is considerably larger than is found in the piano sonatas of Haydn or Mozart. Half of Beethoven's twenty have four movements (the sonatas of Haydn and Mozart never surpass three), and in these cases Beethoven adds a minuet, scherzo, or march as a third movement to enlarge the customary fast/slow/fast three-movement frame. The two sonatas of Opus 27 (the second is the celebrated "Moonlight" Sonata) have the freedom of form characteristic of a **fantasia.** As in the earlier Classical period, most of Beethoven's early piano sonatas are in the major mode, but the six that are in minor keys have an especially passionate character.

One of the most original of the early minor-mode sonatas is the Sonata in C Minor ("Pathétique"), Op. 13, completed in 1798. The title "Pathétique," which was given to the work by Beethoven himself, suggests that the sonata will be emotional and deeply felt, qualities that apparently led Beethoven to introduce many formal novelties. Beethoven's pieces in the key of C minor have certain similarities: most are filled with turbulence and conflict. Frequently—as in the Fifth Symphony and Third Piano Concerto, although not in Opus 13—they end triumphantly in C major. The "Pathétique" Sonata uses the standard sequence of three movements—*allegro* (with slow introduction)/*adagio*/*allegro*—and its first movement is the longest and weightiest of the cycle.

The opening of the first movement was no doubt a surprise for its early listeners. All of the sonatas of Haydn and Mozart, and all of Beethoven's own previous sonatas, begin with a main theme in a fast tempo, but the "Pathétique" Sonata begins instead with a somber and brooding prologue marked *grave.* Haydn's symphonies—an example is his Symphony No. 99 in E♭ Major (see Chapter 46)—often begin with slow introductions that prepare the listener for the principal music to come, but this *grave* is more of an emotive improvisation, one filled with fragmentary ideas, sequences, rapid scales, and harmonies linked by diminished chords. In his opening improvisation, Beethoven uses every inch of the piano keyboard and repeatedly interrupts quiet phrases with *fortissimo* outbursts.

Order is restored at the *allegro molto e con brio*, where a movement in sonata form begins. But Beethoven uses the principle of sonata form in a way that is far from ordinary. An important innovation is his striving for greater continuity throughout the movement and a more seamless integration of its parts, thus avoiding the earlier tendency to compartmentalize a first movement into separate sections. One way that Beethoven achieves this new connectedness is to integrate the slow introduction more fully into the logic of the whole movement. Recall the function of the slow introduction to the first movement of Haydn's Symphony No. 99. Haydn makes the passage introductory, in that its motives only forecast the principal themes that follow in the exposition. They do not explicitly return anywhere in the movement. Beethoven, on the contrary, brings back the *grave* of the "Pathétique" Sonata twice within the body of the movement, just before the development section and before the coda. He also explicitly brings back the first motive from the *grave* within the development section, as shown in Example 49-1, and in this way more fully integrates it into the fabric of the whole movement. In light of these innovations, we must think of the opening *grave* as much a part of the exposition of the sonata form as an introduction to it.

EXAMPLE 49-1

Beethoven's idea of sonata form as a continuous musical argument is also realized in the harmonic dimension, in which the composer finds ways of melding its various parts. For example, in the first movements of Haydn and Mozart, the music normally comes to a full stop at the end of the transition, just before the entrance of the second theme. But, at this point in the "Pathétique" Sonata (measure 51), Beethoven overlays the beginning of the principal second theme with a continuation of harmonic motion that is more characteristic of a transition. As the second theme begins, the fifth degree (B♭) of the new key E♭ is kept in the bass for twelve additional measures as a pedal point, and it arrives on the tonic tone E♭ only at measure 89, with the beginning of another theme.

LISTENING CUE

LUDWIG VAN BEETHOVEN
Piano Sonata in C Minor ("Pathétique," 1798)
First movement, *Grave; Allegro molto e con brio*

CD 8/8
Anthology, No. 139

✤ PIANO CONCERTO NO. 1 IN C MAJOR

In Beethoven's days in Vienna, as earlier in Mozart's, concertos were the primary type of music used by a virtuoso performer in public concerts. These allowed the soloist to show off a command of the instrument, and they revealed the highly prized ability of a player to improvise. For a performer who was also a composer, the genre provided an opportunity to display a full range of creative skills. In each of his major public concerts during his first decade in Vienna, Beethoven played a concerto. During these years he had two of his own concertos at his disposal: Concerto No. 1 in C Major, Op. 15, and Concerto No. 2 in B♭ Major, Op. 19. Confusingly, Concerto No. 2 was composed earlier than Concerto No. 1, but it received the higher number since it was published slightly later. Beethoven gave these early concertos up for publication only after he had used them repeatedly in his concerts, and, after publication, he rarely if ever performed them again.

There are several important differences between the way most modern performers play Beethoven's piano concertos and the way Beethoven himself played them. Judging from the reports of contemporaries, it is likely that Beethoven treated the entire solo part with a greater degree of extemporization than is the case at present, when all performers adhere strictly to the composer's published text and confine improvisation, at most, to cadenzas. Beethoven played his own concertos before they were published, and when he did so, the solo parts were left as incomplete sketches that the composer brought to life in differing ways at the time of a performance. Ignaz von Seyfried recalled turning pages for Beethoven when he first played his Piano Concerto No. 3 in 1803: "He asked me to turn the pages for him; but— heaven help me!—that was easier said than done. I saw almost nothing but empty leaves; at the most on one page or the other a few Egyptian hieroglyphs wholly unintelligible to me scribbled down to serve as clues for him."[4]

Another major difference between then and now is that Beethoven—as well as Mozart and other pianists of the day—played from beginning to end, without falling silent during the passages where the orchestra has the main melodic material. In these tutti sections the soloist became an accompanimental instrument, doubling the basses and playing chords to reinforce the texture. There is much evidence for this practice. Carl Czerny recalled of his first meeting with Beethoven (see Box), during which he played Mozart's Piano Concerto in C Major, K. 503, that Beethoven "played the orchestral melody with his left hand whenever I had purely accompanying passages." This suggests that the normal way of rendering the solo part of a concerto was to play both the principal solo passages and also chords or accompanimental figures during the intervening orchestral moments.

Beethoven's own performances of his concertos were memorable occasions. An impressionable young Czech composer, Václav Tomášek, attended a concert in Prague in 1798 at which Beethoven improvised and performed a concerto. In memoirs published some fifty years later, Tomášek recalled the memories etched by this encounter:

> Beethoven's magnificent playing and particularly the daring flights in his improvisation stirred me strangely to the depths of my soul; indeed I found myself so profoundly bowed down that I did not touch my pianoforte for several days.[5]

The principal work that Tomášek heard at the 1798 concert was Beethoven's Piano Concerto No. 1 in C Major, Op. 15. This composition, like other classical concertos, has three movements—fast/slow/fast—the sequence dominated in weight and length by the first movement. In overall form and character, Beethoven's C-Major Concerto

Carl Czerny Meets Beethoven

Beethoven occasionally taught piano. One of his best students was Carl Czerny (1791–1857), who recalled his initial impressions of Beethoven (Fig. 49-1) when, at the age of ten, he received his first lessons:

art of clavier playing [*Versuch über die wahre Art das Clavier zu spielen*, 1753–1762], which he must have by the time he comes to see me again. . . ."[6]

> . . . His jet-black hair, cut à la Titus, made him look shaggy the way it stood off from his head. Since his beard had not been shaved for several days, the lower part of his swarthy face looked even darker. I also noticed immediately with the power of observation so typical of children that both his ears were stuffed with cotton which seemed to have been dipped in a yellow liquid. But at that time he certainly appeared to be not the least bit hard of hearing. I had to play something right away and since I was too bashful to start with one of his works I played the great C major concerto by Mozart (the one that starts with chords [K. 503]). Beethoven soon took notice, moved close to my chair, and played the orchestral melody with his left hand whenever I had purely accompanying passages. His hands were very hairy and his fingers very broad, especially at the tips. When he expressed satisfaction I felt encouraged enough to play his recently published *Sonate Pathétique* and finally the *Adelaide*, which my father sang with his very respectable tenor voice. When I had finished, Beethoven turned to my father and said, "The boy is talented, I myself want to teach him, and I accept him as my pupil. Let him come several times a week. But most important, get him Emanuel Bach's book on the true

Bridgeman Art Library

❀ **FIGURE 49-1**

Beethoven (age twenty-nine in this engraving) was small in stature and had a dark complexion.

---

is similar to Mozart's piano concertos from the 1780s (see Chapter 47). Like Mozart, Beethoven brings to his early concertos a great variety of expression. By its very medium, one in which an individual performer interacts with an orchestral group, the concerto has the potential to suggest a drama in which the leading role—played by the soloist—can take on a new persona in every movement.

With its march rhythm, trumpets and drums, and a main theme that begins with a fanfare (Ex. 49-2), the opening movement casts a spotlight on the soloist as a military hero who captures our attention with his swaggering virtuosity. In the slow movement, a passionate *largo* in A♭ major, the soloist exchanges his army uniform for the costume of an operatic diva. Her affective and highly florid melody (Ex. 49-3) melts the very soul of her listeners.

EXAMPLE 49-2

EXAMPLE 49-3

A relatively short and high-spirited finale rounds off the C-Major Concerto, and here the soloist becomes a harlequin in a comic opera, impishly clowning, showing off, and defeating our expectations. The finales of all of Beethoven's concertos—like most of those by Mozart—use a rondo form, or, more accurately, **sonata-rondo form.** Recall the general features of rondo form from Chapter 44. An opening theme returns in the tonic key after each in a series of contrasting themes (called **episodes**). The general design of a rondo is thus **ABAC . . . A.** Rondos were especially favored by French composers during the Baroque period. Their popularity continued throughout the Classical period, at which time they were used both in independent compositions and in movements (especially finales) within longer instrumental cycles. By Beethoven's day, the simple rondo had given way to a more complex design that brought in features of sonata form.

Composers in the Classical period were never in complete agreement as to how this amalgamation of the two forms should occur, but the finale of Beethoven's C-Major Concerto offers a typical example. The top of the following diagram charts the rondo-like features of this movement.

Rondo	A		B	A	C		A	B	A	Coda
Sonata	Exposition:	- - - - - - - - - - - - -					Recap	- - - - - -		Coda
	main theme	(trans.)	2nd theme							
Key:	I - - - - - - . . .		V - - - - - -	I - - - - - -	vi - - - - - -		I -			
Measure:	1		66	152	192		311	382	485	505

The rondo theme itself is called **A,** and it is stated four times, each in the tonic key of C major. There are two episodes (**B** and **C**), but only theme **C**—in the minor mode with a dance-like rhythm and heavy beat—has the sharp contrast with its surroundings that we expect of a rondo episode. Compare the beginnings of these three themes in Example 49-4. Theme **B** smoothly fits together with theme **A,** like the two themes in an exposition of a movement in sonata form. But theme **C** makes a clear contrast in comparison to **A,** more in keeping with the tradition of the rondo.

EXAMPLE 49-4

Theme A (mm. 1-6)

Theme B (mm. 65-73, strings only)

Theme C (mm. 191-99, piano only)

ben marcato e sempre stacc.

The outline of sonata form is shown in the lower part of the preceding diagram. Its presence is felt most strongly at the opening and closing of the movement but hardly at all in the middle. Themes **A** and **B** are very similar to the first and second themes of a symphonic exposition, in the tonic and dominant keys, respectively. The middle of the movement has no direct analogy with sonata form, but this reappears at measure 311 with the beginning of a recapitulation of the principal themes **A** and **B,** both in the home key of C major.

Beethoven reminds us that we are hearing a concerto when he adds a cadenza for the pianist near the movement's end. Beethoven writes this cadenza out, unlike the improvised cadenza in the first movement, and after it we hear one final statement of the rondo theme and an extended coda.

LISTENING CUE

LUDWIG VAN BEETHOVEN
Piano Concerto No. 1 in C Major (1795)
Third Movement, *Allegro*

CD 8/9
Anthology, No. 140

❈ THE ONSET OF DEAFNESS

Around 1798, just when his career as a pianist and composer was thriving as never before, Beethoven came to the terrifying realization that he was losing his hearing. He reported a constant buzzing in his ears, an inability to hear high frequencies, a painful discomfort from loud sounds, and a general lack of clarity in making out spoken words. These are all symptoms of neural degeneration of the inner ear, and their cause in Beethoven's case is unknown.

Understanding of deafness and its treatment was primitive during Beethoven's lifetime. His physicians addressed his condition with warm and cold baths, herbal ointments, and by applying a substance to the arms that made the skin blister. Beethoven himself had heard that galvanism (electric shock) was an effective treatment, and he was convinced that his condition stemmed from his chronic digestive disorders.

Like virtually everyone who has faced a disability, Beethoven primarily feared isolation and the threat of social stigma. At this time, he withdrew into himself and came to live solely in his music, which was still crystal clear in his mind, if no longer so in his ears. Finally, in the summer of 1801, he began to discuss his dilemma with his most trusted acquaintances. He wrote to his childhood friend Franz Wegeler (who had become a physician) in June 1801, describing in detail his symptoms and the treatments he had received.[7] An especially affecting letter was addressed at the same time to his friend Karl Amenda:

> A sad resignation must be my refuge, although indeed I am resolved to rise above every obstacle. But how will it be possible? Yes, Amenda, if my infirmity shows itself to be incurable in half a year, I shall appeal to you. You must abandon everything and come to me. Then I shall travel and you must be my companion (my affliction causes me the least trouble in playing and composing, the most in association with others). . . . *I beg of you to keep the matter of my deafness a profound secret to be confided to nobody no matter whom.*[8]

SUMMARY

In their ability to capture and hold the imagination of listeners throughout the world for more than two centuries, the musical works of Ludwig van Beethoven (1770–1827) are unique in the history of music. Beethoven grew up in the city of Bonn, where he showed prodigious gifts as a pianist (especially in improvisation) and composer. In 1792 he moved to Vienna, where he studied with Joseph Haydn and continue to advance in the path of virtuoso and composer. Beethoven's career is customarily divided into three phases: an early period extends from 1792 until about 1802, a middle period from 1802 until 1812 or somewhat later, and the late period from then until 1826.

In his early period, Beethoven consciously attempted to carry on the styles of music that he had encountered in works by Haydn and Mozart, and he concentrated on compositions for his own instrument, the piano. These include many sonatas, of which the "Pathétique" Sonata, Op. 13, shows the wide range of emotion and formal innovation that would characterize his later music. His Piano Concerto No. 1, Op. 15, adheres closely to the form of the Mozartean piano concerto. Its finale is an example of sonata-rondo form (a mixture of elements from these two standard movement plans), and it exhibits the rollicking high spirits typical of a Classical finale.

KEY TERMS

Christian Neefe
Ferdinand Waldstein
WoO numbers

French Revolution
improvisation
Carl Czerny

fantasia
sonata-rondo form
episode (in a rondo form)

Chapter 50

Beethoven's Middle Period: 1802–1814

Beethoven's anxiety over his deafness only worsened after his appeal to his friends in 1801. In the spring of the following year, at the urging of a physician, he spent time in the quiet town of Heiligenstadt, north of Vienna, and here he wrote a will that he addressed to his two brothers. This document, now known as the **Heiligenstadt Testament,** is far from being a simple instruction for the disposition of property after death, and Beethoven's thoughts were directed not so much to his brothers as to all mankind, present and future. The composer pours out his innermost feelings about himself and his future prospects, explaining his moody and withdrawn personality, his life in the shadow of deafness, and his determination to prevail in the face of such a dire adversity. Excerpts from this remarkable document are presented in the box on the next page.

In addition to explaining his frame of mind, Beethoven also touches in the testament on a view of art that breaks with the past. Art is not a means for providing listeners with a simple pleasure, he says; instead, it is something far higher and more basic to life. Art is what held him back from suicide. His life was not his to take, he says, until he had brought forth the artistic works that he was put on earth to create. Compare this elevated idea of art with the definition of music given by Charles Burney in his 1776 *General History of Music*: "Music is an innocent luxury, unnecessary, indeed, to our existence, but a great improvement and gratification of the sense of hearing."[1] We can only wonder if Beethoven would have turned away from self-destruction if music for him was only "an innocent luxury."

BEETHOVEN'S LIFE AND MUSIC DURING THE MIDDLE PERIOD

It is remarkable that Beethoven in his Heiligenstadt Testament says nothing about deafness being an impediment to his work as a composer. The progress of the disease during his middle period, from about 1802 until about 1814, was slow and intermittent. He continued to play piano in public concerts throughout this time, and at no point during these years was his compositional creativity significantly disrupted. His sometimes depressive and vehement states of mind did not, in general, show through into his music, which continued on the forceful and emotive path that he had already blazed in his "Pathétique" Sonata.

The middle years were Beethoven's most productive and successful period as a composer. Between 1802 and 1814 he wrote seven of his nine symphonies, seven new piano sonatas, the opera *Fidelio,* and some of his most respected chamber music. He continued to write concertos, completing three new piano concertos (for a total of five), and also the Violin Concerto (1806) and Triple Concerto for piano, violin, and cello (1804). This last—a concerto with multiple soloists—is the type of work that Mozart and Haydn called a **symphonie concertante.**

Beethoven continued to make his living as an independent composer and pianist. He sold new works to publishers, gave special gala concerts for his own benefit (the Viennese called these **academies**), and taught piano. In March 1809 his financial prospects were further brightened when he received a substantial lifetime salary from three of his aristocratic patrons, who asked only that he remain a citizen of Vienna.

The Heiligenstadt Testament

Oh you men who think or say that I am malevolent, stubborn, or misanthropic, how greatly do you wrong me. You do not know the secret cause which makes me seem that way to you. From childhood on my heart and soul have been full of the tender feeling of goodwill, and I was ever inclined to accomplish great things. But, think that for six years now I have been hopelessly afflicted, made worse by senseless physicians, from year to year deceived with hopes of improvement, finally compelled to face the prospect of *a lasting malady* (whose cure will take years or perhaps be impossible). Though born with a fiery, active temperament, even susceptible to the diversions of society, I was soon compelled to withdraw myself, to live life alone. If at times I tried to forget all this, oh how harshly was I flung back by the doubly sad experience of my bad hearing. Yet it was impossible for me to say to people, "Speak louder, shout, for I am deaf." Ah, how could I possibly admit an infirmity in the *one sense* which ought to be more perfect in me than in others, a sense which I once possessed in the highest perfection, a perfection such as few in my profession enjoy or ever have enjoyed. . . .

For me there can be no relaxation with my fellow men, no refined conversations, no mutual exchange of ideas. I must live almost alone like one who has been banished, I can mix with society only as much as true necessity demands. If I approach near to people a hot terror seizes upon me and I fear being exposed to the danger that my condition might be noticed. . . . But what a humiliation for me when someone standing next to me heard a flute in the distance and *I heard nothing,* or someone heard a *shepherd singing* and again I heard nothing. Such incidents drove me almost to despair, a little more of that and I would have ended my life—it was only *my art* that held me back. Ah, it seemed to me impossible to leave the world until I had brought forth all that I felt was within me. So I endured this wretched existence—truly wretched for so susceptible a body which can be thrown by a sudden change from the best condition to the very worst. . . .

Recommend *virtue* to your children; it alone, not money, can make them happy. I speak from experience; this was what upheld me in time of misery. Thanks to it and to my art, I did not end my life by suicide— Farewell and love each other.[2]

❦ FIGURE 50-1

Isidor Neugass, portrait of Beethoven, c1806. Although Neugass's portrait shows Beethoven elegantly dressed, the composer was famous for his unkempt appearance.

Giraudon/Art Resource

BEETHOVEN'S SYMPHONIES: NEW PATHS

Beethoven approached the genre of the symphony—the stronghold of Haydn and Mozart—with great caution. He completed his Symphony No. 1 in C Major, a work in the vein of Haydn, only in 1800, toward the end of his first period. Symphony No. 2 in D Major followed in 1802, and much of it was composed at the same time that he wrote his Heiligenstadt Testament, although the symphony reveals none of its angst. Six additional symphonies, Nos. 3–8, followed between 1803 and 1812, and his one remaining symphony, No. 9, comes from the late period, which will be described in the next chapter. In addition to symphonies, Beethoven also wrote orchestral overtures that are performed today as concert works. These include overtures for performances of spoken plays—*Egmont* and *Coriolan* (for plays by Goethe and Heinrich von Collin, respectively) are the best known; four overtures for various versions of his opera *Fidelio*; and an overture to his ballet *Die Geschöpfe des Prometheus* (*The Creatures of Prometheus*, 1801).

In many of the works from his middle period, Beethoven made a conscious effort to go beyond the musical forms and styles of Mozart and Haydn, who heretofore provided his principal models for composition. Carl Czerny recalled a remark that Beethoven had made in 1803: "I am not satisfied with what I have composed up to now. From now on I intend to embark on a new path."[3]

Beethoven's "new path" is especially evident in his symphonies of the middle and late periods, during which the composer rethought almost every aspect of the structure, dimension, and expressive content of the genre as it had earlier existed. For example, he progressively expanded and diversified the makeup of the orchestra itself, giving the medium greater resonance and more diverse color. In the finale of the Fifth Symphony (1808), he brought in three trombones—instruments that earlier were used mainly in operas and church music—and he expanded the woodwind choir by the addition of piccolo and contrabassoon. These instruments also appear in the Ninth Symphony (1824), and here the complement of French horns is expanded to four. Most striking of all in this work is Beethoven's unprecedented use of chorus and solo voices.

The new path is also plain to see in Beethoven's Symphony No. 3 in E♭ Major ("Eroica," or "Heroic," 1802–1805). Its differences from the classical norm are evident primarily in two areas: the enlarged scale on which the work is constructed, and a heightened expressivity that extends into nonmusical areas.

The "Eroica" has the customary four symphonic movements (fast/slow/scherzo/fast) and a conventional large tonal plan, but each movement is far longer than in any previous symphony. The first movement lasts nearly a half-hour, about the same duration as an entire symphony by Mozart or Haydn. The added length is produced by a more thorough probing of basic harmonic and melodic materials, which leads to many formal novelties. The second movement—titled *Marcia funebre* (*Funeral March*)—combines elements of ternary and sonata forms into an extended composite, and the third movement contains the familiar scherzo/trio/scherzo, although with unusual proportions and tonal relationships. The finale consists of an ingenious and high-spirited set of variations upon a theme that Beethoven had used in several earlier compositions, including the ballet *The Creatures of Prometheus*.

The "Eroica" Symphony—by its title clearly a work that deals with heroism—also takes an important step foward in the development of **program music,** that is, instrumental music that overtly expresses nonmusical ideas. Orchestral music in earlier periods sometimes depicted extramusical content. In Antonio Vivaldi's violin concertos called *The Four Seasons* (published c1725) each season is described by a poem printed in the score; the music vividly imitates birds chirping, a thunderstorm, and other natural phenomena. Recall that Haydn's Symphony No. 6—titled *Le Matin* (*Morning*)—contains a witty musical depiction of a sunrise. Carl Ditters von Dittersdorf (1739–1799) wrote symphonies that allude to literary works and other nonmusical matters. But such references are not typical of the classical symphony in general, which, on the surface at least, deals with purely musical issues.

Beethoven's expressive resources in the "Heroic" Symphony go beyond the simple illustrative intentions of his predecessors. Beethoven shaped the poetic content of this symphony at a deeper level by reflecting, both objectively and subjectively, on the idea of the hero. Throughout his life, Beethoven was attracted to stories concerning heroes, exceptional individuals who, through struggle and fearless persistence, improve the lot of mankind. During his middle period, he often used such stories as the basis for musical compositions. His ballet *The Creatures of Prometheus* deals with the Greek mythological figure Prometheus, who stole fire from the gods and presented it to mankind despite ghastly punishments. The opera *Fidelio* (discussed momentarily) focuses on the heroine Leonore, who fearlessly frees her husband from an unjust imprisonment.

Beethoven's interest in the hero came into focus, as it did for many European intellectuals and artists of the day, in the figure of Napoleon Bonaparte (1769–1821). Napoleon had attracted widespread admiration as a commander of French armies in the aftermath of the French Revolution, when France was continually at war with its neighboring countries. The composer's imagination was fired by what Napoleon seemed to represent: a fearless warrior and a new type of political leader who could realize for all mankind the ideals of the Revolution, notably "Liberty, Equality, Brotherhood," its most memorable slogan.

Beethoven composed his Third Symphony as a work, not simply dedicated to Napoleon, but one that would bear his name and contain music embodying aspects of his heroism. By the fall of 1803, the symphony was sufficiently advanced for negotiations to begin on its sale to a publisher. These were undertaken on the composer's behalf by his student Ferdinand Ries, who wrote to the publisher Simrock concerning the new symphony: "In his own testimony it is the greatest work he has yet written," Ries assured. "He will entitle it 'Bonaparte.'"

But in 1804 Beethoven's idealism concerning Napoleon was shattered when Napoleon had himself declared Emperor of France. Beethoven eliminated the title "Bonaparte" and, for the first edition of the symphony in 1806, gave its name (in Italian) as the "Heroic Symphony [*Sinfonia eroica*] . . . Composed to celebrate the memory of a great man." The extent to which the music of the symphony deals specifically with Napoleon or with a more general notion of heroism has been endlessly debated. Certainly, the work's epic length, the presence of a funeral march in which mankind evidently mourns a fallen hero, and the re-use of a theme in the finale from *The Creatures of Prometheus*—a ballet dealing with a hero—relate, though in differing ways, to Beethoven's idealized memory of Napoleon and to the subject of heroism. No specific narrative is spelled out in the music.

The second movement, "Funeral March," is one of the symphony's most distinctive parts, especially in its poetic content. Its music vividly paints an objective image, a funeral march, and at the same time it conveys a personal reaction to that image. Shortly before he began to compose the "Eroica" Symphony, Beethoven had written several funeral marches for piano. The "Funeral March on the Death of a Hero"—the title given to the slow movement of the Piano Sonata in A♭ Major, Op. 26 (1801)—is especially relevant. Both this movement and the symphonic one begin with a theme in the low-to-middle register, in minor mode, with a somber dotted march rhythm. Both movements have a large-scale tonal motion from minor to major and back, and they share evocations of the sound of muffled drums.

These are all objective musical attributes of a funeral. But the symphonic movement goes considerably beyond the piano sonata by representing the sorrowful feelings of an observer who contemplates the funeral. This observer's own emotional response shapes the musical content. For example, the principal theme returns at the end, fragmented and dislocated in meter and accompaniment (Ex. 50-1). This transformation suggests the mood, broken and grieving, of one who follows the hero's casket. In this concluding passage, Beethoven does not simply draw a musical portrait of a funeral but reproduces the image of the hero in the mind of the mourner.

EXAMPLE 50-1

Main Theme: Violin I, mm. 1-8

Final Appearance: Violin I, mm. 238-46

Beethoven's use of the orchestral instruments allows him to convey more vividly the images and feelings associated with a funeral. He uncouples the basses from the cellos (in virtually all of his earlier orchestral music they usually double each other at the octave), and this permits him to manipulate the sound of the basses in several distinctive ways, for example, making groaning noises at the movement's opening. He repeatedly gives plaintive melodies to the oboe, which among all the instruments of the orchestra most evokes the human voice, and this contributes to a personalized tone of bereavement. The form of Beethoven's funeral march is irregular, which is not surprising in a work of such protracted scale. It has the general features of a large ternary form whose middle part is in the major mode, while outer parts are in the minor. But prior to the reprise (m. 173), Beethoven inserts an intense fugato passage that is more at home in sonata form than ternary.

The greatly extended dimensions and striking contrasts of the "Eroica" Symphony baffled its early listeners. Following a performance in 1805 one journalist commented: "This reviewer belongs to Herr van Beethoven's sincerest admirers, but in this composition he must confess that he finds too much that is glaring and bizarre, which hinders greatly one's grasp of the whole, and a sense of unity is almost completely lost."[4] After two hundred years of hearing and studying the work, we no longer share this reviewer's perplexity because we have absorbed many of the ways that Beethoven achieves coherence in the work despite its protracted length and diversity. One of the most important of these unifying elements—also present in the C-Major Piano Concerto—is the interlocking of themes throughout the entire four-movement symphony by underlying common elements. Notice, for example, the relation between the principal subject of the fugato in the Funeral March and the first phrase of this movement's main theme (Ex. 50-2). Although outwardly different, the two phrases have a perceptible similarity created by a common intervallic scaffold, which consists of an ascending fourth followed by an ascending minor third (bracketed in the example). Such underlying relationships also connect themes in different movements. Compare the principal theme from the middle part of the Funeral March with the famous opening theme of the first movement (Ex. 50-3). Here the common element is the ascending major triad. The effect of such latent interrelationships is to bring all moments of the symphony together into a coherent, though varied, musical argument and to make the work—to use Richard Wagner's description of his own operas—something spoken in one breath.

EXAMPLE 50-2

Main Theme: Violin I, mm. 1-2

Fugato Subject: Violin II, mm. 114-117

EXAMPLE 50-3

Funeral March: Oboe, mm. 69-71

First Movement: Cello, mm. 3-6

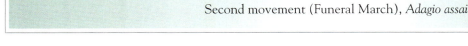

LISTENING CUE

LUDWIG VAN BEETHOVEN
Symphony No. 3 ("Eroica," 1802–1805)
Second movement (Funeral March), *Adagio assai*

CD 8/10
Anthology, No. 141

THE OPERA *FIDELIO*

When he began his second decade in Vienna, Beethoven had conquered the world of instrumental music, and he then turned to the new challenge of composing large vocal genres. First he completed an oratorio *Christus am Oelberge* (*Christ on the Mount of Olives*, 1803), and then he took up the writing of opera—the acid test for an ambitious composer of the early nineteenth century. The operas staged in Vienna around 1800 came from an international repertory in which Italian comic works remained, as in Mozart's day, the most popular. Beethoven had little interest in this genre. He later dismissed the comic operas of Gioachino Rossini for their appeal to "the frivolous and sensuous spirit of the time." Operas in German that continued the tradition of *Singspiel*—such as Mozart's ever-popular *Magic Flute*—were increasingly well-received, and Beethoven was more sympathetic to this type. He was also attracted to new French operas, such as those by Luigi Cherubini (1760–1842), which were successfully produced in German translations in Vienna just after the turn of the century.

Synopsis of *Fidelio*

Fidelio is set in a state prison in Spain. Leonora has disguised herself as a man and taken a job as assistant to the jailer, Rocco, hoping to find her husband, Florestan. He has been wrongly imprisoned by his old rival Don Pizarro, the prison governor. At the very sight of the evil Pizarro, Leonore recoils. "Monster!" she mutters. Compassionately, she asks Rocco to let the prisoners walk freely in the courtyard.

The curtain rises on Act 2 to reveal Florestan's underground cell. Rocco and Leonora descend into the cell to clear out an old well to serve as Florestan's grave, since Pizarro has decided to murder him. Rocco signals Pizarro, who enters wearing a cloak, his dagger drawn. Just as he is about to stab Florestan, Leonora rushes forward, flings herself upon her husband, and cries out "First kill his wife!" As Pizarro runs off, the bewildered Florestan asks Leonora "What have you done for me?" "Nothing, my Florestan," she replies.

All reassemble in the courtyard to greet Don Fernando, a minister of state, who has come, he says, as a brother, not a tyrant. He is astonished to find his old friend Florestan, and Pizarro is led away to answer for his treachery. Everyone praises the goodness of God and the heroic bravery of Leonora.

Beethoven would have been especially familiar with Cherubini's opera *Les deux journées* (*The Two Days*, 1800). It was staged in the summer of 1803 simultaneously in Vienna's two leading opera houses, and Beethoven was then residing in one of them, the Theater-an-der-Wien, where he was at work on an opera text by the theater's owner, Emanuel Schikaneder. The libretto of *Les deux journées*, written by Jean-Nicolas Bouilly, apparently attracted the composer on both a personal and an artistic level. Its story—involving conflict among ruthless aristocrats, helpless political prisoners, and honest workers—conjured up recent memories of the revolutionary years. Its leading characters embody the clear-cut virtues that Beethoven said had sustained him during his suicidal crisis at the time of the Heiligenstadt Testament, and these characters engage in an easily understood morality play in which heroic values win over evil ones. The action is filled with derring-do, which was sure to please its audiences. Beethoven must also have seen himself in Bouilly's character Armand, an innocent man who is wrongly persecuted and ultimately imprisoned, just as Beethoven was hounded by his physical disabilities and imprisoned by deafness.

Beethoven put aside Schikaneder's libretto when he found another one by Bouilly called *Léonore, ou l'amour conjugal* (*Leonore, or Conjugal Love*), that was constructed according to the same formula as *Les deux journées*. Even though *Léonore* had already been set to music by several opera composers, Beethoven had it translated into German for his own use, and it became the basis for his opera *Fidelio*, which he completed in 1805.

Fidelio received its premiere at the Theater-an-der-Wien in November 1805, a time when Vienna was occupied by French troops and many of Beethoven's aristocratic patrons were in hiding. The few who heard the work agreed that it was not successful on stage. One reviewer commented: "As a rule there are no new ideas in the vocal pieces, they are mostly too long, the text repeats itself endlessly, and finally the characterization fails remarkably." Even though Beethoven despised music critics, he must have recognized some truth in these remarks. Before its revival some four months later in 1806, he revised the opera and shortened it from three to two acts. But he was still dissatisfied and withdrew the work after only two performances. A second revision was made before its revival in 1814, and this is the version that is generally performed today.

For each of the three versions of the opera, Beethoven wrote a different overture. The original is now called *Leonore* Overture No. 2 (1805); *Leonore* Overture No. 3

was composed for the 1806 production. Both take the title *Leonore* from Beethoven's provisional title for the opera as a whole. *Leonore* Overture No. 1 was composed around 1808 for a planned revival of the opera in the city of Prague, and the definitive 1814 version is begun by the so-called Overture to *Fidelio*. Today, the brilliant *Leonore* Overture No. 3 usually precedes the opera's second act or the final courtyard scene of Act 2. This is a questionable practice that was adopted by German conductors (including Gustav Mahler) in the late nineteenth century.

The musical form of *Fidelio*—unlike the forms encountered in Beethoven's instrumental music—does not deviate from the late classical model encountered in Mozart's *Magic Flute* and his other German operas. Following an overture, the acts of *Fidelio* are subdivided into a succession of distinct musical numbers, primarily aria-like solos, ensembles (duets, trios, and quartets), and choruses. Between these, spoken dialogue advances the story. The texts of the arias reflect on some static idea or emotion, and these are often introduced by a passage set in orchestrally accompanied recitative. The ensembles present contrasting or conflicting viewpoints among several characters, while the choruses offer a unified viewpoint by a group of like-minded people. The acts are each ended by a longer and sectionalized number called a "finale," in which ensemble singing dominates but choral and soloistic passages are often included. In these, the plot is brought to a point of climax or resolution. At the beginning of Act 2, Beethoven writes **melodrama,** a special type of operatic number associated with French theater. Here the voices speak, alternating with or accompanied by short fragments of orchestral music.

Leonora's principal music occurs in her great aria "Abscheulicher!" ("Monster!") from Act 1. She has overheard Pizarro and Rocco talk about murdering the special prisoner who is kept underground, and she is cast into a state of agitation because she suspects the prisoner is her husband. Imagining a beautiful rainbow, she contains her emotions and invites the star of hope to guide her onward. Finally, she takes command of herself and trusts in her own powers of duty and love.

The aria has a two-part design that came into widespread use in operas of the early nineteenth century. This form has no generally accepted name, although "cavatina and cabaletta," "recitative and aria," "scene and aria," and "double aria" have all been tried. The first part begins with an introductory passage in which Leonore's unsettled emotions are depicted by a recitational melody with wide leaps, disjunct phrases, and sudden shifts in tempo, tonality, and mode (Ex. 50-4a). The music then settles into a firm, slow "first tempo" with a lyrical melody and stable key (Ex. 50-4b). The second part of the aria (the **cabaletta**) is fast, virtuosic, and conclusive, and its main melody is heard twice, with connective materials between (Ex. 50-4c).

EXAMPLE 50-4

(continued on next page)

Come, Hope, let the last star not disappear for the weary one.

I follow an inner drive; I waver not; the duty of true conjugal love strengthens me.

This multipartite form allows for an element of dramatic action to enter into the aria—a musical number that usually brought the action of earlier operas to a standstill. The formal succession recitative/slow tempo/fast cabaletta mirrors the transformation of the character Leonore at this moment, as she moves from a tentative condition, racked by emotion, to a state of resolution from which she will not deviate until her husband is freed.

 ## AFFAIRS OF THE HEART: THE IMMORTAL BELOVED

Throughout his early and middle periods, Beethoven was involved in many love affairs. These were usually short in duration, although several led to proposals of marriage. One such was made to Magdalena Willmann, a singer whom Beethoven had known in Bonn. She declined his offer because—according to the recollections of her niece—"he was so ugly, and half crazy!"[5] Later, Beethoven's marriage proposal to a teenage piano student, Therese Malfatti, met with the same negative outcome.

Beethoven's Letter to the Immortal Beloved

Though still in bed, my thoughts go out to you, my Immortal Beloved [*unsterbliche Geliebte*], now and then joyfully, then sadly, waiting to learn whether or not fate will hear us—I can live only wholly with you or not at all— Yes, I am resolved to wander so long away from you until I can fly to your arms and say that I am really at home with you, and can send my soul enwrapped in you into the land of spirits— Yes, unhappily it must be so— You will be the more contained since you know my fidelity to you. No one else can ever possess my heart—never—never— Oh God, why must one be parted from one whom one so loves. And yet my life in V[ienna] is now a wretched life— Your love makes me at once the happiest and the unhappiest of men— At an age I need a steady, quiet life—can that be so in our connection? . . . Be calm, only by a calm consideration of our existence can we achieve our purpose to live together—Be calm—love me—today—yesterday—what tearful longings for you—you—you—my life—my all—farewell.—Oh continue to love me—never misjudge the most faithful heart of your beloved.

ever thine
ever mine   L[udwig].[6]
ever ours

One of Beethoven's most often played piano pieces, "Für Elise," may have been written for Therese Malfatti and titled "Für Therese"—her name then misread when the piece was published in 1867. (Beethoven's handwriting was sometimes virtually illegible.)

In these early affairs of the heart, Beethoven—consciously or not—seems to have directed his interest toward women with whom no lasting relationship was possible. But around 1811, toward the end of the middle period, he became involved in a far different sort of affair. It is known solely from an extraordinary letter found among his papers after his death. In the letter Beethoven addresses an unnamed woman, whom he refers to as **"Immortal Beloved,"** to whom he speaks in a passionate though conflicted voice that sometimes lapses into incoherence (see Box).

The letter long posed a riddle for Beethoven scholars. It is not certain if it was ever actually mailed, no year for it is given, and its recipient is not identified. Who, then, is the Immortal Beloved? A convincing answer came in 1972 from the Beethoven authority Maynard Solomon, who persuasively identified the lady in question as Antonie Brentano (1780–1869; Fig. 50-2). Solomon also confirmed that the letter was written in the summer of 1812. When she met Beethoven in Vienna in 1810, Antonie Brentano had married into a well-known German literary family and was the mother of four children. Beethoven became a regular visitor to the family's Vienna residence, and Antonie developed a deep admiration for him: "He walks godlike among the mortals," she remarked in a letter to her brother-in-law in 1811. No other details of their relationship are known, although the context of the letter suggests that Brentano was prepared to leave her husband and to live with Beethoven, which the composer seems unwilling to accept despite his passionate response to her. Shortly after writing his impassioned letter, Beethoven had a final reunion with her and her family in the Czech resort of Karlsbad. Then, in the fall of 1812, she moved with her husband to Frankfurt and saw no more of the composer.

The significance of the episode of the Immortal Beloved for Beethoven's music is uncertain. In general—as in the crisis of deafness—Beethoven was adept at separating his personal life from his music. But certainly the

🌸 FIGURE 50-2

Joseph Carl Stieler, portrait of Antonie Brentano (1808). Antonie Brentano was Beethoven's "Immortal Beloved," whose willingness to love the composer unconditionally forced him to a new level of self-realization.

affair was deeply significant for Beethoven's consciousness of himself. From this point onward he accepted the fact that he would live alone, and he had no other romantic contacts with women. The incident caused him more than ever to live in his music, especially as deafness continued to descend upon him. His passionate relation with the Immortal Beloved marked for him a moment of self-realization, and it helped to formulate the emotional background for Beethoven's final period of creativity.

SUMMARY

Beethoven's "middle period" extends from about 1802 to 1814. His music of this time includes symphonies, concertos, sonatas, chamber works, and the opera *Fidelio*. In much of this music—the Symphony No. 3 in E♭ Major ("Eroica"), for example—Beethoven consciously set out to write in a novel style that was not so reliant as before on models from Mozart, Haydn, or other predecessors. The "Eroica" Symphony is far longer than earlier symphonies, which requires many formal innovations, and its intense expressivity encompasses extramusical ideas. Specifically, the work expresses Beethoven's admiration for heroism, which he once believed to be embodied by Napoleon Bonaparte. The original title of the symphony was *Bonaparte*, but this was changed to "Heroic" Symphony ("Sinfonia eroica") after Napoleon declared himself emperor.

Beethoven's opera *Fidelio* went through three versions (1805, 1806, and 1814), of which the last is considered the definitive one. Based on a French libretto, the work takes a conservative approach to form and genre that Beethoven inherited from German opera of the late eighteenth century. *Fidelio* consists of a succession of musical numbers—solos, ensembles, and choruses—separated by spoken dialogue.

KEY TERMS

Heiligenstadt Testament	program music	cabaletta
symphonie concertante	melodrama	"Immortal Beloved"
academy		

Chapter 51

After the Congress of Vienna: Beethoven's Late Music

In the spring of 1814, following twelve years of nearly continuous warfare, the allied forces of Austria, Great Britain, Russia, and Prussia finally conquered the armies of France. The French emperor, Napoleon Bonaparte, abdicated his throne and fled to the Mediterranean island of Elba. To celebrate this long-sought victory, Emperor Francis I, King of Austria, invited leaders from all of Europe to meet in Vienna, where they would redraw the boundaries of their continent and reestablish principles of legitimate rule. This **Congress of Vienna** began in September 1814 and lasted into the following summer.

MUSIC AT THE CONGRESS OF VIENNA

The Congress proved to be as much a gala celebration as a diplomatic conference. It brought more than 100,000 visitors to Vienna, then a city of about 250,000, and entertainment was widely available in the form of concerts, masked balls, banquets, and hunting expeditions. The visiting French poet Auguste de La Garde recalled a concert of an orchestra of a hundred pianos, hosted by Emperor Francis in the Imperial Palace:

> In one of the vastest halls, that of the States, there were a hundred pianos on which professors and amateurs performed a concert. [Antonio] Salieri, the composer of *Les Danaides,* was the conductor of that gigantic orchestra. To tell the truth, however, save for the general scene, which in all these fêtes was always dazzling, that matchless charivari, in spite of the superior talent of the maestro directing it, was more like a huge display of strength and skill than a concert of good taste.[1]

For many of the dignitaries, the trip to Vienna was an opportunity to hear the music of and even personally to meet Beethoven, recognized by this time as the world's greatest living composer. They could attend performances of his opera *Fidelio* at the Kärntnertor Theater, and Beethoven obligingly churned out several new works celebrating the occasion of the congress. He was not at all averse to making money from the festive events. On 29 November 1814, he presented a gala concert for his own benefit that filled the huge Redoutensaal (grand ballroom) in the Imperial Palace. Vienna's leading musicians volunteered to play in the orchestra, which Beethoven conducted in a performance of his Symphony No. 7 and two lesser works appropriate to the occasion—his *Battle Symphony* (a musical depiction of Wellington's victory over the French at Vittoria) and a new cantata titled *Der glorreiche Augenblick* (*The Glorious Moment*). Among the royalty present at the concert was Frederick William III, King of Prussia. Louis Spohr played violin in the orchestra that day, and he recalled Beethoven's eccentric way of conducting, no doubt a product of his near total deafness:

> Beethoven had accustomed himself to give the signs of expression to his orchestra by all manner of extraordinary motions of his body. So often as a *Sforzando* occurred, he tore his arms which he had previously crossed upon his breast, with great vehemence asunder. At a *piano,* he bent himself down, and the lower, the softer he wished to have it. Then when a *crescendo* came, he raised himself again by degrees, and upon the commencement of the *forte* sprang bolt upright. To increase the forte yet more, he would sometimes, also, join in with a shout to the orchestra, without being aware of it.[2]

BEETHOVEN'S LIFE AND WORKS IN HIS LATE PERIOD

The years around the time of the Congress of Vienna were relatively fallow for Beethoven. Beginning about 1816 his creativity reawakened. He began composing piano sonatas, after which he returned to orchestral works, a Mass, and string quartets. Between 1816 and 1822 Beethoven wrote his last five piano sonatas, then in 1823 an imposing set of Thirty-Three Variations on a Waltz by [Anton] Diabelli (Fig. 51-1). As if to counterbalance the massive scale of these compositions, he also wrote two important collections of small pieces, or **bagatelles,** for piano, Opus 119 and Opus 126 (1822–1824). His *Missa solemnis* (High Mass) in D Major was completed in 1823, just before the epic Symphony No. 9 in 1824. For the first time in the history of the genre of the symphony, Beethoven introduces, into the finale of

❋ FIGURE 51-1

Portrait of Beethoven, by Ferdinand Waldmüller, in 1823, the year that Beethoven composed the *Diabelli* Variations. According to his assistant, Anton Schindler, the composer lacked the patience to sit for this portrait. "He would repeatedly stand up, pace the floor irritably, and go to his writing-table in the next room."

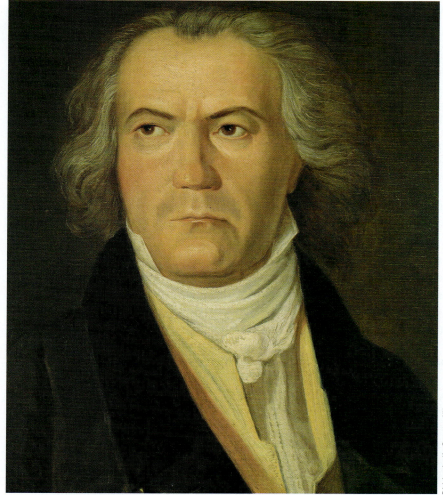

Erich Lessing/Art Resource, NY

the Ninth Symphony, chorus and solo voices. They sing a poem by Friedrich Schiller, "An die Freude" ("To Joy"; the poem is usually referred to as "Ode to Joy"). Beethoven's final compositions were five string quartets, composed from 1824 to 1826. Beethoven left behind no major compositions close to completion, although he had made a few sketches for a string quintet and a symphony. The latter sketches have recently been assembled into a "Symphony No. 10," which was recorded and issued as a work by Beethoven, but in reality has little to do with him.

Beethoven's life during his late period was beset by personal crisis, increased deafness, and failing health. From 1818 his hearing had declined to the point where he could no longer understand speech, so he communicated by way of **conversation books.** A person wishing to speak to him wrote into a notebook and Beethoven responded either orally or, if privacy was desired, in writing. Some one hundred forty of these uniquely important notebooks still exist.

Despite his deafness, the composer still tried to be involved with the making of music. A touching and pathetic incident occurred during the 1824 premiere of his Ninth Symphony, which Beethoven attempted to conduct with an assistant. The pianist Sigismond Thalberg was in the audience, and he related to Alexander Thayer, Beethoven's biographer, that "after the Scherzo of the 9th Symphony B[eethoven] stood turning over the leaves of his score utterly deaf to the immense applause, and [the soloist Caroline] Unger pulled him by the sleeve, and then pointed to the audience, when he turned and bowed."[3]

String Quartet in B♭ Major, Op. 130

Following the premiere of the Ninth Symphony on 7 May 1824, Beethoven devoted his remaining time to the writing of string quartets. Years earlier, between 1800 and 1810, he had written eleven quartets that continued the genre created almost single-handedly by his teacher Haydn, but he had not returned to the quartet medium since. In November 1822 he received a request from one of his Russian admirers, Prince Nicholas Galitzin, to compose "one, two, or three new quartets for which labor I will be glad to pay you what you think proper."

The offer was accepted with a down payment, and by 1825 Beethoven had completed three quartets (in E♭ major, A minor, and B♭ major) that he dedicated to this Russian patron. His interest in quartet writing continued, and in 1826 he completed two additional quartets (in C♯ minor and F major), these being his final compositions.

The last of the Galitzin quartets, Opus 130 in B♭ Major, revives several notable features from Beethoven's earlier music. As in the "Eroica" Symphony, the themes in different movements throughout the quartet are subtly linked by motivic similarities, which compensate below the musical surface for the considerable contrast in character and material above. Like the first movement of the "Pathétique" Sonata, the first movement of the quartet begins with music in a slow tempo that returns repeatedly later in the movement.

There is also much that is new about the B♭ Quartet that is characteristic of Beethoven's late style. The overall design of the work bypasses the classical four-movement norm, which is replaced by six movements each having a different character. The fifth movement, titled **"Cavatina,"** shows the intense lyricism that characterizes many late works, and the original finale, the so-called ***Grosse Fuge (Great Fugue),*** is the grandest of the many imposing fugal compositions from Beethoven's final period, when his interest in reviving the contrapuntal style of such predecessors as J.S. Bach was evidently keen.

The Great Fugue is the quartet's most unusual part. It is nearly twenty minutes long, almost double the first movement, which earlier was the longest and most dominating movement of a quartet or a symphony. The Great Fugue is almost entirely free in form, markedly dissonant, and uniquely dense in texture for a string quartet to this time. Arnold Schoenberg wrote about it later: "I have heard many a good musician, when listening to Beethoven's *Great Fugue*, cry out: 'This sounds like atonal music.'" After the B♭ Quartet was completed, premiered, and sent to the publisher, Beethoven replaced the Great Fugue with an alternate finale that was shorter and lighter. The Great Fugue was then published separately as Opus 133. Depending on which finale is used, there are two equally authentic versions of the B♭ Quartet, something unique in Beethoven's entire oeuvre.

Although our attention is nowadays drawn to the finale of the B♭ Quartet, Beethoven's heart was in the fifth movement, which he titled "Cavatina." Karl Holz, who was Beethoven's personal assistant at the time, and who played violin in the earliest performances of the work, wrote in 1857 to one of Beethoven's biographers: "For him the crown of all of his quartet movements and his very favorite piece was the Cavatina. . . . Truly, he composed it amid tears of sadness, and he assured me that never before had any of his own music had this effect on him and that even the thinking back on it brought him new tears."[4]

The title Cavatina comes from operatic music. For the German composer of the day it denoted an aria that was slow, lyric, and simple in structure. This describes the Cavatina of the quartet, except that the singer's role is taken over by the first violin. Beethoven even gives the instrument places to breathe and to rest, while the melody is echoed at these moments by the second violin. In the middle of its three sections, the music moves into the key of Cb major, at the extreme flat side of the tonal spectrum, which for Beethoven is often a sign of maximal affective content. At this point the emotions seem to overwhelm the singer, whose part is marked *beklemmt* (tormented) and whose line dissolves into a rhythm of sobs above throbbing triplets in the accompaniment (Ex. 51-1). We can readily understand Beethoven's own emotional reaction to this music.

EXAMPLE 51-1

🎵 LISTENING CUE

LUDWIG VAN BEETHOVEN   CD 8/11
String Quartet in Bb Major (1826)   Anthology, No. 142
Fifth movement (Cavatina), *Adagio molto espressivo*

The *Missa solemnis*

In the spring of 1819, Beethoven learned that his student **Archduke Rudolph**—a brother of the Emperor, and long one of Beethoven's most generous patrons—was to be made a cardinal of the Catholic Church and installed as Archbishop of Olomouc, a city north of Vienna. Immediately the composer began planning to honor the Archduke by writing a large-scale Mass—of the type often called "solemn" or "high"—for use at the service of installation, which was to occur on March 9 of the following year. Beethoven wrote to the Archduke: "The day when a high mass of mine shall be performed at the ceremonies for Your Imperial Highness will be for me the most beautiful day of my life."

Of all the major categories of music at this time, however, church music was the one with which Beethoven had the least experience. He had written a Mass in C Major in 1807 and the oratorio *Christ on the Mount of Olives* in 1803, but virtually nothing else. This lack of attention was mainly due to professional circumstances. Unlike Haydn, Beethoven did not work in a situation demanding church music, and his specialities as a composer lay elsewhere. Although nominally a Catholic, Beethoven rarely attended Mass and seemed little interested in enriching music for the liturgy. Still, he maintained an intense and philosophical interest in religions, and he always had a strong spiritual impulse and belief in God as a force in his own life.

As he began to contemplate his new High Mass, or *Missa solemnis,* he apparently studied earlier sacred music—Handel's *Messiah,* Mozart's *Requiem,* works by J.S. Bach, and choral music by Palestrina among other earlier composers—to learn how his predecessors had represented religious ideas musically. His principal formal model was found in the late Masses of Haydn (see Chapter 46), which were large works divided into the five sections of the Ordinary of the Mass (*Kyrie, Gloria, Credo, Sanctus,* and *Agnus dei*). Each of these was subdivided into passages of contrasting tempo, key, and character. The chorus alternates with four solo voices, the latter treated mainly as a small ensemble. Although the richness of orchestral writing suggests a modern style, Haydn often resorts to fugue and counterpoint reminiscent of earlier traditions of church music. Beethoven brought all of these features into his *Missa solemnis.*

Beethoven missed his deadline for the Archduke's service of installation by about three years. The *Missa solemnis* was completed in 1823, and Beethoven—perhaps viewing it as his work for the ages—hatched the idea of holding it back from publication and instead offering manuscript copies to Europe's royalty (at 50 gold ducats each). Louis XVIII of France and Frederick William III of Prussia were among the ten who accepted this offer. Three movements from the *Missa solemnis* were performed at the concert on 7 May 1824, at which the Ninth Symphony also had its premiere, and the first complete performance was arranged a month later by Beethoven's patron, Nicholas Galitzin, in St. Petersburg.

Many listeners to the *Missa solemnis* are first struck by the work's difficulties, sprawling size and tendency toward bombast, and mixture of styles. The *Gloria,* for example, seems almost larger than life, as Beethoven drives the chorus into unrelieved singing in the high register. In the *Agnus dei,* impassioned operatic recitatives stand beside marches and intricate fugatos. Although composed at the same time as the Ninth Symphony and sharing some of the symphony's bravado, the *Missa solemnis* is more complex and idiosyncratic, and for most listeners a harder nut to crack. Beethoven's decidedly experimental frame of mind—always probing the ways that music can relate to the traditional texts of the Mass—mixes unmistakably in this great work with his unrelentingly personal voice. He calls attention to this dichotomy on the very first page of the autograph manuscript (Fig. 51-2). Here he wrote: "Von Herzen—Möge es wieder—zu Herzen gehen!" "From the heart—May it again—go to the heart!"

The first movement, *Kyrie,* is the most conventional of the five. The form is a customary ternary **ABA'**, which follows the tripartite text: Kyrie eleison / Christe eleison / Kyrie eleison (Lord have mercy upon us / Christ have mercy upon us / Lord have mercy upon us). Here and throughout the work, Beethoven uses the interaction of the chorus with the group of four solo voices as a dramatic tool. The chorus suggests the voice of mankind speaking about God—usually exuberant, sometimes full of awe, and almost always unanimous in its sentiments. The solo group represents the voices of individuals, who sometimes echo the excited outcries from the chorus but often produce a more nuanced understanding of God, and seem to teach such thoughts to the chorus.

© Bettmann/CORBIS

❀ FIGURE 51-2
Autograph page from the *Missa solemnis.* Beethoven's musical manuscripts were difficult to read, written in haste and often filled with revisions. The words at the top read "Von Herzen—Möge es wieder—zu [Herzen gehen!]" ("From the heart—May it again—go to the heart!").

💿 LISTENING CUE

LUDWIG VAN BEETHOVEN
Missa solemnis (1823)
Kyrie

CD 8/12
Anthology, No. 143

BEETHOVEN'S DEATH AND FUNERAL

Beethoven's final illness began in December 1826, when his jaundiced appearance suggested liver failure. After writing a will in which he left his entire estate to his nephew, Karl van Beethoven, and after taking the last rites of the Catholic Church, he died in the afternoon of 26 March 1827. On the day of his funeral, a crowd estimated at 20,000 poured into the streets of Vienna to accompany the coffin to the Dreifaltigkeitskirche (Holy Trinity Church) and from there to the cemetery. A funeral oration written by Franz Grillparzer, Austria's leading dramatist, was read:

> . . . He was an artist—and who shall arise to stand beside him? As the rushing behemoth spurns the waves, so did he sweep to the uttermost bounds of his art. From the cooing of the doves to the rolling of thunder, from the craftiest interweaving of well-weighed expedients of art up to that awful pitch where planful design disappears in the lawless whirl of contending natural forces, he had traversed and grasped it all. He who comes after him will not continue him; he must begin anew, for he who went before left off only where art leaves off. [5]

 SUMMARY

Beethoven's final period begins from about the time of the Congress of Vienna (1814–1815), which was a celebration of peace and a political conference intended to redraw the political boundaries of Europe following the fall of Napoleon. After this time, Beethoven wrote fewer compositions, but these were in an idiosyncratic style marked by expanded overall designs, intricate fugal composition, lyricism, and an expressivity so intense that it can no longer be restrained by Classical ideas of balance and symmetry. His late compositions include the Ninth Symphony, the *Missa solemnis*, five piano sonatas, the *Diabelli* Variations for piano, and five string quartets.

Summary of Beethoven's Major Compositions
Orchestral Music
   Symphonies Nos. 1–9 (1800–1824)
   5 piano concertos (1795–1811) and 1 concerto for violin (1806)
   Overtures for plays, opera, and ballet, and concert purposes
Chamber Music
   16 string quartets (1800–1826) and the *Grosse Fuge* (1826)
   7 trios for violin, cello, and piano (1795–1811)
   10 sonatas for violin and piano (1798–1815)
   5 sonatas for cello and piano (1796–1818)
Piano Music (solo)
   32 sonatas (1795–1822)
   Variations (including the *Diabelli* Variations, 1823)
Opera and Ballet
   Fidelio (opera: 1805, revised 1806 and 1814)
   The Creatures of Prometheus (ballet: 1801)
Choral Music
   Masses (in C Major 1807, *Missa solemnis* 1823)
   Oratorio: *Christ on the Mount of Olives* 1803
   Symphony No. 9 finale (1824)

KEY TERMS

Congress of Vienna
bagatelle

conversation books
"Cavatina"

Grosse Fuge (*Great Fugue*)
Archduke Rudolph

THE ROMANTIC PERIOD

*T*he nineteenth century—beginning with the age of Beethoven and Schubert and continuing to the time of Richard Strauss and Gustav Mahler—is commonly called the "Romantic period" in the history of music. The distinctness of this era comes both from a common spirit in music composed during this century and from great social and political upheavals that drew lines through the historical continuum. One such point of demarcation came in 1814, the year in which Napoleon's subjugation of Europe ended. After this time, art was increasingly shaped by the initiatives toward democratic government, the decline in aristocratic privilege, industrialization,

1750	1800	1850

CLASSICAL PERIOD (1750–1820)　　　　　　　　　　　　　　　　**ROMANTIC PERIOD**

Ludwig van Beethoven (1770–1827)

1848–1849 Uprisings throughout Europe

Louis Philippe (1773–1850), French monarch (r. 1830–1848)

Carl Maria von Weber (1786–1826)

Modest Mussorgsky

1789–1799 French Revolution

Peter Ilyich

Giacomo Meyerbeer (1791–1864)

Gioachino Rossini (1792–1868)

Franz Schubert (1797–1828)

Arthur Sullivan

Hector Berlioz (1803–1869)

1804–1814 Napoleonic Wars

Felix Mendelssohn (1809–1847)

Frédéric Chopin (1810–1849)

Robert Schumann (1810–1856)

Franz Liszt (1811–1886)

Richard Wagner (1813–1883)

Giuseppe Verdi (1813–1901)

◆ 1814 Fall of Napoleon

Clara Schumann (1819–1896)

Anton Bruckner (1824–1896)

Johann Strauss, Jr. (1825–1899)

Jacques-Louis David, Napoleon on Horseback at the St. Bernard Pass

Corbis

Corbis

Johannes Brahms (1833–1897)

burgeoning national identity, and other products of Napoleon's legacy. The year 1914, in which World War I began, is another line drawn deeply in the sands of history. After the horrific destruction of this "Great War," people throughout the world felt the need to end the forms of artistic expression that had their origins a hundred years before. Between these two cataclysmic events lies the Romantic period, and its musical features will be the subject of the chapters that follow.

Part

VI

1850   1900   1950

(1820–1914)

◆ c1900 *Belle Époque*

Edward Elgar (1857–1934)

(1839–1881)

   1914–1918 World War I

Tchaikovsky (1840–1893)

Ralph Vaughan Williams (1872–1958)

Alma Mahler (1879–1964)

(1842–1900)

Lili Boulanger (1893–1918)

Gabriel Fauré (1845–1924)

Giacomo Puccini (1858–1924)

Gustav Mahler (1860–1911)

Claude Debussy (1862–1918)

The Mariinsky Theater in St. Petersburg opens in 1860

Arturo Toscanini (1867–1957)

Romanticism

The Romantic period in the history of music designates both a chronological era—corresponding roughly to the nineteenth century—and also a spirit that characterizes music created in that century. People use the terms "romantic" and "romanticism" to designate this distinctive style, although these words are not precise in their meaning. They suffer from the pitfalls of all generalizations about musical style—suggesting similarity where none may exist, and rarely being susceptible to a concrete definition. But, despite these dangers, the idea that much of the music of the nineteenth century is romantic has long persisted, and it fulfills a need for a concept that separates the type of music composed in this century from that before or later.

Early in the nineteenth century, critics began to describe contemporary music as romantic, bringing this and related words over from studies of literature. A "romance" at this time was a work of fiction set in a remote time and place, shrouded in mystery, and often turning more on characters' emotions than on their powers of reason. The writer and musician E.T.A. Hoffmann found these qualities in Beethoven's Symphony No. 5. In an 1813 review of the work, Hoffmann pointed to "that infinite longing which is the essence of romanticism." He continues:

> Beethoven's instrumental music opens up to us also the realm of the monstrous and the immeasurable. Burning flashes of light shoot through the deep night of this realm, and we become aware of giant shadows that surge back and forth, driving us into narrower and narrower confines until they destroy us.[1]

Although Hoffmann does not limit the romantic spirit in music to any one century, he highlights a common feature of music in the 1800s—its tendency toward a vivid expression of feelings and passionate states of mind. As we will see in the chapters ahead, romantic music often embodies complex ideas and strong emotions. Music of this type is no longer only for pleasure, no longer simply an elevated pastime. In the eighteenth century these were widely accepted as the real purpose of music. Mozart said as much in a letter to his father in 1781: "Music, in the most terrible situations, must never offend the ear, but must instead please the hearer, or in other words must never cease to be *music*."[2] Not so with romantic music!

The emotions that characterize romanticism are no mere abstractions, but more often those experienced by the individual composer. A personal voice is heard nowhere so clearly as in music of the Romantic period. In many of his greatest works, Beethoven leads us into his own emotional world, and this element of self-exploration remains in music of Berlioz, Brahms, Mahler, and Strauss later in the century.

The nineteenth century was indeed the era of the individual. The French Revolution, which marked the beginning of this period, was carried forward by the idea of the individual's rights, expressed in the motto *liberté, égalité, fraternité*—"liberty, equality, brotherhood." This was the age when absolute monarchies were overturned throughout western Europe, feudalism was all but ended, and wealth and power passed once and for all from the aristocracy to the middle classes. It was a time when the hero was celebrated and the accomplishments of the individual, whether a military genius such as Napoleon or a virtuoso performer such as Nicolò Paganini or Franz Liszt, commanded the admiration of people from all walks of life.

The emphasis on individualized expression in music produced many innovations in musical style. The melodies and themes in romantic music often reveal asymmetrical shapes that better convey a temperamental content than the balanced and periodic melodies of the Classical period. Harmony becomes more suggestive, especially through an increased use of dissonant chords and modulations to remote keys. Composers of the Romantic era were inclined to greater diversity in the choice of keynotes, indicating that certain keys are inherently more evocative of certain emotional states than other keys. Pieces in the minor mode became much more prevalent as composers delved more deeply into the realm of the subjective. Musicians looked for novel ways of unifying long musical compositions, striving for the same degree of continuity and oneness as in a play by William Shakespeare, whose dramas were appreciated in the nineteenth century as never before. Above all, the music of the nineteenth century wears its heart on its sleeve. It dispenses with classical restraint in favor of overt display, exaggeration, and impetuosity of feeling.

Franz Schubert

Beethoven's funeral in Vienna on 29 March 1827, attended by thousands, began with a great procession that transported Beethoven's casket from his last residence to the nearby Holy Trinity Church. Vienna's leading musicians walked alongside, some carrying candles, others flowers. Beethoven's friends and students—including Carl Czerny and Ignaz Schuppanzigh—were among the candle bearers. Also marching beside the coffin was Franz Schubert (1797–1828), a younger Viennese musician whose reputation was on the rise. Beethoven had heard of Schubert mainly from reports by mutual acquaintances. Beethoven's assistant, Anton Schindler, had brought him some of Schubert's songs and recalled Beethoven's reaction to them: "Truly there is a divine spark in this Schubert."

SCHUBERT'S LIFE

Although Schindler is notorious for his unreliable testimony concerning Beethoven, this recollection is at least accurate—there was unquestionably a divine spark in Schubert. Unlike many of the city's other leading composers, he was a native Viennese, born in a northern suburb only a few blocks from Beethoven's last residence. Beethoven's apartment had eight rooms while Schubert's birthplace had one room, which he shared with his parents and three brothers. His father, an amateur musician, ran an elementary school and provided his son with his first musical and general education.

At the age of eleven Schubert was admitted by audition to the choir of the Court Chapel. Since women were not allowed to sing in this ensemble, boys were needed to sing the alto and soprano parts. (Recall that Haydn, at the age of eight, was enrolled similarly in the choir of the Cathedral of St. Stephen, across town from the

Court Chapel.) The boy choristers were very well treated. They resided free of charge at the City Seminary and were enrolled in a nearby gymnasium, a school with a strong academic program that would prepare them later to enroll in a university.

Schubert had many musical opportunities in addition to choral singing. He played violin in his school's orchestra and studied composition privately with Antonio Salieri. In 1812, after his voice changed, he could no longer sing in the choir. But, unlike Haydn, who was summarily turned out of his choir school to earn his living as best he could, Schubert was allowed to complete his course of study at the gymnasium. Instead of continuing, however, he resigned and in 1813 enrolled in a training school to qualify as an elementary teacher. In the following year he joined the faculty at his father's school. All the while he composed—songs, choral music, chamber music, symphonic works—in astonishing abundance. In 1815 alone he composed some one hundred forty songs; another hundred followed in 1816. Schubert was also absorbed in literature and art, interests developed through regular meetings with a circle of close friends. They created an intellectual atmosphere and social network on which Schubert relied for the remainder of his life.

By 1818, encouraged by his friends, Schubert had quit the career of schoolteacher to become an independent professional musician, and from 1821 he began to have his compositions published. His friend Anselm Hüttenbrenner described his working habits:

> Schubert . . . used to sit down at his writing desk every morning at 6 o'clock and compose straight through until 1 o'clock in the afternoon. . . . Schubert never composed in the afternoon; after the midday meal he went to a coffee house, drank a small portion of black coffee, smoked for an hour or two and read the newspapers at the same time.— In the evening he went to one or other of the theatres.[1]

But there were factors that darkened Schubert's prospects as a professional musician. He was shy, more inclined to make music in intimate surroundings among sympathetic acquaintances than in the harsh public spotlight. Also, he was not a great performer compared to a Beethoven or Mozart in their youth. Schubert was a competent pianist and singer—he often accompanied himself in singing his own songs—but his performing was not at a level that would open doors for him in an era when composition and performance were still closely intertwined.

Nevertheless, Schubert was soon positioned to break into the leading ranks of Viennese composers. By about 1823 he had become reasonably well known as a writer of songs, piano pieces, and church music. He had scored several modest successes as an opera composer, and he was receiving an income from commissions, publications, and public performances. His music was also heard in private gatherings, especially at musical parties called **Schubertiads** that were assembled by his friends, where he could try out new works. The parties typically ended with dining, dancing, and socializing.

Schubert's career and the spread of his reputation were held back, however, by increasingly self-destructive habits, which ultimately brought about his death at the age of only thirty-one. He contracted syphilis in 1822 or 1823, and its effect on his health was only worsened by alcohol and probably narcotics. He fell increasingly into fits of depression, at times showing no interest in his own well-being, at other times acting normally. During his final years he sometimes retreated into isolation to struggle with his demons.

Around 1825 his prospects seemed to brighten as his health improved and his life became better regulated. He was inspired by the beauty of nature during a long stay in the Austrian alps on the Traun Lake near Salzburg, where he composed one of

Schubert's Appearance

Anselm Hüttenbrenner (1794–1868) was an Austrian composer who was an acquaintance of both Schubert and Beethoven. This is an excerpt from a memoir concerning Schubert written in 1854.

. . . . Schubert's outward appearance was anything but striking or prepossessing. He was short of stature, with a full, round face and was rather stout. His forehead was very beautifully domed. Because of his short sight he always wore spectacles, which he did not take off even during sleep. Dress was a thing in which he took no interest whatever: consequently he disliked going into smart society, for which he had to take more trouble with his clothes. As a result many a party anxiously awaited his appearance and would have been only too glad to overlook any negligence in his dress; sometimes, however, he simply could not bring himself to change his everyday coat for a black frock coat; he disliked bowing and scraping, and listening to flattering talk about himself he found downright nauseating. . . .

When the merry musical brotherhood, of whom there were often ten, met together intimately anywhere, each had his own nickname. Our Schubert was called *Schwammerl* [little mushroom]. What a pity that such musical truffles are so rare.— We were young, gay people and, in our dear capital, enjoyed ourselves as much as possible and used to go along arm-in-arm. . . .[2]

FIGURE 52-1
Franz Eybl's 1827 portrait of Schubert shows the composer without his ever-present spectacles.

his very greatest works, the Symphony No. 9 in C Major. His music was being performed in concerts of Vienna's important Gesellschaft der Musikfreunde (Society of the Friends of Music), of which Schubert himself had been elected a member, and publishers were by then competing for his songs and piano pieces.

In March 1828 Schubert finally decided to put himself in the public eye by organizing a concert devoted entirely to his own music—the kind of event, called an "academy," that had so greatly benefited Mozart and Beethoven. The concert was given in the hall of the Gesellschaft, and the program mixed chamber music, songs, and choral works. The concert was a great success and brought the composer a tidy profit, and it was followed by a burst of creativity. Songs including the beautiful "Der Hirt auf dem Felsen" ("The Shepherd on the Rock"), three of his greatest piano sonatas, and the String Quintet in C Major were all composed in little more than two months in the late summer of 1828. But disease then quickly overtook him, and he died on November 19 of that year.

SCHUBERT'S MUSIC: WORKS FOR VOICES

Despite his short life and the battles that he waged with himself, Schubert composed an astoundingly large and diverse body of music. He worked in all of the standard genres of his time with the exception of the concerto, which he never attempted. The sheer quantity of his music makes an accounting of it complex, all the more so because he often left compositions incomplete. Many works—including some of his very greatest ones—were not published during his lifetime. Given these uncertainties, identifying Schubert's music is often done by "D." numbers—similar to Mozart's "K." numbers—which are the numbers assigned to them chronologically in a catalog assembled in 1951 by Otto Erich Deutsch.

Schubert was best known in his own day, as in ours, as a composer of songs (or **Lieder,** the German word for songs), of which there are over six hundred. Most of these are short, independent pieces, but there are also **song cycles,** which are groups of songs that belong together in poetry and music. His two authentic cycles are *Die schöne Müllerin* (*The Lovely Maid of the Mill,* 1823) and *Winterreise* (*Winter's Journey,* 1827). After Schubert's death a publisher created a cycle of fourteen independent songs, called *Schwanengesang* (*Swan Song,* 1828).

Like Mozart and Haydn before him, Schubert composed many works for the Catholic services of worship. These include six Masses and numerous shorter, motet-like pieces for chorus alone or with organ or orchestra accompanying. He wrote about one hundred fifty compositions for chorus, including cantatas and some one hundred pieces for male chorus. He aspired to make a name for himself as an opera composer, but had limited success, in part because of the poor librettos he selected. His incidental music for the play *Rosamunde* (1823) contains some of his most delightful music.

✳ CHAMBER, PIANO, AND ORCHESTRAL COMPOSITIONS

Schubert's chamber music continues the genres developed by Haydn, Mozart, and Beethoven. Schubert composed string quartets, trios, an octet, and two quintets. One of these last—the Quintet for piano, violin, viola, cello, and bass in A major—is fondly called the "Trout" Quintet because Schubert brings the melody from his song "Die Forelle" ("The Trout," Ex. 52-1) into its fourth movement.

EXAMPLE 52-1

In a bright little brook the happy trout darts like an arrow.

Schubert's piano music is among the greatest and most original of its type. He wrote fifteen piano sonatas (some probably incomplete) and a larger number of short **character pieces**—brief compositions that quickly establish a definite mood or atmosphere. These include six *Moments musicaux* (*Musical Moments*) and eight *Impromptus* (*Extemporizations*). There are also many dance pieces for piano—mainly Ecossaises (Scottish Dances), waltzes, waltz-like Ländler (country dances), and "Deutsche" (German dances). Most of these were written by the composer to accompany social dancing, especially at his Schubertiads.

Also like Mozart and Beethoven, Schubert composed several fantasies for piano, works having a nonstandard form and often an improvisatory character. The most imposing and virtuosic of these is the Fantasy in C Major (1822), nicknamed the

"Wanderer" Fantasy because in one section Schubert quotes a melody from his song "The Wanderer." The form of the piano work—which was apparently original with Schubert and very influential upon later composers—continues the tendency already seen in Beethoven's "Eroica" Symphony (see Chapter 50) to achieve continuity rather than compartmentalization throughout a large, multimovement instrumental composition. The "Wanderer" Fantasy has four movements (*allegro/adagio/presto/allegro*) like one of the large piano sonatas of Beethoven. But these are all run together without pause, and each movement has a principal theme that shares motives with the first theme of the first movement. The openings of these themes are shown in Example 52-2.

EXAMPLE 52-2

This large-scale thematic integration also affects the use of formal archetypes. Each movement has its own recognizable form, but the entire four-movement work is built on a single sonata-form plan. The first movement outlines a sonata design of its own, which breaks off within the development section. The development is then continued in the *adagio* and *presto* movements. The fugal finale returns plainly to the theme of the first movement, thus marking the beginning of a large-scale recapitulation.

None of Schubert's symphonies was published in his lifetime, which seems ironic, since these are among the great works of their type. Schubert completed seven symphonies and left several others incomplete or in sketches. The most famous of the latter group is the Symphony in B Minor (1822), nicknamed the "Unfinished" since Schubert left it—for reasons unknown—as a torso, containing only two movements and sketches for a third.

In 1826 Schubert submitted his last symphony, Symphony No. 9 in C Major (1825–1826), to the orchestra of the Gesellschaft der Musikfreunde, which rehearsed it but found it too difficult for a public performance. The work had its premiere only in 1839, under the leadership of Felix Mendelssohn in Leipzig.

This "Great" C-Major Symphony mixes traditional symphonic features with others that look toward the future. It has a standard four-movement form, but, as in Beethoven's "Eroica" Symphony and Symphony No. 9, these are greatly elongated. Schubert uses the standard late eighteenth-century orchestra, expanded only by three trombones, but he gives far more melodic material to the woodwinds and brass than even Beethoven did. The work has many formal novelties. The first movement, for example, begins with a slow passage that is more of an exposition than an introduction since its themes are fully formed and return explicitly later in the movement. The first of these themes, shown in Example 52-3, returns climactically at the end of the first movement.

EXAMPLE 52-3

SCHUBERT'S SONGS

Schubert was the first major composer to put songs front-and-center in his compositional oeuvre. The genre itself had been long cultivated, its history reaching back even to the Middle Ages, where it is found in the settings of love poetry by the French troubadours and trouvères (see Chapter 6). Songs of the modern type—short compositions for solo voice accompanied by piano—were written by Haydn, Mozart, and Beethoven, but these composers considered such works to be sidelights to their larger musical undertakings, such as operas, symphonies, or concertos. Composers of more modest reputation from the same time, such as Johann Friedrich Reichardt (1752–1814), wrote songs in a simplified style for use in the home. An example is Reichardt's 1794 setting of Goethe's poem "Erlkönig" ("Erlking"). The poem has eight stanzas, and Reichardt's music for each is virtually the same, creating a simple **strophic form.** The setting of the first stanza is shown in Example 52-4, in which Reichardt's music, simplified almost to the point of becoming formulaic, can be observed.

EXAMPLE 52-4

Performing Schubert's Songs

There is no reason that we should today perform Schubert's songs precisely as he did himself, even if we could know how he performed them. Still, the modern performer wisely seeks out Schubert's ideas as a guide to the proper realization of these subtly complex works.

To learn about Schubert's own performance practices, we begin with the study of **Johann Michael Vogl** (1768–1840), a singer who was the most important interpreter of Schubert's songs during the composer's lifetime. Schubert met Vogl in 1817, when Vogl was a celebrated Viennese operatic singer. In 1814 Vogl had performed the role of Pizarro in Beethoven's *Fidelio* in Vienna, and toward the end of his career he was one of the first singers to specialize in song recitals. Everyone loved to hear Vogl sing Schubert's songs, although his occasional affectations—"a tonelessly spoken word, a sudden outburst, a falsetto note," to quote one contemporary—were tolerated but not approved by the composer.

Vogl observed many of the practices still used by the modern Lieder singer, including free transpositions of songs. But Schubert would have disagreed with modern singing that becomes too dramatic. He was adamant that a strict tempo must be kept and that vocal mannerisms had to be eliminated. "Schubert always indicated exactly where he wanted or permitted a *ritardando*, an *accelerando* or any kind of freer delivery," wrote his friend Leopold von Sonnleithner. "But where he did not indicate this, he would not tolerate the slightest arbitrariness or the least deviation in tempo."

Unaffected and melodious singing was what Schubert apparently wanted, not melodramatic effects. Sonnleithner continued: "He never allowed violent expression in performance. The Lieder singer, as a rule, only relates experiences and feelings of others; he does not himself impersonate the characters whose feelings he describes. Poet, composer and singer must conceive the song *lyrically*, not *dramatically*."

❧ FIGURE 52-2
Moritz von Schwind, "Schubert Evening at the Home of Joseph von Spaun," 1868. Johann Michael Vogl—the first important interpreter of Schubert's songs—is accompanied by the composer at a Schubertiad.

Bridgeman Art Library

Longer and more complex songs were also written in the late eighteenth century. Those by Johann Zumsteeg (1760–1802), the opera conductor in the city of Stuttgart, were much admired by Schubert. At the time, these were usually called "ballads," "arias," or "cantatas," reserving the term *Gesang* or *Lied* for shorter strophic songs like Reichardt's "Erlkönig." The musical forms encountered in these longer songs were often like scenes from an opera, sometimes mixing tuneful passages with recitatives, and not following any simple repetitive or symmetrical musical plan. This type of song is said to be **through composed.**

Schubert wrote songs of both simple and complex types, and in both he brought to the genre a musical richness and intensity of expression that far surpass the works of a Reichardt or Zumsteeg. A celebrated example of his longer songs is "Erlkönig" (1815), in which he used the same poem as had Reichardt. The poet is **Johann Wolfgang von Goethe** (1749–1832)—the most celebrated German writer of his time—whose poetry stimulated the rise in importance of song writing among composers throughout the German-speaking world. The writings of Goethe (pronounced, approximately, GRR-tuh)—novels, plays (such as *Faust*), opera texts, and poetry—are filled with strophic verse that invites musical treatment. Goethe's poetry was mined repeatedly by the great song composers throughout the nineteenth century.

The text of "Erlkönig" is what at the time was called a **ballad,** which is a poem in stanzas that tells a story and rises quickly to a dramatic climax. Goethe wrote the poem in 1782 for a play with music called *Die Fischerin* (*The Fisher Girl*), in which it was set to music by a Weimar singer and actress named Corona Schröter. It tells an eerie tale, drawn from Danish folklore, of a father riding toward home carrying his sick child. The child sees the sinister erlking, who tries to lure him away and finally takes him by force. When the father arrives at his destination, he finds the child dead in his arms. We can easily understand why Schubert, Reichardt, and numerous other song composers were attracted to the poem. It is strongly musical, with its own strict rhythm and hard consonant sounds that evoke the horse's headlong gallop. It is also tensely dramatic—the erlking speaks seductively to the child who cries out in terror, only to be reassured by the father. The minuscule drama is framed by the impassive words of a narrator.

Schubert composed "Erlkönig" when he was only eighteen years old, but he could find no publisher for it until 1821, shortly after it was performed at a public benefit concert at Vienna's Kärntnertor Theater. It was his first important publication, and marked the beginning of his rise to wider recognition in Vienna's musical circles. While Reichardt had used music only as a neutral backdrop to the poem, Schubert puts the music and words on an equal footing. The form of the song is complex. It is essentially through composed, since each stanza has different music. At the same time, a motive suggesting the child's fear (Ex. 52-5) is repeated in stanzas 4, 6, and 7, each time a half tone higher, which brings into the song an element of strophic form.

EXAMPLE 52-5

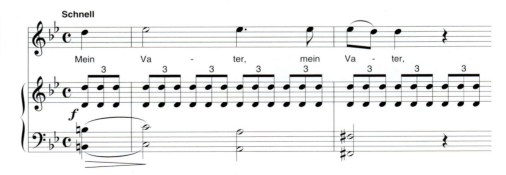

The music is grippingly dramatic. Schubert treats the four characters—narrator, father, son, and erlking—in clearly distinguishable ways. The father sings soothingly in the low register, the son higher in a shrill and repetitive fashion, and the erlking's music is sickly sweet. Schubert brings forward an enriched harmonic palette reminiscent of Beethoven to underscore the emotional state of the child, as in the chain of diminished chords that accompanies its cries. The tonal framework for the song is G minor, although the key becomes unstable, almost disorienting, in the dialogues between the father and son. In the erlking's three stanzas the key is absolutely clear and stable—the erlking knows what he wants.

The role of the piano is far from the simple accompaniment of Reichardt's setting, functioning in Schubert's song as an independent expressive tool. The impetuous triplet figure in the right hand conveys the headlong dash of the horse and rider, which continues throughout the song except in the stanzas where the erlking sings. There it evaporates into a simple lilting accompaniment, and at the very end it comes to a standstill, as the horse reaches its destination.

Schubert saves his most dramatic touch for this last poetic line, which occurs in the last three measures of the song. The horse's hooves fall silent in measure 146, but we know that the song is not finished because the cadential motion is incomplete, having paused on a Neapolitan sixth chord. Now the narrative voice changes to recitative to complete the grim tale—"in his arms the child was dead." The piano then quickly finishes the progression, as though snapping the storybook shut.

LISTENING CUE

FRANZ SCHUBERT
"Erlkönig" (1815)

CD 9/1
Anthology, No. 144

A second example of a song of the longer type is "Ganymed" ("Ganymede," 1817). Like "Erlkönig" it is based on a poem by Goethe, but the two poems are very different in form and emotional content. This poem deals with the Greek legend of Ganymede, a handsome Trojan youth. The god Zeus was so captivated by his beauty that he transformed himself into an eagle, swooped down, and carried the boy off to become a god. The legend has been interpreted as showing a homoerotic practice among the Greek gods, but Goethe's poetic treatment is more spiritualized than worldly. The speaker—who represents Ganymede—is enraptured by the beauty of nature. He embraces it with a sensual passion and finally imagines that he soars upward—just as Ganymede did as he was transformed by Zeus into a god—to become absorbed within nature. In Goethe's pantheistic vision, nature becomes god, the "all-loving father" of the last line.

This symbolic poem must have posed a great challenge to Schubert in the creation of a satisfying song. First of all, its meaning is complex, and it is written in an ecstatic and exalted language that Goethe often used in the 1770s, under the influence of the *Sturm und Drang* style evident in German literature of that period (see Chapter 45). Its poetic structure is entirely irregular and prose-like; it has no consistent stanzas, line lengths, or rhyme. How could Schubert make such a poem into a song?

He does so by approaching the text as though it were a fragment of an opera libretto. The song that results is like a detached operatic passage that moves through contrasting sections, changes from tuneful to recitational melody, and avoids symmetric repetitions or even a concentric tonal plan. The word **scena,** or "scene," is sometimes used to describe a song of this operatic type. Schubert divides Goethe's poem into three groups of lines: in the first the speaker praises the splendor of nature, in the second he feels the morning breeze and hears the song of the nightingale, in the third he soars upward to embrace the god of nature. The three groups are set musically to three distinct musical sections, rather like an aria in an opera of the time. Recall the plan underlying Leonore's aria "Abscheulicher!" from Beethoven's

Fidelio (Chapter 50). It begins in the key of G minor and moves through several contrasting sections, alternating recitative and slow melody. Finally it settles into the key of E major for a fast and conclusive final section in which phrases are repeated for emphasis.

Although Schubert does not exactly follow this order of events, his plan for the song is still related to it. The first group of lines (mm. 1–45) is set to a slow, lyrical melody that begins in the key of A♭ major (Ex. 52-6). The melody for the second group (mm. 46–74) is more recitational and the key is unstable. Finally, the song settles into a stable F major for the third and final group (mm. 75 to end), in which the singer ecstatically repeats musical phrases to extol his union with nature. For Schubert to end his piece in a different key from its beginning is very unusual in the genre of the song, although typical of the progressive key plans in contemporaneous opera arias. In both, the openness of the key plan has a dramatic purpose, showing vividly that the narrating character has been transformed from the beginning to end.

EXAMPLE 52-6

LISTENING CUE

FRANZ SCHUBERT
"Ganymed" (1817)

CD 9/2
Anthology, No. 145

The operatic trappings of "Ganymed" and the condensed drama of "Erlkönig" are generally absent in Schubert's many short songs. These tend to be strophic in structure, often folk-like in their naive sentiments, and reasonably simple and artless. Some of Schubert's short songs take on a heightened degree of artistry within their simple framework. One such is "Nähe des Geliebten" ("Nearness of the Beloved"), which Schubert composed in 1815, again on a poem by Goethe.

The narrator of the poem thinks longingly of a distant beloved, whose image is evoked by the elements of nature. In the narrator's imagination, the beloved seems to come closer and closer as we move through the poem's four stanzas. At first he is only thought of, then seen and heard, and finally he is there. But it is all imagined, and at the end the despondent lover can only cry out "O, would that you were here!" Schubert responds to Goethe's folk-like sentiments and strict poetic regularity by writing a song that is strophic in form. Following a short piano introduction, each of the poem's four stanzas is set to exactly the same music. But just as Goethe brings depth of emotion and artistic subtlety to the poem, Schubert writes a strophic song that is anything but formulaic. The piece begins with a two-measure piano introduction in a mood of scarcely containable excitement, as though representing the mind of the narrator searching feverishly for memories of the beloved (Ex. 52-7). The music begins with throbbing repeated chords, far distant from the tonic harmony, and its top line rises chromatically in increasing anticipation. Finally, the ascending line strikes upon the tonic note, G♭, which seems to force the voice to sing out, "Ich denke dein," "I think of you." Only then does self-control return, as the music moves quickly to a cadence in the home key.

EXAMPLE 52-7

LISTENING CUE

FRANZ SCHUBERT
"Nähe des Geliebten" (1815)

CD 9/3
Anthology, No. 146

SUMMARY

The music of the Viennese composer Franz Schubert (1797–1828) contains most of the genres cultivated by his great forebears, including Beethoven and Mozart, although Schubert placed more emphasis on smaller and more intimate types of music—the character piece for piano and the song. Schubert made the song into a major musical genre. His memorable lyricism and ingenious ways of depicting poetry musically have been models for song composition to the present day. Schubert's songs include short, strophic pieces (as in "Nähe des Geliebten") and longer through-composed types (such as "Erlkönig"). Some of the more complex songs (such as "Ganymed") imitate passages from opera. Schubert's symphonies, piano sonatas, and chamber works continue and expand the forms inherited from earlier Viennese composers.

KEY TERMS

Schubertiad
Lied (pl., Lieder)
song cycle
character piece

strophic form
Johann Michael Vogl
through-composed form

Johann Wolfgang von Goethe
ballad
scena (type of song)

Chapter 53

Music in Paris Under Louis Philippe: Berlioz and Chopin

After the fall of Napoleon in 1814, the Bourbons were restored as the legitimate kings of France, although their powers were then restrained by a constitution that promoted a limited sharing of power with the middle classes. But the Parisian people still remembered the suffering of the Revolution and its aftermath—endured in part for the sake of personal liberty and greater social equality—and they looked with alarm on the actions of their kings, which seemed to be moving France back to the days when monarchs wielded absolute power. King Charles X, who rose to the French throne in 1824, had attempted to restrict the press, limit the right to vote, and return financial privileges to the aristocracy and Church. In July 1830 measures such as these triggered an insurrection among Parisians from all walks of life (Fig. 53-1), and within three days the king was forced to abdicate and flee to England. In his place, **Louis Philippe** (1773–1850), formerly Duke of Orléans, was declared the new monarch and dubbed the "citizen king."

Eugène Delacroix's painting, seen in Figure 53-1, is far from a realistic recording of any single event in the **July Revolution.** It is instead a passionate and larger-than-life allegory concerning the advance of liberty, which is personified by the partially nude female figure at the top center. She strides—armed, fearless, and unstoppable—over barricades and a tangle of bodies, carrying the three-color flag of the French Revolution and leading a motley band of warriors drawn from all stations of Parisian society. To her left is youth, to her right a businessman with top hat (possibly a self-portrait of the artist), and further to the right, a man in worker's clothing carrying a saber. In its emotionality, energy, and dark tone, the painting's style befits its revolutionary subject, and during the reign of King Louis Philippe (1830–1848) these same qualities would increasingly appear in French music.

At this time, Paris displaced Vienna as the center of European musical culture. The profession of music in Paris was entirely different from that of Vienna, reflecting the different social structures of the two cities. In Beethoven's day, the aristocracy in Vienna was still able to provide a haven for musicians; recall the lifetime annuity that Beethoven received in 1809 from a group of music-loving noblemen. An opportunity like this scarcely existed for Parisian musicians. After the Revolution, the wealth of the French aristocracy was largely confiscated, and under Louis Philippe its prerogatives shifted almost completely to the middle classes. Louis Philippe himself had a great interest in the arts, and he often gave sums of money and commissions to deserving artists. But there was no longer a patronage system in existence after the Revolution that could support French musicians. They made their livelihood instead from their

❀ FIGURE 53-1

Liberty Leading the People by Eugène Delacroix (1798–1863) depicts the July Revolution of 1830 in Paris, when the French people deposed their monarch, King Charles X. Delacroix witnessed the event and was reportedly filled with pride to see the tricolor waving above Notre Dame. The cathedral is seen rising above the smoke on the right side of this famous painting.

interaction with a large and faceless audience, which they reached by teaching, organizing concerts, publishing music, and composing operas.

In Vienna, the large churches hired musicians, presented new music, and allowed common people to hear music performed. But this opportunity too was unavailable to the French musician because, following the Revolution, churches had little in the way of music beyond simple chanting. Musical life in Paris was concentrated instead in the opera house and concert hall. Opera was by far the leading genre, and it was fostered by three principal opera companies: the Opéra, the Théâtre-Italien, and the Opéra-Comique. The "Opéra" (actually, the Académie Royale de Musique) presented operas strictly in the French language, and a rule barred works with spoken dialogue. The Opéra theater, which could seat nearly two thousand, was located on the Rue le Peletier, not far from the future site of the great Palais Garnier, which became its home in 1875 and still stands in the center of Paris.

 ## MUSICAL CULTURE IN PARIS

Just when Louis Philippe came to power in 1830, a new operatic style, called **grand opera,** appeared in the repertory of the Opéra. The name came from the grandiose lengths, lavish use of chorus and ballet, and spectacular scenic effects in such works. The Berlin-born **Giacomo Meyerbeer** (1791–1864) was the most successful composer in this style. Meyerbeer first came to European attention as a piano virtuoso, and in the 1820s, while living in Italy, he made a name for himself as a composer of opera.

Meyerbeer's *Robert le diable* (*Robert the Devil*), given triumphantly at the Paris Opéra in 1831, firmly established the identity of the new genre. Meyerbeer followed up on its success with two additional grand operas, *Les Huguenots* (*The Huguenots*, 1836) and *L'africaine* (*The African Girl*, 1865). In these works, Meyerbeer used librettos written for him by **Eugène Scribe** (1791–1861), who was one of the most popular French playwrights of his time. For his grand operas, Scribe adopted historical or legendary subjects, into which he wrote complicated plots full of conflict, action, and surprising turns of events.

The grand operas of Meyerbeer and Scribe astonished contemporary audiences by their realistic and spectacular staging. This was what amazed Frédéric Chopin when he saw Meyerbeer's *Robert le diable* shortly after it opened in Paris in 1831. He wrote about it enthusiastically to a friend in Poland:

> If ever magnificence was seen in a theatre I doubt whether it reached the level of splendour shown in *Robert le diable*, the very latest five-act opera of Meyerbeer. . . Devils (the huge chorus) sing through megaphones and spirits in groups of fifty or sixty rise from their graves. . . . Toward the end, you see the inside of a church and the whole church itself as at Christmas or Easter, all lit up, with monks and congregation seated, with censers and what's more with a grand organ, whose sound, when heard on the stage, enchants and amazes and practically drowns the whole orchestra. No one will ever stage anything like it![1]

Musically, Meyerbeer's grand operas were as up-to-date as their staging. Although ostensibly still "number" operas—divided into a succession of arias, ensembles, and choruses connected by recitatives—the numbers are effectively absorbed into long, action-filled scenes. Each of these contains a fluid alternation of different types of singing, among which choral passages are especially frequent. Meyerbeer further ties his operas together by bringing back prominent melodies to underscore a recurring dramatic idea. Near the beginning of *Robert le diable*, for example, the minstrel

Raimbaut sings a "ballad" that reveals that Robert, the leading character, was born of the devil (Ex. 53-1). In later references to this, as far removed as in the final act, the ballad melody returns.

EXAMPLE 53-1

Once there ruled in Normandy a noble and brave prince. His daughter, the pretty Bertha, rejected all suitors…

Despite his amazement at the scenic wonders of grand opera, Chopin preferred the singing at the Théâtre-Italien. Here, Italian operas, including works by Gioachino Rossini, Vincenzo Bellini, and Gaetano Donizetti, were heard in their original language. The Opéra-Comique put on a mixed repertory of French-language operas whose only distinguishing feature was the inclusion of spoken dialogue.

In addition to opera, Parisians could also hear orchestral music excellently played. The principal orchestra in Paris in 1830 was sponsored by the Société des Concerts du Conservatoire (Society of Conservatory Concerts), led by the violinist-conductor François Habeneck. The precision of this orchestra—comprising mainly students and alumni of the Paris Conservatory—was praised by almost everyone who heard it. Habeneck's programming emphasized the orchestral music of Beethoven, which was virtually unknown in Paris before the Société was founded in 1828.

Pianists also flocked to Paris, where there was a culture for pianism fostered by the piano manufacturers Pleyel and Erard. Erard's instruments had gained a technical advantage over the competition by the invention of a **double escapement action** by which a hammer, after striking a string, falls back first to an intermediary position, from which it can then quickly re-strike the string. This innovation allowed for the rapid repetition of a note, an effect quickly embraced by Paris's crowd of competing virtuoso-composers. Members of the piano fraternity supported themselves by giving public and private concerts, teaching, and publishing piano music.

The competition among them increased in 1824 when the 12-year-old Franz Liszt, born in Hungary, gave his first Paris concert. Typically, Liszt played a concerto

and a set of variations, but then he got down to the more serious business of improvising. He took up the theme of the aria "Non più andrai" from Mozart's *Marriage of
Figaro* (Ex. 53-2), on which he then extemporized to the amazement of everyone. "I
am convinced that the soul and spirit of Mozart have passed into the body of young
Liszt," concluded one critic. Around 1840, Liszt introduced a new type of public
concert, the **recital,** in which a pianist played alone (also see Chapter 57).

EXAMPLE 53-2

🏵 HECTOR BERLIOZ

Perhaps the most distinctive voice in the musical culture in Paris of the 1830s and
1840s was that of Hector Berlioz (pronounced BEAR-lee-ohs, 1803–1869). He was
born in a village in southeastern France, near Grenoble, to the family of a physician. Largely self-taught in music, he learned to play flute and guitar and to compose. In 1821 he moved to Paris, which became his permanent residence, to study
medicine. But he lost interest in this field after witnessing his first autopsy. "When
I entered that fearful human charnel-house," he wrote, "littered with fragments of
limbs, and saw the ghastly faces and cloven heads, the bloody cesspool in which we
stood, with its reeking atmosphere, the swarms of sparrows fighting for scraps, and
the rats in the corners gnawing bleeding vertebrae, such a feeling of horror possessed me that I leapt out of the window, and fled home as though Death and all his
hideous crew were at my heels."[2]

Understandably, he dropped medicine and looked toward music as his desired
profession. He studied with Jean François Lesueur (1760–1837), one of the city's
leading teachers of composition, and in 1830 he won France's most coveted award
for a young composer—the **Prix de Rome** (Rome Prize). Awarded by the Institut de
France until 1968, the Prix de Rome conferred a four-year living stipend and two
years' residency at the Villa Medici in Rome. Among later winners of the prize were
Claude Debussy, Georges Bizet, and Lili Boulanger.

Berlioz returned to Paris from Rome in 1832 and his reputation as a composer
continued to grow. He supplemented his income by writing musical criticism, at
which he was gifted. His musical activities were concentrated upon the organization of concerts—several per year—which showcased his music. When interest in
them flagged among Parisian audiences, Berlioz looked abroad for support. In the
1840s and 1850s he toured repeatedly throughout Europe, giving orchestral concerts of his own music, and his works found approval especially among musicians
and audiences in Germany. He also earned a reputation as a leading conductor.
Near the end of his life, his health and spirits declined. One of his last occupations
was the completion of his *Memoirs,* in which he recounts his life and times in a
uniquely lively and personalized narrative.

Berlioz's Music

Typical of the French composer of his period, Berlioz aspired to make his reputation
in the field of opera. But his three main works of this type—*Benvenuto Cellini*
(1837), *Les Troyens* (*The Trojans*, 1858), and *Béatrice et Bénédict* (1862)—had little

Berlioz as Conductor

By Berlioz's time, the art of conducting had come a long way. In the seventeenth century, in France, conductors often marked time by pounding the floor with a cane or staff, a practice that could have fatal consequences. Recall from Chapter 35 that the great opera composer Jean-Baptiste Lully (1632–1687), while leading a chorus and orchestra in his *Te Deum*, accidentally struck his toe with his staff and two months later died from the gangrenous wound. In the eighteenth century, multiple conductors were common. The orchestra was normally led by its concertmaster, and a keyboardist—whether having an obbligato part or not—was often on hand to join in with the setting of tempos. This was the way that Haydn's symphonies were performed in London in the 1790s; Haydn conducted at the piano and Johann Peter Salomon also conducted from his concertmaster's chair.

Berlioz was one of the first orchestral conductors to modernize these practices. In his treatise "On Conducting" (1855), he insists that conductors use a full score—not just the first violin part, as was done by François Habeneck and

others. He recommends the use of a baton, twenty inches long, and insists that he be watched and followed constantly by his players. His recommendations for the orchestra's seating arrangement seem odd to us now. Berlioz placed the cellos and basses on risers behind the woodwinds and horns, who were themselves seated behind the violins and violas. The brass and percussion were in the back.

Despite these oddities, Berlioz's judgments on the virtues and failings of the conductor are as valid today as in 1850:

> The conductor must *see* and *hear*, he must be resourceful and energetic, he must know the nature and the range of the instruments and be able to read a score. . . . He must have other, almost indefinable gifts, without which the invisible contact between him and the performers cannot be established. Lacking these, he cannot transmit his feelings to the players and has no dominating power or guiding influence. He is no longer a director and leader, but simply a time-beater, provided he is able to beat and divide time regularly.[3]

success with Parisian audiences. Berlioz found more support for his orchestral music and concert works for voices. He wrote four symphonies, each unusual in medium, form, and poetic content. The earliest is *Symphonie fantastique* (1830), which will be discussed presently. Next came *Harold in Italy* (1834), in which Berlioz experiments with joining a programmatic symphony to a concertante treatment of viola. The title refers to the last part of Lord Byron's poem *Childe Harold's Pilgrimage* (1812–1818). Berlioz's third symphony is *Romeo and Juliet* (1839), which depicts scenes from Shakespeare's tragedy and brings in chorus and solo voices. The last symphony, *Grande symphonie funèbre et triomphale* (*Grand Funereal and Triumphal Symphony*, 1840), also uses voices. Berlioz wrote shorter works that he called overtures—including *Waverly*, *King Lear*, *The Roman Carnival*, and *The Corsair*—which he intended for concert purposes rather than as preludes to any longer composition. Pieces of this type are now called **concert overtures,** and they are forerunners of the "symphonic poem" (see Chapter 57).

Berlioz's large choral works include *La damnation de Faust* (*The Damnation of Faust*, 1846), a Requiem Mass (1837), and *L'enfance du Christ* (*The Childhood of Christ*, 1854). The first is a cantata-like composition for solo voices, chorus, and orchestra, using texts from Goethe's drama *Faust*. Berlioz wrote his own text for *L'enfance du Christ*, which tells dramatically of the flight of the Holy Family from the vengeful King Herod. In addition to his large choral works, Berlioz also wrote songs, of which the collection *Les nuits d'été* (*Summer Nights*, 1841) was orchestrated for use in his tours.

Symphonie fantastique

An emerging orchestral culture in Paris in the late 1820s and the impact of Beethoven's symphonies—performed at the Société des Concerts—inspired the youthful Berlioz to turn toward symphonic composition. But, even in his first symphony, which he called *Symphonie fantastique* (literally, *"Fantastic" Symphony*, 1830), he was plainly unwilling to continue with the type of symphony cultivated by the Viennese masters. Instead, he reinterpreted the genre as a fully programmatic type of music, in which dramatic ideas could be made as concrete and coherent as in an opera.

Berlioz's point of departure for this new conception was the tendency in Beethoven, found especially in the "Eroica" Symphony (discussed in Chapter 50) and Symphony No. 6 ("Pastoral"), to imbue an instrumental composition with extramusical meaning. Recall that Beethoven intended his "Eroica" Symphony to "celebrate the memory of a great man," which he did by bringing in musical symbols and allusions to the idea of heroism. Berlioz, whose musical imagination could never be contained by an abstract language of tones, went further, and fully transformed the genre into a musical "novel," to use his own analogy. The term **programmatic symphony** is used today to designate a multi-movement symphonic work of this type.

Another tendency hinted at in Beethoven and brought front and center by Berlioz in his *Symphonie fantastique* is music as autobiography. Certainly, Beethoven's personal voice is heard in many works. The lament for the fallen hero of the Funeral March of the "Eroica" Symphony, for example, is, at least in part, Beethoven's own lament. But typical of composers of an earlier time, this personal voice is muted, spoken in a universalized rather than idiosyncratic tone. The subject of Berlioz's *Symphonie fantastique* is no such timeless vision, but Berlioz himself.

The story that the symphony conveys was written by the composer and originally given the title *Épisode de la vie d'un artiste: Symphonie fantastique en cinq parties* (*Episode in the Life of an Artist: Fantastic Symphony in Five Parts*). It recounts Berlioz's own passionate infatuation for an Irish actress, Harriet Smithson (1800–1854), whom he saw in Shakespearean roles in Paris from 1827 to 1829. Although they never met until after the Symphony was completed, and despite rumors concerning her morality, Berlioz had declared himself hopelessly in love with her. To his friend Ferdinand Hiller he wrote: "Today it is a year since I saw HER for the last time—oh! unhappy woman! how I loved you—trembling I write, HOW I LOVE YOU! If there is another world, shall we find each other again?"[4]

At the first performance of the Symphony in December, 1830, Berlioz distributed the story to the audience. There were five movements (or "parts"), each with a title, and a brief elaboration (here paraphrased):

1. Reveries – Passions. A young musician sees a woman who embodies his ideals, and he falls desperately in love. The mere thought of her brings to his mind an obsessive melody. In the first movement his state of mind progresses from a melancholy reverie to fitful passions.

2. A Ball. Even at a ball the obsessive thought of the beloved and its melody return.

3. Scene in the Country. In the country, the artist's mind is calmed by shepherds piping a folk melody. Suddenly a dark thought comes to him—perhaps the beloved is not as perfect as he has imagined.

4. March to the Scaffold. In despair he takes opium and has a hellish nightmare. He imagines that he has killed his beloved and his punishment is death. A grim march accompanies him to the guillotine, and he thinks one last time of her before the blade falls.

5. Dream of a Witches' Sabbath. He awakens in hell, surrounded by witches. Their number is joined by the beloved, who has come to taunt him in a devilish orgy. Funeral bells and the funeral chant "Dies irae" ("Day of Wrath") are heard, and the witches then dance gleefully around him.

At the 1830 concert, Berlioz informed his audience that the music would not entirely depict this extended narrative, only fill in its gaps by conveying certain emotional states experienced by the artist protagonist. Berlioz used the analogy of an opera with spoken dialogue. The printed program was like the dialogue—realistic and narrational—while the orchestral music was like an operatic number that is static and emotive.

Still, there is much realism and storytelling in Berlioz's music. His main device for making the symphony capable of narration is the recurrent symbolic theme. The obsessive idea of the beloved is symbolized by a melody that is similarly obsessive, since it returns in every movement and changes to mirror the changes in her image in the artist's febrile imagination. Berlioz referred to this recurrent melody as an **idée fixe,** or "obsession."

When it is first heard in the first movement (Ex. 53-3), it embodies her initial qualities, "passionate but at the same time noble and shy." At the end of the second movement's ball, it appears with a waltz rhythm; in the third movement it is passed among woodwinds indecisively. In the grim fourth movement, the *idée fixe* melody returns almost as first heard, only to be chopped off—along with the artist's head—after a few measures. In the finale it is made grotesque and played by the shrill clarinet in E♭, just as the beloved has revealed herself as a vengeful witch. The beginnings of these appearances of the central melody are summarized in Example 53-3.

EXAMPLE 53-3

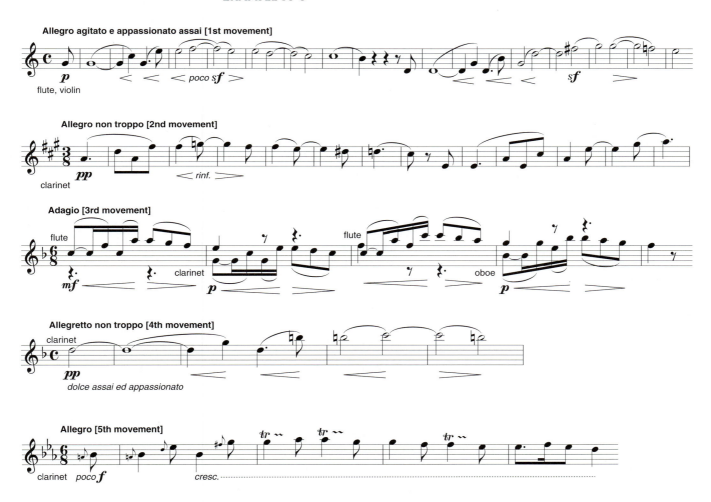

The explicit recurrence of a theme in several movements of a multi-movement composition—called **cyclicism**—has both a formal and a rhetorical function. It serves to unify Berlioz's long and structurally diverse work, and the transformed re-appearances of the theme reinforce its programmatic meaning. Like other aspects of Berlioz's symphony, the cyclic use of themes was forecast in Beethoven's instrumental music (see Chapters 50 and 51), there taking the form of subtle motivic interrelationships among themes in different movements. Berlioz makes explicit what was only hinted at by Beethoven, all in the service of a more concrete expression of ideas.

Many of the additional ways by which Berlioz makes his symphony operatic are encountered in the fourth movement, "March to the Scaffold" (Berlioz's complete programmatic explanation for the movement is given in the Anthology). The formal plan for the march is irregular, although it has features suggesting sonata form. After a short introduction, a main theme begins in G minor; a second theme begins in the relative major, B♭, and the exposition is then repeated (Ex. 53-4). The analogy with sonata form breaks down at this point, although a varied recapitulation of the main theme in G minor occurs at measure 114. The music then becomes almost cinematic, building in intensity as we see the prisoner approach the guillotine. His last thought of the beloved turns briefly to the major mode, then the blade falls and his head bounces down the stairs of the scaffold (Ex. 53-5). A drum roll and G-major chords announce that justice has been served.

EXAMPLE 53-4

First Theme (basses, mm. 17-24)

Second Theme (winds and brass, mm. 62-65)

EXAMPLE 53-5

m. 169 (strings)

Berlioz's orchestra resembles the colorful ensembles of French grand opera far more than the symphony orchestra of Beethoven. Instruments not used in Beethoven's symphonies are brought in—English horn, small clarinets, cornets, and **ophicleides** (keyed brass instruments that are now normally replaced by tubas)—and the entire orchestra is swollen to about ninety players. The composer constantly searches for new combinations of instruments, often played in unusual ways, to create a sound that will make special dramatic effects, as in the bouncing-head music of Example 53-5.

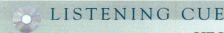

LISTENING CUE

HECTOR BERLIOZ   CD 9/4
Symphonie fantastique (1830)   Anthology, No. 147
Fourth movement, "March to the Scaffold"

Later Developments

The course of Berlioz's life after the premiere of *Symphonie fantastique* in December 1830 would seem far-fetched even as a soap opera. Just as quickly as he had fallen in love with Harriet Smithson, Berlioz transferred his affections to a teenaged pianist, Marie Moke, to whom he became engaged in 1830, before leaving for his sojourn in Rome. There, he received news that his fiancée had married another man. In a rage he left Rome for Paris, intending to murder Mlle. Moke, her husband, and her conniving mother. About halfway to Paris, and after a half-hearted attempt at suicide, he calmed down and returned to Rome. He set about writing a sequel to *Symphonie fantastique* that was at first called *The Return to Life*, later retitled *Lélio*, which calls for solo voices, chorus, and orchestra. Between movements, a narrator impersonates the artist of the symphony, who has awakened from his bad dream and decides to live henceforth for art and music.

Berlioz returned to Paris in the winter of 1832 and organized a concert at which *Symphonie fantastique* (revised during his stay in Italy) was performed together with *The Return to Life*. Harriet Smithson, who had also returned to Paris, was brought to this performance, and she recognized herself as Berlioz's muse. Finally, she met the composer, and Berlioz impetuously declared his love for her, marrying her in the following year. But the soap opera has an unhappy ending, as Berlioz and Smithson quickly drifted apart, their marriage desperately unhappy for both. Following Smithson's death in 1854, Berlioz married a singer, Marie Recio, with whom he had long toured.

"Absence" from *Les nuits d'été*

One of the pieces sung by Marie Recio in her tours with Berlioz was the song "Absence," which shows an understated side of the composer's genius. The song had been composed around 1840 for voice and piano, one of a group of six songs based on poetry by Théophile Gautier (1811–1872) that was published under the title *Les nuits d'été* (*Summer Nights*). They are best known in a later version with orchestral accompaniment. The six pieces form a **song collection** rather than a cycle, since they share no striking musical or poetic ideas, and Berlioz did not insist that they be performed as a group.

The genre of the song was of less interest to French composers of the 1830s and 1840s than it was to the Germans following Schubert. The most popular type of song in France was the **romance,** which was a simple strophic piece with little musical sophistication. Later in the nineteenth century, French composers began to write songs of more complex form and greater artistry that were often called

mélodies (an example from the works of Claude Debussy will be discussed in Chapter 63). Berlioz's songs from *Les nuits d'été* are forerunners of this later type.

In "Absence," Berlioz uses only three stanzas of a longer poem by Gautier that speaks of the pain of separation between lovers. The first stanza opens with the plea, "Come back, come back, my beloved," and Berlioz reinforces this appeal by repeating the first stanza after the second and again after the third. The music follows a similar plan, taking on the rondo shape **A B A B' A.** In addition to the great melodic beauty and poignant atmosphere created by Berlioz's music, the harmonic language is ingenious in its embodiment of the feelings expressed in the poem. As shown in Example 53-6, the voice begins with an upward leap of a fourth, C♯ to F♯, which is stated twice over, on the words "Come back, come back. . . ." The second time, the motive is expanded by the insertion of the leading tone E♯, which meets the bass in a stark tritone—suggesting the bitter feelings of separation—then resolves upward to the tonic note F♯. The melody of section B becomes recitational and harmonically aimless, as the speaker thinks of the distance between herself and her lover.

EXAMPLE 53-6

mm. 1-4

Re-viens, re-viens, ma bien ai - mé - - e!

Come back, come back, my beloved!

LISTENING CUE

HECTOR BERLIOZ
"Absence" from *Les nuits d'été* (1840)

CD 9/5
Anthology, No. 148

❁ FRÉDÉRIC CHOPIN

The wind has blown me here, where one breathes freely; but perhaps for that very reason—because it's so easy—one falls to sighing still more. Paris is whatever you care to make of it. You can enjoy yourself, get bored, laugh, cry, do anything you like, and no one takes any notice because thousands here are doing exactly the same. Everyone goes his own way. Well, I really don't know whether any place contains more pianists than Paris, or whether you can find anywhere more asses and virtuosos.[5]

This was Frédéric Chopin's reaction to the city of Paris, written shortly after his arrival in the fall of 1831 on a leg of a European concert tour. "I may stay longer than I intended," he confessed in another letter, and in fact Paris remained his permanent home.

Chopin (1810–1849) was born in Poland, near Warsaw, and grew up there in the family of a French-born schoolteacher. He was a child prodigy as both pianist and composer, and he attended the conservatory in Warsaw, where his teacher, Józef Elsner, had no trouble describing him on the final report card—"a musical genius," Elsner wrote. Piano concerts in the larger European capitals followed. In these performances Chopin, typical of the virtuoso performer of the day, played much of his own music, especially concertos and other brilliant pieces including rondos and variations. Chopin was especially gifted in the art of improvisation, whose freedom and spontaneity is felt in his compositions. His first public concert in Paris came in February 1832, and its program consisted again of mixed fare—chamber pieces, a piano concerto with orchestra, and vocal music.

Chopin soon tired of the public spotlight and made a comfortable living by teaching, playing privately, and selling piano pieces to publishers. In 1838 he began a nine-year affair with the novelist Aurore Dudevant (1804–1876), who was called by her pen name, **George Sand.** Known to her contemporaries for eccentric dress, leftist politics, and tumultuous love affairs, Sand is now held as one of the most important French writers of her day and a founder of the feminist outlook in literature. She was uniquely positioned to observe Chopin's creative process, its mixture of inspiration and labor:

> His creation was spontaneous, miraculous. He found without search or foresight. It came out of the keyboard, sudden, complete, sublime, or it sang in his head as he sauntered, and he hastened back to cast it on the instrument and hear it aloud. But then began the most crushing labor I have ever witnessed. It was a train of efforts, waverings, frustrated stabs at recapturing certain details of the theme that he had heard; what he had conceived as a unity he now overanalyzed in his desire to get it down, and his chagrin at not being able to rediscover it whole and clear plunged him into a sort of despair. He withdrew into his room for days, weeping, pacing up and down, breaking his pens, playing a measure a hundred times over, changing it each time, then writing it out and erasing it as many times, and beginning all over again on the morrow with painstaking and desperate perseverance.[6]

The couple spent the winter of 1838 on the island of Majorca, where Chopin completed his Preludes for piano, Opus 28, but where his health began a relentless decline due to the effects of tuberculosis. Summers were spent in seclusion at Sand's estate, called Nohant, located in central France. These visits brought the composer in touch with writers and artists from Sand's circle, including the painter Eugène Delacroix, with whom Chopin formed a close friendship. The painter described life at Nohant during a visit in the summer of 1842:

> This is a delightful place and my hosts do everything in their power to make life agreeable. When we are not together for dinner, lunch, billiards or walks, one can read in one's room or sprawl on one's sofa. Every now and then there blows in through your window, opening on to the garden, a breath of the music of Chopin, who is at work in his room, and it mingles with the song of the nightingales and the scent of the roses. You see that so far I am not much to be pitied.[7]

In 1847 Chopin and Sand parted company, and the composer's health continued to decline. He visited London and Scotland to give concerts, but his disease had sapped his energy and spirits. To his childhood friend Julius Fontana he could only compare his condition to that of a worn-out piano:

> The sound board is perfect, only the strings have snapped and a few pegs have jumped out. But the only real trouble is this: we are the creation of some famous maker, in his way a kind of Stradivari, who is no longer there to mend us. In clumsy hands we can-

Chopin and the Musical Hoax

In 1945 the world of Chopin scholarship was churned by the appearance of texts purporting to be copied from letters written by Chopin to Countess Delphine Potocka, a wealthy Polish émigrée living in Paris, whose company Chopin is known to have kept. The language is highly erotic. Chopin repeatedly describes his creative instinct as closely related to sex, which he describes using frank and often vulgar language. This is entirely different from the tactful and reserved tone that Chopin's other correspondence reveals. "My romance with Sandowa [Sand] has taught me quite a lot," he says to the Countess. "You'll see how you will become my pupil and I'll teach you some love tricks which are absolutely new and frightfully *piquant*." Later he adds, "With us creators the process is like child bearing is with you—one woman has a terrible time while another spits out a baby like a plum stone."

Many accepted the Potocka letters as genuine, even though they were only known in copies made by a certain Mme. Czernicka, a more-than-slightly psychotic Chopin groupie who committed suicide in 1949, on the centennial of the composer's own death. Ultimately, the many contradictions contained in these texts proved that they were entirely fraudulent.

not give forth new sounds and we stifle within ourselves those things which no one will ever draw from us, and all for lack of a repairer. I can scarcely breathe—I am just about ready to give up the ghost.[8]

Chopin returned to Paris in the winter of 1848 and died there in October 1849, at the age of thirty-nine.

Chopin's Music

All of Chopin's music involves the piano, and most of it consists of character pieces. Recall from Chapter 52 that these are works of brief or moderate length that establish a particular mood or style. Some of the pieces imitate dances, including waltzes, polonaises, and mazurkas. Chopin concentrated especially on the **mazurka,** composing some sixty such works that reflect his lifelong interest in Polish culture. The mazurka is an old Polish country dance in triple time, with accents often on beats two or three of a measure. Chopin's interpretation of the dance produced pieces of endless variety and imagination.

The compositions called ballades and scherzos are longer, and Chopin also composed three piano sonatas. His **nocturnes,** of which there are twenty-one, have a special character that will be described shortly, and he wrote numerous **études** (studies) that stem from his piano teaching but achieve at the same time a great artistry.

Chopin composed relatively little other music. There are two youthful piano concertos that he composed for his early public performances, a late cello sonata (1846), and some Polish language songs.

Nocturne in D♭ Major

The nocturne was a type of piano character piece made popular in the early nineteenth century by John Field (1782–1837), an Irish player and composer whom Chopin especially admired. In Field's hands the nocturne took on a distinct style—delicate and dreamy in its evocations of the night—which was very different from the brilliant and bombastic variations and rondos that were the stock-in-trade of a touring virtuoso. Field's nocturne style involved a simple, singing melody in the right hand, accompanied by broken chords in the left, the harmonies blended by a liberal use of the sustaining pedal.

Chopin's Nocturne in D♭ Major, Op. 27, No. 2 (1835), conforms in general to this character, although Chopin goes far beyond Field in the originality that he brings to the genre. Our attention is first captured by the beautiful sound that Chopin coaxes from the instrument, as he explores the changing sonorities inherent in the piano's different registers and gauges just the right spacing of chordal tones.

The sound is always rhythmically alive and filled with light and air. Chopin's way of playing his own music involved an almost constant rubato. "Chopin *could* not play in strict time," Berlioz remarked about his friend. We also marvel at the beauty and glittering ornament of the melodies, which may have been suggested to the composer by the operatic singing that he heard at the Théâtre-Italien.

The work uses no standard form, but an improvisatory alternation of two melodic ideas (Ex. 53-7). One appears at the outset and returns twice later in the piece, in rondo fashion. The other, more unstable harmonically and built on sequence, alternates with the first. A coda rounds the piece off from measure 62.

EXAMPLE 53-7

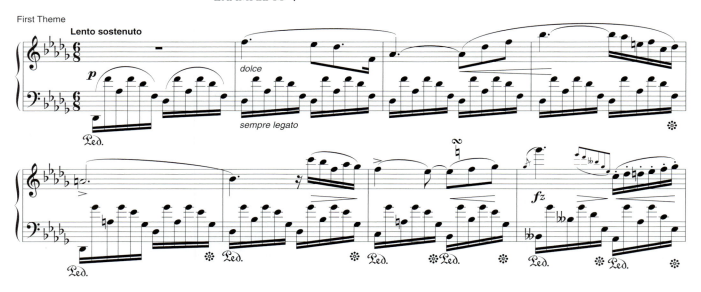

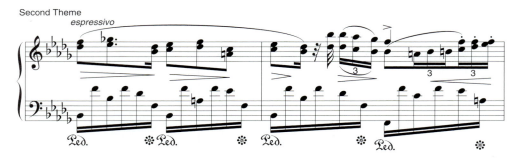

Chopin's originality is expressed especially in his harmonic and tonal language. The key of the work, D♭ major, is at the far flat side of the tonal spectrum, which in music of the nineteenth century often suggests a relaxed and lyrical spirit. Compare it to the yearning and tension implicit in the key of F♯ major, on the far sharp side, in Berlioz's song "Absence." Chopin's entire nocturne remains reasonably close to the home key, although the composer finds imaginative ways of connecting primary chords in that key. Consider, for example, the chords between the tonic harmony in measure 4 and the dominant-seventh chord at the end of measure 8 (see Ex. 53-7). It is futile to try to explain the chords between these two points by roman numerals. Instead, the harmonic coherence of this linking passage is created by a downward stepwise motion in the bass voice, D♭–C–B♭–B♭♭–A♭. The voices above the bass move smoothly by stepwise or common-tone connections.

LISTENING CUE

FRÉDÉRIC CHOPIN
Nocturne in D♭ Major, Op. 27, No. 2 (1835)

CD 9/6
Anthology, No. 149

SUMMARY

Paris in the 1830s and 1840s, during the reign of the monarch Louis Philippe, became the musical capital of Europe. Operas flourished there, and a new type, "grand opera," was characterized by grandiose lengths, lavish use of chorus and ballet, and spectacular scenic effects. The leading composer of grand opera was Giacomo Meyerbeer. Paris was also home to pianists, who arrived from all of Europe. Orchestras were on the rise, stimulated by performances of the symphonies and concertos of Beethoven.

Hector Berlioz and Polish-born Frédéric Chopin were among the leading composers in Paris during this period. Berlioz aspired to success as a composer of opera, but he was better known for his orchestral and choral music. His *Symphonie fantastique* (1830) is an overtly programmatic work, dealing with a narrative that was provoked by Berlioz's own infatuation with an Irish actress. The work explores new ways in which symphonic music can be made concretely dramatic, such as the recurrent appearance of a melody (an *idée fixe*, as the composer called it) that symbolizes an element in the story.

Chopin's compositions were largely for his own instrument, the piano. In addition to a few large works—three piano sonatas and two piano concertos—Chopin wrote character pieces, which were works of brief or moderate length that establish a particular mood. Over twenty of these are called "nocturnes," which are lyrical works that use a distinctive texture made from a singing melody in the right hand and an arpeggiated accompaniment in the left.

KEY TERMS

Louis Philippe	recital	song collection
July Revolution	Prix de Rome	romance (type of song)
grand opera	concert overture	*mélodie*
Giacomo Meyerbeer	programmatic symphony	George Sand
Eugène Scribe	*idée fixe*	mazurka
double escapement action	cyclicism	nocturne
	ophicleide	étude

Chapter 54

Leipzig and the Gewandhaus:
Felix Mendelssohn and the Schumanns

In his tour of Germany in 1843, Hector Berlioz was invited by his old acquaintance Felix Mendelssohn to visit Leipzig—a city in the east-central part of what is now Germany (Map 54-1)—to have his music played by the local orchestra. Berlioz readily accepted the invitation, but during his visit he was surprised by several things. The orchestra seemed limited in its instrumental resources compared to the French orchestras. Berlioz could find no English horn, harp, or ophicleide to cover these parts in the performance of his *Symphonie fantastique*. Even more perplexing to Berlioz was the taste for older music that he found in Leipzig. In this city, new compositions had to share the stage with works from the past, even those going back a hundred years to the time of Bach and Handel. Mendelssohn, Berlioz concluded, was "a little too fond of the dead."

✺ MUSIC IN SAXONY

Unknown to Berlioz in 1843, the mixed taste that prevailed in Leipzig was a harbinger of the present day, in which classical music draws its sustenance from both the past and present. The city's conservatism stemmed in part from the greatness of its musical heritage. After all, this was the city where Johann Sebastian Bach had worked for twenty-seven years (see Chapter 40). Just as Bach in his own music looked both to the past and the present, Leipzig's later musicians found ways of stitching together old and new, often so seamlessly as to defy any distinction between them. In the nineteenth century, Leipzig was home to Robert and Clara Schumann, and, in the twentieth century, to Max Reger (1873–1916), all of whom shared Mendelssohn's multi-stylistic outlook on music.

✺ M A P 5 4 - 1
Europe after the Congress of Vienna.

When Berlioz visited in 1843, Leipzig was a city of some 45,000 people located in the Kingdom of Saxony. This was one of thirty-nine sovereign states that were allied into the so-called German Confederation, which was formed to replace the Holy Roman Empire that Napoleon had eliminated. The president of this alliance was the emperor of Austria, although its most powerful state was the Kingdom of Prussia to the north. Saxony's wealth came mainly from its textile industry, and its high reputation derived from the intellectual and artistic achievements of its people. Robert Schumann commented that the aristocracy of Leipzig was not its wealthy and privileged citizens but its "150 bookstores, 50 printing establishments, and 30 newspapers."

A university was founded there in 1409, and in the eighteenth century this was one of the first institutions where the discipline of *Musikwissenschaft*—"musical science," or roughly what we now call musicology—was taught. One of the first professor-musicologists in

Leipzig was Lorenz Christoph Mizler (1711–1778), who had been a student of Bach at the Saint Thomas School. He had an essentially new idea for teaching music in a university—as a discipline that would "bring science to music and to explore and bring order to its history," as he said. Music theory, in addition to music history, was a part of the new study of musical science, and at the end of the nineteenth century one of the world's leading theorists, **Hugo Riemann** (1849–1919), was on the Leipzig faculty. Riemann developed a simple way of discussing **functional harmony.** Any chord, he said, represents one of only three harmonic functions within a key—that of its tonic, dominant, or subdominant. His theory is the origin of our present-day outlook on harmonic progressions as motions toward tonics and dominants by way of chords functioning as dominant preparations.

Leipzig in the nineteenth and early twentieth centuries was also the world's leading center for music publishing. It was home to the great firms of C. F. Peters and Breitkopf & Härtel. The latter company was the first publisher of important works by Beethoven, Berlioz, Chopin, and Schubert. Beginning in the mid nineteenth century, it pioneered a new type of musical edition, one containing the **complete works** of a great composer of the past. Such editions were primarily intended for study and reference rather than performance, and Leipzig's own J. S. Bach was the first composer whom Breitkopf honored in this way.

Leipzig had an opera house, but its main claim to fame in music of the nineteenth century was its orchestra. This was called the **Gewandhaus Orchestra,** named after the hall in which it performed (Fig. 54-1). The orchestra's small auditorium occupied an upper floor of a building used earlier to display cloth, or *Gewand* in German, from the city's fabric industry. In Mendelssohn's day the women in the audience sat separate from the men—people went to a concert to hear music, not to flirt.

 FIGURE 54-1
Felix Mendelssohn was a skillful painter in addition to being a gifted musician, and here he depicts Leipzig's Gewandhaus in watercolor. The city's orchestra performed in a hall on the second floor.

❋ FELIX MENDELSSOHN: LIFE AND MUSIC

The rise of the Gewandhaus Orchestra to international fame began in 1835, when a gifted musician from Düsseldorf, Felix Mendelssohn (1809–1847; Fig. 54-2), was appointed music director. Mendelssohn grew up in Berlin in the family of an affluent, cultured banker. He received his education at the hands of distinguished private tutors and through carefully organized travel. Mendelssohn and his siblings—including his musically talented sister Fanny (1805–1847)—converted in 1816 from Judaism to Christianity, whereupon they added the name **Bartholdy** to their family name. This was done at a time when many European Jews sought a greater degree of professional and social assimilation by embracing Christianity; later composers to follow the same path include Gustav Mahler and Arnold Schoenberg. Mendelssohn's education continued at the University of Berlin, where he attended lectures on aesthetics given by the great philosopher Georg Friedrich Hegel.

Mendelssohn's principal tutor in music was Carl Friedrich Zelter (1758–1832). He was well known in Berlin as a composer and as the conductor of the city's main choral society, the Singakademie (Singing Academy). This

 **FIGURE 54-2**
Wilhelm von Schadow's portrait of Felix Mendelssohn, 1834, when the composer was in his mid-twenties.

was one of the few organizations during the early nineteenth century that performed choral music by Johann Sebastian Bach, who at this time was remembered primarily as a composer of keyboard music. In 1829 Mendelssohn, with Zelter's support, conducted the Singakademie in a performance of Bach's mammoth *St. Matthew Passion*, a work that one hundred years after its first performance was still unpublished and largely unknown. Mendelssohn's concert was a huge success, and a revelation to German audiences. It provoked the so-called **Bach Revival,** in which Bach's music in its entirety was at last performed, published, and studied.

The later years of Mendelssohn's short life were taken up by the dual careers of composer and conductor. His main position was in Leipzig as *Kapellmeister* (conductor) of the Gewandhaus Orchestra (1835–1847), and from 1840 he divided his time in Leipzig with an appointment as music director in the city of Berlin. He traveled repeatedly to music festivals throughout Germany and made ten highly successful visits to England, where his music was keenly appreciated.

During his twelve years as conductor of the Gewandhaus Orchestra, Mendelssohn selected music for performance in a way that was unusual for its time but similar to the approach of an orchestra in the present day. His programs mixed styles and historical periods of origin, without the uniform emphasis on recently composed works, which was more typical of concert planning at the time. Mendelssohn searched for seemingly timeless works from the past—Handel's *Messiah*, Bach's keyboard concertos, symphonies by Haydn, Mozart, and Beethoven—and mixed these in with new orchestral compositions, such as those of a Berlioz or Robert Schumann. One of his greatest discoveries, made during his search through the orchestra literature of the past, was Schubert's Symphony No. 9 in C Major (see Chapter 52). It had never been performed in public, or published, when its manuscript was sent to Mendelssohn by his friend and fellow Leipziger Robert Schumann. Mendelssohn recognized its greatness and in 1839 conducted its first performance.

Mendelssohn's philosophy of programming took a first step toward the establishment of the **canon,** the term used nowadays for the generally accepted body of musical works, composed almost entirely in the eighteenth and nineteenth centuries, that has come to dominate our serious musical culture.

Piano Trio in D Minor

Mendelssohn's mixed approach to programming is reflected in the style of his own music, which uses elements from the past that he cautiously extends by new thinking. He was one of the great composers of orchestral music of his time, but his works for this medium avoid the experimental aspects of a composer such as Berlioz in favor of a continuation of the classical lines established by Haydn, Mozart, and Beethoven. Mendelssohn composed five mature symphonies, in addition to thirteen symphonies for string orchestra that were written during his student period. He also wrote concertos—two for piano and one for violin—and, like Berlioz, he composed concert overtures (including the ever-popular *Fingal's Cave*). His chamber music includes six string quartets, two piano trios, and several sonatas. An excellent pianist, Mendelssohn composed primarily character pieces for this instrument. He wrote two large oratorios, *St. Paul* (1836) and *Elijah* (1846), in addition to many other works for chorus. Although Mendelssohn wrote no major operas, he often composed incidental music to spoken plays, including music to Shakespeare's *A Midsummer Night's Dream*. This has become Mendelssohn's most often performed work.

Getting into the Canon

Musicians can agree on one thing at least: the world of classical music today is dominated by the works of a relatively small number of composers. Their compositions have taken on such prestige and authority as to be tantamount to a canon, a term also used for the books that make up the Bible and are accepted by the faithful as the word of God.

The musicians whose compositions make up this canon, or "standard repertory," of classical music come from a relatively similar background. All are men, all are Europeans, and virtually all lived in the eighteenth and nineteenth centuries. To many in the present day, this sounds more than a bit objectionable—smacking of elitism, sexism, and similar small-minded thinking. Why is it that Robert Schumann and Felix Mendelssohn are in, while Clara Schumann and Fanny Mendelssohn—female composers of note—are out?

Even today, musicians do not agree on this question. Some believe that the canon is like an exclusive club that needs to be opened to women, minorities, and non-Europeans. Composers in the canon are there arbitrarily, it is said, in part because writers of textbooks return to them in edition after edition.

Other musicians respond that those in the canon are there because they wrote better music. People want to hear Felix Mendelssohn, not Fanny Mendelssohn, they say. But if this is so, what makes Felix's music better than his sister Fanny's? Again, no agreement. Some hold that a close study of musical works can show the superiority of one piece over another. This was an idea that motivated the Austrian theorist Heinrich Schenker (1868–1935), who looked intensely at the harmonic and contrapuntal technique of composers and found about ten European male composers whose music, he concluded, was inherently superior.

His conclusions do not satisfy everyone. Why should an ingenuity of musical structure make a piece good or enduring? Isn't simplicity a good thing? The French composer Maurice Ravel threw up his hands over the whole issue: "I consider it impossible to explain or judge a work of musical art," he declared. For a musician like Ravel, the only objective criterion for judging music is viability. Works in the canon are those that for long periods of time—for whatever reason—have lived; they have been performed, studied, and recorded, and have stimulated people's imagination.

The Trio in D Minor, Op. 49, illustrates the composer's marriage of old and new. Trios for piano, violin, and cello (called simply "piano trios") were an important type of music for the Viennese composers. Beethoven's piano trios, for example, are second in number only to his string quartets among the chamber genres. Mendelssohn's D-Minor Trio, written in 1839, has a classical exterior—four movements in the sequence *allegro/andante/scherzo/allegro*, each using a traditional form. The whole work is concise—about a half-hour in length—and its overall tonal plan is similar to that of a trio composed fifty years earlier.

Comparison of the first movement of Mendelssohn's trio with a movement from Berlioz's *Symphonie fantastique* (see Chapter 53) reveals the varying ways that Beethoven influenced the generation of composers that followed him. Berlioz picks up ideas subtly present in Beethoven—programmaticism, cyclicism, formal liberty—and carries them to such lengths as to create a whole new conception of the symphony. Mendelssohn, on the contrary, takes Beethoven's ideals of musical form and expression only a small and measured step forward.

One feature of Mendelssohn's movement that plainly derives from Beethoven is the presence throughout of a clash between two opposing ideas—one of them stable though passionately lyric, the other agitated and eruptive. This battle of opposites is often seen in Beethoven's first movements, as in his famous Piano Sonata in D Minor, Op. 31, No. 2 (nicknamed "The Tempest"). Beethoven's work opens with a dreamy arpeggio on an A-major triad, followed immediately by an impulsive, downward-moving line in the tonic D minor (Ex. 54-1). These starkly contrasted moods compete for the remainder of the movement.

EXAMPLE 54-1

mm. 1-5

In Mendelssohn's trio movement, also in the key of D minor, the conflict is embodied in two main themes, one in the cello at the beginning and the second following immediately in the piano (Ex. 54-2). The cello's theme is richly melodious, the piano's unstable, agitated, fragmented. These opposites are later represented in the movement by sudden juxtapositions of minor and major, triple versus duple divisions of the beat, and piano set against the strings. Also like Beethoven is the creation of an uninterrupted continuity throughout the entire sonata-form movement. Mendelssohn moves toward this sense of connectedness by omitting the familiar double bar with repeat signs at the end of the exposition, something occasionally done by Beethoven in his first movements. Both composers promote musical unity, despite the contrasts on the musical surface, by subtly carrying over motives from one theme to another.

We will find an example in Mendelssohn's movement by comparing the two principal subsidiary (or "second") themes that arise toward the end of the exposition (Ex. 54-3). Outwardly, these embody the same contrasts seen at the beginning. The first one is lyrical, proceeds in quarter-note values, and is played by the cello; the other erupts into agitated triplets, is not very melodious, and is given to the piano. But beneath these contrasts there is a sameness created by an ascending triadic motive, E - A - C♯ - E, shown by the bracket in the example.

EXAMPLE 54-2

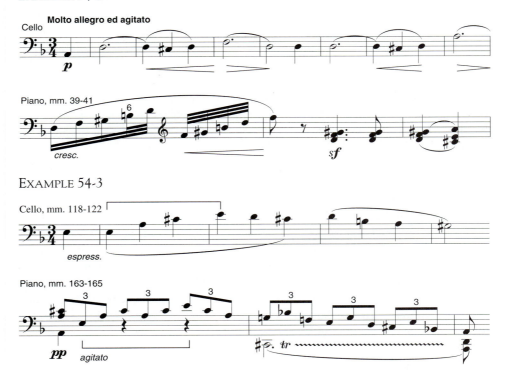

In other ways, Mendelssohn apparently wished to move the music beyond the classical style of Beethoven and bring it closer, however cautiously, to the spirit of his own day. The piano part has some of the flashy virtuosity typical of the age of Chopin and Liszt. The timbre of the music is dark and the first main theme is richly songful, even operatic, in character. Mendelssohn's method of development is entirely different from Beethoven's; he tends to keep his melodies intact, only to lead them through a quickly changing tonal environment. Look at the passage in the development section from measures 250 to 284. Here the first subsidiary theme returns repeatedly, almost intact, although it quickly traverses the keys of B♭ major, G minor, and finally D minor.

The Trio in D Minor thus reveals Mendelssohn's conservative interpretation of the romantic spirit: its first movement maintains Beethoven's approach to sonata form, underscoring Beethoven's ways of promoting motivic and tonal unity beneath an apparent diversity on the surface of the music. At the same time its concentration on a warm and affective melody allies it with contemporary musical trends.

LISTENING CUE

FELIX MENDELSSOHN
Piano Trio in D Minor, Op. 49 (1839)
First movement, *Molto allegro ed agitato*

CD 9/7
Anthology, No. 150

 ## ROBERT SCHUMANN

Mendelssohn's stylistic conservatism was fully supported by his fellow Leipzig musician Robert Schumann (1810–1856). "He is the Mozart of the nineteenth century," wrote Schumann approvingly about Mendelssohn, "the most brilliant musician, the one who sees most clearly through the contradictions of this period and for the first time reconciles them."[1]

Schumann was born in the Saxon town of Zwickau, about forty miles south of Leipzig. As a child his imagination was fired equally by music and literature, and he aspired to be a concert pianist. In 1828 he enrolled at the University of Leipzig in law, although Schumann had no interest in this area, cut classes regularly, and concentrated instead on piano and composition. He studied piano with a well-known teacher in Leipzig, Friedrich Wieck, although his prospects as a player were set back by an injury to his hand. He admired the virtuosity of Wieck's prize student and daughter, Clara, whom Schumann would marry in 1840.

Like Berlioz before him, Schumann combined his talents for literature and music by writing musical criticism. In 1833 he collaborated on the founding of the **Neue [Leipziger] Zeitschrift für Musik** (*New Journal for Music*), which he edited and wrote almost single-handedly until 1844. This journal is still in existence. Music criticism at this time was different from its modern counterpart. Instead of passing judgments on performances like the reviewer of today, Schumann wrote primarily about newly published music, and his opinions were insightful. He immediately recognized the greatness of Chopin: "Hats off, gentlemen, a genius!" he declared in 1831 after examining the score of Chopin's early Variations, Op. 2. After studying a piano reduction of *Symphonie fantastique* he declared Berlioz's art to be a "flaming sword," although he found many eccentricities and was bothered by the explicit program that Berlioz used in the work. In 1853 he recognized the youthful Johannes Brahms as "a young creature over whose cradle graces and heroes stood guard."

After his marriage to Clara Wieck, Schumann often traveled with his wife on her concert tours. The pair moved in 1844 from Leipzig to the nearby city of Dresden—the capital of Saxony—and in 1850 again to Düsseldorf, where Schumann was appointed conductor of the local orchestra and chorus. Schumann waged a lifelong struggle with mental illness—its origins are uncertain—and in Düsseldorf his illness took a dire turn. He suffered several nervous breakdowns and tried studying counterpoint to focus his thoughts. Gradually his mind filled with voices and visions. "He heard entire pieces from beginning to end, as if played by a full orchestra," wrote Clara, "and the sound would remain on the final chord until Robert directed his thoughts to another composition." His psychosis only worsened, and in 1854 he attempted to drown himself in the Rhine River. He was then committed to a mental institution, where he died in 1856.

Schumann's Music

In the 1830s Schumann began his compositional career by writing almost exclusively for piano, something typical of the aspiring piano virtuoso. In addition to sonatas conceived on a large scale, he created miniature character pieces that were often gathered into cycles. *Papillons* (*Butterflies*, 1831), *Carnaval* (*Carnival*, 1835), and *Kinderscenen* (*Scenes from Childhood*, 1838) are some of the best known. These miniature works are fully imbued with the romantic spirit that originated with Schubert. As in Schubert's piano waltzes, impromptus, and "musical moments," Schumann's pieces bring the most intense expressivity and innovative musical materials into miniature dimensions. As with Berlioz's *Symphonie fantastique*, they are personalized and autobiographical, but, unlike Berlioz, this personal element is spoken under the breath, not intended for everyone to hear.

Examples of Schumann's sometimes cryptic allusions to his own world are found in **Carnaval,** a collection of more than twenty small pieces, each bearing a title of a person or event at an imaginary masked ball during carnival season. Musicians including Chopin and Nicolò Paganini—the great violin virtuoso—are at the dance, represented by pieces that bear their names and imitate their styles of composition. We meet Schumann himself in the pieces titled "Florestan" and "Eusebius," which were the names that he gave to the impetuous and the dreamy sides of his personality, respectively. Clara is there in a piece titled "Chiarina," which Schumann marks *passionato*. But his affections were apparently still divided among several women. The alto part of its opening phrase contains a descending line A♭-G-F-E♭-D, which—according to one hypothesis—Schumann used in later music as his private motto for Clara (Ex. 54-4). But the opening three notes in the soprano line, A♭-C-B♮, refer to one of her rivals. In German solfège, these note names are spelled A s-C-H, and Asch was the hometown of Ernestine von Fricken, another of Wieck's female students.

EXAMPLE 54-4

mm. 1-5

In 1840, just before his marriage to Clara in September, Schumann turned his attention from piano music to songs, and in that year alone he poured out some one hundred seventy works of this type, including his great cycles *Dichterliebe* (Poet's Love), *Frauenliebe und -leben* (Women's Love and Life), and *Myrthen* (Myrtles). As with the piano miniatures, his model for song-writing was Schubert, whose deeply expressive approach to the genre of song Schumann adopts and extends.

After their marriage, Clara urged her husband to take up the larger musical forms, and he responded by hurriedly composing the first two of his four symphonies. He later wrote concertos for piano and for cello, three string quartets, and important chamber works with piano—a Quintet, Op. 44, Quartet, Op. 47, and three piano trios. In these later works Schumann partly turns away from the exuberant, affective style of the early piano pieces and songs in order to recapture a more classical form and measured expression. Schumann wrote one opera, *Genoveva* (1849).

Symphony No. 1 in B♭ Major ("Spring")

Schumann's four symphonies have a complex history. The first of them, in B♭ major, was written in a burst of creativity spanning only four days in January 1841. Later in that year he composed another symphony, in D minor, although it was not fully orchestrated until 1851, whereupon it was called Symphony No. 4. In the intervening years he wrote two additional symphonies, one in C major (called Symphony No. 2) and another in E♭ major (Symphony No. 3, nicknamed the "Rhenish" Symphony after the Rhine River). These four are among the greatest works in the entire symphonic literature.

Schumann began his Symphony No. 1 as a subtly programmatic work, much as Beethoven had done in his "Eroica" and "Pastoral" symphonies. His subject would be springtime, and he at first referred to a poem by a Leipzig writer named Adolf Böttger (1815–1870), although the verse has little apparent relevance to the finished work. He gave each of the movements a descriptive subtitle: Spring's Beginning, Evening, Happy Games, Spring Bursting Out. But Schumann was never in favor of the overt programmaticism used by Berlioz, which for Schumann could only limit the freedom of a listener's imagination. "What remains as really important," he wrote, "is whether the music, without text and explanation, has intrinsic value, and especially whether it is imbued with spirit."[2] When his symphony was published later in 1841, Schumann removed all of the verbal references to spring, although the work is still commonly known as the "Spring" Symphony.

There is much about it that is springlike. In the first movement, a triangle is brought in, giving the work a festive sound. The flute twitters like a bird, and the music—as often with Schumann—has the freshness of a spring day. The work has the overall shape of a symphony by Beethoven or Schubert. There are the customary four movements (fast with slow introduction/slow/scherzo/fast) and the whole symphony is moderate in length, about thirty-five minutes. The orchestra is virtually identical to the one used in Schubert's Symphony No. 9 in C Major, which had been played repeatedly by the Gewandhaus Orchestra beginning in 1839, and was certainly in Schumann's ear as he wrote his B♭ symphony.

The audience at the Gewandhaus for the premiere of Schumann's "Spring" Symphony, which Mendelssohn conducted in March 1841, must have noted from the very outset the similarities with Schubert's Ninth. The two works begin similarly, with slow introductions launched by brass motives that underlie later themes (Schumann's opening motive is shown in Ex. 54-5; see Schubert's in Chapter 52). In both works, the motive returns climactically later in the movement, at the beginning of the recapitulation in Schumann, in the coda in Schubert. Both first movements take liberties with the customary sequence of events in sonata form.

EXAMPLE 54-5

Schumann looks to Beethoven's gestures of continuity and large-scale unity in the symphony as a fertile area for development. The slow movement and the scherzo of Symphony No. 1 are played without pause, and they are further linked by a hymn-like figure in the trombones at the end of the slow movement that is immediately transformed into the main scherzo theme (Ex. 54-6a). A theme subtly shared between the outer movements is shown in Example 54-6b.

EXAMPLE 54-6

Schumann's slow movement is unusual in its tempo and lyric character. Symphonic slow movements before this time were normally marked *andante,* but Schumann's is slower—a broad *larghetto*—and its main melody (Ex. 54-7) is unusually intense, reminiscent of an operatic melody, or one by Chopin. A model for this type of slow movement may have been the slow movement, marked *adagio,* of Beethoven's "Pastoral" Symphony, which has a similar character. Beethoven's *Adagio* also shares with Schumann's *Larghetto* a busy accompaniment in the strings, one that always poses a problem in balance.

EXAMPLE 54-7

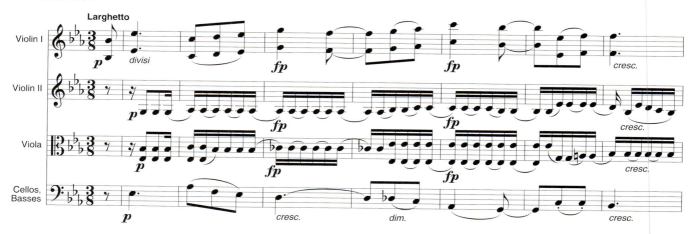

CLARA SCHUMANN

Clara Schumann (1819–1896) was one of the great piano virtuosos of the nineteenth century (Fig. 54-3). Growing up in Leipzig, where she was relentlessly pushed to succeed by her father, she proved herself an extraordinary child prodigy. She played at the Gewandhaus at the age of only nine and in 1831, at the age of eleven, she began to tour throughout Europe. She continued to concertize virtually to the end of her long life, even through numerous pregnancies during her sixteen years of marriage (the Schumanns had eight children).

A special chapter in her life following Robert Schumann's untimely death concerns her friendship with the composer Johannes Brahms. He introduced himself to the Schumanns in 1853 and was warmly embraced by them both. After Schumann's death, Brahms and Clara Schumann continued a platonic, artistic relationship that endured for the remainder of Clara's life. In 1896, as Clara's health began to fail, Brahms composed *Four Serious Songs*, Op. 121, a collection that was his memorial to her and to their 43-year friendship. He sent a copy of the songs to Clara's daughter with a poignant explanation of their content:

Deep in the heart of man something often whispers and stirs, quite unconsciously perhaps, which in time may ring out in the form of poetry or music. . . . I beg you to regard these [songs] as a true memorial to your beloved mother.[3]

FIGURE 54-3
Eduard Kaiser's lithograph of Robert and Clara Schumann, 1847. The Schumanns lived in Dresden when this was made.

CORBIS

The programs that Clara Schumann played spanned a general change in the idea of the piano concert—from a gala event with many players and differing genres, to the recital, in which the pianist plays alone or nearly so. In the earlier type, Clara Schumann played improvisations, her own compositions, flashy studies, variations on opera melodies, and concertos. Later she changed to a more modern soloistic repertory that mixed sonatas by Domenico Scarlatti and Beethoven, fugues by Bach, works by her husband (always), and other modern pieces (especially those by Brahms). These were chosen for their artistry rather than showmanship, for which she had only disdain. She toured far and wide, from Russia to England (where she visited nineteen times), although never to America. She ended her days as a professor of piano playing at the Conservatory in Frankfurt. There are no recordings of her playing.

Clara Schumann also composed, primarily because this was part of the art of the virtuoso in her day. Most of her music—a piano concerto, character works for this instrument, variations, and songs—were pieces intended for her concerts. Her songs show an introspective side of her musical personality, one that was plainly stimulated by the songs of her husband. She wrote "Liebst du um Schönheit" ("If You Love Beauty") in 1841, and it was published in a collection of songs to texts by Friedrich Rückert, some composed by her husband during his great song year of 1840, some by her.

The poetry of Friedrich Rückert (1788–1866) was set to music by many of the greatest nineteenth-century Lieder composers—Schubert, Gustav Mahler, and Robert and Clara Schumann are only a few. In Chapter 60 we will return to Rückert's poem "Um Mitternacht," where it is found in a song by Gustav Mahler. The poem "Liebst du um Schönheit" is frank in its emotionality. Love me only for the sake of love, says the narrator, not for beauty, youth, or wealth, for which you can do better elsewhere. These same direct sentiments are captured in the music, which is unsophisticated and repetitive, although affective in its melodic warmth.

LISTENING CUE

CLARA SCHUMANN
"Liebst du um Schönheit" (1841)

CD 9/9
Anthology, No. 152

SUMMARY

Music in the city of Leipzig in the early nineteenth century had a conservative tone, mixing elements of eighteenth-century music with modern ideas. The city was a center of orchestral music, thanks to its excellent Gewandhaus Orchestra, which was conducted by Felix Mendelssohn from 1835 to 1847. Mendelssohn composed music in a mixed style, close to the models provided by Mozart and Beethoven, but cautiously expanded by more modern notions. His Trio in D Minor, Op. 49, shows this combination of old and new.

Robert Schumann lived in Leipzig from 1831 to 1844, during which he composed piano music, songs, and, beginning in 1841, orchestral music. His symphonies show the same mixture of stylistic elements as in Mendelssohn. His Symphony No. 1 in

B♭ Major ("Spring") uses a form inherited from Beethoven and Schubert, although the four movements are linked together by shared themes and other gestures toward continuity. The slow movement, *Larghetto*, is especially songful.

Clara Wieck Schumann, who married Robert Schumann in 1840, was one of the great piano virtuosos of the nineteenth century. Like most professional pianists, she also composed, and her song "Liebst du um Schönheit" achieves an affecting beauty despite its artlessness and simplicity of form.

KEY TERMS

Hugo Riemann
functional harmony
complete works (type of
    musical edition)

Gewandhaus Orchestra
Bartholdy
Bach Revival
canon

Neue Zeitschrift für Musik
Carnaval

German Opera of the Nineteenth Century: Weber and Wagner

Opera in the early nineteenth century retained its unique importance within the world of music. Like other musical genres, it was partly a diversion, but it also had the special capacity to deal with the real social and historical issues of its time. Mozart's *Marriage of Figaro* attracted attention in part because it questioned the right of the aristocracy to privilege. Beethoven's *Fidelio* touched on the legitimate limits of the power of the state over the individual. Giuseppe Verdi's *Nabucco* alluded to the plight of a people having no homeland, a condition felt by many of Verdi's Italian countrymen when the opera was first heard in 1842.

Opera in the nineteenth century was not only relevant but highly popular. In virtually all of the major European capitals of this time, the genre flourished as never before. New and larger opera houses were being built with updated staging and lighting equipment. Opera singers had become international celebrities, and new ideas about operatic composition flowed, at first from France and Italy, and later from Germany. Fame and fortune awaited the successful opera composer to a degree unknown by composers in any other medium.

But, with a few exceptions such as Mozart and Beethoven, German musicians had been underachievers in the genre. Schubert, Mendelssohn, and Schumann composed operas, but they were never very successful. Recall from Chapter 48 that German opera in the eighteenth century existed primarily in a form called **Singspiel** (literally, "play with singing"). In *Singspiel*, simple musical numbers were inserted into a lighthearted or folkish spoken play. Works of this type continued to be composed after 1800, but in musical terms they seemed unsophisticated and old-fashioned. To most audiences, even in German lands, *Singspiel* paled in comparison to the intensely human comedies found in Gioachino Rossini's Italian operas, or the spectacular French operas by Giacomo Meyerbeer, or the studies in heroism found in the French operas of Gaspare Spontini.

Singspiel was far more modest. Its performers were typically members of a traveling company who performed spoken plays one day and opera the next. The art of purely operatic singing was scarcely known among them. In the eighteenth century, King Frederick the Great had said unkindly that a horse could sing opera better than a German. If so, little had changed by the early nineteenth century. "Where in all our German fatherland are there training schools for higher vocal culture?" asked Richard Wagner in 1834. "The higher vocal art, solo singing, is in manifest decline, and many a mile might we journey before we could assemble a couple of dozen good singers really worthy of the name."[1]

✺ CARL MARIA VON WEBER

German opera took on new vitality and identity in the works of Carl Maria von Weber (pronounced VAY-ber, 1786–1826). He was born in Eutin, a small town in the far north of Germany, and his life was unsettled by almost constant travel and by a career divided among composing, conducting, performing (he excelled at both guitar and piano), writing musical criticism, and managing theaters. In 1817 he was appointed director of an opera troupe in the city of Dresden, the capital of Saxony, where he staged *Singspiele* and French operas in German translation. An Italian opera company was also in residence in the city, and a heated rivalry soon developed between the two. Weber was determined to bring the level of German opera above the Italian, which, except for its excellent singing, he found thin in artistic content. He poked fun at the make-up of a typical Italian work as something where "oboes double the flutes, clarinets double the oboes, flutes double the violins, bassoons double the bass. Second violins double the firsts, viola doubles the bass. Voice ad libitum. Violins double the voice."[2]

In Dresden, Weber composed his greatest opera, *Der Freischütz* (freely, *The Bewitched Marksman*, 1821). It has much in common with Beethoven's *Fidelio* (see Chapter 50). The characters are strictly types, not drawn to the measure of real individuals, and the musical form is an old-fashioned succession of traditional operatic numbers interspersed into a spoken play. In light of these features, both *Der Freischütz* and *Fidelio* are related to *Singspiel*, and both works also incorporate styles from French and Italian operas of their time.

Der Freischütz also has features that look to the future of opera. The libretto, written by **Friedrich Kind** (an amateur writer who lived in Dresden), avoids the more typical themes of contemporary operas of the day—the comic farce or the tragedy stemming from heightened, conflicting human emotions. Instead, Kind adapted a ghost story, making it into a morality play in which good is pitted against the forces of evil. Mysterious events take place and there is an aura of the supernatural, just as in a popular type of literature of the time called the "romance." Because of this similarity, Weber designated his opera, not as old-fashioned *Singspiel*, but by the more up-to-date term, **romantic opera.**

In addition to characters representing everyman (Max), the pure woman (Agathe), religion (the Holy Man), the good ruler (Prince Ottokar), and the fallen individual (Caspar), there is also a strong presence of common people—plain folk—who live in harmony with nature. In their rousing choruses Weber quotes several folk songs, as he wished to give his opera a nationalistic flavor at a time when Germans were discovering patriotism after their long subjugation by the French under Napoleon.

Synopsis of *Der Freischütz*

The hunter Max is dejected over his poor shooting, and he knows that he must do better in tomorrow's shooting match in order to win the hand of his beloved Agathe, daughter of the chief forester. A fellow hunter, Caspar, tells Max that he can supply enchanted, or "free," bullets, that will go wherever the shooter wishes. These can be had if Max meets him that night in the haunted Wolf's Glen. Despite Agathe's premonitions, Max agrees, and the two hunters cast seven magic bullets. But, unknown to Max, the spirit of the devil, Samiel, is lurking near, and he will control the seventh bullet himself.

At the next day's shooting contest, Max is unbeatable. For his seventh and final shot, Prince Ottokar picks an easy target—a dove sitting on a nearby branch. Just as he aims, Agathe darts from behind the tree. "Don't shoot, Max, I am the dove!" But the shot rings out and Agathe falls to the ground. To everyone's relief, she has only fainted and the bullet has instead killed Caspar, who had earlier sold his soul to Samiel. After confessing his crimes and receiving support from a Holy Man, Max is given a year's probation, after which he can marry Agathe. All praise the goodness of God.

Weber's most original accomplishment in *Der Freischütz* is to unify the diverse elements that make up an opera on the basis of its drama. He achieves this especially in the work's orchestral music, which closely follows and underscores the drama. No longer is the orchestra simply an accompaniment to singing, as often in Italian opera. Weber instead elevates its role by a network of musical symbols—specifically, by identifying orchestral motives, tonalities, and specific instruments with certain characters or situations. The idea of using musical elements as explicit dramatic symbols was not entirely new with Weber, but in the context of German opera he brought the notion to a higher and more systematic level than had been done before, and his achievements were carefully studied by later opera composers, including Hector Berlioz and Richard Wagner.

The keys of C major and D major, for example, are used in *Der Freischütz* whenever the good characters—especially Agathe and choruses representing the people—sing. The villainous Caspar sings primarily in B minor and D minor, and the devil, Samiel, doesn't sing at all; instead, he speaks over an unstable diminished chord played by the orchestra. Max, the hero and hunter, is accompanied most often by the French horns; the pure Agathe by the pure sound of the clarinet; Samiel by the devilish timpani.

The most striking, and always the most popular, part of *Der Freischütz* is the finale to Act 2, also called the **Wolf's Glen Scene.** Recall from Chapter 48 that an operatic finale is a longish number occurring at the end of an act. It is made from several contrasting but connected musical sections in differing vocal styles, although ensemble singing usually dominates. Several of the leading singer-actors appear in a finale to bring the plot either to a crisis point or to some resolution. Weber, like Beethoven at the climactic beginning of Act 2 of *Fidelio*, underscores the dramatic tension of his finale by using **melodrama,** in addition to normal singing. In melodrama—which was favored among French composers of the day—the voices speak in alternation with or accompanied by orchestral music.

In the finale of Act 2, Max has foolishly agreed to meet Caspar in the haunted Wolf's Glen to cast magic bullets. Caspar arrives first, greeted by a chorus of invisible spirits in the key of F♯ minor, and he calls on Samiel to appear. We know Samiel arrives when we hear the orchestra play the motive by which he is always accompanied (Ex. 55-1). His motive is no arbitrary symbol. It is made from a sustained diminished-seventh chord, always with the notes A-C-E♭-G♭ regardless of the tonal context, and it is always played quietly with the timpani muttering on offbeats. It has the same shadowy, slippery quality as the diabolical creature that it represents. The key then shifts to C minor, and Caspar asks Samiel for an extension to his time on earth in return for Caspar's bringing him the soul of Max. Samiel seems to agree to this arrangement, and Caspar builds a fire in a forge to cast the magic bullets. The hunting horns announce Max's arrival as the key turns to E♭ major—the key of the hero ever since Beethoven's Symphony No. 3.

EXAMPLE 55-1

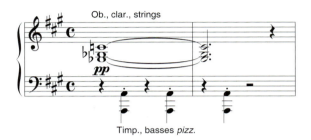

The casting of the seven bullets forms the climactic last section of the finale (Anthology, No. 153). The orchestral music begins in A minor and depicts the furnace's crackling fire. Caspar shouts out the number of each new bullet as it is tossed from its mold, and after each one there is an eerie vision, as though nature protests what is happening. A wild boar crashes through the bushes, the Wild Huntsman (a character from folklore) rides through the air, and finally a great thunderstorm rises. Audiences of the 1820s were fascinated by the dramatic realism of Weber's staging, especially by a wooden owl whose eyes glowed and wings flapped. Like the orchestral music, the scenery was no longer a neutral backdrop but instead an active expressive tool. When the seventh bullet is cast, both Caspar and Max are thrown to the ground, and as the key returns to F♯ minor Samiel reaches out for Max's hand.

In addition to creating a network of musical and visual symbols in this scene, Weber looks for subtle ways of instilling continuity in the music, which is necessary if it is to be as dramatic as the words. He finds in the work's tonal plan a dimension for promoting musical integration. This is unified and concentric, as in a symphony or concerto of the day, but unusual in an opera. The entire opera returns at its end to a home key, here C major, in which it began. The Wolf's Glen Scene—like an inner movement from a symphony—begins and ends in a contrasting key, F♯ minor.

Integration of key and harmony is also felt on the smaller scale, always with reference to the work's drama. In the Wolf's Glen Scene, for example, the succession of principal tonic notes which span the entire passage— F♯, C, E♭, A, then back to F♯ at the end—make up on the large scale the same diminished-seventh chord that represents Samiel in his small motive. By this integration of timespans, Weber shows us that Samiel controls the scene from beginning to end, ruthlessly wielding his power over such frail human beings as Caspar and Max.

LISTENING CUE

CARL MARIA VON WEBER
Der Freischütz (1821)
Act 2, Wolf's Glen Scene, concluding section

CD 9/10
Anthology, No. 153

❋ RICHARD WAGNER

Weber's creation of an opera unified in music and drama was developed later in the nineteenth century by Richard Wagner (pronounced VAHG-ner, 1813–1883; Fig. 55-1). Wagner was born in Leipzig and grew up there and in nearby Dresden. Like his fellow Saxon, Robert Schumann, he was strongly attracted to literature and later wrote voluminously on music. Wagner was largely self-taught as a composer, and at the age of nineteen he had a symphony performed by the Gewandhaus Orchestra. On the same program Clara Wieck, thirteen years old, also played, and she teased her friend Robert Schumann about Wagner's progress: "Listen, Mr. Wagner has got ahead of you. His symphony was performed, and it's said to be almost exactly like Beethoven's Symphony [No. 7] in A Major."[3]

In 1839 Wagner moved to Paris to try to advance his career as a composer of opera in the world's operatic capital. He began to write musical criticism to earn money, but he had no success in finding a stage for his early operas. His breakthrough came in 1842, when his opera *Rienzi*—a work in the style of French grand opera although having a German text—was accepted for production in Dresden. Its success led to Wagner's appointment there as *Kapellmeister*, in a position earlier held by Carl Maria von Weber. His next two operas—*Der fliegende Holländer* (*The Flying Dutchman*, 1841) and *Tannhäuser* (1845)—also had their premieres in Dresden, and his *Lohengrin* (1848) was readied for the 1849 season.

But, in the spring of 1849, Wagner's burgeoning career was derailed by his participation in an uprising in Dresden directed against the rule of Friedrich Augustus II, the king of Saxony and also Wagner's employer. The insurgency was quickly put down, but some two hundred people were killed and a warrant was issued for Wagner's arrest. Using a faked passport, he escaped a possible death sentence by fleeing to Zurich in neutral Switzerland. With an arrest warrant looming permanently over him, Wagner was effectively banished from visiting countries in the German Confederation, and, as a specialist in German opera, his prospects as a composer were in tatters. In 1860 the king of Saxony granted Wagner a limited amnesty, and only then could he return to German lands without fear of arrest.

In Switzerland, Wagner's interests first turned toward literary matters. He wrote aesthetic treatises on the state of opera and its relation to contemporary and future society, and he continued to hatch ideas for new works. Following the breakup of his marriage in 1859, Wagner left Switzerland and began an unsettled period of travel, hounded by increasing debt and frustrated musical ambitions.

In 1864 Wagner was living in a Stuttgart hotel and literally down to his last dollar. He was found there by a secretary to Ludwig II—eighteen years old and newly enthroned as the king of Bavaria—who invited Wagner to meet him in the Bavarian capital of Munich. Needless to say, Wagner accepted the invitation. Although not especially musical, King Ludwig was a passionate admirer of Wagner's writings and music, and he immediately paid off Wagner's debts, gave him a salary and a place to live, and underwrote the expenses for the premier performances of the operas *Tristan und Isolde* (1859) and *Die Meistersinger von Nürnberg* (*The Master Singers of Nuremberg*, 1867).

The large expenses arising from having Wagner as a guest soon made it necessary for the king to ask Wagner to leave Munich, and the composer then returned to Switzerland and lived near Lucerne. In 1870 he married Cosima Liszt, daughter of Franz Liszt and formerly the wife of Liszt's student Hans von Bülow. In Lucerne, Wagner pushed ahead on a longstanding project of epic proportions—*Der Ring des Nibelungen* (*The Ring of the Nibelung*)—a cycle of four related operas.

Bridgeman Art Library

❋ FIGURE 55-1

Portrait of Richard Wagner by Franz von Lenbach. Lenbach, a personal friend of Wagner and his wife, painted many of the leading personalities of his day.

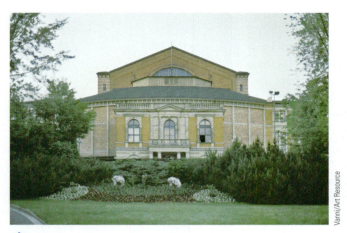

FIGURE 55-2

The Bayreuth Festival Theater is located on a hill on the outskirts of the town of Bayreuth. The auditorium seats about 1,500.

Vanni/Art Resource

For their staging he felt that he needed a special theater where the operas could be performed in a festival-like atmosphere. With King Ludwig's financial help, Wagner purchased property in the Bavarian village of **Bayreuth** and began to raise money to build a theater specifically for the performance of his own works (Fig. 55-2). He also built a permanent residence in Bayreuth, moving there in 1872 to oversee the first complete performances of the *Ring* operas. These took place in the summer of 1876. Wagner then turned his attention to his last opera, *Parsifal* (1882), a work that he thought should only be performed in the Bayreuth theater. In February 1883, while visiting Venice, the composer suffered a fatal heart attack, and he is buried on the grounds of his villa in Bayreuth.

WAGNER'S MUSIC AND THEORIES OF OPERA

Wagner was a specialist in operatic composition, a genre that best combined his literary and musical talents. Not counting a few youthful experiments, he wrote a total of eleven operas, although he did not consider the first of these, *Rienzi*, to be a mature work. There are also a few songs, piano pieces, choral music, and orchestral works such as the delightful *Siegfried Idyll* for chamber orchestra (1870).

All of Wagner's operas use texts that he wrote himself. He developed an idea for a new composition by his literary readings and by calling on his own experiences and ideas. He worked these stimuli into a prose outline and from there into a poetic libretto which was usually published immediately. Composition then followed, and Wagner sometimes returned to a completed work to make substantial revisions.

The first three of the ten principal operas—*The Flying Dutchman, Tannhäuser,* and *Lohengrin*—form a related group, not too distant in style from Weber's *Der Freischütz.* Wagner based their texts on old German legends, and the stories bring in magical and supernatural elements in the same way as *Der Freischütz.* Wagner called each of these a "romantic" opera, using Weber's term. Like *Der Freischütz, The Flying Dutchman* is clearly divided into operatic numbers, although Wagner dispenses with the old-fashioned spoken dialogue of Weber's time. In *Tannhäuser* and *Lohengrin,* the division into numbers is less apparent because they are absorbed into larger divisions, or scenes, in which there is a fluid alternation among soloistic, ensemble, and choral singing. The scenes are all connected without pause, so that there is no encouragement for the audience to break the concentration by applause.

After *Lohengrin,* Wagner went into his Swiss exile and wrote a series of books and articles on the state of opera and its future prospects, and his theories guided him in his later musical works. Wagner believed that opera in his day was out of balance, since the musical element had taken on too much importance and the dramatic part had, he thought, become trivial. He wanted to redress this imbalance by elevating the drama of opera to a more sophisticated level and creating an integrated equilibrium among text, music, and staging. Opera, he said, should become a **Gesamtkunstwerk (total work of art),** not just an occasion for singing. Thinking as always in utopian terms, Wagner proposed that this integrated and dramatic artwork would become the ideal of **music of the future.**

The best subjects for the artwork of the future, Wagner speculated, were drawn from myths, since these were products of a collective imagination and inherently understandable by everyone. Myths, he said, deal with the essential problems facing humanity—the nature of love, the concept of property, the idea of God—and big ideas such as these could become the stuff of opera. But, for this to happen, the artificialities of the genre as it then existed would have to be reformed. The stop-and-go of number opera had to be eliminated in favor of a continuous and uninterrupted form. Melody would have to avoid regular and symmetric phrases and instead continually reshape motives and ride upon an enriched, expressive harmony. The virtuoso singing of opera would be reined in and made to share the burden of expression with the orchestra. The orchestra would not be the "huge guitar" of Italian opera—a mere accompaniment—but a continuation of Weber's idea of the opera orchestra as an independent expressive voice that abstractly communicates the drama through a network of musical symbols.

A model for the operatic artwork of the future, said Wagner, could be found in ancient Greek tragedy. These plays were given in festival-like productions involving an entire community, and they were performed with the combination of poetry, dance, choral chanting, and expressive acting that suggests a total work of art. Using symbolic motives, the orchestra of future opera could be like a Greek chorus, an independent voice that continuously comments on and judges the actions presented on stage. Ultimately, Wagner's ideal for the future of the genre seemed so different from his contemporary opera that he proposed a new name for it, not opera but **music drama** (Wagner eventually found this term also to be misleading).

✵ DAS RHEINGOLD

Many of Wagner's theories on music of the future were realized in the four operas—*Das Rheingold* (*The Rhine Gold*, 1854), *Die Walküre* (*The Valkyrie*, 1856), *Siegfried* (1869), and *Götterdämmerung* (*Twilight of the Gods*, 1874)—that make up the cycle *The Ring of the Nibelung*. Wagner based his sprawling tale on characters and events drawn from Old Norse and medieval German mythology. He even imitated the literary style of his ancient sources by replacing normal rhyme with alliteration (as in "Peter Piper picked a peck of pickled peppers"). He also imitated the old figure of speech called "kenning," by which an object is named by its observed characteristics (for example, a battle becomes a "storm of swords"). As in the old sagas, certain objects—a ring, a sword, a spear—take on a broad symbolic meaning. This affected style makes the *Ring* texts difficult to read now, although they still have a literary value in themselves, and readers will find many similarities with J. R. R. Tolkien's *Lord of the Rings*.

The doings of the old gods and the deeds of medieval heroes in the *Ring* operas are only the outer shell of an underlying statement about the prospects of modern people in a society that Wagner believed to be devoid of compassion and gripped by material values. In general terms, at least, Wagner makes the symbolism of the story plain. The gold and its ring stand for wealth, which, as Alberich says, confers great power but brings with it anxiety and animosity, diminishing the capacity for love. Wealth rightly belongs only to nature, represented by the Rhine River. The magical golden tarnhelm suggests that a person in possession of wealth becomes deceptive and hypocritical, not what he seems. Wotan's dilemma arises because he, like other beings, craves material possessions, such as Valhalla. This weakness prevents him from leading the universe to a peaceful and ethical state where love can exist.

The answer to Wotan's dilemma comes only after four days of opera, during which the gods gradually stand aside and allow humanity to act freely and to discover on its own a capacity for love. The message of the *Ring* operas is both complex and

Synopsis of *The Rhine Gold*

The opera is in four scenes. In the Rhine River, mermaids, or "Rhine Maidens," frolic playfully around a horde of gold, whose beauty delights them. Alberich, one of the dwarfish Nibelungs who live in the earth, swims up and learns from the ladies that a ring made from the gold will allow its wearer to rule the world. But this person would have to renounce love, something that for them is unthinkable. To their horror, Alberich steals the gold. "I renounce love and curse it," he yells as he swims away.

The scene shifts to the mountains, where the chief god, Wotan, lives with his wife, Fricka. He proudly gazes over to his new castle, called Valhalla, which has just been built for him by giants, although Fricka is alarmed to learn that her sister Freia has been promised to the giants in payment. Wotan has no intention of giving Freia to such beasts; he is counting on his ability as a wheeler-dealer to get better terms. His shifty advisor Loge suggests paying off the giants by stealing Alberich's gold. Although Wotan is pledged to maintain ethics in the universe, he sees no alternative.

Loge and Wotan descend into the earth, where they find that Alberich has used the golden ring to enslave his fellow Nibelungs. From the treasure Alberich's brother Mime has made him a "tarnhelm," a magical mask by which he can change identity. It is clear that Alberich plans nothing less than bringing down the gods and dominating the world. To show what the tarnhelm can do, Alberich uses it to turn himself into a toad, and Wotan cleverly traps him with his foot.

Back in the mountains, Wotan demands the entire treasure for Alberich's release. He agrees, but repeats the curse of the ring; it will confer power but its owner will suffer fear and ultimately death. The owner of the ring will actually be its slave. When the giants demand the ring in addition to the rest of the treasure, Wotan refuses. Just then Erda, the mother goddess of the earth, rises up to warn Wotan that all things will perish. Give up the ring, she demands, and Wotan sullenly obeys. As they pack up their treasure, the giants argue over it and one slays the other. The ring has claimed its first victim.

Although relieved to have ransomed Freia, Wotan has a dilemma on his hands. How can he create an orderly universe in which love can flourish when he himself has had continually to break his own moral laws? He picks up a sword left over from the Nibelung's horde, and a great idea comes to him: he will turn over ethical authority to mortals acting of their own free will. In high spirits he leads the gods over a rainbow bridge toward **Valhalla.**

---

disarmingly simple: there are two great forces in the universe, Wagner says, the power of love and the power of wealth. The power of love is shown to be the higher.

To create a musical context appropriate to this titanic message, Wagner resorted to a much expanded medium and time frame. Lasting about three hours, *The Rhine Gold* is the shortest of the four operas (it is a prelude of sorts and there is no intermission); the other three last between four and five hours each. The voice parts—especially the leading male roles, given generally to the tenor voice—demand such strength and endurance that they are mastered by relatively few singers.

True to his theories, Wagner in *The Rhine Gold* dispenses with divisions into operatic numbers and creates instead a relatively continuous musical texture. Even during the changes of scenery, the music keeps going in the form of descriptive orchestral interludes. Except for the ensemble singing by the Rhine Maidens, all of the singing in the opera is soloistic—there are no choruses or other ensembles—nor is there any rigid distinction in the solo singing between recitative and aria. The voices sing in a midway style, the text always clearly audible, with the melody sometimes becoming recitational and at other times lyrical.

One of the great joys of listening to Wagner's operas is their orchestral music. No composer has ever made an orchestra sound better or more expressive than Wagner. The orchestra of the *Ring* operas is enlarged and enriched by new instruments. Wagner writes for eight French horns, and he calls for the other brass and woodwinds in fours. There are six harps and a large percussion section (sixteen anvils are needed in the interlude before Scene 3), and the composer specifies that sixty-four string players should cover the customary five lines. New instruments appear in the brass.

For example, Wagner calls for four mid-range brass instruments now called **Wagner tubas.** These are played by hornists, and together they produce an unusually mellow and dignified tone, creating the precise atmosphere that Wagner wanted us to experience when we first see Valhalla at the beginning of Scene 2.

Wagner greatly expands upon Weber's idea of giving symbolic motives to the orchestra, which allows it to comment upon and narrate elements of the drama directly. These figures are now called **leitmotives** (leading, or associative, motives) although Wagner himself did not use this term. The motives usually appear in the orchestra, sometimes migrating into the voice parts for emphasis. Some of them appear concretely and unchangingly, functioning as a musical label for a person or thing. An example is the motive that identifies the sword found by Wotan as he enters Valhalla at the end of the opera (Ex. 55-2). It is always played by the brass, usually in C major, and it surges upward energetically and climactically—all suggesting the thing that it represents.

EXAMPLE 55-2

Other motives are more flexible in their use and shadowy in their symbolism, making any labeling of them arbitrary or misleading. An example of this more subtle level of symbolism is seen by comparing the motives for the ring and for Valhalla, which are shown in Example 55-3 in their first occurrences in the opera. They are very similar, suggesting that Wagner found some underlying relation between the ring and the castle. In the final scene of *The Rhine Gold*, the so-called Entrance of the Gods into Valhalla, Wagner alternates between them to make a subtle dramatic point. As the gods gaze at the new castle, the Valhalla motive is stated repeatedly. But when Wotan comments that the castle was built from toil and care, from which it will now be a shelter, the Valhalla figure is made to resemble the motive of the ring, which is a symbol suggesting care and anxiety.

EXAMPLE 55-3

In many of Wagner's operas, the final sections of acts and scenes create a memorable climax, and this is certainly the case in the music of *The Rhine Gold* that Wagner composes for the gods as they enter their new home. The scene is unified by a central key, D♭ major, which is generally used by Wagner whenever the drama focuses on Valhalla. The passage begins with an introductory orchestral portrait of a thunderstorm, in B♭ major. Donner and Froh, the gods of thunder and rain, send out a great lightning bolt that clears away the clouds and reveals the magnificent castle in the

Wagner and Anti-Semitism

Wagner's writings contain outright and repeated hostility toward Jews, and this outlook casts a dark shadow over his undeniable greatness as an artist and musician. His first overtly anti-Semitic essay was titled "Judaism in Music," published under a pseudonym in the *Neue Zeitschrift für Musik* in 1850. Here Wagner reinforces many of the invidious stereotypes used against Jews at the time, and his anti-Semitic diatribes only increased in his later writings.

Wagner's unapologetic racism considerably advanced the acceptability in Germany of anti-Semitic thinking, which later contributed to the rise of the Nazis and, ultimately, to the unspeakable tragedy of the Holocaust. Fortunately, none of Wagner's music is overtly polluted by his racist attitudes. But his writings have made it difficult for many in the present day to listen to this music with the whole-hearted sympathy that Wagner himself asked of his audiences. Even today, Wagner's music is virtually never performed in the state of Israel.

There can be no excuse for the anti-Semitic element in Wagner's writings. Still, the modern listener must evaluate Wagner's personal failings in light of a broader range of personal and artistic factors. These include the high-minded content of his operas in general and the likelihood that Wagner would have opposed the violence inflicted upon the Jews during the Nazi period. In *Das Rheingold,* when Wotan is negotiating with the giants, his thuggish lieutenant, Donner, threatens to slay them with his hammer. Wotan—who speaks for Wagner himself—stops Donner cold. "Nothing through force!" he commands.

distance. A spectacular rainbow bridges the valley, and the gods prepare to walk triumphantly over it. But, as usual, something spoils Wotan's pleasure. The Rhine Maidens are heard from the river valley lamenting the loss of their beautiful gold. "Tell those insufferable creatures to be quiet!" he snaps to Loge. But they continue. Only in the river, the depths of nature, is there truth, they say; what is above is false and weak.

These dramatic events are shadowed by vividly descriptive orchestral music and its leitmotives. In addition to the motives already illustrated that represent the sword, the ring, and Valhalla, there are four other important motives that appear in the passage, and these are shown in Example 55-4 in their initial forms.

EXAMPLE 55-4

Rhine gold! Rhine gold! Radiant joy…

LISTENING CUE

RICHARD WAGNER
Das Rheingold (1854)
Entrance of the Gods into Valhalla

CD 9/11
Anthology, No. 154

SUMMARY

In the early nineteenth century, operas in the German language at first lagged behind the sophistication and popularity of such works coming from Italy and France. But in the hands of the composers Carl Maria von Weber and Richard Wagner, German opera became the source of new ideas. In *Der Freischütz,* Weber expands upon the old form of *Singspiel* to create an opera in which the dramatic element takes on a new emphasis. Weber was especially resourceful in making the orchestra not simply an accompaniment but, through its use of a network of musical symbols, directly expressive.

Wagner continued Weber's initiatives and strove toward a conception of opera as a dramatic genre in which text, music, and staging are balanced and integrated. Wagner elevated the literary element of opera and changed its traditional musical form by removing musical numbers in favor of a homogeneity of vocal styles and an uninterrupted continuity. A distinctive feature of his operas is the use of leitmotives in the orchestral music. These are short musical figures that symbolize elements in the drama.

His most imposing realization of his theories about opera is found in *Der Ring des Nibelungen* (*The Ring of the Nibelung*), which is a gigantic cycle of four related operas that uses ideas drawn from ancient German mythology to critique the society in which the composer lived. Since 1876 Wagner's operas have been performed in a special festival theater that he personally had constructed in the Bavarian town of Bayreuth.

KEY TERMS

Singspiel
Friedrich Kind
romantic opera
Wolf's Glen Scene
melodrama (in opera)

Bayreuth
total work of art
    (*Gesamtkunstwerk*)
music of the future
music drama

Valhalla
Wagner tuba
leitmotive

Opera in Italy: Rossini and Verdi

Italian opera in the nineteenth century was more closely linked to operatic traditions than was its German counterpart, and it was more in line with the spirit of its own time than with any utopian "music of the future." During the nineteenth century, the leading Italian composers guardedly expanded upon traditional operatic

🌀 FIGURE 56-1

One of the most popular and influential composers of the nineteenth century, Gioachino Rossini was also an accomplished chef and famous for his wit.

form based on the familiar musical numbers of aria, duet, ensemble, and chorus, all inherited from the eighteenth century. Italian librettos adhered to familiar subjects—especially the tragedy brought on by irreconcilable human desires. Singers continued to rule the genre, just as they had in the eighteenth century. The intention of the Italian opera composer was, as always, to please the audience, and the leading figures were extraordinarily successful in doing this.

The most successful of the early nineteenth-century Italian composers of opera was Gioachino Rossini (1792–1868; Fig. 56-1), whose works were performed and acclaimed all over the world. In 1823 the French novelist Stendhal extravagantly declared Rossini to be a second Napoleon:

> Napoleon is dead; but a new conqueror has already shown himself to the world; and from Moscow to Naples, from London to Vienna, from Paris to Calcutta, his name is constantly on every tongue. The fame of this hero knows no bounds save those of civilization itself.[1]

Later in the century, the operas of Giuseppe Verdi (1813–1901) provoked similar raves. Following the premiere of Verdi's *Otello* in Milan in 1887, the composer's carriage was mobbed by the ecstatic audience, the horses unleashed, and the wagon then partly carried, partly pulled by the composer's admirers to his hotel. Verdi's wife insisted that this enthusiasm came ultimately from an appreciation of the music: "This passionate demonstration comes from a high esteem, an affection that is heavy with understanding," she wrote.

✳ GIOACHINO ROSSINI

Rossini brought the various strands of Italian opera of the early nineteenth century into a classic form that was maintained, at least in general outline, for nearly a hundred years in the hands of his successors Vincenzo Bellini (1801–1835), Gaetano Donizetti (1797–1848), Giuseppe Verdi, and Giacomo Puccini (1858–1924). Rossini was born in Pesaro, on the Adriatic coast, to a family of musicians, and he grew up in Bologna in north central Italy. Here he attended the local conservatory, the Liceo Musicale, and began to compose. His career as a major opera composer was launched when he was only eighteen years old, and over the next ten years he composed no fewer than thirty operas. During this time he traveled almost constantly between cities where his works were staged, especially the Italian opera capitals of Venice, Rome, Milan, and Naples.

His works were soon taken up by opera companies outside of Italy, and his presence was in demand all over Europe. In 1822 he visited Vienna for a festival of his operas and found himself a celebrity there. During his stay in Vienna he met Beethoven. In 1823 Rossini settled in Paris and became director of the Théâtre-Italien (see Chapter 53), and here he wrote operas in French for the Paris Opéra. After *Guillaume Tell* (*William Tell*, 1829), he went into a forty-year retirement, wrote no further operas, and lived alternately in Italy and France.

Rossini specialized in operatic composition. He wrote thirty-nine operas in all, some of which are French revisions of earlier works in Italian. Additionally, he composed music for the church, including several Masses and a *Stabat mater* (1832). Toward the end of his life he wrote a large number of small, lighthearted pieces—mainly songs and piano music—which he called *Péchés de vieillesse* (*Sins of Old Age*).

The Barber of Seville

Early in his meteoric career, Rossini concentrated on comic opera, later on serious opera, although the musical styles and forms in either type had by the nineteenth century become largely interchangeable. The typical early Rossini opera begins with an overture, although this is sometimes omitted in his later works. As in opera of the preceding century, acts are divided into a succession of musical numbers—arias, duets, other ensembles, and choruses. In the early operas, the numbers are connected by **simple recitative** (accompanied by a keyboard instrument, or sometimes by the cello or bass), although Rossini subsequently dropped this old-fashioned element. He retained passages of recitative accompanied by the orchestra, and these usually function as introductions or transitions within a number.

The elimination of simple recitative made it necessary for the narrative aspect of his operas to be absorbed into the regular musical numbers, and this caused Rossini to make these numbers longer and mixed in style. Such complex numbers were already found in earlier Italian opera in the finales of acts, which typically consist of several sections in different tempos, and mix together ensemble, choral, and soloistic singing.

Il barbiere di Siviglia (*The Barber of Seville*, 1816) is by far Rossini's most famous opera. The steps through which it came into existence provide a vivid example of the way the Italian opera business worked at this time. Rossini signed a contract for a new opera with the **impresario** (manager) of a theater in Rome (he agreed on a fee that was less than half that of the company's leading singer). He had only a few weeks to compose the new work (which was plenty of time for Rossini), he had to use whatever libretto the impresario provided, and he agreed to conduct the initial performances from the keyboard.

The impresario hired a local amateur writer, Cesare Sterbini, to come up with a comic libretto. Sterbini then dashed one off by revising two well-known sources—Beaumarchais's French play *Le barbier de Séville* (*The Barber of Seville*, 1775) and the libretto of an Italian comic opera by Giovanni Paisiello (1782) that was itself based on Beaumarchais's famous comedy. Rossini needed only about three weeks to compose the music, in part because the forms making up an opera at the time were well established and because he had no hesitation about borrowing musical passages from earlier works that would be unknown to his audience. In other operas, Rossini occasionally farmed out the composing of some of the music to an assistant (much as film composers do today). Many of the characters of *The Barber of Seville* will be familiar from Mozart's *Marriage of Figaro* (see Chapter 48), because both operas are based on related comedies by Beaumarchais, *Marriage* being a sequel to *Barber*.

Although the first performance of *The Barber of Seville* was greeted by an uproar provoked by various staging mishaps, the work became an instant success, its fame soon spreading over the whole world. The *Barber's* popularity has never waned. Hans von Bülow, long an associate of Richard Wagner, found its greatness in its whole-hearted acceptance of its own genre, needing none of the reform that Wagner found necessary:

> In this work there is an eternal youthfulness that mocks the ravages of time. It is a bouquet of flowers that never fade and keep their full fragrance, a champagne euphoria

---

Synopsis of *The Barber of Seville*

The young Count Almaviva, disguised as a poor student, tries to attract the attention of the lovely Rosina, who lives in Seville with her guardian, Dr. Bartolo. The count turns for advice to his former servant, Figaro, now a barber, who hatches a series of schemes to get Almaviva into Bartolo's house and in touch with Rosina. Bartolo has plans to marry Rosina himself, and he is ready to use any and all means to defeat Almaviva. After a series of ludicrous escapades, misunderstandings, and changes of disguise, the Count reveals his true identity to Rosina and proposes marriage. Seeing that he is defeated, Bartolo blesses their union. (The opera is in two acts, although in some editions and performances the first act is divided in two.)

---

with no morning after. In brief, this *Barber* remains a truly classic opera, since this term describes "whatever pleases everywhere and for all times."[2]

The music for *The Barber of Seville* exemplifies Rossini's early style, which is fairly close to that found in such eighteenth-century models as Mozart's *Marriage of Figaro*. The work is strictly a number opera because it consists musically of self-contained pieces (arias, ensembles, and choruses). These are separated by simple recitative, in which the story is pushed forward. Applause could be expected at the end of each number, bringing the opera to a complete halt, and a number would be repeated immediately if the audience demanded it.

The first number of Act 1 following the overture is an example of a special type of operatic piece called an *introduzione,* or **introduction.** These were regularly found in comic operas of the late eighteenth and early nineteenth centuries (Mozart's *Don Giovanni* and *Magic Flute,* for example, begin with introductions). The introduction balances the finale, the last number of an act, since both are relatively long and multi-sectional, made from a succession of contrasting passages that mix choral, ensemble and solo singing.

The introduction in *Barber* has a symmetric and entirely self-contained **ABA'** form. Brief transitions between the sections are accomplished by recitative accompanied by the orchestra. The first section is devoted mainly to the singing of a chorus of musicians whom Fiorello (a servant of the Count) has quietly positioned in front of Bartolo's house to accompany the Count in singing a serenade below Rosina's window. The second section is aria-like, a love song "Ecco ridente in cielo" ("Look, Smiling in Heaven") that is filled with an overblown sentimentality. The third section begins with a reprise of the melodies of the first section, but this is soon interrupted when the musicians are paid and create a comic hubbub—just what the love-struck Count was hoping to avoid.

Our attention in the introduction is drawn mainly to the second of its three sections, which contains the Count's aria-like serenade. This has a two-part form already encountered in the aria "Abscheulicher!" from Beethoven's *Fidelio* (see Chapter 50), although here the form is shorter and simpler. Rossini calls it a **cavatina,** which is his term for an entrance aria. (Recall that Beethoven had used this term, although in an entirely different way, for the slow movement of his String Quartet in B♭ Major, Op. 130.)

The first of the two parts of the aria covers two stanzas of text. The music is slow in tempo, intensely lyrical, and strophic in form—all typical features of the begin-

The Audience Greets the Barber

The opening night of *The Barber of Seville* in Rome's Teatro Argentina was a fiasco. Rossini's biographer, Alexis-Jacob Azevedo, reports:

... The crowning disaster occurred when, during the wonderful finale [of Act 1], a cat appeared on stage and ran among the singers. The excellent Figaro, Zamboni, shooed it off to one side but it returned from the other and leapt up onto the leg of Bartolo-Botticelli. The hapless pupil of the doctor and respectable Marceline [Berta], fearing a scratch, nimbly avoided the prodigious leaps of the crazed animal, which paid attention only to the sword of the police guard. The charitable audience called to it, imitated its meowing, and with yells and gestures egged it on in its improvised role. An athletic young fellow seated in the middle of the parterre—he wasn't part of the claque, that's for sure—found the finale too serious, climbed up on his seat and called out in a loud voice, 'It's a funeral ....' " [3]

ning of the traditional two-part aria. The second part is fast and full of vocal fireworks, the sort of passage that was called a cabaletta at the time. It covers two additional poetic stanzas, of which the second is extended by repetitions within the text. Here the tenor shows how many notes he can sing (he probably would have extemporaneously added to the already considerable number of ornaments written out by the composer).

The third section begins as a simple reprise of the opening part, but, when the musicians erupt in excitement, the tempo shifts to *allegro vivace* for a climactic final passage called a **stretta.** Rossini sharpens the sense of climax at this point by bringing in one of his trademarks: the so-called **Rossini crescendo.** This is made from a series of crescendos that coincide with repetitions of ever-shorter phrases, a steady thickening of orchestration, and an ever-quicker harmonic motion.

LISTENING CUE

GIOACHINO ROSSINI
The Barber of Seville (1816)
Act 1, No. 1 (*Introduzione*)

CD 9/12–13
Anthology, No. 155

GIUSEPPE VERDI

In a letter of 1898, Giuseppe Verdi reflected on the importance to him of the works of Rossini: "I cannot help believing that *The Barber of Seville,* for abundance of ideas, for comic verve, and for truth of declamation, is the most beautiful comic opera in existence." In Verdi's operas the spirit of Rossini is very much alive as Verdi continues to expand the basic forms inherited from Rossini and makes Rossini's marriage of music and drama ever more intimate. At the same time, Verdi modernized Italian opera, making it into a more realistic dramatic entity and bringing to it the advances in orchestration and harmony that characterize the later nineteenth century.

Verdi was born in a small village, Roncole, in north Italy. Roncole is about fifteen miles from the city of Parma, which was the seat of government of a small duchy that from 1814 was ruled by a relative of the Austrian Hapsburg emperors. Much of Italy during Verdi's life was either directly ruled by or closely allied to Austria, a situation that offended the composer's patriotic sensibilities and formed a subject touched on explosively in his early operas. As a child he showed a prodigious gift for music, and in 1832 he moved to Milan to further his musical education, but at the age of eighteen he was found too old to be accepted at the Conservatory in Milan, so he studied privately instead.

In 1839 Verdi's first opera, *Oberto*, was performed in Milan at the **Teatro alla Scala,** and its impresario, Bartolomeo Merelli, then commissioned additional works. One of these was *Nabucco*, based on the biblical story of King Nebuchadnezzar, which scored a huge success at La Scala in 1842 and launched Verdi's international operatic career. Like Rossini before him, Verdi capitalized on his fame by quickly composing new operas and traveling constantly among theaters to oversee new productions. He lived abroad for long periods, especially in Paris, and then from 1857 settled on a farm near the town in which he was born. From about 1874, after completing a Requiem Mass in honor of the Italian patriot and novelist Alessandro Manzoni (1785–1873), Verdi composed less, although in his final years he returned to the stage with two operas based on Shakespearean subjects, *Otello* (1887) and *Falstaff* (1893).

One of Verdi's last concerns was the founding in the city of Milan of the Casa di Riposo per Musicisti—a retirement home for musicians that still exists. Following his death in 1901, the composer donated his considerable wealth to support this home, and it is where he and his wife, Giuseppina Strepponi, are buried.

❋ VERDI AND THE *RISORGIMENTO*

Verdi composed twenty-eight operas and relatively little else, although his great Requiem is frequently heard. His early operas became symbols of the **Risorgimento** (resurgence), which was the movement toward Italian political and social unification that began after Napoleon's defeat in 1814 and culminated in 1870, when virtually all of Italy was at last brought into a single nation under the leadership of King Victor Emmanuel II. Although Verdi's energies were almost totally claimed by his musical career, he was plainly sympathetic to the objectives of the *Risorgimento*. In his operas, his countrymen found many supportive allusions to their hopes of ridding Italy of Austrian domination. Often the leading characters in his operas choose duty, even death, over personal happiness. Frequently, two nations are at war, one of which is easily identified with the Austrians, the other with the Italians. For example, in the story of the opera *I lombardi alla prima crociata* (*The Lombards at the First Crusade*, 1843), Italians from the region of Lombardy (an ancient kingdom surrounding the city of Milan) battle the Saracens in the crusades. Those in Verdi's audience immediately saw the parallel with Italy and Austria in their own day, and they responded enthusiastically to the leading character's call for war to liberate a Holy Land.

In 1859 Verdi was all the more closely identified with the cause of Italian unification when warfare between the Kingdom of Sardinia (which encompassed not only the island of Sardinia but also much of northern Italy) erupted with Austria. Many in the *Risorgimento* thought that an alliance with Sardinia and its king, Victor Emmanuel II, was the best way of achieving unification for all of Italy. Their patriotic cry was "Viva VERDI!" which evoked both the name of their compatriot composer

Synopsis of *Otello*

The action takes place on the island of Cyprus, an outpost of the Republic of Venice. The fearless soldier Othello ("Otello" is the Italian equivalent) has battled the Turks and, as the opera begins, his ship returns to port in a fearsome storm. The storm abates, the ship arrives, and Othello announces that victory has been won. All are elated except for the soldier Iago, who hates Othello and schemes to bring him down. Iago leads a drinking song, which produces a drunken brawl that Othello quells, after which he sings a love duet with his wife, Desdemona (in Italian, pronounced des-DAY-mona). Iago sings a "credo" in which he asserts that we are the fools of fate, and all is false

and meaningless. Slyly, Iago plants seeds of doubt in Othello's mind, hinting that Desdemona is having an affair with Cassio, Othello's lieutenant. He offers a contrived proof by planting in Cassio's pocket Desdemona's handkerchief, which is seen by the jealous Othello.

Preparing for bed, Desdemona senses that she will be murdered by Othello. She sings the "Willow Song" of a lovelorn girl who sadly faced the grave, then a prayer-like "Ave Maria." Othello silently enters her bedchamber, kisses her, then strangles her despite her avowals of fidelity to him. Her maid calls for help, and Iago's lies are explained to him. Othello stabs himself and dies after one final kiss for his dead wife.

and an acronym for their king, **V**ittorio **E**manuele **R**e d'**I**talia (Victor Emmanuel, King of Italy).

Otello

By the time Italian unification was finally completed in 1870, Verdi (Fig. 56-2) had become cynical about politics, and he turned in his later operas to purely musical and dramatic matters. He closely oversaw the creation of his librettos, favoring tragic subjects drawn from classic literature. In *Otello* Verdi and his librettist, Arrigo Boito (1842–1918), turned to Shakespeare's tragedy *Othello*. As usual in the creation of an opera libretto, the literary model was preserved only in its characters and external action. Little of Shakespeare's memorable poetry or subtlety of characterization is kept, as Boito flattens the roles into types, changes the narrative to allow for traditional operatic numbers, and simplifies the action.

Vestiges of number opera from the days of Rossini are still visible in *Otello*. The first act, for example, consists of four numbers: a chorus depicting the storm in which Othello's boat is caught, a second chorus during which the townsfolk celebrate by a bonfire, a drinking duet for Iago and Cassio (a cliché of Italian opera called a **brindisi**), and a love duet for Othello and Desdemona.

But, unlike an opera by Rossini, these are not free-standing divisions, since they are connected without pause by interludes that push the story forward. The interludes are themselves complex, consisting of a quick alternation of solo singing, ensemble, chorus, and recitation. The numbers themselves are equally complex, not the simple duets and choruses of earlier years but more fluid and dramatic passages that mix together bits of soloistic singing into an ensemble or choral context. It is characteristic of Verdi's later works that he diminishes the importance of the large aria as the principal means of expression, replacing it with duets and choruses. The dramatic role of the orchestra is also much increased by its capacity vividly to depict images and emotions.

🌼 FIGURE 56-2

In 1877, when this portrait was made, Giuseppe Verdi had entered retirement to rest on the laurels of his Requiem Mass and the worldwide success of *Aida*, his last opera. But his creative spark was soon to be fanned by the prospect of composing a new opera based on Shakespeare's *Othello*.

Bridgeman Art Library

The opera's climactic fourth act also has four main musical numbers, and in this instance they agree with the division of the act into four **scenes** (a scene is a passage calling a particular selection of characters to the stage). After introductory measures in the orchestra, the first scene is devoted to an aria-like song for Desdemona, the famous "Willow Song," which is cast in a strophic form with recitational introduction and coda. The second scene follows without pause and contains Desdemona's "Ave Maria," a prayer to the Virgin in simple ternary form. Like the brindisi of Act 1, the prayer scene, or **preghiera,** was a common feature of Verdian opera.

The murder scene follows, and musically it has no precedent in traditional Italian opera because it does not rely primarily on singing to convey its dramatic message. Instead, it is the orchestra—its motivic symbolism, harmonic language, and tonal plan—that takes over the burden of affective communication. The voices are confined to a more rudimentary declamation of their lines.

The scene opens with a gripping orchestral portrait of Othello's inner conflict, incoherence, and confusion. Two fragmentary melodic ideas alternate—one in the basses and the other in the celli (marked A and B in Ex. 56-1)—and these represent Othello's love for Desdemona versus his murderous jealousy. The tonal plan in this virtual tone poem provides no coherence because the keys constantly change and conflict.

EXAMPLE 56-1

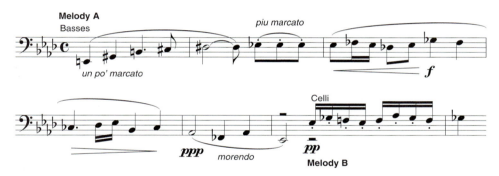

Finally, Othello arrives at the bedside of the sleeping Desdemona, draws back the curtains, and kisses her. At this moment the theme that accompanied their kiss in the love duet of Act 1 returns in the same taut key of E major (Ex. 56-2). Othello's accusations and Desdemona's denials follow, in a tortured crescendo in which the jealousy motive in the orchestra takes complete control.

EXAMPLE 56-2

LISTENING CUE

GIUSEPPE VERDI
Otello (1887)
Act 4, scene 3

CD 10/1
Anthology, No. 156

The fourth scene of Act 4 is like the familiar operatic finale. The singing is mainly devoted to an ensemble of all the remaining characters, and the music moves through several contrasting sections. Here the drama is brought to a denouement.

 ## VERDI AND WAGNER

Many of the new ideas that Verdi introduced to Italian opera in *Otello* are similar to those encountered in the operas of Richard Wagner (see Chapter 55). The murder scene is especially like a scene from Wagner, in which a climactic dramatic action is presented by declamation intensified by orchestration, harmony, motivic symbolism, and key scheme. The continuity in *Otello*—promoted by connecting the sections and by the symbolic motive of the kiss that returns outside of the boundaries of a single number—has an obvious resonance in Wagner's theory of operatic structure. The enriched harmonies of the kiss motive may sound more like those of Wagner than Verdi.

But Verdi was indignant over the idea that he had copied from Wagner. To his publisher, Ricordi, he dismissed the allegation that ". . . after all I was an imitator of Wagner!!! What a fine result after twenty-five years, to end up as an *Imitator*!!!"[4] Although Verdi rarely had anything good to say about Germans, he recognized Wagner's importance. Upon learning of Wagner's death in 1883, he again wrote to Ricordi: "A great individualist has disappeared! A name that leaves a very powerful mark on the history of Art!!! Addio, addio."[5]

It is unlikely that Verdi was directly influenced by Wagner. Instead, both Wagner and Verdi were influenced by a common spirit in music of their time, which encouraged formal continuity, plausible drama, and harmonic intricacy. It is not surprising that their music should have evolved to produce similarities.

SUMMARY

Italian opera of the nineteenth century was closely linked to operatic traditions. The leading composers, including Gioachino Rossini and Giuseppe Verdi, expanded in an orderly way upon traditional operatic form based on a division into familiar musical numbers. Rossini's *The Barber of Seville* (1816) is a comic opera that is especially close to the form of eighteenth-century works. Its libretto is based upon a comic farce by Beaumarchais, and Rossini's music is made from a succession of arias, duets, ensembles, and choruses linked together by simple recitative.

As a "modern" composer of the late nineteenth century, Verdi enriched Rossini's forms. In his opera *Otello*—based on Shakespeare's tragedy—music is used to create a plausible drama. The "kiss motive" heard in the first act recurs in the fourth act, to link the music organically to the drama, and the old operatic numbers, though still in evidence, are made more complex and linked together continuously.

KEY TERMS

simple recitative
impresario
introduction (as an
    operatic number)

cavatina (in Rossini's operas)
stretta
Rossini crescendo
Teatro alla Scala

Risorgimento
brindisi
scene
preghiera

Nationalism and Virtuosity: Franz Liszt

By the middle of the nineteenth century, a new consciousness of national identity began to appear in many parts of the world. The birth of **nationalism**—the love for and allegiance to one's region of birth and its people, culture, and language—occurred in Europe in the aftermath of Napoleonic imperialism. Previously, the concept of nationhood was limited or dim, and personal allegiances were more typically directed to a sovereign ruler rather than to a native land. But this circumstance began to change as Napoleon's conquests in the early nineteenth century placed many distant parts of Europe under French domination. After Napoleon's overthrow in 1814, nationalism became a powerful political factor in the reorganization of European culture.

It was expressed principally in two related movements: one toward political unification of people having a common language, and the other toward independence from foreign rule. The strivings toward unification were felt most strongly on the Italian peninsula and in German lands, and these areas achieved political unification in 1861 and 1871, respectively. Foreign rule of whole nations remained widespread in Europe even by the mid-nineteenth century. Poles and Finns were still governed by Russians, Italians by Austrians, and Rumanians by Hungarians.

The frictions created by these political alignments were especially heated in the Austrian Empire. At the time of the Congress of Vienna (1814–1815), the sprawling lands of the Hapsburg rulers—which formed Austria in the broad sense—came to include most of Italy and Eastern Europe, in addition to the ancestral Hapsburg lands in modern-day Austria. The Hapsburgs themselves were Germans by language, but their kingdom contained many nationalities vying for independence. The most powerful of these were the Hungarians, who in 1867 were granted a privileged status by the formation of the so-called **Austro-Hungarian Monarchy.**

As the century progressed, growing nationalistic sentiments made an important mark on music. We have seen in Chapter 56 how the texts of Verdi's early operas were influenced by the desire, shared by the composer's Italian countrymen, to escape from the rule of Austria and to establish an independent homeland. Other composers used their music to celebrate their nation and its history. This was done on a broad scale by the Czech composer **Bedřich Smetana** (1824–1884) in his cycle of six orchestral works called *Má vlast* (*My Fatherland*, 1874–1879).

Many composers looked into the soul of their own people by collecting and arranging the folk songs of their native lands. These materials, which seemed to embody the spirit of a nation, were often brought into original compositions. In Chapter 59 we will encounter a group of Russian musicians of the late nineteenth century, called the *kuchka* (handful) or "The Five," who demonstrated a special affinity for folk song. One of them, Nicolai Rimsky-Korsakov (1844–1908), arranged and published one hundred forty Russian folk songs, which contained for him "pictures of the ancient pagan period and spirit" of his land. The symphonies and operas of the Czech composer Antonín Dvořák (1841–1904) often evoke the folk songs and dances of his native land. Even the most cosmopolitan of nineteenth-century composers sometimes wrote nationalistic music. One of them is Franz Liszt (1811–1886), probably the greatest pianist of the century and a musician at home virtually anywhere in the world.

✸ LISZT'S LIFE AND WORKS

Liszt was born in the village of Raiding, some fifty miles south of Vienna. This town lies just inside the Hungarian regions of the Hapsburg Empire. Although Liszt's family spoke German, many of his ancestors were Hungarians, and Liszt gradually came to think of Hungary as his true homeland. "I remain from my birth to the grave Magyar in heart and mind," he wrote in 1873.[1]

His father was a good amateur cellist and an employee of the Esterházy family—Haydn's patrons of old. When the young Liszt's prodigious talent as a pianist was revealed, the elder Liszt gave up his position to promote his son's musical development and career. The first step was education. In 1821 the Liszt family moved to Vienna, where Franz became a student of Carl Czerny in piano and Antonio Salieri in composition. Czerny took the 11-year-old wunderkind to play for his own teacher, Beethoven, and Liszt later recalled the occasion:

> Beethoven asked me whether I could play a Bach fugue. I chose the C-minor fugue from the Well-Tempered Clavier. "And could you also transpose the fugue at once into another key?" Beethoven asked me. Fortunately I was able to do so. After my closing chord I glanced up. The great master's darkly glowing gaze lay piercingly upon me. Yet suddenly a gentle smile passed over his gloomy features, and Beethoven came quite close to me, stooped down, put his hand on my head, and stroked my hair several times. "A devil of a fellow," he whispered. . . ."[2]

Next came European tours, during which the child prodigy traveled as far as Paris and London, amazing all who heard him. Liszt and his father settled in Paris in 1823, and his tours continued to take him far and wide. He composed primarily for his own instrument, and in Paris he became a close acquaintance of both Berlioz and Chopin (see Chapter 53).

His personal life proved controversial even in a period when artists often felt unconstrained by accepted principles of morality. In 1834 he began an affair with the French writer Marie d'Agoult (1805–1876; see Box), who left her husband and child to live and travel with Liszt (Fig. 57-1). Although they never married, they had three children, including Cosima Liszt (1837–1930), later the wife of Richard Wagner. Liszt and Marie drifted apart in the 1840s, whereupon Liszt took up with a wealthy Russian-Polish Princess, Carolyne von Sayn-Wittgenstein (1819–1887). She would be his principal companion for the remainder of his life, although the two never married.

During the period from 1839 to 1847, Liszt undertook virtually nonstop touring and performing, which brought him to the four corners of Europe and to a level of fame and adulation never before achieved by a musician. He was swarmed by his admirers in a way now known only to rock stars. Heinrich Heine described his emotional effect on his audiences as **Lisztomania.** Although travel at this time was still done largely by horse-drawn carriage, Liszt performed in more than one hundred seventy cities in this eight-year span.

He retired from his grueling tours in 1848 and settled into a position as conductor of the court orchestra in Weimar. This

 FIGURE 57-1

Ary Scheffer, "Liszt in Geneva," 1835. "He was tall and extremely thin. His face was pale and his large sea-green eyes shone like a wave when the sunlight catches it" (Marie d'Agoult describes her first glimpse of Liszt).

LISZT.

Bridgeman Art Library

Marie d'Agoult

At a musical gathering in Paris in 1833, Countess Marie d'Agoult caught her first glimpse of Franz Liszt. "A wonderful apparition appeared before my eyes," she recalled in her *Memoirs* about the 21-year-old pianist. "I can find no other word to describe the sensation aroused in me by the most extraordinary person I had ever seen. He was tall and extremely thin. His face was pale and his large sea-green eyes shone like a wave when the sunlight catches it." That night, so the Countess recalled, her sleep was disrupted by bizarre dreams.

Her attraction to Liszt was plain enough, but Marie at the time was married and the mother of two small children. She aspired to be a writer, not just a wealthy pa-

troness of the arts, so in 1835 she abandoned her family for a daring artistic alliance with Franz Liszt. The pair lived alternately in Paris, Switzerland, and Italy, and three children were born to them.

Liszt's concertizing made any semblance of family life impossible. Marie returned in 1840 to Paris with the children, and her relationship with Liszt gradually deteriorated. In 1844 the two finally broke up, and Marie worked out her bitterness at Liszt in a novel called *Nélida*, which became a bestseller in France. The heroine, Nélida, is plainly a self-portrait. She falls in love with an artist, Guermann Regnier (Liszt in disguise). Guermann treats her shabbily, dreams only of cheap success, and finally abandons her. With this, his creativity vanishes.

Bridgeman Art Library

✹ FIGURE 57-2
Henri Lehmann, portrait of Marie d'Agoult, 1839.

town in eastern Germany was the seat of government of a small duchy called Saxe-Weimar, and it was earlier home to the great writers Goethe and Friedrich von Schiller (1759–1805), and earlier still to J.S. Bach. Here, Liszt led the orchestra in concerts and operatic performances, and his interests as a composer came to include orchestral music. In his programming he was a stalwart supporter of modern compositions, and he conducted new works by Hector Berlioz and Richard Wagner that at the time were still baffling to many audiences.

In 1861 Liszt resigned from his position in Weimar and moved to Rome, where he found solitude in the company of priests and monks. In 1865 he took the lower orders of the Catholic priesthood, which allowed him to use the title "abbé" but did not seriously interfere with his lifestyle. From 1869 until his death he alternated residences among Rome, Weimar, and Budapest, giving master classes, composing, and occasionally playing the piano in public. He died in 1886 in Bayreuth, where he had gone to hear Wagner's operas and visit with his daughter Cosima. Liszt is buried in Bayreuth.

Liszt composed an astonishingly large amount of music, more than seven hundred compositions in all. More than a hundred pieces are for solo piano, and Liszt also made important contributions to the orchestral, choral, and song literature.

His solo piano music includes a Sonata in B Minor (1853) and character pieces of all types, some gathered into collections with titles such as *Années de pèlerinage* (*Years of Pilgrimage*), *Harmonies poétiques et religieuses* (*Poetic and Religious Harmonies*), and *Légendes* (*Legends*). His études for piano reach to new levels of technical difficulty, and many of his piano works incorporate national or folk-like themes. These include *Hungarian Rhapsodies,* to be discussed momentarily, which are artistic arrangements of Hungarian and Gypsy music.

The arrangement was one of Liszt's most distinctive specialties. From existing songs, symphonies, and operas, he made some two hundred such transcriptions and paraphrases for piano, creating concert pieces out of a hitherto functional type of music. Toward the end of his life he wrote a series of small piano works whose spareness and unusual harmonic materials are unlike anything in music before their time.

His orchestral music includes thirteen **symphonic poems** (discussed below), two programmatic symphonies (*A Faust Symphony*, 1854–1857, and *A Symphony on Dante's "Divine Comedy,"* 1856), and two piano concertos. He found time also to write a large number of songs and works for chorus that include Masses and the oratorios *The Legend of St. Elizabeth* (1862) and *Christus* (1867). Liszt almost entirely avoided chamber music and opera.

 ## LISZT AND THE PIANO

Partly for practical reasons, during his tours from 1839 to 1847 Liszt dispensed with the traditional format of the piano concert, which earlier had required hiring an orchestra and bringing in singers to perform operatic excerpts. Instead, he played either entirely alone or with only a few other performers, creating a new type of concert called the **recital.**

His repertory was broad and highly original. He continued to present the staples of earlier piano concerts, including showy character pieces of his own composition, fantasies and variations upon popular operatic tunes, and improvisations. To these he added his massively virtuosic transcriptions of music originating in other media—the symphonies of Beethoven, for example—and he began to present classics from the past, including Beethoven piano sonatas, fugues by J.S. Bach, and sonatas by Domenico Scarlatti.

Liszt usually played from memory, something still unusual at the time, and he often alternated among several different pianos placed on the stage. His appearance—tall, thin, with shoulder-length black hair, often bedecked with medals and wearing a ceremonial sword—was straight from Hollywood. Between numbers he typically walked into the audience to chat with his fans.

Hungarian Rhapsody No. 15 ("Rákóczy March")

Liszt's music for piano adheres to no uniform style. Some works are lengthy, others relatively short. Some are original compositions, and many others are artistic transcriptions and arrangements of music by other composers. Some are relatively easy to play while others approach the very limits of human dexterity. Some are bombastic and grandiloquent, others understated.

His *Hungarian Rhapsodies* for piano illustrate the virtuosic side of Liszt's musical imagination as well as the element of nationalism that he brought periodically into his works. In 1839 he returned to Hungary to give concerts following an absence of sixteen years, and there he found himself a national hero. His consciousness of

At a Liszt Recital

The Russian journalist Vladimir Stasov heard Liszt play in St. Petersburg in 1842 and reported:

> Just at that moment Liszt, noting the time, walked down from the gallery, elbowed his way through the crowd and moved quickly toward the stage. But instead of using the steps he leaped onto the platform. He tore off his white kid gloves and tossed them on the floor, under the piano. Then after bowing low in all directions to a tumult of applause such as had probably not been heard in Petersburg since 1703 [the year the city was founded], he seated himself at the piano. Instantly the hall became deadly silent. Without any preliminaries Liszt began playing the opening cello phrase of the *William Tell* Overture [by Rossini]. As soon as he finished the overture and while the hall was still rocking with applause, he moved swiftly to a second piano facing the opposite direction. . . . On this occasion Liszt also played the Andante from *Lucia* [*di Lammermoor,* by Gaetano Donizetti], his fantasy on Mozart's *Don Giovanni,* piano transcriptions of Schubert's [songs] "Ständchen" and "Erl-könig," Beethoven's [song] "Adelaide" and in conclusion his own [*Grand*] *Galop chromatique.*
>
> We had never in our lives heard anything like this. We had never been in the presence of such a brilliant, passionate, demonic temperament, at one moment rushing like a whirlwind, at another pouring forth cascades of tender beauty and grace.[3]

Liszt elevated the piano to a new status. In his playing, and in his compositions for the instrument, he showed the piano's capacity to rival the newly expanded orchestra. He demonstrated that pianists could rise above previous limitations of technique and make the instrument create unsus-

pected new sounds and expressive effects. "My piano is to me what his vessel is to the sailor, his horse to the Arab," Liszt wrote:

> Nay even more, till now it has been myself, my speech, my life. It is the repository of all that stirred my nature in the passionate days of my youth. I confided to it all my desires, my dreams, my joys, and my sorrows. Its strings vibrated to my emotions, and its keys obeyed my every caprice.[4]

Bridgeman Art Library

🌸 FIGURE 57-3

An 1845 caricature of Liszt in typical recital mode.

himself as a Hungarian was awakened, and he began to collect Hungarian melodies and make brilliant arrangements of them for use in his concerts.

Liszt came to view these pieces as tantamount to a Hungarian national epic, told in music rather than in words. Just as the *Iliad* and *Odyssey*—the epic stories of ancient Greece and its people—were recited in public by professional orators called rhapsodes, Liszt saw himself as the rhapsode of his Hungarian musical epic. He wrote:

> By the word **"Rhapsody"** the intention has been to designate the fantastically *epic* element which we deem this music to contain. Each one of these productions has always seemed to us to form part of a poetic cycle, remarkable by the unity of its inspiration, eminently national. The conditions of this unity are fulfilled by the music belonging exclusively to the one people whose soul and intimate sentiments it accurately depicts; sentiments moreover which are nowhere else so well expressed and which are cast into a form proper to this one nation; having been invented and practiced exclusively by them.[5]

Between 1851 and 1853 he selected fifteen of his Hungarian arrangements—most of which were revisions of pieces from the 1840s—and published them as a loose cycle of *Hungarian Rhapsodies*. Later in his career he added several more works with this title.

But what is the "Hungarian" music that forms the basis of Liszt's rhapsodies? The composer pondered this question at length. The Magyars—those who spoke Hungarian as their native language—formed only one of many ethnic groups living side by side in the lands thought of as Hungary. The Magyars were primarily farmers who, according to Liszt, showed no particular genius for music.

Living in their midst were Gypsies, nomadic people who were often professional musicians of great skill. Liszt considered them and their music to be just as Hungarian as that of the Magyars. Gypsy bands—typically featuring a solo violin and a dulcimer called the **cimbalom**—were popular throughout Hungary, where they played dance music and flashy improvisations on folk or traditional melodies. Their music, which Liszt had heard even as a child, had many other distinctive features. It was often based on a **Gypsy scale,** which is a minor scale with raised fourth and seventh degrees. These alterations produce two augmented seconds in the scale, as seen in this example on the keynote D: D E F G♯ A B♭ C♯ D. Gypsy music typically had a flexibility of rhythm and meter, and in spirit it could be subdued, or rise to the level of "a furious orgy of wild beasts," as Liszt described it.

In his *Hungarian Rhapsody* No. 15 (published in 1853), we see Liszt mingle together aspects of Gypsy and Magyar music. The piece is an arrangement of the "Rákóczy March," which in Liszt's day had become a patriotic favorite among Hungarians, played by military bands and Gypsy ensembles alike. Liszt described the march to Marie d'Agoult as "a kind of aristocratic Hungarian *Marseillaise*" (the *Marseillaise* is the national anthem of France). The composer of the march has never been conclusively identified, but he was probably a minor Hungarian composer active around the year 1800. The march was named in honor of Francis II Rákóczy (1676–1735), who led Hungarian armies in an uprising against their Hapsburg overlords that in 1707 created a short-lived independent republic.

The "Rákóczy March" is typical of the band march around 1800. It has a duple meter and opens with several themes that are repeated in symmetrical fashion. These lead to a contrasting section, called the **trio,** then to a reprise of the opening music. Its main themes are shown in Example 57-1.

EXAMPLE 57-1

First theme

Tempo di Marcia animato

First trio theme

Un poco meno allegro

Liszt interprets this familiar framework as though the march were played by a Gyspy band (which it frequently was). An introduction lays out a Gypsy scale with its distinctive augmented seconds. Later in the work, in a cadenza that Liszt situates at the end of the trio, the sound of the cimbalom is imitated by glissandos in the pianist's right hand. The flashy ornamentation for which Gypsy musicians were famous is reinterpreted by Liszt as pianistic virtuosity—including a blur of octaves in both hands, gymnastic leaps over the entire keyboard, and free dissonances.

 LISTENING CUE

FRANZ LISZT   CD 10/2
Hungarian Rhapsody No. 15 ("Rákóczy March") (1853)   Anthology, No. 157

 LISZT, WAGNER, AND THE NEW GERMAN SCHOOL

The nationalism apparent in his *Hungarian Rhapsodies* represents only one element of Liszt's remarkable musical career and historical importance. He also played a major role in establishing a modernist faction in the European musical culture of his time, one that was clearly distinct from the conservative approach to nineteenth-century music practiced by Mendelssohn and the Schumanns. Although honoring the classical past in music, Liszt believed that the more important role of leading composers was to prepare for the future. In a letter of 1874 he emphasized this aspiration: "My sole ambition as a musician," he wrote, "has been and shall be to hurl my lance into the infinite expanse of the future."[6]

In his commitment to the future, Liszt found a kindred spirit in Richard Wagner. They met in Paris in 1840, and Liszt came to admire Wagner's early operas. He performed *Tannhäuser* in Weimar in 1849. Later in that year he was helpful in arranging for Wagner's escape from German lands following the Dresden uprisings (see Chapter 55), and he then boldly conducted the premiere of Wagner's *Lohengrin* in 1850, during its composer's forced exile in Switzerland.

While Wagner was banished from German lands, Liszt took over the leadership of the modernist faction in European music, and Weimar became home to critics, composers, and performers of like mind. They proudly used Wagner's term "music of the future" as their slogan and, later, the **New German School** as their name. Their numbers steadily grew and came to include such talented musicians as Hans von Bülow (1830–1894), Carl Tausig (1841–1871), Peter Cornelius (1824–1874), and the American Edward MacDowell (1860–1908).

Their arch rivals were located nearby in Leipzig, later in Vienna. At first there were friendly relations between the two camps, but a split opened up on the question of how the great music of the past should be played. Under Mendelssohn, there was a careful adherence to the letter of the score of a work by Bach, Mozart, or Beethoven. But when Liszt played the classics, there was no such reverence. He freely interpreted, rearranged, and altered the works of the old masters. Mendelssohn remarked on this after hearing Liszt play in Leipzig in 1842: "Here he added six bars, there omitted seven; here he played the wrong chords, and later introduced other similar corruptions, and there in the most gentle passages made a dreadful *fortissimo*, and, in my view, it was all sorry nonsense."[7] Liszt's guideline for performing, on the other hand, was "the letter kills the spirit, a thing to which I will never subscribe."

Younger musicians were also beginning to choose sides. The youthful Johannes Brahms introduced himself to Liszt in 1853 and promptly dozed off while Liszt was playing his own Piano Sonata. In 1860 Brahms and three other musicians were emboldened to publish a manifesto directly attacking the music of "the leaders [Liszt and Wagner] and pupils of the so-called New German School . . . as contrary to the innermost spirit of music."[8]

Liszt's relations with his allies were sometimes as choppy as with his enemies. His life as a pious abbé in Italy was disrupted by the knowledge that his daughter Cosima—since 1857 the wife of his student Hans von Bülow—was engaged in a scandalous affair with his friend Wagner, who was the father of two of Cosima's children (conceived while Wagner and the Bülows lived in a bizarre *ménage à trois*). In the fall of 1867, Liszt traveled to Switzerland to confront Wagner and express his outrage and disapproval. After Father made his obligatory protest, the tensions apparently eased and the two got down to the more serious business of making music. Liszt sightread the orchestra part of *Die Meistersinger* at the keyboard while Wagner sang the vocal roles.

MUSIC FOR ORCHESTRA: THE SYMPHONIC POEM

Liszt's intention to hurl his lance into the future was realized especially in his orchestral music. When he ended his career as a touring piano virtuoso in 1848 and took up the baton as orchestral conductor in Weimar, he turned his composer's attention toward the orchestra. It was a difficult transition, especially since he had little experience in scoring his ideas for orchestra. At first he relied on assistance from other Weimar musicians—August Conradi (1821–1873) and Joseph Joachim Raff (1822–1882)—to orchestrate his music, but later he felt confident to take over this aspect of his craft.

As an orchestral composer, Liszt concentrated first on the one-movement programmatic orchestral piece, a genre that by mid-century had been well established in the concert overtures of Beethoven, Berlioz, and Mendelssohn. Liszt called his works of this type not overtures but "symphonic poems," to emphasize their affinity with the art of poetry.

The programmatic element in them is very different from the one used by Hector Berlioz in a work such as his *Symphonie fantastique*. For Berlioz, the program suggests, step by step, what might occur musically in the course of the piece. For Liszt, on the other hand, the program usually indicates only a certain mood or feeling that can be formulated in words and which runs parallel to the spirit of the music. The program in Liszt's symphonic poems provides at most a means for the listener to interpret correctly the atmosphere or emotional content of a work.

In addition to their programmaticism, Liszt's symphonic poems are highly original in form. The composer often uses a standard design, such as sonata form, but he typically changes the order of events and tonalities in a free way that is better geared to capture the spirit or character that he had in mind. He also tends to draw the work's themes out of a common melodic prototype, heard at the outset, although changing its character at each reappearance. This technique of thematic unity, called **transformation of themes,** had been prefigured by Berlioz in *Symphonie fantastique* (see Chapter 53) and by Schubert in his "Wanderer" Fantasy (see Chapter 52). Liszt was very familiar with both of these works because he had transcribed Berlioz's symphony for piano and arranged Schubert's fantasy for piano and orchestra.

An example of Liszt's approach to the transformation of themes is found in his symphonic poem *Les préludes* (*The Preludes*, 1854), a work that is freely based on a poem of the same name by Alphonse de Lamartine (1790–1869). The melodic prototype for all of the work's main themes is given out in the strings in the opening measures (Ex. 57-2a). Note especially the distinctive head motive (C-B-E) of this theme and also its pentatonic content of pitches. Except for the lower neighbor tone B, all other notes in the theme are drawn from the pentatonic scale G-A-C-(D)-E. These basic materials are then transformed to create the other main themes of the movement.

EXAMPLE 57-2

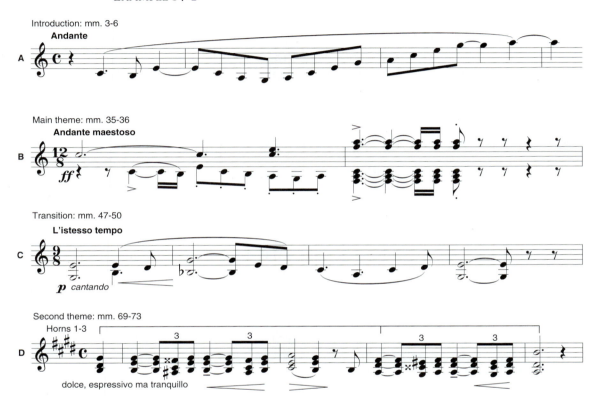

The first transformation occurs in the first theme of the sonata form proper (Ex. 57-2b). Its materials plainly come from the introductory prototype, although its character is made majestic rather than lyric. The transition to the second thematic area begins with a seemingly new theme (Ex. 57-2c), but this too derives from the prototype. Its character takes yet another turn, as it is played *cantando* in the lower strings. Finally, the principal second theme arrives in the horns (Ex. 57-2d). Here the degree of transformation is more extensive, although the head motive of the prototype is apparent in the framing tones G♯-F♯-B, which are marked by a bracket in the example.

 SUMMARY

Musical nationalism was an important factor in nineteenth-century music. This phenomenon is seen in music that celebrates a composer's homeland or embodies elements of its musical folklore or culture. Examples are found in the *Hungarian Rhapsodies* for piano by Franz Liszt (1811–1886). In these works, Liszt transcribes

Hungarian and Gypsy melodies and evokes the playing of Gypsy bands, which the composer had heard in his childhood in Hungary and during his concert tours there in the 1840s.

Liszt's early career was centered on piano playing—he was one of the greatest virtuosos of the instrument—and composing for this instrument. In the late 1840s and 1850s he turned his attention to composing for orchestra, specializing in programmatic music, both multi-movement programmatic symphonies and shorter, one-movement "symphonic poems." The programmatic element in these works is often unrelated to the formal plan of a composition and intended instead to aid the listener in locating a mood or spirit in which the work is best heard. The forms encountered in Liszt's compositions are usually freely—not strictly—derived from classical archetypes. Liszt also practiced an economy of themes (often termed "transformation of themes") by which an initial melodic prototype is apparent in the subsequent melodies in a work, only transformed in character and in details. A similar technique had been used earlier in music by Hector Berlioz and Franz Schubert.

KEY TERMS

nationalism
Austro-Hungarian
  Monarchy
Bedřich Smetana
Lisztomania

symphonic poem
recital
rhapsody
cimbalom
Gypsy scale

trio (of a march)
New German School
transformation of themes

Vienna in the Late Nineteenth Century: Brahms and Bruckner

In 1862 Johannes Brahms (1833–1897) arrived in Vienna for what he expected would be a short stay. By then he was well known as a composer, conductor, and pianist, and he was anticipating an appointment to a good position, probably as conductor of the orchestra in his home town of Hamburg. Although this was not granted to him, he increasingly found Vienna to be a congenial home, and by the later 1860s decided to make it his permanent place of residence.

 ## VIENNA IN THE 1860s

The Vienna that he encountered in 1862 was a far cry from the one in which Beethoven and Schubert had lived thirty-five years before. Under the rule of the Austrian emperor, Franz Joseph, Vienna became a huge and sprawling metropolis whose population had doubled since the 1820s. When Franz Joseph came to power after the uprisings of 1848, the old central city remained much as it had been for centuries, still surrounded by battlements that were themselves circled by a broad esplanade (Fig. 58-1). Beyond this open space, a newer city had grown up as a hodge-podge of suburban villages.

In 1857 the emperor turned the circular open space over to the city government to begin a massive urban renewal, and over the next thirty years the Vienna of the present day was created. On the western flank of the circular band, the city planners built imposing governmental and educational structures—a parliament, city hall, and university—each in a distinctive historical style of architecture. The eastern side was devoted to large commercial and residential buildings, and the southern portion to structures for the arts, including the Kunsthistorisches Museum (Museum for Historical Art), Opera, and a home for the Vienna Philharmonic Orchestra and the city's music conservatory. The complex reconstruction of this part of Vienna was tied together by a broad, tree-lined avenue called the Ringstrasse (Ring Street), which today lends the Austrian capital much of its distinctive charm and grandeur.

The development of the Ringstrasse symbolized the return of Vienna to its old vigor as a musical center. In 1869 a new theater for the Vienna Opera was completed; it was a splendidly ornate, neo-Renaissance structure that seated more than 2,000. Although destroyed during World War II, this imposing theater was rebuilt keeping its old appearance, and it remains today one of the world's great opera houses. In 1870 Vienna's Gesellschaft der Musikfreunde (Society of the Friends of Music)—a name usually shortened to **"Musikverein"** (Music Society)—built a new home near the Opera. The building contains a splendid auditorium (the "Golden Hall") that is still one of Europe's acoustically most perfect concert sites (Fig. 58-2). It is home to the Vienna Philharmonic Orchestra, which began to present regular concerts in 1860, drawing its personnel from the orchestra of the Opera.

In addition to its reputation for higher musical arts, Vienna was also known throughout the nineteenth century for popular music, especially music for the dance. Social dancing had long been a craze among the Viennese, and in the nineteenth century the dance of choice for people from all walks of life was the **waltz.** Dance halls had cropped up across the city, and for a small entrance fee the Viennese could waltz the night away to the accompaniment of a piano or small orchestra (Fig. 58-3).

Waltzing and its music had a questionable reputation early in the century. When Chopin visited Vienna in 1830 he reported to his parents: "Best known among the many Viennese entertainments are those evenings in the beer-halls where Strauss or Lanner . . . play waltzes during supper," he wrote. "The audience is so delighted that they can scarcely contain themselves. It just shows you how corrupted the taste of the Viennese public is."[1]

But by the 1860s the waltz had moved out of Vienna's beer gardens and into its palaces, and it came to embody a sophisticated happi-

FIGURE 58-1
Jakob Alt, "View of Vienna's Karlskirche," 1820. The old city of Vienna was ringed by an open area (called a "glacis") used partly as a park, partly by the military.

FIGURE 58-2
Built in 1870, the "Golden Hall" of the Musikverein is the home of the Vienna Philharmonic Orchestra. Its best-known concert is the one that takes place yearly on New Year's Day.

ness that characterizes Vienna and its people. The leading composer of waltzes was **Johann Strauss, Jr.** (1825–1899)—known as the "Waltz King"—whose dance orchestras played all over the city. When he conducted them, he stood with his violin amid the orchestra and led his musicians in a famously energetic and precise manner. His waltzes—*The Blue Danube, Tales from the Vienna Woods, The Emperor's Waltz,* and a hundred others—continue to delight the whole world.

BRAHMS'S LIFE AND WORKS

Brahms was born to the family of a musician in the city of Hamburg in north central Germany, which then as now is Germany's busiest seaport. He quickly advanced as a pianist and composer, and in 1853 set off on a tour as accompanist to the Hungarian violinist Eduard Reményi. He brought with him his own early compositions, including two piano sonatas, songs, and chamber works, and these attracted the attention of the influential musicians whom he met.

Most important was his encounter in Düsseldorf with Robert and Clara Schumann, who immediately recognized his genius. Robert Schumann was moved to write his final review, titled "New Paths," for the *Neue Zeitschrift für Musik* to call attention to the still unknown Brahms (excerpted in Box). In 1854 Schumann was institutionalized, and Brahms returned to Düsseldorf to assist Clara Schumann and her seven children. The romantic attachment that arose between her and Brahms was touched on in Chapter 54.

Brahms at first aimed for a career that combined conducting and composing, along the lines already laid out by Schumann and Mendelssohn. After moving to Vienna in 1862 he held a position as conductor of a chorus, and following upon the example of Mendelssohn he performed early music (especially the choral works of J.S. Bach) together with modern compositions. From 1872 to 1875 he was the artistic director of the concerts of the Musikverein in Vienna, but after this time he concentrated more fully on composing.

A new chapter in his creative life was opened in 1876 with the premiere of his Symphony No. 1, on which he had worked sporadically for more than twenty years. It was followed quickly by three additional symphonies, which helped to solidify his position as one of the very greatest composers of his or any other time. Following his death from cancer in April 1897, tributes poured in from around the world. In a gesture that may never again be accorded to a classical musician, the flags on the great ships in the port of Hamburg, Brahms's home town, were flown in his honor at half mast.

The body of music composed by Brahms is very different in its finite quantity and orderly status from that of a Schubert or Liszt. Those musicians left behind a far larger amount of music, many pieces incomplete, others existing in multiple versions, and many probably not intended for publication at all. But Brahms destroyed all such imperfect works, self-consciously leaving behind only complete compositions in a definitive form, all of which satisfied him artistically.

Brahms's orchestral music consists of four symphonies (1876–1885), several concert overtures, the popular *Variations on a Theme by Joseph Haydn,* and one concerto for violin, two for piano, and a double concerto for violin and cello. He wrote a

FIGURE 58-3

The waltz, danced here at a court ball, captured the sophisticated pleasure that was prized by the Viennese.

Bridgeman Art Library

New Paths by Robert Schumann

Following a concert tour in the fall of 1853, Johannes Brahms traveled to Düsseldorf to meet Robert and Clara Schumann, and a deep mutual admiration arose immediately among them. Robert Schumann— earlier one of Germany's leading music critics—took up the pen one final time to call attention to the youthful Brahms. Here are excerpts from his article, titled *Neue Bahnen* (*New Paths*):

. . . I have thought that in the course of events there would and must someday suddenly appear one who would be called to utter the highest expression of the time in an ideal manner, someone who presents us with mastery not through a gradual development but like Minerva springing fully armed from the head of Kronion. And he has arrived, a young blood, at whose cradle graces and heroes stood guard. His name is *Johannes Brahms*, from Hamburg, working there in quiet obscurity but under an excellent and enthusiastic teacher (Eduard Marxsen), trained in the strictest rules of art and recommended to

me not long ago by an honored and renowned master. He came just as he was billed, even in appearance. He is a natural. Sitting at the piano he began to reveal wondrous lands. We were drawn ever more into his magical circle. He played ingeniously, coaxing from the piano an orchestra of multicolored and joyous voices—his sonatas were more disguised symphonies. Then there were songs whose poetry one could understand without knowing the words, while a deep lyric melody penetrated everything. Then single piano pieces, some having a demonic character with the most clever form. Then sonatas for violin and piano, next quartets for string instruments. And each so different from the others that they all seemed to flow from some different source. And then he seemed to bring them like a gathering storm together into a waterfall, over whose tumbling waves a peaceful rainbow stretched and at whose edge butterflies flitted about to the song of nightingales. . . .[2]

large amount of chamber music, including instrumental sonatas, string quartets, sextets, and works combining piano and strings. For piano there are three early sonatas and many character pieces, in addition to chorale preludes for organ. His vocal works include songs, choruses and pieces for vocal ensemble. Among the latter are two collections of waltzes, called *Liebeslieder* (*Love Songs*) that have a distinctively Viennese flavor.

After the death of Mendelssohn and Schumann, Brahms took over the leadership of the conservative branch of European musical culture. His traditionalism is seen in his concentration on "absolute" musical genres—those having no explicit programmatic content—as in his chamber works and his symphonies of a classical type. His allegiance to classical forms—sonata form, variations, rondo, and simple ternary—was stronger than in a musician such as Liszt. Brahms did not write opera, thus avoiding comparisons with Wagner.

At the same time, strongly romantic and progressive elements are apparent in virtually all of his music. These include an intensely lyrical impulse, a darkly enriched tone, advanced harmonic and tonal thinking, and a passionately affective content. His forms—on the surface seemingly familiar from the Classical period—are highly intricate beneath and continue the movement toward unity that allies him, albeit in a different way, with the most progressive musicians of the nineteenth century.

Symphony No. 3

During the period 1876–1885 when Brahms completed his four symphonies, orchestral culture was flourishing throughout Europe. Orchestras were on the rise everywhere, as in Vienna, where the Vienna Philharmonic Orchestra had begun its permanent subscription concerts in 1860 and moved into its splendid home in the Musikverein in 1870.

At this time, three types of music were being written specifically for orchestra: symphonies, one-movement programmatic pieces (called overtures or symphonic poems), and concertos. Symphonies came in several types that reflect the split existing at this time between conservative and progressive composers. The symphony preserving the classical form of four movements without program was still the leading genre, with important examples appearing in the 1870s from Anton Bruckner, the Czech composer Antonín Dvořák, and a whole school of Russian symphonists headed by Peter Ilych Tchaikovsky and his teacher, Anton Rubinstein (1829–1894).

An alternative to the classical-type symphony was the programmatic symphony, an example of which has been seen in Berlioz's *Symphonie fantastique*. In addition to the overt presence of a program, this type of symphony is more variable in its form than its classical cousin. It often has more than four movements and these can extend to unusual lengths. Typically, the orchestra is enlarged beyond the classical makeup.

Brahms's approach to the genre of the symphony allied him—at least outwardly—with the traditionalists, and specifically with the genre as it existed in the hands of Beethoven during his middle period (see Chapter 50). All of Brahms's symphonies have four movements with a customary sequence of tempos (fast/slow/lilting/fast), and they are all moderate in length (none as long as Beethoven's "Eroica" Symphony). All use traditional forms—all of the first movements are in sonata form, for example—and all call for an orchestra of moderate size. None of the four is programmatic.

Brahms's Symphony No. 3 in F Major, Op. 90 (1883), illustrates his moderate extension of Beethoven's symphonic style. The first movement is the longest of the work's four, as in the classical model. Other conservative features are plain to see. The movement uses an uncomplicated version of sonata form, including a repeat of the exposition and a long coda, as in most of the symphonic first movements of Beethoven. The orchestra is moderate in size, calling for even fewer instruments than Beethoven did sixty years earlier in his Ninth Symphony.

Progressive features are equally evident. Brahms's tonal plan is far from the classical norm. The home key is F major, but the second theme appears in the mediant key, A major, and this subsidiary material returns in the recapitulation in D major and minor, the submediant key. The metric structure of the movement is unstable, as it contains many hemiola figures and otherwise almost constantly shifts its metric patterns in defiance of the bar line. Here, as in much of his music, Brahms almost completely avoids the regular four- and eight-measure phrases of the classicists.

The work is also tightly unified by recurrences of a small motive that precedes the main theme (Ex. 58-1). The top line of the motive, played by Flute I, contains the ascending melodic figure F - A♭ - F, which Brahms's biographer Max Kalbeck interpreted as a recurrent personal motto in Brahms's music representing the words **Frei aber froh,** "free but happy." Brahms himself was entirely silent about any such idea.

EXAMPLE 58-1

In various shapes, the motive reappears throughout the movement. It is embedded in different themes and turns up frequently in the bass line and in fleeting figures in inner voices. Its multiple appearances at the beginning of the main theme—to cite only one of many such examples of its use—are marked by brackets in Example 58-2. The listener is reminded of a similar phenomenon in works by Beethoven, notably the famous short-short-short-long motto that opens Beethoven's Symphony No. 5. Brahms goes beyond Beethoven's Fifth by explicitly bringing back the central motive in its original form at the end of the fourth movement of the Third Symphony. In this way he brings the symphony closer to the unified, cyclic forms of a composer such as Liszt.

EXAMPLE 58-2

LISTENING CUE

JOHANNES BRAHMS
Symphony No. 3 (1883)
First movement, *Allegro con brio*

CD 10/3
Anthology, No. 158

BRAHMS'S VOCAL MUSIC

Among Brahms's many outstanding works for chorus, his *Ein deutsches Requiem* (*A German Requiem*, 1868) is perhaps the greatest. The piece was begun as early as 1857 and achieved its completed form—with seven movements that call for mixed chorus, orchestra, and solo voices—in 1868. It is not an example of the traditional genre of the requiem (or Requiem Mass) as encountered in Chapter 48 in connection with Mozart's Requiem. That was a composition geared for use in the official Catholic funeral service, but Brahms, like several earlier composers, uses the term "Requiem" to designate a work that more freely addresses the idea of death. His *German Requiem* is more appropriate to the concert hall than to a service of worship.

Brahms selected his texts from the German Bible, choosing passages that speak of comfort for the bereaved, the impermanence of life, and the joyful prospect of the afterlife. The whole composition has a symmetrical form that begins and ends in F major and reaches its crowning center in the fourth movement, "Wie lieblich sind Deine Wohnungen" ("How Lovely Are Thy Dwelling Places"). The music here is blissfully melodious.

Brahms composed nearly two hundred songs for voice and piano, and in these works he brought the genre established by Schubert to new heights of warmth and expressivity. Toward the end of the nineteenth century composers wrote two types of songs: one aspired to be a literary event, the other a musical event. We will encounter literary songs in pieces by Gustav Mahler and Claude Debussy (see Chapters 60 and 63). Brahms's tastes leaned strongly toward the latter type. In his songs a certain simplicity and conservatism reigns. Their affective content resides mainly in a lyric melody in the voice, and the piano is relegated largely to an accompanimental role. The form of Brahms's songs is most often strophic or varied strophic, and these works often have an artlessly folkish flavor. The composer once declared that the folk song was his "ideal" in all song writing.

We see a folk-like simplicity at work in his song "Feldeinsamkeit" ("Alone in the Country"), Op. 86, No. 2 (c1879). This is a setting of an unpretentious poem in two stanzas by Hermann Allmers (1821–1902), a minor German poet. Lying in the grass, the narrator gazes peacefully at the clouds and feels dead to the world. Brahms's setting keeps Allmers's artless tone. The song has a simple varied strophic form, and the piano is confined to the role of accompaniment, with no elaborate prelude or postlude.

Despite these gestures toward a superficial simplicity, the song uses an advanced harmonic language that is filled with chromatic motions. The music also persistently mirrors the text. We experience the narrator's passive gazing into the sky in the long pedal point on the tone F at the beginning. When the narrator finds himself surrounded by crickets, we hear their chirping in a pungent ninth chord, and when the blue sky that he sees above him opens up before our eyes, the tonic minor triad is suddenly transformed into a major triad (Ex. 58-3).

EXAMPLE 58-3

...while crickets around me chirp ceaselessly, with the blue of heaven...

In Chapter 75 we will study another setting of Allmers' poem "Feldeinsamkeit" by the American composer Charles Ives.

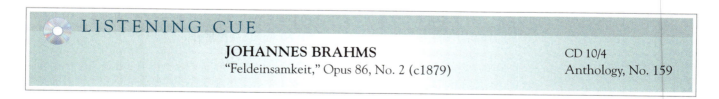

LISTENING CUE

JOHANNES BRAHMS
"Feldeinsamkeit," Opus 86, No. 2 (c1879)

CD 10/4
Anthology, No. 159

ANTON BRUCKNER

The great and immediate success of Brahms's symphonies with audiences all over the world long eluded those of his Viennese contemporary Anton Bruckner (1824–1896). Bruckner was born in a village near the city of Linz, which lies midway between Salzburg and Vienna. Until the age of forty-four, he led the life of a provincial church musician and school teacher. He was an excellent organist, especially known for his improvisations, and in his early years he composed almost exclusively choral music for use in the Catholic liturgy.

In 1868 Bruckner moved to Vienna, where he worked primarily as a music professor, first at the Vienna Conservatory and later also at the University of Vienna. His many students include Gustav Mahler, Arnold Schoenberg, and the theorist Heinrich Schenker. As a composer in Vienna, Bruckner turned decisively to the symphony, ultimately composing nine mature symphonies, of which the ninth was left incomplete when he died in 1896.

These compositions pledge conflicting allegiances in the war of the conservatives versus the futurists. In some ways they exhibit Classical features. None of them is overtly programmatic, all have four movements in a customary succession of tempos and movement types, and, except for the final symphonies, they all use an orchestra of moderate size.

But virtually everything else about them suggests the thinking of a composer from the New German School. They are epic in length, about twice as long as Brahms's symphonies. Most are cyclic, as themes from the first movements are brought back in the finales (although we have seen Brahms hint at this in his Third Symphony). The forms encountered in their individual movements—especially the sonata forms in the first and last movements—are extensively reinterpreted relative to the classical norm, just as Berlioz did in the first movement of his *Symphonie fantastique* or Liszt in his *Les préludes*. Given the unprecedented way that Bruckner organizes and expresses musical ideas, it is not at all surprising that many audiences of his time found his symphonies incoherent rather than original.

In one of the great ironies of music history, Bruckner allowed himself to be persuaded by his friends and students to make radical cuts and other revisions in all of his symphonies, hoping to make them more acceptable to audiences of his day.

Bruckner's symphonies all have trademark features. Their first movements usually open with a gesture reminiscent of the opening of Beethoven's Ninth Symphony. Over mysterious chords in the strings, a melody is gradually pulled up from fragments of open fourths and fifths. A theme then forces its way out at the end of a long and repetitive crescendo. The music that follows is unapologetically full of clichés—rhythms constantly alternating groupings of twos and threes, ostinatos carried out through long crescendos, extended motionless harmonies over pedal points, moments of utter bombast placed beside those of serenity. Bruckner's liberated outlook on musical form and expression found its only approval in the progressive faction of European musicians led by Wagner and Liszt.

Bruckner made several trips to visit Wagner, whom he worshiped in a child-like way. Bruckner traveled to Bayreuth for the premiere of *Parsifal* in 1882, and Wagner greeted him and asked how he liked the new work. "While still holding his hand," Bruckner later recalled, "I knelt down, pressed his precious hand to my lips, and kissed it, saying, 'O master, I worship you!!!' The Master responded, 'Calm down, Bruckner, good night!!!' These were the Master's last words to me. On the following day he sat behind me at the *Parsifal* performance and scolded me for applauding too loudly."[3]

Bruckner's Motets: *Christus factus est*

Bruckner concentrated on only two types of music—symphonies and choral compositions for the Catholic liturgy. His mature works of the latter type consist of three Masses (1864–1868), a *Te Deum* (a Latin text praising God that can be performed at virtually any celebration), a setting of Psalm 150 ("Hallelujah! Praise the Lord in His Holy Place"), and a number of mostly unaccompanied Latin motets.

Christus factus est (1884) is a handsome example of the last of these. Recall from Chapter 21 that a motet, during its heyday in the late Renaissance period, was a setting for unaccompanied chorus of a sacred Latin text. Depending on the words used, such pieces might have been performed within the Catholic liturgy or used outside of the church for private devotion or reflection. Following the Renaissance, major composers continued to write motet-like compositions, but there was increasingly less homogeneity in their styles or purposes. Mozart, for example, often wrote motets—such as his exquisite *Ave verum corpus* (Hail, True Body, 1791). His works of this type are usually for the medium of chorus and orchestra and they were intended for church performance. Among the early nineteenth-century composers, Schubert, Mendelssohn, Berlioz, and Liszt wrote motet-like works, again in a mixed style that preserved some antique features (such as an imitative texture) combined with more modern forms of expression.

Bruckner's *Christus factus est* is appropriate to the Catholic Mass on Maundy Thursday, the Thursday before Easter, when the Church celebrates the founding of the eucharist (a symbolic recreation of the Last Supper). The words are taken from the Gradual for that feast, and in a celebration of Mass in Bruckner's time, the chorus might well have substituted this motet for the more normal chanting of this text:

Christus factus est pro nobis obediens	Christ was for us obedient
usque ad mortem, mortem autem crucis.	unto death, unto death on the cross.
[verse] Propter quod et Deus exaltavit illum,	Therefore God exalted him,
et dedit illi nomen,	and gave him a name
quod est super omne nomen.	that is above every other name.

In Bruckner's day, there was a movement afoot in the Catholic Church in German lands, called **Cecilianism,** that urged a greater uniformity in church music based on the seemingly pure style of religious works from the time of Palestrina (see Chapter 25). To musicians of the nineteenth century, this suggested a serene and uniform mood in which the chorus sang unaccompanied in simplified rhythms with a light counterpoint, sometimes using the church modes and quoting from Gregorian chant. Although Bruckner found Cecilian church music to be unimaginative, the goals of this movement are partly evident in his motet *Christus factus est*.

Echoes of Renaissance polyphony are plain to hear. Bruckner's motet is unaccompanied, simple in rhythm, and it alternates homophonic passages with others using a light imitation. The harmonies consist largely of root-position triads. The words are always clearly audible, and these govern the form of the piece and also trigger word paintings. From measure 7, on the word "obediens" (obedient), the altos and basses obediently follow one another downward through a chain of suspensions. On the word "mortem" (death) the music sinks low and arrives in measure 15 on a dissonant chord with notes separated by whole tones. The voices then repeatedly soar into their highest register on the words "quod est super omne nomen" ("that is above every other name"). All of these features are derived from the motet style of composers of the sixteenth century.

But the tonal language of the work comes straight from Wagner. The voice leading is densely chromatic, dissonances are freely admitted, and the triadic cadence points in the interior of the work have little relevance to the framing tonality of

D minor and major. As in his symphonies, Bruckner in *Christus factus est* pours new wine into old bottles.

LISTENING CUE

ANTON BRUCKNER
Christus factus est (1884)

CD 10/5
Anthology, No. 160

SUMMARY

Vienna in the 1860s regained its preeminence in the world of music. New structures—including a new Opera house and a new concert hall called the "Musikverein" ("Music Society")—were built in that decade, and Vienna continued to be a center for sophisticated popular music, as in the waltzes of Johann Strauss, Jr.

Johannes Brahms emerged in this decade as Vienna's leading composer of serious music. In the public's mind, he was allied with musical conservatives, although his symphonies and choral music (such as his *A German Requiem* of 1868) defy any real distinctions between old and new. In his music there is an intense melodiousness, an advanced harmonic language, irregular phrases—all cast into traditional forms. Many of Brahms's two hundred songs have a folk-like spirit, although their chromatic harmonies link the composer with his most progressive contemporaries.

As a proponent of Wagner and the New German School, Anton Bruckner, a resident of Vienna from 1868 until his death in 1896, was on the other side of the critic's fence. Despite their seemingly classical exterior, his symphonies reveal a profound originality in form and substance. Before (and occasionally after) arriving in Vienna, Bruckner composed mainly choral music for the Catholic liturgy. His motet *Christus factus est* uses a chromatic harmony reminiscent of Wagner's music, although this is placed in a form drawn from motets at the time of Palestrina.

KEY TERMS

"Musikverein"
waltz

Johann Strauss, Jr.
Cecilianism

Chapter 59

Music and Ballet in Nineteenth-Century Russia: Mussorgsky and Tchaikovsky

A native culture for artistic music was slow to develop in Russia. During the reign of Tsar Peter the Great (1682–1725), the artistic life of Russia was placed in the hands of foreigners who came to the capital city of St. Petersburg to design its architectural monuments, occupy court positions in the arts and letters, and make music. During the rule of Catherine the Great (1762–1796) Italian opera flourished in the Russian court. The Queen brought in a succession of leading Italian opera composers—Baldassare Galuppi, Tommaso Traetta, Giovanni Paisiello, and Giuseppe Sarti among others—to compose and to oversee new works, and Italian opera found a devoted following among Russia's aristocracy.

The first significant and original Russian-born composer was **Mikhail Glinka** (1804–1857). He spent his adult life mainly in St. Petersburg, with long sojourns in Paris, Berlin, Milan, and other European cities. He was largely self-taught as a musician and worked as a governmental employee while approaching music as an amateur. Most of his compositions—which include the operas *A Life for the Tsar* and *Ruslan and Lyudmila*, symphonic works, and songs—speak with a Russian accent through the use of national themes and folk-song quotations or imitations. Glinka's basic language, all the same, is that of German and Italian music.

❀ ST. PETERSBURG IN THE LATE NINETEENTH CENTURY

During the reign of Tsar Alexander II (1855–1881) the culture for classical music in St. Petersburg was greatly modernized, and opportunities for native composers brightened. In 1860 the **Mariinsky Theater** (called the Kirov Theater during the Soviet period) was opened and placed at the disposal of a state-supported Russian opera troupe (see Part VI timeline). A rival Italian company gradually lost out in popularity as the native-born Russian musicians revealed a great genius for music. The Mariinsky Theater soon became the focal point for music throughout the city, where a taste for opera and ballet was solidly entrenched. In 1862 a conservatory was established that provided for the training of native performers and composers, the latter including Peter Ilyich Tchaikovsky, Sergei Prokofiev, and Dmitri Shostakovich. Although opera and ballet were supreme, orchestral music began to flourish with the founding of the Russian Musical Society (1859), Russian Symphonic Concerts (1885), and the establishment of a permanent Court Orchestra (1882).

❀ THE *KUCHKA*

As musical culture in St. Petersburg by the 1860s began to produce outstanding native composers, conflict with the older domination by foreigners and by Western musical models became unavoidable. Some of the leaders of musical life at that time, such as the virtuoso pianist Anton Rubinstein (1829–1894), thought that Russian music would best develop by continuing to imitate traditional European values, including accepted styles of composition, strict conservatory training, and a cosmopolitan outlook that could blend with the familiar musical tastes of the Germans, French, and Italians. To these westward-looking Russians, the styles of Schumann, Wagner, Verdi, and Brahms were perfectly acceptable.

Rubinstein's pro-Western philosophy was opposed by a circle of influential St. Petersburg musicians and music critics who gathered around the brilliant pianist and composer **Mily Balakirev** (pronounced Ba-LA-kir-ef, 1837–1910). He distrusted the regimented and doctrinaire teaching of traditional musical conservatories, which he believed restrained new ideas and inhibited creative freedom. He was also a Slavic nationalist who was annoyed by the dominance of European music in Russian concert halls and opera houses. In its place he wanted to hear a distinctively

Russian voice in new music, such as Glinka had achieved by the use of folk songs and stories, and he also encouraged the development of new musical materials that broke with European traditions. Balakirev supported the appearance of oriental themes in music—as in his virtuosic *Islamey* for piano. Such compositions, he thought, celebrated the extension of the Russian empire into Asia.

Younger St. Petersburg musicians were drawn to Balakirev's powerful personality and great musicianship. "His influence over those around him," wrote his student Nicolai Rimsky-Korsakov, "was boundless, and resembled some magnetic or mesmeric force."[1] Following an orchestral concert that Balakirev conducted in St. Petersburg in 1867 featuring his own works and those of others in his circle, the writer Vladimir Stasov pointed approvingly to Balakirev's nationalistic outlook: "How much poetry, feeling, talent, and ability there is," Stasov wrote, "in the small but already mighty handful (*moguchaya kuchka*) of Russian musicians."[2] The epithet **kuchka,** "handful," caught on as a name for Balakirev's circle, whose other principal members were the composers Rimsky-Korsakov, César Cui (1835–1918), Alexander Borodin (1833–1887), and Modest Mussorgsky (1839–1881). (The group is also sometimes called **The Five.**) In 1867 all were still musical amateurs lacking in any systematic musical education, something that Balakirev thought unnecessary. Their background made them all the more sympathetic to rough-and-ready experimentation into new musical resources. All wanted a distinctive Russian profile in their music.

❖ MODEST MUSSORGSKY

Mussorgsky's career characterizes the interests of the group, although his development of a nationalistic, realistic, and non-Westernized musical language went further than his *kuchka* comrades toward a distinctively original and influential style. He was largely self-taught as a composer, receiving guidance from several friends, especially from the magnetic Balakirev. Although passionate about composing, he made his living as an army officer and later as a government worker, and he enjoyed little recognition as an artist during his own lifetime. A self-destructive and manic personality, Mussorgsky died from alcohol poisoning at the age of only forty-two. Even his friends from the *kuchka* could not always take him seriously, given his personal habits and his disdain for conventional modes of composition.

Mussorgky's greatest work is the opera **Boris Godunov,** based on a play by Alexander Pushkin that deals with the life of an early Russian tsar. Mussorgsky completed it in 1869, although he could not arrange for a performance. He revised it in 1872, whereupon it was performed at the Mariinsky Theater. His other principal works are the tone poem *Night on Bald Mountain,* the cycle of piano pieces *Pictures at an Exhibition* (best known in Maurice Ravel's orchestration of 1922), and three song cycles (*The Nursery, Sunless,* and *Songs and Dances of Death*).

The song "Within Four Walls" that opens the cycle *Sunless* (1874) shows Mussorgsky's realism and a novel approach to the genre itself. The poem, written by Arseny Golenishchev-Kutuzov (an amateur poet whom the composer had befriended), consists of a series of melancholy exclamations, made by an individual trapped by life and sustained only by a glimmer of hope for future happiness. Although poetically unsophisticated, the words express a non-sentimental and realistic outlook on life that surely rang true with the composer during his depressive moods.

A gritty realism was at the very root of Russian art of the 1870s (also see Chapter 65), and it was a guiding principle in Mussorgsky's choice of song poetry. The composer explained his attachment to realistic images to the painter Ilya Repin: "It is the people I want to depict: when I sleep I see them, when I eat I think of them, when I drink—I can visualize them, integral, big, unpainted, and without any tinsel. And what an *awful* (in the true sense of the word) richness there is in the people's speech for a musical figure."[3] Repin's own realistic style as a painter is evident in his searing portrait of the composer (Fig. 59-1), made only days before Mussorgsky's untimely death. It shows the subject "without any tinsel," in the final stages of his battle with alcohol and depression.

To match the realistic text, Mussorgsky created music that is stripped bare of artifice. The song has virtually no tune, only an artful imitation of the text as it would be spoken. "My music must be an artistic reproduction of human speech in all its finest shades, that is, *the sounds of human speech*, as the external manifestations of thought and feeling," he wrote in 1868. "That is the ideal toward which I strive."[4]

The piano accompaniment in the song adds bare and loosely connected chords that hover statically around a D-major triad (the opening line is shown in Ex. 59-1). There are no distractions coming from normal harmonic progressions or traditional voice leading. Mussorgsky's partial removal of functional harmonic progressions in songs such as "Within Four Walls" would later prove to be a powerful influence on the music of Claude Debussy (see Chapter 63).

❋ FIGURE 59-1

Ilya Repin painted this portrait of his friend Mussorgsky only days before Mussorgsky's death from the effects of alcoholism.

EXAMPLE 59-1

mm. 1-2

Andante tranquillo

Kom - nat - ka tes - na - ia,   ti - kha - ia,   mi - la - ia;

My room is small, quiet, pleasant; ...

 LISTENING CUE

MODEST MUSSORGSKY
Sunless, "Within Four Walls" (1874)

CD 10/6
Anthology, No. 161

✿ PETER ILYICH TCHAIKOVSKY

Balakirev and his *kuchka* were well-known to Peter Ilyich Tchaikovsky (1840–1893), Russia's greatest composer of the nineteenth century. Tchaikovsky met Balakirev in Moscow in 1867, and Balakirev shortly afterward conducted his music in St. Petersburg.

Tchaikovsky's works from this time had much that appealed to Balakirev, including their quotations of folk songs and other nationalistic gestures. Balakirev freely offered the young composer advice about composing, and he guided Tchaikovsky through the creation of one of his first great works, the concert overture *Romeo and Juliet*. But Tchaikovsky was wary of Balakirev's overbearing personality and the anti-Western element in his aesthetic program. Living in Moscow rather than the *kuchka* stronghold of St. Petersburg, Tchaikovsky always kept a cautious distance from Balakirev's circle.

Born in a mining village near the Ural Mountains, Tchaikovsky as a child moved with his family to St. Petersburg, and in 1865 he was one of the earliest graduates from the city's new conservatory, where he studied composition with Anton Rubinstein. His career path was very different from those of the *kuchka*, since he was determined to be a professional musician, not an amateur. Immediately after leaving the St. Petersburg Conservatory, he was appointed to the faculty of Moscow's new conservatory, where he taught until 1878. His life was otherwise unsettled, as he traveled almost constantly between European cities and various locations in Russia. A remarkable chapter in his life concerns his relationship with a wealthy admirer of his music, Countess Nadezhda von Meck, with whom he exchanged an extensive and highly personal correspondence but whom he never met. For a period, Mme. Meck supported the composer financially.

Tchaikovsky was a master of all of the musical genres of his day. He wrote operas (including *Eugene Onegin* and *The Queen of Spades*), six symphonies, symphonic poems, piano character pieces, songs, three string quartets, and concertos. He was also the first leading composer of the late nineteenth century to write music for ballet, in his *Swan Lake* (1876), *The Sleeping Beauty* (1889), and *The Nutcracker* (1892).

❀ BALLET

A **ballet**—in the modern sense—is a theatrical presentation in which a story or idea is communicated by music, mime, and dancing. The genre has a long history, although it emerged as an independent art form only in the late eighteenth century. Nowhere was it more popular than in Paris, where dancing had long been a principal courtly entertainment (see Chapter 35). Parisian audiences of the 1820s were enchanted by the dancing of **Marie Taglioni** (1804–1884), who was the first ballerina to specialize in dancing *en pointe*, on the toes, which is done with the aid of special shoes (Fig. 59-2). Her graceful and fluent movements fit in well with romantic ballet **scenarios,** or stories, that typically featured supernatural creatures, evoked the passions of unrequited love, and created the atmosphere of fairy tale.

Although a ballet in the nineteenth century was a collaborative creation, the **choreographer** (often called the "ballet master") was the leading figure. He often wrote or adapted the scenario, devised a structure for the work as a whole, commissioned the writing of music, and created the dance steps used in each section.

The layout of a typical ballet in the nineteenth century had much in common with traditional opera. A ballet, like an opera, normally begins with an overture. The story—which in opera is largely told in recitative—is conveyed in ballet by passages in **mime,** where the leading dancers communicate by way of standardized hand movements, poses, and facial expressions. These are interspersed with danced numbers. Some involve the entire company (the *corps de ballet*), rather like a chorus in an opera. Other numbers are ensembles—passages for a few leading dancers such as in a *pas de deux* (for two dancers, normally a man and woman). Still other dances, called **variations,** are for a single performer, comparable to an operatic aria. Ballets often

Marie Taglioni

Marie Taglioni created the art of the modern ballerina. Strictly trained by her father, the choreographer Filippo Taglioni, Marie developed a style of dancing and a stage persona that by the 1830s brought her to the top of her profession and created a model for dancing that still exists today.

She perfected the idea of vertical line for the ballerina—an elegant extension of the body and an elevation that seemed to free her from all gravitational limits. She also emphasized dancing on the points of the toes, which creates the illusion of elongation and detachment from the stage. Although she did not invent this practice, she brought it to the prominence it still enjoys in theatrical dance. Her costumes were also revolutionary. She rejected realistic dress in favor of a bell-shaped skirt made from white tulle, worn with bare arms and shoulders. Her motions were praised for their fluidity and lightness. In all, Marie Taglioni represented the essence of what we now call "classical ballet."

Her greatest role was in the ballet *La sylphide*, whose choreography was created by her father for the Paris Opéra in 1832. Here she impersonated a sylph, one of a band of imaginary winged creatures who frolic in the woods. She falls in love with a mortal, who pursues her through the forest and finally embraces her. With this her wings fall to earth and she dies.

After her initial triumph in Paris, Taglioni traveled throughout Europe to delight ballet audiences everywhere. From 1837 she was in residence at the Mariinsky Theater in St. Petersburg, where she developed a cult-like following. Her departure was the occasion of a bizarre event among her Russian fans. As a memento, she had left behind a pair of ballet slippers, which her following seized upon and had cooked into an edible form. They then devoured the shoes as a culinary delicacy.

Bridgeman Art Library

❋ FIGURE 59-2

Marie Taglioni created the modern art of the ballerina, especially in her refinement of techniques for dancing *en pointe*.

contain interludes called **divertissements** ("entertainments"), which are episodes with dancing and spectacle that have little connection to the surrounding story.

In the traditional nineteenth-century ballet, music has a secondary role. Although occasionally written by accomplished composers such as the Frenchmen Adolphe Adam (1803–1856, composer of the ballet *Giselle*) and Léo Delibes (1836–1891, composer of *Coppélia* and *Sylvia*), the music was more typically written by an obscure composer on the staff of a theater. In writing the music, the composer took strict orders from the choreographer and aspired only to produce a tuneful score that would serve as a backdrop to the dancing. No originality or self-expression was expected.

❂ BALLET IN RUSSIA: *THE NUTCRACKER*

Early in the nineteenth century, visiting French dancers and choreographers firmly established the French style of ballet in St. Petersburg, where an enthusiasm for the genre was as great as in Paris. Toward the end of the century, the leading figure in

Scenario of *The Nutcracker*

Preparations for Christmas are in full swing at the Silberhaus home, where the tree is being trimmed and presents assembled for the children. A family friend, the mysterious Drosselmayer, arrives, bringing life-sized dolls as presents for his godchildren, Clara and Fritz Silberhaus. Father insists that these be safely stored, whereupon Drosselmayer produces another toy, a small nutcracker in the shape of a toy soldier, which Fritz immediately breaks. Clara sadly wraps up the injured toy and places it in her doll bed, whereupon the party ends and the children are sent to bed.

Late at night Clara steals back into the room to check on the nutcracker, and she is astonished to see the tree growing large and all the toys coming alive. Mice do battle with the toy soldiers, and the Mouse King gains the upper hand over the Nutcracker, who has now come alive to lead his army against the mice. He is saved by Clara, who throws her slipper at the Mouse King. Magically, the Nutcracker turns into a charming Prince, who escorts Clara toward the tree, whereupon they disappear into its branches and fly through a snowstorm.

In the second act the Prince brings Clara to his home, where they meet the kindly Sugar Plum Fairy. A divertissement is ordered for Clara's entertainment, at the end of which the Sugar Plum Fairy dances a *pas de deux* with her consort.

Russian ballet was the French émigré **Marius Petipa** (1818–1910), who came to St. Petersburg in 1847 as a dancer and soon rose to the position of the principal choreographer at the Imperial Ballet of the Mariinsky Theater. He collaborated with Tchaikovsky on two ballet scores—*The Sleeping Beauty* and *The Nutcracker*—which remain masterpieces of their type and are among Tchaikovsky's most beloved works.

The Nutcracker was intended for the Christmas season, and it is geared to the enjoyment of children and adults alike. Since its premiere at the Mariinsky Theater in the week before Christmas 1892, it has been given at Christmas by ballet companies around the world, and it is now by far the most often performed work of its genre. Its scenario is loosely based on a children's story, "Nutcracker and Mouse King" (1819), by E.T.A. Hoffmann, although the narrative was extensively rewritten by Petipa to create a ballet scenario.

The story itself begins with a clear narrative, but by the end of Act 1 it dissolves into pure fantasy. The entire second act is devoted to a divertissement, and we never learn more about the mysterious Drosselmayer, the Mouse King, or other characters from the opening. Ballet—far more than opera—can accommodate such inconsistencies, and these have not prevented *The Nutcracker* from achieving its enduring popularity. Another unusual aspect of the work is that the leading roles, Clara and the Nutcracker Prince, were intended to be enacted by children (actually, younger students from the ballet school of the Mariinsky Theater). Their dancing is simple, and the more virtuosic choreography is given to the subsidiary roles of the Sugar Plum Fairy, her consort, and the figures who perform variations in the divertissement of Act 2.

Tchaikovsky wrote the music for the work based on an outline given him by Petipa. In this document the ballet master sketched out the story, which he divided preliminarily into forty-six sections. Typical of the choreographer in his relation with a composer, Petipa instructed Tchaikovsky concerning the length and character of each dance and Tchaikovsky closely adhered to this outline. For example, in a section toward the end of Act 1, just after Clara dispatches the Mouse King with her slipper, Petipa gave these instructions:

> The Nutcracker turns into an enchanting prince. One or two chords. He runs to aid Clara, who regains consciousness. Here begins emotional music, which changes into a

poetic *andante*, and ends in a grandiose fashion. 64 bars. The decor changes. A fir forest in winter. Gnomes with torches are standing around the Christmas tree to pay homage to the Prince, Clara, and the dolls, who are placed around the tree. A grouping. All this takes place within the *andante* of 64 bars.[5]

The music that Tchaikovsky wrote for this passage (Act 1, no. 8) is almost exactly what Petipa ordered. It opens with two measures stating a C major chord and then progresses through a succession of phrases that are *andante* in tempo and, as Petipa instructed, highly poetic and emotional in character. A lesser composer for ballet would probably have followed Petipa's instructions even more explicitly by writing a succession of eight eight-measure phrases, for a total of sixty-four bars. But Tchaikovsky avoids such a purely formulaic plan by introducing asymmetrical extensions to some of the phrases, while still writing music that is generally regular in structure.

Here, as elsewhere in Tchaikovsky's oeuvre, the composer promotes ease of understanding by a high degree of repetitiveness of melodic material. The whole number uses a simple repetitive form (**A B A'** coda), and each of the three main parts begins with a phrase that is then immediately repeated, in the manner of a melodic period. (For some listeners, past and present, the amount of simple repetition is a weakness in Tchaikovsky's music.) The composer achieves the emotionalism that Petipa wanted in a way also commonly seen in his other works: as the music approaches the reprise, the orchestration is thickened, the tempo dramatically broadens, and, with the crash of cymbals at the point of reprise, the melody is thrust grandiosely into the upper register. The music contains no harmonic surprises and remains unambiguously in C major.

In *The Nutcracker*, as in his other ballet scores, Tchaikovsky did not attempt to duplicate the close expressive connection between music and dramatic ideas and characters that was found in opera of the same period. There is instead a far looser and more general resemblance between the music and the drama, conveyed by tempo, meter, length, and spirit ("emotional," "poetic," "grandiose"—the sentiments that were specified by Petipa). There remains enough freedom so that virtually any section of the ballet can subsequently be re-choreographed. In modern productions of Act 1, no. 8, for example, the change to a snowy winter scene envisioned by Petipa is often replaced by a *pas de deux* for the adults now commonly cast in the roles of Clara and the Prince, with a suggestion of romantic interest between the two. There is no incongruity between the music and this revised choreography.

LISTENING CUE

PETER ILYICH TCHAIKOVSKY
The Nutcracker (1892)
Act 1, scene 8

CD 10/7
Anthology, No. 162

Tchaikovsky strengthened the connection between music and character in one area not addressed by Petipa—in the work's orchestration. In *The Nutcracker*, as in his symphonies, Tchaikovsky shows a profound understanding of the orchestra and a resourcefulness in finding new color combinations that evoke images and ideas. When the mysterious Drosselmayer appears in Act 1, no. 4, for example, his music is given to the low strings, trombones, and the horns playing *bouché* (with the tone tightly stopped by a mute or by the hand in the bell). The sound is just right for the character's unnerving eccentricity. Tchaikovsky uses the ethereal sound of the **celesta** to accompany the Sugar Plum Fairy in her variation in the *pas de deux* near the end of the ballet. This bell-like instrument controlled by a keyboard had been invented by Auguste Mustel only shortly before, and it was heard by the composer on a trip to Paris in 1890. Immediately Tchaikovsky asked his Moscow publisher, Peter Jurgenson, to purchase the instrument. "In the meantime I would prefer it to be shown to nobody," he warned, "or I am afraid that [Nicolai] Rimsky-Korsakov and [Alexander] Glazunov will get wind of it and use its unusual effects sooner than me."[6]

Immediately upon completing the score to *The Nutcracker*, Tchaikovsky arranged excerpts into an orchestral **suite,** for use as a concert work. There are also suites of excerpts from the ballets *The Sleeping Beauty* and *Swan Lake*, but these were created by musicians after the composer's death in 1893.

 ## SUMMARY

Russian musical culture until the mid nineteenth century was dominated by foreigners. Native-born Russians began to assert their genius and originality for music in the later part of the century. In the capital city, St. Petersburg, a group of composers know as the *kuchka* (handful), or "The Five," was led by Mily Balakirev. They favored a nationalistic profile in their works (often achieved by quoting Slavic folk songs in original compositions) and a freedom from traditional European styles and musical materials. These qualities are seen especially in the works of one of their number, Modest Mussorgsky, whose opera *Boris Godunov* and songs project a realistic image of Russian life. In Mussorgsky's song "Within Four Walls" from the cycle *Sunless*, this realism is captured by a simple declamatory melody and by chords whose progressions are remote from the central key.

Peter Ilyich Tchaikovsky was sympathetic to the nationalistic aspirations of the *kuchka* group, although he was more strongly connected to developments in the European music of his day. Tchaikovsky was the first major composer of the nineteenth century to write important works for ballet. His final ballet score, *The Nutcracker*, is based on a fanciful Christmas story. His music is memorably tuneful, repetitive, and skilled in orchestration, although he avoids the innovative harmonic experiments of many of his contemporaries.

 ## KEY TERMS

Mikhail Glinka	ballet	divertissement
Mariinsky Theater	Marie Taglioni	Marius Petipa
Mily Balakirev	scenario	celesta
kuchka ("handful")	choreographer	suite
The Five	mime	
Boris Godunov	variations (ballet)	

Vienna at the Turn of the Twentieth Century: Gustav and Alma Mahler

Chapter 60

In the fall of 1875, Gustav Mahler—then fifteen years old—arrived in Vienna to enroll in the Conservatory of the Musikverein (see Chapter 58) and to begin training for the career of a virtuoso pianist. Home to Johannes Brahms and to the waltzes of Johann Strauss, Jr., Vienna by this time had fully regained the greatness of musical culture that it enjoyed during the time of Haydn, Mozart, and Beethoven.

The two main focal points for serious music—the Opera and the Musikverein—were flourishing in 1875 as never before. The repertory of the Opera was filled with important new works coming from all over Europe. In 1875 alone, Verdi traveled to Vienna to conduct his *Aida* and Requiem, Wagner arrived to oversee productions of *Lohengrin* and *Die Meistersinger,* and Georges Bizet's *Carmen* received its Viennese premiere. The Vienna Philharmonic Orchestra continued to play in the magnificent "Golden Hall" of the Musikverein, which opened five years before Mahler's arrival. The membership of the Philharmonic was, and continues to be, drawn from the orchestra of the Opera, although the Vienna Philharmonic Orchestra itself is self-governing. Even the conductor is elected by its members, which ensures a uniquely reciprocal relation between them and their leaders, who have included Hans Richter, Wilhelm Furtwängler, Karl Böhm, Herbert von Karajan, and Leonard Bernstein, in addition to Mahler himself. The repertory of the Philharmonic at this time had a distinctly conservative flavor, although new music was not neglected. Between 1873 and 1881 the Philharmonic gave the premier performances of Bruckner's Symphonies No. 2, 3, and 4, and Brahms was a regular visitor to its concerts, as piano soloist, conductor, and composer of new works.

Mahler's arrival in Vienna in 1875 was itself a testament to the continuing changes in Austrian society. Mahler was born to a Jewish family living in a small village, Kalist, northwest of Vienna, and in an earlier time his legal right to relocate within the Austrian Empire—not to mention his professional opportunities—would have been strictly limited. Beginning with the uprisings of 1848, and finally in 1867, Jews in the empire were accorded full civil liberties, which allowed them to move freely and to enter any profession. These liberal measures resulted in a great migration of Jews from the eastern regions of the empire into the capital city of Vienna, where they were quickly assimilated into a cosmopolitan German-speaking society and became leaders in the arts and sciences.

MAHLER'S LIFE

When Mahler concluded his training at the conservatory, he enrolled at the University of Vienna and attended lectures on a variety of topics. These included harmony, which was taught by Anton Bruckner, with whom he formed a friendly relationship. He soon faced a dilemma shared with other aspiring composers of his day: how to make a living. The solution available to many a composer born near the end of the nineteenth century was to perform as a touring virtuoso, but Mahler had given up on this idea. Others such as Bruckner made teaching their livelihood, but Mahler had no affinity for this profession. His plan, which Richard Strauss was

Bridgeman Art Library

FIGURE 60-1

Mahler in 1902, when this photograph was made, had reached the pinnacle of his fame as conductor at the Vienna Court Opera.

choosing at the same time, was to make his living as a conductor (primarily of opera) and to compose when time permitted, mainly in the summer months. In 1880 he acquired his first conducting position, initiating a career that would lead him ultimately to the very pinnacle of success: his appointment in October 1897 by the emperor himself, as director of the Opera in Vienna (Fig. 60-1). In 1907 Mahler resigned this position to conduct at the Metropolitan Opera in New York, and he ended his career as conductor of the New York Philharmonic Orchestra. Unlike his friend Strauss, however, Mahler never lived to see his music accepted by the public to an extent that allowed him to reduce his grueling schedule of conducting. By his own rueful estimation, he remained a lifelong "summer composer."

MAHLER'S SONGS

Mahler specialized in two of the main musical genres of his day: the song and symphony. At the end of the nineteenth century, the song continued to attract composers of every nationality, much as it had since the time of Schubert and Schumann. Recall from Chapter 58 that songs at this time were sometimes folk-like and relatively simple in musical style, at other times more sophisticated in musical resources and literary in tone.

Although Mahler wrote songs of both types, he increasingly emphasized the literary song. In his works of this type, the poetry attracts our attention nearly as much as the music. The texts are often sophisticated and subtle, written by leading literary figures. The burden of expression is shared between the voice and the accompaniment—piano or orchestra—and principal themes are located mainly in the latter. The harmonic and tonal language is expressive in its own right and highly enriched in sonority, and the form of such songs is usually through composed. Composers like Mahler often linked together several such songs into integrated cycles.

Mahler composed songs throughout his career, often as a way to exteriorize some deeply emotional event in his own life. He wrote the poetry himself for his first important cycle, the *Lieder eines fahrenden Gesellen* (*Songs of a Wayfarer*) of 1884–1885, which speaks about an unhappy love affair. Here, as often in his later songs, Mahler uses an orchestral accompaniment, although all of his songs also exist in authentic versions with piano alone. He believed that poetry of deep emotion could only be interpreted musically through an orchestral medium. "A large-scale composition that plumbs the depths of the subject unconditionally demands the orchestra," he told his friend Natalie Bauer-Lechner.[1] The large medium of the orchestra helped the composer to plumb those depths.

For the songs he composed just after the *Lieder eines fahrenden Gesellen*, Mahler selected song poetry from **Des knaben Wunderhorn** (*The Youth's Magic Horn*), a collection of some seven hundred German folk poems edited by Achim von Arnim and Clemens Brentano that was published in three volumes from 1805 to 1808. This folk poetry, which was freely modified by the editors, had already proved influential upon German romantic literature, but Mahler was the first major composer to explore it extensively as song text. The verses paint a variety of mundane scenes. Conversations between lovers, the dreary life of soldiering, humorous tales, the joys of nature, and stories involving the supernatural are characteristic.

By the turn of the century, Mahler's enthusiasm for the *Wunderhorn* poems waned, and he turned for song texts to the poetry of Friedrich Rückert, whom we have already encountered in Clara Schumann's song "Liebst du um Schönheit" (Chapter 54). In its highly intellectualized and introspective character, Rückert's verse is entirely different from the artless folk style. For his cycle *Kindertotenlieder* (*Songs on the Death of Children*, 1904), Mahler chose five wrenchingly emotional poems written by Rückert in 1834 following the death of his two children. In 1901 and 1902 Mahler composed five additional Rückert songs, including "Liebst du um Schönheit" ("If You Love Beauty"), the one set to music sixty years earlier by Clara Schumann.

Another of Mahler's Rückert songs is "Um Mitternacht" (1901). In this poem, the narrator awakens in the dead of night with a troubled mind. He looks for comfort alternately in the stars and in himself, but he finds none. He thinks next of his fellow man, but there he sees only suffering. Finally, having no other conceivable recourse, he turns to God, in whom he recognizes the guardian of all life.

Mahler's treatment of this sophisticated poem is typical of the literary song of the turn of the century. The accompaniment is provided by an orchestra, and the composer selects only those instruments—brass, woodwinds, piano, harp, and percussion—that seem to fit with the sentiments of the poem. Among the woodwinds he includes a prominent part for **oboe d'amore**—a sometimes ungainly alto oboe that Strauss used in his *Symphonia domestica* at about the same time. (The oboe d'amore is replaced by oboe in some editions.) Throughout his songs and symphonies, Mahler constantly experimented with such new combinations of sound: "Here is the future of all orchestral technique," he told his friend Josef Foerster.

Typical of the literary song, the form of "Um Mitternacht" avoids all simple repetitive patterns and remains close to the model of through composition. Musical materials from the opening stanza recur in each of the later ones, but always in a flexible and developmental manner that allows for the introduction of new ideas. Mahler's principle of form was embodied in the perpetual development of material, never in its simple repetition. He explained this to Bauer-Lechner:

> I have come to recognize a perpetual evolution of content in song, in other words, through-composition as the true principle of music. In my writing, from the very first, you won't find any more repetition from strophe to strophe; for music is governed by the law of eternal evolution, eternal development—just as the world, even in one and the same spot, is always changing, eternally fresh and new.[2]

The through-composed form allows the composer to follow closely upon the ideas of the poem. At the opening, for example, the key and mode are not firmly established, which suggests the narrator's ambivalent frame of mind, and the recurrent descending bass line in the accompaniment suggests his depression (Ex. 60-1). The harmonies of the song deserve careful study, both for their syntactic and expressive meaning. Prior to the fifth stanza, for example, Mahler totally avoids the dominant harmony in the key, again suggesting the narrator's uncertainty. But when his thoughts turn to God, the mode shifts to major and the harmonic progressions become absolutely clear and normative in the principal tonality. (Mahler himself was apparently undecided about the key of "Um Mitternacht." He sketched the song in the key of B♭ and had it published in 1905 in separate editions, one in the key of A, another in the key of B.)

EXAMPLE 60-1

LISTENING CUE

GUSTAV MAHLER   CD 10/8
"Um Mitternacht" (1901)   Anthology, No. 163

MAHLER'S SYMPHONIES

When Mahler completed his Symphony No. 1 in 1888, the genre of the symphony had risen to a position of supreme importance throughout the world of serious music. Surprisingly, its dominance had not been foreseen even by the leading composers of the earlier Romantic period. In his theory concerning "music of the future," formulated at mid-century, Richard Wagner said that the symphony had exhausted itself with Beethoven's Ninth Symphony, and that the future of music would tend toward an integrated musical drama distantly akin to opera. Plainly, Wagner was incorrect in this prediction. By the end of the century the symphony—not opera—was the supreme challenge for a composer. Virtually all of the principal figures of this time wrote symphonies, many of whom (including Brahms, Bruckner, Jean Sibelius, and Mahler himself) neglected opera entirely.

The writing of a new symphony in the 1880s confronted the composer with a number of critical choices. One was the makeup of the orchestra. The symphonists of conservative sentiment, including Brahms, wrote symphonies at this time for an orchestra of moderate size, whose constitution was similar to that of Beethoven's symphonies except for the inclusion of tuba, which was needed to give a bass voice to the brass choir. Symphonic composers of more modernist inclination—Mahler and Richard Strauss are examples—tended to follow Wagner in his expansion and diversification of the orchestra. Beethoven's idea of adding chorus and solo voices to the symphonic medium had waned among composers late in the century, but it was revived by Mahler, who included voices in his Symphonies No. 2, 3, 4, and 8.

Another question concerned the overall form of the symphony, and in this area there was little agreement among even the most successful composers. The conservatives preserved the classical four-movement sequence, consisting of a fast opening movement in sonata form, interior movements that were slow or dance-like, and a fast finale that tended to take on ever more weight. A more experimental solution, associated with Liszt and the New German School and reaching back to the time of Schubert's "Wanderer" Fantasy (see Chapter 52), was to write long and integrated one-movement works. Orchestral works of this type might have been considered tone poems or symphonies per se, and they typically had contrasting sections unified by the reappearance of common themes. Strauss's *Symphonia domestica* (1903) is an example. It has four main sections (a connected sequence fast/scherzo/slow/fast) that suggest a four-movement symphony. A third formal alternative, the one favored by Mahler, was to avoid all accepted plans and to rethink the overall form of the symphony freely and anew for each work.

The most vexing question of all for the aspiring symphonist of the 1880s concerned the content of a new work. Would the composer follow Brahms by avoiding any overt statement of non-musical content? Or would he take a midway position, as did Beethoven in the "Pastoral" Symphony or Schumann in his Symphony No. 1 ("Spring") by suggesting extra-musical ideas through movement titles and a freedom of form? Or would he follow the Berlioz of *Symphonie fantastique* and write an unabashedly programmatic symphony, in which the musical materials were placed directly in the service of a detailed narrative?

In his symphonies, Mahler was always ambiguous about this question. His writings make it clear that he was thoroughly skeptical about attaching programmatic meaning to orchestral music. To Alma Schindler in 1901 he described a program as something "that leads directly to misunderstanding, to a flattening and coarsening, and in the long run to such distortion that the work, and still more its creator, is utterly unrecognizable."[3] He was even more detailed in a letter of 1896 to the Berlin music critic Max Marschalk:

> I know that, so far as I myself am concerned, as long as I can express an experience in words I should never try to put it into music. The need to express myself musically— in symphonic terms—begins only on the plan of *obscure* feelings, at the gate that opens into the "other world," the world in which things no longer fall apart in time and space. — Just as I find it banal to compose programme-music, I regard it as unsatisfactory and unfruitful to try to make programme notes for a piece of music. This remains so despite the fact that the *reason* why a composition comes into being at all is bound to be something the composer has experienced, something real, which might after all be considered sufficiently concrete to be expressed in words.[4]

Despite these reservations, Mahler was aware that programmaticism in symphonic music helped to promote its understanding and acceptance, especially for new works that were unfamiliar in style. This had been proved by the great success of Richard Strauss's symphonic poems, works that were concrete in their programmatic content. Perhaps feeling a rivalry with Strauss, Mahler first presented his Symphonies Nos. 1–4 (composed 1888–1900) as overtly programmatic compositions that deal with the life, aspirations, and fate of a hero who is unnamed, although certainly the composer himself. Mahler's way of making his music relate to this program would have been familiar to audiences at the end of the century, since it included such familiar strategies as quoting from his own earlier music, associating themes with specific elements of the program, creating unusual forms that suggest a narrative, and fashioning irregular tonal plans whose meaning seemed to reside in an extra-musical dimension.

But in 1897, when Mahler began to publish his early symphonies, the programmatic element was strictly suppressed, and, in his symphonies beginning with No. 5, all programmatic allusions were banished. His Symphonies Nos. 5–7 (1902–1905) also eliminate the voices that were present in Nos. 2–4, although the Eighth Symphony (1906, called "Symphony of a Thousand" for its gigantic medium) brings the chorus back to sing texts from Goethe's *Faust* and the Pentecost hymn "Veni creator spiritus" ("Come, Creative Spirit"). Mahler's next major work, *Das Lied von der Erde* (*The Song of the Earth*, 1908–1909), combines the genres of symphony and song. The Ninth Symphony (1909) is remarkable for its abstraction and stylistic advancement, and his Symphony No. 10 was left incomplete upon his death in 1911, although the work is now performed using any of several reconstructions.

Mahler's Symphony No. 5

Mahler's Fifth Symphony (1902) initiated a new phase in the composer's creative life, although it has much about it that still hints at the openly programmatic works of the past. As in his earlier symphonies, he quotes in the first and fifth movements from his own earlier songs (from "Nun will die Sonn' so hell aufgeh'n" ["Now the Sun Will Brightly Rise"] from *Kindertotenlieder* and "Lob des hohen Verstandes" ["In Praise of Lofty Intellect"], a *Wunderhorn* song). The first movement is a grim funeral march, like the first movement of the Second Symphony, and, like the Fourth Symphony, the whole work has a non-concentric tonal plan, here beginning in C♯ minor and ending in D major. Also like Symphony No. 4, the five movements are linked into an integrated cycle by varied recurrence of themes.

A new and more classical direction is also plain to see. The orchestra is moderate in size, and, after the opening funeral march (which Mahler compared to a prelude), the normal sequence of four symphonic movements (fast/scherzo/slow/fast) is apparent. The work is also far shorter than the sprawling Symphonies Nos. 1–3. There is a new spirit present that is less self-conscious and introspective in expression and more given to a delight in pure and virtuosic music making.

The slow fourth movement, titled *Adagietto,* has a lost-to-the-world character that reappears throughout Mahler's oeuvre—notably in the finales of the Third and Ninth Symphonies and also in the orchestral song "Ich bin der Welt abhanden gekommen" ("I've Lost Track of the World"), which Mahler composed concurrently with the Fifth Symphony. Like the interior movements of most of his symphonies, the *Adagietto* has the character of an interlude, little resembling the outer movements in materials or mood. In its reduced orchestration for harp and strings it appears as a relaxed moment before the symphony's main musical issues are taken up again in the finale.

Our attention in the *Adagietto* is drawn most to the melody, which is passed between the violins and cellos. Its phrases are drawn out so leisurely as to make any regular beat or meter seem unapparent and any firm sense of cadence elusive. The principal melody, in a simple **ABA** form, has a teasing relationship to the underlying harmonies. On the downbeat of virtually every measure, the last melodic tone from the preceding measure is suspended over the bar, as though the melody is in no hurry to move on. This lazy hanging back is also evident in the free treatment of non-harmonic tones. At the end of the first phrase, for example, the music in measure 9 settles on the dominant chord (C major) in the key of F, but the third (E) of this chord is displaced by the tone F, suspended over from the preceding measure, and the expected resolution to the chordal tone E is reached only after the next melodic phrase has begun (Ex. 60-2).

EXAMPLE 60-2

mm. 8-11 (strings only)

Sehr langsam

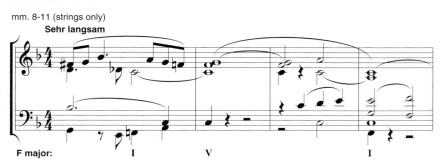

F major: I   V   I

Choosing a Tempo

Mahler marked the tempo of his *Adagietto* movement in the Fifth Symphony simply *Sehr langsam*—"very slow." He left behind nothing more specific, no metronome marking or recordings to help future musicians find the proper tempo. The time signature is a plain $\frac{4}{4}$, so this is not much help, other than to suggest the quarter-note as the unit corresponding to the beat.

It is known that Mahler himself conducted with generally quick tempos. In a letter to Albert Neisser in 1906, he states that the entire Fifth Symphony lasts about 45 minutes. This means that Mahler's tempos in the work were astonishingly fast (virtually no modern recordings of the symphony have a duration of less than an hour). The conductor Bruno Walter (1876–1962)—an associate conductor with Mahler in Vienna and present in Cologne for the premier performance of the Fifth Symphony in 1904 under Mahler's own leadership—later recorded the *Adagietto* with a quick tempo. Under his baton, the movement lasted about 7 minutes, 30 seconds.

The tempos have slowed since Walter's time. Leonard Bernstein's recording of 1964 stretched to 11 minutes, Herbert von Karajan's of 1973 to 12 minutes, and Bernard Haitink in a 1988 recording weighed in at just under 14 minutes, almost twice as long as in Walter's interpretation.

Can any of these tempos be judged absolutely right or wrong? The question itself is ambiguous. Many conductors believe that a tempo even far slower than Mahler's own can be musical, or "right," if other factors support it, especially the rare ability of an orchestra to play convincingly at a slow tempo. But Mahler himself was no relativist when it came to choosing tempos. In his writings he had no hesitation to speak of certain tempos as absolutely right or wrong.

Mahler's thinking on the subject of tempo reflects the ideas of Richard Wagner, especially those recorded in Wagner's landmark discussion in the essay "On Conducting" (1869). In an *Adagio* movement, Wagner writes, the conductor must set the tempo as slow as possible provided that its melodies can still be effectively sung. It is the singer's ability to regulate the breath, to create phrases, and to shape the line that governs tempo—even when the singer is absent!

No one movement—not even one so memorable as the *Adagietto* from the Fifth Symphony—can illustrate the inexhaustible inspiration and diversity of Mahler's symphonies. In his hands the genre became a truly total work of art, able to record nature in all its variety as well as the passions of the human soul in all their depth and subtlety. In a conversation in 1907 with the Finnish symphonic composer Jean Sibelius, Mahler summarized his viewpoint concerning the symphony. "The symphony must be like the world," Mahler insisted. "It must embrace everything."[5]

LISTENING CUE

GUSTAV MAHLER
Symphony No. 5 (1902)
Fourth movement, *Adagietto*

CD 10/9
Anthology, No. 164

 ## ALMA MAHLER: MUSICIAN AND MUSE

In the spring of 1902, Vienna was transfixed by news of the wedding engagement of Gustav Mahler—one of the city's most eligible bachelors—and the beautiful Alma Schindler (1879–1964; Fig. 60-2), daughter of a prominent family of Viennese artists. No one expected it to be a typical marriage. Mahler was known as impatient and domineering, Alma as creative, headstrong, and—nearly twenty years younger than her fiancé—evidently irresistible to men.

Schindler was also a talented musician. She was a good pianist, and when she met Mahler in 1901 she was a student in composition of **Alexander Zemlinsky**

❊ FIGURE 60-2

Alma Schindler, before her marriages to three world-famous men: Gustav Mahler, Walter Gropius, and Franz Werfel.

(1871–1942). She composed primarily piano pieces and songs—a hundred of them, as she later claimed. After Mahler died in 1911, Alma married the architect Walter Gropius and, following their divorce, the novelist Franz Werfel. Most of her musical compositions were lost when she fled from Hitler on an odyssey that ultimately brought her in 1940 to the United States. She lived first in California, later in New York City, until her death in 1964.

Mahler made it a condition of their marriage that she give up composing. "The role of 'composer,' the 'worker's' role falls to me," he insisted, "yours is that of the loving companion and understanding partner."[6] Alma reluctantly complied, although in 1910 Mahler relented in his opposition to her creative work. He then encouraged Alma to return to her earlier compositions and to prepare some of the songs for publication, after both he and Alma had revised them. A total of fourteen of her songs were published between 1910 and 1924.

The song "Die stille Stadt" ("The Quiet City") was placed first in the 1910 publication, suggesting that it was a favorite of both Mahlers. The song reveals melodic and expressive warmth and a daring harmonic originality. The date of composition is unknown, but it was probably in 1900 or 1901, during Alma's period of study with Zemlinsky. The poet of "Die stille Stadt," Richard Dehmel (1863–1920), was admired by Zemlinsky, as he was by many other progressive German musicians of the day. The poem is romantic stuff. A narrator describes a town swallowed by a darkness and fog so dense as to strike fear in the hearts of its visitors. The anxiety is dispelled by the simple sound of a child singing, which is like a ray of light that cannot be dimmed.

The harmonic language of the song brings to it an element of strangeness that matches the disoriented feelings of the narrator as fog descends on the city. Tonic and dominant chords in the keys of D major and minor (the parallel modes are used interchangeably) appear at structural junctures in the song, like the tops of spires and bridges peeping up through the fog in Dehmel's poem. But, between these guideposts, the harmonic motions seem to get lost, arriving on chords that are distant from the harmonic road map, only then suddenly to regain a tonal point of orientation.

Such harmonic detours arise at the very opening of the song (Ex. 60-3). The short piano introduction begins on a tonic triad but by the second beat it has slipped into the fog of a diminished chord. Another try leads only to a greater disorientation, represented on beat four by an augmented-sixth chord (Db-F-Ab-B♮) with no clear function in the home key. The tonic then suddenly reappears on the downbeat of measure 2, and, however briefly, we know where we are.

EXAMPLE 60-3

mm. 1-2

LISTENING CUE

ALMA MAHLER
"Die stille Stadt" (c1901)

CD 10/10
Anthology, No. 165

SUMMARY

New music flourished in Vienna at the time Mahler lived there (1875–1880 as a student, and 1897–1907 as conductor and director of the Opera). His career was divided between conducting and composing, and in the latter capacity he wrote primarily songs and symphonies. For his early songs he drew upon folk poetry from the anthology *Des knaben Wunderhorn*, and later from the works of Friedrich Rückert. The song "Um Mitternacht" is an example of a song with literary emphasis: the music closely interprets the text, the song is accompanied by an orchestra of unusual makeup, and it is through composed and continually developmental.

Mahler wrote ten symphonies (the last one left incomplete) and a "song symphony" called *Das Lied von der Erde*. The first four were presented as autobiographical programmatic works, although these were later published as absolute music with the programmatic apparatus removed. His later symphonies are even more in the absolute vein. Symphony No. 5 is the first of the later group, and, although it shares much in style with the earlier symphonies, its relative brevity, moderate-sized orchestra, and musical virtuosity suggest a new phase in the composer's work. Its fourth movement, *Adagietto*, is celebrated for its melodiousness and spirit of detachment.

Mahler's wife, Alma, was a skillful composer in the late Romantic style of the turn of the twentieth century. She composed mainly songs, of which fourteen were published during her lifetime. Her "Die stille Stadt" is remarkable for its advanced harmonic thinking and intense expressivity.

KEY TERMS

Des knaben Wunderhorn   oboe d'amore   Alexander Zemlinsky

Chapter
61

England at the End of the Romantic Period: Elgar and Vaughan Williams

The great wealth and political might of England in the late nineteenth century supported a thriving musical culture. By 1901 the population of greater London had risen to an astounding 6.6 million residents, and these numbers, together with an affluence generated by industrialization and empire, created in the capital city a uniquely large demand for music. Music also flourished in smaller English cities, where orchestras, choir festivals, and amateur music making had grown in popularity throughout the nineteenth century.

Oddly, this demand for music was satisfied—as it had been for almost two hundred years—primarily by imported music and foreign composers. For reasons that are not at all clear, England after the time of Purcell did not, until the twentieth century, produce native composers who were widely recognized beyond their own land. In the eighteenth century, the leading "English" figures were German immigrants, including George Frideric Handel and John Christian Bach, and other foreigners such as the Rome-born pianist Muzio Clementi (1752–1832) were also leaders in English music.

European composers flocked to London throughout the nineteenth century to organize special concerts and to write works on commission. Carl Maria von Weber composed and conducted his last opera, *Oberon,* for Covent Garden, and Mendelssohn wrote his late oratorio *Elijah* for the Birmingham Festival in 1846. Clara Schumann performed in England no less than nineteen times. The elderly Franz Liszt came to London in 1886 for what proved a triumphant performance of his oratorio *The Legend of St. Elizabeth* at the Crystal Palace. During this stay he was invited to Windsor Castle to meet Queen Victoria, who was herself highly musical. "We asked him to play," she wrote in her diary, "which he did, several of his own compositions. He played beautifully."[1]

Although London held out the promise of financial gain for visiting composers, the complex entrepreneurship that existed in the city could easily cast visiting artists into financial disaster. This was the outcome of Richard Wagner's visit to London in 1877. Hoping to reduce the debt incurred in the first Bayreuth festival and aware of his great popularity in London, he arranged for a series of concerts at the huge Royal Albert Hall. Apparently unknown to Wagner, many of the seats were permanently leased to patrons who could attend any event without additional cost. Wagner's visit was an artistic success but a financial debacle.

The most successful of the native English composers of the late nineteenth century was **Arthur Sullivan** (1842–1900). Following training at the conservatory in Leipzig, he attracted attention in London for his serious choral and orchestral music. But he made his most lasting mark in the genre of **operetta,** a type of light opera that was well established in Paris and Vienna by mid-century. In 1871 he began to collaborate on comic works with the London writer **William Gilbert,** and in 1875 the team of Gilbert and Sullivan scored their first major success with the operetta *Trial by Jury.* Their collaboration endured until 1896, resulting in fourteen works including *H. M. S. Pinafore, The Pirates of Penzance, The Mikado,* and *The Yeomen of the Guard.*

❋ THE ENGLISH CHOIR FESTIVALS

Although known for his light music, Arthur Sullivan spent much of his career as a conductor and composer for **choir festivals.** Summer festivals that featured choral singing took place in Germany and elsewhere during the nineteenth century, but they had a special importance for English musical life. Often lasting for several days at a time, they brought together amateur choruses and church choirs from an entire region to perform choral classics and new works. Their popularity was advanced by the enduring demand throughout England to hear the choral music of Handel and by a longstanding tradition of amateur choral singing. By the end of the nineteenth century, the festivals had taken on their own character, with huge numbers of performers, long programs that mixed choral and symphonic music, and a gala at-mosphere in which entire communities were brought together.

The most famous of these events in London was the **Handel Festival,** which took place every third year beginning in 1857. Similar occasions outside of London also had a great appeal. The Three Choirs Festival figures prominently in the careers of several leading English musicians, especially Edward Elgar. In its early history in the eighteenth century, it brought together the cathedral choirs from Gloucester, Worcester, and Hereford, rotating its location yearly among these three cities. By the mid nineteenth century, the Three Choirs Festival extended for six consecutive days, with participation by amateur choruses throughout the region accompanied by a professional festival orchestra.

The festivals also had importance for English society. The singers, from all walks of life, encountered music not as onlookers but participants in an activity whose importance reinforced a sense of national unity. A reporter at the Leeds Festival of 1898 commented on its galvanizing atmosphere:

> It was here that the crowds—for there was a crowd outside all three main entrances—gaped most, and stared and jostled and pushed in their energetic attempts to see the Festival from without. And in sooth it was a brave sight to see the gaily dressed ladies tripping from the steps of the broughams and up over the red-carpeted steps, with the gentlemen behind shouting directions to the Jehus and giving a final pat for the satisfactory adjustment of their white tie. . . . Hither and thither hurried people—grey-beards, youths, elderly ladies, maidens—with 'scores' rolled under their arms.[2]

EDWARD ELGAR

The choir festivals provoked a broad involvement of the English people in amateur music-making, and they finally contributed to the emergence of one of the great composers of the late Romantic period, Edward Elgar (1857–1934; Fig. 61-1). His early career is typical of such lesser nineteenth-century English musicians as Hubert Parry, Charles Stanford, and Alexander Mackenzie. He grew up in the town of Worcester and frequently attended concerts in London, which by train was four hours distant. His father ran a music shop, and he learned to play violin and keyboard instruments, although his knowledge of composition was entirely self-taught. Until well into his forties he made his living as a freelance violinist, church organist, and music teacher. His compositions did not attract attention far beyond his home town.

His musical career was then rooted in a regional culture whose main institutions were choir festivals, glee club performances, and amateur orchestras. His imagination as a creative musician ultimately could not be contained within this provincial milieu, and he looked beyond it for a musical language that could express more universal matters.

Elgar found in German music a model for his fully romantic spirit. Like many English musicians of the late nineteenth century, Elgar became a staunch Germanist. The cultural interchange between England and German lands had been strong

FIGURE 61-1

Edward Elgar was the outstanding English composer of the late Romantic period.

since 1714, when the Elector of Hanover rose to the English throne as George I. Queen Victoria's mother was German-born, as was her husband, Prince Albert. Elgar was especially attracted to the new works of Brahms and Wagner, as well as to those of younger German progressivists such as Richard Strauss. In Brahms, Elgar noted the absence of a regionalism that was so pronounced in his own musical environment. Brahms's Symphony No. 3, he wrote, was "free from any provincialism or expression of national dialect (the charming characteristic of lesser men: Gade, Dvořák, Grieg)." Brahms, continued Elgar, "writes for the whole world and for all time—a giant—lofty and unapproachable." Wagner was equally esteemed. On his score of *Tristan und Isolde*, Elgar wrote: "The best and the whole of the best of this world and the next."

In the 1890s Elgar and his wife (who shared his admiration for German culture) traveled repeatedly to Munich and Bayreuth to hear Wagner. On one such pilgrimage they were joined by a family friend, Rosa Burley, who recalled the occasion in her memoirs:

> The *Ring* impressed me chiefly by its interminable length, and I was quite unable to understand the Genius's [Elgar's] enthusiasm. But *Tristan* was a shattering experience—Mrs. Elgar, always deeply affected by romantic music, was the most touched . . . but on all of us the heavily erotic melodies worked such a spell as to make sleep impossible for the whole night.[3]

Elgar primarily wrote for chorus and orchestra and for orchestra alone—the two types of music that could be most readily marketed to festivals in the England of his day. In the late 1890s, his music begin to attract attention in London, and finally in 1899 his Variations on an Original Theme (*Enigma*) brought him international celebrity. The work was followed by the oratorio *The Dream of Gerontius* (1900), and by a series of short orchestral compositions including the overtures *Cockaigne* (1901) and *In the South* (1904), and by five orchestral marches titled **Pomp and Circumstance** (see Box). In 1904 he was knighted by King Edward VII, making him "Sir Edward Elgar." The main successes of his later years were works for orchestra: two symphonies (1908 and 1911), and concertos for violin (1910) and cello (1919).

Variations on an Original Theme ("Enigma")

Sets of variations are not especially prominent in the nineteenth-century orchestral literature, although Brahms's *Variations on a Theme by Joseph Haydn* (1873) may have been a model for Elgar when he wrote his "Enigma" Variations, Op. 36, in 1898–1899. Both works proceed through a number of variations having strongly contrasting character and end in a climactic finale. Unlike Brahms's Variations, the "Enigma" Variations is an intensely programmatic composition in the late nineteenth-century German progressive manner. Like Mahler's early symphonies, it concerns the composer's own life in its outward and inward dimensions, although both Elgar and Mahler kept exact details of such programmatic meaning strictly out of sight.

The existence of Elgar's personalized program is hinted at in familiar ways—titles of movements, quotations from pre-existing music (from Mendelssohn's overture *Meeresstille und glückliche Fahrt* [*Calm Seas and Prosperous Journey*] in Variation 13), and the use of a melody in Variation 1 that was sung and played in the Elgar household.

But for public consumption, Elgar gave away only superficial ideas: "This work, commenced in a spirit of humour & continued in deep seriousness, contains

Pomp and Circumstance

There are some few compositions in the history of music that immediately please everyone and continue to do so indefinitely, seemingly impervious to passing time and changing taste. One such is the "Hallelujah" chorus from Handel's *Messiah*. Even though we have all heard it countless times, the "Hallelujah" chorus still brings us to our feet. We stand not just because of a tradition of doing so, but because this music is filled with so much electricity that we cannot stay in our seats. Audiences have always felt its power. After the first performance in Dublin, Ireland, in 1742, a reviewer wrote that *Messiah* "was allowed by the greatest Judges to be the finest composition of Musick that ever was heard."

Edward Elgar's *Pomp and Circumstance* contains another such timeless moment in music. In 1901 Elgar wrote two short marches for orchestra, which he called *Pomp and Circumstance*, drawing the title from a line in Shakespeare's *Othello*. His jealousy aroused by Iago, Othello exclaims, "Farewell the tranquil mind! Farewell . . . pride, pomp, and circumstance of glorious war!"

Elgar knew all along that the melody in the trio of the first of the two marches was something special (its beginning is shown below). He had written about it to his publisher, "Gosh! Man I've got a tune in my head!" The early audiences of the march shared Elgar's enthusiasm. When March No. 1 was first performed at a Promenade concert in London in 1901, the conductor, Henry Wood, had to play it three times before the audience would let the concert continue.

It has never lost its inspiring power. Nowadays the *Pomp and Circumstance* March No. 1 and its famous trio are played at every American high school graduation, regally accompanying the entrance of the proud graduates and always bringing tears of joy to the eyes of their parents.

There is no possibility of explaining the longevity or the uniquely inspiring effect of this work on purely technical grounds. The melody seems simple and unremarkable as it marches down the scale from G to A, accompanied by the simplest of chords. Its appeal may well be in its perfect balance of materials, which seem to achieve just the right mixture of things that are original with others that can be readily anticipated. There is neither too much complication nor simplicity, and a perfect marriage is formed in it between the expected and the unexpected.

sketches of the composer's friends. It may be understood that these personages comment or reflect on the original theme & each one attempts a solution of the Enigma, for so the theme is called."[4]

What is this "enigma" contained in the theme (its beginning is shown in Ex. 61-1)? On this question Elgar was more than a little evasive:

The Enigma I will not explain—its "dark saying" must be left unguessed, and I warn you that the apparent connexion between the Variations and the Theme is often of the slightest texture; further, through and over the whole set another and larger theme "goes", but is not played. . . . So the principal Theme never appears, even as in some late dramas—e.g., Maeterlinck's "L'Intruse" and "Les sept Princesses"—the chief character [Death] is never on the stage.[5]

EXAMPLE 61-1

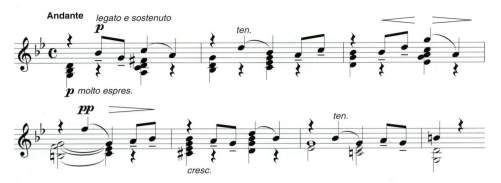

The work consists of a theme in G minor and major followed by fourteen variations, of which the last is marked "Finale." Each of the variations is headed by initials of (or other references to) the name of an acquaintance of the composer, the music being "what I think they w[oul]d have written, if they were asses enough to compose," as he told his publisher. The first variation, for example, refers to Elgar's wife, Alice, and the last one to Elgar himself.

The true nature of the central enigma and the identity of the unplayed "principal theme" have been infinitely debated, with no unanimous agreement about what Elgar might have meant. Some have held that the missing theme is a melody ("Auld Lang Syne" has been suggested) that could form a counterpoint with the actual theme, although many other solutions have also been proposed, involving music that ranges from Mozart's "Prague" Symphony to the **B-A-C-H motive** (B♭-A-C-B♮, the musical letters of Bach's name). Others believe that Elgar referred not to a musical theme but to a musical problem posed by the theme, which the variations then gradually resolve.

In purely musical terms, there is much about the theme that is complex and possibly enigmatic. Although it has a simple ternary form, it opens with phrases that are divided into breathless one-measure units (see Ex. 61-1). Its many leaps suggest that at least two melodic strands exist in it simultaneously, their notes touched alternately to form what is called a **compound melody.** The leaps of a descending-seventh in measures 3 and 4 are especially distinctive.

The centerpiece and longest section of the work is the ninth variation, which is often performed as a separate composition. It is subtitled "**Nimrod,**" the name of the "mighty hunter" from the Book of Genesis. This is a reference to Elgar's friend and editor, August Johannes Jaeger (the German word *Jaeger* means "hunter"— Elgar was fond of puns). Elgar paints a highly sympathetic portrait of Jaeger in this variation. The rich sound of the orchestra comes from Elgar's skillful adaptation of the German style of orchestration, which aimed at a blended sound. When the full orchestra plays, the important primary and subsidiary lines are doubled, so as to mix elements from several of the orchestra's main choirs—strings, woodwinds, and brass. No one sonority is made to stand out, as it does in contemporaneous French and Russian orchestral works from the same period.

The Nimrod variation preserves the ternary form of the theme and clearly paraphrases its opening melodic shapes, including the distinctive downward leaps. But much is changed. The disjointed phrases of the theme are made continuous, and the minor mode that hung clouds over the theme has changed to major and revealed a blissfully blue sky. In these ways it may be that Nimrod has begun to solve Elgar's enigma.

🎵 **LISTENING CUE**

EDWARD ELGAR   CD 10/11–12
"Enigma" Variations (1899)   Anthology, No. 166
Theme and ninth variation ("Nimrod")

❋ ENGLISH MUSIC AFTER ELGAR: RALPH VAUGHAN WILLIAMS

Following the turn of the twentieth century, Edward Elgar's unabashedly romantic music—bursting with emotion and plainly using the nineteenth-century language of Wagner—seemed to many audiences to be out of touch with broader developments in music of the day. It was not a musical style that could be unquestioningly accepted by younger English composers. Ralph Vaughan Williams (1872–1958; Fig. 61-2) continued some of the romantic traits of Elgar's music, especially its expressive melodiousness and emphasis on traditional orchestral and choral forms and genres. But, at the same time, Vaughan Williams looked for alternatives that could stamp his music as English rather than German, and a product of the twentieth century rather than the nineteenth.

Vaughan Williams grew up in London and received his musical education at the Royal College of Music and Cambridge University. His attention as a church organist and choir master was drawn to the hymnody of the Anglican Church, and in 1906 he helped to edit a new collection called the **English Hymnal.** Here he included some of his own hymns ("Hail Thee, Festival Day!," "Down Ampney," and "Sine Nomine"—Ex. 61-2—are especially well known). He also created hymns by joining folk songs to hymn texts and by reviving the music of numerous Renaissance musicians.

❋ FIGURE 61-2
Vaughan Williams brought new ideas to the romantic style of Elgar.

EXAMPLE 61-2

mm. 1-4

As a composer, Vaughan Williams concentrated on symphonies—he wrote nine of these—and works for chorus. He also composed shorter orchestral pieces, such as the *Fantasia on a Theme by Thomas Tallis* (1910). It is based on a hymn that he included in the *English Hymnal,* "When Rising from the Bed of Death," the music from the English composer Thomas Tallis (1505–1585). Vaughan Williams had found Tallis's hymn in a collection of sixteenth-century psalm tunes, where it appears in Phrygian mode with a simple four-part harmonization (see Chapter 26). Its first phrase is shown in Example 61-3, as Vaughan Williams presents Tallis's piece in the *English Hymnal* with the melody in the soprano voice.

EXAMPLE 61-3

Vaughan Williams's interest in English folk song and early English polyphony suggests a new way of thinking about music that differs from the romantic outlook of Elgar and the great nineteenth-century German musicians like Brahms and Wagner. For these composers, music was a universal and timeless language, but Vaughan Williams's works suggest that it can just as well be rooted in a particular place. In his lecture-essay "Should Music Be National?" (1932), Vaughan Williams rejects the notion of music of the future and the cult of the genius, both central to Elgar's aesthetic. He would never have praised Brahms, as did Elgar, for being "for the whole world and for all time." Music, wrote Vaughan Williams, was primarily for the present time and for the composer's region, and only in this context could it project a healthy nationalism. The larger-than-life works of Wagner held little appeal to him.

 ## SUMMARY

Music in England in the late nineteenth century was supplied largely by foreign composers, although the popular choir festivals created a demand for new music, and the operettas of Gilbert and Sullivan were universally admired. Edward Elgar adopted the musical language of German romantic composers, especially Wagner, although he used it in a highly original way in his orchestral and choral works. His first international success was with his so-called "Enigma" Variations for orchestra, in which one striking variation is subtitled "Nimrod," named after the hunter in Genesis. The revival in English music begun by Elgar was continued by his younger contemporaries, including Ralph Vaughan Williams. In his use and imitation of English folk song and Renaissance melodies, Vaughan Williams partly turned away from Elgar's Germanic romanticism and developed a harmonic language based on the old church modes.

 ## KEY TERMS

Arthur Sullivan	Handel Festival	"Nimrod"
operetta	*Pomp and Circumstance*	*English Hymnal*
William Gilbert	B-A-C-H motive	
choir festival	compound melody	

Opera in Milan after Verdi:
Puccini, Toscanini, and *Verismo*

When Verdi's *Otello* received its triumphant premiere at the Teatro alla Scala in Milan in 1887, the city's musical and operatic culture was well on its way to becoming fully modernized and cosmopolitan. How different this was from the situation at La Scala when Verdi's first opera, *Oberto,* was heard there in 1839. The enterprise of opera at La Scala was then almost entirely in the hands of its impresario, Bartolomeo Merelli, and the works in any one season rotated among recent compositions that Merelli commissioned or rented. A successful opera was repeated until the audience for it dwindled, whereupon the composer or his publisher tried to market it to other cities. A notable success by a well-known figure such as a Vincenzo Bellini or Gaetano Donizetti could be revived for as many years as there was a demand for it, but it was thought inevitable that even the most admired opera would fade into oblivion after a few years.

❋ THE OPERA BUSINESS

The economic viability of opera early in the nineteenth century depended on the creation of new works, and the **impresario** was their catalyst. He offered contracts to promising composers, placed them in touch with librettists whom he also hired, and worked closely with a publisher to promote the sale or rental of works to other houses, for which he normally received a commission. The operas performed at La Scala in the 1830s were almost entirely by living Italian composers, as older works seemed woefully outdated and compositions by foreigners were looked on with a good deal of skepticism.

By 1887 the opera business in Italy had changed. The role of the impresario had been taken over by publishing houses, which coordinated the creation and marketing of new works. Verdi's publisher was the powerful Milan firm of **Ricordi,** whose representatives worked directly with the composer—as they did later with Giacomo Puccini—to promote the creation of new works. Verdi's *Otello* (see Chapter 56) came into being largely through Ricordi's urging, and such a major operatic success was no longer merely a local phenomenon but a worldwide event.

The practice of operatic performance by 1887 was also on its way to modern standards. The challenging orchestra part of *Otello,* for example, was played by La Scala's large and excellent orchestra, led by the well-known conductor Franco Faccio. This was a far cry from the first performance of *Oberto,* which had been directed—as was the custom in the 1830s—only by the orchestra's first violinist, with the composer at his side.

The deportment of the opera audience had also changed. In the 1830s the atmosphere at an opera was almost like a sports event in the present day: people cheered, booed, and hurled sarcastic remarks. The booing could bring a performance to an early end if the crowd didn't like what it heard. The audience especially guarded its right to demand an immediate repetition of an enjoyable part of an opera, even though this practice was certain to obscure the coherence of the work as a whole. The performance of encores was finally ended at La Scala only in the 1906–1907 season, when it was officially banned by the management.

The Claque

One of the oddities of nineteenth-century operatic culture was the claque. This was a group of professional applauders (*claquer* is the French word for clapping). They were hired, usually by the opera management, to attend opera performances and to applaud on cue. The effect of their work was just like having canned laughter in a TV comedy.

The claque was most valuable at the premiere of a new opera. In a large theater at such an event, the claque could number more than one hundred clappers, all well-rehearsed and coordinated. Their work was highly prized by composers and performers since they could create enthusiasm, underscore a high point in an unknown work, and guide those in the audience as to when applause was needed and when not.

The institution of the claque reached its heights at the Paris Opéra in the 1830s. Its leader was known simply as Auguste, and his power to make a success or failure out of a new opera was legendary. He had no hesitation to tell a composer what needed to be changed, and he was not inclined to waste his efforts on a work he didn't like. Hector Berlioz recalled Auguste's response to a minor composer who had asked for his support: "I can't do it, sir. It would compromise me in the eyes of the public, of the artists, and of my colleagues. I have my reputation to maintain; . . I cannot allow myself to be hissed."

INNOVATIONS AT LA SCALA

The modernization of operatic culture at La Scala in the 1880s was most evident in the expansion of its repertory to include works by leading foreign composers (always given in Italian translation) and a new readiness to restage classic works from the past. The number of operas and performances in a season was much reduced in comparison to 1839. In that year's playbill, seventeen operas were given no fewer than 221 performances. In 1887, only five operas were in the repertory, and these received a total of sixty-two presentations. Classics of the past were now amply represented: Donizetti—by far the most popular opera composer at La Scala in 1839—was still in the repertory in 1887 with his *Lucrezia Borgia*, which was composed over a half-century earlier. The Milanese audiences long had a taste for French opera (Jules Massenet and Charles Gounod were especially well-liked), and in the 1880s Wagner's works were poised to take the city by storm. In 1889 *Lohengrin* (by "Riccardo Wagner") had seventeen performances, and in the 1890s his works had become staples of the city's operatic diet. Many of Milan's leading younger composers—including Giacomo Puccini and Pietro Mascagni—declared themselves to be Wagnerians.

ARTURO TOSCANINI

The internationalization of La Scala was advanced by the appointment in 1898 of **Arturo Toscanini** (1867–1957) as artistic director and principal conductor. Toscanini began his career as a cellist. He had played in the La Scala orchestra at the premiere of *Otello* in 1887, and even then he was considered one of Italy's rising young conductors. He had many of the same qualities that made Gustav Mahler a controversial success in Vienna: excellent musicianship, high standards, and the willpower to impose a unified artistic conception on a large and often contentious group of musicians.

At La Scala, Toscanini insisted on the highest level of technical excellence from the orchestra and singers, and he also demanded respect from the audience, not just for the singing but for the work as a whole. His career led him increasingly away from Milan to other cities of the world, although he periodically returned to La Scala for important events. One of the most poignant of these followed the death in 1924 of his friend Puccini. At the funeral in Milan's great Duomo (cathedral), Toscanini conducted Puccini's music with La Scala's orchestra. Two years later he led the premier performance of Puccini's last opera, *Turandot*, whose ending the composer did not live to complete. Instead of using Franco Alfano's reconstruction of Puccini's sketches for these concluding minutes, Toscanini ended it with the last measures that Puccini himself had composed—Liù's funeral music—whereupon he turned to the audience to state movingly that the composer had died at that point.

What primarily separated Toscanini from other Italian conductors of the day was his breadth of repertory. He was equally at home with the symphonic literature as with opera, and he was also open to complex modern music. In addition to his great understanding of the works of Verdi and Puccini, Toscanini also specialized in the operas of Wagner. He inaugurated his tenure as music director in Turin in 1895 by conducting Wagner's *Götterdämmerung* and at La Scala with *Die Meistersinger*. In 1930 he was the first non-German to conduct at Bayreuth.

He crossed paths with Gustav Mahler only briefly, in New York in 1909 and 1910, when both were on the staff of the Metropolitan Opera, both competing for the Wagnerian repertory. Just as in Milan and Turin, he wished first to conduct Wagner at the Met, but to his credit he stepped aside when Mahler protested that this would conflict with his own native specialty.

✿ PUCCINI AT LA SCALA

Like Verdi before him, Giacomo Puccini (1858–1924) was closely associated with the city of Milan and its Teatro alla Scala (Fig. 62-1). He attended the Conservatory in Milan from 1880 to 1883, during which time he composed his earliest opera, *Le villi*. His first real success came in 1893 with *Manon Lescaut*, in which he took up a literary source already used by Jules Massenet in the 1884 French opera *Manon*. More oper-

❋ FIGURE 62-1
Puccini and Arturo Toscanini in Paris, where they planned the Metropolitan Opera premiere of *La fanciulla del West*.

atic successes followed: *La Bohème* (1896), *Tosca* (1900), *Madama Butterfly* (1904), *La fanciulla del West* (1910, based on the American play *Girl of the Golden West*) and *Turandot* (1924). Like Wagner and Verdi before him, Puccini specialized strictly in operatic composition. After his student days, he wrote no large-scale works of any other type. He explained in a letter to his librettist Giuseppe Adami: "The Almighty touched me with his little finger and said, 'Write for the theater— only for the theater!' And I have obeyed the supreme command."

Madama Butterfly received a stormy premiere at La Scala in February 1904, after which it underwent a series of extensive revisions. It is based on the play *Madame Butterfly* by the American writer David Belasco and on a short story of the same title by John Luther

Synopsis of *Madama Butterfly*

On a hill overlooking Nagasaki harbor, the marriage broker, Goro, shows a house to the American naval officer Benjamin Franklin Pinkerton. He is to be married to the Japanese girl Cho-Cho-San (called "Butterfly"). In Pinkerton's aria "Dovunque al mondo," he explains that he travels the world sampling the best of local delights, leaving them all quickly behind. The American consul, Sharpless, disapproves of this philosophy. Butterfly arrives with her large family, and just as the marriage ceremony is concluded her uncle, the Bonze, bursts in to chastise Butterfly for marrying outside of her culture and religion. Left alone, Pinkerton and Butterfly profess their love.

When Act 2 opens, three years have passed with no word from Pinkerton, who has left Butterfly and her servant, Suzuki, behind. Butterfly is confident that he will return as he promised, when the robins return to their nests. Sharp-

less and Goro arrive to try to arrange another marriage for Butterfly, to a Japanese-American businessman named Yamadori, but she will hear none of it. Butterfly shows Sharpless the son born after Pinkerton's departure. At last, Pinkerton's ship is seen entering the harbor, and Butterfly elatedly dresses in her wedding gown to greet Pinkerton upon his return.

Act 3 begins at dawn. Pinkerton has still not arrived and Butterfly has fallen asleep. Sharpless, Pinkerton, and his American wife, Kate, quietly enter. Filled with shame and sorrow, Pinkerton leaves Sharpless and Kate to try to convince Butterfly to allow the child to be brought up in America. She agrees, provided that Pinkerton makes the request in person. Behind a screen she stabs herself to death as Pinkerton rushes in. "Butterfly! Butterfly!" he cries.

Long, which was also Belasco's source. As usual in a new opera by Puccini, the libretto was created by multiple hands, including Puccini's own and those of his publisher, Giulio Ricordi. An outline was first made by Luigi Illica, and the poetic text itself was written by Giuseppe Giacosa, both writers working for Ricordi.

The literary sources provided only a shell of what eventually became the musical text (see Box). The librettists freely added episodes and characters, and they had no hesitation to change the entire tone of the work. The first act of the libretto, for example, was created almost entirely by Illica and Giacosa. It has no counterpart in Belasco's play (although some of its episodes are outlined in Long's story). The character of Butterfly is flattened into a one-dimensional type that is far removed from Belasco's character. In the play she is a primitive and almost clownish figure; in the opera, a sensitive victim of exploitation who, typical of Puccini's heroines, sacrifices everything for love.

Puccini's music contains a mixture of styles: the Verdian reliance on emotional expression through vocal melody is still the central element, although the voices also sing for long stretches in a more conversational mode. Puccini—always interested in the new harmonic resources of his day—gives the score pungency by whole-tone and pentatonic passages, the latter reinforcing the Japanese setting. (Puccini also quotes several authentic Japanese folk songs.)

The structure of the opera represents an updating that shows the composer's effort to make opera plausible as drama as well as music. To do this he merges traditional principles of Italian opera with the newer thinking of modern French and German composers. The acts contain numerous operatic numbers—arias, duets, ensembles, and choruses—each of which has a reasonably closed or symmetrical form. These numbers are floated into a more continuous music sung by ensembles with changing numbers of characters. Here the singing is declamatory, and these ensembles fulfill a narrative function provided in earlier opera by recitative.

Puccini's new structural synthesis is apparent at the beginning of Act 1. The work begins without an overture in a narrative ensemble in which the number of characters steadily increases. It begins with Goro and Pinkerton, who are soon joined by Butterfly's servants including Suzuki, then by Sharpless. At each arrival of a new character and at each change of topic, a new section of music begins, usually with a new tempo, key, and melody. The singing has the character of a melodious declamation, musically midway between aria and recitative.

Puccini is plainly interested in promoting continuity throughout these conversational ensembles by bringing back themes and motives at points far distant from one another. For example, the opera opens with the theme shown in Example 62-1, which is first presented in the orchestra as the subject of a four-part fugue. The figure returns frequently throughout the first act, serving to bind the music together.

EXAMPLE 62-1

Puccini also uses a more subtle principle of motivic recurrence that links together several themes on the basis of a common melodic profile. Three of the most important themes heard near the beginning of the opera (Ex. 62-2) are associated in this way. Their affinity comes from their sharing an ascending major triad (bracketed in the example). The second one quotes the opening of the American national anthem, which frames Pinkerton's aria "Dovunque al mondo" (discussed below). The other melodies are sung by Pinkerton and Sharpless, the two principal American characters, Puccini's apparent objective being to give these related figures related melodic material. But the composer does not go so far as to make themes into Wagnerian leitmotives; he does not use them so pervasively or with such clear symbolism as does Wagner.

EXAMPLE 62-2

The opening narrative ensemble is interrupted by the first traditional operatic number, Pinkerton's aria "Dovunque al mondo" ("Wherever in the World"). Typical of the traditional Italian opera, the text is reflective rather than narrative. Here Pinkerton declares his philosophy of life—to travel the world seeking pleasure with no concern about its consequences.

The aria has a symmetrical form: it is framed by the quotations of the American national anthem and it has two stanzas which begin with essentially the same music. Puccini also looks for ways to bring dramatic action even into a self-contained aria. Within the number, Pinkerton continues his conversation with Sharpless. Both of Pinkerton's stanzas lead into recitational music in which Sharpless interrupts to disapprove of Pinkerton's philosophy of life. They cannot resolve their argument, and the music finally breaks off in the middle of a harmonic progression, far from having reached its completion in the home key of G♭ major. Pinkerton then finds an idea on which they can agree: "America forever!" he sings in English. With this the music returns to the tonic chord, Sharpless concurs by singing the same line, and the aria ends.

LISTENING CUE

GIACOMO PUCCINI
Madama Butterfly (1904)
Aria "Dovunque al mondo"

CD 10/13
Anthology, No. 167

❋ VERISMO OPERA

In the 1890s Milan was also prominent in the origin of a new type of Italian opera, called **verismo** (realism). Such operas are short and musically condensed, usually spanning only a single act, and they are typically set among people from the lower social classes who are driven by uncontrollable passions to acts of violence. Musically, the *verismo* opera has a small cast that is dominated by a soprano and tenor. The action moves quickly to its climax, dispensing with all character portraits and subsidiary plots. The traditional operatic numbers are still present, but they are so abbreviated as to appear blended together into a continuous action.

Verismo opera was a response by Italian composers to an ever-growing competition from abroad. Wagner's operas had begun to attract attention in Italy, and French operas were increasingly popular. Georges Bizet's immensely influential French opera *Carmen* (1875) offered the Italians a model for the new direction that led to *verismo*. In Bizet's fast-moving work, the character Don José is driven by love and jealousy to murder his beloved Carmen after seeing her with the dashing bullfighter, Escamillo.

The first *verismo* opera was *Cavalleria rusticana* (*Rustic Chivalry*, 1890) by **Pietro Mascagni** (1863–1945), who was briefly a roommate of Puccini while both were students at the Milan Conservatory. This and other works of a related type were especially in vogue at La Scala in the 1890s, where *Cavalleria rusticana* had twenty-three performances in its first season (1891), more than either Verdi's *Otello* or *Falstaff* in their first seasons.

Cavalleria rusticana is based on a short story and related play by Giovanni Verga (1840–1922). Turiddu returns to his home in Sicily after military service to find his old girlfriend, Lola, married to the working man Alfio. Turiddu takes up with the peasant girl Santuzza, whom he shortly jilts to renew his affair with Lola. He then demands that Alfio fight him to the death, observing a Sicilian custom of biting Alfio's ear as part of the challenge. Word shortly arrives from offstage that Turridu has been killed by his opponent.

Although it is difficult to see much realism in this contrived story, it has an echo in literature of the nineteenth century that focuses objectively on the lives of people from lower social strata. This trend is seen preliminarily in novels such as Charles Dickens's *Oliver Twist* (1837–1838), and later in the century in works of the French writers Gustave Flaubert (1821–1880) and Emile Zola (1840–1902).

In its new formula for opera texts, *verismo* was quickly imitated, as in **Ruggero Leoncavallo**'s *Pagliacci* (*Clowns*, 1892), and it is plain to see in Puccini's later operas, including *Tosca* and *Il tabarro* (*The Cloak*, 1918). Today, *Cavalleria rusticana* and *Pagliacci* are almost always performed back-to-back (opera goers fondly call them "Cav and Pag").

SUMMARY

Italy's most prominent opera house in the late nineteenth century was the Teatro alla Scala in Milan. By the 1880s its repertory had been modernized to consist not only of the newest works of Italian composers but also old favorites and classics, including those of non-Italian origin. A high level of musicianship was achieved by the theater under the leadership of Arturo Toscanini.

The most successful Italian composer of opera in the generation after Verdi was Giacomo Puccini. His *Madama Butterfly* (1904) continues aspects of the older Italian number opera, and Puccini also mixes in modern elements that promote a greater musical continuity and dramatic plausibility. These new features include the use of narrative ensembles to tell the story and to connect the arias, duets, and choruses. Puccini also brings back certain themes outside of the confines of a single number and creates families of related themes to suggest related groups of characters in the libretto.

In the 1890s a new type of opera called *verismo* (realism) emerged in Italy, as a response to competition from such foreign composers as Richard Wagner and Georges Bizet. In *verismo* opera, characters from low social strata are beset by elemental passions that drive them to acts of violence. The first important work of the type was Pietro Mascagni's *Cavalleria rusticana*, and other examples of the idiom were composed by Puccini and Ruggero Leoncavallo.

KEY TERMS

impresario   Arturo Toscanini   Pietro Mascagni
Ricordi   *verismo*   Ruggero Leoncavallo

Chapter 63

Paris in the *Belle Époque*: Debussy, Fauré, and Lili Boulanger

The years straddling the turn of the twentieth century in France are often termed the *Belle époque,* the "beautiful era." The term points to a reigning mood that was at once carefree, high-spirited, and optimistic, all the outcome of a relatively good economy, peace, and satisfaction with a progressive government that had been installed in the 1870s, following France's humiliating defeat by the armies of Prussia. The spirit of the period demanded entertainment and diversion, which were sure to stimulate the arts. Popular culture—cabaret, circus, café-concert, and early cinema—was especially in vogue, and the high arts of literature, painting, and music advanced and prospered.

Music flourished in the Paris of 1900. The Opéra, installed since 1875 in the magnificent Palais Garnier (named for its architect, Charles Garnier), brought the operas of Wagner to an appreciative French audience. Native opera composers largely took their new works to the nearby Opéra-Comique, where Gustave Charpentier's *Louise* premiered in 1900 and Claude Debussy's *Pelléas et Mélisande* in 1902. The operettas of Edmond Audran (1840–1901) and André Messager (1853–1929) increased the great popularity of the genre that had been established in Paris in the 1850s by Jacques Offenbach (1819–1880). There were two major series of orchestral concerts, the Concerts Lamoureux and Concerts Colonne, both named after a founding conductor. New music was supported by the Société Nationale de Musique (National Society of Music), in whose concerts works by Claude Debussy and Maurice Ravel were frequently heard, and wealthy patrons of music, such as the Princesse Edmond de Polignac (an American by birth), sponsored private concerts.

This positive and vibrant atmosphere stimulated the formation of new ideas, which arrived in profusion as younger artists looked for a distinctive tone and method in their work that would be relevant to their own period. Artists in different fields were often closely in touch, egging each other on toward new thinking and new ways in which their disciplines could be brought closer together.

❋ NEW POETRY

The poetry of **Paul Verlaine** (1844–1896) will illustrate this striving for a new tone in French literature of the late nineteenth century and the close affinity that arose between poetry and music. Verlaine's life was disordered and tempestuous, but these qualities are not especially notable in his poetic oeuvre, which is delicate in the extreme. His early style is apparent in the poetic collection *Fêtes galantes* (*Elegant Parties*), which was published in 1869 and later drawn on by Debussy and Gabriel Fauré for song texts. It consists of seventeen short poems that depict fleeting scenes and fragile memories: a momentary conversation between lovers, a comic instant among the clowns at the Comédie-Italienne, a portrait of a silly cleric, an ambiguous dialogue between lovers at the seashore.

The title of the collection gives us a clue to the context in which these fragments arise. A ***fête galante*** was a popular social occasion among the aristocracy of the eighteenth century. In the summer months the courtiers of the day—with precious language, stilted manners, and the finest of dress—met out of doors to converse, flirt, and make music. Such occasions were favorite themes for painters of the eighteenth century, especially for Antoine Watteau (1684–1721), as in his *La gamme d'amour* (*The Scale of Love*; Fig. 63-1). Verlaine's poems resemble the imaginary conversations overheard at such occasions—laden with artifice, but human and emotional beneath a thick layer of masks.

An especially delicate and musical poem from *Fêtes galantes* is "En sourdine" ("Muted"), which was used by Claude Debussy in a song of the same title, to be discussed momentarily. (The

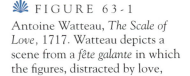

❋ FIGURE 63-1

Antoine Watteau, *The Scale of Love*, 1717. Watteau depicts a scene from a *fête galante* in which the figures, distracted by love, have momentarily forgotten their music.

Bridgeman Art Library

text and its translation are given in full in the Anthology.) The speaker of the poem records a succession of minute and transitory feelings—sensations from the light sifting through the trees and a breeze rustling in the grass, as well as the emotions of love and despair. He is impassive and wishes not to act but to relish the moment, with its network of diverse sensations. Although the structure of the poem is reasonably strict and regular, Verlaine chooses words and creates a syntax that stretch the French language and enrich its sonority.

A comparison with Friedrich Rückert's "Um Mitternacht" (see Chapter 60) points up other distinctive features of Verlaine's poetry. Rückert's narrator speaks from the depths of an anguished soul. He actively searches for calm, and his thoughts have a certain bombast, as when he declares that he has fought the battle of all mankind. Verlaine's poetic imagination is entirely different: his narrator's words are understated, focused on minutiae, and the narrator remains entirely passive, engaged only in the present moment. His inner self is never apparent. These differences between German assertiveness and French refinement are also apparent in the music of these countries at the end of the Romantic period.

IMPRESSIONISM IN PAINTING

Many of the qualities of Verlaine's poetry—its evocation of mood and atmosphere, understatement, passivity, and appeal to the senses—also characterize a new style of painting practiced by a group of French artists of the 1870s and 1880s. The works of these painters—Claude Monet, Auguste Renoir, Camille Pissarro, Edgar Degas, Alfred Sisley among others—were controversial in their day. Their style was dubbed **impressionism** by critics, since it seemed to record mere impressions gained from observing nature rather than advancing the more accepted academic principles and subjects of painting. But, by the turn of the century, impressionism was widely embraced, and in the present such works are among the most celebrated paintings in the entire world of art.

The works of **Claude Monet** are quintessential impressionist paintings. An example is his *Wild Poppies* (1873; Fig. 63-2). The artist depicts a beautiful though unpretentious scene from nature. Like the narrator in Verlaine's "En sourdine," he impassively records what he sees by seeming to float slightly above the landscape. Although the beauty of nature is his main subject, Monet also includes two women with children, who are shown at a distance happily integrated into their natural surroundings. The viewer's eye is drawn to the brilliant red poppies, which are represented with a certain abstraction as flecks of paint that stand out as though electrified by sunlight. A sense of motion is created in the large band of sky, in which clouds seem to sweep toward the viewer. In all, the painting creates a powerful mood of serenity and nostalgia.

✿ NEW REALITIES: CLAUDE DEBUSSY

Claude Debussy (1862–1918), the greatest musician of the *Belle époque*, was flattered to be compared to the leading impressionist

✺ FIGURE 63-2

Claude Monet, *Wild Poppies*, 1873. Monet's landscapes embody the essence of impressionism in their closeness to nature, mood of happy nostalgia, and vision of a world brought alive by sunlight and color.

painters. "You do me a great honor by calling me a pupil of Claude Monet," he told his friend Emile Vuillermoz.[1] Despite the obvious differences between painting and music, there is much that connects his works with impressionist painting: understatement, subtlety, a love of the beauty and freedom of nature, a preference for primary orchestral colors, a sense of free motion, and an originality that bypasses academic formulas. But Debussy, like all great composers, did not wish to have his music reduced to an *-ism*. To his publisher Jacques Durand he complained: "I'm trying to write 'something else'—*realities* in a manner of speaking—what imbeciles call 'impressionism,' a term employed with the utmost inaccuracy."[2]

Debussy spent virtually his entire life in Paris. He entered the Paris Conservatory in 1872, at the tender age of ten, and proved brilliantly talented though implacably rebellious in all areas of his study. For a long time he remained obscure as a composer and made his living by giving lessons, writing reviews, and receiving patronage from several wealthy supporters. His existence, rather like that of Schubert earlier in Vienna, was bohemian and fully devoted to art. He achieved general recognition as a composer only in 1902 with the premiere of his opera *Pelléas et Mélisande*, and even after this he was hounded by debt, failing health, and personal crises. He died from cancer in 1918, at the age of only fifty-five.

Debussy's music was written in the leading genres of the late Romantic period, primarily song, character piece for piano, and the symphonic poem for orchestra. He aspired to write dramatic music but was able to complete only one opera (*Pelléas et Mélisande*) and one ballet (*Jeux*). There is also an early string quartet and three late sonatas (for cello and piano; violin and piano; and flute, viola, and harp).

Debussy's song setting of Verlaine's "En sourdine" reveals a tone that he shared with modern French writers and painters, as well as a far-reaching musical originality. Although this is an early work, composed in 1891, Debussy's principal innovations are already apparent. One of the most important of these is a harmonic language that leaves the sense of key in an ambiguous state. Only in the final four measures of the song is a central tonality, B major, firmly established by the appearance of dominant and tonic chords, and even there the tonic triad is decorated by its major sixth, G♯.

We can see Debussy's ambiguity with functional harmony by looking at the chords in the opening phrase of the song in measures 1–10 (these are shown in a condensed form in Ex. 63-1). The chords themselves are certainly familiar, consisting of several different triads, a half-diminished seventh chord (E♯-G♯-B-D♯), and, near the end, a dominant seventh on the root tone C♯. But the progression into which these chords is placed defines no key concretely. There is no strong motion toward an apparent tonic or dominant chord, and the progression is not framed by harmonies that plainly refer to a tonic.

EXAMPLE 63-1

The harmonic freedom in Debussy's songs may have been inspired by the music of Modest Mussorgsky (recall Mussorgsky's song "Within Four Walls" from Chapter 59). Debussy had high praise for Mussorgsky's music: "Nobody has spoken to that which is best in us with such tenderness and depth," he said.[3]

Debussy's harmonic innovations were of great interest to his contemporaries. "His harmonies, without constructive meaning, often served the coloristic purpose

Debussy on Music and Nature

Between 1901 and 1915 Debussy regularly wrote reviews and opinionated essays for leading Paris journals. For the *Revue musicale* in 1913 he contributed a short speculation on the prospects for music. Here he touched upon two of his favorite themes: the relation of music to nature, and the need for music to be free from laborious complication:

. . . Music is the art that is in fact the closest to Nature, although it is also the one that contains the most subtle pitfalls. Despite their claims to be true representationalists, the painters and sculptors can only present us with the beauty of the universe in their own free, somewhat fragmentary interpretation. They can capture only one of its aspects at a time, preserve only one moment. It is the musicians alone who have the privilege of being able to convey all the poetry of night and day, or earth and sky. Only they can re-create Nature's atmosphere and give rhythm to her heaving breast. . .

Let us purify music! Let us try to relieve its congestion, to find a less cluttered kind of music. And let us be careful that we do not stifle all feeling beneath a mass of superimposed designs and motives: how can we hope to preserve our finesse, our spirit, if we insist on being preoccupied with so many details of composition? We are attempting the impossible in trying to organize a braying pack of tiny themes, all pushing and jostling each other for the sake of a bite out of the poor old sentiment! If they are not careful the sentiment will depart altogether, in an attempt to save its skin. As a general rule, every time someone tries to complicate an art form or a sentiment, it is simply because they are unsure of what they want to say. . . .[4]

of expressing moods and pictures," wrote Arnold Schoenberg. "In this way, tonality was already dethroned in practice, if not in theory."[5] Schoenberg interpreted the function of Debussy's chords for their capacity, not to define a key, but to create colors. The chords, Schoenberg suggests, make attractive sounds and promote the calm and quiet mood established by the poem.

Debussy's innovative harmonic practice is only one of several ways in which the subtlety and understatement of Verlaine's poetry is communicated. Debussy makes sure that the text is always clearly heard, and the listener is never distracted from it by any elaborate vocal melody. Word paintings are also frequently brought in. The rhythm has a freedom from regular beat and rigid meter, just like the free movements of nature mentioned in the poem.

LISTENING CUE

CLAUDE DEBUSSY
Fêtes galantes I (1891)
"En sourdine"

CD 10/14
Anthology, No. 168

HARMONIC CHEMISTRY IN DEBUSSY'S PIANO MUSIC

Debussy's music for piano consists of some eighty character pieces, which include twelve études, twenty-four preludes, and other works gathered into brief programmatic cycles. His treatment of the instrument continues the line established by Chopin in its exploitation of highly animated motions and bright sonorities, a flamboyant use of arpeggiated arabesques, and the exploration of new harmonies. As a composer of the character piece, Debussy extends the ideas of Schumann by finding ways to create the most diverse and vivid images in the least space.

Debussy's "Reflets dans l'eau" ("Reflections in the Water," 1905) paints an ingenious musical portrait of rippling water, often the subject of the paintings of Monet. To achieve his picturesque objectives, Debussy suppresses the melodic element, which at the beginning is reduced to an isolated three-note figure, A♭-F-E♭ (Ex. 63-2, left hand), and melody per se is replaced by arabesques that splash freely into the bright, high register of the instrument.

EXAMPLE 63-2

The work is also notable for its harmonic innovations: Debussy told his publisher, Durand, that it contained "the most recent discoveries of harmonic chemistry."[6] One of these "discoveries," which Debussy uses as a means of contrast, is to select tones from a **whole-tone scale** rather than a diatonic scale. This is apparent especially in the middle of the piece, as in the passage shown in Example 63-3. In these measures, all of the tones are drawn from the whole-tone scale B C♯ D♯ F G A, omitting only D♯. The whole tones make the passage stand apart strikingly from its surrounding sections, which are largely diatonic.

EXAMPLE 63-3

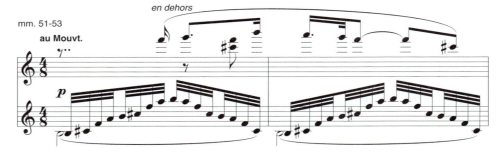

Another innovation is the embellishment of triads and seventh chords with a tone a major sixth above the bass or root of the chord. This was a means of harmonic enrichment that in the 1920s was imitated by American popular composers, including Duke Ellington and George Gershwin.

LISTENING CUE

CLAUDE DEBUSSY

Images I (1905)

"Reflets dans l'eau"

CD 10/15

Anthology, No. 169

 ## DEBUSSY'S ORCHESTRAL MUSIC

A culture for orchestral music flourished in Paris during the *Belle époque*, and the medium attracted all of the leading composers of the day. Most of the prominent Parisian musicians—Camille Saint-Saëns, Ernest Chausson, Paul Dukas, and Vincent d'Indy—wrote symphonies of large proportion, but the inflated scope and necessity for development made the genre unattractive to Debussy after his earliest years. He explained his distaste for developmental forms as a constraint upon his artistic freedom:

> Explorations previously made in the realm of pure music had led me toward a hatred of classical development, whose beauty is solely technical and can interest only the mandarins in our profession. I wanted music to have freedom, that is perhaps more inherent in it than in any other art, for music is not limited to a more or less exact representation of nature, but rather to the mysterious affinity between Nature and the Imagination.[7]

Accordingly, Debussy turned not to the symphony but to the more intimate proportions of the symphonic poem and orchestral character piece. His principal works of this type include the Prelude to *The Afternoon of a Faun* (based on a poem by Stéphane Mallarmé), the cycles *Nocturnes* and *Images*, and the powerful *La mer*, which consists of three symphonic portraits of the sea.

Three short and strongly contrasting pieces—"Nuages" ("Clouds"), "Fêtes" ("Festivals"), and "Sirènes" ("Sirens")—make up *Nocturnes*. The first of them, "Nuages," is strongly evocative and pictorial, and it employs harmonic devices that are far in advance of its time. When it was first performed in 1900 at the Concerts Lamoureux, Debussy tried to explain its immense originality by using ordinary visual analogies. The work, he wrote, "renders the immutable aspect of the sky and the slow solemn motion of clouds, fading away in gray tones lightly tinged with white."[8] But this description scarcely does justice to a work of such profound expressivity and novel structure.

Several of the stylistic features encountered in "En sourdine" and "Reflets dans l'eau" are again apparent in "Nuages": like the song, this piece has a symmetrical **A B A'** form in which normal development is replaced by a more static repetition of short phrases. An emphasis here on ostinato and repetition seems intended to dispel any sense of forward motion or, as Debussy explained it, to portray "the immutable aspect of the sky." As in the piano piece, there is a dim reference to a centric triad (here B minor), but otherwise virtually no functional harmonic progressions.

We saw in "Reflets dans l'eau" the alternation of diatonic passages with others whose tones are drawn from a whole-tone scale. In "Nuages" Debussy continues such experiments by using the octatonic scale and pentatonic scale in addition to the more familiar major and minor. The so-called **octatonic scale,** which consists of an alternation of whole and half steps, had been used frequently by Russian composers of the nineteenth century. In this work by Debussy it appears most prominently in the haunting melody given to the English horn (Ex. 63-4). The **pentatonic scale,** a feature of traditional Asian music, duplicates the intervals of the black keys on the piano, and it underlies the tones of the work's subsidiary melody (Ex. 63-5).

EXAMPLE 63-4

English horn, mm. 5-8

Octatonic scale

EXAMPLE 63-5

Flute, harp, mm. 64-66

Pentatonic scale

It is perhaps the timbre of Debussy's orchestral music that most remains with the listener. Debussy writes for an orchestra of normal constitution, although he omits the brass except for horns. Like French composers throughout the nineteenth century, he tends to segregate the orchestra into distinct choirs, and lines are usually doubled only within a single group. Plainly, the composer did not want the blended or homogeneous sonority of German orchestral music, instead choosing a brighter and more variegated sound. The important thematic elements, which are shortened to appear as mere fragments, are normally given to the contrasting colors of the solo woodwinds, and toward the end Debussy instructs the strings to play with mysterious sonorous effects, including harmonics and tremolos on the fingerboard. Debussy's orchestration was carefully studied by a younger generation of modernist composers—Igor Stravinsky among others—who would shortly put Debussy's orchestrational and harmonic innovations into new and daring contexts.

LISTENING CUE

CLAUDE DEBUSSY
Nocturnes (1900)
"Nuages"

CD 11/1
Anthology, No. 170

GABRIEL FAURÉ

Debussy's innovations went further than most of the progressive French composers of the *Belle époque* were willing to go. One such reluctant contemporary was Gabriel Fauré (1845–1924). "If I like Debussy," he remarked, "I no longer like Fauré. How can I then be Fauré?" Fauré began his career as a church musician and composed religious works for chorus, including his much-admired Requiem (1877). He was later a professor of composition at the Paris Conservatory (his students include Maurice Ravel and Lili Boulanger) and from 1905 was its director. He wrote in all of the major musical genres of his time, of which his songs, piano character pieces, and chamber music with piano are best known.

The song "Dans la forêt de septembre" ("In September's Forest," 1902) reveals Fauré's intensely romantic musical personality. The speaker in the poem by Catulle Mendès (1841–1909) beholds an ancient forest and feels a sympathy with its long and stoic suffering, which he shares. As he enters the forest, a tree sends down a leaf that lights upon his shoulder, which the narrator interprets as a token of their kinship.

Certainly the poem is full of emotion and sentimentality, qualities shared with Fauré's music. Our attention in the song is drawn to its warm melodiousness, which Fauré enhances by the soothing arpeggios in the piano and the enriched harmonies. In form the work is repetitive and symmetrical, cast in a rondo-like design. Fauré's admiration for the music of Wagner is reflected in the harmonic vocabulary, which stretches the key of G♭ major but never disrupts it.

Fauré's music shares with Debussy's its nuance and refinement, but Fauré was more the romantic traditionalist in his love for long and intensely tuneful melodies and a harmonic language that never abandons functional progressions.

LISTENING CUE

GABRIEL FAURÉ
"Dans la forêt de septembre," Opus 85, No. 1 (1902)

CD 11/2
Anthology, No. 171

THE SPREAD OF DEBUSSYISM: LILI BOULANGER

 FIGURE 63-3
Lili Boulanger was the first female composer to win the coveted Prix de Rome.

While Debussy's innovations in harmony and tonality were questioned by the older composer Gabriel Fauré, they were enthusiastically adopted by younger French musicians of the *Belle époque*. One of the most promising of these was Lili Boulanger (1893–1918; Fig. 63-3). She was born in Paris to a family of distinguished musicians. Her older sister, Nadia (1887–1979), became the most renowned French teacher of composition of her day. Lili Boulanger studied composition at the Paris Conservatory, and in 1913 she was the first female composer to be awarded the Prix de Rome, an honor conferred earlier on Hector Berlioz and Claude Debussy, and also on her father, Ernest Boulanger (1815–1900).

Lili Boulanger was plagued throughout her short life by poor health, and she died in 1918 at the age of twenty-four. She left behind primarily choral compositions, including works based on psalm texts such as the imposing *Du fond de l'abîme* (*Out of the Depths*, from Psalm 130). She also composed songs, including the cycle *Clairières dans le ciel* (*Clearings in the Sky*, 1914), and a few piano pieces.

Clairières dans le ciel shows Boulanger's enormous gift as a composer and underscores the tragedy of her untimely death. The work is a cycle of thirteen songs based

on poems in free verse by Francis Jammes (1868–1938). These tell of a blissful love affair, existing close to nature, that is ultimately and inexplicably struck down. Boulanger's songs closely follow the spirit of these words. The thirteen pieces move from major to minor, and in the sixth song Boulanger quotes a motive from the beginning of Wagner's opera *Tristan und Isolde*—a work that tells of another hopeless love affair. In the final poem, the composer brings back motives from earlier in the cycle, just as the poet at the conclusion looks back sadly on what once had been.

"Elle est gravement gaie" ("She Is Solemnly Cheerful") is the second song of the cycle. The music perfectly mirrors the naive and uncomplicated sentiments of the poem. The song has a simple ternary design, and the piano and voice share a warm melodiousness, more like that of Boulanger's teacher Fauré than that of Debussy. But in harmony and tonality, the song speaks clearly in Debussy's language. The tonal context is E major, although there are no functional harmonic progressions, and the tonic triads after the opening are all decorated by nonharmonic tones. The music is painted with colors from Debussy's harmonic palette, which consists mainly of triads, seventh chords, and ninth chords. The music alternates smoothly among pitch fields that are diatonic, pentatonic, and octatonic. Other technical features of the song will be familiar from Debussy's music, including the chain of parallel ninth chords in the middle and the replacement of development by a repetitive mosaic made from small figures.

Boulanger's own musical personality appears most in the treatment of the voice. Written with the French tenor David Devriès in mind, the cycle requires an agile, high voice which can glide effortlessly to sustained high tones. The voice's upper register is repeatedly mined for expressive effects, as on the word *surprendre* ("surprise"), where the voice leaps up a seventh to the tone A, sung *pianissimo*.

LISTENING CUE

LILI BOULANGER

Clairières dans le ciel (1914)
"Elle est gravement gaie"

CD 11/3
Anthology, No. 172

SUMMARY

The *Belle époque* refers to the period in French history before and after 1900 when both popular and serious arts flourished. Poets such as Paul Verlaine introduced a subtle and understated style of poetry that emphasized the creation of mood, and these qualities were often captured in song settings such as in Debussy's "En sourdine." Impressionist painters of the 1870s and 1880s, notably Claude Monet, depicted everyday scenes that reflect the motions and luminosity of the out-of-doors. Monet's fondness for the image of reflecting water has its musical counterpart in Debussy's "Reflets dans l'eau" for piano.

Even in his own lifetime, Debussy was referred to as a "musical impressionist," although he did not accept this term as a good description of his music. Debussy's innovations include the suppression of functional harmonic progressions despite his continued use of triads and seventh and ninth chords. Many of his works alternate diatonic music with passages whose tones are drawn from whole-tone, octatonic, and pentatonic scales. Debussy was a master of orchestral music, as seen in his "Nuages" from *Nocturnes*, in which a motionless sky is depicted by ostinatos and undifferentiated rhythms.

Debussy's older contemporary Gabriel Fauré composed music in a more conventional romantic style, notable for its warmth, lyricism, and harmonies that absorbed the expressive implications of those of Wagner. Younger contemporaries, such as Lili Boulanger, more eagerly adopted Debussy's advances in harmony and tonality, although the melodiousness of Fauré's music also remained a model.

KEY TERMS

Belle époque	impressionism	octatonic scale
Paul Verlaine	Claude Monet	pentatonic scale
fête galante	whole-tone scale	

THE EARLY TWENTIETH CENTURY

*T*he history of music in the first half of the twentieth century is divided into two parts, separated by a major stylistic change that occurred around 1920, just after the end of World War I. Before this dividing point, the Romantic period had come to a blazing end. The longstanding romantic traits of passionate expression, complex ideas, and innovative musical resources drove music at this time to extremes. Gustav Mahler's Symphony No. 8 (1906) is typical of the larger-than-life work of the pre-war years. The sprawling composition lasts for an hour and a half, and its gargantuan orchestra and chorus earned it the

1850	1900

ROMANTIC PERIOD (1820–1914)

Richard Strauss (1864–1949), German composer

Erik Satie (1866–1925), French composer

Scott Joplin (1868–1917), American composer

Alexander Scriabin (1872–1915), Russian composer

Charles Ives (1874–1954), American composer

Arnold Schoenberg (1874–1951), Viennese composer of atonal and twelve-tone music

Maurice Ravel (1875–1937), French composer

Béla Bartók (1881–1945), Hungarian composer

Anton Webern (1883–1945), Austrian composer, student of Schoenberg

Alban Berg (1885–1935), Austrian composer, uses Büchner's play as text

Sergei Prokofiev (1891–1953), Russian piano virtuoso and

Darius Milhaud (1892–1974), French composer

Paul Hindemith (1895–1963), leading German

George Gershwin (1898–1937), American pianist

Kurt Weill (1900–1950), German-American

Aaron Copland (1900–1990), American composer

Ruth Crawford Seeger (1901–1953), American

Richard Rodgers (1902–1979), American

Dmitri Shostakovich (1906–1975),

Samuel Barber (1910–1981),

Leonard Bernstein

*Igor Stravinsky (1882–1971)
Russian-American composer*

Al Jolson, in The Jazz Singer (1927)

nickname *Symphony of a Thousand*. In its music and text Mahler explored no less a subject than man's destiny and capacity for creativity.

Following World War I, this music of extremes was overturned in favor of a lighter and more life-sized style. The new taste of the 1920s had one unmistakable common feature—to be as unlike late Romantic music as possible. Composers after World War I were far less inclined to take up Mahler's metaphysical contemplations or to call on a thousand performers. Moderation and objectivity became the new order of the day. Composers looked for a new simplicity in their music and cast a sympathetic eye on musical styles and forms of the eighteenth century.

Part

VII

1950   2000

TWENTIETH CENTURY

for *Wozzeck*

prodigious composer

neoclassicist composer of twentieth century

and composer

composer

composer

song writer

Russian composer

American composer

(1918–90), American composer of *West Side Story*

Music After 1900

Of all the style periods of Western music history, only the one beginning around 1900 has no generally accepted name. There is no counterpart to a critical term like romanticism, classicism, Enlightenment, or baroque that points to common and distinctive features in music composed since the turn of the twentieth century.

Why this is so takes us to the very core of musical culture of this time. Many of its enduring musical works in fact show certain common traits. A freer-than-ever occurrence of dissonant harmony, the removal or reinterpretation of traditional tonality, a new emphasis on the expressive power of sound in itself, an openness to change and experimentation in musical resources, and a dissolution of traditional genres and media are all common features that bind together works that began to appear after 1900. At the same time, overlapping and sharply opposing styles have counteracted any idea that the century forms one single period, by whatever name.

This ambiguity reaches even into the works of individual composers. In earlier eras, the mature works of a major figure sound reasonably alike. The music of Wagner sounds like Wagner, whether from *The Flying Dutchman*, his first major opera, or *Parisfal*, his final composition. But there is often no such consistency in the music of leading composers of the early twentieth century. Samuel Barber is an example. In his romantic *Adagio for Strings*, his homespun songs *Knoxville: Summer of 1915*, or his angular and dissonant Piano Sonata we encounter such diversity of expression that it is scarcely imaginable that these compositions are products of a single mind. This mixing of styles continues to appear in works by major composers later in the century. George Rochberg's Variations on an Original Theme differs little in style from piano music written a hundred years before, in the early Romantic period. His piano "Blues" from *Carnival Music* differs little in style from an improvisation by the jazz pianist Art Tatum from the 1940s. The Variations movement from Rochberg's String Quartet No. 3 is almost indistinguishable in style from a late quartet by Beethoven. So what is the name of Rochberg's style?

Rochberg's eclecticism cannot mask the fact that there has existed a succession of prevailing tastes in music of the early twentieth century. In its first decade, a continuation of romanticism is apparent. As in the nineteenth century, heightened expressivity was paramount at this time, when composers searched for new themes and for new musical materials by which these could be conveyed.

In the 1920s and 1930s these romantic features were questioned, then rejected, by most composers. Many of the leading musicians of these decades, including Igor Stravinsky, Paul Hindemith, and Kurt Weill, swept aside the sort of music that they had grown up with—works with complex expressivity and larger-than-life emotions. Objectivity and coolness of expression became the order of the day in a new type of music that critics labeled "neoclassicism." Romantic emotionalism in music seemed clearly outdated. Also at this time, thanks to advances in sound-recording technology, popular music claimed the attention of audiences throughout the world. Classical composers of these years, such as Kurt Weill, began to question whether a distinction between popular and art music could be maintained.

But, at the same time that Stravinsky and Hindemith were writing music in the new objective style of the 1920s, other major composers of the day headed in opposite directions. Arnold Schoenberg found in neoclassicism only a movement that had removed "all that was good in the preceding period." His own music of the 1920s maintained the complexity, dissonance, and chromaticism that was being shunned by the neoclassicists. The French composer Charles Koechlin (1867–1950) continued to write evocative and impressionistic music inspired by Fauré and Debussy, and he had no sympathy with the neoclassicists' call for a "return to Bach" as an antidote for romanticism.

The very existence of these overlapping and conflicting attitudes and musical styles became one of the distinctive features of musical culture in the early twentieth century. A multiplicity of styles is unique to this period, just as the century itself is unique in its sharp juxtapositions of peace and war, poverty and wealth. The years from 1900 to 1950 witnessed two world wars, a worldwide economic depression, a Holocaust, and unprecedented wealth and technological advance, and the impact of these titanic events upon musical culture will be traced in the following chapters.

Richard Strauss in Berlin

Chapter 64

The modern nation of Germany came into existence only in 1871. In January of that year, shortly after German armies had defeated the French in the Franco-Prussian War, leaders representing most of the German-speaking states met in the Palace of Versailles near Paris and proclaimed their allegiance to Wilhelm I, King of Prussia. By doing this they created a unified German *Reich* (Empire), which they proudly called the "Second Reich," the first being the medieval Germanic empire founded by Charlemagne. Recall from Chapter 54 that German lands after the fall of Napoleon were loosely allied in the German Confederation, although the rivalry between Prussia and Austria—the two most powerful members—remained keen. In 1866 Prussia defeated Austria in the Austro-Prussian War, and shortly thereafter Austria was excluded from a new "North German Confederation," which replaced the older alliance. The evolving boundaries that led to the emergence of a unified German nation are illustrated in Map 64-1.

The German Empire that was created in 1871 was much larger than the Germany we know today. It extended westward beyond the Rhine River into what is now France. To the east it stretched along the Baltic Sea to modern-day Lithuania and Estonia, and to the southeast its borders reached well into what is now Poland.

❊ BERLIN

The capital of the new empire was Berlin, which earlier had been the capital of the powerful north European state of Prussia. In the early nineteenth century the city was small and isolated, but by 1900 it had become a great metropolis with a population of over 2.7 million. The center of the city (after World War II, part of Communist East Berlin) was bounded on the west by the Brandenburg Gate, an imposing triumphal arch completed in 1791 (Fig. 64-1). By walking eastward from this point

🌸 MAP 64-1

The Unification of Germany, 1866–1871.

along the tree-lined avenue called Unter den Linden, one shortly passed the Royal Library, which was home to the greatest collection of composer's manuscripts anywhere in the world. Next to it was the university, where Hegel had earlier lectured on philosophy and where, at the end of the century, Philipp Spitta—then the world's greatest authority on the music of J.S. Bach—taught musicology. Across the street was the Royal Opera, built by King Frederick the Great in 1742. After passing over the Spree Canal, the walker could view the grandiose Imperial Palace before arriving in residential suburbs to the east.

In 1900 the Royal Opera was the city's most prestigious musical institution. The emperor himself, then Wilhelm II, was directly involved with choosing the repertory and overseeing productions. Two years before, Richard Strauss (1864–1949; Fig. 64-2) was brought in as principal conductor and later made music director, a position that he held until 1918. From 1908 he was also music director of the Berlin Philharmonic Orchestra, which was founded in 1882 and grew to prominence under the leadership of Hans von Bülow and Arthur Nikisch. Its later conductors have included Wilhelm Furtwängler (1886–1954) and Herbert von Karajan (1908–1989).

🌸 FIGURE 64-1

The Brandenburg Gate is a neo-Grecian portal completed in the center of Berlin in 1791; it remains one of the most imposing monuments in the city.

✸ RICHARD STRAUSS

When Strauss came to the Royal Opera in 1898, he was already recognized as one of the world's leading composers, primarily because of a series of brilliant orchestral pieces. These compositions revived the genre of the one-movement programmatic work for orchestra that had been advanced by Franz Liszt at mid-century. Liszt called a composition of this type a "symphonic poem" (see Chapter 57), while Strauss preferred the equivalent term *Tondichtung*, or **tone poem**. By 1889 Strauss had completed three such works—*Don Juan, Macbeth,* and *Tod und Verklärung* (*Death and Transfiguration*)—whereupon he turned to the genre of opera and wrote *Guntram,* a work in the Wagnerian vein. The opera was a failure in the eyes of the public, who dealt Strauss his first major setback as a composer.

He then returned to his strong suit, composing for orchestra, and wrote one brilliant tone poem after another: *Till Eulenspiegels lustige Streiche* (*Till Eulenspiegel's Merry Pranks,* 1895), *Also sprach Zarathustra* (*Thus Spoke Zarathustra,* 1896), *Don Quixote* (1897), and *Ein Heldenleben* (*A Hero's Life,* 1898). Strauss had also attracted attention with his songs, which began to appear in print in 1887 and increased in number in the 1890s, near the time of his marriage to Pauline de Ahna, a singer and interpreter of his vocal music. His production of songs dwindled after her retirement in 1906.

By this time, Strauss had again taken up the challenge of writing opera, although after *Guntram* he looked for a more original operatic style. Following the comic opera *Feuersnot* (*Need for Fire,* 1901), he made a great success with *Salome* (1905), a work in a modern idiom. *Elektra,* an opera in a similar style, followed in 1909, after which Strauss entered into a collaboration with the Viennese writer **Hugo von Hofmannsthal** (1874–1929) on a series of new operas. These include the ever-popular *Der Rosenkavalier* (*The Cavalier of the Rose,* 1910), *Ariadne auf Naxos* (*Ariadne on Naxos*), *Die Frau ohne Schatten* (*The Woman Without Shadow*), and *Arabella.* In these works Strauss abandons the experimental language of *Salome* and *Elektra* and returns to a fully romantic style, conveyed in classical operatic forms.

After his final opera, *Capriccio* (1941), Strauss contemplated retirement, but a great resurgence of creative spirit toward the end of his life led to several memorable late compositions, including the tone poem *Metamorphosen* (*Metamorphoses,* 1945) and orchestral songs published posthumously under the title *Four Last Songs* (1948). For a discussion of Strauss's late works, see Chapter 78.

Bettmann/CORBIS

FIGURE 64-2
Richard Strauss in mid-career.

Salome

Strauss always hoped for success in the genre of opera. More than most other composers of his generation, he accepted Wagner's idea that opera would be at the center of "music of the future," and the genre seemed to be the perfect outlet for his interest in modern theater and his passionate belief in the expressive power of the orchestra and the human voice. But for a composer around 1900, finding the right subject and musical style for a new opera posed a complex challenge. Strauss had failed in his effort to continue the Wagnerian idiom in his first opera, *Guntram,* and the reception of his second opera, the comedy *Feuersnot,* was limited by its bawdy subject. When he saw **Oscar Wilde**'s highly controversial play *Salome* staged in Berlin in 1902, he recognized material that he could transform into an opera having both musical and dramatic originality.

Even in Berlin—a city known for free thinking in theater—*Salome* was strong stuff. Wilde wrote the play in 1891 in French, with the celebrated French actress Sarah Bernhardt in mind for the title role. Using the biblical story of the beheading of John the Baptist by Herod, Wilde creates a fantasy of forbidden love. At its center

Synopsis of *Salome*

King Herod and his queen Herodias are entertaining in their palace on a moonlit night. Soldiers and attendants wait outside, where they can hear the holy man Jochanaan (John the Baptist) issue prophecies from a nearby cistern, in which he is held prisoner. They are joined by Salome, the daughter of Herodias, who commands that Jochanaan be brought before her. Salome finds him disgusting as he spews forth condemnations of her mother. But suddenly she declares herself enamored of him—especially his body, his hair, and, most of all, his red mouth. "I will kiss your mouth, Jochanaan," she swears, whereupon he asks to return to the cistern.

Herod now leads the party outside, seeking Salome, at whom he stares lasciviously. The voice of Jochanaan is again heard, quoting prophecies from the Apocrypha: The hour is at hand, he says, when the earth will turn black, stars will fall

like ripe figs, and the kings of the earth will grow afraid. The strumpet, he says, will die beneath soldiers' shields.

Herod wants to see Salome dance, for which he promises to grant her any wish. After her seductive "Dance of the Seven Veils," she demands that the head of Jochanaan be brought to her on a silver platter. Paralyzed by fear and drink, Herod allows her wish to be carried out. An arm rises from the cistern bearing the decapitated head, which Salome takes and fondles. Filled with disgust and apprehension, Herod commands that all torches be extinguished, and the stage falls totally dark as clouds temporarily screen the moon and stars. From the darkness, Salome luridly declares that she has kissed Jochanaan's lips, which, she says, had a bitter taste. A moonbeam betrays her at this climactic moment, and Herod screams, "Kill that woman!" Soldiers rush forward and crush her beneath their shields.

---

he places Salome, the daughter of Herodias. Compared to tragic heroines of the nineteenth century, she is plainly a new type—lustful, perverse, a bizarre femme fatale to whom nothing in the realm of sensuality is forbidden. The play went into rehearsal in London in 1892, but the censor forced it to be withdrawn, and it was first brought to the stage only in 1896, in Paris. The work has subsequently been known primarily through Strauss's opera.

The apparent sordidness of the play is attenuated by the absurdity of the dialogue and Wilde's unrelenting parody. His reputation as a writer of satiric social comedies, such as the contemporary *Lady Windermere's Fan*, is never entirely forgotten in *Salome*. The characters themselves, beneath their distorted exteriors, are comic types. Herodias is the shrew, Herod the foolish old lecher, Jochanaan a pompous buffoon. Salome herself reminds us of the mad heroine of romantic tragedy, the maiden who has lost her wits on account of love. Even the circumstances of her madness—her sexual arousal by John the Baptist and her ghoulish delight in his decapitation—are so exaggerated as to make her at home with the other clownish figures.

Strauss immediately recognized in Wilde's play the element of parody, which he considered one of his strengths as a composer. In *Till Eulenspiegel* he had used a choir of bassoons in the low register to draw a devastating portrait of a band of stuffy professors; in *Ein Heldenleben* he called on the solo violin to impersonate his wife—alternately happy or moody, and always talkative. Strauss continues this line of parody in parts of *Salome*, as in the music for Herod, whose whining tenor voice lacks any regal character and whose melodic material has a cloying banality. But Wilde's dark humor is largely missing from the opera, lost in part to the German translation and to the riveting power of Strauss's music, which grips the listener in a way that agrees with Wilde's perhaps ironic designation of the play as tragedy.

Strauss's creation of a libretto from Wilde's play was also atypical. He composed directly from its prose text, with no adaptation other than omitting lines from the original. The more typical way of adapting a literary work for an opera (recall Puccini's *Madama Butterfly*, discussed in Chapter 62) was to remove the complexity of the literary model and flatten the characters into simple types. Typically, the librettist segregated narrative text from other moments that suggested musical arias, ensembles, and choruses. By working directly with a spoken play, Strauss avoids all such artificialities and retains a sophisticated literary content for his opera; he was also freed to compose in short, asymmetrical phrases with few apparent divisions into musical numbers.

MUSIC OF THE OPERA

The overall structure of the opera resembles the structure of the play. Both are based on a large-scale symmetry in which passages of text and music near the beginning—notably Salome's love song to Jochanaan's body, hair, and mouth—return in a varied form in Salome's final monologue (discussed below). The music otherwise is continuously developmental, based on recurrent motives and tonalities that symbolize characters and dramatic situations. These resemble the leitmotives of Wagnerian opera, which was plainly a model for Strauss despite the highly un-Wagnerian text. As in Wagner's operas, traditional musical numbers—arias, recitatives, ensembles, and choruses—are rarely evident.

The large orchestra, enriched by such unusual instruments as **xylophone** and **heckelphone** (a member of the clarinet family), is the primary expressive element, as it also is in Wagner. It states most of the principal motives and takes over entirely from the voices at certain crucial moments, such as Salome's seductive **"Dance of the Seven Veils."**

The climax of the whole work is reached in Salome's concluding monologue, during which she fondles, and finally kisses, Jochanaan's decapitated head. The passage contains a complex network of motives that differ from Wagner's leitmotives in their greater number and complexity of presentation. Some are heard prominently on the surface of the music, and occasionally in the voices, but they are given out more typically deep within the orchestra's dense counterpoint, often fleetingly and subject to extensive transformations.

We can appreciate Strauss's intricate use of motives by tracing the evolution of the principal one that identifies the character Salome. This figure makes its first appearance in the clarinet in the very first measure of the opera (Ex. 64-1a). Salome appears on stage for the first time in scene 2, at which point her motive returns in the violin (Ex. 64-1b). The central measures of its earlier form (bracketed in the example) are now embedded into a new and more lyrical melody. In scene 3, where Salome asks about the prisoner who is spouting prophecies, her motive returns in yet another transformation (Ex. 64-1c). It has the same head motive as in (b), but a new continuation that reiterates an ascending and descending minor third. Later, where Salome sees Jochanaan and declares him disgusting, her motive (Ex. 64-1d) sheds its opening from (c) and adds a descending fourth to the minor thirds. In this form it dominates the music of her final monologue.

EXAMPLE 64-1

(continued on next page)

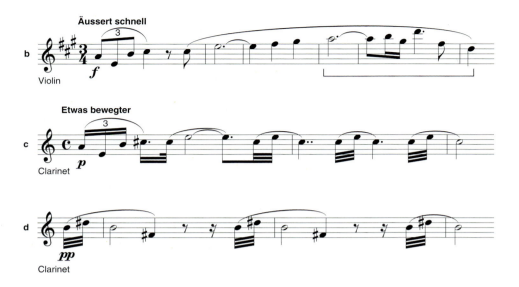

The central tonality of the monologue is C♯ minor and major, but this key appears only sporadically, mainly in moments where Salome gathers her thoughts. Where she drifts off into confusion, Strauss eliminates any unified sense of key. These wavering principles of tonal organization come directly into conflict near the end, after Salome sings her final exultant, "I have kissed your mouth, Jochanaan." As the music approaches a mammoth cadence in C♯ major, the upper instruments outline notes from a dominant chord in the key, but the lower ones go off by a semitone and play an A7 chord (Ex. 64-2). The stridently confused harmony that results is met by Herod's command, "Kill that woman!" This triggers a ten-measure coda in which the key is wrenched down to C minor, and the opera ends with convulsive reiterations of Salome's motive while she is crushed beneath the soldiers' shields.

EXAMPLE 64-2

 LISTENING CUE

RICHARD STRAUSS   CD 11/4
Salome, concluding scene (1905)   Anthology, No. 173

✳ STRAUSS AND "PROGRESS"

The success of *Salome* in 1905 brought an unexpected complexity into prospects for the future of music. Before this time most composers and audiences—at least in the German-speaking world—had settled comfortably into the assumption that there were only two available styles for new compositions. The more conservative one was associated with Brahms, the more progressive with Wagner. The Brahmsian model, as discussed in Chapter 58, balanced modern and traditional elements. It was modern in its extended harmonic language, intensive motivic development, and certain liberties in form, but it was traditional in genre, medium, and absolute rather than programmatic expressivity. The Wagnerian model made fewer overt references to the Classical past. It pushed harmony and tonality into new areas of ambiguity, expanded the orchestra to unprecedented size, and expressed a broad spectrum of extra-musical ideas.

Although we can now see that the differences between the styles of Brahms and Wagner are not so extreme, around 1900 there was very little middle ground separating the partisans of the two. You were either a Brahmsian or a Wagnerian. Gustav Mahler—a stalwart Wagnerian—wrote to his wife in 1904: "I have gone all through Brahms pretty well by now. All I can say of him is that he's a puny little dwarf with a rather narrow chest. Good Lord, if a breath from the lungs of *Richard Wagner* whistled around his ears he would scarcely be able to keep his feet."[1] On the other side was a musician like **Hugo Riemann,** the great German music theorist, who saw Wagner's influence as leading only to decadence. Brahms, said Riemann, was like a great tree that could withstand the winds of change:

> [Brahms is the] lone rugged oak that has endured on the paths swept by destructive tempests, its mighty roots having sunk deep into the earth. Its canopy is intact and spreads forth ever more proudly. It commands the present day, where the salvation of the future lies; it restores new powers to the healthy soil.[2]

Strauss's *Salome* changed this dichotomy by introducing a musical style whose novelties seemed to outweigh any indebtedness to Brahms, Wagner, or other late-Romantic models. For many of the progressive musicians of the day, this amounted to a betrayal. A year after the opera's premiere, **Felix Draeseke**—a composer and staunch advocate of Wagner—published a widely read polemic called "Confusion in Music."[3] In it he dismisses contemporary works that seemed to him intentionally ugly and muddled. Although Draeseke does not mention Strauss by name, he drops enough hints to make it clear that he considered Strauss to be the leader of this "Cult of the Ugly," as he called it.

Draeseke's attack provoked Strauss—who normally was not inclined to write about music—to respond. In his essay "Is There an Avant-Garde in Music?" Strauss professes his belief in the necessity in music of "progress." Music, he says, can never stop evolving, even at such an elevated stage as the one reached by a Brahms or a Wagner. He writes:

> Even a perfect work of art should be considered only as a stage in a great organic development. It should be planted as a seed in the souls of our descendants, to inspire and assist in the birth of even higher and more perfect creations.[4]

At the same time, Strauss placed a heavy restriction upon progress. Great works of any period, he said, must be acclaimed by the public in general. "A great artist is instinctively recognized as a natural genius by the public at large, even if its judgment of details is not at all clear headed."[5] This demand for public acceptance ultimately made Strauss appear to be a reactionary, not a progressive. In the eyes of younger modernist musicians such as Arnold Schoenberg, a truly important work could never be fully understood by a contemporary audience, only by one at some future time.

Strauss's *Salome* transcended the arguments between the Brahmsians and Wagnerians, conservatives and progressives. Although the work contains romantic features—intense expression, exploration of the human psyche, harmony and tonality employed as expressive as well as syntactic tools—it also broaches new ideas, including its hitherto untouchable subject, free use of dissonant harmonies, and a higher level of musical complexity than ever before. These constituted a whole new concept of "progress" that onlookers like Draeseke could only interpret as leading to ugliness. In the years just after 1905, younger composers throughout the world fixed their gaze on these novel features in *Salome* and left behind the romantic ones, ultimately ushering in a new period in the history of music.

 ## SUMMARY

Berlin was the German capital city from the founding of the country in 1871. At the turn of the twentieth century, its central musical institution was the Royal Opera, which was led by Richard Strauss from 1898 to 1918. In addition to conducting, Strauss during this period wrote tone poems and operas, among which *Salome* (1905) was his first major operatic success.

The work introduces a new subject matter for opera, filled with grotesquerie and parody that mix explosively with a biblical story. Based on a play by Oscar Wilde, the opera brings the literary content of the genre to a higher level. Strauss's music is equally innovative. Building upon Wagner's technique of the leitmotive, Strauss introduces motives with a withering complexity that make them sometimes virtually impossible to follow. Their complications are only heightened by the raucous dissonance of much of the score and passages in which key is scarcely evident. Strauss later justified these novelties as the result of a necessary progress in music.

 ## KEY TERMS

tone poem	xylophone	Hugo Riemann
Hugo von Hofmannsthal	heckelphone	Felix Draeseke
Oscar Wilde	"Dance of the Seven Veils"	

Chapter 65

Music in Russia During the Silver Age: Igor Stravinsky

The arts and letters in Russia during the reign of Tsar Nicholas II (1894–1917) entered a prosperous time that is now commonly called the **Silver Age.** Like the Silver Age of literature in ancient Rome of the first century C.E., it was a period of changing tastes. The romantic and melodious style of Tchaikovsky still enjoyed immense prestige in Russia, but to many observers it was a monument to an earlier era rather than a guide for the future. The experimental and nationalistic approach of the *kuchka* (see Chapter 59) held more promise, although the realism of a composer such as Modest Mussorgsky also seemed increasingly dated, as did the anti-Westernism implicit in the aesthetics of these Russian nationalists. For many younger Russian musicians of the Silver Age, the new ideas flowing, especially from France, could not be ignored.

REALISM IN RUSSIAN ART AND LITERATURE

The element of **realism** in Russian literature is well known from the penetrating psychological and social novels of Fyodor Dostoyevsky (1821–1881) and Leo Tolstoy (1828–1910), and it can also be readily seen in the paintings of an artist such as Ilya Repin (1844–1930). His *They Did Not Expect Him* (1884–1888; Fig. 65-1) captures a moment in life. A man unexpectedly returns to his family, whereupon each member registers a different emotion. The painting suggests a moment in a larger story whose full narrative could easily be imagined by any observer.

Compare this painting to Mikhail Vrubel's *The Six-Winged Seraph* (1905; Fig. 65-2). It relies for its effect not on social issues or a readily told story, but on color and form, as the artist reaches back in his theme to some primitive, mystic, and distinctively Russian essence. The artistic visions of Vrubel (1856–1910) point to the new post-realistic tendency in Russian arts of the Silver Age, which emphasizes experimental materials, abstraction more than realism, and an affinity with primitive and ancient Russian themes.

Bridgeman Art Library

FIGURE 65-1

Ilya Repin, *They Did Not Expect Him* (1884–1888). Ilya Repin was a leading Russian realist painter whose direct depictions of everyday life also guided the music of Mussorgsky.

Bridgeman Art Library

FIGURE 65-2

Mikhail Vrubel, *The Six-Winged Seraph* (1905). The paintings of Mikhail Vrubel often depart from the dominant realist style of Repin and use symbolist techniques associated with modern French art and metaphysical or religious themes.

MUSIC DURING THE SILVER AGE

Russian music of the period underwent a similar evolution. Many of the great works of nineteenth-century Russian music have an analogy with the realism of a Tolstoy or a Repin. Realism is especially apparent in the music of Mussorgsky, as in his opera *Boris Godunov* and songs such as "Within Four Walls" (see Chapter 59). Recall how the melody of "Within Four Walls" realistically imitates the depressed muttering of the poem's speaker. Mussorgsky avails himself of unusual musical elements, including aimless chord progressions, changing meters, and the suppression of normal melody, to mimic the spoken word and the poem's underlying emotion.

Although Mussorgsky's experimental musical resources were of interest to the next generation of Russian composers, these younger musicians generally bypassed his realistic attachment to his own world. At the turn of the twentieth century the nationalism that characterized the *kuchka* remained prominent, although this outlook was then expressed by an interest in the mystic or primitive element of the Russian consciousness more than by any anti-Westernism. This orientation led younger Russian musicians of the time to a musical language that relied upon the most contemporary thinking of European musicians.

The Silver Age also witnessed a continued modernization and diversification of Russian musical culture. The amateurism that had characterized native composers in the mid-nineteenth century was diminished, as Russian artists were more readily supported by the aristocracy and also by a rising, wealthy merchant class. The foreign domination of Russian music had also largely ended, and Russian figures, like their Western contemporaries, were all the more ready to export their own ideas abroad.

St. Petersburg continued to be the leading center for music. In addition to the celebrated opera and ballet of the Mariinsky Theater, the city's culture for orchestral and chamber music continued to expand. There were several important new opportunities for modern music to be heard: in 1903 the conductor and piano virtuoso **Alexander Siloti** (1863–1945) founded orchestra concerts that served a mixed fare of new music from both Russian and European figures. The modernist Viennese composer Arnold Schoenberg conducted his tone poem *Pelleas und Melisande* in 1912 with Siloti's orchestra, which he found musically outstanding. In 1901 a group of art-loving amateurs formed a society called the **Evenings of Contemporary Music** specifically to perform new works. Igor Stravinsky and Sergei Prokofiev—the leading young modernists on the Russian musical scene at the time—were both active as players and composers in this organization.

 SERGEI DIAGHILEV AND *THE WORLD OF ART*

The new vistas in Russian art associated with the Silver Age come into focus in the work of the remarkable impresario **Sergei Diaghilev** (1872–1929). Diaghilev was born in Gruzino, southeast of St. Petersburg, where he arrived in 1890 to study law. His interests quickly turned to the arts. He took classes in music at the Conservatory, although after publishing several articles on modern Russian painting he seemed headed for the career of an art critic. In 1898 he founded an art journal called **Mir iskusstva (World of Art)** in which he and his fellow writers expressed sympathy with modern European developments. Under the aegis of his journal, Diaghilev also presented a series of art exhibitions in St. Petersburg, and the Evenings of Contemporary Music were organized by several who collaborated on his journal.

Diaghilev's first taste of the professional world of ballet came near the turn of the century when he was asked to coordinate the design of a new production of Léo Delibes's ballet *Sylvia* for the Mariinsky Theater. Diaghilev's imagination was awakened to the creative possibilities available to an impresario, and he was especially keen on producing an opera or ballet as an integral collaboration among artists representing different fields. On a more practical level, his future as an impresario was brightened by his remarkable skill in raising money for artistic purposes from Russia's aristocracy and wealthy middle classes.

Beginning about 1906, Diaghilev looked to Western Europe—especially to Paris—for an outlet for his artistic initiatives. The Parisian social climate was then optimal for the appearance of Russian art, as France was just then reaching out to Russia on the diplomatic front. In 1907 the Russians, French, and British entered into a **Triple Entente,** by which they hoped collectively to balance the power of an opposing alliance among Germany, Austria, and Italy. Russian music—especially the works of Nicolai Rimsky-Korsakov and Mussorgsky—had long appealed to the French taste for the exotic and colorful.

Diaghilev soon turned his attention to music and dance, intending, as he had with Russian painting, to display the riches of modern Russian culture more fully to the French and other European capitals. In 1907 he organized a season of concerts at the Paris Opéra, featuring Russian composers and performers; the next year he brought a production of Mussorgsky's *Boris Godunov* for the Opéra; and in 1909 he presented ballets, using dancers from the Mariinsky Theater.

✿ THE BALLETS RUSSES

Ballet would be Diaghilev's focus from that time forward. In 1909 he established his own company, later named the **Ballets Russes (Russian Ballet),** which toured Europe and the Americas, with major seasons in Paris, Berlin, Milan, London, and Monte Carlo. The ballets that Diaghilev produced were very different from a typical nineteenth-century ballet such as Tchaikovsky's *The Nutcracker* (see Chapter 59). Those works filled an entire evening, and they told a story by mime, with danced numbers—solos, ensembles, and dances for the full company—periodically inserted. The music had only a loose connection to the story, mainly providing a backdrop to the dancing rather than an expressive enhancement to the drama.

Diaghilev's ballets were entirely different. They were short, and several were needed to fill an evening's entertainment. Their music could come from different sources. Concert works for orchestra (such as Debussy's Prelude to *The Afternoon of a Faun*) were sometimes provided with choreographies, and pastiches of music were specially arranged and orchestrated (as in the ballet *Les sylphides*, based on piano music by Chopin). Diaghilev also commissioned original scores to be joined to original choreographies.

This last type is the most interesting musically and the area in which Diaghilev and his associates exerted their most lasting influence on the history of ballet. Before Diaghilev, ballet music had a mixed reputation. With the exception of Tchaikovsky, music for the genre tended to be written by secondary figures, who provided at most a tuneful and repetitive score that had a limited range of expression and no attempt at originality. By the end of the nineteenth century, these utilitarian features made the entire genre of ballet pale in the eyes of musicians when compared to opera, in which a truer dramatic expression was the norm.

Diaghilev followed up on the achievements of Tchaikovsky by bringing musical respectability back to the genre. He was guided aesthetically by a choreographer from the Mariinsky Theater, **Mikhail Fokine** (1880–1942). Fokine was dismayed by the traditional ballet of his time. It seemed to lack drama, unity, or high artistic intentions, all of which he found being sacrificed to the stock jumps, spins, and poses from classical dance. Ballet, he said in his memoirs, "lacked its most essential element: presentation to the spectator of an artistically created image."[1]

He experienced the same displeasure with his genre that, fifty years earlier, Richard Wagner did with traditional opera, and both had similar ideas for improvement. Fokine insisted that all aspects of a ballet—its scenario, mime, dancing, lighting, costume, stage design, and music—should be integrated into a unified dramatic image. Fokine's prescription was that ballet should become a "total work of art," for which the Wagnerian music drama was plainly a model.

❖ IGOR STRAVINSKY

Igor Stravinsky (1882–1971; see Part VII timeline) rose to fame as a composer by realizing Fokine's conception of the integrated ballet. Fokine was the choreographer of Stravinsky's first two ballets, *The Firebird* (1910) and *Petrushka* (1911), and his ideas concerning the artistic integrity of ballet served Stravinsky well from this time forward.

Stravinsky was born near St. Petersburg to a musical family (his father was a leading singer at the Mariinsky Theater). Typical of the amateuristic tradition of Russian music, he at first did not choose the life of a professional musician. Instead he studied law at the university in St. Petersburg and only at the age of twenty-three began to study music seriously, taking lessons then with Rimsky-Korsakov. Following the death in 1908 of his conservative teacher, Stravinsky deepened his contacts with the modernists of the *World of Art* group, and he was eventually introduced to Diaghilev.

Stravinsky's breakthrough to international celebrity as a composer came in 1910, when Diaghilev presented his new ballet, *The Firebird*, to Parisian audiences. This work was followed by other brilliantly original ballet scores for Diaghilev's company: *Petrushka* (1911), *The Rite of Spring* (1913), *Les noces* (*The Wedding*, 1917, premiere 1923), and *Pulcinella* (1920). During this early period, Stravinsky also composed songs (typically for voice accompanied by small and diverse ensembles of instruments), an opera called *The Nightingale*, and a choral work with large orchestra called *Zvezdoliki* (*King of the Stars*).

During World War I, Stravinsky settled in Switzerland, then later in France, where in the 1920s he became a leader of new thinking in modern music. (His ideas from this time are discussed in Chapter 68.) Between the world wars Stravinsky often toured as pianist, conductor, and composer, and he made several trips to the United States. With the beginning of World War II in 1939, Stravinsky emigrated permanently to America, and in 1940 he settled in California in what is now the city of West Hollywood. He remained there until shortly before his death in 1971, and he is buried in Venice, Italy, near the tomb of his great patron, Sergei Diaghilev.

The Rite of Spring

The basic idea for Stravinsky's *The Rite of Spring* (*Le sacre du printemps*)—his third ballet for Diaghilev—was a re-enactment of spring rituals in prehistoric Russia. A theme drawn from Russian folklore was squarely in the aesthetic spirit of the *World of Art* group, where delving into national roots and the Slavic subconsciousness was considered a way for the Russian artist to reach a higher reality. Russian folklorism also appealed to European audiences for its color and exoticism, and Stravinsky's two earlier ballets—*Firebird* and *Petrushka*—had successfully used folkloric scenarios.

To work this idea into a ballet, Stravinsky collaborated with Fokine (who later dropped out of the project, replaced as choreographer by the dancer **Vaslav Nijinsky**) and with the painter Nicholas Roerich, who specialized in ancient Russian subjects and was considered an authority on Russian ethnography. The ballet that they foresaw was consistent with the dramatic theories of Fokine. They would produce not simply an artistic or stylized evocation of a subject from Russian folklore, but, to the extent possible, an authentic re-creation of one. To this end Roerich designed historically plausible costumes and decor, the dancing imitating realistic movements more than those of classical ballet, and Stravinsky brought authentic and relevant folk melodies into his score.

The scenario for the ballet consists of a series of scenes disposed in two large parts. Unlike Tchaikovsky's *The Nutcracker*, there is no attempt to tell a connected story. The general idea contained within each section is outlined by headings that Stravinsky placed in the score:

Part 1: Adoration of the Earth	Part 2: The Sacrifice
Introduction	Introduction
The Augurs of Spring	Mystic Circles of the Young Girls
Dances of the Young Girls	Glorification of the Chosen One
Ritual of Abduction	Evocation of the Ancestors
Spring Rounds	Ritual Action of the Ancestors
Ritual of the Rival Tribes	Sacrificial Dance (The Chosen One)
Procession of the Sage	
The Sage	
Dance of the Earth	

This outline was considerably fleshed out in an article (excerpted in Box) that appeared in the Parisian journal *Montjoie!* on 29 May 1913, the day of the work's premiere. The first performance was much anticipated by French audiences. Stravinsky's two previous ballets had been warmly received in the French capital, but by 1913 audiences throughout Europe were more inclined than ever to rise up in protest against music that was unfamiliar in style. Only two months before, a concert at the Musikverein in Vienna, with orchestral pieces by Arnold Schoenberg, Anton Webern, and Alban Berg, was brought to an early end by a tumult in the audience.

Apparently not wanting to be outdone, the Parisians had a similar uprising at the first night of *The Rite of Spring*. The American ballet critic Carl Van Vechten was present on that evening, and he reported:

> This first audience would not permit the composer to be heard. Cat-calls and hisses succeeded the playing of the first few bars, and then ensued a battery of screams, countered by a foil of applause. We warred over art (some of us thought it was and some thought it wasn't). . . . Some forty of the protestants were forced out of the theatre but that did not quell the disturbance. The lights in the auditorium were fully turned on but the noise continued and I remember Mlle. Piltz executing her strange dance of religious hysteria on a stage dimmed by the blazing light in the auditorium, seemingly to the accompaniment of the disjointed ravings of a mob of angry men and women.[2]

"What I Wanted to Express in *The Rite of Spring*" by Igor Stravinsky (excerpts)

"The Parisian public has for some years accorded a good reception to my *Firebird* and *Petrushka*. My friends have observed an evolution in their underlying ideas, from a fantastic fable in the one to a generalization concerning all of humanity in the other. I am afraid that *The Rite of Spring*—in which I project an abstraction of a somewhat broader sort, rather than a fairy tale or the sadness and joy of the human condition—may disconcert those who have extended to me to this point a heartfelt sympathy.

"With *The Rite of Spring* I wanted to express the sublime ascent of nature eternally reborn—the total, panic rising of the universal sap.

"In the Prelude, before the curtain, I express in my orchestra that great fear which weighs upon all sentient beings in the face of things that exert power—a 'thing in itself' that has the *capacity* to grow and infinitely develop. A delicate sound, even on the flute, can contain this element of power and spread above the whole orchestra. It is the obscure and immense sensation that everything experiences at the moment when nature renews its forms; it is the vague and deep anxiety of universal puberty. Even in my orchestration and in the play of melodies, I demand that it be evoked. . . . In sum, I wanted to express in the Prelude the panic fear of nature in the face of a rising beauty, a sacred terror in the glare of the midday sun, a sort of cry of Pan. The musical material itself inflates, expands, grows. Each instrument is like a bud that pushes against the husk in an old tree, each becoming part of an imposing whole. . . .

"Now we hear a procession coming near. The Holy Man arrives, the Sage, the High Priest, the oldest of the clan. A great terror sweeps through all gathered. The Sage then gives a blessing to the earth, stretching on his stomach with arms and legs spread, becoming himself as though one with the earth. His blessing is like a signal for a rhythmic outburst. All cover their heads and run in circles, pouring forth in great numbers, as though representing the new energy of nature. This is the Dance of the Earth.

"The Second Tableau begins darkly with the games of the adolescent girls. At the outset, a musical Prelude is based on a mysterious chant that accompanies their dancing. . . . The Chosen One is the one to be consecrated by spring, the one who must yield to spring that force which her youth had hold over. The young girls dance around the Chosen One, who remains motionless in a sort of apotheosis. Then it is the purification of the earth and the evocation of the ancestors. And the ancestors also circle the Chosen One, who begins her Sacrificial Dance. . . ."[3]

Stravinsky himself seemed none too upset by the stormy reaction, and *The Rite of Spring*—both in its original form as ballet music and as an independent orchestral tone poem—was soon recognized as one of the great masterpieces of the early twentieth century.

The music—which reveals both emotionality and extraordinary new materials—is certainly the core of the work's greatness. The orchestra is very large, expanded to over ninety instruments. Woodwinds are in fives, and there are eight horns and a large battery of percussion. Stravinsky calls for instruments not normally heard in the orchestra—the breathy alto flute, strident small trumpet and small clarinet, bass trumpet (played by a trombonist), Wagner tubas, antique cymbals, and gourd—and all of the instruments are driven to the limits of their ranges and instructed to play in many irregular ways. Plainly, the composer wanted to increase the number of sounds that the orchestra could produce and the diversity of ideas and emotions that such sounds could evoke.

The melodic element does not at first attract our attention because it seems reduced to a mosaic of fragments (many drawn from Eastern European folk songs) that are spun out by repetition and ostinato. The harmonic and tonal organization of the work makes no consistent reference to key and, instead, constantly shifts among passages that are diatonic (for example, in the folk song that Stravinsky quotes in the bassoon at the beginning of the ballet), octatonic (as in the flourish in the trumpets that announces the appearance of the Sage), and whole tone in the frenzied "Dance of the Earth." These passages are shown in Example 65-1.

Authenticity in the Writings of Stravinsky

Stravinsky's first important essay on music is the analysis of *The Rite of Spring* that is excerpted in the box on the facing page. It appears to be a highly valuable and authoritative explanation of one of the great works of music of the twentieth century. But the essay is clouded by controversy over its authenticity. Although published solely with Stravinsky's name as author, the composer received some measure of assistance from the editor of *Montjoie!*, Ricciotto Canudo. Its authenticity was further confused when Stravinsky complained in his *Chronicles of My Life* (1935) that it contained "a distortion of my language and even of my ideas."

Should this complaint be taken seriously? We now know that Stravinsky's *Chronicles* were themselves largely ghost written by Walter Nuvel, an old acquaintance of Stravinsky from Diaghilev's *World of Art* group. The composer's deceptions in claiming authorship for other people's words continued for the rest of his life. His *Poetics of Music*—lectures for the 1939 Charles Eliot Norton Lectures at Harvard University—were written by the French critic Roland-Manuel and the Russian émigré Pierre Suvchinsky. They contain an interesting statement *about* Stravinsky's aesthetic of the

1930s, but they are not what they purport to be—a far more important declaration *by* Stravinsky himself.

Stravinsky's unwillingness to speak his own mind has cast doubt upon and created misinformation about his life and musical oeuvre. It has clouded the entire historical record concerning the composer and brought confusion upon the general understanding of his work. Like most plagiarists, Stravinsky was clumsy in his deceptions, sometimes stumbling into ludicrous situations. He was evidently proud of the work done by Roland-Manuel on *Poetics of Music*, and he read one of the lectures to a Parisian gathering of friends that included the poet Paul Valéry. Apparently unknown to the composer, Roland-Manuel had taken ideas from Valéry's own recent college lectures on poetics to put into Stravinsky's mouth, and the composer unwittingly read these to their real author. After the gathering Valéry wrote in his diary: "Stravinsky . . . gets out the text of the lectures he has just written to give at Harvard. He calls them 'poetics' and his main ideas are more than analogous to mine from the course at the Collège."

EXAMPLE 65-1

Diatonic
Solo bassoon, mm. 1-3

Octatonic
Tpts., 2 before reh. 66

(Source octatonic scale)

Whole tone
Bass clar., reh. 75

By 1913 such free harmonic thinking was familiar to the world of new music from the innovations of composers like Richard Strauss and Arnold Schoenberg. It is in rhythmic organization that *The Rite of Spring* breaks new ground. The work contains an unprecedented rhythmic energy, achieved by exploiting a virtual catalog of alternatives to normal rhythmic organization.

In the Introduction to Part 1, for example, there is little sense of beat at all, instead a free intertwining of lines with differing motions. Then in the first scene, "The Augurs of Spring," the rhythm changes to a steady, hypnotic pounding of eighth-note values (Ex. 65-2). These are cut through by irregularly placed accents that dispel any normal or symmetrical meter. Onstage, at this point, a dancer impersonates an old woman who, Stravinsky writes, "runs, bent over the earth, half-woman, half-beast. The adolescents at her side are Augurs of Spring, who mark in their steps the rhythm of spring, the pulse beat of spring."

EXAMPLE 65-2

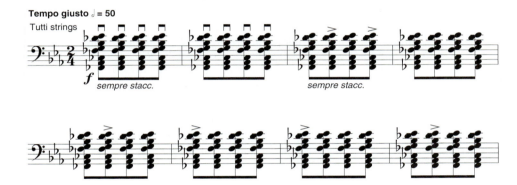

The chord played by the strings in this passage shows Stravinsky's keen ear for dissonant harmonies, which even by themselves can be exciting and rousing. The lower strings play a E-major triad (spelled as F♭) while the upper strings at the same time sound an inversion of an E♭7 chord. The combination arising by a juxtaposition of familiar but unrelated harmonies is often called a **polychord.** Stravinsky's use of key signature (three flats) in this scene may relate to the presence of the E♭ harmonic component, although the scene is not organized by this or any other key. Yet another type of rhythmic organization is found in the concluding "Sacrificial Dance." The meter of this passage changes virtually from one bar to the next, with only a small submetric value (here a sixteenth note) acting as a common element that runs through (Ex. 65-3).

EXAMPLE 65-3

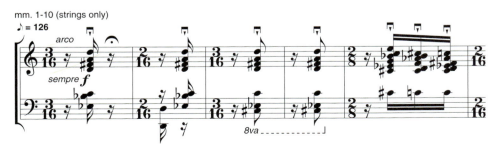

In passages of the "Dance of the Earth," Stravinsky constructs a complex rhythmic canon. At Rehearsal 70 (Ex. 65-4) the part for D-clarinet and D-trumpet contains a repeated rhythm consisting of a quarter-note followed by a dotted half-note, suggesting a meter with four beats; the same figure is heard in the trombones and C-trumpet III but is offset by two beats. Stravinsky notates the passage in $\frac{6}{4}$, which does not conform to the meter expressed in either stratum.

EXAMPLE 65-4

Stravinsky's often brutal rhythms, mesmerizing ostinatos and moments of wrenching tension in *The Rite of Spring* showed once and for all that the new resources and outlook of musical modernism were capable of holding the attention of an audience. They were destined to be the central elements in musical expression of the twentieth century.

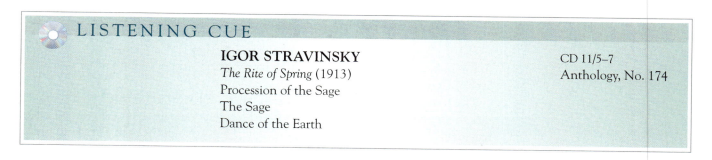

LISTENING CUE

IGOR STRAVINSKY
The Rite of Spring (1913)
Procession of the Sage
The Sage
Dance of the Earth

CD 11/5–7
Anthology, No. 174

THE RUSSIAN REVOLUTION

On 15 March 1917, Tsar Nicholas II abdicated his throne amid uncontrollable strikes, rioting, and military insurgency throughout Russia's largest cities. The crisis was most directly provoked by the disastrous economic and social effects of Russia's participation in World War I, during which the country relentlessly descended into chaos and anarchy. After the tsar's departure, a provisional government was established, but the real power was in hands of councils of workers and soldiers (called "soviets"). Those in St. Petersburg (which in 1914 had been renamed Petrograd) gradually threw their support to the **Bolshevik** faction led by **Vladimir Lenin,** who promised to end Russia's involvement in the war, to distribute land to peasants, and to cede power to the soviets. On the night of 6 November 1917, the Bolsheviks seized control from the provisional government, and thus began a long and violent process of consolidation and centralization of power. In 1922 the older Russian empire was reassembled as the Union of Soviet Socialist Republics (USSR), which endured until its ultimate collapse in 1991.

The effect of the **Russian Revolution** on musical culture was profound. Many artists greeted the change of government with a positive idealism. "I and those associated with me," wrote Sergei Prokofiev, "welcomed it with open arms. I was in the streets of Petrograd while the fighting was going on, hiding behind house corners when the shooting came too close."[4] Lenin immediately placed Anatoli Lunacharsky—a respected writer—in charge of culture and education, and Lunacharsky brought such leading younger artists as Marc Chagall, Vasili Kandinsky, and Alexander Blok into his arts ministry. The writer Blok saw the revolution—despite its excesses and violence—as a necessary step in the progress of Russian society and art.

But the desperate economic conditions into which the country was cast caused many of its leading composers and performers to emigrate to Europe. Even earlier, with the outbreak of World War I, Stravinsky had settled in Switzerland and had become increasingly estranged from his homeland. He would not return to Russia until 1962. Diaghilev and his Ballets Russes were likewise permanently established in Europe. Sergei Prokofiev left in 1918 to try his luck in America; the great pianist and composer Sergei Rachmaninoff quickly departed for Scandinavia, never to return.

SUMMARY

The arts in Russia near the turn of the twentieth century (commonly called the "Silver Age") are characterized by an absorption of modern developments from western Europe and a reduction in the importance accorded to realism or traditional thinking. The nationalistic element of earlier Russian composers remained in force, but this was often redirected into artistic studies of archaic or primitive aspects of Russian society.

The transformation in taste in Russian music and art was furthered by the impresario Sergei Diaghilev, who in 1909 formed a ballet company later called the Ballets Russes (Russian Ballet) that brought new works to audiences in Paris and other Western capitals.

The leading composer in Diaghilev's troupe was Igor Stravinsky, whose five ballet scores for the Ballets Russes, composed between 1910 and 1920, include *The Rite of Spring,* a work notable for original thinking in rhythm, the use of Russian folk melodies, colorful orchestration, and powerful expression of primitive humanity close to nature. The rhythmic innovations in the work include shifting meters, suppression of regular meter by irregular accents, and rhythmic canons. In passages such as "The Augurs of Spring," Stravinsky's harmonies include polychords—dissonant chords made from juxtaposing two familiar though unrelated harmonies.

The Revolution of 1917 marked a break with the past as the leading Russian composers and performers left the country, their place soon to taken by younger figures.

KEY TERMS

Silver Age
realism
Alexander Siloti
Evenings of Contemporary
    Music
Sergei Diaghilev

Mir iskusstva (*World of
    Art*)
Triple Entente
Ballets Russes
    (Russian Ballet)
Mikhail Fokine

Vaslav Nijinsky
polychord
Bolshevik
Vladimir Lenin
Russian Revolution

Chapter

66

Atonality: Schoenberg and Scriabin

Russian-born artist **Vasili Kandinsky** created the painting in Figure 66-1 shortly
after hearing a 1911 concert devoted to the works of the Viennese composer Arnold
Schoenberg (1874–1951). Kandinsky, who was accompanied by several fellow
artists from the Munich area, heard two of Schoenberg's string quartets and a selection of his songs, as well as his Three Piano Pieces, Op. 11. Although Kandinsky
was himself an experienced musician, he was apparently startled by the unusual
music. Schoenberg's String Quartet No. 2 (1908) brought in a soprano voice in its
last two movements to sing poetry by Stefan George—one of Kandinsky's favorite
writers—that speaks of an individual's hope for release from a world containing
only misery. The music expresses these sentiments in new ways. For long passages
its rhythm and texture are turbulent and unsettled, having little sense of regular
pulse or metric symmetry. The harmonies are almost entirely dissonances, and a
sense of key is evident only sporadically. The brief Piano Pieces go even further in
removing normal tonality and banishing triads—long the building blocks of harmony—which are replaced by a large number of unfamiliar dissonances. Despite
these novelties, the works are in certain ways
traditional, especially in their familiar genres
and intense, almost romantic expressivity.

FIGURE 66-1

Vasili Kandinsky, *Impression 3
(Concert)*, 1911. Kandinsky's
partly abstract painting was created shortly after first hearing
Schoenberg's atonal music.

NEW MUSIC AND
ABSTRACT ART

Kandinsky's friends began to speculate on the
meaning of Schoenberg's innovations and
their relevance to modern painting. Franz
Marc, who was with Kandinsky at the concert,
thought that Schoenberg wanted each note
or chord to stand on its own and that the
composer intended to remove all traditional
musical laws, composing entirely through instinct like a primitive artist.[1]

Kandinsky's own reaction was to paint the
"impression." In this powerful work, certain

realistic images—human forms and the black piano lid—are evident, but these are outweighed by abstract shapes and fields of color (such as the strident yellow area on the right side) and by a freely emotional expression that communicates the artist's feelings about the music. Kandinsky was one of the first important abstract artists, a painter who used largely nonrepresentational shapes in his works.

In an article that he wrote in 1912, Kandinsky tried to explain the artistic effect of an abstract shape by using the example of a simple line.[2] In the "real" world, a written line exists mainly to fulfill certain functions or uses. In an essay, for example, it can be called on to underscore, or stress, an important thing or concept. But when the line is placed on the canvas of an abstract painting, all such uses are abandoned and the shape can only represent what Kandinsky—echoing the ideas of philosophers going back to Plato—called the "thing in itself." By this he meant that the line took on a pure value and meaning rather than a meaning defined by its use. But what meaning? Kandinsky could only indicate this by a musical analogy. The line, he said, had a "pure inner sound."

This "thing in itself" is what Kandinsky and his artist friends found revealed in Schoenberg's music. The compositions that they heard seemed to lack other symbols of the real world—a normal or euphonious blending of elements or utilitarian purposes—all of which seemed to have been replaced by direct references to more elemental or inner states. Kandinsky was sufficiently provoked to write to the composer himself. In a letter of 18 January 1911 he told Schoenberg: "What we are striving for and our whole manner of thought and feeling have so much in common that I feel completely justified in expressing my empathy."[3]

Schoenberg responded enthusiastically. To explain his music to Kandinsky he was not so philosophical as the artist had been; instead, he chose to emphasize the ways that his music had come into being—by instinctive and spontaneous choices rather than by applying rules. Relying on instinct, he said, could tap into his unconscious mind and produce the truest image of the self, which he thought to be the goal of all art. "Art belongs to the *unconscious*!" Schoenberg exclaimed. "One must express *oneself*! Express oneself *directly*! Not one's taste, or one's upbringing, or one's intelligence, knowledge or skill. Not all these *acquired* characteristics, but that which is *inborn, instinctive*."[4]

ARNOLD SCHOENBERG

Schoenberg's music had not always been so unusual as were the works heard by Kandinsky in 1911. His earlier compositions—songs, chamber pieces, a tone poem based on Maurice Maeterlinck's play *Pelléas et Mélisande*, and a massive oratorio called *Gurrelieder*—were typical products of the late Romantic period. They were intensely melodious, highly expressive, serious to the point of overstatement, and they used harmony and tonality in the enriched manner of such late nineteenth-century figures as Richard Strauss, Hugo Wolf, and Gustav Mahler.

These were among the musicians who inspired Schoenberg during his youth in Vienna. He was largely self-taught as a composer, and he made his mark as an independent thinker. Until 1933 (see Fig. 66-2) he resided alternately in Vienna and Berlin and earned his living primarily as a teacher of composition, at which he was especially gifted. All the while his music attracted attention for its originality and audacity. Among his private students in composition were such leading composers as Alban Berg and Anton Webern, performers including Rudolf Kolisch and

Edward Steuermann, and the conductors Heinrich Jalowetz and Karl Rankl.

His final sojourn in Berlin began in 1926 as professor of composition at the Berlin Academy of Arts. When Hitler rose to power in Germany in 1933, Schoenberg—born a Jew but long since a convert to Lutheranism—was dismissed from his position. With his family he fled first to Paris where, in an act of defiance, he reconverted to Judaism. He then traveled to America and settled finally in California, where he was later appointed to the music faculty of the University of California, Los Angeles.

Although Schoenberg at first embraced the romantic language of Wagner, Brahms, and their followers, he felt compelled to move beyond it and to find a style that was original—recognizable as his alone. Between 1905 and 1908 he gradually developed this alternative, the main characteristics of which were the absence of tonal center and the pervasive presence of dissonant rather than triadic harmony. He never settled on a term to designate this style, but in describing it he repeatedly pointed to one of its most salient characteristics—that he used dissonance as though it was "emancipated." By the **emancipation of dissonance** he meant that dissonant chords could appear freely, and be just as readily understood and enjoyed as triads had been in earlier music.

THE ATONAL STYLE

Others called Schoenberg's music of this new type **atonal.** The composer himself could never accept this term, which he found inherently negative—something that no composer would want to be known for. The phenomenon of atonality in early twentieth-century music gradually took on a more concrete and positive meaning. Such music has no key, that is, no functional harmonic progressions that extend over and unify large spans of a musical work. Its pitch basis is the entire chromatic scale, each tone of which has, at least theoretically, equal importance. Because of this equality of notes, atonal music normally lacks a key signature (the presence of which suggests that seven notes are natural and the other five only "accidental"). The harmonic basis of atonal music consists primarily of dissonant chords, theoretically of any size and intervallic makeup (although triads and other tertian harmonies occur in passing). Other musical features, such as the choice of forms, melodic styles, and rhythmic motions, are more flexible, depending on the taste of the individual composer.

Schoenberg wrote atonal music until the early 1920s, at which time he abandoned the intuitive and spontaneous processes that were originally at its root and which he had emphasized in his correspondence with Kandinsky. Believing that larger forms were incompatible with the spontaneity of atonality, Schoenberg during this period wrote primarily brief character pieces—for orchestra, piano, and voice. He also composed two short operas, *Erwartung* (*Waiting*) and *Die glückliche Hand* (*The Magic Touch*), and an incomplete symphony with voices.

Despite its great originality in harmony, Schoenberg's atonal style still contains features brought forward from late nineteenth-century music. These include expressive melody, traditional musical textures, irregular phrase lengths, and an intense

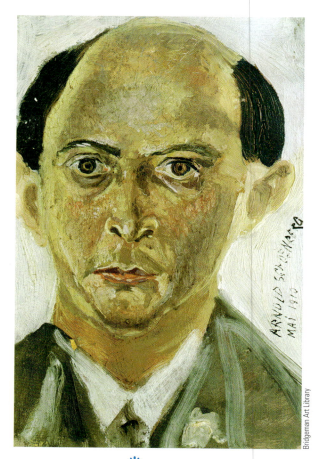

FIGURE 66-2
Arnold Schoenberg, *Self-Portrait* (1910). Schoenberg was a skillful painter in addition to being a musician, and he created many self-portraits.

Schoenberg on Atonal Music

Schoenberg was reluctant to describe his music as "atonal," since he believed that the tones in any composition had some degree of relatedness. In place of this word, he used the term "emancipation of dissonance" to characterize his works written between 1908 and 1923. Here Schoenberg describes this concept:

> The term *emancipation of dissonance* refers to its comprehensibility, which is considered equivalent to the consonance's comprehensibility. A style based on this premise treats dissonances like consonances and renounces a tonal centre. By avoiding the establishment of a key, modulation is excluded, since modulation means leaving an established tonality and establishing *another* tonality.
>
> The first compositions in this new style were written by me around 1908 and, soon afterward, by my pupils,

Anton von Webern and Alban Berg. From the very beginning such compositions differed from all preceding music, not only harmonically but also melodically, thematically, and motivally. But the foremost characteristics of these pieces *in statu nascendi* were their extreme expressiveness and their extraordinary brevity. At that time, neither I nor my pupils were conscious of the reasons for these features. Later I discovered that our sense of form was right when it forced us to counterbalance extreme emotionality with extraordinary shortness. Thus, subconsciously, consequences were drawn from an innovation which, like every innovation, destroys while it produces. New colourful harmony was offered; but much was lost. . . . [5]

development of motives. Still, Schoenberg's innovations most capture our attention. One of the most controversial of these is his banishing of triads from his atonal music. He explained why these were no longer admissible: "I believe they would sound too cold, too dry, expressionless. Or, perhaps, what I mentioned on an earlier occasion applies here. Namely, that these simple chords, which are imperfect imitations of nature, seem to us too primitive."[6]

Schoenberg also believed that a richness of tone color was appropriate to atonal music. He mentions it in his correspondence with Kandinsky in the context of painting: "Color is so important to me (not 'beautiful' color, but color which is expressive in its relationships)." In his *Theory of Harmony* (1911) Schoenberg proposed a new resource for modern music that he called **tone-color melody (*Klangfarbenmelodie*)** in which a succession of differing timbres could take on a structural role in a composition akin to that of normal melody. In a "melody" of this type, each tone or chord could have its own particular timbre.

Piano Piece, Op. 11, No. 1

Schoenberg's Three Piano Pieces, Op. 11 (1909), are among his earliest compositions in the atonal style. Each is a brief character piece having a definite mood. Piece No. 1 is generally somber, and it frequently erupts into momentary outbursts. One of the difficulties that the piece poses for the listener and performer is that these conflicting moods—and the musical figures that embody them—are so abbreviated. They change quickly from one moment to the next, and the melodic ideas themselves tend to dissolve into minute fragments. The quick moving, abbreviated shapes, lack of keynote, and absence of triadic harmonies make Schoenberg's music difficult for most of us to understand. Schoenberg was well aware of this difficulty and thought that it could be overcome only by many years of familiarity. In a letter of 1937 he remarked about his music: "I am content if they do not dislike it when they hear it the fifteenth time," he confessed.

The tonal organization of Piece No. 1 conforms to the general characteristics of atonality. The notes of the full chromatic scale are drawn on equally, the harmonies are almost entirely dissonant, and there are no functional harmonic progressions. Typical also of the atonal composer, Schoenberg subtly coaxes new colors from the piano. One way that he does this is by using **piano harmonics.** In measures 14–17, Schoenberg instructs the player silently to depress the tones F-A-C♯-E, thus releasing the dampers on those strings. The left hand then plays the same notes in a lower register, which makes the partials of these open strings shimmer with a glassy tone.

The form of the work is closest to the ternary model. The music opens with a theme (measures 1–11), itself having a small ternary design. The middle section follows with a succession of contrasting subsections, each of which plainly develops motives from the theme. At measure 53 the theme is brought back in a recognizable though transformed state. The perpetual development of motives in the piece is something shared with nineteenth-century composers (recall from Chapter 58 Brahms's pervasive use of the motto F - A♭ - F in the first movement of his Third Symphony). Schoenberg, like such forebears, at first aimed in his atonal music for a unified and homogeneous substratum that could support a diverse and changeable surface.

LISTENING CUE

ARNOLD SCHOENBERG
Piano Piece, Opus 11, No. 1 (1909)

CD 11/8
Anthology, No. 175

THE EVOLUTION OF SCHOENBERG'S ATONAL STYLE

Shortly after he completed the Piano Piece No. 1 in February 1909, Schoenberg began to experiment with a far more radical type of atonal music having fewer points of contact with traditional styles and structures. He began at this time to compose in a stream of consciousness, without the development of motives that is apparent in the Piano Piece. "I strive for complete liberation from all forms, from all symbols of cohesion and logic," he wrote to Ferruccio Busoni. "Thus, away with 'motivic working out.'"[7] His opera *Erwartung* (1909) was one of several pieces written in this new way.

Schoenberg's experiment soon led him into a compositional crisis in which he lost his confidence and inspiration. In 1911 he wrote to his student Alban Berg: "I've lost all interest in my works. I'm not satisfied with anything any more. I see mistakes and inadequacies in everything. Enough of this; I can't begin to tell you how I feel at such times."[8] Gradually, Schoenberg pulled himself out of his creative doldrums, which he did by rethinking how atonal music could be created. He dispensed with the procedure that he had described to Busoni and Kandinsky—composing as an "unconscious" act—and moved toward an opposite viewpoint by which composing would once again be methodical, leading to familiar musical forms while retaining the more general features of atonality.

He looked back in time to the great works of Bach, Beethoven, and Brahms, and he found all of these composers working consciously with themes and motives to create unified structures. Their motivic craftsmanship was lacking in his stream-of-consciousness pieces, so he decided to return to an earlier formal outlook and use motives even more pervasively and systematically than ever.

Pierrot lunaire

Pierrot lunaire (*Moonstruck Pierrot*, 1912) was the crucial piece that set Schoenberg on this future direction; it is one of his most original creations in the atonal style. *Pierrot lunaire* is a cycle of twenty-one narrations for a female speaker accompanied by a small ensemble of piano, strings, and woodwinds. Its genre is that of the **melodrama,** a composition that combines spoken recitation with instrumental music (in Chapter 55 we encountered an example of the style in the Wolf's Glen Scene in Weber's opera *Der Freischütz*).

The words of *Pierrot lunaire* are drawn from a collection of French poetry of the same title by **Albert Giraud** (1860–1929), translated into German by Otto Erich Hartleben. They deal with the sad-sack, moonstruck clown Pierrot, whose antics range from the comic to the grotesque. Each of the poems, or "rondels," has thirteen lines of which lines 1–2 are repeated as 7–8, and line 1 returns as line 13.

The delivery of the speaking part was not left entirely to the reciter. Schoenberg instead wrote out a recitation, using musical notation that dictates the rhythms precisely and shows approximate pitches. Schoenberg emphasized that he wanted the reciter to speak, not to sing, although the exact interpretation of the reciter's part occupies an indefinite place between speech and song. Schoenberg called this type of recitation **Sprechgesang** (speech song), and he notated it by placing an X through the stems of notes. An example from the eighth recitation is shown in Example 66-1.

EXAMPLE 66-1

Dark, black, giant butterflies killed the sunshine.

Schoenberg's new way of composing systematically with themes and motives is especially evident in the eighth recitation, titled "Nacht (Passacaglia)." The poem contains a grotesque vision of gigantic butterflies sinking to earth and blotting out the sun, which Schoenberg depicts by growling sounds from the bass instruments and by a contrapuntal texture that ranges from strict canon to free imitation.

The music is saturated by a three-note motive—first heard in the piano in the form E-G-E♭—whose many recurrences suggest the term **passacaglia,** which Schoenberg chose for the title of this movement. Recall from Chapter 31 that a passacaglia in the seventeenth century was a work based on continuous repetitions of a short thematic figure.

While the baroque composer usually confined the recurring thematic figure to the bass line, creating a so-called **basso ostinato,** Schoenberg uses the E-G-E♭ figure in all of the lines, and he also spreads it vertically into several interlocking and adjacent parts. We can see how he does this by observing the instrumental introduction in measures 1–3. As seen in Example 66-2, there are six brief lines present in these measures (four in the piano part alone), and each of them descends by semitone except for the single note in the bass clarinet. The basic motive is presented not linearly but vertically, by joining adjacent tones from several lines. For example, in measure 1 the motive E-G-E♭ arises in the two lowest lines of the piano part.

In this way, the composer extends the unifying power of a motive beyond a single linear dimension into the two-dimensional space that music occupies. Schoenberg believed that this verticalized presence of motives represented a "discovery" that was so logical and so closely connected to trends in great music of the past that it would eventually become standard practice among composers. It led him directly to his **twelve-tone method** of composing, which he devised in 1923 (see Chapter 69).

EXAMPLE 66-2

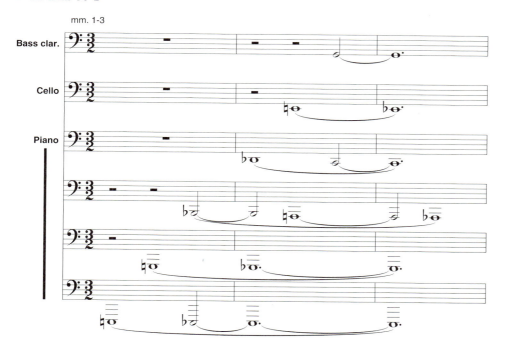

Following the introduction, the basic motive is spread into the two-dimensional texture by means of strict imitation. In measures 4–10, for example, the instruments play a canon on a theme that begins with the three-note motive. In measure 8 the clarinet states the basic motive simultaneously over different spans of time (Ex. 66-3). Here the motive is heard in groups of eighth-notes in three different transpositions; also, the three first notes, three second notes, and three third notes of each eighth-note group state the motive.

EXAMPLE 66-3

Bass clarinet, m. 8

LISTENING CUE

ARNOLD SCHOENBERG
Pierrot lunaire (1912)
No. 8, "Nacht (Passacaglia)"

CD 11/9
Anthology, No. 176

✿ OTHER ATONALISTS: ALEXANDER SCRIABIN

The atonal style emerged in the first decade of the twentieth century, not only with Schoenberg in Vienna but also among progressive composers in many other locations worldwide. Its characteristics are seen in works composed between 1905 and 1910 by Béla Bartók in Hungary, Igor Stravinsky in St. Petersburg, and Charles Ives in New York. One of its most important converts was the Russian composer Alexander Scriabin (1872–1915). He was born in Moscow and educated at the Moscow Conservatory, where he developed skills as a pianist. Typical of the nineteenth-century virtuoso, he composed for his own instrument, mainly sonatas, character pieces, and a piano concerto (1896), which he performed on tours in Europe and America. These compositions were at first romantic in style, with a melodiousness and harmonic vocabulary reminiscent of works by Chopin. He began to compose symphonic music in 1900, and his later symphonies and tone poems are programmatic. His Fifth Symphony ("Prometheus—Poem of Fire," 1910) calls for the projection of colored lights that he associated with certain keys (C major, for example, was red). But Scriabin never devised a practical notation for this idea.

Around 1908 Scriabin began to compose atonal music. The distinctive trademarks of his atonal style—and its differences from Schoenberg's brand of atonality—are apparent in his Five Preludes for Piano, Op. 74. These short pieces were completed in 1914, only months before Scriabin's untimely death. Prelude No. 5 is marked *fier, belliqueux* (proud, warlike) and filled with flamboyant and expressive rhetoric, quite unlike Schoenberg's understated Piano Piece, Op. 11, No. 1. Scriabin repeats themes and motives in this Prelude according to a simple plan (**ABAB**), unlike Schoenberg, who avoids repetition in favor of a constant development of motives.

While Schoenberg avails himself of a large number of dissonant chords drawn from the chromatic scale, Scriabin limits himself, in making up his lines and chords, to only two collections of notes. These systematically underlie the tonal organization of his entire atonal oeuvre. The first of these is the **octatonic scale,** the presence of which is not surprising in Scriabin since it had long been used by Russian composers (it is sometimes called the "Rimsky-Korsakov scale," given that composer's fondness for it). The other is called the **mystic chord,** or alternately "'Prometheus' chord" since it is prominent in Scriabin's "Prometheus" Symphony. The mystic chord appears as the first harmony of "Prometheus," taking the form G-D♯-A-C♯-F♯-B (Ex. 66-4). Scriabin uses it not only as a chord per se, but also as the source for notes in lines and themes.

EXAMPLE 66-4

If we place its tones into a compact scalewise order, such as F♯-G-A-B-C♯-D♯, we see that the mystic collection of pitches is closely related to a whole-tone scale, since only one note (F♯ in the preceding example) deviates from a fully whole-tone pattern. The mystic collection is also closely related to a segment of an octatonic scale. By moving the single tone B to become Bb, it forms six of the eight notes of the octatonic scale F#-G-A-Bb-(C)-C#-D#-(E).

Scriabin has several ways of varying the octatonic and mystic collections of tones when he uses them in a piece of music. He presents them equally as lines and chords, he sometimes omits tones from them, and he freely reorders their notes. He also transposes and symmetrically inverts their pitches. A symmetric **inversion** of a collection of notes results if the intervals formed by those notes *above* the first tone are duplicated *below* it. Consider the mystic collection illustrated above: F#-G-A-B-C#-D#. It can be symmetrically inverted by duplicating its *ascending* intervals instead in a *descending* direction, that is F#-Fᵇ-Eb-Db-Cb-A.

We can see how Scriabin uses these relationships in the very first measure of his Prelude No. 5 (Ex. 66-5). The notes that make up the second half-note beat of this measure, placed in a compact scalewise form, are Bb-A-G-F-Eb-Db. On beat three the tones are D-Eb-F-G-A-B. Apparently, the two collections (both versions of the mystic chord) are related by symmetric inversion followed by transposition. On beat one there are seven notes, C-Db-Eb-F-G-A-Bb, which merge, in a sense, a mystic collection with its inversion, since the first six notes, as shown in the scalewise order, are inversionally related to the last six.

EXAMPLE 66-5

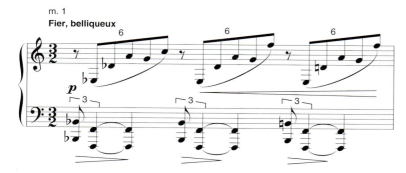

The form of Prelude No. 5 is clarified by shifts between the mystic and octatonic collections. Music A (mm. 1–4 and 9–12) is generally based on mystic collections; music B (mm. 5–8 and 13–17) is almost entirely octatonic. To see how Scriabin uses the octatonic scale, look at measure 5 (Ex. 66-6). The six tones appearing in this measure are drawn from the octatonic scale A-Bb-(C)-C#-D#-(E)-F#-G. The two missing tones (C and E) are supplied in the measures that immediately follow.

EXAMPLE 66-6

 LISTENING CUE

ALEXANDER SCRIABIN   CD 11/10
Piano Prelude, Opus 74, No. 5 (1914)   Anthology, No. 177

SUMMARY

Around 1908, Arnold Schoenberg began to compose "atonal" music, a style characterized by the lack of traditional key and functional harmonic progressions, a free and theoretically equal use of all tones of the chromatic scale, and a free application of dissonant harmonies, which are treated as though equivalent to consonant (triadic) chords. Modern artists of the same time, such as the Russian-born Vasili Kandinsky, recognized similarities between atonal music and their own abstract, nonrepresentational paintings. In his atonal pieces from 1910 and 1911, Schoenberg experimented with composing in a stream of consciousness—very quickly and with a minimum of planning. Beginning with his recitations of *Pierrot lunaire* (1912), he began to compose atonal music more systematically, returning to strict polyphony and reinforcing traditional linear motivic unity by deploying motives throughout a texture.

Schoenberg's Russian contemporary, Alexander Scriabin, also began to compose atonal music around 1908, evolving, as did Schoenberg, from his earlier romantic language. The pitch organization of Scriabin's atonal music is based upon the octatonic scale and the so-called mystic chord, the latter a six-note collection of tones that is close to the whole-tone scale.

KEY TERMS

Vasili Kandinsky
emancipation of
    dissonance
atonal music
tone-color melody
    (*Klangfarbenmelodie*)

piano harmonics
melodrama
Albert Giraud
Sprechgesang
passacaglia
basso ostinato

twelve-tone method of
    composition
octatonic scale
mystic chord
(symmetric) inversion

Chapter 67

French Music at the Time of World War I: Ravel and Satie

The esteem accorded the music of Claude Debussy following the premiere in 1902 of his opera *Pelléas et Mélisande* showed that modernism had reached a considerable degree of acceptance by French audiences. This new work was given no fewer than fourteen performances in its first season at Paris's Opéra-Comique—an extraordinary number for a composition of such complex originality. Its innovations caused a great stir throughout French intellectual and artistic circles; Olivier Messiaen recalled playing the music of *Pelléas* as a child and finding it "a revelation, a thunderbolt." Erik Satie heard the work at the Opéra-Comique shortly after its premiere and described it to his brother as something "absolutely astounding."

Debussy's modernism resided in a great originality of both form and material, and it extended to new ways of presenting melody, a new harmonic and tonal language, and new ideas about rhythmic organization (see Chapter 63). He allied his music with the most recent trends in French painting and literature, and in all of these ways it suggested a certain elitism. It was difficult for his contemporaries to understand and plainly not intended for everyone.

At the same time that Debussy's music appeared triumphant, new or alternative ideas arose among his contemporary composers. Some figures of an older generation—Camille Saint-Saëns (1835–1921) and Vincent d'Indy (1851–1931) are examples—could not accept Debussy's innovations at all, and several younger French composers had their own ideas of how music should progress. Erik Satie (1866–1925) composed in a radically simplified and almost naivist manner. Maurice Ravel (1875–1937), although sharing many of Debussy's romantic inclinations, moved his music into a new relationship with works from the past.

✶ MAURICE RAVEL

Maurice Ravel was the leading younger French contemporary of Debussy. He lived for virtually his entire life in and around Paris. At the age of fourteen he entered the Paris Conservatory, first as a piano student, and later in the composition class of Gabriel Fauré. As a budding composer he at first enjoyed the support of Debussy, who described him as "extraordinarily gifted," although their relations at a later time became strained.

Ravel lived as a freelance musician, primarily from income derived from the sale of his music and from concerts in which he conducted and played piano. He occasionally taught—one of his students was Ralph Vaughan Williams (see Chapter 61), with whom he formed a close friendship—although Ravel never held an institutional teaching appointment. Following World War I, he was recognized internationally as one of the greatest living composers, and he traveled the world giving concerts of his own music. He undertook a triumphant but grueling tour of the United States and Canada in 1928. His last compositions date from 1933, after which he suffered from a degenerative condition that may have been a form of Alzheimer's disease.

Ravel wrote music in all of the important genres of his day—opera, ballet, orchestral tone poems and piano character pieces, songs, chamber music, and concertos. In his early works—those composed before World War I—he concentrated on the piano. After the war he turned decisively to orchestral composition, at which he was especially skilled. Among the orchestral genres he bypassed only the symphony, as did other progressive French composers, including Debussy and Fauré. Among his larger works are the ballets *Daphnis et Chloé* and *Boléro,* the tone poem *La valse* (which was intended as a ballet score), the Piano Concerto, and the monumental piano collections *Miroirs* (*Mirrors*) and *Gaspard de la nuit* (*Gaspard of the Night*).

While the works of Debussy are fairly homogeneous in style, those of Ravel are highly diverse. His early compositions are plainly indebted to Debussy's influence. Ravel generously described Debussy as "the most phenomenal genius in the history of French music," but he added, "I believe that I myself have always followed a direction opposite to that of Debussy's symbolism."[1] Ravel gradually freed himself from Debussy and experimented in a variety of new techniques including jazz adaptations and atonality. Some of these were associated with younger composers, and especially with the music of his friend Igor Stravinsky.

Ravel set off in this "opposite direction" from Debussy primarily by adopting a new outlook on music of the past. This was different from the conservative attitude that was held earlier by a Mendelssohn or Brahms. These composers were concerned mainly with preserving in their music the outlines of Viennese classicism, which they updated and extended in an orderly manner. Ravel was not interested in preserving a particular heritage so much as he was drawing from anywhere and everywhere in the past to create an entirely contemporary musical language. His sources were diverse, some coming from as far back as the Baroque period, others more recent, and others still drawn from such popular musical idioms as American jazz and Spanish flamenco. Ravel revived the forms that he found in his sources and parodied their styles, which he updated with modern harmony.

At the turn of the twentieth century, musicologists in France were hard at work promoting the country's musical past, especially the compositions of Baroque masters such as Jean-Philippe Rameau (1683–1764) and François Couperin (1668–1733). In 1895 the Parisian publisher Durand began to produce an edition of the complete works of Rameau, beginning with his harpsichord music, and in 1903 Durand came out with an edition of Couperin's 1722 *Concerts royaux* (*Royal Concerts*). Ravel apparently studied these sources and drew upon them for ideas for new works.

Le tombeau de Couperin

In the piano suite *Le tombeau de Couperin* (*Couperin's Monument*, 1914–1917), Ravel revives the forms and certain of the styles of harpsichord music from the Baroque period in France, especially as they occur in the works of François Couperin. The word *tombeau* (French for "tomb" or "monument") had been long used by French composers to designate a musical tribute to a great predecessor, especially a deceased teacher.

Recall from Chapter 36 that François Couperin was a harpsichordist and composer employed by King Louis XIV of France. Among his greatest works are twenty-seven dance suites for harpsichord (Couperin called them *ordres*, or "orderings"), and other suites called *Concerts royaux* (*Royal Concerts*) that were playable either by harpsichord alone or with the addition of a few instruments.

Ravel appears to have studied Couperin's fourth *Royal Concert* (c1722) prior to composing his *Tombeau*, and he made it the model for a brilliant and thoroughly modern suite of piano pieces. Ravel's *Tombeau* consists of six movements—Prelude, Fugue, Forlane, Rigaudon, Menuet, and Toccata. These allude to dance types that (with the exception of the Toccata) appear in Couperin's 1722 Royal Concerts. Like Couperin, Ravel writes each of his dances (except for the C-major Rigaudon) in a single key, E minor. Couperin's Fourth Royal Concert is also in E, alternating between minor and major. With some exceptions, Ravel also preserves the binary or rondo forms in which Couperin casts his dance movements. So serious was Ravel's study of Couperin's Fourth Royal Concert at this time that he made an incomplete arrangement for piano of its Forlane movement, probably as a way to absorb Couperin's idiom.

The Rigaudon from Ravel's *Le tombeau de Couperin* is an especially brilliant and festive work. In the seventeenth and eighteenth centuries, a **rigaudon** was a lively social dance in $\frac{2}{4}$ time. It was often imitated in the music of French baroque operas and instrumental suites. The opening of the Rigaudon that appears in Couperin's Fourth Royal Concert is shown in Example 67-1; below it is the beginning of Ravel's Rigaudon. Couperin uses a familiar binary form in his Rigaudon, which is expanded by Ravel into a ternary alternative. Ravel also captures the motoric rhythms of Couperin's baroque style. In harmony, however, Ravel's piece is thoroughly modern. It alludes to the key of C major, although in the interior of the piece chromatic tones are liberally added as the music dashes through a series of conflicting tonal centers.

EXAMPLE 67-1

Couperin's Rigaudon, mm. 1-8

Ravel's Rigaudon, mm. 1-7

Ravel's way of referring to music of the past was influential on composers living in France after World War I. Especially significant was his tendency in *Le tombeau de Couperin* to treat the past as though it were his musical *subject*—to write music, that is, about music. This outlook would shortly become central to the 1920s style called **neoclassicism,** to which we turn in the next chapter.

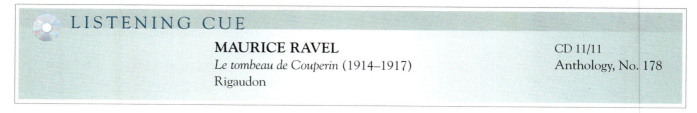

LISTENING CUE

MAURICE RAVEL
Le tombeau de Couperin (1914–1917)
Rigaudon

CD 11/11
Anthology, No. 178

ERIK SATIE

Prior to the end of World War I, the works of Erik Satie were unrelated to any general development in French serious music. Satie played piano as a child and, beginning in 1879, attended the preparatory division of the Paris Conservatory. His advancement there was found unpromising, and he dropped out in 1886. He then worked as cabaret pianist—first at the famous **Chat Noir** in the Montmartre district of Paris—composing and arranging popular songs for the establishment and writing whimsical essays for its publications. Through his appearances in this and other

Cabaret Then and Now

Today **cabaret** is a relaxed form of popular musical entertainment in which a singer croons above the soulful tones of a piano for audiences in a nightclub setting. In Satie's day, in Paris, it was something different. In 1888 Satie was hired as a piano accompanist at the Chat Noir (Black Cat) in Montmartre, the first important modern cabaret. The word "cabaret" comes probably from a small tray on which drinks are served. A show at the Chat Noir usually included dramatic skits, shadow plays (forerunners of cinema), and the singing of poet-songsters. The mood was anything but relaxed, being instead satiric and provocative. The style was intentionally rough and always relevant (at least in the eyes of the performers). For artists of all disciplines in the 1880s, cabaret was a way of bringing average citizens face to face with art.

The singer Yvette Guilbert (1865–1944) introduced a new type of cabaret art, that of the *diseuse*. With piano or small-band accompaniment, she partly sang, partly spoke a poem that ridiculed and poked fun at the society of her day. Her performances may well have been a model for Schoenberg's *Pierrot lunaire*.

The old art of cabaret was exported from Paris around the world. It found a thriving home in Germany—especially in Berlin—where the artistic trappings of the Chat Noir were reconstructed. This is the risqué world of entertainment that was recreated in 1966 in the show *Cabaret*, with music by John Kander. The musical was the basis for a highly successful 1972 film starring Liza Minnelli, which captures the spirit of anything-goes that made German cabaret unique. With the rise of the Nazis in the 1930s, the freethinking cabaret was ruthlessly eliminated.

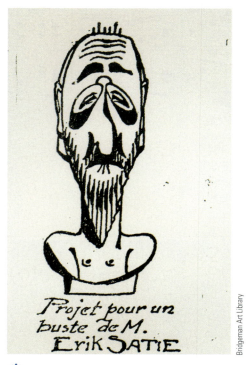

🌸 FIGURE 67-1

Satie frequently drew whimsical portraits, often of himself, as in *Projet pour un buste de M. Erik Satie* (*Project for a Bust of Mr. Erik Satie*). Their humor and understatement are reflected in his music.

Projet pour un buste de M. Erik Satie

Bridgeman Art Library

cabarets, he became acquainted with numerous classical musicians, including Debussy and Ravel, who found him to be an eccentric and irrepressible personality (Fig. 67-1). Finding the life of a cabaret pianist increasingly burdensome, Satie aspired to write classical music, and he returned to school in 1905, at the age of almost forty, to study counterpoint.

Satie's first significant exposure as serious composer came in 1911 when Ravel performed three of his piano pieces at a concert of the Société Musicale Indépendante (of which Ravel was a founder). The performance led to the publication of several collections of piano music, and gradually other Parisian pianists, including the virtuoso Ricardo Viñes, took them up.

Satie's reputation grew steadily, and in 1917 Sergei Diaghilev commissioned him to compose the music for a new ballet, **Parade,** on which he collaborated with the painter Pablo Picasso and writer Jean Cocteau. *Parade* attracted attention for its novelty, unpretentious tunefulness, and absorption of popular musical styles, and these features seemed to forecast a new spirit in the arts, which Satie and Cocteau continued to encourage in the years to come.

Satie wrote mainly short piano pieces, to which he gave eccentric and witty titles such as "Three Pieces in the Shape of a Pear" and "Three Truly Limp Preludes (For a Dog)." The humorous tone was probably a carryover from Satie's work in cabaret, where parody was the order of the day. There are also a few songs and pieces using small orchestra or instrumental ensembles, including the scores for the ballets *Parade*, *Mercure* (1924), and *Relâche* ("Closed," 1924).

One of Satie's piano pieces played by Ravel in 1911 was the Sarabande No. 2, one of three works with this title that Satie had composed in 1887. The piece must have baffled the listeners of 1911 because its complete artlessness was so opposite the highly elaborate new music of the day. The Sarabande resembles a mere improvised succession of chords, presented in a monotonously repetitive form, with very little melody and rhythm and absolutely no counterpoint or development of ideas.

The chords themselves alternate among triads, major sevenths, and major ninths, only occasionally presented with functional harmonic implications. The central sonority is the major ninth chord (for example, E-G♯-B-D-F♯ in m. 18). These harmonies are presented mainly in streams in which the dissonant tones are neither prepared nor resolved, and the chords rarely fulfill tonal harmonic functions. Throughout the piece we can almost hear Satie—wearing his famous wry smile— ask his listeners why harmonies must progress and why dissonances must resolve!

Following World War I, with the onset of a broad reaction against the late Romantic style, Satie's music of simplicity, humor, and naïveté emerged as a precursor of important events and trends. Satie himself relished this newfound significance, and musicians worldwide praised his music for its refreshingly anti-Romantic profile. The American composer and critic **Virgil Thomson,** who while a student in Paris in the 1920s met Satie, became a lifelong admirer. For him Satie's music is "as simple, as straightforward, as devastating as the remarks of a child."

LISTENING CUE

ERIK SATIE
Sarabande No. 2 for Piano (1887)

Thomson-Schirmer Website
Anthology, No. 179

WORLD WAR I

During the summer of 1914, Ravel vacationed on the French coast, working on a new string trio "with an insane certainty and lucidity," as he told his friend Maurice Delage. On 1 August news arrived that Germany had declared war on Russia; two days later Germany declared war on France, and all of Europe then descended into general warfare. The issues that precipitated war—militarism, economic rivalry, and nationalistic hostility, among others—had before 1914 exerted little effect on musical culture. The major concert halls and opera houses of Europe presented a cosmopolitan repertory, and on a personal level European composers of different nationalities got along reasonably well.

Internationalism seemed to be the order of the day throughout the musical world. The Englishman Edward Elgar was an outspoken admirer of German culture, and the German Richard Strauss praised Elgar's progressivism. "I raise my glass to the welfare and success of the first English progressivist, Meister Edward Elgar, and of the young progressivist school of English composers," he said in a 1902 speech. The Austrian Arnold Schoenberg respected Claude Debussy's avant-gardism, and the Russian Igor Stravinsky considered France a second home.

Given these cordial international contacts among leading musicians, the declaration of war took virtually everyone by surprise. Many musicians were on vacation in August, when the announcement of war was made, and most thought that the conflict would be quickly settled. Still, there was great uncertainty. Schoenberg hurriedly returned to Berlin from his vacation, spent with the Russian painter Vasili Kandinsky in the Bavarian resort of Murnau. Ravel returned to Paris from his vacation retreat on the French coast, Elgar from Scotland to London.

Composers had different reactions to the onset of war. Many felt helpless and bewildered by world events, with a dark apprehension about their future as musicians. Debussy wrote to his publisher shortly after war was declared: "I'm nothing more than a wretched atom hurled around by this terrible cataclysm, and what I'm doing seems to me so miserably petty!"[2] Others rethought old allegiances. Ferruccio Busoni—an Italian composer and pianist living in Berlin—cynically reassessed his adopted German identity:

> I used to say: there exist in the world, all in all, either *incipient* or *moribund* cultures. Only the diminutive area between London and Rome, between Paris and Moscow [i.e., Germany], can credit itself with a culture which is florescent and vigorous, mature yet still youthful (I used to say). I declare this opinion to be one of the greatest mistakes I ever made.[3]

Most musicians became rabid patriots, willing to exchange their instruments for rifles. Schoenberg at the age of forty enlisted in the Austrian army; Ravel, despite poor health, joined the French forces. "Vive la France!" he wrote to Cipa Godebski. "But, above all, down with Germany and Austria! Or at least what those two nations represent at the present time. And with all my heart: long live the Internationale and Peace!"[4] Paul Hindemith, whose father would shortly be killed in battle, wrote from Frankfurt: "Many French pretend to be wounded or dead, then shoot our troops in the back. It is entirely the fault of the French if German troops become outraged and act thoughtlessly."[5]

For the duration of the war, 1914 to 1918, musical culture throughout Europe was much reduced. Travel was restricted, and many composers were deprived of an income from foreign royalties. Although efforts existed in most countries to spare artists from combat, many composers, painters, and writers were killed, including the German painters Franz Marc and August Macke, the French composer Albéric Magnard and his countryman, the writer Charles Péguy.

What would be the outcome of this war for music? The question was pondered by musicians everywhere, and most foresaw profound and lasting changes looming on the horizon. In 1914 the English music critic Ernest Newman wrote:

> The war, if it be prolonged, will mean the drawing of a line across the ledger and the commencement of a new account. It is impossible for the Continent to pass through so great a strain as this without a setting free of great funds of dormant emotion, and a turning of old emotions into new channels. These tremendous crises always have a far-reaching nervous effect.[6]

The "new channels" so accurately predicted by Newman will be outlined in chapters to follow.

 ## SUMMARY

Although Debussy's approach to modernism was the most important direction in French music in the decade before World War I (see Chapter 63), alternative styles are seen at the same time in the works of Maurice Ravel and Erik Satie. Ravel began his career as a composer by writing piano music that could not escape Debussy's powerfully evocative Impressionism, but Ravel later tried to distance himself from Debussy by finding his own style. He did so in part by adopting a new approach to music of the past, which he drew upon in the manner of parody. In his piano suite *Le tombeau de Couperin* he derives forms and stylistic ideas—motoric rhythms, ornamented melodic lines, and a percussive treatment of the keyboard—from François Couperin's *Royal Concerts* (1722), which he updates with modern harmonies and tonal organization.

The piano pieces of Erik Satie, such as his Sarabande No. 2 (1887), are highly simplified and primitivized in technique. With a puckish humor, they seem to question hallowed rules of traditional music, such as the necessity for goal-directed harmonic progressions and the preparation and resolution of dissonances.

World War I (1914–1918) marked the end of an era in musical history.

KEY TERMS

rigaudon	Chat Noir	*Parade*
Neoclassicism	cabaret	Virgil Thomson

Chapter
68

New Music in Paris After World War I: Stravinsky and The Six

On 11 November 1918, three German diplomats arrived in the village of Compiègne near Paris to meet Marshal Ferdinand Foch, the commander of the Allied armies during the final stages of World War I. The visitors accepted Foch's terms for German surrender, and all signed an armistice that ended the war. As news of this event swept through France, there was an outpouring of exhilaration and also utter exhaustion. On the positive side for France, their armies had spearheaded the successful Allied war effort, conquering the mighty German Empire and regaining the lands lost to Germany after the humiliating defeat in the Franco-Prussian War of 1870–1871. The war had forged a close alliance between the French and the people of the United States—by 1918 the world's greatest economic power—and cultural interchange soon increased between the two countries. But the French people had suffered greatly. Four years of horrific warfare had been fought largely on French lands, at the staggering cost of 1.4 million of its citizens killed.

 ## MUSICAL LIFE IN PARIS

Although the northern and eastern provinces of France had experienced a drastic level of destruction during the war, Paris was spared, and after the Armistice its musical culture quickly rebounded. Opportunities to hear new music multiplied. The Russian émigré conductor **Serge Koussevitsky** (1874–1951) founded an orchestra in Paris in 1920 that performed new works by French and Russian composers. Stravinsky's Octet (discussed momentarily) and Maurice Ravel's brilliant orchestration of Modest Mussorgsky's *Pictures at an Exhibition* were among the compositions first heard in Koussevitsky's concerts. In 1924 Koussevitsky was appointed director of the Boston Symphony Orchestra, with which he diligently supported new symphonic compositions by American composers.

Ballet companies specializing in new repertory also proliferated following the war. The Ballets Russes, led by Sergei Diaghilev (see Chapter 65), continued to present a season in Paris every year, and after the war they gave the premier performances there of new works by Igor Stravinsky, Sergei Prokofiev, Erik Satie, and younger French-born musicians. In the 1920s Diaghilev had to compete with several new rivals, including the modernistic **Ballets Suédois** (Swedish Ballet) and the **Ballets Ida Rubinstein,** which first presented Maurice Ravel's ballet *Boléro* in 1928.

An important musical discovery in postwar Paris was **jazz.** Immediately after the end of the war, American and English dance bands arrived in Paris to play at casinos and fashionable bars such as Le Boeuf sur le Toit (The Ox on the Roof, named after a trendy 1919 ballet by Darius Milhaud). Their music ignited a craze for dancing and helped to dispel the bitter memories of war. They called their playing "jazz," although it had little in common with what we now call jazz. The typical dance band that came to Paris after 1918 was a large ensemble that mixed strings, woodwinds, brass, piano, plucked instruments, and drums, and it played written arrangements in which improvisation had little if any role. The music was filled with lively syncopations, crisp and polished playing, and the musicians were adept at creating special sound effects by glissandos, mutes, exaggerated vibrato, and the resources of the percussionist's **drum set.**

The high-spirited dance music had a powerful attraction for classical composers. In jazz they discovered a style that was down to earth, something distinctly appealing after a period when grandiosity and complexity in music had left many listeners bewildered. It was also the source of many new musical ideas, especially in its rhythm, whose originality was underscored by the young Parisian composer Darius Milhaud:

> The power of jazz comes from a novelty of technique that extends to all of its elements. In rhythm there is an exploration of resources resulting from the constant use of syncopation, opening up in this music a realm of expression with the simplest means that does not need a rich or varied orchestration.[1]

❋ FIGURE 68-1

Piet Mondrian, *The Winkel Mill in Sunlight*, 1908.

Jazz rhythms were quickly imported into many new works by the leading French classical composers—including Igor Stravinsky, Maurice Ravel, Erik Satie, Georges Auric, and Milhaud himself—as a mingling of the high and popular arts became the order of the day. The pianist **Jean Wiéner** (1896–1982) launched a concert series in Paris in 1920 in which new experimental pieces were performed side-by-side with jazz band music.

❋ REGAINING CONTROL

Jazz dancing was a welcome antidote to the dismal aftermath of war, whose appalling chaos made all Europeans look to regain control. This became an underlying theme in the arts in the decades after 1918, and in music it helped to produce one of the clearest and most definitive stylistic changes in its history.

Like many other shifts in artistic temperament, the change of taste after the war can be most readily assessed in the visual arts. We find examples in the works of the Dutch artist **Piet Mondrian** (1872–1944), who lived in Paris both before and after World War I. His paintings before the war extend the language of the French impressionists (see Chapter 63). An example from 1908 is his *The Winkel Mill in Sunlight* (Fig. 68-1). Here Mondrian, like the impressionists before him, depicts a familiar object found in the countryside. But, unlike the im-

"Some Ideas About My Octuor" by Igor Stravinsky (excerpts)

"My Octuor is a musical object. This object has a form and that form is influenced by the musical matter with which it is composed. The differences of matter determine the differences of form. One does not do the same with marble that one does with wood. My Octuor is made for an ensemble of wind instruments. Wind instruments seem to me to be more apt to render a certain rigidity of the form I had in mind than other instruments—the string instruments, for example, which are less cold and more vague. . . . My Octuor is not an 'emotive' work but a musical composition based on objective elements which are sufficient in themselves. . . . The aim I sought in this Octuor, which is also the aim I sought with the greatest energy in all my recent works, is to realize a musical composition through means which are emotive in themselves. These emotive means are manifested in the rendition by the heterogeneous play of movements and volumes. This play of movements and volumes that puts into action the musical text constitutes the impelling force of the composition and determines its form. . . .

"Form, in my music, derives from counterpoint. I consider counterpoint as the only means through which the attention of the composer is concentrated on purely musical questions. Its elements also lend themselves perfectly to an architectural construction.

"This sort of music has no other aim than to be sufficient in itself. In general, I consider that music is only able to solve musical problems; and nothing else, neither the literary nor the picturesque, can be in music of any real interest. The play of musical elements is the thing. . . ."[6]

The Octet's diminutive medium—hard and clear in sound—is only one of several means by which Stravinsky dispels the mists of romanticism. The work is concise. Its three movements—titled "Sinfonia," "Theme with Variations," and "Finale"— last scarcely thirteen minutes. Its spirit is light, melodious, and witty—there is no angst, no hyper-emotionality, nothing that would make those in the audience listen with their heads in their hands.

Especially in the fast tempos, the controlled rhythmic chaos of Stravinsky's earlier *Rite of Spring* is replaced by an almost motoric sense of beat, which is occasionally draped over changes of meter. The music has a cosmopolitan tone, devoid of regionalisms or folk song quotations and cleansed of anything that could identify the nationality of its creator. The design of the first movement suggests a concise sonata form with slow introduction.

These and other features remind the listener of aspects of the music of the Classical period, although the work has a thoroughly modern harmonic and tonal language. Stravinsky's high spirits suggest that the work's classicism is—as it was for Ravel in *Le tombeau de Couperin*—more of a witty parody than any naive revivalism. The American composer Aaron Copland—who was present at the Paris premier performance of the work in October 1923—aptly described Stravinsky's parody as "art grafted on art."

LISTENING CUE

IGOR STRAVINSKY
Octet (1923)
First movement, "Sinfonia"

CD 11/12
Anthology, No. 180

DARIUS MILHAUD AND "THE SIX"

The lighthearted spirit of Stravinsky's Octet also appeared in the new music of younger native-born French composers during the decades following World War I. An article published in 1920 in a Paris journal identified a group of these figures as **"The French Six,"** and those named—Darius Milhaud, Georges Auric, Francis

Poulenc, Germaine Tailleferre, Louis Durey, and Arthur Honegger—found the term to be good publicity and gave a series of joint concerts. They were encouraged in their efforts by Erik Satie and by the influential French writer **Jean Cocteau** (1889–1963), whose works trumpeted many of the anti-romantic ideals for postwar music also espoused by Stravinsky. In his widely read pamphlet *Le coq et l'arlequin* (*The Cock and Harlequin*, 1918), Cocteau demanded a music of tuneful and entertaining simplicity. It would be the opposite of late Romantic German music, which "grimaces" and "wears a mask."

Darius Milhaud (1892–1974) readily complied with Cocteau's demand. Milhaud (pronounced MEE-OH) was born in the south of France and educated at the Paris Conservatory. He lived in the United States after 1940, and following the end of World War II held teaching positions both at Mills College in Oakland, California, and the Paris Conservatory. He was an immensely prolific composer whose early works, those from about 1915 through the 1920s, are best known. These include ballets and operas, chamber works, and piano pieces.

Milhaud was fascinated by popular music, whose styles he frequently brought into his own compositions. He had a special affinity with American jazz, which he heard on a trip to Harlem in 1922 and then re-created in his ballet *La création du monde* (*Creation of the World*, 1923). During a two-year sojourn with the French diplomatic corps in Rio de Janeiro, he became familiar with Brazilian popular dance music. He remarked on its special rhythmic character:

> I was intrigued and fascinated by the rhythms of this popular music. There was an imperceptible pause in the syncopation, a careless catch in the breath, a slight hiatus which I found very difficult to grasp. So I bought a lot of maxixes and tangoes and tried to play them with their syncopated rhythms that run from one hand to the other. At last my efforts were rewarded and I could both play and analyze this typically Brazilian subtlety.[7]

Milhaud made use of Brazilian dance rhythms in his collection of piano character pieces titled *Saudades do Brazil* (*Longing for Brazil*, 1920). In addition to the presence of syncopated rhythms, these pieces are all studies in **polytonality.** This is a simultaneous presentation of two or more keys or diatonic collections of tones in different strata of a composition, and it was long a Milhaud specialty. He described its attraction for him as a resource for emphasis and expression in new music: "I think that it gives to music a sort of particular brilliancy. It can mean much more powerful fortissimi, much more tender pianissimi. It increases the field of expression that we have at our disposal," he wrote.[8]

"Botafogo" (the name of a beach in Rio), from *Saudades do Brazil*, illustrates Milhaud's imaginative use of his diverse resources. The piece imitates the Brazilian samba, with its comfortable syncopations and simple repetitive form. In the first section (mm. 1–26) the two hands quickly pull apart into a polytonal texture (Ex. 68-1). The right plays in F♯ minor, the left in F minor, and the two come together at cadences. In the middle part (mm. 27–42), the right hand plays mainly white keys, suggesting C major against the left hand's black keys.

EXAMPLE 68-1

LISTENING CUE

DARIUS MILHAUD
Saudades do Brazil (1920)
"Botafogo"

CD 11/13
Anthology, No. 181

SUMMARY

Parisian musical culture quickly returned to life following the end of World War I in 1918, at which time a new spirit emerged throughout the artistic world. An emphasis on simplicity, directness, construction, and objectivity tended to replace the older romantic notions of a warm string sound, a large colorful orchestra, a programmatic agenda, and overt displays of emotion. Many French music critics found the new spirit in music embodied in a return to the styles and forms of the Classical and Baroque periods, and they termed the new musical taste "Neoclassicism." The leading figure of the movement was the Russian émigré Igor Stravinsky, whose Octet (1923) is an example of the leaner, clearer style of Neoclassicism.

A group of younger native-born French composers called "The Six" shared in Stravinsky's Neoclassical style. One of their most adventuresome members was Darius Milhaud, who brought popular music into his original compositions and experimented with new harmonic ideas including polytonality. In this style, differing keys exist simultaneously in different strata of a composition.

KEY TERMS

Serge Koussevitsky
Ballets Suédois
Ballets Ida Rubinstein
jazz

drum set
Jean Wiéner
Piet Mondrian
neoclassicism

The Six (The French Six)
Jean Cocteau
polytonality

Chapter

69

Vienna in the Aftermath of War: Twelve-Tone Methods

> I shall never forget what an opera performance meant in those days of direst need. For lack of coal the streets were only dimly lit and people had to grope their way through; gallery seats were paid for with a bundle of notes in such denominations as would once have been sufficient for a season's subscription to the best box. The theater was not heated, thus the audience kept their overcoats on and huddled together and how melancholy and gray this house was that used to glitter with uniforms and costly gowns![1]

The writer Stefan Zweig made these observations when he returned to Vienna following World War I and found his native city in a state of chaos, its economy shattered, its people in the grip of a famine so severe that many of them literally starved to death.

Zweig discovered that in this time of "direst need" the Viennese turned as never before to music. "The conductor lifted his baton, the curtain parted and it was as glorious as ever," he wrote, "and we strained and listened, receptive as never before, because perhaps it was really the last time. That was the spirit in which we lived, thousands of us, multitudes, giving forth to the limit of our capacity in those weeks and months and years, on the brink of destruction. Never have I experienced in a people and in myself so powerful a surge of life as at that period when our very existence and survival were at stake."[2]

AUSTRIA AFTER 1918

Austria and its empire had been totally transformed by the war. In 1916, after sixty-eight years on the throne, Emperor Franz Joseph died, and with him passed a symbol of Austria's political stability and cultural identity. Shortly after his death, under the burden of war, the Hapsburg Empire itself broke apart. The eastern regions declared their independence and reconstituted themselves as the new nations of Czechoslovakia, Yugoslavia, Hungary, and Poland. On the day of armistice, the Hapsburg monarch, King Charles I, abdicated his throne and fled to Switzerland, leaving behind only a small German-speaking country. Austria on that day was declared a republic.

These political and social changes had important implications for music. The Opera in Vienna was no longer the "Court Opera" but the "State Opera," and it had to rely for its very existence on a subsidy from a faceless city government. Still, music flourished. The management of the Opera scored a coup by bringing in Richard Strauss as co-director. The Vienna Philharmonic Orchestra, then under the leadership of Felix Weingartner, continued to present highly acclaimed concerts in the splendid Musikverein (see Chapter 58). A strict diet of modern music could be had at the concerts of the Society for Private Musical Performances, founded by Arnold Schoenberg in 1918.

ORGANIZING THE TWELVE TONES

Just as in Paris following World War I, in Vienna too composers felt the demand for control and organization in new music. In Paris the call for order had been answered by Igor Stravinsky's turning away from both radical modernism and from the entire musical language of late Romanticism. Stravinsky replaced the older outlook on music with an objective and plainly structured modern music that seemed attuned to the day.

Musicians in Vienna similarly looked for laws and systems that could justify the advances in music that had arisen largely from instinct. Several of the leading Viennese composers of the postwar period looked to the tones of the chromatic scale—which in earlier atonal music had been drawn upon freely and interchangeably—as a resource especially in need of organizational principles. One such musician in Vienna was **Josef Matthias Hauer** (1883–1959). Self-taught as a composer, Hauer wrote songs and brief piano pieces prior to World War I. "I worked by instinct," he recalled, "without any external theory, following only my inspiration with no conscious thought."[3] By 1920 his attitude had changed, and he then announced the discovery of a simple "twelve-tone law" that provided him with the conscious guidance he then desired. "Within a given succession of tones," Hauer proclaimed, "no note may be repeated and none may be omitted."[4]

The way that Hauer applied his twelve-tone law can be gathered from the opening of his Etude for Piano, Op. 22, No. 1 (1922; Ex. 69-1). The melodic line in the work consists of a succession of statements of the twelve tones (Hauer called each one a "building block"), and within each block no tone is repeated and none omitted. Hauer did not extend his law to the chords of the piece, which consist of simple triads and their extensions. Here are the tones in the first four melodic building blocks:

1. E♭ B♭ G G♭ D D♭   G♯ E B F A C   (mm. 1–2)
2. E G B♭ D F♯ C♯   B D♯ G♯ C A F   (m. 3)
3. C♯ G E D B♭ C   G♯ A G♭ E♭ B F   (m. 4)
4. E C C♯ B♭ D A♭   D♯ A G F F♯ B   (mm. 5–6)

EXAMPLE 69-1

Since Hauer does not repeat or omit any tones within a block, he has observed his own twelve-tone law. Writers today often use the term **aggregate** to designate one of Hauer's twelve-tone building blocks. This term—which will be useful for the discussion that follows—refers to a contiguous presentation of all twelve notes, with none repeated except in an immediate context. Reformulated using this more modern terminology, Hauer's twelve-tone law states that the melodic stratum of a composition should consist entirely of a succession of aggregates.

Hauer also had a method for promoting continuity from one aggregate to the next and for allowing twelve-tone organization to govern the form of the work as a whole. Throughout the Etude, the first and second halves (or **hexachords**) of each aggregate share five of the six tones with the corresponding hexachord in the next block. Compare blocks 1 and 2. The first hexachords of both differ in total pitch content only by one tone (E♭ and E are exchanged). Blocks 2 and 3 exchange F♯ and C; blocks 3 and 4, G and A♭. After all twelve tones have been exchanged in this way (which occurs at the end of the seventh block in m. 11), a section of the work ends and music with a new surface design follows.

Hauer's twelve-tone pieces—which enjoyed a measure of prominence in modern music circles during the 1920s—are intentionally primitive in style, as they lack indication of tempo, dynamics, or expressive character, and they have only a limited rhythmic and textural variety. Their austere style comes from Hauer's wish to eliminate traditional expressivity from his music: "The purely physical, sensual, also the trivial and sentimental are, so far as possible, ruled out," he wrote. Plainly, his music embodies a reaction against romanticism and represents the same wish to erase the immediate past that composers such as Stravinsky experienced at the same time.

SCHOENBERG'S TWELVE-TONE METHOD

A more artistic method for organizing the twelve-tones emerged in the works of Arnold Schoenberg following World War I. As we saw in Chapter 66, Schoenberg's earlier atonal compositions drew freely on the full resources of the chromatic scale. In his 1911 *Theory of Harmony*, Schoenberg declared that the chromatic scale was the "conceptual basis" for his new harmonic practices. In a few passages in compositions written before and during World War I, he experimented in forming aggregates, which represents a far more systematic use of tones than before. An instance of this from 1913 is seen in Example 69-2, from an isolated passage in the orchestral song "Seraphita," Op. 22, No. 1. The violins in these two measures play a six-note chord having the tones C♯ F A C E G♯. Against this harmony the clarinets play lines made from these notes transposed down a tone. Since these two hexachords are **complementary** (that is, they share no tones in common) an aggregate is formed. The passage resembles one of Hauer's building blocks, except that Schoenberg has made his twelve-tone structure extend throughout the two-dimensional musical space made from melody plus chord. This desire to integrate musical space is plainly akin to Schoenberg's objective in using the motif E-G-E♭ in "Nacht (Passacaglia)" from *Pierrot lunaire*, discussed in Chapter 66.

EXAMPLE 69-2

For a ten-year period following the composition of "Seraphita," Schoenberg continued to experiment with new methods for bringing order into his hitherto intuitive and freely spontaneous way of composing. In 1923 he consolidated the results of his research into a **twelve-tone method,** which he used in most of his later major compositions.

Schoenberg's twelve-tone method, as it existed in the 1920s and 1930s, contains two entirely different procedures: aggregate formation is one, and the other is a new principle by which melodic phrases are varied. The latter process concerns melodic "shapes," which was Schoenberg's term for what we call phrases—that is, melodic units that can usually be sung in one breath. An example of Schoenberg's innovative way of deriving one shape from another is found within the phrases that make up the main theme of the first movement of his String Quartet No. 4 (the entire movement is given in Anthology, No. 182). This theme, shown in Example 69-3, has three shapes (phrases), which are played in succession by Violin I, Violin II, and Violin I.

EXAMPLE 69-3†

Each of the three phrases embodies an aggregate, since each contains a statement of the twelve tones with none repeated except in an immediate or repetitive context. But this twelve-tone feature is not our main concern at this point. Instead, see how Schoenberg varies the first, or "basic" shape, to create the second and third ones. The variational relation among the three occurs, first of all, in a traditional way by the re-currence of small and plastic motives. Notice, for example, that the motive in mea-sure 2 made from three successive eighth notes on the tone A returns in freely varied forms in measures 3, 4, 6, 8, 11, and 12. It is heard finally in measure 13, where the rhythm has broadened to three successive quarter notes on the tone A.

At the same time, a stricter and more systematic variational process is at work, one that is at the core of Schoenberg's twelve-tone method. This involves only tones and the intervals that separate them—not rhythms, contours, or gestures, as in motivic variation—and it concerns the entire succession of notes as they are pre-sented in a given order in the various shapes. Here are the three ordered succes-sions, or **rows,** of tones as they occur in the three phrases:

Phrase 1 (mm. 1–6)
D C♯ A B♭ F E♭ E C A♭ G F♯ B

Phrase 2 (mm. 6–9)
G A♭ C B E F♯ F A C♯ D E♭ B♭

Phrase 3 (mm. 9–14)
B F♯ G A♭ C E E♭ F B♭ A C♯ D

†Used by permission of Belmont Music Publishers, Pacific Palisades, CA 92072.

The notes in phrase 3 have the same order as in phrase 1, only reversed (presented, that is, in **retrograde**). The order of tones in phrase 2 also derives from phrase 1, but in a more complex fashion. The notes of phrase 1 are first **transposed** up five semitones, to render the row G F♯ D E♭ B♭ A♭ A F D♭ C B E. Next, this transposed row is symmetrically **inverted.** Recall from Chapter 66 that a symmetric inversion of a group of notes occurs if the intervals formed by those notes are duplicated in the opposite direction. For example, the first interval of the transposed row (G - F♯) is a descending minor second. To begin the formation of an inversion, the second note must form an *ascending* minor second, so the F♯ is replaced by A♭. When this process of replacement is carried out on each tone of the transposed row, the notes of phrase 2 result.

To summarize: Schoenberg in his twelve-tone method treats the entire succession of notes in an original shape as an integral, ordered unit, and he reproduces that unit in the notes of later shapes, albeit changing the tones by transposition, inversion, retrogression, or a combination of these. It is also apparent from the opening of the Fourth Quartet that Schoenberg freely repositions tones in different registers when they return. Schoenberg's process of variation is an example of what has come to be known as **serialism** in music, which means that the order of occurrence of some element in a composition (pitches, in this case) is governed by a predetermined plan or arrangement.

There is one additional aspect of this serialized method of variation that Schoenberg himself considered to be of the utmost importance. This is the capacity of variations upon a shape to unify a two-dimensional musical texture. We have already observed Schoenberg moving in this direction in his *Pierrot lunaire* and song "Seraphita." In the twelve-tone method he extended the idea so as to achieve a homogeneous intervallic unity throughout an entire composition—from beginning to end, and in both the linear and harmonic or textural dimensions. We can see his thinking at work in a passage from the first movement of the Fourth Quartet (Ex. 69-4). In these measures, Schoenberg applies a tone row derived from the basic row (the one encountered in the main theme in mm. 1–6) by inversion and transposition to begin on the note C:

C D♭ F E A B B♭ D F♯ G A♭ E♭

EXAMPLE 69-4

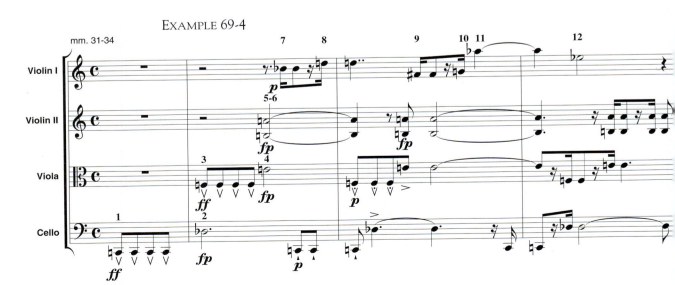

In the measures shown in Example 69-4, Schoenberg does not place this row into any single line or melody but distributes its notes throughout the texture (a process now called **partitioning** the row). The row's distinctive order is still maintained. The first two tones are given to the cello, the next two to the viola. The next two are deployed as a chord in Violin II, and the remaining six are given to the line in Violin I (the notes of the row are numbered in Ex. 69-4). By partitioning the row, the entire four-part texture embodies a variation of the basic shape.

Schoenberg's String Quartet No. 4

Schoenberg's compositional career entered a new phase in 1923, when he established his twelve-tone method. During his earlier period of free atonal composition (1908–1923), he had written primarily short character pieces. But with the twelve-tone method at his disposal, he returned to large instrumental genres, since he then had a structural scaffold on which to build extended compositions. In these works he often uses or approximates Classical forms.

Among Schoenberg's major twelve-tone compositions are his String Quartets No. 3 and 4 (1927 and 1936), String Trio (1946), Woodwind Quintet (1924), Suite for chamber ensemble (1926), concertos for violin (1936) and piano (1942), and Variations for Orchestra (1928). He continued to write melodramas for reciter and instruments, as in the *Ode to Napoleon Buonaparte* and *A Survivor from Warsaw* (this powerful composition is discussed in Chapter 78). Schoenberg also composed numerous twelve-tone works for chorus, and there are two twelve-tone operas—*Von heute auf morgen* (*From One Day to the Next*) and *Moses und Aron* (*Moses and Aaron*). Schoenberg almost entirely abandoned the composing of songs during his twelve-tone period.

Schoenberg's String Quartet No. 4, Op. 37 (1936), is one of his greatest compositions, one that shows that the twelve-tone method is adaptable to music that is inventive and emotionally—as well as intellectually—engaging. The work has four movements, each of which reveals analogies in form and style to quartets from the Classical period.

This Classical tone is especially apparent in the clarity of rhythm and texture in the first movement. The design of the movement is also loosely reminiscent of sonata form, which Schoenberg had not used at all in the diminutive works of his atonal period. Notice the traditional relationship between the bold main theme (see Ex. 69-3) and the lyrical second theme, the beginning of which is shown in Example 69-5. The contrast in character between these themes is often found in Classical movements in sonata form. Also observe in the second theme the underlying tone row, which Schoenberg partitions between the cello and viola. This is the original row transposed up a fifth, just as the second theme in a Classical first movement is normally in a key a fifth above the original one. When Schoenberg brings back the main theme at the recapitulation in measure 239, he returns to the "tonic" by using the original, un-transposed form of the row.

EXAMPLE 69-5

mm. 66-68

In studying the work, we are tempted to focus on the ingenious ways that the composer applies his twelve-tone method. But Schoenberg adamantly rejected this practice. He considered the intricacies of the method itself to be purely a guideline for the composer and virtually irrelevant to the listener. To the violinist Rudolf Kolisch—whose quartet gave the premier performance of the Fourth Quartet—Schoenberg in 1932 commented on twelve-tone analysis:

> This isn't where the aesthetic qualities reveal themselves, or, if so, only incidentally. I can't utter too many warnings against overrating these analyses, since after all they only lead to what I have always been dead against: seeing how it is *done*; whereas I have always helped people to see: what it *is*! . . . My works are twelve-note *compositions*, not *twelve-note* compositions. In this respect people go on confusing me with Hauer, to whom composition is only of secondary importance.[5]

A discovery of what the music "is," in Schoenberg's view, results primarily from listening carefully to the unfolding of themes and motives. Aspects of form, color, pacing, harmony, and contrast all contribute to an understanding of this central thematic element.

LISTENING CUE

ARNOLD SCHOENBERG
String Quartet No. 4 (1936)
First movement, *Allegro molto, energico*

CD 11/14
Anthology, No. 182

 ## ANTON WEBERN

In the 1920s and 1930s, Schoenberg's twelve-tone method was adopted by several of his students, including Alban Berg and Anton Webern, and a few other Viennese composers such as Theodor Adorno and Ernst Krenek. These musicians all developed their own distinctive ways of applying the general idea of the method, and they all created music in different and highly individualized styles. This diversity makes it impossible to speak of any single twelve-tone style in music, or even of any single twelve-tone method.

One of the most distinctive followers of Schoenberg along the twelve-tone road was his student Anton Webern (1883–1945). A lifelong resident of Vienna, Webern received a Ph.D. degree in musicology from the University of Vienna, where he wrote a dissertation on the Renaissance composer Heinrich Isaac (see Chapter 24). In 1904, while at the university, he began to take lessons privately with Schoenberg, with whom he formed a close personal and professional relationship. After a few attempts at tonal composition, Webern began to write atonal music, and in 1924 he adopted a version of Schoenberg's twelve-tone method for his own compositional purposes.

Webern's music received little attention during his lifetime, and he was better known as a conductor than as a composer. He also taught and worked as a consultant for the Austrian radio and for music publishers. He died as the result of a tragic mishap at the very end of World War II. He and his wife had fled from Vienna, which was under bombardment, to live with his daughter and son-in-law in the mountainous western regions of Austria, an area that had recently come under American occupation. On 15 September 1945 he was accidentally shot to death by an Occupation soldier.

Schoenberg Writes to Webern's Widow

18 January 1946
Dear Minna,

For several weeks now I and my friends here have been terribly upset over Anton's death, and we have not been able to understand what took place and how it could have happened to him. And this just now—when at last there are again brilliant prospects for the international recognition of his works. We have all found this tragic in highest measure, and try as I may I cannot convince myself that it is really true that I shall never see him again. We were also shaken by the death of Peter [Webern's son], whom I knew only as a small child and whom I cannot at all imagine as a soldier. This dreadful war has been a frightful disaster for the whole world, and it has brought even greater misery to your family. . . . [Library of Congress]

Arnold Schönberg Center, Vienna

❋ FIGURE 69-1
Anton Webern.

Webern conferred an opus number on works that he considered complete and important to his oeuvre, although many of these were not published in his lifetime. There are thirty-one works with opus numbers, which include songs, choral music (including two cantatas), a variety of chamber pieces, and short orchestral works (including a brief symphony, which will be discussed momentarily). When he fled Vienna in 1945, he left behind an even larger number of compositions in varying states of completion. These were recovered only in 1965 by Webern's biographer Hans Moldenhauer, and many of these additional works have now been published and recorded.

Webern's music bemused everyone—even his teacher Schoenberg—by its extreme brevity, radical understatement, and textures so disjunct that melodic lines sometimes dissolve into a succession of minute splotches of color. These kaleidoscopic surfaces in his works have been compared to the painting technique called **pointillism,** in which dots of pure and contrasting color merge into recognizable images. An example of the pointillistic technique in painting is seen in Camille Pissarro's *Woman in the Meadow at Eragny* (Fig. 69-2).

Webern's musical pointillism, as in the work of painters like Pissarro, represents an art of the greatest concentration and the most subtle refinement. Performers and listeners

❋ FIGURE 69-2
Camille Pissarro, *Woman in the Meadow at Eragny, Spring,* 1887. Using a technique termed "pointillism," Pissarro applied dots of pure color that merge at a distance to create realistic images.

Bridgeman Art Library

must diligently attempt to recreate the element of image and continuity that Webern always intended his music to have but which is almost always hidden beneath its fragmented surfaces.

This quality of concentrated and fragmented image is encountered in his Symphony, Op. 21 (1928). The work is for chamber orchestra, consisting of pairs of clarinets and horns, harp, and a string quartet, in which the composer allowed for either one player on a part or for more normal orchestral doublings. There are two movements, and the whole composition lasts about nine minutes.

In the second movement, "Variations," Webern fits a lively range of expression into a duration of less than three minutes and a variety of moods into a rigid form. The music—which Webern originally wanted as the first movement of the Symphony—consists of a theme, seven variations, and coda, each spanning eleven measures. The theme is played in measures 1–11 by the clarinet (Ex. 69-6), and it states the following twelve-tone row (whose notes are numbered from 1 to 12 in the example):

F A♭ G F♯ B♭ A   E♭ E C C♯ D B

EXAMPLE 69-6

This row has many distinctive features. Its two halves, for example, are symmetrical in that the tones of the second half, transposed to the tritone, are the retrograde of the first half. This symmetrical feature of the row strongly influences the form of the whole movement. An example of this is found in Webern's choice of rhythms and dynamics. The sequence of rhythmic values, dynamic levels, and attack types in the second half of the theme returns in a nearly exact retrograde of that in the first half, just as the notes of the row return in retrograde. This linking of row structure to the order of occurrence of rhythms, dynamics, and attack amounts to a serialization of these non-pitch elements and an integration of them into the twelve-tone structure. The idea of extending the principle of pitch serialism explicitly to other musical elements would become a powerful inspiration to composers following World War II (see Chapter 79).

A comparison of the Variations movement with the first movement of Schoenberg's String Quartet No. 4 will show that the two composers had little in common as to style, form, or even their interpretation of the twelve-tone principle. After the initial presentation of the main theme, Webern tends to avoid conventional themes altogether, allowing his music to explode into a montage of small motives. In comparison, Schoenberg's textures, based on lines and chords, seem entirely traditional.

Webern's way of using tone rows is also very different from Schoenberg's. Recall from Schoenberg's Fourth Quartet that the notes of a row are easily traced in lines and chords, since Schoenberg uses one row (or at most two) at any one time. But Webern tends to interweave numerous forms of the basic row, both within a single line and within the texture. This interlacing often makes it difficult to find the rows and it also usually dispels any straightforward creation of aggregates.

We can see how this happens by studying the second variation (mm. 23–33). The horn part (its beginning is shown in Ex. 69-7) is the easiest to decipher. In this line, Webern alternates tones as they occur in two forms of the row— an inversion beginning on F and a transposition beginning on E:

F D E♭ E C C♯ G F♯ B♭ A A♭ B
(inversion beginning on F)

E G G♭ F A G♯ D D♯ B C C♯ B♭
(transposition beginning on E).

EXAMPLE 69-7

Horn (nontransposing), mm. 23-28

The other instruments in this variation play notes drawn from two additional forms of the basic row (an inversion beginning on E♭ and a transposition beginning on G):

E♭ C C♯ D B♭ B F E G♯ G F♯ A
(inversion beginning on E♭)

G B♭ A G♯ C B F F♯ D D♯ E C♯
(transposition beginning on G).

Webern partitions these two rows into the texture so that segments of no more than two notes of any row are heard one after the other in any line. Plainly, Webern didn't want us to follow the rows, whose role in the music is to provide an abstract unity in the background.

In the Variations movement from the Symphony, Webern generally bypasses Schoenberg's principles of serialized variation and aggregate formation, and he essentially follows his own method of composing.

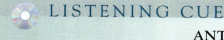

LISTENING CUE

ANTON WEBERN
Symphony, Opus 21 (1928)
Second movement, *Sehr ruhig*

CD 11/15
Anthology, No. 183

SUMMARY

Although Austria was greatly reduced in size following World War I, it continued to be the source of new musical ideas. Several of its progressive composers, including Josef Matthias Hauer, Arnold Schoenberg, and Anton Webern, devised new ways of bringing order into the presentation of tones from the chromatic scale.

Schoenberg's way of doing this was by devising a "twelve-tone method of composition." A work coming from his method has a succession of "aggregates," which are contiguous presentations of the twelve tones with none omitted and none repeated except in an immediate context. The initial melodic phrase in a twelve-tone work is also subject to a new variational process called "serialism," by which its entire succession of notes is reproduced in later phrases and passages, albeit changed by transposition, symmetric inversion, retrogression, or a combination of these. Schoenberg used his twelve-tone method in most of his major new works written after 1923.

Twelve-tone composition was adopted shortly thereafter by Anton Webern, Schoenberg's student. Webern's works are unusually brief and deliberately fragmented in texture, inviting a comparison with the technique of modern French painters called "pointillism." Webern's application of the twelve-tone method is very different from Schoenberg's, with less emphasis on forming aggregates or consistently relying upon serialized variations. Multiple tone rows are often presented simultaneously, tightly interlaced throughout the texture.

KEY TERMS

Josef Matthias Hauer	twelve-tone method	inversion
aggregate	row	serialism
hexachord	retrograde	partitioning
complementary hexachords	transposition	pointillism

Chapter 70

Musical Theater in Germany in the 1920s: Berg and Weill

Theater in Germany in the 1920s enjoyed a popularity surpassing that in any other country in the world. Attending plays, operas, and revues was a passion for the Germans, and in the capital city of Berlin alone the demand for staged entertainment supported some forty professional playhouses, three major opera theaters, and countless "specialty" stages for cabaret, variety, and vaudeville. Berlin's theatergoers could choose from a seemingly infinite variety of plays. The classics—great works of the past from Sophocles to Schiller—were amply available, although these were frequently staged using updated interpretations and technologies.

More recent plays often embodied modern literary styles that also appeared in operas of the day. One such was **naturalism.** Here the playwright looked realistically at the lives of people from the lower social classes, usually underscoring their struggle with the society in which they live. Recall that naturalism (or "realism") is the literary movement that in the 1890s underlay *verismo* opera, such as Pietro Mascagni's *Cavalleria rusticana* (see Chapter 62). In the politicized atmosphere of German theater of the 1920s, these plays often tended toward a proletarian outlook that meshed with Communist ideology by showing class conflicts and laborers struggling to improve their lot in life.

Another modern literary movement with resonance in the world of opera was **expressionism.** Plays of this sort began to appear just before World War I. Typically, they contain a symbolic treatment of characters' irrational impulses, which often lead to grotesque or violent conclusions. An example is August Stramm's *Sancta Susanna* (1914), which deals with the repressed sexual desires of a nun. Aroused by the beauty of a spring night, the nun Susanna tears off her habit and rushes naked to embrace the crucifix. Her performance is interrupted by a huge spider that falls into her hair and leaves her shrieking. As other nuns arrive for prayer, Susanna stands defiant before their cries of "Satan!" The play was made into an opera in 1921 by Paul Hindemith.

GEORG BÜCHNER

Among the major discoveries of Berlin theater culture of the 1920s were the plays of **Georg Büchner** (1813–1837). He was a scientist by profession and an amateur writer who lived in Germany and Switzerland before his death at the age of only twenty-three. Büchner's writings—which include the plays *Woyzeck, Danton's Death* and *Leonce and Lena*, and the novella *Lenz*—were virtually unknown until the end of the nineteenth century, and they first attracted widespread attention even later, in the explosively polarized social climate in Germany and Austria that followed World War I.

Woyzeck was performed repeatedly in Berlin in the 1920s, both as a spoken drama and as the basis for an opera by Alban Berg first given at Berlin's State Opera in 1925. The play itself has a curious history. When Büchner died in 1837 he left it incomplete, consisting of a tangle of disconnected scenes with no title, no clear order of events, and no conclusion. These were all provided by an editor, Karl Emil Franzos, when the play appeared in print in 1879. Franzos titled the drama *Wozzeck*—his reading of the name of its leading character—and he also made up an ending and tried to provide the fragments with a logical order despite the absence of continuity from one to the next.

A later editor, Georg Witkowski, had learned that Büchner's play was based on a historical event: an 1822 trial in Leipzig of a soldier, **Johann Christian Woyzeck,** for the murder of his commonlaw wife. The trial was highly sensational in its day, and reports of it were drawn on extensively by Büchner. During the trial, Woyzeck was examined by Dr. Johann Clarus, who found symptoms of mental disorder, although these did not prevent Woyzeck from being put to death for his crime by a public beheading. The title of Büchner's play in Witkowski's 1920 edition was appropriately changed from *Wozzeck* to *Woyzeck* (in older German handwriting the letter *z* is almost indistinguishable from *y*), and this is the spelling that is now used for the spoken play.

Although a product of the early nineteenth century, Büchner's *Woyzeck* has much about it that is similar to modern German drama of the period following World War I. There is a strong element of naturalism, with a leading character drawn from the lowest levels of a society that brutalizes and ultimately destroys him. It can also be read as a proletarian drama that shows a certain dignity in the laborer Woyzeck, a man with nothing in the world except for Marie, whom he is ultimately driven to murder.

The text also has an uncanny similarity to expressionist plays. Just as in later expressionist writing, some characters have no names (they are called simply "the captain" or "the doctor"), and these figures represent whole social and professional

Synopsis of *Woyzeck* by Georg Büchner

(This synopsis is based on the order of scenes in a 1909 edition by Paul Landau of the Büchner-Franzos text.)

The story of the play unfolds in series of disconnected scenes. The impoverished soldier Wozzeck (Woyzeck in later editions) lives with his commonlaw wife Marie and their child. Marie watches a parade led by the dashing Drum Major, who embraces her. "You're some woman," he says. "We'll have a whole litter of little drum majors!" "If you want," Marie responds. "What's the difference."

At a local tavern, Wozzeck sees Marie dancing with the Drum Major, and his jealousy is aroused. Back in the regimental barracks, Wozzeck hears the Drum Major brag about his pleasures with Marie, and, for good measure, he throttles Wozzeck, who then mutters menacingly "One after the other!"

Village women listen to a folk tale told by an old woman: A poor boy had nothing in the world so he goes into the heavens only to find that the moon is a lump of wood, the sun a withered sunflower, and the stars only gnats. He returns to earth to find that it is an overturned chamber pot, whereupon he sits and cries.

On a walk with Marie by a lake, Wozzeck shrieks out "If not I, then no one else!" whereupon he stabs her to death. Now in a demented state, he returns to the tavern and dances wildly, then returns to the lake and drowns while trying to wash off the blood. The next morning Marie's child is playing in front of his house and other children tell him that his mother is dead, whereupon they leave to see the corpse. Following an autopsy a judge declares that this was the most beautiful murder in a long time.

Theater Museum of the University of Cologne

✿ FIGURE 70-1

Stage painting by Ludwig Sievert (1887–1966) for the murder scene in *Wozzeck*. Sievert was one of the most famous German operatic set designers of his day. He brought ideas of expressionistic painting to the stage.

classes. The grotesque ending, with its murder and suicide, became stock features of expressionist plays (Fig. 70-1). *Woyzeck*, like many plays in Germany following World War I, also has an anti-military theme through its unflattering portrait of a captain and his insensitive dealings with the common soldier Woyzeck.

✿ ALBAN BERG'S WOZZECK

Büchner's play was used as the text of one of the great operas of the twentieth century, *Wozzeck* by Alban Berg (1885–1935). The composer was Viennese, a student of Arnold Schoenberg, and he saw Büchner's drama when it was given in Vienna in 1914. Feeling an empathy with its leading character, Berg was determined to transform the material into an opera text. But his work on it was delayed by service in the Austrian army, and he completed the opera only in 1922. He left the spelling of the title as *Wozzeck*, the same as in pre-1920 editions of the source play.

At the time when he wrote the opera, Berg was still relatively unknown as a composer, having written only songs and a few short chamber and orchestral pieces. Following the premiere of *Wozzeck* in 1925 at Berlin's State Opera, he vaulted to international recognition and gained confidence as a composer, although he continued to work in a painstakingly methodical manner. He subsequently composed a Chamber Concerto for Piano, Violin, and Winds; a passionate string quartet called the *Lyric Suite*, a Violin Concerto, and a second opera, *Lulu*, based on plays by Frank Wedekind.

For *Wozzeck*, Berg himself made up the libretto—much as Richard Strauss had done for *Salome*—by using material directly from the spoken play. Using Paul Landau's 1909 edition (see Box), Berg selected fifteen of Büchner's scenes and distributed these equally into three acts. His choice of which scenes to include and which to omit shows that he wanted the opera text to be interpreted primarily as a social drama that could elicit sympathy for the world's downtrodden, symbolized by the figure of Wozzeck. He eliminated scenes, such as the old woman's bleakly existentialist tale, that suggest alternative readings, and he ended his opera—as did the editor Franzos—with the grotesque and expressionistic image of Marie's child mindlessly following the other children to see his mother's corpse.

The libretto of *Wozzeck* is markedly different from the opera texts used by the great romantic composers. Wagner's texts for *Der Ring des Nibelungen* (see Chapter 55), for example, contain a pointed critique of contemporary European society—so distracted, in his view, by materialism that the higher values of brotherly love have vanished. But in Wagner's works there is always a hero who can lead mankind toward a better future. His operas are filled with clouds that have silver linings; all end optimistically with a world in which love can again flourish, and all glorify compassionate and fearless heroes who will ride to mankind's rescue.

Berg's *Wozzeck* is entirely different. Its central figure, Wozzeck, is the opposite of a hero, instead a crazed murderer who is snuffed out by his world rather than having any capacity to reshape it. At the end of the play and opera, the audience has no sense that the conditions that produced Wozzeck and brought him down have changed. The cynicism and hopelessness that pervade the work will be encountered often in twentieth-century art and music.

When Berg began to compose the music for the opera, he faced a quandary in choosing the form that the work should take. Büchner's scenes were mostly short and unconnected in time and place with their neighboring scenes. Any attempt at the seamless through-composed operatic form used by Wagner would have been impossible given these disjunctions in the narrative. Also, just as Berg was composing the work between 1914 and 1922, the Wagnerian model was itself being set aside by several important German opera composers in favor of a return to the more traditional scheme of "number opera," in which subdivisions into arias, duets, ensembles, recitatives, and choruses are unmistakable.

The leading figure in this retrospectivist movement was Richard Strauss, the composer who in his earlier opera *Salome* (see Chapter 64) had shown himself to be a stalwart adherent to the Wagnerian conception of operatic form. But beginning in the opera *Der Rosenkavalier* (*The Cavalier of the Rose*, 1910) and even more emphatically in his *Ariadne auf Naxos* (*Ariadne on Naxos*, 1912), Strauss returned to the form of number opera, more reminiscent of the age of Mozart than of Wagner.

Although Berg realized that it was futile to try to apply the Wagnerian form to *Wozzeck*, he was no advocate of Strauss's glance toward the operatic past. So his solution to the question of form in *Wozzeck* was to adopt a highly original compromise. In each of the fifteen scenes, Berg employs some unifying element that gives the scene closure and distinguishability from its surroundings. In some scenes Berg uses a genre, form, or style associated with traditional instrumental music; in others he deploys an ever-present musical figure to lend unity.

Each of the five scenes of Act 3, for example, brings in a musical element as a "principle of cohesion," to quote Berg himself. The first scene dwells upon a theme to produce a theme and variations form; the second uses a single note, B♮, as its point of focus. The third introduces a particular rhythmic figure, the fourth a persistent six-note chord, and the last scene is presented over a steady eighth-note rhythm.

At the end of a scene within an act the curtain falls and the orchestra continues to play transitional music until the curtain again rises. The overall impression of Berg's formal compromise is one of musical continuity with an underlying level of architecture characteristic of instrumental music.

The distinguishability of the scenes is bridged over by thematic recurrences that span and help to unify the music of the entire work. These are similar to Wagner's leitmotives in that they often symbolize elements in the drama. Berg's music also mirrors the drama by a flexibility in style. Depending on the text, for example, the voices in the opera speak or sing in ways that range from the "speech melody" that Schoenberg had used in *Pierrot lunaire* (see Chapter 66) to a pronounced lyricism.

The work's harmonic language is equally varied. The general idiom of the opera is atonal, although moments in the key of D minor are heard in the work's final interlude (which Berg said was a musical representation of his own voice commenting on the fate of Wozzeck). In Act 1, scene 4, there is a passacaglia upon a twelve-tone theme.

A climax of intensity in the opera is reached in Act 3, scene 2, in which Wozzeck murders Marie. The form of the scene is among the freest of the opera since it has almost none of the architectural symmetry that is found in other scenes. Instead, Berg in this scene writes through-composed music that meticulously follows the text, and he brings in an ever-present tone, B♮, as a unifying element and musical symbol.

This note had appeared ominously at the end of Act 2, just after Wozzeck had been thrashed by the Drum Major. After watching the fight, the soldiers in the barracks return to their bunks "one after the other," "einer nach dem Andern," according to Berg's staging instruction. Wozzeck mutters these same words to himself (Example 70-1), but the final note—a hushed low B♮—tells us that by this he means murder, Marie first of all. The note is then heard in every measure of Act 3, scene 2, as a sustained pedal point, representing Wozzeck's murderous obsession.

EXAMPLE 70-1

mm. 813–814

Wozzeck

Ei - ner nach dem An - dern!

harp,
tamtam

In his 1929 "Lecture on *Wozzeck*," Berg describes some of the extraordinarily complex methods by which his music represents Marie's murder.[1] He singles out the tangle of her leitmotives—symbols of herself and her world—which race through her mind at the moment of her death (mm. 103–105). He also points to the imaginative way in which the scene-change music (mm. 109–21) at the end of the passage mixes together the unifying tone B♮ with the rhythm that will dominate the next scene. The winds and brass play a great crescendo on the unison tone B (Ex. 70-2), and their entrance points create the rhythm shown on the lower line of the example. This rhythm then becomes the unifying element of Act 3, scene 3, set among dancers in a noisy bar.

EXAMPLE 70-2

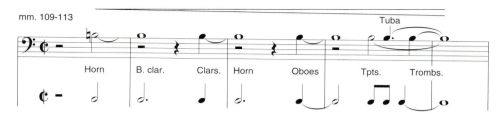

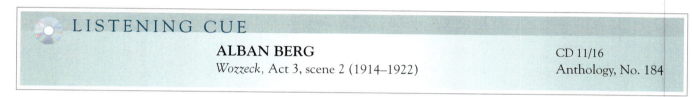

By these and other ingenious ways of linking the music to the drama, Berg in *Wozzeck* showed that the atonal style could be successfully adapted to the genre of opera. His music grippingly expresses even the most human emotions conveyed in Büchner's text.

🔘 LISTENING CUE

ALBAN BERG
Wozzeck, Act 3, scene 2 (1914–1922)

CD 11/16
Anthology, No. 184

✳ KURT WEILL

Shortly after Alban Berg had taken a small step away from the Wagnerian form of opera in *Wozzeck*, Kurt Weill (1900–1950) made a giant leap away from it in his *Die Dreigroschenoper* (*The Threepenny Opera*). Earlier in the 1920s, while still a student of Ferruccio Busoni at Berlin's Academy of Arts, Weill had attracted attention in Berlin as a composer of modernistic instrumental pieces. Shortly following his apprenticeship with Busoni, he turned to opera and wrote a series of successful works collaborating with the playwright Georg Kaiser. For his *The Threepenny Opera* (1928) he worked with the writer Bertolt Brecht to create one of the most successful and influential works in the entire history of musical theater.

With the rise of the Nazis, Weill was forced to flee from Germany. He moved first to Paris and then permanently to New York City. There he established himself as a Broadway composer, creating a series of hits that include *Lady in the Dark* (1940), *One Touch of Venus* (1943), *Street Scene* (1946), and *Lost in the Stars* (1949).

Weill's music represents an extreme stage in the rebellion against romanticism that in the 1920s came to characterize modern music worldwide. In France critics called the new style neoclassicism, and they pointed to Igor Stravinsky as its leading figure. Weill described his own anti-romantic music as **Gebrauchsmusik,** or "music for use." (This word was also mentioned by the German composer Paul Hindemith for practical pieces aimed at young players and singers.) Weill applied the word differently, for pieces that were useful in their capacity to satisfy the need of a mass audience for music of high quality. In both cases, utilitarianism had replaced the ideal of "art for the sake of art," which was characteristic of music from the late Romantic period.

After his youthful essays in instrumental music, Weill turned decisively to the theater as an outlet for his notion of useful music. He was especially attracted to the writings of the Berlin poet and playwright **Bertolt Brecht** (1898–1956). In such early plays as *Drums in the Night* (1923) and *A Man Is a Man* (1926), Brecht assessed German society of the postwar period with a biting cynicism. In 1928, Brecht and

Synopsis of *The Threepenny Opera*

The opera is set in London in the 1700s. Following an overture, a balladeer appears and sings about the legendary highwayman Macheath, known for his evil deeds as "Mac the Knife." Jonathan Peachum runs a supply shop for beggars, whom he organizes and trains. Those that disobey him are impeached (turned in to the law), hence his name (from "Impeach them!"). Mrs. Peachum brings news that Polly, their daughter, has a new boyfriend, and Peachum suspects that he must be the notorious Macheath. As they speak, Macheath is preparing the stable where he has taken shelter for his wedding to Polly. His gang of thieves is on hand, the sheriff Tiger Brown (an old friend, bought off by Macheath) drops by, and Rev. Kimball arrives to perform the ceremony.

In Act 2 Polly confesses to her parents about her intention to marry Macheath, and the news is not well received. He already has several wives, says Mrs. Peachum. Macheath will receive the usual treatment—the Peachums will have him arrested, impeached, and hanged. But Polly tips Macheath off and he flees. Mrs. Peachum pays one of his whores, Jenny—whose part was originally sung by Weill's wife Lotte Lenya—to lead the police to him, and he is arrested and taken to jail. The plot thickens as the sheriff's daughter, Lucy, reveals that she too is married to Macheath and claims to be pregnant. She helps him to escape from jail.

Outraged by sloppy police work, Peachum threatens Sheriff Brown with a disruption of the forthcoming coronation of a new Queen. Brown arrests him for this, but Peachum threatens blackmail and is released. Macheath is again arrested and a hanging now seems sure. But suddenly there arrives a royal messenger: the new Queen has commanded that Macheath be freed and knighted! At Peachum's command, the moral of the story is given out as everyone sings a hymn: "Don't punish every wrong so harshly," they sing. Concentrate instead on making our own world a better place to live.

🌀 FIGURE 70-2

Lotte Lenya (1898–1981) was born in Vienna and studied acting in Switzerland. In 1921 she moved to Berlin, where she met Kurt Weill. They were married in 1926, after which Weill wrote a succession of parts, including that of Jenny in *The Threepenny Opera*, for her distinctively earthy style of singing.

his assistant Elisabeth Hauptmann were planning a revival of John Gay's famous English ballad opera **The Beggar's Opera** (1728). This older work (discussed in Chapter 41) is set among London's thieves and beggars, who act out a devastating satire on the culture and politics of the time, one in which Brecht saw parallels with his own day. Spoken dialogue in *The Beggar's Opera* alternates with songs and other musical numbers that Gay's musical collaborator, Johann Christoph Pepusch, arranged from traditional or well-known tunes.

Brecht and Hauptmann translated the text of *The Beggar's Opera* into German, made certain revisions, and added a few song texts from poetry by François Villon and Rudyard Kipling. Weill was brought in to provide musical tunes that would conform to the light and satiric style of the work as a whole, and the team renamed their work: *The Beggar's Opera* was reborn as *Die Dreigroschenoper*, *The Threepenny Opera*.

The differences separating *The Threepenny Opera* from late Romantic opera reach to the very bedrock of the genre, and they mirror the essential differences separating classical from popular musical theater. The operas of Wagner, for example, were products of the composer's individual imagination, and these arrived at a fixed state that is usually represented by an early performance or edition. The composer could revise this conception at a later time—Wagner did so extensively for several of his operas—but then another fixed and unchanging conception is established. *The Threepenny Opera* is different. It is the product of a collaboration among numerous artists—Weill, Brecht, and Hauptmann, to name only three—and it has no definitive or fixed form. The versions heard in the original performances in Berlin in 1928 were in a constant state of change dictated by circumstances—changes in cast, ad libitum playing and singing, extemporaneous adjustments in length, adding and deleting dialogue and music. The creative team never agreed on a definitive version of the work. Like the score of a later Broadway show, the original editions of Weill's music resemble anthologies of songs rather than a comprehensive record of the thing itself, and Brecht had no hesitation in rewriting the work's dialogue—even changing its meaning—in later published versions of the libretto.

Despite these idiosyncrasies, a general portrait of the work can be drawn. The 1928 staging of *The Threepenny Opera* was especially distinctive and original. There was no attempt to portray the London of 1728 realistically or to transport the audience back in time. The stage was instead plainly a stage and the objects on it were products of the 1920s. A small jazz band sat in plain view in front of the pipes of a barrel organ, and still images and texts were projected on screens to provide the audience with an explanation of the events that they witnessed. The simple vocal parts were performed by actors and operetta stars rather than opera singers, and their pieces tended to interrupt the narrative rather than to advance it. The songs resemble reports on the events and characters in the play more than personalized expressions of individuals in roles.

By these means, Weill and Brecht wanted to avoid normal theatric illusion and to prevent the audience member from being drawn emotionally into an imaginary narrative. Instead, they hoped to detach or "alienate" the listener from the fictitious action so that its relevance to the real world of 1928 could become more apparent. This highly mixed and loose form for a theatric work is now termed **epic theater,** and it is an idea with which Brecht is most closely associated.

Weill's music for the play consists of some twenty numbers, mainly solo songs, duets, and choruses. Larger ensembles ("finales") are situated at the ends of each act, and instrumental music is added here and there. The style of the music evokes jazz—not so much the American variety as the bouncy dance music of tangos, foxtrots, and shimmies that was part of Berlin night life in the 1920s. The accompaniment is for a small jazz band consisting of saxophones and other reeds, brass, plucked instruments, drums, and keyboard instruments played by the conductor. The musical style is highly simplified: the songs are mainly repetitive in form, homophonic in texture, and they use simple triadic harmonic progressions. There is a degree of stridency and linearity in the music that distinguishes it from popular music per se.

The best known of Weill's songs for *The Threepenny Opera* is the very first one, "The Ballad of Mac the Knife." In the 1928 performances it followed the overture, which was played by the band on stage with this message projected on two screens: "Tonight you'll see an opera for beggars. Since this opera is as splendidly conceived as only beggars can do and since it has to be cheap enough for them to pay for it, it'll be called *The Threepenny Opera*."

The curtain was then briefly lowered and, when raised, the actors had taken their places on a darkened stage. The title of the first song, "The Ballad of Mac the Knife," was then projected on the screens, and an actor cast as a balladeer stood to sing the tale of the murderous Mac, accompanied by barrel organ with other instruments gradually added. Weill indicates the character of the strophic song by the words "blues tempo," which suggests something slow and lazy, but the music has no relation to the distinctive form of the American blues song. "Mac the Knife" quickly became a hit song and jazz standard, performed by pop singers including Louis Armstrong, Ella Fitzgerald, and Bobby Darin.

LISTENING CUE

KURT WEILL
The Threepenny Opera (1928)
"Ballad of Mac the Knife"

CD 11/17
Anthology, No. 185

SUMMARY

Opera and spoken theater flourished in Germany in the 1920s and early 1930s. New literary styles in dramas from this time—including naturalism, expressionism, and epic theater—were shared with new operas. *Wozzeck,* by Alban Berg, is based on a play by Georg Büchner and is a literary precursor of both naturalism and expressionism. Its atonal music takes on a novel form by which scenes imitate forms or styles drawn from instrumental music or, in its third act, an ever-present musical element. In this opera, Berg demonstrates that the atonal style could be successful in opera and could express a wide range of emotions.

The Threepenny Opera by Kurt Weill and Bertolt Brecht revives an eighteenth-century English ballad opera in its use of spoken dialogue alternating with musical numbers. It exemplifies Brecht's notion of "epic theater," in which ordinary dramatic illusion is dispelled as the audience is coaxed to focus on the meaning of events for contemporary society. Weill's music consists primarily of songs having a popular flavor, one of which, "The Ballad of Mac the Knife," became a hit song.

KEY TERMS

naturalism
expressionism
Georg Büchner

Johann Christian Woyzeck
Gebrauchsmusik ("music
    for use")

Bertolt Brecht
The Beggar's Opera
epic theater

Chapter 71

Béla Bartók and Hungarian Folk Music

World War I had a disastrous outcome for the nation of Hungary. Prior to the war it enjoyed a position of preeminence within the Austro-Hungarian Monarchy. While recognizing the German-speaking Hapsburg emperor as their king, the Hungarians

MAP 71-1
Austro-Hungarian Empire
before World War I.

formed their own government that ruled over the internal affairs of a large region
east of the Leitha River. The borders of Hungary at this time reached south to the
Adriatic Sea, east into what is now Romania, and north into present-day Russia,
Czech Republic, and Poland (see Map 71-1).

Hungary was a restless kingdom, cobbled together from a hodge-podge of competing enclaves of language and culture. Hungarians—those who spoke the Magyar
language—lived beside Slovenians, Serbians, Croatians, Bulgarians, Armenians,
Ruthenians, Poles, and Germans. After World War I, during which the Austro-
Hungarian Empire dissolved, the country was greatly reduced in size and left as a
small, landlocked nation stripped of its regions of mixed ethnicity. Until World War II
it was ruled by the authoritarian government of Admiral Nicholas Horthy.

The Hungarian capital is Budapest, a city of great beauty that lies
astride the Danube River some one hundred fifty miles east of Vienna.
Since the late nineteenth century, its musical culture has centered on the
Opera House, built in 1884, where conductors including Gustav Mahler
have worked. Nearby is the Academy of Music, with its excellent concert
hall. Since its opening in 1875, the academy has trained many of Europe's
leading performers and composers.

FIGURE 71-1
Béla Bartók's imagination as a
composer was stimulated by simple
Hungarian peasant songs, whose
spirit and materials he brought to
his own original works.

✾ BÉLA BARTÓK

Perhaps the greatest of these musicians is Béla Bartók (1881–1945; Fig.
71-1). He was born in a farming village in what is now Romania, and his
childhood was unsettled. His father died when he was only seven years
old, and he then lived in several different cities with his mother, a piano
teacher, and his sister. He attended the Budapest Academy of Music,
where he concentrated mainly on piano playing, and in 1907 he was
appointed to its piano faculty.

Like many Budapest artists and intellectuals, he was an avid Hungarian nationalist. "For my own part," he wrote to his mother in 1903, "all my life, in every sphere, always and in every way, I shall have one objective: the good of Hungary and the Hungarian nation."[1] While pursuing the career of a touring piano virtuoso and pedagogue he also composed, although he was periodically discouraged by the lack of understanding his works received.

Bartók's nationalistic pride led him to examine the folk music of his country, and from 1905 he traveled repeatedly, often accompanied by his friend **Zoltán Kodály** (1882–1967), to farming regions to record folk songs. He explored the possibilities by which peasant music could be integrated into his own original compositions.

In the 1920s and 1930s, Bartók's music was at last recognized for its originality, and he toured throughout the world, giving concerts that brought him ever greater acclamation. His life in Budapest was unsettled by the rise of the Nazis—"a band of thieves and murderers" he called them—who to his alarm found increasing support in the Hungarian government. In October 1940, well after the outbreak of World War II, Bartók and his wife made an audacious dash across Europe to Lisbon, where they boarded a ship that took them to safety in New York City. The composer spent his last five years there, created some of his greatest works, and continued with his folk music research.

Bartók composed in all of the genres of his day. His music for solo piano includes a Sonata (1926) and various collections of character works, and also a cycle of pedagogical pieces called *Mikrokosmos,* many of which are based on folk songs. Bartók is one of the greatest composers of modern chamber music, and his six string quartets are monuments in the literature. He wrote one opera (*Duke Bluebeard's Castle,* 1911), two ballets (*The Wooden Prince,* 1916, and *The Miraculous Mandarin,* 1919), and his orchestral music includes the dazzling *Music for Strings, Percussion and Celesta* and Concerto for Orchestra. He also wrote two concertos for violin, three for piano, and one (incomplete) for viola.

HUNGARIAN PEASANT MUSIC

Bartók's career as a musician is closely tied to his study of the folk music of peasants of Hungary, Romania, and Slovakia. His interest in this repertory was both musical and scholarly, and it developed into a passion for field research that he described as "the one thing that is as necessary to me as fresh air is to other people."[2] He collected thousands of folk songs and meticulously classified them according to certain stylistic features. His central contribution to the knowledge of this music was to clarify the distinction between an ancient repertory of Hungarian peasant songs and a more modern repertory. He also advanced criteria by which to distinguish the Hungarian songs from those of neighboring regions.

The old Hungarian songs especially attracted his attention. These had been preserved in isolated Hungarian farming villages, and they were relatively untouched by modern European musical styles. Their unaffected artistry, stripped bare of everything superfluous, appealed to the musician in Bartók. Having learned of this ancient type of Hungarian music, Bartók dismissed the importance of other, better-known types, such as the flashy instrumental playing of Gypsies that had been celebrated in Franz Liszt's *Hungarian Rhapsody* No. 15 (see Chapter 57). All of this Bartók disdainfully termed "**popular art music**"; true folk music, he believed, was the product of the peasant uncorrupted by city life and modern culture.

An example of the old Hungarian peasant song is "Fekete főd" ("Black Is the Earth"), which Bartók recorded on a research trip to Transylvania in 1906 or 1907 (Ex. 71-1). The region of Transylvania occupies roughly the northwest quarter of modern Romania, and Bartók found it to be the richest location of all for finding ancient Hungarian songs. They were preserved there in isolated farming communities populated by a Hungarian ethnic group called the Székely.

EXAMPLE 71-1

Black is the earth, snow white is my kerchief. He abandoned me; love's curse falls heavily on me.

The song "Fekete főd" has most of the features that Bartók found characteristic of its type. It is unaccompanied in medium and strophic in form. One stanza (see Ex. 71-1) has two lines of text (four is more typical). Each has the same number of syllables (in this case, eleven), and the musical setting is entirely syllabic. The rhythm of the melody is flexible and free from regular beat—Bartók described it as **parlando-rubato**—although other old Hungarian songs often have a strict beat, a type of rhythm that Bartók called "tempo giusto," which was appropriate for dancing. The short-long rhythm at the beginning is a characteristic rhythmic figure, and the leap of a descending fourth to the final note E is also a common cadential marker. The melody is entirely pentatonic, using only the notes E G A B D.

The terseness and stark simplicity of such music represented for Bartók a pinnacle of artistry. He wrote:

> According to the way I feel, a genuine peasant melody of our land is a musical example of a perfected art. I consider it quite as much a masterpiece, for instance, in miniature, as a Bach fugue or a Mozart sonata movement is a masterpiece in larger form. A melody of this kind is a classic example of the expression of a musical thought in its most conceivably concise form, with the avoidance of all that is superfluous.[3]

✿ BARTÓK'S USE OF FOLK MUSIC

Given his exuberant praise for the artistry of peasant tunes, Bartók naturally wanted to bring such melodies into his own compositions. He was encouraged in this when he found quotations of peasant songs made in passing by Haydn and Beethoven in their symphonies. For the modern composer, the use of folkish materials, Bartók said, could bring an element of nature into new music, promoting ease of understanding.

Bartók also found in the old folk tunes models for progressive thinking about musical materials. The tune "Fekete főd" (see Ex. 71-1), for example, does not outline functional harmonic progressions, so it is not illogical, Bartók said, to harmonize it in a way that bypasses functional harmony. But the peasant melodies are otherwise totally different from new music. They are never chromatic in their pitch content and they always exhibit a tonality based on motion toward a final focal tone. Still, Bartók insisted that there was no inconsistency in absorbing such melodies into a fully atonal style. In an essay of 1931, he defined three ways in which a peasant tune could enrich an original composition:

We may, for instance, take over a peasant melody unchanged or only slightly varied, write an accompaniment to it and possibly some opening and concluding phrases. This kind of work would show a certain analogy with Bach's treatment of chorales. . . . [Second:] The composer does not make use of a real peasant melody but invents his own imitation of such melodies. There is no true difference between this method and the one described above. . . . [Third:] Neither peasant melodies nor imitations of peasant melodies can be found in his music, but it is pervaded by the atmosphere of peasant music. In this case we may say, he has completely absorbed the idiom of peasant music which has become his musical mother tongue.[4]

Bartók's compositions contain examples of all three ways of using folk music. His arrangements of folk tunes—made for voice, chorus, and piano—are especially imaginative. One such is his treatment of "Fekete főd," for voice and piano, which he prepared around 1907 and published in 1922 in his *Eight Hungarian Folksongs*. The voice sings two stanzas of the unadorned tune while the piano adds a subtle accompaniment that preserves the character of the song. The piece opens with billowing arpeggios in the piano, whose tones are limited to those of the pentatonic scale used in the tune. Here Bartók—like Liszt before him in *Hungarian Rhapsody No. 15*—evokes the sound of the **cimbalom,** a Hungarian dulcimer. Gradually the accompaniment adds additional notes to create familiar chords and harmonic progressions, although Bartók entirely avoids the dominant chord in the home key of E minor, presumably since the strong dominant-to-tonic motion is not suggested within the tune itself.

LISTENING CUE

BÉLA BARTÓK
Eight Hungarian Folksongs
"Fekete főd" (c1907)

CD 11/18
Anthology, No. 186

Concerto for Orchestra

Bartók's Concerto for Orchestra (1943) exemplifies his third way of using folk materials. There are no quotations of peasant songs per se, although their influence is often apparent, having been thoroughly absorbed into the composer's "musical mother tongue." The Concerto for Orchestra comes from Bartók's final years, composed while he was living in the United States. This was the most difficult period in his life. He was unable to make a living in any way acceptable to him, and he was plagued by failing health.

A commission for a new orchestral work from Serge Koussevitsky, conductor of the Boston Symphony Orchestra, was a godsend that brought the creative winds back into his sails. Many émigré composers of this time—Paul Hindemith, Arnold Schoenberg, and Igor Stravinsky are other examples—turned to orchestral composition when they arrived in America during World War II. Orchestras were the strong suit of American musical culture, and conductors such as Koussevitsky were ready to reach out to composers for new works.

Bartók's Concerto for Orchestra is a five-movement composition whose form has more in common with the symphony than with the concerto. In his notes for the premier performance in Boston in December 1944, the composer explained the term "concerto" as a reference to a virtuosic treatment of instruments in the orches-

Bartók and the Golden Section

In the visual arts, an aesthetically pleasing point at which to divide a line is one that creates the so-called **Golden Section.** Imagine that the original line has the length *a* and that it is divided into two segments of lengths *b* (the longer of the two) and *c*:

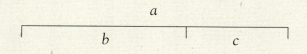

a

b   *c*

The division point forms the pleasing Golden Section if the lengths *b/a = c/b*. In terms of absolute measurements, these ratios form a constant value of about 0.618.

This simple relationship has for centuries fascinated both mathematicians and artists. It is also found in a number series named for the medieval mathematician Leonardo Fibonacci. The Fibonacci series consists of a string of numbers beginning with 0 and 1 and continuing with numbers that equal the sum of the preceding two. The Fibonacci series thus begins 0, 1, 1, 2, 3, 5, 8. . . . Higher up in the series, the ratio formed by any two adjacent terms is roughly 0.618, the same ratio as in the Golden Section.

If artists have found this proportion to be pleasing, so too have musicians. From the Renaissance to the twentieth century, composers have sometimes shaped the proportions of a musical work to equal or approximate those of the Golden Section and the related Fibonacci series. In his *Klavierstück XI* (*Piano Piece XI*, 1956), for example, the German composer Karlheinz Stockhausen explicitly used numbers from the Fibonacci series to govern the lengths of sections.

Did Bartók do the same? Bartók himself was entirely silent on this. Still, the Hungarian scholar Ernő Lendvai has found in his music a pervasive use of Golden Section proportions, both in the divisions of a work into parts and in Bartók's harmonic language. The first movement of Bartók's Sontata for Two Pianos and Percussion (1937), for example, has 443 measures. The Golden Section occurs approximately in measure 274, which is just where Bartók begins the recapitulation of the movement's sonata form. Other scholars find this a provocative accident, not the product of any systematic thinking on Bartók's part.

---

tra, most of which step forward periodically to display their skills. But the principal formal model for the work is the symphony. The first movement is fast with a slow introduction, and it uses Bartók's reinterpretation of sonata form. This is followed by a lighthearted *scherzo* movement, then a slow movement, another *scherzo,* and the work ends with a brilliant finale.

Bartók provided the movements with titles—the third, for example, is called "Elegia" ("Elegy")—that hint at some programmatic meaning. He also alluded to this dimension in his program notes for Boston: "The general mood of the work represents—apart from the jesting second movement—a gradual transition from the sternness of the first movement and the lugubrious death-song of the third, to the life-assertion of the last one."[5]

When he composed the concerto, Bartók was almost certainly aware that he suffered from a fatal disease, the blood disorder polycythemia, and it seems likely that the concerto is a highly personalized reflection upon his fate. The personal voice speaks plainly in the fourth movement, titled "Interrupted Intermezzo," in which Bartók quotes part of a theme from the first movement of the recent Symphony No. 7 by Dmitri Shostakovich—a composer whom Bartók considered kitschy, but who was a great favorite of Koussevitsky's. In Bartók's version, the theme is immediately hooted down by various instruments of the orchestra.

Such high spirits are little in evidence in the somber first movement. It begins with a slow introduction that presents motivic and tonal material that is later reshaped into main themes. An economical interconnection of motives is a distinctive characteristic of the movement, in which development is ever-present and variety among themes is achieved on a relatively superficial level of tempo, character, and instrumentation. Notice how the mysterious opening motive in the cellos and basses—moving by fourths and major seconds to outline a **pentatonic** collection of tones—is linked to these same features in the themes at measures 76 and 134. In Example 71-2, a few of the most obvious such connections among these themes are shown in brackets. Bartók's thematic economy and insistence on a multi-dimensional process of development is also revealed by his use of fugue, as in the virtuosic passage in the brass in measures 316–396.

EXAMPLE 71-2

Pentatonic collections of tones are the principal means by which Bartók relates the music to its Hungarian folk roots. Other folklike materials are also in evidence. The rhythms of the slow introduction remind us of the flexible freedom from beat of a "parlando-rubato" song such as "Fekete főd," and Bartók also resorts—as in the phrase in Violin I in measures 95–101 (Ex. 71-3)—to the short-long rhythmic figure that characterizes Hungarian music.

EXAMPLE 71-3

The style of the piece has certain features in common with the dominant anti-romantic trend of the 1920s, 1930s, and 1940s (see Chapter 68). Bartók's music, even before World War I, anticipated this rejection of romanticism in its spareness and avoidance of romantic extravagance. But after the war he generally held himself aloof from the neoclassic movement led by Stravinsky. Still, a clarity of form in the Concerto for Orchestra, its general melodiousness and ease of understanding, and its use of classic forms and genre suggest a connection between the work and the prevailing artistic spirit of its time.

LISTENING CUE

BÉLA BARTÓK
Concerto for Orchestra (1943)
First movement, *Andante non troppo; Allegro vivace*

CD 11/19
Anthology, No. 187

The Kodály Method

Bartók's research companion on many of his folk song forays into the Hungarian countryside was Zoltán Kodály (1882–1967). His career in music shadowed that of Bartók. Both attended the Academy of Music in Budapest and both were later on its faculty. Both had a passion for folk song research, and their discoveries were largely made together. Both were leading composers, and Bartók was always unstinting in his praise for the new music of his friend.

But Kodály's greatest contribution to the history of music lay in his effort to improve the musical education of children and youth. As early as the 1920s he wrote singing exercises using solfège syllables to promote musicianship and musical literacy. By 1950 these initiatives had coalesced into the "Kodály Method," which is based on the premise that choral and vocal training is basic to the musical awareness and skill of younger students.

His outlook has continued to flourish. Kodály societies now exist in cities around the world and continue to be praised not only for their effectiveness in training pre-professional musicians but also in bringing musical sensitivity to the public at large.

SUMMARY

The nation of Hungary was greatly reduced in size following World War I. At this time its rural people still preserved a rich culture of folk songs, some of which were ancient in origin. The Hungarian composer Béla Bartók collected and studied this musical repertory, and he was able to distinguish between older and newer styles. He especially valued the old Hungarian songs, which tended to be simple in expression, pentatonic in pitch content, and flexible in their freedom from a strict beat.

Bartók often made artistic arrangements of these songs, and his original compositions, such as his Concerto for Orchestra, more subtly reveal elements of the folk style combined with modern harmonic practices. Bartók's Concerto for Orchestra is close to the symphony in form, although the virtuosic treatment of various instruments from the orchestra ties in with the idea of a concerto. The themes and motives of the work are closely unified, and the Concerto also has a classical tone in form and genre that hints at Stravinsky's neoclassicism.

KEY TERMS

Zoltán Kodály	parlando-rubato rhythmic style	Golden Section
"popular art music"	cimbalom	pentatonic

Chapter

Early Jazz

72

What is **jazz**? Even so basic a question defies any simple answer. The word began to appear in print around 1915, and at first it was attached to many different types of popular music that existed then in America. The early writers on jazz seemed themselves baffled about what it was and where it came from, and they gradually tried to give the word a more specific meaning. Aaron Copland, in 1927, defined jazz purely as a musical style. Jazz occurred in popular music, he said, when a rhythmically regular accompaniment is joined to a syncopated or metrically asymmetrical melodic line.[1] In an interview in 1938, Jelly Roll Morton claimed to have used the word "jazz" as early as 1902 to refer to a style of performance that was freer in rhythm than in the strict style of ragtime. In 1958 the pioneering jazz historian Rudi Blesh limited jazz to the playing of African American musicians in New Orleans bands. "To this day," he wrote, "with rare exceptions, only New Orleans Negroes can play real jazz."[2] The jazz authority Gunther Schuller found improvisation to be the central factor in true jazz. This was its "heart and soul," he wrote in 1968.[3]

Today there is still no general agreement on the origin of the term or exactly what music it should designate, and it is now apparent that any but the most general definition is arbitrary. One reason for this impreciseness is the nature of the phenomenon itself. The styles and genres of jazz have constantly intermixed and hybridized, never remaining stable for long. A definition of jazz cannot be limiting because it is a musical phenomenon always in progress. With this reality in mind, our search for the general outlines of jazz can begin by studying the types of music from which it came.

❖ THE SOURCES OF EARLY JAZZ: RAGTIME

Jazz, in its early stages, resulted from an interaction of four principal genres of American popular music that existed around 1900: ragtime, blues, popular songs, and dance music. In the 1890s the term **ragtime** was applied to popular music having a "ragged," or syncopated, rhythm. Gradually the term became associated more exclusively with music for the piano, whereupon it indicated a character piece (each one called a **rag**) that was carefree in spirit, syncopated in melody, and similar to a march in form. Rags were primarily used to accompany march-like dances such as the "two-step" and "cakewalk," the latter being a revival of a dance that had been performed by plantation slaves. The heyday for the composing of piano rags was from about 1895 until 1920, although in more recent times the genre has experienced a revival among both composers and pianists.

We can gather the principal characteristics of a piano rag by studying the most famous composition of its type, "Maple Leaf Rag" by **Scott Joplin** (1868–1917). Joplin was born in Texas and lived primarily in Missouri—a center of ragtime culture at the turn of the twentieth century—and he spent his last decade in New York City. Although known primarily as a composer of rags, he also adapted the ragtime style to classical genres, as in his opera *Treemonisha* (1911).

Joplin's "Maple Leaf Rag" (1899) was named after the Maple Leaf Club, a dance hall where Joplin worked as a pianist in Sedalia, Missouri. Except for the syncopated melody and the medium of piano, the music is similar in almost all ways to a contemporaneous American band march. It has a duple meter and moderate tempo—"Never play ragtime fast," he warned—and it consists of a succession of phrases, or "strains," each of sixteen measures and most immediately repeated. In the middle of the work, at the point marked "trio," the key shifts to the subdominant. The strains in a rag are sometimes brought back to form a repetitive pattern: in "Maple Leaf Rag" the first strain returns just before the trio.

The most distinctive feature of the style is the syncopated melody in the right hand, which is accompanied in the left hand by a rhythm of absolute regularity.

A **syncopation** is a temporary metric irregularity, and several types are encountered in the tunes of ragtime. The one in "Maple Leaf Rag" comes from a metric displacement (Ex. 72-1). At the top of the example the rhythm in the right hand (mm. 1–2) is barred as a regular figure in $\frac{2}{4}$ time. The very same rhythm appears below, but here the bar line is shifted to the left by a sixteenth-note value, which produces the syncopated rhythm as given by the composer.

EXAMPLE 72-1

Such rhythmic figures were strictly interpreted when Joplin played his own rags. He apparently stayed close to the printed music and avoided any extensive embellishment or improvisation. "Each note will be played as it is written," he said in his *School of Ragtime*.[4]

LISTENING CUE

SCOTT JOPLIN
"Maple Leaf Rag" (1899)

CD 12/1
Anthology, No. 188

James P. Johnson's "Carolina Shout" (c1921) shows a later stage in the evolution of ragtime, one in which the process of hybridization among several types of popular music is well underway. Johnson (1894–1955) lived in the New York area amid a highly competitive group of ragtime pianists that also included Willie "The Lion" Smith, Luckey Roberts, and the young Duke Ellington. Like Joplin, he aspired to bring jazz styles into the composition of classical genres, as in his "blues opera" *De Organizer* (1940), on which he collaborated with the Harlem poet Langston Hughes.

The overall form of "Carolina Shout" embodies the ragtime archetype seen in Joplin's "Maple Leaf Rag." Following a four-measure introduction, there is a succession of sixteen-measure strains, of which the fourth begins a trio in the subdominant key (in which the work ends). But differences between the two compositions abound. Johnson's rag is in $\frac{4}{4}$ with a driving tempo, not the moderate march-like $\frac{2}{4}$ of Joplin. Johnson's virtuosic playing imitates styles that are less pianistic than they are vocal, especially those found in the blues songs to be discussed presently. His rhythms are not made from the motoric eighths and sixteenths of Joplin's piece but from a swinging triplet subdivision of the beat that always leans forward and resembles the way that words are normally spoken or sung. On the repeats of phrases, Johnson introduces improvisatory variations upon the harmony and melody of the strain just played.

Listen especially for the bass line and left hand in Johnson's piece (the first four measures of the first strain are shown in Ex. 72-2). Johnson's left hand moves regularly from a tone in the bass to a chord in the middle register, creating a striding motion. This distinctive pattern was common, not only in Johnson's music but also in that of a group of post-ragtime pianists in Harlem in the 1920s. Their style is now called **stride.** Notice also that Johnson overcomes the disruption of the striding motion to create a predominantly stepwise bass line, which takes on a melodic identity that is not heard in Joplin's piece. In this way Johnson forecasts the **walking bass** of jazz combos of the 1930s, 1940s, and 1950s. In these later ensembles (see Chapter 81), the walking bass was adopted by string bass players, who create a stepwise line in quick, even rhythmic values. Finally, listen for Johnson's remarkable rhythmic inventiveness as he departs effortlessly from the regularity of duple meter to insert bass patterns temporarily suggesting triple time.

EXAMPLE 72-2

Ragtime influenced jazz in its syncopated rhythms and in the tension existing between a rhythmically regular accompaniment and irregular melody. The essential form of ragtime—multi-thematic and multi-sectional—also provided jazz with a basic archetype to which it has periodically returned.

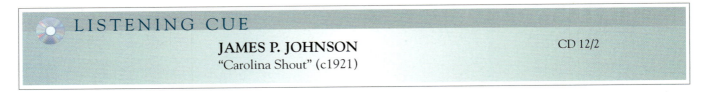

LISTENING CUE

JAMES P. JOHNSON
"Carolina Shout" (c1921)

CD 12/2

BLUES

The early history of **blues** is more shadowy than that of ragtime. Originally, a blues was a type of improvised song that by the early twentieth century had emerged among African Americans of the South. It probably borrowed on styles of folk singing that reach back considerably earlier, although it attained its mature form only after the turn of the twentieth century.

The words of blues are worldly—often sad and dejected, sometimes coarse or vulgar—and the early blues singers made them up on the spot. In their classic form, the words of an entire blues song consist of an open-ended succession of three-line stanzas. In each, the first two lines are identical and the third comments on the first two. Here is a typical blues stanza by the singer Bessie Smith from her 1926 recording of "Lost Your Head Blues":

> I was with you, baby, when you didn't have a dime;
> I was with you, baby, when you didn't have a dime;
> Now that you got plenty money, you done throw'd your good gal down.

Blues singing is highly expressive, and the vocalist often bends and slides between tones to underscore the bittersweet sentiments contained in the words. The expressive lowering of a note by a half-step—especially the third or seventh degree of the major scale—creates so-called **blue notes,** which are distinctive features of the blues style.

The accompaniment of a blues song is sometimes provided by a single instrument such as piano or guitar—played often by the singer—or it might come from a small band. The role of the instruments goes well beyond simple accompaniment. The players often improvise in a way that enriches the harmony and reinforces the emotions and vocal delivery of the singer. Typically, the singer engages in an outright dialogue with at least one of the instruments, which imitates and shadows the singer's melody. Their interchange is reminiscent of the improvised **call-and-response** singing between an individual and a group that is known to have existed among slaves. This closeness between singer and accompaniment made it inevitable that bands quickly took up the playing of blues, dispensing with the singer.

Like all improvised music, blues relies upon a widely understood form to guide and organize the performers' extemporaneous creativity. In the first stanza, the singer **improvises** a melody or uses a preexisting blues tune. In either case, the melody accommodates a simple and standardized harmonic progression that spans twelve measures in $\frac{4}{4}$ time. It has three four-measure phrases, with a line of words situated in each. The first four-measure phrase rests steadily on the tonic chord; the second moves from subdominant to tonic harmonies, and the third begins on the dominant, usually moves then to the subdominant, and arrives for its final two measures back on the tonic chord. Other stanzas (usually called **choruses**) consist of further variations upon these harmonies and, generally, upon the melodic ideas from the main tune in the first stanza.

A handsome example of the early blues song is Bessie Smith's "Lost Your Head Blues" (1926). Bessie Smith (1894–1937) was the most successful professional blues singer of her time; she achieved an unprecedented polish and expressive force in a string of successful recordings that began to appear in 1923. For "Lost Your Head Blues"—recorded in New York in 1926—she is accompanied by the pianist Fletcher Henderson and cornetist Joe Smith. The song has the classic blues form, although its length is limited by the three-minute duration of phonograph discs of this period. There is an introduction, in which the cornetist prefigures the basic melody, then five choruses (stanzas). The emotional power of Smith's singing is enhanced by her bending and sliding between tones and her imaginative variations upon the basic melodic ideas. The cornetist completes the space at the end of each four-measure phrase with a chattering solo (called a **fill**) that imitates the voice and engages sympathetically with the singer's tale of woe.

The blues influenced jazz through its improvisatory and expressive element. Blue notes became the stock in trade of later jazz musicians, and the form of blues—monothematic with variations upon an unchanging harmonic progression—was a basic design to which jazz musicians often returned.

LISTENING CUE

BESSIE SMITH   CD 12/3
"Lost Your Head Blues" (1926)

✿ POPULAR SONGS

Songs played an important role in the musical life of Americans throughout the nineteenth century. Some were written for music-making in middle-class homes, and these were geared to the rudimentary performing skills of amateurs and used homespun and sentimental words. Religious songs, or **spirituals,** were performed in churches and religious meetings, and these were richly developed in African American congregations. Other songs were written for use in traveling **minstrel shows,** a popular form of theatric entertainment that rested on a comic caricature of black dialect and culture and included songs, dances, and skits.

By the later nineteenth century, most popular songs used a common strophic form with refrain. Following an introduction, each stanza was divided into a verse and a chorus. The words of the verse changed from stanza to stanza, the chorus (refrain) remained unchanged in both words and music. In the days of the minstrel shows, the refrain was a true chorus, typically having four voice parts that were sung by the whole minstrel troupe. If multiple singers were not available, then the "chorus" melody could be sung soloistically.

In Chapter 77 we will return to the popular song, with classic examples from the 1920s through the 1950s. In them the traditional **verse-and-refrain form** is still in effect, and it remains in evidence in songs by the Beatles, Elton John, Michael Jackson, and other songsters to the present day.

Popular songs contributed to the history of early jazz by providing its material, its tunes. The familiar song melodies and their harmonies became **jazz standards**—works that jazz musicians could be expected to know from memory and use to accompany dancing, have as a basis for improvisation, or write out in arrangements. They exerted an ever-greater importance on jazz during the Big Band era beginning in the late 1920s (see Chapter 81).

DANCE MUSIC

Like the singing of songs, dancing was an important traditional form of entertainment throughout American history. In the early twentieth century its popularity grew steadily, and in the 1920s social dancing—in clubs, hotels, and restaurants—became a national passion. But, prior to the appearance of the swing bands of the late 1920s, dance pieces had no distinctive musical identity—no particular medium, form, or style beyond a meter and tempo that could accommodate the popular dance steps of the day. At the turn of the century, triple-time dances such as waltzes and "Bostons" were still popular, and music for them could be played by piano or bands of any size, using original compositions or song arrangements. Rags, played by piano or ensembles of varying size, were at the height of their popularity, and these were danced to syncopated march-like steps.

After 1910 the older triple-time dances lost favor at the hands of newer and more vigorous duple-meter dances such as the **foxtrot** and the syncopated **Charleston.** As dancing became more popular, the larger dance halls required larger musical ensembles. The demand was answered primarily by dance orchestras, in which fifty members were not unusual. These groups typically mixed strings, brass, woodwinds, drums, and plucked instruments, and their music relied upon new compositions and arrangements. These works adhered generally to the ragtime prototype, with a succession of melodies freely repeated. Improvisation had little role, although a controlled embellishment of a melody and addition of special playing effects—flutter tongue, glissandos, growls, mute effects—were typical of the style. The "Society Orchestra" led by **James Reese Europe** (1881–1919) was one of the most successful of the New York dance orchestras of this day, and Europe saw a need to keep improvisation out of his band's playing:

> I have to call a daily rehearsal of my band to prevent the musicians from adding to their music more than I wish them to. Whenever possible they all embroider their parts in order to produce new, peculiar sounds. Some of these effects are excellent and some are not, and I have to be continually on the lookout to cut out the results of my musicians' originality.[5]

Music at Congo Square

The American architect Benjamin Latrobe visited New Orleans in 1819 and recorded this account of music-making on Sundays at Congo Square:

> In going up St. Peters Street & approaching the common I heard a most extraordinary noise. . . . It proceeded from a crowd of 5 or 600 persons assembled in an open space or public square. I went to the spot & crowded near enough to see the performance. All those who were engaged in the business seemed to be *blacks*. I did not observe a dozen yellow [i.e., Creole] faces. They were formed into circular groupes in the midst of four of which, which I examined (but there were more of them), was a ring, the largest not 10 feet in diameter. In the first were two women dancing. . . .
>
> The music consisted of two drums and a stringed instrument. An old man sat astride of a cylindrical drum about a foot in diameter, & beat it with incredible quickness with the edge of his hand & fingers. . . . The most curious instrument, however, was a stringed instrument which no doubt was imported from Africa. On the top of the finger board was the rude figure of a man in a sitting posture, & two pegs behind him

to which the strings were fastened. [Latrobe made the accompanying drawings of the two instruments.]

> The women squalled out a burthen [refrain] to the playing at intervals, consisting of two notes, as the negroes, working in our cities, respond to the song of their leader. . . .[6]

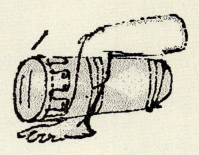

❋ FIGURE 72-1

Benjamin Latrobe, drawings of instruments used by slaves in New Orleans. These instruments were handmade from common materials. The art of drumming is especially sophisticated among African musicians.

NEW ORLEANS AND THE EMERGENCE OF JAZZ

New Orleans musicians near the turn of the twentieth century played a special role in the creation of the new idiom called jazz. It was here that the intermixture of existing popular musical genres—especially band marches, ragtime, and blues—produced, not a simple development of these individual types of music but an amalgamation with its own spirit and character. The term "jazz" was most often used to designate this phenomenon.

Why did jazz first flourish in New Orleans? The presence of riverboats, bordellos in the red-light district of Storyville, festivals such as Mardi Gras, and parades for any and all occasions ensured a demand for music. Much about the city's musical culture was special. Throughout the nineteenth century, slaves living in and around New Orleans were allowed to express themselves musically; in other cities their music-making was generally forbidden. On Sundays, their day of rest, slaves gathered in central New Orleans at Congo Square to dance, sing, and play native African instruments. An eyewitness account of their music can be found in the Box.

New Orleans also had a well-developed tradition of serious music, which promoted musical literacy and supported music teaching. Musical instruments were readily available. Opera was especially advanced in New Orleans by the later nineteenth century, thanks to the existence of the French Opera House, which from 1859 until 1919 produced numerous American premieres of operas by modern French composers.

A distinctive feature of musical culture in New Orleans was the brass band. Bands were popular throughout America around 1900, and especially so in New Orleans. They played for every imaginable social occasion—funerals, weddings, parties—and they had their own informally joyous style. Jelly Roll Morton recalled their spirited playing:

> Those parades were really tremendous things. The drums would start off, the trumpets and trombones rolling into something like *Stars and Stripes* or *The National Anthem* and everybody would strut off down the street, the bass-drum player twirling his beater in the air, the snare drummer throwing his sticks up and bouncing them off the ground, the kids jumping and hollering, the grand marshall and his aides in their expensive uniforms moving along dignified.[7]

To accompany dancing, these bands were pared down and adjusted in their instrumentation, but they kept the spirited freedom of playing that Morton recalled. The typical New Orleans dance band early in the century was small, generally five to seven players. These were divided into two groups: the cornet, clarinet, and trombone were typically entrusted with the melody and the piano, drums, and bass—called the **rhythm section**—played an accompaniment. Many of the bandsmen could only play by ear, others apparently read music, and their tunes included rags, marches, popular songs, and blues-like pieces.

An example of the **New Orleans style** of jazz is "Dippermouth Blues," recorded in 1923 by **Joe "King" Oliver**'s Creole Jazz Band (Fig. 72-2). Oliver (1885–1938) was a leading New Orleans cornetist who, like many musicians following World War I, left the city for greater opportunities in Chicago and New York. The band on the recording is typical of the New Orleans medium. It has seven players consisting of a melody group of two cornets (Oliver and his protégé, Louis Armstrong), clarinet, and trombone, and a rhythm section of piano, bass (doubling on banjo), and drums.

The music has the character of ragtime and the form of blues. After a four-measure introduction, there are nine blues choruses, each with the classic twelve-measure harmonic structure. The playing most characteristic of the New Orleans style occurs in choruses 1, 2, 5, and 9, when all four of the melody instruments improvise in group fashion over the blues harmonies. In these passages there is no distinguishable melody, which is replaced by a comfortably blended polyphony. The group playing alternates with solo choruses. In numbers 3 and 4 the clarinetist Johnny Dodds leads while the band accompanies in **stop time**—playing only on the first three beats of each measure. Oliver's cornet solo in chorus numbers 6 through 8 is especially distinctive in its closeness to the sound of the human voice, which Oliver imitates with blue notes, playing with the valves pushed halfway, and using the mute. At the end of

✹ FIGURE 72-2
King Oliver's Creole Jazz Band, 1923, was formed in Chicago in 1922 and had the makeup of New Orleans bands. Oliver is seated; standing from the left are Baby Dodds, Honoré Dutrey, Bill Johnson, Louis Armstrong, Johnny Dodds, and Lillian Hardin, soon to be Armstrong's wife.

CORBIS

his solo, the band suddenly falls silent (observing a characteristic **break**), and a player shouts out "O shake that thing!"

> ### LISTENING CUE
>
> ## JOE "KING" OLIVER
> "Dippermouth Blues" (1923)
>
> CD 12/4

By the mid-1920s, the New Orleans style was losing focus. Most of the city's leading musicians had moved elsewhere, and the ensemble concept was undergoing a far-reaching transformation (see Chapter 81). Echoes of New Orleans' jazz can still be heard in recordings from the late 1920s by one of New Orlean's greatest musical expatriates, **Louis Armstrong** (1901–1971). Born in dire poverty in New Orleans, Armstrong grew up in the city's Home for Colored Waifs, where he learned to play cornet. His skills advanced under King Oliver, his mentor, and he followed Oliver to Chicago in 1922. In 1925 Armstrong founded his own band, the Hot Five, which conformed in general to the New Orleans concept but which increasingly focused on his own individualized virtuosity rather than the group playing of Oliver's band. By this time Armstrong had dispensed with the cornet—an instrument suited to ensemble playing—in favor of the more brilliant and soloistic trumpet.

His recording of "West End Blues," made by Louis Armstrong and His Hot Five in 1928, shows the new directions in which Armstrong pointed the New Orleans style. Armstrong's band was made up according to New Orleans standards, with a melody group consisting of trumpet, trombone, and clarinet, and a rhythm section of piano, banjo, and drums. The form of the work is the standard instrumental blues, the same as in Oliver's "Dippermouth Blues."

A version of the melody "West End Blues" had shortly before been composed and recorded by the Dixie Syncopators, a New Orleans–type band that Oliver then led. In Armstrong's version, the tune is not basic to the structure of the work, which depends more on true improvisation than on the restrained melodic embellishment that was Oliver's specialty. Armstrong's "West End Blues" is both a tribute to Oliver and the New Orleans style and also a brash declaration of independence from it. The new spirit is heard straightaway in the introduction, played by Armstrong alone as a flamboyant improvisation over a few blues chords. Here Armstrong breaks free from the temporal and harmonic restrictions of the idiom. His playing exploits the high register of his instrument—so different from Oliver's exclusively middle-register playing—and it has an expressive impetuosity, as though Armstrong is demanding that he be listened to as an individual.

The five blues choruses that follow the introduction cover a range of emotions from Armstrong's comfortable **scat singing** in number 3 to the happy ragtime virtuosity of the pianist Earl Hines in number 4. "Scat" is an improvised singing on nonsense syllables that usually imitates the playing of an instrument. It was often used by early New Orleans jazz musicians, and Louis Armstrong was its first important practitioner.

> ### LISTENING CUE
>
> ## LOUIS ARMSTRONG
> "West End Blues" (1928)
>
> CD 12/5

SUMMARY

Jazz refers to several styles of American popular music that emerged in the early twentieth century. The term has always been used imprecisely, although in general it is a type of music that at first mixed together elements from ragtime, blues, popular songs, and dance music. Its roots reach back to earlier types of improvised music of African Americans.

A "rag" is a march-like piano character piece in which a syncopated melody is joined to a rhythmically regular accompaniment. A "blues" was originally an improvised strophic song whose stanzas (or "choruses") span twelve-measure phrases and rest upon a fixed and simple harmonic progression. Popular songs around 1900 were strophic compositions in which each stanza (or "verse") was ended by a refrain (called a chorus because at an earlier time it was sung in group fashion). Dance music prior to the late Big Band phenomenon of the late 1920s had no single identity in medium or form.

The most likely birthplace of jazz is New Orleans, where, following the turn of the twentieth century, the term "jazz" was applied to music played in a free manner by small dance bands. These were subdivided into a group of instruments playing melody (often cornet, clarinet, and trombone) and other instruments playing accompaniment (a "rhythm section" often made up by piano, drums, and bass). A distinctive feature of their music-making was group improvisation, in which all of the melody instruments created a closely knit polyphony.

KEY TERMS

jazz	call-and-response	Charleston
ragtime	improvise	James Reese Europe
rag	chorus	rhythm section
Scott Joplin	fill	New Orleans style
syncopation	spiritual	Joe "King" Oliver
stride	minstrel show	stop time
walking bass	verse-and-refrain form	break
blues	jazz standard	Louis Armstrong
blue notes	foxtrot	scat singing

Chapter 73

Paul Hindemith and Music in Nazi Germany

On 30 January 1933, Paul von Hindenburg, Germany's aging president, made a desperate move to stabilize his country and stave off its political and social collapse: he appointed **Adolf Hitler** (1889–1945) to be Germany's chancellor, its head of state. Hitler was the leader of the country's strongest and most radical political party, the National Socialist German Workers' Party, derisively nicknamed the **Nazis.** During his rise to prominence, Hitler had made no secret of his plans for Germany. He wished to rid the country of Communists and Jews, revive the army after its defeat in World War I, expand the country's borders, and replace its recent attempt at democratic government with a centralized authoritarian rule. Germans, he believed, were a "master race" who were destined to rule over the people of the world that he considered less advanced.

🌸 MUSICAL LIFE UNDER THE NAZIS

Immediately after they came to power, the Nazis began to make their ideas a reality, and the lives of Jewish musicians in Germany were among the first to be disrupted. In April 1933 a new law banned Jews from civil-service positions, which in Germany at the time included virtually all teaching appointments. The effects were immediately felt by composers who were teachers, and Bernhard Sekles, Franz Schreker, and Arnold Schoenberg were only a few of those who lost their jobs.

Schoenberg, for one, had anticipated the dismal outlook for Jews in Germany. In 1924 he had written to the painter Vasili Kandinsky:

> But what is anti-Semitism to lead to if not to acts of violence? Is it so difficult to imagine that? You are perhaps satisfied with depriving Jews of their civil rights. Then certainly Einstein, Mahler, I, and many others will have been got rid of. But one thing is certain: they will not be able to exterminate those much tougher elements thanks to whose endurance Jewry has maintained itself unaided against the whole of mankind for 20 centuries. For these are evidently so constituted that they can accomplish the task that their God has imposed on them: To survive in exile, uncorrupted and unbroken, until the hour of salvation comes![1]

With such thoughts no doubt in mind, Schoenberg in May 1933 fled from Berlin to Paris and then to the United States, where he continued his career as a teacher and composer.

For non-Jewish musicians in Germany, prospects temporarily brightened. The Nazis wanted the arts to flourish in their new empire, which they called the **Third Reich,** and Hitler was himself a devotee of classical music. He once bragged that he had carried a score to Wagner's *Tristan und Isolde* in his backpack during his army service in World War I. **Joseph Goebbels,** the minister of the new Department of Education and Propaganda, which oversaw the arts, held a Ph.D. degree in literature and aspired to be a writer. At first, the cooperation of leading German musicians—including the composers Richard Strauss and Hans Pfitzner and the conductor Wilhelm Furtwängler—was solicited, but later any disagreement with Nazi control or ideology by these or other figures was ruthlessly crushed.

Music by Jewish composers, including romantic pieces by Felix Mendelssohn and Gustav Mahler, was soon effectively banned from performance, and ultramodern directions in new music—such as free dissonance, atonality, and twelve-tone composition—were also ruled out. American jazz was dismissed as decadent.

Goebbels wanted German composers to write music that had traditional materials but that could still be recognized as original and innovative. He was uncertain about the new music of the 1920s and 1930s that mixed elements of old and new and was hard to categorize as tonal or atonal, consonant or dissonant. Such music, which critics alternately termed "neoclassical" or "objective," had much about it that could appeal to the Nazis. Its chords, rhythms, forms, and textures were basically familiar, and it seemed to honor the traditions of past masters—especially the German J.S. Bach. But other features of neoclassical music, such as its tendency to incorporate elements from jazz or an eclecticism that mixed traditional with modern thinking, were less acceptable. Also, composers like Stravinsky had only a few years earlier written compositions—*The Rite of Spring* is an example—that made use of blatant dissonance and atonality, styles that were now dismissed as degenerate or an example of **cultural bolshevism.**

The Nazis' shallowness in understanding the music of their time manifested in their dealings with Paul Hindemith (1895–1963), the leading German neoclassicist composer of the twentieth century. Hindemith's career placed him at the crisis points of music of his day. As much as any major figure in the century, he grappled head on with the essential questions that faced the classical composer of the early twentieth century: Could the basic materials of music—including triadic harmony, consonant intervals, and fluent melody—be set aside in favor of new alternatives? Could composers of the future develop a distinctive style using alternative materials? Could such new musical vocabularies contribute positively to society?

✿ HINDEMITH'S LIFE AND WORKS

Hindemith (pronounced HIN-duh-mit) first made his living as a professional violinist (he was appointed concertmaster of the Frankfurt Opera orchestra at the age of nineteen). Following World War I he gained attention as a composer in a modernistic vein, although he gradually became an adherent of the more conservative anti-romantic artistic movement of the 1920s, one that asserted objectivity, traditionalism, and craft. Like Stravinsky at the same time, he expressed disdain for unrestrained experimentation in music.

In 1927 Hindemith was appointed to the faculty of the Hochschule für Musik (Technical College for Music) in Berlin, and he began an intense study of musical pedagogy, history, and theory. He also searched for ways by which music could establish a stronger presence throughout contemporary society. With this social objective in mind, he composed a series of educational works intended for young players and singers. Given their utilitarian purpose, he called them *Gebrauchsmusik* (music for use)—a term also used by Kurt Weill for a different phenomenon (see Chapter 70).

In 1938 Hindemith emigrated from Germany, first to Switzerland, then to the United States, where in 1941 he was appointed to the faculty of the School of Music at Yale University. He returned to Europe in 1953, where he lived primarily in Switzerland, not Germany, and he increasingly occupied himself as an orchestral conductor.

Hindemith's large musical oeuvre emphasizes the instrumental genres. He wrote concertos, symphonies, pieces for chamber orchestra and band, six string quartets, piano music, and sonatas for virtually every instrument. He was also attracted to opera, and his principal works of this type are *Mathis der Maler* (*Mathis the Painter*, 1935), *Cardillac* (1926, revised 1952), and *Die Harmonie der Welt* (*The Harmony of the World*, 1957). His other major vocal compositions include the monumental song cycle *Das Marienleben* (*The Life of Mary*, 1923, revised 1948), which is based on poetry by Rainer Maria Rilke, and a Mass (1963).

✿ HINDEMITH'S THEORY OF THE TWELVE TONES

Like many composers of the 1920s, Hindemith searched for laws and principles by which the expanded musical resources of the early twentieth century could be organized and put to productive use in new compositions. Stravinsky, for example, said that his Octet was a work concerned primarily with form, counterpoint, and architecture. Schoenberg in the 1920s turned to twelve-tone rows as means of organization, an answer to his wish "to know *consciously* the laws and rules which govern the forms which he has conceived 'as in a dream.'"

Hindemith's exploration for laws led him, first, to study the history of music theory (he taught himself Latin to be able to do this), and then to write his own theory capable of extending traditional thinking on the subject to the new chromatic tonal resources of the modern period.

In 1937 he published his findings in a treatise called *Unterweisung im Tonsatz* (Hindemith's English equivalent was **The Craft of Musical Composition**). Here he presents a theory concerning the twelve tones of the chromatic scale, and his conclusions are all based on the fundamental premise that these tones and the intervals that they form have a hierarchy of differing strengths. A fifth, for example, must always be structurally different from a second. Such differences derive, he asserted, from acoustical laws that could not be denied or ignored by any composer or any musical style.

Plainly, Hindemith's ideas are rooted in musical traditions, not in the liberated thinking about musical structure characteristic of the years before World War I. They differ sharply from notions of earlier atonal composers, for whom all twelve tones and all intervals were available as though essentially equivalent. For Arnold Schoenberg, a consonant interval such as a fifth occurring in new music was not different structurally from a dissonant interval such as a second. One was no more a product of nature than the other, he wrote. They both occurred between adjacent tones in the overtone series, the fifth lower down in the series, the second higher up—differences that for Schoenberg were insignificant and arbitrary. "They are no more opposites than two and ten are opposites," he wrote.

Hindemith was totally opposed to this outlook. For him, all intervals and chords had differing weights and strengths that had to be respected if a musical structure was to stand on its own. He compared composing to designing and building a house:

> Harmonic progressions—governed by [interval] relationships—are laid out in a sort of ground plan that shows, first of all, the structure's main support points, between which the connecting building elements are subsequently added. Devising this ground plan depends on an assessment of the harmonic weight of chords. . . . The outcome of this working procedure, when elaborated with elementary rhythmic effects and ornamental building elements, is the completed composition.[2]

Mathis der Maler

Hindemith began to apply his theory of tones in his masterpiece—the opera *Mathis der Maler*—which he conceived of just when Hitler took power in 1933. This composition ultimately incorporated not only his ideas about musical materials but also his consciousness of the role of the artist in a society that was evidently in crisis. Hindemith wrote the libretto himself, and he chose as his topic a fictionalized account of the life of the Renaissance German painter **Matthias Grünewald** (c1470–1528). Grünewald's greatest works—studied by Hindemith as he wrote the libretto—are the paintings made for a large altarpiece installed in the chapel of a hospital monastery in Isenheim, a village near Colmar, France. These spectacular paintings are now displayed at the Musée d'Unterlinden in Colmar.

When the altarpiece is closed (Fig. 73-1a), the viewer sees a disturbingly realistic view of the crucifixion. Grünewald's conception is both symbolic and passionately

Synopsis of *Mathis der Maler*

The opera is divided into seven scenes, or "tableaux." The painter Mathis is at work at the monastery of the Order of St. Anthony, where he is completing a year's leave from the service of his patron, Albrecht, who is the ruler of the region around Mainz and an archbishop of the Catholic Church. Both Mathis and Albrecht are facing personal dilemmas. The peasants of the region are in revolt against the ruling classes, and Mathis sympathizes with their cause and wonders what value his art can have in a time of social and political turmoil. Albrecht's court is in an uproar between adherents to the Catholic Church and its pope and others who are followers of the reform movement led by Martin Luther. The latter group wants Albrecht to join their cause, and he is tempted to do so. Still, he obeys an order from the pope to burn Lutheran books.

Hans Schwalb, the leader of the peasants' revolt, is brought wounded to the monastery by his daughter, Regina, and Mathis sympathetically gives them his horse with which to escape. Mathis decides to put aside his art and to take up the cause of the rebels, but he is appalled by their brutality. Albrecht meanwhile has resigned his position as ruler and archbishop but remains with the Church, taking on the life of a hermit.

In the climactic sixth tableau, Mathis and Regina have fled for safety into the forest. Here Mathis has a complex dream in which he imagines that he is St. Anthony. In the desert he is tempted by a series of worldly distractions, each embodied by an earlier acquaintance. Now utterly confused, he visits with a holy man, St. Paul of the Desert (represented in the dream by his patron, Albrecht), who advises him to return to his art, by which he can best serve God and his fellow man. "Go forth and create!" commands Paul.

The last scene depicts Mathis at the end of his life as he retires his painting gear and prepares for death, having obeyed the command of Paul.

Bridgeman Art Library

❀ FIGURE 73-1a

Matthias Grünewald, Isenheim altarpiece. Grünewald's masterpiece is the collection of altar paintings created for a hospital monastery in the French-German village of Isenheim near Colmar. Its scenes are duplicated in the sets used in Hindemith's opera *Mathis der Maler*.

dramatic. In the central panel to the left of the crucifix, the Virgin Mary (in white) faints while the anguished figure of Mary Magdalene kneels beside in prayer; to the right, John the Baptist points to Jesus and utters Latin words meaning, "It is fitting that He increase and I diminish." Flanking panels show St. Anthony and St. Sebastian; the entombment of Christ is depicted below the central panel.

The ingeniously constructed altarpiece can be opened, first, to display three scenes from the life of Christ: the annunciation, the birth of Jesus serenaded by an angelic concert (Fig. 73-1b), and the brilliant resurrection. The central panels can be opened yet again to show a depiction of St. Anthony's legendary temptation in the desert and his consultation with St. Paul of the Desert (Fig. 73-1c).

To a considerable extent Hindemith's text is a symbolic representation of contemporary events. The composer wrote much of himself into the character of Mathis—the man who is torn between serving society and serving art. The portrait of an explosively polarized nation that has been driven to the breaking point depicts the Germany of 1933 as much as that of the 1500s. In creating the libretto, Hindemith was also plainly attempting to meet the Nazis halfway, to appeal to their artistic interests, as he understood them, while at the same time exposing false directions. His choice of a great German artist as his central character conformed to the Nazis' worship of nationalism, and Mathis's decision to renounce revolution for art was in line with their ideas of a centralized political authority. But Hindemith's scene in which Lutheran books are burned was an obvious criticism of a recent book burning in Berlin orchestrated by Goebbels, and the open-mindedness of the political leader Albrecht was not at all part of the Nazis' thinking.

Ultimately, the struggle dramatized in *Mathis der Maler* comes not from external forces or characters who represent good and evil, instead an internal conflict within Mathis himself—between art as moral obligation and art as willful indulgence. For Hindemith, as for Mathis, art had to represent a moral dimension if it was to continue to be relevant to modern society.

The music that Hindemith wrote for *Mathis der Maler* (1935) reflects the international neoclassical style of the 1920s and 1930s, as well as Hindemith's attempt to accommodate the Nazis' conservatism in artistic taste. The opera's form continues the departure—already seen in Alban Berg's *Wozzeck*—from the Wagnerian model of through composition. Neither Hindemith or Berg went so far as to return outright to number opera, although Hindemith's music has unmistakable subdivisions into traditional musical forms and operatic media such as choruses, ensembles, arias, and melodious narrations. The composer makes these numbers all the more distinguishable from one another by giving them a symmetrical musical form akin to that in instrumental music as well as a distinct tonality.

An example of his approach to operatic structure is found in the climactic third *Auftritt* ("entrance") of scene 6, in which Mathis, dreaming that he is St. Anthony, seeks advice from Albrecht, whom he imagines to be St. Paul of the Desert. Hindemith directs that the scenery should duplicate the appearance of Grünewald's painting of this meeting (see Fig. 73-1c). The music of the entrance is divided into three connected subsections: a dialogue between Anthony and Paul in rondo form, an aria for Paul in varied strophic form, and a through-composed duet for both characters that is worked out as a two-part contrapuntal invention. The principal themes of the three sections are shown in Example 73-1.

EXAMPLE 73-1

Bridgeman Art Library

❀ FIGURE 73-1b
The concert of angels from Grünewald's Isenheim altarpiece.

❀ FIGURE 73-1c
St. Anthony (left) is advised by St. Paul of the Desert in Grünewald's Isenheim altarpiece.

Bridgeman Art Library

Langsam (reh. F)

Anthony: Mein Bru-der, ent-rei-ße dich der höl-len-tie-fen Qual.
My brother, tear yourself free from hell's agony.

Lebhaft, mit Kraft (reh. G)

Paul: Wenn du de-mü-tig dem Bru-der dich bogst,
When you bow, humbly before your brother,

(3 before reh. 98)

Breit

(Both: Dem Kreis, der uns geboren hat, können wir nicht entrinnen...)
We cannot escape the circumstances of our birth...

Although the three subsections flow into one another without pause, they are made noticeably distinct by their contrasting tonal centers. The rondo touches repeatedly on a D-minor pitch collection and triad, the aria on D♭ minor, and the duet on D major. These subsections are not "in" these keys in any traditional sense, since the music has no significant functional harmonic progressions.

Another distinctive feature of the opera's music is Hindemith's borrowing preexistent melodies from folk songs, Lutheran hymns, and Gregorian chants. These well-known tunes give a work populated by peasants, Lutherans, and Catholics all the more dramatic plausibility, and their presence also allows Hindemith to tie the work more closely to the spirit and substance of Grünewald's altar paintings. For example, Hindemith quotes repeatedly from the chants used at Mass in the Catholic Feast of Corpus Christi. This is the day when the Church celebrates Holy Communion, a Christian sacrament that reenacts the crucifixion, which is the principal subject of Grünewald's altarpiece.

Hindemith apparently felt the need to spread thematic elements beyond the boundary of a single scene or musical number, but he did not adopt Wagner's device of the leitmotive. Instead, he isolates a few motivic fragments within the chants and folksongs that he quotes and then reuses them among the work's melodies. These recurrent motives give the opera a purely musical unity and provide a counterbalance to its subdivision into distinct musical parts. An example comes from the melody that ends scene 6, entrance 3, sung by Anthony and Paul on the word "Alleluia." The tune is taken from Gregorian chant, from the Alleluia used at Mass on the Feast of Corpus Christi. The opening of the two melodies is shown in Example 73-2.

EXAMPLE 73-2

The rising scalar motive C-D-E at the beginning of Hindemith's alleluia melody is embedded in numerous other important melodies in different parts of the opera. Example 72-3, for example, shows the main themes of the opera's Prelude, where the alleluia motive (shown in brackets) figures prominently.

EXAMPLE 73-3

"The Hindemith Case" by Wilhelm Furtwängler (excerpts)

This article by **Wilhelm Furtwängler**—conductor of the Berlin Philharmonic Orchestra and the leading German conductor of his day—appeared in a Berlin newspaper on 25 November 1934. The previous March, Furtwängler had conducted the premiere of the Symphony *Mathis der Maler*, and he now wished to bring out the entire opera, permission for which was still pending from the Nazi authorities. Although reasonable in tone, Furtwängler's article outraged the Nazis for its presumptuousness, and *Mathis* was essentially banished from the stage in Germany. The opera was first given in Zurich, Switzerland, in 1938.

> A campaign has been launched in certain circles against Paul Hindemith on the grounds that he is "not acceptable" to the new Germany. Why? What is he accused of? . . .
>
> His reputation has spread abroad not only because of his skill as a performer but also due to [the] progressive and pioneering quality of his music. He deliberately broke with the emotionalism of the Whilhelmine era, the false romanticism that still lingered after the time of Wagner and Richard Strauss. He has avoided music that serves philosophical ideas or wallows in an indulgent neo-romantic sentimentality, as does the music of many of his contemporaries, and he has instead cultivated the values of straightforwardness, objectivity, and simplicity.

> His most recent work, the Symphony *Mathis der Maler*, has served to confirm these qualities. Since its first performance in March 1934 it has made a deep impression wherever it has been played, notably on those not otherwise particularly well-disposed toward him. This does not signify, I repeat, any ideological change of direction on his part, but instead a return to his beginnings, to his real self.
>
> Eight months ago, when the *Mathis* Symphony was first heard, the authorities made no move against Hindemith, perhaps because of an unconscious reluctance to interfere in the course of the nation's culture. Now, although he has published nothing in the meantime, they have decided to mount a campaign of public vilification against him with the object of forcing him to leave the country. No tactic seems too petty. They have even sunk to the depths of quoting the occasional parody of Wagner and Puccini in his works, completely missing the point of such badinage. Obviously, with a composer who has written so much and whose works are there in published form for everyone to inspect, it is not difficult, years after the event, to find youthful indiscretions. Moreover Hindemith has never engaged in political activity. Where will it lead if we begin to apply the methods of political denunciation to art? . . .[3]

LISTENING CUE

PAUL HINDEMITH
Mathis der Maler (1935)
Scene 6, entrance 3

CD 12/6
Anthology, No. 189

Symphony *Mathis der Maler*

The first music to be completed for the opera was a set of three orchestral passages, each depicting one of Grünewald's altar paintings. Well before he finished the remainder of the opera or even its libretto, Hindemith assembled these into a separate orchestral showpiece in symphonic form that he called Symphony *Mathis der Maler* (1934). The first of the symphonic movements is titled *Engelkonzert* (*Concert of Angels*), and it refers musically to the painting in Figure 73.1b. The second movement, *Grablegung* (*Entombment*), depicts another part of Grünewald's altarpiece, and the third movement, *Versuchung des heiligen Antonius* (*Temptation of St. Anthony*), has its equivalent in the Grünewald's depiction of this legendary event.

The music of the three movements also reappears in the completed opera. The *Engelkonzert* is synonymous with the work's Prelude (overture), the *Grablegung* is situated at the conclusion in scene 7, and the *Versuchung des heiligen Antonius* is distributed into passages at the beginning of scene 6.

Hindemith's music for *Mathis der Maler* shows a new and important development in the spirit of music between the world wars. Hindemith not only embraces the musical language of neoclassicism but also interprets this choice on a moralistic basis. After his time, a composer's adoption of a musical style could convey not merely taste but an embodiment of right versus wrong.

SUMMARY

When the Nazis took over the German government in 1933, they immediately dismissed Jews from employment and banished music by Jewish composers. Atonal and twelve-tone music was also ruled out as an example of "cultural bolshevism," and American jazz was dismissed as decadent. Nazi leaders supported the music of other leading figures such as Richard Strauss and Hans Pfitzner, although they seemed confused over trends in the music of their day. Their attitude toward the music of Paul Hindemith was especially ambivalent, despite Hindemith's efforts to accommodate their wishes.

In addition to his musical compositions, Hindemith was a music theorist who attempted to establish laws based on timeless natural principles for the use of chromatic tones. He applied his ideas in his opera *Mathis der Maler* and in the Symphony *Mathis der Maler*, the latter an orchestral work that pre-dates the opera. Both compositions are based on paintings by the Renaissance German artist Matthias Grünewald.

In the opera, Hindemith continues the general departure from Wagnerian principles that had been begun earlier by Richard Strauss, Alban Berg, and Kurt Weill. Hindemith partly returns to a division of the work into number-like passages suggesting arias, duets, choruses, and ensembles. He abandons Wagner's use of leitmotives, although he reinforces a broad melodic unity throughout the work by shared motives, and he quotes many preexisting chants and folksongs. In his writings, Hindemith justified his stylistic preferences in music on a moral basis.

KEY TERMS

Adolf Hitler	cultural bolshevism	Matthias Grünewald
Nazis	*Gebrauchsmusik*	Wilhelm Furtwängler
Third Reich	*The Craft of Musical*	
Joseph Goebbels	*Composition*	

Chapter 74

Music in Soviet Russia: Prokofiev and Shostakovich

Prospects for music in Russia following the October Revolution of 1917 were uncertain at best. The country was economically devastated by its participation in World War I and by the upheaval of revolution. The future role for classical music—an art long associated with privileged social classes and a product of the individual imagination—was still undefined for a state that professed proletarian and collectivist values. Over the next few years, most of Russia's leading musicians—including Jascha Heifetz, Serge Koussevitsky, Alexander Glazunov, Vladimir Horowitz, Sergei Rachmaninoff, and Sergei Prokofiev—left their homeland for more certain terrain abroad.

SERGEI PROKOFIEV

Many relocated in France, but Sergei Prokofiev (1891–1953) emigrated instead to the United States. When he arrived in New York in 1918, he attracted attention as a piano virtuoso and prodigious composer, one with a whole portfolio of works in a modernist vein. But he found audiences here unprepared for his innovative outlook, although he had praise for America's high performance standards. In his *Autobiography* he recalled these years:

> Discussion of new music, new trends and composers had become an integral part of our musical life. America, on the contrary, had no original composers, apart from those who came from Europe with ready-made reputations, and the whole accent of musical life was concentrated on execution. In this field the standard was rather high.[1]

Between the time of his arrival in America in 1918 and 1932, Prokofiev lived what he later called a "nomadic concert-tour existence." He concertized all over the world, including the Soviet Union, composed all the while in a highly disciplined way, and when not traveling lived alternately in the United States, Germany, and France. Between 1932 and 1936 he shuttled between Moscow and Paris, and finally returned with his family permanently to Russia.

His return came as a surprise to other Russian émigrés such as Stravinsky and Rachmaninoff, who had expressed only disdain for the political developments in their native land and refused at first even to visit Soviet Russia. Prokofiev was of a different mind. He never gave up the idea that he was a Russian musician at heart, and his return was provoked by a homesickness for his mother country, a search for more time to compose, and the presence of a sympathetic Russian audience.

Prokofiev was an immensely prolific composer. Operas and ballets—including the comic opera *Love for Three Oranges* (1919), the epic *War and Peace* (1943), and the ballets *Romeo and Juliet* (1936) and *Cinderella* (1944)—are central to his oeuvre. Orchestral works include his five concertos for piano, two concertos for violin, seven symphonies, and numerous suites. He wrote nine piano sonatas, character piano pieces, sonatas for solo instruments (violin, cello, and flute), two string quartets, songs, and choral works. Prokofiev was especially drawn to composing for cinema, and his scores for the films *Alexander Nevsky* and *Lieutenant Kijé* were also reworked in concert forms. His charming musical narration *Peter and the Wolf* (1936) is known by children worldwide (see Box on pages 681–682).

MUSICAL CULTURE IN THE SOVIET UNION

The year 1932—when Prokofiev began the renewal of his ties to Russia—was a turning point for the country and for its musicians. Before this time there had existed in the Soviet Union a heated debate on the role of music. One faction was open to Western ideas and modernistic styles; another was more ideological in its opposition to Western music and to art music in general. Still, there was considerable openness in the practice of the arts. Traditionalists and experimentalists lived side by side, and new music by major European figures was often heard, especially in Leningrad (the name given in 1924 to the old capital city of St. Petersburg). Lenin's minister for the arts was the respected writer and critic **Anatoli Lunacharsky** (1875–1933), who tried to balance opposing factions while supporting artistic freedom from the threat of political and proletarian ideology.

The atmosphere of tolerance created by Lunacharsky gradually eroded under the rule of Joseph Stalin (1879–1953). Stalin distrusted the West and wanted to centralize control over the arts, which he accomplished partly through organizational means, partly through repression and terror. A resolution issued by the central Communist Party in April 1932 abolished the various proletarian organizations among artists and led to the founding of a "Union of Soviet Composers." For most musicians in the country, this was a positive step, since it seemed to give the musicians themselves—rather than proletarian amateurs—a larger voice in the control of their art. Dmitri Shostakovich spoke out immediately praising the decree: "I personally see the Resolution as a sign of faith in the composer."[2] But the musicians could not have been happy about Stalin's delegation of ultimate control over these organizations to political or military figures, such as his trusted ally **Andrei Zhdanov,** rather than to artists and intellectuals like Lunacharsky. All the same, the decree was apparently a principal reason why Prokofiev felt confident in reestablishing ties with Russia in 1932.

More crucial questions concerned artistic freedom and individual versus collective expression. What type of music would be approved of and supported by the Party? The answer first came in connection with literature. At a meeting in 1934 of the Soviet Writers' Congress, Zhdanov enunciated a policy of **socialist realism** as the single overriding objective in the future. This was not unexpected, since realism had long been a distinguishing feature of Russian literature and music. Recall the song "Within Four Walls" by Modest Mussorgsky (see Chapter 59), in which a text expressing everyday sentiments seems to override the music of the song, which is stripped bare of any elaborate melody or harmonic enrichment.

But realism for Zhdanov was not to be "objective," not a disinterested portrait of life or of working people. Instead it would of necessity be colored by optimism and idealistic thinking. In his 1934 speech he gave these guidelines for the new concept of realism:

> In the first place, it means knowing life so as to be able to depict it truthfully, in works of art, not to depict it in a dead, scholastic way, not simply as "objective reality," but to depict reality in its revolutionary development. In addition to this, the truthfulness and historical concreteness of the artistic portrayal should be combined with the ideological remolding and education of the toiling people in the spirit of socialism. This method in *belles lettres* and literary criticism is what we call the method of socialist realism.[3]

He cautioned writers to avoid subjects that deal with "non-existent life and non-existent heroes" or "a world of utopian dreams." Artists should instead "actively help to remold the mentality of people in the spirit of socialism."

The implications of these statements for music were clear enough. Composers would be urged to concentrate on programmatic or texted works glorifying the Revolution and the worker. Their music would have to be geared to the understanding and enjoyment of the masses. The admonition against utopianism and "non-existent life" could only refer to music that was advanced beyond the understanding of the present day—music, in other words, that deviated from the norm in harmony, rhythm, tonality, and form.

Music of this latter sort was dismissed as **formalism.** The term itself is nebulous, although it suggests a work in which abstract musical elements outweigh programmatic content. But, practically speaking, it was used as a catchall condemnation for any-thing in music—atonality, emancipated dissonance, rhythmic dislocation, disturbing or erotic subject matter—that was difficult for or unsettling to the average listener.

Although Prokofiev was ready to compose "great works" that glorified the Soviet Union and the ideals of the Revolution, he saw the dangers inherent in bureaucrats trying to distinguish between realism and formalism. Shortly after Zhdanov's speech, an interview with Prokofiev was published in the Moscow newspaper *Izvestia*, and here the composer warned against banality in the guise of realism:

> The danger of becoming provincial is unfortunately a very real one for modern Soviet composers. It is not so easy to find the right idiom for this music. To begin with it must be melodious; moreover the melody must be simple and comprehensible, without being repetitive or trivial. . . . The same applies to the technique and the idiom: it must be clear and simple, but not banal. We must seek a new simplicity.[4]

Prokofiev's call for a "new simplicity" touched on an issue not limited to Soviet Russia. It echoed throughout the entire world of music during the 1920s and 1930s. The Soviets' demand for realism, in other words, was a symptom of a broad move-ment in the arts of the time, not a cause of that movement. Given his years of travel, Prokofiev was uniquely placed to understand the direction that music had taken following World War I, especially among the younger composers in France and in the works of Igor Stravinsky. Prokofiev's own music generally followed the same course as these contemporaries, moving toward a relative simplicity and melodious-ness mixed with certain modernistic thinking in harmony and tonality. By person-ality, Prokofiev was not inclined to be a follower of trends, and he was very unmoved by much of the neoclassical music that he had heard in Paris in the 1920s. His rela-tionship to neoclassicism would always be ambiguous.

In an *Autobiography* written in 1941, Prokofiev assessed his own musical style and found in it four principal characteristics: a classical trait represented by the use of classical forms, a modern element seen mainly in an enriched harmonic language, motoric rhythms, and a pronounced lyricism. While his list of characteristics pro-vides an excellent general definition of neoclassicism, Prokofiev was not in favor of any "back to . . ." return to eighteenth-century composers or styles. He regretted his own youthful foray into music of this type—the "Classical" Symphony (Symphony No. 1, 1917)—and he found the retrospectivist outlook to be especially dismaying in recent works by Stravinsky. In a letter to Boris Asafiev in 1925, Prokofiev de-scribed Stravinsky's Concerto for Piano and Wind Instruments as "monkey see, monkey do":

> Stravinsky's concerto is a continuation of the line he adopted in the finale of his Octet—that is, a stylization in imitation of Bach—which I don't approve of, because even though I love Bach and think it's not a bad idea to compose according to his principles, it's not a good idea to produce a stylized version of his style. . . . Unfortu-nately, Stravinsky thinks otherwise; he doesn't see this as a case of "monkey see, mon-key do," and now he's written a piano sonata in the same style. He even thinks this will create a new era.[5]

Piano Sonata No. 7

Prokofiev's attempt to juggle realism, formalism, and the pitfalls of neoclassicism is especially evident in his Seventh Piano Sonata (1939–1942). All four of the traits that the composer described as characteristic of his oeuvre are plainly discernible in it. Classicism is found in the choice of genre and the work's overall form; lyricism is evident in the slow movement, and motoric rhythms and modernistic harmonies are plain to hear in its first and third movements.

The sonata is dominated by its third movement, an impetuous finale. The musical idiom owes much to Stravinsky's brand of neoclassicism, although it avoids the outright "back to Bach" allusions that Prokofiev found objectionable in Stravinsky's contemporaneous music. Still, it is Stravinskian in its driving ostinatos and motoric eighth-note pulse, which is draped over an asymmetrical $\frac{7}{8}$ meter (Ex. 74-1). As in Stravinsky's works of the 1920s and 1930s, Prokofiev mixes together octatonic, diatonic, and freely chromatic pitch fields, and the movement has a cool, witty tone, not unlike Stravinsky's Octet. Also typical of neoclassicism is a parody of jazz, represented at the beginning by the blue note C♯ in the left hand (equivalent to the lowered-third scale degree in the implied B♭ major tonality). Prokofiev, like Stravinsky, was a self-declared fan of American jazz, which he had many opportunities to hear on his American tours.

EXAMPLE 74-1

The Seventh Sonata is the product of a great composer at work in the musical culture and taste of his day, oblivious to bureaucrats' attempts to limit his imagination with labels such as realism and formalism. Certainly the finale of the Sonata is formalistic by the Soviets' definition, but the work was still greeted with great enthusiasm on its first hearing in Moscow in January 1943 at the height of World War II—as functionaries like Zhdanov were apparently too involved with the war to notice.

Still, some explanation for its modern resources had to be given. After Prokofiev's death, its first interpreter—the virtuoso pianist **Sviatoslav Richter** (1915–1997)—offered up an interpretation of the Seventh Sonata that was geared to please the authorities. Despite appearances, Richter claimed, the work is actually a realist composition whose modernism is only an expression of wartime anxiety. Richter writes:

> The sonata immediately throws one into the anxious situation of the world losing its equilibrium. Anxiety and uncertainty reign. Man is witnessing the riot of the violent forces of death and destruction. However what he had lived by before did not cease to exist for him. He feels, loves. Now the full range of his emotions bursts forth. Together with everyone and everything he protests and poignantly shares the common grief. The impetuous, advancing race, full of the will for victory, sweeps away everything in its path. It gains its strength in struggle and develops into a gigantic life-affirming force.[6]

The duplicity apparent in Richter's description became ever more widespread among Russian artists in their effort to cope with a meddlesome government.

LISTENING CUE

SERGEI PROKOFIEV
Piano Sonata No. 7 (1939–1942)
Third movement, *Precipitato*

CD 12/7
Anthology, No. 190

Peter and the Wolf

One of Prokofiev's most beloved and ingenious works is **Peter and the Wolf,** a "symphonic tale" for narrator and orchestra, which the composer wrote in 1936 for the Children's Musical Theater in Moscow. The story, written by Prokofiev himself, is narrated against a musical background. Peter, our youthful hero, ventures out into the meadow and greets the bird and duck, ignoring Grandfather's warnings about the wolf. A prowling cat is outsmarted by a clever bird. Just after Peter returns home at the insistence of Grandfather, the wolf comes out of the forest and swallows up the duck in one gulp. Peter sees this and intrepidly snares the wolf's tail in a noose and hoists him up. Hunters arrive and triumphantly carry the wolf off to the zoo.

Prokofiev's music has a memorable simplicity and warmth, and it demonstrates for children and adults alike the capacity of music to illustrate specific ideas. Each of the characters in the story has its own identifying motive, and these are played on instruments that precisely fit the character's qualities. Peter's motive is played primarily by the strings, in a happy and self-confident manner.

Bridgeman Art Library

❧ FIGURE 74-1

Reg Cartwright's painting shows Peter, the intrepid hero, with the other characters in Prokofiev's timeless musical fable.

EXAMPLE A

The bird is represented by the flute, whose music is filled with a rhythmic effervescence.

EXAMPLE B

The duck's instrument is the oboe, played with a waddling rhythm in the low register where its tone can be more than a bit duck-like.

EXAMPLE C

The cat's motive is taken by the clarinet in an even rhythm that suggests menace beneath a nonchalant exterior.

EXAMPLE D

(continued on next page)

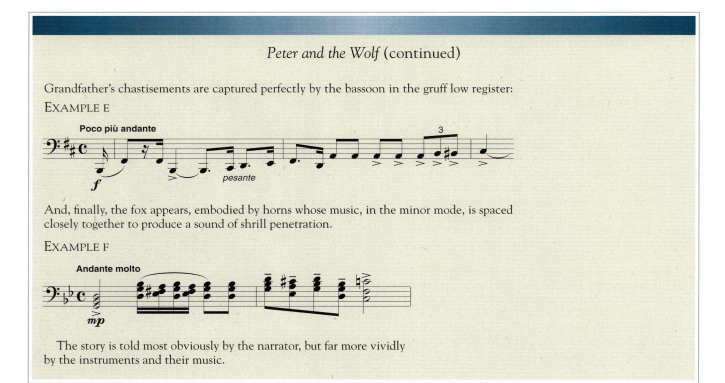

Peter and the Wolf (continued)

Grandfather's chastisements are captured perfectly by the bassoon in the gruff low register:

EXAMPLE E

And, finally, the fox appears, embodied by horns whose music, in the minor mode, is spaced closely together to produce a sound of shrill penetration.

EXAMPLE F

The story is told most obviously by the narrator, but far more vividly by the instruments and their music.

DMITRI SHOSTAKOVICH

The fifteen years in age that separate Dmitri Shostakovich (1906–1975; Fig. 74-2) from Prokofiev ensured that their musical careers would develop differently. Shostakovich was only eleven years old at the time of the Revolution. When he graduated in 1925 from the Conservatory in his home city of Leningrad, he had become a loyal citizen and apparently an idealistic believer in the official objectives of the Soviet state. Like many younger musicians who had remained in Russia, he was optimistic about prospects for its future musical culture. The Soviet economy had been stabilized by Lenin's New Economic Policy, and the arts were flourishing despite ideological debates.

The German conductor Bruno Walter came to Leningrad in 1926, and he too sensed an optimism about the future: "The Leningrad Philharmonic Orchestra, the members of the Opera, and the audiences," he wrote, "made me joyfully aware of that spirit of enthusiasm which imparts to Russia's musical life its pulsating force."[7]

EARLY WORKS AND SUCCESSES

During his 1926 visit, Walter met Shostakovich and heard his Symphony No. 1, written at the age of nineteen while the composer was still a student. Walter performed the work with the Berlin Philharmonic Orchestra, and it was then taken up by orchestras elsewhere in the West and

FIGURE 74-2

The brilliant Soviet composer Dmitri Shostakovich was born in St. Petersburg in 1906, and died in Moscow in 1975.

CORBIS

Shostakovich on Music and Ideology

In this article-interview in *The New York Times* in 1931, Dmitri Shostakovich contends that all music contains a political and social message:

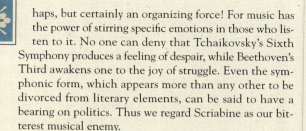

> There can be no music without an ideology. The old composers, whether they knew it or not, were upholding a political theory. Most of them, of course, were bolstering the rule of the upper classes. Only Beethoven was a forerunner of the revolutionary movement. If you read his letters, you will see how often he wrote to his friends that he wished to give new ideas to the public and rouse it to revolt against its masters.
>
> On the other hand, Wagner's biographies show that he began his career as a radical and ended as a reactionary. His monarchistic patriotism had a bad effect upon his mind. Perhaps it is a personal prejudice, but I do not consider Wagner a great composer. It is true he is played rather frequently in Russia today; but we hear him in the same spirit as we go to a museum to study the forms of the old régime. We can learn certain technical lessons from him, but we do not accept him.
>
> We, as revolutionists, have a different conception of music. Lenin himself said that "music is a means of unifying broad masses of people." Not a leader of masses, per-
>
> haps, but certainly an organizing force! For music has the power of stirring specific emotions in those who listen to it. No one can deny that Tchaikovsky's Sixth Symphony produces a feeling of despair, while Beethoven's Third awakens one to the joy of struggle. Even the symphonic form, which appears more than any other to be divorced from literary elements, can be said to have a bearing on politics. Thus we regard Scriabine as our bitterest musical enemy.
>
> Why? Because Scriabine's music tends to an unhealthy eroticism. Also to mysticism and passivity and escape from the realities of life.
>
> Not that the Soviets are always joyous, or supposed to be. But good music lifts and heartens and lightens people for work and effort. It may be tragic but it must be strong. It is no longer an end in itself, but a vital weapon in the struggle. Because of this, Soviet music will probably develop along different lines from any the world has known. There must be a change! After all, we have entered a new epoch and history has proved that every age creates its own language. Precisely what form this development in music will take I cannot say, any more than I can say what the idioms of speech will be fifty years from now. The notes will be same![8]

held up as evidence that music of originality could still come from Russia. Shostakovich was soon recognized as Russia's leading young composer and, like Prokofiev somewhat later, he became a spokesperson for socialist realism in music. "There can be no music without an ideology," he said in an article in *The New York Times* in 1931 (see Box). "Even the symphonic form, which appears more than any other to be divorced from literary elements, can be said to have a bearing on politics."[9]

Symphonic forms were much on Shostakovich's mind in their relation to Soviet artistic policy. Like many Russian composers in the early twentieth century, Shostakovich concentrated on the genre of the symphony. He wrote fifteen symphonies in all, and in them he continues the conception of the genre as it was inherited from the late romantic works of Gustav Mahler. Progressive composers elsewhere in the world had generally abandoned the symphony after the turn of the century, although they returned to it in the 1920s under the aegis of neoclassicism. Like Mahler, Shostakovich frequently uses chorus and solo voices in his symphonies, and most have strongly implied programs.

His most often performed symphony is No. 5 (1937), which uses the traditional classical form and has no explicit program despite the presence of many musical figures—marches, fanfares, bombastic orchestration, surging rhythms—that could plausibly support a programmatic interpretation. Shostakovich encouraged such thinking. Concerning the Fifth Symphony, he wrote: "The central idea of the work is man, with all his sufferings. The finale of the symphony resolves the tragic, tense elements of the first movements on a joyful, optimistic level."[10]

In addition to his fifteen symphonies, Shostakovich's huge oeuvre includes fifteen string quartets, sonatas, concertos, songs, choral music, and over thirty film scores. In his earlier years he had shown an affinity for theatric composition. Between 1928 and 1935 he wrote a series of operas and ballets of which the opera *Lady Macbeth of the Mtsensk District* (1932) proved to be hugely successful both in Russia and abroad. Its text has the realism characteristic of nineteenth-century Russian literature, but little of the revolutionary optimism that Zhdanov had demanded. Katerina, the wife of a merchant, is involved in an affair with a worker. She murders her husband and subsequently her lover, whereupon she commits suicide. Despite the grimness of the libretto, Shostakovich's music is full of parody, especially in the sex scenes, which were daringly explicit for Soviet Russia of the time.

❋ LATER WORKS AND CONTROVERSIES

Following the great success of *Lady Macbeth*, Shostakovich was emboldened to speak out on more sensitive issues, such as the possibility that socialist realism could have a negative effect on artistic creativity. In an article in the newspaper *Izvestia* in 1935, he joined with Prokofiev to warn that realism could easily lapse into banality:

> To brand any work as formalistic on the grounds that its language is complex and perhaps not immediately comprehensible is unacceptably frivolous. Now my main goal is to find my own simple and expressive musical language. Sometimes the aspiration for a simple language is understood rather superficially. Often "simplicity" merges into epigonism [i.e., sterile imitation]. But to speak simply does not mean to speak as people did 50 or 100 years ago. This is a trap into which many modern composers fall, afraid of being accused of formalism. Both formalism and epigonism are harmful to Soviet music.[11]

It may have been such outspoken and independent pronouncements as this that contributed only a few months later to Shostakovich's being taken down a peg. In January 1936 his opera *Lady Macbeth* was the subject of an article, "Chaos Instead of Music," in the Communist Party newspaper *Pravda*. The essay was anonymous, which suggested that it came from the highest Soviet authorities, perhaps even from Stalin, who was reportedly indignant when he had seen the opera in Moscow only days before. In the article, Shostakovich's opera is denounced as "a confused stream of sound," a "distortion" that was filled with "fidgety, screaming, neurotic music." The writer continues:

> The composer has clearly not made it his business to heed what the Soviet public looks for in music and expects of it. As if by design, he has encoded his music and jumbled up all the sounds in such a way that it can only appeal to aesthetes and formalists who have lost all touch with good taste. He has ignored the determination of Soviet culture to banish crassness and crudeness from every corner of Soviet daily life.[12]

"This is a meaningless game," the writer says menacingly, "that may well come to a very bad end." The effect of this attack was immediate and profound, for Shostakovich and for all Russian composers. The year 1936 was the beginning of Stalin's murderous purge of citizens from all walks of life, many of whom were artists and several of whom were personal acquaintances of the composer. Shostakovich would have to watch his step and move even more decisively toward a "simple and expressive musical language." His next major work, the Symphony No. 5, seemed to satisfy his critics and his career was again on track, although the specter of threats from bureaucrats and rivals periodically resurfaced.

Following Stalin's death in 1953, a greater measure of artistic freedom was granted to Soviet composers, and Shostakovich again became an artistic ambassador for the Soviet system. In 1979, some four years after the composer's death, a book called *Testimony*, purporting to contain Shostakovich's memoirs, was published in the United States.[13] Here Shostakovich presents himself as an embittered dissident with no sympathy for Soviet ideology, a composer who communicated his disdain for the Soviet regime through subtle and ironic hints in his music. His complicity with the Soviets, he says, was only a pretense, "a survival tactic that permits you to maintain a minimal decency." The Russian authorities and many Shostakovich specialists dispute the authenticity of these memoirs.

Piano Concerto No. 1

Shostakovich's emphasis on the orchestral medium produced not only fifteen symphonies but also pairs of concertos for piano, violin, and cello. The earliest of these is his Piano Concerto No. 1 (1933), which he wrote "to fill a gap in Soviet instrumental music, which lacks full-scale concerto-type works." The genre of the concerto, like the symphony, was generally shunned by progressive composers following the turn of the century, although it returned to favor in the 1920s, the period of neoclassicism.

The First Concerto plainly shows the influence of this movement. It was composed on the heels of Ravel's Piano Concerto and Prokofiev's Fifth Piano Concerto—both squarely in the vein of Stravinskian neoclassicism. Like Ravel's Concerto, Shostakovich's is high-spirited and full of parody, as much "music about music" as are Stravinsky's neoclassical works from the 1920s (see Chapter 68).

Shostakovich was very enthusiastic about Stravinsky's music and his new aesthetics of the 1920s: "I certainly do not believe that he should be imitated in every respect," Shostakovich wrote, "but he is very interesting and original in that he has opened up new paths in modern music. This is why I single him out among contemporary West European composers." In his 1931 interview for *The New York Times* (see Box) he parrots Stravinsky's well-known dismissal of the music of Wagner and Scriabin, and also Stravinsky's contention that music had in the 1920s entered a new epoch. But Shostakovich, as always, attributed the playful quality of his Concerto not to Stravinsky's "new paths" but to the special role of the Soviet composer. "Our age, as I perceive it, is heroic, spirited and joyful. This is what I wanted to convey in my concerto."[14]

The work has a classical three-movement form, although a prelude to the finale is shown in the score as a separate movement, bringing the total to four. Typical of the Classical style, the work is brief and the orchestra small, calling only for strings and a solo trumpet that banters off and on with the piano.

The first movement is cast into a free sonata form whose main and second themes (both introduced by the piano) are shown in Example 74-2. The movement has many comic touches. References to keys are spoofed, as tonalities careen and collide. In several passages the cellist enters with his own themes, as though mistakenly thinking that it is his concerto. By the end all are exhausted by the madcap antics, and the music seems to deflate into the low register, where it dies.

EXAMPLE 74-2

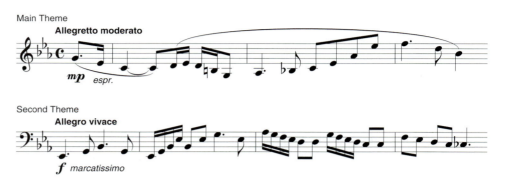

In the music of Shostakovich we see the neoclassical element of parody carried over into outright satire and humor. "I want to fight for the right of laughter to be accepted in so-called serious music," Shostakovich demanded.

 LISTENING CUE

DMITRI SHOSTAKOVICH   CD 12/8
Piano Concerto No. 1 (1933)   Anthology, No. 191
First movement, *Allegro moderato*

SUMMARY

In the early post-revolutionary period (1917–1920), many of Russia's leading musicians emigrated to the West. These include Sergei Prokofiev, who lived in the United States, France, and Germany from 1918 to 1932, during which time he worked as both a concert pianist and composer. Between 1932 and 1936 he gradually strengthened his ties with Soviet Russia and embraced Soviet ideology concerning the role of music, which demanded "socialist realism" rather than "formalism." The former quality is found in works that are understandable by the average listener and positive in outlook; the latter in abstract or difficult works.

The objective of realism in music conforms in general to the musical style of neoclassicism, which was most closely associated with works by Stravinsky from the 1920s and 1930s and influential on Russia's leading composers. Prokofiev did not accept the "back to Bach" element of Stravinsky's music of the time, although he agreed with Stravinsky concerning the need for a return to clarity and simplicity in music, an eclectic harmonic style that mixed diatonicism with alternative pitch resources, and an emphasis on lyrical melody.

Dmitri Shostakovich was the leading younger composer in Soviet Russia in the 1920s and 1930s, although his music was harshly criticized by Soviet authorities for its formalism. Shostakovich, like Prokofiev, attempted to conform to bureaucratic wishes by finding a simple and expressive style rooted in neoclassicism. Shostakovich emphasized parody and satire in his music.

Anatoli Lunacharsky
Andrei Zhdanov

socialist realism
formalism

Sviatoslav Richter
Peter and the Wolf

Chapter

75

Self-Reliance in American Music: Ives, Seeger, Nancarrow

In his landmark 1841 essay "Self-Reliance," **Ralph Waldo Emerson** appeals to his American readers for individualism and independent thinking. "Imitation is suicide," he declares. "Whoso would be a man, must be a nonconformist." Emerson then elaborates: "Insist on yourself; never imitate. Your own gift you can present every moment with the cumulative force of a whole life's cultivation; but of the adopted talent of another you have only an extemporaneous half possession."[1]

Emerson's words have an uncanny relevance to the history of American music, which has been driven by opposing instincts, on the one hand for self-reliance and on the other for an "adopted talent," an imitation of European styles.

 ## MUSIC IN COLONIAL AMERICA

America's first important composer, **William Billings** (1746–1800), was a nonconformist. "I don't think myself confin'd to any Rules for Composition laid down by any that went before me," he proclaimed. "Neither should I think (were I to pretend to lay down Rules) that any who came after me were any ways obligated to adhere to them."[2]

Billings lived in Boston, taught himself music, and worked as a tanner. His compositions consist primarily of unaccompanied choral pieces used in church services and singing schools. Some are **fuguing tunes,** which contain a simple point of imitation usually inserted toward the end, and Billings also composed longer, multisectional pieces that he called "anthems." In addition to his rough-and-ready originality, Billings had a gift for creating a memorable tune. An example is in the rousing "Chester" (c1770; Ex. 75-1). Its words, written by Billings himself, capture the patriotic mood in the colonies just before the American Revolution. The tune appears in the tenor voice, surrounded by simple and direct harmonies.

EXAMPLE 75-1

mm. 1-8

(continued on next page)

and slav-'ry clank___ her gall - ing chains;

✦ NINETEENTH-CENTURY DEVELOPMENTS

In the nineteenth century, a modern musical culture was gradually created in the United States. Its centerpiece was (and continues to be) the symphony orchestra. In New York a permanent orchestra—forerunner of the New York Philharmonic—was founded in 1842. The Boston Symphony Orchestra followed in 1881, and in 1900 occupied its acoustically splendid Symphony Hall (Fig. 75-1). The Chicago Orchestra was formed in 1891, and the Philadelphia Orchestra in 1900. The Philadelphians were brought to great prominence by the English-born conductor **Leopold Stokowski** (1882–1977), who daringly programmed the works of modern composers.

Other types of music also flourished in nineteenth-century America. Pianos appeared in ever-greater numbers in the homes of middle-class families, with excellent instruments provided by American makers including Jonas Chickering, William Knabe, and Henry Steinway. Opera was slower to develop, but flourished in New Orleans and later in New York. The **Metropolitan Opera** was founded in New York in 1883. Alongside the culture for artistic music in nineteenth-century America was an unusually vigorous and diverse popular music, which led early in the twentieth century to the birth of jazz (see Chapter 72). Domestic music-making created a demand for both popular and serious piano music and songs, which was met by a thriving sheet music trade.

Just as William Billings exemplifies the beginnings of self-reliance in American music, **Edward MacDowell** (1860–1908) typifies the adopted talent, the composer who aspired primarily to elevate American musical culture to the level of contemporary European music. MacDowell was born in New York and spent the years from 1876 to 1888 living in Europe, primarily in Germany. There he gave piano concerts, taught, and composed in the style of modern German musicians. He then returned to America and resumed his career. In 1896 he was appointed the first professor of music at Columbia University. His home in Peterborough, New Hampshire, was left as an artists' retreat, the "MacDowell Colony," that still exists today. MacDowell's music includes two piano concertos, orchestral tone poems, songs and choruses, and a large number of compositions for piano, including four sonatas and collections of character pieces.

The "Song" from *Sea Pieces*, Op. 55 (1898), for piano, shows MacDowell's skillful adoption of an existing style. *Sea Pieces* is a collection of eight character piano pieces squarely in the idiom of similar works by Romantic-era composers such as Mendelssohn and Liszt. Each piece depicts an aspect of the sea as seen through the eyes of an imaginary traveler. MacDowell adds poetic lines to

✦ FIGURE 75-1

Boston's Symphony Hall—home of the Boston Symphony Orchestra—was completed in 1900. The building is a symbol of the great importance of orchestras to American musical culture.

CORBIS

the beginning of the pieces to reinforce the image that the music is intended to convey. The "Song" is introduced by these verses:

> A merry song, a chorus brave,
> And yet a sigh regret
> For roses sweet, in woodland lanes—
> Ah, love can ne'er forget!

Each of these thoughts is represented by a theme. The first one—"a merry song, a chorus brave"—imitates a sea **shanty,** a rousing type of work song that MacDowell no doubt encountered among sailors during his own ocean travels. Its beginning is shown in Example 75-2. Although repetitive and more than a bit sentimental, the *Sea Pieces* have a great charm and melodic imagination.

EXAMPLE 75-2

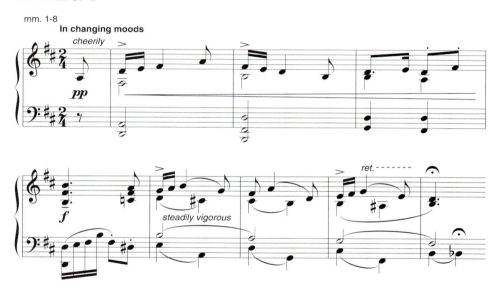

✿ CHARLES IVES

The Emersonian ideal of self-reliance bloomed in American music in the works of Charles E. Ives (1874–1954). He was born in Danbury, Connecticut, the son of a musician. In his youth Ives learned piano and organ and received a good knowledge of European music and its rules from his father, a free-thinking musician who was entirely open to musical experiments. "Father was not against a reasonable amount of 'boy's fooling,'" Ives wrote, "if it were done with some sense behind it (maybe not very much or too good a sense, but something more than just thoughtless fooling)—as playing left-hand accompaniment in one key and tune in right hand in another. . . . He made us stick to the end, and not stop when it got hard."[3]

As a youngster Ives began to compose in a vein that was alternately homespun, humorous, and experimental. He wrote more polished and conventional works during his undergraduate days at Yale University, where he studied composition with **Horatio Parker** (1863–1919), a German-trained composer and teacher who had little sympathy for Ives's experiments.

An especially skillful work that Ives wrote for Parker is the song "Feldeinsamkeit" ("Alone in the Fields," 1897). Parker often asked his students to compose songs to texts that had already been used by the great nineteenth-century musicians, and here Ives takes up a German poem by Hermann Allmers that had been famously set to music by Johannes Brahms (see Chapter 58.)

Ives's treatment of the poem shows a thorough knowledge of the contemporary progressive style of German music, associated more with a Richard Strauss or Hugo Wolf than with Brahms. In the middle section of the song's **ABA** form, where the poetic voice speaks of sailing disembodied through space, Ives's harmony detaches itself from the principal key and moves tonally far afield, finally returning to earth with the reprise of the opening stanza. In his autobiographical *Memos,* Ives recalled Parker playing "Feldeinsamkeit" in the presence of the composer George Chadwick:

> When Chadwick came in Parker was objecting to the too many keys in the middle. . . . C. said, "The melodic line has a natural continuity—it flows . . . as only good songs do. And it's different from Brahms, as in the piano part and the harmony it takes a more difficult and almost opposite aspect to Brahms, for the active tranquility of the outdoor beauty of nature is harder to express than just quietude. In its way it's almost as good as Brahms."[4]

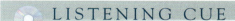

LISTENING CUE

CHARLES IVES   CD 12/9
"Feldeinsamkeit" (1897)   Anthology, No. 192

Following graduation, Ives moved to New York and entered the insurance business, first as an actuary, then as the head of his own agency. He and his partner, Julian Myrick, proved immensely successful, in large part due to Ives's systematic ideas for insurance marketing. Ives is now recognized as a leading figure in the creation of the modern American insurance industry, and he brought the same passion to his business life as he did to his music, seeing many connections between the two worlds. He composed in his spare time and dispensed with the European romantic style demanded by Parker to return to the experimental ideas of his youth, which he enriched with new and original aesthetic intentions. His works had virtually no public performances.

Ives composed little after suffering a heart attack in 1918, following which he turned his attention to making his music known. In 1920, at his own expense, he published his Piano Sonata No. 2 (subtitled *Concord, Mass., 1840–60*) and an explanatory pamphlet titled *Essays Before a Sonata.* Two years later he published a collection of *114 Songs.* Gradually, performances of his music increased, and its scope and originality became better known. In 1939 the "Concord" Piano Sonata was hailed in the *New York Herald-Tribune* as a "masterpiece," and in 1947 Ives won a Pulitzer Prize for his Symphony No. 3.

✱ AESTHETICS

Much about Ives's music resembles traditional European compositions of the late nineteenth and early twentieth century. He composed in traditional genres, and, like the musician of the Romantic era, he made his instrumental music expressive through familiar programmatic strategies such as melodic quotations and free forms. His penchant for novel materials—dissonant chords, polyrhythms, microtones, among others—is not so unusual for this period. But Ives's musical aesthetic was largely his own. Inspired by reading Emerson and recalling his father's free-thinking about music, he developed his own philosophy, which guided him in the creation of a body of compositions that was essentially unlike anything that had come before.

In the Epilogue to *Essays Before a Sonata,* Ives describes what he was aiming for in his music. He proposes that any musical work has two sides: one is its "manner" (its outer aspect, the form in which it is presented), and the other its "substance" (its spiritual or poetic content). "Substance has something to do with character," he writes. "Manner has nothing to do with it. The 'substance' of a tune comes from somewhere near the soul, and the 'manner' comes from— God knows where."[5] Manner is the lesser quality since it relies only on ephemera; substance is higher since it expresses the real world—filled with everyday concerns in addition to higher moral and spiritual insights. Ives insisted that the substance of art was as much the property of the common man as it was the specialist. He foresaw a future "when every man while digging his potatoes will breathe his own Epics, his own Symphonies."[6]

Although other composers have written about this two-sidedness of music— Schoenberg called the distinction "style" versus "idea"—Ives is unusual in that he sees the two as opposites. The more apparent the manner in a composition, Ives says, the less its substance. This reciprocity, he thought, had caused a crisis in late Romantic music. Composers such as Tchaikovsky and Richard Strauss, Ives says, overly emphasize manner in their striving for beauty and perfection of form. For this reason their compositions lose touch with the real world and are diminished in substance. A composer like Debussy, Ives writes, could have improved his music "if he had hoed corn or sold newspapers for a living, for in this way he might have gained a deeper vitality and truer theme to sing at night and of a Sunday."[7] This imbalance in manner and substance was the reason that Ives could not continue to write such sonorous music as "Feldeinsamkeit." In purely musical terms, he saw the truth in Emerson's warning about imitation.

✿ IVES'S MUSIC: VOCAL WORKS

Ives's music exhibits no single style. Some compositions use traditional musical materials, others are dissonant, atonal, microtonal, or otherwise experimental. Some appear to be written in an improvisatory stream of consciousness, while others are carefully planned out to produce unified structures. A recurrent feature of his music is the quotation of tunes that he recalled from his Connecticut childhood.

Ives's vocal works consist of more than one hundred fifty songs plus music for chorus, including psalm settings, *Three Harvest Home Chorales,* and *The Celestial Country* for chorus, orchestra, and organ. In these pieces Ives uses several strategies for bringing his music into contact with the real world and giving it substance. One was to make it depict the musical memories of his own past—thus the quotations of tunes and other evocations of the musical world of his boyhood. At the same time he saw the need for his music to rise above the everyday, to achieve a more timeless level that was worthy of art, while still being rooted in the mundanities of the real world. Just as Emerson believed that universal truth came to the individual through a flash of intuition, Ives wanted to find in the everyday experience some momentary insight that revealed a higher meaning. He then searched for an appropriate musical language to depict the special within the commonplace.

The dichotomy that underlay Ives's outlook on art is apparent in one of his most charming songs, "Charlie Rutlage" (c1920). This is a setting of a ballad by the Montana cowboy and writer, D.J. O'Malley. It tells the supposedly true story of a fellow cowboy, Charlie Rutlage, who was killed in an accident while herding cattle. The image of a common man about his daily work suddenly coming face to face with his destiny was just what Ives was looking for in a musical text, and his setting of the scene finds a musical equivalent of its juxtaposition of opposites.

The work begins with a portrait of Charlie's everyday world, expressed in a quirky folk-like music with a pentatonic melody and an accompaniment that constantly changes key. In the middle part, where Charlie's number is up, Ives looks for a non-conventional style. The vocalist speaks rather than sings, while the pianist impersonates Charlie, crying out "Whoopee ti yi yo, git along little doggies." The music rises to a frenzy, and at the point where Charlie is killed, the pianist uses the fists to pound out **tone clusters** (dissonant groups of adjacent notes; Ex. 75-3). Following this spiritual flash, Charlie goes to heaven to be reunited with his kinfolk and the music returns to the everyday world of the opening.

EXAMPLE 75-3

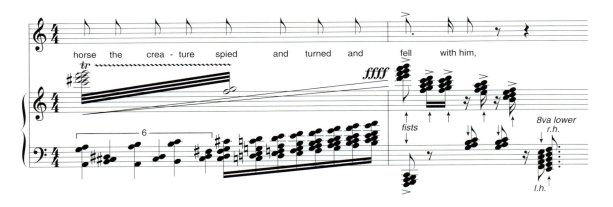

IVES'S INSTRUMENTAL MUSIC: THE UNANSWERED QUESTION

Ives composed four symphonies and numerous tone poems, four violin sonatas and two string quartets, two piano sonatas and a variety of character pieces for piano. Virtually all of his mature instrumental music is programmatic. It deals with topics that include recollections of his boyhood, portraits of people he admired, locations in New England, Americana, and metaphysical speculations. His tone poem *The Unanswered Question* (1906, later revised) is an example of the last. According to a Foreword in the score, the music portrays the universe. We repeatedly hear a question raised concerning the meaning of existence, and mankind's attempts to answer the question are futile, leading only to frustration.

To express this idea Ives uses a spatial device also exploited by late Romantic composers. He instructs the strings to sit offstage, or at least separated from the other instruments. Ives also finds another ingeniously effective way to communicate the idea of the work, one that had not been used by any of his contemporaries. Each of the three elements in the program—the silent universe, the question of existence, and mankind's futile answers—is represented by a distinguishable stratum of music, and these are put together without strict coordination in time. The universe—or as Ives calls it "The Silences of the Druids, Who Know, See, and Hear Nothing"—is represented by soothing and featureless music in the strings. They play diatonically, form consonant chords, and dispense with any strong sense of beat or meter. The "Perennial Question of Existence" is raised repeatedly by a short figure in the solo trumpet (Ex. 75-4). Its motive is chromatic in content and its notes do not duplicate tones of the string chords. Human beings are represented by four flutes (Ives allows for them to be replaced by other woodwinds). After every question they bicker furiously, each time with great animation and stridency. They can never answer the trumpet's question of existence.

EXAMPLE 75-4

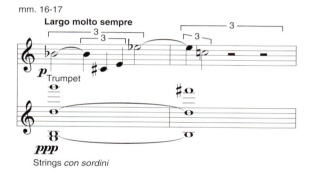

mm. 16-17

Largo molto sempre

p Trumpet

ppp

Strings *con sordini*

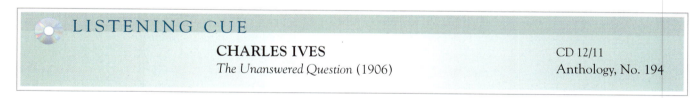

LISTENING CUE

CHARLES IVES

The Unanswered Question (1906)

CD 12/11

Anthology, No. 194

The works of Charles Ives created a new way of thinking about music for composers in the United States. The American composer, Ives seemed to say, need not join in the mainstream of music established by European classical composers. American musicians were instead free to move in new directions, to mix styles, and even to rethink the very laws that composers on the other side of the Atlantic had long accepted.

LATER FIGURES: RUTH CRAWFORD SEEGER AND CONLON NANCARROW

Ives's spirit of self-reliance resurfaced in American music later in the twentieth century. It is plain to hear in the works of **Harry Partch** (1901–1974). Partch had little use for traditional classical music, which he condemned as "abstract," something of interest only to a handful of snobs. What he wanted instead was "corporeal" music:

> The approved Abstraction is a full musical fare for only a small percentage of our people, and the resulting hunger is satisfied by anything that breaks the formal barriers in the direction of Corporeality—hillbilly, cowboy, and popular music, which, whatever its deficiencies, owes nothing to scholastic and academic Europeanisms.[8]

✹ FIGURE 75-2
Ruth Crawford, c1926. Ruth
Crawford (later Ruth Crawford
Seeger) was one of the most origi-
nal voices in American music in
the 1920s and 1930s.

Partch's disdain for "Europeanisms" led him to compose music for home-
made instruments, to which he added earthy recitations.

A more sophisticated expression of the Ivesian spirit is found in the
music of **Ruth Crawford Seeger** (1901–1953; Fig. 75-2). She was born in
Ohio, grew up in Florida, and studied piano in Chicago. There she began
to compose modernistic songs, piano pieces, and chamber music, and her
independence of mind attracted the attention of other free-thinking musicians. In 1929 she moved to New York and began to study with **Charles
Seeger** (1886–1979), whom she married in 1932. Seeger, a man of broad
interests in music, taught composition by a method that he called **dissonant counterpoint.** His idea was to liberate a student's thinking about
music while maintaining its craft. He asked his students to write exercises
in species counterpoint, but he reversed the roles of consonance and dissonance. In his exercises, dissonances became the basic, stable intervals and
consonances were restricted in rhythm and meter. They appeared only in
passing until "resolved" to a dissonance.

In a self-reliant fashion, the Seegers looked for a musical style that was
different from the more established American musical idioms of their day,
such as folklorism and neoclassicism, for which they had no affinity. They
were attracted to the serial music of Arnold Schoenberg, although as always they insisted on finding their own way, independent of the Europeans.

Ruth Crawford Seeger's String Quartet (1931) illustrates their objectives. The
work has four short movements of contrasting character. The third movement, *Andante*, is the most original of the four. The part for each instrument consists of long-
held tones, which create slowly changing and densely chromatic chords. These sound
masses come to life through constantly shifting and subtly overlapping crescendos
and decrescendos, which gather with a wave-like force until reaching a climax in
measure 75, whereupon the music quickly collapses and evaporates.

The movement has only a single melodic line, created as the instruments enter
or change their tones, one by one. The line is highly chromatic. For example, in
measures 1–17 it has the tones C♯-D-C-D♯-F-F♯-A-B♭-G♯-B, covering ten of the
twelve notes before the tone C is repeated on the downbeat of measure 18. The line
weaves its way upward through generally small intervals that avoid the outlining of
familiar chords. The Seegers called a melody of this type "dissonant," not only because it moved through primarily dissonant intervals but also because its diverse and
heterogeneous materials suggested a freedom from familiar patterns. The work's concentration into a single, free melodic line represented for the Seegers a progressive
step toward the future. Charles Seeger wrote:

> The proposition is here advanced that by decreasing the number of lines and increas-
> ing their freedom, two ends are served: first, the correction of the abuses of polyphony;
> second, the reinstatement of the single melodic line, whose return to preference in
> the not too distant future is at least a probability.[9]

An element of counterpoint enters the work, not by any multiple melodies but
by simultaneous strata, each formed from the instruments' distinctive patterns of
dynamics. "This movement," said Ruth Crawford Seeger, "is built on a counterpoint of dynamics. The crescendi and diminuendi should be exactly timed."[10] We
can see what she means by examining a passage near the opening of the movement
(mm. 16–20 in Ex. 75-5). Each instrument repeatedly plays small crescendos and
decrescendos, and within every section of the movement the crescendo in each instrument reaches its high point at a fixed location within the measure. In the sec-

tion shown in Example 75-5, for example, the viola reaches its loudest moment on the downbeat of each measure; Violin II on the second beat of every measure, Violin I on the last beat of the measure, and the cello on the next to last beat. At measure 28 the pattern changes, as though the "counterpoint" has shifted to a new key.

EXAMPLE 75-5

(The dotted tie indicates that the first tone of each new bow is not to be attacked.)

LISTENING CUE

RUTH CRAWFORD SEEGER
String Quartet (1931)
Third movement, *Andante*

CD 12/12
Anthology, No. 195

The Seegers' independent outlook is also found in the music of **Conlon Nancarrow** (1912–1997). He was born in Arkansas to a family that was, by his description, tone deaf. Growing up, he played jazz while he received a good musical education. In the 1930s he began to compose, mainly jazzy instrumental pieces.

In 1940 he emigrated permanently to Mexico City, although he found himself isolated there from a culture for new music. Out of necessity he began to compose for the medium of player piano (see Chapter 77), first sketching out a work and then painstakingly punching a paper roll to encode it in a performable medium. His player-piano pieces—all of them are called simply "studies"—are often jazz inspired, and they exploit the precision of his medium by using complex **polyrhythms,** often far more complex than could be realized by any human performer. His music was long unknown, except to a few musicians such as Elliott Carter who were sensitive to his rhythmic originality, and he went through long periods when he did not compose at all.

His breakthrough to international recognition came only in the 1970s, when recordings of his player-piano studies finally captured the attention of modern music enthusiasts. Except for a small number of pieces for piano and instrumental ensembles, his entire oeuvre is devoted to about fifty player-piano studies, which are remarkable for their imaginative use of the instrument and for their stunning rhythmic complication.

Study 3a for player piano (c1948) has the form of a boogie-woogie piano blues. **Boogie woogie** (or "honky tonk") is a style of blues piano playing developed in the 1920s by Meade "Lux" Lewis and other blues pianists. The most distinctive feature is a fast, driving tempo and a bass line that outlines the blues harmonies through a percussive ostinato. The idiom of boogie woogie lived on into the 1950s and 1960s in the music of **rhythm-and-blues,** which was the direct forerunner of rock 'n' roll.

Nancarrow's Study 3a consists of twenty-two blues choruses. The boogie-woogie bass line (Ex. 75-6) runs unchanged from beginning to end. Above it we hear variations upon several short riff-like motives, the first of which is shown in Example 75-7. As the series of variations continues, new lines are added, each with its own rhythmic and metric organization. The last seven choruses undergo a steady increase in contrapuntal complexity until finally eight separate streams of sound are present. Three of these lines create a mensuration canon. Recall from Chapter 18 that this type of canon is made from simultaneous lines that contain the same music performed at different rates of speed. In the lowest line of Nancarrow's canon (Ex. 75-8), each note of the blues bass has a duration equivalent to two sixteenths. Above it, the blues bass is stated more slowly, with three sixteenths per tone, and higher still it reappears with five sixteenths per note. Other contrapuntal lines add asymmetrical rhythmic ostinatos until the limits of complication are reached, whereupon the piece suddenly ends.

EXAMPLE 75-6

EXAMPLE 75-7

EXAMPLE 75-8

SUMMARY

Throughout its history, classical music in America has alternately imitated European models and broken free from them. The colonial hymn composer William Billings declared himself unrestrained by conventional rules, although nineteenth-century figures such as Edward MacDowell wrote music squarely in the manner of German romantic contemporaries.

Charles E. Ives began in the same imitative mold, but soon broke with the musical traditions of his time and professed a self-reliance in composing that he found in the writings of Ralph Waldo Emerson. He sometimes strove for substance in his music by making it reflect everyday life, into which a glimpse of a higher spirituality is usually granted. Many of his pieces quote tunes that he heard as a child. Other pieces express metaphysical ideas by a variety of innovative means, and Ives music alternates in style between conventional forms and experiments with dissonance, spatiality, and noncoordination among strata.

The music of Ruth Crawford Seeger continues the self-reliant spirit of Ives. In the *Andante* movement of her String Quartet she experiments with a new concept of counterpoint, made not from simultaneous melodies but from distinct patterns of crescendos and decrescendos in the four lines.

Virtually all of the music of Conlon Nancarrow is written for the medium of player piano. His player-piano studies are often jazzy, and they combine layers of sounds having differing metric organization. These create complex polyrhythmic and polymetric textures.

KEY TERMS

Ralph Waldo Emerson	shanty	dissonant counterpoint
William Billings	Horatio Parker	Conlon Nancarrow
fuguing tune	tone cluster	polyrhythm
Leopold Stokowski	Harry Partch	boogie woogie
Metropolitan Opera	Ruth Crawford Seeger	rhythm-and-blues
Edward MacDowell	Charles Seeger	

American Composers Return from Europe: Copland and Barber

In June 1921, Aaron Copland (1900–1990) set off for Europe to continue his musical education. In doing so he was following the pattern of the leading American composers of the later nineteenth century, including George Chadwick and Horatio Parker, mentioned in Chapter 75. But there was an important difference, since Copland was headed for Paris, whereas the earlier musicians had studied composition primarily in Germany. During World War I, Germany had been the enemy and France an ally, and, following the armistice, America's longstanding musical connection with Germany was largely transferred to France.

In the 1920s, Paris became a home away from home for an entire generation of American musicians, writers, and painters. The shift from Germany to Paris was not simply a matter of geography. For the musician it indicated a change of orientation from the German world of complex emotionality to France's up-to-date modernism.

COPLAND'S LIFE AND MUSIC

Copland studied during his first summer at a music school for American students in Fontainebleau, near Paris. Here he met the remarkable teacher **Nadia Boulanger** (1887–1979), who was the older sister of Lili Boulanger (see Chapter 63). Copland immediately recognized Nadia Boulanger's gift as a teacher. "Her sense of involvement in the whole subject of harmony made it more lively than I ever thought it could be," he wrote. "She created a kind of excitement about the subject, emphasizing how it was, after all, the fundamental basis of our music, when one really thought about it. I suspected that first day that I had found my composition teacher."[1] Copland followed "Mademoiselle," as Boulanger was known to her students, to Paris, where for the next three years he studied with her privately, forming a warm friendship.

In 1924 Copland returned to New York and took up the life of a professional composer. Predictably, his early works favored the orchestra, which was the strong suit of American musical culture of the day. He remained for his whole career an independent composer, although he periodically taught (for example, during the summers from 1940 to 1965 at the Berkshire Music Center in Tanglewood, Massachusetts) and wrote books and essays on music. In the 1940s he came repeatedly to Hollywood to write film scores, and in 1949 he received an Oscar for his score for the movie *The Heiress*. He was much involved in arts organizations that supported new American music, and in the 1950s he began the career of an orchestral conductor, specializing in his own music.

Copland's best known works include his three symphonies, ballet scores, orchestral character pieces including *Fanfare for the Common Man* (1942), *El Salón México* (1936), *An Outdoor Overture* (1938), and the patriotic narration *Lincoln Portrait* (1942). His smaller works include a Violin Sonata (1943), Nonet for strings (1960), Piano Sonata (1941), Piano Variations (1930), and the songs *Twelve Poems of Emily Dickinson* (1950). His folksong arrangements, *Old American Songs*, are often performed today.

THE FORMATION OF A STYLE

When Copland arrived in Paris in 1921, his own future language as a composer was still largely unformed. Different from many European musicians of the day, he came from an environment in the United States that did not by itself set him on any particular path. The Brooklyn of his childhood, he wrote, "had little or no connection with serious music. My discovery of music was rather like coming upon an unsuspected city—like discovering Paris or Rome if you had never before heard of their existence."[2] Understandably, Parisian musical culture of the 1920s exerted a powerful and lasting influence, especially through the modern works of Fauré, Debussy, Ravel, and, most of all, the new music of Igor Stravinsky, who then lived in France and was greatly admired by Nadia Boulanger.

But this European connection posed a danger in Copland's mind. He did not want to be a mere follower of his European contemporaries. He found this a failing in nineteenth-century American composers such as Chadwick and Parker: "They were essentially practitioners in the conventional idiom of their own day, and therefore had little to offer us of a younger generation."[3]

Copland instead wanted his music to bring together apparent opposites—Americanism at the same time as universality, and accessibility with the trappings of high art. "We wanted to find a music that would speak of universal things in a vernacular of American speech rhythms," Copland wrote. "We wanted to write music on a level that left popular music far behind—music with a largeness of utterance wholly representative of the country that Whitman had envisaged."[4]

Copland's mention of the poet **Walt Whitman** (1819–1892) was no accident. He was one of Copland's favorite writers, one whose legacy combined the same opposites that Copland wanted to bring to music. Whitman's poetry dealt with American themes but had an international appeal, and his principal subject is America's common men and women, whom he extolled as though the material of high art.

In the preface to his 1855 *Leaves of Grass*, Whitman elaborated on his artistic outlook: "The genius of the United States is not best or most in its executives or legislatures, nor in its ambassadors or authors or colleges or churches or parlors, nor even in its newspapers or inventors . . . but always most in the common people."[5] The role of the artist, Whitman continued, was to be the voice of the common man ("his spirit responds to his country's spirit"), and this could only succeed by adopting a plain and simple style: "The art of art, the glory of expression, and the sunshine of the light of letters," Whitman concluded, "is simplicity. Nothing is better than simplicity . . . nothing can make up for excess or for the lack of definiteness."[6]

These ideas had a powerful influence on Copland, and they reflect the distinctively American emphasis on individuality and self-reliance that we have already encountered in the writings of Ralph Waldo Emerson and the music of Charles Ives (see Chapter 75). Ives had grappled with the same fundamental question that concerned Copland: How can classical music have relevance to American society? Ives's answer was to create a naivist music celebrating everyday experience, but Copland could not accept this outlook. Despite his appreciation for Ives's imagination, Copland found Ives's music lacking in structure, polish, and craft—all things that Ives had dismissed as worthless "manner." Copland would not accept the idea that manner was something insignificant in music, and it was exactly what he found missing in Ives. "At its worst his music is amorphous, disheveled, haphazard—like the music of a man who is incapable of organizing his many different thoughts," wrote Copland about Ives.[7]

Organization—what Copland found so lacking in Ives's music—was the quality that Boulanger most prized in a work. She called this formal element *"la grande ligne"* ("the long line"), and Copland interpreted it to mean continuity and "flow:"

> Every good piece of music must give us a sense of flow—a sense of continuity from first note to last. Every elementary music student knows the principle, but to put it into practice has challenged the greatest minds in music! A great symphony is a man-made Mississippi down which we irresistibly flow from the instant of our leave-taking to a long foreseen destination. Music must always flow, for that is part of its very essence, but the creation of that continuity and flow—that long line—constitutes the be-all and end-all of every composer's existence.[8]

His rejection of Ives's self-reliance in music only increased the dilemma that Copland faced in finding his own style. At first he tried to write compositions that combined modern harmonies with jazz rhythms, an alternative that was encouraged by Mlle. Boulanger and squarely in the French manner of the 1920s. But by 1930 he had abandoned this practice because he believed that jazz was limited in its emotional range. He finally decided to compose alternately in two styles. Some pieces would be modernistic and close to the contemporary neoclassical model; others were made simple, folkloric and American in theme, and musically accessible to almost everyone.

Piano Variations

The Piano Variations (1930) is the first masterpiece of the former type—music taking its departure from Stravinskian neoclassicism but transformed in Copland's own way. The work consists of an eleven-measure theme, twenty connected variations, and a coda. Copland gives his variations distinguishable and contrasting moods: "expressive," "naive," "clangorous," "blurred," "scherzando," and "threatening" are some of the playing instructions. Despite these contrasts, the entire composition is tightly unified by a continuous development of ideas.

Like Stravinsky's neoclassical music of the 1920s, the Piano Variations is relatively brief, contrapuntal in texture, and classical in form and genre. The fast passages display a motoric rhythm set against changing and asymmetrical meters, and the sound of the work is transparent, lean, and hard. The harmonies are modernistically dissonant, as they mix together diatonic, octatonic, and freely chromatic pitch structures. Traditional tonality plays no role, although—as in the music of Stravinsky—triads remain important sonorities and certain pitches are temporarily given priority. There is nothing overtly regional or American about the work.

All of these are features of Stravinsky's music from the 1920s, but Copland departs from his model in several ways. He avoids Stravinsky's witty parody of earlier musical styles, and he writes for the piano with a more rawboned texture and rhythm. Perhaps bearing in mind Boulanger's admonition about the need in music for "the long line," Copland also introduces a principle of unity in the Piano Variations that derives more from Arnold Schoenberg than from Stravinsky.

Copland freely admitted Schoenberg's influence in the work: "I *did* make use to some extent, but in my own way, of the method invented by Arnold Schoenberg that came to be known as 'twelve-tone' and from which developed 'serialism.' The *Variations* incorporates a four-note motive on which the entire piece is based. Almost every note and chord in the piece relate back to these four notes."[9]

Copland's principal tone row consists of the opening four notes: E-C-D♯-C♯ (Ex. 76-1, top). The figure is then expanded into an eleven-measure theme by free development and by the addition of new motivic ideas. The tone row, as well as the other motivic features of the theme, are then continually developed in the variations that follow. Copland brings back the basic four-note row in transpositions, inversions, and retrogrades (see Ex. 76-1), and he promotes variety by placing the notes of a row in different registers. As with Schoenberg's early serial music, Copland at times freely reorders the tones within a row, and row-based passages alternate with others made from free motivic development.

EXAMPLE 76-1

mm. 1-3

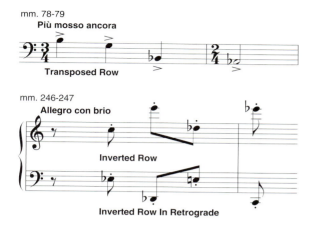

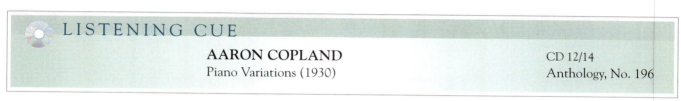

LISTENING CUE

AARON COPLAND
Piano Variations (1930)

CD 12/14
Anthology, No. 196

Appalachian Spring

Copland's ballet scores—*Billy the Kid* (1938), *Rodeo* (1942), and *Appalachian Spring* (1944)—were written in the composer's second style, in which he appealed to the understanding of a large audience through familiar materials, Whitmanesque simplicity, and American themes. The music of *Appalachian Spring* is an especially distinguished example of this style. The work was commissioned by the dancer and choreographer **Martha Graham** (1893–1991) for a performance in the Coolidge Auditorium in the Library of Congress in Washington, D.C. Since this auditorium is small, Copland was limited to a thirteen-piece chamber orchestra of strings, woodwinds, and piano.

Graham's idea for the scenario of the ballet underwent several changes—some made even after Copland had composed the music—and by the time of the 1944 premiere she had settled on this story:

> The action of the ballet concerns "a pioneer celebration in spring around a newly-built farm house in the Pennsylvania hills in the early part of the last century. The bride-to-be [Fig. 76-1] and the young farmer-husband enact the emotions, joyful and apprehensive, their new domestic partnership invites. An older neighbour suggests now and then the rocky confidence of experience. A revivalist and his followers remind the new householders of the strange and terrible aspects of human fate. At the end the couple are left quiet and strong in their new house."[10]

❋ FIGURE 76-1
Martha Graham ecstatically dances the role of the Bride in the premier performance of Copland's *Appalachian Spring* (1944), while the followers of a revivalist minister sit by stoically.

CORBIS

In 1945 Copland reworked the music of *Appalachian Spring* into a suite for full orchestra, and it is in this form that the work is now best known. (Later, Copland also created additional suites, both for full and chamber orchestras, some containing the music of the entire ballet.) The climax of the 1945 Suite comes near the end, in music for a scene that depicts events of everyday farm life. For this passage, Copland took Graham's suggestion to write variations on a song melody, which he chose from an anthology of Shaker hymns. Copland frequently used traditional melodies in his works of the populist type. The Shaker hymn that he chose for *Appalachian Spring*—called **"Simple Gifts"**—provides an appropriate local color in a ballet about pioneering life in America, and its simple tunefulness helps the audience to understand the work. Its opening is shown in Example 76-2.

EXAMPLE 76-2

Copland insisted that the use of such a preexisting melodic source had to be more than decoration, its musical and expressive essence somehow worked out through the entire composition. He explained: "A hymn tune represents a certain order of feeling: simplicity, plainness, sincerity, directness. It is the reflection of those qualities in a stylistically appropriate setting, imaginative and unconventional and not mere quotation, that gives the use of folk tunes reality and importance."[11] The "order of feeling" of the hymn is abundant in Copland's score, with its uncluttered texture, largely triadic harmony, and clear-cut rhythms. The composer also integrates the tune into the work's musical substance by anticipating its triadic head motive in earlier themes.

LISTENING CUE

AARON COPLAND
Appalachian Spring (Suite, 1945)
Variations on a Shaker Hymn

CD 12/15
Anthology, No. 197

Copland pointed to the last section of the 1945 Suite—just following the variations—as containing his favorite music of the entire work. Certainly, it has the touching, Whitmanesque simplicity that he wanted: "I had become convinced that simplicity was the way out of isolation for the contemporary composer," he later wrote.[12] The melody (Ex. 76-3) is harmonized to evoke an African American gospel hymn—blue notes E♭ and B♭ are brought in, there are parallel fifths and octaves, and the V-IV harmonic motion at the cadence recalls the ninth and tenth measures of a typical blues harmonic progression.

Copland on Art and the Affirmative Spirit

In the early 1950s, Copland, together with many other American artists, was attacked in the press and in Congress for alleged Communist sympathies. Copland strenuously denied such accusations, but the climate of fear created by McCarthyism took a toll on his creative spirit. At the end of his book *Music and Imagination* (1952), Copland commented obliquely on this dilemma:

> One of the primary problems for the composer in an industrial society like that of America is to achieve integration, to find justification for the life of art in the life about him. I must believe in the ultimate good of the world and of life as I live it in order to create a work of art. Negative emotions cannot produce art; positive emotions bespeak an emotion about something. I cannot

imagine an art work without implied convictions; and that is true also for music, the most abstract of the arts.

It is this need for a positive philosophy which is a little frightening in the world as we know it. You cannot make art out of fear and suspicion; you can make it only out of affirmative beliefs. This sense of affirmation can be had only in part from one's inner being; for the rest it must be continually reactivated by a creative and yea-saying atmosphere in the life about one. The artist should feel himself affirmed and buoyed up by his community. In other words, art and the life of art must mean something, in the deepest sense, to the everyday citizen. When that happens, America will have achieved a maturity to which every sincere artist will have contributed.[3]

EXAMPLE 76-3

The music of the ballet ends delicately with a special five-note chord that was a favorite Copland harmony. Here it consists of notes of the tonic C-major triad together with those of the dominant G-major triad (Ex. 76-4). This chord, which is heard sporadically throughout the work in differing transpositions, again subtly alludes to the Shaker hymn since, in its simplicity, the melody outlines solely tonic and dominant harmonies.

EXAMPLE 76-4

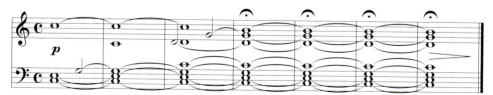

The music of Aaron Copland shows two sides of the American artistic consciousness during the period between the world wars. One is modern, biting in its dissonant harmony and angularity of line, and abstract in meaning; the other is warm, filled with Americana, and traditional in musical materials. In the latter type, Copland succeeded in creating a musical idiom that seemed to many to be the very embodiment of the American spirit.

 SAMUEL BARBER

Samuel Barber (1910–1981) repeatedly visited Europe and acquired a lifelong fascination for its culture and society. His European experiences had a very different effect on his music from those of Copland or most of the other American students of Nadia Boulanger. Barber had no special affinity with French modern music, and he was one of the few major composers of his day who professed to be uninterested in the works of Stravinsky. "With all Stravinsky's talent and imagination," Barber wrote, "his lack of lyricism and utter inability to work in more than small periods weigh heavily against him."[14] Barber's music rarely delves into Americana, and he had no sympathy for the self-made aesthetic of Ives. "He [Ives] was an amateur, a hack, who didn't put pieces together well," Barber wrote.

Barber's sympathies were mostly with German romantic musicians of the nineteenth century. He did not participate in the general rebellion against romanticism that spread throughout the musical world in the 1920s, and he rose to fame as a composer by extending the language of romantic composers, always in his own distinctive way, far into the twentieth century.

BARBER'S LIFE AND WORKS

Barber attended the Curtis Institute of Music in Philadelphia, where he studied composition with Rosario Scalero (1870–1954) and became an accomplished singer. He soon attracted attention with orchestral works such as his Overture to *The School for Scandal* (1933). Following service in the army during World War II, he received numerous prestigious commissions, one of which led to the opera *Antony and Cleopatra*, written for the opening in 1966 of the new Metropolitan Opera house at New York's Lincoln Center.

Like all of the major American composers of his period, Barber wrote for orchestra—symphonies, shorter character pieces, and concertos—and he was also a leading composer of songs. Among his chamber works are a String Quartet (1936), a Piano Sonata (1949), and a Sonata for Cello and Piano (1932). In addition to *Antony and Cleopatra*, he also composed the opera *Vanessa* (1957) and several ballets.

Barber's music has an astonishing diversity of styles. He was most at home in a traditional but still distinctive type of music characterized by lyric and affective melody and by traditional harmony. These features suggest a continuation of values of the Romantic period.

Beginning in the 1940s, Barber apparently became self-conscious about the character of his music and the direction it had taken. He was willing then to experiment in styles associated with other composers, as if to show that he could outdo his contemporaries at their own game. His "Capricorn" Concerto (1944) is an outright adaptation of Stravinsky's neoclassical style; his *Excursions* for piano (1944) use jazz idioms, and his songs *Knoxville: Summer of 1915* suggest the folkloric regionalism of Copland. Gradually, Barber slid into a bleak self-criticism. Fully twenty years after he composed his Symphony No. 2 (1944), he attempted to withdraw and destroy the work (which he was not able to do), and in his later years he fell nearly silent as a composer.

Adagio for Strings

Barber's orchestral music includes three *Essays*, two symphonies, and the ever-popular **Adagio for Strings** (1938). He also wrote concertos for violin (1939), cello (1945), and piano (1962), and a concerto grosso called "Capricorn" Concerto (1944). His essentially romantic spirit is apparent in his most often performed work, the *Adagio for Strings*. The piece had its origin as the slow movement of his String Quartet, which Barber composed in 1936 while living in Austria near Salzburg. At the time, he was studying music by Wagner, especially Wagner's *Siegfried Idyll,* an orchestral character piece whose warm melodiousness, free form, and extended harmonic language are all reflected in the *Adagio.* In 1938 the quartet movement was arranged for string orchestra and performed by Arturo Toscanini with the NBC Symphony Orchestra, an event that helped to establish Barber's standing among the leading American composers. The popularity of the work has never waned, and Barber arranged it again in 1967 for chorus, giving it the traditional *Agnus dei* text from the Catholic Mass.

The *Adagio* contains a skillful adaptation of the Wagnerian style. The piece has a passionate melodiousness, rich texture, and an intensity of expression that is pushed almost to the point of becoming maudlin. The form involves a free development of lines heard in the first eight measures (Ex. 76-5). These gather into ever-increasing waves until the motions reach a climax, whereupon they fall back into an exhausted recapitulation of the opening.

EXAMPLE 76-5

The lasting popularity of the *Adagio* is evidence that importance in music of the twentieth (or any other) century cannot be judged solely by its relation to a dominant style or a musical "mainstream." Certainly, the *Adagio for Strings* stands far apart from the major competing trends in music of the 1930s—Schoenbergian serialism, Stravinskian neoclassicism, and Copland's regionalism, among others. It looks to the past, but not by way of any parody. Copland (Fig. 76-2) found its value to reside in its authenticity: "It's really well felt, it's believable you see, it's not phoney. He's not just making it up because he thinks that would sound well. It comes straight from the heart, to use old-fashioned terms."[15]

Barber's *Hermit Songs*

Barber's songs also come straight from the heart. He wrote some fifty of these, including *Knoxville: Summer of 1915* (1947)

❋ FIGURE 76-2

Samuel Barber and Aaron Copland, photographed together in 1950, were the two leading European-trained American composers of the early twentieth century.

on words by James Agee, a setting of Matthew Arnold's *Dover Beach* for voice and string quartet (1931), and the cycle *Hermit Songs* (1953), which consists of ten settings of medieval Irish poetry translated into modern English.

The texts of the *Hermit Songs* are predominantly religious, although spoken in an entirely worldly and personalized tone. "Sea-Snatch," the sixth of the ten songs, paints a miniature portrait of a boat caught in a violent storm, its planks consumed as though by a great fire, its sailors left to cry out to the all-powerful King of Heaven. The title "Sea-Snatch" was apparently given to the poem by Barber, a "snatch" referring to a succinct song or poetic fragment. The brevity of such poems came from their being entered hurriedly by medieval scribes into the narrow margin of a manuscript.

Barber's music for the song brings the storm alive through a relentless and surging rhythm. There is no regular meter, as the lines toss violently up and down. The voice has no respite from the storm as it moves breathlessly, accompanied by a twisting ostinato in the piano. By repeating the opening lines, Barber makes a concise ternary form out of his diminutive text. The expressive harmonic language of the *Adagio for Strings* is replaced in the *Hermit Songs* by more dissonant sounds, especially chords made from intervals of the fourth. "Sea-Snatch" is strictly limited to the notes of a C-minor scale, which Barber limits further by dwelling on pentatonic collections of tones.

LISTENING CUE

SAMUEL BARBER
Hermit Songs (1953)
"Sea-Snatch"

CD 12/16
Anthology, No. 198

In Barber's works we see a cross-section of the stylistic diversity of mid twentieth-century music. The romanticism evident in the early *Adagio for Strings* gives way in later pieces such as "Sea-Snatch" to a more modernistic harmonic organization.

SUMMARY

Following World War I, American musicians established a stronger contact with French musical culture. Aaron Copland was only one of the leading younger composers of the 1920s who studied in France with Nadia Boulanger. Copland, like many of his fellow American musicians, made his music express distinctively American themes and values, which he accomplished (as in the ballet *Appalachian Spring*) by a simple and traditional style and, as with Ives, by the quotation of folk melodies. Copland also wanted his music to have the universality and sophistication of contemporary European music, and this was his goal in his Piano Variations.

Samuel Barber came to prominence by composing music in a traditional romantic style, although he often tried his hand at other, more contemporary trends in music. His *Adagio for Strings* is an example of his extension of the Wagnerian idiom in its intense expressivity and enriched harmonic language. His *Hermit Songs* (1953), which are settings of medieval Irish poetry, depart from the romanticism of the earlier pieces, although they maintain the traditional values associated with song composition.

KEY TERMS

Nadia Boulanger	Martha Graham	*Adagio for Strings*
Walt Whitman	"Simple Gifts"	

Chapter 77

Tin Pan Alley and the Broadway Musical

Around 1900, popular songs were the type of music most frequently heard by the average American. A piano was installed in many middle-class homes, and one of its main functions was to accompany the singing of parlor songs, providing an enjoyable form of family entertainment before the days of TV and DVDs. A thriving sheet music industry evolved in America to make songs available to amateur players and singers, and a successful new song could produce astonishing sales and instant wealth for its publisher—sometimes also for its composer. Harry Von Tilzer's "A Bird in a Gilded Cage" (1900) sold 2 million copies of sheet music in its first year alone; Charles Harris's "After the Ball" (1892) brought in $25,000 per week— a virtual fortune at this time. George Gershwin's song "Swanee" (1919) earned its still unknown composer $10,000 in royalties during its first year and made his name familiar around the world.

An easy way to perform songs in the home was to purchase a **player piano.** These began to appear in the 1890s, and at first consisted of a cabinet-like apparatus that was placed in front of a normal piano keyboard. A perforated paper roll that encoded the song's piano accompaniment was inserted into the device, and a pneumatic action driven by a pair of pedals activated mechanical fingers that "played" the instrument. After 1900 the player mechanism was most often mounted into the piano itself. Although sometimes used to distribute classical music (rolls were made by Debussy, Ravel, Mahler, Richard Strauss and many other composers and performers of the day), the player piano had its greatest success in bringing popular songs into American homes, allowing families to sing along with the tunes.

✦ THE POPULAR SONG BUSINESS

The explosion in demand for songs near the turn of the century went hand in hand with the rise of new forms of theatric entertainment—especially the **vaudeville show** and **musical play.** Unlike classical or "art" songs, which are independent and free-standing musical works, popular songs at this time were normally functional music that first achieved popularity in a theatric show. Professional singers in shows introduced audiences firsthand to new songs, and sheet music was normally available for purchase on the spot. The vaudeville show and musical play had by 1900 largely replaced the old minstrel shows, whose racial humor had at last been recognized by American audiences as crude and bigoted.

Vaudeville was more attuned to the times. This was a type of variety show consisting of a succession of independent "acts"—comedy routines, short skits, juggling, animal tricks—and songs were essential. Musical plays, which were forerunners of the Broadway musical, consisted of a succession of songs and dances strung together by a simple story line.

The center of the lucrative song-publishing business at the turn of the twentieth century was New York City, in downtown Manhattan. Vaudeville theaters had sprung up there, especially on Broadway, which angled across the center of town. Crossing Broadway near Madison Square Park were 27th and 28th Streets, where so many music publishers were located that their pianos made the neighborhood sound like a jangle of tin pans. **Tin Pan Alley** became the nickname for the whole popular-song industry.

The marketing of songs was done by **song pluggers**—musicians who worked for a publisher and demonstrated its new offerings for the customers. At the age of fifteen, George Gershwin dropped out of high school to became a song plugger for the firm of Jerome H. Remick & Co. He earned only $15 per week, but he thoroughly learned the art and craft of song writing and the business that supported it.

In the 1920s the distribution of popular songs was revolutionized by the new technologies of radio, sound film, and sound recording, which quickly cut into the sale of sheet music. The first commercial radio station in America, KDKA, was founded in 1920 in Pittsburgh, and by the end of the decade radio receivers were in most homes. For the first time, songs could be heard in the home with no active participation on the part of the listener—certainly a mixed blessing for the history of music. The development of radio soon led to a transformation in sound recordings from a primitive acoustical technology to a modern electronic one. The earliest "electronic discs"—superior in sound quality to the older mechanical phonograph recordings—began to appear around 1925, although these were for a long time limited to about three minutes in duration. The first sound film, *The Jazz Singer* starring Al Jolson, appeared in 1927, and many of the movies that followed were of Broadway musicals, bringing the tunes of George Gershwin, Jerome Kern, Irving Berlin, and other leading New York songsmiths to a larger audience than ever before.

✤ FIGURE 77-1
George Gershwin, c1932. In his short life, George Gershwin brought the art and craft of popular song writing to a new level of sophistication.

CORBIS

✤ GEORGE GERSHWIN

The art of the popular song rose to new heights in the works of George Gershwin (1898–1937; Fig. 77-1). Born in Brooklyn, he acquired a solid training in music, became an accomplished pianist, and had a good knowledge of classical works. He began writing songs as a teenaged song plugger, and he composed his first musical (*La-La-Lucille!*) in 1919. In his short career he wrote more than three hundred fifty songs, which were placed into some forty musicals and films. Gershwin also wrote classical works with a popular or jazzy flavor, including three Piano Preludes, *Rhapsody in Blue* for piano and jazz band (1924), a Piano Concerto (1925), the orchestral character pieces *An American in Paris* (1928) and *Cuban Overture* (1932), and the opera *Porgy and Bess* (1935).

The reasons for his success as a songwriter are easy to hear in "The Man I Love" (1924; Fig. 77-2). This was written for the musical *Lady, Be Good* (1924), but withdrawn before its opening and later re-situated in *Strike Up the Band* (1927). The story of *Lady, Be Good*, written by Guy Bolton, tells of a struggling brother-and-sister dance team (roles created for Fred and Adele Astaire), whose cleverness leads ultimately to their success. The lyrics of the song are by Gershwin's brother, Ira, and they are general enough—expressing wistful sentiments of love—to fit into almost any musical of the day.

Gershwin's music for the song is an example of a **ballad,** which in the context of Tin Pan Alley refers to a love song in a slow tempo. Its form agrees with the norm for popular songs of the 1920s. It begins with a four-measure introduction in $\frac{4}{4}$ time, in which a motive from the following section is introduced. Next comes the **verse,** which spans sixteen measures that are divided into two symmetrical eight-measure phrases, both ending on a dominant-seventh chord in the home key of E♭ major. The **chorus** (also called the **refrain**) follows the verse. Both terms are vestiges of earlier songwriting practices. Recall from Chapter 72 that the late nineteenth-century American popular song had a strophic form in which each stanza ended with a true refrain taken by a four-part chorus. By the 1920s the terms remained for this section of the song, but it was then sung by a solo voice rather than a chorus. Since songs by this time had usually been whittled down to a single stanza, there could be no literal refrain.

The weight of Gershwin's song falls in the chorus, which has the most memorable tune and words that state the idea of the song most directly. The verse is left with an introductory function, and this section could be (and often was) omitted. The chorus of "The Man I Love," as in most other songs of the 1920s, covers thirty-two measures that are divided into four eight-measure phrases, each with a line of text. Within the four phrases there are only two different eight-measure musical components (call them **A** and **B**), and these are repeated according to some simple scheme, here **AABA,** the most common plan.

Phrase **A** remains close to the home key of E♭ major, but phrase **B** (sometimes called the **release** of the song) creates tonal contrast by shifting briefly to the key of C minor. Typical of many Gershwin songs, the chorus of "The Man I Love" is performed twice in succession. The words of the song are entirely typical of the genre, with their sentiment of reaching out beyond the drab everyday world for a happiness that is just beyond grasp.

In addition to being an inexhaustible font of memorable tunes, Gershwin left his mark on popular music by bringing to it an enriched harmonic and tonal language—one borrowed from classical music of the late nineteenth century—and also using elements from African American jazz. The main melody in the refrain of "The Man I Love" immediately lights on a blue note, here D♭, the flatted seventh in E♭ major. The points of harmonic arrival and departure throughout the song are all simple tonics and dominants, but Gershwin connects these basic chords with a variety of harmonies that arise through an advanced compositional thinking. Notice the augmented chords in the verse in measures 10 and 11

❄ F I G U R E 77-2

Gershwin's manuscript for the verse of "The Man I Love" suggests that he composed at the piano and first wrote down the music for the piano accompaniment. The vocal line per se, as well as the chorus of the song, was entered only later.

(Ex. 77-1), and listen for the diminished chords and secondary dominants that Gershwin brings in here and there. Such harmonic inventiveness was an important element of expansion in the tradition of song writing. Gershwin's originality brought a new depth to the genre that also found its way into jazz at about the same time.

EXAMPLE 77-1

LISTENING CUE

GEORGE GERSHWIN
"The Man I Love" (1924)

CD 12/17
Anthology, No. 199

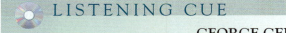 THE BROADWAY MUSICAL

Almost all of Gershwin's songs first became known through their placement in a **musical.** This is a genre of popular musical theater (also called "Broadway musical" or "musical comedy") that emerged in America shortly after 1900. One of its antecedents was **operetta,** a type of opera that had garnered success in Paris and Vienna after 1850. Operettas were made from songs, choruses, and dances—all with a certain operatic pretense—interspersed into a lighthearted spoken play. The American musical did not at first have the artistic aspirations of operetta, since it consisted only of a string of songs and dances hung together on the thinnest of story lines.

The central figure in establishing the identity of the Broadway musical was the songwriter **Jerome Kern** (1885–1945). Like most American composers of classical music of his generation, he received his musical education in Germany, and he returned to New York to work as a song plugger and composer of songs to be inserted in shows given by visiting English troupes. During World War I he began to compose the music for his own new productions, which were instantly successful. Kern's songs include such timeless favorites as "Smoke Gets in Your Eyes," "All the Things You Are," and "Ol' Man River," and these have a solid musical substance that was an inspiration to later songsters like Gershwin and Richard Rodgers.

Kern's *Show Boat* (1927)—his most important work—created a prototype for the classic American musical. Its story is based on a contemporaneous novel by Edna Ferber and makes for more sophisticated drama than is found in earlier musicals. Kern's music is not simply a succession of unrelated songs and dances but an integrated whole that included large choral and ensemble numbers reminiscent of opera.

Synopsis of *Oklahoma!*

Singing as usual, the cowboy Curly McClain pays a visit to the Williams farm on the Oklahoma frontier. Laurey Williams—a headstrong orphan of eighteen—lives there with her Aunt Eller Murphy. Curly has come to invite Laurey to the social that evening at Skidmore's, but he learns that she has already been asked by the new hired man, Jud Fry. Other neighbors arrive: Will Parker has just returned from Kansas City having won $50, and now he wants to marry his girlfriend, Ado Annie, although—unable to say no to a man—she arrives in the company of the slick-talking peddler, Ali Hakim. Curly goes to confront Jud over Laurey.

In a dream ballet, Laurey imagines that she has married Curly, but Jud enters, strangles him, and carries her off. At the party that evening, Curly is in a tense stand-off with Jud while the cowboys are arguing, as always, with the farmers. Jud quarrels with Laurey, who angrily tells him not to come on her farm any more. She runs to Curly, who blurts out a marriage proposal that she accepts.

At Laurey's place after the wedding the neighbors celebrate, and the future looks bright for living in Oklahoma. The menfolk haze the newlyweds by a "shivaree" (a noisy celebration), which is interrupted when Jud arrives. He fights with Curly and is killed as he falls on his knife. A judge and marshall are at the party, and they convene an informal court that finds Curly "not guilty!"

RODGERS AND HAMMERSTEIN: OKLAHOMA!

Kern's classic type of musical was brought to its highest level in the shows of Richard Rodgers (1902–1979). Between 1919 and 1942 he collaborated with the writer Lorenz Hart on more than thirty musicals, including *On Your Toes* (1936), *Babes in Arms* (1937), and *Pal Joey* (1940). Rodgers subsequently teamed with the writer **Oscar Hammerstein II** (1895–1960) on a series of hugely successful musicals including *Oklahoma!* (1943), *Carousel* (1945), *South Pacific* (1949), *The King and I* (1951), *Flower Drum Song* (1958), and *The Sound of Music* (1959). Rodgers also wrote the stirring incidental music for *Victory at Sea* (1952), a televised documentary on naval warfare during World War II.

Oklahoma! was the first show by Rodgers and Hammerstein, and their most successful collaboration of all. Going well beyond the norm for Broadway composers and writers, they worked together like an opera composer and librettist. Earlier, as in the musicals of Gershwin, the story line of a show—the "libretto" that would ultimately be given in spoken dialogue—was made by a writer using some tried-and-true formula. The words for the songs were written by a second writer, the **lyricist,** who was adept in clever rhymes and turns of phrase. Hammerstein wrote both the libretto and the song lyrics for Rodgers, a consolidation of effort that helped to produce a more unified and integrated dramatic effect.

Just as an opera librettist, Hammerstein started with a literary work—the play *Green Grow the Lilacs* (1931) by the Oklahoma playwright Lynn Riggs (1899–1954). The play has certain themes that were promising for a musical in the mold of *Show Boat*—a folkish American subject set among common people, a love story with a happy ending, and plenty of action, local color, and clearly drawn characters. But the play also has many sharp edges. Oklahoma for Riggs was not an idyllic place, but a region on the very edge of civilization. Some of his characters are vulgar and violent beneath their folksy surface, and the play leaves the bleak message that we are all trapped by an existence in which the only certainty is death. Needless to say, Hammerstein removed all of these unsettling features, reinforced the comic situations, and flattened the characters into mainly good-natured types.

Rodgers's music begins with an overture that is a medley of the song melodies to come. The principal music in each act consists of songs, most based on the verse-and-refrain model seen in Gershwin's "The Man I Love." Rodgers cautiously expands this prototype by making the songs strophic and by adding extraneous musical sections. The melody of a song is often elaborated upon in a dance that follows, and song tunes are frequently repeated as fragmentary "reprises" that serve to integrate the music more closely into the spoken play. To accompany Laurey's dream ballet, Rodgers breaks free from the simple confines of the song to write a longer multi-sectional instrumental number, although this music, like the overture, is still a medley of song tunes already heard. The ballet—which is the dramatic high point of the work—was choreographed by **Agnes De Mille,** who was trained in classical dance. A version of her gripping choreography can be seen in the award-winning 1955 film version of *Oklahoma!*

"I Cain't Say No!" shows Rodgers' irrepressible wit and his expansion of the typical verse-and-refrain song. The number is sung by the neighborhood girl Ado Annie, who has taken up with the peddler Hakim while her boyfriend, Will, is in Kansas City. She confesses to Laurey that attention from any man makes her "all shaky from horn to hoof." Except for adding a contrasting section to the song, Rodgers formal plan for "I Cain't Say No!" is virtually the same one used by Gershwin in "The Man I Love." Rodgers begins with an eighteen-measure verse followed by a refrain with the standard **AABA** form, and the refrain is sung twice over.

Between the refrain and its repetition, Rodgers inserts a contrasting section that he calls a "trio," probably because it is in a contrasting key, like the trio of a band march or piano rag. Rodgers takes more liberties than Gershwin with the phrase structure of the song, bringing the music closer to the words and giving it more flexibility and naturalness. The eight-measure phrases are sometimes extended to make the music underscore an important point in the text. For example, the final statement of the A melody is extended to twenty-four measures to allow the voice part chromatically to ascend to a mock-dramatic climax, showing that Ado Annie positively cain't say no.

LISTENING CUE

RICHARD RODGERS AND OSCAR HAMMERSTEIN II
Oklahoma! (1943)
"I Cain't Say No!"

CD 12/18
Anthology, No. 200

❄ LEONARD BERNSTEIN: *WEST SIDE STORY*

The differences that separated opera from musicals in the 1940s dwindled on Broadway following World War II. The growing affinity between opera and musical is especially apparent in one of the great works in the entire genre of the Broadway musical, *West Side Story* by Leonard Bernstein (1918–1990).

Bernstein was a phenomenon in the history of American music, someone equally gifted as a composer, pianist, and conductor, and at home in both classical and popular music. He was a New Englander, educated at Harvard and the Curtis Institute of Music, and he followed the dual careers of orchestral conductor and composer.

Synopsis of *West Side Story*

On a summer evening on the Upper West Side of New York, members of a local gang, the Jets, begin to appear. Their leader is Riff, and they all act tough and cool. Members of the rival Puerto Rican gang, the Sharks, led by Bernardo, appear menacingly, taunting and picking fights. Riff asks his old friend Tony to come to the evening's gym dance, where both gangs will be present and where a challenge will be made for a rumble (a gang fight). Tony agrees, although he has lately shown little interest in his old gang and seeks something new and better in life.

In a Puerto Rican bridal shop, Anita makes a white party dress for her friend Maria, sister of her boyfriend, Bernardo. Bernardo brought Maria to America to marry Chino, but she is not attracted to him. The gangs arrive for the gym dance, and as a tumultuous mambo is played, they dance passionately. Suddenly, Tony and Maria see each other and stand as though transfixed. After only a few words they kiss, whereupon Bernardo pushes Tony away. After the dance Tony rushes to the alley behind Maria's apartment, climbs the fire escape, and they embrace. The gangs meet for a "war council" at Doc's drug store, and despite admonitions to keep cool, they erupt into wild dancing. Finally, Riff and Bernardo agree that the rumble will happen the next evening—using fists only.

Maria tells Tony to stop the fight, but he cannot do so and knives are soon drawn despite the agreement. Tony tries to hold back Riff, only to see him stabbed to death by Bernardo. In a fury, Tony grabs the knife and kills Bernardo. Tony rushes back to Maria and they both sense that they are helplessly trapped by their fate. Tony then goes into hiding, but he overhears Anita say wrongly that Maria has been killed by Chino. With no more reason to hide, he wanders the dark streets, only to be shot dead by Chino. At last stunned and silent, the gangs carry his body away.

Bernstein was the musical director of the New York Philharmonic Orchestra from 1958 to 1969, and later a regular visiting conductor of the Vienna Philharmonic Orchestra. His principal compositions were for Broadway, including the musicals *On the Town* (1944), *Wonderful Town* (1952), *Candide* (1956), and *West Side Story* (1957). He also composed the ballet *Fancy Free* (1944), three symphonies, orchestral suites derived from his musicals, and the choral work *Chichester Psalms* (1965).

West Side Story continued the collaborative creative process that was normal for the genre of the Broadway musical, although ultimately the work is so overwhelmed by its music that it is usually thought of as Bernstein's alone. The initial idea was hatched in 1949 by the choreographer **Jerome Robbins** (1918–1998), who enlisted Bernstein for a musical having a large element of dance, based on Shakespeare's *Romeo and Juliet*. His idea did not progress until 1955, a time of widely publicized gang violence in New York that pitted Puerto Rican youths against others. The playwright Arthur Laurents then rewrote Shakespeare's feuding Montague and Capulet families as New York gangs called the Jets and Sharks. Romeo becomes Tony, a former member of the Jets; Juliet is Maria, sister of the leader of the Sharks. **Stephen Sondheim** (b. 1930)—who later became famous as both a Broadway composer and writer—was brought in to create the lyrics. The idea of basing a musical on Shakespeare's bleakly tragic story was only the first of many innovations in the work, which had its premiere in 1957.

From the very opening curtain, the differences in musical conception between *West Side Story* and *Oklahoma!* are unmistakable. Instead of Rodgers's easy-going overture medley, Bernstein begins with a grippingly dramatic instrumental "Prologue" that accompanies Robbins's choreography, in which the gangs taunt each other with a mixture of ballet and street dancing. The music has a degree of difficulty and complexity exceeding anything seen before on Broadway. Bernstein himself oversaw the orchestration of the work (something unusual for a show composer), and he enlarged the normal Broadway pit orchestra to allow it to evoke different jazz styles—big band swing, combos playing bebop or cool jazz, and the jazz of high-voltage Latin bands.

The musical numbers that follow the Prologue are in a variety of styles and forms. Riff's "Jet Song" or Tony's ballad "Maria" are based on the verse-and-refrain model of the traditional popular song. Other numbers—the extended ballet music for the "Dance at the Gym" or the pseudo-operatic finale in "Tonight"—are essentially new types for a musical, given their complexity.

The song and dance "Cool" illustrates many of these innovative features. In the drugstore where the Jets hang out, their gang members await the arrival of the Sharks to have their war council. Riff tells his men to be cool, but their tension flares up in a frenzied dance, after which calm returns. Structurally, the number has four contrasting sections, all held together by shared motives. The first section is a verse-and-refrain song for Riff. In the verse, Riff and the others speak rather than sing while a jazzy ostinato riff is introduced. The ostinato continues in the refrain, which is conventional in phrase structure, with thirty-two measures arranged in an **ABAB** pattern.

The second section begins when the restless gang members start to dance to the music of a strict fugue. The opening of the fugue subject, a countersubject, and the first fugal answer are shown in Example 77-2. The third section—an orchestral development—follows the fugue, as the dance grows ever more frenzied. This section concentrates on the fugal countersubject, which is stated as an intricate canon between the basses and muted trumpet (Ex. 77-3). Calm returns in the final section, in which the song refrain is brought back and sung in unison by the whole gang. The breathless number is rounded off by a short coda.

EXAMPLE 77-2

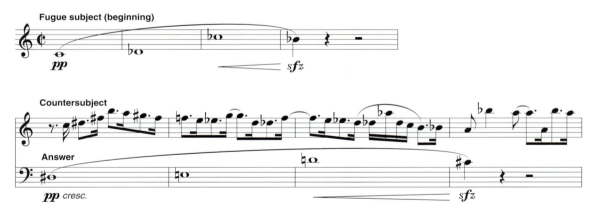

EXAMPLE 77-3

The music for "Cool" defies any distinction between popular and serious art. Bernstein uses advanced harmonic, rhythmic, and structural materials—shared at the time by jazz musicians and by some classical composers, notably Igor Stravinsky—and he brings these into an intimate fusion. "Cool" is ostensibly in the key of

C major, but the harmonies that support this key are altered to produce chords whose common feature is that their tones are all available in an octatonic scale. For example, the first chord in the number has the tones C E♭ E G (Ex. 77-4), which is also the first chord of the Prologue. Certainly, this harmony represents the tonic in C major, but the added E♭ (in addition to evoking a blue note in the key) also suggests an octatonic origin, which is reinforced by the tones added just after the downbeat—F♯ and A. These notes flesh out an almost complete octatonic scale: C (D♭) E♭ E F♯ G A (B♭).

EXAMPLE 77-4

West Side Story is also remarkable for the extent to which a few central motives recur throughout the entire work. These create a unity that is more at home in the genre of opera (think of the recurring motives in a music drama by Wagner) than in a musical, which generally consists of a sequence of largely unrelated numbers.

The ostinato figure C-F♯-G in the left hand of Example 77-4 is an example of one of these central recurring motives. A few of the subtle ways in which Bernstein uses the small figure are shown in Example 77-5. At the top is Tony's outcry "Maria!" from his song of this title (No. 5). Here the motive has the same shape as in "Cool"—an ascending tritone followed by an ascending semitone—although in "Maria" it is transposed and used in a different musical context. Tony's last call to Maria at the end of the song (shown in the middle of the example) finds the notes of the motive transposed and shuffled in order. A still more subtle transformation occurs in the whistle-like figure heard in the Prologue (No. 1), at the point when Bernardo enters (shown at the bottom of the example). Its tones are yet another transposition and reshuffling of the basic figure.

EXAMPLE 77-5

No. 5, mm. 8-9

No. 5, mm. 50-52

No. 1, mm. 41-43

 LISTENING CUE

LEONARD BERNSTEIN   CD 12/19
West Side Story, "Cool" (1957)   Anthology, No. 201

Leonard Bernstein's *West Side Story* revealed the capacity of the musical to rise above comedy and simple entertainment. Many dimensions of the work have such richness and depth that they can only be grasped by repeated listening and study. But *West Side Story* also has songs and dances of immediate appeal, thus honoring the traditions of musical theater established by Kern, Gershwin, and Rodgers.

MUSICALS OF THE 1960s AND BEYOND

Both the classical musical as seen in *Oklahoma!* and Bernstein's sophisticated *West Side Story* have continued to provide models for musicals to the present day. But many innovations have also appeared on Broadway since the 1960s. Musicals nowadays are often sung straight through, without the spoken dialogue of *Oklahoma!* or *West Side Story*. There has also been a diversification of musical styles beyond that of the Tin Pan Alley song. For example, rock began to be imported into Broadway shows beginning in the 1960s. An early example of the rock musical is *Hair* (1967), an anti–Viet Nam War piece in which the music is provided largely by an amplified rock band playing on stage, with Galt MacDermot's songs interspersed.

An even more fundamental innovation was the birth in the 1980s of the so-called **megamusical,** which is a show in which grandiose staging, stunning visual effects, and massive danced or choral numbers are characteristic. Early examples include *Les Misérables* (1980) and *Miss Saigon* (1989), both with music by Claude-Michel Schoenberg and lyrics by Alain Boublil.

The megamusical reached unprecedented acclamation in the shows of **Andrew Lloyd Webber** (b. 1948). Lloyd Webber was born in London and educated at the Royal College of Music. As a composer he is at home in classical and virtually any style of pop music, and the musical types present in his shows range from rock (*Jesus Christ Superstar,* 1971) to opera (*Phantom of the Opera,* 1986). The latter of these and his immensely successful *Cats* (1981) are classic examples of the megamusical.

SUMMARY

The popular song was the type of music most often heard by the average American around 1900. Songs were distributed mainly through sheet music and player-piano rolls, whose sale created a thriving business. The art and industry of the popular song of the early twentieth century is now commonly called "Tin Pan Alley." One of the greatest song composers of the 1920s and 1930s was George Gershwin, whose songs became known in musical comedies and early sound films. Gershwin generally adhered in his songs to a simple verse-and-chorus prototype. To this conventional framework, he added harmonic enrichment and also elements from jazz.

The Broadway musical flourished in America in the early twentieth century in the hands of Jerome Kern, and it reached a classic stage in the 1940s in works such as *Oklahoma!* by Richard Rodgers and the librettist Oscar Hammerstein II. *Oklahoma!* consists of a spoken folk comedy in which Rodgers inserted songs as well as longer instrumental numbers to accompany dancing.

Leonard Bernstein's musical *West Side Story* goes far beyond Rodgers in musical and dramatic complexity. It mingles diatonic and octatonic fields of pitches, and its numbers are unified by small recurring motives. *West Side Story* is based on Shakespeare's *Romeo and Juliet,* which is updated to a contemporary New York setting among West Side gangs. The music mingles elements of jazz with Tin Pan Alley songs.

Musicals since the 1960s regularly bring in rock styles of music and playing, and they often dispense with the spoken dialogue present in earlier shows. Since the 1980s they often use grandiose visual and scenic effects, creating a genre called the "megamusical."

KEY TERMS

player piano	song "release"	Agnes De Mille
vaudeville show	musical (Broadway	Jerome Robbins
musical play	musical)	Stephen Sondheim
Tin Pan Alley	operetta	megamusical
song plugger	Jerome Kern	Andrew Lloyd Webber
ballad	Oscar Hammerstein II	
chorus (refrain)	lyricist	

CONTEMPORARY MUSIC

*M*usic flourishes today as never before. Both live and recorded music seem to be everywhere, and virtually all of music—in every style, from any period—is at our fingertips. The landscape for music also has a different appearance from any time in the past. It has been reshaped by the spectacular rise of popular music and by advances in musical technology that bring the art to more people than ever.

New classical music (art music) shares in this prosperity. In its report on a recent season, the American Symphony Orchestra League noted increases in both concert attendance and endowments for its member orchestras. Composers of classical music are free as never before to follow their imaginations in any and all directions. Like a John Zorn, they can defy the traditional dis-

1900		1950

Fletcher Henderson (1897–1952), central figure in big band phenomenon and swing style

Edward "Duke" Ellington (1899–1974), American composer and big band leader

Elliott Carter (b. 1908), American composer

Benny Goodman (1909–1986), clarinetist and bandleader

Pierre Schaeffer (1910–1995), French radio engineer, inventor of *musique concrète*

John Cage (1912–1992), American composer

Milton Babbitt (b. 1916), American composer

John "Dizzy" Gillespie (1917–1993), trumpeter

Charlie Parker (1920–1955), alto saxophonist, one of founders of bebop

György Ligeti (b. 1923), Hungarian composer

Luciano Berio (1925–2003), Italian composer

Miles Davis (1926–1991), jazz trumpeter

George Crumb (b. 1929), American composer

Terry Riley (b. 1935), American minimalist

Arvo Pärt (b. 1935), Estonian composer

Steve Reich (b. 1936), American

Philip Glass (b. 1937), American

Joan Tower (b. 1938), American

World War II (1939–1945)

Olivier Messiaen (1908–1992), French composer

Bill Haley and Elvis Presley, Germany, 1958

Beatles take America by storm, 1964

tinctions between popular, experimental, and artistic music. Like a Morten Lauridsen, they can re-create the serene harmonies of Renaissance polyphony. Or, like a Brian Ferneyhough, they can write music of withering complexity and abstraction. In classical music of today, anything goes.

This tolerant atmosphere is completely unlike the mood that dominated music following World War II. During the postwar decades, a demand for conformity and abstraction ruled the world of classical music. But, by the mid-1970s, this largely depersonalized context for music had evaporated, to be superseded by the present spirit of openness and eclecticism. The final chapters of this book trace this remarkable transformation.

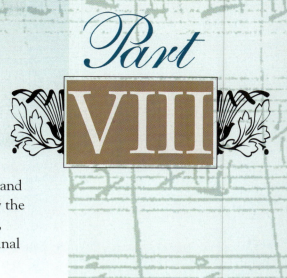

Part

VIII

1950   2000

● 1961 Benjamin Britten (1913–1976) composes *War Requiem*

● 1978 John Adams (b. 1947) appointed new music advisor to San Francisco Symphony

● 1958 Edgard Varèse (1883–1965) creates *Poème électronique*

● 1971 Pierre Boulez (b. 1925) becomes music director of New York Philharmonic

composer

composer

composer

composer

● 1955 Bill Haley's "Rock Around the Clock" vaults to top of charts

● 1960 Krzysztof Penderecki (b. 1933) composes *Threnody for the Victims of Hiroshima*

Musical Interlude 8

After World War II

In the preceding chapters, we encountered music composed after World War I that represented a clean break with the past. These works were created in a world recovering from war, whose horrors made a new order in music seem imperative. If World War I led to an upheaval in the world of music, what could the greater tragedy of World War II have in store? By the early 1950s the answer was evident. At this time the culture for modern music worldwide underwent yet another shift of taste every bit as decisive as the one in 1918.

This new style had three principal characteristics: depersonalization, control, and innovation. Its most typical works were depersonalized by composers' willing removal of their own taste from their music and their own capacity to exercise free choice. These were sacrificed to procedures of composing by system or by chance. Emotionality was hidden behind abstraction and complexity. In the place of a familiar emotional content in music, form became its be-all and end-all. "To write poetry after Auschwitz is barbaric," said Theodor Adorno, and his dictum echoed in the musical world throughout the 1950s and 1960s.

The desire for control was felt in several ways. The first was in a demand for conformity in how to write music. There was little tolerance in the musical world of the 1950s and 1960s. Virtually all ambitious younger composers at this time fell into line with the accepted formalism and abstraction of the day. Control was also exerted by systems of composition—total serialism and phase processes are examples—that reduced free choice.

Finally, the postwar period was one of unprecedented innovation, produced in large part by the desire to efface the past. If musical styles such as neoclassicism were to be rejected, then a whole new order in music would have to be discovered, and composers after World War II were tireless in finding new materials and outlooks, reaching even to elements that earlier had defined music as an art. Younger composers of the 1950s and 1960s tried their hand at creating an entirely new idea of music, sometimes not even involving sound, much less traditional organization, communication, or meaning.

Predictably, a musical style so rigid as that of the postwar period was not destined to last very long. It collapsed as soon as the anxieties that beset society following World War II had eased. In its place yet another taste in music emerged, one that in virtually every way was the opposite of the one immediately before. Beginning in the 1970s, composers replaced the striving for control with tolerance and musical diversity. Individuality and personalized outlooks on music returned to center stage. The constant search for innovation ended as composers returned to known values and materials. The taste of the 1970s and beyond was for a simpler style that embodied and enshrined any and all values from the past, so long as they were familiar and relatively untroubling.

The twentieth century came to its end with a music that embodied the inner spirit of the time and reflected, however indirectly, the society in which it originated. When listening to music of earlier eras, we often find a haven, a respite from our occupations. But when we go to music of the twentieth century, we rarely find a sanctuary from the world. Instead we are brought face to face with all of its realities.

Chapter 78

Reflections on War:
Britten, Penderecki, and Others

On 1 September 1939, German armies swept into Poland in an attack that marks the beginning of **World War II.** Two days later, Britain and France responded by declaring war on Germany, but, using the new technique of "lightning" warfare, Germany's conquest of Europe continued. In 1940 its armies overran Scandinavia, the Lowlands, and, finally, France. By this time Germany had formed an alliance, called the "Axis," with other nations, most importantly Japan, which had used military force to extend its dominion into China and Southeast Asia. In Europe, Great Britain was left virtually alone in opposing Germany's onslaught, as the United States tried to remain neutral. In the fall of 1940, the cities and strategic centers of England came under a withering bombardment, or "blitz," by the German air force, and the English feared an invasion was imminent.

America was finally drawn into the war on 7 December 1941, when Japan attacked the American navy at Pearl Harbor in Hawaii. Germany then declared war on the United States. In both Europe and the Far East, the "Allies," led by America and Great Britain, gradually gained the upper hand against the Axis nations. On 7 May 1945, following massive destruction of its cities, Germany unconditionally surrendered, and on 14 August 1945—after the United States unleashed nuclear weapons on the cities of Hiroshima and Nagasaki—the Japanese likewise capitulated.

The world was profoundly and permanently changed by this devastating conflict. The degree of destruction, loss of life, and general degradation of society was unprecedented. The Nazis had attempted to wipe out the entire Jewish population of Europe through a methodical genocide, now called the **Holocaust.** The world had witnessed the appalling human consequences of nuclear weapons in Hiroshima and Nagasaki, and "the bomb" seemed a permanent and menacing threat to all of civilization. World War II triggered the Cold War, which for nearly fifty years pitted the Communist countries of Eastern Europe and Asia against the West in a bitter and often deadly struggle.

Music—whose direction and character have always been sensitive to the society around it—shared in the upheaval brought by the war. Tragic consequences were plain to see. Talented musicians—Viktor Ullmann, Erwin Schulhoff, Hans Walter David, to name only a few—were sent to their death in Hitler's concentration camps. Others, such as Schoenberg, Bartók, and Stravinsky, left Europe and permanently resettled in America. In Germany and Austria, virtually every major opera house and concert hall was destroyed by war's end. The Prussian State Library in Berlin, which housed the musical manuscripts of Bach, Beethoven, Mozart, and Mendelssohn, was bombed, although its priceless musical documents were saved, in part by the foresight of its music librarian, Georg Schünemann, who hurriedly shipped them out of Berlin. After seeing his library destroyed, Schünemann committed suicide.

The war also changed the inner spirit of music. Neoclassicism—the dominant trend in music between the world wars—appeared to many to be naive and outdated. For most of the younger postwar composers, Stravinsky's witty parody of earlier musical styles could no longer serve in a world that had experienced the Holocaust, and reviving the past only reawakened bleak and unspeakable memories. A new order in music would have to be found, and the search for it is the subject of the following two chapters of this book. In this chapter we explore music that reflects upon war in a direct way, in works that embody the theme of warfare by composers who attempted in them to give artistic expression to its horror.

RICHARD STRAUSS, *METAMORPHOSEN*

Richard Strauss remained in Germany and Austria throughout the war. Strauss was then Germany's most famous living composer, and he tried to continue his career by accommodating the Nazis, who manipulated him and his reputation to serve their own purposes. The fact that his daughter-in-law and grandchildren were Jewish created for him a special level of anxiety and reluctance to speak out against the Nazis.

Strauss was deeply distressed by the destruction of the great musical institutions that had been the centers of his life's work. He was especially affected by the ruin of the National Theater in Munich, his home town. It was the place where his father had served for nearly fifty years as principal hornist, and after the theater was bombed in October 1943, Strauss wrote, "This is the greatest catastrophe that has ever been brought into my life, for which there can be no consolation and in my old age no hope." Most of his operas had received their premiere in the beautiful Semper opera house in Dresden, and on 12 February 1945 this structure, along with the rest of the city, was destroyed in a devastating firestorm following a bombing raid. Hearing the news, Strauss could only exclaim "My beautiful Dresden— Weimar—Munich, all gone!"

In this depressive frame of mind, the 80-year-old composer was forced out of retirement to write songs and one major instrumental work, an orchestral elegy for a destroyed German culture. He titled it *Metamorphosen* (*Metamorphoses*, 1945), with the subtitle "a study for twenty-three solo strings." The half-hour composition calls for ten violins, five violas, five cellos, and three basses, each having its own line of music. This unique orchestration makes for a rich texture and dark sound, which conform to Strauss's romantic musical language, one filled with a poignant melancholy mixed with resignation.

In the *Metamorphosen*, Strauss returns to the orchestra and to the genre of the tone poem, which had brought him international recognition some sixty years earlier but was long since put aside in favor of operatic composition. The title word "**metamorphoses**" refers to changes of form. Although Strauss gave no definitive explanation of what the term meant in the context of this work, he copied into its manuscript a poem by Goethe that speaks of the metamorphoses of history. We cannot hope to understand why things change, Goethe says in this poem, but only to persist.

Another aspect of the idea of metamorphosis is captured by the work's continual development and transformation of its themes. The main theme, heard near the opening, is shown in Example 78-1. It reappears in different guises, becoming ever more insistent toward the end, as though pointing to something positive. Its final metamorphosis occurs in the work's last ten measures, marked in the score "IN MEMORIAM!" Here the theme (Ex. 78-2) evolves to take the shape of the main theme of the Funeral March of Beethoven's "Eroica" Symphony. Recall from Chapter 50 that Beethoven's "Eroica" was itself a work that memorialized what had once existed—it was "composed to celebrate the memory of a great man," as Beethoven wrote on it. By quoting Beethoven, Strauss appears to be saying that civilization— even at its most highly evolved stages—contains the seeds of its own destruction and renewal. Strauss leaves us with an epitaph written by Beethoven, whose tribute to the past is as relevant to the world of 1945 as the one of 1804.

EXAMPLE 78-1

EXAMPLE 78-2

ARNOLD SCHOENBERG: A SURVIVOR FROM WARSAW

Schoenberg was dismissed from his professorship at Berlin's Academy of the Arts immediately after Hitler came to power in 1933 (see Chapter 66). More clearly than many others at the time, he foresaw the threat of extermination that Hitler represented for Jews, and the composer fled with his family to America. In 1934 he settled in Southern California, where he continued to compose and teach, surrounded by a group of friends and émigré artists that included Edward Steuermann, Theodor Adorno, Hanns Eisler, and Alma Mahler.

In August 1947, shortly after the end of the war, Schoenberg composed a short orchestral work, *A Survivor from Warsaw*, that is his tribute to the spirit of European Jews who faced annihilation at the hands of the Nazis. In addition to the orchestra, *A Survivor from Warsaw* calls for narrator and male chorus. The narrator's words were written in English by Schoenberg himself, and they outline a brief drama told by a Jewish survivor of Nazi persecution. Schoenberg reportedly based the story on the recollections of a Jewish refugee who had hidden from the Nazis in Warsaw, only to be sent to a concentration camp. Beaten senseless by a camp guard, the narrator recalled a group of Jewish men who, about to be sent to the gas chamber, spontaneously and defiantly sang the *She'ma*, a central text of Judaism from the Old Testament book of Deuteronomy: "Hear, O Israel, the Lord our God, the Lord is one. And you shall love the Lord your God with all your heart and soul and mind. . . ." Pious Jews often recite these words when facing death.

A Survivor from Warsaw is in two distinct parts. The first is recitational, as the speaker tells the story of his persecution and brutal imprisonment (the opening of the recitation is shown in Ex. 78-3). In this part, the orchestra shadows and underscores the words by adding distorted bugle signals, nervous string tremolos played on the bridge, frantic rhythms, and a fragmented, strident texture. Schoenberg uses his twelve-tone method with great freedom, occasionally creating twelve-tone aggregates (see Chapter 69), but making no strict use of tone rows. The music is dissonant and atonal, and it shares with Strauss's *Metamorphosen* its direct emotional impact.

EXAMPLE 78-3

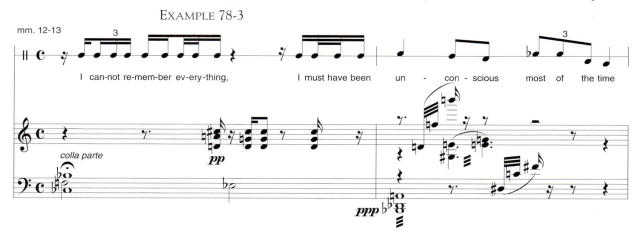

The music becomes more connected and determined in the second part, where the male chorus sings the *She'ma* prayer in a resolute unison to a strict twelve-tone melody. Its beginning is shown in Example 78-4.

EXAMPLE 78-4

✿ BENJAMIN BRITTEN AND THE WAR REQUIEM

The career of Benjamin Britten (1913–1976) was much affected by World War II. He received his musical education at London's Royal College of Music, where he studied composition and piano playing, becoming proficient on this instrument. He attracted attention in the later 1930s primarily for his orchestral music. His first international success came with his *Variations on a Theme of Frank Bridge* for string orchestra, which was heard in Salzburg in 1937 and then played around the world. By 1939 Britten was widely regarded as England's leading younger composer.

As war clouds gathered over Europe, Britten—an avowed pacifist—emigrated to America. During his absence, the war began and the blitz inflicted its ghastly toll on his homeland. His absence was noted by England's musical community. The editor of London's influential *Musical Times* snapped: "Mr. Britten is only one of many thousands of young men who 'wished to continue their work undisturbed'; and if they had all followed him to America, Hitler would have had a walk-over."[1]

Britten returned to England in 1942, making no apologies for his unconditional rejection of warfare, and he soon reestablished his public reputation. Just after the war he began to specialize in composing operas. The seventeen that he ultimately wrote include *Peter Grimes* (1945), *Billy Budd* (1951), *The Turn of the Screw* (1954), and *Death in Venice* (1973). In addition to his operas, he wrote a large number of choral compositions including *A Ceremony of Carols* (1942), *Spring Symphony* (1949), and *War Requiem* (1961). His music for solo voice includes five Canticles, a Serenade for tenor, horn, and strings (1943), and several volumes of folk song arrangements. His music for orchestra includes symphonies, concertos, and his always popular *The Young Person's Guide to the Orchestra* (1946).

Britten's *War Requiem* is one of his very greatest works and the one that most directly embodies his conscientious rejection of warfare. It was commissioned for the consecration of a new St. Michael's Cathedral in Coventry, a city in central England. Prior to the war, Coventry was home to one of the most magnificent gothic churches in the world. Its nave and altar are shown in Figure 78-1a as they once were. On the night of 14 November 1940 the city was attacked by the German air force and the cathedral entirely destroyed (Fig. 78-1b). By 1962 a new cathedral (Fig. 78-1c) was built beside the ruins of the old one, and for its commemoration Britten was commissioned to write a work that became the *War Requiem*.

It is music on a monumental scale, powerful in its emotionality. And, although Britten wrote for a world that had been victimized by warfare, he speaks with a voice that unflinchingly refuses to take sides—instead condemning all war.

Recall from Chapters 48 and 58 the traditional features of the musical Requiem Mass. Since the fifteenth century, composers had written works that drew their Latin texts

(a)

Photograph courtesy of Robert Orland

(b)

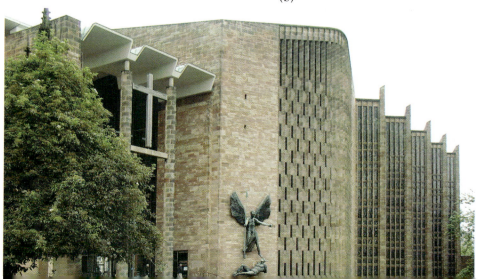

(c)

❈ FIGURE 78-1
The splendid gothic nave and altar of the Cathedral of St. Michael are shown in (a); (b) shows the same cathedral after bombardment in 1940; in (c) is the new church, completed in 1962 and the site of the premiere of Britten's *War Requiem*.

✹ FIGURE 78-2
Wilfred Owen is one of the greatest English poets at the time of World War I, during which he was killed in battle. His poetry was used by Britten in the *War Requiem*.

from, and could be subsequently used for, the Catholic Mass for the Dead, prescribed for funerals and commemorations of the deceased. In the nineteenth century, the musical requiems of Hector Berlioz, Giuseppe Verdi, and others had taken on the dramatic trappings and huge proportions of opera, making them more appropriate to the concert hall than the church. Composers beginning in the Baroque period also wrote "requiems" that do not use words from the Catholic liturgy, but other texts on the subject of death. Brahms's *German Requiem*—a concert work with texts chosen freely from the German Bible (see Chapter 58)—is an example of this nonliturgical type of requiem.

Britten's *War Requiem* refers to these earlier conceptions, but creates an essentially new composite genre. Like the requiems of Berlioz and Verdi, the *War Requiem* is huge in length and medium, and boldly expressive, sharing styles with the composer's own operas. Like Brahms, Britten dispenses with the notion of a requiem as a composition that is limited to certain traditional and preordained texts. He intertwines the war poetry of **Wilfred Owen** (1893–1918; Fig. 78-2) with the Latin texts from the traditional Catholic requiem.

The two textual strands are carefully knit together. Owen's poetry is sometimes situated to expand upon the Latin words, giving their universal sentiments a more personal resonance. At other times, Owen's English poetry is placed so as to question and even contradict the ideas expressed in the Latin words.

Wilfred Owen was a schoolteacher and amateur poet. He enlisted in the English army during World War I and was wounded near Somme. While convalescing in a hospital in Edinburgh, he discovered a great talent for poetry and also a central theme for his writing—warfare—which he condemned unconditionally. His poetry expresses a deep compassion for the individual soldier—enemy as well as ally—and an indignation at social conditions that lead to war. In 1918 Owen returned to combat in France, where he was killed one week before the armistice.

Owen's antiwar sentiments were shared by many people in England during World War I, when the issues underlying the conflict often seemed unclear and not commensurate with its horrible human toll. Britten's decision to bring them forward into a commission dealing with the aftermath of German aggression during World War II proved highly controversial, especially since Owen's poetry allows for no distinction between right and wrong in war—it is all wrong, he says—and attributes the cause of warfare to the warmongering press, misguided national allegiances, and even to the church.

The interweaving of the traditional Latin texts and Owen's personalized visions of war is especially skillful in the fifth movement, Agnus Dei. Here, as elsewhere in the work, the distinctions that separate the English from the Latin words are made even sharper by instrumentation. Throughout Britten's *War Requiem*, the Latin words are sung by mixed chorus, boys' choir, or soprano soloist, accompanied by a large orchestra (the boys are accompanied only by organ). The English poetry is sung by baritone and tenor soloists—who represent the individual voices of soldiers—accompanied by a separate chamber orchestra.

In this fifth movement, the chorus, accompanied by full orchestra, sings the Agnus dei. This text has a special form in the Requiem Mass that is slightly different from its reading in the regular Mass. The sentence "Lamb of God, who takes away the sins of the world, grant them rest" is sung three times, the final repetition ending ". . . grant them eternal rest." These three statements alternate with the tenor voice, accompanied by chamber orchestra, singing Owen's poem "At a Calvary Near the Ancre." In it, the poet compares Jesus at the time of the crucifixion to a soldier in war, separated from his comrades and in the hands of a ruthless enemy. He is cruci-fied with the complicity of smug priests and writers who fan the flames of national-ism. In a short coda the tenor intones "Dona nobis pacem" ("Give us peace"), these words taken from the Agnus dei in the regular Catholic Mass.

The music is haunting, with a disarming simplicity. An ostinato runs throughout, made at first from a figure (Ex. 78-5) with notes of a descending B-minor scale seg-ment followed by a C-major scale. The music itself is a study in opposites—ascend-ing motions placed next to those descending, major triads and scale segments beside those in minor, the tone C placed opposite F♯. The tenor's music constantly changes and evolves, while the music of the chorus is ever the same, and the voice of protest in Owen's words stands in stark contrast to that of unquestioning acceptance in the Latin ones.

EXAMPLE 78-5

In the coda, the unaccompanied tenor, singing the words "give us peace," struggles to overcome the opposites but cannot do so. In one of the most memorable conclu-sions in all of modern music, the voice dies away on the tone F♯, with peace but no resolution (Ex. 78-6).

EXAMPLE 78-6

LISTENING CUE

BENJAMIN BRITTEN
War Requiem (1961)
Agnus dei

CD 13/1
Anthology, No. 202

KRZYSZTOF PENDERECKI, THRENODY FOR THE VICTIMS OF HIROSHIMA

The aftermath of World War II drove Strauss, Schoenberg, and Britten toward a re-newed emotionalism and led them to avoid, each in his own way, the cool emo-tional detachment that characterized much of the modern music between the world wars. This new element of *espressivo* is also found in postwar music by the Polish composer Krzysztof Penderecki (b. 1933), although his musical materials are experi-mental, very different from those of his older contemporaries.

Penderecki (pronounced pen-der-RET-skee) was born in Dębica (south of the Polish capital city of Warsaw), and after World War II he resumed his education at the conservatory in Kraków. His music began to attract attention in the late 1950s, just as Poland was leading the way among Communist Bloc countries in allowing its artists greater freedom of expression. Penderecki's works were heard at the modern musical festival called **Warsaw Autumn,** where younger Polish composers boldly separated themselves from an old-fashioned socialist realism (see Chapter 74) and made contact with new ideas in music among European contemporaries. From 1966 Penderecki lived abroad, mainly in Germany and the United States, although he returned to Poland in 1972.

His music includes the operas *The Devils of Loudon* (1968) and *The Black Mask* (1986), five symphonies and numerous concertos, two string quartets and two violin sonatas, and a large amount of Latin sacred music for chorus. This includes *St. Luke Passion* (1966), *Psalms of David* (1958), *Te Deum* (1980), *Magnificat* (1974), and *Stabat mater* (1962). His *Polish Requiem* (1984) was inspired by the Solidarity uprising in Poland that led to the country's liberation from Soviet domination. Several of his pieces were used by Stanley Kubrick in the 1980 movie *The Shining*.

Threnody for the Victims of Hiroshima (1960) was one of Penderecki's earliest compositions to attract international attention. It calls for fifty-two string instruments, and it was at first given the most neutral of titles, 8'37". The extent to which the music is a **threnody** (a song of lamentation) is not clear, but the shrieking sounds of the violins at the opening, the crackling whip-like noises in the middle, and the sense of disintegration at the end could easily suggest to the listener images of the terrible suffering of Hiroshima's victims. In all likelihood the title—which suggests a protest against the West—was primarily chosen to make the boldly experimental composition more appealing to conservative Polish authorities.

The style of the *Threnody* is based upon ideas drawn from electronic music of the 1950s (see Chapter 80). Penderecki worked in an electronic music studio at the Polish Radio in Warsaw just at the time that he was composing *Threnody*, and he was probably familiar with the 1950s electronic compositions by the Europeans Karlheinz Stockhausen and Iannis Xenakis. The tape works of Xenakis are especially relevant. In his *Concret PH*, written for the Brussels Exposition in 1958 and much publicized at the time (see Chapter 80), Xenakis made up a piece of music by recording the sound of burning charcoal. Its crackling noises were then amplified, edited, and returned to tape as a work of music that was devoid of regular rhythm, line, chord, interval, and all other such traditional building blocks.

These older materials were replaced by **sound masses,** which become the basic elements of the composition. The composer casts the sonorous textures into an artistic shape by molding their density and volume. Xenakis referred to such works as **stochastic** (that is, involving chance and probability) since he could not control individual sounds—these behaved randomly—but only their totality, which he could accurately predict and manipulate.

This is essentially Penderecki's approach in the *Threnody*, although he achieves comparable effects by sounds from the string instruments playing in real time. The basic elements of the piece are not notes, intervals, and rhythms per se, only masses of sounds achieved by giving the orchestra a variety of unusual playing instructions. For example, the instrumentalists are told that at a certain time they should play and sustain the highest note on their instrument. At another point they are instructed to tap on its sound board, or scrape on the wood of the bridge, or noodle on tones and microtones chosen randomly within some fixed interval. Much of what they do is left for them to decide, allowing the players to make sounds that are random incidents—not determined by the composer—much as Xenakis had no control over the individual sounds of his burning charcoal.

Penderecki devises special notational symbols, or **graphic notations,** to guide the players, and he controls their coordination by laying out the score in a succession of blocks, each of a specific duration. See how this works by studying the very beginning of the score (Ex. 78-7). The first graphic figure is a black wedge, which tells the strings to play and sustain their highest possible note, which will be different for every player. During the first block of time, fifteen seconds long, other groups of strings enter, also on their highest tones. The second block lasts for eleven seconds, and here some of the string groups are instructed by the wavy line to play their high tone with a slow, wide vibrato, others with a smaller, faster vibrato.

EXAMPLE 78-7[†]

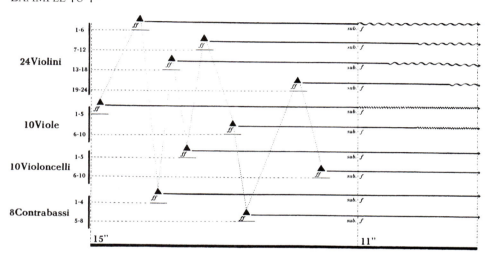

The piece has no form in the traditional sense—no thematic exposition, development, and return—although it has a definite shape as it moves through passages of tension and relaxation. At the opening, the shriek of each instrument's highest tone gradually erodes into a softer dynamic level. This first sound mass soon gives way to one characterized by popping and crackling noises, then by more tranquil tone clusters.

Penderecki's ideas were widely influential on modern music in the 1960s. His insistence on music as an expressive art formed a bridge between the postwar tendency toward abstraction and a return in the 1970s to more traditional values. This transition will be the subject of later chapters.

🎵 LISTENING CUE

KRZYSZTOF PENDERECKI

Threnody for the Victims of Hiroshima (1960)

CD 13/2

Anthology, No. 203

SUMMARY

World War II (1939–1945) was unprecedented in the loss of life, destruction, and upheaval that it brought upon civilization. It produced not only a change of style in modern music but also a group of compositions that deal with the theme of warfare. *Metamorphosen* (1945), by Richard Strauss, is a work of mourning, written in an elegiac romantic style in which the composer at the end quotes the Funeral March theme from Beethoven's "Eroica" Symphony. Arnold Schoenberg's *A Survivor from Warsaw* (1947) calls for orchestra, male chorus, and narrator to present the drama of a survivor of Nazi persecution. The narrator recalls a group of Jewish prisoners, about to be sent to the gas chamber, who break defiantly into the singing of a Hebrew prayer. The work uses a free version of the twelve-tone method and achieves a powerful effect.

Benjamin Britten was a pacifist who refused service in the British military during World War II, and his *War Requiem* (1961) makes a monumental statement in opposition to all warfare. The work is for two orchestras, two choruses, and solo voices, and it uses poetry by Wilfred Owen in addition to Latin texts from the traditional Roman Catholic Requiem Mass. Krzysztof Penderecki's *Threnody for the Victims of Hiroshima* (1960), for large string orchestra, deploys sound masses to communicate the anguished images of the victims of war.

KEY TERMS

World War II	Wilfred Owen	sound mass
Holocaust	Warsaw Autumn Festival	stochastic music
metamorphoses	threnody	graphic notation

Chapter 79

Twelve-Tone Music and Serialism after World War II

As World War II came to an end, most observers of the arts expected that neoclassicism would return to center stage in modern music, just where it was before the war. Stravinsky—the leading figure in this style—was then living on the American West Coast and at the height of his powers. During the war he had composed the magnificent Symphony in C and the Symphony in Three Movements, and he was about to begin one of his most important works of the neoclassical type: the opera *The Rake's Progress* (completed in 1951). This was "an opera of arias and recitatives, choruses and ensembles," as he called it, which would fit into the number opera mold of Mozart's comic Italian operas.

The German neoclassicist Paul Hindemith, living during the war on the East Coast, had been equally productive. Following war's end his music was briskly in demand in Germany. His publisher, Willy Strecker, wrote to him in 1946 to report that the music of other composers could not be obtained: "In consequence Krenek, Schönberg, Bartók, Weill, Berg etc. have been consigned to virtual oblivion. You and Stravinsky are the only ones of the whole former group still left." Stravinsky and Hindemith had ever fewer rivals among established composers. Berg, Webern, and Bartók were dead; Weill died in 1950, and Schoenberg in 1951.

But shortly after the war concluded, the whole style and aesthetic of neoclassicism came under attack in both Europe and America, especially from younger composers. Elliott Carter (b. 1908) found the idiom out of touch with a world that had experienced total warfare. "The whole conception of human nature underlying the neoclassical aesthetic," he said, "amounted to a sweeping under the rug of things that, it seemed to me, we had to deal with in a less oblique and resigned way."[1]

Pierre Boulez (b. 1925) was even more emphatic. In 1951 he asked:

> Can a "universal" language be established now? By means of "neoclassicism"? One scarcely needs to deny it, given the total gratuity of the game thus played, its historical necessity not being at all evident. The distracting sudden movements—as distracted as distracting—from Bach to Tchaikovsky, from Pergolesi to Mendelssohn, from Beethoven to the Renaissance polyphonists, mark off the steps toward an eclectic, miserable insolvency without the smallest embryo of a language being forced into birth.[2]

THE TWELVE-TONE REVIVAL

It was Carter, Boulez, and other younger composers—far more than the older, established figures—who set the agenda for modern music after World War II. They rejected neoclassicism in favor of a dizzying variety of experimental approaches to music. One of the earliest and most striking aspects of their revisionist thinking was the emphasis on and extension of twelve-tone composition and serialism. Recall from Chapter 69 that these terms refer to interrelated compositional procedures put forward in the early 1920s by Arnold Schoenberg and used in different ways by him and his students Alban Berg and Anton Webern.

Recall that a twelve-tone composition by Schoenberg presents a succession of twelve-tone aggregates, which are lines and harmonies that contain all twelve notes of the chromatic scale with none omitted and none repeated out of context. These arise methodically in Schoenberg's music by "serialism" applied to the choice of tones. In general, serialism is a compositional procedure in which choices are influenced or dictated by a pre-compositional ordering of elements. In a twelve-tone piece by Schoenberg, serialism is evident in the use of a basic ordering of the twelve tones—a "tone row," that is—which then governs the choice of pitches throughout the composition.

Prior to the end of World War II, Schoenberg's method had exerted only a minor impact on the musical world outside of his own circle. Twelve-tone music was usually thorny and difficult, full of dissonance and chromaticism, which made it jarring to audiences attuned to the greater simplicity and diatonicism of neoclassical works. During World War II itself, performances of twelve-tone music virtually disappeared in Europe and scores became unavailable. A few composers in the 1930s experimented with aspects of Schoenberg's method—Copland in the *Piano Variations* (see Chapter 76), the Viennese composer **Ernst Krenek,** the Swiss-French composer Frank Martin, and the Italian Luigi Dallapiccola—but Schoenberg's bold prediction that the method would "insure the supremacy of German music for the next hundred years" seemed by 1945 to be an idle boast.

MILTON BABBITT AND "TOTAL SERIALISM"

The impulse to revive twelve-tone and serial composition was strongly felt in the United States after the war. In this country, scores by Schoenberg, Berg, and Webern were readily available for study, and Schoenberg himself occasionally lectured on the workings of the method. An important factor in the dispersal across the United States of information on twelve-tone music was the writing of the émigré composer and scholar Ernst Krenek (1900–1991). Krenek was Viennese, and made his reputation in the 1920s as a composer in a neoclassical vein. In the 1930s he changed his outlook and adopted a version of the twelve-tone method, first in his opera *Karl V* (1933). In 1938 he immigrated to America, where, unlike Schoenberg, he frequently wrote on the subject of twelve-tone composition, even producing a textbook, *Studies in Counterpoint Based on the Twelve-Tone Technique* (1940). His ideas were especially important for the twelve-tone music of his student George Perle (b. 1915) and for the twelve-tone compositions of Igor Stravinsky.

Twelve-tone and serial procedures were taken in an important new direction following World War II by the American composer **Milton Babbitt** (b. 1916). Beginning in the 1930s, Babbitt taught at Princeton University—both in mathematics and music—and his influence was exerted through his teaching and theoretical writings on the twelve-tone idea as well as through his musical compositions. His point of departure as a composer was the twelve-tone music of Schoenberg, which he found uniquely revolutionary "in its nature and implications, the degree to which it imposes new demands of perception and conception upon the composer and listener, and—therefore—the degree to which it admits of further and extensive exploration and discovery."[3]

Babbitt studied the systematic aspects of Schoenberg's method (something never emphasized by Schoenberg himself), with the intention of broadening its applicability and reinforcing its capacity for organization in his own new works. He began to apply this expanded notion of serialism in 1947, in his Three Compositions for Piano (published in 1957). Stylistically, Composition No. 1 reflects several influences: it has the strictly linear texture of a two-part invention, exemplifying the counterpoint that Krenek considered a necessary outcome of the twelve-tone technique. Its syncopated and jazzy flavor may recall Babbitt's own background as a jazz performer, and aspects of the work's twelve-tone method come from Schoenberg.

Composition No. 1 is based on the tone row: Bb-Eb-F -D-C-Db-G-B-F#-A-Ab-E. Babbitt lays out forms of the basic row (transpositions, inversions, and retrogrades) in each of the work's two lines. Except for a few measures in which only one hand plays, the two hands simultaneously state different row forms, and these are always chosen to exhibit a special relationship—also found in Schoenberg's twelve-tone music— that Babbitt called **combinatoriality** (it is sometimes also called "complementarity").

Combinatoriality refers to the capacity of two or more forms of a row to create aggregates when stacked vertically. A simple example of the phenomenon can be observed in the first two measures of Composition No. 1. The left hand states the basic row while the right hand states this row transposed to the tritone:

measure 1		measure 2			

right hand:

E	A	B	Ab	F#	G		Db	F	C	Eb	D	Bb

left hand:

Bb	Eb	F	D	C	Db		G	B	F#	A	Ab	E

Not only does each line contain the twelve tones, but twelve-tone aggregates are also formed in each measure, and thus the twelve tones more completely penetrate the entire two-dimensional texture.

Babbitt also extends the principle underlying the inversion and retrogression of tone rows to the work's rhythms. Recall from Chapter 69 that Anton Webern in his Symphony, Op. 21, had presented a series of rhythmic durations in retrograde when he used a retrograded tone row. Babbitt goes considerably beyond Webern in his own system for serializing such compositional decisions. In Composition No. 1, he begins with a basic rhythmic figure made by grouping together first five, then one, then four, and finally two sixteenth-notes. Look at Example 79-1 (showing the rhythm in the left hand in mm. 1–2) to see how this works. There are four groups of sixteenth-notes, each ended by a rest or by having its last note lengthened, and these groups contain 5, 1, 4, and 2 values, respectively. The rhythmic numbers 5 1 4 2 create a row that can be retrograded, just like a tone row. Whenever a retrograded row of pitches occurs, Babbitt applies the retrograded rhythmic row (2 4 1 5). An example arises in the right hand in measures 3–4, as shown in Example 79-2.

EXAMPLE 79-1

EXAMPLE 79-2

Rhythmic row: 2   4   1   5
pitch row: simple retrograde of the basic row

But how can such a rhythmic row be inverted? Babbitt answers the question by resorting to a simple numerical operation by which a pitch row can be inverted, and he then uses the same operation on the rhythmic numbers. He first represents the notes of the basic series by integers from 0 to 11. He defines 0 as the first note in the row and replaces the other tones by their number of semitones above the first note. In this way the basic row of Composition No. 1 can be represented as this number set:

> 0   5   7   4   2   3   9   1   8   11 10 6
> (B♭ E♭ F   D   C   D♭ G   B   F♯ A   A♭ E)

An inversion of the tone row can be obtained simply by subtracting each number from 12 (the number 12 in the result is replaced by 0):

Inversion:

> 0   7   5   8   10 9   3   11 4   1   2   6
> (B♭ F   E♭ G♭ A♭ G   D♭ A   D   B   C   E)

"Who Cares If You Listen?" by Milton Babbitt (excerpts)

Babbitt's 1958 article "Who Cares If You Listen?" (originally titled "The Composer as Specialist") unequivocally states the composer's reaction to public indifference toward his music. Such works have evolved beyond the understanding of most people, Babbitt writes, so it follows that there is no longer a reason for a composer to present this music to the public at large.

. . . The unprecedented divergence between contemporary serious music and its listeners, on the one hand, and traditional music and its following, on the other, is not accidental and—most probably—not transitory. Rather, it is a result of a half-century of revolution in musical thought, a revolution whose nature and consequences can be compared only with, and in many respects are closely analogous to, those of the mid-nineteenth-century revolution in mathematics and the twentieth-century revolution in theoretical physics. . . .

Why should the layman be other than bored and puzzled by what he is unable to understand, music or anything else? It is only the translation of this boredom and puzzlement into resentment and denunciation that seems to me indefensible. After all, the public does have its own music, its ubiquitous music: music to eat by, to read by, to dance by, and to be impressed by. Why refuse to recognize the possibility that contemporary music has reached a stage long since attained by other forms of activity?

The time has passed when the normally well-educated man without special preparation could understand the most advanced work in, for example, mathematics, philosophy, and physics. Advanced music, to the extent that it reflects the knowledge and originality of the informed composer, scarcely can be expected to appear more intelligible than these arts and sciences to the person whose musical education usually has been even less extensive than his background in other fields. . . .

I say all this not to present a picture of a virtuous music in a sinful world, but to point up the problems of a special music in an alien and inapposite world. And so, I dare suggest that the composer would do himself and his music an immediate and eventual service by total, resolute, and voluntary withdrawal from this public world to one of private performance and electronic media, with its very real possibility of complete elimination of the public and social aspects of musical composition. By so doing the separation between the domains would be defined beyond any possibility of confusion of categories, and the composer would be free to pursue a private life of professional achievement, as opposed to a public life of unprofessional compromise and exhibitionism. . . .[4]

This same operation is then applied to the rhythmic row 5 1 4 2. It is "inverted" by subtracting each number from 6, which produces the row 1 5 2 4. Babbitt brings this rhythmic row into play whenever an inverted pitch row is present, as in the right hand in measures 7–8 (Ex. 79-3).

EXAMPLE 79-3

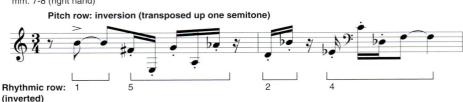

LISTENING CUE

MILTON BABBITT
Composition for Piano No. 1 (1947)

CD 13/3
Anthology, No. 204

In these and related ways, Babbitt in Composition No. 1 takes a step toward what he later termed "total structuralization" (others call it **total serialism**), since a single serial principle has been extended beyond pitch to organize multiple elements of the work. Plainly, total serialism represents a reduction in the free choices available to a composer and a step toward a degree of automatism in the compositional process. These were very much in the spirit of the postwar period, when artists wished to reestablish control in the arts, after a time when all of society seemed out of control. At virtually the same moment—apparently independently from Babbitt—the European composer Olivier Messiaen was experimenting with a similarly automated approach to composing. This will be addressed in the next chapter.

IGOR STRAVINSKY, AGON

The rumblings of serialism among younger composers in both Europe and America in the late 1940s broke into a loud roar in 1952, with the premiere of Stravinsky's *Cantata*. The fourth movement of this work begins with a tenor soloist singing the melody shown in Example 79-4. The brackets (which were placed into the score by Stravinsky himself, as though marking something not to be missed) show tone rows: the first is a basic series, the second its retrograde, the third its inversion, and the fourth the inversion in retrograde. The strictly linear presentation of these units and their overlap—the final one or two tones of one row become the first such in the next row—had been a distinctive features of row usage in the music of Anton Webern, which Stravinsky is said to have studied while composing the work.

EXAMPLE 79-4

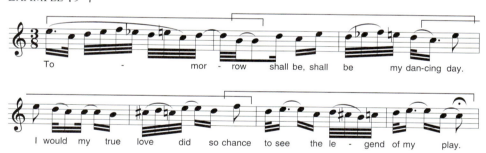

To - mor - row shall be, shall be my dan-cing day.

I would my true love did so chance to see the le - gend of my play.

In his new music, composed between 1952 and 1958, Stravinsky (Fig. 79-1) gradually reinforced the use of serialism and, later, the formation of twelve-tone aggregates. These changes of technique mark one of the most important moments in the history of twentieth-century music. Stravinsky's new procedures signaled a partial abandonment of the neoclassical style by its leading figure and an indication that serialism and twelve-tone composition were poised to become the new common practices of the postwar period.

Why did Stravinsky change his way of composing? He never wrote in detail about this matter, although he insisted that he did not

FIGURE 79-1
Stravinsky in 1956, during which time he composed *Agon*.

calculate a style: "I can follow only where my musical appetites lead me," he wrote. He held also that the ideas in his serial music were not so different from those of his neoclassical works, only expressed in a more evolved language: "A step in this evolution does not cancel the one before."

Certainly, the critical writings of authors such as Boulez—already cited for his attack upon neolassicism—must have influenced the older composer, who understandably did not wish to be left behind in the new postwar order. Boulez grew ever more strident on the issue: "I, in turn, assert that any musician who has not experienced—I do not say understood, but, in all exactness, experienced—the necessity for the dodecaphonic language is USELESS. For his whole work is irrelevant to the needs of his epoch," Boulez wrote in 1952.[5]

Other writers of the day were relentless in asserting the priority of Schoenberg over Stravinsky. Theodor Adorno in his influential *Philosophie der neuen Musik* (*Philosophy of New Music*, 1949) dismissed Stravinsky as the composer of "fashionable commercial music," something for "listeners who wish their music to be familiar, but at the same time to be labeled modern."[6] The twelve-tone method, Adorno continued, grew from the bedrock of music itself: "Among the rules of twelve-tone technique, there is not one which does not proceed necessarily out of compositional experience—out of the progressive illumination of the natural material of music."[7]

Stravinsky may have read such polemics as harbingers of a new taste, to which he decided to conform. The stages in his conversion from neoclassicist to twelve-tone composer are apparent in the sections of his ballet *Agon* (1953–1957). In creating this twenty-minute work, Stravinsky collaborated with the Russian-American choreographer **George Balanchine** (1904–1983). The ballet calls for twelve dancers—four men and eight women—who dance twelve short numbers that suggest an abstract competition (*agon* is the Greek word for a contest). There is no plot. Some of the dance types, like the *pas de deux* (see Chapter 59), are customary in modern ballet; others—a sarabande, galliard, and three branles—are in the style of old French court dances. The score is tied together by recurrent instrumental passages, and some of the dances share musical materials with their neighboring ones.

This continuity from dance to dance is especially evident in the center of the work, in the series of three branles. These were among the last parts of the ballet to be composed, and they contain a fairly strict serialism and, in the last of the three, also twelve-tone organization. This is unlike the sections of the ballet composed earlier, which have a diatonicism reminiscent of the neoclassical style.

The name of the old French dance called the **branle** (or bransle) comes from the verb *branler,* to shake or swing. The seventeenth-century lexicographer Randle Cotgrave—apparently searching for just the right word—described it as "a totter, swing, or swindge; a shake, shog, or shocke." It was a dance, Cotgrave continued, "wherein many (men and women) holding by the hands sometimes in a ring, and otherwise at length, move all together."[8] There were several different types of branles, distinguished by character, meter, and phrasing, and Stravinsky chose ones called "simple," "gay," and "double" for his group of three. Although he consulted a seventeenth-century dance treatise, he seems to have been concerned with historical authenticity only in general features of tempo and meter.

There is much about the Bransle Double—the last of the group—that still reminds us of Stravinsky's earlier neoclassical music. It has a rigidity of beat that suggests the motoric rhythms of his earlier works and a hard, clear sound made from an orchestra that juxtaposes small groups of brass, woodwinds, and strings. But the movement has many new features. It is chromatic rather than diatonic, dissonant rather than triadic, and it has none of the witty parody and leisurely tunefulness of neoclassicism. All such features are replaced by a tone of concise abstraction.

The pitch structure of the movement is entirely serialized, based on this twelve-tone row:

C D E♭ F E A G A♭ B♭ C♭ D♭ G♭

As in the *Cantata*, the row forms are laid out linearly—not partitioned into the accompanimental texture, as was Schoenberg's preference. Again, Stravinsky links rows together so that they overlap by one or two notes. This can be observed in the main theme, shown in Example 79-5, which is made from the basic series followed by its retrograde inversion, the two elided on the note G♭. Also like Webern's technique is Stravinsky's placement of tones of the row into widely distant registers, which weakens the sense of line. The accompaniment of the main theme—in the brass and, later, in the string instruments—does not use full twelve-tone rows, instead, only half-rows.

EXAMPLE 79-5

LISTENING CUE

IGOR STRAVINSKY
Agon (1953–1957)
Bransle Double

CD 13/4
Anthology, No. 205

Several important conclusions concerning the history of twentieth-century music can be drawn from Stravinsky's conversion to serial and twelve-tone composition. It confirmed, first of all, that a new style period had dawned on the musical world in the 1950s and that serial composition would be one of its principal features. It underscored the primary relevance of the Viennese School of composers—especially Schoenberg and Webern—for the larger direction of music in this century. Since it represented the third major style embraced by Stravinsky—unquestionably one of the leading composers of the century—it showed that the evolution of musical taste and idiom had taken on a quicker pace in the twentieth century than ever before. In the past, a few major composers stood astride two eras in music history. Claudio Monteverdi, for example, bridged both the Renaissance and Baroque periods; Beethoven, the Classic and Romantic periods. Now, in the twentieth century, Stravinsky's career and music spanned fully three major periods, and a sorting out of overlapping styles would be more difficult than ever in the past.

✺ PIERRE BOULEZ, *LE MARTEAU SANS MAÎTRE*

While Stravinsky and Babbitt turned in the 1950s to twelve-tone music in a form that was reasonably close to the ways that Schoenberg and Webern had used this technique, many European composers of the 1950s hatched their own highly idiosyncratic interpretations of serialism that had little to do with their Viennese forebears. Many of Europe's younger composers learned about twelve-tone composition and shared ideas for its reinterpretation at the International Summer Courses for New Music, founded in 1946 in the German town of **Darmstadt** (near Frankfurt). With established composers including René Leibowitz and Olivier Messiaen looking on approvingly, the younger musicians Luigi Nono (1924–1990), Karlheinz Stockhausen (b. 1928), and Pierre Boulez (b. 1925) led discussions, study sessions, and concerts that soon linked the name Darmstadt with a doctrinaire outlook on the need for serialism in new music.

Pierre Boulez was closely associated with Darmstadt beginning in the mid-1950s. He had come to Paris as a student in 1942 and entered the conservatory, where he studied with Olivier Messiaen, among others. He learned about twelve-tone music in private study with René Leibowitz, and began to compose serial pieces from 1945 onward. In the early 1950s, in works such as his *Structures* for two pianos, Boulez arrived at a highly automated system of total serialism. Shortly thereafter he became active as a conductor, and in 1971 rose to the position of music director of the New York Philharmonic Orchestra (Fig. 79-2). Since 1974 he has directed the Institut de Recherche et Coordination Acoustique/Musique (Institute for Musical Research and Collaboration, called **IRCAM**) in Paris, which is devoted to explorations into and performance of new music.

Boulez has always been outspoken in his demand that modern music must wipe the slate clean of styles from the past—and not only those inherited from the neoclassicists. Only months after Schoenberg's death in 1951, Boulez published an inflammatory article titled "Schoenberg Is Dead." This did not contain the heartfelt eulogy that everyone expected. Instead, Boulez lashed out at Schoenberg's traditionalism—especially his familiar textures made from melody and accompaniment—and also against his limited use of the serial principle. Schoenberg's twelve-tone music, Boulez asserted, was a "catastrophe," heading in "a direction as wrong as any in the history of music." "So let us not hesitate to say," he concluded, "without any silly desire for scandal, but equally without shamefaced hypocrisy or pointless melancholy: SCHOENBERG IS DEAD."[9]

But by the mid-1950s Boulez had backed away from his dogmatism concerning the necessity for strict serial composition, and he looked for freer ways of composing. He stopped writing totally serialized music and created his own private method for tonal organization. He began to admit chance procedures into his music (see Chapter 80), and he looked for ways to balance "freedom of invention and the need for discipline in invention," as he wrote.

The interchange between freedom and discipline is apparent in Boulez's most often performed work, *Le marteau sans maître* (*The Hammer Without a Master*, 1955). This half-hour composition calls for alto voice and six instrumentalists: viola,

✺ FIGURE 79-2

The outspoken Pierre Boulez served as music director of the New York Philharmonic Orchestra from 1971 to 1977. He continues to compose and conduct today.

CORBIS

alto flute, guitar, vibraphone, xylorimba (a xylophone with an extended low register), and one percussionist playing multiple instruments. The voice sings in four of the work's nine movements, using poetry by **René Char** (1907–1988), and (like Schoenberg's *Pierrot lunaire*) each movement has a different instrumentation.

The overall structure of the work is complex. The nine movements are intertwined into three cycles, each containing a setting of one of Char's surrealistic poems and also instrumental commentaries upon these poems. The three cycles are summarized in this diagram:

↓*Cycle 1* (based on the text "The raging proletariat")

　　↓*Cycle 2* (based on "Hangmen of loneliness")

　　　　↓*Cycle 3* (based on "Beautiful edifice and forebodings")

1. Before "The raging proletariat" (instruments)

　　2. Commentary I to "Hangmen of loneliness" (instruments)

3. "The raging proletariat" (voice and instruments)

　　4. Commentary II to "Hangmen of loneliness" (instruments)

　　　　5. "Beautiful edifice and forebodings" (voice and instruments)

6. "Hangmen of loneliness" (voice and instruments)

7. After "The raging proletariat" (instruments)

　　8. Commentary III to "Hangmen of loneliness" (instruments)

　　　　9. Counterpart to "Beautiful edifice and forebodings" (voice and instruments)

The third movement, "L'artisanat furieux" ("The raging proletariat"), for voice and alto flute, is by far the simplest and most conventional part of this immensely complicated work. The poem is drawn from a 1934 collection of Char's poetry, also titled *Le marteau sans maître*, that stemmed from the literary movement called **surrealism.** Here a poet gives out images, feelings, and memories, often disconnected and incongruous, that seem to spill from the unconscious mind. "L'artisanat furieux" is a poem in prose that uncovers a grotesque and fantastic dream:

> La roulotte rouge au bord du clou
> Et cadavre dans le panier
> Et chevaux de labours dans le fer à cheval
> Je rêve la tête sur la pointe de mon couteau le Pérou
>
> The red caravan beside the prison
> And a body in the basket
> And work horses in the horseshoe
> I dream with my head on the point of my Peruvian knife.

Boulez does not set the poem to music in a traditional way, in which its ideas are underscored by music. Instead, the words create sounds as though detached from meaning, and these are floated into a freely ornamental dialogue with the alto flute. One of the composer's stated premises in the work is to synthesize word sounds with instrumental tones and to find a common sound shared by both instruments and voice, all leading to a unity on the basis of sound alone. (In Chapter 82 we will see Italian composer Luciano Berio continue with this experiment.)

Boulez removes all feeling of beat or regular rhythm, allowing the music to float without a sense of moving from beginning to end. There are no musical themes or motives in the normal sense. These are dispelled through the avoidance of a connected line and the absence of any thematic development or return.

The work's tonal organization is the product of Boulez's own private system. It takes its departure from serial and twelve-tone procedures, but these lead to music that has virtually nothing in common with traditional twelve-tone or serialized structures. In composing *Le marteau sans maître* Boulez began with a twelve-tone row that he divided into segments of different sizes. These were then "multiplied" with one another. In simple terms, multiplication reproduces the intervals of one segment of the row on each note of some other segment, and the products are treated as pitch collections without any inherent ordering. They are deployed in the composition in a way that is partly predetermined, partly free. There is no possibility in Boulez's system for a tone row being identified with a theme—something that he found objectionable in earlier twelve-tone music.

 LISTENING CUE

PIERRE BOULEZ	CD 13/5
Le marteau sans maître (1955)	Anthology, No. 206
"L'artisanat furieux"	

 THE WANING OF THE TWELVE-TONE METHOD

Stravinsky's adoption of twelve-tone and serial procedures in his music was soon matched by other established figures. Aaron Copland, William Walton, Benjamin Britten, and Roger Sessions all wrote twelve-tone music of some type shortly thereafter. But Boulez's rejection of doctrinaire twelve-tone and serial procedures in *Le marteau sans maître* was the harbinger of a general turning away from these methods.

Stravinsky persisted in writing strictly twelve-tone music to the end of his composing career in 1966, but by then the method had been dropped by most other musicians, both young and old. Increasingly, serialism represented a mentality about composition that came under attack. Krzysztof Penderecki wrote: "Anyone can learn to write twelve-tone music—you don't even have to be a composer. There were no standards. Anyone who had been in Darmstadt for one or two weeks thought that he could compose."[10] For Luciano Berio, serialism was close to fascism, something that could only produce music that was "dull on the outside and empty inside." By 1960 it was clear that other alternatives would have to be found for music in a postwar society.

 SUMMARY

Following World War II, younger composers in Europe and America rejected neoclassicism, which before the war had been the dominant style of modern music worldwide. It its place they at first proposed a revival of twelve-tone and serial composition, extending the thinking that underlay these methods to encompass not only the selection of pitch but also rhythm and other variables in a composition, thus producing "total serialism." In America, Milton Babbitt used a mathematical model to create a common procedure by which both rhythms and pitches could be inverted.

Babbitt's interest in serial procedures received a boost when they were adopted in the 1950s by Igor Stravinsky, who took the twelve-tone music of Webern as his principal model. Stravinsky's use of the twelve-tone method confirmed the existence of a new style period in the 1950s, with serial composition as one of its principal features.

Pierre Boulez began his career as a composer of strictly serialized music, but in *Le marteau sans maître* (1955) he reinterpreted its methods for tonal organization in a far freer manner. This was the harbinger of a general rejection of the twelve-tone method and other strict serial procedures.

KEY TERMS

Ernst Krenek
Milton Babbitt
combinatoriality
total serialism
George Balanchine

branle (bransle)
Darmstadt
IRCAM (Institut de
  Recherche et Coordination
  Acoustique/Musique)

René Char
surrealism

Alternatives to Serialism: Chance, Electronics, Textures

Chapter 80

During the quarter-century that followed the end of World War II in 1945, serialism was one of many approaches to music that seemed appropriate to a time of international readjustment. Total serialism—with its tendency to automate the compositional process—had the effect of imposing a strict control on music, something that seemed fitting after a wartime period when society lacked control. The postwar years were also filled with a great anxiety that found expression, often indirectly, in music. Warfare continued sporadically in Southeast Asia—first in Korea, then in Viet Nam—and the threat of nuclear destruction now hung over mankind. The spread of Communism and the prospect of a renewed worldwide conflict between America and the Soviet Union were also in people's minds. What type of classical music could have meaning in such a world?

Composers during the quarter-century after 1945 found no unanimous answer to this question. Pierre Boulez was one of numerous musicians who had loudly insisted on the necessity of twelve-tone and serial music, but by 1955 he had backed away from a strict serialism and opted instead for greater freedom (see Chapter 79). Others could not accept serialism at all. Elliott Carter commented in 1960 on twelve-tone music: "I have found that it is apparently inapplicable to what I am trying to do, and is more of a hindrance than a help."[1] These composers experimented with drastically different types of music, in which the only apparent common feature is a rejection of the past and a search for novelty.

In this chapter we turn to three such innovative outlooks that were prominent in the 1950s and 1960s: chance music, electronic music, and experiments with new musical textures. For each of these we will focus on one of its most representative composers.

✿ CHANCE MUSIC: JOHN CAGE

The most radical of all the postwar experiments was the composing of music by **chance,** that is, making compositional choices at random rather than basing them on taste, musical laws, or traditions. Its most vigorous proponent was the American composer John Cage (1912–1992).

Cage was born in Los Angeles, and in the 1930s he began to compose in an independently modern fashion. He was briefly a student of Arnold Schoenberg, who advised him to give up music since he showed no feeling for harmony. Not discouraged by this advice, Cage went on to write music without harmony. In the 1940s he attracted attention with pieces for percussion ensemble—a medium explored earlier in music by the French-American composer Edgard Varèse (discussed later in this chapter).

At first, Cage composed in a highly systematic way—just the opposite of his later reliance on chance. To organize the durations and sectional divisions in his music, he devised a numerical system that would have made a serialist proud. See how it works in his Sonata No. 5, from *Sonatas and Interludes* (1948; Ex. 80-1). A series of numbers, 4 4 5 5, controls the formal durations and phrasing in both the large and small dimensions of the piece. On the large scale, the work has an **AABB** form, and the length of each section measured in numbers of half-notes is 36, 36, 45, and 45, which reduces to 4 4 5 5. The same number sequence also influences the division into smaller units. Look, for example, at the first phrase of the **B** section (mm. 19–27, marked off by double bars). Within this smaller segment, the four notes in the right hand have durations equivalent to 4, 4, 5, and 5 half-notes.

EXAMPLE 80-1[†]

[†]John Cage, Sonata No. 5, from *Sonatas and Interludes.* Copyright © C. F. Peters Corp. Reprinted by permission of Hemar Press, Inc.

The piece is stunningly original in its diversity of sound. Cage composed here for what he called **prepared piano,** which is a piano that has been transformed into a one-person percussion ensemble by inserting screws, bolts, and rubber erasers between the instrument's strings. Except in rhythm and an occasional unprepared string, the appearance of the notation is very unlike the sound of the work. In other ways, Sonata No 5 is a reasonably traditional composition. Cage chose its sounds intuitively, and he worked out the piece by improvising at the keyboard. The sonata has a regular rhythm, a normal repetitive form, and in it the composer intended to communicate emotions to the listener.

Around 1950, inspired by his readings in Zen, Cage began to replace these familiar features with various applications of the principle of chance. His *Music of Changes* (1951) takes a first step toward this new orientation, by which a composer willingly relinquishes control over the details or even the entire substance of a new work.

Music of Changes is a lengthy composition for piano, in four large parts. A sequence of numbers, comparable to that in Sonata No. 5, is still operative in *Music of Changes,* but let us turn our attention instead to the way that Cage creates the musical material itself—its tones, rhythms, dynamics, and textures. In Sonata No. 5, Cage had chosen these elements based on taste. He picked the notes, rhythms, and sounds, he said, because he liked them. In *Music of Changes* this element of composer's taste is largely removed because the materials are selected by processes involving chance.

Cage began by constructing charts showing a variety of sounds, durations, and dynamics. Each of the sound charts, for example, contained sixty-four figures with one or a few tones in each. Fully half of the sixty-four figures in each sound chart are left void, containing only silence. Cage then tossed coins to choose a figure, which was given a rhythm selected from another chart by a similarly random process. The tempo, dynamics, and polyphonic density of a passage were chosen by comparable routines.

The result is music having **indeterminacy of composition,** as Cage called it, because the choice of musical materials is not directly controlled by the composer. "Value judgments are not in the nature of this work as regards either composition, performance, or listening," Cage concluded. "A 'mistake' is beside the point, for once anything happens it authentically is."[2]

LISTENING CUE

JOHN CAGE   CD 13/6
Music of Changes (1951)   Anthology, No. 207
Part 1

Soon after *Music of Changes,* Cage went even further in the removal of compositional order and personal taste from his music. In these later compositions, "silence"—the absence of a musical sound—grows in importance and, ironically, becomes the context in which a different kind of sound—unpredictable ambient noise—occurs. In Cage's music, these "silences" are occasions during which the listener can meditate upon unintended sounds of nature and environment, by which we are always surrounded. He was exuberant about them—about their inevitability and closeness to life and nature—and for him they held out the possibility for the "sudden enlightenment" of Zen. Silence, he contended, is "urgent, unique, uninformed about history and theory, beyond the imagination, central to a sphere without surface, its becoming is unimpeded, energetically broadcast. There is no escape from its actions."[3]

Cage's most emphatic silent work is the famous *4' 33"* (1952), in which a pianist sits before the instrument and audience for four minutes, thirty-three seconds without playing at all. (Cage insists that the piece is in three movements.) *4' 33"* is not a musical "work" in the normal sense, only an occasion for a Zen-like meditation. Its existence led the writer Paul Griffiths to the witty conclusion that if you're not listening to anything else, you're listening to Cage.

In other compositions following *Music of Changes,* Cage creates pieces that are **indeterminate of performance,** meaning that the performers share with the composer in making decisions about what and how to play. Cage writes most pieces of this type in graphic notation, using visual symbols other than conventional musical notations. Recall from Chapter 78 that Krzysztof Penderecki used graphic notation in his *Threnody for the Victims of Hiroshima,* although Cage's visual materials are far more imprecise in their musical implications than are Penderecki's.

An example is found in the score for Cage's *Concert for Piano and Orchestra* (1958) shown in Example 80-2. To the graphic design, Cage adds only this minimal instruction:

> Any pitch area having at least 20 chromatic tones. Space
> vertically = frequency. Horizontally = time. Horizontal lines =
> duration of single tones. Vertical lines = clusters or legati.
> Points = short tones.

John Cage on Chance Music

In 1958, John Cage was invited to lecture at the Darmstadt Summer School, a center for the rationalized music of serialism. His subject was "experimental" music in the United States, but it soon became evident to his audience that by this term he referred primarily to his own chance music. Experimental music, Cage said, was the outcome of an action whose result is not foreseen, thus quite the opposite of the works that the Darmstadters thought experimental. Cage's witty language and juggling of ideas is seen in this excerpt from his talk:

. . . . Actually America has an intellectual climate suitable for radical experimentation. We are, as Gertrude Stein said, the oldest country of the twentieth century. And I like to add: in our air way of knowing nowness. Buckminster Fuller, the dymaxion architect, in his three-hour lecture on the history of civilization, explains that men leaving Asia to go to Europe went against the wind and developed machines, ideas, and Occidental philosophies in accord with a struggle against nature; that, on the other hand, men leaving Asia to go to America went with the wind, put up a sail, and developed ideas and Oriental philosophies in accord with the acceptance of nature. These two tendencies met in America, producing a movement into the air, not bound to the past, traditions, or whatever. Once in Amsterdam, a Dutch musician said to me, "It must be very difficult for you in America to write music, for you are so far away from the centers of tradition." I had to say, "It must be very difficult for you in Europe to write music, for you are so close to the centers of tradition."[4]

EXAMPLE 80-2[†]

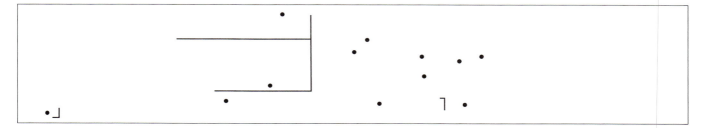

In other works, Cage communicates with the performers by way of a **verbal score**—a short narration of what the performer is intended to do. Here is the score for *4' 33" No. 2* (1962): "In a situation provided with maximum amplification (no feedback), perform a disciplined action."

The music of John Cage moved to an extreme point in the postwar rethinking about what music could become. Although to many his innovations are pure absurdity, he dramatically represents the spirit of the 1950s and 1960s, when experimentation in music seemed to be both relevant and limitless.

ELECTRONIC MUSIC: EDGARD VARÈSE

Postwar developments in audio technology led in the 1950s to the creation of a whole new genre—**electronic music.** This term refers to works whose sounds are directly realized by a composer using electronic equipment. Music of this type was

[†]John Cage, *Concert for Piano and Orchestra*, pp. 30–31. Copyright © 1960 Henmar Press (a division of C. F. Peters Corp.).

nourished by the liberated thinking of the 1950s concerning musical materials, but it became practical only with the development and distribution of the tape recorder.

The technology for the tape recorder was created primarily in Germany before and during World War II, and the first commercial versions were marketed to the public in the late 1940s. The ease of editing sounds on tape lured musicians of the day to experiment with a type of music that could admit any and all sounds, produce wholly new forms and textures, and give the composer total control over the musical outcome.

The first important type of electronic music was **musique concrète** (concrete music), which is electronic music made from recordings of natural or man-made sounds. This was the brainchild of **Pierre Schaeffer** (1910–1995), a French radio engineer. Beginning in 1948, Schaeffer used sound-effects discs available at his radio station to create a series of musical "studies." He called his genre "concrete" music because he worked directly with sounds, rather than abstractly through musical notation. He began with recordings of everyday sounds—pots and pans, musical instruments, a locomotive—and then edited and manipulated them so that they would take on musical features including regular rhythm and motivic recurrences.

Trained musicians soon took notice of his experiments, and Pierre Boulez, Olivier Messiaen, and Edgard Varèse were among those who composed in his Paris studio in the 1950s. They approached the idiom with far more freedom than had Schaeffer, typically disguising the source of the sounds and bypassing the elements from traditional music that Schaeffer had thought necessary.

Around 1952, the New York composers Vladimir Ussachevsky (1911–1990) and Otto Luening (1900–1996) created what they called **tape music,** which was a variant of Schaeffer's musique concrète. They composed and recorded their own instrumental pieces on tape and then modified the sound—especially by adding reverberation, or "feedback," which was easily provided by the tape recorder itself.

A different type of electronic music was created at about the same time by German musicians including Herbert Eimert (1897–1972) and Karlheinz Stockhausen (b. 1928) at West German Radio in Cologne. Their point of departure was not acoustical sound but tones and noises generated by electronic equipment, and they called their idiom "electronic music," although this term was soon used to refer to a more general phenomenon. The source sounds of purely electronic music were manipulated and reassembled as musical works on tape, often organized with the structural trappings of serialism.

In 1958 Edgard (or Edgar) Varèse (1883–1965) brought together several of these directions into one of the earliest important pieces of electronic music, *Poème électronique* (*Electronic Poem*). Varèse was born in Paris and lived alternately in France and Germany, working as a composer and conductor. In 1915 he emigrated to the United States and settled in New York, where he continued to compose and teach. He helped to found the **International Composers' Guild,** an organization devoted to performing new music. His compositions written before coming to America are almost entirely lost, and Varèse is now known for a small number of orchestral and chamber works that he composed after about 1920. These include *Ionisation* (1931) for percussion ensemble, *Déserts* (1954) for instruments alternating with sounds on tape, and the purely electronic *Poème électronique*.

Varèse pursued a career in music that was always outside of the establishment. His dissonant and atonal music of the 1920s and 1930s made no concessions to the neoclassical taste that reigned in Europe and America at the time. "In neoclassicism, tradition is reduced to the level of a bad habit," he quipped.[5] He argued in favor of a music in which sound per se—more than intervals, lines, or accompaniments—became the central element. In a lecture in 1936 he said:

> When new instruments will allow me to write music as I conceive it, taking the place of the linear counterpoint, the movement of sound-masses, of shifting planes, will be clearly perceived. When these sound-masses collide the phenomena of penetration or repulsion will seem to occur. Certain transmutations taking place on certain planes will seem to be projected onto other planes, moving at different speeds and at different angles. There will no longer be the old conception of melody or interplay of melodies.[6]

The "new instruments" that he foresaw finally became available to him in the context of electronic music. Varèse considered the elimination of live performance, implicit in the electronic medium, to be a progressive step. "The interpreter will disappear like the storyteller after the invention of printing," he predicted.[7]

A music of colliding sound masses became a reality in Varèse's *Poème électronique*. It was written for use in the Philips Pavilion at the 1958 World's Fair in Brussels, where it was part of a visionary multimedia display, also called "Poème Électronique," that was conceived of by the Swiss-French architect **Le Corbusier** (1887–1965). Le Corbusier intended it to "show the new resources that electronic technology has placed at the disposition of the arts, sound, color, image, and rhythm." To realize his vision of an electronic poem, Le Corbusier brought together a team of artists and technicians. **Iannis Xenakis** (1922–2001) designed the pavilion itself, which was a spectacular structure (Fig. 80-1) that was destroyed after the fair. In addition to being an architect and engineer, Xenakis was also a prominent composer.

Visitors to the pavilion experienced an eight-minute multimedia event in which Varèse's electronic composition swept through the space on hundreds of loudspeakers. At the same time, a film by Philippe Agostini was projected on the structure's inner walls, showing images that represented the advance of civilization. Colored lights and additional projections added to the sensory barrage, and Xenakis composed a short electronic work, *Concret PH* (discussed in Chapter 78) that was played while the audiences departed.

In *Poème électronique* (Fig. 80-2), Varèse adopted several of the styles of electronic music in existence in the early 1950s. Some of his raw materials—as in the musique concrète studies of Schaeffer—are drawn from easily identified acoustic sources. The bells at the opening, the human voice at 3:40, and the organ at 7:15, provide familiar milestones for the listener. Also like Schaeffer, Varèse adds formal elements from traditional music, most obviously a recurrent motive made from three tones ascending by half-steps (heard at 0:56, 1:34, and 7:31). Following the example of Ussachevsky and Luening, Varèse quotes from music that he had earlier composed and recorded—specifically, percussion music from his Study for *Espace* (1947),

❋ FIGURE 80-1

Le Corbusier and Iannis Xenakis, Philips Pavilion, Brussels World's Fair, 1958. The visionary pavilion was the site of Le Corbusier's "Poème électronique," an eight-minute multimedia display for visitors to the fair. Edgard Varèse composed an electronic piece, also called *Poème électronique*, for use in this display.

❋ FIGURE 80-2

Sketch for *Poème électronique* by Edgard Varèse.

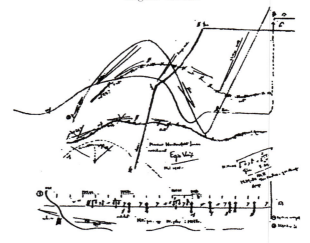

which appears at 2:10 and later. Like Eimert and Stockhausen, Varèse also adds a variety of purely electronic sounds, and these seem to merge seamlessly into the percussion sounds.

Varèse initially thought that the music would illustrate the film, but this plan was abandoned, and there was ultimately no coordination between Varèse's sound and visual images. Still, the music is expressive and dramatic—quite different in this respect from the 1950s tendency toward abstraction and depersonalization in much new music. Sound images suggesting the church (the bells, the organ, a chorus at 7:02) run throughout the piece, and the purely electronic sounds conjure up many human images. The interplay at 1:39 may well remind us of the antics of R2-D2 and C-3PO from *Star Wars*. The dramatic high point occurs at 3:40, when the human voice enters with its unearthly cry, "Hu-gah!" Varèse himself was never explicit about the meaning of the work, although he remarked that it was intended "to express tragedy and inquisition."

LISTENING CUE

EDGARD VARÈSE   CD 13/7
Poème électronique (1958)

Electronic music continued to hold a place in modern music circles after the time of Varèse. Composers were stimulated by the appearance of new equipment—synthesizers, computer programs, and sampling devices—that widened the avenues toward new sounds and textures. But by the 1970s the phenomenon began to wane among classical composers. Electronic music in the 1950s and 1960s was sustained by widespread support for experimentation in the arts and by a sense that exploration was necessary. By the 1970s these sentiments began to evaporate as composers reawakened to traditional musical values. Electronics suggested novelty and academicism—features that gradually became remote to the evolving culture for new music.

From the 1970s onward, electronic music was also increasingly swallowed up by commercial music and popular culture. The Beatles were the first to bring advanced electronic music into their recordings. Songs like "Tomorrow Never Knows" and "Revolution 9" include sounds developed in electronic music studios of the 1950s. Since the Beatles, bands such as Velvet Underground, Talking Heads, and Tangerine Dream have been on the leading edge of electronic music. Today, in addition to experimental rock, the technology for electronic music has found a greater outlet in computer games, MTV, and heavy-metal bands than in the world of classical music.

NEW MUSICAL TEXTURES: OLIVIER MESSIAEN

The experience with electronic music in the 1950s and 1960s opened two principal avenues for further developments—a greater range of sounds admissible to music, and textures based on sound masses rather than on lines and chords. The second of these, new textures, was especially important for the postwar period and was worked out by composers in virtually every medium.

The revolutionary expansion in musical materials earlier in the century had almost entirely bypassed textures. Polyphonic and homophonic patterns created by lines and chords continued to exist in music that otherwise had audaciously over-thrown traditional resources. In some of the music of Anton Webern (see Chapter 69) the texture is so spare, the notes so disjunct in register, and the musical fabric so permeated with silences that the distinguishability of lines and chords is blurred. But these are relatively superficial appearances, and Webern himself claimed that familiar textures would emerge in his music provided it received a sensitive performance. In the experimental atmosphere in music following World War II, texture at last became a focal point for new ideas and experiments. The music of Webern was studied and imitated precisely for its originality in this area, as well as for its sense of abstraction and strict use of serial and twelve-tone thinking.

Olivier Messiaen (1908–1992) was one of the first major postwar composers to seek alternatives to the familiar patterns of lines and chords. He was born in Avignon in the south of France and educated at the Paris Conservatory. From 1931 he was organist at the Church of the Trinity in Paris, and he became one of the major composers of twentieth-century organ music. His influence was exerted also through his teaching, which he did both privately and at the Paris Conservatory. Pierre Boulez and Karlheinz Stockhausen are among his students.

Messiaen, like Varèse, was relatively little involved with the neoclassical movement that dominated French modern music in the 1930s and 1940s. Messiaen's music was generally chromatic, colorfully dissonant, and always expressive—features that did not conform to the dominant prewar taste for musical objectivity. In the 1950s Messiaen attracted attention with works that incorporated melodic ideas inspired by **bird song.** He had become an avid ornithologist, and he attempted to capture bird songs in musical notation, even though this could only be done by an often-remote approximation. The bird songs stimulated his musical imagination and gave him "the right to be a musician," he said. "Nature is always beautiful, always grand, always new, inexhaustible in colors and sounds, forms and rhythms—an unequalled model for total development and perpetual change. Nature is the supreme resource!"[8]

Just before turning to nature for guidance, Messiaen in 1949 and 1950 explored an opposite sort of music—abstract in tone, partly automated in composition, and utterly original in texture. In these years he composed four "rhythmic studies" for piano, which proved highly influential upon the younger composers of the day. The second of these is called "Mode de valeurs et d'intensités" ("Mode of Durations and Dynamics," 1949)—the very title suggesting a spirit of abstraction and formalism. For Messiaen a "mode" is a fixed collection of musical elements to which the composer limits himself in a composition. The mode in this piece contains exactly thirty-six different pitches, twenty-four durations, twelve attack types, and seven dynamic levels.

In composing the study, Messiaen chose the pitches freely and intuitively, and he laid them out in three simultaneous strata—high, middle, and low—each given its own staff in the score. There are certain motivic recurrences in the music, but no sense of thematic exposition, development, or return. All twelve chromatic tones were available to him in each stratum. To this extent, the work is a fairly traditional atonal character piece for piano. But Messiaen worked out the composition in a highly original fashion. Virtually all compositional decisions outside of the choice of pitch were automated, as Messiaen assigned a predetermined and unchanging register, duration, attack type, and dynamic level to each of the twelve notes in each stratum.

This system integrates the compositional process and exerts the control that composers of the time apparently desired. The integration of elements is somewhat akin to the system used by Milton Babbitt in his Composition for Piano, No. 1 (see Chapter 79), although Babbitt structures his piece in units corresponding to full twelve-tone rows, while Messiaen thinks in terms of the individual tone.

To see how Messiaen's system works, look at the middle stratum of "Modes de valeurs et d'intensités." The register, duration, attack type, and dynamic level of each of the twelve tones is established in advance, as shown in Example 80-3. Whenever the note G is used in this part, for example, it will be placed an octave and a fifth above middle C, have a duration of one sixteenth-note, be attacked *sforzando* with an accent and staccato dot, and played *fortissimo*.

EXAMPLE 80-3

Messiaen's system exerts its effect mainly on the resulting musical texture. Although the score suggests three polyphonic lines, these are not apparent when the piece is played because any sense of line is dispelled by the maximal diversity in register, dynamics, attack quality, and duration from one note to the next. The texture becomes almost entirely pointillistic—made from an array of individualized tones rather than from lines and chords. Recall from Chapter 69 that the term "pointillism" is also used to describe the music of Webern.

LISTENING CUE

OLIVIER MESSIAEN
"Mode de valeurs et d'intensités" (1949)

CD 13/8
Anthology, No. 208

 SUMMARY

Following World War II, modern music took on a variety of styles and compositional methods in addition to serialism. One of the most novel was the making of compositional choices by chance, an approach associated with the music of the American composer John Cage around 1950. A work such as *Music of Changes* for piano is notated in detail, but the compositional choices are made from a number of options by chance routines. Earlier, Cage had written more traditional types of music, often for "prepared piano"—an instrument converted into a virtual percussion ensemble. In works composed later in the 1950s, Cage used a style that he termed "indeterminacy of performance," with which he turned decisions about what to play almost entirely over to performers. His involvement with a "composition" dwindled to brief graphic notations and verbal scores.

Another postwar alternative to serialism was the composition of electronic music. An early version was "musique concrète," which is electronic music made from recordings of natural or man-made sounds that are manipulated electronically and reassembled on disc or tape in a musical form. Other composers opted for pure electronic music, in which the source sounds were produced by electronic devices. Edgard Varèse's *Poème électronique* (1958) uses both approaches.

Composers following World War II also experimented with new musical textures, alternatives to the traditional homophony and polyphony. Varèse praised the value of "sound masses"—conglomerations of sound in which no single tones or intervals are apparent. Olivier Messiaen, in his piano study "Mode de valeurs et d'intensités" (1949), linked together the choice of register, duration, dynamic level, and attack type to produce a "pointillistic" texture in which individual tones seem to leap out without association into lines or chords.

 KEY TERMS

chance music	verbal score	International
prepared piano	electronic music	Composers' Guild
indeterminacy of	musique concrète	Le Corbusier
composition	Pierre Schaeffer	Iannis Xenakis
indeterminacy of	tape music	bird song
performance		

Harlem in the 1930s, 1940s, and 1950s: Big Bands, Bebop, and Cool Jazz

By 1930 New York City had become the world's capital for jazz. During the teens and twenties this constantly changing type of music had spread from points of origin such as New Orleans, Kansas City, and Chicago (see Chapter 72) to cities in the West, North, and East. It found its most vibrant home in Harlem, which was then the center of African American culture in the United States.

 JAZZ IN HARLEM

Around the time of World War I, African Americans from the South and East migrated in large numbers to **Harlem**—a district in north-central Manhattan—where they hoped to find greater economic prosperity and a more sympathetic environment. In the 1920s Harlem became a center for the arts, and writers including Langston Hughes, James Weldon Johnson, and W. E. B. Du Bois fostered the **Harlem Renaissance** in literature that focused on the black experience in America. At the same time Harlem became a mecca for the lighter entertainments of dancing, theater, and nightclub, for which popular music was needed. Some of the most famous venues in the history of jazz were opened in Harlem during this period. The Apollo Theatre on 125th Street at first presented shows and reviews and later brought the leading names of jazz on stage to perform. At the Cotton Club on Lenox

Darius Milhaud Recalls a Visit to Harlem in 1922

The French composer Darius Milhaud came to New York in 1922 to give concerts, and he eagerly visited Harlem to hear jazz. He recalled the experience:

. . . Harlem had not yet been discovered by the snobs and aesthetes: we were the only white folk there. The music I heard was absolutely different from anything I had ever heard before, and it was a revelation to me. Against the beat of the drums, the melodic lines criss-crossed in a breathless pattern of broken and twisted rhythms. A Negress whose grating voice seemed to come from the depths of the centuries, sang in front of the various tables.

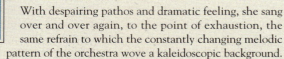

With despairing pathos and dramatic feeling, she sang over and over again, to the point of exhaustion, the same refrain to which the constantly changing melodic pattern of the orchestra wove a kaleidoscopic background.

This authentic music had its roots in the darkest corners of the Negro soul, the vestigial traces of Africa no doubt. Its effect on me was so overwhelming that I could not tear myself away. From then on, I frequented other Negro theatres and dance-halls. In some of their shows, the singers were accompanied by a flute, a clarinet, two trumpets, a trombone, a complicated percussion section played by one man, a piano, and a string quintet. . . .[1]

Avenue, Duke Ellington's band was in residence from 1927 until 1931, after which the bands of Cab Calloway and Jimmie Lunceford could be heard. The Savoy Ballroom, the largest dance hall in Harlem, was only a block away. With two jazz bands alternating, the dancing never stopped. The Harlem Stompers, led by the drummer Chick Webb, was one of the most popular bands at the Savoy, and Webb brought in the still-unknown Ella Fitzgerald as a vocalist, to launch her career as the "First Lady" of jazz.

The diversity of popular music available in Harlem by 1930 seemed endless. A group of virtuoso pianists—James P. Johnson, Luckey Roberts, Fats Waller, Willie "The Lion" Smith, among others—were active in Harlem developing a post-ragtime style called **stride.** The name comes from the striding motions of the pianist's left hand, from chord roots in the low register of the instrument on strong beats of the measure to inner voices on weak beats. An example of the style is heard in James P. Johnson's "Carolina Shout" (see Chapter 72).

Dance music played by bands and orchestras was increasingly in demand as social dancing in the 1920s became a virtual craze. Small bands playing in the New Orleans style (see Chapter 72) seemed old fashioned in comparison to larger dance orchestras made from strings, winds, and brass, playing arrangements in an eclectic style sometimes called "symphonic jazz." In the late 1920s and early 1930s, several dance bands in New York took on a clearer identity. These new groups were soon dubbed **big bands,** and they led to a new style, marked by impulsive energy, called **swing,** which dominated jazz into the 1940s.

THE BIG BANDS: FLETCHER HENDERSON AND DUKE ELLINGTON

Although no one musician can be credited with the emergence of the big band phenomenon and the swing style, a central figure in their development was **Fletcher Henderson** (1897–1952; Fig. 81-1). Born in Georgia, Henderson arrived in New York in 1920, whereupon he worked as a song-plugger and later as a band leader. In 1924 his band was hired to play at the Roseland Ballroom on 51st Street, the most prestigious dance hall in the city, and his distinctive style was soon widely imitated. His band often went uptown to play at the Savoy Ballroom in Harlem.

Shortly after arriving at Roseland, Henderson's band was invigorated by the addition to the trumpet section of Louis Armstrong, who brought to the group an improvised solo playing that was more forceful than usual in the sedate style of symphonic jazz. Don Redman (1900–1964), who played reed instruments in Henderson's band, wrote arrangements in a style that would later be widely imitated.

Henderson's initiatives laid the groundwork for the emergence of one of jazz's greatest musicians, **Edward "Duke" Ellington** (1899–1974; Fig. 81-2). Ellington grew up in Washington, D.C., where he was largely self-taught in music and where he learned to play piano in the stride style. Like Henderson (also a pianist), he moved to New York and formed his own band. His group entered the spotlight in 1927 when it became the resident band at Harlem's Cotton Club, where Ellington played for dancing and as back-up to production numbers and floor shows. To accompany imitation African dances, Ellington players evoked the menacing sounds of the jungle: the brass players growled and the drummer played tom-toms, all creating a **jungle style** which became an Ellington specialty.

Duke Ellington devoted his entire career to this ensemble. He composed, arranged, and played piano for the group, toured the world over, and made a series of celebrated recordings and films. In addition to such big band hits as "Take the A Train," "Mood Indigo," and "Satin Doll," Ellington also composed film scores, musicals, and longer concert works—including concertos, suites, and programmatic music—for his jazz orchestra.

Ellington rose to prominence in the 1920s on the tide of big band music, a functional genre which he advanced, transformed, and ultimately surpassed. By the 1930s his orchestra had reached a size of fourteen or fifteen instrumentalists (sometimes adding a vocalist), which was a number typical of other big bands. The players were divided into four basic groups—saxophones (doubling on clarinets), trumpets, trombones, and "rhythm" (an accompanying group consisting of piano, drums, bass, and guitar). The Ellington orchestra's music, like that of other bands, used a form based on the variations model inherited distantly from the blues. Melodic material was taken from (or imitated) the popular songs of the day, and these were molded into shape by arrangers such as Redman and Ellington's assistant, **Billy Strayhorn** (1915–1967).

The musical styles and forms of big bands can be studied in their classic state in "Take the A Train" (1941). Named after a familiar subway line in New York, "Take the A Train" became Ellington's signature work and his orchestra's greatest hit. After a four-measure introduction in $\frac{4}{4}$ time, the

FIGURE 81-1
Henderson in the 1930s led a typical big band, made from saxophones, trumpets, and trombones, with a rhythm section of guitar, drums, bass, and piano (Henderson's own instrument).

FIGURE 81-2
Duke Ellington brought a composer's outlook to jazz, and with it helped to enrich the big band style.

band plays the first chorus (i.e., section), which contains the main theme. It is entirely written out, involving no improvisation. The melody is given to the saxophones, accompanied by crisp and syncopated chords in the trumpets and trombones, while the rhythm group plays unobtrusive chords in the background. The melody spans thirty-two measures, laid out in the form **AABA**—a pattern that will be recognized as the standard form for the chorus of a popular song of the day (see Chapter 77). Phrase A is shown in Example 81-1.

EXAMPLE 81-1

In the big band era, the main themes of dance pieces were usually borrowed from preexisting popular song choruses, which were considered **jazz standards** and the common property of all dance bands and their arrangers. These songs could be played instrumentally (as in "Take the A Train") or sung by a vocalist—in either case functioning primarily as an accompaniment to dancing. In "Take the A Train," the melody was not preexistent, nor was it literally a song, having been composed by Billy Strayhorn expressly for use in this instrumental piece.

The remainder of "Take the A Train" consists of two variations (choruses) on the song melody, this number limited by the roughly three-minute duration of sound recordings at the time. The first variation features a relaxed improvised solo for muted trumpet, its accompaniment entirely written out (probably by Strayhorn). In a four-measure interlude before the second variation, the key changes from C major to E♭ major, in which key the remainder of the piece is played. The second variation has a more intricate and forceful character than the first, as the solo trumpet alternates with the saxophone section. The arrangement builds to a climactic chord at 2:15, just before the final statement of the A phrase. The end of this variation is extended by two additional statements of phrase A during which the band fades out, just beating the three-minute limit.

Additional elements of the big band style are also evident. Improvisation is strictly limited to a few solo variations, as the music is essentially a written arrangement of a song-like melody. The arranger pits the saxophones against the brass in a crisp and lively dialogue, and the beat is a steady and regular $\frac{4}{4}$. The entire work has a polished surface with an energy geared to dancing.

The swing band pieces of Ellington and Strayhorn, such as "Take the A Train," go beyond other works of their type in their wholeness and symmetry. There is no arbitrariness as to the number or character of variations and no ideas that are left undeveloped. Listen, for example, for how Ellington on piano brings back the descending whole-tone motive from the introduction (Ex. 81-2) in the very last statement of the A phrase (at 2:45), and notice the relation of this whole-tone figure to the augmented chord in measures 3–4 of the main melody (see Ex. 81-1).

EXAMPLE 81-2

Maurice Ravel Visits America, 1928

Maurice Ravel, like most French composers of the 1920s, was a fan of American jazz. In Paris he was a regular at Le Boeuf sur le Toit, a nightclub where jazz was played. On his 1928 tour of the United States Ravel gladly accepted George Gershwin's invitation to join him on a trip to Harlem to hear authentic American jazz. He gave his opinion about it in this interview:

> . . . You Americans take jazz too lightly. You seem to feel that it is cheap, vulgar, momentary. In my opinion it is bound to lead to the national music of the United States.

Aside from it you have no veritable idiom as yet. Most of your compositions show European influences, either Spanish, Russian, French, or German—rather than American individuality. Nor do I believe those who claim that this is due to the admixture of foreign peoples who comprise the American people. *Pas du tout. C'est ridicule, ça!* [Not at all—that's ridiculous!]. . . . I am also happy to have come to America at last and although I have hardly been out of doors I can testify that Broadway After Dark is *ravissant* [delightful].[2]

The form of the piece is not an open-ended series of variations; instead, it is a concentric design that creates a unified whole. The theme in the first chorus constitutes an exposition of materials, which are then developed in the variations following. In this development the melody itself does not explicitly reappear, only its harmonies, and these coherently support a massing of ever-new melodic ideas that grow in intensity. After the climactic chord at 2:15, a reprise occurs, as the melodic phrase A reemerges plainly in the saxophones, its energy quickly dispelled as the band fades out in a short coda.

It is often said that jazz is essentially improvisatory—a performer's art—but the long-range formal unity and integration of materials of Ellington and Strayhorn in a piece like "Take the A Train" plainly come from the thinking of a composer.

LISTENING CUE

EDWARD "DUKE" ELLINGTON   CD 13/9
"Take the A Train" (1941)

In the 1930s and early 1940s, the big band phenomenon became virtually synonymous with the word jazz. By virtue of radio and sound recordings it achieved the status of a national style, associated with no single city or regional audience. By the late 1930s the country's most successful big band was the one led by clarinetist **Benny Goodman** (1909–1986). His organization was based in New York, and his band occasionally played in Harlem, although it was known nationwide through its radio broadcasts. Goodman recorded both with his big band and with smaller ensembles, and he favored the intense and driving style that was the essence of swing. The character of his music was shaped in part by Fletcher Henderson, who provided Goodman's bands with many of their most celebrated arrangements. Goodman was one of the first major band leaders to promote racial integration in his musical organizations, and his popularity led to his receiving the nickname "King of Swing."

❋ FIGURE 81-3
Charlie Parker was one of
the founders of bebop.

 BEBOP

As World War II neared its end in the 1940s, many jazz musicians began to tire of the big band style, which, except in a few orchestras such as Ellington's and Goodman's, had become mired in predictable musical formulas. A rebellion against its clichés was fomented not so much by the famous band leaders themselves, but by their players, or **sidemen.** They met after hours at Harlem jazz clubs, such as Minton's Playhouse on 118th Street, to play informally for their own enjoyment, in **jam sessions** involving smaller groups in which new ideas could be tried out. By about 1945 a new style, called **bebop** (or simply **bop**) had emerged that would move to a central position in the history of jazz as the swing bands lost popularity after World War II.

The two musicians most closely identified with the origins of bop are the trumpeter John "Dizzy" Gillespie (1917–1993) and alto saxophonist Charlie Parker (1920–1955; Fig. 81-3). Both musicians established their reputations in big bands. In the 1930s and early 1940s Gillespie played in the bands of Teddy Hill and Cab Calloway, among others. Parker, who hailed from Kansas City, played in the bands of Earl Hines and Billy Eckstine at the same time as did Gillespie. In the mid-1940s the two collaborated on recordings that helped to establish the identity of bebop and, with it, change the direction of jazz.

The bebop style carried over many elements from the big bands; at the same time it rebelled against the big band style. The typical bebop ensemble was not the large dance orchestra of fourteen or fifteen players, instead a much smaller ensemble, or **jazz combo,** made from one or a few melody instruments and a rhythm section usually having piano, drums, and bass. The music played by bop combos used the same form as the big band arrangement—introduction, theme (usually a blues in twelve measures or a song chorus in thirty-two), and a succession of variations on the theme's harmonies.

Improvisation, strictly limited in the big band arrangement, returned to central importance in bebop, and the texture of such works was thin, focused on solo improvisations with rhythm section accompaniment. The improvisations, especially when done by a Gillespie or Parker, were virtuosic, often exploding torrents of sound that were scarcely held in check by a heavy beat, strict harmonic progression, or familiar melody.

The most distinctive feature of bebop—the element most unlike the big band arrangement—is its rhythm. Recall the role of the bass and drum set in Ellington's "Take the A Train." They play almost entirely in the background, and unvaryingly on the beat in a moderate $\frac{4}{4}$. In bebop, by contrast, the typical tempo is headlong fast, and the beat is kept mainly by the "walking" bass, which plays a stepwise line with even rhythmic values. The drum set is freed from marking the beat and instead creates impulsive sound textures on the cymbals and other percussion instruments. The piano typically **comps,** that is, plays irregularly spaced chords. Bebop numbers were often used for dancing, but they invited a deeper level of attention to themselves as pure music than did the more rhythmically regular big band arrangements.

Many of these characteristics of bebop may be heard in "Koko," a celebrated 1945 recording featuring Parker and Gillespie (who plays trumpet and is also credited with playing piano). They are joined by the bassist Curly Russell and drummer Max Roach. The piece is based on the jazz standard "Cherokee," written by Ray Noble and often arranged for use by big bands. The main theme of "Cherokee" spans sixty-four measures laid out in the standard **AABA** form. Phrase **A** is shown in Example 81-3. The familiar pentatonic melody of the song plays no role in "Koko." Only its harmonies are retained, which are played quietly by the pianist. The tempo is amazingly fast, with the half note at the rate of about 150.

EXAMPLE 81-3

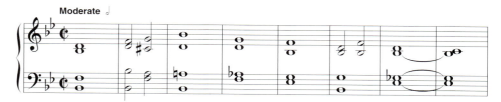

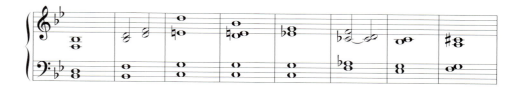

The introduction spans thirty-two measures in the fast tempo, creating music that was apparently worked out in rehearsals as a **head arrangement,** that is, an entirely composed but unwritten musical conception. Gillespie and Parker first play eight measures in a precise unison (a typical gambit in bebop), they then improvise eight measures each, and the final eight measures is another unison. Parker then takes charge, playing two successive sixty-four-measure choruses in a breathlessly virtuosic improvisation, free from any preexistent melody and imaginatively extending the harmonies of "Cherokee." A high-voltage drum interlude follows with little apparent sense of strict beat, and the work ends with a return to the music of the introduction, concluding on the dominant harmony in the key of Bb major.

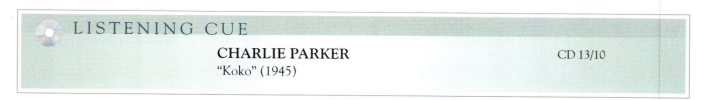

LISTENING CUE

CHARLIE PARKER   CD 13/10
"Koko" (1945)

COOL AND FREE JAZZ

The modernism and rebellion embodied in bebop led in the 1950s and 1960s to a splintering of jazz styles. An important new direction that emerged in the 1950s is a style called **cool jazz.** In many ways cool jazz is close to bebop, but without the breakneck tempos or aggressive virtuosity heard in "Koko." The mood of cool jazz is instead relaxed and homogeneous, the tempos moderate, and the dynamics calm. An early example of the style is heard in "Boplicity," recorded in 1949 by Miles Davis and His Orchestra. Miles Davis (1926–1991) grew up in St. Louis, learned trumpet, and in 1944 moved to New York, where he played in the big bands of Benny Carter and Billy Eckstine. He was closely associated with Charlie Parker in the early development of bebop, and he began to make recordings with his own groups in the late 1940s. Always of an experimental temperament, Davis was an originator of the cool style and, in the late 1960s, of jazz-rock fusions.

"Boplicity" looks backward to the music of the big bands and bebop combos as well as forward to the future of jazz. Davis's orchestra has nine members, larger than the typical bop combo. The brass include French horn and tuba, unusual instruments in a jazz ensemble, and there are two saxophones plus a standard bop rhythm section of piano, drums, and bass. The instruments are used by Davis's arranger, Gil Evans (1912–1988), to produce a mellow sound, not the thin or linear texture of bebop. The playing of the rhythm section is totally unlike bebop, as the drummer, Kenny Clarke, restricts himself to the hi-hat cymbal with a regularity that would be at home in a big band arrangement. Some aspects of the piece still recall bebop, especially the opening melody, which is played in a near unison by the trumpet and saxophone.

Other features have the relaxation of cool jazz. Davis plays his trumpet in the middle register with an airy tone that has none of the drive or sharpness of a Gillespie or a big band section player. Note also the differences separating Gerry Mulligan's baritone saxophone solo at 0:58, played with a relaxed confidence, from the aggressive virtuosity of Charlie Parker in "Koko."

The form of "Boplicity" mixes the regular and irregular. The piece begins with a thirty-two measure theme (composed apparently by Davis) in the predictable **AABA** form. The opening is shown in Example 81-4. The second chorus (from 0:57), begins with Mulligan's improvisation, but the clear eight-measure phrases of jazz and its simple variational form soon dissolve into a freer development, leading to a recapitulation of the theme's phrase **A** at 2:40.

EXAMPLE 81-4

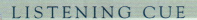

LISTENING CUE

MILES DAVIS   CD 13/11
"Boplicity" (1949)

Gradually, the preeminence of Harlem as a source of new ideas in jazz began to diminish. Cool jazz was as much a product of the West Coast as it was the East, and, from the 1960s, jazz musicians traveled on different paths with no evidence of a dominant style. Many jazz performers began to look backward to revive earlier types of jazz, including ragtime and New Orleans ("Dixieland") band styles. Some performers, such as Ornette Coleman and Cecil Taylor, have experimented with styles drawn from contemporary artistic music, including atonality, in an idiom called **free jazz.** The composer Gunther Schuller wrote what he called **third stream music,** in which the two mainstreams of jazz and classical music flowed together. New alliances were built between jazz and rock, opening up a style called **fusion.**

    SUMMARY

In the 1920s and 1930s Harlem, an African American district in New York City, became the world's capital of jazz. Musicians from all other centers of jazz—New Orleans, Chicago, Kansas City—migrated there, and a native group of pianists explored a type of playing called "stride," which was loosely based on the model of ragtime.

In the late 1920s Harlem witnessed the development of "big bands"—dance bands numbering some fourteen or fifteen players, divided into choirs of trumpets, trombones, and saxophones, with a rhythm section typically consisting of piano, drums, bass, and guitar. Under the leadership of musicians including Fletcher Henderson, Duke Ellington, and Benny Goodman, dance music took on a standard form based on a theme (usually a blues melody or the chorus section of a popular song) followed by soloistic variations. The music of Duke Ellington's orchestra regularly went beyond this formula to create unified and integrated jazz compositions.

The big bands lost popularity shortly after World War II, and their place was taken by a more experimental style called bebop. This type of music was played by a small combo of instruments, it was often extremely fast in tempo, and it was based on virtuosic improvisations that were largely freed from a strict adherence to a preexisting melody and its harmonies. A branch of bebop popular in the 1950s was "cool jazz," in which the aggressive virtuosity of bebop was replaced by a relaxed and homogeneous type of playing.

KEY TERMS

Harlem	jungle style	jazz combo
Harlem Renaissance	Billy Strayhorn	comp
stride	jazz standards	head arrangement
big bands	Benny Goodman	cool jazz
swing	sidemen	free jazz
Fletcher Henderson	jam sessions	third stream music
Edward "Duke" Ellington	bebop (bop)	fusion

Musical Interlude

The Birth of Rock

9

For a decade following World War II, the popular song industry in America rolled in the same traces that had been formed in the 1920s. The most successful songs were still composed in the style of Tin Pan Alley, and many of the most popular recordings were still made from jazz standards that had been around for decades. Sheet-music editions of new songs remained a profitable source of income. The most popular song in America for the year 1953 was the sentimental and quasi-religious "I Believe," sung by Frankie Laine to music by Ervin Drake. Among the older standards, "Tea for Two," composed in 1923 by Vincent Youmans for the show *No, No, Nanette*, was still a substantial money-maker.[1] The leading singers of the day—Bing Crosby, Perry Como, and Frank Sinatra, among others—had risen to fame during the Big Band era.

All of this changed in 1955 when the song "Rock Around the Clock" vaulted to the top of the charts in a recording made by Bill Haley and The Comets. Music for this song had been composed several years earlier by Jimmy deKnight and it had already been recorded, but it was Haley's "cover" (a new recording of a previously known song) that garnered attention. Haley's rendition had a drive and intensity that is completely unlike the sedate crooning of a Bing Crosby or Perry Como. The accompaniment was provided not by satin strings but by a lean combo that featured a walking bass, amplified guitars, and drum set playing relentlessly on beats 2 and 4 in a fast $\frac{4}{4}$ time. The form of "Rock Around the Clock" is a straightforward blues filled with the driving ostinatos of boogie-woogie and the saucy twang of blue notes. The words ("We're gonna rock around the clock tonight; we're gonna rock rock rock till the broad day light") refer obliquely to sex, something kept politely out of sight in songs such as "Tea for Two." Plainly, Haley's recording was music for a rebellious youth for whom cute and sentimental songs were merely emblems of a stodgy older generation.

The style of music heard in "Rock Around the Clock" was certainly known by 1955, but before this year it was marketed mainly to African American audiences, not to the white middle-class listeners who bought recordings of Crosby and Como. The trade journal *Billboard* categorized recordings targeted to African Americans as "rhythm and blues" (or "R&B"); those for the white working-class listener as "country and western" ("C&W"). Music of the former type—including recordings by Big Joe Turner, Fats Domino, and Little Willie Littlefield—was closest to "Rock Around the Clock," with its astringent medium, driving tempo, and blues-based form. Country and western recordings made by Hank Williams, Eddie Arnold, and Jimmy Dean (later of sausage fame) were more relaxed and mellifluous, and their lyrics usually told a story that resonated with the working class.

The revolution begun by "Rock Around the Clock" was not so much the appearance of a new style as it was the crossing over of existing styles to new audiences. The music that earlier had appealed mainly to blacks and working-class whites was now ecstatically embraced by the burgeoning young and privileged white audience.

❋ FIGURE 1

Chuck Berry was one of the founders of rock 'n' roll.

© Neal Preston/CORBIS

Disk jockeys, such as Cleveland's Alan Freed, began to use the term "rock 'n' roll" to designate this music of mixed tastes, and with it a new era in the history of popular music was born. Bill Haley's success with "Rock Around the Clock" was soon matched by other performers from the worlds of R&B and C&W. The early rock 'n' roll recordings of African American performers like Chuck Berry (Fig. 1) and Little Richard reached not only the R&B charts but also those earlier dominated by white performers. Elvis Presley's recordings, which ranged in style over R&B, gospel, country, and older-type ballads, achieved their unprecedented level of success by transcending racial and social divisions.

The birth of rock 'n' roll was in large measure a product of the social and economic upheaval of the postwar period in America. It coincided with the decision of the U.S. Supreme Court that racial segregation in public schools is unconstitutional, and also with the civil rights movement that would ultimately transform all of American society. It came at the same time as older social patterns in this country were being disrupted by massive suburbanization and relocation between rural and urban areas. It was a harbinger of the ascendancy of youth, dramatically symbolized by the election in 1960 of John F. Kennedy, then only forty-three years old, as President of the United States.

Although rock was a product of its time, it proved very controversial in musical terms. Many performers in the jazz world admired Elvis's revival of blues singing with a country twang and his success in bridging racial divisions, but they uniformly condemned the commercialism of rock that drove Elvis to try to be all things to all people. This was the assessment made in 1958 by Rudi Blesh, who praised Elvis's musical origins but lamented his forays into styles of pure entertainment. "He is [now] singing mainly Tin Pan Alley trash," snorted Blesh, "and his preeminence is being threatened by sophisticated 'folk' singers, the breed that infests the cities today with their guitars and their crooning. Exactly thus, in 1926, was New Orleans jazz replaced."[2]

Classical musicians had equally mixed feelings about early rock 'n' roll. The American composer John Harbison found rock recordings to be musically empty when compared to the older compositions of Tin Pan Alley:

> It isn't *Heartbreak Hotel* or *Hound Dog* that survives as a cultural artifact, it is *Elvis Presley* or his posthumous doubles singing them. Sheet music disappeared or became hopelessly primitive. The *song* became the *record*: few tunes circulated among performers; they were instead identified definitely with a single recorded performance, which that performer tried to duplicate exactly in live performance or "lip-synched" to the record. The beat, the harmonies, and the forms emphasized clear reiterated shapes ("hooks"), root position chords, and hypnotic, crushing pulsations, physicality and presence above all.[3]

Other classical musicians, especially those who had tired of the abstractions of postwar modernism, found much to praise in the energy and inventiveness of rock 'n' roll. The composer and critic Ned Rorem valued the Beatles' songs for their sense of fun, something he thought had been driven from classical music by the abstractions of Boulez and Babbitt. "They have removed sterile martyrdom from art, revived the sensual," Rorem wrote. "Their sweetness lies in that they doubtless couldn't care less about these pedantic explications."[4]

The infancy of rock 'n' roll came to an end in the 1960s, when the Beatles took America by storm. Although their early songs sprang from the same roots as the recordings of Bill Haley and Elvis Presley, their music soon diversified and began to suggest a new and broadly unpredictable future for popular songs. So different was their eclecticism from early rock 'n' roll that many journalists began to call their idiom simply "rock." By whatever name, the pioneers of rock 'n' roll—Haley, Presley, Berry, Jerry Lee Lewis among others—began a movement that ultimately changed the entire landscape of American musical culture.

Music in the 1960s and 1970s: Live Processes, Minimalism, Metric Modulations

Chapter 82

By 1960 modern music seemed to be trapped in an identity crisis. After World War II the impulse to forget the past had driven it in so many opposing directions that agreement among musicians was hard to find and the audience for new music ever more scarce. Total serialism, chance, electronic music, sound masses, stochastic textures, and pointillism (see Chapters 79 and 80) were musical responses to the spirit of the time, but they seemed to have little in common except for an audacious novelty.

Almost no one was happy. Leonard Bernstein declared the year 1966 to be "a low point in the musical course of our century":

> Pop music seems to be the only area where there is to be found unabashed vitality, the fun of invention, the feeling of fresh air. Everything else suddenly seems old-fashioned: electronic music, serialism, chance music—they have already acquired the musty odor of academicism. Even jazz seems to have ground to a painful halt. And tonal music lies in abeyance, dormant.[1]

Composers of this time bickered furiously among themselves. Elliott Carter proclaimed that total serialism "produces disastrous results, from any artistic standpoint." John Cage found that Carter's ideas only build "a new wing on the academy." Cage's use of chance in composing was dismissed by the composer Luigi Nono as "a method for those who fear decisions and the freedom that they entail." Nono's countryman Luciano Berio judged serialism—Nono's compositional method—to be close to fascism.

Such opposing viewpoints suggest that music of the 1960s and early 1970s was in a state of transition. Composers during this period tried to find their place within an unstable musical culture, often repeatedly changing their allegiances to achieve affirmation for their work. Although they continued to experiment with new ideas, they gradually dispensed with the doctrinaire attitudes of the 1950s and looked instead for consensus and new avenues toward acceptance.

We turn in this chapter to musical styles of the 1960s and early 1970s that embody this transitional outlook. In works by Luciano Berio and George Crumb we find new ways of using the voice and of joining words to tones. Both composers intended their music to speak to a larger audience than had existed hitherto for new compositions. Steve Reich was one of several American musicians of the 1960s who developed an influential style called "minimalism," which held a special appeal for younger listeners attuned to pop music. In his music of the early 1970s, Elliott Carter simplified the complex principles of rhythmic organization of his earlier works. In all of the compositions studied in this chapter we will see a continuation of the search for novelty, but at the same time an effort to find a basis for communication and broader appeal.

✤ NEW USES OF THE VOICE: LUCIANO BERIO AND GEORGE CRUMB

The music of Luciano Berio (1925–2003) typifies the conflicting viewpoints of the 1960s. Berio was devoted to **modernism**—he wanted to expand his inherited musical language, to find new materials and novel principles of organization. But he was dissatisfied with the musical culture that had been created by modernism, especially by serialism, which produced a music that seemed to him sterile and lifeless. Music could expand its language, he thought, so long as it remained a "live process"— a product, that is, of people making musical sounds that could communicate to listeners.

Berio was born in the town of Oneglia, on the Italian Riviera near San Remo, to a family of musicians. Following the end of World War II, he enrolled at the conservatory in Milan, and in the 1950s he regularly attended the courses for modern music in Darmstadt. He rose to prominence as a composer of serial music, and he was also one of the first Italians to write electronic works. But by the late 1950s Berio had become disenchanted with much of the thinking associated with Darmstadt. "Serial procedures in themselves guarantee absolutely nothing," he wrote. "No idea is so wretched that it cannot be *serialized*, just as ideas and images that have no interest can always be versified."[2] What was needed in the place of sterile serialism was "a living and permanent contact with sound material."

In the 1960s Berio composed music that rejected rigid formalisms in favor of the live processes he had come to favor. One group of pieces, each called a *Sequenza*, explored the capacity of a single instrumentalist or singer to sustain an entire composition. Another group consists of "songs" in which Berio addresses the apparent incompatibility between ultramodern poetry—works by writers such as James Joyce, e. e. cummings, Samuel Beckett, and Edoardo Sanguineti—and traditional musical forms and principles of expression. In these latter works, Berio creates a new type of song involving **extended techniques** of singing, such as singing with the mouth closed, on the breath, with phonetic symbols instead of words, or using imprecise pitch. In these ways Berio's songs become soundscapes like those of electronic music, and they invoke a new aesthetic concerning the relation between words and tones. His use of the voice was influenced by the virtuosic skills of the American soprano Cathy Berberian (1928–1983), to whom Berio was married in the 1950s. He also owed a debt to Pierre Boulez's *Le marteau sans maître* (see Chapter 79), in which the voice and text are treated in novel ways.

One of the most influential of Berio's song-like compositions from this period is *Circles* (1960) for soprano, harp, and two percussionists. The work uses poetry by e. e. cummings (1894–1962), which is laid out in five song-like sections connected by instrumental interludes. The overall form of the composition is made from a variety of symmetric or circular gestures, as suggested by the title word. For example, the text in the fourth song is the same as the second (but with new music); the text of the fifth is the same as the first. The two percussionists are instructed to place their instruments in circles, around which they move. The singer takes differing positions as the cycle progresses, again partly outlining a circle. The cycle rises to a climax in the third song, where words are entirely replaced by resonant nonsense syllables that are accompanied by an explosion of sounds in the percussion instruments.

Berio's point of departure in this highly imaginative work is cummings' poetry. The writer experiments playfully with the sounds of words, their odd juxtapositions, and new rhythms suggested by how the words are placed on the page. In cummings' poetry the reader often encounters a succession of unrelated images and musical effects that override any narrative or logical meaning.

An example is the poem "stinging" (from cummings' collection *Tulips and Chimneys*, 1923), which Berio uses in the first and fifth sections of *Circles*:

> stinging
> gold swarms
> upon the spires
> silver
>
>   chants the litanies the
> great bells are ringing with rose
> the lewd fat bells
>   and a tall

(continued on next page)

> wind
>
> is dragging
>
> the
>
> sea
>
> with
>
> dream
>
> -S

A poem like this is not a good choice for a traditional song. The music of song, by its very nature, projects ideas and emotions. Music expands upon the poem and reinforces its atmosphere and elements of continuity. None of these characteristics have analogies in this poem. There is no continuity of thought, no apparent emotion, no unifying ideas upon which the music might expand.

Like a true modernist, Berio brushes such problems aside. He focuses on two aspects of the poem—its sounds (especially the recurrent hissing *s*'s and the nasal *-ing*'s), and its formal disposition on the page, which suggests a certain rhythm, pacing, and two-dimensional form. Berio shapes these word sounds as though composing *musique concrète*. Recall from Chapter 80 that musique concrète is a type of electronic music in which the composer begins with recorded natural or man-made sounds. These raw materials are then manipulated into soundscapes. The harp in Berio's song creates sounds and noises that echo and punctuate those of the voice. Berio's medium also retains some elements from the traditional song. The voice is often lyrical and melismatic, and certain words are subtly painted in music. Note the "stinging" of tones at the opening and the bell-like sound tolled by the harp on the words "great bells are ringing." Cummings's spatial arrangement of words on the page also has an analogy in Berio's composition, in which the movements of the players and their position on stage are part of the expressive content of the work.

LISTENING CUE

LUCIANO BERIO
Circles (1960)
"stinging"

CD 13/12
Anthology, No. 209

Berio's new approach to the genre of song was continued later in the 1960s by the American composer George Crumb (b. 1929). Crumb was born in West Virginia and followed an academic path in music. He received graduate degrees from the University of Illinois and University of Michigan, and for more than thirty years was a professor of music at the University of Pennsylvania.

As a composer, Crumb attracted attention beginning in 1963 with a series of settings of Spanish poetry by Federico García Lorca (1898–1936) for voice and various chamber ensembles. He collaborated in these works with the American soprano Jan DeGaetani (1933–1989), whose virtuosity and extended singing techniques inspired Crumb in much the same way that Berberian did Berio.

Crumb's *Ancient Voices of Children* (1970) is one of the most celebrated of his García Lorca settings. It calls for soprano, boy soprano, oboe, mandolin, harp, amplified piano, toy piano, and a grand assortment of percussion instruments that include Japanese temple bells, Tibetan prayer stones, and a musical saw. *Ancient Voices* has five vocal movements, each using an excerpt from García Lorca's poetry, and there are also two instrumental interludes that may optionally be danced.

The five García Lorca poems outline a cycle of life and death in which the central symbolic image is that of the child. The first two poems use vivid metaphors to situate the spirit of the child in a fantasy world, presumably before birth. In the central third poem, "¿De dónde vienes?" ("Where Are You From?"), the child becomes a personification of love who converses with the woman who will give it birth. The child of love comes to her from afar, delights in nature, and demands sensuality. "What do you ask for, child, from afar?" demands the woman. "The white mountains of your breast," responds the child. Finally the child inflicts the pain of birth upon the woman. The cyclic view of life continues in the final two poems. In the fourth, the child dies, and in the fifth its spirit goes beyond the stars to regain its child-like soul, ready then to begin the cycle anew.

Crumb represents the symbolic and ritualistic poetry through a great mixture of means in which no sonorous or expressive device is ruled out. Motives from the first song, for example, are brought back at the end of the work to reinforce the connection between the beginning and end of the poetic cycle. Crumb also quotes from earlier music, in different historical styles, suggesting that the cycle of creation lies outside of any definite or historic time. In the fourth piece, where the child dies and returns to the spirit world, Crumb quotes from J.S. Bach's harmonization of the song "Bist du bei mir," BWV 508, whose unspoken words read "If you remain with me I will go gladly to death and to my rest." The quotation is played by a toy piano, the instrument of the child (Ex. 82-1). In the fifth movement, in which the speaker departs the earth for heaven, Crumb quotes the oboe solo in "The Farewell" movement of Gustav Mahler's *Das Lied von der Erde* (Ex. 82-2), music that deals with the departure of the soul at the time death.

EXAMPLE 82-1

EXAMPLE 82-2

The third piece, "¿De dónde vienes?"—subtitled "Dance of the Sacred Life-Cycle"—lies at the center of *Ancient Voices*, the point in the cycle representing creation itself. Crumb's notation of the music is laid out partly as a circle, symbolizing the content of García Lorca's poetry. The music begins with the soprano singing inarticulate syllables into an amplified piano, whereupon the percussionists begin an ostinato **bolero rhythm** (Ex. 82-3). The bolero is a sensual and erotic Spanish dance (one by Maurice Ravel was used with this effect in the film *10*, starring Bo Derek and Dudley Moore), so it is appropriate to this text.

EXAMPLE 82-3

The soprano, impersonating the woman, then begins her dialogue with the child, represented by a boy soprano situated offstage. The performers move three times around the notational circle, finally reaching the coda in the lower right corner of the score. In this piece, as in Berio's, our attention is drawn most directly to its sounds, as the composer devises an endless variety of ways in which the performers can create new and engaging colors. Note the shimmering effect of the soprano singing into the amplified piano, and the exuberance of her vocalization as well as the startling shouts from the percussionists as they play their bolero.

LISTENING CUE

GEORGE CRUMB   CD 13/13
Ancient Voices of Children (1970)   Anthology, No. 210
"¿De dónde vienes?"

❀ ELLIOTT CARTER

The movement from an abstract modernism toward a more accessible style is also seen in the career of Elliott Carter (b. 1908). Carter was born in New York City, educated at Harvard University and the École Normale de Musique in Paris, where he studied for three years with Nadia Boulanger (recall that she was also the teacher of Aaron Copland and numerous other American composers). Carter returned to New York in 1935 and taught, wrote essays on music, and made his way as a composer in a neoclassical vein.

Around 1950 Carter sharply changed the style of his music, bringing it closer to the modernist spirit of the period and greatly increasing its complexity. Carter's new musical rhetoric and method were self-made—typically American in their independence from trends. "I feel that my music is really something developed by myself," he wrote, "and whatever value and character it has is a result of the way I've thought about it. . . . That may be an American way of thinking in itself."[3]

But, at the same time that he joined the modernist movement, Carter expressed only disdain for most of the -isms of the 1950s. He wrote:

The neo-avant-garde has a very great preoccupation with the physical materials of music. . . . There seems to be very little concern with the perception of these sounds, their possibilities of intellectual interrelation by the listener, and, therefore, their possibilities of communication on a high level. Most of the time the possibility of communication is denied, or, if admitted, kept on the primitive level of any music that has only a sensuous effect.[4]

This "communication on a high level" is what Carter aimed for beginning in the 1950s in his new music. This consisted almost entirely of instrumental compositions in traditional genres—string quartets, concertos, symphonies, character pieces. Despite the composer's praise for communication in new music, these works are uncompromisingly complex in texture and material.

A celebrated example of Carter's music from this time is his String Quartet No. 2 (1959). This is a twenty-minute work having four movements in a traditional sequence, fast/*scherzo*/slow/fast, the whole framed by a brief introduction and conclusion. The movements are played without pause, and each movement is connected to the one following by a cadenza (for viola, cello, and violin, respectively).

The Introduction and first movement (*Allegro fantastico*) illustrates Carter's attempt to communicate on a high level. We are first confronted by the work's difficulties and complexities. The texture is densely contrapuntal and the harmonic language entirely dissonant and atonal. There are no themes, developments, or recapitulations in the normal sense. Our attention turns instead to a high-speed interaction among the four instruments, each of which has its own character. Notice in Example 82-4 the independence of the four lines. In addition to its own "behavior," to use Carter's term, each line has its own distinct musical materials. The first violin is "fantastic, ornate, and mercurial," to quote the composer, and it tends to dominate the other lines. Violin II has a "laconic, orderly character which is sometimes humorous." The viola is expressive, the cello impetuous. Together, the four instruments act out a wordless drama. At one moment, a musical character struts pompously on stage and ignores the others; the next moment there is an exchange of ideas and an attempt to get along, only to dissolve into furious confrontations. This fast-moving drama creates the form of the composition, which lacks traditional recurrences and symmetries.

EXAMPLE 82-4

(*continued on next page*)

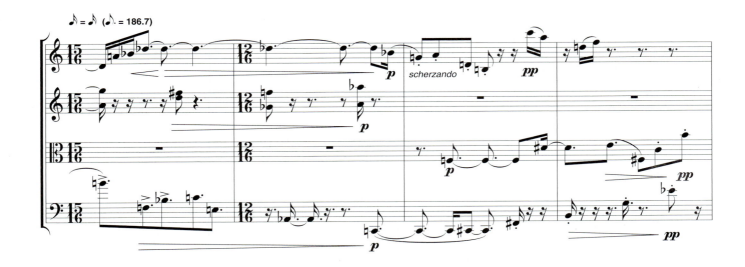

The distinctions in character among the four musical actors are reinforced by their different intervals and rhythms. Look, for example, at the passage near the beginning of the first movement, shown in Example 82-4. Violin I in these measures moves entirely by step, minor third, and perfect fifth. Violin II has different intervals. The notes of its chords are separated by major thirds, major sixths, and major sevenths—fewer intervals than in the flashy first violin and more appropriate to its stodgy persona.

The contrasts and interrelationships in rhythmic structure among the four parts are especially complex and inventive. In general, the lines in a work by Carter each have quickly changing tempos and unstable (or sometimes negligible) metric organization. The rhythmic structure of one line is normally not shared with the other lines.

To understand this element of Carter's language, we must first recognize an additional player in the drama—the notation of the score itself—which is clearly seen by the string-playing actors on stage as they struggle through their parts, but entirely unseen by the audience. We can observe notation playing the role of devil's advocate in the first few measures of Example 82-4. Here, it seems that a beat is marked by the first violin—showing off as always—with its sixteenth-note quintuplets at a tempo of 112. The other parts seem left behind, perplexed as to beat and meter.

But the notation has laid down a smoke screen, beneath which the rhythm is simpler and more regular than it appears. Its basic simplicity is shown by the re-notation in Example 82-5, where the two violins are seen to proceed hand-in-hand at a tempo of the quarter-note at 140, not 112. The impetuous cello and emotive viola at first cannot conform, as they press ahead irregularly. Finally, the cello gets the rhythmic upper hand in measure 60, where it establishes a regular pulse for itself at the rate of 186.7 for each note, and at this tempo it shortly joins hands with the viola. Carter's notation—the appearance of which often does not conform to the music's rhythmic organization—keeps all of the musical actors in a state of motion.

EXAMPLE 82-5

The rapid-fire changes in tempo—112 to 140 to 186.7 in only a few measures—are not arbitrarily selected, but based on simple numerical proportions. The rate of 140, taken by Violin II in measure 58, is exactly ¾ of the first violin's 112; the cello's 186.7 is ⅓ of the second violin's 140. Carter referred to a proportional change of tempo such as this as a **metric modulation,** which is a change of tempo produced when a small division of a beat is regrouped as part of a new beat. An example is found in measures 59–60. The sixteenth-note in measure 59 (which spans one-fifth of a beat in the tempo of 112), is regrouped in measure 60 as one-third of a new beat, producing a new tempo of 186.7 (that is, ⅗ of 112).

LISTENING CUE

ELLIOTT CARTER
String Quartet No. 2 (1959)
Introduction and first movement (*Allegro fantastico*)

CD 13/14
Anthology, No. 211

By the mid-1970s, Carter may have sensed that he had set the level of communication too high in a work such as the String Quartet No. 2. Just then a broadly based reaction against postwar modernism, with its complication and abstraction, was becoming apparent. Carter turned away from the complexities of the String Quartet No. 2 and began to write music for solo voice that communicates on a far more immediate plane. In works including *A Mirror on Which to Dwell* (1975, for soprano and nine instruments), *Syringa* (1978, for mezzo-soprano, baritone, and eleven instruments), and *In Sleep, in Thunder* (1981, for tenor and fourteen instruments) only a shadow of the audacious rhythmic complications of the Second String Quartet remains.

MINIMALISM: STEVE REICH

Carter's retreat from the no-holds-barred modernism of the Second String Quartet followed the path taken by a group of younger American composers of the 1960s and 1970s who mixed innovation with a return to recognizable melody, counterpoint, and harmony. These musicians—Steve Reich (b. 1936), Terry Riley (b. 1935), La Monte Young (b. 1935), and Philip Glass (b. 1937)—experimented in the mid-to-late 1960s with a style having a minimum of materials (a simple beat, a few tones) that are spun out—often to great lengths—by repetition varied by gradual change. Although some precedents for their type of music can be found—in John Cage's static and slowly evolving *String Quartet in Four Parts* (1950), for example—the group worked in a distinctly American, self-reliant manner, bolstered by direct personal contact and mutual collaboration.

An early example of their type of music is Terry Riley's *In C* (1964). The score consists of fifty-three short melodic fragments, each made from a few notes of a C-major scale (some F♯'s crop up in the middle, a few B♭'s at the end). The first four of the figures are shown in Example 82-6. A piano sets a pulse by repeatedly playing octave C's, and an ensemble of any makeup begins by repeating figure 1 in unison. Gradually everyone moves to figure 2, which is similarly repeated. The piece ends when everyone has played all fifty-three motives and decides to stop. *In C* is obviously novel and experimental—it resonates with the spirit of the 1960s—but, different from most other modernist developments of the time, it also has the familiar elements of simple pulse, normal rhythm, and tones from a major scale.

EXAMPLE 82-6

In the 1970s, the style of pieces like Riley's was dubbed **minimalism,** a term borrowed from art criticism. Another type of minimalism arose in the mid-1960s in the music of Steve Reich. He was born in New York and educated in music at Cornell University, the Juilliard School, and Mills College in Oakland, California, where he studied with Luciano Berio. Typical of the times, he began as a composer of twelve-tone and serial works, but he could sustain no affinity for such music.

In the mid-1960s, while experimenting with taped musique concrète, Reich discovered an acoustic phenomenon that led him in a new direction. By putting a phrase of speech on a tape loop (by which it is sounded over and over as an ostinato) and by playing the loop on two tape recorders, Reich noticed that a succession of new rhythms would emerge if the two tape players turned at slightly different speeds, as the coordination of the looped ostinatos came further and further apart. He termed the phenomenon **phasing** and used it in his *concrète* pieces *It's Gonna Rain* (1965) and *Come Out* (1966).

These works were audaciously modernistic, squarely in the spirit of the 1960s. They were as completely depersonalized as the chance pieces by John Cage and as strictly controlled as an automated composition by Milton Babbitt. Reich considered them not so much compositions as processes, which, when set in motion, generate an entire musical substance on their own. The objective of the phasing process was the creation of an evolving series of secondary rhythmic patterns, arising and then evaporating as the ostinatos came ever further out of phase.

The phenomenon had similarities with a movement in the graphic arts of the 1960s called "**conceptual art**" (or sometimes "minimal art"). An example, *Arcs from Corners and Sides* by the New York artist Sol LeWitt (b. 1928), is shown in Figure 82-1. The design, like Reich's phase music, is made from a minimum of materials—semicircular arcs—and a simple plan by which the arcs radiate from the four sides of a square. The design that results is enriched by other symmetrical patterns created by areas of varying densities of lines. These additional patterns—like the secondary rhythmic figures in Reich's music—are a by-product of the artist's concept and process.

✿ FIGURE 82-1
Sol LeWitt, *Arcs from Corners and Sides* (in various venues, 1968–1993). LeWitt's graphic works—like a phase composition by Steve Reich—are the product of a relatively simple process. The radiating arcs also produce interlocking rose-like designs, just as Reich's phase works produce secondary rhythmic patterns.

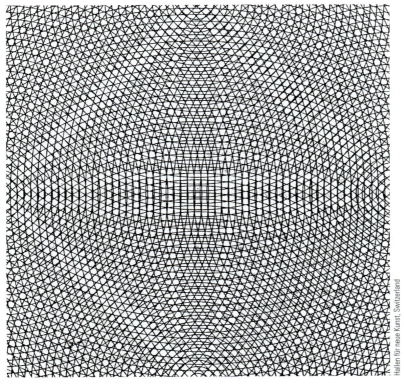

Hallen für neue Kunst, Switzerland

Reich later transferred his idea of phasing to a live medium, replacing the tape loop and concrète sound with a performed ostinato. This led him to pieces such as *Clapping Music* (1972), which is for two performers using only their hands to clap out rhythms. The two clappers start in unison with the figure shown in Example 82-7, which is repeated numerous times. The first clapper continues this pattern from beginning to end, but the second player at the beginning of each measure leaps ahead by an eighth-note. The figure has twelve eighth-note values, so in the thirteenth measure the two come back into unison, whereupon the piece ends. The phase process creates many unexpected rhythmic patterns. For example, rests in both parts occur only on the fourth, seventh, ninth, and twelve eighth-notes within any measure. Although the metric pattern arising in most measures is asymmetric and irregular, in the seventh measure the clouds suddenly part to reveal a perfectly regular $\frac{3}{8}$ meter (Example 82-8).

EXAMPLE 82-7

EXAMPLE 82-8

m. 7 (composite)

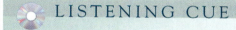

 LISTENING CUE

STEVE REICH

Clapping Music (1972)

CD 13/15

Anthology, No. 212

Minimalism proved to be the most enduring new musical style of the postwar decades. It was born from the audacious spirit of innovation that was dominant during this time, and it spread to composers in Europe, influencing experimental rock as well as classical music. Minimalism outlived the waning of this experimental phase in the history of postwar music, a phenomenon that will be taken up again in the next chapter.

SUMMARY

The 1960s and early 1970s were a transitional period in the history of music, during which composers continued to explore and search for new styles but dropped doctrinaire attitudes to look for ways that modern music could communicate and regain the interest of audiences. The song-like compositions of Luciano Berio and George Crumb are examples of this thinking. Both composers rely on sound per se to enhance the poetry that they set to music, and Crumb adds additional expressive techniques such as quotations from preexisting music.

Elliott Carter's music of the 1950s and 1960s was unrelentingly complex, especially in its multiple and changeable tempos and the complex counterpoint of lines. The composer intended these features to create a wordless drama in his instrumental music. In the 1970s, in works such as the songs *A Mirror on Which to Dwell,* he simplified his music's texture and returned to a more traditional model of song composition.

The mixture of audacious novelty and traditional materials is also seen in minimalist music, composed from the mid-1960s by a group of American composers including La Monte Young, Terry Riley, Philip Glass, and Steve Reich. Minimalism is a style that uses a minimum of materials that are spun out by repetition with gradual change. It is seen in the music of the 1960s and early 1970s by Steve Reich as the result of a "phasing" process by which an ostinato begun in unison by two or more sources of sound (performers or taped sounds) gradually moves out of synchrony, thus producing a changing series of secondary rhythmic patterns.

 KEY TERMS

modernism	metric modulation	phasing
extended techniques	minimalism	conceptual art
bolero rhythm		

Returning to the Known: Music of the Recent Past

By 1975 a rejection of postwar modernism in music and a return to more familiar musical values were in full swing. This change of taste was accompanied and provoked by changes in the society that supported music. The unspeakable memories of World War II had lost some of their jagged edge and the anxieties that attended the Cold War had eased. People were wealthier than ever before. Popular culture had grown exponentially in importance all over the world, and with it came the expectation for simple and immediate entertainment—things that were scarce in the classical music that had dominated the 1950s and 1960s. The factors that nourished postwar musical modernism—a desire among artists to forget the past and to hide the personality behind complexity, abstraction, and intricate form—had by 1975 largely evaporated.

As often in the twentieth century when styles have changed, new thinking was accompanied by a forceful rejection of the immediate past. Pierre Boulez in the 1950s had demanded conformity to the principle of serialism, so composers after 1975 tended to go in the very opposite direction by preaching tolerance for any and all styles and procedures. While Elliott Carter wrote music of daunting complexity in the 1960s, composers of the 1970s and later brought simplicity to their music. In a lecture in 1984, the American composer John Harbison assured his students that it was then acceptable to write simple diatonic music:

In the early seventies it took more nerve, it was more out of step to explore a nonchromatic language than now. The chromatic revolution had been certified by the universities, was socially and academically acceptable. . . . Younger composers [today] are fortunate that they confront in their early years an unpressured multiplicity of options; the rewards will be clear.[1]

The modernists' demand that composers wipe out the musical past seemed especially undesirable. In the 1950s, Pierre Boulez had insisted that new music should have historical amnesia: "Strong expanding civilizations have no memory," he said. "They reject and forget the past. They feel strong enough to be destructive because they know they can replace what has been destroyed."[2] By the later 1970s this outlook was discredited by almost everyone. Embracing all of music—old and new, popular and classical, Western and non-Western—had become the order of the day. In 1972 the American composer George Rochberg spoke for this new outlook: "Unlike Boulez, I will not praise amnesia," he wrote.

> The desperate search in the second half of the twentieth century for a way out of cultural replication, i.e., being influenced by others, borrowing, leapfrogging, etc., has let loose a veritable Pandora's box of aberrations which have little or nothing to do with art.[3]

Composers, wrote Rochberg, must once again frankly express their personalities and emotions: "There can be no justification for music, ultimately, if it does not convey eloquently and elegantly the passions of the human heart," he wrote.[4]

In this chapter we turn to representative compositions from the last quarter of the twentieth century, in which the new taste of these years is apparent. In all of them we will see a greater simplicity and accessibility than before, a free use of styles from the past, and non-doctrinaire thinking on how to write music. György Ligeti's *Hungarian Rock* joins disparate musical styles into a happy amalgam. John Adams's opera *Nixon in China* reveals the evolution of minimalism from a thorny experimental music to a friendly and agreeable one. Joan Tower's *Fanfare for the Uncommon Woman*, No. 1, calls to mind Aaron Copland's *Fanfare for the Common Man*—one of the best-known pieces of classical music in the entire twentieth century. Arvo Pärt's *Berlin Mass* revives the outwardly serene features of Renaissance vocal music, although it also preserves aspects of minimalist and serial methods of composition.

MIXING STYLES: GYÖRGY LIGETI

The career of the composer György Ligeti (pronounced JERGE LI-geti, b. 1923) illustrates the changes of direction in modern music during the 1970s. Ligeti was born to Hungarian parents in a village in Romania and, as a Jew, only miraculously survived World War II while living in Budapest. Following the war he enrolled at the Budapest Academy of Music—the institution where Béla Bartók had earlier studied and taught—and Ligeti too served on its faculty from 1950 to 1956.

During the Hungarian Revolution against the Soviet Union in 1956, Ligeti fled to Vienna and then settled in Cologne, Germany, where he composed electronic works and met important figures in the world of contemporary European music. From 1959 he was active at the Darmstadt Summer Courses for New Music, and he established a reputation as an essayist on technical aspects of avant-garde composition.

Ligeti burst into view as a composer in 1960 and 1961 with his orchestral works *Apparitions* and *Atmosphères*. These pieces—somewhat similar to the orchestral works of Krzysztof Penderecki from the same time (see Chapter 78)—use sound masses made from what Ligeti calls **micropolyphony.** This is a texture created by large numbers of lines, so many that the individual lines, intervals, and rhythms are not distinguishable and are absorbed instead into a web-like mass. An example of micropolyphony can be seen in a few measures from *Atmosphères*, shown in Example 83-1. Here, twenty-eight violins, ten violas, ten celli, and eight basses have their own distinct lines, each playing chromatically in uncoordinated and complex rhythms. The individual lines cannot be heard, only a texture made from a sound mass that has a certain color and dynamic level.

EXAMPLE 83-1[†]

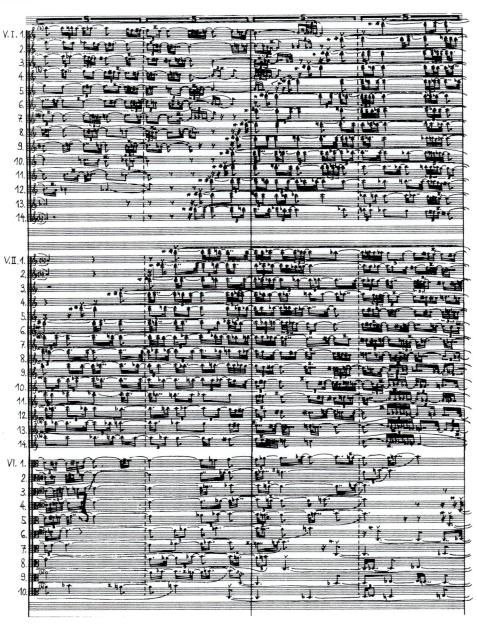

†György Ligeti, *Atmosphères*, study score, p. 9. Copyright © 1963 Universal Edition (no. 13590), Vienna.

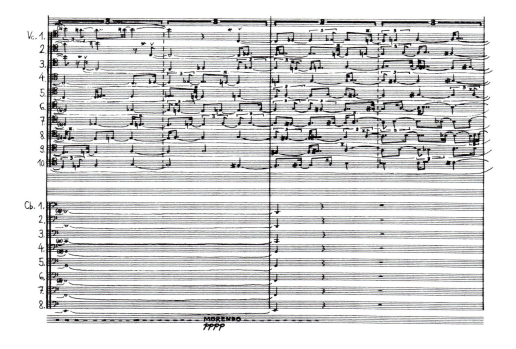

By the 1970s Ligeti had moved beyond textural composition into an eclectic style that was more clearly connected to familiar earlier models. He explained this change of outlook:

> If 30 or even 20 years ago I may have belonged to some group of composers that considered itself "avant-garde," today I adhere to no group ideology. The avant-garde protest action was a political gesture of an elite. With the collapse of the socialistic utopia and with the change in civilization's technology, brought by the spread of microelectronics, the time for an artistic avant-garde is past. Since for me "beautiful" postmodernism is only an illusion, I am looking for some "other" modernism, neither a "back to" nor a modish protest or "criticism." [5]

One of Ligeti's "other modernisms" in the 1970s was to combine disparate styles, which is evident in his *Hungarian Rock* (1978) for harpsichord. The work cleverly intertwines aspects of jazz, baroque keyboard music, and modern harmony. The baroque element comes from the use of harpsichord and from the form of the chaconne. Recall from Chapter 31 that the form of the chaconne, which appeared in both instrumental and vocal music of the Baroque period and is virtually synonymous with the form of the passacaglia, is characterized by continuous variations on a short ostinato figure in the bass, a short harmonic progression, or both simultaneously. Often the tones of the bass of a chaconne leap by intervals of the fourth and fifth, as in Claudio Monteverdi's celebrated chaconne "Zefiro torna" of 1632 (Example 83-2). Ligeti's bass figure shares the fourths and fifths of the baroque model, although the composer compresses the motive into a single measure with an asymmetrical rhythm (Example 83-3).

EXAMPLE 83-2

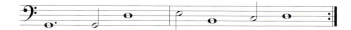

EXAMPLE 83-3

Ligeti's next step is to use the ostinato figure like a jazz musician constructing a blues. A four-measure harmonic progression is made by repeating the bass figure four times in succession, each time with different chords (Ex. 83-4), and this phrase is played in the left hand forty-four times, with no alterations. Above it, the right hand—like a bebop saxophonist—adds an ever more complex series of melodic variations. These begin with only a few tones and adhere to the 2 + 2 + 3 + 2 rhythm of the bass, but gradually the right hand becomes more complex and chromatic, and it imposes changing rhythms, meters, and irregular phrase patterns above the bass. Eight measures before the end, the breathless motion grinds to a halt and an improvisatory coda completes the piece.

EXAMPLE 83-4

One whole bar = mm. 50

LISTENING CUE

GYÖRGY LIGETI

Hungarian Rock (1978)

CD 13/16

Anthology, No. 213

THE TRANSFORMATION OF MINIMALISM: JOHN ADAMS

The change of taste in music in the late 1970s is apparent also in the evolution of minimalism. Recall from Chapter 82 that minimalism is a musical style that arose in America in the 1960s. In it, a minimum of musical material—often contained in a short ostinato figure—is expanded, often to great lengths, by repetition with gradual change. At its time of origin the style reflected the spirit of the avant-garde—minimalistic pieces tended to be automated, depersonalized, and unprecedented in their materials (recall the hand clapping in Reich's *Clapping Music*). But, in the 1970s and 1980s, minimalism was defanged, losing its modernistic bite and gaining footholds in the world of rock. The minimalistic ostinatos were then often shunted into an accompaniment, to which normal melodies and rock lyrics were readily added.

The transformation of minimalism is apparent in the music of John Adams (b. 1947). Adams was educated at Harvard, and in 1978 appointed **new music advisor** to the San Francisco Symphony Orchestra. Many American orchestras of the 1970s created a position of this type, which has proved to be an important alternative to academic employment for the modern American composer. In addition to longer orchestral works such as *Harmonielehre* (1985), Adams also revitalized the genre of the short orchestral character piece in compositions such as *Short Ride in a Fast Machine* (1986) and *The Chairman Dances* (1985). Works of this type, typically bright and lively, are often programmed by orchestras nowadays at the beginning of a concert, to give the audience a relatively painless dose of modern music.

Adams's early music is minimalistic in concept, but with important differences from the minimalism of ten years before. This distinction can be observed in his *China Gates* for piano (1977), the opening measures of which are seen in Example 83-5. The work is plainly minimalistic, as it uses relatively few materials that are spun into ostinatos that undergo—in the middle voice—gradual change.

EXAMPLE 83-5

Several distinctive features of Adams's style can also be observed in this piece. The first is the presence of what the composer calls **gates,** which are points at which pitch collections change, akin to modulations in earlier music. The first gate occurs

Synopsis of *Nixon in China*

Richard M. Nixon, President of the United States, arrives with his wife, Pat, and national security advisor Henry Kissinger, in the Chinese capital of Peking, to make direct diplomatic contact with the Chinese government. They meet the Chinese premier, Chou En-lai, and the elderly Chairman Mao Tse-Tung, whose conversation Nixon finds mysterious. At the evening's banquet, spirits are high and many toasts are proposed. In the second act, Pat Nixon visits monuments of the city and in the evening attends a performance of the ballet "The Red Detachment of Women," which has been devised by Mao's wife, Chiang Ch'ing. Many misunderstandings occur during the performance. Although a staging or context is not specified for the third act, the principals reminisce nostalgically about their earlier years and differing aspirations while a band plays old-fashioned dance music.

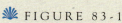 FIGURE 83-1
The Finnish graphic artist Pekka Loiri created this poster for a performance of Adams's *Nixon in China*.

Photograph courtesy of Pekka Loiri

---

in measure 16, where the previous collection of tones, all drawn from a D♭-major scale, shifts to tones from a B-major scale. (The term "gate" comes from a device used by electronic composers to create sudden shifts in the amplitude of an electronic signal.)

Another distinctive feature of the piece is in its layering of textures. There are three strata, each containing an ostinato, but each distinguishable by rhythmic motion and register. The top level moves in eighth notes, the middle in longer values, and the lowest is a simple drone. Note especially the differences separating *China Gates* from an earlier minimalistic piece like Steve Reich's *Clapping Music* (see Chapter 82). Adams's minimalism has become beautiful—relaxing, sonorous, comfortable—not difficult or unsettling, as was often true of 1960s minimalism.

Gates and layers are still present in the music of Adams's opera *Nixon in China* (1987), but the shadows of minimalism have receded even further, relegated to the musical accompaniment. The opera is distinctly unusual in its subject matter, which is drawn from current events. The libretto, by the poet Alice Goodman, deals with the visit of President Richard Nixon to Mainland China in February 1972. This occasion was of immense historical importance, as it helped to defuse the hostile relations that had long existed between China and the West and proved a milestone in the waning of the Cold War.

Goodman's focus is not so much on historical fact as on the personalities involved. The librettist intended to make these realistic and "heroic," but since contemporary political figures are known almost entirely by one-dimensional portrayals in the media, any true realism in such an opera is largely an illusion. Nixon is drawn, predictably, as paranoid, someone who slips easily off the track into trivial nostalgia. Pat Nixon is the long-suffering wife, Mao is inscrutable, Henry Kissinger is bureaucratic. Given these one-sided character types and certain ludicrous situations into which they are placed, the work most resembles the archetype of traditional comic opera. Also like comic opera is the form, which is made from a succession of distinct arias, narrations, choruses, and ensembles. Finally, there is a comic parody of traditional operatic forms.

Nixon's aria "News" is the first major musical number of the opera. Just after arriving in Peking and greeting Premier Chou, the President becomes transfixed by the importance of the moment. Historic news is being made at this very time, he thinks, and he compares the event to the Apollo astronauts walking on the moon. He imagines that his arrival is just then being broadcast on the evening news, its importance consecrated by this uniquely American ritual. But his thoughts then dart toward his enemies, those ungrateful for his achievements. But he will ignore them: "My hand is as steady as a rock," he declares. His reverie is finally interrupted by Henry Kissinger—his part sung in this scene by a male chorus—who brings word that a meeting with Chairman Mao has been arranged.

The overall form of the aria is free, following the shifting ideas of the text, although an element of da capo form (see Chapter 32) is present as the opening music returns at measure 582. Nixon sings in a partly repetitive, partly lyrical style to a minimalistic accompaniment.

LISTENING CUE

JOHN ADAMS
Nixon in China (1987)
Act 1, scene 1, "News"

Nonesuch CD 79177 or
Nonesuch CD 79193
Anthology, No. 214

 ## REVIVING THE RECENT PAST: JOAN TOWER

The music of Joan Tower (b. 1938; Fig. 83-2) reflects the change of taste by which musical modernism in the 1970s was swept aside. Her earlier works were serialized and abstract, but from the mid-1970s they became simpler, more eclectic, and more familiar in material. She describes this change:

> When I first got out of school, I hung around a lot of serial composers and was into the twelve-tone stuff, heavily, I was playing it, so my music was fairly twelve-tone based at that time. But after about ten years I found my own voice. . . . This was at a time [earlier on] when you didn't do anything simple. [Later] it was a real door-opener for me, because after that my own voice started to take shape.[6]

Tower was born in New York State and attended Bennington College and Columbia University. A pianist, she specialized in performing modern music with her own ensemble, the Da Capo Chamber Players, for which she has written numerous works. She composes primarily instrumental music, including orchestral character pieces, concertos, and chamber compositions.

Her *Fanfare for the Uncommon Woman*, No. 1 (1986), is an example of the short orchestral character piece that has increasingly become the stock-in-trade of the serious American composer. It is made not only from familiar pitch materials and expressive gestures, but in its title and in musical content refers explicitly to Aaron Copland's ever-popular *Fanfare for*

❀ FIGURE 83-2
Joan Tower is a leading voice in contemporary American music.

the Common Man (1942). Written during World War II, Copland's Fanfare is a patriotic work that evokes the sound of cannons and bugles, all leading to a triumphant conclusion.

Tower's Fanfare has a different context. Although written for the same medium as Copland's Fanfare—orchestral brass and percussion—Copland's war-like allusions are replaced by a more lilting and festive spirit. "It is dedicated," Tower writes about the Fanfare, "to women who take risks and who are adventurous."

Tower's fanfare, like Copland's, begins with a trumpet figure based on a pentatonic scale and chords made from fourths and fifths (Ex. 83-6). Copland's opening figure (top) imitates the intervals available on a valveless bugle, while Tower's opening material (bottom) is more pervasively quartal. In the middle of Tower's fanfare, the lines become complex in makeup, based alternately on diatonic, whole-tone, and chromatic scales, and the opening music and its pentatonicism return near the end.

EXAMPLE 83-6

LISTENING CUE

JOAN TOWER   CD 13/17
Fanfare for the Uncommon Woman, No. 1 (1986)   Anthology, No. 215

❋ THE RENAISSANCE REBORN: ARVO PÄRT

As composers of the 1970s searched the past for new alliances with the present, they found an especially fruitful source of inspiration in Renaissance choral music. Recall from Chapters 21 and 25 the features of this body of music, which achieves a balance and serenity that seemed appropriate to the relaxed spirit of the 1970s and also an antidote to the complex dissonances of the immediate musical past. Renaissance choral music became the stylistic framework for the works of Arvo Pärt (pronounced PAIRT). Pärt was born in Estonia in 1935, when this small country, lying on the Baltic Sea just below Finland, was an independent republic. Following World War II, Estonia was absorbed into the Soviet Union, although its independence was recovered in 1991. Pärt attended the conservatory in Tallinn, the capital city, and established a reputation in the Soviet Union as a rebellious composer writing complex serialized music. Even in 1980 he was little known in the West; in that year he emigrated from Russia, first to Vienna, and settled finally in Berlin.

Pärt's compositional evolution neatly shows a cross section of the broad changes in modern music following World War II. In the 1960s he was a serialist, although he found this idiom unsatisfying. Composers at Darmstadt, he said later, were like children playing in a sandbox. He then turned to an eclectic style that mixed modern elements with quotations from the past (recall a similar feature in George Crumb's *Ancient Voices of Children*, see Chapter 82). Finally, in the later 1970s, Pärt developed a personalized idiom that outwardly imitates Renaissance choral music. Since 1980 he has composed primarily for voices, using Latin texts from the Roman Catholic liturgy. These pieces include Masses, motets, passions, and a Magnificat.

Pärt calls the style of his works after 1976 **tintinnabuli** (Latin for "bells"), which refers to his method for constructing a polyphonic texture. A work in the tintinnabuli style has one or more pairs of polyphonic lines. In each pair one line is melodic, the other harmonic (or bell-like) in nature. The melodic line resembles a Gregorian chant, progressing largely stepwise in a diatonic motion that tends to focus on a keynote. The harmonic line is restricted to the notes of the tonic triad.

An example of a tintinnabuli pair of lines is shown in Example 83-7, music that is drawn from the *Credo* of Pärt's *Berlin Mass* (1990). The lower line is the melodic voice. It is entirely diatonic, in the key of E major, and it moves predominantly by step. The upper voice is the bell line. Its notes are limited to those of an E-major triad, and these tones are chosen to meet the melodic line only at the intervals of the fourth, fifth, sixth, and octave.

EXAMPLE 83-7

mm. 1-11 (Bass and tenor, text omitted)

Pärt's *Berlin Mass* shows other aspects of his revival of Renaissance music. Like the Mass in the fifteenth and sixteenth centuries, Pärt's *Berlin Mass* is functional music, intended to be performed in a Catholic service of worship. With its primarily consonant harmony and clear declamation of the text, the work has a serenity reminiscent of a Mass by Palestrina or a motet by Josquin. The second tintinnabuli pair (made by the altos and sopranos) relates to the first (bass-tenor) by a strict canon.

Pärt deviates from his ancient model by adding an instrumental accompaniment to the chorus; also, his music is more static than a Renaissance work because it contains an unchanging triad in the harmonic lines. The work has many subtly modernistic touches—a repetitiveness suggesting minimalism and even a few holdovers from the days of serialism—but with Pärt these all contribute to a personalized and expressive objective.

LISTENING CUE

ARVO PÄRT
Berlin Mass (1990)
Credo

CD 13/18
Anthology, No. 216

✿ MUSIC IN THE TWENTY-FIRST CENTURY

Arvo Pärt's tying the past together with the present is an appropriate theme with which to end this study of music in Western civilization. Pärt's outlook on the past would be impossible if music throughout our history did not possess so many recurrences and symmetries, so many similar patterns of change provoked by recurring conditions. The liberation of dissonance that characterizes Monteverdi's "second practice" in 1600 has an uncanny similarity to the emancipation of dissonance proclaimed by Arnold Schoenberg around 1908. Both were declared to sharpen the expressive resources available to the musician, and both initiated a new period in musical history that followed on a time when musical expression had become limited and predictable. Stravinsky's attacks of the 1920s on music of the recent past reminds us strikingly of Johannes Tinctoris' complaint, made in 1477, that no music composed more than forty years earlier "is thought by the learned as worthy of performance."

Given these cycles and symmetries of music history, can we look with any confidence at what music will be in the future? The near future appears clear enough. Now, at the beginning of the twenty-first century, classical music retains its allegiance to known values, its tolerant embracing of all music of the past, and its basic simplicity. We can be fairly sure that classical composers will continue in the near future to seek as large an audience as possible and continue to find alliances with popular music, non-Western music, film, and all earlier styles of classical works.

But beyond this, the crystal ball for music grows dim. Although we cannot reliably predict what music will be in the future, we can with reasonable certainty say *why* it will become what it will. The first factor is contained within music itself. Music changes in part because of its own life cycles. In the nineteenth century, for example, the trend toward ever-greater expressivity led to greater and greater lengths and grandiosity. Finally, these had reached their own limit. How could music be longer than Wagner's operas or more grandiose than Mahler's symphonies? The late romantic style collapsed under its own weight and a new style grew from it.

Music also changes because of non-musical factors, especially the character and course of the society in which it exists. The muscular impulsiveness of Beethoven's music was shaped, in part, by the era in which he lived, a time of continuous warfare, when the exploits of heroic individuals were praised. In the twentieth century, the two world wars produced sharp changes in musical styles as artists struggled to regain control by rejecting a past filled with unsustainable memories.

What will music be in the future? Almost certainly it will be an outgrowth of its own evolution, expansion, and ultimate exhaustion. With equal certainty it will be a product of the society around it and, as such, a reflection of our own experiences, brought back to those of us who listen and study with a greater clarity and meaning.

SUMMARY

Around 1975 a major change of style occurred in the world of classical music. The complexity, desire for control, and experimentation of the preceding decades were replaced by a simpler and more familiar style. Composers no longer rejected the past but embraced it, in all its dimensions. György Ligeti's *Hungarian Rock* combines disparate styles from the past—jazz and baroque chaconnes—into an eclectic mixture. John Adams's music, as in his opera *Nixon in China*, transforms minimalism from an experimental type of music to one with familiar features and comforting sonorities. Joan Tower's *Fanfare for the Uncommon Woman*, No. 1, alludes to a specific earlier composition by Aaron Copland. Arvo Pärt's music after 1976, which uses what this composer calls the "tintinnabuli" (bells) style, imitates Renaissance vocal counterpoint.

KEY TERMS

micropolyphony   gate
new music advisor   *tintinnabuli* style

NOTES

Abbreviations

History in Documents   *Music in the Western World: A History in Documents*, ed. Piero Weiss and Richard Taruskin (New York, 1984).

JAMS   *Journal of the American Musicological Society*

Letters of Mozart   Emily Anderson, *The Letters of Mozart and His Family*, ed. and trans. Emily Anderson, 3 vols. (London, 1966).

NG   *The New Grove Dictionary of Music and Musicians*, ed. S. Sadie and J. Tyrrell (London, 2001).

PART I

Chapter 1   1. Thomas J. Mathiesen, *Apollo's Lyre: Greek Music and Music Theory in Antiquity and the Middle Ages* (Lincoln, NE, 1999), 145. 2. Anicius Manlius Severinus Boethius, *Fundamentals of Music*, trans. Calvin M. Bower, ed. Claude V. Palisca (New Haven, CT 1989), Book I, Chapter 1. 3. Aristotle, *Politics*, 8:1340s.

Chapter 2   none

Chapter 3   none

Chapter 4   none

Chapter 5   none

Chapter 6   1. This translation is drawn from Paris, Bibliothèque nationale, fonds français, MS 12473, fol. 15. 2. Translated from Jean Boutière and Irénée-Marcel Cluzel, *Biographies des troubadours; textes provençaux des XIIIe et XIVe siècles*, 2nd ed. (Paris, 1973), 29.

Chapter 7   1. *Hucbald, Guido, and John on Music: Three Medieval Treatises*, trans. Warren Babb, ed. Claude V. Palisca (New Haven, CT 1978), 159.

Chapter 8   1. Edmond de Coussemaker, ed., *Scriptorum de Musica Medii Aevi*, 4 vols. (Paris, 1864–1876; rpt. 1931), I, 342. See also, Jeremy Yudkin, *The Music Treatise of Anonymous IV: A New Translation*, vol. 41 of Musicological Studies and Documents (Rome, 1985), 39.

Chapter 9   1. *The Letters of Abelard and Heloise*, trans. Betty Radice (London, 1974), Letter No. 1, p. 115.

Chapter 10   1. Adapted from Robert F. Hayburn, *Papal Legislation on Sacred Music: 95 A.D. to 1977 A.D.* (Collegeville, MN, 1979), 20–21.

Chapter 11   1. Margaret Bent and Andrew Wathey, "Philippe de Vitry," *NG*, 26:804. 2. Timothy J. McGee, *Medieval Instrumental Dances* (Bloomington and Indianapolis, 1989), 20. 3. McGee, *Medieval Instrumental Dances*, 26.

Chapter 12   none

Chapter 13   1. Francesco Petrarch, quoted in many translations and many sources including Marcel Frémiot and Charles Pitt, "Avignon," *NG*, 2:251.

Musical Interlude 1   1. Isidore of Seville, *Etymologies*, as given in *Source Readings in Music History*, ed. Oliver Strunk; rev. ed. Leo Treitler (New York and London, 1998), 149. 2. Jan Herlinger, ed. *Prosdocimus de' Beldomandi: Contrapunctus* (Lincoln, NE, 1984), p. 83 and especially footnote 11.

PART II

Chapter 14   1. Coluccio Salutati, *Le "consulte" e "pratiche" della Repubblica fiorentina* (1403), quoted in part in Michael Levey, *Florence: A Portrait* (Cambridge, MA, 1996), 68. 2. Giovanni Gherardi da Prato, *Il Paradiso degli Alberti*, ed. Antonio Lanza (Rome, 1975), 165. 3. Prato, *Il Paradiso degli Alberti*, 176. 4. *Giovanni Boccaccio's Decameron*, trans. Mark Musa and Peter Bondanella (New York, 1982), 6. 5. *Giovanni Boccaccio's Decameron*, 3.

Chapter 15   1. The correct dimensions of the cathedral of Florence and their symbolic significance are discussed in a splendid article by Marvin Trachtenberg, "Architecture and Music Reunited: A New Reading of Dufay's *Nuper Rosarum Flores* and the Cathedral of Flo-

rence," *Renaissance Quarterly*, 54 (2001): 740–75. 2. Giannozzo Manetti, *Oratio*, cited in Craig Wright, "Dufay's *Nuper Rosarum Flores*, King Solomon's Temple, and the Veneration of the Virgin," *JAMS*, 47 (1994): 430.

Chapter 16   1. Geraldus Cambrensis, *Descriptio Cambriae* (1198), as given in and adapted from Frederick Sternfeld, *Music from the Middle Ages to the Renaissance* (New York, 1973), 264; also cited in *History in Documents*, 61.

Chapter 17   1. Mathieu d'Escouchy, *Chronique*, quoted in and translated from Jeanne Marix, *Les Musiciens de la cour de Bourgogne au XVe siècle* (Strasbourg, 1937), 41.

Chapter 18   1. Leeman L. Perkins, "Ockeghem," *NG*, 18:315. 2. Heinrich Glarean, *Dodecachordon* (1547), trans. Clement Miller, 2 vols. (Rome, 1965), II, 284. Glarean, publishing in 1547, identifies the king as Louis XII; the sole musical source (St. Gall, Switzerland, Stiftsarchiv, MS 462), written around 1515, identifies him as Louis XI. The most recent bibliographical discoveries about Josquin suggest that the earlier king (Louis XI) is the royal monotone in question.

Chapter 19   none

PART III

Musical Interlude 2   none

Chapter 20   1. The following discussion draws heavily on part one of Patrick Macey's excellent study, *Bonfire Songs: Savonarola's Musical Legacy* (Oxford, 1998). 2. *The Book of the Courtier: A New Translation*, trans. Charles S. Singleton (Garden City, NJ, 1959), Book II, p. 13.

Chapter 21   1. Patrick Macey, "Josquin," *NG*, 13:229. 2. Translated from Cosimo Bartoli, *Ragionamenti accademici* (1567); a similar translation can be found in "Josquin," *NG*, 13:229. 3. Patrick Macey, "Josquin," *NG*, 13:225. 4. Macey, "Josquin," 13:225. 5. This thesis was first developed in a superb article by Patrick Macey, "Savonarola and the Sixteenth-Century Motet," *JAMS*, 36 (1983): 422–52. 6. This and the preceding remark are cited in Patrick Macey, "Josquin," in *NG*, 13:228.

Musical Interlude 3   none

Chapter 22   1. Thoinot Arbeau, *Orchesography*, trans. Mary Steward Evans (New York, 1967), 118–19. 2. Arbeau, *Orchesography*, 121.

Chapter 23   none

Musical Interlude 4   none

Chapter 24   1. Translated from the preface of Walter's *Geistliche Gesangbüchlein* (1524); a similar translation can be found in Carl Schalk, *Music in Early Lutheranism* (St. Louis, 2001), 31.

Chapter 25   1. Lewis Lockwood, ed. *Palestrina: Pope Marcellus Mass* (New York, 1975), 14. 2. Gustave Reese, *Music in the Renaissance* (New York, 1954), 449.

Chapter 26   1. Simon Schama, *A History of Britain* (New York, 2000), 334.

Chapter 27   1. For this and the previous quote, see Craig Monson, "Elizabethan London," in Iain Fenlon, ed., *The Renaissance: From the 1470s to the End of the 16th Century* in the series *Man and Music*, ed. Stanley Sadie (Englewood Cliffs, NJ, 1989), 319, 321. 2. Quoted by Monson, "Elizabethan London," 331. 3. Later in the Fitzwilliam Virginal Book there is an identical setting of this piece with an eighth variation ascribed to John Mundy.

Chapter 28   1. This and the previous quote are found in Anthony Newcomb, *The Madrigal at Ferrara 1579–1597*, 2 vols. (Princeton, 1980), I, 55, 67. 2. This passage has been adapted from the translation of Glenn Watkins given in *Gesualdo, The Man and His Music* (Chapel Hill, 1973), 44–46. 3. This passage is a slight rearrangement of the translation of Gary Tomlinson in *Source Readings in Music History*, ed. Oliver Strunk; rev. ed. Leo Treitler (New York and London, 1998), 528.

PART IV

Chapter 29   none

Chapter 30   1. This translation to Peri's preface of the score of Euridice was kindly provided by Pietro Moretti. 2. The words of Marco da Gagliano (1582-1643) as quoted in *History in Documents*, 176.

Chapter 31   1. Translated from Monteverdi's preface to his eighth book of madrigals as given in the introduction to vol. 8 of G. Francesco Malipiero, ed., *Tutte le opere di Claudio Monteverdi* (Bologna, 1929). 2. *History in Documents*, 185.

Chapter 32   1. Letter of Leopold Mozart of 14 April 1770 as given in *Letters of Mozart*, I, 187.

Chapter 33   1. Michael Talbot, *Vivaldi* (New York, Oxford, Singapore, and Sidney, 1993), 42. 2. Correspondence of Charles de Brosses, translated in H.C. Robbins Landon, *Vivaldi: Voice of the Baroque* (London, 1993), 30. 3. Talbot, *Vivaldi*, 40.

Chapter 34   1. Translated from the preface of Georg Muffat's *Armonico tributo* (Salzburg, 1682). 2. In Froberger's original manuscripts the gigue usually, but not always, precedes the sarabande. Publishers of his music, however, invariably grouped them in the sequence allemande, courante, sarabande, and gigue. It was these posthumous publications that firmly established this as the "standard" order for the dance suite. 3. *The Philosophical Works of Descartes Rendered into English*, by Elizabeth S. Haldane and G.R.T. Ross, 2 vols. (Cambridge, 1973), I, 372, 377. 4. *History in Documents*, 218. 5. Kerala J. Snyder, *Dieterich Buxtehude: Organist in Lübeck* (New York, 1987), 57. 6. Snyder, *Dieterich Buxtehude*, 57–58.

Chapter 35   1. James Anthony, *French Baroque Music from Beaujoyeulx to Rameau* (Portland 1997), 66. 2. Evrard Titon du Tillet, *Second Supplément du Parnasse françois* (Paris, 1755), 791–92. 3. *Dictionnaire universel françois et latin*, 6 vols. (Paris, 1743), I, 1670.

Chapter 36   1. Most fixed-pitched instruments, such as harpsichord and organ, did not use equal temperament in this period, but one kind or another of "mean-tone" temperament which began by adjusting the fifth on C (or perhaps G or F) and proceeding by fifths from there. Thus the keys around C were generally well in tune, but those very far away from them around the circle of fifths, such as F♯, were unpleasantly out of tune. Whether the lute in seventeenth-century France was tuned in mean-tone temperament or equal temperament is not certain. 2. Davitt Moroney, "Prélude non mésuré," *NG*, 20:294. 3. Translated from the French as given in Margery Halford, ed., *L'Art de toucher le clavecin* (Port Washington, NY, 1974), 49.

Musical Interlude 5   1. Handel's letter to Mattheson, cited in Joel Lester, "Recognition of Major and Minor in Germany Music: 1680–1730," *Journal of Music Theory*, 22 (1978): 91–92. 2. Translated from *Traité de l'harmonie* (1722), preface, no page.

Chapter 37   1. An account reported by Sir John Hawkins and reproduced in Michael Burden, *Purcell Remembered* (Portland, OR, 1995), 71–72.

Chapter 38   1. Translated from Johann Mattheson, *Das neu-eröffnete Orchestre* (Hamburg, 1713), 211. 2. H.C. Robins Landon, *Handel and his World* (London, 1984), 88. 3. Charles Burney, *An Account of the Musical Performances in Westminster-Abbey* (New York and London, 1775; rpt. 1979), 27.

Chapter 39   1. *The New Bach Reader*, ed. Hans T. David and Arthur Mendel, rev. Christoph Wolff (New York, 1998), 92–93.

Chapter 40   1. Earlier, when Bach was at Mühlhausen in 1708, the town council sponsored the publication of his Cantata *Gott ist mein König* (BWV 71), but only because the work was in honor of the town council. This was Bach's sole vocal work to be published during his lifetime. 2. *The New Bach Reader*, 399.

PART V

Chapter 41   1. Benjamin Franklin, *Writings*, ed. Albert Henry Smyth, 10 vols. (New York, 1907), VII, 207. 2. Hedwig and E. H. Mueller von Asow, eds., *The Collected Correspondence and Papers of Christoph Willibald Gluck* (London, 1962), 22-24. A slightly different translation is given by Bruce Brown, "Gluck," NG, 10:48. 3. Patricia Howard, *C.W. von Gluck: Orfeo* (Cambridge, 1981), 107.

Chapter 42   1. As translated from the German by Robert Gutman, *Mozart: A Social Biography* (New York, 1999), 188. 2. Remark of Charles Burney quoted in Roland Würtz and Eugene K. Wolf, "Mannheim," *NG*, 15:772. Leopold Mozart's assessment is contained in a letter written from Mannheim in July 1763.

Chapter 43   1. Matthew Head, "'If the Pretty Little Hand Won't Stretch': Music for the Fair Sex in Eighteenth-Century Germany," *JAMS*, 52 (1999): 218. 2. Carl Philipp Emanuel Bach, *Essay on the True Art of Playing Keyboard Instruments*, trans. and ed. William J. Mitchell (New York, 1949), 15–16. 3. *Dr. Burney's Musical Tours in Europe*, ed. Percy A. Scholes, 2 vols. (London, 1959), II, 219. 4. Translated from the German given in Arthur Loesser, *Men, Women and Pianos: A Social History* (New York, 1954), 60–61. 5. Robert Marshall, *Mozart Speaks* (New York, 1991), 322. 6. Charles Burney as quoted in Daniel Heartz, *Music in European Capitals: The Galant Style, 1720–1780* (New York, 2003), 907. 7. Charles Burney as quoted in James Parakilas, *Piano Roles* (New Haven and London, 1999), 39.

Chapter 44   1. Some scholars have rightly questioned the use of the term *classical music*, believing it to be an overly simple label for a complex stylistic development. There is more than a kernel of truth to this view. Nonetheless, like all chronological labels, the expressions *Classical period* and *classical music* are useful terms that help us to identify and focus upon common musical traits. 2. *Mémoires ou Essais sur la musique*, 3 vols. (Paris, 1797), III, 356.

Chapter 45   1. Craig Wright, *Listening to Music* (Belmont, CA, 2004), 174; a slightly different translation is given in James Webster, "Haydn," NG, 11:176. 2. Webster, "Haydn," NG, 11:192. 3. A.C. Dies, *Biographische Nachrichten* translated in Vernon Gotwalls, *Joseph Haydn, Eighteenth-Century Gentleman and Genius* (Madison, 1963), 111. 4. A paraphrase of G.A. Griesinger's *Biographische Notizen*, as given in Gotwalls, *Joseph Haydn*, 20.

Chapter 46   1. A.C. Dies, *Biographische Nachrichten*, translated in Gotwalls, *Joseph Haydn*, 119. 2. Dies, *Biographische Nachrichten*, 130. 3. H.C. Robbins Landon, *The Symphonies of Joseph Haydn* (London, 1955), 509. 4. Dies, *Biographische Nachrichten*, translated in Gotwalls, *Joseph Haydn*, 123–24. 5. James Webster, "Haydn," NG, 11:189.

Chapter 47   1. Cliff Eisen and Stanley Sadie, "Mozart," NG, 17:276. 2. In fact, Mozart composed nearly sixty symphonies. The first complete edition of them, however, done in the nineteenth century, counted only forty-one. It omitted nearly two dozen early symphonies but counted three that were not by him. Nonetheless, the nineteenth-century numbering for Mozart symphonies remains with us today. 3. Letter of 26 May 1781, *Letters of Mozart*, III, 1095. 4. Letter of 14 February 1785, *Letters of Mozart*, III, 1321. 5. Letter of 13 February 1782, *Letters of Mozart*, III, 1187. 6. Translated from Cramer's *Magazin der Musik*, Hamburg, 9 May 1783. A similar rendering can be found in Otto Erich Deutsch, *Mozart: A Documentary Biography* (Stanford, CA, 1965), 215.

Chapter 48   1. These words were attributed to Mozart by an early biographer in connection with the first performance of his opera *Die Entführung aus dem Serail*; see Neal Zaslaw with William Cowdery, *The Compleat Mozart: A Guide to the Musical Works of Wolfgang Amadeus Mozart* (New York, 1990), 55.

Chapter 49   1. *Thayer's Life of Beethoven*, ed. Elliot Forbes (Princeton, 1970), 105. 2. *Thayer's Life of Beethoven*, 115. 3. *Thayer's Life of Beethoven*, 368. 4. *Thayer's Life of Beethoven*, 329. 5. *Thayer's Life of Beethoven*, 207. 6. Carl Czerny, "Recollections from My Life," *Musical Quarterly* 42 (1956): 306–307. 7. *Selected Letters of Beethoven*, trans. Emily Anderson, ed. Alan Tyson (New York, 1967), 31–36. 8. *Selected Letters of Beethoven*, 38.

Chapter 50   1. Charles Burney, *A General History of Music* (1776), ed. Frank Mercer 2 vols. (New York, 1935), I, 21. 2. Maynard

Solomon, *Beethoven,* 2nd ed. (New York, 1998), 151–53. 3. Carl Czerny, *On the Proper Performance of All Beethoven's Works for the Piano,* ed. Paul Badura-Skoda (Vienna, 1970), 13. 4. *Thayer's Life of Beethoven,* ed. Elliot Forbes (Princeton, 1970), 375. 5. *Thayer's Life of Beethoven,* 232. 6. Solomon, *Beethoven,* 210–11.

Chapter 51   1. Auguste de La Garde-Chambonas, *Anecdotal Recollections of the Congress of Vienna* (London, 1902), 68. 2. *Louis Spohr's Autobiography* (London, 1865), 186. 3. *Thayer's Life of Beethoven,* ed. Elliot Forbes (Princeton, 1970), 909. 4. Georg Kinsky and Hans Halm, *Das Werk Beethovens: Thematisch-bibliographisches Verzeichnis seiner sämtlichen vollendeten Kompositionen* (Munich, 1955), 393. 5. *Thayer's Life of Beethoven,* 1057.

PART VI

Musical Interlude 6   1. E.T.A. Hoffmann, "Beethoven's Instrumental Music," ed. Oliver Strunk, in *Source Readings in Music History: The Romantic Era* (New York, 1965), 37. 2. Letter of 26 September 1781 in *the Letters of Mozart and his Family,* ed. Emily Anderson, 3 vols. (London, 1938), III, 1144.

Chapter 52   1. Anselm Hüttenbrenner, "Fragments from the Life of the Song Composer Franz Schubert" (1854), in Otto Erich Deutsch, *Schubert: Memoirs by his Friends,* trans. Rosamond Ley and John Nowell (New York, 1958), 182–83. 2. Deutsch, *Schubert,* 178–79, 185–86. 3. Deutsch, *Schubert,* 337.

Chapter 53   1. *Selected Correspondence of Fryderyk Chopin,* trans. Arthur Hedley (New York, 1963), 100–101. 2. Hector Berlioz, *Memoirs,* trans. Rachel Holmes and Eleanor Holmes, rev. Ernest Newman (New York, 1932), 19. 3. Berlioz, "On Conducting" (1856), in Hector Berlioz and Richard Strauss, *Treatise on Instrumentation,* trans. Theodore Front (New York, 1991), 410. 4. Hector Berlioz, *A Selection from his Letters,* ed. and trans. Humphrey Searle (New York, 1973), 27. 5. *Selected Correspondence of Fryderyk Chopin,* 97–98. 6. George Sand, *My Life,* trans. Dan Hofstadter (New York, 1979), 236–37. 7. *Selected Correspondence of Fryderyk Chopin,* 220. 8. *Selected Correspondence of Fryderyk Chopin,* 329–30. 9. Quoted and discussed by Arthur Hedley in *Selected Correspondence of Fryderyk Chopin,* 377–87.

Chapter 54   1. *Neue Zeitschrift für Musik,* 13 (19 December 1840): 198. 2. Robert Schumann, "A Symphony by Berlioz," in Berlioz *Fantastic Symphony,* Norton Critical Score, ed. Edward T. Cone (New York, 1971), 248. 3. Letters of Clara Schumann and Johannes Brahms, 1853–1896, ed. Berthold Litzmann, 2 vols. (New York, 1973), II, 300.

Chapter 55   1. Richard Wagner, "Pasticcio" (1834), in *Richard Wagner's Prose Works,* vol. 8, trans. William Ashton Ellis (London, 1899), 60. 2. From Weber's *Tonkünstlerleben,* quoted in John Warrack, *Carl Maria von Weber,* 2nd ed. (Cambridge, 1976), 97. 3. *The Complete Correspondence of Clara and Robert Schumann,* ed. Eva Weissweiler, trans. Hildegard Fritsch and Ronald L. Crawford, 2 vols. (New York, 1994), I, 3.

Chapter 56   1. Stendhal, *Life of Rossini* (1824), trans. Richard N. Coe (New York, 1970), 3. 2. Hans von Bülow, *Briefe und Schriften,* 8 vols.(Leipzig, 1896), III, 357. 3. Alexis-Jacob Azevedo, G. *Rossini: Sa vie et ses oeuvres* (Paris, 1864), 114. 4. Quoted in Mary Jane Phillips-Matz, *Verdi: A Biography* (Oxford, 1993), 612. 5. Phillips-Matz, *Verdi,* 669.

Chapter 57   1. Letter of 7 May, 1873 to Antal Augusz, in Franz Liszt, *Briefe aus ungarischen Sammlungen, 1835–1886,* ed. Margit Prahács (Kassel, 1966), 160. 2. From memoirs of Ilka Horowitz-Barnay, cited by Alan Walker, *Franz Liszt,* 3 vols. (New York, 1983), I, 83. 3. Vladimir Stasov, *Selected Essays on Music,* trans. Florence Jonas (New York, 1968), 121. 4. Letter of 1837 to Adolphe Pictet, in Franz Liszt, *Gesammelte Schriften,* ed. Lina Ramann, 6 vols. (Leipzig, 1888), II, 151. 5. Franz Liszt, *The Gipsy in Music* (1859), trans. Edwin Evans, 2 vols. (London, n.d.), II, 337. 6. *Franz Liszts Briefe,* ed. La Mara, 8 vols. (Leipzig, 1902), VII, 57–58. 7. Felix Mendelssohn-Bartholdy, *Briefe*

aus Leipziger Archiven, ed. Hans-Joachim Rothe and Reinhard Szeskus (Leipzig, 1972), 174. 8. The text of the manifesto is given in full in Peter Latham, *Brahms* (London, 1975), 31.

Chapter 58   1. *Selected Correspondence of Fryderyk Chopin,* trans. Arthur Hedley (New York, 1963), 72. 2. Robert Schumann, "Neue Bahnen," *Neue Zeitschrift für Musik,* 39 (28 October 1853): 185–86. 3. Letter to Hans von Wolzogen, in Bruckner, *Gesammelte Briefe,* ed. Max Auer (Regensburg, 1924), 168.

Chapter 59   1. Nikolay Rimsky-Korsakov, *My Musical Life,* trans. Judah A. Joffe (London, 1974), 28. 2. Quoted in Francis Maes, *A History of Russian Music: From "Kamarinskaya" to "Babi Yar,"* trans. Arnold J. Pomerans and Erica Pomerans (Berkeley, 2002), 43. 3. *The Musorgsky Reader,* ed. Jay Leyda and Sergei Bertensson (New York, 1947), 215. 4. *The Musorgsky Reader,* 112. 5. From Roland John Wiley, *Tchaikovsky's Ballets* (Oxford, 1985), 373–74. 6. Wiley, *Tchaikovsky's Ballets,* 229.

Chapter 60   1. Natalie Bauer-Lechner, *Recollections of Gustav Mahler,* trans. Dika Newlin (Cambridge, 1980), 130. 2. Bauer-Lechner, *Recollections of Gustav Mahler,* 130. 3. Alma Mahler, *Gustav Mahler: Memories and Letters,* ed. Donald Mitchell, trans. Basil Creighton, 3d ed. (Seattle, 1975), 217–18. 4. *Selected Letters of Gustav Mahler,* eds. Alma Mahler and Knud Martner, trans. Eithne Wilkins, Ernst Kaiser, and Bill Hopkins (New York, 1979), 179. 5. Alma Mahler, *Gustav Mahler,* 297. 6. Letter of 19 December 1901. The text is given in full in Henry-Louis de La Grange, *Gustav Mahler,* 3 vols. (Oxford and New York, 1995), II, 448–52.

Chapter 61   1. Quoted in Alan Walker, *Franz Liszt,* 3 vols. (Ithaca, 1996), III, 486. 2. *Leeds Mercury,* 6 October 1898, cited in Jerrold Northrop Moore, *Edward Elgar: A Creative Life* (Oxford, 1984), 244. 3. Rosa Burley and Frank C. Carruthers, *Edward Elgar: The Record of a Friendship* (London, 1972), 68–69. 4. Cited in Moore, *Edward Elgar,* 260. 5. From program notes for the premier performance, 19 June 1899, quoted in Moore, *Edward Elgar,* 270.

Chapter 62   none

Chapter 63   1. Letter of 25 January 1916, in *Debussy Letters,* ed. François Lesure and Roger Nichols, trans. Roger Nichols (Cambridge, MA, 1987), 313. 2. *Debussy Letters,* 188. 3. Claude Debussy, "*The Nursery,* Poem and Music by M. Moussorgsky" (1901), in *Debussy on Music,* trans. and ed. Richard Langham Smith (Ithaca, 1988), 20. 4. *Debussy on Music,* 295–97. 5. Arnold Schoenberg, "Composition with Twelve Tones" (1941), in *Style and Idea,* ed. Leonard Stein, trans. Leo Black (Berkeley, 1984), 216. 6. *Debussy Letters,* 155. 7. *Debussy on Music,* 74. 8. Quoted in Léon Vallas, *Claude Debussy: His Life and Works,* trans. Maire and Grace O'Brien (London, 1933), 112.

PART VII

Chapter 64   1. Alma Mahler, *Gustav Mahler: Memories and Letters,* ed. Donald Mitchell, trans. Basil Creighton, 3d ed. (Seattle, 1975), 239. 2. Hugo Riemann, "Degeneration und Regeneration in der Musik" (1908), in *Die Konfusion in der Musik: Felix Draesekes Kampfschrift von 1906 und ihre Folgen,* ed. Susanne Shigihara (Bonn, 1990), 248. 3. *Die Konfusion in der Musik,* 41–62. 4. Richard Strauss, *Recollections and Reflections,* ed. Willi Schuh, trans. L. J. Lawrence (Westport, CT, 1974), 16. 5. Strauss, *Recollections and Reflections,* 13.

Chapter 65   1. Michel Fokine, *Fokine: Memoirs of a Ballet Master,* trans. Vitale Fokine (Boston and Toronto, 1961), 49. 2. Carl Van Vechten, "Music and Bad Manners," in *Music and Bad Manners* (New York, 1916), 34. 3. Igor Stravinsky, "Ce que j'ai voulu exprimer dans Le Sacre du Printemps" (1913), in *Le Sacre du Printemps: Dossier de Presse,* ed. François Lesure (Geneva, 1980), 13–15. 4. Sergei Prokofiev, "Autobiography," in *Soviet Diary 1927 and Other Writings,* trans. Oleg Prokofiev (Boston, 1992), 258.

Chapter 66   1. August Macke and Franz Marc, *Briefwechsel* (Cologne, 1964), 40. 2. Vasili Kandinsky, "Über die Formfrage," in

Der blaue Reiter (Munich, 1912), 74–100. 3. *Arnold Schoenberg, Wassily Kandinsky: Letters, Pictures and Documents,* ed. Jelena Hahl-Koch, trans. John C. Crawford (London and Boston, 1984), 21. 4. *Arnold Schoenberg, Wassily Kandinsky,* 23. 5. Arnold Schoenberg, "Composition with Twelve Tones" (1941), in *Style and Idea,* ed. Leonard Stein, trans. Leo Black (Berkeley, 1984), 217. 6. Arnold Schoenberg, *Theory of Harmony,* trans. Roy E. Carter (Berkeley and Los Angeles, 1978), 420. 7. Letter to Ferruccio Busoni, ca. August 1909, in *Busoni, Selected Letters,* ed. and trans. Antony Beaumont (New York, 1987), 389. 8. *The Berg-Schoenberg Correspondence: Selected Letters,* ed. Juliane Brand, Christopher Hailey, and Donald Harris (New York and London, 1987), 60.

Chapter 67 1. Maurice Ravel, "Contemporary Music" (1928), in *Composers on Modern Musical Culture,* ed. Bryan R. Simms (New York, 1999), 92. 2. *Debussy Letters,* ed. François Lesure and Roger Nichols, trans. Roger Nichols (Cambridge, MA, 1987), 291. 3. Ferruccio Busoni, *Selected Letters,* trans. and ed. Antony Beaumont (New York, 1987), 186. 4. 20 August 1914, in *A Ravel Reader: Correspondence, Articles, Interviews,* ed. Arbie Orenstein (New York, 1990), 152. 5. Letter to Familie Weber, 23 September 1914, in *Paul Hindemith Briefe,* ed. Dieter Rexroth (Frankfurt, 1982), 35. 6. Ernest Newman, "The War and the Future of Music," *Musical Times,* 55 (1 September 1914): 571.

Chapter 68 1. Darius Milhaud, "The Evolution of the Jazz Band and Music of the Negroes of North America" (1923), in *Composers on Modern Musical Culture,* ed. and trans. Bryan R. Simms (New York, 1999), 239. 2. Igor Stravinsky, *An Autobiography* (New York, 1962), 53. 3. Stravinsky, *An Autobiography,* 97. 4. Edward Evans, "Igor Stravinsky: Contrapuntal Titan," *Musical America* (February 12, 1921). 5. Igor Stravinsky and Robert Craft, *Dialogues* (Berkeley and Los Angeles, 1982), 40. 6. Igor Stravinsky, "Some Ideas About my Octuor," *The Arts* 5/1 (January 1924): 5–6. 7. Darius Milhaud, *My Happy Life,* trans. Donald Evans, George Hall, and Christopher Palmer (London and New York, 1995), 70–71. 8. Darius Milhaud, "The Composer on His Work: 'I am always interested in what is coming,'" *Christian Science Monitor,* May 20, 1968.

Chapter 69 1. Stefan Zweig, *The World of Yesterday* (Lincoln, NE, 1964), 295–96. 2. Zweig, *The World of Yesterday,* 296. 3. Josef Matthias Hauer, "Die Tropen," *Musikblätter des Anbruch* 6/1 (1924): 18. 4. Josef Hauer, *Vom Wesen des Musikalischen* (Vienna, 1920), 53. 5. Arnold Schoenberg, *Letters,* ed. Erwin Stein, trans. Eithne Wilkins and Ernst Kaiser (New York, 1965), 164–65.

Chapter 70 1. "Berg's Lecture on 'Wozzeck'" (1929), in H. F. Redlich, *Alban Berg: The Man and his Music* (London, 1957), 261–85.

Chapter 71 1. Béla Bartók, *Letters,* ed. János Demény, trans. Péter Balabán, István Farkas (New York, 1971), 29. 2. Bartók, *Letters,* 153. 3. Béla Bartók, "The Folk Songs of Hungary" (1928), in *Béla Bartók Essays,* ed. Benjamin Suchoff (Lincoln and London, 1976), 333. 4. Béla Bartók, "The Influence of Peasant Music on Modern Music" (1931), in *Béla Bartók Essays,* 341–44. 5. Béla Bartók, "Explanation to Concerto for Orchestra," in *Béla Bartók Essays,* 431.

Chapter 72 1. Aaron Copland, "Jazz Structure and Influence," *Modern Music* 4/2 (1927): 9–14. 2. Rudi Blesh, *Shining Trumpets: A History of Jazz* (New York, 1958), 176. 3. Gunther Schuller, *Early Jazz: Its Roots and Musical Development* (New York and Oxford, 1968), 58. 4. Scott Joplin, *School of Ragtime: Exercises for Piano* (New York, 1908), 3. 5. James Reese Europe, "A Negro Explains 'Jazz'" (1919), in *Readings in Black American Music,* ed. Eileen Southern (New York, 1971), 225. 6. Benjamin Latrobe, *Impressions Respecting New Orleans,* ed. Samuel Wilson, Jr. (New York, 1951), 49–50. 7. Alan Lomax, *Mister Jelly Roll: The Fortunes of Jelly Roll Morton, New Orleans Creole and "Inventor of Jazz,"* 2nd ed. (Berkeley, 1973), 12.

Chapter 73 1. Arnold Schoenberg, *Letters,* ed. Erwin Stein, trans. Eithne Wilkins and Ernst Kaiser (New York, 1965), 92–93. 2. Paul Hindemith, "Sterbende Gewässer" (1963), in *Aufsätze, Vorträge,*

Reden, ed. Giselher Schubert (Zurich and Mainz, 1994), 326–27. 3. Wilhelm Furtwängler, "The Hindemith Case," in *Furtwängler on Music: Essays and Addresses,* ed. and trans. Ronald Taylor (Brookfield, VT, 1991), 117–20.

Chapter 74 1. Sergei Prokofiev, "Autobiography" (1941) in *Soviet Diary 1927 and Other Writings,* trans. Oleg Prokofiev (Boston, 1991), 264. 2. *Dmitri Shostakovich About Himself and his Times,* trans. Angus and Neilian Roxburgh (Moscow, 1981), 33. 3. Andrei Zhdanov, "Soviet Literature: The Richest in Ideas, the Most Advanced Literature," in *Problems of Soviet Literature: Reports and Speeches at the First Soviet Writers' Congress,* ed. H. G. Scott (New York, 1935), 21. 4. Sergei Prokofiev, "Autobiography," 297. 5. *Selected Letters of Sergei Prokofiev,* ed. and trans. Harlow Robinson (Boston, 1998), 94–95. 6. Sviatoslav Richter, "On Prokofiev," in *Sergei Prokofiev: Materials, Articles, Interviews* (Moscow, 1978), 193. 7. Bruno Walter, *Theme and Variations: An Autobiography,* trans. James A. Galston (New York, 1946), 277–78. 8. Rose Lee, "Dimitri Szostakovich: Young Russian Composer Tells of Linking Politics with Creative Work," *New York Times,* 20 December 1931. 9. Lee, "Dimitri Szostakovich." 10. From an article in *Vechernaya Moskva,* 11 December 1940, in *Dmitri Shostakovich About Himself and His Times,* 83. 11. From an article in *Izvestia,* 3 April 1935, in *Dmitri Shostakovich About Himself and His Times,* 58. 12. The entire essay is found in Francis Maes, *A History of Russian Music from "Kamarinskaya" to "Babi Yar,"* trans. Arnold J. Pomerans, Erica Pomerans (Berkeley, 2002), 299–300. 13. *Testimony: The Memoirs of Dmitri Shostakovich,* ed. Solomon Volkov, trans. Antonina W. Bouis (New York, 1979). 14. From an article in *Sovetskoye Iskusstvo,* 14 December 1933, in *Dmitri Shostakovich About Himself and His Times,* 43.

Chapter 75 1. Ralph Waldo Emerson, "Self-Reliance," in *Selected Essays, Lectures, and Poems,* ed. Robert D. Richardson, Jr. (New York, 1990), 168. 2. William Billings, *The New-England Psalm-Singer: or American Chorister* (Boston, 1770). 3. Charles E. Ives, *Memos,* ed. John Kirkpatrick (New York, 1972), 46. 4. Ives, *Memos,* 183–84. 5. Charles E. Ives, *Essays Before a Sonata,* in *Three Classics in the Aesthetic of Music* (New York, 1962), 162. 6. Charles E. Ives, "Notes to 114 Songs," in *Composers on Modern Musical Culture,* ed. Bryan R. Simms (New York, 1999), 213. 7. Ives, *Essays Before a Sonata,* 166. 8. Harry Partch, *Genesis of a Music: An Account of a Creative Work, Its Roots and Its Fulfillment,* 2nd ed. (New York, 1974), 52. 9. Charles Seeger, "Tradition and Experiment in (the New) Music," in *Studies in Musicology II: 1929–1979,* ed. Ann M. Pescatello (Berkeley, 1994), 211. 10. Cited in Matilda Gaume, *Ruth Crawford Seeger: Memoirs, Memories, Music* (Metuchen, NJ, and London, 1986), 204.

Chapter 76 1. Aaron Copland and Vivian Perlis, *Copland: 1900 Through 1942* (New York, 1984), 50. 2. Aaron Copland, *Music and Imagination* (New York, 1959), 104. 3. Copland, *Music and Imagination,* 108. 4. Copland, *Music and Imagination,* 111. 5. *Walt Whitman's Leaves of Grass: The First (1855) Edition,* ed. Malcolm Cowley (New York, 1959), 5–6. 6. *Walt Whitman's Leaves of Grass,* 12. 7. Copland, *Music and Imagination,* 112. 8. Aaron Copland, *What to Listen For in Music,* rev. ed. (New York, 1957), 30. 9. *Copland 1900 Through 1942,* 182. 10. Aaron Copland, *Appalachian Spring—Ballet for Martha,* full score (New York and London, 1945), Preface. 11. Copland, *Music and Imagination,* 110–11. 12. *Copland 1900 Through 1942,* 279. 13. Copland, *Music and Imagination,* 117–18. 14. Quoted in Barbara B. Heyman, *Samuel Barber: The Composer and His Music* (New York and Oxford, 1992), 244. 15. Cited in Heyman, *Samuel Barber,* 174.

Chapter 77 none

PART VIII
Chapter 78 1. Editor's note, *Musical Times* (London), 82 (no. 1182: August 1941), 308.
Chapter 79 1. Allen Edwards, *Flawed Words and Stubborn Sounds: A Conservation with Elliott Carter* (New York, 1971), 61. 2. Pierre Boulez,

"A Time for Johann Sebastian Bach" (1951), in *Notes of an Apprenticeship*, trans. Herbert Weinstock (New York, 1968), 14. 3. Milton Babbitt, "Twelve-Tone Invariants as Compositional Determinants," *Musical Quarterly* 46 (1960): 246. 4. Milton Babbitt, "Who Cares If You Listen (The Composer as Specialist)" (1958), in *Composers on Modern Musical Culture*, ed. Bryan R. Simms (New York, 1999), 153–59. 5. Pierre Boulez, "Eventually . . ." (1952), in *Notes of an Apprenticeship*, 148. 6. Theodor W. Adorno, *Philosophy of Modern Music*, trans. Anne G. Mitchell and Wesley V. Blomster (New York, 1973), 203. 7. Adorno, *Philosophy of Modern Music*, 68. 8. Randle Cotgrave, *A Dictionarie of the French and English Tongues* (London, 1611), s.v. *Bransle*. 9. Pierre Boulez, "Schönberg Is Dead, *Score* (May 1952): 22. 10. Thomas Meyer, "'Man kann nur einmal Avantgardist sein': Gespräche mit Krzysztof Penderecki," *Neue Zeitschrift für Musik* 150 (December 1989): 19.

Chapter 80 1. Elliott Carter, "Shop Talk by an American Composer" (1960), in *The Writings of Elliott Carter*, eds. Else Stone and Kurt Stone (Bloomington and London, 1977), 206. 2. John Cage, "Composition" (1952), in *Silence* (Middletown, CT, 1961), 59 3. John Cage, "Experimental Music: Doctrine" (1955), in *Silence*, 14. 4. John Cage, "History of Experimental Music in the United States" (1959), in *Silence*, 73. 5. Louise Varèse, *Varèse: A Looking-Glass Diary* (New York, 1972), 257. 6. Edgard Varèse, "New Instruments and New Music" (1936), in "The Liberation of Sound," *Perspectives of New Music* 5 (1966–67): 11. 7. Louise Varèse, *Varèse*, 276. 8. Olivier Messiaen, "Musikalisches Glaubensbekenntnis," *Melos* 25 (1958): 385.

Chapter 81 1. Darius Milhaud, *My Happy Life: An Autobiography*, trans. Donald Evans, George Hall, and Christopher Palmer (New York

and London, 1995), 110. 2. Maurice Ravel, "Take Jazz Seriously!," *Musical Digest* 13/3 (March 1928): 49–50.

Musical Interlude 9
1. Based on "Peatman's Annual Survey of Song Hits on Radio and TV," *Variety* (13 January 1954): 50. 2. Rudi Blesh, *Shining Trumpets: A History of Jazz* (New York, 1958), 352. 3. John Harbison, "Uses of Popular Music" (1984), reprinted in *Composers on Modern Musical Culture*, ed. Bryan R. Simms (New York, 1999), 200. 4. Ned Rorem, "The Beatles," in *Music and People* (New York, 1968), 18.

Chapter 82 1. Leonard Bernstein, *The Unanswered Question: Six Talks at Harvard* (Cambridge, MA, and London 1976), 420–21. 2. Luciano Berio, "Poesia e musica: Un' esperienza," from the German version in *Darmstädter Beiträge zur neuen Musik* 2 (1959); 44–45. 3. Jonathan Bernard, "An Interview with Elliott Carter," *Perspectives of New Music* 28/2 (1990): 190. 4. Elliott Carter, "Letter from Europe" (1963), in *The Writings of Elliott Carter*, ed. Else Stone and Kurt Stone (Bloomington and London, 1977), 220.

Chapter 83 1. John Harbison, "Two Tanglewood Talks" (1984), in *Composers on Modern Musical Culture*, ed. Bryan R. Simms (New York, 1999), 204. 2. Pierre Boulez, *Conversation with Célestin Deliège* (London, 1976), 33. 3. George Rochberg, "Reflections on the Renewal of Music" (1972), *Composers on Modern Musical Culture*, 193–94. 4. Rochberg, "Reflections on the Renewal of Music," 195. 5. György Ligeti, "Rhapsodische, unausgewogene Gedanken über Musik, besonders über meine eigenen Kompositionen" (1991), *Neue Zeitschrift für Musik* 154 (January 1993): 28. 6. Quoted in Ann McCutchan, *The Music That Sings: Composers Speak About the Creative Process* (New York and Oxford, 1999), 58–59.

BIBLIOGRAPHY

What follows is a brief, preliminary bibliography. Far more comprehensive bibliographies are included in the Student Workbook and Instructor's Manual for *Music in Western Civilization*, and are also available on the Thomson-Schirmer website (where they are updated). These bibliographies cite only works in the English language. Each of the books and articles contains either its own bibliography or copious footnotes that suggest still more useful sources for research. For help in the challenging task of writing about the ephemeral art of music, see the essay "Writing a Research Paper on a Musical Topic" by Sterling Murray that is included in the Workbook.

❀ DICTIONARIES AND ENCYCLOPEDIAS

By far the most useful tool for research in music—both for scholars and students—is **The New Grove Dictionary of Music and Musicians,** 2nd edition (London: Macmillan, 2001). It is available both in a 29-volume printed edition and online (www.grovemusic.com). Many colleges and universities subscribe to the online version, making it accessible to students at many locations on campus and at home. The online version is continually updated, as contemporary scholarship requires. In addition, the online version includes articles from the more specialized *The New Grove Dictionary of Opera* and *The New Grove Dictionary of Jazz*. Almost every subject dealing with classical and popular, Western and non-Western music, can be found in *The New Grove Dictionary*. Each entry is written by a world-renowned scholar and is followed by its own detailed bibliography. For major composers, a complete list of compositions is given, along with the date of publication or first performance, as well as references to scholarly editions in which a specific piece may be found. Other, much smaller but nonetheless useful, reference tools include:

Baker's Biographical Dictionary of Musicians. New York: Schirmer Books, 2001.

The Harvard Biographical Dictionary of Music. Cambridge, MA: Harvard University Press, 1996.

The Harvard Dictionary of Music, 4th ed., ed. Don Randel. Cambridge, MA: Harvard University Press, 2003.

The Norton/Grove Concise Encyclopedia of Music, ed. Stanley Sadie and Alison Lathan. New York and London: Norton, 1988.

The Norton/Grove Dictionary of Women Composers, ed. Julie Anne Sadie and Rhian Samuel. London and New York: MacMillan and Norton, 1994.

The Oxford Companion to Music, ed. Alison Lathan. Oxford: Oxford University Press, 2002.

❀ PRIMARY-SOURCE DOCUMENTS FOR WESTERN MUSIC

Music in the Western World: A History in Documents, ed. Piero Weiss and Richard Taruskin. New York: Schirmer Books, 1984.

Opera: A History in Documents, ed. Piero Weiss. Oxford: Oxford University Press, 2002.

Readings in the History of Musical Performance, ed. Carol MacClintock. Bloomington, IN: Indiana University Press, 1979.

Source Readings in Music History, ed. Oliver Strunk; rev. edition ed. Leo Treitler. New York and London: Norton, 1998.

❀ HISTORICAL SURVEYS OF WESTERN MUSIC

Part I: Antiquity and the Middle Ages

Caldwell, John. *Medieval Music.* Bloomington, IN: Indiana University Press, 1978.

Hoppin, Richard H. *Medieval Music.* New York: Norton, 1978.

Wilson, David Fenwick. *Music of the Middle Ages: Style and Structure.* New York: Schirmer Books, 1990.

Yudkin, Jeremy. *Music in Medieval Europe.* Englewood Cliffs, NJ: Prentice Hall, 1989.

Part II: The Late Middle Ages and Early Renaissance

See later chapters of books listed in Part I, as well as:

Atlas, Allan W. *Renaissance Music: Music in Western Europe, 1400–1600.* New York and London: Norton, 1998.

Brown, Howard Mayer. *Music in the Renaissance,* 2nd ed. (with Louis K. Stein). Saddle River, NJ: Prentice Hall, 1999.

Perkins, Leeman. *Music in the Age of the Renaissance.* New York: Norton, 1999.

Strohm, Reinhard. *The Rise of European Music 1380–1500.* Cambridge: Cambridge University Press, 1993.

Part III: The Late Renaissance

Atlas, Allan W. *Renaissance Music: Music in Western Europe, 1400–1600.* New York and London: Norton, 1998.

Brown, Howard Mayer. *Music in the Renaissance,* 2nd ed. (with Louis K. Stein). Saddle River, NJ: Prentice Hall, 1999.

Carter, Tim. *Music in Late Renaissance and Early Baroque Italy.* London: Batsford, 1992.

Perkins, Leeman. *Music in the Age of the Renaissance.* New York: Norton, 1999.

Part IV: Baroque Music

Buelow, George J. *A History of Baroque Music.* Bloomington, IN: Indiana University Press, 2004.

Hill, John Walter. *Baroque Music: Music in Western Europe, 1580–1750.* New York: Norton, 2005.

Palisca, Claude V. *Baroque Music,* 3rd ed. Englewood Cliffs, NJ: Prentice Hall, 1991.

Schulenberg, David. *Music of the Baroque.* Oxford: Oxford University Press, 2001.

Part V: The Enlightenment and the Classical Era

Downs, Philip G. *Classical Music: The Era of Mozart, Haydn, and Beethoven.* New York: Norton, 1992.

Heartz, Daniel. *Haydn, Mozart and the Viennese School: 1740–1780.* New York and London: Norton, 1995.

———. *Music in European Capitals: The Galant Style, 1720–1780.* New York and London: Norton, 2003.

Rushton, Julian. *Classical Music: A Concise History from Gluck to Beethoven.* London: Thames and Hudson, 1986.

Part VI: The Romantic Period

Dahlhaus, Carl. *Nineteenth-Century Music,* trans. J. Bradford Robinson. Berkeley and Los Angeles: University of California Press, 1989.

Palantinga, Leon. *Romantic Music.* New York: Norton, 1984.

Whittall, Arnold. *Romantic Music: A Concise History from Schubert to Sibelius.* London: Thames and Hudson, 1987.

Part VII: The Early Twentieth Century

Cook, Nicholas and Anthony Pople, eds. *The Cambridge History of Twentieth-Century Music.* Cambridge: Cambridge University Press, 2004.

Morgan, Robert P. *Twentieth-Century Music: A History of Musical Style in Modern Europe and America.* New York: Norton, 1992.

Salzman, Eric. *Twentieth-Century Music: An Introduction.* Upper Saddle River, NJ: Prentice Hall, 2002.

Simms, Bryan R. *Music of the Twentieth Century: Style and Structure.* New York and London: Schirmer Books, 1996.

Part VIII: Contemporary Music

Griffiths, Paul. *Modern Music and After.* New York: Oxford University Press, 1995.

Nyman, Michael. *Experimental Music: Cage and Beyond.* Cambridge: Cambridge University Press, 1999.

Schwartz, Elliott and Daniel Godfrey. *Music Since 1945: Issues, Materials, and Literature.* New York: Schirmer Books, 1993.

MUSIC JOURNALS

There are hundreds of journals (periodicals containing scholarly articles) dealing with various aspects of the history and performance of Western classical music. Some of these journals regularly publish an index to the articles found in previous issues, but most do not. There are, however, three useful indexes to journals that encompass English as well as foreign-language journals: *Music Index, International Index to Music Periodicals,* and *RILM* (acronym for *Répertoire international de littérature musicale*). All three

are available online, usually through a university or college computer network, for a quick search of specific topics. Thus, to find out more about Mozart's *Don Giovanni* or Copland's *Appalachian Spring,* for example, simply go to one of these sites and type in the title in the appropriate search box. *RILM,* perhaps the most useful of the three, often provides helpful abstracts that allow the reader to determine if the article in question will be of use. For dissertations about musical topics, *Dissertations and Theses—Full Text* has not merely abstracts but, as the title states, entire dissertations and theses online (those written after 1997). Finally, more than forty of the most important music journals now also have back issues online through a link called JSTOR (*Journal Storage: The Scholarly Journal Archive*). Most university and college libraries subscribe to this online service.

ONLINE SEARCH ENGINES FOR ARTICLES, DISSERTATIONS, AND THESES ABOUT MUSIC

Music Index (Warren, MI: Harmony Park Press) http://www.hppmusicindex.com

International Index to Music Periodicals (Alexandria, VA: Chadwyck-Healey Inc.) http://iimpft.chadwyck.com/home

RILM (*Répertoire international de littérature musicale*; New York: International Musicological Society) http://www.rilm.org

Dissertations and Theses—Full Texts (Cambridge: ProQuest Company) *http://proquest.umi.com*

JSTOR (*Journal Storage: The Scholarly Journal Archive*; New York: JSTOR) http://www.jstor.org

IMPORTANT ENGLISH LANGUAGE MUSIC JOURNALS

Journal (earlier *Proceedings*) *of the Royal Musical Association* (British, 1874–)

Musical Quarterly (American, 1915–)

Music and Letters (British, 1920–)

Journal (earlier *Bulletin*) *of the American Musicological Society* (American, 1948–)

Ethnomusicology (American, 1953–)

Journal of Music Theory (American, 1957–)

Perspectives of New Music (American, 1963–)

Early Music (British, 1973–)

19-Century Music (American, 1977–)

Music Theory Spectrum (American, 1979–)

Early Music History (British, 1981–)

Journal of Musicology (American, 1981–)

Popular Music (British, 1981–)

American Music (American, 1983–)

CREDITS

xxxii CORBIS; xxxii CORBIS; xxxiii Angel playing a clavichord, detail from the vault of the crypt (fresco), French School, (15th century) Collegiale Saint-Bonnet-le-Chateau, France, Jean-Francois Claustre.Bridgeman Art Library, London, UK/www.bridgeman.co.uk; 003 Réunion des Musées Nationaux/Art Resource, NY; 004 Réunion des Musées Nationaux/Art Resource, NY; 006 The Metropolitan Museum of Art, Fletcher Fund, 1956, (56.171.38) Photograph © 1998 The Metropolitan Museum of Art; 013 Photograph © 2005 Museum of Fine Arts, Boston. Trumpet (salpinx), Greek, Hellenistic or Roman Imperial period, Greece, Bone with bronze rings and bell, 155 x 7.8 cm (61 x 3 1/16 inch), Museum of Fine Arts Boston, Frederick Brown Fund, 37.301; 014 Cambridge University Library. Manuscript Ii.3.12, fol. 61v; 016 Cathedral de Leon, Spain. Antifonario visigotico mozarabe, fol. 29 r; 019 Stiftsbibliothek St. Gallen. Abbey Library of St. Gall, Cod. Sang. 375, p. 235; 023 Photograph by Reverend Mother Dolores Hart, Order of St. Benedict. Courtesy of the Abbey of Regina Archives; 031 Bildarchiv d. ÖNB, Wein. Vienna, National Library, Codex 51, fol. 35v; 033 Biblioteca Ambrosiana, Milan. MS D. 75. INF; 036 Biblioteka Jagiellonska. MS. Berol. Theol Lat. Quart. 11f. f. 144r. From the collections of the former Prussian State Library in Berlin preserved at the Jagiellonian Library; 040 Otto Miller Verlages, Salzburg; 045 Three Plantagenet Tombs: Henry II (1133–1189), Eleanor of Aquitaine (c.1122–1204) and Richard I (1157–1199) in Fontevrault Abbey, 12th Century. Bridgeman Art Library, London, UK/www.bridgeman.co.uk; 046 Arixu MAS; 050 Bibliothèque Nationale, Paris. MS Latin 3549, fols. 151v; 051 Library of the Cathedral de Santiago de Compostela, Spain. "Codex Calixtinus," fol. 185r; 053 East end of Notre Dame, 1163–1345 (photo) French School/Paris, France, Paul Maeyaert. Bridgeman Art Library, London, UK/www.bridgeman.co.uk; 056 Biblioteca Laurenziana, Florence; 062 Detail from a map of Paris in the reign of Henri II showing the quartier des Ecoles, 1552 (engraving), French School, (16th century) Musee de la Ville de Paris, Musee Carnavalet, Paris, France, Lauros. Bridgeman Art Library, London, UK/www.bridgeman.co.uk; 066 University of Montpellier, France, Bibliothèque de la Faculté de Médecine, MS H196, fol. lxiiii; 075 Ms Fr 146 f.34 'Le Charivari', discordant musicians from a manuscript written by Gervais du Bois (vellum), French School, (14th century) Bibliotheque Nationale, Paris, France, Flammarion. Bridgeman Art Library, London, UK/www.bridgeman.co.uk; 079 (above) Ms 6465 fol. 444v Banquet given by Charles V (1338–80) in honour of his uncle Emperor Charles IV (1316–78) in 1378, c.1460 (vellum), Fouquet, Jean (c.1420–80) Bibliothèque Nationale, Paris, France, Giraudon. Bridgeman Art Library, London, UK/www.bridgeman.co.uk; 079 (below) Bodleian Library, University of Oxford. Dance in the Garden of Mirth, MS E Mus.65, fol.3v; 080 The Pierpont Morgan Library/Art Resource, NY; 081 Positive Organ (engraving) (b/w photo), Meckenem, Israhel van, the younger (fl.1450–1503) Private Collection. Bridgeman Art Library, London, UK/www.bridgeman.co.uk; 082 Bibliothèque Nationale, Paris fonds francais, MS 1584; 090 (above) View of the entrance facade of the Palace (photo), French School, (14th century) Palais des Papes, Avignon, France, Peter Willi. Bridgeman Art Library, London, UK/www.bridgeman.co.uk; 091 Ms 564/1047 fol.12, 'Tout Par Compas Suy Composee . . . , illuminated composition by Baude Cordier, from a collection of Medieval ballads, motets, and songs (ink on vellum), French School, (15th century) Musee Conde, Chantilly, France, Giraudon. Bridgeman Art Library, London, UK/www.bridgeman.co.uk; 102 (left) New College, Oxford, from 'Oxonia Illustrata', published 1675 (engraving), Loggan, David (1633/35–92) Courtesy of the Warden and Scholars of New College, Oxford. Bridgeman Art Library, London, UK/www.bridgeman.co.uk; 102 (right) Portrait of Petrarch (Francesco Petrarca) (1304–74) (oil on panel), Italian School, (16th century) Private Collection, Lauros/Giraudon. Bridgeman Art Library, London, UK/www.bridgeman.co.uk; 105 Biblioteca Medicea Laurenziana, ms. Med. Palat. 87, fol. 121v; 109 Bibliothèque Nationale, Paris,MS It. 63, fol. 10v; 111 CORBIS; 116 British Library. MS Harley 978, fol. 11v. Reproduce by permission; 120 British Library. MS 57950, fol.121v. Reproduced by permission; 125 (above) Bibliothèque Nationale, Paris; 125 (below) Bibliothèque Nationale, Paris, MS Rothchilde 2973, fol. 19v-20r; 132 Ms Fr 1537 f.58v Illustration from 'Chants Royaux sur la Conception Couronnee du Puy de Rouan', depicting the choir singing the Gloria, conducted by Jean Ockeghem (1410–97), 1519–26 (vellum), French School, (16th century) Bibliotheque Nationale, Paris, France. Bridgeman Art Library, London, UK/www.bridgeman.co.uk; 139 Harl 4425 f.12v Garden scene, the lover and dame Oyeuse without, illuminated by the Master of the Prayer Books of c.1500, Bruges (vellum) British Library, London, UK. Bridgeman Art Library, London, UK/www.bridgeman.co.uk; 142 Bibliothèque Nationale, Paris, MS Latin 7295; 143 Bibliothèque Nationale, Paris, MS f. fr. 5073, fol. 117v; 144 Bibliothèque Royale, Brussels, MS 9085, fol. 20v; 146 (center) Portrait of Martin Luther (1483–1546) 1529 (oil on panel), Cranach, Lucas, the Elder (1472–1553) Galleria degli Uffizi, Florence, Italy. Bridgeman Art Library, London, UK/www.bridgeman.co.uk; 146 (left) CORBIS; 146 (right) Christ Clasping the Cross, Greco, El (Domenico Theotocopuli) (1541–1614) Prado, Madrid, Spain. Bridgeman Art Library, London, UK/www.bridgeman.co.uk; 148 David by Michelangelo Buonarroti, 1501–04. Galleria dell' Accademia, Florence, Italy/Bridgeman Art Library, London/New York; 149 © Scala/Art Resource; 151 Biblioteca Riccardiana, Florence, Ed. r.276; 153 The Torture of Savonarola (1452–98) (oil on panel), Italian School, (15th century) Museo di San Marco, Florence, Italy. Bridgeman Art Library, London, UK/www.bridgeman.co.uk; 154 Lira da braccio by Francesco Linarol, Venice, 1563. (NMM 4230) Ex coll W.F. Hill & Sons, London. Rawlins Fund, 1988. National Music Museum, University of South Dakota. photography by Bill Willroth, Sr.; 159 © The British Library, London; 160 © Alinari/Art Resource, NY; 165 Bibliothèque Nationale, Paris; 166 Bibliothèque Nationale, Paris; 167 Boston Athenaeum. Image X8F At8.h.Moulton's Mass 1531, Attaignant Viginti Massarum; 168 Francois I (1494–1547) (oil on panel), Clouet, Jean (1485/90–1540) Louvre, Paris, France, Giraudon. Bridgeman Art Library, London, UK/www.bridgeman.co.uk; 169 The Rustic Concert, the Song (oil on panel) (pair of 19949), Italian School, (16th century) Musee de l'Hotel Lallemant, Bourges, France, Giraudon. Bridgeman Art Library, London, UK/www.bridgeman.co.uk; 173 The Prodigal Son among the Courtesans, 97CAR1594, V005. © Photothèque des Musées de la Ville de Paris; 178 Bayerische Staatsbibliothek, Munich. Cim 352b, fol. 40; 179 © Foto Marburg/Art Resource, NY; 180 The Concert (see also 51374), Master of Female Half Lengths (c.1490–c.1540) Private Collection. Bridgeman Art Library, London, UK/www.bridgeman.co.uk; 181 Orpheus Playing Music (woodcut) (b/w photo), Spanish School/Private Collection. Bridgeman Art Library, London, UK/www.bridgeman.co.uk; 182 © Museo del Prado, Madrid; 195 © Foto Marburg/Art Resource, NY; 199 Bayerische Staatsbibliothek, Munich. Mus. MS A II, fol. 187; 200 Bayerische Staatsbibliothek, Munich. Mus. MS A II, fol. 81; 205 Sistine Chapel, Vatican, Rome, Italy/ Fratelli Alinari/SuperStock; 206 Scala/Art Resource; 212 CORBIS; 217 © Penshurst, Kent; 227 Portrait of Isabella d'Este (1474–1539) (red chalk & pierre noire on paper) (see also 223606), Vinci, Leonardo da (1452–1519) Louvre, Paris, France, Giraudon. Bridgeman Art Library, London, UK/www.bridgeman.co.uk; 228 Tiroler Landesmuseum Ferdinandeum, Innsbruck; 229 Albi Rosenthal; 232 (above) © CORBIS; 232 (center) CORBIS; 232 (left) The Collection of William H. Scheide, Princeton, New Jersey; 232 (right) Staats-und Universitätsbibliothek Hamburg; 234 Archiv fur Kunst und Geschichte, Berlin; 235 (above) The chair of St. Peter, 1665 (bronze), Bernini, Giovanni Lorenzo (1598-1680) St. Peter's, Vatican, Rome, Italy, Joseph Martin. Bridgeman Art Library, London, UK/www.bridgeman.co.uk; 235 (below) Glorification of the Reign of Pope Urban VIII, in the Great Hall, 1633–39, Cortona, Pietro da (Berrettini) (1596–1669) Palazzo Barberini, Rome, Italy. Bridgeman Art Library, London, UK/www.bridgeman.co.uk; 237 Columbus Museum of Art, Ohio: Schumacher Fund Purchase 1963.033; 241 © Foto Marburg/Art Resource, NY; 252 The Choir Singing in St. Mark's Basilica, Venice, 1766 (pen, ink and wash on paper), Canaletto, (Giovanni Antonio Canal) (1697–1768) Hamburg Kunsthalle, Hamburg, Germany. Bridgeman Art Library, Lon-

GLOSSARY

a cappella: singing without instrumental accompaniment

Abendmusik: an hour-long concert of sacred music with arias and recitatives—something akin to a sacred opera or oratorio; a single religious theme unfolded in music over the course of five late-afternoon performances on the Sundays immediately before and during Advent in the city of Lübeck, Germany

Académie royale de musique: in effect, a French national opera company directly licensed and indirectly financed by the king; it performed in the center of Paris at the Palais Royal

academy: a learned society, sometimes devoted to presenting concerts; in Germany in the eighteenth century the term often referred to a public concert

acciaccatura: a technique of crunching dissonant chords used by Domenico Scarlatti

accompanied recitative: a recitative that features a full orchestral accompaniment; it appears occasionally in the sacred vocal music of Bach, but was used more extensively in the operas of Gluck and later composers.

Aeolian: the first of the four new modes added to the canon of eight medieval church modes by Heinrich Glarean in 1547; first official recognition of the minor mode

aggregate: in twelve-tone composition, a contiguous statement of the twelve notes with none repeated except in an immediate or repetitive context

agréments: French word for ornaments, or embellishments

air de cour: the French term for a simple, strophic song for a single voice or a small group of soloists

Alberti bass: an animation of simple triads brought about by playing the notes successively and in a pattern; a distinctive component of the style of keyboard composer Domenico Alberti (c1710–1746)

allemande: French for the "German" dance and usually the first dance in a Baroque suite; a stately dance in $\frac{4}{4}$ meter at a moderate tempo with upbeat and gracefully interweaving lines that create an improvisatory-like style

alternatim technique: a technique in which the verses of a chant are assigned to alternating performing forces, such as an organ and a choir

Ambrosian chant: a body of chant created by Ambrose (340?–397 C.E.) for the church of Milan in northern Italy

Amen cadence: a final phrase setting the word "Amen"; more specifically, a pla-

gal cadence that English composers in particular employed to set "Amen" giving a piece an emphatic conclusion

antecedent phrase: the opening, incomplete-sounding phrase of a melody; often followed by a consequent phrase that brings closure to the melody

anthem: a sacred vocal composition, much like a motet but sung in English, in honor of the Lord or invoking the Lord to preserve and protect the English king or queen

antiphon: in antiphonal singing the short chant sung before and after a psalm and its doxology

antiphonal singing: a method of musical performance in which a divided choir alternately sings back and forth

Aquitanian polyphony: a repertory of about sixty-five pieces of two-voice organum surviving today from various monasteries in Aquitaine in southwestern France

arcicembalo: a sixteenth-century harpsichord constructed in Ferrara, Italy, that had two keyboards, each with three rows of keys

aria: an elaborate, lyrical song for solo voice more florid, more expansive, and more melodious than a recitative or arioso; an aria invariably sets a short poem made up of one or more stanzas

arioso style: an expressive manner of singing somewhere between a recitative and a full-blown aria

Ars antiqua: the music of the thirteenth century characterized by a uniform pace and clear ternary units (as contrasted with the *Ars nova* of the early fourteenth century)

Ars nova: musical *avant garde* of the early fourteenth century characterized by duple as well as triple relationships and a wide variety of note values (as contrasted with the *Ars antiqua* of the thirteenth century)

Ars subtilior: (more subtle art) a style of music exhibited by composers working in Avignon and other parts of southern France and northern Italy during the late fourteenth century; marked by the most subtle, sometimes extreme, rhythmic relationships

Artusi-Monteverdi Controversy: the conflict between Claudio Monteverdi, who composed in a new style inspired by a text-driven approach to musical composition, and Giovanni Maria Artusi, a churchman and conservative music theorist who advocated the older style of music that followed traditional rules of harmony and counterpoint, and who characterized Monteverdi's music as harsh and offensive to the ear

atonal music: twentieth-century harmony lacking consistent tonal center; atonal music normally has no large-scale functional harmonic progressions, uses tones of the full chromatic scale as though structurally equivalent, and emphasizes dissonant chords of any size and intervallic make-up

atonality: see atonal music

aulos: an ancient Greek wind instrument played in pairs that produced a high, clear, penetrating sound

authentic mode: in the eight church modes the authentic is the first of each of the four pairs of modes; each authentic mode has a corresponding lower mode (plagal), but both modes of the pair end on the same final pitch

BACH motive: a motive consisting of the tones B♭ A C B♮ (the musical letters in Bach's name, according to German usage); found in compositions by J.S. Bach himself and many later composers

Bach Revival: a movement originating in Germany in the early nineteenth century by which Bach's entire compositional oeuvre was published and performed

Bach-Abel concerts: a series of public concerts begun in London in 1764 by J.C. Bach (son of J.S.) and another German musician, Carl Abel; the concerts featured the most recent works of Bach and Abel as well as other fashionable composers; continuing for nearly twenty years, they became a model for the public concert series in London and on the Continent

bagatelle: a short instrumental composition

ballad: (1) a narrative poem or its musical setting; (2) a traditional, usually strophic, song that tells a lengthy story; in popular music, a love song in a slow tempo

ballad opera: a type of popular eighteenth-century English musical theater using re-texted ballads (or other popular songs) and spoken dialogue rather than recitative

ballade: one of the three French *formes fixes* that originated in the Middle Ages; a song always with the form AAB setting a poem with from one to three stanzas, or strophes; employs a lyrical melody accompanied by one or two voices or instruments

ballata: a dance song with a choral refrain; one of the three *formes fixes* of secular music in trecento Italy

ballet: a theatrical genre made from regulated dancing and mime, accompanied by orchestra

ballet de cour: (court ballet) a type of elaborate ballet with songs and choruses danced at the French royal court from the late sixteenth to the late seventeenth century in which members of the court appeared alongside professional dancers

ballet variations: passages in a ballet featuring soloistic dancing

Baroque: the term used generally to describe the art, architecture, and music of the period 1600–1750

baryton: a *viola da gamba*-like instrument with six strings

bas instruments: (soft instruments) one of the two classifications of instruments in the fifteenth century; constituted no set group but could include recorder, vielle, lute, harp, psaltery, portative organ, and harpsichord, individually or in combination

basse danse: the principal aristocratic dance of court and city during the early Renaissance; a slow and stately dance in which the dancers' feet glided close to the ground

basso continuo: a bass line that provided a never-ending foundation, or "continuous bass," for the melody above; also a small ensemble of usually two instruments that played this support

basso ostinato: a bass line that insistently repeats, note for note

bebop: a style of jazz originating in the 1940s for small improvising ensembles, often in fast tempos

Bebung: German term for the vibrating sound produced by the clavichord technique of holding and "wiggling" a key up and down

Belle époque: (beautiful era) name often given to the years straddling the turn of the twentieth century in France

big band: the dominant medium of jazz during the 1930s and 1940s; big bands typically numbered about fifteen players, divided into a rhythm section (usually piano, bass, guitar, and drums) and choirs of saxophones (doubling on clarinets), trumpets, and trombones

binary form: a structure consisting of two complementary parts, the first moving to a closely related key and the second beginning in that new key but soon returning to the tonic

blue note: a lowered scale degree (usually the third and seventh) in the major mode in blues and other jazz styles

blues: originally an improvised strophic folk song containing a succession of three-line stanzas, each sung to a twelve-measure phrase and using a standard recurrent harmonic progression; the blues form is also applicable to instrumental jazz

blues chorus: a principal subsection of a jazz work in blues form, usually twelve-measures in duration

bolero: Spanish dance in triple meter

boogie woogie: a style of piano blues with a driving ostinato accompaniment

bop: see bebop

branle (bransle): a fifteenth- and sixteenth-century group dance

break: in jazz, a sudden and momentary pause during which a player introduces an improvised solo

breve: one of the three basic note values and shapes recognized by Franco of Cologne around 1280 in his classification of musical durations

bridge: see transition

brindisi: a drinking song, often found in nineteenth-century Italian opera

Broadway musical: see musical

broken consort: a mixed ensemble of different types of instruments

burden: the refrain with which an English carol begins and which is repeated after each stanza

Burgundian cadence: (octave-leap cadence) when three voices are present, the contratenor often jumps an octave at a cadence to avoid parallel fifths and dissonances and to fill in the texture of the final chord

Buxheim Organ Book: one of the largest sources of Renaissance organ music; written about 1470, it contains 256 mostly anonymous compositions notated in tablature for organ, almost all of which are arrangements of sacred and secular vocal music

BWV (Bach Werke Verzeichnis): Bach Work List; an identifying system for the works of Johann Sebastian Bach, which functions much like the "K" numbers used for Mozart's works

Byzantine chant: the special dialect of chant developed by the Byzantine Church; it was eventually notated and a body of music theory emerged to explain it

cabaletta: the fast, virtuosic concluding part of an aria or duet, often found in nineteenth-century Italian opera

cabaret: a popular entertainment including songs, skits, and dancing

caccia: a piece involving a musical canon in the upper two voices supported by a slower moving tenor; one of the three *formes fixes* of secular music in trecento Italy

cadenza: a technically demanding, rhapsodic, improvisatory passage for a soloist near the end of a movement

call and response: a style of African-American song alternating phrases between two individuals, or between an individual leader and a group

canon: imitation of a complete subject at a fixed interval and time delay; in a canon (round) the following voice(s) must duplicate exactly the pitches and rhythms of the first, as for example in "Row, row, row your boat"

canonical hours (liturgical offices): a set of eight periods of worship occurring throughout the day and observed in monasteries and convents; first prescribed in the Rule of St. Benedict (c530 C.E.)

canso: the name for a song in southern medieval France, in langue d'oc (occitan)

cantata: the primary genre of vocal chamber music in the Baroque era; it was "something sung" as opposed to a sonata, which was "sounded" on an instrument; in its mature state it consisted of several movements, including one or more arias and recitatives; cantatas can be on secular subjects, but those of J.S. Bach are primarily sacred in content

cantate française: virtually identical to the late seventeenth-century Italian chamber cantata except that it set a French rather than an Italian text

canticle: a particularly lyrical and memorable passage of scripture usually drawn from the New Testament of the Bible

cantiga: a medieval Spanish or Portuguese monophonic song; hundreds were created on subjects of love, epic heroism, and everyday life

cantor: the practitioner who performs music, as distinguished from the *musicus*; in a medieval monastery or nunnery the person specially trained to lead the music of the community who sat with one of the two groups and led the singing

cantrix in a convent, the main female singer and, in effect, the director of the choir

cantus: the highest vocal part in an early polyphonic composition, what would later come to be called the superius and finally the soprano

cantus firmus: a well-established, previously existing melody, be it a sacred chant or a secular song, that usually sounds in long notes and provides a structural framework for a polyphonic composition

cantus firmus Mass: a cyclic Mass in which the five movements of the Ordinary are unified by means of a single cantus firmus

canzona: a freely composed instrumental piece, usually for organ or instrumental ensemble, which imitated the lively rhythms and lightly imitative style of the Parisian chanson

cappella: (1) a building consecrated for religious worship; (2) an organized group of highly trained musicians who sang at the services in such a chapel

cappella pontificia sistina: the pope's private vocal ensemble as it came to be called in the early seventeenth century and that sang in the Sistine Chapel

carnival song: a short, homophonic piece associated with carnival season, the text of which usually deals with everyday life on the streets

carol: a strophic song for one to three voices setting a religious text, usually associated with Christmas

carole: one of two main types of dances of the Middle Ages; a song and dance that often made use of the musical form called strophe plus refrain, in which a series of stanzas would each end with the same refrain; singers and dancers grouped in a circle and a soloist sang each successive strophe of text, while everyone else joined in for the refrain

castrato: an adult male singer who had been castrated as a boy to keep his voice from changing so that it would remain in the soprano or alto register

cauda (pl., caudae): in the vocabulary of the medieval musical theorist, a long melisma on a single syllable; used in a conductus to set off key words

cavatina: in eighteenth- and nineteenth-century Italian opera, an entrance aria; in German opera a simple aria in a slow or moderate tempo

Cecilianism: movement in Catholic Church music in Germany in the nineteenth century that favored the reintroduction of a pure style based on sixteenth-century principles

celesta: a small keyboard instrument on which tones are sounded by hammers striking metal bars

chamber cantata: a cantata performed before a select audience in a private residence; intimate vocal chamber music, principally of the Baroque era

chance music: twentieth-century music in which compositional decisions are made by chance procedures

chanson: the French word for song, monophonic or polyphonic

chansonnier: a book of songs, as created by musicians in the Middle Ages and Renaissance; a collected anthology of chansons

chant: monophonic religious music that is sung in a house of worship

character piece: a short instrumental work (especially for piano or orchestra) that establishes a particular mood

Charleston: a popular dance of the 1920s, fast in tempo with a distinctive asymmetrical rhythm

chekker: original name for the clavichord in England

choir: the eastern end of a cathedral or large church; contained the high altar and was the area in which most music was made; an ensemble of singers

choir festival: special occasion for the performance of choral and orchestral music; especially prominent in Germany and England during the nineteenth and twentieth centuries

choir school: a school that took boys at about the age of six, gave them an education with a strong emphasis on music, especially singing, and prepared them for a lifetime of service within the church

choirbook format: a layout common for writing religious music from the late Middle Ages onward in which the soprano voice was on the upper left, the alto or tenor on bottom left, alto or tenor in upper right, and the bass on the bottom right; contrasted with written music today where all the parts are superimposed on one another

chorale: a monophonic spiritual melody or religious folksong of the Lutheran church, what today is called by many Christian denominations a "hymn"

chorale cantata: a genre of sacred vocal music that employs the text and tune of a pre-existing Lutheran chorale in all or several of its movements

chorale fantasia: a lengthy composition for organ that takes a chorale tune as a point of departure but increasingly gives free rein to the composer's imagination

chorale prelude: an ornamental setting of a pre-existing chorale tune intended to be played on the organ before the singing of the chorale by the full congregation

Choralis Constantinus: a collection of nearly three hundred fifty motet-like compositions of Heinrich Isaac (c1450–1518) setting polyphonically all the Proper chants of the Catholic Mass; the first systematic attempt to provide polyphony for the entire church year since the twelfth century

chord inversion: a revolutionary principal codified by Jean-Philippe Rameau in his *Treatise on Harmony* holding that a triad may have different pitches other than the root in the bass but without changing the identity of the triad

choreographer: in ballet, the creator of the dance steps

chorus: a group of singers performing together; in jazz, a basic phrase in blues

(usually spanning twelve measures), or a refrain in a popular song

chromatic genus: a tetrachord employed by the ancient Greeks consisting of two semi-tones and a minor third

chronos: in ancient Greek musical notation the basic unit of time—a short value

church modes: the eight melodic patterns into which medieval theorists categorized the chants of the church; the four principal ones are Dorian, Phrygian, Lydian, and Mixolydian

ciaconna (chaconne): originally a separate and distinct bass melody, but during the seventeenth century the term came to mean almost any repeating bass pattern of short duration

cimbalom: a Hungarian dulcimer

circle of fifths: an arrangement of the tonic pitches of the twelve major and minor keys by ascending or descending perfect fifths, C-G-D-A etc., for example, which, because of the enharmonic equivalency of F♯ and G♭, ultimately come full circle back to C

clarino register: the very high register of the trumpet; playing in this register was a special technique of Baroque trumpeters that was exploited by Baroque composers

clausula (pl., clausulae): section, phrase, or "musical clause" in a medieval composition

clavecin: French word for harpsichord; the favorite chamber keyboard instrument in the late seventeenth and early eighteenth centuries

clavichord: a keyboard instrument that makes sound when a player depresses a key and thereby pushes a small metal tangent in the shape of a "T" upward to strike a string; the sound produced is very quiet, the softest of any musical instrument

closed ending: the term used in the Middle Ages for what we today call a second ending

coda: the musical section appended to a piece to add extra weight to the end to give it a feeling of conclusion

Codex Calixtinus: manuscript that survives today at the cathedral at Santiago de Compostela, Spain, written around 1150 and once believed to be the work of Pope Calixtus II; contains a service for St. James, which includes twenty polyphonic pieces; important in the history of Western music because it is the first manuscript to ascribe composers' names to particular pieces

colla parte: a technique in which all the instrumental parts double the vocal lines

collegium musicum: an association of musicians in eighteenth-century Germany, consisting usually of university students, who came together voluntarily to play the latest music in a public setting such as a large café or beer hall

color: the melodic unit that serves as a structural backbone in an isorhythmic composition

coloratura: florid figuration assigned to the soprano voice in an opera; also the high female voice capable of singing such a florid part

colossal Baroque: name for the style of large-scale sacred music employing multiple choirs of voices and instruments and sung in largest churches in Rome, Venice, Vienna, and Salzburg

combinatoriality: the capacity of two forms of a twelve-tone row to create multidimensional aggregates

combo: a small jazz ensemble

comic opera: a simple, direct type of musical theater that made use of comic characters, dealt with everyday social issues, and emphasized values more in step with those of the middle class

comping: the playing of accompanimental chords by a pianist or other instrumentalist in jazz

complementary hexachords: two collections of notes, each having six tones, which together contain all tones of the chromatic scale

complete works edition: a musical edition containing the complete oeuvre of a composer

compound melody: a melody made from two or more simultaneous stepwise strands whose tones are touched alternately

conceptual art: a loosely defined movement in art of the 1960s and 1970s in which the artist calls attention to ideas by which the art work is created rather than to traditional artistic objects

concert overture: an orchestral piece in one movement, usually programmatic in content, and intended for concert purposes

Concert spirituel: one of the first and foremost public concert series founded in Paris in 1725; originally formed to give a public hearing to religious music sung in Latin, its repertory soon came to emphasize instrumental symphonies and concertos as well

concert symphony: a three- or four-movement instrumental work projecting the unified sounds of an orchestra; has its origins in the Enlightenment

concertante: a special orchestral style; a concerto-like approach to the use of the orchestra in which individual instruments regularly emerge from the orchestral texture to function as soloists

concerted madrigal: a madrigal in the concertato style with strong contrasts in textures and timbres involving voices and instruments

concerted motet: a motet in the concertato style with strong contrasts in textures and timbres involving voices and instruments

concertino: the small group of solo performers in a concerto grosso

concerto: a purely instrumental piece for ensemble in which one or more soloists both complement and compete with a full orchestra

concerto delle donne: (ensemble of ladies) a group of female singers employed by the duke of Ferrara at the end of the sixteenth century; they constituted the first professional ensemble of women employed by a court

concerto grosso: a concerto in which a larger body of performers, namely the full orchestra (the ripieno, or tutti), contrasts with a smaller group of soloists (the concertino)

concerto-sonata form: a form, originating in the concerto of the Classical period, in which first the orchestra and then the soloist present the primary thematic material; much like sonata form but with two expositions

concrete music: see musique concrète

conductus: an extra-liturgical piece written for one, two, three, or occasionally four voices with texts that are metrical Latin poems arranged in successive stanzas; although not part of the canonical liturgy, most were serious and moralistic in tone; often used to accompany the movement of the clergy from one place to another in and around the church

confraternity: a Christian society of laymen emphasizing religious devotion and charity; in Florence performing laude was an essential part of their fraternal life

Congress of Vienna the meeting called by Emperor Francis I, King of Austria—after Napoleon Bonaparte abdicated his throne and fled France—inviting all the leaders of Europe to meet to redraw the boundaries of their continent and reestablish principles of legitimate rule

consequent phrase: the second phrase of a two-part melodic unit that brings a melody to a point of repose and closure

consort: an ensemble of instruments all of one family

consort song: one of two forms of the solo art song that flourished in England around 1600; the voice is accompanied by a group of independent instruments, usually a consort of viols

contenance angloise: the "English manner" of composition that fifteenth-century Continental musicians admired and adopted, though the exact nature of this style is not known

contrafactum (pl., contrafacta): the transformation of a piece of music from a secular piece to a sacred one, or (less often) from a sacred to a secular one

contralto: a low alto (a low female voice)

contratenor altus the upper of the two contratenor voices (the other being the bass); the medieval equivalent of our alto voice

contratenor bassus: the lower of the two contratenor voices (the other being the alto); the medieval equivalent of our bass voice

conversation books: notebooks used (by Beethoven and others with a hearing impairment) to communicate; one hundred forty of Beethoven's conversation books survive today

cool jazz: a style of jazz of the 1950s characterized by subdued playing and moderate tempos

Coptic chant: the music of the Christian Church of Egypt, which still exists today, passed along for nearly 2000 years entirely by oral tradition

cori spezzati: music for two, three, or four choirs placed in different parts of a building

cornett: a wooden instrument with fingerholes that is played with a mouthpiece and sounds in the soprano range with a tone something like a soft trumpet

Council of Trent: (1545–1563) a congress of bishops and cardinals held at the small town of Trento in the Italian Alps; the institutionalization of the spirit of the Counter-Reformation; its decision regarding music insisted that music must never interfere with the comprehension of the sacred word

counterpoint: from the Latin punctus contra punctum (one note moving against another note); the harmonious opposition of two or more independent musical lines

counterpoint, dissonant: see dissonant counterpoint

Counter-Reformation: the movement that fostered reform in the Roman Church in response to the challenge of the Protestant Reformation

countersubject: in a fugue, a unit of thematically distinctive material that serves as a counterpoint to the subject

countertenor: a male performer who sings in the alto or soprano range in falsetto voice

couplet: a term used in the rondo form of the seventeenth and eighteenth centuries to indicate an intermediate section (episode) distinctly different from the refrain

courante: a lively dance in triple meter characterized by intentional metrical ambiguity created by means of hemiola; one of the four dances typically making up a Baroque dance suite

Credo: a profession of faith formulated as the result of the Council of Nicaea in 325; one of the five parts of the Ordinary of the Mass

crook: a small piece of pipe that could be inserted in a horn if the player needed to change key; it altered the length of tubing within the instrument and consequently its pitch

crumhorn: a capped double-reed wooden instrument with a curving shape; has the range of a tenth and makes a sound like a kazoo

cultural bolshevism: a catch phrase used by Nazi ideologues to condemn art that was considered decadent on account of its association with foreign, Jewish, or Communist influences

cyclic Mass: a Mass in which all of the movements are linked together by a common musical theme; the first was Machaut's *Mass of Our Lady* composed in the mid fourteenth century

cyclicism: the recurrence of melodic ideas (often transformed) throughout a multimovement or multisectional composition

da camera: (of the chamber) a seventeenth-century designation for music that was not intended primarily for the church

da capo **aria:** an aria in two sections with an obligatory return to and repeat of the first (hence ABA); the reprise was not written out but signaled by the inscription "da capo" meaning "take it from the top"

da chiesa: (of the church) a seventeenth-century designation for music that was intended primarily for the church

dance suite: an ordered set of dances for solo instrument or ensemble, all written in the same key and intended to be performed in a single sitting

development: in sonata form, the middle-most section in which the themes of the exposition are varied or developed in some fashion; it is often the most confrontational and unstable portion of the movement

diabolus in musica: (devil in music) the dissonant, or disagreeable tritone such as F-B

diatonic genus: the basic genus within the ancient Greek musical system; reflects the primary tetrachord spanning the intervals S-T-T

Dies irae: (*Day of Wrath*) an anonymous thirteenth-century sequence; today the most famous of all medieval sequences, one which serves as the sequence of the requiem Mass

discant: a style of music in which the voices move at roughly the same rate and are written in clearly defined modal rhythms (as compared to organum purum)

diseme: in ancient Greek musical notation a long value of time—formed by two chronoi

dissonant counterpoint: term coined by Charles Seeger to refer to counterpoint in which the traditional roles of consonance and dissonance are reversed

dithyramb: in ancient Greece, a wild choral song, mingled with shouts, that honored Dionysus; a term applied today to any poem with these characteristics

divertimento: originally simply a musical diversion, it came to imply a lighter style of music and a five-movement format: fast/minuet and trio/slow/minuet and trio/fast; the term was used interchangeably with serenade

divertissement: (1) a lavishly choreographed diversionary interlude with occasional singing set within French *ballet de cour*; (2) an "entertainment" in an opera or ballet, only loosely connected to its surrounding scenes

Doctrine of Affections: a theory of the Baroque era that held that different musical moods could and should be used to influence the emotions, or affections, of the listeners

dot: following a note, a dot adds fifty percent to the value of the note; this concept entered music history in the early fourteenth century

double escapement action: a piano action in which a hammer falls back only halfway after striking a string, allowing the hammer to restrike more quickly

double leading-tone cadence a cadence with two leading tones in the penultimate chord, one pulling upward to the primary tone of the final chord and the other upward to the fifth degree

double verse structure: a distinctive feature of the sequence; each musical phrase is sung twice to accommodate a pair of verses

doxology: a standard formula of praise to the Holy Trinity

drum set: a collection of percussion instruments in a jazz ensemble that can be wielded by a single player

duplum: second voice in two- three- or four-voice organa

electronic music: works whose sounds are directly realized by a composer using electronic equipment

emancipation of dissonance: term used by Arnold Schoenberg to refer to a phenomenon in modern music by which dissonant chords and intervals are used as though equivalent to consonant ones

empfindsamer Stil: term applied to the hyper-expressivity that affected northern European, and particularly German, arts generally in the second half of the eighteenth century

emulation technique: see parody technique

English cross (false) relation: the simultaneous or adjacent appearance in different voices of two conflicting notes with the same letter name

English discant: a general term for the technique in fifteenth-century English music, both written and improvised, of using parallel 6/3 chords and root position triads in a homorhythmic style

English Madrigal School, The: the name given to the composers who fashioned the great outpouring of English secular music vocal music, mostly madrigals, in London between 1588 and 1627

enharmonic genus: a tetrachord found in ancient Greek music consisting of a major third and two quarter-tones; used for music demanding more subtle variations of pitch than that of the diatonic or chromatic genera

Enlightenment: a philosophical, scientific, and political movement that dominated eighteenth-century thought

ensemble finale: an energetic finish to an operatic act that is sung by a vocal ensemble rather than a soloist

envoi: one or more lines of verse added to the end of a chanson to suggest a leave taking

epic theater: a theatric style, associated with the plays of Bertolt Brecht, that dispels normal theatric illusion and "alienates" the audience from the narrative

episode: a passage in a musical work occurring between other passages that have more central thematic importance (as in a rondo form); in a fugue, a section full of modulation and free counterpoint that is based on motives derived from the subject

equal temperament: a division of the octave into twelve equal half-steps, each with the ratio of approximately 18:17; first advocated by some musicians in the early sixteenth century

estampie: one of two main dance types of the Middle Ages; originally a dance-song in which the dancers also sang a text, usually a poem about love; however, during the thirteenth and fourteenth centuries it evolved into a purely instrumental piece

étude: a study; a work intended to build a player's technique and often also having artistic value

Evensong: the final service of the day in the Anglican religion, an amalgam of Vespers and Compline

exposition: in sonata form the first main section in which the primary thematic material of the movement is presented or exposed; of a fugue, an opening section in which each voice presents the subject in turn

expressionism: a movement in twentieth-century literature and art in which symbolic means are used to explore irrational states of mind and grotesque actions

extended techniques: playing and singing in unusual ways in order to expand the sounds available in a musical work

faburden: a style of English medieval choral music that arose when singers improvised around a given chant placed in the middle voice; it is important because English composers began to incorporate this improvisatory style into their more formal written work

falsobordone: an improvisatory technique used by church singers that originated in Spain and Italy around 1480; at first three voices chanted along with the psalm tone making simple chant sound more splendid; by the seventeenth century, psalm tone and improvisation were abandoned and it became a newly composed piece for four or five voices but with the same simple, chordal style

fantasia: an imaginative composition the exact nature of which depends on the period of origin; in earlier eras these were usually contrapuntal works; later, the term suggested an improvisatory piece in free form, or sometimes pieces incorporating preexisting themes

fauxbourdon: the Continental style related to the English faburden; in fauxbourdon singers of sacred music improvised at pitches a fourth and a sixth below a given plainsong

fête galante: a popular social occasion among the French aristocracy of the eighteenth century

figured bass: a numerical shorthand placed with the bass line that tells the player which unwritten notes to fill in above the written bass note

fill: in jazz, a brief figure added between phrases performed by the principal soloist or singer

fin'amors: the theme of ideal love, an important value in chivalric society, as expressed in the poetry of the troubadours

flat trumpet: a slide trumpet, but one for which the sliding tube extended backward over the player's left shoulder, rather than extending forward from the right; had the capacity to play in minor keys more easily

formalism: in general, emphasis on strict formal principles or patterns in music; more specifically, a pejorative term used in the Soviet Union for music that seemed abstract or difficult, not in tune with the taste of the masses or with Soviet artistic ideology

formes fixes: the three fixed forms—ballade, rondeau, virelai—in which nearly all French secular art songs of the fourteenth and early fifteenth centuries were written

foxtrot: a social dance in $\frac{4}{4}$ time, popular in America in the 1920s

free jazz: a type of jazz of the 1950s and 1960s characterized by the removal or reinterpretation of key, normal harmonic progressions, and familiar jazz forms

French horn: the English term for the instrument that in other languages is simply called a horn; introduced into English ensembles only after 1700

French overture: a distinctive type of instrumental prelude created by the composer Jean-Baptiste Lully; came to be understood as an overture in two sections, the first slow in duple meter with dotted note values, the second fast in triple meter and with light imitation

frottola (pl., frottole): a catch-all word used to describe a polyphonic setting of a wide variety of strophic Italian poetry; the frottola flourished between 1470 and 1530 but had its origins in the improvisatory, solo singing that arose in Italy during the 1400s

fugue: a contrapuntal composition for two, three, four, or five voices, which begins with a presentation of a subject in imitation in each voice (exposition), continues with modulating passages of free counterpoint (episodes) and further appearances of the subject, and ends with a strong affirmation of the tonic key

fuguing tune: a hymn, often composed by American musicians of the eighteenth century, having fugal passages

functional harmony: a theory of harmonic syntax that defines the role of a chord as a point of departure or arrival (a tonic), a secondary point of arrival or moment of harmonic tension (a dominant), or a prefix to a dominant

fusion: a style of popular music that mixes elements of jazz and rock

galant style: French term used by music historians (rather than "Enlightenment style") to describe eighteenth-century music that is graceful, light in texture, and generally symmetrical in melodic structure

galliard: a fast leaping dance in triple meter especially popular during the Renaissance

Gallican chant: the Christian music of early-medieval Gaul; it later mixed with chant coming from Rome and that fusion formed the basis of what we call Gregorian chant

gate: in electronic music, a device allowing for shifts in amplitude in an electronic signal; in the music of John Adams a point of modulation from one collection of tones to another

Gebrauchsmusik: (music for use) a term used in the 1920s by Paul Hindemith to designate his compositions for amateurs or for everyday settings; also used by Kurt Weill for music of artistic value that was accessible to a general audience

German flute: what is today called the flute (the transverse flute)

gigue: a fast dance in $\frac{6}{8}$ or $\frac{12}{8}$ with a constant eighth-note pulse that produces a galloping sound; the gigue is sometimes lightly imitative and in the Baroque era was often used to conclude a suite

Gloria: a hymn of praise originating in early Christian times; one of the five parts of the Ordinary of the Mass

Golden Section: the division of a line into two parts such that the ratio of lengths of the smaller to the larger division equals the larger to the whole

Gothic architecture: the style of architecture that emerged in Paris and surrounding territories in the twelfth century; a lighter style than its Romanesque predecessor, it was characterized by greater height, greater light, and an almost obsessive application of repeating geometrical patterns

Gradual: the first of the two melismatic, responsorial chants of the Proper of the Mass that are sung between the *Gloria* and the *Credo*; consists of two parts: a respond and a psalm verse

grand opera: a style of opera originating around 1830 in France characterized by lavish use of chorus and ballet and elaborate spectacle

grand piano: a term that first appeared in England toward the end of the eighteenth century that denoted a large piano with sturdy legs and strings running roughly in the same direction as the keys

graphic notation: in twentieth-century compositions, musical notation that includes unusual graphic designs

Greater Perfect System: the framework of the Greek two-octave scale formed by four tetrachords and the proslambanomenos

Gregorian chant (plainsong): a vast body of monophonic religious music setting Latin texts and intended for use in the Roman Catholic Church; the music sung daily at the eight canonical hours of prayer and at Mass

ground bass: the English term for *basso ostinato*

Guidonian hand: ascribed to Guido of Arezzo that involves a system of using the left hand to inscribe mentally all the notes of the Guidonian scale and thus provide a portable mnemonic aid for the musical staff and the notes set upon it

Gypsy scale: a scale used by Gypsy musicians of the nineteenth and twentieth centuries containing two augmented seconds (such as C D E♭ F♯ G A♭ B C)

hand-crossing: a technique in keyboard playing in which the left hand must cross over the right to create an exciting three-level texture (left hand, right hand, and left over)

hard hexachord: in the Guidonian system, the hexachord—six-note pattern of TTSTT—set on G

Harlem Renaissance: a literary and artistic movement of the 1920s in Harlem (an African-American district in New York City)

harmonics: overtones, or frequencies, that are components of a fundamental tone

Harmonie: German name for an eighteenth-century independent wind band; called thus because winds played mostly harmony and not melody in the symphony of the day

Harmoniemusik: music written for an eighteenth-century *Harmonie*, or independent wind band

harpsichord: a string keyboard instrument that first appeared in the West in the fifteenth century; it utilized a key-jack mechanism to pluck the taut wire strings; during the Baroque era it was the principal keyboard instrument for realizing the basso continuo, but it lost favor as the piano grew in popularity during the second half of the eighteenth century

hautboys: another name for the shawm; the term was in use in England and France in the sixteenth century, and in England was eventually transformed into "oboe"

hauts instruments: (loud instruments) one of the two classifications of instruments in the fifteenth century; included trumpets, sackbuts, shawms, bagpipes, drums, and tambourine

head arrangement: a jazz arrangement rehearsed and memorized by musicians, but not written down

heckelphone: a double-reed woodwind instrument in the bass range sounding as notated

Heiligenstadt Testament: Beethoven's will that he prepared while staying in Heiligenstadt, Austria, in 1802; ostensibly addressed to his two brothers, it is actually an expression of his innermost feelings for all posterity

hexachord: a collection of six pitches

Hoboken (Hob.) number: number by which Josef Haydn's individual works may be identified following the catalogue prepared by the Dutch musicologist Anthony Hoboken

hocket: a contrapuntal technique and a musical genre; it occurs when the sounds of two voices are staggered by the careful placement of rests, thereby creating a highly syncopated piece

Hofkapelle: the group of singers responsible for the religious music at the Hapsburg court of Emperor Maximilian I; they were the center of religious and musical life at the court

horn fifths: a characteristic musical figure assigned to the French horns in which the instruments slide back and forth through sixths, fifths, and thirds, sometimes ornamenting along the way

hot jazz: an intense and exciting style of jazz

hymn: a relatively short chant with a small number of phrases, often four, and a rather narrow vocal range; hymns are invariably strophic, the usual hymn having three or four stanzas

idée fixe: (obsession): term used by Hector Berlioz to describe a recurrent melody in his *Symphonie fantastique*; the *idée fixe* melody symbolizes the beloved in the work's program

imitation: duplication of the notes and rhythms in one voice by a following voice; from the mid fifteenth century onward it became an oft used technique to enliven polyphonic music and sacred polyphonic music in particular

impresario: a manager, as of a ballet or opera company

impressionism: a realistic style of French painting of the late nineteenth century using everyday subjects (especially sea- and landscapes) and emphasizing the effects of sunlight upon colors; used in music to designate the style of Claude Debussy and others composing evocative music partially freed from strict beat and normative harmonic progressions

improvisation: playing or singing without reference to an existing musical composition

indeterminacy: see chance music

indeterminacy of composition: term associated with the composer John Cage by which compositional decisions are largely determined by chance routines; see also chance music and indeterminacy of performance

indeterminacy of performance: term associated with the composer John Cage by which music results from spontaneous decisions made by players, not strictly dictated by a composer; see also chance music

intabulation: a piece of music notated in tablature and specifically for certain solo instruments such as lute or keyboard; an intabulation implies that a preexisting polyphonic vocal piece has been arranged for a single instrument

intermezzo: a musical diversion between the acts of an opera or a play

introduction: a passage at the beginning of a composition or movement that prepares for and is often slower in tempo than the music to come; in nineteenth-century opera, a musical number (usually called an *introduzione*) at the beginning of the first act that is multisectional and composite in medium

Introit: an introductory chant for the entrance of the celebrating clergy; the first item of the Proper of the Mass

inversion: (1) in traditional harmony, the placement of a bass tone into an upper voice; a melody is inverted if its contour is replaced by its mirror image; (2) a tone row in a twelve-tone composition (or set of pitches in freely atonal music) is inverted if each interval separating the notes is replaced by the octave complement—sometimes said to be a "symmetric" inversion

invertible counterpoint: counterpoint carefully written so that the vertical position of two or more voices can be switched without violating the rules of counterpoint or creating undue dissonance

Ionian: added to the canon of eight medieval church modes by Glarean in

1547; first official recognition of the major mode

isorhythm: in isorhythm (same rhythm) a rhythmic pattern is repeated again and again in a line, usually in the tenor voice; a technique introduced by composers in the early fourteenth century

jam session: in jazz, an informal making of music by improvisation

jazz: a collective term for various types of twentieth-century popular music originating among African-American musicians and often involving improvisation; see also swing, hot jazz, free jazz, cool jazz

jazz break: see break

jazz combo: a small jazz ensemble

jazz dance bands: bands of moderate to large size and flexible makeup, freely incorporating jazz idioms, that played for dancing in the period from about 1915 to 1925

jazz standard: see standard

jubilus: the melisma on the final syllable of the word Alleluia; called this because at that moment the full choir and community celebrates with jubilation the redemptive life of Christ

jungle style: a big band style, associated especially with Duke Ellington in the 1920s and 30s, evoking African or primitive musical effects

just tuning: a system in which, in addition to the ratios required by Pythagorean tuning, the major and minor thirds were also tuned according to strict ratios (5:4 and 6:5)

Kapellmeister: chief of music at court; the German equivalent of *maestro di cappella* (chapel master) in Italy

keyboard tablature: a combination of note symbols (for the fast-moving upper part) and pitch-letter names (for the lower parts)

kithara: the largest of all ancient Greek string instruments (an especially large lyre) usually fitted with seven strings and a resonator of wood

Köchel (K) number: an identifying number assigned to each of the works of Mozart, in roughly chronological order, by German botanist and mineralogist Ludwig von Köchel (1800–1877)

kuchka: (handful) the sobriquet given in 1867 to a group of Russian composers living in St. Petersburg: Mily Balakirev (the mentor of the group), Nicolai Rimsky-Korsakov, César Cui, Alexander Borodin, and Modest Mussorgsky; the group is sometimes called "The Five"

Kyrie: an ancient Greek text and the only portion of the traditional Mass not sung in Latin; in this the first section of the Ordinary of the Mass the congregation petitions the Lord for mercy in threefold exclamations

La Guerre des Bouffons: (The War of the Buffoons) a paper war over the relative merits of Italian and French musical style; it raged, on and off, for several years in Paris during the 1750s and centered on the question of what sort of opera was appropriate for the French stage

lament bass: a descending tetrachordal *basso ostinato* employed during the Baroque era as a musical signifier of grief

Landini cadence: the name for a cadential gesture used frequently by Francesco Landini in which he ornamented a cadence by adding a lower neighbor-tone to the upper voice as it moves up to the octave

langue d'oc (occitan): the vernacular language of southern France in the high Middle Ages; the language of the troubadours and trobairitz

langue d'oïl: the vernacular language of northern France in the high Middle Ages; the language of the trouvères

lauda (pl., laude): Italian for a song of praise; a simple, popular sacred song written, not in church Latin but in the local dialect of Italian; from its beginning in the thirteenth century, the lauda had been sung by members of a confraternity

Le nuove musiche: (*The New Music*, 1602) published by Giulio Caccini; an anthology of solo madrigals and strophic solo songs gathered over time, rather than all new music as was implied; the preface contains invaluable information on vocal performance practices of the early Baroque era

leitmotive: a musical motive, normally occurring in the orchestral part of an opera, which symbolizes a character or dramatic entity; associated primarily with the operas of Richard Wagner, and also used by later composers

libretto: the text of an opera or an oratorio written in poetic verse

Lied (pl., Lieder): (song) a German art song or popular song

ligature: in early notation a group of two, three, or four individual notes

lira da braccio: a Renaissance fiddle; a bowed five-string instrument tuned in fifths and played on the shoulder

Lisztomania: Heinrich Heine's term for the emotional effect that Liszt had on his audiences

liturgical drama: a religious play with music intended to be performed as an adjunct to the liturgy, sometimes before Mass

liturgical offices: see canonical hours

liturgy: the collection of prayers, chants, readings, and ritual acts by which the theology of the church, or any organized religion, is practiced

long: one of the three basic note values and shapes recognized by Franco of Cologne around 1280 in his classification of musical durations

lute: a pear-shaped instrument with six sets of strings called courses, as well as frets created with thin strips of leather wrapped around the fingerboard at measured intervals, and a distinctive peg box that turns back at a right angle to the fingerboard; during the sixteenth century the most popular of all musical instruments

lute ayre: one of two forms of the solo art song that flourished in England around 1600; the soloist is accompanied by a lute and possibly a bass instrument such as the *viola da gamba*; a strophic piece that depended on the solo singer to employ the expressive nuances of the voice to make each stanza sound distinctive

lute tablature: a special type of notation for lute music that directs the fingers to stop strings at specific frets so as to produce sounds

lyre: in ancient Greece a medium-sized instrument usually fitted with seven strings of sheep gut and a resonator of turtle shell; plucked with a metal or bone plectrum and used most often to accompany a solo singer

lyricist: the writer of the words of a popular song, especially the songs in a musical

madrigal: (fourteenth century) originally a poem in the vernacular to which music was added for greater emotional effect; having the form AAB, it was one of the three *formes fixes* of secular music in trecento Italy; (sixteenth century) like the frottola, a catch-all term used to describe settings of Italian verse; sixteenth-century madrigals were through composed rather than strophic and employed a variety of textures and compositional techniques

madrigalism: the term for a musical cliché in which the music tries to sound out the meaning of the text, such as a drooping melody that signals a sigh or a dissonance to intensify a "harsh" word

magister cappellae: musician who is leader of the chapel

Mannheim *crescendo*: a gradual increase from very soft to very loud with a repeating figure over a pedal point; a specialty of the highly disciplined orchestra at the court of Mannheim

Mannheim rocket: a triadic theme that bursts forth as a rising arpeggio; another specialty of the highly disciplined orchestra at the court of Mannheim

masque: an elaborate courtly entertainment using music, dance, and drama to portray an allegorical story that shed a favorable light on the royal family

Mass: the central and most important religious service each day in the traditional liturgy of the Roman Catholic Church

Matins: the night office of the canonical hours, required much singing, and on high feasts such as Christmas or Easter, might go on for four hours

mazurka: a triple-time Polish dance

megamusical: a type of musical appearing in the 1980s with large cast and lavish spectacle

melisma: a lengthy vocal phrase setting a single syllable of text

melismatic chant: chants in which there are many notes per syllable of text; Matins, Vespers, and the Mass have the most melismatic chants

mélodie: (melody or song) a French art song of the nineteenth century

melodrama: a musical genre in which spoken text is accompanied by, or alternates with, instrumental music

mensural notation: symbol specific notation developed in the late thirteenth century; the direct ancestor of the system of notation used today (in contrast to modal notation, a contextual notation system used prior to the late thirteenth century)

mensuration canon: a canon in which two voices perform the same music at different rates of speed, the corresponding notes of which grow progressively distant from one another

metamorphoses: changes in form; used by Richard Strauss as the title of his final orchestral tone poem (1945)

metric modulation: a term associated with the composer Elliott Carter designating a proportional change of tempo by which a small division of a beat is regrouped into a new beat so that a new tempo results

Micrologus: (Little Essay) music theory treatise written c1030 by Guido of Arezzo setting forth all that a practicing church musician needed to know to sing the liturgy

micropolyphony: a term associated with the composer György Ligeti designating a texture in which a large number of lines merge into a sound mass

mime: the art of portraying a character or narrative solely by bodily movements and facial gestures

minim: a new short note value recognized by the fourteenth-century theorists of the *Ars nova*; a subdivision of the semibreve

minimalism: a musical style originating in the United States in the 1960s in which works are created by repetition and gradual change enacted upon a minimum of basic materials

Minnesang: (a song of love in old high German) a song created by a Minnesinger

Minnesinger: in the high Middle Ages the name for a German poet-musician writing love songs

minstrel show: a theatric entertainment originating in the United States in the middle of the nineteenth century, containing skits, songs, and dancing, which parodies the language and manners of African Americans

minuet: originally a triple-meter dance that was often added toward the end of the Baroque dance suite; in the Classical period it was invariably written in rounded binary form and coupled with a matching rounded binary movement called a trio

minuet and trio: a pair of movements with each usually constructed in rounded binary form; the trio was often scored for fewer instruments, sometimes only three (thus the name); often served as the third movement of a symphony or piece of chamber music

modal notation: a new type of notation that came into music gradually around 1150–1170 and that allowed composers to specify rhythmic duration as well as pitch; in modal notation the context determines the rhythm as opposed to the modern system of mensural notation in which each sign (note) indicates a specific duration

mode: (*modus*) the division of the long into two or three breves

modernism: in general, a style that departs from traditional norms of musical materials and aesthetic principles in the name of contemporaneity and progress; the term is often encountered in musical criticism of the twentieth century, especially for music arising in its early years and in the decades following World War II

monochord: a ancient device with a single string stretched over a wooden block and anchored at each end; distances were carefully measured on the string to correspond to specific pitches

monody: the overarching term for solo madrigals, solo arias, and solo recitatives written during the early Baroque era

Morning Prayer: the first service of the day in the Anglican religion, an amalgam of Matins and Lauds

motet: (thirteenth century) originally a discant clausula to which sacred words were added; in a motet each of the upper voices declaims its own poetic text that comments on the significance of the single Latin word being sung by the tenor; (later) the term generally used to connote a sacred choral composition, either accompanied by instruments or sung *a cappella*

motet-chanson: (fifteenth century) a hybrid of a motet and a chanson; a genre in which a vernacular text in an upper voice is sung simultaneously with a Latin chant in the tenor

motetus: the second voice (immediately above the tenor) in the thirteenth-century motet

movable type: individual small pieces of metal type cut with the letters of the alphabet or musical symbols that can be arranged to form words or music; once a sheet using the type has been printed the pieces of type can then be "moved"—rearranged to create a completely different page

Mozarabic chant: the old Christian church music as sung by Christians living in Spain under Moslem rule; survives today in more than twenty manuscripts but is nearly impossible to transcribe and perform

multiple cantus firmus Mass: when two or more cantus firmi sound simultaneously or successively in a Mass

multiple stops: on a violin (or other bowed string instruments) playing two or more notes simultaneously as chords

multiple-impression printing: a process for printing musical notation in which the lines of the staff are first printed horizontally across the sheet, then the sheet is pressed a second time to place the notes on the staff, finally a third pressing adds the text, title, composer's name, and any written instructions

murky bass: German name for a rumbling octave bass, created by repeating a bass note in alternating octaves, that became a favorite technique of both Italian and German keyboard composers of the eighteenth century

muses: in ancient Greek mythology, the nine goddesses who attended Apollo and presided over the arts and sciences; root of our word "music"

music drama: a term associated with the operas of Richard Wagner, who rejected the genre term "opera" for his mature works; Wagner preferred the word "drama"—sometimes "music drama"—for his operas to stress their heightened literary value; but in his essay "On the Name 'Music Drama'" (1872) Wagner also rejected this term as misleading

music of the future: a slogan derived from the writings of Richard Wagner that points to a utopian state in which the various arts coalesce into an integrated or "total" work of art

music of the spheres: part of the ancient Greek world-view of music, which held that when the stars and planets rotated in balanced proportions they made heavenly music

***Musica enchiriadis* (*Music Handbook*):** a music theory treatise that dates from the 890s and is ascribed to Abbot Hoger; it describes a type of polyphonic singing called organum and aimed to teach church singers how to improvise polyphonic music

musica ficta: accidentals not found on the Guidonian scale but that had to be added by medieval performers because, being theoretically "off the scale," they had to be imagined

musica humana: music of the human body—one of the three harmonies Boethius posited as part of his cosmology of music

musica instrumentalis: earthly vocal and instrumental music—one of the three harmonies Boethius posited as part of his cosmology of music

musica mundana: music of the spheres—one of the three harmonies Boethius posited as part of his cosmology of music; the belief that all the universe resonates with music as sounding number

musica reservata: text-sensitive music reserved for a small circle of connoisseurs

musica secreta: (*musica reservata*) progressive chamber music reserved for a small, elite audience; used to describe the performances by the *concerto delle donne* before the ducal family in Ferrara

musical: a form of popular musical theater of the twentieth century, normally with spoken dialogue alternating with songs, dances, ensembles, and choruses; synonymous with musical comedy, musical play, and Broadway musical

musical play: see musical

musicologist: a scholar of music

musicus: as defined by Boethius, the musicologist who studies and understands music; as distinguished from the *cantor*, who is a practitioner

musique concrète: (concrete music) electronic music (q.v.) made from recordings of natural or man-made sounds

mystic chord: a collection of six tones used in the later music of Alexander Scriabin; an example of the mystic

chord, placed into a compact scalewise order, is B C D E F♯ G♯

nationalism: in general, the love for or allegiance to a region of birth and its people, culture, and language; in music, nationalism is often expressed by the quotation of folk songs and dances or the use of folk stories

natural hexachord: in the Guidonian system, the hexachord—six-note pattern of TTSTT —set on C

naturalism: a movement in literature of the late nineteenth century that depicts society in an objective and truthful manner

nave: the western end of a cathedral or large church; the public part of the church, which functioned as town hall and civic auditorium as well as a space for religious processions and votive prayers

neoclassical architecture: term for the architecture of the eighteenth century that copied classical Roman qualities of balance, harmonious proportions, and an absence of ornate decoration

neoclassicism: a critic's term designating a dominant musical style of the 1920s through 1940s, especially associated with the music of Igor Stravinsky of that time; characteristics of neoclassical music include parody-like references to earlier music (especially works of Baroque and Classical periods), motoric rhythms, changing meters, a cool and detached tone, modernistic harmony, and an international tone rather than regional allegiances

neumatic chant: chants in which there are three, four, or five notes for each syllable of text

neume: in medieval musical notation, a sign used to delineate single pitches or groups of pitches; originally, around 900 C.E., neumes were just laid out on the parchment above text as a reminder of how it should be sung

New German School: a group of musicians gathering around Franz Liszt in Weimar and supporting the artistic outlook of Liszt and Richard Wagner

new music advisor: a position existing since the 1970s with many American symphony orchestras; the new music advisor typically composes new works for the orchestra and recommends other contemporary compositions

New Orleans style of jazz: a jazz style emerging in New Orleans in the early twentieth century characterized by small bands, an energetic ("hot") style of playing, and group improvisation

Nimrod variation: ninth variation in Edward Elgar's *Enigma* Variations for

orchestra; a musical portrait of Elgar's publisher, August Jaeger

nocturne: a type of piano character piece appearing in the nineteenth century distinguished by a dreamy mood, a lyric melody in the right hand, and widely-spaced, arpeggiated chords in the left hand

nota: (Latin for note) a symbol on a line or space representing a single, precise pitch

notes inégales: in which a succession of equal notes moving rapidly up or down the scale are played somewhat unequally, such as "long-short, long-short"

Notre Dame School: the name given by historians to the composers Leoninus, Perotinus, and their colleagues who created a huge musical repertory of more than a thousand pieces during the period 1160–1260 at and around Notre Dame of Paris

number symbolism: a system prevalent during the Middle Ages and Renaissance in which meaning in music was conveyed by the use of numbers representing religious themes and concepts; a composition might have certain structural proportions such as 6:4:2:3 in Dufay's motet that mirror the proportions of the cathedral of Florence

obbligato: indication that a composer has written a specific part for an instrument and intends it to be played as written

obbligato recitative: recitative in which the full orchestra is necessary to the desired effect (also known as accompanied recitative)

oblique motion: motion occurring when one voice repeats or sustains a pitch while another moves away or toward it; used in medieval organum as a way to avoid dissonant tritones

oboe d'amore: an oboe-like instrument in A, slightly lower in range than the oboe; used by J.S. Bach and revived in works by Gustav Mahler and Richard Strauss

occitan: see langue d'oc

occursus: a running together, Guido of Arezzo's term for cadence

octatonic scale: a symmetric scale alternating half and whole steps

ode: a multi-movement hymn of praise to a person or ideal usually lasting about twenty minutes and containing an instrumental introduction, choruses, duets, and solo arias, but no recitative because there is no story

Odhecaton: the first book of polyphonic music printed from movable type; although published in Venice, most of the nearly one-hundred compositions in it were the works of the great northern masters of counterpoint

open ending: the term used in the Middle Ages for what we today call a first ending

opera: a dramatic work, or play, set to music; in opera the lines of the actors and actresses are sung, not spoken, and music, poetry, drama, scenic design, and dance combine to produce a powerful art form

opera buffa: the name for Italian comic opera but which, unlike most other forms of comic opera, uses rapid-fire recitative rather than spoken dialogue

opéra comique: similar to Italian *opera buffa*, has characters from the everyday world, singing in a fresh, natural style, and the dialogue is generally spoken or sometimes delivered in recitative; the principals sing either simple airs or popular melodies

opera seria: serious, not comic, opera; the term is used to designate the heroic, fully sung Italian opera that dominated the stage at the courts of Europe during the eighteenth century

operetta: a genre of light or comic opera with spoken dialogue and traditional operatic numbers originating in the mid nineteenth century

ophicleide: an early nineteenth-century bass brass instrument, forerunner of the tuba

opus dei: "work of the lord"; the services of the canonical hours as referred to in the Rule of St. Benedict

oratorio: a genre of religious music developed in the seventeenth century to satisfy the desire for dramatic music during Lent; a musical setting of a dramatic text in Latin or Italian or, later, other languages that usually elaborates upon an event in the Old Testament; uses the essential processes of opera but without the lavish sets, costumes, or acting

oratory: a prayer hall set aside just for praying, preaching, and devotional singing

Orchésographie: lengthy treatise on dance published by Thoinot Arbeau in 1589; it details all the popular dances of the day with their steps, tells what is in fashion and what is not, and provides unexpected information about performance practices of the day

Ordinary of the Mass: chants of the Mass with unvarying texts that can be sung almost every day of the year; *Kyrie, Gloria, Credo, Sanctus,* and *Agnus dei*

ordre: the term used by François Couperin to designate a group of pieces loosely associated by feeling and key; similar to

what other composers of the Baroque era would call a dance suite

organ Mass: a Mass in which an organ alternates with, or entirely replaces, the choir

organ verset: an independent organ section in an *alternatim* organ Mass; a short piece that replaces a liturgical item otherwise sung by the choir

organum (pl., organa): a type of polyphonic religious music of the Middle Ages; the term came to be used generally to connote all early polyphony of the church

organum purum: florid two-voice organum of medieval Paris continuing the tradition of earlier Aquitanian polyphony in sustained-tone style

ostinato: see *basso ostinato*

overdotting: practice in which a dotted note is made longer than written, while its complementary short note(s) is made shorter

paean: in ancient Greece, a hymn that celebrated the deeds of primary gods such as Zeus or Apollo; today any poetic hymn of praise

pan-consonance: music in which almost every note is a member of a triad or a triadic inversion and not a dissonance

pan-isorhythm: a technique whereby isorhythm is applied to all voices, not just the tenor in an isorhythmic piece

parallel organum: organum in which all voices move in lockstep, up or down, with the intervals between voices remaining the same

paraphrase Mass: a Mass in which the movements are united by a single paraphrased chant

paraphrase motet: a motet that contains a paraphrased chant throughout

paraphrase technique: when a composer takes a preexisting plainsong and embellishes it somewhat, imparting to it a rhythmic profile; the elaborated chant then serves as the basic melodic material for a polyphonic composition

Parisian chanson: a newer (after 1500) style of French chanson in which the rhythm of the text begins to animate the rhythm of the music; almost every note has its own syllable and the duration of that note is often determined by the length or stress of the syllable; subject matter was also more "down to earth" and might include lusty lovers or drinking scenes

parlando-rubato rhythm: term used by Béla Bartók to describe the flexible rhythm of most ancient Hungarian peasant songs

parody technique (emulation technique): when one composer emulates another

by borrowing entire polyphonic sections of an earlier work

part book: a volume that contains the music of one voice part and only one voice part

partita: term used by J.S. Bach as a synonym for suite

partitioning: in twelve-tone music, the distribution of the notes of a tone row into several strands in a texture

partsong: a strophic song with English text intended to be sung by three or four voices in a predominantly homophonic musical style

passacaglia: (1) a musical form involving continuous variations upon a *basso ostinato*, originating in the Baroque period and virtually synonymous with the term chaconne; (2) originally a separate and distinct bass melody but during the seventeenth century it came to mean almost any repeating bass pattern of short duration

passion: a large-scale musical depiction of Christ's crucifixion as recorded in the Gospels; an oratorio on the subject of the passion

pastoral aria: a slow aria with several distinctive characteristics: parallel thirds that glide mainly in step-wise motion, a lilting rhythm in compound meter, and a harmony that changes slowly and employs many subdominant chords

patter-song: the rapid delivery of text on repeated notes

pavane: a slow gliding dance in duple meter performed by couples holding hands; replaced the fifteenth-century *basse danse* as the primary slow dance of the court

pedal point: on the organ, a sustained or continually repeated pitch, usually placed in the bass and sounding while the harmonies change around it

Penitential Psalms: the seven of the one hundred fifty psalms of the Psalter that are especially remorseful in tone and sung in the rites of the Catholic Church surrounding death and burial

pentatonic scale: a scale with five tones per octave; specifically, a scale having the form C D E G A (or a transposition or reordering of these tones); "pentatonic music" makes use of pentatonic scales

pes: (Latin for foot) the English name for a bottom voice that continually repeats throughout a polyphonic composition

phasing: a term associated with composer Steve Reich; a phase piece is one that begins with two sources of sound giving forth an identical ostinato; one sound source gradually pulls ahead, creating a constantly-changing rhythmic interaction with the other source

pianoforte: original name for the piano because, unlike the harpsichord, its mechanism allowed the player to control the force of a blow to the string and thus could play piano or forte

Picardy third: a shift from minor to major in the final chord of a piece

plagal cadence: a IV-I chordal movement with the bass in root position falling down by the interval of a fourth or rising up by a fifth

plagal mode in the eight church modes the plagal is the second of each of the four pairs of modes; plagal means "derived from" and each plagal mode is a fourth below its authentic counterpart; the Dorian mode, for example, has its plagal counterpart in the Hypodorian mode

plainsong: see Gregorian chant

player piano: a piano provided with a mechanical device that "plays" the instrument according to musical instructions entered on a perforated paper roll

point of imitation: a distinctive motive that is sung or played in turn by each voice or instrumental line

pointillism: an artistic style of the late nineteenth century in which dots of color merge into recognizable images in the eye of the viewer; a similar phenomenon occurs in music by modern composers including Anton Webern and Olivier Messiaen in which notes seem isolated and detached from larger context

polychord: a chord made by juxtaposing two familiar harmonies

polymeter: two or more meters sounding simultaneously

polyrhythm: the simultaneous appearance in a musical work of two or more rhythmic patterns or principles of rhythmic organization

polytonality: the simultaneous appearance in a musical work of two or more keys

popular art music: a term coined by Béla Bartók to describe songs composed by nineteenth-century composers, of low artistic value, that had been accepted by the populace as folk songs

portative organ: a small movable instrument that sounded at courtly entertainments, usually to accompany singers rather than dancers

positive organ: a large stationary instrument that began to appear in large numbers in churches in the West shortly after 1300; considered one of the technological wonders of its day, it was usually attached high on the wall in the nave of the church and was the only instrument sanctioned for use in the church

preghiera: a prayer scene, often found in nineteenth-century Italian opera

prelude: a preliminary piece, one that comes immediately before and introduces the main musical event

prepared piano: a piano whose sound is modified by the introduction of mutes and other objects between strings

prima donna: leading lady

prima pratica: a traditional style for church music that is in contrast to the freer writing found in some madrigals of the late sixteenth century; the musical embodiment of the restrained spirit of the Counter-Reformation

program music: instrumental music that explicitly embodies extra-musical content

programmatic symphony: a multimovement symphony that is explicitly programmatic

prolation: (*prolatio*) the division of the semibreve into two or three minims

Proper of the Mass: chants of the Mass whose texts change each day to suit the religious theme, or to honor a particular saint on just that one day

proportions: time signatures often written as fractions that modify the normal value of notes

proslambanomenos: term used by the ancient Greeks to indicate the lowest sounding pitch in their Greater Perfect System

psalm tone: eight simple recitation formulas (simple repeating patterns) to which psalms were chanted

psalmody: act or process of singing the psalms (of the Psalter); done each week during the services of the canonical hours

Psalter: the book of one hundred fifty psalms found in the Old Testament

punctum (pl., puncta): a pair of musical phrases (couplet) usually associated with medieval instrumental music

Pythagorean tuning: a process in which the octaves, fifths, and fourths are tuned in perfect 2:1, 3:2, and 4:3 ratios

quadrivium: the four scientific disciplines of the seven liberal arts—arithmetic, geometry, astronomy, and music— that used number and quantitative reasoning to arrive at the truth

quadruplum: fourth voice in four-voice organa

quattrocento: Italian for what we refer to as "the 1400s"

quodlibet: a genre of music created when several secular tunes are brought together and sound together or in immediate succession

rag see ragtime

ragtime: a style of American popular music, especially found in piano character pieces (called "rags"), in which a syncopated melody is joined to a rhythmically-regular accompaniment

rank: each group of similar sounding pipes in an organ

realism: in Russian music of the nineteenth century a style portraying people objectively and truthfully, often using a melodic style that is close to speech

recapitulation: in sonata form, the return of the first theme and the tonic key following the development; although essentially a revisiting of previous material it is usually by no means an exact repeat

recital: a concert given by a single performer or a small number of musicians

récitatif ordinaire: a style of recitative, developed by French composer Jean-Baptiste Lully, noteworthy for its length, vocal range, and generally dramatic quality

recitation tone: a constantly repeating pitch followed by a mediation or a termination; the recitation tone is the heart of the psalm tone

recitative: a musically heightened speech, often used in an opera, oratorio, or cantata to report dramatic action and advance the plot

reform opera: first created in the 1760s by Christoph Willibald Gluck and Ranieri Calzabigi in an attempt to combine the best features of the Italian and French operatic traditions, to yoke Italian lyricism to the French concern for intense dramatic expression

Reformation: the religious revolution that began as a movement to reform Catholicism and ended with the establishment of Protestantism

release: a contrasting phrase in a popular song refrain

requiem Mass: the burial Mass of the Roman Catholic Church

respond: the opening chant in responsorial singing; usually sung by the full choir, it is followed by a verse sung by a soloist, and is repeated by the full choir

responsorial singing: when the full choir prefaces and responds to the psalm verse, which is sung by a soloist (choral respond, solo verse, choral respond)

retransition: in sonata form, the point near the end of the development where tonal stability returns, often in the form of a dominant pedal point, in preparation for the return of the first theme (in the tonic key) and the beginning of the recapitulation

retrograde: backward in motion, as in twelve-tone music where a tone row is deployed with its tones in reverse order

reverberation time: the time it takes a sound to die out

rhapsody: a type of character piece of the nineteenth century, usually for piano, having no established form or mood

rhythm and blues: a style of American popular songs appearing in the 1940s that use the traditional blues form; forerunner of rock

rhythm section: in jazz, an accompanimental group of instruments

rhythmic imitation: process in which each voice in turn sings the same rhythmic motive, but to melodic motives that differ slightly in pitch

rhythmic modes: simple patterns of repeating rhythms employed in the polyphony created in Paris during the twelfth and thirteenth centuries; modal notation evolved into a system of six rhythmic modes

ricercar: (sixteenth century) an instrumental piece, usually for lute or keyboard, similar in style to the imitative motet; (seventeenth century) Frescobaldi perfected a tightly organized, monothematic ricercar that influenced the later fugal writing of J.S. Bach

rigaudon: a Baroque dance in duple meter

ripieno: the larger ensemble (full orchestra) in a concerto grosso

ripresa: a refrain

Risorgimento: (resurgence) the movement toward Italian political and social unification that began in 1814 and culminated in 1861 when much of Italy was brought together as a single nation under King Victor Emmanuel II

ritornello: a return or refrain

ritornello form: a carefully worked out structure for a concerto grosso, which employs regular reappearances of the ritornello

Robertsbridge Codex: the earliest surviving collection of keyboard music; preserves various pieces typically heard at the French royal court in the mid fourteenth century

rock 'n roll (or rock): a type of popular song, gaining prominence in America in the 1950s, accompanied typically by amplified guitars, drums, and a few other instruments; early rock songs often had the form of a blues, elements of country music, and sexually-suggestive lyrics

rococo: term used to describe the decorative arts and the music of mid eighteenth-century France, with all their lightness, grace and highly ornate surfaces

Roman chant: the dialect of chant sung in the early churches of Rome; the principal repertory from which Gregorian chant would later emerge

romance: in nineteenth-century French music, a simple strophic song

romantic opera: a genre term used by Carl Maria von Weber for certain of his operas and by Richard Wagner for his early operas; the term suggests that the texts stressed mysterious or supernatural elements, as in the contemporary literary genre of the "romance"

Romantic period: a basic period in the history of Western music extending from the early nineteenth to the early twentieth century; although the music of this time is too diverse to admit meaningful generalizations about its style, there is a recurring impulse toward intense expressivity, which often drives the music to free forms expressed through innovative materials

romanticism: the general style of music of the Romantic period

rondeau: (fourteenth and fifteenth centuries) one of the three French *formes fixes* that originated as a dance-song with the troubadours and trouvères; its musical and textual form is ABaAabAB; (seventeenth and eighteenth centuries) a composition based on the alternation of a main theme (refrain) with subsidiary sections called *couplets* to allow musical diversity

rondellus: a distinctly English musical technique in which two or three voices engage in voice exchange, or more correctly, phrase exchange

rondo: one of the main musical forms of the Classical period; a Classical rondo sets a refrain (A) against contrasting material (B, C, or D) to create a pattern such as ABACA, ABACABA, or even ABACADA; it usually projects a playful, exuberant mood, and is often used as the last movement of a sonata or symphony, to bid a happy farewell to the audience

Rossini crescendo: a characteristic feature in operas by Gioachino Rossini in which a long crescendo is accompanied by ever shorter phrases, a thickening of orchestration, and quicker harmonic motions

rota: the English name for a canon that endlessly circles back to the beginning

rotulus: an oblong sheet of paper or parchment on which chansons were inscribed; the sheet music of the late Middle Ages and the Renaissance

Royal Academy of Music: George Frideric Handel's London opera company started in 1719; a publicly held stock company, its principal investor being the king

Russian Revolution: an uprising in the major cities of Russia in 1917 during which Tsar Nicholas II abdicated and power was seized by the Bolshevik political faction

sackbut: a slide trumpet common in the fifteenth and sixteenth centuries; precursor of the modern trombone

sarabande: a slow, stately dance in $\frac{3}{4}$ with a strong accent on the second beat; one of four dances typically found within a Baroque dance suite

Sarum chant: England's special dialect of Gregorian chant; called that from the old Latin name of the cathedral town of Salisbury; melodies and texts were somewhat different from the chant sung on the Continent

scat singing: in jazz, singing on nonsense syllables

scena: a passage of a nineteenth-century opera given largely in recitative and often leading to an aria or duet

scenario: the story outline of a ballet

scene: a passage in an opera or ballet calling to the stage a particular selection of characters

scherzo: (Italian for joke) an exuberant triple-meter dance that frequently replaced the more stately minute as the third movement in symphonies and chamber works of the Classical period; was favored first by Haydn (in his Opus 33 quartets) and then especially by Beethoven in his symphonies

scholasticism: the mode of thinking that rose to prominence at the University of Paris in the thirteenth century; it managed information by constructing chains of hierarchical categories and relationships

Schubertiad: a social gathering organized within the circle of Franz Schubert at which his music was performed

scordatura: tuning a string instrument to something other than standard tuning

seconda pratica: Claudio Monteverdi's term for the new text-driven approach to musical composition that he practiced; it allowed for "deviations" from conventional counterpoint if these moments were inspired by an especially expressive text

semibreve: one of the three basic note shapes recognized by Franco of Cologne around 1280 in his classification of musical durations

semi-opera: a spoken play in which the more exotic, amorous, or even supernatural moments in the story were sung or danced

sequence: a Gregorian chant, sung on high feasts during the Proper of the Mass immediately after the Alleluia, in which successive verses were paired into double verses; the most famous sequence today is the *Dies irae*

serenade: a piece of outdoor music for a small ensemble usually in at least five movements; the term was used interchangeably with divertimento

serialism: a compositional method in which the choice and ordering of elements is governed by a precompositional arrangement or system; see also total serialism

seven liberal arts: a framework of seven intellectual disciplines set forth by Martianus Capella (c435 C.E.) composed of the trivium and the quadrivium

shanty: a sailor's work song

shawm: a double-reed instrument with a loud penetrating tone, used to provide dance music during the Middle Ages and Renaissance; the ancestor of the modern oboe

sideman: in jazz, a section player

Silver Age: (in Russian art) common designation for an artistic period in Russia during the reign of Tsar Nicholas II (1894–1917); a time of changing tastes

simple recitative: a basic form of recitative in operas of the eighteenth and nineteenth centuries: narrative in text, speech-like in melody, and accompanied solely by keyboard or a minimal number of instruments; a recitative accompanied only by a basso continuo

sincopa: the medieval term for syncopation, a temporary shift of the downbeat

sinfonia: (Italian for symphony) a three-section or three-movement instrumental work that might preface an opera or stand alone as an independent concert symphony

single-impression printing: utilizes individual pieces of movable type that are both the note and a small vertical section of the staff; required only one pressing and was thus much more economical than multiple-impression printing

Singspiel: (sung play) a genre of German opera appearing in the eighteenth and nineteenth centuries using a folkish or comic spoken play with musical numbers inserted

Six, The: a critic's sobriquet given in 1920 to a group of six French neoclassical composers: Darius Milhaud, Arthur Honegger, Germaine Tailleferre, Georges Auric, Francis Poulenc, and Louis Durey

skolion: a song setting an aphoristic poem; the primary musical entertainment at an ancient Greek symposium

socialist realism: an officially-approved doctrine guiding the arts in Soviet Russia that promoted a style geared to the understanding of the masses

soft hexachord: in the Guidonian system, the hexachord—six-note pattern of TTSTT—set on F

soggetto cavato: soggetto cavato dale vocali—a cantus firmus extracted from the vowels of a name

solfege: the system of singing different pitches to the syllables "do (ut), re, mi, fa, sol, la, ti (si), do (ut)"

solo concerto: a concerto composed for only one solo instrument

solo sonata: a sonata played by a single melody instrument such as a violin, flute or oboe usually accompanied, in the Baroque era, by a basso continuo

sonata: originally "something sounded" on an instrument as opposed to something sung (a "cantata"); later a multi-movement work for solo instrument or ensemble

sonata form: the most important formal innovation of the Classical period, used by composers most often when writing a fast first movement of a sonata, quartet, or symphony; an expansion of rounded binary form, it consists of an exposition, development, and recapitulation, with optional introduction and coda

sonata-rondo form: a design often found in the finales of symphonies and concertos of the eighteenth and nineteenth centuries that merges elements of sonata and rondo forms

sonatina: a name sometimes used for the easiest and shortest sonatas

song "release": see release

song collection: a group of art songs having a loose connection, such as that coming from a single poet or literary theme

song cycle: a group of songs intended by the composer to be performed as a unit, having definite musical and textual interconnections

Song of Songs: (also called the Song of King Solomon) a particularly lyrical book in the Old Testament of the Bible portions of which have often been set to music over the centuries

song plugger: in the American popular song industry of the early twentieth century, a musician who demonstrated new works for a publisher

sound mass: a basic element in a modern composition made from a conglomerate of tones, lines, and rhythms

Spanish guitar: see *vihuela*

spiccato: designation requiring performers to play in a detached fashion, but not quite as short as *staccato*

spiritual: an American religious song

Sprechgesang: (speech song) a term coined by Arnold Schoenberg to describe the recitational part of his melodrama *Pierrot lunaire* (1912); in *Sprechgesang*, rhythms are notated exactly and pitches are only approximated; a synonym is *Sprechmelodie* (speech melody); the reciter herself is called the *Sprechstimme* (speaking voice); the style was later used in the operas of Alban Berg

square piano: a small box-shape piano with strings running at right angles to the keys, which could be set upon a table or simple stand

standard: in jazz, a popular song that is frequently arranged or used as the basis for improvisation; also called a "jazz standard"

stile antico: the name given to the conservative music emanating from the papal chapel in the seventeenth century

stile concertato: Italian for concerted style; a term broadly used to identify Baroque music marked by grand scale and strong contrast, either between voices and instruments, between separate instrumental ensembles, between separate choral groups, or even between soloist and choir

stile concitato: an agitated style particularly suited to warlike music; Claudio Monteverdi used this term for a new style of music he created that was more direct and insistent than previous martial music

stile rappresentativo: (dramatic or theater style) a type of vocal expression somewhere between song and declaimed speech

stochastic music: a term brought to music from probability theory by the composer Iannis Xenakis to designate works in which individual sonic events are not controlled by the composer, who focuses instead on shaping only their aggregate appearance and behavior

stop: a small wooden knob on an organ that activates a rank of pipes when pulled out

stop time: in jazz, a temporarily simplified rhythm in the accompaniment, which allows for a soloist briefly to improvise

stretta: the climactic section of a number in a nineteenth-century opera, often in a fast tempo; the masculine form *stretto* usually alludes to a passage in a fugue in which a subject is imitated at a shorter than normal time span

stride: a style of ragtime piano playing and composing in which the pianist's left hand moves regularly from chord tones in a low register to harmonies in the middle register

strophe plus refrain: a common musical form in which the strophe, or stanza, is sung by a soloist while all the singers join in with the burden, or refrain

strophic form: a song form in which the music composed for the initial stanza of text is repeated for each additional stanza

strophic variation aria: an aria in which the same melodic and harmonic plan appears, with slight variation, in each successive strophe

Sturm und Drang: (German for "Storm and Stress") as a musical term it refers to a small but significant group of works written around 1770 that are marked by agitated, impassioned writing, such as Mozart's Symphony No. 25 (K. 183) of 1773

style brisé: a modern term for a type of discontinuous texture in which chords are broken apart and notes enter one by one; such a style is inherent in lute music because the sounds of the lute are delicate and quickly evaporate

subject: in a fugue, the theme

substitute clausula: one clausula written in discant style intended to replace another

suite: a musical work that consists of a succession of short pieces, especially dances; also used for a concert work made from excerpts from an opera, ballet, or film score

surrealism: twentieth-century literary and artistic movement that confounds superficial reality or logic in order to evoke unconscious states of mind

sustained-tone organum: organum in which the bottom voice holds a note while the faster-moving top voice embellishes it in a florid fashion

swing: in jazz, a rhythm that drives forward in a triplet pattern; also a style of jazz of the 1930s and 1940s often involving big bands that play in an impulsive and dynamic mood

syllabic chant: chants in which there is usually only one note and only one note for each syllable of text

symmetric inversion: see inversion

symphonic poem: a one-movement programmatic orchestral work; roughly synonymous with tone poem

symphonie concertante: a concerto-like composition of the Classical period with two or more soloists

symposium: in ancient Greece, a tightly organized social gathering of adult male citizens for conversation and entertainment

syncopation: a temporary metric irregularity or dislocation by which beats or divisions of beats do not conform to their normal placement within the meter

syncope: the Renaissance term for a suspension

tablature: directs a performer's fingers to a specific spot on an instrument

tactus: the term used to indicate the beat by music theorists of the Renaissance

Tafelmusik: German name for chamber music, both vocal and instrumental, for the dinner table

talea: a rhythmic pattern, or unit appearing in an isorhythmic composition

tape music: a style of electronic music associated with Vladimir Ussachevsky and Otto Luening in which compositions are recorded and subsequently distorted (especially by reverberating feedback)

temperament: the tuning of intervals in something slightly more or less than strict mathematical ratios

tenor: one of the standard four voice parts; in early medieval polyphony the bottom most voice, often a preexisting chant, upon which the composition is built; called that because in these early works it holds or draws out the notes

Tenorlied: a polyphonic German song in which a preexisting tune is placed in the tenor and two or three other voices enhance it with lightly imitative polyphony

tetrachord: a succession of four pitches

text painting (word painting): the use of striking chord shifts, musical repetition, controlled dissonance, and abrupt textural changes to highlight the meaning of the text; a very popular technique with sixteenth-century madrigal composers

theorbo: a large lute-like instrument with a full octave of additional bass strings descending in a diatonic pattern

third stream: a term coined by the composer Gunther Schuller to describe a musical style merging jazz and classical elements

threnody: a musical lament

through composed: containing new music for every stanza of text, as opposed to strophic form in which the music is repeated for each successive stanza

tibia: Roman name for the aulos

time: (*tempus*) the division of the breve into two or three semibreves

Tin Pan Alley: the art and business of the American popular song of the early twentieth century

tintinnabuli style: (bells style) a term coined by the composer Arvo Pärt for a polyphony in which a melodic line is joined to a "bells" line limited to the three tones of the tonic triad

toccata: an instrumental piece, for keyboard or other instruments, requiring the performer to touch the instrument with great technical dexterity; designed to show off the creative spirit of the composer as well as the technical skill of the performer

tombeau: an instrumental piece commemorating someone's death

tonal answer: a following voice that imitates the subject at the interval of a fifth above or fourth below and changes the subject so as to keep the music in the home tonality

tone cluster: a dissonant chord made from sounding all of the tones within a boundary interval

tone poem: a one-movement programmatic work, usually for orchestra, and roughly synonymous with symphonic poem

tone-color melody (Klangfarbenmelodie): a term coined by Arnold Schoenberg to designate a melody-like line made from changing tone colors

tonos (pl., tonoi): ancient Greek term for a scale

total serialism: a compositional method in which the choice of most of the principal elements of a composition (including pitches, rhythms, and dynamics) is governed precompositionally by an integrated system or arrangement

total work of art (Gesamtkunstwerk): a term used by Richard Wagner to designate a goal for art in which its various branches are merged into a integrated and dramatic whole

tragédie lyrique: the term used to designate French opera in the late seventeenth and eighteenth centuries, which was a fusion of classical French tragedy with traditional French ballet (*ballet de cour*)

transformation of themes: a technique of thematic unity throughout a multi-sectional work by which one or a few initial themes recur, albeit changed in character

transition (bridge): in sonata form the passage of modulation between the tonic and the new key

treble: the highest of the three voices for which much late-medieval English polyphony was written; evolved in general musical terminology to mean the top part as well as the top clef (G clef), the highest clef in music

trecento: short for *mille trecento*, or the century of the 1300s, in Italian

trio: a composition for three solo instruments; also, a contrasting section of a work originally played by a trio of instruments; in minuets, band marches, and rags, the term refers to a contrasting section or episode, with no implications for medium

trio sonata: comprised a line for two treble instruments (usually two violins) and basso continuo

triplum: third voice in a piece of three- or four-voice organum of the Middle Ages

triseme: a triple unit long value of time in ancient Greek musical notation—formed by three chronoi

trivium: the three verbal disciplines of the seven liberal arts—grammar, logic, and rhetoric—which deal with language, logic, and oratory

trobairitz: a female troubadour (poet-musician)

trope: an addition of music or text, or both, to a preexisting chant; they more fully explain the theology inherent in the chants to which they are added

troubadour: a poet-musician of the courtly art of vernacular sung poetry that developed in the Middle Ages in southern France

trouser role: an opera role designed to be sung by a woman dressed as a man

trouvère: a poet-musician of the courtly art of vernacular sung poetry that developed in northern France during the late twelfth and thirteenth centuries

tuba: Roman name for the trumpet; a long, straight instrument with a cylindrical bore and a bell at the end, which originated with the Etruscans

Turkish music: the noise of Turkish military percussion instruments, which were introduced into Western European music in the eighteenth century during the Turkish Wars; some pianos of the day were equipped with special devices to effect the sounds of "Turkish" music, such as bass drum, cymbals, and the like

twelve-tone composition: a composition in which the twelve tones of the chromatic scale are systematically recirculated; the term usually refers to works using Arnold Schoenberg's "twelve-tone method," formulated in 1923, in which the recirculation of tones is joined to a serialized principle of order

unmeasured prelude: an opening piece without specific indications for rhythmic duration or metrical organization

variation technique: a procedure in which successive statements of a theme are changed or presented in altered musical surroundings

variations: a work, movement of a work, or a form in which an initial theme is subject to a series of modifications or paraphrases; see also ballet variations

vaudeville show: a popular theatric entertainment in America made from acts including dances, songs, and skits

verbal score: a musical composition represented not by conventional musical notation but by verbal instructions to the performers

verismo: (realism) a style of Italian opera appearing in the 1890s in short works in which characters from lower social strata are driven by the passions to violent acts

verse and refrain: a form for popular songs in which each stanza (sometimes only a single stanza) is divided into an introductory passage (the verse) followed by a more tuneful refrain

Vespers: the late-afternoon service, and most important of the eight canonical hours for the history of music; not only were psalms and a hymn sung but also the Magnificat

vida: a brief biographical sketch of a troubadour or trouvère; appears along with a small portrait of the artist in some French chansonniers

vielle: a large five-string fiddle capable of playing the entire Guidonian scale; often provided dance music during the thirteenth and fourteenth centuries

Viennese School: historians' term for composers Haydn, Mozart, Beethoven, and Schubert who capped their careers in Vienna and knew one another personally, however indirectly

vihuela **(Spanish guitar):** a plucked string instrument with a waisted body, and a long pole-neck that serves as a fingerboard; the direct ancestor of the modern classical guitar

Vingt-quatre violons du roi: twenty-four instruments of the violin family that formed the string core of the French court orchestra under Louis XIV (six violins, twelve violas, and six *basse de violons*)

viol: a six-string instrument fretted and tuned like the lute and *vihuela,* but bowed and not plucked; it came in three sizes—treble, tenor, and bass—and was played with the instrument resting on the lap or legs

viola da gamba: Italian name for the bass viol, so called because it was held between each leg (*gamba* in Italian)

violino: (little viol) original name for the violin

violino piccolo: a small violin usually tuned a minor third higher than the normal violin

virelai: one of the three French *formes fixes* of the Middle Ages yet more playful than a serious ballade; originated with the troubadours and trouvères as a monophonic dance that involved choral singing; the form is AbbaA

virginal: a diminutive harpsichord possessing a single keyboard with the strings placed at right angles to the keys

vox organalis: (organal voice) one of the two voice parts in an early organum; it is a newly created line added to the preexisting chant

vox principalis: (principal voice) one of the two voice parts in an early organum; it is a preexisting chant that served as a foundation for another newly created line

Wagner tuba: nickname for a tenor-range tuba used by Richard Wagner in his *Der Ring des Nibelungen*

walking bass: a bass line, especially in jazz, with a predominantly stepwise motion and steady rhythm (for example, entirely quarter or eighth notes)

waltz: a triple-time dance for couples that rose to great popularity in the nineteenth century

whole-tone scale: a scale with six notes per octave separated entirely by whole tones

Winchester Troper: a troper—chant manuscript mainly preserving additions to the liturgy called tropes—dating from c1000 C.E. from a Benedictine Monastery at Winchester, England; shows that the singers had a repertory of about 150 two-voice organa, but the troper was a memory aid and is not a prescriptive document that allows singers today to perform the music with confidence

Wolf's Glen Scene: the finale to Act 2 of Carl Maria von Weber's *Der Freischütz,* its most striking and most popular scene

WoO numbers: (*Werk ohne Opuszahl,* or work without opus number) a number given in a catalog of a composer's works designating those pieces lacking a traditional opus number; first used in the 1955 catalog of Beethoven's works compiled by Georg Kinsky and Hans Halm

word painting: see text painting

xylophone: a percussion instrument in which wooden bars are sounded with a mallet

INDEX